admirador *m,*

campeón *m,*

salvapantallas

ronquido *m* sn

sg

enemigo 1 *adj* e   ormation

  enemigo de *fig*

lleno *adj* full **(de**

  with)

---

debatir ⟨3a⟩ **1** *v/t* debate, discuss **2** *v/i* struggle **3** *v/r* **debatirse:** ***debatirse entre la vida y la muerte*** fight for one's life

    ● Entries divided into grammatical categories

---

uva *f* BOT grape; ***estar de mala uva*** F be in a foul mood; ***tener mala uva*** F be a nasty piece of work F

fiambre *m* cold cut, *Br* cold meat; P *(cadáver)* stiff P

profiláctico 1 *adj* preventive, prophylactic *fml* **2** *m* condom

    ● Register labels

---

acomedido *adj* *L.Am.* obliging, helpful

acomedirse ⟨3l⟩ *v/r* *Méx* offer to help

residencial 1 *adj* residential **2** *f* *Arg, Chi* boarding house

sablear ⟨1a⟩ *v/t & v/i* *L.Am.* F scrounge (*a* from)

    ● Latin American Spanish

---

riñonera *f* fanny pack, *Br* bum bag

rotonda *f* traffic circle, *Br* roundabout

    ● British variants

A B C D E F G H I J K L M N Ñ O P Q R S T U V W X Y Z

Langenscheidt
Pocket Dictionary

Spanish

Spanish – English
English – Spanish

Langenscheidt

Compiled by LEXUS with José A. Gálvez, Roy Russell, Jane Goldie, Peter
Terrell, Monica Tamariz-Martel Mirêlis, Rafael Alarcón Gaeta Andrew
Wilkes, Stephanie Parker, Mike Gonzalez
Activity section by Heather Bonikowski

1. Auflage 2015 (1,02 - 2020)
© PONS GmbH, Stöckachstraße 11, 70190 Stuttgart 2015
All Rights Reserved.

www.langenscheidt.com

Print: Druckerei C. H. Beck Nördlingen
Printed in Germany

ISBN 978-3-12-514030-1

Preface

This new dictionary of English and Spanish is a tool with 50,000 references for learners of the Spanish language at beginner's or intermediate level.

Thousands of colloquial and idiomatic expressions have been included. The user-friendly layout with all headwords in blue allows the user to have quick access to all the words, expressions and their translations.

Clarity of presentation has been a major objective. Is the *mouse* you need for your computer, for example, the same in Spanish as the *mouse* you don't want in the house? This dictionary is rich in sense distinctions like this – and in translation options tied to specific, identified senses.

Vocabulary needs grammar to back it up. In this dictionary you will find extra grammar information on Spanish conjugation and on irregular verb forms.

The additional activity section provides the user with an opportunity to develop language skills with a selection of engaging word puzzles. The games are designed specifically to improve vocabulary, spelling, grammar and comprehension in an enjoyable style.

Designed for a wide variety of uses, this dictionary will be of great value to those who wish to learn Spanish and have fun at the same time.

Contents

How to use the dictionary

To get the most out of your dictionary you should understand how and where to find the information you need. Whether you are yourself writing text in a foreign language or wanting to understand text that has been written in a foreign language, the following pages should help.

1. How and where do I find a word?

1.1 Spanish and English headwords.
The word list for each language is arranged in alphabetical order and also gives irregular forms of verbs and nouns in their correct alphabetical order.

Sometimes you might want to look up terms made up of two separate words, for example **shooting star**, or hyphenated words, for example **absent-minded**. These words are treated as though they were a single word and their alphabetical ordering reflects this.

The only exception to this strict alphabetical ordering is made for English phrasal verbs - words like **go off**, **go out**, **go up**. These are positioned directly after their main verb (in this case **go**), rather than being scattered around in alphabetical positions.

Spanish words beginning with **ch** and **ll** are positioned in their alphabetical position in letters C and L. Words beginning with **ñ** are listed after N.

1.2 Spanish feminine headwords are shown as follows:

> **abogado** *m*, **-a** *f* lawyer
> **fumador** *m*, **fumadora** *f* smoker
> **bailarín** *m*, **-ina** *f* dancer
> **pibe** *m*, **-a** *f Rpl* F kid F
> **edil** *m*, **edila** *f* council(l)or

The feminine forms of these headwords are: **abogada**, **fumadora**, **bailarina**, **piba** and **edila**.

When a Spanish headword has a feminine form which translates differently from the masculine form, the feminine is entered as a separate headword in alphabetical order:

> **empresaria** *f* businesswoman; **empresa-rio** *m* businessman

1.3 Running heads

If you are looking for a Spanish or English word you can use the **running heads** printed in bold in the top corner of each page. The running head on the left tells you the *first* headword on the left-hand page and the one on the right tells you the *last* headword on the right-hand page.

1.4 How is the word spelt?

You can look up the spelling of a word in your dictionary in the same way as you would in a spelling dictionary. British spelling variants are marked *Br*.

2. How do I split a word?

Spanish speakers find English hyphenation very difficult. All you have to do with this dictionary is look for the bold dots between syllables. These dots show you where you can split a word at the end of a line but you should avoid having just one letter before or after the hyphen as in **a·mend** or **thirst·y**. In such cases it is better to take the entire word over to the next line.

3. Long dashes

In the Spanish-English part of the dictionary, when a headword is repeated in a phrase or compound with an altered form, a long dash is used:

> **escaso** *adj* ... **-as posibilidades de** not
> much chance of, little chance of

Here **-as posibilidades** means **escasas posibilidades**.

4. What do the different typefaces mean?

4.1 All Spanish and English headwords and the Arabic numerals differentiating between parts of speech appear in **bold**:

> **neoyorquino 1** *adj* New York *atr* **2** *m*, **-a**
> New Yorker
> **splin·ter** ['splɪntər] **1** *n* astilla *f* **2** *v/i* astil-
> larse

4.2 Italics are used for:

a) abbreviated grammatical labels: *adj*, *adv*, *v/i*, *v/t* etc

b) gender labels: *m*, *f*, *mpl* etc

c) all the indicating words which are the signposts pointing to the correct translation for your needs:

> **sport·y** ['spɔːrtɪ] *adj person* deportista;
> *clothes* deportivo
> ◆ **work out 1** *v/t problem*, *puzzle* resol-
> ver; *solution* encontrar, hallar **2** *v/i at*
> *gym* hacer ejercicios; *of relationship etc*
> funcionar, ir bien
> **completo** *adj* complete; *autobús*, *teatro* full
> **grano** *m* grain; *de café* bean; *en la piel*
> pimple, spot

4.3 All phrases (examples and idioms) are given in **_secondary bold italics_**:

> **sym·pa·thet·ic** [sɪmpəˈθetɪk] *adj* (*show-ing pity*) compasivo; (*understanding*) comprensivo; **_be sympathetic toward a person / an idea_** simpatizar con una persona / idea
> **salsa** *f* GASTR sauce; *baile* salsa; **_en su salsa_** *fig* in one's element

4.4 The normal typeface is used for the translations.

4.5 If a translation is given in italics, and not in the normal typeface, this means that the translation is more of an *explanation* in the other language and that an explanation has to be given because there just is no real equivalent:

> **'walk-up** *n apartamento en un edificio sin ascensor*
> **adobera** *f Méx type of mature cheese*

5. Stress

To indicate where to put the **stress** in English words, the stress marker appears before the syllable on which the main stress falls:

> **mo·tif** [mouˈtiːf] motivo *m*
> **rec·ord**[1] [ˈrekɔːrd] *n* MUS disco *m*; SP *etc* récord *m*
> **re·cord**[2] [rɪˈkɔːrd] *v/t electronically* grabar; *in writing* anotar

Stress is shown either in the pronunciation or, if there is no pronunciation given, in the actual headword or compound itself:

> **'rec·ord hold·er** plusmarquista *m/f*

6. What do the various symbols and abbreviations tell you?

6.1 A solid blue diamond is used to indicate a phrasal verb:

> ◆ **call off** *v/t* (*cancel*) cancelar; *strike* desconvocar

6.2 A white diamond is used to divide up longer entries into more easily digested chunks of related bits of text:

> **de** *prp* ◇ *origen* from; **_de Nueva York_** from New York; **_de a_** from to ◇ *posesión* of; **_el coche de mi amigo_** my friend's car ◇ *material* (made) of; **_un anillo de oro_** a gold ring ◇ *contenido* of; **_un vaso de agua_** a glass of water ◇ *cualidad:* **_una mujer de 20 años_** 20 year old woman ◇ *causa* with; **_temblaba de miedo_** she was shaking with fear …

6.3 The abbreviation F tells you that the word or phrase is used colloquially rather than in formal contexts. The abbreviation V warns you that a word or phrase is vulgar or taboo. Words or phrases labeled P are slang. Be careful how you use these words.

These abbreviations, F, V and P, are used both for headwords and phrases (placed after) and for the translations of headwords and phrases (placed after). If there is no such label given, then the word or phrase is neutral.

6.4 A colon before an English or Spanish word or phrase means that usage is restricted to this specific example (at least as far as this dictionary's translation is concerned):

> catch-22 [kætʃtwentɪ'tuː]: *it's a catch-22
> situation* es como la pescadilla que se
> muerde la cola
> co·au·thor [koʊɒθər] … 2 *v/t:* *co-author
> a book* escribir un libro conjuntamente
> decantarse ⟨1a⟩ *v/r:* *decantarse por* opt
> for

7. Does the dictionary deal with grammar too?

7.1 All English headwords are given a part of speech label:

> tooth·less ['tuːθlɪs] *adj* desdentado
> top·ple ['tɑːpl̩] 1 *v/i* derrumbarse 2 *v/t
> government* derrocar

But if a headword can only be used as a noun (in ordinary English) then no part of speech is given, since none is needed:

> 'tooth·paste pasta *f* de dientes, dentífrico
> *m*

7.2 Spanish headwords have part of speech labels. Spanish gender markers are given:

> barbacoa *f* barbecue
> bocazas *m/f inv* F loudmouth F
> budista *m/f & adj* Buddhist

7.3 If an English translation of a Spanish adjective can only be used in front of a noun, and not after it, this is marked with *atr*:

> bursátil *adj* stock market *atr*
> campestre *adj* rural, country *atr*

7.4 If the Spanish, unlike the English, doesn't change form if used in the plural, this is marked with *inv*:

> cortacircuitos *m inv* circuit breaker
> metrópolis *f inv* metropolis

7.5 If the English, in spite of appearances, is not a plural form, this is marked with *nsg*:

> **bil·li·ards** ['bɪljərdz] *nsg* billar *m*
> **mea·sles** ['mi:zlz] *nsg* sarampión *m*

English translations are given a *pl* or *sg* label (for plural or singular) in cases where this does not match the Spanish:

> **acciones** *pl* COM stock *sg*, *Br* shares
> **entarimado** *m* (*suelo*) floorboards *pl*

7.6 Irregular English plurals are identified:

> **the·sis** ['θi:sɪs] (*pl* **theses** ['θi:si:z]) tesis
> *f inv*
> **thief** [θi:f] (*pl* **thieves** [θi:vz]) ladrón
> (-ona) *m(f)*
> **trout** [traʊt] (*pl* **trout**) trucha *f*

7.7 Words like **physics** or **media studies** have not been given a label to say if they are singular or plural for the simple reason that they can be either, depending on how they are used.

7.8 Irregular and semi-irregular verb forms are identified:

> **sim·pli·fy** ['sɪmplɪfaɪ] *v/t* (*pret & pp* **-ied**)
> simplificar
> **sing** [sɪŋ] *v/t & v/i* (*pret* **sang**, *pp* **sung**)
> cantar
> **la·bel** ['leɪbl] **1** *n* etiqueta *f* **2** *v/t* (*pret &*
> *pp* **-ed**, *Br* **-led**) bags etiquetar

7.9 Cross-references are given to tables of Spanish conjugations:

> **gemir** ⟨31⟩ *v/i* moan, groan
> **esconder** ⟨2a⟩ *v/t* hide, conceal ...

7.10 Grammatical information is provided on the prepositions you'll need in order to create complete sentences:

> **'switch·o·ver** *to new system* cambio *m* (**to**
> a)
> **sneer** [snɪːr] **1** *n* mueca *f* desdeñosa **2** *v/i*
> burlarse (**at** de)
> **escindirse** ⟨3a⟩ *v/r* (*fragmentarse*) split
> (**en** into); (*segregarse*) break away (**de**
> from)
> **enviciarse** ⟨1b⟩ *v/r* get addicted (**con** to)

Abbreviations

and	&	y		electronics,	ELEC	electrónica,
see	→	véase		electronic		electrotecnia
registered	®	marca		engineering		
trademark		registrada		Spain	*Esp*	España
abbreviation	*abbr*	abreviatura		especially	*esp*	especialmente
abbreviation	*abr*	abreviatura		euphemistic	*euph*	eufemismo
adjective	*adj*	adjetivo		familiar,	F	familiar
adverb	*adv*	adverbio		colloquial		
agriculture	AGR	agricultura		feminine	*f*	femenino
anatomy	ANAT	anatomía		feminine noun	*f/adj*	sustantivo
architecture	ARCHI	arquitectura		and adjective		femenino y
Argentina	*Arg*	Argentina				adjetivo
architecture	ARQUI	arquitectura		railroad	FERR	ferrocarriles
article	*art*	artículo		figurative	*fig*	figurativo
astronomy	AST	astronomía		financial	FIN	finanzas
astrology	ASTR	astrología		physics	FÍS	física
attributive	*atr*	atributivo		formal	*fml*	formal
motoring	AUTO	automóvil		photography	FOT	fotografía
civil aviation	AVIA	aviación		feminine plural	*fpl*	femenino
biology	BIO	biología				plural
Bolivia	*Bol*	Bolivia		feminine	*fsg*	femenino
botany	BOT	botánica		singular		singular
British English	*Br*	inglés		gastronomy	GASTR	gastronomía
		británico		geography	GEOG	geografía
Central	*C.Am.*	América		geology	GEOL	geología
America		Central		geometry	GEOM	geometría
chemistry	CHEM	química		grammatical	GRAM	gramática
Chile	*Chi*	Chile		historical	HIST	histórico
Colombia	*Col*	Colombia		humorous	*hum*	humorístico
commerce,	COM	comercio		IT term	INFOR	informática
business				interjection	*int*	interjección
comparative	*comp*	comparativo		interrogative	*interr*	interrogativo
computers,	COMPUT	informática		invariable	*inv*	invariable
IT term				ironic	*iron*	irónico
conjunction	*conj*	conjunción		ironic	*irón*	irónico
Southern Cone	*CSur*	Cono Sur		law	JUR	jurisprudencia
sports	DEP	deporte		Latin	*L.Am.*	América
contemptuous	*desp*	despectivo		America		Latina
determiner	*det*	determinante		law	LAW	jurisprudencia
Ecuador	*Ecuad*	Ecuador		linguistics	LING	lingüística
education	EDU	educación,		literary	*lit*	literario
(schools,		enseñanza		masculine	*m*	masculino
universities)		(sistema		masculine	*m/adj*	sustantivo
		escolar y		noun and		masculino y
		universitario)		adjective		adjetivo
electronics,	EL	electrónica,		nautical	MAR	navegación,
electronic		electrotecnia				marina
engineering				mathematics	MAT	matemáticas

mathematics	MATH	matemáticas
medicine	MED	medicina
meteorology	METEO	meteorología
Mexico	*Mex*	México
Mexico	*Méx*	México
masculine and feminine	*m/f*	masculino y femenino
masculine and feminine plural	*m/fpl*	masculino y femenino plural
military	MIL	militar
mineralogy	MIN	mineralogía
motoring	MOT	automóvil
masculine plural	*mpl*	masculino plural
music	MUS	música
music	MÚS	música
mythology	MYTH	mitología
noun	*n*	sustantivo
nautical	NAUT	navegación, náutica
negative	*neg*	negativo
noun plural	*npl*	sustantivo plural
noun singular	*nsg*	sustantivo singular
ornithology	ORN	ornitología
oneself	o.s.	sí mismo
popular, slang	P	popular
painting	PAINT	pintura
Paraguay	*Parag*	Paraguay
past participle	*part*	participio pasado
Peru	*Pe*	Perú
pejorative	*pej*	peyorativo
photography	PHOT	fotografía
physics	PHYS	física
painting	PINT	pintura
plural	*pl*	plural
politics	POL	política
possessive	*pos*	posesivo
possessive	*poss*	posesivo
past participle	*pp*	participio pasado
predicative usage	*pred*	predicativo
prefix	*pref*	prefijo
preposition	*prep*	preposición

preterite (past tense)	*pret*	pretérito
pronoun	*pron*	pronombre
preposition	*prp*	preposición
psychology	PSI	psicología
psychology	PSYCH	psicología
chemistry	QUÍM	química
radio	RAD	radio
railroad	RAIL	ferrocarriles
relative	*rel*	relativo
religion	REL	religión
River Plate	*Rpl*	Río de la Plata
South America	*S.Am.*	América del Sur
singular	*sg*	singular
someone	s.o.	alguien
sports	SP	deporte
Spain	*Span*	España
something	*sth*	algo, alguna cosa
subjunctive	*subj*	subjuntivo
superlative	*sup*	superlativo
bullfighting	TAUR	tauromaquia
also	*tb*	también
theater, theatre	TEA	teatro
technology	TÉC	técnica
technology	TECH	tecnología
telecommunications	TELEC	telecomunicaciones
theater	THEA	teatro
typography, typesetting	TIP	tipografía
transportation	TRANSP	transportes
television	TV	televisión
vulgar	V	vulgar
auxiliary verb	*v/aux*	verbo auxiliar
verb	*vb*	verbo
Venezuela	*Ven*	Venezuela
intransitive verb	*v/i*	verbo intransitivo
impersonal verb	*v/impers*	verbo impersonal
reflexive verb	*v/r*	verbo reflexivo
transitive verb	*v/t*	verbo transitivo
West Indies	*W.I.*	Antillas
zoology	ZO	zoología

The pronunciation of Spanish

Stress

1. If a word ends in a vowel, or in *n* or *s*, the penultimate syllable is stressed: esp**a**da, bibliot**e**ca, h**a**blan, telef**o**nean, edif**i**cios.
2. If a word ends in a consonant other than *n* or *s*, the last syllable is stressed: dificul**ta**d, hab**la**r, lau**re**l, ni**ñe**z.
3. If a word is to be stressed in any way contrary to rules 1 and 2, an acute accent is written over the stressed vowel: rub**í**, m**á**quina, cr**í**menes, car**á**cter, contin**ú**a, autob**ú**s.
4. **Diphthongs and syllable division**. Of the 5 vowels *a, e, o* are considered "strong" and *i* and *u* "weak":

   a) A combination of weak + strong forms a diphthong, the stress falling on the stronger element: r**ei**na, b**ai**le, cosmon**au**ta, t**ie**ne, b**ue**no.
   b) A combination of weak + weak forms a diphthong, the stress falling on the second element: v**iu**da, r**ui**do.
   c) Two strong vowels together remain two distinct syllables, the stress falling according to rules 1 and 2: ma/**e**stro, atra/**e**r.
   d) Any word having a vowel combination not stressed according to these rules has an accent: tra**í**do, o**í**do, b**a**úl, r**í**o.

Sounds

Since the pronunciation of Spanish is (unlike English) adequately represented by the spelling of words, Spanish headwords have not been given a phonetic transcription. The sounds of Spanish are described below.

The pronunciation described is primarily that of the educated Spaniard. But the main features of Latin American pronunciation are also covered.

Vowels

a   As in English *father*: paz, pata.

e   Like *e* in English *they* (but without the following sound of *y*): grande, pelo. A shorter sound when followed by a consonant in the same syllable, like *e* in English *get*: España, renta.

i   Like *i* in English *machine*, though somewhat shorter: pila, rubí.

o   As in English *November, token*: solo, esposa. A shorter sound when followed by a consonant in the same syllable, like *au* in English *fault* or the *a* in *fall*: costra, omba.

u   Like *oo* in English *food*: pura, luna. Silent after **q** and in **gue, gui**, unless marked with a dieresis (antigüedad, argüir).

y   When occurring as a vowel (in the conjunction **y** or at the end of a word), is pronounced like *i*.

Diphthongs

ai   like *i* in English *right*: **baile**, **vaina**.

ei   like *ey* in English *they*: **reina**, **peine**.

oi   like *oy* in English *boy*: **boina**, **oigo**.

au   like *ou* in English *bout*: **causa**, **audacia**.

eu   like the vowel sounds in English *may-you*, without the sound of the *y*: **deuda**, **reuma**.

Semiconsonants

i, y   like *y* in English *yes*: **yerno**, **tiene**; in some cases in *L.Am*. this *y* is pronounced like the *s* in English *measure*: **mayo**, **yo**.

u   like *w* in English *water*: **huevo**, **agua**.

Consonants

b, v   These two letters represent the same value in Spanish. There are two distinct pronunciations:
1. At the start of a word and after *m* and *n* the sound is like English *b*: **batalla**, **ventaja**; **tromba**, **invierno**.
2. In all other positions the sound is what is technically a "bilabial fricative". This sound does not exist in English. Go to say a *b* but do not quite bring your lips together: **estaba**, **cueva**, **de Vigo**.

c   1. *c* before *a*, *o*, *u* or a consonant is like English *k*: **café**, **cobre**.
2. *c* before *e*, *i* is like English *th* in *thin*: **cédula**, **cinco**. In *L.Am*. this is pronounced like an English *s* in *chase*.

ch   like English ch in church: **mucho**, **chocho**.

d   Three distinct pronunciations:
1. At the start of a word and after *l* and *n*, the sound is like English *d*: **doy**, **aldea**, **conde**.
2. Between vowels and after consonants other than *l* and *n* the sound is relaxed and approaches English *th* in *this*: **codo**, **guardar**; in parts of Spain it is further relaxed and even disappears, particularly in the **-ado** ending.
3. In final position, this type 2 is further relaxed or omitted altogether: **usted**, **Madrid**.

f   like English *f*: **fuero**, **flor**.

g   Three distinct pronunciations:
1. Before *e* and *i* it is the same as the Spanish **j** (below): **coger**, **general**.
2. At the start of a word and after *n*, the sound is that of English *g* in *get*: **granada**, **rango**.
3. In other positions the sound is like 2 above, but much softer, the *g* almost disappearing: **agua**, **guerra**. N.B. In the group **gue**, **gui** the **u** is silent (**guerra**, **guindar**) unless marked with a dieresis (**antigüedad**, **argüir**). In the group **gua** all letters are sounded.

14

h   always silent: **honor**, **búho**.

j   A strong guttural sound not found in English, but like the *ch* in Scots *loch*, German *Achtung*: **jota**, **ejercer**.

k   like English *k*: **kilogramo**, **ketchup**.

l   like English *l*: **león**, **pala**.

ll   approximating to English *lli* in *million*: **millón**, **calle**. In *L.Am.* like the *s* in English *measure*.

m   like English *m*: **mano**, **como**.

n   like English *n*: **nono**, **pan**; except before **v**, when the group is pronounced like *mb*: **enviar**, **invadir**.

ñ   approximating to English *ni* in *onion*: **paño**, **ñoño**.

p   like English *p*: **Pepe**, **copa**.

q   like English *k*; always in combination with *u* , which is silent: **que**, **quiosco**.

r   a single trill stronger than any *r* in English, but like Scots *r*: **caro**, **querer**. Somewhat relaxed in final position. Pronounced like **rr** at the start of a word and after **l**, **n**, **s**: **rata**.

rr   strongly trilled: **carro**, **hierro**.

s   like *s* in English *chase*: **rosa**, **soso**. But before **b**, **d**, hard **g**, **l**, **m** and **n** it is like English *s* in *rose*: **desde**, **mismo**, **asno**. Before "impure **s**" in recent loan-words, an extra *e*-sound is inserted in pronunciation: **e-sprint**, **e-stand**.

t   like English *t*: **patata**, **tope**.

v   see *b*.

w   found in a few recent loan-words only and pronounced pretty much as the English *w*, but sometimes with a very slight *g* sound before it: **whisky**, **windsurf**. In one exceptional case it is pronounced like an English *v* or like Spanish **b** and **v**: **wáter**.

x   like English *gs* in *big sock*: **máximo**, **examen**. Before a consonant like English *s* in *chase*: **extraño**, **mixto**.

z   like English *th* in *thin*: **zote**, **zumbar**. In *L.Am.* like English *s* in *chase*.

The Spanish Alphabet

a [ah]	g [ʜeh]	m ['emeh]	rr ['erreh]	x ['ekees]
b [beh]	h ['acheh]	n ['eneh]	s ['eseh]	y [eegree-eh-ga]
c [theh]	i [ee]	ñ ['en-yeh]	t [teh]	z ['theh-ta]
ch [cheh]	j ['ḥota]	o [oh]	u [oo]	
d [deh]	k [ka]	p [peh]	v ['ooveh]	ʜ *is pronounced*
e [eh]	l ['eleh]	q [koo]	w ['ooveh	*as in the Scottish*
f ['ef-feh]	ll ['el-yeh]	r ['ereh]	doh-bleh]	*way of saying loch*

Written Spanish

I. Capitalization

The rules for capitalization in Spanish largely correspond to those for the English language. In contrast to English, however, adjectives derived from proper nouns are not capitalized (*americano* American, *español* Spanish).

II. Word division

Spanish words are divided according to the following rules:

1. If there is a **single consonant** between two vowels, the division is made between the first vowel and the consonant (*di-ne-ro, Gra-na-da*).

2. **Two consecutive consonants** may be divided (*miér-co-les, dis-cur-so*). If the second consonant is an *l* or *r*, however, the division comes before the two consonants (*re-gla, nie-bla; po-bre, ca-bra*). This also goes for *ch, ll* and *rr* (*te-cho, ca-lle, pe-rro*).

3. In the case of **three consecutive consonants** (usually including an *l* or *r*), the division comes after the first consonant (*ejem-plo, siem-pre*). If the second consonant is an *s*, however, the division comes after the *s* (*cons-tan-te, ins-ti-tu-to*).

4. In the case of **four consecutive consonants** (the second of these is usually an *s*), the division is made between the second and third consonants (*ins-tru-men-to*).

5. **Diphthongs** and **triphthongs** may not be divided (*bien, buey*). Vowels which are part of different syllables, however, may be divided (*frí-o, acre-e-dor*).

6. **Compounds**, including those formed with prefixes, are divided morphologically (*nos-otros, des-ali-ño, dis-cul-pa*).

III. Punctuation

In Spanish a comma is often placed after an adverbial phrase introducing a sentence (*sin embargo, todos los esfuerzos fueron inútiles* however, all efforts were in vain). A subsidiary clause beginning a sentence is also followed by a comma (*si tengo tiempo, lo haré* if I have time, I'll do it, **but**: *lo haré si tengo tiempo* I'll do it if I have time).

Questions and exclamations are introduced by an inverted question mark and exclamation point respectively, which immediately precedes the question or exclamation (*Dispense usted, ¿está en casa el señor Pérez?* Excuse me, is Mr. Pérez at home?; *¡Qué lástima!* What a shame!).

English pronunciation

Vowels

[ɑː]	*father*	['fɑːðər]
[æ]	*man*	[mæn]
[e]	*get*	[get]
[ə]	*about*	[ə'baut]
[ɜ]	*absurd*	[əb'sɜːrd]
[ɪ]	*stick*	[stɪk]
[iː]	*need*	[niːd]
[ɒː]	*in-laws*	['ɪnlɒːz]
[ɔː]	*more*	[mɔːr]
[ʌ]	*mother*	['mʌðər]
[ʊ]	*book*	[bʊk]
[uː]	*fruit*	[fruːt]

Diphthongs

[aɪ]	*time*	[taɪm]
[au]	*cloud*	[klaud]
[eɪ]	*name*	[neɪm]
[ɔɪ]	*point*	[pɔɪnt]
[ou]	*oath*	[ouθ]

Consonants

[b]	*bag*	[b] [æ]
[d]	*dear*	[dɪr]
[f]	*fall*	[fɔːl]
[g]	*give*	[gɪv]
[h]	*hole*	[houl]
[j]	*yes*	[jes]
[k]	*come*	[kʌm]
[l]	*land*	[lænd]
[m]	*mean*	[miːn]
[n]	*night*	[naɪt]
[p]	*pot*	[pɑːt]
[r]	*right*	[raɪt]
[s]	*sun*	[sʌn]
[t]	*take*	[teɪk]
[v]	*vain*	[veɪn]
[w]	*wait*	[weɪt]
[z]	*rose*	[rouz]
[ŋ]	*bring*	[brɪŋ]
[ʃ]	*she*	[ʃiː]
[tʃ]	*chair*	[tʃer]
[dʒ]	*join*	[dʒɔɪn]
[ʒ]	*leisure*	['liːʒər]
[θ]	*think*	[θɪŋk]
[ð]	*the*	[ðə]

['] means that the following syllable is stressed: *ability* [ə'bɪlətɪ]

Part 1

Spanish-English Dictionary

A

a *prp* ◇ *dirección* to; **al este de** to the east of; **a casa** home; **ir a la cama / al cine** go to bed / to the movies; **vamos a Bolivia** we're going to Bolivia; **voy a casa de Marta** I'm going to Marta's (house)
◇ *situación*: **a la mesa** at the table; **al lado de** next to; **a la derecha** on the right; **a la izquierda** on the left
◇ *modo*: **a la española** the Spanish way; **a mano** by hand; **a pie** on foot; **a 50 kilómetros por hora** at fifty kilometers (*Br* kilometres) an hour
◇ *precio*: **¿a cómo** or **cuánto está?** how much is it?
◇ *objeto indirecto*: **dáselo a tu hermano** give it to your brother
◇ *objeto directo*: **vi a mi padre** I saw my father
◇ *en perífrasis verbal*: **empezar a** begin to; **jugar a las cartas** play cards; **a decir verdad** to tell the truth
◇ *para introducir pregunta*: **¿a que no lo sabes?** I bet you don't know; **a ver ... OK ...**, right ...

ábaco *m* abacus

abadía *f* abbey

abajo 1 *adv situación* below, underneath; *en edificio* downstairs; **ponlo ahí abajo** put it down there; **el cajón de abajo siguiente** the drawer below; *último* the bottom; **el último de abajo** the bottom drawer ◇ *dirección* down; *en edificio* downstairs; **cuesta abajo** downhill; **empuja hacia abajo** push down
◇ *con cantidades*: **de diez para abajo** ten or under, ten or below **2** *int*: **¡abajo los traidores!** down with the traitors!

abalanzarse ⟨1f⟩ *v/i* rush *o* surge forward; **abalanzarse sobre algo / alguien** leap *o* pounce on sth/s.o.

abalear ⟨1a⟩ *v/t S. Am.* shoot

abandonar ⟨1a⟩ **1** *v/t lugar* leave; *objeto, a alguien* abandon; *a esposa, hijos* desert; *idea* give up, abandon; *actividad* give up **2** *v/r* **abandonarse** let o.s. go; **abandonarse a** abandon o.s. to

abanicar ⟨1g⟩ **1** *v/t* fan **2** *v/r* **abanicarse** *v/r* fan o.s.

abanico *m* fan; *fig* range; **abanico eléctrico** *Méx* electric fan

abaratar ⟨1a⟩ *v/t* reduce or lower the price of; *precio* reduce, lower

abarcar ⟨1g⟩ *v/t territorio* cover; *fig* comprise, cover; *L.Am. (acaparar)* hoard, stockpile; **el libro abarca desde ... hasta ...** the book covers the period from ... to ...; **abarcar con la vista** take in

abarrotado *adj* packed

abarrotar ⟨1a⟩ **1** *v/t lugar* pack; *L.Am.* COM buy up, stockpile **2** *v/r* **abarrotarse** *L.Am. del mercado* become glutted

abarrotes *mpl L.Am. (mercancías)* groceries; **(tienda de) abarrotes** grocery store, *Br* grocer's

abarrotería *f Méx, C.Am.* grocery store, *Br* grocer's

abarrotero *m*, **-a** *f Méx, C.Am.* storekeeper, shopkeeper

abastecer ⟨2d⟩ **1** *v/t* supply **(de** with) **2** *v/r* **abastecerse** stock up **(de** on *o* with)

abastecimiento *m* supply

abasto *m*: **no dan abasto** they can't cope **(con** with)

abatí *m Rpl* corn, *Br* maize; *Parag. fermented* maize drink

abatible *adj* collapsible, folding *atr*

abatido *adj* depressed

abatimiento *m* gloom

abatir ⟨3a⟩ *v/t edificio* knock *o* pull down; *árbol* cut down, fell; AVIA shoot *o* bring down; *fig* kill; *(deprimir)* depress

abdicación *f* abdication

abdicar ⟨1g⟩ *v/t* abdicate

abdomen *m* abdomen

abdominal *adj* abdominal

abdominales *mpl* sit-ups

abecedario *m* alphabet

abedul *m* birch

abeja *f* zo bee

abejorro *m* bumblebee

aberración *f* aberration

abertura *f* opening

abeto *m* fir (tree)

abiertamente *adv* openly

abierto 1 *part* → **abrir 2** *adj tb persona* open; **está abierto a nuevas ideas** *fig* he's open to new ideas

abigarrado *adj* multicolo(u)red

abismo *m* abyss; *fig* gulf

ablandar ⟨1a⟩ **1** *v/t tb fig* soften **2** *v/r*

ablandarse soften, get softer; *fig* relent

ablande *m Arg* AUTO running in

abnegación *f* self-denial

abnegado *adj* selfless

abocado *adj* doomed; *abocado al fracaso* doomed to failure, destined to fail

abochornar ⟨1a⟩ **1** *v/t* embarrass **2** *v/r* **abochornarse** feel embarrassed

abogacía *f* law

abogaderas *fpl L.Am.* F *(discusiones)* arguments

abogado *m*, **-a** *f* lawyer; *en tribunal superior* attorney, *Br* barrister; *no le faltaron abogados fig* there were plenty of people who defended him

abogar ⟨1h⟩ *v/i*: *abogar por alguien* defend; *algo* advocate

abolición *f* abolition

abolir ⟨3a⟩ *v/t* abolish

abollado *adj* dented

abolladura *f* dent

abollar ⟨1a⟩ *v/t* dent

abombado *adj S. Am.* F *comida* rotten, bad; F *(tonto)* dopey F

abombarse *S. Am. de comida* go off, go bad

abominable *adj* abominable

abominar ⟨1a⟩ *v/t* detest, loathe

abonado *m*, **-a** *f* subscriber; *a teléfono, gas, electricidad* customer; *a ópera, teatro* season-ticket holder

abonar ⟨1a⟩ **1** *v/t* COM pay; AGR fertilize; *Méx* pay on account; *abonar el terreno fig* sow the seeds **2** *v/r* **abonarse** *a espectáculo* buy a season ticket (*a* for); *a revista* take out a subscription (*a* to)

abono *m* COM payment; AGR fertilizer; *para espectáculo, transporte* season ticket

abordar ⟨1a⟩ *v/t* MAR board; *tema, asunto* broach, raise; *problema* tackle, deal with; *a una persona* approach

aborigen **1** *adj* native, indigenous **2** *m/f* native

aborrecer ⟨2d⟩ *v/t* loathe, detest

abortar ⟨1a⟩ **1** *v/i* MED *espontáneamente* miscarry; *de forma provocada* have an abortion **2** *v/t* *plan* foil

abortivo *adj* abortion *atr*; *píldora* **-a** abortion pill

aborto *m espontáneo* miscarriage; *provocado* abortion; *fig* F freak F; *tener un aborto* have a miscarriage

abotonar ⟨1a⟩ *v/t* button up

abra *f L.Am.* clearing

abrasador *adj* scorching (hot)

abrasar ⟨1a⟩ **1** *v/t* burn **2** *v/i del sol* burn, scorch; *de bebida, comida* be boiling hot **3** *v/r* **abrasarse**: *abrasarse de sed* F be parched F; *abrasarse de calor* F be swel-

tering F; *abrasarse de pasión lit* be aflame with passion *lit*

abrazar ⟨1f⟩ **1** *v/t* hug **2** *v/r* **abrazarse** embrace

abrazo *m* hug; *dar un abrazo a alguien* hug s.o., give s.o. a hug; *un abrazo en carta* best wishes; *más íntimo* love

abrebotellas *m inv* bottle opener

abrelatas *m inv* can opener; *Br tb* tin opener

abreviar ⟨1b⟩ *v/t* shorten; *palabra* abbreviate; *texto* abridge

abreviatura *f* abbreviation

abridor *m* bottle opener

abrigado *adj* warmly dressed

abrigar ⟨1h⟩ *v/t* wrap up; *esperanzas* hold out; *duda* entertain **2** *v/r* **abrigarse** wrap up warm; *abrigarse del frío* (take) shelter from the cold

abrigo *m* coat; *(protección)* shelter; *ropa de abrigo* warm clothes; *al abrigo de* in the shelter of

abril *m* April

abrir ⟨3a; *part abierto* ⟩ **1** *v/t* open; *túnel* dig; *grifo* turn on; *le abrió el apetito* it gave him an appetite **2** *v/i de persona* open up; *de ventana, puerta* open; *en un abrir y cerrar de ojos* in the twinkling of an eye **3** *v/r* **abrirse** open; *abrirse a algo fig* open up to sth; *abrirse paso entre* make one's way through

abrochar ⟨1a⟩ **1** *v/t* do up; *cinturón de seguridad* fasten **2** *v/r* **abrocharse** do up; *cinturón de seguridad* fasten; *tendremos que abrocharnos el cinturón* we'll have to tighten our belts

abrumador *adj* overwhelming

abrumar ⟨1a⟩ *v/t* overwhelm (*con or de* with); *abrumado de or con trabajo* snowed under with work

abrupto *adj* *terreno* rough; *pendiente* steep; *tono, respuesta* abrupt; *cambio* sudden

absentismo *m* absenteeism; *absentismo escolar* truancy

absolución *f* absolution

absolutamente *adv* absolutely; *no entendió absolutamente nada* he didn't understand a thing

absolutismo *m* absolutism

absoluto *adj* absolute; *en absoluto* not at all

absolver ⟨2h; *part absuelto* ⟩ *v/t* JUR acquit; REL absolve

absorbente *adj* absorbent

absorber ⟨2a⟩ *v/t* absorb; *(consumir)* take; *(cautivar)* absorb

absorto *adj* absorbed (*en* in), engrossed (*en* in)

abstemio 1 *adj* teetotal **2** *m*, **-a** *f* teetotal-(l)er

abstención *f* abstention

abstenerse ⟨2l⟩ *v/r* refrain (**de** from); POL abstain

abstinencia *f* abstinence; **síndrome de abstinencia** MED withdrawal symptoms *pl*

abstracto *adj* abstract

abstraerse ⟨2p; *part* **abstraído**⟩ > *v/r* shut o.s. off (**de** from)

abstraído 1 *adj* preoccupied; **abstraído en algo** engrossed in sth **2** *part* → **abstraerse**

absuelto *part* → **absolver**

absurdo 1 *adj* absurd **2** *m*: **es un absurdo que** it's absurd that

abuchear ⟨1a⟩ *v/t* boo

abucheo(s) *m* (*pl*) booing *sg*, boos *pl*

abuela *f* grandmother; F *persona mayor* old lady; **¡cuéntaselo a tu abuela!** F don't try to put one over on me! F, *Br* pull the other one! F

abuelo *m* grandfather; F *persona mayor* old man; **abuelos** grandparents

abultado *adj* bulging; *derrota* heavy

abultamiento *m* bulge

abultar ⟨1a⟩ *v/t* be bulky; **no abulta casi nada** it takes up almost no room at all

abundancia *f* abundance; **había comida en abundancia** there was plenty of food

abundante *adj* plentiful, abundant

abundar ⟨1a⟩ *v/i* be plentiful *o* abundant

aburguesarse ⟨1a⟩ *v/r* desp become bourgeois *o* middle class

aburrido *adj* (*que aburre*) boring; (*que se aburre*) bored; **aburrido de algo** bored *o* fed up F with sth

aburrimiento *m* boredom

aburrir ⟨3a⟩ **1** *v/t* bore **2** *v/t* **aburrirse** get bored; **aburrirse de algo** get bored *o* fed up F with sth; **aburrirse como una ostra** F get bored stiff F

abusado *adj Méx* F smart, clever; **¡abusado!** look out!

abusar ⟨1a⟩ *v/i*: **abusar de** *poder, confianza* abuse; *persona* take advantage of; **abusar del alcohol** drink too much; **abusar sexualmente de alguien** sexually abuse s.o.

abusivo *adj* JUR unfair

abuso *m* abuse; **abusos** *pl* **deshonestos** indecent assault *sg*

A.C. *abr* (= **antes de Cristo**) BC (= before Christ)

acá *adv* here; **de acá para allá** from here to there; **de entonces para acá** since then

acabado *m* finish

acabar ⟨1a⟩ **1** *v/t* finish **2** *v/i de persona* finish; *de función, acontecimiento* finish, end; **acabé haciéndolo yo** I ended up doing it myself; **acabar con** put an end to; *caramelos* finish off; *persona* destroy; **acabar de hacer algo** have just done sth; **va a acabar mal** F *persona* he'll come to no good; **esto va a acabar mal** F this is going to end badly **3** *v/r* **acabarse** *de actividad* finish, end; *de pan, dinero* run out; **se nos ha acabado el azúcar** we've run out of sugar; **¡se acabó!** that's that!

acacia *f* acacia

academia *f* academy; **academia de idiomas** language school; **academia militar** military academy

académico 1 *adj* academic **2** *m*, **-a** *f* academician

acalenturarse ⟨1a⟩ *v/r L.Am.* (*afiebrarse*) get a temperature *o* fever

acallar ⟨1a⟩ *v/t tb fig* silence

acalorarse ⟨1a⟩ *v/r* (*enfadarse*) get worked up; (*sofocarse*) get embarrassed

acampada *f* camp; **ir de acampada** go camping

acampar ⟨1a⟩ *v/i* camp

acantilado *m* cliff

acaparar ⟨1a⟩ *v/t* hoard, stockpile; *tiempo* take up; *interés* capture; (*monopolizar*) monopolize

acápite *m L.Am.* section; (*párrafo*) paragraph

acaramelado *adj fig* F lovey-dovey F

acariciar ⟨1b⟩ *v/t* caress; *perro* stroke; **acariciar una idea** *fig* contemplate an idea

acarrear ⟨1a⟩ *v/t* carry; *fig* give rise to, cause

acaso *adv* perhaps; **por si acaso** just in case

acatar ⟨1a⟩ *v/t* comply with, obey

acatarrarse ⟨1a⟩ *v/r* catch a cold

acaudalado *adj* wealthy, well-off

acceder ⟨2a⟩ *v/i* (*ceder*) agree (**a** to), accede (**a** to) *fml*; **acceder a lugar** gain access to; *cargo* accede to *fml*

accesible *adj* accessible

acceso *m tb* INFOR access; *de fiebre* attack, bout; *de tos* fit; **de difícil acceso** inaccessible

accesorio 1 *adj* incidental **2** *m* accessory

accidentado 1 *adj terreno, camino* rough; *viaje* eventful **2** *m*, **-a** *f* casualty

accidental *adj* (*no esencial*) incidental; (*casual*) chance *atr*

accidente *m* accident; (*casualidad*) chance; GEOG feature; **accidente de tráfico** *or* **de circulación** road traffic accident, RTA; **accidente laboral** industrial accident

acción f action; **acciones** pl COM stock sg, Br shares; **poner en acción** put into action

accionar ⟨1a⟩ v/t activate

accionista m/f stockholder, Br shareholder

acebo m holly

acechar ⟨1a⟩ v/t lie in wait for

acecho m: **al acecho** lying in wait

aceite m oil; **aceite de girasol / oliva** sunflower / olive oil; **aceite lubricante** lubricating oil

aceitera f oilcan; GASTR cruet

aceitoso adj oily

aceituna f olive

aceleración f acceleration

acelerador m accelerator

acelerar ⟨1a⟩ **1** v/t motor rev up; fig speed up; **aceleró el coche** she accelerated **2** v/i accelerate **3** v/r **acelerarse** L.Am. F (enojarse) lose one's cool

acelgas fpl BOT Swiss chard sg

acento m en ortografía, pronunciación accent; (énfasis) stress, emphasis; **poner el acento en** fig stress, emphasize

acentuar ⟨1e⟩ **1** v/t stress; fig accentuate, emphasize **2** v/r **acentuarse** become more pronounced

acepción f sense, meaning

aceptable adj acceptable

aceptación f acceptance; (éxito) success

aceptar ⟨1a⟩ v/t accept

acequia f irrigation ditch

acera f sidewalk, Br pavement; **ser de la otra acera, ser de la acera de enfrente** F be gay

acerca adv: **acerca de** about

acercar ⟨1g⟩ **1** v/t bring closer; **acercar a alguien a un lugar** give s.o. a ride (Br lift) somewhere **2** v/r **acercarse** approach; (ir) go; de grupos, países come closer together; de fecha draw near; **se acercó a mí** she came up to me o approached me; **acércate** come closer; **no te acerques a la pared** don't get close to the wall

acero m steel; **acero inoxidable** stainless steel

acertado adj comentario apt; elección good, wise; **estar muy acertado** be dead right

acertar ⟨1k⟩ **1** v/t respuesta get right; **al hacer una conjetura** guess **2** v/i be right; **acertar con algo** get sth right

acertijo m riddle, puzzle

achacar ⟨1g⟩ v/t attribute (**a** to)

achantarse ⟨1a⟩ v/r F keep quiet, keep

one's mouth shut F

achaque m ailment

achatado adj flattened

achatarse ⟨1a⟩ v/r be flattened

achicharrar ⟨1a⟩ v/t **1** burn **2** v/r **achicharrarse** fig roast F

achinado adj L.Am. oriental-looking

achinero m C.Am. vendedor peddler

achiquitarse ⟨1a⟩ v/r L.Am. become frightened o scared

achisparse ⟨1a⟩ v/r F get tipsy F

acholar ⟨1a⟩ v/t S. Am. embarrass

achuchar ⟨1a⟩ v/t fig F pester, nag

achuchón m F squeeze, hug; (empujón) push; **le dio un achuchón** desmayo she felt faint

achuras fpl S. Am. variety meat sg, Br offal sg

aciago adj fateful

acicalarse ⟨1a⟩ v/r get dressed up

acidez f acidity; **acidez de estómago** heartburn

ácido 1 adj tb fig sour, acid **2** m acid

acierto m idea good idea; respuesta correct answer; habilidad skill

aclamación f acclaim

aclamar ⟨1a⟩ v/t acclaim

aclaración f clarification

aclarar ⟨1a⟩ **1** v/t duda, problema clarify, clear up; ropa, vajilla rinse **2** v/i de día break, dawn; del tiempo clear up **3** v/r **aclararse: aclararse la voz** clear one's throat; **no me aclaro** F I don't understand; por cansancio, ruido etc I can't think straight

aclimatarse ⟨1a⟩ v/r acclimatize, become acclimatized

acné m acne

ACNUR abr (= **Alto Comisionado de las Naciones Unidas para los Refugiados**) UNHCR (= United Nations High Commission for Refugees)

acobardar ⟨1a⟩ **1** v/t daunt **2** v/r **acobardarse** get frightened, lose one's nerve

acodarse ⟨1a⟩ v/r lean (one's elbows) (**en** on)

acogedor adj welcoming; lugar cozy, Br cosy

acoger ⟨2c⟩ **1** v/t receive; en casa take in; **acoger con satisfacción** welcome, greet with satisfaction **2** v/r **acogerse: acogerse a algo** have recourse to sth

acogida f reception; **tener buena acogida** get a good reception, be well received

acojonar ⟨1a⟩ **1** v/t V (asustar) scare the shit out of P; (asombrar) knock out F, blow away P **2** v/r **acojonarse** V be shit scared P

acolchado adj Rpl quilted

acolchonar ⟨1a⟩ v/t Rpl quilt
acomedido adj L.Am. obliging, helpful
acomedirse ⟨3l⟩ v/r Méx offer to help
acometer ⟨2a⟩ 1 v/t attack; tarea, proyecto
undertake, tackle 2 v/i attack; **acometer
contra algo** attack sth
acomodado adj well-off
acomodador m usher
acomodadora f usherette
acomodar ⟨1a⟩ 1 v/t (adaptar) adapt; a alguien accommodate 2 v/r acomodarse
make o.s. comfortable; (adaptarse) adapt
(a to)
acompañamiento m accompaniment
acompañante m/f companion; MÚS ac-
companist
acompañar ⟨1a⟩ v/t (ir con) go with, accompany fml; (permanecer con) keep
company; MÚS, GASTR accompany
acompaño m C.Am. (reunión) meeting
acomplejar ⟨1a⟩ 1 v/t: **acomplejar a alguien** give s.o. a complex 2 v/r acomple-
jarse get a complex
acondicionar ⟨1a⟩ v/t un lugar equip, fit
out; pelo condition
acongojar ⟨1a⟩ v/t lit grieve lit, distress
aconsejable adj advisable
aconsejar ⟨1a⟩ v/t advise
acontecer ⟨2d⟩ v/i take place, occur
acontecimiento m event
acopio m: **hacer acopio de** gather, mus-
ter
acoplar ⟨1a⟩ 1 v/t piezas fit together 2 v/r
acoplarse de persona fit in (a with); de
nave espacial dock (a with); de piezas
fit together
acorazado adj armo(u)red
acordar ⟨1m⟩ 1 v/t agree 2 acordarse v/r
remember; ¿te acuerdas de él? do you
remember him?
acorde 1 adj: **acorde con** appropriate to,
in keeping with 2 m MÚS chord
acordeón m accordion
acordeonista m/f accordionist
acordonar ⟨1a⟩ v/t cordon off
acorralar ⟨1a⟩ v/t tb fig corner
acortar ⟨1a⟩ 1 v/t shorten 2 v/i take a short
cut 3 v/r acortarse get shorter
acosar ⟨1a⟩ v/t hound, pursue; con preguntas bombard (con with)
acosijar ⟨1a⟩ v/t Méx badger, pester
acoso m fig hounding, harrassment; **acoso sexual** sexual harrassment
acostar ⟨1m⟩ 1 v/t put to bed 2 v/r acostarse go to bed; (tumbarse) lie down;
acostarse con alguien go to bed with
s.o., sleep with s.o.
acostumbrado adj (habitual) usual; **estar
acostumbrado a algo** be used to sth

acostumbrar ⟨1a⟩ 1 v/t get used (a to) 2
v/i: acostumbraba a venir a este café
todas las mañanas he used to come
to this café every morning 3 v/r acostumbrarse get used (a to); **se acostum-
bró a levantarse temprano** he got used
to getting up early
ácrata m/f & adj anarchist
acre adj olor acrid; crítica biting
acrecentar ⟨1k⟩ 1 v/t increase 2 v/r acre-
centarse increase, grow
acreditar ⟨1a⟩ 1 v/t diplomático etc ac-
credit (como as); (avalar) prove; **un documento que lo acredita como el propietario** a document that is proof of his
ownership 2 v/r acreditarse acquire a
good reputation
acreedor m, acreedora f creditor
acreencia f L.Am. credit
acribillar ⟨1a⟩ v/t: **acribillar a alguien a
balazos** riddle s.o. with bullets; **acribillar a alguien a preguntas** bombard
s.o. with questions
acrílico m/adj acrylic
acristalar ⟨1a⟩ v/t glaze
acróbata m/f acrobat
acrobático adj acrobatic; **vuelo acrobático** stunt flight
acta(s) f (pl) minutes pl
actitud f (disposición) attitude; (posición)
position
activar ⟨1a⟩ v/t activate; (estimular) stimulate
actividad f activity
activista m/f POL activist
activo 1 adj active; **en activo** on active
service; **población -a** labo(u)r force 2
m COM assets pl
acto m (acción), TEA act; ceremonia ceremony; **acto sexual** sexual intercourse;
acto seguido immediately afterward(s);
en el acto instantly, there and then
actor m actor
actriz f actress
actuación f TEA performance; (intervención) intervention
actual adj present, current; **un tema muy
actual** a very topical issue
actualidad f current situation; **en la actualidad** at present, presently; (hoy en
día) nowadays; **actualidades** current affairs
actualizar ⟨1f⟩ v/t bring up to date, update
actualmente adv currently
actuar ⟨1e⟩ v/i (obrar, ejercer), TEA act;
MED work, act
acuarela f watercolo(u)r
acuario m aquarium

Acuario m/f inv ASTR Aquarius
acuático adj aquatic; **deporte acuático** water sport
acuchillar ⟨1a⟩ v/t stab
acuciante adj pressing, urgent
acudir ⟨3a⟩ v/i come; **acudir a alguien** turn to s.o.; **acudir a las urnas** go to the polls
acueducto m aqueduct
acuerdo m agreement; **estar de acuerdo con** agree with; **llegar a un acuerdo, ponerse de acuerdo** come to o reach an agreement (**con** with); **de acuerdo con algo** in accordance with sth; **¡de acuerdo!** all right!, OK!
acumulación f accumulation
acumular ⟨1a⟩ **1** v/t accumulate **2** v/r acumularse accumulate
acunar ⟨1a⟩ v/t rock
acuñar ⟨1a⟩ v/t monedas mint; término, expresión coin
acuoso adj watery
acupuntura f acupuncture
acurrucarse ⟨1g⟩ v/r curl up
acusación f accusation
acusado m, -a f defendant
acusar ⟨1a⟩ v/t accuse (**de** of); JUR charge (**de** with); (manifestar) show; **acusar recibo de** acknowledge receipt of
acuse m: **acuse de recibo** acknowledg(e)ment
acusetas m/f inv S. Am. F tattletale F, Br tell-tale F
acusica m/f F tattletale F, Br tell-tale F
acústica f acoustics
acústico adj acoustic
adaptable adj adaptable
adaptación f adaptation; **adaptación cinematográfica** screen o movie version
adaptador m adaptor
adaptar ⟨1a⟩ **1** v/t adapt **2** adaptarse v/r adapt (**a** to)
A. de C. abr (= año de Cristo) AD (= Anno Domini)
adecentar ⟨1a⟩ v/t straighten up, tidy up
adecuadamente adv properly
adecuado adj suitable, appropriate
adecuar ⟨1d⟩ **1** v/t adapt (**a** to) **2** v/r adecuarse fit in (**a** with)
adefesio m fig F monstrosity F; persona freak F; **estar hecho un adefesio** look a sight
a. de J.C. abr (= antes de Jesucristo) BC (= before Christ)
adelantado adj advanced; **por adelantado** in advance; **ir adelantado** de un reloj be fast
adelantamiento m AUTO passing maneuver, Br overtaking manoeuvre
adelantar ⟨1a⟩ **1** v/t mover move forward;

reloj put forward; AUTO pass, Br overtake; dinero advance; (conseguir) achieve, gain **2** v/i de un reloj be fast; (avanzar) make progress; AUTO pass, Br overtake **3** v/r adelantarse mover move forward; (ir delante) go on ahead; de estación, cosecha be early; de un reloj gain; **se me adelantó** she beat me to it, she got there first
adelante adv en espacio forward; **seguir adelante** carry on, keep going; **¡adelante!** come in; **más adelante** en tiempo later on; **de ahora** o **de aquí en adelante** from now on; **salir adelante** fig: de persona succeed; de proyecto go ahead
adelanto m tb COM advance
adelfa f BOT oleander
adelgazante adj weight-reducing, slimming atr
adelgazar ⟨1f⟩ **1** v/t lose **2** v/i lose weight
ademán m gesture; **hacer ademán de** make as if to
además adv as well, besides **2** prp: **además de** as well as
adentrarse ⟨1a⟩ v/r: **adentrarse en** territorio penetrate; tema go into
adentro 1 adv inside; **¡adentro!** get inside!; **mar adentro** out to sea; **adentro de** L.Am. inside **2** mpl: **para sus adentros** to oneself
adepto m follower; fig supporter
aderezar ⟨1f⟩ v/t con especias season; ensalada dress; fig liven up
adeudar ⟨1a⟩ v/t owe
adherente adj adhesive
adherir ⟨3i⟩ **1** v/i stick, adhere fml **2** v/t stick **3** v/r adherirse a superficie stick (**a** to), adhere (**a** to) fml; **adherirse a una organización** become a member of o join an organization; **adherirse a una idea** support an idea
adhesivo m/adj adhesive
adicción f addiction; **adicción a las drogas** drug addiction
adicional adj additional
adictivo adj additive
adicto 1 adj addicted (**a** to); **ser adicto al régimen** be a supporter of the regime **2** m, -a f addict
adiestrar ⟨1a⟩ v/t train
adinerado adj wealthy
adiós 1 int goodbye, bye; al cruzarse hello **2** m goodbye; **decir adiós** say goodbye (**a** to)
aditivo m additive
adivinanza f riddle
adivinar ⟨1a⟩ v/t guess; de adivino foretell
adjetivo m adjective
adjudicar ⟨1g⟩ **1** v/t award **2** v/r adjudi-

carse win
adjuntar ⟨1a⟩ *v/t* enclose
adm. *abr* (= **administración**) admin (= administration)
administración *f* administration; *de empresa etc* management; (*gobierno*) administration, government; **administración pública** civil service
administrador *m*, **administradora** *f* administrator; *de empresa etc* manager
administrar ⟨1a⟩ *v/t medicamento, sacramentos* administer, give; *empresa* run, manage; *bienes* manage
administrativo 1 *adj* administrative **2** *m*, **-a** *f* administrative assistant
admirable *adj* admirable
admiración *f* admiration; **signo de admiración** exclamation mark
admirador *m*, **admiradora** *f* admirer
admirar ⟨1a⟩ **1** *v/t* admire; (*asombrar*) amaze **2** *v/r* **admirarse** be amazed (**de** at *o* by)
admisible *adj* admissible
admisión *f* admission; **derecho de admisión** right of admission
admitir ⟨3a⟩ *v/t* (*aceptar*) accept; (*reconocer*) admit
admón. *abr* (= **administración**) admin (= administration)
ADN *abr* (= **ácido desoxirribonucleico**) DNA (= deoxyribonucleic acid)
adobar ⟨1a⟩ *v/t* GASTR marinate
adobera *f Méx type of mature cheese*
adobo *m* GASTR marinade
adoctrinar ⟨1a⟩ *v/t* indoctrinate
adolecer ⟨2d⟩ *v/i* suffer (**de** from)
adolescencia *f* adolescence
adolescente *m/f* adolescent
adonde *adv* where
adónde *interr* where
adopción *f* adoption
adoptar ⟨1a⟩ *v/t* adopt
adoptivo *adj padres* adoptive; *hijo* adopted
adoquín *m* paving stone
adorable *adj* lovable, adorable
adoración *f* adoration
adorar ⟨1a⟩ *v/t* love, adore; REL worship
adormecer ⟨2d⟩ **1** *v/t* make sleepy **2** *v/r* **adormecerse** doze off
adormidera *f* BOT poppy
adormilado *adj* sleepy
adormilarse ⟨1a⟩ *v/r* doze off
adornar ⟨1a⟩ *v/t* decorate
adorno *m* ornament; *de Navidad* decoration
adosar ⟨1a⟩ *v/t*: **adosar algo a algo** put sth (up) against sth
adquirir ⟨3i⟩ *v/t* acquire; (*comprar*) buy

adquisición *f* acquisition; **hacer una buena adquisición** make a good purchase
adquisitivo *adj*: **poder adquisitivo** purchasing power
adrede *adv* on purpose, deliberately
adrenalina *f* adrenaline
aduana *f* customs
aduanero 1 *adj* customs *atr* **2** *m*, **-a** *f* customs officer
aducir ⟨3o⟩ *v/t razones, argumentos* give, put forward; (*alegar*) claim
adueñarse ⟨1a⟩ *v/r*: **adueñarse de** take possession of
adulación *f* flattery
adular ⟨1a⟩ *v/t* flatter
adulón 1 *adj S. Am.* fawning **2** *m*, **-ona** *f* flatterer
adúltera *f* adulteress
adulterar ⟨1a⟩ *v/t* adulterate
adulterio *m* adultery; **cometer adulterio** commit adultery
adúltero 1 *adj* adulterous **2** *m* adulterer
adultez *f* adulthood
adulto 1 *adj* adult; **edad -a** adulthood **2** *m*, **-a** *f* adult
adusto *adj paisaje* harsh; *persona* stern, severe; *L.Am.* (*inflexible*) stubborn
adverbio *m* adverb
adversario *m*, **-a** *f* adversary, opponent
adverso *adj* adverse
advertencia *f* warning
advertir ⟨3i⟩ *v/t* warn (**de** about, of); (*notar*) notice
adyacente *adj* adjacent
aéreo *adj air atr*; *vista, fotografía* aerial; **compañía -a** airline
aerobic, aeróbic *m* aerobics
aerodinámico *adj* aerodynamic
aeroespacial *adj* aerospace *atr*
aerolínea *f* airline
aeromozo *m*, **-a** *f L.Am.* flight attendant
aeronáutico *adj* aeronautical
aeropuerto *m* airport
aerosol *m* aerosol
afable *adj* pleasant, affable
afamado *adj* famous
afán *m* (*esfuerzo*) effort; (*deseo*) eagerness; **sin afán de lucro** *organización* not-for-profit, non-profit (*making*)
afanar ⟨1a⟩ **1** *v/i C.Am.* (*ganar dinero*) make money **2** *v/t C.Am. dinero* make; *Rpl* F (*robar*) pinch F **3** *v/r* **afanarse** make an effort
afección *f* MED complaint, condition
afectado *adj* (*afligido*) upset (**por** by); (*amanerado*) affected
afectar ⟨1a⟩ *v/t* (*producir efecto en*) affect; (*conmover*) upset, affect; (*fingir*)

feign
afectivo adj emotional
afecto m affection; **tener afecto a alguien** be fond of s.o.
afectuoso adj affectionate
afeitada f shave
afeitado m shave
afeitadora f electric razor
afeitar ⟨1a⟩ **1** v/t shave; barba shave off **2** v/r afeitarse shave, have a shave
afeminado adj effeminate
aferrarse ⟨1k⟩ v/r fig cling (**a** to)
Afganistán Afghanistan
afianzar ⟨1f⟩ **1** v/t fig strengthen **2** v/r afianzarse become consolidated
afición f love (**por** of); (pasatiempo) pastime, hobby; **la afición** DEP the fans
aficionado 1 adj: **ser aficionado a** be interested in, Br tb be keen on **2** m, -a f enthusiast; **no profesional** amateur; **un partido de aficionados** an amateur game
aficionarse ⟨1a⟩ v/r become interested (**a** in)
afiebrarse ⟨1a⟩ v/r L.Am. develop a fever
afilado adj sharp
afilador m sharpener
afilalápices m inv pencil sharpener
afilar ⟨1a⟩ **1** v/t sharpen; L.Am. F (halagar) flatter, butter up F; S. Am. (seducir) seduce **2** v/r afilarse S. Am. F (prepararse) get ready
afiliarse ⟨1a⟩ v/r: **afiliarse a un partido** become a member of a party, join a party
afinar ⟨1a⟩ v/t MÚS tune; punta sharpen; fig perfect, fine-tune
afincarse ⟨1g⟩ v/r settle
afinidad f affinity
afirmación f statement; declaración positiva affirmation
afirmar ⟨1a⟩ v/t state, declare
afirmativo adj affirmative
afligido adj upset
afligir ⟨3c⟩ **1** v/t afflict; (apenar) upset; L.Am. F (golpear) beat up **2** v/r afligirse get upset
aflojar ⟨1a⟩ **1** v/t nudo, tornillo loosen; F dinero hand over **2** v/i de tormenta abate; de viento, fiebre drop **3** v/r aflojarse come o work loose
afluente m tributary
afmo. abr (= **afectísimo**): **su afmo** Yours truly
afónico adj: **está afónico** he has lost his voice
aforo m capacity
afortunado adj lucky, fortunate
afrecho f Arg bran
África Africa; **África del Sur** South Afri-

ca
africano 1 adj African **2** m, -a f African
afrodisíaco m aphrodisiac
afrontar ⟨1a⟩ v/t face (up to)
afuera adv outside
afueras fpl outskirts
agachar ⟨1a⟩ **1** v/i duck **2** v/r agacharse bend down; (acuclillarse) crouch down; L.Am. (rendirse) give in
agalla f zo gill; **tener agallas** F have guts F
agarrado adj fig F mean, stingy F
agarrar ⟨1a⟩ **1** v/t (asir) grab; L.Am. (tomar) take; L.Am. (atrapar, pescar), resfriado catch; L.Am. velocidad gather, pick up; **agarrar una calle** L.Am. go up o along a street **2** v/i (asirse) hold on; de planta take root; L.Am. por un lugar go; **agarró y se fue** he upped and went **3** v/r agarrarse (asirse) hold on; L.Am. a golpes get into a fight
agarrón m Rpl P (pleito) fight, argument; L.Am. (tirón) pull, tug
agarrotado adj stiff
agarrotarse ⟨1a⟩ v/r de músculo stiffen up; TÉC seize up
agasajar ⟨1a⟩ v/t fête
agazaparse ⟨1a⟩ v/r crouch (down); (ocultarse) hide
agencia f agency; **agencia inmobiliaria** real estate office, Br estate agency; **agencia de viajes** travel agency
agenciarse ⟨1b⟩ v/r F get hold of
agenda f diario diary; programa schedule; de mitin agenda
agente 1 m agent **2** m/f agent; **agente de cambio y bolsa** stockbroker; **agente de policía** police officer
ágil adj agile
agilidad f agility
agilizar ⟨1f⟩ v/t speed up
agitación f POL unrest
agitar ⟨1a⟩ **1** v/t shake; brazos, pañuelo wave; fig stir up **2** v/r agitarse become agitated o worked up
aglomeración f de gente crowd
aglomerar ⟨1a⟩ v/t pile up
aglutinar ⟨1a⟩ v/t fig bring together
agobiante adj oppressive
agobiar ⟨1b⟩ **1** v/t de calor oppress; de problemas get on top of, overwhelm **2** v/r agobiarse F feel overwhelmed
agobio m: **es un agobio** it's unbearable, it's a nightmare F
agolparse ⟨1a⟩ v/r crowd together
agonía f agony; **la espera fue una agonía** the wait was unbearable
agonizante adj dying
agonizar ⟨1f⟩ v/i de persona be dying; de régimen be crumbling

agorero *adj* ominous

agosto *m* August; *hacer su agosto* F make a fortune

agotado *adj* (*cansado*) exhausted, worn out; (*terminado*) exhausted; (*vendido*) sold out

agotador *adj* exhausting

agotar ⟨1a⟩ 1 *v/t* (*cansar*) wear out, exhaust; (*terminar*) use up, exhaust 2 *v/r* agotarse (*cansarse*) get worn out, exhaust o.s.; (*terminarse*) run out, become exhausted; (*venderse*) sell out

agraciado *adj persona* attractive

agradable *adj* pleasant, nice

agradar ⟨1a⟩ *v/i*: *me agrada la idea fml* I like the idea; *nos agradaría mucho que ... fml* we would be delighted *o* very pleased if ...

agradecer ⟨2d⟩ *v/t*: *agradecer algo a alguien* thank s.o. for sth; *te lo agradezco* I appreciate it

agradecimiento *m* appreciation

agrado *m*: *ser del agrado de alguien* be to s.o.'s liking

agrandar ⟨1a⟩ 1 *v/t* make bigger 2 *v/r* agrandarse get bigger

agrario *adj* land *atr*, agrarian; *política* agricultural

agravar ⟨1a⟩ 1 *v/t* make worse, aggravate 2 *v/r* agravarse get worse, deteriorate

agravio *m* offense, *Br* offence

agredir ⟨3a⟩ *v/t* attack, assault

agregado *m*, -a *f* en universidad senior lecturer; *en colegio* senior teacher; POL attaché; *agregado cultural* cultural attaché

agregar ⟨1h⟩ *v/t* add

agresión *f* aggression

agresividad *f* aggression

agresivo *adj* aggressive

agresor *m*, agresora *f* aggressor

agreste *adj terreno* rough; *paisaje* wild

agriarse ⟨1b *or* 1c⟩ *v/r de vino* go sour; *de carácter* become bitter

agrícola *adj* agricultural, farming *atr*

agricultor *m*, agricultora *f* farmer

agricultura *f* agriculture

agridulce *adj* bittersweet

agriera *f L.Am.* heartburn

agrietarse ⟨1a⟩ *v/r* crack; *de manos, labios* chap

agringarse ⟨1h⟩ *v/r L.Am.* become Americanized

agrio *adj fruta* sour; *disputa, carácter* bitter

agrios *mpl* BOT citrus fruit *sg*

agropecuario *adj* farming *atr*, agricultural

agrupar ⟨1a⟩ 1 *v/t* group, put into groups

2 *v/r* agruparse gather

agua *f* water; *agua corriente* running water; *agua dulce* fresh water; *agua mineral* mineral water; *agua oxigenada* (hydrogen) peroxide; *agua potable* drinking water; *es agua pasada* it's water under the bridge; *está con el agua al cuello con problemas* he's up to his neck in problems F; *con deudas* he's up to his neck in debt F; *se me hace la boca agua* it makes my mouth water

aguas waters; *aguas pl residuales* effluent *sg*, sewage *sg*

aguacate *m* BOT avocado

aguacero *m* downpour

aguachento *adj CSur* watery

aguafiestas *m/f inv* partypooper F, killjoy

aguaitar ⟨1a⟩ *v/t S. Am.* spy on

aguamala *f S. Am.* jellyfish

aguamiel *f L.Am.* mixture of water and honey; *Méx* (*jugo de maguey*) agave sap

aguanieve *f* sleet

aguantar ⟨1a⟩ 1 *v/t un peso* bear, support; *respiración* hold, (*soportar*) put up with, *no lo puedo aguantar* I can't stand *o* bear it 2 *v/i* hang on, hold out 3 *v/r* aguantarse *contenerse* keep quiet; *me tuve que aguantar conformarme* I had to put up with it

aguante *m* patience; *física* stamina, endurance

aguar ⟨1a⟩ *v/t fiesta* spoil

aguardar ⟨1a⟩ 1 *v/t* wait for, await 2 *v/i* wait

aguardiente *m fruit-based alcoholic spirit*

aguarrás *m* turpentine, turps F

aguatero *m*, -a *f S. Am.* water-seller

agudeza *f de voz, sonido* high pitch; MED intensity; (*perspicacia*) sharpness; *agudeza visual* sharp-sightedness

agudizar ⟨1f⟩ *v/t un sentido* sharpen; *agudizar un problema* make a problem worse 2 *v/r* agudizarse MED get worse; *de un sentido* become sharper

agudo *adj* acute; (*afilado*) sharp; *sonido* high-pitched; (*perspicaz*) sharp

agüero *m* omen; *ser de mal agüero* be an ill omen

aguijón *m* zo sting; *fig* spur

águila *f* eagle; *¿águila o sol? Méx* heads or tails?; *ser un águila fig* be very sharp

aguilucho *m* eaglet

agüita *f L.Am.* F (*agua*) water; (*infusión*) infusion

aguja *f* needle; *de reloj* hand; *buscar una aguja en un pajar fig* look for a needle in a haystack

agujerear ⟨1a⟩ 1 *v/t* make holes in 2 *v/r* agujerearse develop holes

agujero *m* hole

agujetas *fpl* stiffness *sg*; **tener agujetas** be stiff

aguzar ⟨1f⟩ *v/t* sharpen; **aguzar el ingenio** sharpen one's wits; **aguzar el oído** prick up one's ears

ah *int* ah!

ahí *adv* there; **está por ahí** it's (somewhere) over there; *dando direcciones* it's that way

ahijada *f* goddaughter

ahijado *m* godson

ahínco *m* effort; **trabajar con ahínco** work hard

ahogado *adj en agua* drowned

ahogar ⟨1h⟩ **1** *v/t (asfixiar)* suffocate; *en agua* drown; AUTO flood; *protestas* stifle **2** *v/r ahogarse* choke; *(asfixiarse)* suffocate; *en agua* drown; AUTO flood; **ahogarse en un vaso de agua** *fig* F get in a state over nothing

ahondar ⟨1a⟩ *v/i:* **ahondar en algo** go into sth in depth

ahora *adv (en este momento)* now; *(pronto)* in a moment; **ahora mismo** right now; *por ahora* for the present, for the time being; **ahora bien** however; **desde ahora, de ahora en adelante** from now on; **¡hasta ahora!** see you soon

ahorcar ⟨1g⟩ **1** *v/t* hang **2** *v/r ahorcarse* hang o.s.

ahorita *adv L.Am. (en este momento)* (right) now; *Méx, C.Am. (pronto)* in a moment; *Méx, C.Am. (hace poco)* just now

ahorrar ⟨1a⟩ **1** *v/t* save; **ahorrar algo a alguien** save s.o. (from) sth **2** *v/i* save (up) **3** *v/r ahorrarse dinero* save; *fig* spare o.s., save o.s.

ahorro *m* saving; **ahorros** *pl* savings; **caja de ahorros** savings bank

ahulado *m C.Am., Méx* oilskin

ahumar ⟨1a⟩ *v/t* smoke

ahuyentar ⟨1a⟩ **1** *v/t* scare off *o* away **2** *v/r ahuyentarse L.Am.* run away

AI *abr (= Amnistía Internacional)* AI (= Amnesty International)

airado *adj* angry

airbag *m* AUTO airbag

aire *m* air; **aire acondicionado** air-conditioning; **al aire libre** in the open air; **a mi aire** in my own way; **estar en el aire** *fig* F be up in the air F; **hace mucho aire** it is very windy

airear ⟨1a⟩ *v/t tb fig* air

airoso *adj:* **salir airoso de algo** do well in sth

aislado *adj* isolated

aislante 1 *adj* insulating, insulation *atr* **2** *m* insulator

aislar ⟨1a⟩ **1** *v/t* isolate; EL insulate **2** *v/r aislarse* cut o.s. off

ajardinado *adj* landscaped; **zona -a** area with parks and gardens

a. J.C. *abr (= antes de Jesucristo)* BC (= before Christ)

ajedrez *m* chess

ajeno *adj propiedad, problemas etc* someone else's; **me era totalmente ajeno** it was completely alien to me; **estar ajeno a** be unaware of, be oblivious to; **por razones -as a nuestra voluntad** for reasons beyond our control

ajete *m* BOT young garlic

ajetreo *m* bustle

ají *m S. Am.* chili, *Br* chilli

ajiaco *m Col* spicy potato stew

ajillo *m:* **al ajillo** with garlic

ajo *m* BOT garlic; **estar** *or* **andar en el ajo** F be in the know F

ajuar *m de novia* trousseau

ajustar ⟨1a⟩ **1** *v/t máquina etc* adjust; *tornillo* tighten; *precio* set; **ajustar cuentas** *fig* settle a score **2** *v/i* fit **3** *v/r ajustarse el cinturón* tighten; **ajustarse a algo** *fig* keep up/with sth; **ajustarse a la ley** comply with the law

ajuste *m:* **ajuste de cuentas** settling of scores

ajusticiar ⟨1b⟩ *v/t* execute

al *prp* **a** *y art el*; **al entrar** on coming in, when we / they etc came in

ala *f* wing; MIL flank; **ala delta** hang glider; **cortar las alas a alguien** clip s.o.'s wings

alabanza *f* acclaim

alabar ⟨1a⟩ *v/t* praise, acclaim

alacena *f* larder

alacrán *m* ZO scorpion

alambrada *f* wire fence

alambrar ⟨1a⟩ *v/t* fence

alambre *m* wire; **alambre de espino** *or* **de púas** barbed wire

álamo *m* BOT poplar; **álamo temblón** aspen

alarde *m* show, display; **hacer alarde de** make a show of

alardear ⟨1a⟩ *v/i* show off *(de* about)

alargador *m* TÉC extension cord, *Br* extension lead

alargar ⟨1h⟩ **1** *v/t* lengthen; *prenda* let down; *en tiempo* prolong; *mano, brazo* stretch out **2** *v/r alargarse de sombra, día* get longer, lengthen

alarido *m* shriek; **dar alaridos** shriek

alarma *f (mecanismo, miedo)* alarm; **dar la voz de alarma** raise the alarm

alarmante *adj* alarming

alarmar ⟨1a⟩ **1** v/t alarm **2** v/r alarmarse become alarmed

alba f dawn

albahaca f BOT basil

Albania Albania

albañil m bricklayer

albaricoque m BOT apricot

albatros m inv ZO albatross

albedrío m: **libre albedrío** free will

alberca f reservoir; *Méx* (swimming) pool

albergar ⟨1h⟩ v/t (*hospedar*) put up; (*contener*) house; *esperanzas* hold out

albergue m refuge, shelter; **albergue juvenil** youth hostel

albino m, **-a** f albino

albóndiga f meatball

albornoz m bathrobe

alborotador m, **alborotadora** f rioter

alborotar ⟨1a⟩ **1** v/t stir up; (*desordenar*) disturb **2** v/i make a racket **3** v/r alborotarse get excited; (*inquietarse*) get worked up

alboroto m commotion

álbum m album

alcachofa f BOT artichoke; *de ducha* shower head

alcalde m, **-esa** f mayor

alcalino adj alkaline

alcance m reach; *de arma etc* range; *de medida* scope; *de tragedia* extent, scale; **al alcance de la mano** within reach; **¿está al alcance de tu bolsillo?** can you afford it?; **dar alcance a alguien** catch up with s.o.; **poner al alcance de alguien** put within s.o.'s reach

alcancía f L.Am. piggy bank

alcantarilla f sewer; (*sumidero*) drain

alcanzar ⟨1f⟩ **1** v/t a alguien catch up with; *lugar* reach, get to; *en nivel* reach; *cantidad* amount to; *objetivo* achieve **2** v/i en altura reach; *en cantidad* be enough; **alcanzar a oír / ver** manage to hear / see

alcaparra f BOT caper

alcayata f hook

alcázar m fortress

alce m ZO elk

alcista adj en bolsa rising, bull atr; **tendencia alcista** upward trend

alcoba f S. Am. bedroom

alcohol m alcohol; MED rubbing alcohol, *Rr* surgical spirit; **alcohol de quemar** denatured alcohol, *Br* methylated spirits sg

alcoholemia f blood alcohol level; **prueba de alcoholemia** drunkometer test, *Br* Breathalyzer® test

alcohólico 1 adj alcoholic **2** m, **-a** f alcoholic

alcoholismo m alcoholism

alcornoque m BOT cork oak; **pedazo de alcornoque** F blockhead F

alcurnia f ancestry

aldea f (small) village

aleación f alloy

aleatorio adj random

aleccionar ⟨1a⟩ v/t instruct; (*regañar*) lecture

aledaños mpl surrounding area sg; *de ciudad* outskirts

alegador adj L.Am. argumentative

alegar ⟨1h⟩ **1** v/t motivo, razón cite; **alegar que** claim o allege that **2** v/i L.Am. (*discutir*) argue; (*quejarse*) moan, gripe

alegrar ⟨1a⟩ **1** v/t make happy; (*animar*) cheer up **2** v/r alegrarse cheer up; F *bebiendo* get tipsy; **alegrarse por alguien** be pleased for s.o. (*de* about)

alegre adj (*contento*) happy; *por naturaleza* happy, cheerful; F *bebido* tipsy

alegría f happiness

alejar ⟨1a⟩ **1** v/t move away **2** v/r alejarse move away (**de** from); *de situación, ámbito* get away (**de** from); **¡no te alejes mucho!** don't go too far away!

alelar ⟨1a⟩ v/t stupefy

aleluya m & int hallelujah

alemán 1 m/adj German **2** m, **-ana** f persona German

Alemania Germany

alentado adj L.Am. encouraged

alentar ⟨1k⟩ **1** v/t (*animar*) encourage, *esperanzas* cherish **2** v/r alentarse L.Am. get better

alergia f allergy

alérgico adj allergic (**a** to)

alerta 1 adv: **estar alerta** be on the alert **2** f alert; **dar la alerta** raise the alarm; **poner en alerta** alert

alertar ⟨1a⟩ v/t alert (**de** to)

aleta f ZO fin; *de buzo* flipper; *de la nariz* wing

aletargarse ⟨1h⟩ v/r feel lethargic

aletear ⟨1a⟩ v/i flap one's wings

alevosía f treachery

alfabético adj alphabetical

alfabetizar ⟨1f⟩ v/t lista etc put into alphabetical order; **alfabetizar a alguien** teach s.o. to read and write

alfabeto m alphabet

alfalfa f BOT alfalfa

alfanumérico adj alphanumeric

alfarero m, **-a** f potter

alfil m bishop

alfiler m pin; **alfiler de gancho** *Arg* safety pin; **no cabe un alfiler** fig F there's no room for anything else

alfiletero m (*cojín*) pincushion; (*estuche*) needlecase

alfombra f carpet; *más pequeña* rug

alfombrado m L.Am. carpeting, carpets pl

alfombrar ⟨1a⟩ v/t carpet

alfombrilla f mouse mat

alga f BOT alga; *marina* seaweed

álgebra f algebra

álgido adj fig decisive

algo 1 pron en frases afirmativas something; en frases interrogativas o condicionales anything; *algo es algo* it's something, it's better than nothing **2** adv rather, somewhat

algodón m cotton; *criado entre algodones* F mollycoddled, pampered

alguacil m, **alguacilesa** f bailiff

alguien pron en frases afirmativas somebody, someone; en frases interrogativas o condicionales anybody, anyone

algún adj en frases afirmativas some; en frases interrogativas o condicionales any; *algún día* some day

alguno 1 adj en frases afirmativas some; en frases interrogativas o condicionales any; *no la influyó de modo alguno* it didn't influence her in any way; *¿has estado alguna vez en …?* have you ever been to …? **2** pron: persona somebody; *algunos opinan que …* some people think that …; *alguno se podrá usar* objeto we'll be able to use some of them

alhaja f piece of jewel(le)ry; fig gem; *alhajas* jewelry sg

alhelí m BOT wallflower

aliado m, **-a** f ally

alianza f POL alliance; (anillo) wedding ring

aliarse ⟨1c⟩ v/r form an alliance (*con* with)

alias m inv alias

alicaído adj F down F

alicatar ⟨1a⟩ v/t tile

alicates mpl pliers

aliciente m (estímulo) incentive; (atractivo) attraction

alienar ⟨1a⟩ v/t alienate

alienígena m/f alien

aliento m breath; fig encouragement

aligerar ⟨1a⟩ v/t carga lighten; *aligerar el paso* quicken one's pace

alijo m MAR consignment

alimentación f (dieta) diet; acción feeding; EL power supply

alimentar ⟨1a⟩ **1** v/t tb TÉC, fig feed; EL power **2** v/i be nourishing **3** v/r alimentarse feed o.s.; *alimentarse de algo* de persona, animal live on sth; de máquina run on sth

alimento m (comida) food; *tiene poco alimento* it has little nutritional value; *alimentos dietéticos (de régimen)* slimming aids

alineación f DEP line-up

alinear ⟨1a⟩ **1** v/t align **2** v/r alinearse (ponerse en fila) line up; POL align o.s. (*con* with)

aliñar ⟨1a⟩ v/t dress

aliño m dressing

alioli m GASTR garlic mayonnaise

alisar ⟨1a⟩ v/t smooth

alistarse ⟨1a⟩ v/r MIL enlist

aliviar ⟨1b⟩ v/t alleviate, relieve

alivio m relief

allá adv de lugar (over) there; *allá por los años veinte* back in the twenties; *más allá* further on; *más allá de* beyond; *el más allá* the hereafter; *allá él / ella* F that's up to him / her

allanamiento m: *allanamiento de morada* JUR breaking and entering

allanar ⟨1a⟩ v/t (alisar) smooth; (aplanar) level (out); obstáculos overcome

allegado m, **-a** f relation, relative

allí adv there; *por allí* over there; dando direcciones that way; *¡allí está!* there it is!

alma f soul; *se me cayó el alma a los pies* F my heart sank; *llegar al alma* conmover move deeply; herir hurt deeply; *no se ve un alma* there isn't a soul to be seen; *lo siento en el alma* I am truly sorry

almacén m warehouse; (tienda) store, shop; *grandes almacenes* pl department store sg

almacenamiento m storage; *almacenamiento de datos* data storage

almacenar ⟨1a⟩ v/t tb INFOR store

almacenero m, **-a** f storekeeper, shopkeeper

almanaque m almanac

almeja f ZO clam

almenas fpl battlements

almendra f almond

almendro m almond tree

almíbar m syrup; *en almíbar* in syrup

almibarado adj fig syrupy

almidón m starch

almirante m admiral

almirez m mortar

almohada f pillow; *consultarlo con la almohada* sleep on it

almohadilla f small cushion; TÉC pad

almohadón m large cushion

almorranas fpl piles

almorzada f Méx lunch

almorzar ⟨1f & 1m⟩ **1** v/i al mediodía have

lunch; *a media mañana* have a mid-morning snack **2** *v/t: almorzar algo al mediodía* have sth for lunch; *a media mañana* have sth as a mid-morning snack

almuerzo *m al mediodía* lunch; *a media mañana* mid-morning snack; *almuerzo de trabajo* working lunch

¿ aló? *L.Am.* hello?

alocado 1 *adj* crazy **2** *m, -a f* crazy fool

áloe *m* BOT aloe

alojamiento *m* accommodations *pl, Br* accommodation

alojar ⟨1a⟩ **1** *v/t* accommodate **2** *v/r* alojarse stay (**en** in)

alojo *m L.Am.* → *alojamiento*

alondra *f* ZO lark

alopecia *f* MED alopecia

alpaca *f animal, lana* alpaca

alpargata *f Esp* espadrille

alpinismo *m* mountaineering

alpinista *m/f* mountaineer, climber

alpiste *m* birdseed

alquilar ⟨1a⟩ *v/t de usuario* rent; *de dueño* rent out

alquiler *m acción: de coche etc* rental; *de casa* renting; *dinero* rental, *Br* rent; *alquiler de coches* car rental, *Br tb* car hire

alquitrán *m* tar

alrededor 1 *adv* around **2** *prp: alrededor de* around

alrededores *mpl* surrounding area *sg*

alta *f* MED discharge; *dar de alta* MED discharge; *darse de alta en organismo* register

altanero *adj* arrogant

altar *m* altar; *llevar al altar* marry

altavoz *m* loudspeaker

alteración *f* alteration

alterar ⟨1a⟩ **1** *v/t (cambiar)* alter; *a alguien* upset; *alterar el orden público* cause a breach of the peace **2** *v/r* alterarse get upset (**por** because of)

altercado *m* argument, altercation *fml*

alternar ⟨1a⟩ **1** *v/t* alternate; *alternar el trabajo con el descanso* alternate work and study **2** *v/i* mix **3** *v/r* alternarse alternate, take turns

alternativa *f* alternative

alternativo *adj* alternative

alterno *adj* alternate; *corriente -a* EL alternating current; *en días alternos* on alternate days

Alteza *f título* Highness

altibajos *mpl* ups and downs

altillo *m (desván)* attic; *en armario* top (part of the) closet

altiplano *m* high plateau

aitisonante *adj* high-flown

altitud *f* altitude

altivo *adj* haughty

alto[1] **1** *adj persona* tall; *precio, número, montaña* high; *-as presiones* high pressure; *alto horno* blast furnace; *clase -a* high class; *en -a mar* on the high seas; *en voz -a* out loud **2** *adv volar, saltar* high; *hablar alto* speak loudly; *pasar por alto* overlook; *poner más alto* TV, RAD turn up; *por todo lo alto* F lavishly **3** *m (altura)* height; *Chi* pile

alto[2] *m* halt; *(pausa)* pause; *hacer un alto* stop; *alto el fuego* ceasefire; *¡alto!* halt!

altoparlante *m L.Am.* loudspeaker

altozano *m* hillock

altramuz *m planta* lupin; *semilla* lupin seed

altruismo *m* altruism

altruista *adj* altruistic

altura *f* MAT height; MÚS pitch; AVIA altitude, height; GEOG latitude; *a estas alturas* by this time, by now; *estar a la altura de algo* be up to sth F

alubia *f* BOT kidney bean

alucinación *f* hallucination

alucinado *adj* F gobsmacked F

alucinante *adj* F incredible

alucinar ⟨1a⟩ **1** *v/i* hallucinate **2** *v/t* F amaze

alucine *m: de alucine* F amazing

alucinógeno *m* hallucinogen

alud *m* avalanche

aludir ⟨3a⟩ *v/i: aludir a algo* allude to sth

aludido: darse por aludido take it personally

alumbrar ⟨1a⟩ **1** *v/t (dar luz a)* light (up) **2** *v/i* give off light

aluminio *m* aluminum, *Br* aluminium; *papel de aluminio* aluminum (*Br* aluminium) foil

alumno *m, -a f* student

alusión *f* allusion (**a** to); *hacer alusión a* refer to, allude to

aluvión *m* barrage

alza *f* rise; *en alza* rising

alzado *m, -a f L.Am.* insurgent

alzar ⟨1f⟩ **1** *v/t barrera, brazo* lift, raise; *precios* raise **2** *v/r* alzarse rise; *en armas* rise up

alzo *m C.Am.* theft

a. m. *abr* (= *ante meridiem*) a. m. (= ante meridiem)

ama *f (dueña)* owner; *ama de casa* housewife, homemaker; *ama de llaves* housekeeper; *ama de leche* or *cría* L.Am. wetnurse

amabilidad *f* kindness

amable *adj* kind (**con** to)

amaestrar ⟨1a⟩ *v/t* train

amago *m* threat; **hizo amago de levantarse** she made as if to get up; **amago
de infarto** minor heart attack

amainar ⟨1a⟩ *v/i de lluvia, viento* ease up,
slacken off

amalgamar ⟨1a⟩ **1** *v/t fig* combine **2** *v/r*
amalgamarse amalgamate

amamantar ⟨1a⟩ *v/t bebé* breastfeed; *cría*
feed

amanecer **1** ⟨2d⟩ *v/i* get light; *de persona*
wake up **2** *m* dawn

amanerado *adj* affected

amante **1** *adj* loving; **es amante de la
buena vida** he's fond of good living **2**
m/f en una relación lover; **los amantes
de la naturaleza** nature lovers

amañar ⟨1a⟩ *v/t* F rig F; *partido* fix F

amapola *f* BOT poppy

amar ⟨1a⟩ *v/t* love

amargar ⟨1h⟩ **1** *v/t día, ocasión* spoil;
amargar a alguien make s.o. bitter **2**
v/r amargarse get bitter; **amargarse
la vida** get upset

amargo *adj tb fig* bitter

amargura *f tb fig* bitterness

amarillento *adj* yellowish

amarillo *m/adj* yellow

amarrar ⟨1a⟩ *v/t L.Am. (atar)* tie

amasar ⟨1a⟩ *v/t pan* knead; *fortuna* amass

amatista *f* amethyst

amazona *f* horsewoman

amazónico *adj* GEOG Amazonian

Amazonas: **el Amazonas** the Amazon

ambages *mpl*: **decirlo sin ambages** say
it straight out

ámbar *m* amber; **el semáforo está en
ámbar** the lights are yellow, *Br* the lights
are at amber

ambición *f* ambition

ambicioso *adj* ambitious

ambidextro, ambidiestro *adj* ambidex-
trous

ambientador *m* air freshener

ambiental *adj* environmental

ambientar ⟨1a⟩ **1** *v/t película, novela* set **2**
v/r ambientarse

ambiente **1** *adj*: **medio ambiente** environment; **temperatura ambiente** room
temperature **2** *m (entorno)* environment;
(situación) atmosphere

ambigüedad *f* ambiguity

ambiguo *adj* ambiguous

ámbito *m* area; *(límite)* scope

ambo *m Arg* two-piece suit

ambos, ambas **1** *adj* both **2** *pron* both (of
us / you / them)

ambulancia *f* ambulance

ambulante **1** *adj* travel(l)ing; **venta ambulante** peddling, hawking **2** *m/f*

L.Am. (vendedor) street seller

ambulatorio **1** *adj* MED out-patient *atr* **2** *m*
out-patient clinic

amedrentar ⟨1a⟩ *v/t* terrify

amén **1** *m* amen **2** *prp*: **amén de** as well as

amenaza *f* threat; **amenaza de bomba**
bomb scare

amenazador *adj* threatening

amenazante *adj* threatening

amenazar ⟨1f⟩ **1** *v/t* threaten (**con, de**
with) **2** *v/i*: **amenazar con** threaten to;
amenaza tempestad there's a storm
brewing

amenizar ⟨1f⟩ *v/t*: **amenizar algo** make
sth more entertaining *o* enjoyable

ameno *adj* enjoyable

América America; **América del Norte**
North America; **América del Sur** South
America

americana *f* American (woman); *prenda*
jacket

americano *m/adj* American

amerizar ⟨1f⟩ *v/i de nave espacial* splash
down

ametralladora *f* machine gun

amianto *m* MIN asbestos

amígdala *f* ANAT tonsil

amigdalitis *f* MED tonsillitis

amigo **1** *adj* friendly; **ser amigo de algo**
be fond of sth **2** *m*, **-a** *f* friend; **hacerse
amigos** make friends

aminorar ⟨1a⟩ *v/t* reduce; **aminorar la
marcha** slow down

amistad *f* friendship; **amistades** friends

amistosamente *adv* amicably

amistoso *adj* friendly; *partido amistoso*
DEP friendly (game)

amnesia *f* amnesia

amnistía *f* amnesty

amo *m (dueño)* owner; HIST master

amoblado *S. Am.* **1** *adj* furnished **2** *m* furniture

amodorrarse ⟨1a⟩ *v/r* feel sleepy

amoldarse ⟨1a⟩ *v/r* adapt (**a** to)

amonestación *f* warning; DEP caution

amonestar ⟨1a⟩ *v/t reñir* reprimand; DEP
caution

amoníaco, amoniaco *m* ammonia

amontonar ⟨1a⟩ **1** *v/t* pile up **2** *v/r* amontonarse *de objetos, problemas* pile up; *de
gente* crowd together

amor *m* love; **amor mío** my love, darling;
amor propio self-respect; **por amor al
arte** *fig* just for the fun of it; **por amor
de Dios** for God's sake; **hacer el amor**
make love

amoral *adj* amoral

amoratado *adj* bruised

amordazar ⟨1f⟩ *v/t* gag; *animal, la prensa*

muzzle
amorfo *adj* shapeless
amoroso *adj* amorous
amortajar ⟨1a⟩ *v/t* shroud
amortiguador *m* AUTO shock absorber
amortiguar ⟨1i⟩ *v/t impacto* cushion; *sonido* muffle
amortizar ⟨1f⟩ *v/t* pay off; COM *bienes* charge off, *Br* write off
amotinarse ⟨1a⟩ *v/r* rebel
amp. *abr* (= *amperios*) amp (= amperes)
amparar ⟨1a⟩ **1** *v/t* protect; (*ayudar*) help **2** *v/r* **ampararse** seek shelter (*de* from); *ampararse en algo* seek protection in sth
amparo *m* protection; (*cobijo*) shelter; *al amparo de* under the protection of
ampliación *f de casa, carretera* extension; FOT enlargement; *ampliación de capital* COM increase in capital
ampliadora *f* FOT enlarger
ampliamente *adv* widely
ampliar ⟨1c⟩ *v/t plantilla* increase; *negocio* expand; *plazo, edificio* extend; FOT enlarge **2** *v/r* **ampliarse** broaden
amplio *adj casa* spacious; *gama, margen* wide; *falda* full
amplitud *f* breadth
ampolla *f* MED blister; (*botellita*) vial, *Br* phial
ampolleta *f Arg, Chi* light bulb
ampuloso *adj* pompous
amputación *f* amputation
amputar ⟨1a⟩ *v/t brazo, pierna* amputate
amueblar ⟨1a⟩ *v/t* furnish
amuermar ⟨1a⟩ *v/t* F bore
amuleto *m* charm
anabolizante *m* anabolic steroid
anacardo *m* BOT cashew
anaconda *f* ZO anaconda
anacoreta *m/f* hermit
anacrónico *adj* anachronistic
ánade *m* ZO duck
anagrama *m* anagram
anal *adj* anal
anales *mpl* annals
analfabeto **1** *adj* illiterate **2** *m*, -a *f* illiterate
analgésico **1** *adj* painkilling, analgesic **2** *m* painkiller, analgesic
análisis *m inv* analysis; *análisis de mercado* market research; *análisis de sangre* blood test; *análisis de sistemas* INFOR systems analysis
analista *m/f* analyst
analizar ⟨1f⟩ *v/t* analyze
analogía *f* analogy

analógico *adj* analog, *Br* analogue
análogo *adj* analogous
ananá(s) *m S. Am.* BOT pineapple
anarquía *f* anarchy
anárquico *adj* anarchic
anarquista **1** *adj* anarchist *atr* **2** *m/f* anarchist
anatema *m* anathema
anatomía *f* anatomy
anatómico *adj* anatomical; *asiento anatómico* AUTO anatomically designed seat
anca *f* haunch; *ancas pl de rana* GASTR frogs' legs
ancestral *adj* ancestral
ancho **1** *adj* wide, broad; *a sus -as* at ease, relaxed; *quedarse tan ancho* F carry on as if nothing had happened **2** *m* width; *ancho de vía* FERR gauge; *dos metros de ancho* two meters (*Br* metres) wide
anchoa *f* anchovy
anchura *f* width
anciana *f* old woman
anciano **1** *adj* old **2** *m* old man
ancla *f* MAR anchor
anclar ⟨1a⟩ *v/i* MAR anchor
andadas *fpl*: *volver a las andadas* F fall back into one's old ways
andador *m para bebé* baby walker; *para anciano* walker, Zimmer®
andamio *m* scaffolding
andanzas *fpl* adventures
andar ⟨1q⟩ **1** *v/i* (*caminar*) walk; (*funcionar*) work; *andando* on foot; *andar bien / mal* fig go well / badly; *andar con cuidado* be careful; *andar en algo* (*buscar*) rummage in sth; *andar tras algo* be after sth F; *andar haciendo algo* be doing sth; *¡anda!* come on! **2** *v/t* walk **3** *v/r* andarse; *andarse con bromas* kid around F
andas *fpl*: *llevar en andas* carry on one's shoulders
andén *m* platform; *L.Am.* sidewalk, *Br* pavement
Andes *mpl* Andes
andinismo *m L.Am.* mountaineering, climbing
andinista *m/f L.Am.* mountaineer, climber
andino *adj* Andean
Andorra Andorra
andrajoso *adj* ragged
andurriales *mpl*: *por estos andurriales* F around here
anécdota *f* anecdote
anegar ⟨1h⟩ **1** *v/t* flood **2** *v/r* anegarse *de campo, terreno* be flooded; *anegarse en llanto* dissolve into tears

anemia f MED an(a)emia

anémico adj an(a)emic

anestesia f MED an(a)esthesia

anestesiado adj an(a)esthetized, under F

anestesiar ⟨1b⟩ v/t an(a)esthetize

anexión f POL annexation

anexionar ⟨1a⟩ v/t POL annex

anexo 1 adj attached **2** m edificio annex, Br annex(e)

anfeta F, **anfetamina** f MED amphetamine

anfibio m/adj amphibian

anfiteatro m TEA amphitheater, Br amphitheatre; de teatro dress circle

anfitrión m host

anfitriona f hostess

ánfora f L.Am. POL ballot box; HIST amphora

ángel m angel; **ángel custodio** or **de la guarda** guardian angel

angelical adj angelic

angina f MED: **anginas** pl sore throat sg, strep throat sg; **angina de pecho** angina

anglicano 1 adj Anglican **2** m, -a f Anglican

anglicismo m Anglicism

anglófono adj English-speaking

anglosajón 1 adj Anglo-Saxon **2** m, -ona f Anglo-Saxon

angora f angora

angosto adj narrow

anguila f ZO eel

angula f ZO, GASTR elver

ángulo m MAT, fig angle

angustia f anguish

angustiado adj distraught

angustiante adj distressing

angustiar ⟨1b⟩ **1** v/t distress **2** v/r angustiarse agonize (**por** over)

angustioso adj agonizing

anhelar ⟨1a⟩ v/t long for

anhelo m longing, desire (**de** for)

anhídrido m QUÍM anhydride; **anhídrido carbónico** carbon dioxide

anidar ⟨1a⟩ v/i nest

anilla f ring; **cuaderno de anillas** ring binder; **anillas** pl DEP rings

anillo m ring; **te viene como anillo al dedo** F it suits you perfectly

animación f liveliness; en películas animation; **hay mucha animación** it's very lively

animado adj lively

animador m host; **animador turístico** events organizer

animadora f hostess; DEP cheerleader

animal 1 adj animal atr; fig stupid **2** m tb fig animal; **animal doméstico** mascota pet; de granja domestic animal

animalada f: **decir / hacer una animala-**

da F say / do something nasty

animar ⟨1a⟩ **1** v/t cheer up; (alentar) encourage **2** v/r animarse cheer up

anímico adj mental; **estado anímico** state of mind

ánimo m spirit; (coraje) encouragement; **estado de ánimo** state of mind; **con ánimo de** with the intention of; **¡ánimo!** cheer up!

animosidad f animosity

aniquilar ⟨1a⟩ v/t annihilate

anís m BOT aniseed; bebida anisette

aniversario m anniversary

ano m ANAT anus

anoche adv last night; **antes de anoche** the night before last

anochecer ⟨2d⟩ **1** v/i get dark; **anocheció** night fell, it got dark **2** m dusk

anodino adj anodyne; fig bland

anómalo adj anomalous

anonadar ⟨1a⟩ v/t: **anonadar a alguien** take s.o. aback

anónimo 1 adj anonymous **2** m poison pen letter

anorak m anorak

anorexia f MED anorexia

anoréxico adj anorexic

anormal adj abnormal

anotar ⟨1a⟩ v/t note down

anquilosarse ⟨1a⟩ v/r get stiff

ansia f yearning; (inquietud) anxiousness

ansiar ⟨1b⟩ v/t yearn for, long for

ansiedad f anxiety

ansioso adj anxious; **está ansioso por verlos** he's longing to see them

anta f L.Am. ZO tapir

antagonista m/f antagonist

antaño adv long ago

antártico adj Antarctic

Antártida Antarctica

ante[1] m suede; ZO moose; Méx (postre) egg and coconut dessert

ante[2] prp posición before; dificultad faced with; **ante todo** above all

anteayer adv the day before yesterday

antebrazo m forearm

antecedente m precedent; **antecedentes penales** previous convictions; **poner a alguien en antecedentes** put s.o. in the picture

antecesor m, **antecesora** f predecessor

antediluviano adj prehistoric hum

antelación f: **con antelación** in advance

antemano: **de antemano** beforehand

antena f de radio, televisión antenna, Br aerial; ZO antenna; **antena parabólica** satellite dish

anteojos mpl binoculars

antepasado m, -a f ancestor

antepenúltimo *adj* third last

anteponer ⟨2r⟩ *v/t*: *anteponer algo a algo* put sth before sth

anteproyecto *m* draft

anterior *adj* previous, former

antes **1** *adv* before; *cuanto antes, lo antes posible* as soon as possible; *poco antes* shortly before; *antes que nada* first of all **2** *prp*: *antes de* before

antesala *f* lobby

antiadherente *adj* non-stick

antiaéreo *adj* anti-aircraft *atr*

antibala(s) *adj* bulletproof

antibelicista *adj* anti-war

antibiótico *m* antibiotic

anticiclón *m* anticyclone

anticipado *adj pago* advance *atr*; *elecciones* early; *por anticipado* in advance

anticipar ⟨1a⟩ **1** *v/t sueldo* advance; *fecha, viaje* move up, *Br* bring forward; *información, noticias* give a preview of **2** *v/r* anticiparse *de suceso* come early; *anticiparse a alguien* get there ahead of s.o.

anticonceptivo **1** *adj* contraceptive *atr* **2** *m* contraceptive

anticongelante *m* antifreeze

anticonstitucional *adj* unconstitutional

anticuado *adj* antiquated

anticuario *m* antique dealer

anticuerpo *m* BIO antibody

antideslizante *adj* non-slip

antidisturbios *adj*: *policía antidisturbios* riot police

antidoping *adj*: *control antidoping* dope test, drug test

antídoto *m* MED antidote; *fig* cure

antifaz *m* mask

antiguamente *adv* in the past

antigüedad *f* age; *en el trabajo* length of service; *antigüedades* antiques

antiguo *adj* old; *del pasado remoto* ancient; *su antiguo novio* her old *o* former boyfriend

antiinflamatorio *adj* MED anti-inflammatory

Antillas *fpl* West Indies

antílope *m* ZO antelope

antinatural *adj* unnatural

antinuclear *adj* anti-nuclear

antioxidante *m/adj* antioxidant

antipatía *f* antipathy, dislike

antipático *adj* disagreeable, unpleasant

antípodas *mpl* antipodes

antirreglamentario *adj* DEP *posición* offside; *una jugada -a* a foul

antirrobo *m* AUTO antitheft device

antisemitismo *m* anti-Semitism

antiséptico *m/adj* antiseptic

antisocial *adj* antisocial

antiterrorista *adj brigada* antiterrorist; *la lucha antiterrorista* the fight against terrorism

antítesis *f inv* antithesis

antojarse ⟨1a⟩ *v/r*: *se le antojó salir* he felt like going out; *se me antoja que ...* it seems to me that ...

antojo *m* whim; *de embarazada* craving; *a mi antojo* as I please

antología *f* anthology; *de antología fig* fantastic, incredible F

antonomasia *f*: *por antonomasia* par excellence

antorcha *f* torch

antro *m* F dive F, dump F

antropófago *m*, *-a f* cannibal

antropología *f* anthropology

anual *adj* annual

anualidad *f* annual payment

anualmente *adv* yearly

anudar ⟨1a⟩ *v/t* knot

anular¹ ⟨1a⟩ *v/t* cancel, *matrimonio* annul; *gol* disallow

anular² *adj* ring-shaped; *dedo anular* ring finger

anunciante *m* COM advertiser

anunciar ⟨1b⟩ *v/t* announce; COM advertise

anuncio *m* announcement; (*presagio*) sign; COM advertisement; *anuncio luminoso* illuminated sign; *anuncios por palabras, pequeños anuncios* classified advertisements

anzuelo *m* (fish) hook; *morder o tragar el anzuelo fig* F take the bait

añadidura *f*: *por añadidura* in addition

añadir ⟨3a⟩ *v/t* add

añejo *adj* mature

añicos *mpl*: *hacer añicos* F smash to smithereens F

año *m* year; *año bisiesto* leap year; *año fiscal* fiscal year, *Br* financial year; *año luz* light year; *año nuevo* New Year; *¿cuándo cumples años?* when's your birthday?; *¿cuántos años tienes?* how old are you?; *a los diez años* at the age of ten; *los años veinte* the twenties

añorar ⟨1a⟩ *v/t* miss

aorta *f* ANAT aorta

apabullante *adj* overwhelming

apabullar ⟨1a⟩ *v/t* overwhelm

apacible *adj* mild-mannered

apaciguar ⟨1i⟩ **1** *v/t* pacify, calm down **2** *v/r* apaciguarse calm down

apadrinar ⟨1a⟩ *v/t* be godparent to; *político* support, back; *artista etc* sponsor; *apadrinar a la novia* give the bride away

apagado *adj fuego* out; *luz* off; *persona*

dull; *color* subdued

apagar ⟨1h⟩ **1** v/t *televisor, luz* turn off; *fuego* put out **2** v/r **apagarse** *de luz* go off; *de fuego* go out

apagón m blackout

apaisado adj landscape atr

apalabrar ⟨1a⟩ v/t agree (verbally)

apalancar ⟨1g⟩ **1** v/t lever **2** v/r **apalancarse** F settle

apalear ⟨1a⟩ v/t beat

apañar ⟨1a⟩ **1** v/t tidy up; *aparato* repair; *resultado* rig F, fix F; *estamos apañados* F we've had it F **2** v/r **apañarse** manage; *apañárselas* manage, get by

apaño m fig F makeshift repair

aparador m sideboard; *Méx (escaparate)* shop window

aparato m piece of equipment; *doméstico* appliance; BIO, ANAT system; *de partido político* machine; *aparato respiratorio* respiratory system; *al aparato* TELEC speaking

aparatoso adj spectacular

aparcacoches m inv valet

aparcamiento m parking lot, Br car park; *aparcamiento subterráneo* underground parking garage, Br underground car park

aparcar ⟨1g⟩ **1** v/t park; *tema, proyecto* shelve **2** v/i park

aparearse ⟨1a⟩ v/r zo mate

aparecer ⟨2d⟩ **1** v/i appear **2** v/r **aparecerse** turn up

aparejador m, **aparejadora** f architectural technician, Br quantity surveyor

aparejo m: *aparejos* pl *de pesca* fishing gear sg

aparentar ⟨1a⟩ v/t pretend; *no aparenta la edad que tiene* she doesn't look her age

aparente adj *(evidente)* apparent; *L.Am. (fingido)* feigned

aparentemente adv apparently

aparición f appearance; *(fantasma)* apparition; *hacer su aparición* make one's appearance

apariencia f appearance; *en apariencia* outwardly; *las apariencias engañan* appearances can be deceptive

apartado m section; *apartado de correos* PO box

apartamento m apartment, Br flat

apartamiento m separation; *L.Am. (apartamento)* apartment, Br flat

apartar ⟨1a⟩ **1** v/t separate; *para después* set o put aside; *de un sitio* move away *(de* from); *apartar a alguien de hacer algo* dissuade s.o. from doing sth **2** v/r **apartarse** move aside *(de* from); *apartarse*

del tema stray from the subject

aparte adv to one side; *(por separado)* separately; *aparte de* aside from, Br apart from; *punto y aparte* new paragraph

apasionado 1 adj passionate **2** m/f enthusiast

apasionante adj fascinating

apasionar ⟨1a⟩ v/t fascinate

apatía f apathy

apático adj apathetic

apdo. abr *(= apartado (de correos))* PO Box *(= Post Office Box)*

apearse ⟨1a⟩ v/r get off, alight fml; *apearse de algo* get off sth, alight from sth fml

apechugar ⟨1h⟩ v/i: *apechugar con algo* cope with sth

apego m attachment

apelación f JUR appeal

apelar ⟨1a⟩ v/t tb JUR appeal *(a* to)

apellidarse ⟨1a⟩ v/r: *¿cómo se apellida?* what's your / his / her surname?; *se apellida Ocaña* his / her surname is Ocaña

apellido m surname; *apellido de soltera* maiden name

apelmazarse ⟨1f⟩ v/r *de lana* get matted; *de arroz* stick together

apelotonarse ⟨1a⟩ v/r crowd together

apenado adj sad; *L.Am. (avergonzado)* ashamed; *L.Am. (incómodo)* embarrassed; *L.Am. (tímido)* shy

apenar ⟨1a⟩ **1** v/t sadden **2** v/r **apenarse** be upset o distressed; *L.Am. (avergonzarse)* be ashamed; *L.Am. (sentir incómodo)* be embarrassed; *L.Am. (ser tímido)* be shy

apenas 1 adv hardly, scarcely **2** conj as soon as

apéndice m appendix

apendicitis f MED appendicitis

apercibirse ⟨3a⟩ v/r: *apercibirse de algo* notice sth

apergaminado adj fig wrinkled

aperitivo m *comida* appetizer; *bebida* aperitif

apero m *utensilio* implement; *L.Am. (arneses)* harness; *aperos de labranza* farming implements

apertura f opening; FOT aperture; POL opening up

apesadumbrado adj heavy-hearted

apestar ⟨1a⟩ v/t stink out F **2** v/i reek *(a* of); *huele que apesta* it reeks

apestoso adj smelly

apetecer ⟨2d⟩ v/i: *me apetece ir a dar un paseo* I feel like going for a walk; *¿qué te apetece?* what do you feel like?

apetito m appetite

apetitoso *adj* appetizing

apiadarse ⟨1a⟩ *v/r* take pity (**de** on)

ápice *m*: **ni un ápice** *fig* not an ounce; **no ceder ni un ápice** *fig* not give an inch

apicultura *f* beekeeping

apilar ⟨1a⟩ *v/t* pile up

apiñarse ⟨1a⟩ *v/r* crowd together

apio *m* BOT celery

apisonadora *f* steamroller

aplacar ⟨1g⟩ *v/t hambre* satisfy; *sed* quench; *a alguien* calm down, placate *fml*

aplanar ⟨1a⟩ **1** *v/t* level, flatten; **aplanar las calles** *C.Am., Pe* hang around the streets **2** *v/r* **aplanarse** *fig* (*descorazonarse*) lose heart

aplastante *adj* overwhelming; *calor* suffocating

aplastar ⟨1a⟩ *v/t tb fig* crush

aplaudida *f L.Am.* applause

aplaudir ⟨3a⟩ **1** *v/i* applaud, clap **2** *v/t tb fig* applaud

aplauso *m* round of applause

aplazamiento *m de visita, viaje* postponement

aplazar ⟨1f⟩ *v/t visita, viaje* put off, postpone; *Arg* fail

aplicación *f* application

aplicar ⟨1g⟩ **1** *v/t* apply; *sanciones* impose **2** *v/r* **aplicarse** apply o.s.

aplomo *m* composure, aplomb *fml*

apocalíptico *adj* apocalyptic

apócrifo *adj* apocryphal

apodar ⟨1a⟩ *v/t* nickname, call

apoderado *m* COM agent

apoderar ⟨1a⟩ **1** *v/t* authorize **2** *v/r* **apoderarse** take possession *o* control (**de** of)

apodo *m* nickname

apogeo *m fig* height, peak; **estar en su apogeo** be at its height

apolillarse ⟨1a⟩ *v/r* get moth-eaten

apolítico *adj* apolitical

apología *f* defense, *Br* defence

apoltronarse ⟨1a⟩ *v/r en asiento* settle down; *en trabajo, rutina* get into a rut

apoplejía *f* MED apoplexy; **ataque de apoplejía** MED stroke

aporrear ⟨1a⟩ *v/t* pound on

aportación *f* contribution; COM investment

aportar ⟨1a⟩ *v/t* contribute; **aportar pruebas** JUR provide evidence

apósito *m* dressing

aposta *adv* on purpose, deliberately

apostar ⟨1m⟩ **1** *v/t* bet (**por** on) **2** *v/i* bet; **apostar por algo** opt for sth **3** *v/r* **apostarse** bet; MIL position o.s.

apóstata *m/f* apostate

apóstol *m* apostle

apóstrofe, apóstrofo *m* apostrophe

apoteosis *f fig* climax

apoyar ⟨1a⟩ **1** *v/t* lean (**en** against), rest (**en** against); (*respaldar, confirmar*) support **2** *v/r* **apoyarse** lean (**en** on; **contra** against); *en persona* rely (**en** on); **¿en qué te apoyas para decir eso?** what are you basing that comment on?

apoyo *m fig* support

apreciable *adj* (*visible*) appreciable, noticeable; (*considerable*) considerable, substantial

apreciar ⟨1b⟩ *v/t* appreciate; (*sentir afecto por*) be fond of, think highly of

aprecio *m* respect

apremiar ⟨1b⟩ **1** *v/t* pressure, put pressure on **2** *v/i*: **el tiempo apremia** time is pressing

aprender ⟨2a⟩ **1** *v/t* learn **2** *v/r* **aprenderse** learn; **aprenderse algo de memoria** learn sth (off) by heart

aprendiz *m*, **aprendiza** *f* apprentice, trainee

aprendizaje *m* apprenticeship

aprensión *f* (*miedo*) apprehension; (*asco*) squeamishness

apresar ⟨1a⟩ *v/t nave* seize; *ladrón, animal* catch, capture

aprestarse ⟨1a⟩ *v/r*: **aprestarse a** get ready to

apresurar ⟨1a⟩ **1** *v/t* hurry **2** *v/r* **apresurarse** hurry up; **apresurarse a hacer algo** hurry *o* rush to do sth

apretado *adj* tight; **iban muy apretados en el coche** they were very cramped *o* squashed in the car

apretar ⟨1k⟩ **1** *v/t botón* press; (*pellizcar, pinzar*) squeeze; *tuerca* tighten; **apretar el paso** quicken one's pace; **apretar los puños** clench one's fists **2** *v/i de ropa, zapato* be too tight **3** *v/r* **apretarse** squeeze *o* squash together; **apretarse el cinturón** *fig* tighten one's belt

apretón *m* squeeze; **apretón de manos** handshake

apretujar ⟨1a⟩ **1** *v/t* F squeeze, squash **2** *v/r* **apretujarse** F squash *o* squeeze together

aprieto *m* predicament

aprisa *adv* quickly

aprisionar ⟨1a⟩ *v/t fig* trap

aprobación *f* approval; *de ley* passing

aprobado *m* EDU pass

aprobar ⟨1m⟩ *v/t* approve; *comportamiento, idea* approve of; *examen* pass

apropiado *adj* appropriate, suitable

apropiarse ⟨1b⟩ *v/r*: **apropiarse de algo** take sth

aprovechado 1 *adj desp* opportunistic **2** *m*, **-a** *f desp* opportunist

aprovechar ⟨1a⟩ **1** v/t take advantage of; *tiempo, espacio* make good use of; **quiero aprovechar la ocasión para** ... I would like to take this opportunity to ... **2** v/i take the opportunity (**para** to); **¡que aproveche!** enjoy your meal! **3** v/r **aprovecharse** take advantage (**de** of)

aprovisionarse ⟨1a⟩ v/r stock up (**de** on)

aproximadamente adv approximately

aproximado adj approximate

aproximar ⟨1a⟩ **1** v/t bring closer **2** v/r **aproximarse** approach

aptitud f aptitude (**para** for), flair (**para** for)

apto adj suitable (**para** for); *para servicio militar* fit; EDU pass

apuesta f bet

apuesto adj handsome

apunado adj Pe, Bol suffering from altitude sickness

apunarse ⟨1a⟩ v/r S. Am. get altitude sickness

apuntador m, **apuntadora** f TEA prompter

apuntalar ⟨1a⟩ v/t *edificio* shore up; *fig* prop up

apuntar ⟨1a⟩ **1** v/t (*escribir*) note down, make a note of; TEA prompt; *en curso, para viaje etc* put down (**en, a** on, **para** for); **apuntar con el dedo** point at o to **2** v/i *con arma* aim **3** v/r **apuntarse** put one's name down (**para, en** o **a** for); **¡me apunto!** count me in!

apunte m note

apuñalar ⟨1a⟩ v/t stab

apurado adj L.Am. (*con prisa*) in a hurry; (*pobre*) short (of cash)

apurar ⟨1a⟩ **1** v/t *vaso* finish off; *a alguien* pressure, put pressure on **2** v/i *Chi:* **no me apura** I'm not in a hurry for it **3** v/r **apurarse** worry; L.Am. (*darse prisa*) hurry (up)

apuro m predicament, tight spot F; *vergüenza* embarrassment; L.Am. rush; **me da apuro** I'm embarrassed

aquejado adj: **estar aquejado de** be suffering from

aquel, aquella, aquellos, aquellas det *singular* that; *plural* those

aquél, aquélla, aquéllos, aquéllas pron *singular* that (one); *plural* those (ones)

aquello pron that

aquí adv *en el espacio* here; *en el tiempo* now; **desde aquí** from here; **por aquí** here

árabe 1 m/f & adj Arab **2** m *idioma* Arabic

Arabia Saudí Saudi Arabia

arado m plow, Br plough

arancel m tariff

arancelario adj tariff atr

arándano m blueberry

arandela f washer

araña f ZO spider; *lámpara* chandelier

arañar ⟨1a⟩ v/t scratch

arañazo m scratch

arar ⟨1a⟩ v/t plow, Br plough

arbitraje m arbitration

arbitrar ⟨1a⟩ v/t *en fútbol, boxeo* referee; *en tenis, béisbol* umpire; *en conflicto* arbitrate

arbitrario adj arbitrary

árbitro m *en fútbol, boxeo* referee; *en tenis, béisbol* umpire; *en conflicto* arbitrator

árbol m tree; **árbol genealógico** family tree

arboleda f grove

arbusto m shrub, bush

arca f chest; **arca de Noé** Noah's Ark

arcada f MED: **me provocó arcadas** it made me retch o heave F

arcaico adj archaic

arce m BOT maple

arcén m shoulder, Br hard shoulder

archidiócesis f inv archdiocese

archipiélago m archipelago

archivador m filing cabinet

archivar ⟨1a⟩ v/t *papeles, documentos* file; *asunto* shelve

archivo m archive; INFOR file

arcilla f clay

arco m ARQUI arch; MÚS bow; L.Am. DEP goal; **arco iris** rainbow

arder ⟨2a⟩ v/i burn; *estar muy caliente* be exceedingly hot; **la reunión está que arde** F the meeting is about to erupt F

ardilla f ZO squirrel

ardor m *entusiasmo* fervo(u)r; **ardor de estómago** heartburn

arduo adj arduous

área f area; DEP **área de castigo** or **de penalty** penalty area; **área de descanso** pull-in (at the side of the road); **área de servicio** service area

arena f sand; **arenas** pl **movedizas** quicksand sg

arenga f morale-boosting speech; (*sermón*) harangue

arenque m herring

arepa f C.Am., Ven cornmeal roll

arete m L.Am. *joya* earring

Argelia Algeria

Argentina Argentina

argentino 1 adj Argentinian **2** m, **-a** f Argentinian

argolla f L.Am. ring

argot m slang

argucia f clever argument

argüir ⟨3g⟩ v/t & v/i argue

argumentar ⟨1a⟩ v/t argue
argumento m razón argument; de libro, película etc plot
árido adj arid, dry; fig dry
Aries m/f inv ASTR Aries
arisco adj unfriendly
aristocracia f aristocracy
aristócrata m/f aristocrat
aristocrático adj aristocratic
aritmética f arithmetic
arma f weapon; **arma blanca** knife; **arma de doble filo** or **de dos filos** fig two-edged sword; **arma de fuego** firearm; **alzarse en armas** rise up in arms
armada f navy
armadillo m zo armadillo
armado adj armed
armadura f armo(u)r
armamento m armaments pl
armar ⟨1a⟩ 1 v/t MIL arm; TÉC assemble, put together; **armar un escándalo** F kick up a fuss F, make a scene F 2 v/r **armarse** arm o.s.; **la que se va a armar** F all hell will break loose F; **armarse de valor** pluck up courage
armario m closet, Br wardrobe; de cocina cabinet, Br cupboard
armazón f skeleton, framework
armisticio m armistice
armonía f harmony
armónica f harmonica, mouth organ
armonioso adj harmonious
armonizar ⟨1f⟩ 1 v/t harmonize; diferencias reconcile 2 v/i de color, estilo blend (**con** with); de persona get on (**con** with)
arnés m harness; para niños leading strings pl, Br leading reins pl
aro m hoop; L.Am. (pendiente) earring; **entrar** or **pasar por el aro** fig F bite the bullet, take the plunge
aroma m aroma; de flor scent
arpa f harp
arpía f harpy
arpón m harpoon
arquear ⟨1a⟩ v/t espalda arch; cejas raise
arqueología f arch(a)eology
arqueológico adj arch(a)eological
arqueólogo m, -a f arch(a)eologist
arquero m archer; L.Am. en fútbol goalkeeper
arquetipo m archetype
arquitectónico adj architectural
arquitecto m, -a f architect
arquitectura f architecture
arrabal m poor outlying area
arraigado adj entrenched
arraigar ⟨1h⟩ 1 v/i take root 2 v/r arraigarse de persona settle (**en** in); de costumbre, idea take root

arramblar ⟨1a⟩ v/t (destruir) destroy
arrancar ⟨1g⟩ 1 v/t planta, página pull out; vehículo start (up); (quitar) snatch 2 v/i de vehículo, máquina start (up); INFOR boot (up); Chi (huir) run away 3 v/r **arrancarse** Chi run away
arranque m AUTO starting mechanism; (energía) drive; (ataque) fit
arrasar ⟨1a⟩ 1 v/t devastate 2 v/i F be a big hit
arrastrar ⟨1a⟩ 1 v/t por el suelo, INFOR drag (**por** along); (llevarse) carry away 2 v/i por el suelo trail on the ground 3 v/r **arrastrarse** crawl; fig (humillarse) grovel (**delante de** to)
arrastre m: **estar para el arrastre** fig F be fit to drop F
arreada f Rpl round-up
arrebatar ⟨1a⟩ v/t snatch (**a** from)
arrebato m fit
arrebujarse ⟨1a⟩ v/r F wrap o.s. up; en cama snuggle up
arreciar ⟨1b⟩ v/i get worse; de viento get stronger
arrecife m reef
arredrarse ⟨1a⟩ v/r be intimidated (**ante** by)
arreglar ⟨1a⟩ 1 v/t (reparar) fix, repair; (ordenar) tidy (up); (solucionar) sort out; MÚS arrange; **arreglar cuentas** settle up; fig settle scores 2 v/r **arreglarse** get (o.s.) ready; de problema get sorted out; (apañarse) manage; **arreglárselas** manage
arreglo m (reparación) repair; (solución) solution; (acuerdo) arrangement, agreement; MÚS arrangement; **arreglo de cuentas** settling of scores; **con arreglo a** in accordance with; **esto no tiene arreglo** there's nothing to be done
arrellanarse ⟨1a⟩ v/r settle
arremangarse ⟨1h⟩ v/r roll up one's sleeves
arremeter ⟨2a⟩ v/i: **arremeter contra** charge (at); fig (criticar) attack
arremolinarse ⟨1a⟩ v/r mill around
arrendamiento m renting
arrendar ⟨1k⟩ v/t L.Am. (dar en alquiler) rent (out), let; (tomar en alquiler) rent; **se arrienda** for rent
arreo m Rpl driving, herding; (manada) herd
arrepentimiento m repentance; (cambio de opinión) change of heart
arrepentirse ⟨3i⟩ v/r be sorry; (cambiar de opinión) change one's mind; **arrepentirse de algo** regret sth
arrestar ⟨1a⟩ v/t arrest
arresto m arrest

arriba 1 *adv* ◇ *situación* up; *en edificio* upstairs; ***ponlo ahí arriba*** put it up there; ***el cajón de arriba*** *siguiente* the next drawer up, the drawer above; *último* the top drawer; ***arriba del todo*** right at the top
◇ *dirección* up; *en edificio* upstairs; ***sigan hacia arriba*** keep going up; ***me miró de arriba abajo*** *fig* she looked me up and down
◇ *con cantidades*: ***de diez para arriba*** ten or above **2** *int* long live

arribeño *m*, **-a** *f L.Am.* uplander, highlander

arribista *m/f* social climber

arriesgado *adj* adventurous

arriesgar ⟨1h⟩ **1** *v/t* risk **2** *v/r* **arriesgarse** take a risk; ***arriesgarse a hacer algo*** risk doing sth

arrimar ⟨1a⟩ **1** *v/t* move closer; ***arrimar el hombro*** F pull one's weight **2** *v/r* **arrimarse** move closer (**a** to)

arrinconar ⟨1a⟩ *v/t* (*acorralar*) corner; *libros etc* put away; *persona* cold-shoulder

arroba *m* INFOR 'at' symbol, @

arrodillarse ⟨1a⟩ *v/r* kneel (down)

arrogancia *f* arrogance

arrogante *adj* arrogant

arrojar ⟨1a⟩ **1** *v/t* (*lanzar*) throw; *resultado* produce; (*vomitar*) throw up **2** *v/r* **arrojarse** throw o.s.

arrollador *adj* overwhelming

arropar ⟨1a⟩ *v/t* wrap up; *fig* protect

arrope *m Rpl, Chi, Pe* fruit syrup

arroyo *m* stream; ***sacar a alguien del arroyo*** *fig* lift s.o. out of the gutter

arroz *m* rice; ***arroz con leche*** rice pudding

arruga *f* wrinkle

arrugar ⟨1h⟩ **1** *v/t* wrinkle; **2** *v/r* **arrugarse** *de piel, ropa* get wrinkled

arruinado *adj* ruined, broke F

arruinar ⟨1a⟩ **1** *v/t* ruin **2** *v/r* **arruinarse** be ruined

arrullo *m de paloma* cooing; *para niño* lullaby

arsenal *m* arsenal

arsénico *m* arsenic

art *abr* (= ***artículo***) art. (= article)

art.° *abr* (= ***artículo***) art. (= article)

arte *m* (*pl f*) art; ***arte dramático*** dramatic art; ***bellas artes*** *pl* fine art *sg*; ***malas artes*** *pl* guile *sg*

artefacto *m* (*dispositivo*) device

arteria *f* artery

arterio(e)sclerosis *f* arteriosclerosis

artesana *f* craftswoman

artesanía *f* (handi)crafts *pl*

artesano *m* craftsman

Ártico *zona, océano* Arctic

articulación *f* ANAT, TÉC joint; *de sonidos* articulation

artículo *m de periódico*, GRAM, JUR article; COM product, item

artificial *adj* artificial

artillería *f* artillery; ***artillería ligera / pesada*** light / heavy artillery

artilugio *m aparato* gadget

artimaña *f* trick

artista *m/f* artist

artístico *adj* artistic

artritis *f* MED arthritis

arveja *f Rpl, Chi, Pe* BOT pea

arzobispo *m* archbishop

as *m* tb *fig* ace

asa *f* handle

asado 1 *adj* roast *atr* **2** *m* roast

asalariado *m*, **-a** *f* wage earner; *de empresa* employee

asaltante *m/f* assailant

asaltar ⟨1a⟩ *v/t persona* attack; *banco* rob

asalto *m a persona* attack (**a** on); *robo* robbery, raid; *en boxeo* round

asamblea *f reunión* meeting; *ente* assembly

asar ⟨1a⟩ **1** *v/t* roast; ***asar a la parrilla*** broil, *Br* grill **2** *v/r* **asarse** *fig* F be roasting F

ascender ⟨2g⟩ **1** *v/t a empleado* promote **2** *v/i de precios, temperatura etc* rise; *de montañero* climb; DEP, *en trabajo* be promoted (**a** to)

ascensión *f* ascent

ascenso *m de temperatura, precios* rise (**de** in); *de montaña* ascent; DEP, *en trabajo* promotion

ascensor *m* elevator, *Br* lift

ascético *adj* ascetic

asco *m* disgust; ***me da asco*** I find it disgusting; ***¡qué asco!*** how revolting *o* disgusting!

ascua *f* ember; ***estar en*** *or* ***sobre ascuas*** be on tenterhooks

asearse ⟨1a⟩ *v/r* wash up, *Br* have a wash

asediar ⟨1b⟩ *v/t* tb *fig* besiege

asedio *m* MIL siege, blockade; *a alguien* hounding

aseguradora *f* insurance company

asegurar ⟨1a⟩ **1** *v/t* (*afianzar*) secure; (*prometer*) assure; (*garantizar*) guarantee; COM insure **2** *v/r* **asegurarse** make sure

asentamiento *m* settlement

asentarse ⟨1k⟩ *v/r* settle

asentir ⟨3i⟩ *v/i* agree (**a** to), consent (**a** to); *con la cabeza* nod

aseo *m* cleanliness; (*baño*) restroom, toilet

aséptico *adj* aseptic

asequible *adj precio* affordable; *obra* accessible

aserrar ⟨1k⟩ *v/t* saw

aserrín *m L.Am.* sawdust

asesinar ⟨1a⟩ *v/t* murder; POL assassinate

asesinato *m* murder; POL assassination

asesino *m*, -a *f* murderer; POL assassin

asesor *m*, asesora *f* consultant, advisor, *Br* adviser; **asesor fiscal** financial advisor (*Br* adviser); **asesor de imagen** public relations consultant

asesorar ⟨1a⟩ *v/t* advise

asesoría *f* consultancy

asestar ⟨1a⟩ *v/t golpe* deal (**a** to); **me asestó una puñalada** he stabbed me

asfaltar ⟨1a⟩ *v/t* asphalt

asfalto *m* asphalt

asfixia *f* asphyxiation

asfixiante *adj* asphyxiating, suffocating

asfixiar ⟨1b⟩ **1** *v/t* asphyxiate, suffocate **2** *v/r* asfixiarse asphyxiate, suffocate

así **1** *adv* (*de este modo*) like this; (*de ese modo*) like that; **así no más** *S. Am.* just like that; **así pues** so; **así que** so; **así de grande** this big **2** *conj*: **así como** *al igual que* while, whereas

Asia Asia

asiático **1** *adj* Asian **2** *m*, -a *f* Asian

asiduidad *f* frequency; **con asiduidad** *con frecuencia* regularly

asiduo *adj* regular

asiento *m* seat; **tomar asiento** take a seat

asignación *f acción* allocation; *dinero* allowance

asignar ⟨1a⟩ *v/t* allocate; *persona, papel* assign

asignatura *f* subject

asilarse ⟨1a⟩ *v/r* take refuge, seek asylum

asilo *m* home, institution; POL asylum; **asilo de ancianos** old people's home

asimétrico *adj* asymmetrical

asimilar ⟨1a⟩ *v/t* assimilate

asimismo *adv* (*también*) also; (*igualmente*) in the same way, likewise

asistencia *f* (*ayuda*) assistance; *a lugar* attendance (**a** at); **asistencia en carretera** AUTO roadside assistance; **asistencia médica** medical care

asistenta *f* cleaner, cleaning woman

asistente *m/f* (*ayudante*) assistant; **asistente social** social worker; **los asistentes** those present

asistir ⟨3a⟩ **1** *v/t* help, assist **2** *v/i* be present; **asistir a una boda** attend a wedding

asma *f* asthma

asmático *adj* asthmatic

asno *m* ZO donkey; *persona* idiot

asociación *f* association

asociar ⟨1b⟩ **1** *v/t* associate; **asociar a alguien con algo** associate s.o. with sth **2** *v/r* asociarse team up (**con** with), go into partnership (**con** with); **asociarse a grupo, club** become a member of

asolar ⟨1m⟩ *v/t* devastate

asoleada *f*: **pegarse una asoleada** *Bol, Pe* sunbathe

asomar ⟨1a⟩ **1** *v/t* put *o* stick out **2** *v/i* show **3** *v/r* asomarse lean out; **asomarse a** *or* **por la ventana** lean out of the window

asombrado *adj* amazed

asombrar ⟨1a⟩ **1** *v/t* amaze, astonish **2** *v/r* asombrarse be amazed *o* astonished

asombro *m* amazement, astonishment

asombroso *adj* amazing

asomo *m*: **ni por asomo** no way

asorocharse ⟨1a⟩ *v/r Pe, Bol* get altitude sickness

aspecto *m de persona, cosa* look, appearance; (*faceta*) aspect; **tener buen aspecto** look good

áspero *adj superficie* rough; *sonido* harsh; *persona* abrupt

aspersor *m* sprinkler

aspiraciones *fpl* aspirations

aspirador *m*, aspiradora *f* vacuum cleaner

aspirante *m/f a cargo* candidate (**a** for); *a título* contender (**a** for)

aspirar ⟨1a⟩ **1** *v/t* suck up; *al respirar* inhale, breathe in **2** *v/i*: **aspirar a** aspire to

aspirina *f* aspirin

asqueado *adj* disgusted

asquear ⟨1a⟩ *v/t* disgust

asqueroso **1** *adj* (*sucio*) filthy; (*repugnante*) revolting, disgusting **2** *m*, -a *f* creep

asterisco *m* asterisk

astigmatismo *m* astigmatism

astilla *f* splinter; **astillas** *pl para fuego* kindling *sg*; **hacer astillas algo** *fig* smash sth to pieces

astillero *m* shipyard

astral *adj* astral

astringente *m/adj* astringent

astro *m* AST, *fig* star

astrología *f* astrology

astrólogo *m*, -a *f* astrologer

astronauta *m/f* astronaut

astronave *f* spaceship

astronomía *f* astronomy

astronómico *adj* astronomical

astrónomo *m*, -a *f* astronomer

astucia *f* shrewdness, astuteness

astuto *adj* shrewd, astute

asumir ⟨3a⟩ *v/t* assume; (*aceptar*) accept, come to terms with

asunto *m* matter; F (*relación*) affair; **asuntos exteriores** foreign affairs; **no es asunto tuyo** it's none of your business

asustar ⟨1a⟩ **1** *v/t* frighten, scare **2** *v/r* **asustarse** be frightened *o* scared

atacar ⟨1g⟩ *v/t* attack

atajar ⟨1a⟩ **1** *v/t* check the spread of, contain; *L.Am.* **pelota** catch **2** *v/i* take a short cut

atajo *m L.Am.* short cut

atañer ⟨2f⟩ *v/i* concern

ataque *m* (*agresión*) attack; (*acceso*) fit; **ataque cardíaco** *or* **al corazón** MED heart attack; **le dio un ataque de risa** she burst out laughing

atar ⟨1a⟩ *v/t* tie (up); *fig* tie down

atardecer ⟨2d⟩ **1** *v/i* get dark **2** *m* dusk

atareado *adj* busy

atascar ⟨1g⟩ **1** *v/t* block **2** *v/r* **atascarse de** cañería get blocked; *de mecanismo* jam, stick; *al hablar* dry up

atasco *m* traffic jam

ataúd *m* coffin, casket

atemorizar ⟨1f⟩ *v/t* frighten

atención *f* attention; (*cortesía*) courtesy; **¡atención!** your attention, please!; **llamar la atención a alguien** tell s.o. off; *por ser llamativo* attract s.o.'s attention; **prestar atención** pay attention (**a** to)

atender ⟨2g⟩ **1** *v/t a enfermo* look after; *en tienda* attend to, serve **2** *v/i* pay attention (**a** to)

atenerse ⟨2l⟩ *v/r*: **atenerse a normas** abide by; *consecuencias* face, accept; **saber a qué atenerse** know where one stands

atentado *m* attack (**contra, a** on); **atentado terrorista** terrorist attack

atentamente *adv* attentively; *en carta* sincerely, *Br* Yours sincerely

atentar ⟨1k⟩ *v/i*: **atentar contra** *vida* make an attempt on; *moral etc* be contrary to

atento *adj* attentive; **estar atento a algo** pay attention to sth

atenuante *adj* JUR extenuating; **circunstancia atenuante** JUR extenuating circumstance

atenuar ⟨1e⟩ *v/t* lessen, reduce

ateo 1 *adj* atheistic **2** *m*, **-a** *f* atheist

aterciopelado *adj tb fig* velvety

aterido *adj* frozen

aterrador *adj* frightening

aterrar ⟨1a⟩ *v/t* terrify

aterrizaje *m* AVIA landing; **aterrizaje forzoso** *or* **de emergencia** emergency landing

aterrizar ⟨1f⟩ *v/i* land

aterrorizado *adj* terrified, petrified F

aterrorizar ⟨1f⟩ *v/t* terrify; (*amenazar*) terrorize

atestado *adj* overcrowded

atestiguar ⟨1i⟩ *v/t* JUR testify; *fig* bear witness to

atiborrarse ⟨1a⟩ *v/r* F stuff o.s. F (**de** with)

ático *m piso* top floor; *apartamento* top floor apartment (*Br* flat); (*desván*) attic

atinar ⟨1a⟩ *v/i* manage (**a** to); **no atinó con la respuesta correcta** she couldn't come up with the right answer

atípico *adj* atypical

atisbo *m* sign

atizar ⟨1f⟩ *v/t fuego* poke; *pasiones* stir up; **le atizó un golpe** she hit him

Atlántico *m/adj*: **el** (**océano**) **Atlántico** the Atlantic (Ocean)

atlas *m inv* atlas

atleta *m/f* athlete

atlético *adj* athletic

atletismo *m* athletics

atmo. *abr* (= **atentísimo**): **su atmo** Yours truly

atmósfera *f* atmosphere

atole *m Méx* flavored hot drink made with maize flour

atolladero *m*: **sacar a alguien del atolladero** *fig* F get s.o. out of a tight spot

atolondrado *adj* scatterbrained

atómico *adj* atomic

átomo *m* atom; **ni un átomo de** *fig* not an iota of

atónito *adj* astonished, amazed

atontar ⟨1a⟩ *v/t* make groggy *o* dopey; *de golpe* stun, daze; (*volver tonto*) turn into a zombie

atorar ⟨1a⟩ *L.Am.* **1** *v/t* cañería etc block (up) **2** *v/r* **atorarse** choke; *de cañería etc* get blocked (up)

atormentar ⟨1a⟩ *v/t* torment

atornillar ⟨1a⟩ *v/t* screw on

atorrante *m Rpl*, *Chi* F bum F, *Br* tramp; (*holgazán*) layabout

atosigar ⟨1h⟩ *v/t* pester

atrabancado *adj Méx* clumsy

atracar ⟨1g⟩ **1** *v/t banco*, *tienda* hold up; *a alguien* mug; *Chi* F make out with F, neck with *Br* F **2** *v/i* MAR dock

atracción *f* attraction

atraco *m de banco*, *tienda* robbery; *de persona* mugging

atracón *m*: **darse un atracón de** stuff o.s. with F

atractivo 1 *adj* attractive **2** *m* appeal, attraction

atraer ⟨2p⟩ *v/t* attract

atragantarse ⟨1a⟩ *v/r* choke (**con** on); **se**

le ha atragantado *fig* she can't stand *o* stomach him

atrancar ⟨1g⟩ **1** *v/t puerta* barricade **2** *v/r* **atrancarse** *fig* get stuck

atrapar ⟨1a⟩ *v/t* catch, trap

atrás *adv para indicar posición* at the back, behind; *para indicar movimiento* back; **años atrás** years ago *o* back; **hacia atrás** back, backwards; **quedarse atrás** get left behind

atrasado *adj en estudios, pago* behind (**en** in *o* with); *reloj* slow; *pueblo* backward; **ir atrasado** *de un reloj* be slow

atrasar ⟨1a⟩ **1** *v/t reloj* put back; *fecha* postpone, put back **2** *v/i de reloj* lose time

atraso *m* backwardness; COM **atrasos** arrears

atravesar ⟨1k⟩ *v/t* cross; *(perforar)* go through, pierce; *crisis* go through

atrevido *adj* daring

atreverse ⟨2a⟩ *v/r* dare

atribuir ⟨3g⟩ **1** *v/t* attribute (**a** to) **2** *v/r* **atribuirse** claim

atrincherarse ⟨1a⟩ *v/r* MIL dig o.s. in, entrench o.s.; **se atrincheró en su postura** *fig* he dug his heels in

atrocidad *f* atrocity

atrofiado *adj* atrophied

atrofiarse ⟨1b⟩ *v/r* atrophy

atropellar ⟨1a⟩ *v/t* knock down

atroz *adj* appalling, atrocious

ATS *abr* (= **ayudante técnico sanitario**) registered nurse

atte. *abr* (= **atentamente**) sincerely (yours)

atuendo *m* outfit

atufar ⟨1a⟩ *v/t* F stink out F

atún *m* tuna (fish)

aturdido *adj* in a daze

aturdir ⟨3a⟩ *de golpe, noticia* stun, daze; *(confundir)* bewilder, confuse **2** *v/r* **aturdirse** be stunned *o* dazed; *(confundirse)* be bewildered *o* confused

aturullar ⟨1a⟩ **1** *v/t* confuse **2** *v/r* **aturullarse** get confused

audacia *f* audacity

audaz *adj* daring, bold, audacious

audición *f* TEA audition; JUR hearing

audiencia *f* audience; JUR court; **índice de audiencia** TV ratings *pl*

audífono *m para sordos* hearing aid

audiovisual *adj* audiovisual

auditivo *adj* auditory; *problema* hearing *atr*

auditor *m*, **auditora** *f* auditor

auditoría *f* audit

auditorio *m* *(público)* audience; *sala* auditorium

auge *m* peak; **estar en auge** *aumento* be

enjoying a boom

augurar ⟨1a⟩ *v/t de persona* predict, foretell; *de indicio* augur

augurio *m* omen, sign; **un buen / mal augurio** a good / bad omen

aula *f* classroom; *en universidad* lecture hall, *Br* lecture theatre

aullido *m* howl

aumentar ⟨1a⟩ **1** *v/t* increase; *precio* increase, raise, put up **2** *v/i de precio, temperatura* rise, increase, go up

aumento *m de precios, temperaturas etc* rise (**de** in), increase (**de** in); *de sueldo* raise, *Br* rise; **ir en aumento** be increasing

aun *adv* even; **aun así** even so

aún *adv en oraciones no negativas* still; *en oraciones negativas* yet; *en comparaciones* even; **aún no** not yet

aunar ⟨1a⟩ *v/t* combine

aunque *conj* although, even though; + *subj* even if

auricular *m de teléfono* receiver; **auriculares** headphones, earphones

aurora *f* dawn; **aurora boreal** northern lights *pl*

auscultar ⟨1a⟩ *v/t*: **auscultar a alguien** listen to s.o.'s chest

ausencia *f de persona* absence; *no existencia* lack (**de** of); **brillaba por su ausencia** he was conspicuous by his absence

ausente *adj* absent

auspicio *m* sponsorship; **bajo los auspicios de** under the auspices of

austeridad *f* austerity

austero *adj* austere

austral *adj* southern

Australia Australia

australiano 1 *adj* Australian **2** *m*, **-a** *f* Australian

Austria Austria

austriaco 1 *adj* Austrian **2** *m*, **-a** *f* Austrian

auténtico *adj* authentic

autentificar ⟨1g⟩ *v/t* authenticate

autismo *m* autism

auto *m* JUR order; *L.Am.* AUTO car

autoadhesivo *adj* self-adhesive

autoayuda *f* self-help

autobiografía *f* autobiography

autobombo *m* F self-glorification

autobús *m* bus

autocar *m* bus

autocaravana *f* camper van

autocontrol *m* self-control

autocrítica *f* self-criticism

autóctono *adj* indigenous, native

autodefensa *f* self-defense, *Br* self-de-

fence
autodeterminación f self-determination
autodidacta 1 adj self-taught **2** m/f self-taught person
autoedición f desktop publishing, DTP
autoescuela f driving school
autoestima f self-esteem
autoestop m hitchhiking
autoestopista m/f hitchhiker
autógrafo m autograph
automático adj automatic
automatizar ⟨1f⟩ v/t automate
automedicación f self-medication
automóvil m car, automobile
automovilismo m driving
automovilista m/f motorist
autonomía f autonomy; *en España* autonomous region
autónomo adj autonomous
autopista f freeway, *Br* motorway; ***autopista de la información** or **de la comunicación*** INFOR information (super)highway
autopsia f post mortem, autopsy
autor m, **autora** f author; *de crimen* perpetrator
autoridad f authority
autoritario adj authoritarian
autorización f authority
autorizar ⟨1f⟩ v/t authorize
autorradio m car radio
autorretrato m self-portrait
autoservicio m supermarket; *restaurante* self-service restaurant
autostop m hitchhiking; ***hacer autostop*** hitch(hike)
autosuficiencia f self-sufficiency; *desp* smugness
autosuficiente adj self-sufficient; *desp* smug
autovía f divided highway, *Br* dual carriageway
auxiliar 1 adj auxiliary; *profesor* assistant **2** m/f assistant; ***auxiliar de vuelo*** stewardess, flight attendant **3** ⟨1b⟩ v/t help
auxilio m help; ***primeros auxilios*** pl first aid sg
Av. abr (= **Avenida**) Ave (= Avenue)
aval m guarantee; ***aval bancario*** bank guarantee
avalancha f avalanche
avalar ⟨1a⟩ v/t guarantee; *fig* back
avance m advance
avanzado adj advanced
avanzar ⟨1f⟩ **1** v/t move forward, advance **2** v/i advance, move forward; MIL advance (*hacia* on); *en trabajo* make progress
avaricia f avarice

avaro 1 adj miserly **2** m, **-a** f miser
avasallar ⟨1a⟩ v/t subjugate; ***no dejes que te avasallen*** fig don't let them push you around
Av.ᵈᵃ abr (= **Avenida**) Ave (= Avenue)
ave f bird; *S. Am.* (*pollo*) chicken; ***ave de presa*** or ***de rapiña*** bird of prey
avecinarse ⟨1a⟩ v/r approach
avejentar ⟨1a⟩ v/t age
avellana f BOT hazelnut
avellano m BOT hazel
avena f oats pl
avenida f avenue
avenirse ⟨3s⟩ v/r agree (**a** to)
aventajar ⟨1a⟩ v/t be ahead of
aventura f adventure; *riesgo* venture; *amorosa* affair
aventurar ⟨1a⟩ **1** v/t risk; *opinión* venture **2** v/r **aventurarse** venture; ***aventurarse a hacer algo*** dare to do sth
aventurero adj adventurous
avergonzar ⟨1n & 1f⟩ **1** v/t (*aborchornar*) embarrass; ***le avergüenza*** algo reprensible she's ashamed of it **2** v/r **avergonzarse** be ashamed (**de** of)
avería f TÉC fault; AUTO breakdown
averiarse ⟨1c⟩ v/r break down
averiguar ⟨1i⟩ v/t find out
aversión f aversion
avestruz m ZO ostrich; ***del avestruz*** política, táctica head-in-the-sand
aviación f aviation; MIL air force
avicultor m, **avicultora** f poultry farmer
avidez f eagerness
ávido adj eager (**de** for), avid (**de** for)
avinagrarse ⟨1a⟩ v/r *de vino* turn vinegary; *fig* become bitter o sour
avión m plane; ***por avión*** mandar una carta (by) airmail
avioneta f light aircraft
avisar ⟨1a⟩ v/t notificar let know, tell; *de peligro* warn; (*llamar*) call, send for
aviso m comunicación notice; (*advertencia*) warning; *L.Am.* (*anuncio*) advertisement; ***hasta nuevo aviso*** until further notice; ***sin previo aviso*** unexpectedly, without any warning
avispa f ZO wasp
avivar ⟨1a⟩ v/t fuego revive; *interés* arouse
avizor adj: ***estar ojo avizor*** be alert
axila f armpit
axioma m axiom
ay *int de dolor* ow!, ouch!; *de susto* oh!
ayer adv yesterday; ***ayer por la mañana*** yesterday morning
ayuda f help; ***ayuda al desarrollo*** development aid o assistance
ayudante m/f assistant
ayudar ⟨1a⟩ v/t help

ayunas: *estoy en ayunas* I haven't eaten anything

ayuno *m* fast

ayuntamiento *m* city council, town council; *edificio* city hall

azabache *m* MIN jet

azadón *m* mattock

azafata *f* flight attendant; *azafata de congresos* hostess

azafrán *m* BOT saffron

azalea *f* BOT azalea

azar *m* fate, chance; *al azar* at random

azorarse ⟨1a⟩ *v/r* be embarrassed

azotar ⟨1a⟩ *v/t con látigo* whip, flog; *con mano* smack; *de enfermedad, hambre* grip; *Méx puerta* slam

azote *m con látigo* lash; *con mano* smack;

fig scourge; *dar un azote a alguien* F smack s.o.

azotea *f* flat roof; *estar mal de la azotea fig* F be crazy F

azteca *m/f* & *adj* Aztec

azúcar *m (also f)* sugar; *azúcar glas* confectioner's sugar, *Br* icing sugar; *azúcar moreno* brown sugar

azucarero *m* sugar bowl

azucena *f* BOT Madonna lily

azufre *m* sulfur, *Br* sulphur

azul 1 *adj* blue; *azul celeste* sky-blue; *azul marino* navy(-blue) 2 *m* blue

azulejo *m* tile

azuzar ⟨1f⟩ *v/t*: *azuzar los perros a alguien* set the dogs on s.o.; *fig* egg s.o. on

B

B.A. *abr* (= *Buenos Aires*) Buenos Aires

baba *f* drool, dribble; *se le caía la baba* F he was drooling F (*con* over)

babear ⟨1a⟩ *v/i* dribble

babero *m* bib

Babia *f*: *estar en Babia* be miles away

babor *m* MAR port

babosa *f* ZO slug

babosada *f L.Am.* F stupid thing to do / say

baboso *adj L.Am.* F stupid

baca *f* AUTO roof rack

bacalao *m* cod; *cortar el bacalao* F call the shots F

bache *m* pothole; *fig* rough patch

bachicha *m/f Rpl, Chi desp* wop *desp* 2 *f Méx* cigarette stub

bachillerato *m Esp* high school leaver's certificate

bacón *m* bacon

bacteria *f* bacteria

bádminton *m* badminton

bafle *m* loudspeaker

bahía *f* bay

bailaor *m*, bailaora *f* flamenco dancer

bailar ⟨1a⟩ 1 *v/i* dance; *de zapato* be loose 2 *v/t* dance; *se lo bailó Méx* F he pinched F *o* swiped F it

bailarín *m*, -ina *f* dancer

baile *m* dance; *fiesta formal* ball; *baile de salón* ballroom dancing; *baile de San Vito fig* St. Vitus's dance

baja *f descenso* fall, drop; *estar de baja (por enfermedad)* be off sick; *bajas* MIL casualties

bajada *f* fall

bajar ⟨1a⟩ 1 *v/t voz, precio* lower; *escalera* go down; *bajar algo de arriba* get sth down 2 *v/i* go down; *de intereses* fall, drop 3 *v/r* bajarse get down; *de automóvil* get out (*de* of); *de tren, autobús* get off (*de* sth)

bajío *m L.Am.* lowland

bajo 1 *adj* low; *persona* short; *por lo bajo* at least 2 *m* MÚS bass; *piso* first floor, *Br* ground floor 3 *adv* cantar, hablar quietly, softly; *volar* low 4 *prp* under; *tres grados bajo cero* three degrees below zero

bajón *m* sharp decline; *dar un bajón* decline sharply, slump

bala *f* bullet; *como una bala* like lightning; *ni a bala L.Am.* F no way

balaceo *m L.Am.*, balacera *f L.Am.* shooting

balada *f* ballad

balance *m* COM balance

balancearse ⟨1a⟩ *v/r* swing, sway

balanza *f* scales *pl*; *balanza comercial* balance of trade; *balanza de pagos* balance of payments

balaustrada *f* balustrade

balazo *m* shot

balbucear ⟨1a⟩, balbucir ⟨3f; *defective*⟩ 1 *v/i* stammer; *de niño* babble 2 *v/t* stam-

mer
Balcanes *mpl* Balkans
balcánico *adj* Balkan
balcón *m* balcony
baldado *adj fig* F bushed F
balde *adv*: **de balde** for nothing; **en balde** in vain
baldosa *f* floor tile
balear ⟨1a⟩ *v/t L.Am.* shoot
baleo *m L.Am.* shooting
Baleares *fpl* Balearic Islands
baleárico *adj* Balearic
baliza *f* MAR buoy
ballena *f* ZO whale
ballet *m* ballet
balneario *m* spa
balón *m* ball
baloncesto *m* basketball
balonmano *m* handball
balonvolea *m* volleyball
balsa *f* raft; **como una balsa de aceite** *fig* like a mill pond
bálsamo *m* balsam
baluarte *m* stronghold; *persona* pillar, stalwart
balumba *f L.Am.* F heap, pile; F (*ruido*) noise, racket F
bambolearse ⟨1a⟩ *v/r* sway
bambolla *f L.Am.* F fuss
bambú *m* BOT bamboo
banal *adj* banal
banana *f L.Am., Rpl, Pe, Bol* banana
banca *f actividad* banking; *conjunto de bancos* banks *pl*; *en juego* bank; DEP, *Méx* (*asiento*) bench
bancal *m* terrace; *división de terreno* plot
bancario *adj* bank *atr*
bancarrota *f* bankruptcy; **estar en bancarrota** be bankrupt
banco *m* COM bank; *para sentarse* bench; **banco de arena** sand bank; **banco de datos** data bank
banda *f* MÚS, (*grupo*) band; *de delincuentes* gang; (*cinta*) sash; *en fútbol* touchline; **banda sonora** soundtrack
bandada *f* de pájaros flock
bandazo *m*: **dar bandazos** *de coche* swerve
bandeja *f* tray; **servir en bandeja** hand on a plate
bandera *f* flag; (*lleno*) **hasta la bandera** packed (out); **bajar la bandera** *de taxi* start the meter running
banderilla *f* TAUR banderilla (*dart stuck into bull's neck during bullfight*)
bandido *m*, **-a** *f* bandit
bando *m* edict; *en disputa* side
bandolero *m*, **-a** *f* bandit
banjo *m* MÚS banjo

banquero *m*, **-a** *f* banker
banqueta *f L.Am.* stool; *L.Am.* (*acera*) sidewalk, *Br* pavement; **banqueta trasera** AUTO back seat
banquete *m* banquet; **banquete de bodas** wedding reception
banquillo *m* JUR dock; DEP bench
bañadera *f Rpl* (*baño*) bath
bañador *m* swimsuit
bañar ⟨1a⟩ **1** *v/t de sol, mar* bathe; *a un niño, un enfermo* bathe, *Br* bath; GASTR coat (**con** with, **en** in) **2** *v/r* bañarse have a bath; *en el mar* go for a swim
bañera *f* (bath)tub, bath
bañista *m/f* swimmer
baño *m* bath; *en el mar* swim; *esp L.Am.* bathroom; TÉC plating; **baño de sangre** blood bath; **baño María** bain-marie
baptisterio *m* baptistry
baquiano *L.Am.* **1** *adj* expert *atr* **2** *m*, **-a** *f* guide
bar *m* bar
baraja *f* deck of cards
barandilla *f* handrail, banister
barata *f Méx* bargain counter; (*saldo*) sale
baratero *m*, **-a** *f Chi tendero* junk-shop owner
baratija *f* trinket
barato *adj* cheap
barba *f tb* BOT beard; **por barba** F a head, per person
barbacoa *f* barbecue
barbaridad *f* barbarity; **costar una barbaridad** cost a fortune; **decir barbaridades** say outrageous things; **¡qué barbaridad!** what a thing to say / do!
bárbaro 1 *adj* F tremendous, awesome F; **¡qué bárbaro!** amazing!, wicked! F **2** *m*, **-a** *f* F punk F
barbería *f* barber's shop
barbero *m* barber
barbilla *f* chin
barbitúrico *m* barbiturate
barbo *m pescado* barbel
barca *f* boat
barcaza *f* MAR barge
barco *m* boat; *más grande* ship; **barco de vela** sailing ship
baremo *m* scale
barniz *m para madera* varnish
barnizar ⟨1f⟩ *v/t* varnish
barómetro *m* barometer
barquero *m* boatman
barquillo *m* wafer; *Méx, C.Am.* ice-cream cone
barra *f de metal, en bar* bar; *de cortinas* rod; **barra de labios** lipstick; **barra de pan** baguette; **barra espaciadora** space-bar; **barra de herramientas** INFOR

tool bar; **barra invertida** backslash

barraca f (*chabola*) shack; *de tiro* stand; *de feria* stall; L.Am. (*deposito*) shed; **barracas** pl L.Am. shanty town sg

barracón f MIL barrack room

barranco m ravine

barrenar ⟨1a⟩ v/t drill

barrendero m, -a f street sweeper

barreno m drill hole

barreño m washing up bowl

barrer ⟨2a⟩ v/t sweep

barrera f barrier; **barrera del sonido** sound barrier

barriada f C.Am. (*barrio marginal*) slum, shanty town

barrial m L.Am. bog

barricada f barricade

barrida f L.Am. sweep; L.Am. (*redada*) police raid

barriga f belly; **rascarse la barriga** fig F sit on one's butt F

barrigón adj F pudgy F

barril m barrel

barrio m neighbo(u)rhood, area; **barrio de chabolas** Esp shanty town; **irse al otro barrio** F kick the bucket P

barro m mud

barroco m/adj baroque

barrote m bar

bártulos mpl F things, gear sg F

barullo m uproar, racket

basar ⟨1a⟩ **1** v/t base (*en* on) **2** v/r **basarse** be based (*en* on)

báscula f scales

base f QUÍM, MAT, MIL base; **base de datos** INFOR database; **bases** de concurso etc conditions; **a base de** by dint of

básico adj basic

basílica f basilica

básquetbol m L.Am. basketball

bastante 1 adj enough; *número o cantidad considerable* plenty of; **quedan bastantes plazas** there are plenty of seats left **2** adv quite, fairly; **bebe bastante** she drinks quite a lot

bastar ⟨1a⟩ v/i be enough; **basta con uno** one is enough; **¡basta!** that's enough!

bastardo 1 adj bastard atr **2** m bastard

bastidor m: **entre bastidores** F behind the scenes

bastión m bastion

basto 1 adj rough, coarse **2** mpl: **bastos** (*en naipes*) suit in Spanish deck of cards

bastón m stick

basura f th fig trash, Br rubbish; **cubo de la basura** trash can, Br rubbish bin

basural m L.Am. dump, Br tip

basurero m garbage collector, Br dustman

bata f robe, Br dressing gown; MED (white) coat; TÉC lab coat

batacazo m F bump

batalla f battle

batallón m battalion

batata f BOT sweet potato

bate m DEP bat

batería f MIL, EL, AUTO battery; MÚS drums, drum kit; **batería de cocina** set of pans; **aparcar en batería** AUTO parallel park

batido 1 adj camino well-trodden **2** m GASTR milkshake

batidora f mixer

batir ⟨3a⟩ v/t beat; *nata* whip; *récord* break

baúl m chest, trunk; L.Am. AUTO trunk, Br boot

bautismo m baptism, christening; **bautismo de fuego** baptism of fire

bautizar ⟨1f⟩ v/t baptize, christen; *barco* name; *vino* F water down

bautizo m baptism, christening

baya f berry

bayeta f cloth

bayoneta f bayonet

bayunco adj C.Am. P silly, stupid

baza f en naipes trick; fig trump card; **meter baza** F interfere

bazar m hardware and fancy goods store; *mercado* bazaar

bazo m ANAT spleen

bazofia f fig F load of trash F

beatífico adj beatific

beatitud f beatitude

beato 1 adj desp overpious **2** m, -a f desp over-pious person

bebé m baby

bebedor m, **bebedora** f drinker

beber ⟨2a⟩ **1** v/i & v/t drink **2** v/r **beberse** drink up

bebida f drink

beca f scholarship; (*del estado*) grant

becerro m calf

béchamel f GASTR béchamel (sauce)

bedel m porter

beige adj beige

béisbol m baseball

belén m nativity scene

belga m/f & adj Belgian

Bélgica Belgium

Belice Belize

belicista m/f warmonger

bélico adj war atr

beligerante adj belligerent

bellaco m, -a f Arg rascal

belleza f beauty

bello adj beautiful

bellota f BOT acorn

bemol m MÚS flat; **mi bemol** E flat; **tener**

bemoles *fig* F be tricky F

bencina *f* benzine; *Pe, Bol (gasolina)* gas, *Br* petrol

bendecir ⟨3p⟩ *v/t* bless

bendición *f* blessing

bendito *adj* blessed

benefactor *adj* charitable

beneficencia *f* charity

beneficiar ⟨1b⟩ **1** *v/t* benefit; *Rpl ganado* slaughter **2** *v/r* **beneficiarse** benefit (**de, con** from)

beneficio *m* benefit; COM profit; *Rpl* slaughterhouse; *C.Am.* coffee-processing plant; *en beneficio de* in aid of

beneficioso *adj* beneficial

benéfico *adj* charity *atr*; *función -a* charity function *o* event

beneplácito *m* approval

benévolo *adj* benevolent, kind; *(indulgente)* lenient

bengala *f* flare

benigno *adj* MED benign

benjamín *m* youngest son

benjamina *f* youngest daughter

beodo *adj* drunk

berberecho *m* ZO cockle

berenjena *f* BOT egg plant, *Br* aubergine

berenjenal *m*: *meterse en un berenjenal* *fig* F get o.s. into a jam F

bermudas *mpl, fpl* Bermuda shorts

berrear ⟨1a⟩ *v/i* bellow; *de niño* bawl, yell

berrido *m* bellow; *de niño* yell

berrinche *m* F tantrum; *coger un berrinche* F throw a tantrum

berro *m* BOT watercress

berza *f* BOT cabbage

besamel *f* GASTR béchamel (sauce)

besar ⟨1a⟩ **1** *v/t* kiss **2** *v/r* **besarse** kiss

beso *m* kiss

bestia **1** *f* beast **2** *m/f fig* F brute F, swine F; *mujer* bitch F; *conducir a lo bestia* F drive like a madman

besugo *m* ZO bream; *fig* F idiot

betún *m* shoe polish

biberón *m* baby's bottle

Biblia *f* Bible

bibliografía *f* bibliography

biblioteca *f* library; *mueble* bookcase

bibliotecario *m*, *-a* *f* librarian

bicarbonato *m*: *bicarbonato (de sodio)* bicarbonate of soda, bicarb F

bíceps *mpl* biceps

bicho *m* bug, *Br tb* creepy-crawly; *(animal)* creature; *fig* F *persona* nasty piece of work; *¿qué bicho te ha picado?* what's eating you?

bici *f* F bike

bicicleta *f* bicycle; *ir o montar en bicicleta* go cycling; *bicicleta de montaña* mountain bike

BID *abr* (= *Banco Interamericano de Desarrollo*) IADB (= Inter-American Development Bank)

bidé *m* bidet

bidón *m* drum

bien **1** *m* good; *por tu bien* for your own good; *bienes* *pl* goods, property *sg*; *bienes de consumo* consumer goods *o* durables; *bienes inmuebles* real estate *sg* **2** *adv* well; *(muy)* very; *más bien* rather; *o bien ... o ...* either ... or ...; *¡está bien!* it's OK!, it's alright!; *estoy bien* I'm fine, I'm OK; *¿estás bien aquí?* are you comfortable here?; *¡bien hecho!* well done!

bienestar *m* well-being

bienvenida *f* welcome; *dar la bienvenida a alguien* welcome s.o.

bienvenido *adj* welcome

bife *m* *Rpl* steak

bifocal *adj* bifocal

bifurcación *f* fork; *de línea férrea* junction

bifurcarse ⟨1g⟩ *v/r* fork

bigamia *f* bigamy

bigote *m* m(o)ustache; *bigotes de gato etc* whiskers

bikini *m* bikini

bilateral *adj* bilateral

bilingüe *adj* bilingual

bilis *f* bile; *fig* F bad mood

billar *m* billiards; *billar americano* pool

billete *m* ticket; *billete abierto* open ticket; *billete de autobús* bus ticket; *billete de banco* bill, *Br* banknote; *billete de ida, billete sencillo* one-way ticket, *Br* single (ticket); *billete de ida y vuelta* round-trip ticket, *Br* return (ticket)

billetera *f* *L.Am.*, **billetero** *m* billfold, *Br* wallet

billón *m* trillion

binario *adj* binary

bingo *m* bingo; *lugar* bingo hall

biodegradable *adj* biodegradable

biodiversidad *f* biodiversity

biografía *f* biography

biología *f* biology

biológico *adj* biological; AGR organic

biólogo *m*, *-a* *f* biologist

biombo *m* folding screen

biopsia *f* MED biopsy

bioquímica *f* biochemistry

bipartidismo *m* POL two-party system

biquini *m* bikini

birlar ⟨1a⟩ *v/t* F lift F, swipe F

birome *m* *Rpl* ballpoint (pen)

birria *f* F piece of junk F; *va hecha una birria* F she looks a real mess

bis *m* encore; *9 bis* 9A

bisabuela *f* great-grandmother

bisabuelo *m* great-grandfather

bisagra *f* hinge

biscote *m* rusk

bisexual *adj* bisexual

bisiesto *adj*: **año bisiesto** leap year

bisnieta *f* great-granddaughter

bisnieto *m* great-grandson

bisonte *m* zo bison

bisoñé *m* hairpiece, toupee

bisté, bistec *m* steak

bisturí *m* MED scalpel

bisutería *f* costume jewel(le)ry

bit *m* INFOR bit

bizco *adj* cross-eyed

bizcocho *m* sponge (cake)

blanca *f persona* white; MÚS half-note, *Br* minim; **estar sin blanca** *fig* F be broke F

blanco 1 *adj* white; *(sin escrito)* blank; **arma -a** knife 2 *m persona* white; *(diana)*, *fig* target; **dar en el blanco** hit the nail on the head; **ser el blanco de todas las miradas** be the center *(Br* centre*)* of attention

blando *adj* soft

blanquear ⟨1a⟩ *v/t* whiten; *pared* whitewash; *dinero* launder

blanqueo *m* whitewashing; **blanqueo de dinero** money laundering

blanquillo *m* Méx egg

blasfemar ⟨1a⟩ *v/i* curse, swear; REL blaspheme

blasfemia *f* REL blasphemy

blindado *adj* armo(u)red; *puerta* reinforced; EL shielded

bloc *m* pad

blof *m* L.Am. bluff

bloque *m* block; POL bloc; **bloque de apartamentos** apartment building, *Br* block of flats; **en bloque** en masse

bloquear ⟨1a⟩ *v/t* block; DEP obstruct; *(atascar)* jam; MIL blockade; COM freeze

bloqueo *m* blockade

blusa *f* blouse

boa *f* zo boa constrictor

bobada *f* piece of nonsense

bobina *f* bobbin; FOT reel, spool; EL coil

bobo 1 *adj* silly, foolish 2 *m*, -*a f* fool

boca *f* mouth; **boca a boca** mouth to mouth; **boca de metro** subway entrance; **boca abajo** face down; **boca arriba** face up; **dejar con la boca abierta** leave open-mouthed; **se me hace la boca agua** my mouth is watering

bocacalle *f* side street

bocadillo *m* sandwich

bocado *m* mouthful, bite

bocana *f* river mouth

bocanada *f* mouthful; *de viento* gust

bocata *m* F → **bocadillo**

bocazas *m/f inv* F loudmouth F

boceto *m* sketch

bochar ⟨1a⟩ *v/t* Rpl F *en examen* fail, flunk F; *Méx* cold-shoulder, rebuff

bochinche *m* Méx uproar

bochorno *m* sultry weather; *fig* embarrassment

bocina *f* MAR, AUTO horn

bocio *m* MED goiter, *Br* goitre

boda *f* wedding

bodega *f* wine cellar; MAR, AVIA hold; *L.Am.* bar; *C.Am., Pe, Bol* grocery store

bodeguero *m*, -*a f* C.Am., Pe, Ven storekeeper

body *m prenda* body

bofetada *f* slap

bofetear ⟨1a⟩ *v/t* L.Am. slap

bofia *f* F cops *pl* F

boga *f*: **estar en boga** *fig* be in fashion

bogavante *m* zo lobster

bohemio 1 *adj* bohemian 2 *m*, -*a f* bohemian

bohío *m* Cuba, Ven hut

boicot *m* boycott

boicotear ⟨1a⟩ *v/t* boycott

boicoteo *m* boycotting

boina *f* beret

bojote *m* L.Am. fig bundle

bol *m* bowl

bola *f* ball; TÉC ball bearing; *de helado* scoop; F *(mentira)* fib F; **bola de nieve** snowball; **no dar pie con bola** get everything wrong

bolada *f* L.Am. throw; *(suerte)* piece of luck

bolado *m* S. Am. deal; L.Am. F *(mentira)* fib F

boleada *f* Arg hunt

boleador *m*, boleadora *f* Méx bootblack

boleadoras *fpl* L.Am. bolas

bolear ⟨1a⟩ 1 *v/i* L.Am. DEP have a knockabout 2 *v/t* L.Am. DEP bowl; *Rpl con boleadoras* bring down; *Méx zapatos* shine 3 *v/r* **bolearse** *Rpl* fall; *(aperarse)* get embarrassed

bolera *f* bowling alley

bolero 1 *m* MÚS bolero 2 *m/f* Méx F bootblack

boleta *f* L.Am. ticket; L.Am. *(pase)* pass, permit; L.Am. *(voto)* ballot paper

boletería *f* L.Am. ticket office; *en cine, teatro* box office

boletero *m*, -*a f* L.Am. ticket clerk; *en cine, teatro* box office employee

boletín *m* bulletin, report; **boletín de evaluación** report card; **boletín meteorológico** weather report

boleto *m* L.Am. ticket; **boleto de autobús** bus ticket; **boleto de ida y** *vuelta* *L.Am.*, **boleto redondo** *Méx* round-trip ticket, *Br* return

boliche *m* AUTO jack; *CSur* grocery store, *Br* grocer's

bólido *m* fig racing car

bolígrafo *m* ball-point pen

bolillo *m* bobbin; *Méx* bread roll; **encaje de bolillos** handmade lace

Bolivia Bolivia

boliviano 1 adj Bolivian **2** *m*, -a *f* Bolivian

bollo *m* bun; *(abolladura)* bump

bolo *m* pin; *C.Am.*, *Méx* christening present

bolos *mpl* bowling *sg*

bolsa *f* bag; COM stock exchange; *L.Am.* *(bolsillo)* pocket; **bolsa de agua caliente** hot-water bottle

bolsero *m*, -a *f* *Méx* F scrounger

bolsillo *m* pocket; **meterse a alguien en el bolsillo** F win s.o. over

bolso *m* purse, *Br* handbag

bolsón *m* *Arg*, *Pe* traveling bag, *Br* holdall

bomba *f* bomb; TÉC pump; *S. Am.* gas station; **bomba de relojería** time bomb; **caer como una bomba** fig F come as a bombshell; **pasarlo bomba** F have a great time

bombacha *f* *Arg* panties *pl*, *Br tb* knickers *pl*

bombacho *m*: **bombachos** *pl*, **pantalón bombacho** baggy pants *pl*

bombardear ⟨1a⟩ *v/t* bomb

bombero *m*, -a *f* firefighter; **llamar a los bomberos** call the fire department

bombilla *f* light bulb; *Rpl* metal straw for the mate gourd

bombillo *m* *C.Am.*, *Pe*, *Bol* light bulb

bombita *f* *Arg* light bulb

bombo *m* MÚS bass drum; TÉC drum

bombón *m* chocolate; *fig* F babe F

bombona *f* cylinder

bonaerense 1 adj of Buenos Aires, Buenos Aires *atr* **2** *m/f* native of Buenos Aires

bonanza *f* fig boom, bonanza

bondad *f* goodness, kindness; **tenga la bondad de** please be so kind as to

bondadoso adj caring

bongo *m* *L.Am.* bongo

boniato *m* BOT sweet potato

bonito 1 adj pretty **2** *m* zo tuna

bono *m* voucher; COM bond

bonsái *m* bonsai

boñiga *f* dung

boom *m* boom

boquerón *m* zo anchovy

boquete *m* hole

boquiabierto adj fig F speechless

borbotón *m*: **salir a borbotones** de agua

gush out; **hablaba a borbotones** fig it all came out in a rush; **hablar borbotón** burble, splutter

borda *f* MAR gunwale; **echar** *or* **tirar por la borda** throw overboard

bordado 1 adj embroidered **2** *m* embroidery

bordar ⟨1a⟩ *v/t* embroider; **bordar algo** fig do sth brilliantly

borde¹ adj F rude, uncouth

borde² *m* edge; **al borde de** fig on the verge *o* brink of

bordear ⟨1a⟩ *v/t* border

bordillo *m* curb, *Br* kerb

bordo *m*: **a bordo** MAR, AVIA on board

borona *f* corn, *Br* maize

borrachera *f* drunkenness; **agarrar una borrachera** get drunk

borrachería *f* *Méx*, *Rpl* → **borrachera**

borracho 1 adj drunk **2** *m*, -a *f* drunk

borrador *m* eraser; *de texto* draft; *(boceto)* sketch

borrar ⟨1a⟩ *v/t* erase; INFOR delete; *pizarra* clean; *recuerdo* blot out

borrasca *f* area of low pressure

borrego *m* zo lamb; *fig*: *persona* sheep

borrico *m*, -a *f* donkey; *fig* dummy

borrón *m*: blot; *mancha extendida* smudge; **hacer borrón y cuenta nueva** fig wipe the slate clean

borroso adj blurred, fuzzy

Bosnia Bosnia

bosque *m* wood; **grande** forest

bosquejo *m* sketch; *fig* outline

bostezar ⟨1f⟩ *v/i* yawn

bostezo *m* yawn

bota *f* boot; **bota de montar** riding boot; **ponerse las botas** *fig* F coin it F, rake it in F; *(comer mucho)* make a pig of o.s. F

botado *L.Am.* F **1** adj *(barato)* dirt cheap **2** *m*, -a *f* abandoned child

botana *f* *Méx* snack

botánica *f* botany

botar ⟨1a⟩ **1** *v/t* MAR launch; *pelota* bounce; *L.Am.* *(echar)* throw; *L.Am.* *(desechar)* throw out; *L.Am.* *(despedir)* fire **2** *v/i* *de pelota* bounce

bote *m* *(barco)* boat; *L.Am.* *(lata)* can, *Br tb* tin; *(tarro)* jar; **pegar un bote** jump; **bote de la basura** *Méx* trash can, *Br* rubbish bin; **bote salvavidas** lifeboat; **chupar del bote** *fig* F line one's pockets F; **tener a alguien en el bote** *fig* F have s.o. in one's pocket F; **de bote en bote** packed out

botella *f* bottle

botijo *m* container with a spout for drinking from

botín *m* loot; *calzado* ankle boot

botiquín *m* medicine chest; *estuche* first-aid kit

botón *m en prenda*, TÉC button; BOT bud

botones *m inv en hotel* bellhop, bellboy

boutique *f* boutique

bóveda *f* vault

bovino *adj* bovine

boxeador *m*, boxeadora *f* boxer

boxear ⟨1a⟩ *v/i* box

boxeo *m* boxing

boya *f* buoy; *de caña* float

boyante *adj fig* buoyant

bragas *fpl* panties, *Br tb* knickers

bragueta *f* fly

bramido *m* roar, bellow

brandy *m* brandy

branquia *f* zo gill

brasa *f* ember; *a la brasa* GASTR charbroiled, *Br* char-grilled

brasero *m* brazier; *eléctrico* electric heater

Brasil Brazil

brasileño 1 *adj* Brazilian 2 *m*, -a *f* Brazilian

bravata *f* boast; *(amenaza)* threat

bravo *adj animal* fierce; *mar* rough, choppy; *persona* brave; *L.Am. (furioso)* angry; *¡bravo!* well done!; *en concierto etc* bravo!

bravucón *m*, -ona *f* F boaster, blowhard F

braza *f* breaststroke

brazalete *m* bracelet; *(banda)* armband

brazo *m* arm; *brazo de gitano* GASTR jelly roll, *Br* Swiss roll; *con los brazos abiertos* with open arms; *dar su brazo a torcer* give in

brebaje *m desp* concoction

brecha *f* breach; *fig* F gap; MED gash; *seguir en la brecha* F hang on in there F

brécol *m* broccoli

breva *f* BOT early fig; *no caerá esa breva fig* F no such luck!

breve *adj* brief; *en breve* shortly

brevedad *f* briefness, shortness

brevemente *adv* briefly

brezo *m* BOT heather

bribón *m*, -ona *f* rascal

bricolaje *m* do-it-yourself, DIY

brigada *f* MIL brigade; *en policía* squad

brillante 1 *adj* bright; *fig* brilliant 2 *m* diamond

brillar ⟨1a⟩ *v/i fig* shine

brillo *m* shine; *de estrella, luz* brightness; *dar or sacar brillo a algo* polish sth

brincar ⟨1g⟩ *v/i* jump up and down

brinco *m* F leap, bound; *dar brincos* jump

brindar ⟨1a⟩ **1** *v/t* offer **2** *v/i* drink a toast *(por* to)

brindis *m inv* toast

brío *m fig* F verve, spirit

brisa *f* MAR breeze

brisera *f L.Am.* windshield, *Br* windscreen

británico **1** *adj* British **2** *m*, -a *f* Briton, Brit F

broca *f* TÉC drill bit

brocha *f* brush

broche *m* brooch; *(cierre)* fastener; *L.Am. (pinza)* clothes pin

brocheta *f* skewer

brócoli *m* broccoli

broma *f* joke; *en broma* as a joke; *gastar bromas* play jokes; *tomar algo a broma* take sth as a joke

bromear ⟨1a⟩ *v/i* joke

bromista *m/f* joker

bronca *f* F telling off F; *Méx* P fight; *armar una bronca Méx* get into a fight; *echar bronca a alguien* F give s.o. a telling off, tell s.o. off

bronce *m* bronze

bronceado **1** *adj* tanned **2** *m* suntan

bronceador *m* suntan lotion

broncearse ⟨1a⟩ *v/r* get a tan

bronquitis *f* MED bronchitis

brotar ⟨1a⟩ *v/i* BOT sprout, bud; *fig* appear, arise

brote *m* BOT shoot; MED, *fig* outbreak; *brotes de bambú* bamboo shoots; *brotes de soja* beansprouts

bruces: *caer de bruces* F fall flat on one's face

bruja *f* witch

brujo *m* wizard

brújula *f* compass

bruma *f* mist

bruñir ⟨3h⟩ *v/t* burnish, polish; *C.Am.* F *(molestar)* annoy

brusco *adj* sharp, abrupt; *respuesta, tono* brusque, curt

Bruselas Brussels

brutalidad *f* brutality

bruto **1** *adj* brutish; *(inculto)* ignorant; *(torpe)* clumsy; COM gross **2** *m*, -a *f* brute, animal

buceador *m*, buceadora *f* diver

bucear ⟨1a⟩ *v/i* dive; *fig* delve *(en* into)

bucólico *adj* bucolic

budista *m/f & adj* Buddhist

buen *adj* → **bueno**

buenaventura *f* fortune

bueno *adj* good; *(bondadoso)* kind; *(sabroso)* nice; *por las -as* willingly; *de -as a primeras* without warning; *ponerse bueno* get well; *¡bueno!* well!; *¿bueno? Méx* hello; *-a voluntad* goodwill; *¡-as!* hello!; *buenos días* good morning;

-as noches good evening; **-as tardes** good evening

buey m ZO ox

búfalo m ZO buffalo

bufanda f scarf; fig F perk

bufete m lawyer's office

buffet m GASTR buffet

bufón m buffoon, fool

buganvilla f BOT bougainvillea

buhardilla f attic, loft

búho m ZO owl

buitre m ZO vulture

bulbo m BOT bulb

bulevar m boulevard

Bulgaria Bulgaria

bulimia f MED bulimia

bulla f din, racket

bullicio m hubbub, din; (*actividad*) bustle

bullir ⟨3h⟩ v/i fig: *de sangre* boil; *de lugar* swarm, teem (**de** with)

bulo m F rumo(u)r

bulto m package; MED lump; *en superficie* bulge; (*silueta*) vague shape; (*pieza de equipaje*) piece of baggage

bumerán m boomerang

buque m ship; **buque de guerra** warship

burbuja f bubble

burdel m brothel

burdo adj rough

burgués 1 adj middle-class, bourgeois **2** m, **-esa** f middle-class person, member of the bourgeoisie

burguesía f middle class, bourgeoisie

burla f joke; (*engaño*) trick; **hacer burla de alguien** F make fun of s.o.

burlar ⟨1a⟩ **1** v/t F get round **2** v/r **burlarse** make fun (**de** of)

burlete m L.Am. draft excluder, Br draught excluder

buró m bureau

burocracia f bureaucracy

burócrata m/f bureaucrat

burocrático adj bureaucratic

burrada f fig F piece of nonsense; **hay una burrada** there's loads F; **costar una burrada** cost a packet F

burro m ZO donkey; **no ver tres en un burro** be as blind as a bat

bursátil adj stock market atr

bus m bus

busca 1 f search; **en busca de** in search of **2** m F pager

buscador m searcher; INFOR search engine

buscapersonas m inv pager

buscapleitos m/f inv F troublemaker

buscar ⟨1a⟩ v/t search for, look for

búsqueda f search

busto m bust

butaca f armchair; TEA seat

butano m butane

butifarra f type of sausage

buzo m diver

buzón m mailbox, Br postbox; **buzón de voz** TELEC voicemail

byte m INFOR byte

C

C abr (= **Centígrado**) C (= Centigrade); (= **compañía**) Co. (= Company); c (= **calle**) St. (= Street); (= **capítulo**) ch. (= chapter)

cabal adj: **no estar en sus cabales** not be in one's right mind

cabalgar ⟨1h⟩ v/i ride

cabalgata f procession

caballa f ZO mackerel

caballada f Rpl: **decir / hacer una caballada** say / do sth stupid

caballería f MIL cavalry; (*caballo*) horse

caballero 1 adj gentlemanly, chivalrous **2** m hombre gentleman, man; *hombre educado* gentleman; HIST knight; *trato* sir; (**servicio de**) **caballeros** pl men's room, gents; *en tienda de ropa* menswear

caballeroso adj gentlemanly, chivalrous

caballito m: **caballito del diablo** ZO dragonfly; **caballito de mar** ZO seahorse; **caballitos** pl carousel sg, merry-go-round sg

caballo m horse; *en ajedrez* knight; **caballo balancín** rocking horse; **a caballo entre** halfway between; *montar or andar* Rpl **a caballo** ride (a horse); **me gusta montar a caballo** I like riding; **ir a caballo** go on horseback

cabaña f cabin

cabaret m cabaret

cabecear ⟨1a⟩ **1** v/i nod **2** v/t *el balón* head

cabecera f *de mesa, cama* head; *de periódico* masthead; *de texto* top cabecero *m de cama* headboard

cabecilla *m/f* ringleader

cabello *m* hair

caber ⟨2m⟩ *v/i* fit; *caben tres litros* it holds three liters *o Br* litres; *cabemos todos* there's room for all of us; *no cabe duda fig* there's no doubt; *no me cabe en la cabeza* I just don't understand

cabestrillo *m* MED sling

cabeza 1 *f* ANAT head; *cabeza de ajo* bulb of garlic; *cabeza (de ganado)* head of (cattle); *cabeza nuclear* nuclear warhead; *el equipo a la cabeza* or *en cabeza* the team at the top; *por cabeza* per head, per person; *estar mal* or *no estar bien de la cabeza* F not be right in the head F 2 *m/f*: *cabeza de familia* head of the family; *cabeza de turco* scapegoat; *cabeza rapada* skinhead

cabezada *f*: *echar una cabezada* have a nap

cabezonería *f* pigheadedness

cabezota 1 *adj* pig-headed 2 *m/f* pig-headed person

cabida *f* capacity; *dar cabida a* hold

cabildo *m* POL council

cabina *f* cabin; *cabina telefónica* phone booth

cabizbajo *adj* dejected, downhearted

cable *m* EL cable; MAR line, rope; *echar un cable a alguien* give s.o. a hand

cabo *m* end; GEOG cape; MAR rope; MIL corporal; *al cabo de* after; *de cabo a rabo* F from start to finish; *atar cabos* F put two and two together F; *llevar a cabo* carry out

cabra *f* ZO goat; *estar como una cabra* F be nuts F

cabrear ⟨1a⟩ 1 *v/t* P bug F 2 *v/r* cabrearse P get mad F

cabriola *f*: *hacer cabriolas de niño* jump around

cabro *m* Chi boy; *cabro chico* Chi baby

cabrón *m* V bastard P, son of a bitch V

caca *f* F poop F, Br pooh F; *cosa mala* piece of trash F; *hacer caca* F poop F, Br do a pooh F

cacahuate *m* Méx peanut

cacahuete *m* peanut

cacalote *m* C.Am., Cuba, Méx crow

cacao *m* cocoa; *de labios* lip salve; *no valer un cacao* L.Am. fig F not be worth a bean F

cacatúa *f* ZO cockatoo

cacería *f* hunt

cacerola *f* pan

cachar ⟨1a⟩ *v/t* L.Am. (*engañar*) trick; L.Am. (*sorprender*) catch out; *¿me cachas?* Chi get it?

cacharro *m* pot; Méx, C.Am. F (*trasto*) piece of junk; Méx, C.Am. F coche junkheap; *lavar los cacharros* Méx, C.Am. wash the dishes

cachear ⟨1a⟩ *v/t* frisk

cachemira *f* cashmere

cachetada *f* L.Am. slap

cachete *m* cheek

cachetear ⟨1a⟩ *v/t* L.Am. slap

cachimba *f* pipe

cachivache *m* thing; *cachivaches pl* (*cosas*) things, stuff *sg* F; (*basura*) junk *sg*

cacho *m* F bit; Rpl (*cuerno*) horn; Ven, Col F (*marijuana*) joint F; *jugar al cacho* Bol, Pe play dice; *ponerle cachos a alguien* cheat on sb

cachondeo *m*: *estar de cachondeo* F be joking; *tomar a cachondeo* F take as a joke; *¡vaya cachondeo!* F what a laugh! F

cachondo *adj* F (*caliente*) horny F; (*gracioso*) funny

cachorro *m* ZO pup

cacique *m* chief; POL *local political boss*; *fig* F tyrant

cacle *m* Méx shoe

caco *m* F thief

cactus *m inv* BOT cactus

cada *adj* considerado por separado each; con énfasis en la totalidad every; *cada cosa en su sitio* everything in its place; *cada uno, cada cual* each one; *cada vez* every time, each time; *cada vez más* more and more, increasingly; *cada tres días* every three days; *uno de cada tres* one out of every three

cadáver *m* (dead) body, corpse

cadena *f* chain; *de perro* leash, Br lead; TV channel; *cadena perpetua* life sentence

cadencia *f* MÚS rhythm, cadence

cadera *f* hip

caducado *adj* out of date

caducar ⟨1g⟩ *v/i* expire

caducidad *f*: *fecha de caducidad* expiry date; *de alimentos, medicinas* use-by date

caer ⟨2o⟩ 1 *v/i* fall; *me cae bien / mal fig* I like / don't like him; *dejar caer algo* drop sth; *estar al caer* be about to arrive; *caer enfermo* fall ill; *caer en lunes* fall on a Monday; *¡ahora caigo! fig* now I get it! 2 *v/r* caerse fall (down)

café *m* coffee; (*bar*) café; *café con leche* white coffee; *café descafeinado* decaffeinated coffee; *café instantáneo* instant coffee; *café solo* black coffee

cafeína *f* caffeine

cafetera f coffee maker; *para servir* coffee pot

cafetería f coffee shop

cagar ⟨1h⟩ V **1** v/i have a shit P **2** v/r cagarse shit o.s. P; *cagarse de miedo* shit o.s. P

caguama f Méx (*tortuga*) turtle

caída f fall

caigo vb → *caer*

caimán m zo alligator; Méx, C.Am. útil monkey wrench

Cairo: *El Cairo* Cairo

caja f box; *de reloj, ordenador* case, casing; COM cash desk; *en supermercado* checkout; *caja de ahorros* savings bank; *caja de cambios* gearbox; *caja de caudales, caja fuerte* safe, strongbox; *caja de cerillas* matchbox; *caja de música* music box; *caja postal* post office savings bank; *caja registradora* cash register; *echar a alguien con cajas destempladas* F send s.o. packing

cajero m, -a f cashier; *de banco* teller; *cajero automático* ATM, Br tb cash point

cajeta f Méx caramel spread

cajón m drawer; *L.Am.* casket, coffin

cajuele f Méx AUTO trunk, Br boot

cal f lime

cala f cove

calabacín m BOT zucchini, Br courgette

calabaza f pumpkin; *dar calabazas a alguien* F *en examen* fail s.o., flunk s.o. F; *en relación* give s.o. the brush off F

calabozo m cell

calada f puff

calado adj soaked; *calado hasta los huesos* soaked to the skin

calamar m zo squid

calambre m EL shock; MED cramp

calamidad f calamity

calaña f desp sort, type

calar ⟨1a⟩ **1** v/t (*mojar*) soak; *techo, tela* soak through; *persona, conjura* see through **2** v/i *de zapato* leak; *de ideas, costumbres* take root; *calar hondo en* make a big impression on **3** v/r calarse *de motor* stall; *calarse hasta los huesos* get soaked to the skin

calato adj Chi, Pe naked

calavera f skull

calcar ⟨1g⟩ v/t trace

calceta f: *hacer calceta* knit

calcetín m sock

calcinado adj burnt

calcio m calcium

calcomanía f decal, Br transfer

calculador adj fig calculating

calculadora f calculator

calcular ⟨1a⟩ v/t tb fig calculate

cálculo m calculation; MED stone; *cálculo biliar* gallstone; *cálculo renal* kidney stone

caldear ⟨1a⟩ v/t warm up; *ánimos* inflame

caldera f boiler; Rpl, Chi kettle

calderilla f small change

caldero m (small) boiler

caldillo m Méx GASTR stock

caldo m GASTR stock; *caldo de cultivo* fig breeding ground

caldoso adj watery

calefacción f heating; *calefacción central* central heating

calefactor m heater

calendario m calendar; (*programa*) schedule

caléndula f BOT marigold

calentador m heater; *calentador de agua* water heater

calentamiento m: *calentamiento global* global warming

calentar ⟨1k⟩ **1** v/t heat (up); *calentar a alguien* fig provoke s.o. **2** v/i DEP warm up **3** v/r calentarse warm up; *fig: de discusión, disputa* become heated

calentura f fever

calibrar ⟨1a⟩ v/t gauge; fig weigh up

calibre m tb fig caliber, Br calibre

calidad f quality; *calidad de vida* quality of life; *en calidad de médico* as a doctor

cálido adj tb fig warm

caliente adj hot; F (*cachondo*) horny F; *en caliente* in the heat of the moment

calificable adj gradable

calificación f description; EDU grade, Br mark

calificar ⟨1g⟩ v/t describe, label (*de* as); EDU grade, Br mark

caligrafía f calligraphy

caliza f limestone

callado adj quiet

callar ⟨1a⟩ **1** v/i (*dejar de hablar*) go quiet; (*guardar silencio*) be quiet, keep quiet; *¡calla!* be quiet!, shut up! **2** v/t silence **3** v/r callarse (*dejar de hablar*) go quiet; (*guardar silencio*) be quiet, keep quiet; *callarse algo* keep sth quiet

calle f street; DEP lane; *echar a alguien a la calle* fig throw s.o out onto the street

callejón m alley; *callejón sin salida* blind alley; fig dead end

callo m callus; *callos* pl GASTR tripe sg

calma f calm

calmante 1 adj soothing **2** m MED sedative

calmar ⟨1a⟩ **1** v/t calm (down) **2** v/r calmarse calm down

calor m heat; fig warmth; *hace mucho calor* it's very hot; *tengo calor* I'm hot

caloría f calorie

calumnia f oral slander; por escrito libel
calumniar ⟨1b⟩ v/t oralmente slander; por escrito libel
caluroso adj hot; fig warm
calva f bald patch
calvario m fig calvary
calvicie f baldness
calvo 1 adj bald **2** m bald man
calzada f road (surface)
calzado m footwear
calzador m shoe horn
calzar ⟨1f⟩ **1** v/t zapato, bota etc put on; mueble, rueda wedge **2** v/r **calzarse** zapato, bota etc put on
calzón m DEP shorts pl; L.Am. de hombre shorts pl, Br (under)pants pl; L.Am. de mujer panties pl, Br tb knickers pl; **calzones** L.Am. shorts, Br (under)pants
calzoncillos mpl shorts, Br (under)pants
cama f bed; **cama de matrimonio** double bed; **hacer la cama** make the bed; **irse a la cama** go to bed
camaleón m chameleon
cámara f FOT, TV camera; (sala) chamber; **cámara de comercio e industria** chamber of commerce and industry; **a cámara lenta** in slow motion; **cámara de vídeo** video camera
camarada m/f comrade; de trabajo colleague, co-worker
camaradería f camaraderie, comradeship
camarera f waitress
camarero m waiter
camarógrafo m, -a f L.Am. camera operator
camarón m L.Am. zo shrimp, Br prawn
camarote m MAR cabin
camarotero m L.Am. steward
cambalache m Arg F second-hand shop
cambiar ⟨1b⟩ **1** v/t change (por for); compra exchange (por for) **2** v/i change; **cambiar de lugar** change places; **cambiar de marcha** AUTO shift gear, Br change gear **3** v/r **cambiarse** change; **cambiarse de ropa** change (one's clothes)
cambio m change, COM exchange rate; **cambio climático** climate change; **cambio de marchas** AUTO gear shift, Br gear change; **cambio de sentido** U-turn; **a cambio de** in exchange for; **en cambio** on the other hand
camelia f BOT camellia
camello 1 m zo camel **2** m/f F (vendedor de drogas) pusher F, dealer
camelo m F con F; (broma) joke
camilla f stretcher
caminar ⟨1a⟩ **1** v/i walk; fig move; **caminando** on foot **2** v/t walk

camino m (senda) path; (ruta) way; **a medio camino** halfway; **de camino a** on the way to; **por el camino** on the way; **abrirse camino** fig make one's way; **ir por buen / mal camino** fig be on the right / wrong track; **ponerse en camino** set out
camión m truck, Br tb lorry; Méx bus
camionero m, -a f truck driver, Br tb lorry driver; Méx bus driver
camioneta f van
camisa f shirt
camiseta f T-shirt
camisón m nightdress
camorra f F fight; **armar camorra** F cause trouble
campal adj: **batalla campal** pitched battle
campamento m camp
campana f bell; **campana extractora** extractor hood
campanada f chime; **dar la campanada** cause a stir
campanario m bell tower
campanazo m L.Am. warning
campanilla f small bell; ANAT uvula
campante adj: **tan campante** F as calm as anything F
campaña f campaign; **campaña electoral** election campaign
campechano adj down-to-earth
campeón m, -ona f champion
campeonato m championship; **de campeonato** F terrific F
campera f L.Am. jacket
campesino 1 adj peasant atr **2** m, -a f peasant
campestre adj rural, country atr
camping m campground, Br tb campsite
campo m field; DEP field, Br tb pitch; (estadio) stadium, Br tb ground; **el campo** (área rural) the country; **campo de batalla** battlefield; **campo de concentración** concentration camp; **campo de golf** golf course; **campo visual** MED field of vision; **a campo traviesa, campo a través** cross-country
campus m inv: **campus universitario** university campus
camuflaje m camouflage
camuflar ⟨1a⟩ v/t camouflage
cana f gray (Br grey) hair
Canadá Canada
canadiense m/f & adj Canadian
canal m channel; TRANSP canal
canalete m paddle
canalizar ⟨1f⟩ v/t channel
canalla m swine F, rat F
canalón m gutter

canapé *m* (*sofá*) couch; *para cama* base; GASTR canapé

Canarias *fpl* Canaries

canario 1 *adj* Canary *atr* **2** *m* ZO canary

canasta *f* basket; *juego* canasta

cancela *f* (wrought-iron) gate

cancelación *f* cancellation

cancelar ⟨1a⟩ *v/t* cancel; *deuda, cuenta* settle, pay

cáncer *m* MED, *fig* cancer; *Cáncer m/f inv* ASTR Cancer

cancerígeno *adj* carcinogenic

canceroso *adj* cancerous

cancha *f* DEP court; *L.Am. de fútbol* field, *Br* th; pitch; *cancha de tenis* tennis court; *¡cancha! Rpl* F gangway! F; *abrir or hacer cancha Rpl* make room

canchear ⟨1a⟩ *v/i L.Am.* climb

canciller *m* Chancellor; *S. Am. de asuntos exteriores* Secretary of State, *Br* Foreign Minister

canción *f* song; *siempre la misma canción* F the same old story F

candado *m* padlock

candela *f L.Am.* fire; *¿me das candela?* have you got a light?

candelabro *m* candelabra

candelero *m*: *estar en el candelero de persona* be in the limelight

candente *adj* red-hot; *tema* topical

candidato *m*, *-a f* candidate

candidatura *f* candidacy

cándido *adj* naive

candor *m* innocence; (*franqueza*) cando(u)r

canela *f* cinnamon

canelones *mpl* GASTR cannelloni *sg*

cangrejo *m* ZO crab

canguro 1 *m* ZO kangaroo **2** *m/f* F baby-sitter

caníbal 1 *adj* cannibal *atr* **2** *m/f* cannibal

canica *f* marble

caniche *m* poodle

canícula *f* dog days *pl*

canijo *adj* F puny

canilla *f L.Am.* faucet, *Br* tap

canillita *m/f Arg* newspaper vendor

canjear ⟨1a⟩ *v/t* exchange (*por* for)

canoa *f* canoe

canónico *adj* canonical

canónigo *m* canon

canonizar ⟨1f⟩ *v/t* canonize

cansado *adj* tired

cansancio *m* tiredness

cansar ⟨1a⟩ **1** *v/t* tire; (*aburrir*) bore **2** *v/t* cansarse get tired; (*aburrirse*) get bored; *cansarse de algo* get tired of sth

cantante *m/f* singer

cantar ⟨1a⟩ *v/i* sing; *de delincuente* squeal P **2** *v/t* sing **3** *m*: *ése es otro cantar fig* F that's a different story

cántaro *m* pitcher; *llover a cántaros* F pour (down)

cantautor *m*, **cantautora** *f* singer-songwriter

cante *m*: *cante hondo or jondo* flamenco singing

cantera *f* quarry

cantidad *f* quantity; amount; *había cantidad de* there was (*pl* were) a lot of

cantimplora *f* water bottle

cantina *f* canteen

canto[1] *m* singing; *de pájaro* song

canto[2] *m* edge; (*roca*) stone; *canto rodado* boulder; *darse con un canto en los dientes* count o.s. lucky

canturrear ⟨1a⟩ *v/t* sing softly

canutas: *las pasé canutas* F it was really tough F

caña *f* BOT reed; (*tallo*) stalk; *cerveza* small glass of beer; *L.Am.* straw; *muebles de caña* cane furniture; *caña de azúcar* sugar cane; *caña de pescar* fishing rod; *dar or meter caña a alguien* wind s.o. up F; *¡dale caña!* F get off your butt! F

cañada *f* ravine; *L.Am.* (*arroyo*) stream

cáñamo *m* hemp; *L.Am.* marijuana plant

cañería *f* pipe

cañero *adj L.Am.* sugar-cane *atr*

caño *m* pipe; *de fuente* spout

cañón 1 *m* HIST cannon; *antiaéreo, antitanque etc* gun; *de fusil* barrel; GEOG canyon **2** *adj* F great, fantastic F

cañonazo *m* gunshot

caoba *f* mahogany

caos *m* chaos

caótico *adj* chaotic

cap *abr* (= *capítulo*) ch. (= chapter)

capa *f* layer; *prenda* cloak; *capa de ozono* ozone layer; *capa de pintura* coat of paint

capacidad *f* capacity; (*aptitud*) competence; *capacidad de memoria o de almacenamiento* INFOR memory / storage capacity

capacitar ⟨1a⟩ *v/t* prepare; *capacitar alguien para hacer algo* qualify s.o. to do sth

capar ⟨1a⟩ *v/t* castrate

caparazón *m* ZO shell

capataz *m* foreman

capataza *f* forewoman

capaz *adj* able (*de* to); *ser capaz de* be capable of

capcioso *adj*: *pregunta -a* trick question

capear ⟨1a⟩ *v/t temporal* weather

capellán *m* chaplain

capicúa *adj*: **número capicúa** reversible number

capilar 1 *adj* capillary *atr*; **loción** hair *atr* **2** *m* capillary

capilla *f* chapel; **capilla ardiente** chapel of rest

capirotada *f Méx* type of French toast with honey, cheese, raisins etc

capital 1 *adj* importancia prime; **pena capital** capital punishment **2** *f de país* capital **3** *m* COM capital

capitalismo *m* capitalism

capitalista 1 *adj* capitalist *atr* **2** *m/f* capitalist

capitán *m* captain

capitanear ⟨1a⟩ *v/t* captain

capitel *m* ARQUI capital

Capitolio *m* Capitol

capitulación *f* capitulation, surrender; (*pacto*) agreement

capitular ⟨1a⟩ *v/i* surrender, capitulate

capítulo *m* chapter

capó *m* AUTO hood, *Br* bonnet

capón *m Rpl* mutton

capota *f* AUTO top, *Br* hood

capote *m* cloak; MIL greatcoat

capotera *f L.Am.* coat stand

capricho *m* whim

caprichoso *adj* capricious

Capricornio *m/f inv* ASTR Capricorn

cápsula *f* capsule; **cápsula espacial** space capsule

captar ⟨1a⟩ *v/t* understand; RAD pick up; *negocio* take

capturar ⟨1a⟩ *v/t* capture

capucha *f* hood

capuchino *m* cappuccino

capullo *m* ZO cocoon; BOT bud

caqui 1 *adj* khaki **2** *m* BOT persimmon

cara *f* face; (*expresión*) look; *fig* nerve; **cara a algo** facing sth; **cara a cara** face to face; **do oara a** facing; *fig* with regard to; **dar la cara** face the consequences; **echar algo en cara a alguien** remind s.o. of sth; **tener cara dura** have a nerve; **tener buena/mala cara** *de comida* look good/bad; *de persona* look well/sick; **cara o cruz** heads or tails

carabinero *m* GASTR (large) shrimp, *Br* prawn; (*agente de aduana*) border guard

caracol *m* snail; **¡caracoles!** wow! F; *enfado* damn! F

caracola *f* ZO conch

carácter *m* character; (*naturaleza*) nature

característica *f* characteristic

característico *adj* characteristic (**de** of)

caracterizar ⟨1f⟩ **1** *v/t* characterize; TEA play (the part of) **2** *v/r* **caracterizarse** be characterized (**por** by)

caradura *m/f* F guy/woman with a nerve, *Br* cheeky devil F

carajillo *m* coffee with a shot of liquor

carajo *m*: **irse al carajo** F go down the tubes F

caramba *int* wow!; *enfado* damn! F

carambola *f* billar carom, *Br* cannon; **por** or **de carambola** F by sheer chance

caramelo *m dulce* candy, *Br* sweet; (*azúcar derretida*) caramel

carantoña *f* caress

caraqueño 1 *adj* of/from Caracas, Caracas *atr* **2** *m*, **-a** *f* native of Caracas

carátula *f de disco* jacket, *Br tb* sleeve; *L.Am. de reloj* face

caravana *f* (*remolque*) trailer, *Br* caravan; *de tráfico* queue of traffic, traffic jam; *Méx* (*reverencia*) bow

caray *int* F wow! F; *enfado* damn! F

carbón *m* coal

carboncillo *m* charcoal

carbonizar ⟨1f⟩ *v/t* char

carbono *m* QUÍM carbon

carburador *m* AUTO carburet(t)or

carburante *m* fuel

carca *m/f & adj* F reactionary

carcajada *f* laugh, guffaw; **reír a carcajadas** roar with laughter

carcajearse ⟨1a⟩ *v/r* have a good laugh (**de** at)

cárcel *f* prison

carcelero *m*, **-a** *f* warder, jailer

carcinoma *f* MED carcinoma

carcoma *f* ZO woodworm

carcomer ⟨2a⟩ **1** *v/t* eat away; *fig: de envidia* eat away at, consume **2** *v/r* **carcomerse** be eaten away; **carcomerse de** *fig* be consumed with

cardamomo *m* BOT cardamom

cardenal *m* REL cardinal; (*hematoma*) bruise

cardíaco, cardiaco *adj* cardiac

cardinal *adj* cardinal; **número cardinal** cardinal number; **puntos cardinales** points of the compass, cardinal points

cardiólogo *m*, **-a** *f* cardiologist

cardo *m* BOT thistle

carecer ⟨2d⟩ *v/i*: **carecer de algo** lack sth

carencia *f* lack (**de** of)

carente *adj*: **carente de** lacking in

careta *f* mask

carga *f* load; *de buque* cargo; MIL, EL charge; (*responsabilidad*) burden; **carga explosiva** explosive charge; **carga fiscal** or **impositiva** tax burden; **ser una carga para alguien** be a burden to s.o.; **volver a la carga** return to the attack

cargado *adj* loaded (**de** with); *aire* stuffy; *ambiente* tense; *café* strong

cargamento *m* load

cargante *adj* F annoying

cargar ⟨1h⟩ **1** *v/t arma, camión* load; *batería, acusado* charge; COM charge (**en** to); *L.Am.* (*traer*) carry; *esto me carga L.Am.* P I can't stand this **2** *v/i* (*apoyarse*) rest (**sobre** on); (*fastidiar*) be annoying; *cargar con algo* carry sth; *cargar con la culpa fig* shoulder the blame; *cargar contra alguien* MIL, DEP charge (at) s.o. **3** *v/r* **cargarse con peso, responsabilidad** weigh o.s. down; F (*matar*) bump off F; F (*romper*) wreck F

cargo *m* position; JUR charge; *alto cargo* high-ranking position; *persona* high-ranking official; *a cargo de la madre* in the mother's care; *está a cargo de Gómez* Gómez is in charge of it; *hacerse cargo de algo* take charge of sth

cariarse ⟨1b⟩ *v/r* decay

Caribe *m* Caribbean

caribeño *adj* Caribbean

caricatura *f* caricature

caricaturizar ⟨1f⟩ *v/t* caricature

caricia *f* caress

caridad *f* charity

caries *f* MED caries

cariño *m* affection, fondness; *hacer cariño a alguien L.Am.* (*acariciar*) caress s.o.; (*abrazar*) hug s.o.; *¡cariño!* darling!; *con cariño* with love

cariñoso *adj* affectionate

carisma *m* charisma

carismático *adj* charismatic

caritativo *adj* charitable

cariz *m* look; *tomar mal cariz* start to look bad

carmín *m de labios* lipstick

carnaval *m* carnival

carne *f* meat; *de persona* flesh; *carne de gallina fig* goose bumps *pl*, *Br* gooseflesh; *carne picada* ground meat, *Br* mince; *de carne y hueso* flesh and blood; *sufrir algo en sus propias carnes fig* go through sth oneself

carné *m* → **carnet**

carnear ⟨1a⟩ *v/t L.Am.* slaughter

carnero *m* ram

carnet *m* card; *carnet de conducir* driver's license, *Br* driving licence; *carnet de identidad* identity card

carnicería *f* butcher's; *fig* carnage

carnicero *m*, *-a f* butcher

carnívoro *adj* carnivorous

carnoso *adj* fleshy

caro *adj* expensive, dear; *costar caro fig* cost dear

carozo *m Chi, Rpl* pit

carpa *f de circo* big top; ZO carp; *L.Am.*

para acampar tent; *L.Am. de mercado* stall

carpeta *f* file

carpintero *m* carpenter; *de obra* joiner; *pájaro carpintero* woodpecker

carpir ⟨3a⟩ *v/t L.Am.* hoe

carraspear ⟨1a⟩ *v/i* clear one's throat

carraspera *f* hoarseness

carrera *f* race; EDU degree course; *profesional* career; *carrera de armamento* arms race; *a las carreras* at top speed; *con prisas* in a rush; *hacer la carrera* F *de prostituta* turn tricks F; *carreras pl de coches* motor racing *sg*

carrerilla *f*: *tomar carrerilla* take a run up; *decir algo de carrerilla* reel sth off

carreta *f* cart

carrete *m* FOT (roll of) film; *carrete de hilo* reel of thread

carretera *f* highway, (main) road; *carretera de circunvalación* ring road

carretilla *f* wheelbarrow

carril *m* lane; *carril-bici* cycle lane; *carril-bus* bus lane

carrillo *m* cheek; *comer a dos carrillos* F stuff oneself

carrito *m* cart, *Br* trolley; *carrito de bebé* buggy, *Br* pushchair

carro *m* cart; *L.Am.* car; *L.Am.* (*taxi*) taxi, cab; *carro de combate* tank; *carro-patrulla L.Am.* F patrol car

carrocería *f* AUTO bodywork

carroña *f* carrion

carruaje *m* carriage

carta *f* letter; GASTR menu; (*naipe*) playing card; (*mapa*) chart; *carta certificada* or *registrada* registered letter; *carta urgente* special-delivery letter; *a la carta* a la carte; *dar carta blanca a alguien* give s.o. carte blanche *o* a free hand; *poner las cartas boca arriba fig* put one's cards on the table; *tomar cartas en el asunto* intervene in the matter

cartearse ⟨1a⟩ *v/r* write to each other

cartel *m* poster; *estar en cartel de película, espectáculo* be on

cártel *m* cartel

cartelera *f* billboard; *de periódico* listings, entertainments section

cartera *f* wallet; (*maletín*) briefcase; COM, POL portfolio; *de colegio* knapsack, *Br* satchel; *L.Am.* purse, *Br* handbag; *mujer* mailwoman, *Br* postwoman

carterista *m/f* pickpocket

cartero *m* mailman, *Br* postman

cartílago *m* cartilage

cartilla *f* reader; *Méx* identity card; *cartilla de ahorros* savings book; *leerle a alguien la cartilla* F give s.o. a telling off F

C

cartógrafo *m*, **-a** *f* cartographer
cartón *m* cardboard; *de tabaco* carton; **cartón piedra** pap(i)er- mâché
cartuchera *f* cartridge belt
cartucho *m de arma* cartridge
cartulina *f* sheet of card; **cartulina roja** DEP red card
casa *f* house; (*hogar*) home; **en casa** at home; **como una casa** F huge F; **casa cuna** children's home; **casa de huéspedes** rooming house, *Br* boarding house; **casa matriz** head office; **casa de socorro** first aid post; **casa adosada, casa pareada** → **chalet**
casaca *f* cassock
casado *adj* married; **recién casado** newly-wed
casamentero *m*, **-a** *f* matchmaker
casar ⟨1a⟩ **1** *v/i fig* match (up); **casar con** go with F; *v/r* **casarse** get married; **casarse con alguien** marry s.o.; **no casarse con nadie** *fig* refuse to compromise
cascabel *m* small bell
cascada *f* waterfall
cascado *adj voz* hoarse; F *persona* worn out F
cascanueces *m inv* nutcracker
cascar ⟨1g⟩ *v/t* crack; *algo quebradizo* break; *fig* F whack F; **cascarla** peg out F
cáscara *f de huevo* shell; *de naranja, limón* peel
cascarón *m* shell; **salir del cascarón** hatch (out)
cascarrabias *m inv* F grouch F
casco *m* helmet; *de barco* hull; (*botella vacía*) empty (bottle); *edificio* empty building; *de caballo* hoof; *de vasija* fragment; **casco urbano** urban area; **cascos azules** MIL blue berets, UN peace-keeping troops
cascote *m* piece of rubble
casera *f* landlady
casero 1 *adj* home-made; **comida -a** home cooking **2** *m* landlord
caseta *f* hut; *de feria* stall
casete *m* (*also f*) cassette
casi *adv* almost, nearly; *en frases negativas* hardly
casilla *f en formulario* box; *en tablero* square; *de correspondencia* pigeon hole; *S. Am.* post office box; **sacar a alguien de sus casillas** drive s.o. crazy
casino *m* casino
caso *m* case; **en caso de que, caso de** in the event that, in case of; **hacer caso** take notice; **ser un caso** F be a real case F; **no venir al caso** be irrelevant; **en todo caso** in any case, in any event; **en el peor de los casos** if the worst comes to

the worst; **en último caso** as a last resort
caspa *f* dandruff
caspiroleta *f S. Am.* eggnog
casquillo *m de cartucho* case; ELbulb holder; *L.Am.* horseshoe
cassette *m* (*also f*) cassette; **cassette virgen** blank cassette
casta *f* caste
castaña *f* chestnut; **sacar las castañas del fuego a alguien** *fig* F pull s.o.'s chestnuts out of the fire F
castaño 1 *adj color* chestnut, brown **2** *m* chestnut (tree); *color* chestnut, brown; **ya pasa de castaño oscuro** F it's gone too far, it's beyond a joke
castañuela *f* castanet; **estar como unas castañuelas** F be over the moon F
castellano *m* (Castilian) Spanish
castidad *f* chastity
castigar ⟨1h⟩ *v/t* punish
castigo *m* punishment
castillo *m* castle; **castillo de fuegos artificiales** firework display
castizo *adj* pure
casto *adj* chaste
castor *m* ZO beaver
castrar ⟨1a⟩ *v/t* castrate; *fig* emasculate
castrense *adj* army *atr*
casual *adj* chance *atr*
casualidad *f* chance, coincidence; **por** or **de casualidad** by chance
cataclismo *m* cataclysm, catastrophe
catalán 1 *adj* Catalan **2** *m*, **-ana** *f* Catalan
catalejo *m* telescope
catalizador *m* catalyst; AUTO catalytic converter
catalizar ⟨1f⟩ *v/t* catalyze
catalogar ⟨1h⟩ *v/t* catalog(ue); *fig* class
catálogo *m* catalog(ue)
catamarán *m* MAR catamaran
cataplasma *f* MED poultice; *fig: persona* bore
catapulta *f* slingshot, *Br* catapult
catapultar ⟨1a⟩ *v/t* catapult
catar ⟨1a⟩ *v/t* taste
catarata *f* GEOG waterfall; MED cataract
catarro *m* cold; *inflamación* catarrh
catástrofe *f* catastrophe
catastrófico *adj* catastrophic
cate *m* EDU F fail
catear ⟨1a⟩ *v/t* F flunk F
catecismo *m* catechism
catedral *f* cathedral; **una mentira como una catedral** F a whopping great lie F
catedrático *m*, **-a** *f* EDU head of department
categoría *f* category; *social* class; *fig: de local, restaurante* class; (*estatus*) standing; **actor de primera categoría** first-rate ac-

tor

categórico *adj* categorical

catequesis *f* catechism

catéter *m* MED catheter

catolicismo *m* (Roman) Catholicism

católico 1 *adj* (Roman) Catholic **2** *m*, **-a** *f* (Roman) Catholic

catorce *adj* fourteen

catre *m* bed

cauce *m* riverbed; *fig* channel; **volver a su cauce** fig get back to normal

caucho *m* rubber; *L.Am.* (*neumático*) tire, *Br* tyre

caudal *m de río* volume of flow; *fig* wealth

caudillo *m* leader

causa *f* cause; (*motivo*) reason; JUR lawsuit; **a causa de** because of

causante *m* cause

causar ⟨1a⟩ *v/t* cause

cáustico *adj tb fig* caustic

cautela *f* caution

cauteloso *adj* cautious

cauterizar ⟨1f⟩ *v/t* cauterize

cautivar ⟨1a⟩ *v/t fig* captivate

cautiverio *m*, **cautividad** *f* captivity

cautivo 1 *adj* captive **2** *m*, **-a** *f* captive

cauto *adj* cautious

cava *m* cava, sparkling wine

cavar ⟨1a⟩ *v/t* dig

caverna *f* cavern

cavernícola *m/f* caveman; *mujer* cavewoman

caviar *m* caviar

cavidad *f* cavity

cavilar ⟨1a⟩ *v/t* meditate on

cayó *vb* → **caer**

caza 1 *f* hunt; *actividad* hunting; **caza mayor / menor** big / small game; **andar a la caza de algo / alguien** be after sth/s.o. **2** *m* AVIA fighter

cazador *m* hunter

cazadora *f* hunter; *prenda* jacket

cazar ⟨1f⟩ **1** *v/t animal* hunt; *fig: información* track down; (*pillar, captar*) catch; **cazar un buen trabajo** get o.s. a good job **2** *v/i* hunt; **ir a cazar** go hunting

cazo *m* saucepan

cazuela *f pan*; *de barro, vidrio* casserole

cazurro *adj* stubborn; (*basto*) coarse; (*lento de entender*) dense F, thick F

c.c. *abr* (= **centímetro cúbico**) c.c. (= cubic centimeter)

c/c *abr* (= **cuenta corriente**) C/A(= checking account)

CD *m* (= **disco compacto**) CD (= compact disc); *reproductor* CD-player

CD-ROM *m* CD-ROM

cebada *f* barley

cebar ⟨1a⟩ **1** *v/t* fatten; *anzuelo* bait; TÉC

prime; *L.Am.* mate prepare **2** *v/r* **cebarse** feed (**en** on); **cebar con alguien** vent one's fury on s.o.

cebo *m* bait

cebolla *f* onion

cebra *f* zebra; **paso de cebra** crosswalk, *Br* zebra crossing

ceceo *m* pronunciation *of 's' with 'th' sound*

cecina *f* cured meat

cedazo *m* sieve

ceder ⟨2a⟩ **1** *v/t* give up; (*traspasar*) transfer, cede; **ceder el paso** AUTO yield, *Br* give way **2** *v/i* give way, yield; *de viento, lluvia* ease off

cedro *m* BOT cedar

cédula *f L.Am.* identity document

cegar ⟨1h & 1k⟩ *v/t* blind; *tubería* block

ceguera *f tb fig* blindness

ceja *f* eyebrow; **lo tiene entre ceja y ceja** F she can't stand him F

cejar ⟨1a⟩ *v/i* give up; **no cejar en** not let up in

celador *m*, **celadora** *f* orderly; *de cárcel* guard; *de museo* attendant

celda *f* cell

celebración *f* celebration

celebrar ⟨1a⟩ *v/t misa* celebrate; *reunión, acto oficial* hold; *fiesta* have, hold

célebre *adj* famous

celeste *adj* light blue, sky blue

celestial *adj* celestial; *fig* heavenly

celibato *m* celibacy

celo *m* zeal; (*cinta adhesiva*) Scotch® tape, *Br* Sellotape®; **en celo** zo in heat; **celos** *pl* jealousy *sg*; **tener celos de** be jealous of

celofán *m* cellophane

celoso *adj* jealous (**de** of)

célula *f* cell

celular *adj* cellular

celulitis *f* cellulite

celulosa *f* cellulose

cementerio *m* cemetery

cemento *m* cement

cena *f* dinner; *más tarde* supper

cenagoso *adj* boggy

cenar ⟨1a⟩ **1** *v/t*: **cenar algo** have sth for dinner **2** *v/i* have dinner

cencerro *m* cowbell

cenicero *m* ashtray

cenit *m* AST zenith; *fig* peak

ceniza *f* ash; **cenizas** ashes

censo *m* census; **censo electoral** voting register, electoral roll

censura *f* censorship

censurar ⟨1a⟩ *v/t* censor; *tratamiento* condemn

cent *abr* (= **céntimo**) cent

centavo m cent
centellear ⟨1a⟩ v/i sparkle; de estrella twinkle
centena f hundred
centenar m hundred; **regalos a centenares** hundreds of gifts
centenario **1** adj hundred-year-old atr **2** m centennial, Br centenary
centeno m BOT rye
centígrado adj centigrade; **dos grados centígrados** two degrees centigrade
centímetro m centimeter, Br centimetre
céntimo m cent; **estar sin un céntimo** not have a red cent F
centinela m/f sentry; de banda criminal lookout
central **1** adj central; (principal) main, central **2** f head office; **central atómica** or **nuclear** nuclear power station; **central eléctrica** power station; **central térmica** thermal power station
centralismo m POL centralism
centralita f TELEC switchboard
centralizar ⟨1f⟩ v/t centralize
centrar ⟨1a⟩ v/t DEP center, Br centre; esfuerzos focus (**en** on) **2** v/r centrarse concentrate (**en** on)
céntrico adj central
centrifugar ⟨1h⟩ v/t spin
centro m center, Br centre; **centro comercial** (shopping) mall, Br shopping centre; **centro urbano** en señal town center (Br centre)
Centroamérica Central America
centroamericano adj Central American
ceñido adj tight
ceñirse ⟨3h & 3l⟩ v/r: **ceñirse a algo** fig stick to sth
ceño m: **fruncir el ceño** frown
cepa f de vid stock
cepillar ⟨1a⟩ **1** v/t brush **2** v/r cepillarse brush; F (comerse) polish off F; F (matar) kill, knock off F
cepillo m brush; **cepillo de dientes** toothbrush
cera f wax
cerámica f ceramics
cerca¹ f fence
cerca² adv near, close; **de cerca** close up; **cerca de** near, close to; (casi) nearly
cercanía f: **tren de cercanías** suburban train
cercano adj nearby; **cercano a** close to, near to
cercar ⟨1g⟩ v/t surround; con valla fence in
cerciorarse ⟨1a⟩ v/r make sure (**de** of)
cerco m ring; de puerta frame; L.Am.

fence; **poner cerco a** lay siege to
cerda f animal sow; fig F persona pig F; de brocha bristle
cerdo m hog, Br pig; fig F persona pig F
cereal m cereal; **cereales** pl (breakfast) cereal sg
cerebro m ANAT brain; fig: persona brains sg
ceremonia f ceremony
cereza f cherry
cerezo m cherry (tree)
cerilla f match
cernerse ⟨2g⟩ v/r: **cernerse sobre** fig hang over
cernícalo m ZO kestrel
cero m EDU zero, Br tb nought; en fútbol etc zero, Br nil; en tenis love; **bajo / sobre cero** below / above zero; **empezar desde cero** fig start from scratch; **vencer por tres a cero** win three-zero (Br nil)
cerrado adj closed; persona narrow-minded; (tímido) introverted; cielo overcast; **curva -a** tight curve
cerradura f lock; **ojo de la cerradura** keyhole
cerrajero m, -a f locksmith
cerrar ⟨1k⟩ **1** v/t close; para siempre close down; tubería block; grifo turn off; **cerrar con llave** lock **2** v/i close; para siempre close down **3** v/r cerrarse close; de cielo cloud over; de persona shut o.s. off (**a** from); **cerrarse de golpe** slam shut
cerrazón f fig narrow-mindedness
cerrero adj L.Am. persona rough
cerril adj animal wild; (terco) stubborn, pig-headed F; (torpe) F dense F
cerro m hill
cerrojo m bolt; **echar el cerrojo** bolt the door
certamen m competition
certeza f certainty
certidumbre f certainty
certificado **1** adj carta registered **2** m certificado
certificar ⟨1g⟩ v/t certify; carta register
cerval adj: **miedo cerval** terrible fear
cervecería f bar
cerveza f beer; **cerveza de barril** or **de presión** draft, Br draught (beer); **cerveza negra** stout; **cerveza rubia** lager; **fábrica de cerveza** brewery
cesante adj Chi unemployed, jobless; **dejar cesante a alguien** let s.o. go
cesar ⟨1a⟩ v/i stop; **no cesar de hacer algo** keep on doing sth; **sin cesar** non-stop
cesárea f MED C(a)esarean
cese m cessation
cesión f transfer

césped m lawn

cesta f basket; **cesta de la compra** shopping basket

cesto m large basket

C.F. abr (= **Club de Fútbol**) FC (= Football Club)

cfc abr (= **clorofluorocarbono**) CFC (= chlorofluorocarbon)

cg. abr (= **centigramo**) centigram

ch/ abr (= **cheque**) check

chabacano adj vulgar, tacky F

chabola f shack; **barrio de chabolas** shanty town

chacal m zo jackal

chacarero m, **-a** f Rpl, Chi smallholder, farmer

chacha f F maid

chácharas fpl L.Am. junk sg, bits and pieces

chachi adj F great F

chacra f L.Am. AGR smallholding

chafar ⟨1a⟩ v/t squash; cosa erguida flatten; F planes etc ruin F

chaflán m corner

chal m shawl

chalado adj F crazy F (por about)

chalé m → **chalet**

chaleco m de traje waistcoat; de sport gilet, bodywarmer; **chaleco salvavidas** life vest; **chaleco antibalas** bulletproof vest

chalet m chalet; **chalet adosado** house sharing one or more walls with other houses; **chalet pareado** semi-detached house

chalupa f MAR small boat; Méx stuffed tortilla

chamaca f C.Am., Méx girl

chamaco m C.Am., Méx boy

chamarra f Méx (saco) (short) jacket

chamba f Méx F job

chambón m, **-ona** f Méx F clumsy idiot F

champán m, **champaña** m champagne

champiñón m BOT mushroom

champú m shampoo

chamuscar ⟨1g⟩ v/t scorch; pelo singe

chamusquina f: **oler a chamusquina** smell fishy F

chance 1 m L.Am. chance; **dame chance** let me have a go 2 conj Méx perhaps, maybe

chanchería f L.Am. pork butcher's shop

chancho m L.Am. hog, Br pig; carne pork

chanchullo m F trick, scam F

chancla f thong, Br flip-flop; Méx, C.Am. (zapato) slipper

chancleta f thong, Br flip-flop; S. Am. F baby girl

chándal m tracksuit

changa f Rpl odd job

chango 1 adj Méx F sharp, smart 2 m, **-a** f Méx monkey

chanquetes mpl GASTR whitebait sg

chantaje m blackmail; **hacer chantaje a alguien** blackmail s.o.

chantajear ⟨1a⟩ v/t blackmail

chantajista m/f blackmailer

chanza f wisecrack

chao int bye

chapa f (tapón) cap; (plancha) sheet (of metal); (insignia) badge; AUTO bodywork

chapado adj plated; **chapado a la antigua** old-fashioned; **chapado en oro** gold-plated

chapar ⟨1a⟩ v/t plate; Arg, Pe catch

chaparro adj Méx small

chaparrón m downpour; fig F de insultos barrage

chapotear ⟨1a⟩ v/i splash

chapucero 1 adj shoddy, slapdash 2 m, **-a** f shoddy worker

chapurrear ⟨1a⟩ v/t: **chapurrear el francés** speak poor French

chapuza f (trabajo mal hecho) shoddy piece of work; (trabajo menor) odd job

chapuzón m dip; **darse un chapuzón** go for a dip

chaqué m morning coat

chaqueta f jacket; **chaqueta de punto** cardigan

chaquetero m, **-a** f F turncoat

chaquetón m three-quarter length coat

charango m Pe, Bol five string guitar

charca f pond

charco m puddle

charcutería f delicatessen

charla f chat; organizada talk

charlar ⟨1a⟩ v/i chat

charlatán 1 adj talkative 2 m, **-ana** f chatterbox

charol m patent leather; **zapatos de charol** patent leather shoes

charqui m L.Am. beef jerky

charro 1 adj desp garish, gaudy 2 m Méx (Mexican) cowboy

chasco m joke; **llevarse un chasco** be disappointed

chasis m inv AUTO chassis

chasquear ⟨1a⟩ v/t click; látigo crack

chasquido m click; de látigo crack

chatarra f scrap

chato adj nariz snub; L.Am. nivel low

chau int Rpl bye

chaucha f Rpl French bean

chaval m kid F, boy

chavala f F kid F, girl

chavalo m C.Am. F kid F, boy

che int Rpl hey!, look!

checar ⟨1g⟩ v/t Méx check

checo **1** adj Czech **2** m, **-a** f Czech

chef m chef

chelo m MÚS cello

chepa f F hump; **subírsele a la chepa** get too familiar

cheque m check, Br cheque; **cheque cruzado** crossed check (Br cheque); **cheque sin fondos** bad check (Br cheque); **cheque de viaje** traveler's check, Br traveller's cheque

chequear ⟨1a⟩ v/t check; C.Am. equipaje check (in)

chequeo m MED check-up

chequera f checkbook, Br chequebook

chica f girl

chicha f L.Am. corn liquor; **no ser ni chicha ni limonada** F be neither one thing nor the other

chícharo m Méx pea

chiche **1** adj C.Am. F (fácil) easy **2** m S. Am. (juguete) toy; (adorno) trinket

chichera f C.Am. jail

chichería f L.Am. bar selling corn liquor

chichón m bump

chicle m chewing gum

chico **1** adj small, little **2** m boy

chifa m Pe Chinese restaurant; (comida china) Chinese food

chifla f Méx whistling

chiflado adj F crazy F (**por** about), nuts F (**por** about)

chiflar ⟨1a⟩ **1** v/t boo **2** v/i whistle; **me chifla ...** F I'm crazy about ... F

chiflido m scream, shriek; de cerdo squeal

chillar ⟨1a⟩ v/i scream, shriek; de cerdo squeal

chillido m scream, shriek; de cerdo squeal

chillón adj voz shrill; color loud **2** m, **-ona** f loudmouth

chilote m C.Am. baby corn

chimenea f chimney; de salón fireplace

chimichurri m Rpl hot sauce

chimpancé m ZO chimpanzee

China China

china¹ f Chinese woman

china² f piedra small stone

chincheta f thumbtack, Br drawing pin

chinchorro m hammock

chinear ⟨1a⟩ v/t C.Am. niños look after

chingar ⟨1h⟩ v/t Méx V screw V, fuck V; **¡chinga tu madre!** screw you! V, fuck you! V; **no chingues** don't screw me around V

chino **1** adj Chinese **2** m Chinese man; idioma Chinese; L.Am. desp half-breed desp; **trabajo de chinos** F hard work; **me suena a chino** F it's all Chinese o double

Dutch to me F

chip m INFOR chip

chipirón m baby squid

chiquilla f girl, kid

chiquillo m boy, kid

chirimoya f BOT custard apple

chiringuito m beach bar

chiripa f: **de chiripa** F by sheer luck

chirona f: **en chirona** F in the can F, inside F

chirriar ⟨1c⟩ v/i squeak

chirrido m squeak

chisme m F bit of gossip; objeto doodad F, Br doodah F

chismografía f F gossip

chismorrear ⟨1a⟩ v/i F gossip

chismoso **1** adj gossipy **2** m, **-a** f F gossip

chispa f spark; (cantidad pequeña) spot; fig F wit

chispear ⟨1a⟩ v/i spark; fig sparkle; de lluvia spit

chistar ⟨1a⟩ v/i: **sin chistar** without saying a word

chiste m joke

chiva f L.Am. goat; C.Am., Col bus

chivarse ⟨1a⟩ v/r F rat F (**a** to)

chivato m, **-a** f F stool pigeon F

chivo m zo kid; C.Am., Méx wages pl

chocante adj (sorprendente) startling; que ofende shocking; (extraño) odd; L.Am. (antipático) unpleasant

chocar ⟨1g⟩ **1** v/t: **¡choca esos cinco!** P give me five! P, put it there! P **2** v/i crash (**con, contra** into), collide (**con** with); **chocarle a alguien** (sorprender) surprise s.o.; (ofender) shock s.o.; **me choca ese hombre** F that guy disgusts me; **chocar con un problema** come up against a problem

chocho adj F senile; **estar chocho con** dote on

choclo m Rpl corn, Br corn on the cob

chocolate m chocolate; F (hachís) hashish, hash F

chocolatina f chocolate bar

chófer, L.Am. chofer m driver

chollo m F bargain

cholo m L.Am. half-caste desp

chompa f S. Am. jumper, sweater

chop m L.Am. large beer

chopo m BOT poplar

choque m collision, crash; DEP, MIL clash; MED shock

chorizo m chorizo (spicy cured sausage); F thief; Rpl (filete) rump steak

chorlito m: **cabeza de chorlito** F featherbrain F

chorrada f F piece of junk; **decir chorradas** F talk garbage, Br talk rubbish

chorrear ⟨1a⟩ v/i gush out, stream; (*gotear*) drip

chorro m líquido jet, stream; *fig* stream; *C.Am.* faucet, *Br* tap

chovinista m/f chauvinist

choza f hut

chubasco m shower

chubasquero m raincoat

chuchería f knick-knack; (*golosina*) candy, *Br* sweet

chucho **1** adj *C.Am.* mean **2** m F (*perro*) mutt F, mongrel; *Chi* (*cárcel*) can F, prison

chueco adj *L.Am.* (*torcido*) twisted

chulería f bragging

chuleta f GASTR chop

chulo F **1** adj fantastic F, great F; *Méx* (*guapo*) attractive; (*presuntuoso*) cocky F **2** m pimp F

chumbera f *C.Am.* prickly pear

chumpipe m *C.Am.* turkey

chupa f jacket

chupado adj (*delgado*) skinny F; F (*fácil*) dead easy F; *L.Am.* F drunk

chupar ⟨1a⟩ **1** v/t suck; (*absorber*) soak up **2** v/r **chuparse**: *chuparse algo* suck sth; *fig* F put up with sth; *chuparse los dedos* F lick one's fingers

chupete m de bebé pacifier, *Br* dummy; (*sorbete*) Popsicle®, *Br* ice lolly

chupi adj F great F, fantastic F

churrasco m *Rpl* steak

churro m fritter; (*chapuza*) botched job

chusma f desp rabble desp

chutar ⟨1a⟩ v/i DEP shoot; *esto va que chuta* F this is working out fine; *y vas que chutas* F and that's your lot! F

chuzo m *Chi* F persona dead loss F; *caer chuzos de punta* F pelt down F

Cía. abr (= *Compañía*) Co. (= Company)

ciberespacio m cyberspace

cibernauta m/f Internet surfer

cibernética f cybernetics

cicatriz f scar

cicatrizar ⟨1f⟩ scar

cíclico adj cyclical

ciclismo m cycling

ciclista m/f cyclist

ciclo m cycle; *de cine* season

ciclomotor m moped

ciclón m cyclone

cicloturismo m bicycle touring

ciega f blind woman

ciego **1** adj blind; *a -as* blindly **2** m blind man

cielito m *Rpl* folk dance

cielo m sky; REL heaven; *ser un cielo* F be an angel F; *cielo raso* ceiling

ciempiés m inv zo centipede

cien adj a o one hundred

ciencia f science; *ciencia ficción* science fiction; *a ciencia cierta* for certain, for sure

científico **1** adj scientific **2** m, **-a** f scientist

ciento pron a o one hundred; *cientos de* hundreds of; *el cinco por ciento* five percent

ciernes: *en ciernes* fig potential, in the making

cierre m fastener; de negocio closure; *cierre centralizado* AUTO central locking; *cierre relámpago* L.Am. zipper, *Br* zip

cierto adj certain; *hasta cierto punto* up to a point; *un cierto encanto* a certain charm; *es cierto* it's true; *cierto día* one day; *por cierto* incidentally; *estar en lo cierto* be right

ciervo m zo deer; *ciervo volante* zo stag beetle

c.i.f. abr (= *costo, seguro y flete*) cif (= cost, insurance, freight)

cifra f figure

cigala f zo crayfish

cigarra f zo cicada

cigarrería f *L.Am. shop selling cigarettes etc*

cigarrillo m cigarette

cigarro m cigar; *L.Am.* cigarette

cigüeña f zo stork

cigüeñal m AUTO crankshaft

cilantro m BOT coriander

cilindrada f AUTO cubic capacity

cilíndrico adj cylindrical

cilindro m cylinder

cima f summit; fig peak

cimarrón adj *L.Am. animal* wild; *esclavo* runaway; *mate cimarrón Arg* unsweetened maté

cimentar ⟨1k⟩ v/t lay the foundations of; fig base (*en* on)

cimientos mpl foundations

cinc m zinc

cincel m chisel

cinco **1** adj five **2** m five; *no tener ni cinco* F not have a red cent F

cincuenta adj fifty

cincuentón m man in his fifties

cincuentona f woman in her fifties

cine m movies pl, cinema

cineasta m/f film-maker

cinéfilo m, **-a** f movie buff

cinematográfico adj movie atr

cinético adj kinetic

cínico **1** adj cynical **2** m, **-a** f cynic

cinismo m cynicism

cinta f ribbon; de música, vídeo tape; *cinta adhesiva* adhesive tape; *cinta aislante* electrical tape, friction tape, *Br* insulating tape; *cinta métrica* tape measure; *cinta de vídeo* video tape

cintura *f* waist

cinturón *m* belt; *cinturón de seguridad* AUTO seatbelt

cíper *m Méx* zipper, *Br* zip

ciprés *m* BOT cypress

circo *m* circus

circuito *m* circuit; *corto circuito* EL short circuit

circulación *f* movement; FIN, MED circulation; AUTO traffic; *poner en circulación* put into circulation

circular 1 *adj* circular **2** ⟨1a⟩ *v/i* circulate; AUTO drive, travel; *de persona* move (along)

círculo *m* circle; *círculo vicioso* vicious circle

circuncisión *f* circumcision

circundante *adj* surrounding

circunferencia *f* circumference

circunscribir ⟨3a; *part* **circunscrito**⟩ *v/t* limit (*a* to)

circunscripción *f* POL electoral district, *Br* constituency

circunspecto *adj* circumspect, cautious

circunstancia *f* circumstance

circunstancial *adj* circumstantial

circunvalación *f*: (*carretera de*) *circunvalación* beltway, *Br* ring-road

cirio *m* candle; *armar or montar un cirio* F kick up a fuss F

ciruela *f* plum; *ciruela pasa* prune

cirugía *f* surgery; *cirugía estética* cosmetic surgery

cirujano *m*, **-a** *f* surgeon

cisco *m*: *hacer cisco* smash

cisne *m* ZO swan

cisterna *f de WC* cistern

cistitis *f* MED cystitis

cita *f* appointment; *de texto* quote, quotation

citar ⟨1a⟩ **1** *v/t a reunión* arrange to meet; *a juicio* summon; (*mencionar*) mention; *de texto* quote **2** *v/r* **citarse** arrange to meet

citología *f* smear test

cítrico *adj* citrus fruit

ciudad *f* town; *más grande* city; *ciudad universitaria* university campus

ciudadano *m*, **-a** *f* citizen

cívico *adj* civic

civil *adj* civil; *casarse por lo civil* have a civil wedding

civilización *f* civilization

civismo *m* civility

cizaña *f*: *sembrar or meter cizaña* cause trouble

cl. *abr* (= *centilitro*) cl. (= centiliter)

clamar ⟨1a⟩ *v/i*: *clamar por algo* clamo(u)r for sth, cry out for sth

clamor *m* roar; *fig* clamo(u)r

clan *m* clan

clandestino *adj* POL clandestine, underground

claqué *m* tap-dancing

clara *f de huevo* white; *bebida* beer with lemonade, *Br* shandy

claraboya *f* skylight

claridad *f* light; *fig* clarity

clarificar ⟨1g⟩ *v/t* clarify

clarinete *m* clarinet

clarividente *m/f* clairvoyant

claro *adj tb fig* clear; *color* light; (*luminoso*) bright; *salsa* thin; *¡claro!* of course!; *hablar claro* speak plainly

clase *f* class; (*variedad*) kind, sort; *clase particular* private class; *dar clase (s)* teach

clásico *adj* classical

clasificación *f* DEP league table

clasificar ⟨1g⟩ *v/t* classify **2** *v/r* **clasificarse** DEP qualify

claudicar ⟨1g⟩ *v/i* give in

claustro *m* ARQUI cloister

claustrofobia *f* claustrophobia

cláusula *f* clause

clausurar ⟨1a⟩ *v/t acto oficial* close; *por orden oficial* close down

clavadiste *m/f Méx* diver

clavado *adj*: *ser clavado a alguien* be the spitting image of s.o. F

clavar ⟨1a⟩ **1** *v/t* stick (*en* into); *clavos, estaca* drive (*en* into); *uñas* sink (*en* into); *clavar los ojos en alguien* fix one's eyes on s.o.; *clavar a alguien por algo* F overcharge s.o. for sth **2** *v/r* **clavarse: clavarse un cuchillo en la mano** stick a knife into one's hand

clave 1 *f* key; *en clave* in code **2** *adj* (*importante*) key

clavel *m* BOT carnation

clavícula *f* ANAT collarbone

clavija *f* EL pin

clavo *m de metal* nail; GASTR clove; *CSur F persona* dead loss F; *dar en el clavo* hit the nail on the head

claxon *m* AUTO horn

clemencia *f* clemency, mercy

clementina *f* BOT clementine

clérigo *m* priest, clergyman

clero *m* clergy

clic *m* INFOR click; *hacer clic en* click on

cliché *m* cliché

clienta, **cliente** *m/f de tienda* customer; *de empresa* client

clientela *f* clientele, customers *pl*

clima *m* climate

climatizado *adj* air-conditioned
climatizar ⟨1f⟩ *v/t* air-condition
clímax *m fig* climax
clínica *f* clinic
clínico *adj* clinical
clip *m para papeles* paperclip; *para el pelo* bobby pin, *Br* hairgrip
cloaca *f tb fig* sewer
clon *m* BIO clone
clonación *f* BIO cloning
clonar ⟨1a⟩ *v/t* clone
cloro *m* QUÍM chlorine
clóset *m L.Am.* closet, *Br* wardrobe
club *m* club; *club náutico* yacht club
cm *abr* (= *centímetro*) cm (= centimeter)
coacción *f* coercion
coaccionar ⟨1a⟩ *v/t* coerce
coagular ⟨1a⟩ **1** *v/t* coagulate; *sangre* clot **2** *v/r* **coagularse** coagulate; *de sangre* clot
coágulo *m* clot
coala *m* ZO koala
coalición *f* coalition
coaligarse ⟨1h⟩ *v/r tb* POL work together, join forces
coartada *f* JUR alibi
coba *f*: *dar coba a alguien* F soft-soap s.o. F
cobarde 1 *adj* cowardly **2** *m/f* coward
cobaya *f* guinea pig
cobertizo *m* shed
cobertor *m* (*manta*) blanket
cobertura *f* cover; TV *etc* coverage
cobija *f L.Am.* blanket
cobijar ⟨1a⟩ **1** *v/t* give shelter to; (*acoger*) take in **2** *v/r* **cobijarse** take shelter
cobijo *m* shelter, refuge
cobra *f* ZO cobra
cobrador *m*, **cobradora** *f a domicilio* collector
cobrar ⟨1a⟩ **1** *v/t* charge; *subsidio, pensión* receive; *deuda* collect; *cheque* cash; *salud, fuerzas* recover; *importancia* acquire **2** *v/i* be paid, get paid; *vas a cobrar* F (*recibir un palo*) you're going to get it!
cobre *m* copper
cobro *m* charging; *de subsidio* receipt; *de deuda* collection; *de cheque* cashing
coca *f F droga* coke F; *de coca Méx* free
cocacho *m S. Am.* F whack on the head F
cocada *f L.Am.* coconut cookie
cocaína *f* cocaine
cocainómano *m*, **-a** *f* cocaine addict
cocción *f* cooking; *en agua* boiling; *al horno* baking
cocer ⟨2b & 2h⟩ **1** *v/t* cook; *en agua* boil; *al horno* bake **2** *v/r* **cocerse** cook; *en agua* boil; *al horno* bake; *fig F de persona*

be roasting F
cochambroso *adj* F filthy
coche *m* car; *Méx* (*taxi*) cab, taxi; *coche de caballos* horse-drawn carriage; *coche cama* sleeping car; *coche comedor L.Am.* dining car; *coche de línea* (long-distance) bus
cochecito *m*: *cochecito de niño* stroller, *Br* pushchair
cochera *f* garage; *de trenes* locomotive shed
cochina *f* sow; F *persona* pig F
cochino 1 *adj fig* filthy, dirty; (*asqueroso*) disgusting **2** *m* hog, *Br* pig; F *persona* pig F
cocido 1 *adj* boiled **2** *m* stew
cociente *m* quotient
cocina *f habitación* kitchen; *aparato* cooker, stove; *actividad* cooking; *cocina de gas* gas cooker *o* stove
cocinar ⟨1a⟩ **1** *v/t* cook; *fig* F plot **2** *v/i* cook
cocinero *m*, **-a** *f* cook
coco *m* BOT coconut; *monstruo* bogeyman F; *comer el coco a alguien* F softsoap s.o.; *más fuerte* brainwash s.o.
cocodrilo *m* crocodile
cocoliche *m Arg* pidgin Spanish
cocotazo *m L.Am.* F whack on the head F
cocotero *m* coconut palm
cóctel *m* cocktail; *cóctel Molotov* Molotov cocktail
cód *abr* (= *código*) code
codazo *m*: *darle a alguien un codazo* elbow s.o.
codearse ⟨1a⟩ *v/r*: *codearse con alguien* rub shoulders with s.o.
codicia *f* greed
codiciar ⟨1b⟩ *v/t* covet
codicioso *adj* greedy
codificado *adj* TV encrypted
código *m* code; *código de barras* COM barcode; *código postal* zip code, *Br* postcode
codo *m* ANAT elbow; *codo con codo fig* F side by side; *hablar por los codos* F talk nineteen to the dozen F
codorniz *f* ZO quail
coeficiente *m* coefficient
coetáneo *m*, **-a** *f* contemporary
coexistir ⟨3a⟩ *v/i* coexist (*con* with)
cofradía *f* fraternity; (*gremio*) guild
cofre *m de tesoro* chest; *para alhajas* jewel(le)ry box
coger ⟨2c⟩ **1** *v/t* (*asir*) take (hold of); *del suelo* pick up; *ladrón, enfermedad* catch; TRANSP catch, take; (*entender*) get; *L.Am.* V screw V **2** *v/i* fit; *L.Am.* V screw V; *coger por la prime-*

ra a la derecha take the first right **3** v/r **cogerse** hold on (tight); **cogerse de algo** hold on to sth

cogorza f: **agarrar una cogorza** F get plastered F

cogote m F nape of the neck

cohabitar ⟨1a⟩ v/i live together, cohabit

cohecho m JUR bribery

coherencia f coherence

coherente adj coherent; **ser coherente con** be consistent with

cohesión f cohesion

cohete m rocket

cohibir ⟨3a⟩ v/t inhibit

COI abr (= **Comité Olímpico Internacional**) IOC (= International Olympic Committee)

coima f L.Am. bribe

coincidencia f coincidence

coincidir ⟨3a⟩ v/i coincide

coito m intercourse

cojear ⟨1a⟩ v/i de persona limp, hobble; de mesa, silla wobble

cojera f limp

cojín m cushion

cojo adj persona lame; mesa, silla wobbly

cojón m V ball V

cojonudo adj P awesome F, brilliant

col. abr (= **columna**) col. (= column)

col f cabbage; **col de Bruselas** Brussels sprout

cola[1] f (pegamento) glue

cola[2] f (de animal) tail; de gente line, Br queue; L.Am. F de persona butt F, Br bum F; **hacer cola** stand in line, Br queue; **estar a la cola** be in last place

colaboración f collaboration

colaborador m, **colaboradora** f collaborator; en periódico contributor

colaborar ⟨1a⟩ v/i collaborate

colación f: **traer** or **sacar a colación** bring up

colada f: **hacer la colada** do the laundry o washing

colado adj: **estar colado por alguien** F be nuts about s.o. F

colador m colander; para té etc strainer

colapsar ⟨1a⟩ **1** v/t paralyze; **colapsar el tráfico** bring traffic to a standstill **2** v/r **colapsarse** grind to a halt

colapso m collapse; **provocar un colapso en la ciudad** bring the city to a standstill

colar ⟨1m⟩ **1** v/t líquido strain; billete falso pass; **colar algo por la aduana** F smuggle sth through customs **2** v/i fig F: **no cuela** I'm not buying it F **3** v/r **colarse** F en un lugar get in; en una fiesta gatecrash; en una cola cut in line, Br push in

colcha f L.Am. bedspread

colchón m mattress; fig buffer

colchoneta f DEP mat; hinchable air bed

cole m F school

colección f collection

coleccionar ⟨1a⟩ v/t collect

coleccionista m/f collector

colecta f collection

colectivero m, **-a** f Arg bus driver

colectivo 1 adj collective **2** m L.Am. bus; Méx, C.Am. taxi

colega m/f colleague; F pal

colegiado m, **-a** f DEP referee

colegial m student, schoolboy

colegiala f student, schoolgirl

colegio m school; **colegio electoral** electoral college; **colegio profesional** professional institute

cólera 1 f anger; **montar en cólera** get in a rage **2** m MED cholera

colesterol m cholesterol

coleta f ponytail; **coletas de pelo** bunches

colgado adj: **dejar colgado a alguien** F let s.o. down

colgador m L.Am. hanger

colgante 1 adj hanging **2** m pendant

colgar ⟨1h & 1m⟩ **1** v/t hang; TELEC put down **2** v/i hang (de from); TELEC hang up **3** v/r **colgarse** hang o.s.; INFOR F lock up; **colgarse de algo** hang from sth; **colgarse de alguien** hang onto s.o.

colibrí m ZO hummingbird

cólico m MED colic

coliflor f cauliflower

colilla f cigarette end

colina f hill

colindante adj adjoining

colirio m MED eye drops pl

colisión f collision; fig clash

colisionar ⟨1a⟩ v/i collide (**con** with)

colitis f MED colitis

collar m necklace; para animal collar

colleras fpl Chi cuff links

colmar ⟨1a⟩ v/t deseos, ambición etc fulfill; **colmar un vaso** fill a glass to the brim; **colmar a alguien de elogios** heap praise on s.o.

colmena f beehive

colmillo m ANAT eye tooth; de perro fang; de elefante, rinoceronte tusk

colmo m: **¡es el colmo!** this is the last straw!; **para colmo** to cap it all

colocación f positioning, placing; (trabajo) position

colocar ⟨1g⟩ **1** v/t put, place; **colocar a alguien en un trabajo** get s.o. a job **2** v/r **colocarse de persona** position o.s.; **se colocó a mi lado** he stood next to me; **se colocaron en primer lugar** they

C

moved into first place
colofón *m fig* culmination
Colombia Colombia
colombiano 1 *adj* Colombian **2** *m*, **-a** *f* Colombian
Colón Columbus
colonia *f* colony; *de viviendas* subdivision, *Br* estate; *perfume* cologne; **colonia de verano** summer camp
colonial *adj* colonial
colonización *f* colonization
colonizar ⟨1f⟩ *v/t* colonize
coloquial *adj* colloquial
coloquio *m* talk
color *m* colo(u)r; **color café** coffee-colo(u)red; *L.Am.* brown
colorado *adj* red
colorante *m* colo(u)ring
colorear ⟨1a⟩ *v/t* colo(u)r
colorete *m* blusher
colorido *m* colo(u)rs *pl*
colosal *adj* colossal
columna *f* column; **columna vertebral** ANAT spinal column
columnista *m/f* columnist
columpiar ⟨1b⟩ **1** *v/t* swing **2** *v/r* **columpiarse** swing
columpio *m* swing
colza *f* BOT rape
coma 1 *f* GRAM comma **2** *m* MED coma
comadre *f L.Am.* godmother
comadrear ⟨1a⟩ *v/i* F gossip
comadrona *f* midwife
comandante *m* MIL commander; *rango* major; AVIA captain
comarca *f* area
comba *f* jump rope, *Br* skipping rope; **jugar** *or* **saltar a la comba** jump rope, *Br* skip
combate *m acción* combat; MIL engagement; DEP fight; **fuera de combate** out of action
combatir ⟨3a⟩ *v/t & v/i* fight
combi *m Méx* minibus
combinación *f* combination; *prenda* slip; **hacer combinación** TRANSP change
combinar ⟨1a⟩ *v/t* combine
combustible *m* fuel
combustión *f* combustion
comedia *f* comedy
comedianta *f* actress
comediante *m* actor
comedido *adj* moderate
comedor *m* dining room
comején *m* termite
comensal *m/f* diner
comentar ⟨1a⟩ *v/t* comment on
comentario *m* comment; **comentario de texto** textual analysis; **comentarios** *pl*

gossip *sg*
comentarista *m/f* commentator
comenzar ⟨1f & 1k⟩ *v/t* begin
comer ⟨2a⟩ **1** *v/t* eat; *a mediodía* have for lunch **2** *v/i* eat; *a mediodía* have lunch; **dar de comer a alguien** feed s.o. **3** *v/r* **comerse** *tb fig* eat up; **se comió una palabra** she missed out a word; **está para comértela** F she's really tasty F
comercial 1 *adj* commercial; *de negocios* business *atr*; **el déficit comercial** the trade deficit **2** *m/f* representative
comercializar ⟨1f⟩ *v/t* market, sell; *desp* commercialize
comerciante *m/f* trader; **comerciante al por menor** retailer
comercio *m actividad* trade; *local* store, shop; **comercio exterior** foreign trade
comestible 1 *adj* eatable, edible **2** *m* foodstuff; **comestibles** *pl* food *sg*
cometa 1 *m* comet **2** *f* kite
cometer ⟨2a⟩ *v/t* commit; *error* make
cometido *m* task
comezón *f* itch
cómic *m* comic
comicios *mpl* elections *pl*
cómico 1 *adj* comical **2** *m*, **-a** *f* comedian
comida *f* (*comestibles*) food; *ocasión* meal
comienzo *m* beginning
comillas *fpl* quotation marks, inverted commas
comino *m* BOT cumin; **me importa un comino** F I don't give a damn F
comisaría *f* precinct, *Br* police station
comisario *m* commissioner; *de policía* captain, *Br* superintendent
comisión *f* committee; *de gobierno* commission; (*recompensa*) commission
comité *m* committee
comitiva *f* retinue
como 1 *adv* as; **así como** as well as; **había como cincuenta** there were about fifty **2** *conj* if; **como si** as if; **como no bebas vas a enfermar** if you don't drink you'll get sick; **como no llegó, me fui solo** as *o* since she didn't arrive, I went by myself
cómo *adv* how; **¿cómo estás?** how are you?; **¡cómo me gusta!** I really like it; **me gusta cómo habla** I like the way he talks; **¿cómo dice?** what did you say?; **¡cómo no!** *Méx* of course!
cómoda *f* chest of drawers
comodidad *f* comfort
comodín *m en naipes* joker
cómodo *adj* comfortable
comp. *abr* (= **compárese**) cf (= confer)
compacto *adj* compact
compadecer ⟨2d⟩ **1** *v/t* feel sorry for **2** *v/r*

compadecerse feel sorry (**de** for)
compadre m L.Am. F buddy F
compadrear ⟨1a⟩ v/i Arg F brag
compadrito m Arg F show-off
compaginar ⟨1a⟩ v/t fig combine
compañero m, **-a** f companion; *en una relación, un juego* partner; **compañero de trabajo** coworker, colleague; **compañero de clase** classmate
compañía f company; **hacer compañía a alguien** keep s.o. company
comparación f comparison; **en comparación con** in comparison with
comparado adj: **comparado con** compared with
comparar ⟨1a⟩ v/t compare
comparecencia f JUR appearance
comparecer ⟨2d⟩ v/i appear
compartir ⟨3a⟩ v/t share (**con** with)
compás m MAT compass; MÚS rhythm; **al compás** to the beat
compasión f compassion
compatibilidad f compatibility
compatible adj INFOR compatible
compatriota m/f compatriot
compendio m summary
compenetrado adj: **están muy compenetrados** they are very much in tune with each other
compenetrarse ⟨1a⟩ v/r: **compenetrarse con alguien** reach a good understanding with s.o.
compensación f compensation
compensar ⟨1a⟩ **1** v/t compensate (**por** for) **2** v/i fig be worthwhile
competencia f (*habilidad*) competence; *entre rivales* competition; (*incumbencia*) area of responsibility, competency; **competencia desleal** unfair competition
competente adj competent
competición f DEP competition
competir ⟨3l⟩ v/i compete (**con** with)
competitivo adj competitive
compilar ⟨1a⟩ v/t compile
compinche m/f F buddy F; *desp* crony F
complacencia f (*placer*) pleasure; (*tolerancia*) indulgence
complacer ⟨2x⟩ v/t please
complaciente adj obliging, helpful
complejidad f complexity
complejo 1 adj complex **2** m PSI complex; **complejo de inferioridad** inferiority complex
complementar ⟨1a⟩ v/t complement
complemento m complement, object; GRAM **complementos de moda** fashion accessories
completar ⟨1a⟩ v/t complete
completo adj complete; *autobús, teatro* full; **por completo** completely
complicación f complication
complicado adj complicated
complicar ⟨1g⟩ **1** v/t complicate **2** v/r **complicarse** get complicated; **complicarse la vida** make things difficult for o.s.
cómplice m/f accomplice
complot m plot
componente m component
componer ⟨2r; *part* **compuesto** ⟩**1** v/t make up, comprise; *sinfonía, poema etc* compose; *algo roto* fix, mend **2** v/r **componerse** be made up (**de** of); L.Am. MED get better
comportamiento m behavio(u)r
comportarse ⟨1a⟩ v/r behave
composición f composition
compositor m, **compositora** f composer
compostura f fig composure
compota f compote
compra f *acción* purchase; (*cosa comprada*) purchase, buy; **ir de compras** go shopping
comprar ⟨1a⟩ v/t buy, purchase
compraventa f buying and selling
comprender ⟨2a⟩ v/t understand; (*abarcar*) include
comprensión f understanding; *de texto, auditiva* comprehension
comprensivo adj understanding
compresa f sanitary napkin, Br sanitary towel
compresión f tb INFOR compression
comprimido m MED pill
comprimir ⟨3a⟩ v/t compress
comprobación f check
comprobar ⟨1m⟩ v/t check; (*darse cuenta de*) realize
comprometer ⟨2a⟩ **1** v/t compromise; (*obligar*) commit **2** v/r **comprometerse** promise (**a** to); *a una causa* commit o.s.; *de novios* get engaged
comprometido adj committed; **estar comprometido en algo** be implicated in sth; **estar comprometido de novios** be engaged
compromiso m commitment; (*obligación*) obligation; (*acuerdo*) agreement; (*apuro*) awkward situation; **sin compromiso** COM without commitment; **soltero y sin compromiso** F footloose and fancy-free
compuesto 1 part → **componer 2** adj composed; **estar compuesto de** be composed of
compulsar ⟨1a⟩ v/t certify
compulsivo adj PSI compulsive
computación f L.Am. computer science

C

computadora f *L.Am.* computer; ***computadora de escritorio*** desktop (computer); ***computadora personal*** personal computer; ***computadora portátil*** laptop

computarizar ⟨1f⟩ v/t computerize

comulgar ⟨1h⟩ v/i take communion; ***comulgar con alguien (en algo)*** *fig* F think the same way as s.o. (on sth)

común *adj* common; ***por lo común*** generally

comuna f commune; *L.Am.* (*población*) town

comunicación f communication; TRANSP link

comunicado 1 *adj* connected; ***el lugar está bien comunicado*** the place has good transport links 2 *m* POL press release, communiqué

comunicar ⟨1g⟩ 1 v/t TRANSP connect, link; ***comunicar algo a alguien*** inform s.o. of sth 2 v/i communicate; TELEC busy, *Br tb* be engaged 3 v/r **comunicarse** communicate

comunidad f community; ***comunidad autónoma*** autonomous region

comunión f REL communion

comunismo m Communism

comunista m/f & *adj* Communist

comunitario *adj* POL EU *atr*, Community *atr*

con *prp* with; ***voy con ellos*** I'm going with them; ***pan con mantequilla*** bread and butter; ***con todo eso*** in spite of all that; ***con tal de que*** provided that, as long as; ***con hacer eso*** by doing that

conato m: ***conato de violencia*** minor outbreak of violence; ***conato de incendio*** small fire

cóncavo *adj* concave

concebir ⟨3l⟩ v/t conceive

conceder ⟨2a⟩ v/t concede; *entrevista, permiso* give; *premio* award

concejal m, **concejala** f council(l)or

concentración f concentration; *de personas* gathering

concentrar ⟨1a⟩ 1 v/t concentrate 2 v/r **concentrarse** concentrate (***en*** on); *de gente* gather

concepto m concept; ***en concepto de algo*** COM (in payment) for sth; ***bajo ningún concepto*** on no account

concernir ⟨3i⟩ v/i concern; ***en lo que concierne a X*** as far as X is concerned

concertar ⟨1k⟩ v/t *cita* arrange; *precio* agree; *esfuerzos* coordinate

concesión f concession; COM dealership; ***hacer concesiones*** make concessions

concesionario m dealer

concha f ZO shell

conchabar ⟨1a⟩ 1 v/t *L.Am. trabajador* hire 2 v/r **conchabarse** F plot

conciencia f conscience; ***a conciencia*** conscientiously; ***con plena conciencia de*** fully conscious of

concienciar ⟨1b⟩ 1 v/t: ***concienciar a alguien de algo*** make s.o. aware of sth 2 v/r **concienciarse** realize (***de*** sth)

concienzudo *adj* conscientious

concierto m MÚS concert; *fig* agreement

conciliador *adj* conciliatory

conciliar ⟨1b⟩ v/t reconcile; ***conciliar el sueño*** get to sleep

conciso *adj* concise

concluir ⟨3g⟩ v/t & v/i conclude

conclusión f conclusion; ***en conclusión*** in short

concretar ⟨1a⟩ 1 v/t specify; (*hacer concreto*) realize 2 v/r **concretarse** materialize; *de esperanzas* be fulfilled

concreto 1 *adj* specific; (*no abstracto*) concrete; ***en concreto*** specifically 2 *m L.Am.* concrete

concurrencia f audience; *de circunstancias* combination

concurrido *adj* crowded

concursante m/f competitor

concursar ⟨1a⟩ v/i compete

concurso m competition; COM tender

conde m count

condecoración f decoration

condecorar ⟨1a⟩ decorate

condena f JUR sentence; (*desaprobación*) condemnation

condenar ⟨1a⟩ v/t JUR sentence (***a*** to); (*desaprobar*) condemn

condensación f condensation

condensado *adj* condensed

condensar ⟨1a⟩ 1 v/t condense; *libro* abridge 2 v/r **condensarse** condense

condesa f countess

condescendiente *adj actitud* accommodating; *desp* condescending

condición f condition; ***a condición de que*** on condition that; ***estar en condiciones de*** be in a position to

condimentar ⟨1a⟩ flavo(u)r

condimento m seasoning

condón m condom

cóndor m ZO condor

conducir ⟨3o⟩ 1 v/t *vehículo* drive; (*dirigir*) lead (***a*** to); EL, TÉC conduct 2 v/i drive; *de camino* lead (***a*** to)

conducta f conduct, behavio(u)r

conducto m pipe; *fig* channel; ***por conducto de*** through

conductor m, **conductora** f driver; ***conductor de orquesta*** *L.Am.* conductor

condujo vb → **conducir**

conectar ⟨1a⟩ *v/t* connect, link; EL connect

conejillo *m*: **conejillo de Indias** *tb fig* guinea pig

conejo *m* rabbit

conexión *f tb* EL connection

confabularse ⟨1a⟩ *v/r* plot

confección *f* making; *de vestidos* dressmaking; *de trajes* tailoring

confeccionar ⟨1a⟩ *v/t* make

confederación *f* confederation

conferencia *f* lecture; *(reunión)* conference; TELEC long-distance call

conferenciante *m/f* lecturer

conferencista *m/f L.Am.* lecturer

conferir ⟨3i⟩ *v/t* award

confesar ⟨1k⟩ **1** *v/t* REL confess; *delito* confess to, admit **2** *v/i* JUR confess **3** *v/r* **confesarse** confess; *(declararse)* admit to being

confesión *f* confession

confeti *m* confetti

confiado *adj* trusting

confianza *f* confidence; **confianza en sí mismo** self-confidence; **de confianza** *persona* trustworthy; **amigo de confianza** good friend

confiar ⟨1c⟩ **1** *v/t secreto* confide (*a* to); **confiar algo a alguien** entrust s.o. with sth, entrust sth to s.o. **2** *v/i* trust (*en* in); *(estar seguro)* be confident (*en* of)

confidencia *f* confidence

confidencial *adj* confidential

configuración *f* configuration; INFOR set-up, configuration

configurar ⟨1a⟩ *v/t* shape; INFOR set up, configure

confinar ⟨1a⟩ *v/t* confine

confirmación *f* confirmation

confirmar ⟨1a⟩ *v/t* confirm

confiscar ⟨1g⟩ *v/t* confiscate

confitería *f* confectioner's

confitura *f* preserve

conflagración *f* conflagration; *(guerra)* war

conflicto *m* conflict

conformarse ⟨1a⟩ *v/r* make do (*con* with)

conforme 1 *adj* satisfied (*oon* with) **2** *prp*: **conforme a** in accordance with

confortable *adj* comfortable

confrontación *f* confrontation

confundir ⟨3a⟩ **1** *v/t* confuse; *(equivocar)* mistake (*con* for) **2** *v/r* **confundirse** make a mistake; **confundirse de calle** get the wrong street

confusión *f* confusion

confuso *adj* confused

congelación *f* freezing; **congelación de precios / de salarios** price / wage freeze

congelado *adj* frozen

congelador *m* freezer

congelar ⟨1a⟩ **1** *v/t* freeze **2** *v/r* **congelarse** freeze

congeniar ⟨1b⟩ *v/i* get on well (*con* with)

congénito *adj* congenital

congestión *f* MED congestion; **congestión del tráfico** traffic congestion

congestionar ⟨1a⟩ *v/t* congest

congoja *f* anguish

congregar ⟨1h⟩ *v/t* bring together

congresal *m/f L.Am.*, **congresista** *m/f* conference *o* convention delegate, conventioneer

congreso *m* conference, convention; **Congreso** *en EE.UU* Congress; **congreso de los diputados** *lower house of Spanish parliament*

congrio *m* ZO conger eel

conjetura *f* conjecture

conjugar ⟨1h⟩ *v/t* GRAM conjugate; *fig* combine

conjunción *f* GRAM conjunction

conjuntivitis *f* MED conjunctivitis

conjunto 1 *adj* joint **2** *m de personas, objetos* collection; *de prendas* outfit; MAT set; **en conjunto** as a whole

conllevar ⟨1a⟩ *v/t* entail

conmemorar ⟨1a⟩ *v/t* commemorate

conmigo *pron* with me

conmoción *f* shock; *(agitación)* upheaval

conmocionar ⟨1a⟩ *v/t* shock

conmovedor *adj* moving

conmover ⟨2h⟩ **1** *v/t* move **2** *v/r* **conmoverse** be moved

conmutador *m* EL switch; *L.Am.* TELEC switchboard

connotación *f* connotation

cono *m* cone

conocer ⟨2d⟩ **1** *v/t* know; *por primera vez* meet; *tristeza, amor etc* experience, know; *(reconocer)* recognize; **dar a conocer** make known **2** *v/r* **conocerse** know one another; *por primera vez* meet one another; *a sí mismo* know o.s.; **se conoce que** it seems that

conocido 1 *adj* well-known **2** *m*, **-a** *f* acquaintance

conocimiento *m* knowledge; MED consciousness; **perder el conocimiento** lose consciousness

conquista *f* conquest

conquistar ⟨1a⟩ *v/t* conquer; *persona* win over

consabido *adj* usual

consagrar ⟨1a⟩ **1** *v/t* REL consecrate; *(hacer famoso)* make famous; *vida* devote **2** *v/r* **consagrarse** devote o.s. (*a* to)

consciente *adj* MED conscious; **conscien-**

te de aware of, conscious of
consecuencia f consequence; *a consecuencia de* as a result of; *en consecuencia* consequently
consecuente adj consistent
consecutivo adj consecutive; *tres años consecutivos* three years in a row
conseguir ⟨3l & 3d⟩ v/t get; *objetivo* achieve
consejero m, **-a** f adviser; COM director
consejo m piece of advice; *consejo de administración* board of directors; *consejo de ministros* grupo cabinet; *reunión* cabinet meeting
consenso m consensus
consentido adj spoilt
consentimiento m consent
consentir ⟨3i⟩ 1 v/t allow; *a niño* indulge 2 v/i: *consentir en algo* agree to sth
conserje m/f superintendent, Br caretaker
conserva f: *en conserva* canned, Br tinned; *conservas* pl canned (Br tinned) food sg
conservación f de alimentos preservation; de edificios, especies conservation
conservador adj conservative
conservante m preservative
conservar ⟨1a⟩ 1 v/t conserve; *alimento* preserve 2 v/r *conservarse* survive
conservatorio m conservatory
considerable adj considerable
consideración f consideration
considerar ⟨1a⟩ v/t consider
consigna f order; de equipaje baggage room, Br left-luggage
consigo pron with him / her; (con usted, con ustedes) with you; (con uno) with you, with one fml
consiguiente adj consequent; *por consiguiente* and so, therefore
consistencia f consistency
consistente adj consistent; (sólido) solid
consistir ⟨3a⟩ v/i consist (*en* of)
consola f INFOR console
consolar ⟨1m⟩ v/t console
consolidar ⟨1a⟩ 1 v/t consolidate 2 v/r *consolidarse* strengthen
consomé m GASTR consommé
consonancia f: *en consonancia con* in keeping with
consonante f consonant
consorte m/f spouse
conspiración f conspiracy
conspirar ⟨1a⟩ v/i conspire
constancia f constancy; *dejar constancia de* leave a record of
constante adj constant
constar ⟨1a⟩ v/i be recorded; *constar de*

consist of
constatación f verification
constatar ⟨1a⟩ v/t verify
constelación f AST constellation
consternar ⟨1a⟩ v/t dismay
constipado 1 adj: *estar constipado* have a cold **2** m cold
constiparse ⟨1a⟩ v/r get a cold
constitución f constitution
constituir ⟨3g⟩ v/t constitute, make up; *empresa, organismo* set up
construcción f construction; (edificio) building
construir ⟨3g⟩ v/t build, construct
consuelo m consolation
cónsul m/f consul
consulado m consulate
consulta f consultation; MED local office, Br surgery
consultar ⟨1a⟩ v/t consult
consultor m, **consultora** f consultant
consultoría f consultancy
consultorio m MED office, Br surgery
consumidor m, **consumidora** f COM consumer
consumir ⟨3a⟩ 1 v/t consume 2 v/r *consumirse* waste away
consumo m consumption; *de bajo consumo* economical
contabilidad f accountancy; *llevar la contabilidad* do the accounts
contable m/f accountant
contactar ⟨1a⟩ v/i: *contactar con alguien* contact s.o.
contacto m contact; AUTO ignition; *ponerse en contacto* get in touch (*con* with)
contado adj: *al contado* in cash
contador 1 m meter **2** m, **contadora** f L.Am. accountant
contagiar ⟨1b⟩ 1 v/t: *contagiar la gripe a alguien* give s.o. the flu; *nos contagió su entusiasmo* he infected us with his enthusiasm **2** v/r *contagiarse* become infected
contagioso adj contagious
contaminación f de agua etc contamination; de río, medio ambiente pollution
contaminar ⟨1a⟩ v/t contaminate; *río, medio ambiente* pollute
contar ⟨1m⟩ 1 v/t count; (narrar) tell 2 v/i count; *contar con* count on
contemplación f: *sin contemplaciones* without ceremony
contemplar ⟨1a⟩ v/t (mirar) look at, contemplate; *posibilidad* consider
contemporáneo 1 adj contemporary **2** m, **-a** f contemporary
contenedor m TRANSP container; *conte-*

nedor de basura dumpster, Br skip;
contenedor de vidrio bottle bank
contener ⟨2l⟩ v/t contain; *respiración* hold; *muchedumbre* hold back **2** v/r **contenerse** control o.s.
contenido m content
contentarse ⟨1a⟩ v/r be satisfied (**con** with)
contento *adj (satisfecho)* pleased; *(feliz)* happy
contestación f answer
contestador m: **contestador automático** TELEC answer machine
contestar ⟨1a⟩ **1** v/t answer, reply to **2** v/i reply (**a** to), answer (**a** sth); *de forma insolente* answer back
contexto m context
contigo pron with you
contiguo *adj* adjoining, adjacent
continental *adj* continental
continente m continent
continuación f continuation; **a continuación** *(ahora)* now; *(después)* then
continuar ⟨1e⟩ **1** v/t continue **2** v/i continue; **continuar haciendo algo** continue o carry on doing sth
continuidad f continuity
continuo *adj (sin parar)* continuous; *(frecuente)* continual
contorno m outline
contra prp against; **en contra de** against
contraataque m counterattack
contrabajo m double bass
contrabandista m/f smuggler
contrabando m contraband, smuggled goods pl; *acción* smuggling; **hacer contrabando** smuggle; **pasar algo de contrabando** smuggle sth in
contracción f contraction
contraceptivo m/adj contraceptive
contradecir ⟨3p⟩ v/t contradict
contradicción f contradiction
contradictorio *adj* contradictory
contraer ⟨2p; part **contraído**⟩ **1** v/t contract; *músculo* tighten; **contraer matrimonio** marry **2** v/r **contraerse** contract
contraindicación f MED contraindication
contraluz f: **a contraluz** against the light
contrapartida f COM balancing entry; **como contrapartida** fig in contrast
contrapeso m counterweight
contraposición f: **en contraposición a** in comparison to
contraproducente *adj* counterproductive
contrariedad f setback; *(disgusto)* annoyance
contrario 1 *adj* contrary; *sentido* opposite; *equipo* opposing; **al contrario,**

por el contrario on the contrary; **de lo contrario** otherwise; **ser contrario a algo** be opposed to sth; **llevar la -a a alguien** contradict s.o. **2** m, **-a** f adversary, opponent
contrarreloj f DEP time trial
contrarrestar ⟨1a⟩ v/t counteract
contraseña f password
contrastar ⟨1a⟩ v/t & v/i contrast (**con** with)
contraste m contrast
contratar ⟨1a⟩ v/t contract; *trabajadores* hire
contratiempo m setback
contrato m contract
contravenir ⟨3s⟩ v/i contravene
contribución f contribution; *(impuesto)* tax
contribuir ⟨3g⟩ v/t contribute (**a** to)
contribuyente m/f taxpayer
contrincante m/f opponent
control m control; *(inspección)* check; **control remoto** remote control
controlador m, **controladora** f: **controlador aéreo** air traffic controller
controlar ⟨1a⟩ **1** v/t control; *(vigilar)* check **2** v/r **controlarse** control o.s.
controversia f controversy
contundente *adj arma* blunt; *fig:* derrota overwhelming
contusión f MED bruise
convalecencia f convalescence
convaleciente m/f convalescent
convalidar ⟨1a⟩ v/t recognize
convencer ⟨2b⟩ v/t convince
convención f convention
convencional *adj* conventional
conveniencia f *de hacer algo* advisability; **hacer algo por conveniencia** do sth in one's own interest
conveniente *adj* convenient; *(útil)* useful; *(aconsejable)* advisable
convenio m agreement
convenir ⟨3s⟩ **1** v/t agree **2** v/i be advisable; **no te conviene** it's not in your interest; **convenir a alguien hacer algo** be in s.o.'s interests to do sth
conventillo m CSur tenement
convento m *de monjes* monastery; *de monjas* convent
converger ⟨2c⟩ v/i converge
conversación f conversation
conversar ⟨1a⟩ v/i make conversation
conversión f conversion
convertible 1 *adj* COM convertible **2** m L.Am. convertible
convertir ⟨3i⟩ **1** v/t convert **2** v/r **convertirse**: **convertirse en algo** turn into sth
convexo *adj* convex

convicción f conviction

convidar ⟨1a⟩ v/t invite (**a** to)

convincente adj convincing

convivencia f living together

convivir ⟨3a⟩ v/i live together

convocar ⟨1g⟩ v/t summon; *huelga* call; *oposiciones* organize

convocatoria f announcement; *de huelga* call

convoy m convoy

convulsión f convulsion; *fig* upheaval

conyugal adj conjugal

cónyuge m/f spouse

coña f: **decir algo de coña** F say sth as a joke; **darle la coña a alguien** F bug s.o. F; **¡ni de coña!** F no way! F

coñac m (pl ~s) brandy, cognac

coño V cunt V

cooperación f cooperation

cooperar ⟨1a⟩ v/i cooperate

cooperativa f cooperative

coordinación f coordination

coordinar ⟨1a⟩ v/t coordinate

copa f *de vino etc* glass; DEP cup; **tomar una copa** have a drink; **copas** pl (*en naipes*) suit in Spanish deck of cards

copia f copy; **copia pirata** pirate copy

copiar ⟨1b⟩ v/t copy

copiloto m/f copilot

copioso adj copious

copla f verse; (*canción*) popular song

copo m flake; **copo de nieve** snowflake; **copos de maíz** cornflakes

copropietario m, -a f co-owner, joint owner

coquetear ⟨1a⟩ v/i flirt

coquetería f flirtatiousness

coqueto adj flirtatious; *lugar* pretty

coraje m courage; **me da coraje** fig F it makes me mad F

corajudo adj L.Am. brave

coral¹ m zo coral

coral² f mús choir

Corán m Koran

coraza f cuirasse; zo shell; fig shield

corazón m heart; *de fruta* core

corazonada f hunch

corbata f tie

corcho m cork

cordel m string

cordero m lamb

cordial adj cordial

cordillera f mountain range

cordón m cord; *de zapato* shoelace; **cordón umbilical** ANAT umbilical cord

cordura f sanity; (*prudencia*) good sense

Corea Korea

coreano 1 adj Korean 2 m, -a f Korean

coreografía f choreography

cormorán m zo cormorant

cornada f TAUR goring

corneja f zo crow

córner m *en fútbol* corner (kick)

corneta f MIL bugle

cornisa f ARQUI cornice

cornudo 1 adj horned 2 m cuckold

coro m MÚS choir; *de espectáculo, pieza musical* chorus; **a coro** together, in chorus

corona f crown; **corona de flores** garland

coronar ⟨1a⟩ v/t crown

coronario adj MED coronary

coronel m MIL colonel

coronilla f ANAT crown; **estoy hasta la coronilla** F I've had it up to here F

corotos mpl L.Am. F bits and pieces

corporación f corporation

corporal adj *placer, estética* physical; *fluido* body *atr*

corpulento adj solidly built

corral m farmyard

correa f lead; *de reloj* strap

corrección f correction; *en el trato* correctness

correcto adj correct; (*educado*) polite

corredizo adj sliding

corredor 1 m, corredora f DEP runner; COM agent; **corredor de bolsa** stockbroker 2 m ARQUI corridor

corregir ⟨3c & 3l⟩ v/t correct

correlación f correlation

correligionario m, -a f: **sus correligionarios republicanos** his fellow republicans

correntada f L.Am. current

correntoso adj L.Am. fast-flowing

correo m mail, Br tb post; **correos** pl post office sg; **correo aéreo** airmail; **correo electrónico** e-mail; **por correo** by mail; **echar al correo** mail, Br tb post

correr ⟨2a⟩ 1 v/i run; (*apresurarse*) rush; *de tiempo* pass; *de agua* run, flow; **correr con los gastos** pay the expenses; **a todo correr** at top speed 2 v/t run; *cortinas* draw; *mueble* slide, move; **correr la misma suerte** suffer the same fate 3 v/r correrse move; *de tinta* run

correspondencia f correspondence; FERR connection (**con** with)

corresponder ⟨2a⟩ v/i: **corresponder a alguien** *de bienes* be for s.o., be due to s.o.; *de responsabilidad* be up to s.o.; *de asunto* concern s.o.; *a un favor* repay s.o. (**con** with); **actuar como corresponde** do the right thing

correspondiente adj corresponding

corresponsal m/f correspondent

corretear ⟨1a⟩ v/i run around

corrida f: **corrida de toros** bullfight

corrido adj: **decir algo de corrido** fig say sth parrot-fashion

corriente **1** adj (actual) current; (común) ordinary; **corriente y moliente** F run-of-the-mill; **estar al corriente** be up to date **2** f EL, de agua current; **corriente de aire** draft, Br draught

corro m ring

corroborar ⟨1a⟩ v/t corroborate

corroer ⟨2za⟩ v/t corrode; fig eat up

corromper ⟨2a⟩ **1** v/t corrupt **2** v/r corromperse become corrupted

corrosión f corrosion

corrosivo adj corrosive; fig caustic

corrupción f decay; fig corruption; **corrupción de menores** corruption of minors

corrupto adj corrupt

corsetería f lingerie store

cortacésped m lawnmower

cortacircuitos m inv circuit breaker

cortada f L.Am. cut

cortado **1** adj cut; calle closed; leche curdled; persona shy; **quedarse cortado** be embarrassed **2** m coffee with a dash of milk

cortar ⟨1a⟩ **1** v/t cut; electricidad cut off; calle close **2** v/i cut **3** v/r cortarse cut o.s.; fig F get embarrassed; **cortarse el pelo** have one's hair cut

cortaúñas m inv nail clippers pl

corte[1] m cut; **corte de luz** power outage; **corte de pelo** haircut; **corte de tráfico** F road closure; **me da corte** F I'm embarrassed

corte[2] f court; L.Am. JUR (law) court; **las Cortes** Spanish parliament

cortejar ⟨1a⟩ v/t court

cortés adj courteous

cortesía f courtesy

corteza f de árbol bark; de pan crust; de queso rind

cortina f curtain

corto adj short; **corto de vista** near-sighted; **ni corto ni perezoso** as bold as brass; **quedarse corto** fall short

cortocircuito m EL short circuit

corzo m ZO roe deer

cosa f thing; **como si tal cosa** as if nothing had happened; **decir a alguien cuatro cosas** give s.o. a piece of one's mind; **eso es otra cosa** that's another matter; **¿qué pasa? – poca cosa** what's new? – nothing much

coscorrón m bump on the head

cosecha f harvest

cosechar ⟨1a⟩ v/t harvest; fig gain, win

coser ⟨2a⟩ v/t sew; **ser coser y cantar**

be dead easy F

cosmético m/adj cosmetic

cósmico adj cosmic

cosmonauta m/f cosmonaut

cosmopolita adj cosmopolitan

cosmos m cosmos

cosmovisión f L.Am. world view

cosquillas fpl: **hacer cosquillas a alguien** tickle s.o.; **tener cosquillas** be ticklish

cosquilleo m tickle

costa[1] f: **a costa de** at the expense of; **a toda costa** at all costs

costa[2] f GEOG coast

costado m side; **por los cuatro costados** fig throughout, through and through

costar ⟨1m⟩ **1** v/t en dinero cost; trabajo, esfuerzo etc take; **¿cuánto cuesta?** how much does it cost? **2** v/i en dinero cost; **me costó** it was hard work; **cueste lo que cueste** at all costs; **costar caro** fig cost dear

Costa Rica Costa Rica

costarricense m/f & adj Costa Rican

coste m → **costo**

costear ⟨1a⟩ v/t pay for

costero adj coastal

costilla f ANAT rib; GASTR sparerib

costo m cost; **costo de la vida** cost of living

costoso adj costly

costra f MED scab

costumbre f custom; de una persona habit; **de costumbre** usual

costura f sewing

costurear ⟨1a⟩ v/t L.Am. sew

cotarro m: **manejar el cotarro** F be the boss F

cotejar ⟨1a⟩ v/t compare

cotidiano adj daily

cotilla m/f F gossip

cotillear ⟨1a⟩ v/i F gossip

cotizado adj COM quoted; fig sought after

cotizar ⟨1f⟩ v/t de trabajador pay social security, Br pay National Insurance; de acciones, honos be listed (**a** at); **cotizar en bolsa** be listed on the stock exchange

coto[1] m: **coto de caza** hunting reserve; **poner coto a algo** fig put a stop to sth

coto[2] m S. Am. MED goiter, Br goitre

cotorra f ZO parrot; F persona motormouth F

coyote m ZO coyote

coyuntura f situation; ANAT joint

C.P. abr (= **código postal**) zip code, Br post code

cráneo m ANAT skull, cranium

cráter m crater

creación f creation

creador *m*, **creadora** *f* creator
crear ⟨1a⟩ *v/t* create; *empresa* set up
creativo *adj* creative
crecer ⟨2d⟩ *v/i* grow
creces *fpl*: **con creces** *superar* by a comfortable margin; *pagar* with interest
creciente *adj* growing; *luna* waxing
crecimiento *m* growth
credencial *f* document
credibilidad *f* credibility
crédito *m* COM credit; **a crédito** on credit; **no dar crédito a sus oídos / ojos** F not believe one's ears / eyes
credo *m* REL, *fig* creed
crédulo *adj* credulous
creencia *f* belief
creer ⟨2e⟩ **1** *v/i* believe (**en** in) **2** *v/t* think; (*dar por cierto*) believe; **no creo que esté aquí** I don't think he's here; **¡ya lo creo!** F you bet! F **3** *v/r* **creerse**: **creerse que …** believe that …; **se cree muy lista** she thinks she's very clever
crema *f* GASTR cream
cremallera *f* zipper, *Br* zip; TÉC rack
crematorio *m* crematorium
cremoso *adj* creamy
crepe *f* GASTR crêpe, pancake
crepitar ⟨1a⟩ *v/i* crackle
crepúsculo *m tb fig* twilight
cresta *f* crest
cretino *m*, -a *f* F cretin F, moron F
creyente 1 *adj*: **ser creyente** REL believe in God **2** *m* REL believer
creyó *vb* → **creer**
cría *f acción* breeding; *de zorro, león* cub; *de perro* puppy; *de gato* kitten; *de oveja* lamb; **sus crías** her young
criada *f* maid
criado *m* servant
criar ⟨1c⟩ **1** *v/t niños* raise, bring up; *animales* breed **2** *v/r* **criarse** grow up
criatura *f* creature; F (*niño*) baby, child
crimen *m* crime
criminal *m/f & adj* criminal
crío *m*, -a *f* F kid F
criollo 1 *adj* Creole **2** *m*, -a *f* Creole
cripta *f* crypt
crisantemo *m* BOT chrysanthemum
crisis *f inv* crisis
crismas *m inv* Christmas card
crispar ⟨1a⟩ *v/t* irritate; **crisparle a alguien los nervios** get on s.o.'s nerves
cristal *m* crystal; (*vidrio*) glass; (*lente*) lens; *de ventana* pane; **cristal líquido** liquid crystal
cristalizar ⟨1f⟩ *v/i* crystallize; *de idea, proyecto* jell
cristianismo *m* Christianity
cristiano 1 *adj* Christian **2** *m*, -a *f* Christian

Cristo Christ
criterio *m* criterion; (*juicio*) judg(e)ment
crítica *f* criticism; **muchas críticas** a lot of criticism
criticar ⟨1g⟩ *v/t* criticize
crítico 1 *adj* critical **2** *m*, -a *f* critic
Croacia Croatia
crol *m* crawl
cromo *m* QUÍM chrome; (*estampa*) picture card, trading card
crónica *f* chronicle; *en periódico* report
crónico *adj* MED chronic
cronológico *adj* chronological
cronometrar ⟨1a⟩ *v/t* DEP time
cronómetro *m* stopwatch
croqueta *f* GASTR croquette
croquis *m inv* sketch
cross *m* DEP cross-country (running); **con motocicletas** motocross
cruce *m* cross; *de carreteras* crossroads *sg*; **cruce en las líneas** TELEC crossed line
crucero *m* cruise
crucial *adj* crucial
crucificar ⟨1g⟩ *v/t* crucify
crucifijo *m* crucifix
crucigrama *m* crossword
crudo 1 *adj alimento* raw; *fig* harsh **2** *m* crude (oil)
cruel *adj* cruel
cruento *adj* bloody
crujiente *adj* crunchy
crujir ⟨3a⟩ *v/i* creak; *al arder* crackle; *de grava* crunch
cruz *f* cross; **Cruz Roja** Red Cross
cruzar ⟨1f⟩ **1** *v/t* cross **2** *v/r* **cruzarse** pass one another; **cruzarse de brazos** cross one's arms; **cruzarse con alguien** pass s.o.
c.s.f. *abr* (= **costo, seguro, flete**) cif (= cost, insurance, freight)
cta, c.ta *abr* (= **cuenta**) A/C (= account)
cuaderno *m* notebook; EDU exercise book
cuadra *f* stable; *L.Am.* (*manzana*) block
cuadrado 1 *adj* square **2** *m* square; **al cuadrado** squared
cuadrilla *f* squad, team
cuadro *m* painting; (*grabado*) picture; (*tabla*) table; DEP team; **cuadro de mandos** or **de instrumentos** AUTO dashboard; **de** or **a cuadros** checked
cuádruple, cuádruplo *m* quadruple
cuajada *f* GASTR curd
cuajar ⟨1a⟩ *v/i de nieve* settle; *fig: de idea, proyecto etc* come together, jell F
cuajo *m*: **de cuajo** by the roots
cual 1 *pron rel*: **el cual, la cual** etc *cosa* which; *persona* who; **por lo cual** (and)

so **2** *adv* like

cuál *interr* which (one)

cualidad *f* quality

cualificar ⟨1g⟩ *v/t* qualify

cualquier *adj* any; *cualquier día* any day; *cualquier cosa* anything; *de cualquier modo* or *forma* anyway

cualquiera *pron persona* anyone, anybody; *cosa* any (one); *un cualquiera* a nobody; *¡cualquiera lo comprende!* nobody can understand it!

cuando 1 *conj* when; *condicional* if; *cuando quieras* whenever you want **2** *adv* when; *de cuando en cuando* from time to time; *cuando menos* at least

cuándo *interr* when

cuantía *f* amount, quantity; *fig* importance

cuantificar ⟨1g⟩ *v/t* quantify

cuantioso *adj* substantial

cuanto 1 *adj*: *cuanto dinero quieras* as much money as you want; *unos cuantos chavales* a few boys **2** *pron* all, everything; *se llevó cuanto podía* she took all o everything she could; *le dio cuanto necesitaba* he gave her everything she needed; *unas -as* a few; *todo cuanto* everything **3** *adv*: *cuanto antes, mejor* the sooner the better; *en cuanto* as soon as; *en cuanto a* as for

cuánto 1 *interr adj* how much; *pl* how many; *¿cuánto café?* how much coffee?; *¿cuántos huevos?* how many eggs? **2** *pron* how much; *pl* how many; *¿cuánto necesita Vd.?* how much do you need?; *¿cuántos ha dicho?* how many did you say?; *¿a cuánto están?* how much are they?; *¿a cuántos estamos?* what's the date today? **3** *exclamaciones*: *¡cuánta gente había!* there were so many people!; *¡cuánto me alegro!* I'm so pleased!

cuarenta *adj* forty

Cuaresma *f* Lent

cuartear ⟨1a⟩ **I** *v/t* cut up, quarter **2** *v/r* **cuartearse** crack

cuartel *m* barracks *pl*; *cuartel general* headquarters *pl*

cuartelazo *m L.Am.* military uprising

cuartilla *f* sheet of paper

cuarto 1 *adj* fourth **2** *m* (*habitación*) room; (*parte*) quarter; *cuarto de baño* bathroom; *cuarto de estar* living room; *cuarto de hora* quarter of an hour; *cuarto de kilo* quarter of a kilo; *de tres al cuarto* F third-rate; *las diez y cuarto* quarter past ten, quarter after ten; *las tres menos cuarto* a quarter to o of three

cuarzo *m* quartz

cuatro *adj* four; *cuatro gotas* F a few drops

cuatrocientos *adj* four hundred

cuba *f*: *estar como una cuba* F be plastered F

Cuba Cuba

cubano 1 *adj* Cuban **2** *m*, *-a f* Cuban

cubierta *f* MAR deck; AUTO tire, *Br* tyre

cubierto 1 *part* → *cubrir* **2** *m* piece of cutlery; *en la mesa* place setting; *cubiertos pl* cutlery *sg*

cubito *m*: *cubito de hielo* ice cube

cubo *m* cube; *recipiente* bucket; *cubo de la basura* garbage can, *Br* rubbish bin; *fuera* garbage can, *Br* dustbin

cubrir ⟨3a; *part* *cubierto* ⟩ **1** *v/t* cover (*de* with) **2** *v/r* **cubrirse** cover o.s.

cucaracha *f* ZO cockroach

cuchara *f* spoon; *meter su cuchara L.Am.* F stick one's oar in F

cucharada *f* spoonful

cucharilla *f* teaspoon

cucharón *m* ladle

cuchichear ⟨1a⟩ *v/i* whisper

cuchilla *f* razor blade

cuchillo *m* knife

cuclillas: *en cuclillas* squatting

cuco 1 *m* ZO cuckoo; *reloj de cuco* cuckoo clock **2** *adj* (*astuto*) sharp

cucurucho *m de papel etc* cone; *sombrero* pointed hat

cuece *vb* → *cocer*

cuelgo *vb* → *colgar*

cuello *m* ANAT neck; *de camisa etc* collar

cuelo *vb* → *colar*

cuenca *f* GEOG basin

cuenco *m* bowl

cuenta *f* (*cálculo*) sum; *de restaurante* check, *Br* bill; COM account; *cuenta atrás* countdown; *cuenta bancaria* bank account; *cuenta corriente* checking account, *Br* current account; *más de la cuenta* too much; *caer en la cuenta* realize; *darse cuenta de algo* realize sth; *pedir cuentas a alguien* ask s.o. for an explanation; *perder la cuenta* lose count; *tener* or *tomar en cuenta* take into account; *corre por mi* / *su cuenta* I'll / he'll pay for it

cuentagotas *m inv* dropper

cuentakilómetros *m inv* odometer, *Br* mileometer

cuentista *m/f* story-teller; F (*mentiroso*) fibber F

cuento *m* (*short*) story; (*pretexto*) excuse; *cuento chino* F tall story F; *venir a cuento* be relevant

cuerda *f* rope; *de guitarra, violín* string;

C

dar cuerda al reloj wind the clock up;
dar cuerda a algo fig F string sth out
F; **cuerdas vocales** ANAT vocal chords
cuerdo adj sane; (sensato) sensible
cuerno m horn; de caracol feeler; **irse al
cuerno** F fall through, be wrecked; **poner los cuernos a alguien** F be unfaithful to s.o.
cuero m leather; Rpl (fuete) whip; **en
cueros** F naked
cuerpo m body; de policía force; **cuerpo
diplomático** diplomatic corps sg; **a
cuerpo de rey** like a king; **en cuerpo
y alma** body and soul
cuervo m zo raven, crow
cuesta f slope; **cuesta abajo** downhill;
cuesta arriba uphill; **a cuestas** on one's
back
cuestión f question; (asunto) matter,
question; **en cuestión de ...** in a matter
of ...
cuestionar ⟨1a⟩ v/t question
cuestionario m questionnaire
cueva f cave
cuidado m care; **¡cuidado!** look out!; **andar con cuidado** tread carefully; **me tiene sin cuidado** I could o Br couldn't
care less; **tener cuidado** be careful
cuidadora f Méx nursemaid
cuidadoso adj careful
cuidar ⟨1a⟩ **1** v/t look after, take care of **2**
v/i: **cuidar de** look after, take care of **3**
v/r **cuidarse** look after o.s., take care
of o.s.; **cuidarse de hacer algo** take care
to do sth
culebra f zo snake
culebrón m TV soap
culinario adj cooking atr, culinary
culminación f culmination
culminante adj: **punto culminante** peak,
climax
culminar ⟨1a⟩ **1** v/i culminate (**en** in); fig
reach a peak o climax **2** v/t finish
culo m V ass V, Br arse V; F butt F, Br bum
F; **ser culo de mal asiento** fig F be restless, have ants in one's pants F
culpa f fault; **echar la culpa de algo a alguien** blame s.o. for sth; **ser por culpa
de alguien** be s.o.'s fault; **tener la culpa**
be to blame (**de** for)
culpabilidad f guilt
culpable 1 adj guilty **2** m/f culprit
culpar ⟨1a⟩ v/t: **culpar a alguien de algo**
blame s.o. for sth
cultivar ⟨1a⟩ v/t AGR grow; tierra farm; fig
cultivate
cultivo m AGR crop; BIO culture
culto 1 adj educated **2** m worship
cultura f culture

cultural adj cultural; **un nivel cultural
muy pobre** a very poor standard of education
cumbre f tb POL summit
cumpleaños m inv birthday
cumplido m compliment; **no andarse
con cumplidos** not stand on ceremony
cumplimentar ⟨1k⟩ v/t trámite carry out
cumplir ⟨3a⟩ **1** v/t orden carry out; promesa fulfill; condena serve; **cumplir diez
años** reach the age of ten, turn ten **2**
v/i: **cumplir con algo** carry sth out; **cumplir con su deber** do one's duty; **te invi-
ta sólo por cumplir** he's only inviting
you out of politeness **3** v/r **cumplirse**
de plazo expire
cúmulo m (montón) pile, heap
cuna f tb fig cradle
cundir ⟨3a⟩ v/i spread; (dar mucho de sí)
go a long way
cuneta f ditch
cuñada f sister-in-law
cuñado m brother-in-law
cuota f share; de club, asociación fee
cupón m coupon
cúpula f dome; esp POL leadership
cura 1 m priest **2** f cure; (tratamiento)
treatment; Méx, C.Am. F hangover; **tener cura** be curable
curado adj Méx, C.Am. F drunk
curandero m, -a f faith healer
curar ⟨1a⟩ **1** v/t tb GASTR cure; (tratar)
treat; herida dress; pieles tan **2** v/i MED
recover (**de** from) **3** v/r **curarse** MED recover; Méx, C.Am. F get drunk
curda f: **agarrarse una curda** F get plastered F
curiosidad f curiosity
curioso 1 adj curious; (raro) curious, odd,
strange **2** m, -a f onlooker
curita f L.Am. Band-Aid®, Br Elasto-
plast®
currar ⟨1a⟩ v/i F work
currículum vitae m résumé, Br CV, Br
curriculum vitae
curry m GASTR curry
cursi adj F persona affected
cursillo m short course
cursiva f italics pl
curso m course; **curso a distancia** or **por
correspondencia**   correspondence
course; **en el curso de** in the course of
cursor m INFOR cursor
curtir ⟨3a⟩ v/t tan; fig harden
curva f curve
curvo adj curved
cúspide f de montaña summit; de fama
etc height
custodia f JUR custody

custodiar ⟨1b⟩ *v/t* guard
cususa *f C.Am.* corn liquor
cutre *adj* F shabby, dingy

cuyo, -a *adj* whose
CV *m* resumé, *Br* CV

D

D

D. *abr* (**= Don**) Mr
Dª. *abr* (**= Doña**) Mrs
dactilar *adj* finger *atr*
dadivoso *adj* generous
dado¹ *m* dice
dado² **1** *part* → **dar 2** *adj* given; **ser dado a algo** be given to sth **3** *conj*: **dado que** since, given that
dalia *f* BOT dahlia
daltónico *adj* colo(u)r-blind
daltonismo *m* colo(u)r-blindness
dama *f* lady; **dama de honor** bridesmaid; **(juego de) damas** checkers *sg*, *Br* draughts *sg*
damasco *m* damask; *L.Am.* fruta apricot
damnificado **1** *adj* affected **2** *m*, **-a** *f* victim
danés **1** *adj* Danish **2** *m*, **-esa** *f* Dane
danza *f* dance
danzar ⟨1f⟩ *v/i* dance
dañar ⟨1a⟩ **1** *v/t* harm; *cosa* damage **2** *v/r* **dañarse** harm o.s.; *de un objeto* get damaged
dañino *adj* harmful; *fig* malicious
daño *m* harm; *fig* malicious; **hacer daño** hurt; **daños** *pl* damage *sg*; **daños y perjuicios** damages
dar ⟨1r; *part* **dado** ⟩ **1** *v/t* give; *beneficio* yield; *luz* give off; *fiesta* give, have; **dar un golpe a** hit; **dar un salto / una patada / miedo** jump / kick / frighten; **el jamón me dió sed** the ham made me thirsty **2** *v/i*: **dame** give it to me, give me it; **dar a** *de ventana* look onto; **dar con algo** come across sth; **dar de comer a alguien** feed s.o.; **dar de beber a alguien** give s.o. something to drink; **dar de sí** *de material* stretch, give; **le dio por insultar a su madre** F she started insulting her mother; **¡qué más da!** what does it matter!; **da igual** it doesn't matter **3** *v/r* **darse** *de una situación* arise; **darse a algo** take to sth; **esto se me da bien** I'm good at this; **dárselas de algo** make o.s. out to be sth, claim to be sth
dardo *m* dart

datar ⟨1a⟩ *v/i*: **datar de** date from
dátil *m* BOT date
dato *m* piece of information; **datos** *pl* information *sg*, data *sg*; **datos personales** personal details
D.C. *abr* (**= después de Cristo**) AD (= Anno Domini)
dcho, dcha *abr* (**= derecho, derecha**) r (= right)
d. de J.C. *abr* (**= después de Jesucristo**) AD (= Anno Domini)
de *prp* ◇ *origen* from; **de Nueva York** from New York; **de ... a** from ... to
◇ *posesión* of; **el coche de mi amigo** my friend's car
◇ *material* (made) of; **un anillo de oro** a gold ring
◇ *contenido* of; **un vaso de agua** a glass of water
◇ *cualidad*: **una mujer de 20 años** a 20 year old woman
◇ *causa* with; **temblaba de miedo** she was shaking with fear
◇ *hora*: **de noche** at night, by night; **de día** by day
◇ *en calidad de* as; **trabajar de albañil** work as a bricklayer
◇ *agente* by; **de Goya** by Goya
◇ *condición* if; **de haberlo sabido** if I'd known
dé *vb* → **dar**
deambular ⟨1a⟩ *v/i* wander around
debajo **1** *adv* underneath **2** *prp*: **(por) debajo de** under; **un grado por debajo de lo normal** one degree below normal
debate *m* debate, discussion
debatir ⟨3a⟩ **1** *v/t* debate, discuss **2** *v/i* struggle **3** *v/r* **debatirse**: **debatirse entre la vida y la muerte** fight for one's life
deber **1** *m* duty; **deberes** *pl* homework *sg* **2** ⟨2a⟩ *v/t* owe **3** *v/i* *en presente* must, have to; *en pretérito* should have; *en futuro* (will) have to; *en condicional* should; **debe de tener quince años** he must be about 15 **4** *v/r* **deberse**: **deberse a** be due to, be caused by

debido 1 *part* → **deber 2** *adj*: **como es debido** properly; **debido a** owing to, on account of

débil *adj* weak

debilitar ⟨1a⟩ **1** *v/t* weaken **2** *v/r* **debilitarse** weaken, become weak; *de salud* deteriorate

debut *m* debut

década *f* decade

decadencia *f* decadence; *de un imperio* decline

decaer ⟨2o; *part* **decaído** ⟩ *v/i tb fig* decline; *de rendimiento* fall off, decline; *de salud* deteriorate

decaído 1 *part* → **decaer 2** *adj fig* depressed, down F

decantarse ⟨1a⟩ *v/r*: **decantarse por** opt for

decapitar ⟨1a⟩ *v/t* behead, decapitate

decenio *m* decade

decente *adj* decent

decepción *f* disappointment

decepcionado *adj* disappointed

decepcionante *adj* disappointing

decepcionar ⟨1a⟩ *v/t* disappoint

decidido 1 *part* → **decidir 2** *adj* decisive; **estar decidido** be determined (**a** to)

decidir ⟨3a⟩ **1** *v/t* decide **2** *v/r* **decidirse** make up one's mind, decide

decimal *adj* decimal *atr*

décimo 1 *adj* tenth **2** *m de lotería* share of a lottery ticket

decir ⟨3p; *part* **dicho** ⟩ **1** *v/t* say; (*contar*) tell; **querer decir** mean; **decir que sí** say yes; **decir que no** say no; **es decir** in other words; **no es rico, que digamos** let's say he's not rich; **¡no me digas!** you're kidding!; **¡quién lo diría!** who would believe it!; **se dice que ...** they say that ..., it's said that ... **2** *v/i*: **¡diga!**, **¡dígame!** *Esp* TELEC hello

decisión *f* decision; *fig* decisiveness

decisivo *adj* critical, decisive

declaración *f* declaration; **declaración de la renta** *o* **de impuestos** tax return; **prestar declaración** JUR testify, give evidence

declarar ⟨1a⟩ **1** *v/t* state; *bienes* declare; **declarar culpable** find guilty **2** *v/i* JUR give evidence **3** *v/r* **declararse** declare o.s.; *de incendio* break out; **declararse a alguien** declare one's love for s.o.

declinar ⟨1a⟩ *v/t & v/i* decline

declive *m fig* decline; **en declive** in decline

decodificador *m* → **descodificador**

decodificar ⟨1g⟩ *v/t* → **descodificar**

decolaje *m L.Am.* takeoff

decolar ⟨1a⟩ *v/i L.Am.* take off

decolorar ⟨1a⟩ *v/t* bleach

decoración *f* decoration

decorado *m* TEA set

decorador *m*, **decoradora** *f*: **decorador (de interiores)** interior decorator

decorar ⟨1a⟩ *v/t* decorate

decorativo *adj* decorative

decreciente *adj* decreasing, diminishing

decrépito *adj* decrepit

decretar ⟨1a⟩ *v/t* order, decree

decreto *m* decree

dedicación *f* dedication

dedicar ⟨1g⟩ *v/t* dedicate; *esfuerzo* devote **2** *v/r* **dedicarse** devote o.s. (**a** to); **¿a qué se dedica?** what do you do (for a living)?

dedicatoria *f* dedication

dedillo *m*: **conocer algo al dedillo** know sth like the back of one's hand; **saber algo al dedillo** F know sth off by heart

dedo *m* finger; **dedo del pie** toe; **dedo gordo** thumb; **dedo índice** forefinger; **no tiene dos dedos de frente** F he doesn't have much commonsense

deducción *f* deduction

deducir ⟨3o⟩ *v/t* deduce; COM deduct

defecar ⟨1g⟩ *v/i* defecate

defecto *m* defect; *moral* fault; INFOR default

defectuoso *adj* defective, faulty

defender ⟨2g⟩ **1** *v/t* defend **2** *v/r* **defenderse** defend o.s. (**de** against); *fig* F manage, get by; **defenderse del frío** ward off the cold

defenestrar ⟨1a⟩ *v/t fig* F oust

defensa 1 *f* JUR, DEP defense, *Br* defence; *L.Am.* AUTO fender, *Br* bumper; **defensas** MED defenses, *Br* defences **2** *m/f* DEP defender

defensivo *adj* defensive

defensor *m*, **defensora** *f* defender, champion; JUR defense counsel; **defensor del pueblo** *en España* ombudsman

deficiente 1 *adj* deficient; (*insatisfactorio*) inadequate **2** *m/f* handicapped person

déficit *m* deficit

definición *f* definition; **de alta definición** TV high definition

definir ⟨3a⟩ **1** *v/t* define **2** *v/r* **definirse** come down (**por** in favor of)

definitivo *adj* definitive; *respuesta* definite; **en -a** all in all

deforestación *f* deforestation

deformar ⟨1a⟩ *v/t* distort; MED deform

deforme *adj* deformed

defraudar ⟨1a⟩ *v/t* disappoint; (*estafar*)

D

defraud; **defraudar a Hacienda** evade taxes

defunción f death, demise fml

degenerar ⟨1a⟩ v/i degenerate (**en** into)

degollar ⟨1n⟩ v/t cut the throat of

degradante adj degrading

degradar ⟨1a⟩ **1** v/t degrade; MIL demote; PINT gradate **2** v/r **degradarse** demean o.s.

degustar ⟨1a⟩ v/t taste

dejadez f slovenliness; (**negligencia**) neglect

dejar ⟨1a⟩ **1** v/t leave; (**permitir**) let, allow; (**prestar**) lend; **beneficios** yield; **déjame en la esquina** drop me at the corner; **dejar para mañana** leave until tomorrow; **dejar caer algo** drop sth **2** v/i: **dejar de hacer algo** (**parar**) stop doing sth; **no deja de fastidiarme** he keeps (on) annoying me **3** v/r **dejarse** let o.s. go; **dejarse llevar** let o.s. be carried along

del prp **de** y art **el**

delantal m apron

delante adv in front; (**más avanzado**) ahead; (**enfrente**) opposite; **por delante** ahead; **se abrocha por delante** it does up at the front; **tener algo por delante** have sth ahead of o in front of one; **delante de** in front of; **el asiento de delante** the front seat

delantera f DEP forward line; **llevar la delantera** be ahead of, lead

delantero m, -a f DEP forward

delatar ⟨1a⟩ v/t: **delatar a alguien** inform on s.o.; fig give s.o. away

delegación f delegation; (**oficina**) local office; **delegación de Hacienda** tax office

delegado m, -a f delegate; COM representative

delegar ⟨1h⟩ v/t delegate

deleitar ⟨1a⟩ **1** v/t delight **2** v/r **deleitarse** take delight

deletrear ⟨1a⟩ v/t spell

delfín m ZO dolphin

delgado adj slim; **lámina, placa** thin

deliberado adj deliberate

deliberar ⟨1a⟩ v/i deliberate (**sobre** on)

delicadeza f gentleness; **de acabado, tallado** delicacy; (**tacto**) tact

delicado adj delicate

delicia f delight; **hacer las delicias de alguien** delight s.o.

delicioso adj delightful; **comida** delicious

delimitar ⟨1a⟩ v/t delimit

delincuente m/f criminal

delineante m/f draftsman, Br draughtsman; **mujer** draftswoman, Br draughtswoman

delinear ⟨1a⟩ v/t draft; fig draw up

delirar ⟨1a⟩ v/i be delirious; **¡tú deliras!** fig you must be crazy!

delirio m MED delirium; **tener delirio por el fútbol** fig be mad about soccer; **delirios de grandeza** delusions of grandeur

delito m offense, Br offence

demacrado adj haggard

demagógico adj demagogic

demanda f demand (**de** for); JUR lawsuit, claim

demandar ⟨1a⟩ v/t JUR sue

demás **1** adj remaining **2** adv: **lo demás** the rest; **los demás** the rest, the others; **por lo demás** apart from that

demasiado **1** adj too much; antes de pl too many; **demasiada gente** too many people; **hace demasiado calor** it's too hot **2** adv antes de adj, adv too; con verbo too much

demencia f MED dementia; fig madness; **demencia senil** MED senile dementia

demencial adj fig crazy, mad

demente **1** adj demented, crazy **2** m/f mad person

democracia f democracy

demócrata **1** adj democratic **2** m/f democrat

democrático adj democratic

demografía f demographics

demoler ⟨2h⟩ v/t demolish

demoníaco, demóníaco adj demonic

demonio m demon; **¡demonios!** F hell! F, damn! F

demora f delay; **sin demora** without delay

demorar ⟨1a⟩ **1** v/i stay on; L.Am. (**tardar**) be late; **no demores** don't be long **2** v/t delay **3** v/r **demorarse** be delayed; **¿cuánto se demora de Concepción a Santiago?** how long does it take to get from Concepción to Santiago?

demostración f proof; **de método** demonstration; **de fuerza, sentimiento** show

demostrar ⟨1m⟩ v/t prove; (**enseñar**) demonstrate; (**mostrar**) show

denegar ⟨1h & 1k⟩ v/t refuse

denigrante adj degrading; **artículo** denigrating

denigrar ⟨1a⟩ v/t degrade; (**criticar**) denigrate

denominación f name; **denominación de origen** guarantee of quality of a wine

denominador m: **denominador común** fig common denominator

denominar ⟨1a⟩ **1** v/t designate **2** v/r **denominarse** be called

denotar ⟨1a⟩ v/t show, indicate

densidad f density

denso *adj bosque* dense; *fig* weighty

dentadura *f:* **dentadura postiza** false teeth *pl*, dentures *pl*

dental *adj* dental

dentera *f:* **darle dentera a alguien** set s.o.'s teeth on edge

dentífrico *m* toothpaste

dentista *m/f* dentist

dentro 1 *adv* inside; *por dentro* inside; *de dentro* from inside **2 dentro de** *en espacio* in, inside; *en tiempo* in, within

denuncia *f* report; *poner una denuncia* make a formal complaint

denunciar ⟨1b⟩ *v/t* report; *fig* condemn, denounce

departamento *m* department; *L.Am.* (*apartamento*) apartment, *Br* flat

depender ⟨2a⟩ *v/i* depend (*de* on); *depender de alguien en una jerarquía* report to s.o.; *eso depende* that all depends

dependiente 1 *adj* dependent **2** *m*, *-a f* sales clerk, *Br* shop assistant

depilación *f* hair removal; *con cera* waxing; *con pinzas* plucking

depilar ⟨1a⟩ *v/t con cera* wax; *con pinzas* pluck

deplorar ⟨1a⟩ *v/t* deplore

deportar ⟨1a⟩ *v/t* deport

deporte *m* sport

deportista *m/f* sportsman; *mujer* sportswoman

depositar ⟨1a⟩ *v/t tb fig* put, place; *dinero* deposit (*en* in)

depósito *m* COM deposit; (*almacén*) store; *de agua*, AUTO tank; *depósito de cadáveres* morgue, *Br* mortuary

depravado *adj* depraved

depravar ⟨1a⟩ *v/t* deprave

depreciación *f* depreciation

depreciar ⟨1b⟩ **1** *v/t* lower the value of **2** *v/r* **depreciarse** depreciate, lose value

depredador 1 *adj* predatory **2** *m* ZO predator

depresión *f* MED depression

deprimente *adj* depressing

deprimir ⟨3a⟩ **1** *v/t* depress **2** *v/r* **deprimirse** get depressed

depuradora *f* purifier

depurar ⟨1a⟩ *v/t* purify; *agua* treat; POL purge

derecha *f tb* POL right; *la derecha* the right(-hand); *a la derecha posición* on the right; *dirección* to the right

derecho 1 *adj lado* right; (*recto*) straight; *C.Am. fig* straight, honest **2** *adv* straight **3** *m* (*privilegio*) right; JUR law; *del derecho* on the right side; *derecho de asilo* right to asylum; *derechos de autor* roy-

alties; *derechos humanos* human rights; *derecho de voto* right to vote; *no hay derecho* it's not fair, it's not right; *tener derecho a* have a right to **4** *mpl:* **derechos** fees; *derechos de inscripción* registration fee *sg*

derechura *f* straightness; *C.Am.*, *Pe* (*suerte*) luck; *en derechura* straight away

deriva *f:* **ir a la deriva** MAR, *fig* drift

derivar ⟨1a⟩ **1** *v/i* derive (*de* from); *de barco* drift **2** *v/r* **derivarse** be derived (*de* from)

dermatólogo *m*, *-a f* dermatologist

derogar ⟨1h⟩ *v/t* repeal

derramar ⟨1a⟩ **1** *v/t* spill; *luz*, *sangre* shed; (*esparcir*) scatter **2** *v/r* **derramarse** spill; *de gente* scatter

derrame *m* MED: *derrame cerebral* stroke

derrapar ⟨1a⟩ *v/i* AUTO skid

derrengado *adj* exhausted

derretir ⟨3l⟩ **1** *v/t* melt **2** *v/r* **derretirse** melt; *fig* be besotted (*por* with)

derribar ⟨1a⟩ *v/t edificio*, *persona* knock down; *avión* shoot down; POL bring down

derrocar ⟨1g⟩ *v/t* POL overthrow

derrochador *m*, **derrochadora** *f* spendthrift

derrochar ⟨1a⟩ *v/t* waste; *salud*, *felicidad* exude, burst with

derroche *m* waste

derrota *f* defeat

derrotar ⟨1a⟩ *v/t* MIL defeat; DEP beat, defeat

derruir ⟨3g⟩ *v/t edificio* demolish

derrumbar ⟨1a⟩ **1** *v/t* knock down **2** *v/r* **derrumbarse** collapse, fall down; *de una persona* go to pieces

desabrido *adj* (*soso*) tasteless; *persona* surly; *tiempo* unpleasant

desabrochar ⟨1a⟩ *v/t* undo, unfasten

desacato *m* JUR contempt

desaceleración *f* deceleration

desacertado *adj* misguided

desaconsejar ⟨1a⟩ *v/t* advise against

desacreditado *adj* discredited

desacreditar ⟨1a⟩ *v/t* discredit

desactivar ⟨1a⟩ *v/t bomba etc* deactivate

desacuerdo *m* disagreement; *estar en desacuerdo con* disagree with

desafiar ⟨1c⟩ *v/t* challenge; *peligro* defy

desafinar ⟨1a⟩ *v/i* MÚS be out of tune

desafío *m* challenge; *al peligro* defiance

desafortunado *adj* unfortunate, unlucky

desagradable *adj* unpleasant, disagreeable

desagradar ⟨1a⟩ *v/i:* **me desagrada tener que ...** I dislike having to ...

desagradecido *adj* ungrateful; *una tarea -a* a thankless task

desagrado *m* displeasure

desagravio *m* apology

desagüe *m* drain; *acción* drainage; *(cañería)* drainpipe

desahogar ⟨1h⟩ **1** *v/t sentimiento* vent **2** *v/r* **desahogarse** *fig* F let off steam F, get it out of one's system F

desahogo *m* comfort; **con desahogo** comfortably

desahuciar ⟨1b⟩ *v/t:* **desahuciar a alguien** declare s.o. terminally ill; *(inquilino)* evict s.o.

desairar ⟨1a⟩ *v/t* snub

desajustar ⟨1a⟩ *v/t tornillo, pieza* loosen; *mecanismo, instrumento* affect, throw out of balance

desajuste *m* disruption; COM imbalance

desalentar ⟨1k⟩ *v/t* discourage

desaliento *m* discouragement

desalinización *f* desalination

desaliñado *adj* slovenly

desalojar ⟨1a⟩ *v/t ante peligro* evacuate; *(desahuciar)* evict; *(vaciar)* vacate

desamparar ⟨1a⟩ *v/t:* **desamparar a alguien** abandon s.o.

desangelado *adj lugar* soulless

desangrarse ⟨1a⟩ *v/r* bleed to death

desanimar ⟨1a⟩ **1** *v/t* discourage, dishearten **2** *v/r* **desanimarse** become discouraged o disheartened

desánimo *m* discouragement

desapacible *adj* nasty, unpleasant

desaparecer ⟨2d⟩ **1** *v/i* disappear, vanish **2** *v/t L.Am.* disappear F

desaparecido *m*, **-a** *f L.Am.:* **un desaparecido** one of the disappeared

desaparición *f* disappearance

desapego *m* indifference; *(distancia)* distance, coolness

desapercibido *adj* unnoticed; **pasar desapercibido** go unnoticed

desaprensivo *adj* unscrupulous

desaprobar ⟨1m⟩ *v/t* disapprove of

desaprovechar ⟨1a⟩ *v/t oportunidad* waste

desarmado *adj* unarmed

desarmar ⟨1a⟩ *v/t* MIL disarm; TÉC take to pieces, dismantle

desarme *m* MIL disarmament

desarraigo *m fig* rootlessness

desarreglar ⟨1a⟩ *v/t* make untidy; *horario* disrupt

desarrollar ⟨1a⟩ **1** *v/t* develop; *tema* explain; *trabajo* carry out **2** *v/r* **desarrollarse** evolve; *(ocurrir)* take place

desarrollo *m* development

desarticular ⟨1a⟩ *v/t banda criminal* break up; MED dislocate

desaseado *adj* F scruffy

desasirse ⟨3a⟩ *v/r* get free, free o.s.

desasosiego *m* disquiet, unease

desastre *m tb fig* disaster

desastroso *adj* disastrous

desatar ⟨1a⟩ **1** *v/t* untie; *fig* unleash **2** *v/r* **desatarse** *de animal, persona* get free; *de cordón* come undone; *fig* be unleashed, break out

desatascar ⟨1g⟩ *v/t* unblock

desatender ⟨2g⟩ *v/t* neglect; *(ignorar)* ignore

desatino *m* mistake

desatornillador *m esp L.Am.* screwdriver

desatornillar ⟨1a⟩ *v/t* unscrew

desatrancar ⟨1g⟩ *v/t cañería* unblock

desavenencia *f* disagreement

desaventajado *adj* unfavo(u)rable

desayunar ⟨1a⟩ **1** *v/i* have breakfast **2** *v/t:* **desayunar algo** have sth for breakfast

desayuno *m* breakfast

desazón *f (ansiedad)* uneasiness, anxiety

desazonar ⟨1a⟩ *v/t* worry, make anxious

desbancar ⟨1g⟩ *v/t fig* displace, take the place of

desbandarse ⟨1a⟩ *v/r* disband; *de un grupo de personas* scatter

desbarajuste *m* mess

desbaratar ⟨1a⟩ *planes* ruin; *organización* disrupt

desbarrancar ⟨1g⟩ *L.Am.* **1** *v/t* push over the edge of a cliff **2** *v/r* **desbarrancarse** go over the edge of a cliff

desbocarse ⟨1g⟩ *v/r de un caballo* bolt

desbordante *adj energía, entusiasmo etc* boundless; **desbordante de** bursting with, overflowing with

desbordar ⟨1a⟩ **1** *v/t de un río* overflow, burst; *de un multitud* break through; *de un acontecimiento* overwhelm; *fig* exceed **2** *v/i* overflow **3** *v/r* **desbordarse** *de un río* burst its banks, overflow; *fig* get out of control

descabellado *adj:* **idea -a** F hare-brained idea F

descabellar ⟨1a⟩ *v/t* TAUR kill with a knife-thrust in the neck

descabello *m* fatal knife thrust

descafeinado *adj* decaffeinated; *fig* watered-down

descalabro *m* calamity, disaster

descalificar ⟨1g⟩ *v/t* disqualify

descalzarse ⟨1f⟩ *v/r* take one's shoes off

descalzo *adj* barefoot

descaminado *adj fig* misguided; **andar** or **ir descaminado** be on the wrong track

descamisado *adj* shirtless; *fig* ragged

descampado *m* open ground

descansar ⟨1a⟩ *v/i* rest, have a rest; **¡que descanses!** sleep well

descansillo *m* landing

descanso *m* rest; DEP half-time; TEA interval; *sin descanso* without a break

descapotable *m* AUTO convertible

descarado *adj* rude, impertinent

descarga *f* EL, MIL discharge; *de mercancías* unloading

descargar ⟨1h⟩ *v/t arma*, EL discharge; *fig: ira etc* take out (*en, sobre* on); *mercancías* unload; *de responsabilidad, culpa* clear (*de* of)

descaro *m* nerve

descarriado *adj: ir descarriado* go astray

descarrilar ⟨1a⟩ *v/t* derail

descartar ⟨1a⟩ *v/t* rule out

descastado *adj* cold, uncaring

descender ⟨2g⟩ **1** *v/i para indicar alejamiento* go down, descend; *para indicar acercamiento* come down, descend; *fig* go down, decrease, diminish; *descender de* descend from **2** *v/t escalera* go down; *para indicar acercamiento* come down

descendiente 1 *adj* descended **2** *m/f* descendant

descenso *m de precio etc* drop; *de montaña*, AVIA descent; DEP relegation; *la prueba de descenso en esquí* the downhill (race *o* competition)

descentralizar ⟨1f⟩ *v/t* decentralize

descentrar ⟨1a⟩ *v/t fig* shake

descifrar ⟨1a⟩ *v/t* decipher; *fig* work out

descodificación *f* decoding

descodificador *m* decoder

descodificar ⟨1g⟩ *v/t* decode

descolgar ⟨1h & 1m⟩ *v/t* take down; *teléfono* pick up **2** *v/r* **descolgarse** *por una cuerda* lower o.s.; *de un grupo* break away

descollar ⟨1m⟩ *v/i* stand out (*sobre* among)

descolonización *f* decolonization

descolorido *adj* faded; *fig* colo(u)rless

descomponer ⟨2r; *part* **descompuesto**⟩ **1** *v/t* (*dividir*) break down; (*pudrir*) cause to decompose; *L.Am.* (*romper*) break **2** *v/r* **descomponerse** (*pudrirse*) decompose, rot; TÉC break down; *Rpl* (*emocionarse*) break down (in tears); *se le descompuso la cara* he turned pale

descomposición *f* breaking down; *putrefacción* decomposition; (*diarrea*) diarrh(o)ea

descompuesto 1 *part* → **descomponer 2** *adj alimento* rotten; *cadáver* decomposed; *persona* upset; *L.Am.* tipsy; *L.Am. máquina* broken down

descomunal *adj* huge, enormous

desconcertar ⟨1k⟩ *v/t a persona* disconcert

desconchado, desconchón *m place where the paint is peeling; en porcelana* chip

desconcierto *m* uncertainty

desconectar ⟨1a⟩ **1** *v/t* EL disconnect **2** *v/i fig* switch off **3** *v/r* **desconectarse** *fig* lose touch (*de* with)

desconfiar ⟨1c⟩ *v/i* be mistrustful (*de* of), be suspicious (*de* of)

descongelar ⟨1a⟩ *v/t comida* thaw, defrost; *refrigerador* defrost; *precios* unfreeze

descongestionar ⟨1a⟩ *v/t* MED clear; *descongestionar el tráfico* relieve traffic congestion

desconocer ⟨2d⟩ *v/t* not know

desconocido 1 *adj* unknown **2** *m*, **-a** *f* stranger

desconsiderado *adj* inconsiderate

desconsolado *adj* inconsolable

desconsuelo *m* grief

descontado 1 *part* → **descontar 2** *adj*: *dar por descontado* take for granted; *por descontado* certainly

descontaminar ⟨1a⟩ *v/t* decontaminate

descontar ⟨1m⟩ *v/t* COM deduct, take off; *fig* exclude

descontento 1 *adj* dissatisfied **2** *m* dissatisfaction

descontrol *m* chaos

descontrolarse ⟨1a⟩ *v/r* get out of control

desconvocar ⟨1g⟩ *v/t* call off

descorazonar ⟨1a⟩ **1** *v/t* discourage **2** *v/r* **descorazonarse** get discouraged

descorchar ⟨1a⟩ *v/t botella* uncork

descortés *adj* impolite, rude

descoserse ⟨2a⟩ *v/r de costura, dobladillo etc* come unstitched; *de prenda* come apart at the seams

descosido *m*: *como un descosido* F like mad F

descoyuntar ⟨1a⟩ *v/t* dislocate

descremado *adj* skimmed

describir ⟨3a; *part* **descrito**⟩ *v/t* describe

descripción *f* description

descrito *part* → **describir**

descuajaringarse ⟨1h⟩ *v/r* F fall apart, fall to bits

descuartizar ⟨1f⟩ *v/t* quarter

descubierto 1 *part* → **descubrir 2** *adj* uncovered; *persona* bareheaded; *cielos* clear; *piscina* open-air; *al descubierto* in the open; *quedar al descubierto* be exposed **3** *m* COM overdraft

descubrimiento *m* discovery; (*revelación*) revelation

descubrir ⟨3a; *part* **descubierto**⟩ **1** *v/t* discover; *poner de manifiesto* uncover, reveal; *estatua* unveil **2** *v/r* **descubrirse**

take one's hat off; *fig* give o.s. away

descuento *m* discount; DEP stoppage time

descuerar ⟨1a⟩ *v/t L.Am.* skin; **descuerar a alguien** *fig* tear s.o. to pieces

descuidado *adj* careless

descuidar ⟨1a⟩ **1** *v/t* neglect **2** *v/i*: **¡descuida!** don't worry! **3** *v/r* **descuidarse** get careless; *en cuanto al aseo* let o.s. go; (*despistarse*) let one's concentration drop

descuido *m* carelessness; (*error*) mistake; (*omisión*) oversight; **en un descuido** *L.Am.* in a moment of carelessness

desde 1 *prp en el tiempo* since; *en el espacio* from; *en escala* from; **desde 1993** since 1993; **desde hace tres días** for three days; **desde ... hasta ...** from ... to ... **2** *adv*: **desde luego** of course; **desde ya** *Rpl* right away

desdén *m* disdain, contempt

desdeñable *adj* contemptible; **nada desdeñable** far from insignificant

desdeñar ⟨1a⟩ *v/t* scorn

desdibujado *adj* blurred

desdichado 1 *adj* unhappy; (*sin suerte*) unlucky **2** *m*, **-a** *f* poor soul

desdoblar ⟨1a⟩ *v/t* unfold; (*dividir*) split

desear ⟨1a⟩ *v/t* wish for; *suerte etc* wish; **¿qué desea?** what would you like?

desecar ⟨1g⟩ *v/t* dry

desechable *adj* disposable

desechar ⟨1a⟩ *v/t* (*tirar*) throw away; (*rechazar*) reject

desechos *mpl* waste *sg*

desembalar ⟨1a⟩ *v/t* unpack

desembarazarse ⟨1f⟩ *v/r*: **desembarazarse de** get rid of

desembarazo *m* ease

desembarcadero *m* MAR landing stage

desembarcar ⟨1g⟩ *v/i* disembark

desembocadura *f* mouth

desembocar ⟨1g⟩ *v/i* flow (**en** into); *de calle* come out (**en** into); *de situación* end (**en** in)

desembolsar ⟨1a⟩ *v/t* pay out

desembuchar ⟨1a⟩ *v/i fig* F spill the beans F, come out with it F

desempacar ⟨1g⟩ *v/t* unpack

desempaquetar ⟨1a⟩ *v/t* unwrap

desempatar ⟨1a⟩ *v/i* DEP, POL decide the winner

desempeñar ⟨1a⟩ *v/t deber, tarea* carry out; *cargo* hold; *papel* play

desempleado 1 *adj* unemployed **2** *m*, **-a** *f* unemployed person

desempleo *m* unemployment

desencadenar ⟨1a⟩ **1** *v/t fig* trigger **2** *v/r* **desencadenarse** *fig* be triggered

desencajarse ⟨1a⟩ *v/r de una pieza* come out; **se me ha desencajado la mandíbula** I dislocated my jaw

desencantado *adj fig* disenchanted (**con** with)

desencanto *m fig* disillusionment

desenchufar ⟨1a⟩ *v/t* EL unplug

desenfadado *adj* self-assured; *programa* light, undemanding

desenfocado *adj* FOT out of focus

desenfrenado *adj* frenzied, hectic

desenfreno *m* frenzy

desenfundar ⟨1a⟩ *v/t arma* take out, draw

desengañarse ⟨1a⟩ *v/r* become disillusioned (**de** with); (*dejar de engañarse*) stop kidding o.s.

desengaño *m* disappointment

desenlace *m* outcome, ending

desenmascarar ⟨1a⟩ *v/t fig* unmask, expose

desenredar ⟨1a⟩ *v/t* untangle; *situación confusa* straighten out, sort out

desenrollar ⟨1a⟩ *v/t* unroll

desenroscar ⟨1g⟩ *v/t* unscrew

desentenderse ⟨2g⟩ *v/r* not want to know (**de** about)

desentendido *adj*: **hacerse el desentendido** F pretend not to notice

desentonar ⟨1a⟩ *v/i* MÚS go off key; **desentonar con** *fig* clash with; **decir algo que desentona** say sth out of place

desentrañar ⟨1a⟩ *v/t fig* unravel

desenvoltura *f* ease

desenvolverse ⟨2h; *part* **desenvuelto** ⟩ *v/r fig* cope

desenvuelto 1 *part* → **desenvolverse 2** *adj* self-confident

deseo *m* wish

desequilibrar ⟨1a⟩ *v/t* unbalance; **desequilibrar a alguien** throw s.o. off balance

desequilibrio *m* imbalance; **desequilibrio mental** mental instability

desertar ⟨1a⟩ *v/i* MIL desert

desertor *m*, **desertora** *f* deserter

desértico *adj* desert *atr*

desertización *f* desertification

desesperación *f* despair

desesperado *adj* in despair

desesperante *adj* infuriating, exasperating

desesperar ⟨1a⟩ **1** *v/t* infuriate, exasperate **2** *v/i* give up hope (**de** of), despair (**de** of) **3** *v/r* **desesperarse** get exasperated

desestabilizar ⟨1f⟩ *v/t* POL destabilize

desfachatez *f* impertinence

desfalco *m* embezzlement

desfallecer ⟨2d⟩ *v/i* faint

desfase *m fig* gap

desfavorable *adj* unfavo(u)rable

desfavorecer ⟨2d⟩ *v/t* (*no ser favorable*) not favo(u)r, be disadvantageous to; *de ropa etc* not suit

desfigurar ⟨1a⟩ *v/t* disfigure

desfiladero *m* ravine

desfilar ⟨1a⟩ *v/i* parade

desfile *m* parade; ***desfile de modelos** or **de modas*** fashion show

desfogarse ⟨1h⟩ *v/r fig* vent one's emotions

desforestación *f* deforestation

desgana *f* loss of appetite; ***con desgana*** *fig* reluctantly, half-heartedly

desgañitarse ⟨1a⟩ *v/r* F shout one's head off F

desgarbado *adj* F ungainly

desgarrador *adj* heartrending

desgarrar ⟨1a⟩ *v/t* tear up; *fig: corazón* break

desgastar ⟨1a⟩ *v/t* wear out; *defensas* wear down

desgaste *m* wear (and tear)

desglose *m* breakdown, itemization

desgracia *f* misfortune; *suceso* accident; ***por desgracia*** unfortunately

desgraciadamente *adv* unfortunately

desgraciado 1 *adj* unfortunate; (*miserable*) wretched **2** *m*, **-a** *f* wretch; (*sinvergüenza*) swine F

desgravar ⟨1a⟩ **1** *v/t* deduct **2** *v/i* be tax-deductible

desguazar ⟨1f⟩ *v/t* scrap

deshabitado *adj* uninhabited

deshacer ⟨2s; *part* **deshecho** ⟩ **1** *v/t* undo; *maleta* unpack; *planes* wreck, ruin; ***eso los obligó a deshacer todos sus planes*** this forced them to cancel their plans **2** *v/r* **deshacerse** *de nudo de corbata, lazo etc* come undone; *de hielo* melt; ***deshacerse de*** get rid of

deshecho 1 *part* → **deshacer 2** *adj* F *anímicamente* devastated F; *de cansancio* beat F, exhausted

desheredar ⟨1a⟩ *v/t* disinherit

deshice *vb* → **deshacer**

deshidratar ⟨1a⟩ *v/t* dehydrate

deshielo *m* thaw

deshinchar ⟨1a⟩ **1** *v/t globo* deflate, let down **2** *v/r* **deshincharse** deflate, go down; *fig* lose heart

deshonesto *adj* dishonest

deshonra *f* dishono(u)r

deshonroso *adj* dishono(u)rable

deshora *f*: ***a deshora (s)*** at the wrong time

desidia *f* apathy, lethargy

desierto 1 *adj lugar* empty, deserted; ***isla -a*** desert island **2** *m* desert

designar ⟨1a⟩ *v/t* appoint, name; *lugar* select

designio *m* plan

desigual *adj* unequal; *terreno* uneven, irregular

desigualdad *f* inequality

desilusión *f* disappointment

desilusionado *adj* disappointed

desilusionar ⟨1a⟩ **1** *v/t* disappoint; (*quitar la ilusión*) disillusion **2** *v/r* **desilusionarse** be disappointed; (*perder la ilusión*) become disillusioned

desinfectante *m* disinfectant

desinfectar ⟨1a⟩ *v/t* disinfect

desinflar ⟨1a⟩ **1** *v/t globo, neumático* let the air out of, deflate **2** *v/r* **desinflarse** *de neumático* deflate; *fig* lose heart

desinformación *f* disinformation

desinhibir ⟨3a⟩ **1** *v/t*: ***desinhibir alguien*** get rid of s.o.'s inhibitions **2** *v/r* **desinhibirse** lose one's inhibitions

desintegrar ⟨1a⟩ **1** *v/t* cause to disintegrate; *grupo de gente* break up **2** *v/r* **desintegrarse** disintegrate; *de grupo de gente* break up

desinterés *m* lack of interest; (*generosidad*) unselfishness

desinteresado *adj* unselfish

desintoxicación *f* detoxification; ***hacer una cura de desintoxicación*** go into detox F, have treatment for drug / alcohol abuse

desistir ⟨3a⟩ *v/i* give up; ***tuvo que desistir de hacerlo*** I had to stop doing it

deslealtad *f* disloyalty

desligar ⟨1h⟩ **1** *v/t* separate (*de* from); *fig persona* cut off (*de* from) **2** *v/r* **desligarse** *fig* cut s.o. off (*de* from)

desliz *m fig* F slip-up F

deslizar ⟨1f⟩ **1** *v/t* slide, run (*por* along); *idea, frase* slip in **2** *v/i* slide **3** *v/r* **deslizarse** slide

deslomarse ⟨1a⟩ *v/r fig* kill o.s.

deslucido *adj* tarnished; *colores* dull, drab

deslucir ⟨3f⟩ *v/t* tarnish; *fig* spoil

deslumbrante *adj* dazzling

deslumbrar ⟨1a⟩ **1** *v/t fig* dazzle **2** *v/r* **deslumbrarse** *fig* be dazzled

desmadre *m* F chaos

desmandarse ⟨1a⟩ *v/r de animal* break loose

desmantelar ⟨1a⟩ *v/t fortificación, organización* dismantle

desmañado *adj* clumsy

desmaquillar ⟨1a⟩ *v/t* remove makeup from **2** *v/r* **desmaquillarse** remove one's makeup

desmarcarse ⟨1g⟩ *v/r* DEP lose one's

marker; **desmarcarse de** distance o.s. from

desmayarse ⟨1a⟩ v/r faint

desmayo m fainting fit; **sin desmayo** without flagging

desmedido adj excessive

desmelenarse ⟨1a⟩ v/r fig F let one's hair down F; (enfurecerse) hit the roof F

desmembrar ⟨1k⟩ v/t dismember

desmemoriado adj forgetful

desmentido m denial

desmentir ⟨3i⟩ v/t deny; *a alguien* contradict

desmenuzar ⟨1f⟩ v/t crumble up; fig break down

desmerecer ⟨2d⟩ 1 v/t not do justice to 2 v/i be unworthy (**con** of); **desmerecer de** not stand comparison with; **no desmerecer de** be in no way inferior to

desmesurado adj excessive

desmilitarización f demilitarization

desmitificar ⟨1g⟩ v/t demystify, demythologize

desmontar ⟨1a⟩ 1 v/t dismantle, take apart; *tienda de campaña* take down 2 v/i dismount

desmoralizado adj demoralized

desmoralizar ⟨1f⟩ v/t demoralize

desmoronamiento m tb fig collapse

desmoronarse ⟨1a⟩ v/r tb fig collapse

desnatado adj skimmed

desnaturalizado adj QUÍM denatured

desnivel m unevenness; *entre personas* disparity

desnivelar ⟨1a⟩ v/t upset the balance of

desnucarse ⟨1g⟩ v/r break one's neck

desnudar ⟨1a⟩ 1 v/t undress; fig fleece 2 v/r desnudarse undress

desnudo 1 adj naked; (sin decoración) bare 2 m PINT nude

desnutrición f undernourishment

desobedecer ⟨2d⟩ v/t disobey

desobediencia f disobedience

desobediente adj disobedient

desocupación f L.Am. unemployment

desocupado 1 adj apartamento vacant, empty; L.Am. sin trabajo unemployed 2 mpl: **los desocupados** the unemployed

desocupar ⟨1a⟩ v/t vacate

desodorante m deodorant

desoído part → desoír

desoír ⟨3q; part desoído⟩ v/t ignore, turn a deaf ear to

desolado adj desolate; fig griefstricken, devastated

desolar ⟨1m⟩ v/t tb fig devastate

desollar ⟨1m⟩ v/t skin

desorbitado adj astronomical; **con ojos**

desorbitados pop-eyed

desorden m disorder

desordenado adj untidy, messy F; fig disorganized

desordenar ⟨1a⟩ v/t make untidy

desorganización f lack of organization

desorganizado adj disorganized

desorientar ⟨1a⟩ 1 v/t disorient; (confundir) confuse 2 v/r desorientarse get disoriented, lose one's bearings; fig get confused

despabilado adj fig bright

despabilar ⟨1a⟩ 1 v/t wake up; **¡despabila!** get your act together! 2 v/r despabilarse fig get one's act together

despachar ⟨1a⟩ 1 v/t a persona, cliente attend to; problema sort out; (vender) sell; (enviar) send, dispatch 2 v/i meet (**con** with) 3 v/r despacharse F polish off F; **despacharse a su gusto** speak one's mind

despacho m office; diplomático dispatch; **despacho de billetes** ticket office

despacio adv slowly; L.Am. (en voz baja) in a low voice

desparpajo m self-confidence

desparramar ⟨1a⟩ 1 v/t scatter; líquido spill; dinero squander 2 v/r desparramarse spill; fig scatter

despavorido adj terrified

despecho m spite; **a despecho de** in spite of

despectivo adj contemptuous; GRAM pejorative

despedazar ⟨1f⟩ v/t tear apart

despedida f farewell; **despedida de soltero** stag party; **despedida de soltera** hen party

despedir ⟨3l⟩ 1 v/t see off; empleado dismiss; perfume give off; de jinete throw 2 v/r despedirse say goodbye (**de** to)

despegar ⟨1h⟩ 1 v/t remove, peel off 2 v/i AVIA, fig take off 3 v/r despegarse come unstuck (**de** from), come off (**de** sth); de persona distance o.s. (**de** from)

despegue m AVIA, fig take-off

despeinar ⟨1a⟩ v/t: **despeinar a alguien** muss s.o.'s hair

despejado adj cielo, cabeza clear

despejar ⟨1a⟩ 1 v/t clear; persona wake up 2 v/r despejarse de cielo clear up; fig wake o.s. up

despellejar ⟨1a⟩ v/t skin; **despellejar a alguien** fig tear s.o. to pieces

despenalizar ⟨1f⟩ v/t decriminalize

despensa f larder

despeñarse ⟨1a⟩ v/r throw o.s. off a cliff

desperdiciar ⟨1b⟩ v/t oportunidad waste

desperdicio *m* waste; **desperdicios** *pl* waste *sg*; **no tener desperdicio** be worthwhile

desperdigar ⟨1h⟩ *v/t* scatter

despertador *m* alarm (clock)

despertar ⟨1k⟩ **1** *v/t* wake, waken; *apetito* whet; *sospecha* arouse; *recuerdo* reawaken, trigger **2** *v/i* wake up **3** *v/r* **despertarse** wake (up)

despiadado *adj* ruthless

despido *m* dismissal

despierto *adj* awake; *fig* bright

despilfarrar ⟨1a⟩ *v/t* squander

despistado *adj* scatterbrained

despistarse ⟨1a⟩ *v/r* get distracted

despiste *m* distraction; **tener un despiste** become distracted

desplante *m*: **hacer un desplante a alguien** *fig* be rude to s.o.

desplazar ⟨1f⟩ **1** *v/t* move; (*suplantar*) take over from **2** *v/r* **desplazarse** travel

desplegar ⟨1h & 1k⟩ *v/t* unfold, open out; MIL deploy

despliegue *m* MIL deployment; **con gran despliegue de** *fig* with a great show of

desplomarse ⟨1a⟩ *v/r* collapse

desplome *m* collapse

despojar ⟨1a⟩ **1** *v/t* strip (**de** of) **2** *v/r* **despojarse**: **despojarse de** *prenda* take off

despojos *mpl* (*restos*) left-overs; (*desperdicios*) waste *sg*; *fig* spoils; *de animal* offal *sg*

desposeídos *mpl*: **los desposeídos** the dispossessed

déspota *m/f* despot

despotricar ⟨1g⟩ *v/i* F rant and rave F (**contra** about)

despreciar ⟨1b⟩ *v/t* look down on; *propuesta* reject

desprecio *m* contempt; (*indiferencia*) disregard; *acto* slight

desprender ⟨2a⟩ **1** *v/t* detach, separate; *olor* give off **2** *v/r* **desprenderse** come off; **desprenderse de** *fig* part with; **de este estudio se desprende que ...** what emerges from the study is that ...

despreocupación *f* indifference

despreocuparse ⟨1a⟩ *v/r* not worry (**de** about)

desprestigio *m* loss of prestige

desprevenido *adj* unprepared; **pillar** *or* L.Am. **agarrar desprevenido** catch unawares

desproporcionado *adj* disproportionate

despropósito *m* stupid thing

desprotegido *adj* unprotected

desprovisto *adj*: **desprovisto de** lacking in

después *adv* (*más tarde*) afterward, later;

seguido en orden next; *en el espacio* after; **yo voy después** I'm next; **después de** after; **después de todo** after all; **después de que se vaya** after he's gone

desquiciar ⟨1b⟩ *v/t fig* drive crazy **2** *v/r* **desquiciarse** *fig* lose one's mind

desquitarse ⟨1a⟩ *v/r* get one's own back (**de** for)

desrielar ⟨1a⟩ *v/t Chi* derail

destacado *adj* outstanding

destacar ⟨1g⟩ **1** *v/i* stand out **2** *v/r* **destacarse** stand out (**por** because of); (*ser excelente*) be outstanding (**por** because of)

destajo *m*: **a destajo** piecework

destapar ⟨1a⟩ **1** *v/t* open, take the lid off; *fig* uncover **2** *v/r* **destaparse** take one's coat off; *en cama* kick off the bedcovers; *fig* strip (off)

destartalado *adj vehículo, casa* dilapidated

destello *m de estrella* twinkling; *de faros* gleam; *fig* brief period, moment

destemplarse ⟨1a⟩ *v/r fig* become unwell

desteñir ⟨3h & 3l⟩ **1** *v/t* discolo(u)r, fade **2** *v/r* **desteñirse** fade

desternillante *adj* F hilarious

desterrar ⟨1k⟩ *v/t* exile

destiempo *m*: **a destiempo** at the wrong moment

destierro *m* exile

destilar ⟨1a⟩ *v/t* distill; *fig* exude

destinar ⟨1a⟩ *v/t fondos* allocate (**para** for); *a persona* post (**a** to)

destino *m* fate; *de viaje etc* destination; *en el ejército etc* posting

destituir ⟨3g⟩ *v/t* dismiss

destornillador *m* screwdriver

destornillar ⟨1a⟩ *v/t* unscrew

destreza *f* skill

destrozar ⟨1f⟩ *v/t* destroy; *emocionalmente* shatter, devastate

destrozos *mpl* damage *sg*

destrucción *f* destruction

destruir ⟨3g⟩ *v/t* destroy; (*estropear*) ruin, wreck

desunir ⟨3a⟩ *v/t* divide

desuso *m* disuse; **caer en desuso** fall into disuse

desvaído *adj color, pintura* faded

desvalido *adj* helpless

desvalijar ⟨1a⟩ *v/t* rob; *apartamento* burglarize, burgle

desván *m* attic

desvanecimiento *m* MED fainting fit

desvarío *m* delirium; **desvaríos** ravings

desvelar ⟨1a⟩ **1** *v/t* keep awake; *secreto* reveal **2** *v/r* **desvelarse** stay awake; *fig* do one's best (**por** for)

desvelo *m* sleeplessness; **desvelos** ef-

forts
desventaja f disadvantage
desventura f misfortune
desvergonzado adj shameless
desvergüenza f shamelessness
desvestir ⟨3l⟩ 1 v/t undress 2 v/r desvestirse get undressed, undress
desviar ⟨1c⟩ 1 v/t golpe deflect, parry; tráfico divert; río alter the course of; **desviar la conversación** change the subject; **desviar la mirada** look away; **desviar a alguien del buen camino** lead s.o. astray 2 v/r desviarse (girar) turn off; (bifurcarse) branch off; (apartarse) stray (**de** from)
desvincular ⟨1a⟩ 1 v/t dissociate (**de** from) 2 v/r desvincularse dissociate o.s. (**de** from)
desvío m diversion
detallar ⟨1a⟩ v/t explain in detail, give details of; COM itemize
detalle m detail; fig thoughtful gesture; **al detalle** retail
detección f detection
detectar ⟨1a⟩ v/t detect
detective m/f detective; **detective privado** private detective
detector m detector; **detector de mentiras** lie detector
detención f detention; **orden de detención** arrest warrant
detener ⟨2l⟩ 1 v/t stop; de policía arrest, detain 2 v/r detenerse stop
detenido 1 adj held up; (minucioso) detailed 2 m, -a f person under arrest
detenimiento m: **con detenimiento** thoroughly
detentar ⟨1a⟩ v/t hold
detergente m detergent
deteriorar ⟨1a⟩ 1 v/t damage 2 v/r deteriorarse deteriorate
deterioro m deterioration
determinado adj certain
determinar ⟨1a⟩ 1 v/t determine 2 v/r determinarse decide (**a** to)
detestar ⟨1a⟩ v/t detest
detonación f detonation
detonante m explosive; fig trigger
detonar ⟨1a⟩ 1 v/i detonate, go off 2 v/t detonate, set off
detractor m, detractora f detractor, critic
detrás adv behind; **por detrás** at the back; fig behind your / his etc back; **detrás de** behind; **uno detrás de otro** one after the other; **estar detrás de algo** fig be behind sth
detrimento m: **en detrimento de** to the detriment of
detritus m detritus

detuvo vb → **detener**
deuda f debt; **estar en deuda con alguien** fig be in s.o.'s debt, be indebted to s.o.
deudor m, deudora f debtor
devaluación f devaluation
devaluar ⟨1e⟩ v/t devalue
devanarse ⟨1a⟩ v/r: **devanarse los sesos** F rack one's brains F
devaneo m affair
devastar ⟨1a⟩ v/t devastate
devoción f tb fig devotion
devolver ⟨2h; part **devuelto** ⟩ 1 v/t give back, return; fig: visita, saludo return; F (vomitar) throw up F 2 v/r devolverse L.Am. go back, return
devorar ⟨1a⟩ v/t devour
devuelto part → **devolver**
D.F. abr Méx (= **Distrito Federal**) Mexico City
dg. abr (= **decigramo**) decigram
di vb → **dar**
día m day; **día de fiesta** holiday; **día festivo** holiday; **día hábil** or **laborable** work day; **poner al día** update, bring up to date; **a los pocos días** a few days later; **algún día, un día** some day, one day; **de día** by day, during the day; **de un día a or para otro** from one day to the next; **el día menos pensado** when you least expect it; **hace mal día** tiempo it's a nasty day; **hoy en día** nowadays; **todo el santo día** all day long; **todos los días** every day; **un día sí y otro no** every other day; **ya es de día** it's light already; **¡buenos días!** good morning
diabetes f diabetes
diabético 1 adj diabetic 2 m, -a f diabetic
diablesa f F she-devil
diablo m devil; **un pobre diablo** fig a poor devil; **mandar a alguien al diablo** tell s.o. to go to hell
diablura f prank, lark
diabólico adj diabolical
diadema f tiara; **para el pelo** hair-band
diáfano adj clear
diafragma m diaphragm
diagnosticar ⟨1g⟩ v/t diagnose
diagnóstico 1 adj diagnostic 2 m diagnosis
diagonal 1 adj diagonal 2 f diagonal (line)
diagrama m diagram
dialecto m dialect
dialogar ⟨1h⟩ v/i talk (**sobre** about), discuss (**sobre** sth); (negociar) hold talks (**con** with)
diálogo m dialog(ue)
diamante m diamond
diametralmente adv: **diametralmente**

opuesto diametrically opposed

diámetro *m* diameter

diana *f* MIL reveille; *(blanco)* target; *para jugar a los dardos* dartboard; *(centro de blanco)* bull's eye; *dar en la diana fig* hit the nail on the head

diantre *int* F hell! F

diapositiva *f* FOT slide, transparency

diariero *m*, **-a** *f* Arg newspaper vendor

diario 1 *adj* daily **2** *m* diary; *(periódico)* newspaper; *a diario* daily

diarrea *f* MED diarrh(o)ea

dibujante *m/f* draftsman, *Br* draughtsman; *mujer* draftswoman, *Br* draughtswoman; *de viñetas* cartoonist

dibujar ⟨1a⟩ **1** *v/t* draw; *fig* describe **2** *v/r* **dibujarse** *fig* appear

dibujo *m* arte drawing; *ilustración* drawing, sketch; *estampado* pattern; *dibujos animados* cartoons; *película de dibujos animados* animation

diccionario *m* dictionary

dic.ᵉ *abr (= diciembre)* Dec. (= December)

dice *vb* → **decir**

díceres *mpl* L.Am. sayings

dicharachero *adj* chatty; *(gracioso)* witty

dicho 1 *part* → **decir 2** *adj* said; *dicho y hecho* no sooner said than done; *mejor dicho* or rather **3** *m* saying

dichoso *adj* happy; F *(maldito)* damn F

diciembre *m* December

diciendo *vb* → **decir**

dictado *m* dictation

dictador *m*, **dictadora** *f* dictator

dictadura *f* dictatorship

dictaminar ⟨1a⟩ *v/t* state

dictar ⟨1a⟩ *v/t* lección, texto dictate; *ley* announce; *dictar sentencia* JUR pass sentence

didáctico *adj* educational

diecinueve *adj* nineteen

dieciocho *adj* eighteen

dieciséis *adj* sixteen

diecisiete *adj* seventeen

diente *m* tooth; *diente de ajo* clove of garlic; *diente de león* BOT dandelion; *poner los dientes largos a alguien* make s.o. jealous

diesel *m* diesel

diestro 1 *adj*: *a diestro y siniestro fig* F left and right **2** *m* TAUR bullfighter

dieta *f* diet; *estar a dieta* be on a diet; *dietas* travel(l)ing expenses

dietético *adj* dietary

diez *adj* ten

diezmar ⟨1a⟩ *v/t* decimate

difamar ⟨1a⟩ *v/t* slander, defame; *por escrito* libel, defame

difamatorio *adj* defamatory

diferencia *f* difference; *a diferencia de* unlike; *con diferencia fig* by a long way

diferenciar ⟨1b⟩ **1** *v/t* differentiate **2** *v/r* **diferenciarse** differ *(de* from); *no se diferencian en nada* there's no difference at all between them

diferente *adj* different

diferido *adj* TV: *en diferido* prerecorded

difícil *adj* difficult

dificultad *f* difficulty; *poner dificultades* make it difficult

dificultar ⟨1a⟩ *v/t* hinder

difundir ⟨3a⟩ **1** *v/t* spread; *(programa)* broadcast **2** *v/r* **difundirse** spread

difunto 1 *adj* late **2** *m*, **-a** *f* deceased

difuso *adj* idea, conocimientos vague, sketchy

digerir ⟨3i⟩ *v/t* digest; F *noticia* take in

digestión *f* digestion

digital *adj* digital

digitalizar ⟨1f⟩ *v/t* INFOR digitalize

dígito *m* digit

dignarse ⟨1a⟩ *v/r* deign

dignidad *f* dignity

digno *adj* worthy; *trabajo* decent; *digno de mención* worth mentioning

digo *vb* → **decir**

digresión *f* digression

dije *vb* → **decir**

dilación *f*: *sin dilación* without delay

dilapidar ⟨1a⟩ *v/t* waste

dilatar ⟨1a⟩ **1** *v/t* dilate; *(prolongar)* prolong; *(aplazar)* postpone **2** *v/i* Méx *(tardar)* be late; *no me dilato* I won't be long

dilema *m* dilemma

diligencia *f* diligence; *vehículo* stagecoach; *diligencias* JUR procedures, formalities

diligente *adj* diligent

dilucidar ⟨1a⟩ *v/t* clarify

diluir ⟨3g⟩ *v/t* dilute

diluviar ⟨1b⟩ *v/i* pour down

diluvio *m* downpour; *fig* deluge

dimensión *f* dimension; *fig* size, scale; *dimensiones* measurements

diminutivo *m* diminutive

diminuto *adj* tiny, diminutive

dimisión *f* resignation

dimitir ⟨3a⟩ *v/t* resign

Dinamarca *f* Denmark

dinámico *adj* fig dynamic

dinamita *f* dynamite

dinastía *f* dynasty

dinero *m* money; *dinero en efectivo, dinero en metálico* cash

dinosaurio *m* dinosaur

dio *vb* → **dar**

Dios *m* God; *hazlo como Dios manda* do

it properly; **¡Dios mío!** my God!; **¡por Dios!** for God's sake!; **sabe Dios lo que dijo** God knows what he said

dios *m* tb fig god

diosa *f* goddess

diploma *m* diploma

diplomacia *f* diplomacy

diplomático 1 *adj* diplomatic **2** *m*, -a *f* diplomat

diputado *m*, -a *f* representative, *Br* Member of Parliament

dique *m* dike, *Br* dyke

dirá *vb* → **decir**

diré *vb* → **decir**

dirección *f tb* TEA, *de película* direction; COM management; POL leadership; *de coche* steering; *en carta* address; **en aquella dirección** that way; **dirección asistida** AUTO power steering; **dirección de correo electrónico** e-mail address

directiva *f* board of directors; POL executive committee

directivo 1 *adj* governing; COM managing **2** *m*, -a *f* COM manager

directo *adj* direct; **en directo** TV, RAD live

director 1 *adj* leading **2** *m*, directora *f* manager; EDU principal, *Br* head (teacher); TEA, *de película* director; **director de orquesta** conductor

directriz *f* guideline

dirigir ⟨3c⟩ *v/t* TEA, *película* direct; COM manage, run; MÚS conduct; **dirigir una carta a** address a letter to; **dirigir una pregunta a** direct a question to **2** *v/r* **dirigirse** make, head (**a, hacia** for)

discapacidad *f* disability

discapacitado 1 *adj* disabled **2** *m*, -a *f* disabled person

discar ⟨1g⟩ *v/t L.Am.* TELEC dial

discernir ⟨3i⟩ *v/t* distinguish, discern

disciplina *f* discipline

disciplinar ⟨1a⟩ *v/t* discipline

discípulo *m*, -a *f* REL, fig disciple

disco *m* disk, *Br* disc; MÚS record; (*discoteca*) disco; DEP discus; **disco compacto** compact disc; **disco duro**, *L.Am.* **disco rígido** INFOR hard disk

discordante *adj* discordant

discordia *f* discord; (*colección de discos*) record collection

discreción *f* discretion; **a discreción** *disparar* at will; **a discreción de** at the discretion of

discrepancia *f* discrepancy; (*desacuerdo*) disagreement

discrepar ⟨1a⟩ *v/i* disagree

discreto *adj* discreet

discriminación *f* discrimination

discriminar ⟨1a⟩ *v/t* discriminate against;

(*diferenciar*) differentiate

disculpa *f* apology

disculpar ⟨1a⟩ **1** *v/t* excuse **2** *v/r* **disculparse** apologize

discurrir ⟨3a⟩ *v/i de tiempo* pass; *de acontecimiento* pass off; (*reflexionar*) reflect (**sobre** on)

discurso *m* speech; *de tiempo* passage, passing

discusión *f* discussion; (*disputa*) argument

discutir ⟨3a⟩ **1** *v/t* discuss **2** *v/i* argue (**sobre** about)

diseminar ⟨1a⟩ *v/t* scatter; fig spread

disentir ⟨3i⟩ *v/i* disagree (**de** with)

diseñador *m*, **diseñadora** *f* designer

diseñar ⟨1a⟩ *v/t* design

diseño *m* design; **diseño gráfico** graphic design

disfraz *m para ocultar* disguise; *para fiestas* costume, fancy dress

disfrazarse ⟨1f⟩ *v/r para ocultarse* disguise o.s. (**de** as); *para divertirse* dress up (**de** as)

disfrutar ⟨1a⟩ **1** *v/t* enjoy **2** *v/i* have fun, enjoy o.s.; **disfrutar de buena salud** be in *o* enjoy good health

disgregarse ⟨1h⟩ *v/r* disintegrate

disgustar ⟨1a⟩ **1** *v/t* upset **2** *v/r* **disgustar se** get upset

disgusto *m*: **me causó un gran disgusto** I was very upset; **llevarse un disgusto** get upset; **a disgusto** unwillingly

disidente *m/f* dissident

disimular ⟨1a⟩ **1** *v/t* disguise **2** *v/i* pretend

disimulo *m*: **con disimulo** unobtrusively

disipar ⟨1a⟩ **1** *v/t duda* dispel **2** *v/r* **disiparse** *de niebla* clear; *de duda* vanish

diskette *m* diskette, floppy (disk)

dislexia *f* dyslexia

dislocar ⟨1g⟩ *v/t* dislocate

disminución *f* decrease

disminuido 1 *adj* handicapped **2** *m*, -a *f* handicapped person; **disminuido físico** physically handicapped person

disminuir ⟨3g⟩ **1** *v/t gastos, costos* reduce, cut; *velocidad* reduce **2** *v/i* decrease, diminish

disociar ⟨1b⟩ *v/t* separate

disolvente *m* solvent

disolver ⟨1h; *part* **disuelto** ⟩ *v/t* dissolve; *manifestación* break up

disparada *f L.Am.*: **a la disparada** in a rush

disparar ⟨1a⟩ **1** *v/t tiro, arma* fire; *foto* take; *precios* send up **2** *v/i* shoot, fire **3** *v/r* **dispararse** *de arma, alarma* go off; *de precios* rise dramatically, rocket F

disparatado *adj* absurd

disparate m F piece of nonsense; *es un disparate hacer eso* it's crazy to do that

disparo m shot

dispendio m waste

dispensar ⟨1a⟩ v/t dispense; *recibimiento* give; (*eximir*) excuse (*de* from)

dispensario m MED clinic

dispersar ⟨1a⟩ **1** v/t disperse **2** v/r **dispersarse** disperse

disperso adj scattered

displicente adj disdainful

disponer ⟨2r; part **dispuesto**⟩ **1** v/t (*arreglar*) arrange; (*preparar*) prepare; (*ordenar*) stipulate **2** v/i: **disponer de algo** have sth at one's disposal **3** v/r **disponerse** get ready (*a* to)

disponibilidad f COM availability

disponible adj available

disposición f disposition; *de objetos* arrangement; **disposición de ánimo** state of mind; **estar a disposición de alguien** be at s.o.'s disposal

dispositivo m device

dispuesto 1 part → **disponer 2** adj ready (*a* to)

disputa f dispute

disputar ⟨1a⟩ **1** v/t dispute; *partido* play **2** v/i argue (*sobre* about) **3** v/r **disputarse** compete for

disquería f L.Am. record store

disquete m INFOR diskette, floppy (disk)

disquetera f disk drive

distancia f tb fig distance

distanciarse ⟨1b⟩ v/r distance o.s. (*de* from)

distante adj tb fig distant

distar ⟨1a⟩ v/i be far (*de* from)

distinción f distinction; **a distinción de** unlike

distinguido adj distinguished

distinguir ⟨3d⟩ v/t distinguish (*de* from); (*divisar*) make out; *con un premio* hono(u)r

distintivo m emblem; MIL insignia

distinto adj different; **distintos** (*varios*) several

distorsión f distortion

distracción f distraction; (*descuido*) absent-mindedness; (*diversión*) entertainment; (*pasatiempo*) pastime; **por distracción** out of absent-mindedness

distraer ⟨2p; part **distraído**⟩ **1** v/t distract; **la radio la distrae** she enjoys listening to the radio **2** v/r **distraerse** get distracted; (*disfrutar*) enjoy o.s.

distraído 1 part → **distraer 2** adj absent-minded; *temporalmente* distracted

distribución f COM, *de película* distribution

distribuir ⟨3g⟩ v/t distribute; *beneficio* share out

distrito m district

disturbio m disturbance

disuadir ⟨3a⟩ v/t dissuade; POL deter; **disuadir a alguien de hacer algo** dissuade s.o. from doing sth

disuelto part → **disolver**

disyuntiva f dilemma

diurético adj diuretic

diurno adj day atr

divagar ⟨1h⟩ v/i digress

diván m couch

diversidad f diversity

diversión f fun; (*pasatiempo*) pastime; **aquí no hay muchas diversiones** there's not much to do around here

diverso adj diverse; **diversos** several, various

divertido adj funny; (*entretenido*) entertaining

divertir ⟨3i⟩ **1** v/t entertain **2** v/r **divertirse** have fun, enjoy o.s.

dividendo m dividend

dividir ⟨3a⟩ v/t divide

divinamente adv fig wonderfully

divinidad f divinity

divino adj tb fig divine

divisa f currency; **divisas** pl foreign currency sg

divisar ⟨1a⟩ v/t make out

división f MAT, MIL, DEP division; **hubo división de opiniones** there were differences of opinion

divorciado 1 adj divorced **2** m, **-a** f divorcee

divorciarse ⟨1b⟩ v/r get divorced

divorcio m divorce

divulgación f spread

divulgar ⟨1h⟩ **1** v/t spread **2** v/r **divulgarse** spread

d. J.C. abr (= **después de Jesucristo**) A.D. (= Anno Domini)

dl. abr (= **decilitro**) deciliter

dm. abr (= **decímetro**) decimeter

dobladillo m hem

doblado adj película dubbed

doblaje m de película dubbing

doblar ⟨1a⟩ **1** v/t fold; *cantidad* double; *película* dub; MAR round; *pierna, brazo* bend; *en una carrera* pass, Br overtake; **doblar la esquina** go round o turn the corner **2** v/i: **doblar a la derecha** turn right **3** v/r **doblarse** bend; *fig* give in

doble 1 adj double; *nacionalidad* dual; **doble clic** m double click **2** m: **el doble** twice as much (*de* as); **el doble de gente** twice as many people; **dobles** tenis doubles **3** m/f en película double

doblegar ⟨1h⟩ v/t fig: *voluntad* break; *orgullo* humble

doblez 1 m fold **2** f fig deceit

doce adj twelve

docena f dozen

docente adj teaching atr

dócil adj docile

doctor m, **doctora** f doctor; *doctor honoris causa* honorary doctor

doctorado m doctorate

doctrina f doctrine

documentación f documentation; *de una persona* papers

documental m documentary

documento m document; *documento nacional de identidad* national identity card

dogma m dogma

dogo m zo mastiff

dólar m dollar

dolencia f ailment

doler ⟨2h⟩ v/i tb fig hurt; *me duele el brazo* my arm hurts; *le dolió que le mintieran* fig she was hurt that they had lied to her

dolor m tb fig pain; *dolor de cabeza* headache; *dolor de estómago* stomach-ache; *dolor de muelas* toothache

dolorido adj sore, aching; fig hurt

doloroso adj tb fig painful

domador m, **domadora** f tamer

domesticar ⟨1g⟩ v/t domesticate

doméstico 1 adj domestic, household atr **2** m, -a f servant

domiciliación f *de sueldo* credit transfer; *de pagos* direct billing, Br direct debit

domicilio m address; *repartir a domicilio* do home deliveries

dominante adj dominant; *desp* domineering

dominar ⟨1a⟩ **1** v/t dominate; *idioma* have a good command of **2** v/i dominate **3** v/r *dominarse* control o.s.

domingo m Sunday; *domingo de Ramos* Palm Sunday

dominguero m, -a f F weekender, Sunday tripper

dominical adj Sunday atr

dominicano GEOG **1** adj Dominican **2** m, -a f Dominican

dominio m control; fig command; *ser del dominio público* be in the public domain

dominó m dominoes pl

don[1] m gift; *don de gentes* way with people

don[2] m Mr; *don Enrique* Mr Sanchez *English uses the surname while Spanish uses the first name*

donación f donation; *donación de sangre* blood donation; *donación de órganos* organ donation

donante m/f donor; *donante de sangre* blood donor

donar ⟨1a⟩ v/t *sangre, órgano, dinero* donate

donativo m donation

doncella f maid

donde 1 adv where **2** prp esp L.Am.: *fui donde el médico* I went to the doctor's

dónde interr where; *¿de dónde eres?* where are you from?; *¿hacia dónde vas?* where are you going?

dondequiera adv wherever

doña f Mrs; *doña Estela* Mrs Sanchez *English uses the surname while Spanish uses the first name*

dopaje, doping m doping

dorada f zo gilthead

dorado adj gold; *montura* gilt

dormido adj asleep; *quedarse dormido* fall asleep

dormir ⟨3k⟩ **1** v/i sleep; *(estar dormido)* be asleep **2** v/t put to sleep; *dormir a alguien* MED give s.o. a general an(a)esthetic **3** v/r *dormirse* go to sleep; *(quedarse dormido)* fall asleep; *(no despertarse)* oversleep; *no podía dormirme* I couldn't get to sleep

dormitorio m bedroom

dorso m back

dos adj two; *de dos en dos* in twos; *los dos* both; *anda con ojo con los dos* watch out for the pair of them; *cada dos por tres* all the time, continually

doscientos adj two hundred

dosificar ⟨1g⟩ v/t cut down on

dosis f inv dose

dotar ⟨1a⟩ v/t equip (*de* with); *fondos* provide (*de* with); *cualidades* endow (*de* with)

dote f a novia dowry; *tener dotes para algo* have a gift for sth

doy vb → **dar**

dpto. abr (= *departamento*) dept (= department)

Dr. abr (= *Doctor*) Dr (= Doctor)

Dra. abr (= *Doctora*) Dr (= Doctor)

dragar ⟨1h⟩ v/t dredge

dragón m dragon; MIL dragoon

drama m drama

dramático adj dramatic; *arte dramático* dramatic art

dramatizar ⟨1f⟩ v/t dramatize

drástico adj drastic

drenaje m drainage

droga f drug; *droga de diseño* designer drug

drogadicto 1 *adj*: *una mujer -a* a woman addicted to drugs **2** *m*, *-a f* drug addict
drogarse 〈1h〉 *v/r* take drugs
drogodependencia *f* drug dependency
droguería *f* store selling cleaning and household products
dromedario *m* zo dromedary
d.º *abr* (= *descuento*) discount
ducha *f* shower; *ser una ducha de agua fría* fig come as a shock
ducharse 〈1a〉 *v/r* have a shower, shower
duda *f* doubt; *sin duda* without doubt; *poner en duda* call into question
dudar 〈1a〉 **1** *v/t* doubt **2** *v/i* hesitate (*en* to)
dudoso *adj* doubtful; (*indeciso*) hesitant
duele *vb* → **doler**
duelo *m* grief; (*combate*) duel
duende *m* imp
dueño *m*, *-a f* owner
duermo *vb* → **dormir**
dulce 1 *adj* sweet; *fig* gentle **2** *m* candy, *Br* sweet
dulzura *f tb fig* sweetness
dumping *m* dumping
duna *f* dune

duo *m* mús duo
duodécimo *adj* twelfth
dúplex *m* duplex (apartment)
duplicado 1 *adj* duplicate; *por duplicado* in duplicate **2** *m* duplicate
duplicar 〈1g〉 *v/t* duplicate
duque *m* duke
duquesa *f* duchess
duración *f* duration
duradero *adj* lasting; *ropa*, *calzado* hard-wearing
durante *prp indicando duración* during; *indicando período* for; *durante seis meses* for six months
durar 〈1a〉 *v/i* last
duraznero *m L.Am.* bot peach (tree)
durazno *m L.Am.* bot peach
Durex® *m Méx* Scotch tape®, *Br* Sellotape®
duro 1 *adj* hard; *carne* tough; *clima*, *fig* harsh; *duro de oído* F hard of hearing; *ser duro de pelar* be a tough nut to crack **2** *adv* hard **3** *m* five peseta coin
DVD *abr* (= *Disco de Vídeo Digital*) DVD (= Digital Versatile o Video Disc)

E

E *abr* (= *este*) E (= East(ern))
e *conj* (*instead of y before words starting with i, hi*) and
ebanista *m* cabinetmaker
ébano *m* ebony
ebrio *adj* drunk
ebullición f: *punto de ebullición* boiling point
eccema *m* eczema
echar 〈1a〉 **1** *v/t* (*lanzar*) throw; (*poner*) put; *de un lugar* throw out; *humo* give off; *carta* mail, *Br tb* post; *lo han echado del trabajo* he's been fired; *echar abajo* pull down, destroy; *echar la culpa a alguien* blame s.o., put the blame on s.o.; *me echó 40 años* he thought I was 40 **2** *v/i*: *echar a* start to, begin to; *echar a correr* start o begin to run, start running **3** *v/r echarse* (*tirarse*) throw o.s.; (*tumbarse*) lie down; (*ponerse*) put on; *echarse a llorar* start o begin to cry, start crying
eclesiástico *adj* ecclesiastical, church *atr*
eclipsar 〈1a〉 *v/t* eclipse

eclipse *m* eclipse
eco *m* echo; *tener eco* fig make an impact
ecografía *f* (ultrasound) scan
ecología *f* ecology
ecológico *adj* ecological; *alimentos* organic
ecologista *m/f* ecologist
economato *m* co-operative store
economía *f* economy; *ciencia* economics; *economía de mercado* market economy; *economía sumergida* black economy
económico *adj* economic; (*barato*) economical
economista *m/f* economist
economizar 〈1f〉 *v/t* economize on, save
ecosistema *m* ecosystem
ecoturismo *m* ecotourism
ecuación *f* equation
ecuador *m* equator
Ecuador Ecuador
ecuánime *adj* (*sereno*) even-tempered; (*imparcial*) impartial

ecuatorial *adj* equatorial
ecuatoriano 1 *adj* Ecuadorean **2** *m*, *-a f* Ecuadorean
eczema *m* eczema
ed. *abr* (**= edición**) ed (= edition)
edad *f* age; **la Edad Media** the Middle Ages *pl*; **la tercera edad** the over 60s; **estar en la edad del pavo** be at that awkward age; **a la edad de** at the age of; **¿qué edad tienes?** how old are you?
edición *f* edition
edificar ⟨1g⟩ *v/t* construct, build
edificio *m* building
edil *m*, **edila** *f* council(l)or
editar ⟨1a⟩ *v/t* edit; (*publicar*) publish
editor *m*, **editora** *f* editor
editorial 1 *m* editorial, leading article **2** *f* publishing company *o* house, publisher
edredón *m* eiderdown
educación *f* (*crianza*) upbringing; (*modales*) manners; **educación física** physical education, PE
educado *adj* polite, well-mannered; **mal educado** rude, ill-mannered
educar ⟨1g⟩ *v/t* educate; (*criar*) bring up; **voz** train
educativo *adj* educational
edulcorante *m* sweetener
EE. UU. *abr* (**= Estados Unidos**) US(A) (= United States (of America))
efectista *adj* theatrical, dramatic
efectivamente *adv* indeed
efectivo 1 *adj* effective; **hacer efectivo** COM cash **2** *m*: **en efectivo** (in) cash
efecto *m* effect; **efecto invernadero** greenhouse effect; **efectos secundarios** side effects; **en efecto** indeed; **surtir efecto** take effect, work
efectuar ⟨1e⟩ *v/t* carry out
efervescente *adj* effervescent; *bebida* carbonated, sparkling
eficacia *f* efficiency
eficaz *adj* (*efectivo*) effective; (*eficiente*) efficient
eficiencia *f* efficiency
eficiente *adj* efficient
efímero *adj* ephemeral, short-lived
efusivo *adj* effusive
egipcio 1 *adj* Egyptian **2** *m*, **-a** *f* Egyptian
Egipto Egypt
ego *m* ego
egocéntrico *adj* egocentric, self-centered (*Br* -centred)
egoísmo *m* selfishness, egoism
egoísta 1 *adj* selfish, egoistic **2** *m/f* egoist
egresar ⟨1a⟩ *v/i* *L.Am.* *de universidad* graduate; *de colegio* graduate from high school, *Br* leave school
egreso *m* *L.Am.* graduation

eh *int* *para llamar atención* hey!; **¿eh?** eh?
eje *m* axis; *de auto* axle; *fig* linchpin
ejecución *f* (*realización*) implementation, carrying out; *de condenado* execution; MÚS performance
ejecutar ⟨1a⟩ *v/t* (*realizar*) carry out, implement; *condenado* execute; INFOR run, execute; MÚS play, perform
ejecutiva *f* executive
ejecutivo 1 *adj* executive; **el poder ejecutivo** POL the executive **2** *m* executive; **el Ejecutivo** the government
ejemplar 1 *adj* *alumno, padre etc* model *atr*, exemplary **2** *m* *de libro* copy; *de revista* issue; *animal, planta* specimen
ejemplo *m* example; **dar buen ejemplo** set a good example; **por ejemplo** for example
ejercer ⟨2b⟩ **1** *v/t cargo* practice, *Br* practise; *influencia* exert **2** *v/i de profesional* practice, *Br* practise; **ejerce de médico** he's a practicing (*Br* practising) doctor
ejercicio *m* exercise; COM fiscal year, *Br* financial year; **hacer ejercicio** exercise
ejercitar ⟨1a⟩ **1** *v/t músculo, derecho* exercise **2** *v/r* **ejercitarse** train; **ejercitarse en** practice, *Br* practise
ejército *m* army
ojido *m* *Méx* traditional rural communal farming unit
ejote *m* *L.Am.* green bean
el 1 *art* the **2** *pron*: **el de ...** that of ...; **el de Juan's**; **el más grande** the biggest (one); **el que está ...** the one who is ...
él *pron sujeto* he; *cosa* it; *complemento* him; *cosa* it; **de él** his
elaborar ⟨1a⟩ *v/t* produce, make; *metal etc* work; *plan* devise, draw up
elasticidad *f* elasticity
elástico 1 *adj* elastic **2** *m* elastic; (*goma*) elastic band, *Br* rubber band
elección *f* choice
eleccionario *adj* *L.Am.* election *atr*, electoral
elecciones *fpl* election *sg*
elector *m* voter
electorado *m* electorate
electoral *adj* election *atr*, electoral
electricidad *f* electricity
electricista *m/f* electrician
eléctrico *adj luz, motor* electric; *aparato* electrical
electrocutar ⟨1a⟩ **1** *v/t* electrocute **2** *v/r* **electrocutarse** be electrocuted, electrocute o.s.
electrodo *m* electrode
electrodoméstico *m* electrical appliance
electrón *m* electron
electrónica *f* electronics

electrónico *adj* electronic

elefante *m* ZO elephant; **elefante marino** elephant seal, sea elephant

elegancia *f* elegance, stylishness

elegante *adj* elegant, stylish

elegantoso *adj* L.Am. F stylish, classy F

elegía *f* elegy

elegible *adj* eligible

elegir ⟨3c & 3l⟩ *v/t* choose; *por votación* elect

elemental *adj* (*esencial*) fundamental, essential; (*básico*) elementary, basic

elemento *m* element

elevado *adj* high; *fig* elevated

elevador *m* hoist; *L.Am.* elevator, *Br* lift

elevar ⟨1a⟩ *v/t* raise 2 *v/r* **elevarse** rise; *de monumento* stand

eliminación *f* elimination; *de desperdicios* disposal

eliminar ⟨1a⟩ *v/t* eliminate; *desperdicios* dispose of

eliminatoria *f* DEP qualifying round, heat

élite *f* elite

elitista *adj* elitist

elixir *m* elixir; **elixir bucal** mouthwash

ella *pron sujeto* she; *cosa* it; *complemento* her; *cosa* it; *de ella* her; *es de ella* it's hers

ellas *pron sujeto* they; *complemento* them; *de ellas* their; *es de ellas* it's theirs

ello *pron* it

ellos *pron sujeto* they; *complemento* them; *de ellos* their; *es de ellos* it's theirs

elocuente *adj* eloquent

elogiar ⟨1b⟩ *v/t* praise

elogio *m* praise

elote *m* L.Am. corncob; *granos* corn, *Br* sweetcorn

El Salvador El Salvador

eludir ⟨3a⟩ *v/t* evade, avoid

emanar ⟨1a⟩ *v/i fml* emanate (**de** from) *fml*; *fig* stem (**de** from), derive (**de** from) 2 *v/t* exude, emit

emancipación *f* emancipation

emanciparse ⟨1a⟩ *v/r* become emancipated

embadurnar ⟨1a⟩ *v/t* smear (**de** with)

embajada *f* embassy

embajador *m*, embajadora *f* ambassador

embalaje *m* packing

embalar ⟨1a⟩ 1 *v/t* pack 2 *v/r* **embalarse** *de persona* get excited; **el coche se embaló** the car went faster and faster; **no te embales** don't go so fast

embalse *m* reservoir

embarazada 1 *adj* pregnant 2 *f* pregnant woman

embarazo *m* pregnancy; **interrupción del embarazo** termination, abortion

embarazoso *adj* awkward, embarrassing

embarcación *f* vessel, craft

embarcadero *m* wharf

embarcar ⟨1g⟩ 1 *v/t pasajeros* board, embark; *mercancías* load 2 *v/i* board, embark 3 *v/r* **embarcarse** *en barco* board, embark; *en avión* board; **embarcarse en** *fig* embark on

embargo *m* embargo; JUR seizure; **sin embargo** however

embarque *m* boarding; *de mercancías* loading

embarrancar ⟨1g⟩ 1 *v/i* MAR run aground 2 *v/r* **embarrancarse** MAR run aground

embaucador 1 *adj* deceitful 2 *m*, embaucadora *f* trickster

embeberse ⟨2a⟩ *v/r* get absorbed *o* engrossed (**en** in)

embelesar ⟨1a⟩ *v/t* captivate

embestir ⟨3l⟩ 1 *v/t* charge 2 *v/i* charge (**contra** at)

emblema *m* emblem

embobar ⟨1a⟩ *v/t* fascinate

embolarse ⟨1a⟩ *v/r* C.Am., Méx F get plastered F

émbolo *m* TÉC piston

embolsar ⟨1a⟩ 1 *v/t* pocket 2 *v/r* **embolsarse** pocket

emborrachar ⟨1a⟩ 1 *v/t* make drunk, get drunk 2 *v/r* **emborracharse** get drunk

emborronar ⟨1a⟩ *v/t* blot, smudge

emboscada *f* ambush

embotar ⟨1a⟩ *v/t* blunt

embotellamiento *m* traffic jam

embotellar ⟨1a⟩ *v/t* bottle

embrague *m* AUTO clutch

embriagar ⟨1h⟩ *v/t fig* intoxicate

embriaguez *f* intoxication

embrión *m* embryo; **en embrión** in an embryonic state, in embryo

embrollar ⟨1a⟩ *v/t* tangle; *fig* mess, muddle

embrollo *m* tangle; *fig* mess, muddle

embromar ⟨1a⟩ *v/t Rpl* F (*molestar*) annoy

embrujar ⟨1a⟩ *v/t tb fig* bewitch

embrutecer ⟨2d⟩ 1 *v/t* brutalize 2 *v/r* **embrutecerse** become brutalized

embudo *m* funnel

embustero 1 *adj* deceitful 2 *m*, -a *f* liar

embutido *m* GASTR *type of dried sausage*

emergencia *f* emergency

emerger ⟨2c⟩ *v/i* emerge

emigración *f* emigration

emigrante *m* emigrant

emigrar ⟨1a⟩ *v/i* emigrate; ZO migrate

eminente *adj* eminent

emirato *m* emirate

emisario *m* emissary

emisión f emission; COM issue; RAD, TV broadcast

emisora f radio station

emitir ⟨3a⟩ v/t calor, sonido give out, emit; moneda issue; opinión express, give; veredicto deliver; RAD, TV broadcast; voto cast

emoción f emotion; **¡qué emoción!** how exciting!

emocionado adj excited

emocionante adj (excitante) exciting; (conmovedor) moving

emocionarse ⟨1a⟩ v/r get excited; (conmoverse) be moved

emotivo adj emotional; (conmovedor) moving

empacar ⟨1g⟩ **1** v/t & v/i L.Am. pack **2** v/r **empacarse** L.Am. (ponerse tozudo) dig one's heels in; tragar devour

empacharse ⟨1a⟩ v/r F get an upset stomach (de from); **empacharse de** fig overdose on

empacho m F upset stomach; fig bellyful F; **sin empacho** unashamedly

empadronar ⟨1a⟩ **1** v/t register **2** v/r **empadronarse** register

empalagoso adj sickly; fig sickly sweet, cloying

empalizada f palisade

empalmar ⟨1a⟩ **1** v/t connect, join **2** v/i connect (con with), join up (con with); de idea, conversación run o follow on (con from)

empanada f pie

empanadilla f pasty

empanar ⟨1a⟩ v/t coat in breadcrumbs

empantanarse ⟨1a⟩ v/r become swamped o waterlogged; fig get bogged down

empañado adj misty

empañar ⟨1a⟩ **1** v/t steam up, mist up; fig tarnish, sully **2** v/r **empañarse** de vidrio steam up, mist up

empapado adj soaked, dripping wet

empapar ⟨1a⟩ **1** v/t soak; (absorber) soak up; **2** v/r **empaparse** get soaked o drenched; **empaparse de algo** immerse o.s. in sth

empapelar ⟨1a⟩ v/t wallpaper

empaque m presencia; (seriedad) solemnity

empaquetar ⟨1a⟩ v/t pack

emparedado m sandwich

emparejar ⟨1a⟩ v/t personas pair off; calcetines match up

emparentado adj related

empastador m, **empastadora** f L.Am. bookbinder

empastar ⟨1a⟩ v/t muela fill; libro bind

empaste m filling

empatar ⟨1a⟩ v/i tie, Br draw; (igualar) tie the game, Br equalize

empate m tie, draw; **gol del empate** en fútbol equalizer

empecinarse ⟨1a⟩ v/r get an idea into one's head; **empecinarse en algo** insist on sth

empedernido adj inveterate, confirmed

empedrado m paving

empeine m instep

empellón m shove; **entró a empellones** he shoved his way in

empelotarse ⟨1a⟩ v/r L.Am. P take one's clothes off, strip off

empeñado adj (endeudado) in debt; **estar empeñado en hacer algo** be determined to do sth

empeñar ⟨1a⟩ **1** v/t pawn **2** v/r **empeñarse** (endeudarse) get into debt; (esforzarse) strive (en to), make an effort (en to); **empeñarse en hacer** obstinarse insist on doing, be determined to do

empeñero Méx **1** adj determined **2** m, -a f determined person

empeño m (obstinación) determination; (esfuerzo) effort; Méx fig pawn shop

empeñoso adj L.Am. hard-working

empeorar ⟨1a⟩ **1** v/t make worse **2** v/i deteriorate, get worse

empequeñecer ⟨2d⟩ v/t fig diminish

emperador m emperor; pez swordfish

emperatriz f empress

emperrarse ⟨1a⟩ v/r F: **emperrarse en hacer algo** have one's heart set on doing sth; **emperrarse con algo** set one's heart on sth

empezar ⟨1f & 1k⟩ **1** v/t start, begin **2** v/i start, begin; **empezar a hacer algo** start to do sth, start doing sth; **empezar por hacer algo** start o begin by doing sth

empiezo m S. Am. start, beginning

empinado adj steep

empinar ⟨1a⟩ v/t raise; **empinar el codo** F raise one's elbow F

empírico adj empirical

emplazamiento m site, location; JUR subpoena, summons

empleado 1 adj: **le está bien empleado** it serves him right **2** m, -a f employee; **-a de hogar** maid

emplear ⟨1a⟩ v/t (usar) use; persona employ

empleo m employment; (puesto) job; (uso) use; **modo de empleo** instructions for use pl, directions pl

emplomar ⟨1a⟩ v/t S. Am. fill

empobrecer ⟨2d⟩ **1** v/t impoverish, make poor **2** v/i become impoverished, become poor **3** v/r **empobrecerse** become

impoverished, become poor
empobrecimiento *m* impoverishment
empollar ⟨1a⟩ *v/i* F cram F, *Br* swot F
empollón *m* F grind F, *Br* swot F
emporio *m L.Am. almacén* department store
empotrado *adj* built-in, fitted
empotrarse ⟨1a⟩ *v/r* crash (**contra** into)
emprendedor *adj* enterprising
emprender ⟨2a⟩ *v/t* embark on, undertake; **emprenderla con alguien** F take it out on s.o.
empresa *f* company; *fig* venture, undertaking; **empresa de trabajo temporal** temping agency
empresaria *f* businesswoman
empresarial *adj* business *atr*; **ciencias empresariales** business studies
empresario *m* businessman
empujar ⟨1a⟩ *v/t* push; *fig* urge on, spur on
empujón *m* push, shove; **salían a empujones** F they were pushing and shoving their way out
empuñar ⟨1a⟩ *v/t* grasp
emular ⟨1a⟩ *v/t* emulate
emulsión *f* emulsion
en *prp* (*dentro de*) in; (*sobre*) on; **en un mes** in a month; **en la mesa** on the table; **en inglés** in English; **en la calle** on the street, *Br tb* in the street; **en casa** at home; **en coche / tren** by car / train
enajenación *f* JUR transfer; **enajenación mental** insanity
enajenar ⟨1a⟩ *v/t* JUR transfer; (*trastornar*) drive insane
enamorado *adj* in love (**de** with)
enamorar ⟨1a⟩ **1** *v/t*: **lo enamoró** she captivated him **2** *v/r* **enamorarse** fall in love (**de** with)
enano 1 *adj* tiny; *perro, árbol* miniature, dwarf *atr* **2** *m* dwarf; **trabajar como un enano** fig F work like a dog F
enarbolar ⟨1a⟩ *v/t* hoist, raise
encabezamiento *m* heading
encabezar ⟨1f⟩ *v/t* head; *movimiento, revolución* lead
encabritarse ⟨1a⟩ *v/r de caballo* rear up
encadenar ⟨1a⟩ **1** *v/t* chain (up); *fig* link o put together **2** *v/r* **encadenarse** chain oneself (**a** to)
encajar ⟨1a⟩ **1** *v/t piezas* fit; *golpe* take **2** *v/i* fit (**en** in; **con** with)
encaje *m* lace
encalado *m* whitewashing
encalar ⟨1a⟩ *v/t* whitewash
encallar ⟨1a⟩ *v/i* MAR run aground
encaminarse ⟨1a⟩ *v/r* set off (**a** for), head (**a** for); *fig* be aimed o directed (**a** at)

encandilar ⟨1a⟩ *v/t* dazzle
encantado *adj* (*contento*) delighted; *castillo* enchanted; **¡encantado!** nice to meet you
encantador *adj* charming
encantar ⟨1a⟩ *v/t*: **me / le encanta** I love / he loves it
encanto *m* (*atractivo*) charm; **como por encanto** as if by magic; **eres un encanto** you're an angel
encapricharse ⟨1a⟩ *v/r* fall in love (**de** with)
encapuchado *adj* hooded
encaramarse ⟨1a⟩ *v/r* climb
encarar ⟨1a⟩ *v/t* approach; *desgracia etc* face up to
encarcelar ⟨1a⟩ *v/t* put in prison, imprison
encarecer ⟨2d⟩ **1** *v/t* put up the price of, make more expensive **2** *v/r* **encarecerse** become more expensive; *de precios* increase, rise
encarecidamente *adv*: **le ruego encarecidamente que ...** I beg o urge you to ...
encargado *m*, **-a** *f* person in charge; *de un negocio* manager
encargar ⟨1h⟩ **1** *v/t* (*pedir*) order; **le encargué que me trajera ...** I asked him to bring me ... **2** *v/r* **encargarse** (*tener responsabilidad*) be in charge; **yo me encargo de la comida** I'll take care of o see to the food
encargo *m* job, errand; COM order; **¿te puedo hacer un encargo?** can I ask you to do something for me?; **hecho por encargo** made to order
encariñarse ⟨1a⟩ *v/r*: **encariñarse con alguien / algo** grow fond of s.o/sth, become attached to s.o./sth
encarnado *adj* red
encarnar ⟨1a⟩ *v/t cualidad etc* embody; TEA play
encarnizado *adj* bitter, fierce
encarrilar ⟨1a⟩ *v/t fig* direct, guide
encasillar ⟨1a⟩ *v/t* class, classify; (*estereotipar*) pigeonhole
encasquetar ⟨1a⟩ *v/t gorro etc* pull down; **me lo encasquetó** F he landed me with it F
encasquillarse ⟨1a⟩ *v/r de arma* jam
encauzar ⟨1f⟩ *v/t tb fig* channel
encefalopatía *f*: **encefalopatía espongiforme bovina** bovine spongiform encephalitis, BSE
encendedor *m* lighter
encender ⟨2g⟩ **1** *v/t fuego* light; *luz, televisión* switch on, turn on; *fig* inflame, arouse, stir up **2** *v/r* **encenderse de luz, televisión** come on

encendido 1 adj luz, televisión (switched) on; fuego lit; cara red **2** m AUTO ignition

encerado m blackboard

encerar ⟨1a⟩ v/t polish, wax

encerrar ⟨1k⟩ **1** v/t lock up, shut up; (contener) contain **2** v/r **encerrarse** shut o.s. up

encerrona f tb fig trap

encestar ⟨1a⟩ v/i score

encharcado adj flooded, waterlogged

enchicharse ⟨1a⟩ v/r L.Am. (emborracharse) get drunk; Rpl P (enojarse) get angry, get mad F

enchilada f Méx GASTR enchilada (tortilla with a meat or cheese filling)

enchiloso adj C.Am., Méx hot

enchufado m: **es un enchufado** F he has connections, he has friends in high places

enchufar ⟨1a⟩ v/t EL plug in

enchufe m EL macho plug; hembra socket; **tener enchufe** fig F have pull F, have connections F

enchufismo m string-pulling

encía f gum

enciclopedia f encyclop(a)edia

encierro m protesta sit-in; de toros bull running

encima adv on top; **encima de** on top of, on; **por encima de** over, above; **por encima de todo** above all; **lo ayudo, y encima se queja** I help him and then he goes and complains; **hacer algo muy por encima** do sth very quickly; **no lo llevo encima** I haven't got it on me; **ponerse algo encima** put sth on

encimera f sábana top sheet; Esp mostrador worktop

encina f BOT holm oak

encinta adj pregnant

enclaustrarse ⟨1a⟩ v/r fig shut o.s. away

enclave m enclave

enclenque 1 adj sickly, weak **2** m/f weakling

encoger ⟨2c⟩ **1** v/t shrink; las piernas tuck in **2** v/i de material shrink **3** v/r **encogerse** de material shrink; fig: de persona be intimidated, cower; **encogerse de hombros** shrug (one's shoulders)

encolar ⟨1a⟩ v/t glue, stick

encolerizarse ⟨1f⟩ v/r get angry

encomienda f L.Am. HIST grant of land and labor by colonial authorities after the Conquest

enconado adj fierce, heated

encontrar ⟨1m⟩ **1** v/t find **2** v/r **encontrarse** (reunirse) meet; (estar) be; **encontrarse con alguien** meet s.o., run into s.o.; **me encuentro bien** I'm fine, I feel

fine

encontronazo m smash, crash

encorvar ⟨1a⟩ v/t hunch; estantería cause to buckle

encrespar ⟨1a⟩ **1** v/t pelo curl; mar make rough o choppy; fig arouse, inflame **2** v/r **encresparse** del mar turn choppy; fig become inflamed

encrucijada f crossroads; fig dilemma

encuadernar ⟨1a⟩ v/t bind

encuadrar ⟨1a⟩ v/t en marco frame; en grupo include, place

encuartelar ⟨1a⟩ v/t L.Am. billet

encubierto part → **encubrir**

encubrir ⟨3a; part **encubierto** ⟩ v/t delincuente harbo(u)r; delito cover up, conceal

encuentro m meeting, encounter; DEP game; **salir** or **ir al encuentro de alguien** meet s.o., greet s.o.

encuerado adj L.Am. naked

encuesta f survey; (sondeo) (opinion) poll

encuestar ⟨1a⟩ v/t poll

encumbrarse ⟨1a⟩ v/r fig rise to the top

encurtidos mpl pickles

ende adv: **por ende** therefore, consequently

endeble adj weak, feeble

endémico adj endemic

endemoniado adj possessed; fig F terrible, awful

enderezar ⟨1f⟩ **1** v/t straighten out **2** v/r **enderezarse** straighten up, stand up straight; fig straighten o.s. out, sort o.s. out

endeudarse ⟨1a⟩ v/r get (o.s.) into debt

endiablado adj fig (malo) terrible, awful; (difícil) tough

endibia f BOT endive

endilgar ⟨1h⟩ v/t: **me lo endilgó a mí** F he landed me with it F; **endilgar un sermón a alguien** F lecture s.o., give s.o. a lecture

endosar ⟨1a⟩ v/t COM endorse; **me lo endosó a mí** F she landed me with it F

endrina f BOT sloe

endrogarse ⟨1h⟩ v/r Méx, C.Am. get into debt

endulzar ⟨1f⟩ v/t sweeten; (suavizar) soften

endurecer ⟨2d⟩ **1** v/t harden; fig toughen up **2** v/r **endurecerse** harden, become harder; fig become harder, toughen up

enebro m BOT juniper

enema m MED enema

enemigo 1 adj enemy atr **2** m enemy; **ser enemigo de** fig be opposed to, be against

enemistarse ⟨1a⟩ v/r fall out

E

energético *adj* crisis energy *atr*; *alimento* energy-giving

energía *f* energy; *energía eólica* wind power; *energía nuclear* nuclear power, nuclear energy; *energía solar* solar power, solar energy

enérgico *adj* energetic; *fig* forceful, strong

energúmeno *m* lunatic; *ponerse hecho un energúmeno* go crazy F, blow a fuse F

ene. *abr* (= *enero*) Jan. (= January)

enero *m* January

enervar ⟨1a⟩ *v/t* irritate, get on the nerves of

enésimo *adj* nth; *por -a vez* for the umpteenth time

enfadado *adj* annoyed (*con* with); (*encolerizado*) angry (*con* with)

enfadar ⟨1a⟩ **1** *v/t* (*molestar*) annoy; (*encolerizar*) make angry, anger **2** *v/r* **enfadarse** (*molestarse*) get annoyed (*con* with); (*encolerizarse*) get angry (*con* with)

enfado *m* (*molestia*) annoyance; (*cólera*) anger

enfangarse ⟨1h⟩ *v/r* get muddy; *enfangarse en* *fig* get (o.s.) mixed up in

énfasis *m* emphasis; *poner énfasis en* emphasize, stress

enfático *adj* emphatic

enfermar ⟨1a⟩ **1** *v/t* drive crazy **2** *v/i* get sick, *Br tb* get ill

enfermedad *f* illness, disease

enfermería *f sala* infirmary, sickbay; *carrera* nursing

enfermero *m*, *-a f* nurse

enfermizo *adj* unhealthy

enfermo **1** *adj* sick, ill **2** *m*, *-a f* sick person

enfermoso *adj* L.Am. sickly, unhealthy

enfiestarse ⟨1a⟩ *v/r* L.Am. F party F, live it up F

enfocar ⟨1g⟩ *v/t cámara* focus; *imagen* get in focus; *fig: asunto* look at, consider

enfoque *m fig* approach

enfrentamiento *m* clash, confrontation

enfrentar ⟨1a⟩ **1** *v/t* confront, face up to **2** *v/r* **enfrentarse** DEP meet; *enfrentarse con alguien* confront s.o.; *enfrentarse a algo* face (up to) sth

enfrente *adv* opposite; *enfrente del colegio* opposite the school, across (the street) from the school

enfriar ⟨1c⟩ **1** *v/t vino* chill; *algo caliente* cool (down); *fig* cool **2** *v/r* **enfriarse** (*perder calor*) cool down; (*perder demasiado calor*) get cold, go cold; *fig* cool, cool off; MED catch a cold, catch a chill

enfurecer ⟨2d⟩ **1** *v/t* infuriate, make furious **2** *v/r* **enfurecerse** get furious, get into a rage **enfurecido** *adj* furious, enraged

enfurruñado *adj* F sulky

enfurruñarse ⟨1a⟩ *v/r* F go into a huff F

engalanar ⟨1a⟩ *v/t* decorate, deck

enganchar ⟨1a⟩ **1** *v/t* hook; F *novia, trabajo* land F **2** *v/r* **engancharse** get caught (*en* on); MIL sign up, enlist; *engancharse a la droga* F get hooked on drugs F

engañar ⟨1a⟩ **1** *v/t* deceive, cheat; (*ser infiel a*) cheat on, be unfaithful to; *te han engañado* you've been had **2** *v/r* **engañarse** (*mentirse*) deceive o.s., kid o.s. F; (*equivocarse*) be wrong

engaño *m* (*mentira*) deception, deceit; (*ardid*) trick

engarzar ⟨1f⟩ *v/t joya* set

engatusar ⟨1a⟩ *v/t* F sweet-talk F

engendrar ⟨1a⟩ *v/t* father; *fig* breed, engender *fml*

engendro *m fig* eyesore

englobar ⟨1a⟩ *v/t* include, embrace *fml*

engordar ⟨1a⟩ **1** *v/t* put on, gain **2** *v/i de persona* put on weight, gain weight; *de comida* be fattening

engorrar ⟨1a⟩ *v/t Méx, W.I.* F annoy

engorroso *adj* tricky

engranaje *m* TÉC gears *pl*; *fig* machinery

engrasar ⟨1a⟩ *v/t* grease, lubricate

engrase *m* greasing, lubrication

engreído *adj* conceited

engrosar ⟨1m⟩ **1** *v/t* swell, increase **2** *v/i* put on weight, gain weight

engrudo *m* (flour and water) paste

engullir ⟨3h⟩ *v/t* bolt (down)

enhebrar ⟨1a⟩ *v/t* thread, string

enhiesto *adj lit persona* erect, upright; *torre, árbol* lofty

enhorabuena *f* congratulations *pl*; *dar la enhorabuena* congratulate (*por* on)

enigma *m* enigma

enigmático *adj* enigmatic

enjabonar ⟨1a⟩ *v/t* soap

enjambre *m tb fig* swarm

enjoyado *adj* bejewel(l)ed

enjuagar ⟨1h⟩ *v/t* rinse

enjugar ⟨1h⟩ *v/t deuda etc* wipe out; *líquido* mop up; *lágrimas* wipe away

enjuiciar ⟨1b⟩ *v/t* JUR institute proceedings against; *fig* judge

enlace *m* link, connection; *enlace matrimonial* marriage

enlatar ⟨1a⟩ *v/t* can, *Br tb* tin

enlazar ⟨1f⟩ **1** *v/t* link (up), connect; *L.Am. con cuerda* rope, lasso **2** *v/i de carretera* link up (*con* with); AVIA, FERR connect (*con* with)

enloquecer ⟨2d⟩ **1** *v/t* drive crazy *o* mad **2** *v/i* go crazy *o* mad

enmarañar ⟨1a⟩ **1** v/t pelo tangle; asunto complicate, muddle **2** v/r **enmarañarse de pelo** get tangled; **enmarañarse en algo** get entangled o embroiled in sth

enmarcar ⟨1g⟩ v/t frame

enmascarar ⟨1a⟩ v/t hide, disguise

enmendar ⟨1k⟩ **1** v/t asunto rectify, put right; JUR, POL amend; **enmendarle la plana a alguien** find fault with what s.o. has done **2** v/r **enmendarse** mend one's ways

enmienda f POL amendment

enmicar ⟨1g⟩ v/t L.Am. laminate

enmudecer ⟨2d⟩ **1** v/t silence **2** v/i fall silent

ennoblecer ⟨2d⟩ v/t ennoble

enojado adj L.Am. angry

enojar ⟨1a⟩ **1** v/t (molestar) annoy; L.Am. (encolerizar) make angry **2** v/r **enojarse** L.Am. (molestarse) get annoyed; (encolerizarse) get angry

enojo m L.Am. anger

enojón adj L.Am. F irritable, touchy

enojoso adj (delicado) awkward; (aburrido) tedious, tiresome

enorgullecer ⟨2d⟩ **1** v/t make proud, fill with pride **2** v/r **enorgullecerse** be proud (**de** of)

enorme adj enormous, huge

enrarecido adj aire rarefied; relaciones strained

enredadera f BOT creeper, climbing plant

enredar ⟨1a⟩ **1** v/t tangle, get tangled; fig complicate, make complicated **2** v/r **enredarse** get tangled; fig get complicated; **enredarse en algo** get mixed up o involved in sth

enredo m tangle; (confusión) mess, confusion; (intriga) intrigue; amoroso affair

enrevesado adj complicated, involved

enriquecer ⟨2d⟩ **1** v/t make rich; fig enrich **2** v/r **enriquecerse** get rich; fig be enriched

enrojecer ⟨2d⟩ **1** v/t turn red **2** v/i blush, go red

enrolarse ⟨1a⟩ v/r MIL enlist

enrollar ⟨1a⟩ **1** v/t roll up; cable coil; hilo wind; **me enrolla** F I like it, I think it's great **2** v/r **enrollarse** F hablar go on and on F; **se enrolló mucho con nosotros** (se portó bien) he was great to us; **¡no te enrolles!** F get to the point!; **enrollarse con alguien** fig F neck with s.o.

enroscar ⟨1g⟩ v/t tornillo screw in; cable, cuerda coil **2** v/r **enroscarse** coil up

ensaimada f GASTR pastry in the form of a spiral

ensalada f GASTR salad

ensaladera f salad bowl

ensaladilla f: **ensaladilla rusa** GASTR Russian salad

ensalmo m: **como por ensalmo** as if by magic

ensalzar ⟨1f⟩ v/t extol, praise

ensamblar ⟨1a⟩ v/t assemble

ensanchar ⟨1a⟩ **1** v/t widen; prenda let out **2** v/r **ensancharse** widen, get wider; de prenda stretch

ensangrentar ⟨1k⟩ v/t stain with blood, cover with blood

ensañarse ⟨1a⟩ v/r show no mercy (**con** to)

ensartar ⟨1a⟩ **1** v/t en hilo string; aguja thread; L.Am. (engañar) trick, trap **2** v/r **ensartarse** L.Am. en discusión get involved, get caught up

ensayar ⟨1a⟩ v/t test, try (out); TEA rehearse

ensayo m TEA rehearsal; escrito essay; **ensayo general** dress rehearsal

enseguida adv immediately, right away

ensenada f inlet, cove

enseñanza f teaching; **enseñanza primaria** elementary education, Br primary education; **enseñanza secundaria** or **media** secondary education; **enseñanza superior** higher education

enseñar ⟨1a⟩ v/t (dar clases) teach; (mostrar) show

ensillar ⟨1a⟩ v/t saddle

ensimismarse ⟨1a⟩ v/r become lost in thought; L.Am. F get conceited o big-headed F

ensombrecer ⟨2d⟩ v/t cast a shadow over

ensordecedor adj deafening

ensuciar ⟨1b⟩ **1** v/t (get) dirty; fig sully, tarnish **2** v/r **ensuciarse** get dirty; fig get one's hands dirty

ensueño m: **de ensueño** fig fairy-tale atr, dream atr

entablar ⟨1a⟩ v/t strike up, start

entablillar ⟨1a⟩ v/t splint, put in a splint

entarimado m (suelo) floorboards pl; (plataforma) stage, platform

ente m (ser) being, entity; F (persona rara) oddball F; (organización) body

entejar ⟨1a⟩ v/t L.Am. tile

entender ⟨2g⟩ v/t understand; **dar a entender a alguien** give s.o. to understand **2** v/i understand; **entender de algo** know about sth **3** v/r **entenderse** communicate; **a ver si nos entendemos** let's get this straight; **yo me entiendo** I know what I'm doing; **entenderse con alguien** get along with s.o., get on with s.o. **4** m: **a mi entender** in my opinion, to my mind

entendido 1 adj understood; **¿entendi-**

do? do you understand?, understood?;
tengo entendido que I gather *o* understand that **2** *m*, *-a f* expert, authority
entendimiento *m* understanding; (*inteligencia*) mind
enterado *adj* knowledgeable, well-informed; **estar enterado de** know about, have heard about; **darse por enterado** get the message, take the hint
enterarse ⟨1a⟩ *v/r* find out, hear (**de** about); **¡para que te enteres!** F so there! F; **¡se va a enterar!** F he's in for it! F
entereza *f* fortitude
enternecer ⟨2d⟩ *v/t* move, touch
entero 1 *adj* (*completo*) whole, entire; (*no roto*) intact, undamaged; **por entero** completely, entirely **2** *m* (*punto*) point
enterrar ⟨1k⟩ *v/t* bury; **enterrar a todos** *fig* outlive everybody
entidad *f* entity, body
entierro *m* burial; (*funeral*) funeral
entonar ⟨1a⟩ **1** *v/t* intone, sing; *fig* F perk up **2** *v/i* sing in tune **3** *v/r* **entonarse con bebida** get tipsy
entonces *adv* then; **desde entonces** since, since then; **por entonces, en aquel entonces** in those days, at that time
entornar ⟨1a⟩ *v/t puerta* leave ajar; *ojos* half close
entorno *m* environment
entorpecer ⟨2d⟩ *v/t* hold up, hinder; *paso* obstruct; *entendimiento* dull
entrada *f acción* entry; *lugar* entrance; *localidad* ticket; *pago* deposit, down payment; *de comida* starter; **de entrada** from the outset, from the start
entrañable *adj amistad* close, deep; *amigo* close, dear; *recuerdo* fond
entrañar ⟨1a⟩ *v/t* entail, involve
entrañas *fpl* entrails
entrar ⟨1a⟩ **1** *v/i para indicar acercamiento* come in, enter; *para indicar alejamiento* go in, enter; *caber* fit; **me entró frío / sueño** I got cold / sleepy, I began to feel cold / sleepy; **no me entra en la cabeza** I can't understand it **2** *v/t para indicar acercamiento* bring in; *para indicar alejamiento* take in
entre *prp dos cosas, personas* between; *más de dos* among(st); *expresando cooperación* between; **la relación entre ellos** the relationship between them; **entre nosotros** among us; **lo pagamos entre todos** we paid for it among *o* between us
entreabierto 1 *part* → **entreabrir 2** *adj* half-open; *puerta* ajar
entreabrir ⟨3a; *part* **entreabierto** ⟩ *v/t*
half-open
entreacto *m* TEA interval
entrecejo *m*: **fruncir el entrecejo** frown
entrecomillar ⟨1a⟩ *v/t* put in quotation marks
entrecortado *adj habla* halting; *respiración* difficult, labo(u)red
entrecot *m* entrecote
entredicho *m*: **poner en entredicho** call into question, question
entrega *f* handing over; *de mercancías* delivery; (*dedicación*) dedication, devotion; **entrega a domicilio** (home) delivery; **entrega de premios** prize-giving, presentation; **hacer entrega de algo a alguien** present s.o. with sth
entregar ⟨1h⟩ **1** *v/t* give, hand over; *trabajo, deberes* hand in; *mercancías* deliver; *premio* present **2** *v/r* **entregarse** give o.s. up; **entregarse a** *fig* devote o.s. to, dedicate o.s. to
entrelazar ⟨1f⟩ *v/t* interweave, intertwine
entremeses *mpl* GASTR appetizers, hors d'oeuvres
entremezclar ⟨1a⟩ *v/t* intermingle, mix **2** *v/r* **entremezclarse** intermingle, mix
entrenador *m*, **entrenadora** *f* coach
entrenamiento *m* coaching
entrenar ⟨1a⟩ **1** *v/t* train **2** *v/r* **entrenarse** train
entrepierna *f* ANAT crotch
entresacar ⟨1g⟩ *v/t* extract, select
entresijos *mpl fig* details, ins and outs F
entresuelo *m* mezzanine; TEA dress circle
entretanto *adv* meanwhile, in the meantime
entretecho *m Arg, Chi* attic
entretener ⟨2l⟩ **1** *v/t* (*divertir*) entertain, amuse; (*retrasar*) keep, detain; (*distraer*) distract **2** *v/i* be entertaining **3** *v/r* **entretenerse** (*divertirse*) amuse o.s.; (*distraerse*) keep o.s. busy; (*retrasarse*) linger
entretenido *adj* (*divertido*) entertaining, enjoyable; **estar entretenido** *ocupado* be busy
entretenimiento *m* entertainment, amusement
entrevero *m S. Am.* (*lío*) mix-up, mess; *Chi* (*discusión*) argument
entrevista *f* interview
entrevistar ⟨1a⟩ **1** *v/t* interview **2** *v/r* **entrevistarse**: **entrevistarse con alguien** meet (with) s.o.
entristecer ⟨2d⟩ **1** *v/t* sadden **2** *v/r* **entristecerse** grow sad
entrometerse ⟨2a⟩ *v/r* meddle (**en** in)
entrometido 1 *part* → **entrometerse 2** *adj* meddling *atr*, interfering **3** *m* meddler, busybody

entronizar ⟨1f⟩ v/t fig instal(l)

entumecer ⟨2d⟩ **1** v/t numb **2** v/r **entumecerse** go numb, get stiff

enturbiar ⟨1b⟩ v/t tb fig cloud

entusiasmado adj excited, delirious

entusiasmar ⟨1a⟩ v/t excite, make enthusiastic

entusiasmo m enthusiasm

entusiasta **1** adj enthusiastic **2** m/f enthusiast

enumerar ⟨1a⟩ v/t list, enumerate

enunciar ⟨1b⟩ v/t state

envalentonarse ⟨1a⟩ v/r become bolder o more daring; (insolentarse) become defiant

envanecerse ⟨2d⟩ v/r become conceited o vain

envasar ⟨1a⟩ v/t en botella bottle; en lata can; en paquete pack

envase m container; botella (empty) bottle; **envase de cartón** carton; **envase no retornable** nonreturnable bottle

envejecer ⟨2d⟩ **1** v/t age, make look older **2** v/i age, grow old

envejecimiento m aging, ageing

envenenar ⟨1a⟩ v/t tb fig poison

envergadura f AVIA wingspan; MAR breadth; fig magnitude, importance; **de gran** or **mucha envergadura** fig of great importance

enviado m, -a f POL envoy; de un periódico reporter, correspondent; **enviado especial** POL special envoy; de un periódico special correspondent

enviar ⟨1c⟩ v/t send

enviciarse ⟨1b⟩ v/r get addicted (con to)

envidia f envy, jealousy; **me da envidia** I'm envious o jealous; **tener envidia a alguien** or **de algo** envy s.o. sth

envidiar ⟨1b⟩ v/t envy; **envidiar a alguien por algo** envy s.o. sth

envidioso adj envious, jealous

envilecer ⟨2d⟩ **1** v/t degrade, debase **2** v/r **envilecerse** degrade o.s., debase o.s.

envío m shipment

enviudar ⟨1a⟩ v/i be widowed

envoltorio m wrapper

envoltura f cover, covering; de regalo wrapping; de caramelo wrapper

envolver ⟨2h; part envuelto⟩ **1** v/t wrap (up); (rodear) surround, envelop; (involucrar) involve; **envolver a alguien en algo** involve s.o. in sth **2** v/r **envolverse** wrap o.s. up; **envolverse en** fig become involved in

envuelto part → **envolver**

enyesado m plastering

enzarzarse ⟨1f⟩ v/r get involved (en in)

eólico adj wind atr

épico adj epic

epidemia f epidemic

epilepsia f MED epilepsy

epílogo m epilog(ue)

episcopal adj episcopal

episodio m episode

epistolar adj epistolary

epitafio m epitaph

época f time, period; parte del año time of year; GEOL epoch; **hacer época** be epoch-making

epopeya f epic, epic poem

equidad f fairness

equidistante adj equidistant

equilibrado adj well-balanced

equilibrar ⟨1a⟩ v/t balance

equilibrio m balance; FÍS equilibrium

equino adj equine

equinoccio m equinox

equipaje m baggage; **equipaje de mano** hand baggage

equipamiento m: **equipamiento de serie** AUTO standard features pl

equipar ⟨1a⟩ v/t equip (con with)

equiparar ⟨1a⟩ v/t put on a level (a or con with); **equiparar algo con algo** fig compare o liken sth to sth

equipo m DEP team; accesorios equipment; **equipo de música** or **de sonido** sound system

equitación f riding

equitativo adj fair, equitable

equivalente m/adj equivalent

equivaler ⟨2q⟩ v/i be equivalent (a to)

equivocación f mistake; **por equivocación** by mistake

equivocado adj wrong; **estar equivocado** be wrong, be mistaken

equivocar ⟨1g⟩ **1** v/t: **equivocar a alguien** make s.o. make a mistake **2** v/r **equivocarse** make a mistake; **te has equivocado** you are wrong o mistaken; **equivocarse de número** TELEC get the wrong number

equívoco **1** adj ambiguous, equivocal **2** m misunderstanding; (error) mistake

era f era

erección f erection

eres vb → **ser**

ergonómico adj ergonomic

erguir ⟨3n⟩ **1** v/t raise, lift; (poner derecho) straighten **2** v/r **erguirse** de persona stand up, rise; de edificio rise

erial m uncultivated land

erigir ⟨3c⟩ **1** v/t erect **2** v/r **erigirse: erigirse en** set o.s. up as

erizarse ⟨1f⟩ v/r de pelo stand on end

erizo m ZO hedgehog; **erizo de mar** ZO sea urchin

ermita f chapel

ermitaño 1 m zo hermit crab **2** m, -a f hermit

erogación f Méx, S. Am. expenditure, outlay

erógeno adj erogenous

erosión f erosion

erosionar ⟨1a⟩ v/t GEOL erode

erótico adj erotic

erotismo m eroticism

erradicar ⟨1g⟩ v/t eradicate, wipe out

errante adj wandering

errar ⟨1l⟩ **1** v/t miss; **errar el tiro** miss **2** v/i miss; **errar es humano** to err is human

equivocarse be wrong, be mistaken

errata f mistake, error; **de imprenta** misprint

erre f: **erre que erre** F doggedly, stubbornly

erróneo adj wrong, erroneous fml

error m mistake, error; **error de cálculo** error of judg(e)ment

eructar ⟨1a⟩ v/i belch F, burp F

eructo m belch F, burp F

erudito 1 adj learned, erudite **2** m scholar

erupción f GEOL eruption; MED rash

esbelto adj slim, slender

esbozar ⟨1f⟩ v/t sketch; idea, proyecto etc outline

esbozo m sketch; de idea, proyecto etc outline

escabeche m type of marinade

escabroso adj rough; problema tricky; relato indecent

escabullirse ⟨3h⟩ v/r escape, slip away

escala f tb MÚS scale; AVIA stopover; **escala de cuerda** rope ladder; **escala de valores** scale of values; **a escala** to scale, life-sized

escalada f DEP climb, ascent; **escalada de los precios** increase in prices, escalation of prices

escalador m, **escaladora** f climber

escalafón m fig ladder

escalar ⟨1a⟩ **1** v/t climb, scale **2** v/i climb

escaldar ⟨1a⟩ v/t GASTR blanch; manos scald

escalera f stairs pl, staircase; **escalera de caracol** spiral staircase; **escalera de incendios** fire escape; **escalera de mano** ladder; **escalera mecánica** escalator

escalfar ⟨1a⟩ v/t poach

escalofriante adj horrifying

escalofrío m shiver

escalón m step; de escalera de mano rung

escalonar ⟨1a⟩ v/t en tiempo stagger; terreno terrace

escalope m escalope

escama f zo scale; de jabón, piel flake

escamar ⟨1a⟩ **1** v/t scale, remove the scales from; fig make suspicious **2** v/r **escamarse** become suspicious

escamotear ⟨1a⟩ v/t (ocultar) hide, conceal; (negar) withhold

escampar ⟨1a⟩ v/i clear up, stop raining

escanciar ⟨1b⟩ v/t fml pour

escandalizar ⟨1f⟩ **1** v/t shock, scandalize **2** v/r **escandalizarse** be shocked

escándalo m (asunto vergonzoso) scandal; (jaleo) racket, ruckus; **armar un escándalo** make a scene

escandaloso adj (vergonzoso) scandalous, shocking; (ruidoso) noisy, rowdy

Escandinavia Scandinavia

escanear ⟨1a⟩ v/t scan

escáner m scanner

escaño m POL seat

escapar ⟨1a⟩ **1** v/t escape (de from); **dejar escapar** oportunidad pass up, let slip; suspiro let out, give **2** v/r **escaparse** (huir) escape (de from); de casa run away (de from); **escaparse de** situación get out of

escaparate m store window

escapatoria f: **no tener escapatoria** have no way out

escape m de gas leak; AUTO exhaust; **salir a escape** rush out

escarabajo m beetle

escaramuza f skirmish

escarbadientes m inv toothpick

escarbar ⟨1a⟩ **1** v/i tb fig dig around (en in) **2** v/t dig around in

escarceos mpl forays, dabbling sg; **escarceos amorosos** romantic o amorous adventures

escarcha f frost

escardar ⟨1a⟩ v/t hoe

escarmentar ⟨1k⟩ **1** v/t teach a lesson to **2** v/i learn one's lesson; **escarmentar en cabeza ajena** learn from other people's mistakes

escarmiento m lesson; **le sirvió de escarmiento** it taught him a lesson

escarnio m ridicule, derision

escarola f endive, escarole

escarpado adj sheer, steep

escarpia f hook

escasear ⟨1a⟩ v/i be scarce, be in short supply

escasez f shortage, scarcity

escaso adj recursos limited; **andar escaso de algo** falto be short of sth; **-as posibilidades de** not much chance of, little chance of; **falta un mes escaso** it's barely a month away

escatimar ⟨1a⟩ v/t be mean with, be very sparing with; **no escatimar esfuerzos**

be unstinting in one's efforts, spare no effort

escayola f (plaster) cast

escayolar ⟨1a⟩ v/t put in a (plaster) cast

escena f scene; *escenario* stage; *entrar en escena* come on stage; *hacer una escena* fig make a scene

escenario m stage; fig scene

escénico adj stage atr

escenificar ⟨1g⟩ v/t stage

escepticismo m skepticism, Br scepticism

escéptico 1 adj skeptical, Br sceptical **2** m, **-a** f skeptic, Br sceptic

escindirse ⟨3a⟩ v/r (*fragmentarse*) split (*en* into); (*segregarse*) break away (*de* from)

escisión f (*fragmentación*) split; (*segregación*) break

esclarecer ⟨2d⟩ v/t throw o shed light on; *misterio* clear up

esclarecimiento m clarification; *de misterio* solving

esclavitud f slavery

esclavizar ⟨1f⟩ v/t enslave; fig tie down

esclavo m slave

esclerosis f MED: *esclerosis múltiple* multiple sclerosis

escoba f broom

escobilla f small brush; AUTO wiper blade

escocer ⟨2b & 2h⟩ v/i sting, smart; *todavía escuece la derrota* he's still smarting from the defeat

escocés 1 adj Scottish **2** m Scot, Scotsman

escocesa f Scot, Scotswoman

Escocia Scotland

escoger ⟨2c⟩ v/t choose, select

escogido adj select

escolar 1 adj school atr **2** m/f student

escolarización f education, schooling; *escolarización obligatoria* compulsory education

escolarizar ⟨1f⟩ v/t educate, provide schooling for

escolástico adj scholarly

escollera f breakwater

escollo m MAR reef; (*obstáculo*) hurdle, obstacle

escolta 1 f escort **2** m/f motorista outrider; (*guardaespaldas*) bodyguard

escoltar ⟨1a⟩ v/t escort

escombros mpl rubble sg

esconder ⟨2a⟩ **1** v/t hide, conceal **2** v/r *esconderse* hide

escondidas fpl S. Am. hide-and-seek sg; *a escondidas* in secret, secretly

escondite m lugar hiding place; *juego* hide-and-seek

escondrijo m hiding place

escopeta f shotgun; *escopeta de aire comprimido* air gun, air rifle

escopetado adj: *salir escopetado* F shoot o dash off F

escopetazo m gunshot

escorbuto m scurvy

escoria f slag; desp dregs pl

Escorpio m/f inv ASTR Scorpio

escorpión m zo scorpion

escotado adj low-cut

escote m neckline; *de mujer* cleavage

escotilla f MAR hatch

escozor m burning sensation, stinging; fig bitterness

escribir ⟨3a; part *escrito*⟩ v/t write; (*deletrear*) spell; *escribir a mano* handwrite, write by hand; *escribir a máquina* type

escrito 1 part → **escribir 2** adj written; *por escrito* in writing **3** m document; *escritos* writings

escritor m, **escritora** f writer, author

escritorio m desk; *artículos de escritorio* stationery

escritura f writing; JUR deed; *Sagradas Escrituras* Holy Scripture

escrúpulo m scruple; *sin escrúpulos* unscrupulous

escrupuloso adj (*cuidadoso*) meticulous; (*honrado*) scrupulous; (*aprensivo*) fastidious

escrutar ⟨1a⟩ v/t scrutinize; *votos* count

escrutinio m *de votos* count; (*inspección*) scrutiny

escuadrón m squadron

escuálido adj skinny, emaciated

escucha f: *estar a la escucha* be listening out; *escuchas pl telefónicas* wiretapping sg, Br tb phone-tapping sg

escuchar ⟨1a⟩ **1** v/t listen to; L.Am. (*oír*) hear **2** v/i listen

escuchimizado adj F puny F, scrawny F

escudarse ⟨1a⟩ v/r fig hide (*en* behind)

escudería f stable

escudilla f bowl

escudo m *arma* shield; *insignia* badge; *moneda* escudo; *escudo de armas* coat of arms

escudriñar ⟨1a⟩ v/t (*mirar de lejos*) scan; (*examinar*) scrutinize

escuela f school; *escuela de comercio* business school; *escuela de idiomas* language school; *escuela primaria* elementary school, Br primary school

escuelero 1 adj L.Am. school atr **2** m, **-a** f L.Am. (*maestro*) teacher; Pe, Bol (*alumno*) student

escueto adj succinct, concise

escuincle *m/f Méx, C.Am.* F kid
esculpir ⟨3a⟩ *v/t* sculpt
escultor *m*, **escultora** *f* sculptor
escultura *f* sculpture
escupidera *f* spitoon; *L.Am.* chamber pot
escupir ⟨3a⟩ **1** *v/i* spit **2** *v/t* spit out
escupitajo *m* F gob of spit F
escurreplatos *m inv* plate rack
escurridizo *adj* slippery; *fig* evasive
escurridor *m* (*colador*) colander; (*escurreplatos*) plate rack
escurrir ⟨3a⟩ **1** *v/t ropa* wring out; *platos, verduras* drain **2** *v/i de platos* drain; *de ropa* drip-dry **3** *v/r* **escurrirse** *de líquido* drain away; (*deslizarse*) slip; (*escaparse*) slip away
escusado *m* bathroom
ese, esa, esos, esas *det singular* that; *plural* those
ése, ésa, ésos, ésas *pron singular* that (one); *plural* those (ones); **le ofrecí dinero pero no por ésas** I offered him money but even that wasn't enough; **no soy de ésos que** I'm not one of those who
esencia *f* essence
esencial *adj* essential
esfera *f* sphere; **esfera de actividad** *fig* field *o* sphere (of activity)
esférico 1 *adj* spherical **2** *m* DEP F ball
esfinge *f* sphinx
esforzarse ⟨1f & 1m⟩ *v/r* make an effort, try hard
esfuerzo *m* effort; **hacer un esfuerzo** make an effort; **sin esfuerzo** effortlessly
esfumarse ⟨1a⟩ *v/r* F *tb fig* disappear
esgrima *f* fencing
esgrimir ⟨3a⟩ *v/t arma* wield; *fig: argumento* put forward, use
esguince *m* sprain
eslabón *m* link; **el eslabón perdido** the missing link
eslavo 1 *adj* Slavic, Slavonic **2** *m*, **-a** *f* Slav
eslogan *m* slogan
eslora *f* length
Eslovaquia Slovakia
Eslovenia Slovenia
esmalte *m* enamel; **esmalte de uñas** nail polish, nail varnish
esmerado *adj* meticulous
esmeralda *f* emerald
esmerarse ⟨1a⟩ *v/r* take great care (**en** over)
esmerilado *adj*: **cristal esmerilado** frosted glass
esmero *m* care; **con esmero** carefully
esmirriado *adj* F skinny F, scrawny F
esmoquin *m* tuxedo, *Br* dinner jacket
esnifar ⟨1a⟩ *v/t* F *pegamento* sniff F; *cocaína* snort F

esnob 1 *adj* snobbish **2** *m* snob
esnobismo *m* snobbishness
eso *pron* that; **en eso** just then, just at that moment; **eso mismo, eso es** that's it, that's the way; **a eso de las dos** at around two; **por eso** that's why; **¿y eso?** why's that?; **y eso que le dije que no se lo contara** and after I told him not to tell her
esotérico *adj* esoteric
espabilado *adj* (*listo*) bright, smart; (*vivo*) sharp, on the ball F
espabilar ⟨1a⟩ **1** *v/t* (*quitar el sueño*) wake up, revive; **lo ha espabilado** (*avivado*) she's got him to wise up **2** *v/i* (*darse prisa*) hurry up, get a move on; (*avivarse*) wise up **3** *v/r* **espabilarse** *del sueño* wake oneself up; (*darse prisa*) hurry up, get a move on; (*avivarse*) wise up
espacial *adj cohete, viaje* space *atr*; FÍS, MAT spatial
espaciarse ⟨1a⟩ *v/r* become more (and more) infrequent
espacio *m* space; TV program, *Br* programme; **espacios verdes** green spaces; **espacio de tiempo** space of time; **espacio vital** living space
espacioso *adj* spacious, roomy
espada *f* sword; **espadas** *pl* (*en naipes*) suit in Spanish deck of cards; **estar entre la espada y la pared** be between a rock and a hard place
espadachín *m* skilled swordsman
espaguetis *mpl* spaghetti *sg*
espalda *f* back; **a espaldas de alguien** behind s.o.'s back; **de espaldas a** with one's back to you; **por la espalda** from behind; **caerse de espaldas** fall flat on one's back; **no me des la espalda** don't sit with your back to me; **nadar a espalda** swim backstroke; **tener cubiertas las espaldas** *fig* keep one's back covered; **volver la espalda a alguien** *fig* turn one's back on s.o.
espaldarazo *m* slap on the back; (*reconocimiento*) recognition
espalderas *fpl* wall bars
espantajo *m* scarecrow; *fig* sight
espantapájaros *m inv* scarecrow
espantar ⟨1a⟩ **1** *v/t* (*asustar*) frighten, scare; (*ahuyentar*) frighten away, shoo away; F (*horrorizar*) horrify, appal(l) **2** *v/r* **espantarse** get frightened, get scared; F (*horrorizarse*) be horrified, be appal(l)ed
espanto *m* (*susto*) fright; *L.Am.* (*fantasma*) ghost; **nos llenó de espanto** *desagrado* we were horrified; **¡qué espanto!** how awful!; **de espanto** terrible

esquelético

espantoso *adj* horrific, appalling; *para enfatizar* terrible, dreadful; *hace un calor espantoso* it's terribly hot, it's incredibly hot

España Spain

español 1 *adj* Spanish **2** *m idioma* Spanish **3** *m*, **-a** *f* Spaniard; *los españoles* the Spanish

esparadrapo *m* Band-Aid®, *Br* plaster

esparcimiento *m* relaxation

esparcir ⟨3b⟩ **1** *v/t papeles* scatter; *rumor* spread **2** *v/r* **esparcirse** *de papeles* be scattered; *de rumor* spread

espárrago *m* BOT asparagus; *espárrago triguero* wild asparagus; *¡vete a freír espárragos!* F get lost! F

espartano *adj* spartan

esparto *m* BOT esparto grass

espasmo *m* spasm

espátula *f* spatula; *en pintura* palette knife

especia *f* spice

especial *adj* special; *(difícil)* fussy; *en especial* especially

especialidad *f* specialty, *Br* speciality

especialista *m/f* specialist, expert; *en cine* stuntman; *mujer* stuntwoman

especializarse ⟨1f⟩ *v/r* specialize (*en* in)

especie *f* BIO species, *(tipo)* kind, sort

especiero *m* spice rack

especificar ⟨1g⟩ *v/t* specify

específico *adj* specific

espectacular *adj* spectacular

espectáculo *m* TEA show; *(escena)* sight; *dar el espectáculo* fig make a spectacle of o.s.

espectador *m*, **espectadora** *f en cine etc* member of the audience; DEP spectator; *(observador)* on-looker, observer

espectro *m* FÍS spectrum; *(fantasma)* ghost

especulación *f* speculation

especular ⟨1a⟩ *v/i* speculate

especulativo *adj* speculative

espejismo *m* mirage

espejo *m* mirror; *espejo retrovisor* rear-view mirror

espeleólogo *m* spelunker, *Br* pot-holer

espeluznante *adj* horrific, horrifying

espera *f* wait; *sala de espera* waiting room; *en espera de* pending; *estar a la espera de* be waiting for

esperanza *f* hope; *esperanza de vida* life expectancy

esperar ⟨1a⟩ **1** *v/t (aguardar)* wait for; *con esperanza* hope; *(suponer, confiar en)* expect **2** *v/i (aguardar)* wait

esperma *f* sperm

espesar ⟨1a⟩ **1** *v/t* thicken **2** *v/r* **espesar-**

se thicken, become thick

espeso *adj* thick; *vegetación, niebla* thick, dense

espesor *m* thickness

espesura *f* dense vegetation

espía *m/f* spy

espiar ⟨1c⟩ **1** *v/t* spy on **2** *v/i* spy

espiga *f* BOT ear, spike

espina *f de planta* thorn; *de pez* bone; *espina dorsal* spine, backbone; *dar mala espina a alguien* F make s.o. feel uneasy

espinacas *fpl* BOT spinach *sg*

espinazo *m* spine, backbone; *doblar el espinazo* fig *(trabajar mucho)* work o.s. into the ground; *(humillarse)* kowtow (*ante* to)

espinilla *f de la pierna* shin; *en la piel* pimple, spot

espinoso *adj* thorny, prickly; *fig* thorny, knotty

espionaje *m* spying, espionage

espiral 1 *adj* spiral *atr* **2** *f* spiral

espirar ⟨1a⟩ *v/t & v/i* exhale

espiritismo *m* spiritualism

espíritu *m* spirit

espiritual *adj* spiritual

espléndido *adj* splendid, magnificent; *(generoso)* generous

esplendor *m* splendo(u)r

espliego *m* lavender

espolear ⟨1a⟩ *v/t* tb fig spur on

espolvorear ⟨1a⟩ *v/t* sprinkle

esponja *f* sponge

esponjoso *adj bizcocho* spongy; *toalla* soft, fluffy

espónsor *m/f* sponsor

esponsorizar ⟨1f⟩ *v/t* sponsor

espontáneo *adj* spontaneous

esporádico *adj* sporadic

esposa *f* wife

esposar ⟨1a⟩ *v/t* handcuff

esposas *fpl (manillas)* handcuffs *pl*

esposo *m* husband

esprint *m* sprint

espuela *f* spur

espuerta *f: ganar dinero a espuertas* F make money hand over fist F

espuma *f* foam; *de jabón* lather; *de cerveza* froth; *espuma de afeitar* shaving foam; *espuma moldeadora* styling mousse

espumadera *f* slotted spoon, skimmer

espumarajo *m* froth, foam

espumilla *f C.Am.* GASTR meringue

espumoso *adj* frothy, foamy; *caldo* sparkling

esqueje *m* cutting

esquela *f aviso* death notice, obituary

esquelético *adj* skeletal

esqueleto *m* skeleton; *Méx, C.Am., Pe, Bol fig* blank form; **mover** or **menear el esqueleto** F dance

esquema *m* (*croquis*) sketch, diagram; (*sinopsis*) outline, summary

esquemático *adj dibujo* schematic, diagrammatic; *resumen* simplified

esquí *m tabla* ski; *deporte* skiing; **esquí de fondo** cross-country skiing; **esquí náutico** o **acuático** waterskiing

esquiador *m*, **esquiadora** *f* skier

esquiar ⟨1a⟩ *v/i* ski

esquilar ⟨1a⟩ *v/t* shear

esquilmar ⟨1a⟩ *v/t* overexploit; *a alguien* suck dry

esquina *f* corner

esquinazo *m Arg, Chi* serenade; **dar esquinazo a alguien** F give s.o. the slip F

esquirol *m/f* strikebreaker, scab F

esquite *m C.Am., Méx* popcorn

esquivar ⟨1a⟩ *v/t* avoid, dodge F

esquivo *adj* (*huraño*) unsociable; (*evasivo*) shifty, evasive

esquizofrenia *f* schizophrenia

esquizofrénico *adj* schizophrenic

esta *det* this

está *vb* → **estar**

estabilidad *f* stability

estabilizante *m* stabilizer

estabilizar ⟨1f⟩ *v/t* stabilize

estable *adj* stable

establecer ⟨2d⟩ **1** *v/t* establish; *negocio* set up **2** *v/r* **establecerse** *en lugar* settle; *en profesión* set up

establecimiento *m* establishment

establo *m* stable

estaca *f* stake

estacada *f*: **dejar a alguien en la estacada** F leave s.o. in the lurch

estación *f* station; *del año* season; **estación espacial** o **orbital** space station; **estación de invierno** or **invernal** winter resort; **estación de servicio** service station; **estación de trabajo** INFOR work station

estacional *adj* seasonal

estacionamiento *m* AUTO parking; *L.Am.* parking lot, *Br* car park

estacionar ⟨1a⟩ **1** *v/t* AUTO park **2** *v/r* **estacionarse** stabilize

estacionómetro *m Méx* parking meter

estadio *m* DEP stadium

estadística *f cifra* statistic; *ciencia* statistics

estado *m* state; MED condition; **estado civil** marital status; **estado de guerra** state of war; **en buen estado** in good condition; **el Estado** the State; **estado del bienestar** welfare state; **los Estados Unidos (de América)** the United States (of America)

estadounidense 1 *adj* American, US *atr* **2** *m/f* American

estafa *f* swindle, cheat

estafador *m*, **estafadora** *f* con artist F, fraudster

estafar ⟨1a⟩ *v/t* swindle, cheat (**a** out of), defraud (**a** of)

estalactita *f* stalactite

estalagmita *f* stalagmite

estallar ⟨1a⟩ *v/i* explode; *de guerra* break out; *de escándalo* break; **estalló en llanto** she burst into tears

estallido *m* explosion; *de guerra* outbreak

estamento *m* stratum, class

estampa *f de libro* illustration; (*aspecto*) appearance; REL prayer card

estampado *adj tejido* patterned

estampar ⟨1a⟩ *v/t sello* put; *tejido* print; *pasaporte* stamp; **le estampó una bofetada en la cara** F she smacked him one F

estampido *m* bang

estampilla *f L.Am.* stamp

estancado *adj agua* stagnant; *fig* at a standstill

estancar ⟨1g⟩ **1** *v/t río* dam up, block; *fig* bring to a standstill **2** *v/r* **estancarse** stagnate; *fig* come to a standstill

estancia *f* stay; *Rpl* farm, ranch

estanciero *m*, **-a** *f Rpl* farmer, rancher

estanco 1 *adj* watertight **2** *m* shop selling cigarettes etc

estándar *m* standard

estandarizar ⟨1f⟩ *v/t* standardize

estandarte *m* standard, banner

estanque *m* pond

estante *m* shelf

estantería *f* shelves *pl*; *para libros* bookcase

estaño *m* tin

estar ⟨1p⟩ **1** *v/i* be; **¿está Javier?** is Javier in?; **estar haciendo algo** be doing sth; **estamos a 3 de enero** it's January 3rd; **el kilo está a cien pesetas** they're a hundred pesetas a kilo; **te está grande** it's too big for you; **estar con alguien** agree with s.o.; (*apoyar*) support s.o.; **ahora estoy con Vd.** I'll be with you in just a moment; **estar a bien / mal con alguien** be on good / bad terms with s.o.; **estar de** *ocupación* work as, be; **estar en algo** be working on sth; **estar para hacer algo** be about to do sth; **no estar para algo** not be in a mood for sth; **estar por algo** be in favo(u)r of sth; **está por hacer** it hasn't been done yet; **estar sin dinero** have no money; **¿cómo está Vd.?** how are you?; **estoy mejor** I'm (feeling) better; **¡ya estoy!** I'm ready!; **¡ya está!** that's it! **2** v/r **estarse** stay; **estarse quieto** keep still

estárter m choke

estatal adj state atr

estático adj static

estatua f statue

estatura f height

estatutario adj statutory

estatuto m statute; **estatutos** articles of association

estatus m status

este[1] m east

este[2], **esta**, **estos**, **estas** det singular this; plural these

éste, **ésta**, **éstos**, **éstas** pron singular this (one); plural these (ones)

estela f MAR wake; AVIA, fig trail

estelar adj star atr

estepa f steppe

estera f mat

estercolero m dunghill, dung heap

estéreo adj stereo

estereofónico adj stereophonic

estereotipo m stereotype

estéril adj MED sterile; trabajo, esfuerzo etc futile

esterilidad f sterility

esterilizar ⟨1f⟩ v/t ib persona sterilize

esterilla f mat

esterlina adj: **libra esterlina** pound sterling

esternón m breast bone, sternum

estero m Rpl marsh

estertor m death rattle

esteticista m/f beautician

estético adj esthetic, Br aesthetic

estetoscopio m MED stethoscope

estibador m stevedore

estiércol m dung; (abono) manure

estilarse ⟨1a⟩ v/r be fashionable

estilista m/f stylist; de modas designer

estilo m style; **al estilo de** in the style of; **algo por el estilo** something like that; **son todos por el estilo** they're all the same

estilográfica f fountain pen

estima f esteem, respect; **tener a alguien en mucha estima** hold s.o. in high regard o esteem

estimación f (cálculo) estimate; (estima) esteem, respect

estimar ⟨1a⟩ v/t respect, hold in high regard; **estimo conveniente que** I consider it advisable to

estimulante 1 adj stimulating **2** m stimulant

estimular ⟨1a⟩ v/t stimulate; (animar) encourage

estímulo m stimulus; (incentivo) incentive

estío m lit summertime

estipular ⟨1a⟩ v/t stipulate

estirado adj snooty F, stuck-up F

estirar ⟨1a⟩ v/t stretch; (alisar) smooth out; dinero stretch, make go further; **estirar la pata** F kick the bucket F; **estirar las piernas** stretch one's legs

estirpe f stock

estival adj summer atr

esto pron this; **esto es** that is to say; **por esto** this is why; **a todo esto** (mientras tanto) meanwhile; (a propósito) incidentally

estofa f: **de baja estofa** desp low-class desp

estofado adj stewed

estofar ⟨1a⟩ v/t stew

estoico 1 adj stoic(al) **2** m, **-a** f stoic

estómago m stomach

estor m blind

estorbar ⟨1a⟩ **1** v/t (dificultar) hinder; **nos estorbaba** he was in our way **2** v/i get in the way

estorbo m hindrance, nuisance

estornino m zo starling

estornudar ⟨1a⟩ v/i sneeze

estornudo m sneeze

estoy vb → **estar**

estrado m platform

estrafalario adj F eccentric; ropa outlandish

estragón m BOT tarragon

estragos mpl devastation sg; **causar estragos entre** wreak havoc among

estrambótico adj F eccentric; ropa outlandish

estrangular ⟨1a⟩ v/t strangle

estraperlo m black market; **de estraperlo** on the black market

estratagema f stratagem

estrategia f strategy

estratégico adj strategic

estrato m fig stratum

estrechar ⟨1a⟩ **1** v/t ropa take in; mano shake; **estrechar entre los brazos** hug, embrace **2** v/r **estrecharse** narrow, get narrower

estrechez f fig hardship; **estrechez de miras** narrow-mindedness; **pasar estrecheces** suffer hardship

estrecho 1 adj narrow; (apretado) tight; amistad close; **estrecho de miras** narrow-minded **2** m strait, straits pl

estrella f tb de cine etc star; **estrella fugaz** falling star, shooting star; **estrella de mar** zo starfish; **estrella polar** Pole star

estrellar ⟨1a⟩ **1** v/t smash; **estrellar algo**

contra algo smash sth against sth; **estrelló el coche contra un muro** he smashed
the car into a wall **2** v/r **estrellarse** crash
(**contra** into)

estrellón m Pe, Bol crash
estremecer ⟨2d⟩ **1** v/t shock, shake F **2** v/r
estremecerse shake, tremble; de frío
shiver; de horror shudder
estrenar ⟨1a⟩ **1** v/t ropa wear for the first
time, christen F; objeto try out, christen
F; TEA, película premiere; **a estrenar**
brand new **2** v/r **estrenarse** make one's
debut
estreno m TEA, de película premiere; de
persona debut; **estar de estreno** be
wearing new clothes
estreñimiento m constipation
estrépito m noise, racket
estrés m stress
estresar ⟨1a⟩ v/t: **estresar alguien** cause
s.o. stress, subject s.o. to stress
estría f en piel stretch mark
estribar ⟨1a⟩ v/i: **estribar en** stem from,
lie in
estribillo m chorus, refrain
estribo m stirrup; **perder los estribos** fig
fly off the handle F
estrictez f S. Am. strictness
estricto adj strict
estridente adj shrill, strident
estrofa f stanza, verse
estropajo m scourer
estropajoso adj persona wiry; boca dry;
camisa scruffy
estropeado adj (averiado) broken
estropear ⟨1a⟩ **1** v/t aparato break; plan
ruin, spoil **2** v/r **estropearse** break
down; de comida go off, go bad; de plan
go wrong
estructura f structure
estructurar ⟨1a⟩ v/t structure, organize
estruendo m racket, din
estrujar ⟨1a⟩ v/t F crumple up, scrunch up
F; trapo wring out; persona squeeze, hold
tightly
estuario m estuary
estuche m case, box
estuco m stuccowork
estudiante m/f student
estudiantil adj student atr
estudiar ⟨1b⟩ v/t & v/i study
estudio m disciplina study; apartamento
studio, Br studio flat; de cine, música studio
estudioso adj studious
estufa f heater
estupefaciente m narcotic (drug)
estupefacto adj stupefied, speechless
estupendo adj fantastic, wonderful

estupidez f cualidad stupidity; acción stupid thing
estúpido 1 adj stupid **2** m, -a f idiot
estupor m astonishment, amazement;
MED stupor
esturión m ZO sturgeon
estuve vb → **estar**
estuvo vb → **estar**
etapa f stage; **por etapas** in stages
etarra m/f member of ETA
etc abr (= **etcétera**) etc (= etcetera)
etcétera m etcetera, and so on; **y un largo
etcétera de ...** and a long list of ..., and
many other ...
etéreo adj ethereal
eternidad f eternity
eterno adj eternal; **la película se me hizo
-a** the movie seemed to go on for ever
ética f en filosofía ethics; comportamiento
principles pl
ético adj ethical
etimología f etymology
Etiopía f Ethiopia
etiqueta f label; (protocolo) etiquette
etiquetar ⟨1a⟩ v/t tb fig label
étnico adj ethnic
eucalipto m BOT eucalyptus
eucaristía f Eucharist
eufemismo m euphemism
euforia f euphoria
eufórico adj euphoric
euro m euro
eurodiputado m, -a f MEP, member of
the European Parliament
Europa Europe
europeísta m/f pro-European
europeo 1 adj European **2** m, -a f European
eusquera m/adj Basque
eutanasia f euthanasia
evacuación f evacuation
evacuar ⟨1d⟩ v/t evacuate
evadir ⟨3a⟩ **1** v/t avoid; impuestos evade **2**
v/r **evadirse** tb fig escape
evaluación f evaluation, assessment;
(prueba) test
evaluar ⟨1e⟩ v/t assess, evaluate
evangelio m gospel
evangelizar ⟨1f⟩ v/t evangelize
evaporación f evaporation
evaporarse ⟨1a⟩ v/r evaporate; fig F vanish into thin air
evasión f tb fig escape; **evasión de capi-
tales** flight of capital; **evasión fiscal** tax
evasion
evasiva f evasive reply
evento m event
eventual adj possible; trabajo casual, temporary; **en el caso eventual de** in the

event of
eventualidad f eventuality
evidencia f evidence, proof; **poner en evidencia** demonstrate; **poner a alguien en evidencia** show s.o. up
evidente adj evident, clear
evitar ⟨1a⟩ v/t avoid; (impedir) prevent; molestias save; **no puedo evitarlo** I can't help it
evocar ⟨1g⟩ v/t evoke
evolución f BIO evolution; (desarrollo) development
evolucionar ⟨1a⟩ v/t BIO evolve; (desarrollar) develop
ex 1 pref ex- **2** m/f ex F
exabrupto m sharp remark
exacerbar ⟨1a⟩ v/t exacerbate, make worse; (irritar) exasperate
exacto adj medida exact, precise; informe accurate; **¡exacto!** exactly!, precisely!
exageración f exaggeration
exagerado adj exaggerated
exagerar ⟨1a⟩ v/t exaggerate
exaltación f (alabanza) exaltation; (entusiasmo) agitation, excitement
exaltar ⟨1a⟩ v/t excite, get worked up
examen m test, exam; MED examination; (análisis) study; **examen de conducir** driving test
examinar ⟨1a⟩ **1** v/t examine **2** v/r **examinarse** take an exam
exasperar ⟨1a⟩ **1** v/t exasperate **2** v/r **exasperarse** get exasperated
excarcelar ⟨1a⟩ v/t release (from prison)
excavación f excavation
excavadora f digger
excavar ⟨1a⟩ v/t excavate; túnel dig
excedencia f extended leave of absence
excedente 1 adj surplus; empleado on extended leave of absence **2** m surplus
exceder ⟨2a⟩ **1** v/t exceed **2** v/r **excederse** go too far, get carried away
excelencia f excellence; **Su Excelencia la señora embajadora** Her Excellency the Ambassador; **por excelencia** par excellence
excelente adj excellent
excéntrico 1 adj eccentric **2** m, -a f eccentric
excepción f exception; **a excepción de** except for; **sin excepción** without exception
excepcional adj exceptional
excepto prp except
exceptuar ⟨1e⟩ v/t except; **exceptuando** with the exception of, except for
excesivo adj excessive
exceso m excess; **exceso de equipaje** excess baggage; **exceso de velocidad** speeding; **en exceso** in excess, too much
excitación f excitement, agitation
excitante 1 adj exciting; **una bebida excitante** a stimulant **2** m stimulant
excitar ⟨1a⟩ **1** v/t excite; sentimientos, sexualmente arouse **2** v/r **excitarse** get excited; sexualmente become aroused
exclamación f exclamation
exclamar ⟨1a⟩ v/t exclaim
excluir ⟨3g⟩ v/t leave out (**de** of), exclude (**de** from); posibilidad rule out
exclusiva f privilegio exclusive rights pl (**de** to); reportaje exclusive
exclusivo adj exclusive
excomunión f excommunication
excremento m excrement
exculpar ⟨1a⟩ v/t exonerate
excursión f trip, excursion
excursionista m/f excursionist
excusa f excuse; **excusas** apologies
excusado m bathroom
excusar ⟨1a⟩ v/t excuse
execrable adj abominable, execrable fml
exención f exemption; **exención fiscal** tax exemption
exento adj exempt (**de** from); **exento de impuestos** tax-exempt, tax-free
exhalación f: **salir como una exhalación** fig rush o dash out
exhaustivo adj exhaustive
exhausto adj exhausted
exhibición f display, demonstration; de película screening, showing
exhibicionista m/f exhibitionist
exhibir ⟨3a⟩ **1** v/t show, display; película screen, show; cuadro exhibit **2** v/r **exhibirse** show o.s., let o.s. be seen
exhumar ⟨1a⟩ v/t exhume
exigencia f demand
exigente adj demanding
exigir ⟨3c⟩ v/t demand; (requirir) call for, demand; **le exigen mucho** they ask a lot of him
exiguo adj meager, Br meagre
exiliado 1 adj exiled, in exile pred **2** m, -a f exile
exiliar ⟨1a⟩ **1** v/t exile **2** v/r **exiliarse** go into exile
exilio m exile; **en el exilio** in exile
eximir ⟨3a⟩ v/t exempt (**de** from)
existencia f existence; (vida) life; **existencias** COM supplies, stocks
existencialista m/f & adj existentialist
existir ⟨3a⟩ v/i exist; **existen muchos problemas** there are a lot of problems
éxito m success; **éxito de taquilla** box office hit; **tener éxito** be successful, be a success
exitoso adj successful

Exmo. *abr* (= *Excelentísimo*) Your / His Excellency

exonerar ⟨1a⟩ *v/t* exonerate; **exonerar a alguien de algo** exempt s.o. from sth

exorbitante *adj* exorbitant

exorcista *m/f* exorcist

exótico *adj* exotic

expandir ⟨3a⟩ **1** *v/t* expand **2** *v/r* **expandirse** expand; *de noticia* spread

expansión *f* expansion; (*recreo*) recreation

expatriarse ⟨1b⟩ *v/r* leave one's country

expectación *f* sense of anticipation

expectativa *f* (*esperanza*) expectation; **estar a la expectativa de algo** be waiting for sth; **expectativas** (*perspectivas*) prospects

expedición *f* expedition

expediente *m* file, dossier; (*investigación*) investigation, inquiry; **expediente académico** student record; **expediente disciplinario** disciplinary proceedings *pl*; **abrir un expediente a alguien** take disciplinary action against s.o.

expedir ⟨3l⟩ *v/t documento* issue; *mercancías* send, dispatch

expeditar ⟨1a⟩ *v/t* L.Am. (*apresurar*) hurry; (*concluir*) finish, conclude

expeditivo *adj* expeditious

expendedor *adj*: **máquina expendedora** vending machine

expendio *m* L.Am. store, shop

expensas *fpl*: **a expensas de** at the expense of

experiencia *f* experience

experimentado *adj* experienced

experimentar ⟨1a⟩ **1** *v/t* try out, experiment with **2** *v/i* experiment (**con** on)

experimento *m* experiment

experto 1 *adj* expert; **experto en hacer algo** expert *o* very good at doing sth **2** *m* expert (**en** on)

expiar ⟨1c⟩ *v/t* expiate, atone for

expirar ⟨1a⟩ *v/i* expire

explanada *f* open area; *junto al mar* esplanade

explayarse ⟨1a⟩ *v/r* speak at length; (*desahogarse*) unburden o.s.; (*distraerse*) relax, unwind; **explayarse sobre algo** expound on sth

explicación *f* explanation

explicar ⟨1g⟩ **1** *v/t* explain **2** *v/r* **explicarse** (*comprender*) understand; (*hacerse comprender*) express o.s.; **no me lo explico** I can't understand it, I don't get it F

explícito *adj* explicit

explorador *m*, **exploradora** *f* explorer; MIL scout

explorar ⟨1a⟩ *v/t* explore

explosión *f* explosion; **explosión demográfica** population explosion; **hacer explosión** go off, explode

explosionar ⟨1a⟩ *v/t & v/i* explode

explosivo *m/adj* explosive

explotación *f de mina, tierra* exploitation, working; *de negocio* running, operation; *de trabajador* exploitation

explotar ⟨1a⟩ **1** *v/t tierra, mina* work, exploit; *situación* take advantage of, exploit; *trabajador* exploit **2** *v/i* go off, explode; *fig* explode, blow a fuse F

expoliar ⟨1b⟩ *v/t* plunder, pillage

exponente *m* exponent

exponer ⟨2r; *part* **expuesto**⟩ **1** *v/t idea, teoría* set out, put forward; (*revelar*) expose; *pintura, escultura* exhibit, show; (*arriesgar*) risk **2** *v/r* **exponerse a algo** (*arriesgarse*) lay o.s. open to sth

exportación *f* export

exportar ⟨1a⟩ *v/t* export

exposición *f* exhibition

expresar ⟨1a⟩ **1** *v/t* express **2** *v/r* **expresarse** express o.s.

expresión *f* expression

expresivo *adj* expressive

expreso 1 *adj express atr;* **tren expreso** express (train) **2** *m tren* express (train); *café* espresso

exprimidor *m* lemon squeezer; *eléctrico* juicer

exprimir ⟨3a⟩ *v/t* squeeze; (*explotar*) exploit

ex profeso *adv* (*especialmente*) expressly; (*a propósito*) deliberately

expropiar ⟨1b⟩ *v/t* expropriate

expuesto *part* → **exponer**

expugnar ⟨1a⟩ *v/t* take by storm

expulsar ⟨1a⟩ *v/t* expel, throw out F; DEP expel from the game, Br send off

expulsión *f* expulsion; DEP sending off

exquisito *adj comida* delicious; (*bello*) exquisite; (*refinado*) refined

extasiarse ⟨1c⟩ *v/r* be enraptured, go into raptures

éxtasis *m tb droga* ecstasy

extender ⟨2g⟩ **1** *v/t brazos* stretch out; (*untar*) spread; *tela, papel* spread out; (*ampliar*) extend; **me extendió la mano** she held out her hand to me **2** *v/r* **extenderse** *de campos* stretch; *de influencia* extend; (*difundirse*) spread; (*durar*) last; *explayarse* go into detail

extendido 1 *part* → **extender 2** *adj costumbre* widespread; *brazos* outstretched; *mapa* spread out

extensión *f tb* TELEC extension; *superficie* expanse, area; **por extensión** by exten-

sion
extenso *adj* extensive, vast; *informe* lengthy, long
extenuar ⟨1e⟩ **1** *v/t* exhaust, tire out **2** *v/r* **extenuarse** exhaust o.s., tire o.s. out
exterior 1 *adj aspecto* external, outward; *capa* outer; *apartamento* overlooking the street; POL foreign; *la parte exterior del edificio* the exterior *o* the outside of the building **2** *m* (*fachada*) exterior, outside; *aspecto* exterior, outward appearance; *viajar al exterior* (*al extranjero*) travel abroad
exteriorizar ⟨1f⟩ *v/t* externalize
exterminar ⟨1a⟩ *v/t* exterminate, wipe out
externo 1 *adj aspecto* external, outside; *influencia* external, outside; *capa* outer; *deuda* foreign **2** *m*, **-a** *f* EDU *student who attends a boarding school but returns home each evening*, Br day boy / girl
extinción *f*: *en peligro de extinción* in danger of extinction
extinguidor *m L.Am.*: *extinguidor* (*de incendios*) (fire) extinguisher
extinguir ⟨3d⟩ **1** *v/t* BIO, ZO wipe out; *fuego* extinguish, put out **2** *v/r* **extinguirse** BIO, ZO become extinct, die out; *de fuego* go out; *de plazo* expire
extintor *m* fire extinguisher
extirpar ⟨1a⟩ *v/t* MED remove; *vicio* eradicate, stamp out
extorsión *f* extortion
extorsionar ⟨1a⟩ *v/t* extort money from
extra 1 *adj excelente* top quality; *adicional* extra; *horas extra* overtime; *paga extra* extra month's pay **2** *m/f de cine* extra **3** *m gasto* additional expense
extracto *m* extract; (*resumen*) summary; GASTR, QUÍM extract, essence; *extracto de cuenta* bank statement
extractor *m* extractor; *extractor de humos* extractor fan
extradición *f* extradition

extraditar ⟨1a⟩ *v/t* extradite
extraer ⟨2p⟩ *v/t* extract, pull out; *conclusión* draw
extrajudicial *adj* out-of-court
extralimitarse ⟨1a⟩ *v/r* go too far, exceed one's authority
extramatrimonial *adj* extramarital
extranjería *f*: *ley de extranjería* immigration laws *pl*
extranjero 1 *adj* foreign **2** *m*, **-a** *f* foreigner; *en el extranjero* abroad
extranjis: *de extranjis* F on the quiet F, on the sly F
extrañar ⟨1a⟩ **1** *v/t L.Am.* miss **2** *v/r* **extrañarse** be surprised (*de* at)
extraño 1 *adj* strange, odd **2** *m*, **-a** *f* stranger
extraordinario *adj* extraordinary
extrapolar ⟨1a⟩ *v/t* extrapolate
extrarradio *m* outlying districts *pl*, outskirts *pl*
extraterrestre *adj* extraterrestial, alien
extravagante *adj* outrageous
extravertido *adj* extrovert
extraviar ⟨1c⟩ **1** *v/t* lose, mislay **2** *v/r* **extraviarse** get lost, lose one's way
extremadamente *adv* extremely
extremado *adj* extreme
extremar ⟨1a⟩ *v/t* maximize
extremidad *f* end; *extremidades* extremities
extremista 1 *adj* extreme **2** *m/f* POL extremist
extremo 1 *adj* extreme **2** *m* extreme; *parte primera o última* end; *punto* point; *llegar al extremo de* reach the point of **3** *m/f*: *extremo derecho / izquierdo* DEP right / left wing; *en extremo* in the extreme
extrovertido *adj* extrovert
exuberante *adj* exuberant; *vegetación* lush
exultante *adj* elated
eyacular ⟨1a⟩ *v/t* ejaculate

F

fabada *f* GASTR *Asturian stew with pork sausage, bacon and beans*
fábrica *f* plant, factory
fabricación *f* manufacturing
fabricante *m* manufacturer, maker
fabricar ⟨1g⟩ *v/t* manufacture

fábula *f* fable; (*mentira*) lie
fabuloso *adj* fabulous, marvel(l)ous
facción *f* POL faction; *facciones pl* (*rasgos*) features
faceta *f fig* facet
facha 1 *f* look; (*cara*) face **2** *m/f desp* fas-

cist

fachada f tb fig façade

facial adj facial

fácil adj easy; **es fácil que** it's likely that

facilidad f ease; **con facilidad** easily; **tener facilidad para algo** have a gift for sth; **facilidades de pago** credit facilities, credit terms

facilitar ⟨1a⟩ v/t facilitate, make easier; (*hacer factible*) make possible; *medios, dinero etc* provide

factible adj feasible

factor m factor

factoría f esp L.Am. plant, factory

factura f COM invoice; *de luz, gas etc* bill

facturación f COM invoicing; (*volumen de negocio*) turnover; AVIA check-in

facturar v/t COM invoice, bill; *volumen de negocio* turn over; AVIA check in

facultad f faculty; (*autoridad*) authority

faena f task, job; **hacer una faena a alguien** play a dirty trick on s.o.

fagot m MÚS bassoon

faisán m ZO pheasant

faja f prenda interior girdle

fajarse ⟨1a⟩ v/r Méx, Ven F get into a fight

fajo m wad; *de periódicos* bundle

falacia f fallacy; (*engaño*) fraud

falange f ANAT phalange; MIL phalanx

falda f skirt; *de montaña* side

faldero adj: **perro faldero** lap dog

falla f fault; *de fabricación* flaw

fallar ⟨1a⟩ v/i fail; (*no acertar*) miss; *de sistema etc* go wrong; JUR find (**en favor de** for; **en contra de** against); **fallar a alguien** let s.o. down **2** v/t JUR pronounce judg(e)ment in; *pregunta* get wrong; **fallar el tiro** miss

fallecer ⟨2d⟩ v/i pass away

fallecimiento m demise

fallo m mistake; TÉC fault; JUR judg(e)ment; **fallo cardiaco** heart failure

falsedad f falseness; (*mentira*) lie

falsificación f de moneda counterfeiting; *de documentos, firma* forgery

falsificar ⟨1g⟩ v/t moneda counterfeit; *documento, firma* forge, falsify

falso adj false; *joyas* fake; *documento, firma* forged; **jurar en falso** commit perjury

falta f (*escasez*) lack, want; (*error*) mistake; (*ausencia*) absence; *en tenis* fault; *en fútbol* foul; (*tiro libre*) free kick; **hacerle falta a alguien** foul s.o.; **falta de** lack of, shortage of; **sin falta** without fail; **buena falta le hace** it's about time; **echar en falta a alguien** miss s.o.; **hacer falta** be necessary

faltar ⟨1a⟩ v/i be missing; **falta una hora** there's an hour to go; **faltan 10 kilómetros** there are 10 kilometers to go; **sólo falta hacer la salsa** there's only the sauce to do; **faltar a** be absent from; **faltar a clase** miss class, be absent from class; **faltar a alguien** be disrespectful to s.o.; **faltar a su palabra** not keep one's word

falto adj: **falto de** lacking in, devoid of; **falto de recursos** short of resources

fama f fame; (*reputación*) reputation; **tener mala fama** have a bad reputation

familia f family; **sentirse como en familia** feel at home

familiar 1 adj family atr; (*conocido*) familiar; LING colloquial **2** m/f relation, relative

familiaridad f familiarity

familiarizarse ⟨1f⟩ v/r familiarize o.s. (**con** with)

famoso 1 adj famous **2** m, -a f celebrity

fan m/f fan

fanático 1 adj fanatical **2** m, -a f fanatic

fanatismo m fanaticism

fanfarrón 1 adj boastful **2** m, -ona f boaster

fanfarronear ⟨1a⟩ v/i boast, brag

fango m tb fig mud

fantasear ⟨1a⟩ v/i fantasize

fantasía f fantasy; (*imaginación*) imagination; **joyas de fantasía** costume jewel(l)ery

fantasma m ghost

fantástico adj fantastic

farándula f show business

fardar ⟨1a⟩ v/i: **fardar de algo** F boast about sth, show off about sth

fardo m bundle

faringitis f MED inflammation of the pharynx, pharyngitis

fariña f S. Am. manioc flour, cassava

farmacéutico 1 adj pharmaceutical **2** m, -a f pharmacist, Br chemist

farmacia f pharmacy, Br chemist's; *estudios* pharmacy; **farmacia de guardia** 24-hour pharmacist, Br emergency chemist

fármaco m medicine

farmacología f pharmacology

faro m MAR lighthouse; AUTO headlight, headlamp; **faro antiniebla** fog light

farol m lantern; (*farola*) streetlight, streetlamp; *en juegos de cartas* bluff

farola f streetlight, streetlamp

farolillo m: **ser el farolillo rojo** fig F be bottom of the league

farragoso adj texto dense

farrear ⟨1a⟩ v/i L.Am. F go out on the town F

farrista *adj L.Am.* F hard-drinking

farsa *f tb fig* farce

farsante *m/f* fraud, fake

fascículo *m* TIP instal(l)ment

fascinación *f* fascination

fascinante *adj* fascinating

fascinar ⟨1a⟩ *v/t* fascinate

fascismo *m* fascism

fascista *m/f & adj* fascist

fase *f* phase

fastidiar ⟨1b⟩ **1** *v/t* annoy; F (*estropear*) spoil **2** *v/r* **fastidiarse** grin and bear it

fastidio *m* annoyance; **¡qué fastidio!** what a nuisance!

fastuoso *adj* lavish

fatal 1 *adj* fatal; (*muy malo*) dreadful, awful **2** *adv* very badly

fatídico *adj* fateful

fatiga *f* tiredness, fatigue

fatigar ⟨1h⟩ **1** *v/t* tire **2** *v/r* **fatigarse** get tired

fatuo *adj* conceited; (*necio*) fatuous

fauces *fpl* ZO jaws

fauna *f* fauna

favor *m* favo(u)r; **a favor de** in favo(u)r of; **por favor** please; **hacer un favor** do a favo(u)r

favorecer ⟨2d⟩ *v/t* favo(u)r; *de ropa, color* suit

favoritismo *m* favo(u)ritism

favorito 1 *adj* favo(u)rite **2** *m*, **-a** *f* favo(u)rite

fax *m* fax; **enviar un fax a alguien** send s.o. a fax, fax s.o.

fayuca *f Méx* smuggling

fayuquero *m*, **-a** *f Méx* dealer in smuggled goods

F.O. *abr* (= **Fútbol Club**) FC (= Football Club)

fdo. *abr* (= **firmado**) signed

fe *f* faith (**en** in); **fe de erratas** errata

fealdad *f* ugliness

feb. *abr* (= **febrero**) Feb. (= February)

febrero *m* February

fecal *adj* f(a)ecal

fecha *f* date; **fecha límite de consumo** best before date; **fecha de nacimiento** date of birth

fechador *m Chi, Méx* postmark

fécula *f* starch

fecundación *f* fertilization; **fecundación in vitro** MED in vitro fertilization

fecundar ⟨1a⟩ *v/t* fertilize

fecundo *adj* fertile

federación *f* federation

federal *adj* federal

felicidad *f* happiness; **¡felicidades!** congratulations!

felicitación *f* letter of congratulations;

¡felicitaciones! congratulations!

felicitar ⟨1a⟩ *v/t* congratulate (**por** on)

felino *adj tb fig* feline

feliz *adj* happy; **¡feliz Navidad!** Merry Christmas!

felpa *f* towel(l)ing

felpudo *m* doormat

femenino *adj* feminine; *moda, equipo* women's **2** GRAM feminine

femin(e)idad *f* femininity

feminismo *m* feminism

feminista *m/f & adj* feminist

fenomenal 1 *adj* F fantastic F, phenomenal F **2** *adv*: **lo pasé fenomenal** F I had a fantastic time F

fenómeno 1 *m* phenomenon; *persona* genius **2** *adj* F fantastic F, great F

feo 1 *adj* ugly; *fig* nasty **2** *m*: **hacer un feo a alguien** F snub s.o.

féretro *m* casket, coffin

feria *f* COM fair; *L.Am.* (*mercado*) market; *Méx* (*calderilla*) small change; **feria de muestras** trade fair

feriado 1 *adj L.Am.*: **día feriado** (public) holiday **2** *m L.Am.* (public) holiday; **abierto feriados** open on public holidays

ferial 1 *adj*: **recinto ferial** fairground **2** *m* fair

fermentación *f* fermentation

fermentar ⟨1a⟩ *v/t* ferment

fermento *m* ferment

ferocidad *f* ferocity

feroz *adj* fierce; (*cruel*) cruel

férreo *adj tb fig* iron *atr*; **del ferrocarril** rail *atr*

ferretería *f* hardware store

ferrocarril *m* railroad, *Br* railway

ferrocarrilero *m L.Am.* railroad o *Br* railway worker

ferroviario *adj* rail *atr*

ferry *m* ferry

fértil *adj* fertile

fertilidad *f* fertility

fertilizante *m* fertilizer

ferviente *adj fig* fervent

fervor *m* fervo(u)r

festejar ⟨1a⟩ *v/t persona* wine and dine; *L.Am.* celebrate

festejo *m* celebration; **festejos** festivities

festín *m* banquet

festival *m* festival; **festival cinematográfico** film festival

festividad *f* feast; **festividades** festivities

festivo *adj* festive

fetal *adj* fetal

fetiche *m* fetish

fétido *adj* fetid

feto *m* fetus

feudal *adj* feudal

feudo *m fig* domain

FF. AA. *abr* (= **fuerzas armadas**) armed forces

FF. CC. *abr* (= **ferrocarriles**) railroads

fiable *adj* trustworthy; *datos, máquina etc* reliable

fiambre *m* cold cut, *Br* cold meat; P (*cadáver*) stiff P

fiambrera *f* lunch pail, *Br* lunch box

fiambrería *f L.Am.* delicatessen

fianza *f* deposit; JUR bail; **bajo fianza** on bail

fiar ⟨1c⟩ **1** *v/i* give credit **2** *v/r* **fiarse: fiarse de alguien** trust s.o.; **no me fío** I don't trust him / them *etc*

fiasco *m* fiasco

fibra *f* en tejido, alimento fiber, *Br* fibre; **fibra óptica** optical fiber (*Br* fibre); **fibra de vidrio** fiberglass, *Br* fibreglass

fibroso *adj* fibrous

ficción *f* fiction

ficha *f* file card, index card; *en juegos de mesa* counter; *en un casino* chip; *en damas* checker, *Br* draught; *en ajedrez* man, piece; TELEC token

fichar ⟨1a⟩ **1** *v/t* DEP sign; JUR open a file on **2** *v/i* DEP sign (**por** for)

fichero *m* file cabinet, *Br* filing cabinet; INFOR file

ficticio *adj* fictitious

fidedigno *adj* reliable

fidelidad *f* fidelity

fideo *m* noodle

fiebre *f* fever; (*temperatura*) temperature; **fiebre del heno** hay fever

fiel 1 *adj* faithful; (*leal*) loyal **2** *mpl:* **los fieles** REL the faithful *pl*

fieltro *m* felt

fiera *f* wild animal; **ponerse hecho una fiera** F go wild F

fiero *adj* fierce

fierro *m L.Am.* iron

fiesta *f* festival; (*reunión social*) party; (*día festivo*) public holiday; **estar de fiesta** be in a party mood

fifí *m L.Am.* P afeminado sissy F

figura *f* figure; (*estatuilla*) figurine; (*forma*) shape; *naipes* face card, *Br* picture card; **tener buena figura** have a good figure

figurado *adj* figurative; **sentido figurado** figurative sense

figurar ⟨1a⟩ **1** *v/i* appear (**en** in); **aquí figura como ...** she appears *o* is down here as ... **2** *v/r* **figurarse** imagine; **¡figúrate!** just imagine!

fijar ⟨1a⟩ **1** *v/t* fix; *cartel* stick; *fecha, objetivo* set; *residencia* establish; *atención*

focus 2 *v/r* **fijarse** (*establecerse*) settle; (*prestar atención*) pay attention (**en** to); **fijarse en algo** (*darse cuenta*) notice sth

fijo *adj* fixed; *trabajo* permanent; *fecha* definite

fila *f* line, *Br* queue; *de asientos* row; **en fila india** in single file; **filas** MIL ranks

filatelia *f* philately, stamp collecting

filete *m* GASTR fillet

filial 1 *adj* filial **2** *f* COM subsidiary

Filipinas *fpl* Philippines

film(e) *m* movie, film

filmación *f* filming, shooting

filmar ⟨1a⟩ *v/t* film, shoot

filo *m* edge; *de navaja* cutting edge; **al filo de las siete** *fig* around 7 o'clock

filología *f* philology; **filología hispánica** EDU Spanish language and literature

filólogo *m,* **-a** *f* philologist

filón *m* vein, seam; *fig* goldmine

filoso *adj L.Am.* sharp

filosofía *f* philosophy

filosófico *adj* philosophical

filósofo *m,* **-a** *f* philosopher

filtración *f* leak

filtrar ⟨1a⟩ **1** *v/t* filter; *información* leak **2** *v/r* **filtrarse** filter (**por** through); *de agua, información* leak

filtro *m* filter

fin *m* end; (*objetivo*) aim, purpose; **fin de semana** weekend; **a fines de mayo** at the end of May; **al fin y al cabo** at the end of the day, after all; **en fin** anyway

final *f* adj final

finalidad *f* purpose, aim

finalista 1 *adj:* **las dos selecciones finalistas** the two teams that reached the final **2** *m/f* finalist

finalización *f* completion

finalizado *adj* complete

finalizar ⟨1f⟩ *v/t & v/i* end, finish

finalmente *adv* eventually

financiación *f* funding

financiar ⟨1b⟩ *v/t* finance, fund

financista *m/f L.Am.* financier

finanzas *fpl* finances

finca *f* (*bien inmueble*) property; *L.Am.* (*granja*) farm

fingido *adj* false

fingir ⟨3c⟩ **1** *v/t* feign *fml*; **fingió no haberlo oído** I pretended I hadn't heard **2** *v/r* **fingirse: fingirse enfermo** pretend to be ill, feign illness *fml*

finlandés 1 *adj* Finnish **2** *m,* **-esa** *f* Finn

Finlandia *f* Finland

fino *adj* calidad fine; *libro, tela* thin; (*esbelto*) slim; *modales, gusto* refined; *sentido de humor* subtle

firma *f* signature; *acto* signing; COM firm

firmamento *m* firmament

firmar ⟨1a⟩ *v/t* sign

firme *adj* firm; (*estable*) steady; **en firme** COM firm

fiscal 1 *adj* tax *atr*, fiscal **2** *m/f* district attorney, *Br* public prosecutor

fisgar ⟨1h⟩ *v/i* F snoop F; **fisgar en algo** snoop around in sth

fisgón *m*, **-ona** *f* snoop

fisgonear ⟨1a⟩ *v/i* F snoop around F (**en** in)

física *f* physics

físico 1 *adj* physical **2** *m*, **-a** *f* physicist **3** *m de una persona* physique

fisiología *f* physiology

fisión *f* fission

fisioterapeuta *m/f* physical therapist, *Br* physiotherapist

fisioterapia *f* physical therapy, *Br* physiotherapy

fisonomía *f* features *pl*

fisura *f* crack; MED fracture

flác(c)ido *adj* flabby

flaco *adj* thin; **punto flaco** weak point

flacuchento *adj L.Am.* F skinny

flagelar ⟨1a⟩ *v/t* flagellate

flagrante *adj* flagrant; **en flagrante delito** red-handed, in flagrante delicto

flamante *adj* (*nuevo*) brand-new

flamenco 1 *adj* MÚS flamenco **2** *m* MÚS flamenco; ZO flamingo

flan *m* crème caramel

flanco *m* flank

flaquear ⟨1a⟩ *v/i* weaken; *de entusiasmo* flag

flaqueza *f fig* weakness

flash *m* FOT flash

flato *m* MED stitch

flatulencia *f* MED flatulence

flauta *f* flute; *Méx* fried taco; **flauta dulce** recorder; **flauta travesera** (transverse) flute

flautista *m/f* flautist

flecha *f* arrow

flechazo *m fig* love at first sight

flecos *mpl* fringe *sg*

flema *f fig* phlegm

flemático *adj* phlegmatic

flemón *m* MED gumboil

flequillo *m del pelo* fringe

fletar ⟨1a⟩ *v/t* charter; (*embarcar*) load

flete *m L.Am.* freight, cost of transport

fletero *adj L.Am.* hire *atr*, charter *atr*

flexibilidad *f* flexibility

flexible *adj* flexible

flexión *f en gimnasia* push-up, *Br* press-up; *de piernas* squat; *de la voz* inflection

flexionar ⟨1a⟩ **1** *v/t* flex **2** *v/r* **flexionarse** bend

flexo *m* desk lamp

flipar ⟨1a⟩ *v/i*: **le flipa el cine** P he's mad about the movies F

flirtear ⟨1a⟩ *v/i* flirt (**con** with)

flojo *adj* loose; *café, argumento* weak; COM *actividad* slack; *novela, redación* poor; *L.Am.* lazy

flojera *f L.Am.* laziness; **me da flojera** I can't be bothered

flor *f* flower

flora *f* flora

florear ⟨1a⟩ **1** *v/t* decorate with flowers; *Méx* (*halagar*) flatter, compliment **2** *v/i* flower, bloom

florecer ⟨2d⟩ *v/i* BOT flower. bloom; *de negocio, civilización etc* flourish

floreciente *adj* flourishing

florero *m* vase

florista *m/f* florist

floristería *f* florist's, flower shop

flota *f* fleet

flotación *f* flotation

flotador *m* float

flotar ⟨1a⟩ *v/i* float

flote MAR: **a flote** afloat

fluctuación *f* fluctuation

fluctuar ⟨1e⟩ *v/i* fluctuate

fluidez *f* fluidity

fluido 1 *adj* fluid; *tráfico* free flowing; *lenguaje* fluent **2** *m* fluid

fluir ⟨3g⟩ *v/i* flow

flujo *m* flow

fluorescente 1 *adj* fluorescent **2** *m* strip light

fluvial *adj* river *atr*

FM *abr* (= **frecuencia modulada**) FM (= frequency modulation)

FMI *abr* (= **Fondo Monetario Internacional**) IMF (= International Monetary Fund)

fobia *f* phobia

foca *f* ZO seal

foco *m* focus; TEA, TV spotlight; *de infección* center, *Br* centre; *de incendio* seat; *L.Am.* (*bombilla*) lightbulb; *de auto* headlight; *de calle* streetlight

fofo *adj* flabby

fogata *f* bonfire

fogoso *adj* fiery, ardent

foie-gras *m* foie gras

folclore *m* folklore

fólico *adj*: **ácido fólico** folic acid

folio *m* sheet (of paper)

folklore *m* folklore

follaje *m* foliage

folleto *m* pamphlet

follón *m* argument; (*lío*) mess; **armar un follón** kick up a fuss

fomentar ⟨1a⟩ *v/t* foster; COM promote; *re-*

belión foment, incite

fomento *m* COM promotion

fonda *f* L.Am. cheap restaurant; (*pensión*) boarding house

fondear ⟨1a⟩ **1** *v/t* MAR anchor **2** *v/r* **fondearse** L.Am. get rich

fondero *m*, **-a** *f* L.Am. restaurant owner

fondista *m/f* DEP long-distance runner

fondo *m* bottom; *de sala, cuarto* etc back; *de pasillo* end; (*profundidad*) depth; PINT, FOT background; *de un museo* etc collection; COM fund; **fondo de inversión** investment fund; **fondo de pensiones** pension fund; **Fondo Monetario Internacional** International Monetary Fund; **fondos** *pl* money *sg*, funds; **tiene buen fondo** he's got a good heart; **en el fondo** deep down; **tocar fondo** *fig* reach bottom

fonética *f* phonetics

fontanería *f* plumbing

fontanero *m* plumber

footing *m* DEP jogging; **hacer footing** go jogging, jog

forastero 1 *adj* foreign **2** *m*, **-a** *f* outsider, stranger

forcejear ⟨1a⟩ *v/i* struggle

forcejeo *m* struggle

forense 1 *adj* forensic **2** *m/f* forensic scientist

forestación *f* afforestation

forestal *adj* forest *atr*

forestar ⟨1a⟩ *v/t* L.Am. afforest

forjar ⟨1a⟩ *v/t* metal forge

forma *f* form; (*apariencia*) shape; (*manera*) way; **de todas formas** in any case, anyway; **estar en forma** be fit

formación *f* formation; (*entrenamiento*) training; **formación profesional** vocational training

formal *adj* formal; *niño* well-behaved; (*responsable*) responsible

formalizar ⟨1f⟩ *v/t* formalize; *relación* make official

formar ⟨1a⟩ **1** *v/t* form; (*educar*) educate **2** *v/r* **formarse** form

formatear ⟨1a⟩ *v/t* INFOR format

formato *m* format

formidable *adj* huge; (*estupendo*) tremendous

fórmula *f* formula

formular ⟨1a⟩ *v/t teoría* formulate; *queja* make, lodge

formulario *m* form

fornicar ⟨1g⟩ *v/i* fornicate

fornido *adj* well-built

foro *m* forum

forofo *m*, **-a** *f* F fan

forrado *adj prenda* lined; *libro* covered;

fig F loaded F

forraje *m* fodder

forrar ⟨1a⟩ **1** *v/t prenda* line; *libro, silla* cover **2** *v/r* **forrarse** F make a fortune F

forro *m de prenda* lining; *de libro* cover

fortalecer ⟨2d⟩ **1** *v/t tb fig* strengthen **2** *v/r* **fortalecerse** strengthen

fortaleza *f* strength of character; MIL fortress

fortificar ⟨1g⟩ *v/t* MIL fortify

fortuito *adj* chance *atr*, accidental

fortuna *f* fortune; (*suerte*) luck; **por fortuna** fortunately, luckily

forzar ⟨1f & 1m⟩ *v/t* force; (*violar*) rape

forzoso *adj aterrizaje* forced

forzudo *adj* brawny

fosa *f* pit; (*tumba*) grave; **fosa común** common grave; **fosas nasales** nostrils

fósforo *m* QUÍM phosphorus; L.Am. (*cerilla*) match

fósil 1 *adj* fossilized **2** *m* fossil

foso *m* ditch; TEA, MÚS pit; *de castillo* moat

foto *f* photo

fotocopia *f* photocopy

fotocopiadora *f* photocopier

fotocopiar ⟨1a⟩ *v/t* photocopy

fotogénico *adj* photogenic

fotografía *f* photography

fotografiar ⟨1c⟩ *v/t* photograph

fotógrafo *m*, **-a** *f* photographer

FP *f* (= **formación profesional**) vocational training

frac *m* tail coat

fracasado 1 *adj* unsuccessful **2** *m*, **-a** *f* loser

fracasar ⟨1a⟩ *v/i* fail

fracaso *m* failure

fracción *f* fraction; POL faction

fraccionamiento *m* L.Am. (housing) project, *Br* estate

fraccionar ⟨1a⟩ *v/t* break up; FIN pay in instal(l)ments

fractura *f* MED fracture

fracturar ⟨1a⟩ *v/t* MED fracture

fragancia *f* fragrance

frágil *adj* fragile

fragmentar ⟨1a⟩ *v/t* fragment

fragmento *m* fragment; *de novela, poema* excerpt, extract

fraguar ⟨1i⟩ *v/t* forge; *plan* devise; *complot* hatch

fraile *m* friar, monk

frambuesa *f* raspberry

francés 1 *adj* French **2** *m* Frenchman; *idioma* French

francesa *f* Frenchwoman

Francia France

franco *adj* (*sincero*) frank; (*evidente*) dis-

tinct, marked; COM free
francotirador m sniper
franela f flannel
franja f fringe; *de tierra* strip
franquear ⟨1a⟩ v/t *carta* pay the postage on; *camino, obstáculo* clear
franqueo m postage
franqueza f frankness
franquicia f *(exención)* exemption; COM franchise
frasco m bottle
frase f phrase; *(oración)* sentence; *frase hecha* set phrase
fraternal adj brotherly
fraternidad f brotherhood, fraternity
fraternizar ⟨1f⟩ v/i POL fraternize
fraude m fraud
fraudulento adj fraudulent
frazada f L.Am. blanket
frecuencia f frequency; *frecuencia modulada* RAD frequency modulation; *con frecuencia* frequently
frecuentar ⟨1a⟩ v/t frequent
frecuente adj frequent; *(común)* common
frecuentemente adv often, frequently
fregadero m sink
fregar ⟨1h & 1k⟩ v/t *platos* wash; *el suelo* mop; *L.Am.* F bug F
fregón 1 adj annoying **2** m L.Am. F nuisance, pain in the neck F
fregona f mop; *L.Am.* F nuisance, pain in the neck F
freidora f deep fryer
freidura f frying
freír ⟨3m; *part frito* ⟩ v/t fry; F *(matar)* waste P
frenada f *esp L.Am.*: *dar una frenada* F slam the brakes on, hit the brakes F
frenar ⟨1a⟩ **1** v/i AUTO brake **2** v/t *fig* slow down; *impulsos* check
frenazo m: *pegar or dar un frenazo* F slam the brakes on, hit the brakes F
frenesí m frenzy
frenético adj frenetic
freno m brake; *freno de mano* parking brake, Br handbrake
frente 1 f forehead **2** m MIL, METEO front; *de frente* colisión head-on; *de frente al grupo* L.Am. facing the group; *hacer frente a* face up to **3** prp: *frente a* opposite
fresa f strawberry
fresco 1 adj cool; *pescado etc* fresh; *persona* F fresh F, Br cheeky F **2** m, -a f: *¡eres un fresco!* F you've got nerve! F, Br you've got a cheek! F **3** m fresh air; C.Am. fruit drink
frescor m freshness
frescura f freshness; *(frío)* coolness; *fig*

nerve
fresno m BOT ash tree
fresón m strawberry
frialdad f *tb fig* coldness
fricción f TÉC, *fig* friction
friccionar ⟨1a⟩ v/t rub
friega f L.Am. F hassle F, drag F
frígido adj MED frigid
frigorífico 1 adj refrigerated **2** m fridge
frijol m, **frijol** m L.Am. bean
frío 1 adj *tb fig* cold **2** m cold; *tener frío* be cold
friolento L.Am., **friolero** adj: *es friolento* he feels the cold
fritar ⟨1a⟩ v/t L.Am. fry
frito 1 part → **freír 2** adj fried **3** mpl: *fritos* fried food *sg*
fritura f fried food
frívolo adj frivolous
frondoso adj leafy
frontal adj frontal; *ataque etc* head-on; *(delantero)* front *atr*
frontera f border
fronterizo adj border *atr*
frontón m DEP pelota; *cancha* pelota court
frotar ⟨1a⟩ v/t rub
fructífero adj fruitful, productive
frugal adj *persona* frugal
fruncir ⟨3b⟩ v/t *material* gather; *fruncir el ceño* frown
frustración f frustration
frustrante adj frustrating
frustrar ⟨1a⟩ v/t frustrate; *plan* thwart **2** v/r **frustrarse** fail
fruta f fruit
frutal 1 adj fruit *atr* **2** m fruit tree
frutería f fruit store, Br greengrocer's
frutilla f S. Am. strawberry
fruto m *tb fig* fruit; *nuez, almendra etc* nut; *frutos secos* nuts
fucsia adj fuchsia
fue vb → **ir, ser**
fuego m fire; *¿tienes fuego?* do you have a light?; *fuegos artificiales* fireworks; *pegar or prender fuego a* set fire to
fuel(-oil) m fuel oil
fuelle m bellows *pl*
fuente f fountain; *recipiente* dish; *fig* source
fuera 1 vb → **ir, ser 2** adv outside; *(en otro lugar)* away; *(en otro país)* abroad; *por fuera* on the outside; *¡fuera!* get out! **3** prp: *fuera de* outside; *¡sal fuera de aquí!* get out of here!; *está fuera del país* he's abroad, he's out of the country
fuero m: *en el fuero interno* deep down
fuerte 1 adj strong; *dolor* intense; *lluvia* heavy; *aumento* sharp; *ruido* loud; *fig* P incredible F **2** adv hard **3** m MIL fort

fuerza f strength; (*violencia*) force; EL power; **fuerza aérea** air force; **fuerza de voluntad** willpower; **fuerzas armadas** armed forces; **fuerzas de seguridad** security forces; **a fuerza de ...** by (dint of)

fuese vb → **ir, ser**

fuete m *L.Am.* whip

fuga f escape; *de gas, agua* leak; **darse a la fuga** flee

fugarse ⟨1h⟩ v/r run away; *de la cárcel* escape

fugaz adj fig fleeting

fugitivo 1 adj runaway atr **2** m, **-a** f fugitive

fui vb → **ir, ser**

fuimos vb → **ir, ser**

fulano m so-and-so

fulgor m brightness

fulgurante adj fig dazzling

fulminante adj sudden

fulminar ⟨1a⟩ v/t: **lo fulminó un rayo** he was killed by lightning; **fulminar a alguien con la mirada** look daggers at s.o. F

fumador m, **fumadora** f smoker

fumar ⟨1a⟩ **1** v/t smoke **2** v/i smoke; **prohibido fumar** no smoking **3** v/r **fumarse** smoke; **fumarse una clase** F skip a class F

fumigar ⟨1h⟩ v/t fumigate

función f purpose, function; *en el trabajo* duty; TEA performance; **en función de** according to

funcional adj functional

funcionamiento m working

funcionar ⟨1a⟩ v/i work; **no funciona** out of order

funcionario m, **-a** f government employee, civil servant

funda f cover; *de gafas* case; *de almohada* pillowcase

fundación f foundation

fundador m, **fundadora** f founder

fundamental adj fundamental

fundamentalismo m fundamentalism

fundamentalista m/f fundamentalist

fundamentalmente adv essentially

fundamento m foundation; **fundamentos** (*nociones*) fundamentals

fundar ⟨1a⟩ **1** v/t fig base (*en* on) **2** v/r **fundarse** be based (*en* on)

fundición f smelting; (*fábrica*) foundry

fundir ⟨3a⟩ **1** v/t *hielo* melt; *metal* smelt; COM merge **2** v/r **fundirse** melt; *de bombilla* fuse; *de plomos* blow; COM merge; *L.Am. fig: de empresa* go under

fúnebre adj funeral atr; *fig: ambiente* gloomy

funeral m funeral

funeraria f funeral parlo(u)r, *Br* undertaker's

funesto adj disastrous

funicular m funicular; (*teleférico*) cable car

furcia f P whore P

furgón m van; FERR boxcar, *Br* goods van; **furgón de equipajes** baggage car, *Br* luggage van

furgoneta f van

furia f fury; **ponerse hecho una furia** go into a fury o rage

furibundo adj furious

furioso adj furious

furor m: **hacer furor** fig be all the rage F

furtivo adj furtive

fuselaje m fuselage

fusible m EL fuse

fusil m rifle

fusilar ⟨1a⟩ v/t shoot; *fig* F (*plagiar*) lift F

fusión f FÍS fusion; COM merger

fusionar ⟨1a⟩ **1** v/t COM merge **2** v/r **fusionarse** merge

fusta f riding crop

fútbol m soccer, *Br* football; **fútbol americano** football, *Br* American football; **fútbol sala** five-a-side soccer (*Br* football)

futbolín m Foosball®, table football

futbolista m/f soccer player, *Br* footballer, *Br* football player

fútil adj trivial

futre m *Chi* dandy

futuro 1 adj future atr **2** m future

futurólogo m, **-a** f futurologist

G

g. *abr* (= *gramo* (*s*)) gr(s) (= gram(s))
gabardina *f prenda* raincoat; *material* gabardine
gabinete *m* (*despacho*) office; *en una casa* study; POL cabinet; *L.Am. de médico* office, *Br* surgery
gacela *f* ZO gazelle
gaceta *f* gazette
gachas *fpl* porridge *sg*
gachupín *m Méx desp* Spaniard
gacilla *f C.Am.* safety pin
gafas *fpl* glasses; ***gafas de sol*** sunglasses
gafe 1 *adj* jinxed **2** *m* jinx **3** *m/f*: ***es un gafe*** he's jinxed
gaita *f* MÚS bagpipes *pl*
gajes *mpl*: ***gajes del oficio*** *iron* occupational hazard
gajo *m* segment
gala *f* gala; ***traje de gala*** formal dress
galante *adj* gallant
galápago *m* ZO turtle
galardonar ⟨1a⟩ *v/t*: ***fue galardonado con*** … he was awarded …
galaxia *f* galaxy
galería *f* gallery; ***galería de arte*** art gallery
Gales Wales
galés Welsh
galgo *m* greyhound
gallera *f L.Am.* cockpit
galleta *f* cookie, *Br* biscuit
gallina 1 *f* hen **2** *m* F chicken
gallinazo *m L.Am.* turkey buzzard
gallo *m* rooster, *Br* cock
galón *m adorno* braid; MIL stripe; *medida* gallon
galope *m* gallop
galpón *m L.Am.* large shed; *W.I.* HIST slave quarters *pl*
gama *f* range
gamba *f* ZO GASTR shrimp, *Br* prawn
gamberro *m*, **-a** *f* troublemaker
gamín *m*, **-ina** *f Col* street kid
gamo *m* ZO fallow deer
gamonal *m Pe, Bol desp* chief
gamuza *f* chamois
gana *f*: ***de mala gana*** unwillingly, grudgingly; ***no me da la gana*** I don't want to; … ***me da ganas de*** … makes me want to; ***tener ganas de (hacer) algo*** feel like (doing) sth
ganadería *f* stockbreeding
ganadero *m*, **-a** *f* stockbreeder
ganado *m* cattle *pl*

ganador *m* winner
ganancia *f* profit
ganar ⟨1a⟩ **1** win; *mediante el trabajo* earn **2** *v/i mediante el trabajo* earn; (*vencer*) win; (*mejorar*) improve **3** *v/r* ***ganarse*** earn; *a alguien* win over; ***ganarse la vida*** earn one's living
ganchillo *m* crochet
gancho *m* hook; *L.Am., Arg fig* F sex-appeal; ***hacer gancho*** *L.Am.* (*ayudar*) lend a hand; ***tener gancho*** F *de un grupo, una campaña* be popular; *de una persona* have that certain something
gandul *m* lazybones *sg*
gandulear ⟨1a⟩ *v/i* F loaf around F
ganga *f* bargain
gangrena *f* MED gangrene
gángster *m* gangster
ganso *m* goose; *macho* gander
garabatear ⟨1a⟩ *v/i & v/t* doodle
garabato *m* doodle
garaje *m* garage
garantía *f* guarantee
garantizar ⟨1f⟩ *v/t* guarantee
garapiña *f Cuba, Méx* pineapple squash
garbanzo *m* BOT chickpea
garbo *m al moverse* grace
gardenia *f* BOT gardenia
garete *m*: ***irse al garete*** *fig* F go to pot F
garfio *m* hook
gargajo *m* piece of phlegm
garganta *f* ANAT throat; GEOG gorge
gargantilla *f* choker
gárgaras *fpl*: ***hacer gárgaras*** gargle
garito *m* gambling den
garra *f* claw; *de ave* talon; ***caer en las garras de alguien*** *fig* fall into s.o.'s clutches, ***tener garra*** F be compelling
garrafa *f* carafe
garrafal *adj error etc* terrible
garrapata *f* ZO tick
garrote *m palo* club, stick; *tipo de ejecución* garrotte
garúa *f L.Am.* drizzle
garuar ⟨1e⟩ *v/i L.Am.* drizzle
garzón *m Rpl* (*mesero*) waiter
garza *f* ZO heron
gas *m* gas; ***gas natural*** natural gas; ***gases*** *pl* MED gas *sg*, wind *sg*; ***con gas*** sparkling, carbonated; ***sin gas*** still
gasa *f* gauze
gaseosa *f* lemonade
gasfitero *m Pe, Bol* plumber
gasoducto *m* gas pipeline

gasoil, gasóleo m oil; *para motores diesel* tic F, great F

gasolina f gas, *Br* petrol

genialidad f brilliance

gasolinera f gas station, *Br* petrol station

genio m *talento, persona* genius; *(carácter)* temper; **tener mal genio** be bad-tempered

gastar ⟨1a⟩ **1** v/t *dinero* spend; *energía, electricidad etc* use; *(llevar)* wear; *(desperdiciar)* waste; *(desgastar)* wear out; **¿qué número gastas?** what size do you take?, what size are you? **2** v/r **gastarse** *dinero* spend; *gasolina, agua* run out of; *pila* run down; *ropa, zapatos* wear out

genital adj genital

genitales mpl genitals

genocidio m genocide

gente f people pl; *L.Am. (persona)* person

gentileza f kindness; **por gentileza de** by courtesy of

gasto m expense

gastronomía f gastronomy

gata f (female) cat; *Méx* servant, maid; **a gatas** F on all fours; **andar a gatas** F crawl

gentío m crowd

genuino adj genuine, real

geografía f geography

geográfico adj geographical

gatear ⟨1a⟩ v/i crawl

geología f geology

gatillo m trigger

geológico adj geological

gato m cat; AUTO jack; **aquí hay gato encerrado** F there's something fishy going on here F; **cuatro gatos** a handful of people

geólogo m, -a f geologist

geometría f geometry

geométrico adj geometric(al)

geranio m BOT geranium

gaucho m *Rpl* gaucho

gerente m/f manager

gaviota f (sea)gull

geriatría f geriatrics sg

gay **1** adj gay **2** m gay (man)

germen m germ

gazpacho m gazpacho (*cold soup made with tomatoes, peppers, garlic etc*)

germinar ⟨1a⟩ v/i tb fig germinate

gerundio m GRAM gerund

gel m gel

gestación f gestation

gelatina f gelatin(e); GASTR Jell-O®, *Br* jelly

gesticular ⟨1a⟩ v/i gesticulate

gestión f management; **gestiones** pl *(trámites)* formalities, procedure sg

gélido adj icy

gema f gem

gestionar ⟨1a⟩ v/t *trámites* take care of; *negocio* manage

gemelo **1** adj twin atr; **hermano gemelo** twin brother **2** mpl: **gemelos** twins; *de camisa* cuff links; *(prismáticos)* binoculars

gesto m *movimiento* gesture; *(expresión)* expression

gestoría f *Esp* agency offering clients help with official documents

gemido m moan, groan

Géminis m/f inv ASTR Gemini

gigante **1** adj giant atr **2** m giant

gemir ⟨3l⟩ v/i moan, groan

gilipollas m/f inv P jerk P

gen m gene

gilipollez f *Esp* V bullshit V

genealógico adj: **árbol genealógico** family tree

gimnasia f gymnastics; **hacer gimnasia** do exercises

generación f generation

gimnasio m gym

generador m EL generator

gimnasta m/f gymnast

general **1** adj general; **en general** in general; **por lo general** usually, generally **2** m general

gimotear ⟨1a⟩ v/i whine, whimper

ginebra f gin

generalización f generalization

ginecólogo m, -a f gyn(a)ecologist

generalizar ⟨1f⟩ **1** v/t spread **2** v/i generalize **3** v/r **generalizarse** spread

gin-tonic m gin and tonic, G and T F

gira f tour

generalmente adv generally

girar ⟨1a⟩ **1** v/i *(dar vueltas, torcer)* turn; *alrededor de algo* revolve; *fig (tratar)* revolve (**en torno a** around) **2** v/t COM transfer

generar ⟨1a⟩ v/t generate

género m *(tipo)* type; *de literatura* genre; GRAM gender; COM goods pl, merchandise

generosidad f generosity

girasol m BOT sunflower

generoso adj generous

giro m turn; GRAM idiom; **giro postal** COM money order

genética f genetics

gis m *L.Am.* chalk

genético adj genetic

gitano **1** adj gypsy atr **2** m, -a f gypsy

genial adj brilliant; F *(estupendo)* fantastic

glacial adj icy

glaciar m glacier

glándula f ANAT gland

global adj (de todo el mundo) global; vi-sión, resultado overall; cantidad total

globo m aerostático, de niño balloon; te-rrestre globe; **globo terráqueo** globe

gloria f glory; (delicia) delight; **estar en la gloria** F be in seventh heaven

gloriado m Pe, Bol, Ecuad type of punch

glorieta f traffic circle, Br roundabout

glorioso adj glorious

glosario m glossary

glotón 1 adj greedy 2 m, **-ona** f glutton

glucosa f glucose

gnomo m gnome

gobernador m governor

gobernante m leader

gobernar ⟨1k⟩ v/t & v/i rule, govern

gobierno m government

goce m pleasure, enjoyment

gofre m waffle

gol m DEP goal

goleador m DEP (goal-)scorer

golf m DEP golf

golfista m/f golfer

golfo 1 m GEOG gulf **2** m, **-a** f good-for--nothing; niño little devil

Golfo de México m Gulf of Mexico

golondrina f ZO swallow

golosina f candy, Br sweet

goloso adj sweet-toothed

golpe m knock, blow; **golpe de Estado** coup d'état; **de golpe** suddenly; **no da golpe** F she doesn't do a thing

golpear ⟨1a⟩ v/t cosa bang, hit; persona hit

goma f (caucho) rubber; (pegamento) glue; (banda elástica) rubber band; F (preservativo) condom, rubber P; C.Am. (resaca) hangover; **goma (de borrar)** eraser; **goma espuma** foam rub-ber

gomina f hair gel

gominola f jelly bean

góndola f Chi bus

gong m gong

gordinflón m, **-ona** f F fatso F

gordo 1 adj fat; **me cae gordo** F I can't stand him; **se va a armar la -a** all hell will break loose F **2** m, **-a** f fat person **3** m pre-mio jackpot

gorila m ZO gorilla

gorjeo m de pájaro chirping, warbling; de niño gurgling

gorra f cap; **de gorra** F for free F

gorrino m fig pig

gorrión m ZO sparrow

gorro m cap; **estar hasta el gorro de algo** F be fed up to the back teeth with sth F

gorrón m, **-ona** f F scrounger

gorronear ⟨1a⟩ v/t & v/i F scrounge F

gota f drop; **ni gota** F de cerveza, leche etc not a drop; de pan not a scrap

gotear ⟨1a⟩ v/i drip; filtrarse leak

gotera f leak; (mancha) stain

gotero m MED drip; L.Am. (eye)dropper

gozar ⟨1f⟩ v/i (disfrutar) enjoy o.s.; **gozar de** (disfrutar de) enjoy; (poseer) have, enjoy

gozo m (alegría) joy; (placer) pleasure

grabación f recording

grabado m engraving

grabadora f tape recorder

grabar ⟨1a⟩ v/t record, video etc record; PINT, fig engrave

gracia f: **tener gracia** (ser divertido) be funny; (tener encanto) be graceful; **me hace gracia** I think it's funny, it makes me laugh; **no le veo la gracia** I don't think it's funny; **dar las gracias a al-guien** thank s.o.; **gracias** thank you

grácil adj graceful

gracioso adj funny

gradas fpl DEP stands, grandstand sg

graderío m stands pl

grado m degree; **de buen grado** with good grace, readily

graduación f TÉC etc adjustment; de alco-hol alcohol content; EDU graduation; MIL rank

gradual adj gradual

gradualmente adv gradually

graduarse ⟨1e⟩ v/r graduate, get one's de-gree

gráfica f graph

gráfico 1 adj graphic; **artes -as** graphic arts **2** m MAT graph; INFOR graphic

gragea f tablet, pill

grajo m ZO rook

Gral. abr (= **General**) Gen (= General)

gramática f grammar

gramatical adj grammatical

gramo m gram

gran short form of **grande** before a noun

granada f BOT pomegranate; **granada de mano** MIL hand grenade

granangular m wide-angle lens

granate adj dark crimson

Gran Bretaña f Great Britain

grande 1 adj big; **a lo grande** in style **2** m/f L.Am. (adulto) grown-up, adult; (mayor) eldest; **pasarlo en grande** F have a great time

grandeza f greatness

grandiosidad f grandeur

grandioso adj impressive, magnificent

granel m: **vender a granel** COM sell in bulk; **había comida a granel** F there

was loads of food F
granero m granary
granito m granite
granizada f hailstorm
granizado m type of soft drink made with crushed ice
granizar ⟨1f⟩ v/i hail
granizo m hail
granja f farm
granjearse ⟨1a⟩ v/r win, earn
granjero m, **-a** f farmer
grano m grain; de café bean; en la piel pimple, spot; **ir al grano** get (straight) to the point
granuja m rascal
grapa f staple
grapadora f stapler
grapar ⟨1a⟩ v/t staple
grasa f BIO, GASTR fat; lubricante, suciedad grease
grasiento adj greasy, oily
graso adj greasy; carne fatty
gratificación f gratification
gratificar ⟨1g⟩ v/t reward
gratinar ⟨1a⟩ v/t cook au gratin
gratis adj & adv free
gratitud f gratitude
gratuito adj free
grava f gravel
gravar ⟨1a⟩ v/t tax
grave adj serious; tono grave, solemn; nota low; voz deep; **estar grave** be seriously ill
gravedad f seriousness, gravity; FÍS gravity
gravemente adv seriously
gravilla f grave
Grecia f Greece
gremio m HIST guild; fig F (oficio manual) trade; (profesión) profession
griego 1 adj Greek **2** m, **-a** f Greek
grieta f crack
grifo m adj Méx F high **2** m faucet, Br tap; Pe (gasolinera) gas station, Br petrol station
grillo m ZO cricket
grima f: **me da grima** Esp de ruido, material etc it sets my teeth on edge; de algo asqueroso it gives me the creeps F; **en grima** Pe alone
gringo m L.Am. desp gringo desp, foreigner
gripe f flu, influenza
gris adj gray, Br grey
gritar ⟨1a⟩ v/t & v/i shout, yell
griterío m shouting
grito m cry, shout; **a grito pelado** at the top of one's voice; **pedir algo a gritos** F be crying out for sth

grosella f redcurrant
grosero 1 adj rude **2** m, **-a** f rude person
grosor m thickness
grotesco adj grotesque
grúa f crane; AUTO wrecker, Br breakdown truck
grueso adj thick; persona stout
grulla f ZO crane
grumo m lump
gruñido m grunt; de perro growl
gruñir ⟨3h⟩ v/i (quejarse) grumble, moan F; de perro growl; de cerdo grunt
gruñón 1 adj F grumpy **2** m, **-ona** f F grouch
grupo m group
gruta f cave; artificial grotto
guacamol, guacamole m guacamole
guachimán m Chi watchman
guacho 1 adj S. Am. (sin casa) homeless; (huérfano) orphaned **2** m, **-a** f S. Am. sin casa homeless person; (huérfano) orphan
guadaño m Cuba, Méx small boat
guagua f W.I., Ven, Canaries bus; Pe, Bol, Chi (niño) baby
guajolote m Méx, C.Am. turkey
guanaco 1 adj L.Am. F dumb F, stupid **2** m ZO guanaco **3** m, **-a** f persona idiot
guantazo m slap
guante m glove
guantera f AUTO glove compartment
guapo adj hombre handsome, good-looking; mujer beautiful; S. Am. gutsy
guaracha f W.I. street band
guarache → huarache
guarapo m L.Am. alcoholic drink made from sugar cane and herbs
guarda m/f keeper; **guarda jurado** security guard
guardabosques m/f inv forest ranger
guardacostas m inv coastguard vessel
guardaespaldas m/f inv bodyguard
guardameta m/f inv DEP goalkeeper
guardar ⟨1a⟩ **1** v/t keep; poner en un lugar put (away); recuerdo have; apariencias keep up; INFOR save; **guardar silencio** remain silent, keep silent **2** v/r guardarse keep; **guardarse de** refrain from
guardarropa m checkroom, Br cloakroom; (ropa, armario) wardrobe
guardería f nursery
guardia 1 f guard; **de guardia** on duty; **bajar la guardia** fig lower one's guard **2** m/f MIL guard; (policía) police officer; **guardia civil** Esp civil guard; **guardia de seguridad** security guard; **guardia de tráfico** traffic warden
guardián 1 adj: **perro guardián** guard dog **2** m, **-ana** f guard; fig guardian

guarecer ⟨2d⟩ **1** v/t shelter **2** v/r **guarecerse** shelter, take shelter (**de** from)

guarida f zo den; **de personas** hideout

guarnición f GASTR accompaniment; MIL garrison

guaro m C.Am. sugar-cane liquor

guarro 1 adj F sucio filthy **2** m tb fig F pig

guarura m Méx (guardaespaldas) bodyguard; F (gamberro) thug

guasa f L.Am. joke; **de guasa** as a joke

guaso 1 adj S. Am. rude **2** m Chi peasant

guata f L.Am. F paunch

Guatemala Guatemala

guatemalteco 1 adj Guatemalan **2** m, -a f Guatemalan

guatón adj L.Am. F pot-bellied, big-bellied

guay int Esp F cool F, neat F

guayaba f L.Am. BOT guava

guayabera f Méx, C.Am., W I loose embroidered shirt

gubernamental adj governmental, government atr

guepardo m zo cheetah

güero 1 adj Méx, C.Am. fair, light-skinned **2** m, -a f Méx, C.Am. blond(e)

guerra f war; **guerra civil** civil war; **guerra fría** cold war; **guerra mundial** world war; **dar guerra a alguien** F give s.o. trouble

guerrero 1 adj warlike **2** m warrior

guerrilla f guerillas pl

guerrillero m guerilla

gueto m ghetto

guevear v/i → **huevear**

guevón → **huevón**

guía 1 m/f guide; **guía turístico** tourist guide **2** f libro guide (book); **guía telefónica** or **de teléfonos** phone book

guiar ⟨1c⟩ **1** v/t guide **2** v/r **guiarse**: **guiarse por** follow

guijarro m pebble

guillotina f guillotine

güinche m L.Am. winch, pulley

guinda 1 L.Am. purple **2** f fresca morello cherry; en dulce glacé cherry

guindilla f GASTR chil(l)i

guiñar ⟨1a⟩ v/t: **le guiñó un ojo** she winked at him

guiño m wink

guión m de película script; GRAM corto hyphen; largo dash

guionista m/f scriptwriter

guiri m Esp P (light-skinned) foreigner

guirnalda f garland

guisante m pea

guisar ⟨1a⟩ v/t GASTR stew, casserole

guiso m GASTR stew, casserole

guitarra f guitar

guitarrista m/f guitarist

gula f gluttony

gusano m worm

gustar ⟨1a⟩ v/i: **me gusta viajar** I like to travel, I like travelling; **¿te gusta el ajo?** do you like garlic?; **no me gusta** I don't like it

gusto m taste; (placer) pleasure; **a gusto** at ease; **con mucho gusto** with pleasure; **de buen gusto** in good taste, tasteful; **de mal gusto** in bad taste, tasteless; **da gusto …** it's a pleasure …; **mucho** or **tanto gusto** how do you do

gutural adj guttural

H

ha vb → **haber**

haba f broad bean; **en todas partes se cuecen habas** it's the same the world over

Habana: **La Habana** Havana

habanero m, -a f citizen of Havana

habano m Havana (cigar)

haber ⟨2k⟩ **1** v/aux have; **hemos llegado** we've arrived; **he de levantarme pronto** I have to o I've got to get up early; **de haberlo sabido** if I'd known; **has de ver** Méx you ought to see it **2** v/impers: **hay** there is sg, there are pl; **hubo un incendio** there was a fire; **¿qué hay?**, Méx **¿qué hubo?** how's it going?, what's happening?; **hay que hacerlo** it has to be done; **no hay de qué** not at all, don't mention it; **no hay más que decir** there's nothing more to be said **3** m asset; pago fee; **tiene en su haber 50.000 ptas** she's 50,000 pesetas in credit

habichuela f kidney bean

hábil adj skilled; (capaz) capable; (astuto) clever, smart

habilidad f skill; (*capacidad*) ability; (*astucia*) cleverness

habilitar ⟨1a⟩ v/t *lugar* fit out; *persona* authorize

habitación f room; (*dormitorio*) bedroom; **habitación doble / individual** double / single room

habitante m/f inhabitant

habitar ⟨1a⟩ v/i live (*en* in)

hábitat m habitat

hábito m tb REL habit; (*práctica*) knack; **colgar los hábitos** fig de sacerdote give up the priesthood

habitual 1 adj usual, regular **2** m/f regular

habituar ⟨1e⟩ v/t: **habituar a alguien a algo** get s.o. used to sth **2** v/r **habituarse: habituarse a algo** get used to sth

habla f speech; **¡al habla!** TELEC speaking; **quedarse sin habla** fig be speechless

hablada f L.Am. piece of gossip; **habladas** pl gossip sg

hablador adj talkative; *Méx* boastful

habladurías fpl gossip sg

hablante m/f speaker

hablar ⟨1a⟩ v/i speak; (*conversar*) talk; **hablar claro** fig say what one means; **hablar con alguien** talk to s.o., talk with s.o.; **hablar de** libro etc be about, deal with; **hablar por hablar** talk for the sake of it; **¡ni hablar!** no way! **2** v/r **hablarse** speak to one another; **no se hablan** they're not speaking (to each other)

hacendado 1 adj land-owing **2** m, **-a** f land-owner

hacendoso adj hardworking

hacer ⟨2s; part **hecho**⟩ **1** v/t (*realizar*) do; (*elaborar, crear*) make; **¡haz algo!** do something!; **hacer una pregunta** ask a question; **¿qué le vamos a hacer!** that's life; **no hace más que quejarse** all he does is complain; **le hicieron ir** they made him go; **tengo que hacer los deberes** I have to do my homework **2** v/i: **haces bien / mal en ir** you are doing the right / wrong thing by going; **me hace mal** it's making me ill; **esto hará de mesa** de objeto this will do as a table; **hacer como que** or **como si** act as if; **no le hace** L.Am. it doesn't matter; **se me hace qué** L.Am. it seems to me that **3** v/impers: **hace calor / frío** it's hot / cold; **hace tres días** three days ago; **hace mucho** (*tiempo*) a long time; **desde hace un año** for a year **4** v/r **hacerse** *traje* make; *casa* build o.s.; (*cocinarse*) cook; (*convertirse, volverse*) get, become; **hacerse viejo** get old; **hacerse de noche** get dark; **se hace tarde** it's getting late; **hacerse el sordo / el tonto** pretend to

be deaf / stupid; **hacerse a algo** get used to sth; **hacerse con algo** get hold of sth

hacha f ax, *Br* axe; **ser un hacha para algo** F be brilliant at sth

hachís m hashish

hacia prp toward; **hacia adelante** forward; **hacia abajo** down; **hacia arriba** up; **hacia atrás** back(ward); **hacia las cuatro** about four (o'clock)

Hacienda f ministerio Treasury Department, *Br* Treasury; oficina Internal Revenue Service, *Br* Inland Revenue

hacienda f L.Am. (*granja*) ranch, estate

hacinar ⟨1a⟩ v/t stack

hada f fairy

haga vb → **hacer**

hago vb → **hacer**

Haití Haiti

hala int come on!; *sorpresa* wow!

halagar ⟨1h⟩ v/t flatter

halago m flattery

halar ⟨1a⟩ v/t L.Am. haul, pull

halcón m zo falcon

halitosis f MED halitosis, bad breath

hall m hall

hallar ⟨1a⟩ **1** v/t find; (*descubrir*) discover; *muerte, destino* meet **2** v/r **hallarse** be; (*sentirse*) feel

hallazgo m find; (*descubrimiento*) discovery

halógeno adj halogen

halterofilia f DEP weight-lifting

hamaca f hammock; (*tumbona*) deck chair; L.Am. (*mecedora*) rocking chair

hamacar ⟨1g⟩ v/t L.Am. swing

hamaquear ⟨1a⟩ v/t L.Am. swing

hambre f hunger; **morirse de hambre** fig be starving; **pasar hambre** be starving

hambriento adj tb fig hungry (*de* for)

hambruna f famine

hamburguesa f GASTR hamburger

hamburguesería f hamburger bar

hampa f underworld

hámster m zo hamster

hangar m hangar

haragán m, **-ana** f shirker

harapo m rag

hardware m INFOR hardware

haré vb → **hacer**

harina f flour

harinoso adj floury

hartar ⟨1a⟩ **1** v/t: **hartar a alguien con algo** tire s.o. with sth; **hartar a alguien de algo** give s.o. too much of sth **2** v/r **hartarse** get sick (*de* of) F, get tired (*de* of); (*llenarse*) stuff o.s. (*de* with)

harto 1 adj fed up F; (*lleno*) full (up); **había hartos pasteles** there were cakes in abundance; **hace harto frío** L.Am. it's very cold, **estar harto de algo** be sick of sth F, be fed up with sth F **2** *adv* very much; *delante del adjetivo* extremely; *me gusta harto* L.Am. F I like it a lot

hartón 1 *adj* L.Am. greedy **2** *m*: **darse un hartón de algo** overdose on sth

has *vb* → **haber**

hasta 1 *prp* until, till; **llegó hasta Bilbao** he went as far as Bilbao; **hasta ahora** so far; **hasta aquí** up to here; **¿hasta cuándo?** how long?; **hasta que** until; **¡hasta luego!** see you (later); **¡hasta la vista!** see you (later) **2** *adv* even

hastiar ⟨1c⟩ *v/t* tire; (*aburrir*) bore

hastío *m* boredom

hatajo *m* bunch

hato *m* L.Am. bundle

hay *vb* → **haber**

haya 1 *vb* → **haber 2** *f* BOT beech

haz 1 *m* bundle; *de luz* beam **2** *vb* → **hacer**

hazaña *f* achievement

hazmerreír *m* fig F laughing stock

he *vb* → **haber**

hebilla *f* buckle

hechicero 1 *adj* bewitching, captivating **2** *m* sorcerer; *de tribu* witch-doctor

hechizado *adj* spellbound

hechizar ⟨1f⟩ *v/t* fig bewitch, captivate

hechizo *m* spell, charm

hecho 1 *part* → **hacer**; **hecho a mano** hand-made; **¡bien hecho!** well done!; **muy hecho** *carne* well-done **2** *adj* finished; **un hombre hecho y derecho** a fully grown man **3** *m* fact; **de hecho** in fact

hectárea *f* hectare (*10,000 sq m*)

hedor *m* stink, stench

helada *f* frost

heladera *f* Rpl fridge

heladería *f* ice-cream parlo(u)r

helado 1 *adj* frozen; *fig* icy; **quedarse helado** be stunned **2** *m* ice cream

helar ⟨1k⟩ **1** *v/t* freeze **2** *v/i* freeze; **anoche heló** there was a frost last night **3** *v/r* **helarse** *tb* fig freeze

helecho *m* BOT fern

hélice *f* propeller

helicóptero *m* helicopter

hematoma *m* bruise

hembra *f* ZO, TÉC female

hemiplejía *f* MED hemiplegia

hemisferio *m* hemisphere

hemofilia *f* MED h(a)emophilia

hemorragia *f* MED h(a)emorrhage, bleeding

hemorroides *fpl* MED h(a)emorrhoids, piles

hendidura *f* crack

heno *m* hay

hepatitis *f* MED hepatitis

herbicida *m* herbicide, weed-killer

herboristería *f* herbalist

hercúleo *adj* Herculean

heredar ⟨1a⟩ *v/t* inherit (**de** from)

heredera *f* heiress

heredero *m* heir

hereditario *adj* hereditary

hereje *m* heretic

herencia *f* inheritance

herida *f* *de arma* wound; (*lesión*) injury; *mujer* wounded woman; *mujer lesionada* injured woman

herido 1 *adj* *de arma* wounded; (*lesionado*) injured **2** *m de bala* wounded man; (*lesionado*) injured man

herir ⟨3i⟩ *v/t con arma* wound; (*lesionar*) injure; *fig* (*ofender*) hurt

hermana *f* sister

hermanastra *f* stepsister

hermanastro *m* stepbrother

hermano *m* brother

hermético *adj* airtight, hermetic; *fig: persona* inscrutable

hermoso *adj* beautiful

hernia *f* MED hernia

héroe *m* hero

heroico *adj* heroic

heroína *f* *mujer* heroine; *droga* heroin

heroinómano *m*, *-a* *f* heroin addict

herpes *m* MED herpes

herradura *f* horseshoe

herramienta *f* tool

hervidero *m* fig hotbed

hervido *m* S. Am. stew

hervir ⟨3i⟩ **1** *v/i* boil; *fig* swarm, seethe (**de** with) **2** *v/t* boil

heterodoxo *adj* unorthodox

heterogéneo *adj* heterogeneous

hez *f* scum, dregs *pl*

hibernar ⟨1a⟩ *v/i* hibernate

híbrido 1 *adj* hybrid *atr* **2** *m* hybrid

hice *vb* → **hacer**

hicimos *vb* → **hacer**

hidratante *adj* moisturizing; **crema hidratante** moisturizing cream

hidratar ⟨1a⟩ *v/t* hydrate; *piel* moisturize

hidrato *m*: **hidrato de carbono** carbohydrate

hidráulico *adj* hydraulic

hidroavión *m* seaplane

hidroeléctrico *adj* hydroelectric

hidrógeno *m* hydrogen

hiedra *f* BOT ivy

hielo *m* ice; **romper el hielo** *fig* break the ice

hiena *f* ZO hyena

hierba *f* grass; **mala hierba** weed

hiere *vb* → **herir**

hierro *m* iron

hierve *vb* → **hervir**

hígado *m* liver; **ser un hígado** *C.Am.*, *Méx* F be a pain in the butt F

higiene *f* hygiene

higiénico *adj* hygienic

higo *m* BOT fig

higuera *f* BOT fig tree

hija *f* daughter

hijastra *f* stepdaughter

hijastro *m* stepson

hijo *m* son; **hijos** children *pl*; **hijo de puta** P son of a bitch V, bastard P; **hijo único** only child

hilachos *mpl Méx* rags

hilera *f* row, line

hilo *m* thread; **hilo dental** dental floss; **sin hilos** TELEC cordless; **colgar** *o* **pender de un hilo** *fig* hang by a thread; **perder el hilo** *fig* lose the thread

himno *m* hymn; **himno nacional** national anthem

hincapié *m*: **hacer hincapié** put special emphasis (**en** on)

hincar ⟨1g⟩ **1** *v/t* thrust, stick (**en** into); **hincar el diente** F sink one's teeth (**en** into) **2** *v/r* **hincarse**: **hincarse de rodillas** kneel down

hincha *m* F fan, supporter

hinchado *adj* swollen

hinchar ⟨1a⟩ **1** *v/t* inflate, blow up; *Rpl* P annoy **2** *v/r* **hincharse** MED swell; *fig* stuff o.s (**de** with); (*mostrarse orgulloso*) swell with pride

hinchazón *f* swelling

hiperactivo *adj* hyperactive

hipermercado *m* hypermarket

hipertensión *f* MED high blood pressure, hypertension

hipertexto *m* hypertext

hípico *adj* equestrian; **concurso hípico** show-jumping event; **carrera -a** horse race

hipnosis *f* hypnosis

hipnotizar ⟨1f⟩ *v/t* hypnotize

hipo *m* hiccups *pl*, hiccoughs *pl*; **quitar el hipo** F take one's breath away

hipocondríaco 1 *adj* hypochondriac **2** *m*, **-a** *f* hypochondriac

hipocresía *f* hypocrisy

hipócrita 1 *adj* hypocritical **2** *m/f* hypocrite

hipódromo *m* racetrack

hipopótamo *m* ZO hippopotamus

hipoteca *f* COM mortgage

hipotecar ⟨1g⟩ *v/t* COM mortgage; *fig* compromise

hipótesis *f* hypothesis

hipotético *adj* hypothetical

hispánico *adj* Hispanic

hispano 1 *adj* (*español*) Spanish; (*hispanohablante*) Spanish-speaking; *en EE.UU.* Hispanic **2** *m*, **-a** *f* (*español*) Spaniard; (*hispanohablante*) Spanish speaker; *en EE.UU.* Hispanic

hispanohablante *adj* Spanish-speaking

histeria *f* hysteria

histérico *adj* hysterical

historia *f* history; (*cuento*) story; **una historia de drogas** F some drugs business; **déjate de historias** F stop making excuses

historiador *m*, **historiadora** *f* historian

historial *m* record

histórico *adj* historical; (*importante*) historic

historieta *f* anecdote; (*viñetas*) comic strip

hito *m tb fig* milestone

hizo *vb* → **hacer**

Hnos. *abr* (= **Hermanos**) Bros (= Brothers)

hobby *m* hobby

hocico *m* snout; *de perro* muzzle

hockey *m* field hockey, *Br* hockey; **hockey sobre hielo** hockey, *Br* ice hockey

hogar *m fig* home

hogareño *adj* home *atr*; *persona* home-loving

hoguera *f* bonfire

hoja *f* BOT leaf; *de papel* sheet; *de libro* page; *de cuchillo* blade; **hoja de afeitar** razor blade; **hoja de cálculo** INFOR spreadsheet

hojalata *f* tin

hojaldre *m* GASTR puff pastry

hojear ⟨1a⟩ *v/t* leaf through, flip through

hola *int* hello, hi F

Holanda Holland

holandés 1 *adj* Dutch **2** *m* Dutchman

holandesa *f* Dutchwoman

holding *m* holding company

holgado *adj* loose, comfortable; **estar holgado de tiempo** have time to spare

holgazán *m* idler

holgazanear ⟨1a⟩ *v/i* laze around

holgura *f* ease; *de ropa* looseness; TÉC play; **vivir con holgura** live comfortably

hollín *m* soot

holocausto *m* holocaust

hombre *m* man; **el hombre** (*la humanidad*) man, mankind; **hombre lobo** werewolf; **hombre de negocios** businessman; **hombre rana** frogman; *¡claro, hombre!* you bet!, sure thing!; *¡hombre, qué alegría!* that's great!

hombro *m* shoulder; **hombro con hombro** shoulder to shoulder; **encogerse**

de hombros shrug (one's shoulders)
homenaje *m* homage; **rendir homenaje a alguien** pay tribute to s.o.
homeopatía *f* hom(o)eopathy
homicidio *m* homicide
homogéneo *adj* homogenous
homologación *f* approval; *de título, diploma* official recognition
homólogo *m*, **-a** *f* counterpart, opposite number
homosexual *m/f & adj* homosexual
hondo *adj* deep
Honduras Honduras
hondureño 1 *adj* Honduran **2** *m*, **-a** *f* Honduran
honesto *adj* hono(u)rable, decent
hongo *m* fungus
honor *m* hono(u)r; **en honor a** in hono(u)r of; **hacer honor a** live up to; **palabra de honor** word of hono(u)r
honorarios *mpl* fees
honra *f* hono(u)r; **¡a mucha honra!** I'm hono(u)red
honradez *f* honesty
honrado *adj* honest
hora *f* hour; **horas** *pl* **extraordinarias** overtime *sg*; **hora local** local time; **hora punta** rush hour; **a la hora de ...** figwhen it comes to ...; **a última hora** at the last minute; **¡ya era hora!** about time too!; **tengo hora con el dentista** I have an appointment with the dentist; **¿qué hora es?** what time is it?
horario *m* schedule, *Br* timetable; **horario comercial** business hours *pl*; **horario flexible** flextime, *Br* flexitime; **horario de trabajo** (working) hours *pl*
horca *f* gallows *pl*
horcajadas *fpl*: **a horcajadas** astride
horchata *f* drink made from tiger-nuts
horda *f* horde
horizontal *adj* horizontal
horizonte *m* horizon
hormiga *f* ant
hormigón *m* concrete; **hormigón armado** reinforced concrete
hormigueo *m* pins and needles *pl*
hormiguero *m* ant hill; **la sala era un hormiguero de gente** the hall was swarming with people
hormona *f* hormone
hornilla *f* ring
horno *m* oven; *de cerámica* kiln; **alto horno** blast furnace
horóscopo *m* horoscope
horqueta *f* *L.Am. de camino* fork
horquilla *f* *para pelo* hairpin
horrendo *adj* horrendous
horrible *adj* horrible, dreadful

horripilante *adj* horrible
horror *m* horror (**a** of); **tener horror a** be terrified of; **me gusta horrores** F I like it a lot; **¡qué horror!** how awful!
horrorizar ⟨1f⟩ *v/t* horrify
horroroso *adj* terrible; *(de mala calidad)* dreadful; *(feo)* hideous
hortaliza *f* vegetable
hortensia *f* BOT hydrangea
hortera 1 F *adj* tacky F **2** *m/f* F tacky person F
horterada *f* F tacky thing F; **es una horterada** it's tacky F
horticultor *m*, **horticultora** *f* horticulturist
horticultura *f* horticulture
hosco *adj* sullen
hospedaje *m* accommodations *pl*, *Br* accommodation; **dar hospedaje a alguien** put s.o. up
hospedarse ⟨1a⟩ *v/r* stay (**en** at)
hospital *m* hospital
hospitalario *adj* hospitable; MED hospital *atr*
hospitalidad *f* hospitality
hospitalizar ⟨1f⟩ *v/t* hospitalize
hostal *m* hostel
hostelera *f* landlady
hostelería *f* hotel industry
hostelero 1 *adj* hotel *atr* **2** *m* landlord
hostia *f* REL host; P *(golpe)* sock F, wallop F; **¡hostias!** P Christ! P
hostigar ⟨1h⟩ *v/t* pester; MIL harass; *caballo* whip
hostil *adj* hostile
hostilidad *f* hostility
hotel *m* hotel
hotelero *m*, **-a** *f* hotelier
hoy *adv* today; **de hoy** of today; **los padres de hoy** today's parents, parents today; **de hoy en adelante** from now on; **por hoy** for today; **hoy por hoy** at the present time; **hoy en día** nowadays
hoya *f* hole; *de tumba* grave; GEOG plain; *S. Am.* river basin
hoyo *m* hole; *(depresión)* hollow
hoyuelo *m* dimple
hoz *f* sickle
huachafo *adj* *Pe (cursi)* affected, pretentious
huarache *m* *Méx* rough sandal
huayno *m* *Pe, Bol* Andean dance rhythm
hubo *vb* → **haber**
hucha *f* money box
hueco 1 *adj* hollow; *(vacío)* empty; *fig*: *persona* shallow **2** *m* gap; *(agujero)* hole; *de ascensor* shaft
huele *vb* → **oler**
huelga *f* strike; **huelga de celo** work-to-

rule; **huelga general** general strike;
huelga de hambre hunger strike; **declararse en huelga, ir a la huelga** go on
strike

huelguista *m/f* striker

huella *f* mark; *de animal*: track; **huellas dactilares** finger prints

huelo *vb* → **oler**

huérfano 1 *adj* orphan *atr* **2** *m*, **-a** *f* orphan

huero *adj fig* empty; *L.Am.* blond

huerta *f* truck farm, *Br* market garden

huerto *m* kitchen garden; **llevar a alguien al huerto** F put one over on s.o. F

huesear ⟨1a⟩ *v/t C.Am.* beg

huesillo *m S. Am.* sun-dried peach

hueso *m* bone; *de fruta* pit, stone; *persona* tough nut; *Méx* F cushy number F; *Méx* F **duro de roer** *fig* F hard nut to crack; **estar en los huesos** be all skin and bone

huésped *m/f* guest

huesudo *adj* bony

huevas *fpl* roe *sg*

huevear ⟨1a⟩ *v/i Chi* P mess around F

huevo *m* egg; P *(testículo)* ball V; **huevo duro** hard-boiled egg; **huevo escalfado** poached egg; **huevo frito** fried egg; **huevo pasado por agua** soft-boiled egg; **huevos revueltos** scrambled eggs; **un huevo de** P a load of F

huevón *m*, **-ona** *f Chi* P idiot; *L.Am.* F *(flojo)* idler F

huida *f* flight, escape

huir ⟨3g⟩ *v/i* flee, escape *(de* from); **huir de algo** avoid sth

hulado *m C.Am., Méx* rubberized cloth

hule *m* oilcloth; *L.Am. (caucho)* rubber

humanidad *f* humanity; **humanidades** humanities

humanismo *m* humanism

humanitario *adj* humanitarian

humanizar ⟨1f⟩ *v/t* humanize

humano *adj* human

humareda *f* cloud of smoke

humear ⟨1a⟩ *v/i con humo* smoke; *con vapor* steam

humedad *f* humidity; *de una casa* damp (-ness)

humedecer ⟨2d⟩ *v/t* dampen

húmedo *adj* humid; *toalla* damp

humildad *f* humility

humilde *adj* humble; *(sin orgullo)* modest; *clase social* lowly

humillación *f* humiliation

humillante *adj* humiliating

humillar ⟨1a⟩ *v/t* humiliate

humita *f S. Am. meat and corn paste wrapped in leaves*

humo *m* smoke; *(vapor)* steam; **tener muchos humos** F be a real bighead F

humor *m* humo(u)r; **estar de buen / mal humor** be in a good / bad mood; **sentido del humor** sense of humo(u)r

humorista *m/f* humo(u)rist; *(cómico)* comedian

humus *m* GASTR hummus

hundido *adj fig: persona* depressed

hundir ⟨3a⟩ **1** *v/t* sink; *fig: empresa* ruin, bring down; *persona* devastate **2** *v/r* **hundirse** sink; *fig: de empresa* collapse; *de persona* go to pieces

húngaro 1 *adj* Hungarian **2** *m*, **-a** *f* Hungarian

Hungría Hungary

huracán *m* hurricane

huraño *adj* unsociable

hurgar ⟨1h⟩ **1** *v/i* rummage *(en* in) **2** *v/r* **hurgarse: hurgarse la nariz** pick one's nose

hurón *m* zo ferret

hurtadillas *fpl*: **a hurtadillas** furtively

hurtar ⟨1a⟩ *v/t* steal

hurto *m* theft

husmear ⟨1a⟩ *v/i* F nose around F *(en* in)

huy *int sorpresa* wow!; *dolor* ouch!

huyo *vb* → **huir**

I

I+D *abr (= investigación y desarrollo)* R&D (= research and development)

iba *vb* → **ir**

ibérico *adj* Iberian

iberoamericano *adj* Latin American

iceberg *m* iceberg

icono *m tb* INFOR icon

ida *f* outward journey; *(billete de)* **ida y vuelta** round trip (ticket), *Br* return (ticket)

idea *f* idea; **hacerse a la idea de que ...** get used to the idea that ...; **no tener ni**

idea not have a clue
ideal *m/adj* ideal
idealista 1 *adj* idealistic **2** *m/f* idealist
idear *v/t* ⟨1a⟩ think up, come up with
idéntico *adj* identical
identidad *f* identity
identificación *f* identification
identificar ⟨1g⟩ **1** *v/t* identify **2** *v/r* **identificarse** identify o.s.
ideología *f* ideology
idílico *adj* idyllic
idilio *m* idyll; (*relación amorosa*) romance
idioma *m* language
idiota 1 *adj* idiotic **2** *m/f* idiot
idiotez *f* stupid thing to say / do
ido 1 *part* → **ir 2** *adj* (*chiflado*) nuts F; **estar ido** be miles away F
idolatrar ⟨1a⟩ *v/t tb fig* worship
ídolo *m tb fig* idol
idóneo *adj* suitable
iglesia *f* church
ignominioso *adj* ignominious
ignorancia *f* ignorance
ignorante *adj* ignorant
ignorar ⟨1a⟩ *v/t* not know, be not aware of; **ignoro cómo sucedió** I don't know how it happened
igual 1 *adj* (*idéntico*) same (**a, que** as); (*proporcionado*) equal (**a** to); (*constante*) constant; **al igual que** like, the same as; **me da igual** I don't mind **2** *m/f* equal; **no tener igual** have no equal
igualado *adj* even
igualar ⟨1a⟩ **1** *v/t precio, marca* equal, match; (*nivelar*) level off; **igualar algo** MAT make sth equal (**con, a** to) **2** *v/i* DEP tie the game, *Br* equalize
igualdad *f* equality; **igualdad de oportunidades** equal opportunities
igualitario *adj* egalitarian
igualmente *adv* equally
iguana *f* zo iguana
ilegal *adj* illegal
ilegible *adj* illegible
ilegítimo *adj* unlawful; *hijo* illegitimate
ileso *adj* unhurt
ilícito *adj* illicit
ilimitado *adj* unlimited
Ilmo. *abr* (= **ilustrísimo**) His / Your Excellency
ilógico *adj* illogical
iluminación *f* illumination
iluminar ⟨1a⟩ *v/t edificio, calle etc* light, illuminate; *monumento* light up, illuminate; *fig* light up
ilusión *f* illusion; (*deseo, esperanza*) hope
ilusionarse ⟨1a⟩ *v/r* get one's hopes up; (*entusiasmarse*) get excited (**con** about)
ilustración *f* illustration

ilustrar ⟨1a⟩ *v/t* illustrate; (*aclarar*) explain
ilustre *adj* illustrious
imagen *f tb fig* image; **ser la viva imagen de** be the spitting image of
imaginable *adj* imaginable
imaginación *f* imagination
imaginar ⟨1a⟩ **1** *v/t* imagine **2** *v/r* **imaginarse** imagine; **¡ya me lo imagino!** I can just imagine it!
imaginativo *adj* imaginative
imán *m* magnet
imbatible *adj* unbeatable
imbécil 1 *adj* stupid **2** *m/f* idiot, imbecile
imbecilidad *f* stupidity; **¡qué imbecilidad decir eso!** what a stupid thing to say!
imitación *f* imitation
imitar ⟨1a⟩ *v/t* imitate
impaciencia *f* impatience
impacientar ⟨1a⟩ **1** *v/t* make impatient **2** *v/r* **impacientarse** lose (one's) patience
impaciente *adj* impatient
impactar ⟨1a⟩ *v/t* hit; (*impresionar*) have an impact on
impacto *m tb fig* impact; **impacto de bala** bullet wound; **impacto ecológico** ecological
impar *adj número* odd
imparcial *adj* impartial
imparcialidad *f* impartiality
impasible *adj* impassive
impávido *adj* fearless, undaunted
impecable *adj* impeccable
impedimento *m* impediment
impedir ⟨3l⟩ *v/t* prevent; (*estorbar*) impede
imperante *adj* ruling; *fig* prevailing
imperar ⟨1a⟩ *v/i* rule; *fig* prevail
imperativo 1 *adj* GRAM imperative; *obligación* pressing **2** *m* GRAM imperative
imperdible *m* safety pin
imperdonable *adj* unpardonable, unforgivable
imperfecto *m/adj* imperfect
imperial *adj* imperial
imperio *m* empire
imperioso *adj necesidad* pressing; *persona* imperious
impermeable 1 *adj* waterproof **2** *m* raincoat
impersonal *adj* impersonal
impertérrito *adj* unperturbed, unmoved
impertinente 1 *adj* impertinent **2** *m/f*: **¡eres un impertinente!** you've got nerve! F, *Br* you've got a cheek! F
ímpetu *m* impetus
impetuoso *adj* impetuous
implacable *adj* implacable

implemento *m* implement

implicar ⟨1g⟩ *v/t* mean, imply; (*involucrar*) involve; **en un delito** implicate (**en** in)

implícito *adj* implicit

implorar ⟨1a⟩ *v/t* beg for

imponente *adj* impressive, imposing; F terrific

imponer ⟨2r⟩ **1** *v/t* impose; *miedo, respeto* inspire; *impuesto* impose, levy **2** *v/i* be imposing *o* impressive **3** *v/r* **imponerse** (*hacerse respetar*) assert o.s.; DEP win; (*prevalecer*) prevail; (*ser necesario*) be imperative; **imponerse una tarea** set o.s. a task

importación *f* import, importation; *artículo* import

importancia *f* importance; **dar importancia a** attach importance to; **darse importancia** give o.s. airs; **tener importancia** be important

importante *adj* important

importar ⟨1a⟩ *v/i* matter; **no importa** it doesn't matter; **eso a ti no te importa** that's none of your business; **¿qué importa?** what does it matter?; **¿le importa ...?** do you mind ...?

importe *m* amount; (*coste*) cost

importuno *adj* inopportune

imposibilitar ⟨1a⟩ *v/t*: **imposibilitar algo** make sth impossible, prevent sth

imposible *adj* impossible

impostor *m*, **impostora** *f* impostor

impotencia *f* impotence, helplessness; MED impotence

impotente *adj* helpless, powerless, impotent; MED impotent

impreciso *adj* imprecise

impredecible *adj* unpredictable

impregnar ⟨1a⟩ *v/t* saturate (**de** with); TÉC impregnate (**de** with)

imprenta *f taller* printer's; *arte, técnica* printing; *máquina* printing press

imprescindible *adj* essential; *persona* indispensable

impresión *f* impression; *acto* printing; (*tirada*) print run; **la sangre le da impresión** he can't stand the sight of blood

impresionante *adj* impressive

impresionar ⟨1a⟩ *v/t*: **impresionarle a alguien** impress s.o.; (*conmover*) move s.o.; (*alterar*) shock s.o.

impresionismo *m* impressionism

impreso *m* form; **impresos** *pl* printed matter *sg*

impresora *f* INFOR printer; **impresora de chorro de tinta** inkjet (printer); **impresora de inyección de tinta** inkjet (printer); **impresora láser** laser (printer)

imprevisible *adj* unpredictable

imprevisto 1 *adj* unforeseen, unexpected **2** *m* unexpected event

imprimir ⟨3a⟩ *v/t tb* INFOR print; *fig* transmit

improbable *adj* unlikely, improbable

improcedente *adj* improper

improductivo *adj* unproductive

impropio *adj* inappropriate

improvisar ⟨1a⟩ *v/t* improvise

improviso *adj*: **de improviso** unexpectedly

imprudencia *f* recklessness, rashness

imprudente *adj* reckless, rash

impuesto *m* tax; **impuesto sobre el valor añadido** sales tax, *Br* value-added tax; **impuesto sobre la renta** income tax

impugnar ⟨1a⟩ *v/t* challenge

impulsar ⟨1a⟩ *v/t* TÉC propel; COM boost

impulsivo *adj* impulsive

impulso *m* impulse; (*empuje*) impetus; COM boost; *fig* urge, impulse; **tomar impulso** take a run up

impunidad *f* impunity

impureza *f* impurity

imputar ⟨1a⟩ *v/t* attribute

inacabable *adj* endless, never-ending

inaccesible *adj* inaccessible

inaceptable *adj* unacceptable

inactivo *adj* inactive

inadaptado *adj* maladjusted

inadecuado *adj* inadequate

inadmisible *adj* inadmissible

inadvertido *adj*: **pasar inadvertido** go unnoticed

inagotable *adj* inexhaustible

inaguantable *adj* unbearable

inalámbrico 1 *adj* TELEC cordless **2** *m* TELEC cordless telephone

inamovible *adj* immovable

inanición *f* starvation

inapreciable *adj* (*valioso*) priceless; (*insignificante*) negligible

inaudito *adj* unprecedented

inauguración *f* official opening, inauguration

inaugurar ⟨1a⟩ *v/t* (officially) open, inaugurate

inca *m/f & adj* HIST Inca

incalculable *adj* incalculable

incalificable *adj* indescribable

incandescente *adj* incandescent

incansable *adj* tireless

incapacidad *f* disability; (*falta de capacidad*) inability; (*ineptitud*) incompetence

incapacitar ⟨1a⟩ *v/t* JUR disqualify

incapaz *adj* incapable (**de** of)

incautarse ⟨1a⟩ v/r: **incautarse de** seize
incauto adj unwary
incendiar ⟨1b⟩ **1** v/t set fire to **2** v/r **incendiarse** burn
incendio m fire; **incendio forestal** forest fire
incentivo m incentive
incertidumbre f uncertainty
incesante adj incessant
incesto m incest
incidencia f (efecto) effect; (frecuencia) incidence; (incidente) incident
incidente m incident
incidir ⟨3a⟩ v/i: **incidir en** (afectar) have an effect on, affect; (recalcar) stress; **incidir en un error** make a mistake
incienso m incense
incierto m uncertain
incineración f de cadáver cremation
incinerador adj incinerator
incinerar ⟨1a⟩ v/t incinerate; cadáver cremate
incipiente adj incipient
incitante adj provocative
incitar ⟨1a⟩ v/t incite
inclemencia f del tiempo inclemency
inclinación f inclination; de un terreno slope; muestra de respeto bow; fig tendency
inclinar ⟨1a⟩ **1** v/t tilt; **inclinar la cabeza** nod (one's head); **me inclina a creer que ...** it makes me think that ... **2** v/r **inclinarse** bend (down); de un terreno slope; desde la vertical lean; en señal de respeto bow; **inclinarse a** fig tend to, be inclined to
incluido prp inclusive
incluir ⟨3g⟩ v/t include
inclusive adv inclusive
incluso adv, prp & conj even
incógnita f unknown factor; MAT unknown (quantity)
incógnito adj: **de incógnito** incognito
incoherente adj incoherent
incombustible adj fireproof
incomodidad f uncomfortableness; (fastidio) inconvenience
incómodo adj uncomfortable; (fastidioso) inconvenient
incomparable adj incomparable
incompatibilidad f incompatibility
incompatible adj tb INFOR incompatible
incompetencia f incompetence
incompetente adj incompetent
incompleto adj incomplete
incomprendido adj misunderstood
incomprensible adj incomprehensible
incomunicado adj isolated, cut off; JUR in solitary confinement

inconcebible adj inconceivable
incondicional adj unconditional;
inconexo adj unconnected
inconfesable adj shameful
inconformista m/f nonconformist
inconfundible adj unmistakable
incongruente adj incongruous
inconsciencia f MED unconsciousness; (desconocimiento) lack of awareness, unawareness; (irreflexión) thoughtlessness
inconsciente adj MED unconscious; (ignorante) unaware; (irreflexivo) thoughtless
inconsecuente adj inconsistent
inconsistente adj flimsy, weak
inconsolable adj inconsolable
inconstante adj fickle
incontable adj uncountable
incontinencia f MED incontinence
incontrolable adj uncontrollable
inconveniente 1 adj (inoportuno) inconvenient; (impropio) inappropriate **2** m (desventaja) drawback, disadvantage; (estorbo) problem; **no tengo inconveniente** I don't mind
incordiar ⟨1b⟩ v/t annoy
incordio m nuisance
incorporar ⟨1a⟩ **1** v/t incorporate **2** v/r **incorporarse** sit up; **incorporarse a** MIL join
incorrecto adj incorrect, wrong; comportamiento impolite
incorregible adj incorrigible
incorruptible adj incorruptible
incredulidad f disbelief, incredulity
incrédulo adj incredulous
increíble adj incredible
incrementar ⟨1a⟩ **1** v/t increase **2** v/r **incrementarse** increase
incremento m growth
incriminar ⟨1a⟩ v/t incriminate
incruento adj bloodless
incrustar ⟨1a⟩ **1** v/t incrust (de with) **2** v/r **incrustarse** de la suciedad become ingrained
incubación f incubation
incubadora f incubator
incubar ⟨1a⟩ v/t incubate
incuestionable adj unquestionable
inculcar ⟨1g⟩ v/t instil(l) (en in)
inculpar ⟨1a⟩ v/t JUR accuse
inculto adj ignorant, uneducated
incultura f ignorance, lack of education
incumbencia f responsibility, duty; **no es de mi incumbencia** it's not my responsibility
incumplimiento m non-fulfillment (de of), non-compliance (de with)
incumplir ⟨3a⟩ v/t break
incurable adj incurable

incurrir ⟨3a⟩ v/i: **incurrir en un error** make a mistake; **incurrir en gastos** incur costs

incursión f MIL raid; fig foray

indagar ⟨1h⟩ v/i investigate

indecente adj indecent; película obscene

indecisión f indecisiveness

indeciso adj undecided; por naturaleza indecisive

indefenso adj defenseless, Br defenceless

indefinidamente adv indefinitely

indefinido adj (impreciso) vague; (ilimitado) indefinite

indemnización f compensation

indemnizar ⟨1f⟩ v/t compensate (**por** for)

independencia f independence

independentismo m POL pro-independence movement

independiente adj independent

independizarse ⟨1f⟩ v/r become independent

indescriptible adj indescribable

indeseable adj undesirable

indestructible adj indestructible

indeterminado adj indeterminate; (indefinido) indefinite

India: **la India** India

indiada f L.Am. group of Indians

indicación f indication; (señal) sign; **indicaciones** para llegar directions; (instrucciones) instructions

indicado adj (adecuado) suitable; **lo más / menos indicado** the best / worst thing; **hora -a** specified time

indicador m indicator

indicar ⟨1g⟩ v/t show, indicate; (señalar) point out; (sugerir) suggest

índice m index; **dedo índice** index finger; **índice de precios al consumo** consumer price index, Br retail price index

indicio m indication, sign; (vestigio) trace

indiferencia f indifference

indiferente adj indifferent; (irrelevante) immaterial

indígena 1 adj indigenous, native 2 m/f native

indigente adj destitute

indigestión f indigestion

indigesto adj indigestible

indignación f indignation

indignado adj indignant

indignar ⟨1a⟩ 1 v/t: **indignar a alguien** make s.o. indignant 2 v/r **indignarse** become indignant

indigno adj unworthy (**de** of)

indio 1 adj Indian 2 m, -a f Indian; **hacer el indio** F clown around F, play the fool F

indirecta f insinuation; (sugerencia) hint

indirecto adj indirect

indiscreción f indiscretion, lack of discretion; (declaración) indiscreet remark

indiscreto adj indiscreet

indiscriminado adj indiscriminate

indiscutible adj indisputable

indispensable adj indispensable

indisponerse ⟨2r⟩ v/r become unwell; **indisponerse con alguien** fall out with s.o.

indisposición f indisposition

indispuesto adj indisposed, unwell

indistinto adj forma indistinct, vague; noción vague; sonido faint

individual adj individual; cama, habitación single

individualismo m individualism

individualista m/f individualist

individuo m individual

indivisible adj indivisible

indocumentado adj: **un hombre indocumentado** a man with no identity papers

índole f nature

indolente adj lazy

indoloro adj painless

indómito adj indomitable

Indonesia Indonesia

inducir ⟨3o⟩ v/t (persuadir) lead, induce (**a** to); EL induce

indudable adj undoubted

indudablemente adv undoubtedly

indulgente adj indulgent

indultar ⟨1a⟩ v/t pardon

indulto m pardon

indumentaria f clothing

industria f industry; (esfuerzo) industriousness, industry

industrial 1 adj industrial 2 m/f industrialist

industrializar ⟨1f⟩ 1 v/t industrialize 2 v/r **industrializarse** industrialize

inédito adj unpublished; fig unprecedented

ineficacia f inefficiency; de un procedimiento ineffectiveness

ineficaz adj inefficient; procedimiento ineffective

ineficiencia f inefficiency

ineficiente adj inefficient

ineludible adj unavoidable

inepto 1 adj inept, incompetent 2 m, -a f incompetent fool

inequívoco adj unequivocal

inercia f inertia

inerte adj fig lifeless; FÍS inert

inesperado adj unexpected

inestabilidad f instability

inestable adj unstable; tiempo unsettled

inestimable adj invaluable

inevitable adj inevitable

inexacto adj inaccurate
inexcusable adj inexcusable
inexistente adj non-existent
inexperto adj inexperienced
inexplicable adj inexplicable
infalible adj infallible
infame adj vile, loathsome; (terrible) dreadful
infancia f infancy
infantería f MIL infantry
infantil adj children's atr; naturaleza childlike; desp infantile, childish
infarto m MED heart attack
infección f MED infection
infeccioso adj infectious
infectar ⟨1a⟩ **1** v/t infect **2** v/r **infectarse** become infected
infecundo adj infertile
infeliz **1** adj unhappy, miserable **2** m/f poor devil
inferior **1** adj inferior (**a** to); en el espacio lower (**a** than) **2** m/f inferior
inferioridad f inferiority
inferir ⟨3i⟩ v/t infer (**de** from); daño do, cause (**a** to)
infernal adj ruido infernal; (muy malo) diabolical
infertilidad f infertility
infestar ⟨1a⟩ v/t infest; (invadir) overrun
infidelidad f infidelity
infiel **1** adj unfaithful **2** m/f unbeliever
infierno m hell
infiltrarse v/r: **infiltrarse en** infiltrate; de agua seep into
infinidad f: **infinidad de** countless
infinitivo m GRAM infinitive
infinito **1** adj infinite **2** m infinity
inflación f COM inflation; **tasa de inflación** inflation rate
inflacionista adj inflationary
inflamable adj flammable
inflamación f MED inflammation
inflamar ⟨1a⟩ **1** v/t tb fig inflame **2** v/r **inflamarse** MED become inflamed
inflar ⟨1a⟩ **1** v/t inflate **2** v/r **inflarse** swell (up); fig F get conceited
infligir ⟨3c⟩ v/t inflict
inflexible adj tb fig inflexible
influencia f influence; **tener influencias** have contacts
influenciar ⟨1b⟩ v/t influence
influir ⟨3g⟩ v/i: **influir en alguien / algo** influence s.o./sth, have an influence on s.o./sth
influjo m influence
influyente adj influential
infografía f computer graphics pl
información f information; (noticias) news sg

informal adj informal; persona unreliable
informar ⟨1a⟩ **1** v/t inform (**de, sobre** about) **2** v/r **informarse** find out (**de, sobre** about)
informática f information technology
informático **1** adj computer atr **2** m, -a f IT specialist
informativo **1** adj informative; programa news atr **2** m TV, RAD news sg
informatizar ⟨1f⟩ v/t computerize
informe **1** adj shapeless **2** m report; **informes** (referencias) references
infracción f offense, Br offence
in fraganti adv F in the act F
infraestructura f infrastructure
infrahumano adj subhuman
infrarrojo adj infra-red
infravalorar ⟨1a⟩ v/t undervalue
infrecuente adj infrequent
infringir ⟨3c⟩ v/t JUR infringe, violate
infructuoso adj fruitless
infundado adj unfounded, groundless
infundir ⟨3a⟩ v/t inspire; terror instil(l); sospechas arouse
infusión f infusion; de tila, manzanilla tea
ingeniarse ⟨1b⟩ v/r: **ingeniárselas para** manage to
ingeniería f engineering
ingeniero m, -a f engineer
ingenio m ingenuity; (aparato) device; **ingenio azucarero** L.Am. sugar refinery
ingenioso adj ingenious
ingenuidad f naivety
ingenuo **1** adj naive **2** m, -a f naive person, sucker F
ingerir ⟨3i⟩ v/t swallow
Inglaterra England
ingle f groin
inglés **1** adj English **2** m Englishman; idioma English
inglesa f Englishwoman
ingrato adj ungrateful; tarea thankless
ingrediente m ingredient
ingresar ⟨1a⟩ **1** v/i: **ingresar en** universidad go to; en asociación, cuerpo join; en hospital be admitted to **2** v/t cheque pay in, deposit
ingreso m entry; en una asociación joining; en hospital admission; COM deposit; **ingresos** pl income sg; **examen de ingreso** entrance exam
inhabitable adj uninhabitable
inhalar ⟨1a⟩ v/t inhale
inherente adj inherent
inhibición f inhibition; JUR disqualification
inhibir ⟨3a⟩ v/t inhibit
inhóspito adj inhospitable
inhumano adj inhuman

iniciación f initiation
inicial f/adj initial
iniciar ⟨1b⟩ v/t initiate; *curso* start, begin
iniciativa f initiative; **tomar la iniciativa** take the initiative
inicio m start, beginning
inigualable adj incomparable; *precio* unbeatable
inimaginable adj unimaginable
inimitable adj inimitable
ininteligible adj unintelligible
ininterrumpido adj uninterrupted
injerencia f interference
injertar ⟨1a⟩ v/t graft
injerto m graft
injuriar ⟨1b⟩ v/t insult
injusticia f injustice
injustificado adj unjustified
injusto adj unjust
inmaculado adj immaculate
inmaduro adj immature
inmediaciones fpl immediate area sg (**de** of), vicinity sg (**de** of)
inmediatamente adv immediately
inmediato adj immediate; **de inmediato** immediately
inmejorable adj unbeatable
inmenso adj immense
inmersión f immersion; **de submarino** dive
inmerso adj fig immersed (**en** in)
inmigración f immigration
inmigrante m/f immigrant
inmigrar ⟨1a⟩ v/i immigrate
inminente adj imminent
inmiscuirse ⟨3g⟩ v/r meddle
inmobiliaria f realtor's office, Br estate agency
inmoderado adj excessive, immoderate
inmoral adj immoral
inmoralidad f immorality
inmortal adj immortal
inmóvil adj *persona* motionless; *vehículo* stationary
inmovilizar ⟨1f⟩ v/t immobilize
inmueble m building
inmundo adj filthy
inmune adj immune
inmunidad f MED, POL immunity
inmunizar ⟨1f⟩ v/t immunize
inmutarse ⟨1a⟩ v/r: **no inmutarse** not bat an eyelid; **sin inmutarse** without batting an eyelid
innato adj innate, inborn
innecesario adj unnecessary
innegable adj undeniable
innovación f innovation
innumerable adj innumerable, countless
inocencia f innocence

inocente adj innocent
inocuo adj harmless, innocuous; *película* bland
inodoro m toilet
inofensivo adj inoffensive, harmless
inoficioso adj L.Am. (*inútil*) useless
inolvidable adj unforgettable
inopia f: **estar en la inopia** F (*distraído*) be miles away F; (*alejado de la realidad*) be on another planet F
inoportuno adj inopportune; (*molesto*) inconvenient
inorgánico adj inorganic
inoxidable adj: **acero inoxidable** stainless steel
inquietar ⟨1a⟩ 1 v/t worry 2 v/r **inquietarse** worry, get anxious o anxious
inquieto adj worried, anxious
inquietud f worry, anxiety; *intelectual* interest
inquilino m tenant
inquisitivo adj inquisitive
insaciable adj insatiable
insatisfacción f dissatisfaction
insatisfactorio adj unsatisfactory
insatisfecho adj dissatisfied
inscribir ⟨3a⟩ 1 v/t (*grabar*) inscribe; *en lista, registro* register, enter; *en curso, concurso* enrol(l), enter 2 v/r **inscribirse** *en un curso* enrol(l), register; *en un concurso* enter
inscripción f inscription; *en lista, registro* registration, entry; *en curso, concurso* enrol(l)ment, registration;
insecticida m insecticide
insecto m insect
inseguro adj insecure; *estructura* unsteady; (*peligroso*) dangerous, unsafe
inseminación f insemination; **inseminación artificial** artificial insemination
insensato adj foolish
insensible adj insensitive (**a** to)
inseparable adj inseparable
insertar ⟨1a⟩ v/t insert
inservible adj useless
insidia f treachery; **actuar con insidia** act treacherously
insignia f insignia
insignificante adj insignificant
insinuante adj suggestive
insinuar ⟨1e⟩ 1 v/t insinuate 2 v/r **insinuarse**: **insinuarse a alguien** make advances to s.o.
insípido adj insipid
insistencia f insistence
insistir ⟨3a⟩ v/i insist; **insistir en hacer algo** insist on doing sth; **insistir en algo** stress sth
insociable adj unsociable
insolación f MED sunstroke

insolente adj insolent
insólito adj unusual
insolvente adj insolvent
insomnio m insomnia
insondable adj unfathomable
insonorizar ⟨1f⟩ v/t soundproof
insoportable adj unbearable, intolerable
insospechado adj unexpected
inspección f inspection
inspeccionar ⟨1a⟩ v/t inspect
inspector m, **inspectora** f inspector
inspiración f inspiration; MED inhalation
inspirar ⟨1a⟩ v/t inspire; MED inhale
instalación f acto installation; **instalaciones deportivas** sports facilities
instalar ⟨1a⟩ v/t instal(l); (colocar) put; **un negocio** set up **2** v/r **instalarse en un sitio** instal(l) o.s.
instancia f JUR petition; (petición por escrito) application; **a instancias de** at the request of
instantáneo adj immediate, instantaneous
instante m moment, instant; **al instante** right away, immediately
instar ⟨1a⟩ v/t urge, press
instaurar ⟨1a⟩ v/t establish
instigar ⟨1h⟩ v/t incite (**a** to)
instinto m instinct
institución f institution
instituto m institute; Esp high school, Br secondary school; **instituto de belleza** beauty salon; **instituto de educación secundaria** high school, Br secondary school
instrucción f education; (formación) training, MIL drill, INFOR instruction, statement; JUR hearing; **instrucciones de uso** instructions, directions (for use)
instructor m, **instructora** f instructor
instruido adj educated
instruir ⟨3g⟩ v/t educate; (formar) train; JUR **pleito** hear
instrumental 1 adj instrumental **2** m MED instruments pl
instrumento m instrument; (herramienta) tool, instrument; fig tool; **instrumento musical** musical instrument
insubordinación f insubordination
insubordinarse ⟨1a⟩ v/r con un superior be insubordinate; (rebelarse) rebel
insuficiente 1 adj insufficient, inadequate **2** m EDU **nota** fail
insufrible adj insufferable
insulina f insulin
insulso adj bland, insipid
insultada f L.Am. (insultos) string of insults
insultar ⟨1a⟩ v/t insult

insulto m insult
insumiso m person who refuses to do military service
insuperable adj insurmountable
insurrección f insurrection
insustancial adj conferencia lightweight; estructura flimsy
intachable adj faultless
intacto adj intact; (sin tocar) untouched
integración f integration
integral adj complete; alimento whole
integrar ⟨1a⟩ v/t integrate; equipo make up
íntegro adj whole, entire; **un hombre íntegro** fig a man of integrity
intelectual m/f & adj intellectual
inteligencia f intelligence
inteligente adj intelligent
inteligible adj intelligible
intemperie f: **a la intemperie** in the open air
intempestivo adj untimely
intención f intention; **doble** or **segunda intención** ulterior motive
intencionado adj deliberate
intendente m Rpl military governor; (alcalde) mayor
intensidad f intensity; (fuerza) strength
intensificar ⟨1g⟩ **1** v/t intensify **2** v/r intensificarse intensify
intensivo adj intensive
intenso adj intense; (fuerte) strong
intentar ⟨1a⟩ v/t try, attempt
intento m attempt, try; Méx (intención) aim
interacción f interaction
interactivo adj interactive
intercalar ⟨1a⟩ v/t insert
intercambiar ⟨1a⟩ v/t exchange, swap
intercambio m exchange, swap
interceder ⟨2a⟩ v/i intercede (**por** for)
interceptar ⟨1a⟩ v/t tb DEP intercept
intercesión f intercession
interés m tb COM interest; desp self-interest; **sin interés** interest free; **intereses** (bienes) interests
interesante adj interesting
interesar ⟨1a⟩ **1** v/t interest **2** v/r interesarse: **interesarse por** take an interest in
interface m, **interfaz** f INFOR interface
interferencia f interference
interferir ⟨3i⟩ **1** v/t interfere with **2** v/i interfere (**en** in)
interino adj substitute atr, replacement atr; (provisional) provisional, acting atr
interior 1 adj interior; bolsillo inside atr; COM, POL domestic **2** m interior; DEP inside-forward; **en su interior** fig inwardly
interiorista m/f interior designer

interjección f GRAM interjection

interlocutor m, **interlocutora** f speaker; **mi interlocutor** the person I was talking to

intermediario m COM intermediary, middle-man

intermedio 1 adj nivel intermediate; tamaño medium; calidad average, medium **2** m intermission

interminable adj interminable, endless

intermitente 1 adj intermittent **2** m AUTO turn signal, Br indicator

internacional adj international

internado m boarding school

internarse ⟨1a⟩ v/r: **internarse en** go into

internauta m/f INFOR Internet user, Net surfer

Internet f INFOR Internet

interno 1 adj internal; POL domestic, internal **2** m, -a f EDU boarder; (preso) inmate; MED intern, Br houseman

interpelar ⟨1a⟩ v/t question

interplanetario adj interplanetary

interpolar ⟨1a⟩ v/t insert, interpolate fml

interponerse ⟨2r⟩ v/r intervene

interpretación f interpretation; TEA performance (**de** as)

interpretar ⟨1a⟩ v/t interpret; TEA play

intérprete m/f interpreter

interrogación f interrogation; **signo de interrogación** question mark

interrogante 1 adj questioning **2** m (also f) question; fig question mark, doubt

interrogar ⟨1h⟩ v/t question; de policía interrogate, question

interrogatorio m questioning, interrogation

interrumpir ⟨3a⟩ **1** v/t interrupt; servicio suspend; reunión, vacaciones cut short, curtail **2** v/i interrupt

interrupción f interruption; de servicio suspension; de reunión, vacaciones curtailment; **sin interrupción** non-stop

interruptor m EL switch

intersección f intersection

intervalo m tb MÚS interval; (espacio) gap

intervención f intervention; en debate, congreso participation; en película, espectáculo appearance; MED operation

intervenir ⟨3s⟩ **1** v/i intervene; en debate, congreso take part, participate; en película, espectáculo appear **2** v/t TELEC tap; contrabando seize; MED operate on

intestino m intestine

intimar ⟨1a⟩ v/i (hacerse amigos) become friendly (**con** with); (tratar) mix (**con** with)

intimidad f intimacy; (lo privado) privacy; **en la intimidad** in private

intimidar ⟨1a⟩ v/t intimidate

íntimo adj intimate; (privado) private; **somos íntimos amigos** we're close friends

intolerable adj intolerable, unbearable

intolerante adj intolerant

intoxicación f poisoning

intranquilidad f unease; (nerviosismo) restlessness

intranquilo adj uneasy; (nervioso) restless

intransferible adj non-transferable

intransigente adj intransigent

intransitable adj impassable

intransitivo adj GRAM intransitive

intrascendente adj unimportant

intravenoso adj MED intravenous

intrépido adj intrepid

intriga f intrigue; de novela plot

intrigante 1 adj scheming; (curioso) intriguing **2** m/f schemer

intrigar ⟨1h⟩ **1** v/t (interesar) intrigue **2** v/i plot, scheme

intrincado adj intricate

intrínseco adj intrinsic

introducción f introduction; acción de meter insertion; INFOR input

introducir ⟨3o⟩ v/t introduce; (meter) insert; INFOR input **2** v/r: **introducirse: introducirse en** get into; **introducirse en un mercado** gain access to o break into a market

intromisión f interference

introvertido adj introverted

intruso m intruder

intuición f intuition

intuir ⟨3g⟩ v/t sense

intuitivo adj intuitive

inundación f flood

inundadizo adj L.Am. prone to flooding

inundar ⟨1a⟩ v/t flood

inusitado adj unusual, uncommon

inusual adj unusual

inútil 1 adj useless; MIL unfit **2** m/f: **es un inútil** he's useless

inutilidad f uselessness

inutilizar ⟨1f⟩ v/t: **inutilizar algo** render sth useless

inútilmente adv uselessly

invadir ⟨3a⟩ v/t invade; de un sentimiento overcome

invalidar ⟨1a⟩ v/t invalidate

invalidez f disability

inválido 1 adj persona disabled; documento, billete invalid **2** m, -a f disabled person

invasión f MIL invasion

invasor m, **invasora** f invader

invencible adj invincible; miedo insur-

mountable
invención f invention
inventar ⟨1a⟩ v/t invent
inventario m inventory
invento m invention
inventor m inventor
invernada f Rpl winter pasture
invernadero m greenhouse
invernal adj winter atr
inverosímil adj unlikely
inversión f reversal; COM investment
inverso adj opposite; orden reverse; **a la -a** the other way round
inversor m, **inversora** f investor
invertir ⟨3i⟩ v/t reverse; COM invest (**en** in)
invertebrado m invertebrate
investigación f investigation; EDU, TÉC research; **investigación y desarrollo** research and development
investigador m, **investigadora** f researcher
investigar ⟨1h⟩ v/t investigate; EDU, TÉC research
inviable adj nonviable
invidente m/f blind person
invierno m winter
inviolable adj inviolable
invisible adj invisible
invitación f invitation
invitado m, **-a** f guest
invitar ⟨1a⟩ v/t invite (**a** to); (convidar) treat (**a** to)
invocar ⟨1g⟩ v/t invoke
involucrar ⟨1a⟩ v/t involve (**en** in)
involuntario adj involuntary
invulnerable adj invulnerable
inyección f MED, AUTO injection
inyectar ⟨1a⟩ v/t tb TÉC inject
IPC abr (= **índice de precios al consumo**) CPI (= consumer price index), Br RPI (= retail price index)
ir ⟨3t⟩ 1 v/i go (**a** to); ra pie walk, go on foot; **ir en avión** fly; **¡ya voy!** I'm coming!; **ir a por algo** go and fetch sth; **ir bien / mal** go well / badly; **iba de amarillo / de uniforme** she was wearing yellow/a uniform; **van dos a dos** DEP the score is two all; **¿de qué va la película?** what's the movie about?; **¡qué va!** you must be joking! F; **¡vamos!** come on!; **¡vaya!** well! 2 v/aux: **va a llover** it's going to rain; **ya voy comprendiendo** I'm beginning to understand; **ir para viejo** be getting old 3 v/r **irse** go (away), leave; **¡vete!** go away!; **¡vámonos!** let's go
ira f anger
Irak Iraq, Irak
Irán Iran
iraní m/f & adj Iranian

iraquí m/f & adj Iraqi, Iraki
iris m inv ANAT iris; **arco iris** rainbow
Irlanda Ireland
irlandés 1 adj Irish **2** m Irishman
irlandesa f Irishwoman
ironía f irony
irónico adj ironic
irracional adj tb MAT irrational
irradiar ⟨1b⟩ v/t radiate; MED irradiate
irreal adj unreal
irrealizable adj unattainable; proyecto unfeasible
irreconciliable adj irreconcilable
irrecuperable adj irretrievable
irrefutable adj irrefutable
irregular adj irregular; superficie uneven
irregularidad f irregularity; **de superficie** unevenness
irrelevante adj irrelevant
irremediable adj fig irremediable
irreparable adj irreparable
irreprochable adj irreproachable
irresistible adj irresistible
irrespetuoso adj disrespectful
irresponsable adj irresponsible
irreverente adj irreverent
irreversible adj irreversible
irrevocable adj irrevocable
irrigar ⟨1h⟩ v/t MED, AGR irrigate
irrisorio adj laughable, derisory
irritación f tb MED irritation
irritante adj tb MED irritating
irritar ⟨1a⟩ **1** v/t tb MED irritate **2** v/r **irritarse** get irritated
irrompible adj unbreakable
irrumpir ⟨3a⟩ v/i burst in
irrupción f: **hacer irrupción en** burst into
isla f island
islam m Islam
islámico adj Islamic
islamismo m Islam
isleño 1 adj island atr **2** m, **-a** f islander
Israel Israel
israelí m/f & adj Israeli
Italia Italy
italiano 1 adj Italian **2** m, **-a** f Italian
itinerario m itinerary
ITV abr Esp (= **inspección técnica de vehículos**) compulsory annual test of motor vehicles of a certain age, Br MOT
IVA abr (= **impuesto sobre el valor añadido**) sales tax, Br VAT (= value-added tax)
izar ⟨1f⟩ v/t hoist
izdo., izda abr (= **izquierdo, izquierda**) l (= left)
izquierda f tb POL left; **por la izquierda** on the left
izquierdo adj left

J

jabalí *m* zo wild boar

jabalina *f* javelin

jabón *m* soap; **jabón de afeitar** shaving soap

jabonera *f* soap dish

jabonoso *adj* soapy

jacinto *m* hyacinth

jactancia *f* boasting

jactancioso *adj* boastful

jactarse ⟨la⟩ *v/r* boast (**de** about), brag (**de** about)

jacuzzi *m* jacuzzi®

jade *m* MIN jade

jadear ⟨la⟩ *v/i* pant

jadeo *m* panting

jaguar *m* zo jaguar

jalar ⟨la⟩ **1** *v/t* L.Am. pull; **con esfuerza** haul; (*atraer*) attract; *Méx* (*dar aventón*) give a ride *o Br* a lift to; **¿te jala el arte?** *Méx* do you feel drawn to art? **2** *v/i* L.Am. pull; (*trabajar mucho*) work hard; *Méx* F (*tener influencia*) have pull F; **jalar hacia** F head toward; **jalar para la casa** F clear off home F **3** *v/r* **jalarse** *Méx* (*irse*) go, leave; F (*emborracharse*) get plastered F

jalea *f* jelly; **jalea real** royal jelly

jaleo *m* (*ruido*) racket, uproar; (*lío*) mess, muddle; **armar jaleo** F kick up a fuss F

jalón *m* pull; **dar un jalón a algo** pull sth; **de un jalón** *Méx fig* in one go

jalonar ⟨la⟩ *v/t fig* mark out

Jamaica Jamaica

jamás *adv* never; **jamás te olvidaré** I'll never forget you; **¿viste jamás algo así?** did you ever see anything like it?; **nunca jamás** never ever; **por siempre jamás** for ever and ever

jamón *m* ham; **jamón de York** cooked ham; **jamón serrano** cured ham; **¡y un jamón!** F (*¡no!*) no way! F; (*¡bromeas!*) come off it! F

jangada *f* S. Am. F dirty trick

Japón Japan

japonés **1** *adj* Japanese **2** *m*, **-esa** *f* Japanese

jaque *m* check; **jaque mate** checkmate; **dar jaque a** checkmate

jaqueca *f* MED migraine

jarabe *m* syrup; *Méx* type of folk dance

jardín *m* garden; **jardín botánico** botanic(al) gardens; **jardín de infancia** kindergarten

jardinería *f* gardening

jardinero *m*, **-a** *f* gardener

jarra *f* pitcher, *Br* jug; **en jarras** with hands on hips

jarro *m* pitcher, *Br* jug; **un jarro de agua fría** *fig* a total shock, a bombshell

jarrón *m* vase

jauja *f*: **¡esto es jauja!** this is the life!

jaula *f* cage

jauría *f* pack

jazmín *m* BOT jasmine

J.C. *abr* (= **Jesucristo**) J.C. (= Jesus Christ)

jefatura *f* headquarters; (*dirección*) leadership; **jefatura de policía** police headquarters

jefe *m*, **-a** *f* de departamento, organización head; (*superior*) boss; POL leader; *de tribu* chief; **jefe de cocina** (head) chef; **jefe de estado** head of state

jengibre *m* BOT ginger

jeque *m* sheik

jerarquía *f* hierarchy

jerez *m* sherry

jerga *f* jargon; (*argot*) slang

jeringa *f* MED syringe

jeringuilla *f* MED syringe; **jeringuilla desechable** *or* **de un solo uso** disposable syringe

jeroglífico *m* hieroglyphic; *rompecabezas* puzzle

jersey *m* sweater

Jesucristo *m* Jesus Christ

Jesús *m* Jesus; **¡Jesús!** good grief!; *por estornudo* bless you!

jet **1** *m* AVIA jet **2** *f*: **jet (set)** jet set

jeta *f* F face, mug F; **¡qué jeta tiene!** F he's got nerve! F, *Br* what a cheek! F

jíbia *f* zo cuttlefish

jícara *f* *Méx* drinking bowl

jícaro *m* L.Am. BOT calabash

jilguero *m* zo goldfinch

jilote *m* C.Am., *Méx* young corn

jineta *f* zo civet

jinete *m* rider; **en carrera** jockey

jirafa *f* zo giraffe

jitomate *m* *Méx* tomato

JJ.OO *abr* (= **Juegos Olímpicos**) Olympic Games

jocoso *adj* humorous, joking

joder ⟨2a⟩ **1** *v/i* V screw V, fuck V **2** *v/t* V (*follar*) screw V, fuck V; (*estropear*) screw up V, fuck up V; L.Am. F (*fastidiar*) annoy, irritate; **¡joder!** V fuck! V; **me jode**

un montón V it really pisses me off P
jolgorio *m* F partying F
jolín *int* wow! F, jeez! F
jornada *f* (working) day; *distancia* day's journey; **media jornada** half-day; **jornada laboral** work day; **jornada partida** split shift
jornal *m* day's wage
jornalero *m*, **-a** *f* day labo(u)rer
joroba *f* hump; *fig* pain F, drag F
jorobado *adj* hump-backed; *fig* F in a bad way F
jorobar ⟨la⟩ *v/t* F (*molestar*) bug F; *planes* ruin
jorongo *m* *Méx* poncho
jota *f letter 'j'*; **no saber ni jota** F not have a clue F
joven 1 *adj* young **2** *m/f* young man; *mujer* young woman; **los jóvenes** young people
jovial *adj* cheerful
joya *f* jewel; *persona* gem; **joyas** *pl* jewelry *sg*, *Br* jewellery *sg*
joyería *f* jewelry store, *Br* jeweller's
joyero 1 *m*, **-a** *f* jewel(l)er **2** *m* jewelry (*Br* jewellery) box
juanete *m* MED bunion
jubilación *f* retirement; **jubilación anticipada** early retirement
jubilado 1 *adj* retired **2** *m*, **-a** *f* retiree, *Br* pensioner
jubilar ⟨la⟩ **1** *v/t* retire; (*desechar*) get rid of **2** *v/r* **jubilarse** retire; *C.Am.* play hooky F, play truant
júbilo *m* jubilation
jubiloso *adj* jubilant
judaísmo *m* Judaism
judía *f* BOT bean; **judía verde** green bean, runner bean
judicial *adj* judicial
judío 1 *adj* Jewish **2** *m*, **-a** *f* Jew
judo *m* DEP judo
juego *m* game; *acción* play; *por dinero* gambling; (*conjunto de objetos*) set; **juego de azar** game of chance; **juego de café** coffee set; **juego de manos** conjuring trick; **juego de mesa** board game; **juego de rol** role-playing game; **juego de sociedad** game; **Juegos Olímpicos** Olympic Games; **estar en juego** *fig* be at stake; **fuera de juego** DEP offside; **hacer juego con** go with, match
juerga *f* F partying F; **irse de juerga** F go out on the town F, go out partying F
jueves *m inv* Thursday
juez *m/f* judge; **juez de línea** *en fútbol* assistant referee; *en fútbol americano* line judge
jueza *f* → **juez**

jugada *f* play, *Br* move; *en ajedrez* move; **hacerle una mala jugada a alguien** play a dirty trick on s.o.
jugador *m*, **jugadora** *f* player
jugar ⟨1o⟩ **1** *v/t* play **2** *v/i* play; *con dinero* gamble; **jugar al baloncesto** play basketball **3** *v/r* **jugarse** risk; **jugarse la vida** risk one's life; **jugársela a alguien** do the dirty on s.o.
jugarreta *f* F dirty trick F
jugo *m* juice; **sacar jugo a algo** get the most out of sth
jugoso *adj tb fig* juicy
juguete *m* toy
juguetear ⟨la⟩ *v/i* play
juicio *m* judg(e)ment; JUR trial; (*sensatez*) sense; (*cordura*) sanity; **a mi juicio** in my opinion; **estar en su juicio** be in one's right mind; **perder el juicio** lose one's mind
julio *m* July
junco *m* BOT reed
jungla *f* jungle
junio *m* June
júnior *adj tb* DEP junior
junta *f* POL (regional) government; *militar* junta; COM board; (*sesión*) meeting; TÉC joint; **junta directiva** board of directors; **junta general anual** annual general meeting
juntar ⟨la⟩ **1** *v/t* put together; *gente* gather together; *bienes* collect, accumulate **2** *v/r* **juntarse** (*reunirse*) meet, assemble; *de pareja: empezar a salir* start going out; *empezar a vivir juntos* move in together; *de caminos, ríos* meet, join; **juntarse con alguien** *socialmente* mix with s.o.
junto 1 *adj* together **2** *prp*: **junto a** next to, near; **junto con** together with
juntura *f* TÉC joint
iupa *f* *C.Am., Méx fig* F head, nut F
jurado *m* JUR jury
juramento *m* oath; **bajo juramento** under oath
jurar ⟨la⟩ *v/i* swear
jurídico *adj* legal
jurisdicción *f* jurisdiction
jurisprudencia *f* jurisprudence
justamente *adv* fairly; (*precisamente*) precisely
justicia *f* justice; **la justicia** (*la ley*) the law; **hacer justicia a** do justice to
justificable *adj* justifiable
justificación *f tb* TIP justification
justificante *m de pago* receipt; *de ausencia, propiedad* certificate
justificar ⟨1g⟩ *v/t tb* TIP justify; *mala conducta* justify, excuse
justo *adj* just, fair; (*exacto*) right, exact;

J

lo justo just enough; *¡justo!* right!, exactly!

juvenil *adj* youthful

juventud *f* youth

juzgado 1 *part* → *juzgar* **2** *m* court

juzgar ⟨1h⟩ *v/t* JUR try; (*valorar*) judge; *considerar* consider, judge; *a juzgar por* to judge by, judging by

K

kárate *m* DEP karate

kayak *m* DEP kayak

ketchup *m* ketchup

kg. *abr* (= *kilogramo*) kg (= kilogram)

kilo *m* kilo; *fig* F million

kilogramo *m* kilogram, *Br* kilogramme

kilómetro *m* kilometer, *Br* kilometre

kiosco *m* kiosk

kiwi *m* BOT kiwi (fruit)

kleenex® *m* kleenex, tissue

km. *abr* (= *kilómetro*) km (= kilometer)

km./h. *abr* (= *kilómetros por hora*) kph (= kilometers per hour)

kv. *abr* (= *kilovatio*) kw (= kilowatt)

L

la 1 *art* the **2** *pron complemento directo sg* her; *a usted* you; *algo* it; *la que está embarazada* the one who is pregnant; *la más grande* the biggest (one); *dame la roja* give me the red one

laberinto *m* labyrinth, maze

labia *f*: *tener mucha labia* have the gift of the gab

labio *m* lip

labor *f* work; (*tarea*) task, job; *hacer labores* do needlework; *no estar por la labor* F not be enthusiastic about the idea

laborable *adj*: *día laborable* workday

laboral *adj* labo(u)r *atr*

laboratorio *m* laboratory, lab F

laborioso *adj* laborious; *persona* hardworking

labrador *m* farm labo(u)rer, farm worker

labranza *f de la tierra* cultivation

labrar ⟨1a⟩ *v/t tierra* work; *piedra* carve

labriego *m* farm labo(u)rer, farm worker

laca *f* lacquer; *para el cabello* hairspray; *laca de uñas* nail varnish *o* polish

lacear ⟨1a⟩ *v/t Rpl* lasso

lacio *adj* limp; *pelo* lank

lacónico *adj* laconic

lacra *f* scar; *L.Am.* (*llaga*) sore; *la corrupción es una lacra social* corruption is a blot on society

lacre *m* sealing wax

lacrimógeno *adj fig* tear-jerking

lactancia *f* lactation

lácteo *adj*: *Vía Láctea* Milky Way; *productos lácteos* dairy products

ladear ⟨1a⟩ *v/t* tilt

ladera *f* slope

ladino 1 *adj* cunning, sly **2** *m C.Am. Indian who has become absorbed into white culture*

lado *m* side; (*lugar*) place; *al lado* nearby; *al lado de* beside, next to; *de lado* sideways; *ir por otro lado* go another way; *por un lado ... por otro lado* on the one hand ... on the other hand; *hacerse a un lado tb fig* stand aside

ladrar ⟨1a⟩ *v/i* bark

ladrillo *m* brick

ladrón *m* thief

lagartija *f* ZO small lizard

lagarto *m* ZO lizard

lago *m* lake

lágrima *f* tear

laguna *f* lagoon; *fig* gap

laico *adj* lay

lamentable *adj* deplorable

lamentablemente *adv* regretfully

lamentar ⟨1a⟩ **1** *v/t* regret, be sorry about; *muerte* mourn **2** *v/r* **lamentarse** complain (**de** about)

lamento *m* whimper; *por dolor* groan

lamer ⟨2a⟩ *v/t* lick

lámina *f* sheet

lámpara *f* lamp; **lámpara halógena** halogen lamp; **lámpara de pie** floor lamp, *Br* standard lamp

lamparón *m* F grease mark

lana *f* wool; *Méx* P dough F; **pura lana virgen** pure new wool

lancha *f* launch; **lancha fueraborda** outboard

langosta *f* ZO *insecto* locust; *crustáceo* spiny lobster

langostino *m* ZO king prawn

languidecer ⟨2d⟩ *v/i* languish

lánguido *adj* languid

lanza *f* lance

lanzadera *f* shuttle; **lanzadera espacial** space shuttle

lanzado 1 *adj* fig go-ahead; **es muy lanzado con las chicas** he's not shy with girls **2** *part* → **lanzar**

lanzamiento *m* MIL, COM launch; **lanzamiento de disco / de martillo** discus / hammer (throw); **lanzamiento de peso** shot put

lanzar ⟨1f⟩ **1** *v/t* throw; *cohete, producto* launch; *bomba* drop **2** *v/r* **lanzarse** throw o.s. (**en** into); (*precipitarse*) pounce (**sobre** on); **lanzarse a hacer algo** rush into doing sth

lapa *f* ZO limpet

lapicera *f* Rpl, Chi (ballpoint) pen; **lapicera fuente** L.Am. fountain pen

lapicero *m* automatic pencil, *Br* propelling pencil

lápida *f* memorial stone

lapidario *adj* memorable

lápiz *m* pencil; **lápiz de ojos** eyeliner; **lápiz labial** *or* **de labios** lipstick; **lápiz óptico** light pen

lapso *m* de tiempo space, period

lapsus *m* inv slip; **tener un lapsus** have a momentary lapse

larga *f*: **poner la** (**s**) **larga** (**s**) put the headlights on full beam; **dar largas a alguien** F put s.o. off

largar ⟨1h⟩ **1** *v/t* drive away **2** *v/r* **largarse** F clear off *o* out F

largo 1 *adj* long; *persona* tall; **a la -a** in the long run; **a lo largo del día** throughout the day; **a lo largo de la calle** along the street; **¡largo!** F scram! F; **esto va para largo** this will take some time; **pasar de largo** go (straight) past **2** *m* length

largometraje *m* feature film

larguero *m* DEP crossbar

laringe *f* larynx

laringitis *f* MED laryngitis

larva *f* ZO larva

las 1 *art fpl* the **2** *pron complemento directo pl* them; *a ustedes* you; **llévate las que quieras** take whichever ones you want; **las de ...** those of ...; **las de Juan** Juan's; **las que llevan falda** the ones *o* those that are wearing dresses

lasaña *f* GASTR lasagne

lascivo *adj* lewd

láser *m* laser; **rayo láser** laser beam

lástima *f* pity, shame; **me da lástima no usarlo** it's a shame *o* pity not to use it; **¡qué lástima!** what a pity *o* shame!

lastimar ⟨1a⟩ **1** *v/t* (*herir*) hurt **2** *v/r* **lastimarse** hurt o.s.

lastimoso *adj* pitiful; (*deplorable*) shameful

lastre *m* ballast; *fig* burden

lata *f* can, *Br* tb tin; *fig* F drag F, pain F; **dar la lata** F be a drag F *o* a pain F

latente *adj* latent

lateral 1 *adj* side *atr*; **cuestiones laterales** side issues **2** *m* DEP: **lateral derecho / izquierdo** right / left back

latería *f* L.Am. tin works

latero *m*, **-a** *f* L.Am. tinsmith

latido *m* beat

latifundio *m* large estate

latigazo *m* lash; (*chasquido*) crack

látigo *m* whip

latín *m* Latin

latino *adj* Latin

Latinoamérica Latin America

latinoamericano 1 *adj* Latin American **2** *m*, **-a** *f* Latin American

latir ⟨3a⟩ *v/i* beat

latitud *f* GEOG latitude

latón *m* brass

laucha *f* S. Am. mouse

laurel *m* BOT laurel; **dormirse en los laureles** fig rest on one's laurels

lava *f* lava

lavable *adj* washable

lavabo *m* washbowl

lavada *f* L.Am. wash

lavado *m* washing; **lavado de cerebro** fig brainwashing

lavadora *f* washing machine

lavamanos *m* inv L.Am. → **lavabo**

lavanda *f* BOT lavender

lavandería *f* laundry

lavaplatos *m* inv dishwasher; *L.Am.* sink

lavar ⟨1a⟩ **1** *v/t* wash; **lavar los platos** wash the dishes; **lavar la ropa** do the laundry, *Br tb* do the washing; **lavar en seco** dry-clean **2** *v/i* (*lavar los platos*) do the dishes; **de detergente** clean **3** v/r **lavarse** wash up, Br have a wash; **lavarse los dientes** brush one's teeth; **lavarse las manos** wash one's hands; **yo me lavo las manos** fig I wash my hands of it

lavarropas m inv L.Am. washing machine

lavavajillas m inv líquido dishwashing liquid, Br washing-up liquid; **electrodoméstico** dishwasher

laxante m/adj MED laxative

laxo adj relaxed; (poco estricto) lax

lazada f bow

lazarillo m guide; **perro lazarillo** seeing eye dog, Br guide dog

lazo m knot; de adorno bow; **para atrapar animales** lasso

le pron sg complemento indirecto (to) him; (a ella) (to) her; (a usted) (to) you; (a algo) (to) it; complemento directo him; (a usted) you

leal adj loyal

lealtad f loyalty

lección f lesson; **esto le servirá de lección** that will teach him a lesson

lechar ⟨1a⟩ v/t L.Am. (ordeñar) milk

leche f milk; **leche condensada** condensed milk; **leche entera** whole milk; **leche en polvo** powdered milk; **estar de mala leche** P be in a foul mood; **tener mala leche** P be out to make trouble

lechería f dairy

lechero 1 adj dairy atr **2** m milkman

lecho m tb de río bed

lechón m suckling pig

lechuga f lettuce; **ser más fresco que una lechuga** F have a lot of nerve

lechuza f zo barn-owl; Cuba, Méx P hooker F

lectivo adj: **día lectivo** school day

lector m, **~a** f reader

lectura f reading

leer ⟨2e⟩ v/t read

legado m legacy; persona legate

legal adj legal; fig F persona great F, terrific F

legalidad f legality

legalizar ⟨1f⟩ v/t legalize

legaña f: **tener legañas en los ojos** have sleep in one's eyes

legar ⟨1h⟩ v/t leave

legendario adj legendary

legible adj legible

legión f legion

legislación f legislation

legislar ⟨1a⟩ v/i legislate

legislativo adj legislative

legislatura f cuerpo legislature; periodo term of office

legitimar ⟨1a⟩ v/t justify; documento authenticate

legítimo adj legitimate; (verdadero) authentic

lego adj lay atr; fig ignorant

legua f: **se ve a la legua** fig F you can see it a mile off F; **hecho** it's blindingly obvious F

legumbre f BOT pulse

leída f L.Am. reading

lejanía f distance; **en la lejanía** in the distance

lejano adj distant

lejía f bleach

lejos 1 adv far, far away; **Navidad queda lejos** Christmas is a long way off; **a lo lejos** in the distance; **ir demasiado lejos** fig go too far, overstep the mark; **llegar lejos** fig go far **2** prp: **lejos de** far from

lele adj C.Am. stupid

lema m slogan

lencería f lingerie

lengua f tongue; **lengua materna** mother tongue; **con la lengua fuera** fig with one's tongue hanging out; **irse de la lengua** let the cat out of the bag; **sacar la lengua a alguien** stick one's tongue out at s.o.; **lo tengo en la punta de la lengua** it's on the tip of my tongue

lenguado m zo sole

lenguaje m language; **lenguaje de programación** INFOR programming language

lenguaraz adj foul-mouthed

lengüeta 1 f de zapato tongue **2** adj: **ser lengüeta** S. Am. F be a gossip

lenitivo m balm

lente f lens; **lentes de contacto** contact lenses, contacts

lentes mpl L.Am. glasses

lenteja f BOT lentil

lentejuela f sequin

lentillas fpl contact lenses

lentitud f slowness

lento adj slow; **a fuego lento** on a low heat

leña f (fire)wood; **echar leña al fuego** fig add fuel to the fire

leñador m woodcutter

leño m log

Leo m/f inv ASTR Leo

león m zo lion; L.Am. puma; **león marino** sealion

leona f lioness

leonera f lion's den; jaula lion's cage; Rpl, Chi fig F habitación desordenada etc pigsty F; L.Am. F para prisioneros bullpen F, Br communal cell for holding prisoners temporarily

leopardo *m* zo leopard
leotardo *m de gimnasta* leotard; **leotardos** tights, *Br* heavy tights
lépero *adj C.Am., Méx* coarse
lerdo *adj (torpe)* slow(-witted)
les *pron pl complemento indirecto* (to) them; *(a ustedes)* (to) you; *complemento directo* them; *(a ustedes)* you
lesbiana *f* lesbian
lesión *f* injury
lesionado *adj* injured
lesionar ⟨1a⟩ *v/t* injure
letal *adj* lethal
letanía *f* litany
letárgico *adj* lethargic
letra *f* letter; *de canción* lyrics *pl;* **letra de cambio** COM bill of exchange; **letra de imprenta** block letter; **letra mayúscula** capital letter; **al pie de la letra** word for word
letrero *m* sign
letrina *f* latrine
leucemia *f* MED leuk(a)emia
levadura *f* yeast
levantamiento *m* raising; *(rebelión)* rising; *de embargo* lifting
levantar ⟨1a⟩ **1** *v/t* raise; *bulto* lift (up); *del suelo* pick up; *edificio, estatua* put up, erect; *embargo* lift; **levantar sospechas** arouse suspicion; **¡levanta los ánimos!** cheer up!; **levantar la voz** raise one's voice **2** *v/r* **levantarse** get up; *(ponerse de pie)* stand up; *de un edificio, una montaña* rise; *en rebelión* rise up
levante *m* east
levar ⟨1a⟩ *v/t:* **levar anclas** weigh anchor
leve *adj* slight; *sonrisa* faint
levedad *f* lightness
levitar ⟨1a⟩ *v/i* levitate
léxico *m* lexicon
ley *f* law; **con todas las de la ley** fairly and squarely
leyenda *f* legend
leyendo *vb* → **leer**
leyó *vb* → **leer**
liana *f* BOT liana, creeper
liar ⟨1c⟩ **1** *v/t* tie (up); *en papel* wrap (up); *cigarrillo* roll; *persona* confuse **2** *v/r* **liarse de una persona** get confused; **liarse a hacer algo** get tied up doing sth; **liarse con alguien** F get involved with s.o.
Líbano Lebanon
libélula *f* zo dragonfly
liberación *f* release; *de un país* liberation
liberal *adj* liberal
liberalización *f* liberalization
liberalizar ⟨1f⟩ *v/t* liberalize
liberar ⟨1a⟩ **1** *v/t* (set) free, release; *país* liberate; *energía* release **2** *v/r* **liberarse:**

liberarse de algo free o.s. of sth
libertad *f* freedom, liberty; **libertad bajo fianza** JUR bail; **libertad condicional** JUR probation; **dejar a alguien en libertad** release s.o., let s.o. go
libertinaje *m* licentiousness
Libia Libya
líbido *f* libido
libio(-a) *m/f & adj* Libyan
libra *f* pound; **libra esterlina** pound (sterling)
Libra *m/f inv* ASTR Libra
librar ⟨1a⟩ **1** *v/t* free (**de** from); *cheque* draw; *batalla* fight **2** *v/i:* **libro los lunes** I have Mondays off **3** *v/r* **librarse: librarse de algo** get out of sth; **de buena nos hemos librado** F that was lucky
libre *adj* free; *tiempo* spare, free; **eres libre de** you're free to
librecambio *m* free trade
librera *f* bookseller
librería *f* book store
librero *m* bookseller; *L.Am. mueble* bookcase
libreta *f* notebook; **libreta de ahorros** bankbook, passbook
libro *m* book; **libro de bolsillo** paperback (book); **libro de cocina** cookbook, cookery book; **libro de familia** booklet recording family births, marriages and deaths; **libro de reclamaciones** complaints book
licencia *f* permit, license, *Br* licence; *(permiso)* permission; MIL leave; **licencia (de manejar** *or* **conducir)** *L.Am.* driver's license, *Br* driving licence; **tomarse demasiadas licencias** take liberties
licenciado *m,* -**a** *f* graduate
licenciar ⟨1b⟩ **1** *v/t* MIL discharge **2** *v/r* licenciarse graduate; MIL be discharged
licenciatura *f* EDU degree
liceo *m* *L.Am.* high school, *Br* secondary school
licitación *f* *L.Am.* bidding
licitador *m,* **licitadora** *f* *L.Am.* bidder
licitar ⟨1a⟩ *v/t* *L.Am. en subasta* bid for
lícito *adj* legal; *(razonable)* fair, reasonable
licor *m* liquor, *Br* spirits *pl*
licuado *m* *Méx* fruit milkshake
licuadora *f* blender
licuar ⟨1d⟩ *v/t* blend, liquidize
líder *m/f* leader **2** *adj* leading
liderar ⟨1a⟩ *v/t* lead
liderazgo *m* leadership
lidia *f* bullfighting
lidiar ⟨1b⟩ **1** *v/i fig* do battle, struggle **2** *v/t* *toro* fight
liebre *f* zo hare

L

lienzo *m* canvas
liga *f* POL, DEP league; *de medias* garter
ligamento *m* ANAT ligament
ligar ⟨1h⟩ **1** *v/t* bind; (*atar*) tie **2** *v/i*: *ligar con* F pick up F
ligereza *f* lightness; (*rapidez*) speed; *de movimiento* agility; *de carácter* shallowness, superficiality
ligero **1** *adj* (*de poco peso*) light; (*rápido*) rapid, quick; *movimiento* agile, nimble; (*leve*) slight; *ligero de ropa* scantily clad; *a la -a* (*sin pensar*) lightly, casually; *tomar algo a la -a* not take sth seriously **2** *adv* quickly
ligón *m* F: *es un ligón* he's a real Don Juan F
ligue *m* F: *estar de ligue* be on the pick-up F, *Br* be on the pull F
liguero *m* garter belt; *Br* suspender belt
lija *f*: *papel de lija* sandpaper
lijar ⟨1a⟩ *v/t* sand
lila *f* BOT lilac
lima *f* lime; BOT lime; *lima de uñas* nail file
limar ⟨1a⟩ *v/t* file; *fig* polish
limitado *adj* limited **2** *part* → *limitar*
limitar ⟨1a⟩ **1** *v/t* limit **2** *v/i*: *limitar con* border on **3** *v/r* limitarse limit *o* restrict o.s. (*a* to)
límite **1** *m* limit; (*línea de separación*) boundary; *límite de velocidad* speed limit **2** *adj*: *situación límite* life-threatening situation
limítrofe *adj* neighbo(u)ring
limón *m* lemon
limonada *f* lemonade
limosna *f*: *una limosna, por favor* can you spare some change?
limpiabotas *m/f sg* bootblack
limpiacristales *m inv* window cleaner
limpiada *f L.Am.* clean
limpiamanos *m inv L.Am.* hand towel
limpiaparabrisas *m inv* AUTO windshield wiper, *Br* windscreen wiper
limpiar ⟨1b⟩ *v/t* clean; *con un trapo* wipe; *fig* clean up; *limpiar a alguien* F clean s.o. out F
limpieza *f estado* cleanliness; *acto* cleaning; *limpieza general* spring cleaning; *limpieza en seco* dry-cleaning; *hacer la limpieza* do the cleaning
limpio *adj* clean; (*ordenado*) neat, tidy; *político* honest; *gana $5.000 limpios al mes* he takes home $5,000 a month; *quedarse limpio S. Am.* F be broke F; *sacar algo en limpio* *fig* make sense of sth
limusina *f* limousine
linaje *m* lineage
lince *m* ZO lynx; *ojos or vista de lince* *fig*

eyes like a hawk
linchar ⟨1a⟩ *v/t* lynch
lindar ⟨1a⟩ *v/i*: *lindar con algo* adjoin sth; *fig* border on sth
lindo *adj* lovely; *de lo lindo* a lot, a great deal
línea *f* line; *línea aérea* airline; *mantener la línea* watch one's figure; *de primera línea* *fig* first-rate; *tecnología de primera línea* state-of-the art technology; *entre líneas* *fig* between the lines
lineal *adj* linear
linfático *adj* lymphatic
lingote *m* ingot; *lingote de oro* gold bar
lingüista *m/f* linguist
lingüística *f* linguistics
lingüístico *adj* linguistic
linier *m* DEP assistant referee, linesman
lino *m* linen; BOT flax
linterna *f* flashlight, *Br* torch
lío *m* bundle; F (*desorden*) mess; F (*jaleo*) fuss; *lío amoroso* F affair; *estar hecho un lío* be all confused; *hacerse un lío* get into a muddle; *meterse en líos* get into trouble
liposucción *f* MED liposuction
lipotimia *f* MED blackout
liquen *m* BOT lichen
liquidación *f* COM *de cuenta, deuda* settlement; *de negocio* liquidation; *liquidación total* clearance sale
liquidar ⟨1a⟩ *v/t cuenta, deuda* settle; COM *negocio* wind up, liquidate; *existencias* sell off; F (*matar*) liquidate F, bump off F
liquidez *f* COM liquidity
líquido **1** *adj* liquid; COM net **2** *m* liquid
lira *f* lira
lírico *adj* lyrical
lirio *m* BOT lily
lirón *m* ZO dormouse; *dormir como un lirón* *fig* F sleep like a log
lisiado **1** *adj* crippled **2** *m* cripple
liso *adj* smooth; *terreno* flat; *pelo* straight; (*sin adornos*) plain; *-a y llanamente* plainly and simply
lisonja *f* flattery
lista *f* list; *lista de boda* wedding list; *lista de espera* waiting list; *pasar lista* take the roll call, *Br* call the register
listado *m* INFOR printout
listín *m*: *listín* (*telefónico*) phone book
listo *adj* (*inteligente*) clever; (*preparado*) ready; *pasarse de listo* try to be too smart F
listón *m de madera* strip; DEP bar; *poner el listón muy alto* *fig* set very high standards
lisura *f Rpl, Pe* curse, swearword

litera f bunk; *de tren* couchette
literal adj literal
literario adj literary
literatura f literature
litigante m/f & adj JUR litigant
litigar ⟨1h⟩ v/i JUR go to litigation
litigio m lawsuit
litografía f lithography
litoral 1 adj coastal **2** m coast
litro m liter, Br litre
liturgia f REL liturgy
liviano adj light; (*de poca importancia*) trivial
lívido adj pale
llaga f ulcer; **poner** or **meter el dedo en la llaga** fig put one's finger on it
llama f flame; zo llama
llamada f call; *en una puerta* knock; *en timbre* ring; **llamada a cobro revertido** collect call; **llamada de auxilio** distress call
llamado m L.Am. call
llamador m (door) knocker
llamamiento m call; **hacer un llamamiento a algo** call for sth
llamar ⟨1a⟩ v/t call; TELEC call, Br tb ring **2** v/i TELEC call, Br tb ring; **llamar a la puerta** knock at the door; *con timbre* ring the bell; **el fútbol no me llama nada** football doesn't appeal to me in the slightest **3** v/r **llamarse** be called; **¿cómo te llamas?** what's your name?
llamarada f flare-up
llamativo adj eyecatching; *color* loud
llamón adj Méx moaning
llano 1 adj *terreno* level; *trato* natural; *persona* unassuming **2** m flat ground
llanta f wheel rim; *C.Am., Méx (neumático)* tire, Br tyre
llanto m sobbing
llanura f plain
llave f key; *para tuerca* wrench, Br tb spanner; **llave de contacto** AUTO ignition key; **llave inglesa** TÉC monkey wrench; **llave de paso** stop cock; **llave en mano** available for immediate occupancy; **bajo llave** under lock and key; **cerrar con llave** lock
llavero m key ring
llegada f arrival
llegar ⟨1h⟩ **1** v/i arrive; (*alcanzar*) reach; **la comida no llegó para todos** there wasn't enough food for everyone; **me llega hasta las rodillas** it comes down to my knees; **el agua me llegaba a la cintura** the water came up to my waist; **llegar a saber** find out; **llegar a ser** get to be; **llegar a viejo** live to a ripe old age **2** v/r **llegarse: llégate al vecino** F run over

to the neighbo(u)r's
llenar ⟨1a⟩ **1** v/t fill; *impreso* fill out o in **2** v/i be filling **3** v/r **llenarse** fill up; **me he llenado** I have had enough (to eat)
lleno adj full (**de** of); *pared* covered (**de** with); **de lleno** fully
llevadero adj bearable
llevar ⟨1a⟩ **1** v/t take; *ropa, gafas* wear; *ritmo* keep up; **llevar a alguien en coche** drive s.o., take s.o. in the car; **llevar dinero encima** carry money; **llevar las de perder** be likely to lose; **me lleva dos años** he's two years older than me; **llevo ocho días aquí** I've been here a week; **llevo una hora esperando** I've been waiting for an hour **2** v/i lead (**a** to) **3** v/r **llevarse** take; *susto, sorpresa* get; **llevarse bien / mal** get on well / badly; **se lleva el color rojo** red is fashionable
llorar ⟨1a⟩ v/i cry, weep
lloriquear ⟨1a⟩ v/i snivel, whine
lloro m weeping, crying
llorón 1 adj: **ser llorón** be a crybaby F **2** m F crybaby F
llovedera f L.Am., **llovedero** m L.Am. rainy season
llover ⟨2h⟩ v/i rain; **llueve** it is raining
llovizna f drizzle
lloviznar ⟨1a⟩ v/i drizzle
llueve vb → **llover**
lluvia f rain; Rpl (*ducha*) shower; **lluvia ácida** acid rain
lluvioso adj rainy
lo 1 art sg the; **lo bueno** the good thing; **no sabes lo difícil que es** you don't know how difficult it is **2** pron sg: *a él* him; *a usted* you; *algo* it; **lo sé** I know **3** pron rel sg: **lo que** what; **lo cual** which
loable adj praiseworthy, laudable
lobo m wolf; **lobo marino** seal; **lobo de mar** fig sea dog
lóbrego adj gloomy
lóbulo m lobe; **lóbulo de la oreja** earlobe
loca f madwoman
locador m S. Am. landlord
local 1 adj local **2** m premises pl; **local comercial** commercial premises pl
localidad f town; TEA seat
localización f location
localizar ⟨1f⟩ v/t locate; *incendio* contain, bring under control
loción f lotion
loco 1 adj mad, crazy; **a lo loco** F (*sin pensar*) hastily; **es para volverse loco** it's enough to drive you mad o crazy **2** m madman
locomoción f locomotion; **medio de locomoción** means of transport
locomotora f locomotive

L

locro *m* S. Am. stew of meat, corn and potatoes

locuaz *adj* talkative, loquacious *fml*

locución *f* phrase

locura *f* madness; *es una locura* it's madness

locutor *m*, **locutora** *f* RAD, TV presenter

locutorio *m* TELEC phone booth

lodazal *m* quagmire

lodo *m* mud

lógica *f* logic

lógico *adj* logical

logística *f* logistics

logopeda *m/f* speech therapist

logotipo *m* logo

logrado *adj* excellent

lograr ⟨1a⟩ *v/t* achieve; (*obtener*) obtain; *lograr hacer algo* manage to do sth; *lograr que alguien haga algo* (manage to) get s.o. to do sth

logrero *m* L.Am. F profiteer

logro *m* achievement

loma *f* L.Am. small hill

lombriz *f*: *lombriz de tierra* earthworm

lomo *m* back; GASTR loin; *a lomos de burro* on a donkey

lona *f* canvas

loncha *f* slice

lonche *m* L.Am. afternoon snack

lonchería *f* L.Am. diner, luncheonette

londinense **1** *adj* London *atr* **2** *m/f* Londoner

Londres London

longaniza *f* type of dried sausage

longevidad *f* longevity

longevo *adj* long-lived

longitud *f* longitude; (*largo*) length

longitudinal *adj* longitudinal

lonja *f* de pescado fish market; (*loncha*) slice

loquera *f* L.Am. F shrink F; *enfermera* psychiatric nurse

loquero *m* L.Am. F persona shrink F; *enfermero* psychiatric nurse; (*manicomio*) mental hospital, funny farm F

loro *m* parrot; *estar al loro* F (*enterado*) be clued up F, be on the ball F

los *mpl* **1** *art* the **2** *pron complemento directo pl* them; *a ustedes* you; *llévate los que quieras* take whichever ones you want; *los de ...* those of ...; *los de Juan* Juan's; *los que juegan* the ones *o* those that are playing

losa *f* flagstone

lote *m* en reparto share, part; L.Am. (*solar*) lot

lotería *f* lottery

loto **1** *m* BOT lotus **2** *f* F lottery

loza *f* china

lozano *adj* healthy-looking

lubina *f* ZO sea bass

lubri(fi)cación *f* lubrication

lubri(fi)cante **1** *adj* lubricating **2** *m* lubricant

lubri(fi)car ⟨1g⟩ *v/t* lubricate

lucero *m* bright star; (*Venus*) Venus

lucha *f* fight, struggle; DEP wrestling; *lucha libre* DEP all-in wrestling

luchador **1** *adj* espíritu fighting **2** *m*, **luchadora** *f* fighter

luchar ⟨1a⟩ *v/i* fight (*por* for)

lúcido *adj* lucid, clear

luciérnaga *f* ZO glow-worm

lucimiento *m* (*brillo*) splendo(u)r; *le ofrece oportunidades de lucimiento* it gives him a chance to shine

lucio *m* ZO pike

lucir ⟨3f⟩ **1** *v/i* shine; L.Am. (*verse bien*) look good **2** *v/t* ropa, joya wear **3** *v/r* *lucirse tb* irón excel o.s., surpass o.s.

lucrativo *adj* lucrative

lucro *m* profit; *afán de lucro* profit-making; *sin ánimo de lucro* non-profit (making), not-for-profit

ludopatía *f* compulsive gambling

luego **1** *adv* (*después*) later; *en orden, espacio* then; L.Am. (*en seguida*) right now; *luego luego* Méx straight away; *¡desde luego!* of course!; *¡hasta luego!* see you (later) **2** *conj* therefore; *luego que* L.Am. after

lugar *m* place; *lugar común* cliché; *en lugar de* instead of; *en primer lugar* in the first place, first(ly); *fuera de lugar* out of place; *yo en tu lugar* if I were you, (if I were) in your place; *dar lugar a* give rise to; *tener lugar* take place

lúgubre *adj* gloomy

lujo *m* luxury

lujoso *adj* luxurious

lujuria *f* lust

lujurioso *adj* lecherous

lumbago *m* MED lumbago

lumbre *f* fire

lumbrera *f* genius

luminoso *adj* luminous; *lámpara, habitación* bright

luna *f* moon; *de tienda* window; *de vehículo* windshield, Br windscreen; *luna de miel* honeymoon; *luna llena / nueva* full / new moon; *media luna* L.Am. GASTR croissant; *estar en la luna* F have one's head in the clouds F

lunar **1** *adj* lunar **2** *m* en la piel mole; *de lunares* spotted, polka-dot

lunático *adj* lunatic

lunes *m inv* Monday

luneta *f*: *luneta térmica* AUTO heated

windshield, *Br* heated windscreen
lunfardo *m Arg* slang used in Buenos Aires
lupa *f* magnifying glass; *mirar algo con lupa* fig go through sth with a fine tooth-comb
lustrabotas *m/f inv L.Am.* bootblack
lustrador *m*, **lustradora** *f L.Am.* bootblack
lustrar ⟨1a⟩ *v/t* polish
lustre *m* shine; *fig* luster, *Br* lustre; *dar lustre a fig* give added luster (*Br* lustre) to
lustro *m* period of five years

lustroso *adj* shiny
luto *m* mourning; *estar de luto por alguien* be in mourning for s.o.
luxación *f* MED dislocation
luz *f* light; *luz trasera* AUTO rear light; *luces de carretera* or *largas* AUTO full *o* main beam headlights; *luces de cruce* or *cortas* AUTO dipped headlights; *luz verde* tb fig green light; *arrojar luz sobre algo fig* shed light on s.th.; *dar a luz* give birth to; *salir a la luz fig* come to light; *a todas luces* evidently, clearly; *de pocas luces* fig F dim F, not very bright

M

m *abr* (= **metro**) m (= meter); (= **minuto**) m (= minute)
macabro 1 *adj* macabre **2** *m*, **-a** *f* ghoul
macaco *m* ZO macaque
macana *f L.Am.* billyclub, *Br* truncheon; F (*mentira*) lie, fib F; *hizo / dijo una macana* he did / said something stupid; *¡qué macana! Rpl* P what a drag!
macanear ⟨1a⟩ *v/t L.Am.* (*aporrear*) beat
macanudo *S. Am.* F great F, fantastic F
macarra 1 *m* P pimp **2** *adj* F: *ser macarra* be a bastard P
macarrones *mpl* macaroni *sg*
macedonia *f*: *macedonia de frutas* fruit salad
macerar ⟨1a⟩ *v/t* GASTR soak
maceta *f* flowerpot
macetero *m* flowerpot holder; *L.Am.* flowerpot
machacar ⟨1g⟩ *v/t* crush; *fig* thrash
machete *m* machete
machismo *m* male chauvinism
machista 1 *adj* sexist **2** *m* sexist, male chauvinist
macho 1 *adj* male; (*varonil*) tough; *desp* macho **2** *m* male; *apelativo* F man F, *Br* mate F; *L.Am.* (*plátano*) banana
macizo 1 *adj* solid; *estar macizo* F be a dish F **2** *m* GEOG massif; *macizo de flores* flower bed
macuto *m* backpack
madeja *f* hank
madera *f* wood; *tener madera de* have the makings of
maderera *f* timber merchant

madero *m* P cop P
madrastra *f* step-mother
madre 1 *f* mother; *madre soltera* single mother; *dar en la madre a alguien* F hit s.o. where it hurts; *¡me vale madre! Méx* V I don't give a fuck! V **2** *adj Méx*, *C.Am.* F great F, fantastic
madreselva *f* BOT honeysuckle
Madrid Madrid
madriguera *f* (*agujero*) burrow; (*guarida*) tb fig den
madrileño 1 *adj* of / from Madrid, Madrid *atr* **2** *m*, **-a** *f* native of Madrid
madrina *f* godmother
madrugada *f* early morning; (*amanecer*) dawn; *de madrugada* in the small hours
madrugador *m*, **madrugadora** *f* early riser
madrugar ⟨1h⟩ *v/i L.Am.* (*quedar despierto*) stay up till the small hours; (*levantarse temprano*) get up early
madurar ⟨1a⟩ **1** *v/t fig: idea* think through **2** *v/i de persona* mature; *de fruta* ripen
madurez *f mental* maturity; *edad* middle age; *de fruta* ripeness
maduro *adj mentalmente* mature; *de edad* middle-aged; *fruta* ripe
maestría *f* mastery; *Méx* EDU master's (degree)
maestro 1 *adj* master *atr* **2** *m*, **-a** *f* EDU teacher; MÚS maestro
mafia *f* mafia
mafioso 1 *adj* mafia *atr* **2** *m* mafioso, gangster
magdalena *f* cupcake, *Br* tb fairy cake

magia f tb fig magic

mágico adj magic

magisterio m teaching profession

magistrado m judge

magistral adj masterly

magnanimidad f magnanimity

magnánimo adj magnanimous

magnate m magnate, tycoon

magnesio m magnesium

magnético adj magnetic

magnetofón m tape recorder

magnífico adj wonderful, magnificent

magnitud f magnitude

magnolia f BOT magnolia

mago m tb fig magician; **los Reyes Magos** the Three Wise Men, the Three Kings

magrear ⟨1a⟩ v/t F feel up F

Magreb Maghreb

magro adj carne lean

magulladura f bruise

magullar ⟨1a⟩ v/t bruise

magullón m L.Am. bruise

mahometano 1 adj Muslim **2** m, -a f Muslim

mahonesa f mayonnaise

maillot m DEP jersey

maíz m corn

majada f CSur flock of sheep

majaderear ⟨1a⟩ L.Am. F **1** v/t bug F **2** v/i keep going on F

majadería f: **decir / hacer una majadería** say / do something stupid

majadero F 1 adj idiotic, stupid **2** m, -a f idiot

majareta adj F nutty F, screwy F

majestad f majesty

majestuoso adj majestic

majo adj F nice; (bonito) pretty

mal 1 adj → **malo 2** adv badly; **mal que bien** one way or the other; **¡menos mal!** thank goodness!; **ponerse a mal con alguien** fall out with s.o.; **tomarse algo a mal** take sth badly **3** m MED illness; **el mal menor** the lesser of two evils

malabar m/adj: (juegos) **-es** pl juggling sg

malabarista m/f juggler

malacrianza f L.Am. rudeness

malaria f MED malaria

malcriadez f L.Am. bad upbringing

malcriado adj spoilt

malcrianza f L.Am. rudeness

malcriar ⟨1c⟩ v/t spoil

maldad f evil; **es una maldad hacer eso** it's a wicked thing to do

maldecir ⟨3p⟩ **1** v/i curse; **maldecir de alguien** speak ill of s.o. **2** v/t curse

maldición f curse

maldito adj F damn F; **¡-a sea!** (god)damn it!

maleante m/f & adj criminal

malecón m breakwater

maleducado adj rude, bad-mannered

maleficio m curse

maléfico adj evil

malentendido m misunderstanding

malestar m MED discomfort; social unrest

maleta f bag, suitcase; L.Am. AUTO trunk, Br boot; **hacer la maleta** pack one's bags

maletero m trunk, Br boot

maletín m briefcase

malévolo adj malevolent

maleza f undergrowth

malformación f MED malformation

malgastar ⟨1a⟩ v/t waste

malgenioso adj Méx bad-tempered

malhablado adj foul-mouthed

malhechor m, **malhechora** f criminal

malherir ⟨3i⟩ v/t hurt badly

malhumorado adj bad-tempered

malicia f (mala intención) malice; (astucia) cunning, slyness; **no tener malicia** F be very naive

malicioso adj (malintencionado) malicious; (astuto) cunning, sly

maligno adj harmful; MED malignant

malinchismo m Méx treason

malla f mesh; Rpl swimsuit

malo 1 adj bad; calidad poor; (enfermo) sick, ill; **por las buenas o por las -as** whether he / she etc likes it or not; **por las -as** by force; **lo malo es que** unfortunately; **ponerse malo** fall ill **2** m hum bad guy, baddy F

malogrado adj muerto dead before one's time

malograr ⟨1a⟩ **1** v/t waste; trabajo spoil, ruin **2** v/r malograrse fail; de plan come to nothing; fallecer die before one's time; S. Am. (descomponerse) break down; (funcionar mal) go wrong

maloliente adj stinking

malparado adj: **quedar** or **salir malparado de algo** come out badly from sth

malpensado adj: **ser malpensado** have a nasty mind

malsano adj unhealthy

malsonante adj rude

malta f malt

maltratar ⟨1a⟩ v/t mistreat

maltrato m abuse, harsh words pl

maltrecho adj weakened, diminished; cosa damaged

malva f mauve

malvado adj evil

malversación f: **malversación de fondos** embezzlement

nalversar ⟨1a⟩ *v/t* embezzle

Malvinas: *las Malvinas* the Falklands, the Falkland Islands

nalvivir ⟨3a⟩ *v/i* scrape by

mamá *f* mom, *Br* mum

nama *f* breast

namadera *f L.Am.* feeding bottle

namar ⟨1a⟩ *v/i* suck; *dar de mamar* (breast)feed

namarracho *m*: *vas hecho un mamarracho* F you look a mess F

mamífero *m* mammal

mamila *f Méx* feeding bottle

namografía *f* MED mammography

namón 1 *adj Méx* P cocky **2** *m* P bastard P

namona *f* P bitch P

namotreto *m* F *libro* hefty tome

nampara *f* screen

namporro *m* F punch

namposteria *f* masonry

naná *m fig* manna

manada *f* herd; *de lobos* pack

manantial *m* spring

manar ⟨1a⟩ *v/i* flow

manatí *m* zo manatee

manaza *f*: *ser un manazas* F be ham-handed F

nancebo *m* youth

Mancha: *Canal de la Mancha* English Channel

mancha *f* (*dirty*) mark; *de grasa, sangre etc* stain

manchar ⟨1a⟩ **1** *v/t* get dirty; *de grasa, sangre etc* stain **2** *v/r* **mancharse** get dirty

mancillar ⟨1a⟩ *v/t fig* sully

manco *adj de mano* one-handed; *de brazo* one-armed

mancornas *fpl Pe,* E cufflinks

mancuernas *fpl C.Am.* cufflinks

mandamás *m inv* F big shot F

mandado *m Méx, C.Am.*: *los mandados pl* the shopping *sg*

mandamiento *m* order; JUR warrant; REL commandment

mandar ⟨1a⟩ **1** *v/t* order; (*enviar*) send; *a mí no me manda nadie* nobody tells me what to do; *mandar hacer algo* have sth done F *v/i* be in charge; *¿mande?* Méx can I help you?; *Méx* TELEC hallo?; (*¿cómo?*) what did you say?, excuse me?

mandarina *f* mandarin (orange)

mandatario *m* leader; *primer mandatario Méx* President

mandato *m* order; POL mandate

mandíbula *f* ANAT jaw; *reírse a mandíbula batiente* F laugh one's head off F

mandioca *f* cassava

mando *m* command; *alto mando* high command; *mando a distancia* TV remote control; *tablero de mandos* AUTO dashboard

mandolina *f* MÚS mandolin

mandón *adj* F bossy F

manecilla *f* hand

manejable *adj* easy to handle; *automovil* maneuverable, *Br* manoeuvrable

manejar ⟨1a⟩ **1** *v/t* handle; *máquina* operate; *L.Am.* AUTO drive **2** *v/i L.Am.* AUTO drive **3** *v/r* **manejarse** manage, get by

manejo *m* handling; *de una máquina* operation

manera *f* way; *esa es su manera de ser* that's the way he is; *maneras* manners; *lo hace a su manera* he does it his way; *de manera que* so (that); *de ninguna manera* certainly not; *no hay manera de* it is impossible to; *de todas maneras* anyway, in any case

manga *f* sleeve; *manga de riego* hosepipe; *en mangas de camisa* in shirtsleeves; *sin mangas* sleeveless; *sacarse algo de la manga fig* make sth up; *traer algo en la manga* F have sth up one's sleeve

manganeso *m* manganese

mangar ⟨1h⟩ *v/t* P swipe F, pinch F

mangle *m* BOT mangrove

mango *m* BOT mango; *CSur* F (*dinero*) dough F, cash; *estoy sin un mango CSur* F I'm broke F, I don't have a bean F

mangonear ⟨1a⟩ **1** *v/i* F boss people around; (*entrometerse*) meddle **2** *v/t* F: *mangonear a alguien* boss s.o. around

manguera *f* hose(pipe)

maní *m S. Am.* peanut

manía *f* (*costumbre*) habit, mania; (*antipatía*) dislike; (*obsesión*) obsession; *manía persecutoria* persecution complex; *tiene sus -s* she has her little ways; *tener manía a alguien* F have it in for s.o. F

maníaco *m* maniac

maniatar ⟨1a⟩ *v/t*: *maniatar a alguien* tie s.o.'s hands

maniático *adj* F fussy

manicomio *m* lunatic asylum

manicura *f* manicure; *hacerse la manicura* have a manicure

manido *adj fig* clichéd, done to death F

manifestación *f de gente* demonstration; (*muestra*) show; (*declaración*) statement

manifestante *m/f* demonstrator

manifestar ⟨1k⟩ **1** *v/t* (*demostrar*) show; (*declarar*) declare, state **2** *v/r* **manifestarse** demonstrate

manifiesto 1 *adj* clear, manifest; *poner*

de manifiesto make clear **2** *m* manifesto

manigua *f* W.I. thicket, bush

manija *f* L.Am. (asa) handle

manillar *m* handlebars *pl*

maniobra *f* maneuver, *Br* manoeuvre; *hacer maniobras* maneuver, *Br* manoeuvre

maniobrar ⟨1a⟩ *v/i* maneuver, *Br* manoeuvre

manipulación *f* manipulation; (*manejo*) handling

manipular ⟨1a⟩ *v/t* manipulate; (*manejar*) handle

maniquí 1 *m* dummy **2** *m/f* model

manirroto 1 *adj* extravagant **2** *m*, **-a** *f* spendthrift

manisero *m*, **-a** *f* W.I., S. Am. peanut seller

manitas *fpl*: *ser un manitas* be handy

manito *m* Méx pal, buddy

manivela *f* handle

manjar *m* delicacy

mano *f* hand; *mano de obra* labo(u)r, manpower; *mano de pintura* coat of paint; *¡manos arriba!* hands up!; *a mano derecha / izquierda* on the right/left; *atar las manos a alguien* fig tie s.o.'s hands; *de segunda mano* second-hand; *echar una mano a alguien* give s.o. a hand; *estar a mano* L.Am. F be even, be quits; *hecho a mano* handmade; *poner la mano en el fuego* fig swear to it; *poner manos a la obra* get down to work; *se le fue la mano con* fig he overdid it with; *tener a mano* have to hand; *traerse algo entre manos* be plotting sth **2** *m* Méx F pal F, buddy F

manojo *m* handful; *manojo de llaves* bunch of keys; *manojo de nervios* fig bundle of nerves

manopla *f* mitten

manosear ⟨1a⟩ *v/t fruta* handle; *persona* F grope F

manotazo *m* slap

manotear ⟨1a⟩ **1** *v/t Arg, Méx* grab **2** *v/i Arg, Méx* wave one's hands around

mansalva *f*: *a mansalva* in vast numbers; *bebida, comida* in vast amounts

mansedumbre *f* docility; *de persona* mildness

mansión *f* mansion

manso *adj* docile; *persona* mild

manta *f* blanket; *tirar de la manta* fig uncover the truth

manteca *f* fat; *Rpl* butter; *manteca de cacao* cocoa butter; *manteca de cerdo* lard

mantel *m* tablecloth; *mantel individual* table mat

mantelería *f* table linen; *una mantelería* a set of table linen

mantención *f* L.Am. → **manutención**

mantener ⟨2l⟩ **1** *v/t* (*sujetar*) hold; *techo etc* hold up; (*preservar*) keep; *conversación, relación* have; *económicamente* support; (*afirmar*) maintain **2** *v/r* **mantenerse** (*sujetarse*) be held; *económicamente* support o.s.; *en forma* keep

mantenimiento *m* maintenance; *económico* support; *gimnasia de mantenimiento* gym

mantequilla *f* butter

mantequillera *f* L.Am. butter dish

mantilla *f de bebé* shawl; *estar en mantillas* fig F be in its infancy

mantuvo *vb* → **mantener**

manual *m/adj* manual

manualidades *fpl* handicrafts

manubrio *m* handle; *S. Am.* handlebars *pl*

manufacturar ⟨1a⟩ *v/t* manufacture

manuscrito 1 *adj* handwritten **2** *m* manuscript

manutención *f* maintenance

manzana *f* apple; *de casas* block; *manzana de la discordia* fig bone of contention

manzanilla *f* camomile tea

manzano *m* apple tree

maña *f* skill; *darse* or *tener maña para* be good at; *tiene muchas mañas* L.Am. she's got lots of tricks up her sleeve F

mañana 1 *f* morning; *por la mañana* in the morning; *mañana por la mañana* tomorrow morning; *de la mañana a la noche* from morning until night; *de la noche a la mañana* fig overnight; *esta mañana* this morning; *muy de mañana* very early (in the morning) **2** *adv* tomorrow; *pasado mañana* the day after tomorrow

mañanita *f* shawl

mañero *adj Rpl*

mañoso *adj* (*animal: terco*) stubborn; (*nervioso*) skittish, nervous

mañoso *adj* skil(l)ful; *L.Am. animal* stubborn

mapa *m* map; *mapa de carreteras* road map

mapache *m* raccoon

mapamundi *m* map of the world

maqueta *f* model

maquillador *m*, **maquilladora** *f* make-up artist

maquillaje *m* make-up

maquillar ⟨1a⟩ **1** *v/t* make up **2** *v/r* **maquillarse** put on one's make-up

máquina *f* machine; *FERR* locomotive; *C.Am., W.I.* car; *máquina de afeitar* (electric) shaver; *máquina de coser*

153

martes

sewing machine; *máquina de fotos* camera; *máquina recreativa* arcade game; *pasar algo a máquina* type sth; *a toda máquina* at top speed

maquinaciones *fpl* scheming *sg*

maquinador 1 *adj* scheming **2** *m*, **maquinadora** *f* schemer

maquinal *adj fig* mechanical

maquinar ⟨1a⟩ *v/t* plot

maquinaria *f* machinery

maquinilla *f*: *maquinilla de afeitar* razor; *maquinilla eléctrica* electric razor

maquinista *m/f* FERR engineer, *Br* train driver

mar *m (also f)* GEOG sea; *sudaba a mares* *fig* F the sweat was pouring off him F; *llover a mares* *fig* F pour, bucket down F; *alta mar* high seas *pl*; *la mar de bien* (*muy bien*) really well

maraca *f* MÚS maraca

maraña *f de hilos* tangle; (*lío*) jumble

marasmo *m fig* stagnation

maratón *m (also f)* marathon

maratoniano *adj* marathon *atr*

maravilla *f* marvel, wonder; BOT marigold; *de maravilla* marvellously, wonderfully; *a las mil maravillas* marvellously, wonderfully

maravillar ⟨1a⟩ **1** *v/t* amaze, astonish **2** *v/r* **maravillarse** be amazed *o* astonished (*de* at)

maravilloso *adj* marvellous, wonderful

marca *f* mark; COM brand; *marca registrada* registered trademark; *de marca* brand-name *atr*

marcador *m* DEP scoreboard

marcaje *m* DEP marking

marcapasos *m inv* MED pacemaker

marcar ⟨1g⟩ *v/t* mark; *número de teléfono* dial; *gol* score; *res* brand; *de termómetro, contador etc* read, register

marcha *f* (*salida*) departure; (*velocidad*) speed; (*avance*) progress; MIL march; AUTO gear; DEP walk; *marcha atrás* AUTO reverse (gear); *a marchas forzadas* *fig* flat out; *a toda marcha* at top speed; *hacer algo sobre la marcha* do sth as one goes along; *ponerse en marcha* get started, get going; *tener mucha marcha* F be very lively

marchante *m* L.Am. regular customer

marchar ⟨1a⟩ **1** *v/i* (*progresar*) go; (*funcionar*) work; (*caminar*) walk; MIL march **2** *v/r* **marcharse** leave, go

marchitarse ⟨1a⟩ *v/r* wilt

marcial *adj* martial; *artes marciales* martial arts

marciano *m* Martian

marco *m moneda* mark; *de cuadro, puerta* frame; *fig* framework

marea *f* tide; *marea alta* high tide; *marea baja* low tide; *marea negra* oil slick

mareado *adj* dizzy

marear ⟨1a⟩ **1** *v/t* make feel nauseous, *Br* make feel sick; *fig* (*confundir*) confuse **2** *v/r* **marearse** feel nauseous, *Br* feel sick

marejada *f* heavy sea

maremoto *m* tidal wave

mareo *m* seasickness

marfil *m* ivory

margarina *f* margarine

margarita *f* BOT daisy

margen *m tb fig* margin; *al margen de eso* apart from that; *mantenerse al margen* keep out

marginación *f* marginalization

marginal *adj* marginal

marginar ⟨1a⟩ *v/t* marginalize

mariachi 1 *m* mariachi band **2** *m/f* mariachi player

marica *m* F fag P, *Br* poof P

maricón *m* P fag P, *Br* poof P

marido *m* husband

marihuana *f* marijuana

marimacho *m* F butch woman

marimba *f* Rpl MÚS marimba

marina *f* navy; *marina mercante* merchant navy

marinar ⟨1a⟩ *v/t* GASTR marinade

marinero 1 *adj* sea *atr* **2** *m* sailor

marino 1 *adj* *brisa* sea *atr*; *planta, animal* marine; *azul marino* navy blue **2** *m* sailor

marioneta *f tb fig* puppet

mariposa *f* butterfly

mariquita *f* ladybug, *Br* ladybird

marisco *m* seafood

marisma *f* salt marsh

marítimo *adj* maritime

marketing *m* marketing

marmita *f* pot, pan

mármol *m* marble

marmota *f*: *dormir como una marmota* F sleep like a log

marqués *m* marquis

marquesa *f* marchioness

marquesina *f* marquee, *Br* canopy

marranada *f* F dirty trick

marrano 1 *adj* filthy **2** *m* hog, *Br* pig; F *persona* pig F

marras *adv*: *el ordenador de marras* the darned computer F

marrón *m/adj* brown

marroquinería *f* leather goods

Marruecos Morocco

marta *f* ZO marten

Marte *m* AST Mars

martes *m inv* Tuesday

martillero *m S. Am.* auctioneer

martillo *m* hammer; **martillo neumático** pneumatic drill

martín *m*: **martín pescador** zo kingfisher

mártir *m/f* martyr

martirio *m tb fig* martyrdom

martirizar ⟨1f⟩ *v/t tb fig* martyr

marzo *m* March

mas *conj* but

más 1 *adj* more 2 *adv comp* more; *sup* most; MAT plus; **más grande / pequeño** bigger / smaller; **el más grande / pequeño** the largest / smallest; **trabajar más** work harder; **más bien** rather; **más que, más de lo que** more than; **más o menos** more or less; **¿qué más?** what else?; **más L.Am. → nomás; por más que** however much; **sin más** without more ado; **más lejos** further

masa *f* mass; GASTR dough; **pillar a alguien con las manos en la masa** F catch s.o. red-handed

masacrar ⟨1a⟩ *v/t* massacre

masacre *f* massacre

masaje *m* massage

masajista *m/f* masseur; *mujer* masseuse

mascar ⟨1g⟩ 1 *v/t* chew 2 *v/i L.Am.* chew tobacco

máscara *f* mask

mascarilla *f* mask; *cosmética* face pack

mascota *f* mascot; *animal doméstico* pet

masculino *adj* masculine

mascullar ⟨1a⟩ *v/t* mutter

masificación *f* overcrowding

masilla *f* putty

masita *f L.Am. small sweet cake or bun*

masivo *adj* massive

masón *m* mason

masoquismo *m* masochism

masoquista 1 *adj* masochistic 2 *m/f* masochist

máster *m* master's (degree)

masticación *f* chewing

masticar ⟨1g⟩ *v/t* chew

mástil *m* mast; *de tienda* pole

mastín *m* zo mastiff

mastodóntico *adj* colossal, enormous

mastuerzo *m* BOT cress

masturbarse ⟨1a⟩ *v/r* masturbate

mata *f* bush

matadero *m* slaughterhouse

matador *m* TAUR matador

matanza *f de animales* slaughter; *de gente* slaughter, massacre

matar ⟨1a⟩ 1 *v/t* kill; *ganado* slaughter 2 *v/r* matarse kill o.s.; *morir* be killed; **matarse a trabajar** work o.s. to death

matarratas *m* rat poison

matasanos *m/f inv* F quack F

matasellos *m inv* postmark

mate 1 *adj* matt 2 *m en ajedrez* mate; *L.Am. (infusión)* maté

matear ⟨1a⟩ 1 *v/t CSur* checkmate 2 *v/i L.Am.* drink maté

matemáticas *fpl* mathematics

matemático 1 *adj* mathematical 2 *m*, -a *f* mathematician

materia *f* matter; *(material)* material; *(tema)* subject; **materia prima** raw material; **en materia de** as regards

material *m/adj* material

materialismo *m* materialism

materializar ⟨1f⟩ *v/t*: **materializar algo** make sth a reality

maternal *adj* maternal

matero *m*, -a *f L.Am.* maté drinker

matinal *adj* morning *atr*

matiz *m de ironía* touch; *de color* shade

matizar ⟨1f⟩ *v/t comentarios* qualify

matón *m* bully; *(criminal)* thug

matorral *m* thicket

matrícula *f* AUTO license plate, *Br* numberplate; EDU enrol(l)ment, registration

matricular ⟨1a⟩ 1 *v/t* register 2 *v/r* matricularse EDU enrol(l), register

matrimonial *adj* marriage *atr*, marital

matrimonio *m* marriage; *boda* wedding

matriz *f* matrix; ANAT womb

matrona *f (comadrona)* midwife

matutino *adj* morning *atr*

maullar ⟨1a⟩ *v/i* miaow

maullido *m* miaow

mausoleo *m* mausoleum

máxima *f* maxim

máxime *adv* especially

máximo *adj* maximum

mayo *m* May

mayonesa *f* GASTR mayonnaise

mayor 1 *adj comp*: *en tamaño* larger, bigger; *en edad* older; *en importancia* greater; **ser mayor de edad** be an adult; **al por mayor** COM wholesale 2 *adj sup*: **el mayor** *en edad* the oldest *o* eldest; *en tamaño* the largest *o* biggest; *en importancia* the greatest; **los mayores** adults; **la mayor parte** the majority

mayordomo *m* butler

mayoreo *m*: **vender al mayoreo** *Méx* sell wholesale

mayoría *f* majority; **alcanzar la mayoría de edad** come of age; **la mayoría de** the majority of, most (of); **en la mayoría de los casos** in the majority of cases, in most cases

mayorista *m/f* wholesaler

mayoritario *adj* majority *atr*

mayúscula *f* capital (letter), upper case letter

mazamorra *f* S. Am. kind of porridge made from corn

mazapán *m* marzipan

mazmorra *f* dungeon

mazo *m* mallet

mazorca *f* cob

me *pron pers complemento directo* me; *complemento indirecto* (to) me; *reflexivo* myself; *me dio el libro* he gave me the book, he gave the book to me

mear ⟨1a⟩ F 1 *v/i* pee F 2 *v/r* **mearse** pee o.s. F; *mearse de risa* wet o.s. (laughing) F

meca *f fig* mecca

mecachis *int* F blast! F

mecánica *f* mechanics

mecánico 1 *adj* mechanical 2 *m*, -a *f* mechanic

mecanismo *m* mechanism

mecanizar ⟨1f⟩ *v/t* mechanize

mecanógrafo *m*, -a *f* typist

mecanografiar ⟨1c⟩ *v/t* type

mecate *m* Méx string, cord

mecedora *f* rocking chair

mecenas *m inv* patron, sponsor

mecer ⟨2b⟩ 1 *v/t* rock 2 *v/r* **mecerse** rock

mecha *f* wick; *de explosivo* fuse; *del pelo* highlight; *Méx* F fear

mechero *m* cigarette lighter

mechón *m de pelo* lock

medalla *f* medal

medallista *m/f* medal(l)ist

media *f* stocking; *medias pl* pantyhose *pl*, *Br* tights *pl*

mediación *f* mediation

mediado *adj*: *a mediados de junio* in mid-June, halfway through June

mediador *m*, **mediadora** *f* mediator

mediana *f* AUTO median strip, *Br* central reservation

mediano *adj* medium, average

medianoche *f* midnight

mediante *prp* by means of

mediar ⟨1b⟩ *v/i* mediate

mediático *adj* media *atr*

medicación *f* medication

medicamento *m* medicine, drug

medicina *f* medicine

medicinal *adj* medicinal

médico 1 *adj* medical 2 *m/f* doctor; *médico de cabecera* or *de familia* family physician, *Br* GP, *Br* general practitioner; *médico de urgencia* emergency doctor

medida *f* measure; *acto* measurement; *(grado)* extent; *hecho a medida* made to measure; *a medida que* as; *tomar medidas fig* take measures o steps

medidor *m* S. Am. meter

medieval *adj* medi(a)eval

medio 1 *adj* half; *tamaño* medium; *(de promedio)* average; *las tres y -a* half past three, three-thirty 2 *m* environment; *(centro)* middle; *(manera)* means; *medio ambiente* environment; *por medio de* by means of; *en medio de* in the middle of; *medios dinero* means, resources; *medios de comunicación* or *de información* (mass) media; *medios de transporte* means of transport 3 *adv* half; *hacer algo a -as* half do sth; *ir a -as* go halves; *día por medio* L.Am. every other day; *quitar de en medio algo* F move sth out of the way

medioambiental *adj* environmental

mediocre *adj* mediocre

mediodía *m* midday; *a mediodía (a las doce)* at noon, at twelve o'clock; *(a la hora de comer)* at lunchtime

medir ⟨3l⟩ 1 *v/t* measure 2 *v/i*: *mide 2 metros de ancho / largo / alto* it's 2 meters (o *Br* metres) wide / long / tall

meditación *f* meditation

meditar ⟨1a⟩ 1 *v/t* ponder 2 *v/i* meditate

Mediterráneo *m/adj*: *(mar) Mediterráneo* Mediterranean (Sea)

médium *m/f* medium

médula *f* marrow; *médula espinal* spinal cord; *hasta la médula fig* through and through, to the core

medusa *f* ZO jellyfish

megafonía *f* public-address o PA system

megáfono *m* bullhorn, *Br* loud-hailer

megalomanía *f* megalomania

mejicano 1 *adj* Mexican 2 *m*, -a *f* Mexican

Méjico Mexico, *Méx DF* Mexico City

mejilla *f* cheek

mejillón *m* ZO mussel

mejor *adj comp* better; *el mejor sup* the best, *lo mejor* the best thing; *lo mejor posible* as well as possible; *a lo mejor* perhaps, maybe; *tanto mejor* all the better

mejora *f* improvement

mejorana *f* BOT marjoram

mejorar ⟨1a⟩ 1 *v/t* improve 2 *v/i* improve; *¡que te mejores!* get well soon!

mejoría *f* improvement

mejunje *m desp* concoction

melancolía *f* melancholy

melancólico *adj* gloomy, melancholic

melena *f* long hair; *de león* mane

melindroso *adj* affected

mella *f*: *hacer mella en alguien* have an effect on s.o., affect s.o.

mellado *adj* gap-toothed

mellizo 1 *adj* twin *atr* 2 *m*, -a *f* twin

melocotón *m* peach

melocotonero m peach tree

melodía f melody

melodrama m melodrama

melón m melon

membrana f membrane

membrillo m quince; *dulce de membrillo* quince jelly

memela f *Méx* corn tortilla

memo 1 adj F dumb F **2** m, **-a** f F idiot

memorable adj memorable

memoria f tb INFOR memory; (*informe*) report; *de memoria* by heart; *memorias* (*biografía*) memoirs

memorizar ⟨1f⟩ v/t memorize

mención f: *hacer mención de* mention

mencionar ⟨1a⟩ v/t mention

mendigar ⟨1h⟩ v/t beg for

mendigo m beggar

menear ⟨1a⟩ **1** v/t shake; *las caderas* sway; *menear la cola* wag its tail **2** v/r menearse fidget

menestra f vegetable stew

mengano m, **-a** f F so-and-so F

menguante adj decreasing, diminishing; *luna* waning

menguar ⟨1i⟩ v/i decrease, diminish; *de la luna* wane

meningitis f MED meningitis

menopausia f MED menopause

menor adj comp less; *en tamaño* smaller; *en edad* younger; *ser menor de edad* be a minor; *al por menor* COM retail; *el menor* sup: *en tamaño* the smallest; *en edad* the youngest; *el número menor* the lowest number

menos 1 adj en cantidad less; *en número* fewer **2** adv comp en cantidad less; sup en cantidad least; MAT minus; *es menos guapa que Ana* she is not as pretty as Ana; *tres menos dos* three minus two; *a menos que* unless; *al menos, por lo menos* at least; *echar de menos* miss; *eso es lo de menos* that's the least of it; *ni mucho menos* far from it; *son las dos menos diez* it's ten of two, it's ten to two

menoscabar ⟨1a⟩ v/t autoridad diminish; (*dañar*) harm

menospreciar ⟨1b⟩ v/t underestimate; (*desdeñar*) look down on

mensaje m message

mensajero m courrier

menstruación f menstruation

menstruar ⟨1h⟩ v/i menstruate

mensual adj monthly

mensualidad f monthly instal(l)ment, monthly payment

mensualmente adv monthly

menta f BOT mint

mental adj mental

mentalidad f mentality

mentalizar ⟨1f⟩ **1** v/t: *mentalizar a alguien* make s.o. aware **2** v/r mentalizarse mentally prepare o.s.

mente f mind

mentecato 1 adj F dim F **2** m F fool

mentir ⟨3i⟩ v/i lie

mentira f lie

mentiroso 1 adj: *ser muy mentiroso* tell a lot of lies **2** m, **-a** f liar

mentón m chin

mentor m mentor

menú m tb INFOR menu; *menú de ayuda* help menu

menudencias fpl *Méx* giblets

menudeo m *L.Am.* retail trade

menudo 1 adj small; *¡-a suerte!* fig F lucky devil!; *¡-as vacaciones!* irón F some vacation!; *a menudo* often **2** m *L.Am.* small change; *menudos* GASTR giblets

meñique m/adj: (*dedo*) *meñique* little finger

meollo m fig heart

mercader m trader

mercadería f *L.Am.* merchandise

mercadillo m street market

mercado m market; *Mercado Común* Common Market; *mercado negro* black market

mercadotecnia f marketing

mercancía f merchandise

mercantil adj commercial

merced f: *estar a merced de alguien* be at s.o.'s mercy

mercenario m/adj mercenary

mercería f notions pl, Br haberdashery

MERCOSUR abr (= *Mercado Común del Sur*) Common Market including Argentina, Brazil, Paraguay and Uruguay

mercurio m mercury

merecer ⟨2d⟩ v/t deserve; *no merecer la pena* it's not worth it

merecido m just deserts pl

merendar ⟨1k⟩ **1** v/t: *merendar algo* have sth as an afternoon snack **2** v/i have an afternoon snack

merengue m GASTR meringue

meridiano m/f meridian

meridional 1 adj southern **2** m southerner

merienda f afternoon snack

mérito m merit

merluza f ZO hake; *agarrar una merluza* fig F get plastered F

mermar ⟨1a⟩ **1** v/t reduce **2** v/i diminish

mermelada f jam

mero 1 adj mere; *el mero jefe* *Méx* F the big boss **2** m ZO grouper

merodear ⟨1a⟩ *v/i* loiter
mes *m* month
mesa *f* table; **mesa redonda** *fig* round table; **poner / quitar la mesa** set / clear the table
mesera *f L.Am.* waitress
mesero *m L.Am.* waiter
meseta *f* plateau
mesilla, mesita *f*: **mesilla (de noche)** night stand, *Br* bedside table
mesón *m* traditional restaurant decorated in rustic style
mestizo *m* person of mixed race
mesura *f*: **con mesura** in moderation
meta *f* en *fútbol* goal; *en carrera* finishing line; *fig (objetivo)* goal, objective
metabolismo *m* metabolism
metafísica *f* metaphysics
metáfora *f* metaphor
metal *m* metal
metálico 1 *adj* metallic **2** *m*: **en metálico** (in) cash
metalúrgico *adj* metallurgical
metamorfosis *f inv* transformation, metamorphosis
metedura *f*: **metedura de pata** F blunder
meteorito *m* meteorite
meteorológico *adj* weather *atr*, meteorological; **pronóstico meteorológico** weather forecast
meteorólogo *m*, **-a** *f* meteorologist
meter ⟨2a⟩ **1** *v/t gen* put (**en** in, into); *(involucrar)* involve (**en** in); **meter a alguien en un lío** get s.o. into a mess **2** *v/r* **meterse: meterse en algo** get into sth; *(involucrarse)* get involved in sth, **meterse con alguien** pick on s.o.; **meterse de administrativo** get a job in admin; **¿dónde se ha metido?** where has he got to?
meticuloso *adj* meticulous
metido *adj* involved; *L.Am.* F nosy F; **estar muy metido en algo** be very involved in sth
metódico *adj* methodical
método *m* method
metomentodo *m/f* F busybody F
metralleta *f* sub-machine gun
métrico *adj* metric
metro *m medida* meter, *Br* metre; *para medir* rule; *transporte* subway, *Br* underground
metrópolis *f inv* metropolis
metropolitano *adj* metropolitan
mexicano 1 *adj* Mexican **2** *m*, **-a** Mexican
México Mexico; *Méx DF* Mexico City
mezcal *m Méx* mescal
mezcla *f sustancia* mixture; *de tabaco, café etc* blend; *acto* mixing; *de tabaco, café*

etc blending
mezclar ⟨1a⟩ **1** *v/t* mix; *tabaco, café etc* blend; **mezclar a alguien en algo** get s.o. mixed up *o* involved in sth **2** *v/r* **mezclarse** mix; **mezclarse en algo** get mixed up *o* involved in sth
mezquinar ⟨1a⟩ *v/t L.Am.* skimp on
mezquino *adj* mean
mezquita *f* mosque
mg. *abr* (*= miligramo*) mg (= milligram)
mi, mis *adj pos* my
mí *pron* me; *reflexivo* myself; **¿y a mí qué?** so what?, what's it to me?
michelín *m* F spare tire, *Br* spare tyre
mico *m* zo monkey
micro *m or f Chi* bus
microbio *m* microbe
microbús *m* minibus
microchip *m* (micro)chip
microfilm(e) *m* microfilm
micrófono *m* microphone; **micrófono oculto** bug
microondas *m inv* microwave
microordenador *m* microcomputer
microprocesador *m* microprocessor
microscópico *adj* microscopic
microscopio *m* microscope
mide *vb* → **medir**
miedo *m* fear (**a** of); **dar miedo** be frightening; **me da miedo la oscuridad** I'm frightened of the dark; **tener miedo de que** be afraid that; **por miedo a** for fear of; **de miedo** F great F, awesome F
miedoso *adj* timid; **¡no seas tan miedoso!** don't be scared!
miel *f* honey
miembro *m* member; *(extremidad)* limb, member *fml*
mientras 1 *conj* while; **mientras que** whereas **2** *adv*: **mientras tanto** in the meantime, meanwhile
miércoles *m inv* Wednesday
mierda *f* P shit P, crap P; **una mierda de película** a crap movie P; **¡una mierda!** no way! F
miga *f de pan* crumb; **migas** crumbs; **hacer buenas / malas migas** *fig* F get on well / badly
migraña *f* MED migraine
migratorio *adj* migratory
mijo *m* BOT millet
mil *adj* thousand
milagro *m* miracle; **de milagro** miraculously, by a miracle
milagroso *adj* miraculous
milano *m* zo kite
milenio *m* millennium
mili *f* F military service
milicia *f* militia

M

milico *m S. Am. desp* soldier

milímetro *m* millimeter, *Br* millimetre

militante *m/f & adj* militant

militar 1 *adj* military **2** *m* soldier; *los militares* the military **3** ⟨1a⟩ *v/i* POL: *militar en* be a member of

milla *f* mile

millar *m* thousand

millón *m* million; (*mil millones*) billion

millonario *m* millionaire

milpa *f Méx, C.Am.* corn, *Br* maize; *terreno* cornfield, *Br* field of maize

mimar ⟨1a⟩ *v/t* spoil, pamper

mimbre *m* BOT willow; *muebles pl de mimbre* wicker furniture *sg*

mímica *f* mime

mimo *m* TEA mime

mimosa *f* BOT mimosa

mimoso *adj*: *ser mimoso* be cuddly

mina *f* MIN mine; *Rpl* F broad F, *Br* bird F; *mina antipersonal* MIL antipersonnel mine

minar ⟨1a⟩ *v/t* mine; *fig* undermine

mineral *m/adj* mineral

minería *f* mining

minero 1 *adj* mining **2** *m* miner

miniatura *f* miniature

minifalda *f* miniskirt

minimizar ⟨1f⟩ *v/t* minimize

mínimo 1 *adj* minimum; *como mínimo* at the very least **2** *m* minimum

minino *m* F puss F, pussy (cat) F

ministerio *m* POL department; *ministerio de Asuntos Exteriores, L.Am. ministerio de Relaciones Exteriores* State Department, *Br* Foreign Office; *ministerio de Hacienda* Treasury Department, *Br* Treasury; *ministerio del Interior* Department of the Interior, *Br* Home Office

ministro *m*, *-a f* minister; *ministro del Interior* Secretary of the Interior, *Br* Home Secretary; *primer ministro* Prime Minister

minoría *f* minority

minorista COM **1** *adj* retail *atr* **2** *m/f* retailer

minoritario *adj* minority *atr*

mintió *vb* → *mentir*

minucia *f* minor detail

minucioso *adj* meticulous, thorough

minúscula *f* small letter, lower case letter

minúsculo *adj* tiny, minute

minusvalía *f* disability

minusválido 1 *adj* disabled **2** *m*, *-a f* disabled person; *los minusválidos* the disabled

minutero *m* minute hand

minuto *m* minute

mío, mía *pron* mine; *el mío / la -a* mine

miope *adj* near-sighted, short-sighted

miopía *f* near-sightedness, short-sightedness

mira *f*: *con miras a* with a view to

mirada *f* look; *echar una mirada* take a look (*a* at)

mirador *m* viewpoint

mirar ⟨1a⟩ **1** *v/t* look at; (*observar*) watch; *L.Am.* (*ver*) see; *¿qué miras desde aquí?* what can you see from here? **2** *v/i* look; *mirar al norte de una ventana etc* face north; *mirar por la ventana* look out of the window

mirilla *f* spyhole

mirlo *m* ZO blackbird

misa *f* REL mass

misántropo *m* misanthropist

miserable *adj* wretched

miseria *f* poverty; *fig* misery

misericordia *f* mercy, compassion

mísero *adj* wretched; *sueldo* miserable

misil *m* missile

misión *f* mission

misionero *m*, *-a f* missionary

mismo 1 *adj* same; *lo mismo que* the same as; *yo mismo* I myself; *da lo mismo* it doesn't matter, it's all the same; *me da lo mismo* I don't care, it's all the same to me **2** *adv*: *aquí mismo* right here; *ahora mismo* right now, this very minute

misógino *adj* misogynistic

misterio *m* mystery

misterioso *adj* mysterious

místico *adj* mystic(al)

mitad *f* half; *a mitad del camino* halfway; *a mitad de la película* halfway through the movie; *a mitad de precio* half-price

mítico *adj* mythical

mitigar ⟨1h⟩ *v/t* mitigate; *ansiedad, dolor etc* ease

mitin *m* POL meeting

mito *m* myth

mitología *f* mythology

mixto *adj* mixed; *comisión* joint

mm. *abr* (= *milímetro*) mm (= millimeter)

mobiliario *m* furniture

mochila *f* backpack

mochilero *m*, *-a f* backpacker

mochuelo *m* ZO little owl

moción *f* POL motion; *moción de confianza /censura* vote of confidence / no confidence

moco *m*: *tener mocos* have a runny nose

mocoso *m*, *-a f* F snotty-nosed kid F

moda *f* fashion; *de moda* fashionable, in fashion; *estar pasado de moda* be out of fashion

modales *mpl* manners

modalidad f form; DEP discipline; *modalidad de pago* method of payment
modelar ⟨1a⟩ v/t model
modelismo m model making
modelo 1 m model **2** m/f persona model
nódem m INFOR modem
moderado 1 adj moderate **2** m, -a f moderate
moderador m, **moderadora** f TV presenter
moderar ⟨1a⟩ **1** v/t moderate; *impulsos* control, restrain; *velocidad, gastos* reduce; *debate* chair **2** v/r **moderarse** control o.s., restrain o.s.
modernización f modernization
modernizar ⟨1f⟩ v/t modernize
moderno adj modern
modestia f modesty; *modestia aparte* though I say so myself
modesto adj modest
módico adj precio reasonable
modificación f modification
modificar ⟨1g⟩ v/t modify
modista m/f dressmaker; *diseñador* fashion designer
modo m way; *a modo de* as; *de modo que* so that; *de ningún modo* not at all; *en cierto modo* in a way o sense; *de todos modos* anyway
modorra f drowsiness
módulo m module
mofarse ⟨1a⟩ v/r: *mofarse de* make fun of
mofeta f zo skunk
mofletes m/pl chubby cheeks
mogollón m F (*discusión*) argument; *mogollón de* F loads of F
moho m mo(u)ld
moisés m inv Moses basket
mojado adj (*húmedo*) damp, moist; (*empapado*) wet
mojar ⟨1a⟩ **1** v/t (*humedecer*) dampen, moisten; (*empapar*) wet; *galleta* dunk, dip **2** v/r **mojarse** get wet
mojigato 1 adj prudish **2** m, -a f prude
mojón m tb fig milestone
molar ⟨2h⟩ **1** v/t: *me mola ese tío* P I like the guy a lot **2** v/i P be cool F
molcajete m Méx, C.Am. (*mortero*) grinding stone
molde m mo(u)ld; *para bizcocho* (cake) tin; *romper moldes* fig break the mo(u)ld
moldear ⟨1a⟩ v/t mo(u)ld
moldura f ARQUI mo(u)lding
mole 1 f mass **2** m Méx mole (*spicy sauce made with chilies and tomatoes*)
molécula f molecule
moler ⟨2h⟩ v/t grind; *fruta* mash; *carne*

molida ground meat, Br mince; *moler a alguien a palos* fig beat s.o. to a pulp
molestar ⟨1a⟩ v/t bother, annoy; (*doler*) trouble; *no molestar* do not disturb **2** v/r **molestarse** get upset; (*ofenderse*) take offense (Br offence); (*enojarse*) get annoyed; *molestar en hacer algo* take the trouble to do sth
molestia f nuisance; *molestias* pl MED discomfort sg
molesto adj annoying; (*incómodo*) inconvenient
molestoso adj L.Am. annoying
molido adj F bushed F
molinillo m: *molinillo de café* coffee grinder o mill
molino m mill; *molino de viento* windmill
mollera f ⊢ head; *duro de mollera* F pigheaded F
molusco m zo mollusk, Br mollusc
momento m moment; *al momento* at once; *por el momento, de momento* for the moment
momia f mummy
momificar ⟨1g⟩ v/t mummify
monada f: *su hija es una monada* her daughter is lovely; *¡qué monada!* how lovely!
monaguillo m altar boy
monarca m monarch
monarquía f monarchy
monasterio m monastery
mondadientes m inv toothpick
mondar ⟨1a⟩ **1** v/t peel; *árbol* prune **2** v/r **mondarse**: *mondarse de risa* F split one's sides laughing
mondongo m tripe
moneda f coin; (*divisa*) currency
monedero m change purse, Br purse
monetario adj monetary
monigote m rag doll; F (*tonto*) idiot
monitor¹ m TV, INFOR monitor
monitor² m, **monitora** f (*profesor*) instructor
monja f nun
monje m monk
mono 1 m zo monkey; *prenda* coveralls pl, Br boilersuit **2** adj pretty, cute
monógamo adj monogamous
monólogo m monolog(ue)
monopatín m skateboard
monopolio m monopoly
monopolizar ⟨1f⟩ v/t tb fig monopolize
monosílabo adj monosyllabic
monotonía f monotony
monótono adj monotonous
monovolumen m AUTO minivan, Br people carrier, MPV

monsergas *fpl*: **déjate de monsergas** F stop going on F

monstruo *m* monster; (*fenómeno*) phenomenon

monstruosidad *f* eyesore, monstrosity

monstruoso *adj* monstrous

monta *f*: **de poca monta** unimportant

montacargas *m inv* hoist

montada *f L.Am.* mounted police

montaje *m* TÉC assembly; *de película* editing; TEA staging; *fig* F con F

montante *m* COM total

montaña *f* mountain; **montaña rusa** rollercoaster

montañero *m*, **-a** *f* mountaineer

montañismo *m* mountaineering

montañoso *adj* mountainous

montaplatos *m inv* dumb waiter

montar ⟨1a⟩ **1** *v/t* TÉC assemble; *tienda* put up; *negocio* set up; *película* edit; *caballo* mount; **montar la guardia** mount guard **2** *v/i*: **montar en bicicleta** ride a bicycle; **montar a caballo** ride a horse

monte *m* mountain; (*bosque*) woodland

montículo *m* mound

montón *m* pile, heap; **ser del montón** *fig* be average, not stand out; **montones de** F piles of F, loads of F

montura *f* de gafas frame

monumento *m* monument

moño *m* bun

moqueta *f* (wall-to-wall) carpet

mora *f* BOT *de zarza* blackberry; *de morera* mulberry

morada *f* dwelling

morado *adj* purple; **pasarlas -as** F have a rough time

moral 1 *adj* moral **2** *f* (*moralidad*) morals *pl*; (*ánimo*) morale

moraleja *f* moral

moralidad *f* morality

moralista *m/f* moralist

moratón *m* bruise

moratoria *f* moratorium

morbo *m* F perverted kind of pleasure

morboso *adj* perverted

morcilla *f* blood sausage, *Br* black pudding

mordaz *adj* biting

mordaza *f* gag

morder ⟨2h⟩ *v/t* bite

mordida *f Méx* F bribe

mordisco *m* bite

mordisquear ⟨1a⟩ *v/t* nibble

morena *f* ZO moray eel

moreno *adj pelo, piel* dark; (*bronceado*) tanned

morera *f* BOT white mulberry tree

moretón *m L.Am.* bruise

morfina *f* morphine

morfología *f* morphology

moribundo *adj* dying

morir ⟨3k; *pari muerto* ⟩ **1** *v/i* die (**de** of); **morir de hambre** die of hunger, starve to death **2** *v/r* **morirse** die; **morirse de** *fig* die of; **morirse por** *fig* be dying for

morisco *adj* Moorish

mormón *m* Mormon

moro 1 *adj* North African **2** *m* North African; **no hay moros en la costa** F the coast is clear

morocho *adj S. Am. persona* dark

moronga *f C.Am., Méx* blood sausage, *Br* black pudding

morralla *f Méx* small change

morriña *f* homesickness

morro *m* ZO snout; **tener mucho morro** F have a real nerve

morrongo *m* F pussycat F

morsa *f* ZO walrus

mortaja *f* shroud; *L.Am.* cigarette paper

mortal 1 *adj* mortal; *accidente, herida* fatal; *dosis* lethal **2** *m/f* mortal

mortalidad *f* mortality

mortalmente *adv* fatally

mortero *m* tb MIL mortar

mortífero *adj* lethal

mortificar ⟨1g⟩ **1** *v/t* torment **2** *v/r* **mortificarse** *fig* distress o.s.; *Méx* (*apenarse*) be embarrassed *o* ashamed

mosaico *m* mosaic

mosca *f* fly; **por si las moscas** F just to be on the safe side

moscada *adj*: **nuez moscada** nutmeg

moscardón *m* hornet

Moscú Moscow

mosquear ⟨1a⟩ **1** *v/t Esp* F rile **2** *v/r* **mosquearse** F get hot under the collar F; (*sentir recelo*) smell a rat F

mosquitero *m* mosquito net

mosquito *m* mosquito

mostaza *f* mustard

mosto *m* grape juice

mostrador *m* counter; *en bar* bar; **mostrador de facturación** check-in desk

mostrar ⟨1m⟩ **1** *v/t* show **2** *v/r* **mostrarse**; **mostrarse contento** seem happy

mota *f* speck; *en diseño* dot

mote *m* nickname; *S. Am.* boiled corn *o Br* maize

motel *m* motel

motín *m* mutiny; *en una cárcel* riot

motivación *f* motivation

motivar ⟨1a⟩ *v/t* motivate

motivo *m* motive, reason; MÚS, PINT motif; **con motivo de** because of

moto *f* motorcycle, motorbike; **moto acuática** *or* **de agua** jet ski motocicleta f motorcycle

motociclismo m motorcycle racing

motociclista m/f motorcyclist

motocross m motocross

motor m engine; eléctrico motor

motora f motorboat

motorista m/f motorcyclist

motosierra f chain saw

motriz adj motor

mover ⟨2h⟩ **1** v/t move; (agitar) shake; (impulsar, incitar) drive **2** v/r moverse move; ¡muévete! get a move on! F, hurry up!

movida f F scene

móvil **1** adj mobile **2** m TELEC cellphone, Br mobile (phone)

movilidad f mobility

movilizar ⟨1f⟩ v/t mobilize

movimiento m movement; COM, fig activity

moza f girl; camarera waitress

mozo **1** adj: en mis años mozos in my youth **2** m boy; camarero waiter

mucama f Rpl maid

mucamo m Rpl servant

muchacha f girl

muchachada f Arg group of youngsters

muchacho m boy

muchedumbre f crowd

mucho **1** adj cantidad a lot of, lots of; esp neg much; no tengo mucho dinero I don't have much money; muchos a lot of, lots of, many; esp neg many; no tengo muchos amigos I don't have many friends; tengo mucho frío I am very cold; es mucho coche para mí it's too big a car for me **2** adv a lot; esp neg much; no me gustó mucho I didn't like it very much; ¿dura / tarda mucho? does it last / take long?; como mucho at the most; ni mucho menos far from it; por mucho que however much **3** pron a lot, much; muchos a lot of people, many people

muda f de ropa change of clothes

mudanza f de casa move

mudarse ⟨1a⟩ v/r: mudarse de casa move house; mudarse de ropa change (one's clothes)

mudo adj mute; letra silent

mueble m piece of furniture

mueca f de dolor grimace; hacer muecas make faces

muela f tooth; ANAT molar; muela del juicio wisdom tooth

muelle m TÉC spring; MAR wharf

muérdago m BOT mistletoe

muerde vb → morder

muere vb → morir

muermo m fig F boredom; ser un muermo fig F be a drag F

muerte f death; de mala muerte fig F lousy F, awful F

muerto **1** part → morir **2** adj dead **3** m, -a f dead person

muestra f sample; (señal) sign; (exposición) show

muestrario m collection of samples

mueve vb → mover

mugir ⟨3c⟩ v/i moo

mugre f filth

mugriento adj filthy

mugroso adj dirty

mújol m ZO gray o Br grey mullet

mula f mule; Méx trash, Br rubbish

mulato m mulatto

muleta f crutch; TAUR cape

mullido adj soft

mullir ⟨3h⟩ v/t almohada plump up

multa f fine

multar ⟨1a⟩ v/t fine

multicine m multiscreen

multicolor adj multicolo(u)red

multilateral adj multilateral

multimedia f/adj multimedia

multimillonario m multimillionaire

multinacional f multinational

múltiple adj multiple

multiplicación f multiplication

multiplicar ⟨1g⟩ **1** v/t multiply **2** v/r multiplicarse multiply

múltiplo m MAT multiple

multipropiedad f timeshare

multitud f crowd; multitud de thousands of

multitudinario adj mass atr

multiuso adj multipurpose

mundano adj society atr, REL worldly

mundial **1** adj world atr **2** m: el mundial de fútbol the World Cup

mundo m world; el otro mundo the next world; nada del otro mundo nothing out of the ordinary; todo el mundo everybody, everyone

munición f ammunition

municipal adj municipal

municipio m municipality

muñeca f doll; ANAT wrist

muñeco m doll; fig puppet; muñeco de nieve snowman

muñón m MED stump

mural **1** adj wall atr **2** m mural

muralla f de ciudad wall

murciélago m ZO bat

murga f: dar la murga a alguien F bug s.o. F

M

murió *vb* → **morir**
murmullo *m* murmur
murmurar ⟨1a⟩ *v/i hablar* murmur; *criticar* gossip
muro *m* wall
musa *f* muse
musaraña *f* zo shrew; **pensar en las musarañas** F daydream
muscular *adj* muscular
músculo *m* muscle
musculoso *adj* muscular
museo *m* museum; *de pintura* art gallery
musgo *m* BOT moss
música *f* music

musical *m/adj* musical
músico *m*, -a *f* musician
musitar ⟨1a⟩ *v/i* mumble
muslo *m* thigh
mustio *adj* withered; *fig* down F
musulmán 1 *adj* Muslim 2 *m*, -ana *f* Muslim
mutilado *m*, -a *f* disabled person
mutilar ⟨1a⟩ *v/t* mutilate
mutualidad *f* benefit society, *Br* friendly society
mutuo *adj* mutual
muy *adv* very; (*demasiado*) too; **muy valorado** highly valued

N, Ñ

N *abr* (= **norte**) N (North(ern))
nabo *m* 1 *adj Arg* F dumb F 2 *m* turnip
nácar *m* mother-of-pearl
nacatamal *m C.Am., Méx* meat, rice and corn in a banana leaf
nacer ⟨2d⟩ *v/i* be born; *de un huevo* hatch; *de una planta* sprout; *de un río, del sol* rise; (*surgir*) arise (**de** from)
naciente *adj país, gobierno* newly formed; *sol* rising
nacimiento *m* birth; *de Navidad* crèche, nativity scene
nación *f* nation
nacional *adj* national
nacionalidad *f* nationality
nacionalismo *m* nationalism
nacionalización *f* COM nationalization
nacionalizar ⟨1f⟩ 1 *v/t* COM nationalize; *persona* naturalize 2 *v/r* **nacionalizarse** become naturalized
naco *m Col* purée
nada 1 *pron* nothing; **no hay nada** there isn't anything; **¡nada de eso!** F you can put that idea out of your head; **nada más** nothing else; **nada menos que** no less than; **lo dices como si nada** you talk about it as if it was nothing; **¡de nada!** you're welcome, not at all; **no es nada** it's nothing 2 *adv* not at all; **no ha llovido nada** it hasn't rained 3 *f* nothingness
nadador *m*, nadadora *f* swimmer
nadar ⟨1a⟩ *v/i* swim
nadería *f* trifle
nadie *pron* nobody, no-one; **no había nadie** there was nobody there, there wasn't

anyone there
nado: **atravesar a nado** swim across
nafta *f Arg* gas(oline), *Br* petrol
naftalina *f* naphthalene
nailon *m* nylon
naipe *m* (playing) card
nalga *f* buttock
nana *f* lullaby; *Rpl* F (*abuela*) grandma
napias *fpl* F schnozzle *sg* F, *Br* hooter *sg* F
naranja 1 *f* orange; **media naranja** F (*pareja*) other half 2 *adj* orange
naranjada *f* orangeade
naranjo *m* orange tree
narciso *m* BOT daffodil
narcótico *m/adj* narcotic
narcotráfico *m* drug trafficking
nariz *f* nose; **¡narices!** F nonsense!; **estar hasta las narices de algo** F be sick of sth F, be up to here with sth F; **meter las narices en algo** F stick one's nose in sth F
narración *f* narration
narrador *m*, narradora *f* narrator
narrar ⟨1a⟩ *v/t*: **narrar algo** tell the story of sth
nasal *adj* nasal
nata *f* cream; **nata montada** whipped cream
natación *f* swimming
natal *adj* native; **ciudad natal** city of one's birth, home town
natalidad *f* birthrate
natillas *fpl* custard *sg*
nativo *m*, -a *f* native
nato *adj* born
natural 1 *adj* natural; **ser natural de** come

from; **es natural** it's only natural **2** *m*:
fruta al natural fruit in its own juice
naturaleza *f* nature
naturalidad *f* naturalness
naturalmente *adv* naturally
naturista 1 *adj* nudist, naturist; *medicina*
natural **2** *m/f* nudist, naturist
naufragar ⟨1h⟩ *v/i* be shipwrecked; *fig* fail
naufragio *m* shipwreck
náufrago 1 *adj* shipwrecked **2** *m*, -a *f* shipwrecked person
náuseas *fpl* nausea *sg*
nauseabundo *adj* nauseating
náutico *adj* nautical
navaja *f* knife
navajazo *m* knife wound, slash
navajero *m*: **le asaltó un navajero** he was
attacked by a man with a knife
naval *adj* naval
nave *f* ship; *de iglesia* nave; **nave espacial**
spacecraft
navegación *f* navigation; **navegación a**
vela sailing
navegador *m* INFOR browser
navegante *m/f* navigator
navegar ⟨1h⟩ **1** *v/i* sail; *por el aire, espacio*
fly; **navegar por la red** *or* **por Internet**
INFOR surf the Net **2** *v/t* sail
Navidad *f* Christmas
navideño *adj* Christmas *atr*
navío *m* ship
nazi *m/f* & *adj* Nazi
nazismo *m* Nazi(i)sm
N. B. *abr* (= *nótese bien*) NB (= *nota*
bene)
neblina *f* mist
nebuloso *adj fig* hazy, nebulous
necesario *adj* necessary
neceser *m* toilet kit, *Br* toilet bag
necesidad *f* need; *(cosa esencial)* necessity, **de primera necesidad** essential, **en**
caso de necesidad if necessary; **hacer**
sus -es F relieve o.s.
necesitado *adj* needy
necesitar ⟨1a⟩ *v/t* need
necio *adj* brainless
necrológica *f* obituary
nefasto *adj* harmful
negación *f* negation; *de acusación* denial
negar ⟨1h & 1k⟩ **1** *v/t acusación* deny; *(no*
conceder) refuse **2** *v/r* **negarse** refuse (**a**
to)
negativa *f* refusal; *de acusación* denial
negativo 1 *adj* negative **2** *m* FOT negative
negligencia *f* JUR negligence
negociable *adj* negotiable
negociación *f* negotiation; **negociacio-**
nes talks
negociador *m*, **negociadora** *f* negotiator

negociante *m/f* businessman; *mujer* businesswoman; *desp* money-grubber
negociar ⟨1b⟩ *v/t* negotiate
negocio *m* business; *(trato)* deal
negra *f* black woman; MÚS quarter note,
Br crotchet; *L.Am. (querida)* honey,
dear
negrita *f* bold
negro 1 *adj* black; **estar negro** F be furious **2** *m* black man; *L.Am. (querido)*
honey, dear
nena *f* F little girl, kid F
nene *m* F little boy, kid F
nenúfar *m* BOT water lily
neocelandés *m*, **-esa** *f* New Zealander
neón *m* neon
neoyorquino 1 *adj* New York *atr* **2** *m*, -a *f*
New Yorker
nepotismo *m* nepotism
nervio *m* ANAT nerve
nerviosismo *m* nervousness
nervioso *adj* nervous; **ponerse nervioso**
get nervous; *(agitado)* get agitated; **po-**
ner a alguien nervioso get on s.o.'s
nerves
neto *adj* COM net
neumático 1 *adj* pneumatic **2** *m* AUTO tire,
Br tyre
neumonía *f* MED pneumonia
neurocirujano *m*, **-a** *f* brain surgeon
neurólogo *m*, **-a** *f* neurologist
neurosis *f inv* neurosis
neurótico *adj* neurotic
neutral *adj* neutral
neutralidad *f* neutrality
neutralizar ⟨1f⟩ *v/t* neutralize
neutro *adj* neutral
nevada *f* snowfall
nevar ⟨1k⟩ *v/i* snow
nevazón *f Arg, Chi* snowstorm
nevera *f* refrigerator, fridge; **nevera**
portátil cooler
nevería *f Méx, C.Am.* ice-cream parlo(u)r
nevero *m* snowdrift
nexo *m* link; GRAM connective
ni *conj* neither; **ni ... ni** neither ... nor; **ni**
siquiera not even; **no di ni una** I made a
real mess of things
Nicaragua Nicaragua
nicaragüense *m/f* & *adj* Nicaraguan
nicho *m* niche
nicotina *f* nicotine; **bajo en nicotina** low
in nicotine
nido *m* nest
niebla *f* fog
nieta *f* granddaughter
nieto *m* grandson; **nietos** grandchildren
nieva *vb* → **nevar**
nieve *f* snow; *Méx* water ice, sorbet

nihilismo *m* nihilism

nimiedad *f* triviality

nimio *adj* trivial

ningún *adj* → **ninguno**

ninguno *adj* no; **no hay -a razón** there's no reason why, there isn't a reason why

niña *f* girl; *forma de cortesía* young lady

niñato *m*, **-a** *f* brat

niñera *f* nanny

niñería *f*: **una niñería** a childish thing

niñez *f* childhood

niño 1 *adj* young; *desp* childish **2** *m* boy; *forma de cortesía* young man; **niños** children *pl*; **niño de pecho** infant

níquel *m* nickel

níspero *m* BOT loquat

nítido *adj* clear; *imagen* sharp

nitrógeno *m* nitrogen

nitroglicerina *f* nitroglycerin

nivel *m* level; *(altura)* height; **nivel del mar** sea level; **nivel de vida** standard of living

nivelar ⟨1a⟩ *v/t* level

nixtamal *m* *Méx, C.Am. dough from which corn tortillas are made*

n.º *abr* (= **número**) No. (= number)

no *adv* no; *para negar verbo* not; **no entiendo** I don't understand, I do not understand; **no te vayas** don't go; **no bien** as soon as; **no del todo** not entirely; **ya no** not any more; **no más** *L.Am.* = **nomás**; **así no más** *L.Am.* just like that; **te gusta, ¿no?** you like it, don't you?; **te ha llamado, ¿no?** he called you, didn't he?; **¿a que no?** I bet you don't/can't etc

nobiliario *adj* noble

noble *m/f* & *adj* noble

nobleza *f* nobility

noche *f* night; **de noche, por la noche** at night; **de la noche a la mañana** *fig* overnight; **¡buenas noches!** *saludo* good evening; *despedida* good night

Nochebuena *f* Christmas Eve

nochecita *f* *L.Am.* evening

nochero *m* *L.Am.* night watchman

Nochevieja *f* New Year's Eve

noción *f* notion

nocivo *adj* harmful

noctámbulo *m*, **-a** *f* sleepwalker

nocturno *adj* night *atr*; ZO nocturnal; **clase -a** evening class

nogal *m* BOT walnut

nómada 1 *adj* nomadic **2** *m/f* nomad

nomás *adv L.Am.* just, only; **llévaselo nomás** just take it away; **nomás llegue, te avisaré** as soon as he arrives, I'll let you know; **siga nomás** just carry on; **nomás lo vio, echó a llorar** as soon as she saw him she started to cry

nombramiento *m* appointment

nombrar ⟨1a⟩ *v/t* mention; *para un cargo* appoint

nombre *m* name; GRAM noun; **nombre de pila** first name; **no tener nombre** *fig* be inexcusable

nomenclatura *f* nomenclature

nomeolvides *f inv* BOT forget-me-not

nómina *f* pay slip

nominal *adj* nominal

nominar ⟨1a⟩ *v/t* nominate

non *adj* odd

nono *adj* ninth

nopal *m L.Am.* BOT prickly pear

nor(d)este *m* northeast

noria *f de agua* waterwheel; *en feria* ferris wheel

norma *f* standard; *(regla)* rule, regulation

normal *adj* normal

normalidad *f* normality

normalizar ⟨1f⟩ *v/t* standardize

normativa *f* rules *pl*, regulations *pl*

noroeste *m* northwest

norte *m* north

Norteamérica North America

norteamericano 1 *adj* North American **2** *m*, **-a** *f* North American

norteño 1 *adj* northern **2** *m*, **-a** *f* northerner

Noruega Norway

noruego 1 *adj* Norwegian **2** *m*, **-a** *f* Norwegian

nos *pron complemento directo* us; *complemento indirecto* (to) us; *reflexivo* ourselves; **nos dio el dinero** he gave us the money, he gave the money to us

nosotros, nosotras *pron* we; *complemento* us; **ven con nosotros** come with us; **somos nosotros** it's us

nostalgia *f* nostalgia; *por la patria* homesickness

nostálgico *adj* nostalgic

nota *f tb* MÚS note; EDU grade, mark; **nota a pie de página** footnote; **tomar nota de algo** make a note of sth

notable *adj* remarkable, notable

notar ⟨1a⟩ *v/t* notice; *(sentir)* feel; **hacer notar algo a alguien** point sth out to s.o.; **se nota que** you can tell that; **hacerse notar** draw attention to o.s.

notaría *f* notary's office

notario *m*, **-a** *f* notary

noticia *f* piece of news; *en noticiario* news story, item of news; **noticias** *pl* news *sg*

noticiario *m* RAD, TV news *sg*

notificación *f* notification

notificar ⟨1g⟩ *v/t* notify

notorio *adj* famous, well-known

novatada *f* practical joke

novato *m*, **-a** *f* beginner, rookie F
novecientos *adj* nine hundred
novedad *f* novelty; *cosa* new thing; *(noticia)* piece of news; *acontecimiento* new development; *llegar sin novedad* arrive safely
novedoso *adj* novel, new; *invento* innovative
novela *f* novel; *novela negra* crime novel; *novela rosa* romantic novel
novelista *m/f* novelist
noveno *adj* ninth
noventa *adj* ninety
novia *f* girlfriend; *el día de la boda* bride
noviazgo *m* engagement
noviembre *m* November
novillada *f* bullfight featuring novice bulls
novillero *m* novice (bullfighter)
novillo *m* zo young bull; *vaca* heifer; *hacer novillos* F play hooky F, play truant
novio *m* boyfriend; *el día de la boda* bridegroom; *los novios* the bride and groom; *(recién casados)* the newly-weds
nube *f* cloud; *estar en las nubes* fig be miles away; *estar por las nubes* fig F be incredibly expensive
nublado 1 *adj* cloudy, overcast **2** *m* storm cloud
nublarse ⟨1a⟩ *v/r* cloud over
nuboso *adj* cloudy
nuca *f* nape of the neck
nuclear *adj* nuclear
núcleo *m* nucleus; *de problema* heart
nudillo *m* knuckle
nudista *m/f* nudist; *playa nudista* nudist beach
nudo *m* knot; *se me hace un nudo en la garganta* F I get a lump in my throat
nuera *f* daughter-in-law
nuestro 1 *adj pos* our **2** *pron* ours
nueva *f* lit piece of news
nuevamente *adv* again
Nueva York New York
Nueva Zelanda New Zealand

nueve *adj* nine
nuevo *adj* new; *(otro)* another; *de nuevo* again
nuez *f* BOT walnut; ANAT Adam's apple
nulidad *f* nullity; *fig* F dead loss F
nulo *adj* null and void; F *persona* hopeless; *(inexistente)* non-existent, zero
núm. *abr (= número)* No. (= number)
numerar ⟨1a⟩ *v/t* number
numérico *adj* numerical; *teclado numérico* numeric keypad, number pad
número *m* number; *de publicación* issue; *de zapato* size; *número complementario* en lotería bonus number; *número secreto* PIN (number); *en números rojos* fig in the red; *montar un número* F make a scene
numeroso *adj* numerous
numismática *f* numismatics
nunca *adv* never; *nunca jamás* or *más* never again; *más que nunca* more than ever
nupcial *adj* wedding *atr*
nutria *f* zo otter
nutrición *f* nutrition
nutrido *adj* fig large
nutriente *m* nutrient
nutrir ⟨3a⟩ *v/t* nourish; *fig: esperanzas* cherish
nutritivo *adj* nutritious, nourishing
nylon *m* nylon
ñandú *m* zo rhea
ñandutí *m Parag* type of lace
ñapa *f S. Am.* extra, bonus; *le di dos de ñapa* I threw in an extra two
ñato *adj Rpl* snub-nosed
ñeque *m S. Am.* strength, *de ñeque* gutsy F; *tener mucho ñeque* F have a lot of guts F
ñoñería *f* feebleness F, wimpish behavio(u)r F
ñoño 1 *adj* feeble F, wimpish F **2** *m*, **-a** *f* drip F, wimp F
ñu *m* zo gnu

O

O *abr (= oeste)* W (= West(ern))
o *conj* or; *o ... o* either ... or; *o sea* in other words
oasis *m inv* oasis
obcecación *f* obstinacy

obcecarse ⟨1g⟩ *v/r* stubbornly insist
obedecer ⟨2d⟩ **1** *v/t* obey **2** *v/i* obey; *de una máquina* respond; *obedecer a* fig be due to
obediencia *f* obedience

obediente *adj* obedient

obelisco *m* obelisk

obesidad *f* obesity

obeso *adj* obese

obispo *m* bishop

objeción *f* objection; *objeción de conciencia* conscientious objection

objetar ⟨1a⟩ **1** *v/t* object; *tener algo que objetar* have any objection **2** *v/i* become a conscientious objector

objetividad *f* objectivity

objetivo **1** *adj* objective **2** *m* objective; MIL target; FOT lens

objeto *m* object; *con objeto de* with the aim of

objetor *m*, objetora *f* objector; *objetor de conciencia* conscientious objector

oblicuo *adj* oblique, slanted

obligación *f* obligation, duty; COM bond

obligar ⟨1h⟩ *v/t*: *obligar a alguien* oblige o force s.o. (*a* to); *de una ley* apply to s.o.

obligatorio *adj* obligatory, compulsory

obnubilar ⟨1a⟩ *v/t* cloud

oboe *m* MÚS oboe

obra *f* work; *obras pl de construcción* building work *sg*; *en la vía pública* road works; *obra de arte* work of art; *obra maestra* masterpiece; *obra de teatro* play

obraje *m* Méx butcher's

obrar ⟨1a⟩ *v/i* act

obrero **1** *adj* working **2** *m*, -a *f* worker

obsceno *adj* obscene

obsequiar ⟨1b⟩ *v/t*: *obsequiar a alguien con algo* present s.o. with sth

obsequio *m* gift

obsequioso *adj* attentive

observación *f* observation; JUR observance

observador **1** *adj* observant **2** *m*, observadora *f* observer

observar ⟨1a⟩ *v/t* observe; (*advertir*) notice, observe; (*comentar*) remark, observe

observatorio *m* observatory

obsesión *f* obsession

obsesionar ⟨1a⟩ **1** *v/t* obsess **2** *v/r* obsesionarse become obsessed (*con* with)

obsesivo *adj* obsessive

obsoleto *adj* obsolete

obstaculizar ⟨1f⟩ *v/t* hinder, hamper

obstáculo *m* obstacle

obstante: *no obstante* nevertheless

obstetra *m/f* obstetrician

obstetricia *f* obstetrics

obstinación *f* obstinacy

obstinado *adj* obstinate

obstinarse ⟨1a⟩ *v/r* insist (*en* on)

obstrucción *f* obstruction, blockage

obstruir ⟨3g⟩ *v/t* obstruct, block

obtener ⟨2l; *part* obtuvo ⟩ *v/t* get, obtain *fml*

obturador *m* shutter

obtuvo *vb* → obtener

obvio *adj* obvious

oca *f* goose

ocasión *f* occasion; (*oportunidad*) chance, opportunity; *con ocasión de* on the occasion of; *de ocasión* COM cut-price, bargain *atr*; *de segunda mano* second-hand, used

ocasional *adj* occasional

ocasionar ⟨1a⟩ *v/t* cause

ocaso *m del sol* setting; *de un imperio, un poder* decline

occidental **1** *adj* western **2** *m/f* Westerner

occidente *m* west

OCDE *abr* (= *Organización de Cooperación y Desarrollo Económico*) OECD (= Organization for Economic Cooperation and Development)

océano *m* ocean

oceanógrafo *m*, -a *f* oceanographer

ocelote *m* ZO ocelot

ochenta *adj* eighty

ocho *adj* eight

ochocientos *adj* eight hundred

ocio *m* leisure time, free time; *desp* idleness

ociosear ⟨1a⟩ *v/i* S. Am. laze around

ocioso *adj* idle

ocre *m/adj* ocher, Br ochre

oct.° *abr* (= *octubre*) Oct. (= October)

octavilla *f* leaflet

octavo **1** *adj* eighth **2** *m* eighth; DEP *octavos de final* last 16

octógono *m* octagon

octubre *m* October

ocular *adj* eye *atr*

oculista *m/f* ophthalmologist

ocultación *f* concealment

ocultar ⟨1a⟩ *v/t* hide, conceal

ocultismo *m* occult

oculto *adj* hidden; (*sobrenatural*) occult

ocupación *f tb* MIL occupation; (*actividad*) activity

ocupado *adj* busy; *asiento* taken

ocupante *m/f* occupant

ocupar ⟨1a⟩ **1** *v/t espacio* take up, occupy; (*habitar*) live in, occupy; *obreros* employ; *periodo de tiempo* spend, occupy; MIL occupy **2** *v/r* ocuparse: *ocuparse de* deal with; (*cuidar de*) look after

ocurrencia *f* occurrence; (*chiste*) quip, funny remark

ocurrir ⟨3a⟩ *v/i* happen, occur; *se me ocurrió* it occurred to me, it struck me

odiar ⟨1b⟩ *v/t* hate

odio *m* hatred, hate

odioso *adj* odious, hateful

odisea *f fig* odyssey

odontólogo *m* odontologist

OEA *abr* (= *Organización de los Estados Americanos*) OAS (= Organization of American States)

oeste *m* west

ofender ⟨2a⟩ **1** *v/t* offend **2** *v/r* **ofenderse** take offense (*por* at)

ofensa *f* insult

ofensiva *f* offensive

ofensivo *adj* offensive

oferta *f* offer; *oferta pública de adquisición* takeover bid

oficial 1 *adj* official **2** *m/f* MIL officer

oficialista *adj* L.Am. pro-government

oficina *f* office; *oficina de correos* post office, *oficina de empleo* employment office; *oficina de turismo* tourist office

oficinista *m/f* office worker

oficio *m trabajo* trade

oficioso *adj* unofficial

ofimática *f* INFOR office automation

ofrecer ⟨2d⟩ **1** *v/t* offer **2** *v/r* **ofrecerse** volunteer, offer one's services (*de* as); (*presentarse*) appear; *¿qué se le ofrece?* what can I do for you?

ofrecimiento *m* offer

ofrenda *f* offering

oftalmólogo *m*, **-a** *f* ophthalmologist

ofuscar ⟨1g⟩ *v/t tb fig* blind

ogro *m fig* ogre

oída *f*: *conocer algo de oídas* have heard of sth

oído *m* hearing; *hacer oídos sordos* turn a deaf ear; *ser todo oídos fig* be all ears

oigo *vb* → **oír**

oír ⟨3q⟩ *v/t tb* JUR hear; (*escuchar*) listen to; *¡oye!* listen!, hey! F; *como quien oye llover*, *salió sin él* F he turned a deaf ear and went off without it

OIT *abr* (= *Organización Internacional de Trabajo*) ILO (= International Labor Organization)

ojal *m* buttonhole

ojalá *int*: *¡ojalá!* let's hope so; *¡ojalá venga!* I hope he comes; *¡ojalá tuvieras razón!* I only hope you're right

ojeada *f* glance; *echar una ojeada a alguien* glance at s.o.

ojeras *fpl* bags under the eyes

ojo *m* ANAT eye; *¡ojo!* F watch out!, mind! F; *ojo de la cerradura* keyhole; *a ojo* roughly; *andar con ojo* F keep one's eyes open F; *costar un ojo de la cara* F cost an arm and a leg F; *no pegar ojo* F not sleep a wink F

ojota *f* C.Am., Méx sandal

okupa *m/f Esp* F squatter

ola *f* wave; *ola de calor* heat wave; *ola de frío* cold spell

oleada *f fig* wave, flood

oleaje *m* swell

óleo *m* oil

oleoducto *m* (oil) pipeline

oler ⟨2i⟩ **1** *v/i* smell (*a* of) **2** *v/t* smell **3** *v/r*: *me huelo algo fig* there's something fishy going on, I smell a rat

olfatear ⟨1a⟩ *v/t* sniff

olfato *m* sense of smell; *fig* nose

olimpíada, olimpiada *f* Olympics *pl*

olímpico *adj* Olympic

olisquear ⟨1a⟩ *v/t* sniff

oliva *f* BOT olive

olivo *m* olive tree

olla *f* pot; *olla exprés or a presión* pressure cooker

olmo *m* BOT elm

olor *m* smell; *agradable* scent; *olor corporal* body odo(u)r, BO

oloroso *adj* scented

OLP *abr* (= *Organización para la Liberación de Palestina*) PLO (= Palestine Liberation Organization)

olvidadizo *adj* forgetful

olvidar ⟨1a⟩ **1** *v/t* forget **2** *v/r* **olvidarse**: *olvidarse de algo* forget sth

olvido *m* oblivion

ombligo *m* ANAT navel

OMC *abr* (= *Organización Mundial de Comercio*) WTO (= World Trade Organization)

omisión *f* omission

omiso *adj*: *hacer caso omiso de algo* ignore sth

omitir ⟨3a⟩ *v/t* omit, leave out

omnipotente *adj* omnipotent

omóplato, omoplato *m* ANAT shoulder blade

OMS *abr* (= *Organización Mundial de la Salud*) WHO (= World Health Organization)

once *adj* eleven

oncología *f* MED oncology

onda *f* wave; *estar en la onda* F be with it F; *¿qué onda? Méx* F what's happening? F

ondulado *adj* wavy; *cartón* corrugated

ONG *abr* (= *Organización no Gubernamental*) NGO (= non-governmental organization)

onomatopeya *f* onomatopœia

ONU *abr* (= *Organización de las Naciones Unidas*) UN (= United Nations)

onza *f* ounce

OPA *abr* (= *oferta pública de adquisición*) takeover bid

O

opaco *adj* opaque

opción *f* option, choice; (*posibilidad*) chance

opcional *adj* optional

OPEP *abr* (= *Organización de Países Exportadores de Petróleo*) OPEC (= Organization of Petroleum Exporting Countries)

ópera *f* MÚS opera; *ópera prima* first work

operación *f* operation

operador *m*, operadora *f* TELEC, INFOR operator; *operador turístico* tour operator

operar ⟨1a⟩ 1 *v/t* MED operate on; *cambio* bring about 2 *v/i* operate; COM do business (*con* with) 3 *v/r* operarse MED have an operation (*de* on); *de un cambio* occur

operario *m*, -a *f* operator, operative

operativo 1 *adj* operational; *sistema operativo* INFOR operating system 2 *m* L.Am. operation

opereta *f* MÚS operetta

opinar ⟨1a⟩ 1 *v/t* think (*de* about) 2 *v/i* express an opinion

opinión *f* opinion; *la opinión pública* public opinion; *en mi opinión* in my opinion

opio *m* opium

opíparo *adj* sumptuous

oponente *m/f* opponent

oponer ⟨2r; *part* opuesto ⟩ 1 *v/t* resistencia put up (*a* to), offer (*a* to); razón, argumento put forward (*a* against) 2 *v/r* oponerse be opposed (*a* to); (*manifestar oposición*) object (*a* to)

oporto *m* port

oportunidad *f* opportunity

oportunista 1 *adj* opportunistic 2 *m/f* opportunist

oportuno *adj* timely; *momento* opportune; *respuesta, medida* suitable, appropriate

oposición *f* POL opposition; *oposiciones* official entrance exams

opresión *f* oppression

opresor 1 *adj* oppressive 2 *m*, opresora *f* oppressor

oprimir ⟨3a⟩ *v/t* oppress; *botón* press; *de zapatos* be too tight for

optar ⟨1a⟩ *v/i* (*elegir*) opt (*por* for); *optar a* be in the running for; *optar por hacer algo* opt to do sth

optativo *adj* optional

óptica *f* optician's; FÍS optics; *fig* point of view

óptico 1 *adj* optical 2 *m*, -a *f* optician

optimismo *m* optimism

optimista 1 *adj* optimistic 2 *m/f* optimist

optimizar ⟨1f⟩ *v/t* optimize

óptimo *adj* ideal

opuesto 1 *part* → oponer 2 *adj* opposite; *opinión* contrary

opulencia *f* opulence

opuso *vb* → oponer

oquedad *f* cavity

oración *f* REL prayer; GRAM sentence

orador *m*, oradora *f* orator

oral *adj* oral; *prueba de inglés oral* English oral (exam)

orangután *m* ZO orangutan

orar ⟨1a⟩ *v/i* pray (*por* for)

oratoria *f* oratory

órbita *f* orbit; *colocar or poner en órbita* put into orbit

orca *f* ZO killer whale

órdago *m*: *de órdago* F terrific F

orden 1 *m* order; *orden del día* agenda; *por orden alfabético* in alphabetical order; *poner en orden* tidy up 2 *f* (*mandamiento*) order; *¡a la orden!* yes, sir; *por orden de* by order of, on the orders of

ordenado *adj* tidy

ordenador *m* INFOR computer; *ordenador de escritorio* desktop (computer); *ordenador personal* personal computer; *ordenador portátil* portable (computer); laptop; *asistido por ordenador* computer aided

ordenanza 1 *f* by-law 2 *m* office junior, gofer F; MIL orderly

ordenar ⟨1a⟩ *v/t* habitación tidy up; *alfabéticamente* arrange; (*mandar*) order

ordeñar ⟨1a⟩ *v/t* milk

ordinario *adj* ordinary; *desp* vulgar; *de ordinario* usually, ordinarily

orégano *m* BOT oregano

oreja *f* ear; *aguzar las orejas* L.Am. prick one's ears up; *ver las orejas al lobo* *fig* F wake up to the danger

orejeras *fpl* earmuffs

orfanato *m* orphanage

orfebrería *f* goldsmith / silversmith work

orfelinato *m* orphanage

orgánico *adj* organic

organigrama *m* flow chart; *de empresa* organization chart, tree diagram

organillo *m* barrel organ

organismo *m* organism; POL agency, organization; *organismo modificado genéticamente* genetically modified organism

organización *f* organization; *Organización de Cooperación y Desarrollo Económico* Organization for Economic Co-operation and Development; *Organización de las Naciones Unidas* United Nations; *Organización de los Estados Americanos* Organization of American

States; **Organización del Tratado del Atlántico Norte** North Atlantic Treaty Organization; **Organización de Países Exportadores de Petróleo** Organization of Petroleum Exporting Countries; **Organización Internacional de Trabajo** International Labor Organization; **Organización Mundial de Comercio** World Trade Organization; **Organización Mundial de la Salud** World Health Organization; **Organización para la Liberación de Palestina** Palestine Liberation Organization

organizador 1 *adj* organizing 2 *m*, organizadora *f* organizer; **organizador personal** personal organizer

organizar ⟨1f⟩ 1 *v/t* organize 2 *v/r* organizarse *de persona* organize one's time

órgano *m* MÚS, ANAT, *fig* organ

orgasmo *m* orgasm

orgía *f* orgy

orgullo *m* pride

orgulloso *adj* proud (**de** of)

orientación *f* orientation; (*ayuda*) guidance; **sentido de la orientación** sense of direction

orientador *m*, orientadora *f* counsel(l)or

oriental 1 *adj* oriental, eastern 2 *m/f* Oriental

orientar ⟨1a⟩ 1 *v/t* (*aconsejar*) advise; **orientar algo hacia algo** turn sth toward sth 2 *v/r* orientarse get one's bearings; *de una planta* turn (*hacia* toward)

oriente *m* east; **Oriente** Orient; **Oriente Medio** Middle East; **Extremo** or **Lejano Oriente** Far East

orificio *m* hole; *en cuerpo* orifice

origen *m* origin; **dar origen a** give rise to

original *m/adj* original

originalidad *f* originality

originar ⟨1a⟩ 1 *v/t* give rise to 2 *v/r* originarse originate; *de un incendio* start

originario *adj* original; (*nativo*) native (**de** of)

orilla *f* shore; *de un río* bank

orina *f* urine

orinal *m* urinal

orinar ⟨1a⟩ *v/i* urinate

oriundo *adj* native (**de** to)

ornamental *adj* ornamental

ornitología *f* ornithology

ornitólogo *m*, -a *f* ornithologist

oro *m* gold; **guardar como oro en paño** *con mucho cariño* treasure sth; *con mucho cuidado* guard sth with one's life; **prometer el oro y el moro** promise the earth; **oros** (*en naipes*) suit in Spanish deck of cards

orondo *adj* fat; *fig* smug

oropéndola *f* ZO golden oriole

orquesta *f* orchestra

orquestar ⟨1a⟩ *v/t fig* orchestrate

orquídea *f* BOT orchid

ortiga *f* BOT nettle

ortodoncia *f* MED orthodontics

ortodoxo *adj* orthodox

ortografía *f* spelling

ortopédico 1 *adj* orthop(a)edic 2 *m*, -a *f* orthop(a)edist

oruga *f* ZO caterpillar; TÉC (caterpillar) track

orujo *m* liquor made from the remains of grapes

orzuelo *m* MED stye

os *pron complemento directo* you; *complemento indirecto* (to) you; *reflexivo* yourselves; **os lo devolveré** I'll give you it back, I'll give it back to you

osa *f* AST: **Osa Mayor** Great Bear; **Osa Menor** Little Bear

osadía *f* daring; (*descaro*) audacity

osamenta *f* bones *pl*

osar ⟨1a⟩ *v/i* dare

oscilación *f* oscillation; *de precios* fluctuation

oscilar ⟨1a⟩ *v/i* oscillate; *de precios* fluctuate

oscurecer ⟨2d⟩ 1 *v/t* darken; *logro, triunfo* overshadow 2 *v/i* get dark 3 *v/r* oscurecerse darken

oscuridad *f* darkness

oscuro *adj* dark; *fig* obscure; **a -as** in the dark

óseo *adj* bone *atr*

osezno *m* cub

osito *m*: **osito de peluche** teddy bear

oso *m* bear; **oso hormiguero** anteater; **oso panda** panda; **oso polar** polar bear

ostensible *adj* obvious

ostentación *f* ostentation; **hacer ostentación de** flaunt

ostentar ⟨1a⟩ *v/t* flaunt; *cargo* hold

ostentoso *adj* ostentatious

osteoporosis *f* MED osteoporosis

ostra *f* ZO oyster; **¡ostras!** F hell! F

ostrero *m* ZO oyster-catcher

OTAN *abr* (= **Organización del Tratado del Atlántico Norte**) NATO (= North Atlantic Treaty Organization)

otitis *f* MED earache

otoño *m* fall, *Br* autumn

otorgar ⟨1h⟩ *v/t* award; *favor* grant

otorrino F, otorrinolaringólogo *m* MED ear, nose and throat *o* ENT specialist

otro 1 *adj* (*diferente*) another; **con el, la** other; **otros** other; **otros dos libros** another two books 2 *pron* (*adicional*) another (one); (*persona distinta*) someone

o somebody else; (*cosa distinta*) another one, a different one; **otros** others; **entre otros** among others 3 *siguiente:* **¡hasta -a!** see you soon 4 *pron recíproco:* **amar el uno al otro** love one another
ovación *f* ovation
ovacionar ⟨1a⟩ *v/t* cheer, give an ovation to
ovalado *adj* oval
óvalo *m* oval
ovario *m* ANAT ovary
oveja *f* sheep; **oveja negra** *fig* black sheep
overol *m* Méx overalls *pl*, Br dungarees *pl*
ovillo *m* ball; **hacerse un ovillo** *fig* curl up (into a ball)
ovino 1 *adj* sheep *atr* 2 *m* sheep; **ovinos** sheep *pl*

OVNI *abr* (= **objeto volante no identificado**) UFO (= unidentified flying object)
ovulación *f* ovulation
óvulo *m* egg
oxidado *adj* rusty
oxidar ⟨1a⟩ 1 *v/t* rust 2 *v/r* **oxidarse** rust, go rusty
óxido *m* QUÍM oxide; (*herrumbre*) rust
oxigenarse ⟨1a⟩ *v/r* *fig* get some fresh air
oxígeno *m* oxygen
oye *vb* → **oír**
oyendo *vb* → **oír**
oyente *m/f* listener
oyó *vb* → **oír**
ozono *m* ozone; **capa de ozono** ozone layer

P

pabellón *m* pavilion; *edificio* block; MÚS bell; MAR flag
pachanga *f:* **ir de pachanga** Méx, W.I., C.Am. F go on a spree F
pachocha *L.Am.*, pachorra *f* F slowness
pachucho *adj* MED F poorly
paciencia *f* patience
paciente *m/f* & *adj* patient
pacificador *m*, pacificadora *f* peace-maker
pacificar ⟨1g⟩ *v/t* pacify
pacífico 1 *adj* peaceful; *persona* peaceable; **el océano Pacífico** the Pacific Ocean 2 *m:* **el Pacífico** the Pacific
pacifista 1 *adj* pacifist *atr* 2 *m/f* pacifist
paco *m*, -a *f* L.Am. F (*policía*) cop F
pacotilla *f:* **de pacotilla** third-rate, lousy F
pacotillero *m*, -a *f* L.Am. street vendor
pactar ⟨1a⟩ 1 *v/t* agree; **pactar un acuerdo** reach (an) agreement 2 *v/i* reach (an) agreement
pacto *m* agreement, pact
padecer ⟨2d⟩ 1 *v/t* suffer 2 *v/i* suffer; **padecer de** have trouble with
padrastro *m* step-father
padre *m* father; REL Father; **de padre y muy señor mío** terrible; **padres** parents; **¡qué padre!** Méx F brilliant!
padrenuestro *m* Lord's Prayer
padrillo *m* Rpl stallion
padrino *m* *en bautizo* godfather; (*en boda*) man who gives away the bride

padrón *m* *register of local inhabitants*
paella *f* GASTR paella
pág. *abr* (= **página**) p. (= page)
paga *f* pay; *de niño* allowance, Br pocket money
pagado *adj* paid
pagano *adj* pagan
pagar ⟨1h⟩ 1 *v/t* pay; *compra, gastos, crimen* pay for; *favor* repay; **¡me las pagarás!** you'll pay for this! 2 *v/i* pay; **pagar a escote** F go Dutch F
pagaré *m* IOU
página *f* page; **página web** web page; **páginas amarillas** yellow pages
pago *m* payment; *Rpl* (*quinta*) piece of land; **pago al contado** or **en efectivo** payment in cash; **en pago de** in payment for; **por estos pagos** F in this neck of the woods F
país *m* country; **país en vías de desarrollo** developing country; **los Países Bajos** the Netherlands
paisaje *m* landscape
paisano *m:* **de paisano** MIL in civilian clothes; *policía* in plain clothes
paja *f* straw; **hacerse una paja** V jerk off V
pajar *m* hayloft
pajarería *f* pet shop
pajarita *f* corbata bow tie; **de papel** paper bird
pájaro *m* bird; *fig* ugly customer F, nasty piece of work F; **pájaro carpintero**

woodpecker; *matar dos pájaros de un tiro* kill two birds with one stone

Pakistán Pakistan

pakistaní *m/f & adj* Pakistani

pala *f* spade; *raqueta* paddle; *para servir* slice; *para recoger* dustpan

palabra *f tb fig* word; *palabra de honor* word of hono(u)r; *bajo palabra* on parole; *en una palabra* in a word; *tomar la palabra* speak

palabrota *f* swearword

palacete *m* small palace

palaciego *adj* palace *atr*

palacio *m* palace; *palacio de deportes* sports center (*Br* centre); *palacio de justicia* law courts

paladar *m* palate

palanca *f* lever; *palanca de cambios* AUTO gearshift, *Br* gear lever; *tener palanca* *Méx fig* F have pull F *o* clout F

palangana *f* plastic bowl for washing dishes, *Br* washing-up bowl

palanganear ⟨1a⟩ *v/i* S. Am. show off

palanqueta *f* crowbar

palco *m* TEA box

palenque *m* L.Am. cockpit (*in cock fighting*)

Palestina Palestine

palestino 1 *adj* Palestinian **2** *m*, *-a f* Palestinian

palestra *f* arena; *salir o saltar a la palestra* *fig* hit the headlines

paleta *f* PINT palette; TÉC trowel

paletilla *f* GASTR shoulder

paleto F 1 *adj* hick *atr* F, provincial **2** *m*, *-a f* hick F, *Br* yokel F

paliar ⟨1b⟩ *v/t* alleviate; *dolor* relieve

paliativo *m/adj* palliative

palidecer ⟨2d⟩ *v/i de persona* turn pale

palidez *f* paleness

pálido *adj* pale

palillo *m para dientes* toothpick; *para comer* chopstick

palique *m*: *estar de palique* F have a chat

paliza *f* beating; (*derrota*) thrashing F, drubbing F; (*pesadez*) drag F **2** *m/f* F drag F

palma *f* palm; *dar palmas* clap (one's hands)

palmada *f* pat; (*manotazo*) slap

palmar ⟨1a⟩ *v/t*: *palmarla* P kick the bucket F

palmera *f* BOT palm tree; (*dulce*) heart-shaped pastry

palmito *m* BOT palmetto; GASTR palm heart; *fig* F attractiveness

palmo *m* hand's breadth; *palmo a palmo* inch by inch

palo *m de madera etc* stick; MAR mast; *de portería* post, upright; *palo de golf* golf club; *palo mayor* MAR mainmast; *a medio palo* L.Am. half-drunk; *a palo seco* whisky straight up; *ser un palo* L.Am. F be fantastic; *de tal palo tal astilla* a chip off the old block F

paloma *f* pigeon; *blanca* dove; *paloma mensajera* carrier pigeon

palomar *m* pigeon loft

palometa *f* ZO pez pompano

palomilla *f* C.Am., Méx F gang

palomita *f Méx* checkmark, *Br* tick; *palomitas pl de maíz* popcorn *sg*

palpable *adj fig* palpable

palpar ⟨1a⟩ *v/t con las manos* feel, touch; *fig* feel

palpitación *f* palpitation

palpitante *adj corazón* pounding; *cuestión* burning

palpitar ⟨1a⟩ *v/i de corazón* pound; *Rpl fig* have a hunch F, have a feeling

palta *f S. Am.* BOT avocado

palto *m S. Am.* jacket

paludismo *m* MED malaria

palurdo 1 *adj* F hick *atr* F, provincial **2** *m*, *-a f* F hick F, *Br* yokel F

pamela *f* picture hat

pampa *f* GEOG pampa, prairie; *a la pampa* *Rpl* in the open

pamplinas *fpl* nonsense *sg*

pan *m* bread; *un pan* a loaf; *pan francés* L.Am. French bread; *pan integral* wholemeal bread; *pan de molde* sliced bread; *pan de barra* French bread; *pan rallado* breadcrumbs *pl*; *pan tostado* toast; *ser pan comido* F be easy as pie F

pana *f* corduroy

panacea *f* panacea

panadería *f* baker's shop

panadero *m*, *-a f* baker

panal *m* honeycomb

Panamá Panama; *el Canal de Panamá* the Panama Canal; *Ciudad de Panamá* Panama city

panameño 1 *adj* Panamanian **2** *m*, *-a f* Panamanian

pancarta *f* placard

panceta *f* belly pork

páncreas *m inv* ANAT

panda *m* ZO panda

pandereta *f* tambourine

pandilla *f* group; *de delincuentes* gang

panecillo *m* (bread) roll

panel *m tb grupo de personas* panel; *panel solar* solar panel

panela *f* L.Am. brown sugar loaf

panera *f* bread basket

panfleto *m* pamphlet

P

pánico m panic; **sembrar el pánico** spread panic

panocha, panoja f ear

panoli adj F dopey F

panorama m panorama

panorámico adj: **vista -a** panoramic view

panqueque m L.Am. pancake

pantalla f TV, INFOR screen; de lámpara shade; **pequeña pantalla** fig small screen

pantalón m, **pantalones** mpl pants pl, Br trousers pl; **llevar los pantalones** fig F wear the pants (Br trousers) F

pantano m reservoir

panteón m pantheon

pantera f ZO panther

pantomima f pantomime

pantorrilla f ANAT calf

pantufla f slipper

panty m pantyhose pl, Br tights pl

panza f de persona belly

pañal m diaper, Br nappy

paño m cloth; **paño de cocina** dishtowel

pañuelo m handkerchief; **el mundo es un pañuelo** fig F it's a small world

papa 1 m Pope 2 f L.Am. potato

papá m F pop F, dad F; **papás** L.Am. parents; **Papá Noel** Santa Claus

papada f double chin

papagayo m ZO parrot

papal 1 adj papal 2 m L.Am. potato field

papalote m Méx kite

papanatas m/f inv F dope F, dimwit F

paparruchas fpl F baloney sg F

papaya f BOT papaya

papel m paper; **trozo de papel** piece of paper; TEA, fig role; **papel de aluminio** foil; **papel de envolver** wrapping paper; **papel de regalo** giftwrap; **papel higiénico** toilet paper o tissue; **papel reciclado** recycled paper; **perder los papeles** lose control; **ser papel mojado** fig not be worth the paper it's written on

papelada f L.Am. farce

papeleo m paperwork

papelera f wastepaper basket

papelería f stationer's shop

papelerío m L.Am. F muddle, mess

papeleta f de rifa raffle ticket; fig chore; **papeleta de voto** ballot paper

paperas fpl MED mumps

papilla f para bebés baby food; para enfermos puree; **hacer papilla a alguien** F beat s.o. to a pulp F

papista adj: **ser más papista que el papa** hold extreme views

paquete m package, parcel; de cigarrillos packet; F **en moto** (pillion) passenger

Paquistán Pakistan

paquistaní m/f & adj Pakistani

par 1 f par; **es bella a la par que inteligente** she is beautiful as well as intelligent, she is both beautiful and intelligent 2 m pair; **abierto de par en par** wide open; **un par de** a pair of

para prp for ◇ dirección toward(s); **ir para** a head for; **va para directora** she's going to end up as manager

◇ tiempo for; **listo para mañana** ready for tomorrow; **para siempre** forever; **diez para las ocho** L.Am. ten of eight, ten to eight

◇ finalidad: **lo hace para ayudarte** he does it (in order) to help you; **para que** so that; **¿para qué te marchas?** what are you leaving for?; **para mí** for me; **lo heredó todo para morir a los 30** he inherited it all, only to die at 30

parabólica f satellite dish

parabrisas m inv AUTO windshield, Br windscreen

paracaídas m inv parachute

paracaidista m/f parachutist; MIL paratrooper

parachoques m inv AUTO fender, Br bumper

parada f stop; **parada de autobús** bus stop; **parada de taxis** taxi rank

paradero m whereabouts sg; L.Am. → **parada**

parado 1 adj unemployed; L.Am. (de pie) standing (up); **salir bien / mal parado** come off well / badly 2 m, -a f unemployed person

paradoja f paradox

paradójico adj paradoxical

parador m Esp parador (state-run luxury hotel)

parafernalia f F paraphernalia

parafina f kerosene, Br paraffin

paraguas m inv umbrella

Paraguay Paraguay

paraguayo 1 adj Paraguayan 2 m, -a f Paraguayan

paraíso m paradise; **paraíso fiscal** tax haven

paralelismo m parallel

paralelo m/adj parallel

parálisis f tb fig paralysis

paralítico 1 adj paralytic 2 m, -a f person who is paralyzed

paralización f tb fig paralysis

paralizar ⟨1f⟩ v/t MED paralyze; actividad bring to a halt; país, economía paralyze, bring to a standstill

parámetro m parameter

paramilitar adj paramilitary

parangón m: **sin parangón** incompara-

ble
paranoia f paranoia
paranoico 1 adj MED paranoid **2** m, -a f
MED person suffering from paranoia
paranormal adj paranormal
parapente m hang glider; **actividad** hang
gliding
parapeto m parapet
parapléjico 1 adj MED paraplegic **2** m, -a f
paraplegic
parar ⟨1a⟩ **1** v/t stop; L.Am. (poner de pie)
stand up **2** v/i stop; en alojamiento stay;
parar de llover stop raining; **ir a parar**
end up **3** v/r **pararse** stop; L.Am. (ponerse de pie) stand up
pararrayos m inv lightning rod
parásito m parasite
parcela f lot, Br plot
parchar ⟨1a⟩ v/t L.Am. patch; (arreglar)
repair
parche m patch
parcial adj (partidario) bias(s)ed
pardo 1 adj color dun; L.Am. desp half-
-breed desp, Br tb half-caste desp **2** m color dun; L.Am. desp half-breed desp
parecer 1 m opinion, view; **al parecer** apparently **2** ⟨2d⟩ v/i seem, look; **me parece que** I think (that), it seems to me that;
me parece bien it seems fine to me;
¿qué te parece? what do you think? **3**
v/r **parecerse** resemble each other; **parecerse a alguien** resemble s.o.
parecido 1 adj similar **2** m similarity
pared f wall; **subirse por las paredes** F
hit the roof F
pareja f (conjunto de dos) pair; en una relación couple; de una persona partner;
de un objeto other one
parejo adj L.Am. suelo level, even; **andar
parejos** be neck and neck; **llegaron parejos** they arrived at the same time
paréntesis m inv parenthesis; fig break;
entre paréntesis fig by the way
pareo m wrap-around skirt
parida f P stupid thing to say / do
pariente m/f relative
paripé m: **hacer el paripé** F put on an act
F
parir ⟨3a⟩ **1** v/i give birth **2** v/t give birth to
París Paris
parisino 1 adj Parisian **2** m, -a f Parisian
parka f parka
parking m parking lot, Br car park
parlamentario 1 adj parliamentary **2** m,
-a f member of parliament
parlamento m parliament
parlanchín adj chatty
parlante m L.Am. loudspeaker
parlotear ⟨1a⟩ v/i chatter

parmesano m/adj Parmesan
paro m unemployment; **estar en paro** be
unemployed; **paro cardíaco** cardiac arrest
parodia f parody
parpadear ⟨1a⟩ v/i blink
parpadeo m blinking
párpado m eye lid
parque m park; para bebé playpen; **parque de atracciones** amusement park;
parque de bomberos fire station; **parque nacional** national park; **parque natural** nature reserve; **parque temático**
theme park
parqué m → **parquet**
parquear ⟨1a⟩ v/t L.Am. park
parquet m parquet
parquímetro m parking meter
parra f (grape) vine
párrafo m paragraph
parranda f: **andar** or **irse de parranda** F
go out on the town F
parricidio m parricide
parrilla f broiler, Br grill; **a la parrilla**
broiled, Br grilled
parrillada f L.Am. barbecue
párroco m parish priest
parroquia f REL parish; COM clientele, customers pl
parsimonia f parsimony
parte 1 m report; **parte meteorológico**
weather report; **dar parte a alguien** inform s.o. **2** f trozo part; JUR party; **alguna
parte** somewhere; **ninguna parte** nowhere; **otra parte** somewhere else; **de
parte de** on behalf of; **en parte** partly;
en or **por todas partes** everywhere; **la
mayor parte de** the majority of, most
of; **por otra parte** moreover; **estar de
parte de alguien** be on s.o.'s side; **formar parte de** form part of; **tomar parte
en** take part in
participación f participation
participante m/f participant
participar ⟨1a⟩ **1** v/t una noticia announce
2 v/i take part (**en** in), participate (**en** in)
participio m GRAM participle
partícula f particle
particular 1 adj clase, propiedad private;
asunto personal; (específico) particular;
(especial) peculiar; **en particular** in particular **2** m (persona) individual; **parti-
culares** particulars
particularidad f peculiarity
partida f en juego game; (remesa) consignment; documento certificate; **partida de nacimiento** birth certificate
partidario 1 adj: **ser partidario de** be in
favo(u)r of **2** m, -a f supporter

P

partidismo *m* partisanship

partido *m* POL party; DEP game; *sacar partido de* take advantage of; *tomar partido* take sides

partir ⟨3a⟩ **1** *v/t* (*dividir, repartir*) split; (*romper*) break open, split open; (*cortar*) cut **2** *v/i* (*irse*) leave; *a partir de hoy* (starting) from today; *a partir de ahora* from now on; *partir de* fig start from **3** *v/r partirse* (*romperse*) break; *partirse de risa* F split one's sides laughing F

partitura *f* MÚS score

parto *m* birth; fig creation

parvulario *m* kindergarten

pasa *f* raisin

pasable *adj* passable

pasada *f con trapo* wipe; *de pintura* coat; *de pasada* in passing; *¡qué pasada!* F that's incredible! F

pasadizo *m* passage

pasado **1** *adj tiempo* last; *el lunes pasado* last Monday; *pasado de moda* old-fashioned **2** *m* past

pasaje *m* (*billete*) ticket; MÚS, *de texto* passage

pasajero **1** *adj* temporary; *relación* brief **2** *m*, *-a f* passenger

pasamano(s) *m* handrail

pasamontañas *m inv* balaclava (helmet)

pasaporte *m* passport

pasar ⟨1a⟩ **1** *v/t* pass; *el tiempo* spend; *un lugar* go past; *frontera* cross; *problemas, dificultades* experience; AUTO (*adelantar*) pass, Br overtake; *una película* show; *para pasar el tiempo* (in order) to pass the time; *pasar la mano por* run one's hand through; *pasarlo bien* have a good time **2** *v/i* (*suceder*) happen; *en juegos* pass; *pasar de alguien* F not want anything to do with s.o.; *paso de coger el teléfono* F I can't be bothered to pick up the phone; *pasé a visitarla* I dropped by to see her; *pasar de moda* go out of fashion; *pasar por* go by; *pasé por la tienda* I stopped off at the shop; *pasa por aquí* come this way; *dejar pasar oportunidad* miss; *hacerse pasar por* pass o.s. off as; *pasaré por tu casa* I'll drop by your house; *¡pasa!* come in; *¿qué pasa?* what's happening?, what's going on?; *¿qué te pasa?* what's the matter?; *pase lo que pase* whatever happens, come what may **3** *v/r pasarse* *tb* fig go too far; *del tiempo* pass, go by; (*usar el tiempo*) spend; *de molestia, dolor* go away; *pasarse al enemigo* go over to the enemy; *se le pasó llamar* he forgot to call

pasarela *f* catwalk

pasatiempo *m* pastime

Pascua *f* Easter; *¡felices Pascuas!* Merry Christmas!

pase *m tb* DEP, TAUR pass; *en el cine* showing; *pase de modelos* fashion show

pasear ⟨1a⟩ **1** *v/t* take for a walk; (*exhibir*) show off **2** *v/i* walk **3** *v/r pasearse* walk

paseo *m* walk; *paseo marítimo* seafront; *dar un paseo* go for a walk; *mandar a alguien a paseo* fig F tell s.o. to get lost

pasillo *m* corridor; *en avión, cine* aisle

pasión *f* passion

pasividad *f* passivity

pasivo *adj* passive

pasmar ⟨1a⟩ *v/t* amaze, astonish

paso *m* step; (*manera de andar*) walk; (*ritmo*) pace, rate; *de agua* flow; *de tráfico* movement; (*cruce*) crossing; *de tiempo* passing; (*huella*) footprint; *paso a nivel* grade crossing, Br level crossing; *paso de peatones* crosswalk, pedestrian crossing; *a este paso* fig at this rate; *de paso* on the way; *estar de paso* be passing through

pasta *f sustancia* paste; GASTR pasta; P (*dinero*) dough P; *pasta de dientes* toothpaste; *pastas de té* type of cookie (Br biscuit)

pastel *m* GASTR cake; *pintura, color* pastel

pastelería *f* cake shop

pastelero *m*, *-a f* pastry cook

paste(u)rizar ⟨1f⟩ *v/t* pasteurize

pastilla *f tablet; de jabón* bar; *a toda pastilla* F at top speed F, flat out F

pasto *m* (*hierba*) grass; *a todo pasto* F for all one is worth F

pastor *m* shepherd; REL pastor; *pastor alemán* German shepherd

pata[1] *m/f Pe* F pal F, buddy F

pata[2] *f* leg; *a cuatro patas* on all fours; *meter la pata* F put one's foot in it F; *tener mala pata* F be unlucky

patada *f* kick; *dar una patada* kick

patalear ⟨1a⟩ *v/i* stamp one's feet; fig kick and scream

patata *f* potato; *patatas fritas de sartén* French fries, Br chips; *de bolsa* chips, Br crisps

patatús *m*: *le dio un patatús* F he had a fit F

paté *m* paté

patear ⟨1a⟩ *v/t & v/i L.Am. de animal* kick

patentar ⟨1a⟩ *v/t* patent

patente **1** *adj* clear, obvious **2** *f* patent; L.Am. AUTO license plate, Br number-plate

paternidad *f* paternity, fatherhood

paterno *adj* paternal

patético *adj* pitiful

patíbulo m scaffold
patilla f de gafas arm; **patillas** barba sideburns
patín m skate; **patín (de ruedas) en línea** rollerblade®, in-line skate
patinador m, **patinadora** f skater
patinaje m skating; **patinaje artístico** figure skating; **patinaje sobre hielo** ice-skating; **patinaje sobre ruedas** roller-skating
patinar ⟨1a⟩ v/i skate
patinazo m skid; fig F blunder; **dar un patinazo** skid
patinete m scooter
patio m courtyard, patio; **patio de butacas** TEA orchestra, Br stalls pl
pato m ZO duck; **pagar el pato** F take the rap F, Br carry the can F
patojo adj Chi F squat
patológico adj pathological
patoso adj clumsy
patraña f tall story
patria f homeland
patriarca m patriarch
patrimonio m heritage; **patrimonio artístico** artistic heritage
patriota m/f patriot
patriótico adj patriotic
patriotismo m patriotism
patrocinador m, **patrocinadora** f sponsor
patrocinar ⟨1a⟩ v/t sponsor
patrocinio m sponsorship
patrón m (jefe) boss; REL patron saint; para costura pattern; (modelo) standard; MAR skipper
patrona f (jefa) boss; REL patron saint
patronal employers pl
patrulla f patrol
patrullar ⟨1a⟩ v/t patrol
patrullero m patrolman
paulatino adj gradual
pausa f pause; en una actividad break; MÚS rest; **pausa publicitaria** commercial break
pausado adj slow, deliberate
pavimento m pavement, Br road surface
pavo m pej L.Am. F stupid **2** m ZO turkey; **pavo real** peacock
pavonearse ⟨1a⟩ v/r boast (de about)
pavor m terror; **me da pavor** it terrifies me
payada f Rpl improvized ballad
payador m Rpl gaucho singer
payasadas fpl antics; **hacer payasadas** fool o clown around
payaso m clown

paz f peace; **dejar en paz** leave alone
pe: **de pe a pa** F from start to finish
PC abr (= **Partido Comunista**) CP (= Communist Party)
P.D. abr (= **posdata**) PS (= postscript)
peaje m dinero, lugar toll
peatón m pedestrian
peatonal adj pedestrian atr
pebete m, **-a** f Rpl F kid F
peca f freckle
pecado m sin
pecador m, **pecadora** f sinner
pecaminoso adj sinful
pecar ⟨1g⟩ v/i sin; **pecar de ingenuo / generoso** be very naive / generous
pecera f fish tank, aquarium
pecho m (caja torácica) chest; (mama) breast; **tomar algo a pecho** take sth to heart
pechuga f GASTR breast; L.Am. fig F (caradura) nerve F
pecoso adj freckled
pectoral adj ANAT pectoral
peculiar adj peculiar, odd; (característico) typical
peculiaridad f (característica) peculiarity
pedagogía f education
pedagogo m, **-a** f teacher
pedal m pedal
pedalear ⟨1a⟩ v/i pedal
pedante 1 adj pedantic; (presuntuoso) pretentious **2** m/f pedant; (presuntuoso) pretentious individual
pedantería f pedantry; (presunción) pretentiousness
pedazo m piece, bit; **pedazo de bruto** F blockhead F, **hacer pedazos** F smash to bits F
pederasta m pederast
pedestal m pedestal
pediatra m/f p(a)ediatrician
pedicura f pedicure
pedicuro m, **-a** f pedicurist, Br chiropodist
pedido m order
pedigrí m pedigree
pedigüeño m, **-a** f person who is always asking to borrow things, moocher F
pedir ⟨3l⟩ **1** v/t ask for; (necesitar) need; en bar, restaurante order; **me pidió que no fuera** he asked me not to go **2** v/i mendigar beg; en bar, restaurante order
pedo 1 adj drunk **2** m F fart F; **agarrarse un pedo** F get plastered F; **tirarse** o **echar un pedo** F fart F
pedorreta f F Bronx cheer F, Br raspberry F
pedrada f blow with a stone; **me dio una pedrada en la cabeza** he hit me over the

head with a stone
pedregal *m* stony ground
pedregoso *adj* stony
Pedro *m*: *como Pedro por su casa* fig F as if he / she owned the place
pega f F snag F, hitch F; *poner pegas* raise objections
pegadizo *adj* catchy
pegado *adj* (*adherido*) stuck (*a* to); *estar pegado a* (*cerca de*) be right up against; *estar pegado a alguien* fig follow s.o. around, be s.o.'s shadow
pegajoso *adj* sticky; *fig: persona* clingy
pegamento *m* glue
pegar ⟨1h⟩ **1** *v/t* (*golpear*) hit; (*adherir*) stick, glue; (*bofetada, susto, resfriado*) give; *pegar un grito* shout; *no me pega la gana Méx* F I don't feel like it **2** *v/i* (*golpear*) hit; (*adherir*) stick; *del sol* beat down; (*armonizar*) go (together) **3** *v/r* *pegarse resfriado* catch; *acento* pick up; *susto* give o.s.; *pegarse un golpe / un tiro* hit / shoot o.s.; *pegársela a alguien* F con s.o.
pegatina f sticker
pegote *m* F (*cosa fea*) eyesore
peinado *m* hairstyle
peinador *m*, **peinadora** f *L.Am.* hairdresser
peinar ⟨1a⟩ **1** *v/t* tb fig comb; *peinar a alguien* comb s.o.'s hair **2** *v/r* *peinarse* comb one's hair
peine *m* comb
p. ej. *abr* (= *por ejemplo*) e.g. (= exempli gratia, for example)
Pekín Beijing
pela f F peseta
peladero *m* *L.Am.* vacant lot
peladilla f sugared almond
pelado *adj* peeled; *fig* bare; F (*sin dinero*) broke F
pelar ⟨1a⟩ **1** *v/t* *manzana, patata etc* peel; *hace un frío que pela* F it's freezing **2** *v/r* *pelarse* (*cortarse el pelo*) have a haircut; *Rpl* F (*chismear*) gossip
pelazón f *C.Am.* backbiting
peldaño *m* step
pelea f fight
pelear ⟨1a⟩ **1** *v/i* fight **2** *v/r* *pelearse* fight
pelele *m* puppet
peleón *adj* argumentative; *vino peleón* F jug wine, *Br* plonk F
peletería f furrier's
peliagudo *adj* tricky
pelícano *m* zo pelican
película f movie, film; FOT film; *película del Oeste* Western; *de película* F awesome F, fantastic F
peligrar ⟨1a⟩ *v/i* be at risk

peligro *m* danger; *correr peligro* be in danger; *poner en peligro* endanger, put at risk
peligroso *adj* dangerous
pelillo *m*: *¡pelillos a la mar* F let's bury the hatchet
pelín: *un pelín* F a (little) bit
pelirrojo *adj* red-haired, red-headed
pellejo *m* *de animal* skin, hide; *salvar el pellejo* fig F save one's (own) skin F
pellizcar ⟨1g⟩ *v/t* pinch
pellizco *m* pinch; *un buen pellizco* F a tidy sum F
pelma **1** *adj* annoying **2** *m/f* pain F
pelmazo *m*, **-a** f F pain F
pelo *m* *de persona, de perro* hair; *de animal* fur; *tiene el pelo muy largo* he has very long hair; *a pelo* (*sin preparación*) unprepared; *montar a pelo* ride bareback; *por los pelos* F by a whisker F, by the skin of one's teeth F; *tomar el pelo a alguien* F pull s.o.'s leg F
pelota **1** f ball; *pelotas* F nuts F, balls F; *en pelotas* P stark naked; *hacer la pelota a alguien* suck up to s.o. F **2** *m/f* F creep F
pelotazo *m*: *rompió el cristal de un pelotazo* he smashed the window with a ball
pelotero *m*, **-a** f *L.Am.* (base)ball player
pelotón *m* MIL squad; DEP bunch, pack
peluca f wig
peluche *m* soft toy; *oso de peluche* teddy bear
peludo *adj* *persona* hairy; *animal* furry
peluquearse ⟨1a⟩ *v/r* *L.Am.* get one's hair cut
peluquería f hairdresser's
peluquero *m*, **-a** f hairdresser
peluquín *m* toupee, hairpiece
pelusa f fluff
pelvis f *inv* ANAT pelvis
pena f (*tristeza*) sadness, sorrow; (*congoja*) grief, distress; (*lástima*) pity; JUR sentence; *pena capital* death penalty, capital punishment; *pena de muerte* death penalty; *no vale o no merece la pena* it's not worth it; *¡qué pena!* what a shame *o* pity!; *a duras penas* with difficulty; *me da pena L.Am.* I'm ashamed
penal *adj* penal; *derecho penal* criminal law
penalidad f fig hardship
penalización f *acción* penalization; DEP penalty
penalizar ⟨1f⟩ *v/t* penalize
penalty *m* DEP penalty
penca **1** *adj* *Chi* soft, weak **2** f *L.Am.* (*nopal*) leaf of the prickly pear plant

pendejada f L.Am. stupid thing to do
pendejo 1 m (pelea) fight **2** m, -a f L.Am. F dummy F
pendenciero adj troublemaker
pendiente 1 adj unresolved, unfinished; cuenta unpaid **2** m earring **3** f slope
pendón 1 adj swinging F **2** m, -ona f F swinger F
péndulo m pendulum
pene m ANAT penis
penetración f penetration
penetrante adj mirada penetrating; sonido piercing; frío bitter; herida deep; análisis incisive
penetrar ⟨1a⟩ v/i penetrate; (entrar) enter; de un líquido seep in
penicilina f penicillin
península f peninsula; **península Ibérica** Iberian Peninsula
penique m penny
penitencia f penitence
penitenciado m L.Am. prisoner, convict
penitenciario adj penitentiary atr, prison atr
penoso adj distressing; trabajo laborious
pensamiento m thought; BOT pansy
pensar ⟨1k⟩ **1** v/t think about; (opinar) think; **¡ni pensarlo!** don't even think about it **2** v/i think (**en** about)
pensativo adj thoughtful
pensión f hotel rooming house, Br guesthouse; dinero pension; **pensión alimenticia** child support, Br maintenance; **pensión completa** American plan, Br full board
pensionista m/f pensioner
pentagrama m MÚS stave
pentatlón m DEP pentathlon
penúltimo adj penultimate
penumbra f half-light
penuria f shortage (**de** of); (pobreza) poverty
peña f crag, cliff; (roca) rock; F de amigos group, circle
peñasco m boulder
peñón m: **el Peñón de Gibraltar** the Rock of Gibraltar
peón m en ajedrez pawn; trabajador labo(u)rer
peor adj comp worse; **de mal en peor** from bad to worse
pepa f L.Am. (semilla) seed; **soltar la pepa** F spill the beans
pepinillo m gherkin
pepino m cucumber; **me importa un pepino** F I don't give a damn F
pepita f pip
pequeño 1 adj small, little; **de pequeño** when I was small o little **2** m, -a f little

one
pequinés m zo Pekinese, Peke F
pera f pear
peral m pear tree
perca f pez perch
percance m mishap
percatarse ⟨1a⟩ v/r notice; **percatarse de algo** notice sth
percebe m zo barnacle
percepción f perception; COM acto receipt
percha f coat hanger; gancho coat hook
perchero m coat rack
percibir ⟨3a⟩ v/t perceive; COM sueldo receive
percusión f MÚS percussion
perdedor m, perdedora f loser
perder ⟨2g⟩ **1** v/t objeto lose; tren, avión etc miss; el tiempo waste **2** v/i lose; **echar a perder** ruin; **echarse a perder** de alimento go bad **3** v/r **perderse** get lost
perdición f downfall
pérdida f loss
perdido adj lost; **ponerse perdido** get filthy
perdigón m pellet
perdiz f zo partridge
perdón m pardon; REL forgiveness; **pedir perdón** say sorry, apologize; **¡perdón!** sorry
perdonar ⟨1a⟩ v/t forgive; JUR pardon; **perdonar algo a alguien** forgive s.o. sth; **¡perdone!** sorry; **perdone, ¿tiene hora?** excuse me, do you have the time?
perdurar ⟨1a⟩ v/i endure
perecedero adj perishable
perecer ⟨2d⟩ v/i perish
peregrinación f pilgrimage
peregrinar ⟨1a⟩ v/i go on a pilgrimage
peregrino m, -a f pilgrim
perejil m BOT parsley
perenne adj BOT perennial
perentorio adj (urgente) urgent, pressing; (apremiante) peremptory
pereza f laziness
perezoso 1 adj lazy **2** m zo sloth
perfección f perfection; **a la perfección** perfectly, to perfection
perfeccionamiento m perfecting
perfeccionar ⟨1a⟩ v/t perfect
perfeccionista m/f perfectionist
perfecto adj perfect
pérfido adj treacherous
perfil m profile; **de perfil** in profile, from the side
perforación f puncture
perforadora f punch
perforar ⟨1a⟩ v/t pierce; calle dig up
perfumar ⟨1a⟩ v/t perfume
perfume m perfume

P

perfumería f perfume shop
pergamino m parchment
pergenio m, **-a** f Rpl F kid F
pericia f expertise
pericote m Chi, Pe zo large rat
periferia f periphery; **de ciudad** outskirts pl
perilla f goatee; **me viene de perilla** F that'll be very useful; **tu visita me viene de perilla** F you've come at just the right time
perímetro m perimeter
periódico 1 adj periodic **2** m newspaper
periodismo m journalism
periodista m/f journalist
período, periodo m period
peripecia f adventure
periquete m: **en un periquete** F in a second, in no time F
periquito m zo budgerigar
periscopio m periscope
perito 1 adj expert **2** m, **-a** f expert; COM **en seguros** loss adjuster
perjudicar ⟨1g⟩ v/t harm, damage
perjudicial adj harmful, damaging
perjuicio m harm, damage; **sin perjuicio de** without affecting
perjurio m perjury
perla f pearl; **nos vino de perlas** F it suited us fine F
permanecer ⟨2d⟩ v/i remain, stay
permanente 1 adj permanent **2** f perm
permeable adj permeable
permisible adj permissible
permisivo adj permissive
permiso m permission; **documento** permit; **permiso de conducir** driver's license, Br driving licence; **permiso de residencia** residence permit; **con permiso** excuse me; **estar de permiso** be on leave
permitir ⟨3a⟩ **1** v/t permit, allow **2** v/r permitirse afford; **permitirse el lujo de** permit o.s. the luxury of
pernicioso adj harmful
pernoctar ⟨1a⟩ v/i spend the night
pero 1 conj but **2** m flaw, defect; **no hay peros que valgan** no excuses
perogrullada f platitude
peronismo m Peronism
peronista m/f Peronist
perorata f F lecture
perpendicular adj perpendicular
perpetrar ⟨1a⟩ v/t crimen perpetrate, commit
perpetuar ⟨1e⟩ v/t perpetuate
perpetuidad f: **a perpetuidad** in perpetuity
perpetuo adj fig perpetual

perplejidad f perplexity
perplejo adj puzzled, perplexed
perra f dog; **el perro y la perra** the dog and the bitch; **perras** F pesetas
perrera f kennels pl
perrería f F dirty trick
perrito m: **perrito caliente** GASTR hot dog
perro m dog; **perro callejero** stray; **perro guardián** guard dog; **perro lazarillo** seeing eye dog, Br guide dog; **perro pastor** sheepdog; **llevarse como el perro y el gato** fig fight like cat and dog; **hace un tiempo de perros** F the weather is lousy F
persecución f pursuit; (acoso) persecution
perseguidor m, **perseguidora** f persecutor
perseguir ⟨3l & 3d⟩ v/t pursue; delincuente look for; (molestar) pester; (acosar) persecute
perseverancia f perseverance
perseverar ⟨1a⟩ v/i persevere (**en** with)
persiana f blind
pérsico adj Persian
persignarse ⟨1a⟩ v/r cross o.s.
persistente adj persistent
persistir ⟨3a⟩ v/i persist
persona f person; **quince personas** fifteen people
personaje m TEA character; famoso celebrity
personal 1 adj personal **2** m personnel, staff
personalidad f personality
personalizar ⟨1f⟩ v/t personalize
personificar ⟨1g⟩ v/t personify, embody
perspectiva f perspective; fig point of view; **perspectivas** pl outlook sg, prospects
perspicacia f shrewdness, perspicacity
persuadir ⟨3a⟩ v/t persuade
persuasión f persuasion
persuasivo adj persuasive
pertenecer ⟨2d⟩ v/i belong (**a** to)
pertenencias fpl belongings
pértiga f pole; **salto con pértiga** DEP pole vault
pertinaz adj persistent; (terco) obstinate
pertinente adj relevant, pertinent
pertrechos mpl MIL equipment sg
perturbar ⟨1a⟩ v/t disturb; reunión disrupt
Perú Peru
peruano 1 adj Peruvian **2** m, **-a** f Peruvian
perversión f perversion
perverso adj perverted
pervertido m, **-a** f pervert
pervertir ⟨3i⟩ v/t pervert

pesa f para balanza weight; DEP shot; C.Am., W.I. butcher's shop
pesadez f fig drag F
pesadilla f nightmare
pesado 1 adj objeto heavy; libro, clase etc tedious, boring; trabajo tough **2** m, -a f bore; **¡qué pesado es!** F he's a real pain F
pésame m condolences pl
pesar ⟨1a⟩ **1** v/t weigh **2** v/i be heavy; (influir) carry weight; fig weigh heavily (**sobre** on); **me pesa tener que informarle ...** I regret to have to inform you ... **3** m sorrow; **a pesar de** in spite of, despite
pesca f actividad fishing; (peces) fish pl
pescadería f fish shop
pescadero m, -a f fishmonger
pescadilla f pez whiting
pescado m GASTR fish
pescador m fisherman
pescar ⟨1g⟩ **1** v/t un pez, resfriado etc catch; (intentar tomar) fish for; trabajo, marido etc land **2** v/i fish
pescuezo m neck
pese: pese a despite
pesero m L.Am. minibus; Méx (collective) taxi
peseta f peseta
pesetero adj F money-grubbing F
pesimismo m pessimism
pesimista 1 adj pessimistic **2** m/f pessimist
pésimo adj sup awful, terrible
peso m weight; moneda peso; **de peso** fig weighty
pesquero 1 adj fishing atr **2** m fishing boat
pesquisa f investigation
pestaña f eyelash
pestañear ⟨1a⟩ v/i flutter one's eyelashes; **sin pestañear** fig without batting an eyelid
peste f MED plague; F olor stink F; **echar pestes** F curse and swear
pesticida m pesticide
pestilente adj foul-smelling
pestillo m (picaporte) door handle, (cerradura) bolt
petaca f para tabaco tobacco pouch; para bebida hip flask; C.Am. F insecto ladybug, Br ladybird
pétalo m petal
petanca f type of bowls
petardo 1 m firecracker **2** m, -a f F nerd F
petate m kit bag; L.Am. F en el suelo mat
petición f request; **a petición de** at the request of
petirrojo m ZO robin
petiso L.Am. **1** m, -a f F shorty F **2** m pony

peto m bib; **pantalón de peto** overalls pl, Br dungarees pl
petrificado adj petrified
petróleo m oil, petroleum
petrolero 1 adj oil atr **2** m MAR oil tanker
petrolífero adj oil atr
petroquímica f petrochemical
petulante adj smug
peyorativo adj pejorative
pez m ZO fish; **pez espada** swordfish; **pez gordo** F big shot F; **estar pez en algo** be clueless about sth F
pezón m nipple
pezuña f ZO hoof
piadoso adj pious
pianista m/f pianist
piano m piano; **piano de cola** grand piano
piar ⟨1c⟩ v/i tweet, chirrup
PIB abr (= producto interior bruto) GDP (= gross domestic product)
pibe m, -a f Rpl F kid F
picada f de serpiente bite; de abeja sting; L.Am. para comer snacks pl, nibbles pl; Rpl (camino) path
picadero m escuela riding school
picado 1 adj diente decayed; mar rough, choppy; carne ground, Br minced; verdura minced, Br finely chopped; fig offended **2** m L.Am. dive; **caer en picado de precios** nosedive, plummet
picadora f en cocina mincer
picadura f de reptil, mosquito bite; de avispa sting; tabaco cut tobacco
picaflor m L.Am. ZO hummingbird; fig womanizer
picante 1 adj hot, spicy; chiste risqué **2** m hot spice
picaporte m door handle
picar ⟨1g⟩ **1** v/t de mosquito, serpiente bite; de avispa sting, de ave peck; carne grind, Br mince; verdura mince, Br finely chop; TAUR jab with a lance; (molestar) annoy; la curiosidad pique **2** v/i tb fig take the bait; L.Am. de la comida be hot; (producir picor) itch; del sol burn
picardía f (astucia) craftiness, slyness; (travesura) mischievousness; Méx (taco, palabrota) swearing, swearwords pl
pícaro adj persona crafty, sly; comentario mischievous
picarón m Méx, Chi, Pe (buñuelo) fritter
picatoste m piece of fried bread
picha f V prick V
pichicato m Pe, Bol P coke P
pichincha f L.Am. bargain
pichón m L.Am. ORN chick; F (novato) rookie F
Picio: más feo que Picio F as ugly as sin F

picnic *m* (*pl* ~s) picnic
pico *m* ZO beak; F (*boca*) mouth; *de montaña* peak; *herramienta* pickax(e); **a las tres y pico** some time after three o'clock; **cerrar el pico** F shut one's mouth F
picor *m* itch
picota *f* bigarreau (*type of sweet cherry*)
picotazo *m* peck
picotear ⟨1a⟩ *v/t* peck
pido *vb* → **pedir**
pie *m* foot; *de estatua, lámpara* base; **a pie** on foot; **de pie** standing; **no tiene ni pies ni cabeza** it doesn't make any sense at all, I can't make head nor tail of it
piedad *f* pity; (*clemencia*) mercy
piedra *f tb* MED stone; **piedra preciosa** precious stone; **quedarse de piedra** *fig* be stunned
piel *f de persona, fruta* skin; *de animal* hide, skin; (*cuero*) leather; **abrigo de pieles** fur coat
pienso[1] *vb* → **pensar**
pienso[2] *m* animal feed
pierdo *vb* → **perder**
pierna *f* leg; **dormir a pierna suelta** sleep like a log
pieza *f de un conjunto*, MÚS piece; *de aparato* part; TEA play; (*habitación*) room; **pieza de recambio** spare (part); **quedarse de una pieza** F be amazed
pifia *f* F (*error*) booboo F; *Chi, Pe, Rpl* defect
pigmento *m* pigment
pigmeo *m*, **-a** *f* pigmy
pijama *m* pajamas *pl*, *Br* pyjamas *pl*
pijo 1 *adj* posh **2** *m* V (*pene*) prick V **3** *m*, **-a** *f* F *persona* rich kid F
pila *f* EL battery; (*montón*) pile; (*fregadero*) sink
pilar *m tb fig* pillar
píldora *f* pill
pileta *f* Rpl sink; (*alberca*) swimming pool
pillaje *m* pillage
pillar ⟨1a⟩ *v/t* (*tomar*) seize; (*atrapar*) catch; (*atropellar*) hit; *chiste* get
pillo 1 *adj* mischievous **2** *m*, **-a** *f* rascal
pilón *m* Méx: **me dio dos de pilón** he gave me two extra
pilotar ⟨1a⟩ *v/t* AVIA fly, pilot; AUTO drive; MAR steer
piloto *m* AVIA, MAR pilot; AUTO driver; EL pilot light; **piloto automático** autopilot
piltrafa *f*: *piltrafas* rags; **estar hecho una piltrafa** *fig* be a total wreck
pimentón *m* paprika
pimienta *f* pepper
pimiento *m* pepper; **me importa un pimiento** F I couldn't care less F

pimpón *m* ping-pong
PIN *m* PIN
pinar *m* pine forest
pincel *m* paintbrush
pinchadiscos *m/f* F disc jockey, DJ
pinchar ⟨1a⟩ **1** *v/t* prick; AUTO puncture; TELEC tap; F (*molestar*) bug F, needle F; **pincharle a alguien** MED give s.o. a shot **2** *v/i* prick; AUTO get a flat tire, *Br* get a puncture **3** *v/r* **pincharse** *con aguja etc* prick o.s.; F (*inyectarse*) shoot up F; **se nos pinchó una rueda** we got a flat (tire) *o Br* a puncture
pinchazo *m herida* prick; *dolor* sharp pain; AUTO flat (tire), *Br* puncture; F flop F
pinche[1] *m* cook's assistant
pinche[2] *adj* Méx F rotten F; *C.Am., Méx* (*tacaño*) tight-fisted
pincho *m* GASTR bar snack
pingajo *m* F rag
ping-pong *m* ping-pong
pingüino *m* zo penguin
pino *m* BOT pine; **hacer el pino** do a handstand
pinol(e) *m* C.Am., Méx cornstarch, *Br* cornflour; *L.Am.* roasted corn
pinta *f* pint; *aspecto* looks *pl*; **tener buena pinta** *fig* look inviting
pintalabios *m* lipstick
pintar ⟨1a⟩ **1** *v/t* paint; **no pintar nada** *fig* F not count **2** *v/r* **pintarse** put on one's makeup
pintor *m*, **pintora** *f* painter; **pintor (de brocha gorda)** (house) painter
pintoresco *adj* picturesque
pintura *f sustancia* paint; *obra* painting
pinza *f clothes* pin, *Br* clothes peg; ZO claw; *pinzas* tweezers; *L.Am.* (*alicates*) pliers
piña *f del pino* pine cone; *fruta* pineapple
piñón *m* BOT pine nut; TÉC pinion
piojo *m* ZO louse; *piojos pl* lice *pl*
piola *f* L.Am. cord, twine
piolín *m* Arg cord, twine
pionero 1 *adj* pioneering **2** *m*, **-a** *f tb fig* pioneer
pipa *f* pipe; *pipas semillas* sunflower seeds; **pasarlo pipa** F have a great time
pipí *m* F pee F; **hacer pipí** F pee F
pipiolo *m* C.Am., Méx F kid F; *pipiolos pl* C.Am. F (*dinero*) cash *sg*
pique *m* resentment; (*rivalidad*) rivalry; **irse a pique** *fig* go under, go to the wall
piqueta *f herramienta* pickax(e); *en camping* tentpeg
piquete *m* POL picket
pirado *adj* F crazy F
piragua *f* canoe

piragüista *m/f* DEP canoeist
pirámide *f* pyramid
piraña *f* zo piranha
pirarse ⟨1a⟩ *v/r* F (*marcharse*) clear off F;
  pirarse por alguien F lose one's head
  over s.o. F
pirata *m/f* pirate; **pirata informático**
  hacker
piratear ⟨1a⟩ *v/t* INFOR pirate
pirenaico *adj* Pyrenean
Pirineos *mpl* Pyrenees
pirómano *m*, **-a** *f* pyromaniac; JUR arsonist
piropo *m* compliment
pirotécnico *adj* fireworks *atr*
piruleta *f*, **pirulí** *m* lollipop
pis *m* F pee F; **hacer pis** F have a pee F
pisada *f* footstep; *huella* footprint
pisapapeles *m* paperweight
pisar ⟨1a⟩ *v/t* step on; *uvas* tread, *fig* (*maltratar*) walk all over; *idea* steal; **pisar a**
  alguien step on s.o.'s foot
piscifactoría *f* fish farm
piscina *f* swimming pool
Piscis *m/f inv* ASTR Pisces
piso *m* apartment, *Br* flat; (*planta*) floor
pisotear ⟨1a⟩ *v/t* trample
pista *f* track, trail; (*indicio*) clue; *de atletismo* track; **pista de aterrizaje** AVIA runway; **pista de baile** dance floor; **pista de**
  tenis / squash tennis / squash court; **seguir la pista a alguien** be on the trail of
  s.o.
pistacho *m* BOT pistachio
pisto *m* GASTR mixture of tomatoes, peppers etc cooked in oil; *C.Am., Méx* F (*dinero*) cash, dough F
pistola *f* pistol
pistón *m* piston
pitada *f* (*abucheo*) whistle; *S. Am.* de cigarillo puff
pitar ⟨1a⟩ **1** *v/i* whistle; *con bocina* beep,
  hoot; *L.Am.* (*fumar*) smoke; **salir pitando** F dash off F **2** *v/t* (*abuchear*) whistle
  at; *penalti, falta* etc call, *Br* blow for; *silbato* blow
pitazo *m* *L.Am.* whistle
pitear ⟨1a⟩ *v/i* *L.Am.* blow a whistle
pitido *m* whistle; *con bocina* beep, hoot
pitillo *m* cigarette; *hecho a mano* roll-up
pito *m* whistle; (*bocina*) horn; **me importa un pito** F I don't give a hoot F
pitón *m* zo python
pitonisa *f* fortune-teller
pitorrearse ⟨1a⟩ *v/r*: **pitorrearse de alguien** F make fun of s.o.
pivot *m* en baloncesto center, *Br* centre
piyama *m* *L.Am.* pajamas *pl*, *Br* pyjamas
  pl
pizarra *f* blackboard; *piedra* slate

pizca *f* pinch; *Méx* AGR harvest; **ni pizca**
  de not a bit of
pizza *f* pizza
placa *f* (*lámina*) sheet; (*plancha*) plate;
  (*letrero*) plaque; *Méx* AUTO license plate,
  Br number plate; **placa madre** INFOR
  motherboard; **placa (dental)** plaque;
  placa de matrícula AUTO license plate,
  Br number plate
placer ⟨2x⟩ **1** *v/i* please; **siempre hace lo**
  que le place he always does as he pleases
  2 *m* pleasure
plácido *adj* placid
plaga *f* AGR pest; MED plague; *fig* scourge;
  (*abundancia*) glut
plagado *adj* infested; (*lleno*) full; **plagado de gente** swarming with people
plagiar ⟨1b⟩ *v/t* plagiarize; *L.Am.* (*secuestrar*) kidnap
plagio *m* plagiarism
plan *m* plan
plana *f*: **primera plana** front page
plancha *f* para planchar iron; *en cocina*
  broiler, *Br* grill; *de metal* sheet; F (*metedura de pata*) goof F; **a la plancha** GASTR
  broiled, *Br* grilled
planchar ⟨1a⟩ *v/t* iron; *Méx* F (*dar plantón*) stand up F; *L.Am.* (*lisonjear*) flatter
planeador *m* glider
planear ⟨1a⟩ **1** *v/t* plan **2** *v/i* AVIA glide
planeta *m* planet
planetario *m* planetarium
planificación *f* planning; **planificación familiar** family planning
planificar ⟨1g⟩ *v/t* plan
plano 1 *adj* flat **2** *m* ARQUI plan; *de ciudad*
  map; *en cine* shot; MAT plane; *fig* level
planta *f* BOT plant; (*piso*) floor; **planta del**
  pie sole of the foot
plantación *f* plantation
plantado *adj*: **dejar a alguien plantado** F
  stand s.o. up F
plantar ⟨1a⟩ **1** *v/t* árbol etc plant; *tienda de*
  campaña put up; **plantar a alguien** F
  stand s.o. up F **2** *v/r* **plantarse** put one's
  foot down
planteamiento *m* de problema posing;
  (*perspectiva*) approach
plantear ⟨1a⟩ *v/t* dificultad, problema
  pose, create; *cuestión* raise
plantel *m* (*equipo*) team; *L.Am.* staff
plantilla *f* para zapato insole; (*personal*)
  staff; DEP squad; *para cortar*, INFOR template
plantón *m*: **dar un plantón a alguien** F
  stand s.o. up F
plasma *m* plasma
plasmar ⟨1a⟩ *v/t* (*modelar*) shape; *fig* (*representar*) express

P

plasta 182

plasta 1 *m/f* F pain F, drag F **2** *adj:* **ser plasta** F be a pain *o* drag F
plástica *f* EDU handicrafts
plástico *m* plastic
plastificado *adj* laminated
plastificar ⟨1g⟩ *v/t documento* laminate
plastilina *f* Plasticine®
plata *f* silver; *L.Am.* F (*dinero*) cash, dough F
plataforma *f tb* POL platform; **plataforma petrolífera** oil rig
platal *m L.Am.* fortune
plátano *m* banana
plateado *adj Méx* wealthy
plática *f Méx* chat, talk
platicar ⟨1g⟩ **1** *v/t L.Am.* tell **2** *v/i Méx* chat, talk
platillo *m:* **platillo volante** flying saucer; **platillos** MÚS cymbals
platino *m* platinum
plato *m* plate; GASTR dish; **plato principal** main course; **plato preparado / precocinado** ready meal; **plato sopero / hondo** soup dish; **pagar los platos rotos** F carry the can F
plató *m de película* set; TV studio
platónico *adj* platonic
platudo *adj Chi* rich
plausible *adj* plausible
playa *f* beach; **playa de estacionamiento** *L.Am.* parking lot, *Br* car park
playeras *fpl* canvas shoes
playo *adj Rpl* shallow
plaza *f* square; (*vacante*) job opening, *Br* vacancy; *en vehículo* seat; *de trabajo* position; **plaza de toros** bull ring
plazo *m* period; (*pago*) instal(l)ment; **a corto / largo plazo** in the short / long term; **a plazos** in instal(l)ments
plebiscito *m* plebiscite
plegable *adj* collapsible, folding
plegar ⟨1h & 1k⟩ **1** *v/t* fold (up) **2** *v/r* **plegarse** *fig* submit (**a** to)
plegaria *f* prayer
pleito *m* JUR lawsuit; *fig* dispute; **poner un pleito a alguien** sue s.o.
pleno 1 *adj* full; **en pleno día** in broad daylight **2** *m* plenary session
pliego 1 *vb* → **plegar 2** *m* (*hoja de papel*) sheet (of paper); (*carta*) sealed letter *o* document
pliegue *m* fold, crease
plomería *f Méx* plumbing
plomero *m Méx* plumber
plomo *m* lead; EL fuse; *fig* F drag F; **sin plomo** AUTO unleaded
pluma *f* feather; *para escribir* fountain pen
plumaje *m* plumage

plumero *m para limpiar* feather duster; *CSur para maquillaje* powder puff; **vérsele el plumero a alguien** *fig* F see what s.o. is up to F
plumífero *m* F down jacket
plural 1 *adj* plural **2** *m* GRAM plural
pluralismo *m* POL pluralism
pluriempleo *m* having more than one job
plus *m* bonus
plusmarquista *m/f* record holder
plusvalía *f* COM capital gain
plutonio *m* QUÍM plutonium
pluviosidad *f* rainfall
PNB *abr* (= **producto nacional bruto**) GNP (= gross national product)
P.º *abr* (= **Paseo**) Ave (= Avenue)
p.o. *abr* (= **por orden**) p. p. (per procurationem, by proxy)
población *f gente* population; (*ciudad*) city, town; (*pueblo*) village; *Chi* shanty town
poblado 1 *adj* populated; *barba* bushy; **poblado de** *fig* full of **2** *m* (*pueblo*) settlement
poblador *m,* **pobladora** *f Chi* shanty town dweller
poblar ⟨1m⟩ *v/t* populate
pobre 1 *adj económicamente, en calidad* poor **2** *m/f* poor person; **los pobres** the poor
pobreza *f* poverty
pocilga *f* pigpen
pócima *f* concoction
poción *f* potion
poco 1 *adj sg* little, not much; *pl* few, not many; **un poco de** a little; **unos pocos** a few **2** *adv* little; **trabaja poco** he doesn't work much; **ahora se ve muy poco** it's seldom seen now; **estuvo poco por aquí** he wasn't around much; **poco conocido** little known; **poco a poco** little by little; **dentro de poco** soon, shortly; **hace poco** a short time ago, not long ago; *por* **poco** nearly, almost; **¡a poco no lo hacemos!** *Méx* don't tell me we're not doing it; **de a poco me fui tranquilizando** *Rpl* little by little I calmed down **3** *m:* **un poco** a little, a bit
podar ⟨1a⟩ *v/t* AGR prune
poder ⟨2t⟩ **1** *v/aux capacidad* can, be able to; *permiso* can, be allowed to; *posibilidad* may, might; **no pude hablar con ella** I wasn't able to talk to her; **¿puedo ir contigo?** can *o* may I come with you?; **¡podías habérselo dicho!** you could have *o* you might have told him **2** *v/i:* **poder con** (*sobreponerse a*) manage, cope with; **me puede** he can beat me; **es franco a más no poder** F he's as frank as

they come F; *comimos a más no poder* F we ate to bursting point F; *no puedo más* I can't take any more, I've had enough; *puede ser* perhaps, maybe; *puede que* perhaps, maybe; *¿se puede?* can I come in?, do you mind if I come in? **3** *m tb* POL power; *en poder de alguien* in s.o.'s hands

poderoso *adj* powerful

podio *m* podium

podólogo *m, -a f* MED podiatrist, *Br* chiropodist

podrido *adj tb fig* rotten

poema *m* poem

poesía *f género* poetry; (*poema*) poem

poeta *m/f* poet

poético *adj* poetic

poetisa *f* poet

polaco 1 *adj* Polish **2** *m, -a f* Pole

polar *adj* polar

polea *f* TÉC pulley

polémica *f* controversy

polémico *adj* controversial

polen *m* BOT pollen

poleo *m* BOT pennyroyal

polera *f Chi* turtle neck (sweater)

poli *m/f* F cop F; *la poli* F the cops *pl* F

policía 1 *f* police **2** *m/f* police officer, policeman; *mujer* police officer, policewoman

policíaco, policiaco *adj* detective *atr*

policial *adj* police *atr*

polideportivo *m* sports center, *Br* sports centre

poliéster *m* polyester

polifacético *adj* versatile, multifaceted

poligamia *f* polygamy

poliglota *m/f* polyglot

polígono *m* MAT polygon; *polígono industrial* industrial zone, *Br* industrial estate

polilla *f* ZO moth

polio *f* MED polio

poliomielitis *f* MED poliomyelitis

política *f* politics

políticamente *adv*: *políticamente correcto* politically correct

político 1 *adj* political **2** *m, -a f* politician

póliza *f* policy; *póliza de seguros* insurance policy

polizón *m/f* stowaway

polla *f* V prick V, cock V

pollera *f L.Am.* skirt

pollería *f* poulterer's

pollito *m* chick

pollo *m* ZO, GASTR chicken

polluelo *m* ZO chick

polo *m* GEOG, EL pole; *prenda* polo shirt; DEP polo; *Polo Norte* North Pole; *Polo Sur* South Pole

polola *f Chi* girlfriend

pololear ⟨1a⟩ *v/i Chi* be going steady

pololo *m Chi* boyfriend

Polonia Poland

poltrona *f* easy chair

polución *f* pollution; *polución atmosférica* air pollution, atmospheric pollution

polucionar ⟨1a⟩ *v/t* pollute

polvo *m* dust; *en química, medicina etc* powder; *polvos pl de talco* talcum powder *sg*; *echar un polvo* V have a screw V; *estar hecho polvo* F be all in F

pólvora *f* gunpowder

polvorín *m almacén* magazine; *fig* powder keg

polvorón *m* GASTR *type of small cake*

pomada *f* cream

pomelo *m* BOT grapefruit

pómez *f*: *piedra pómez* pumice stone

pomo *m* doorknob

pompa *f* pomp; *pompa de jabón* bubble; *pompas pl fúnebres* ceremonia funeral ceremony *sg*; *establecimiento* funeral parlo(u)r *sg*

pomposo *adj* pompous

pómulo *m* ANAT cheekbone

pon *vb* → **poner**

ponchadura *f Méx* flat, *Br* puncture

ponchar ⟨1a⟩ **1** *v/t L.Am.* puncture **2** *v/r* **poncharse** *Méx* get a flat *o Br* puncture

ponche *m* punch

poncho *m* poncho; *pisarse el poncho* S. Am. be mistaken

ponderación *f mesura* deliberation; *en estadísticas* weighting

ponencia *f* presentation; EDU paper

poner ⟨2r; *part puesto*⟩ **1** *v/t* put; (*añadir*) put in; RAD, TV turn on, switch on; *la mesa* set; *ropa* put on; *telegrama* send; (*escribir*) put down; *en periódico, libro etc* say; *negocio* set up; *huevos* lay; *poner a alguien furioso* make s.o. angry; *ponerle a alguien con alguien* TELEC put s.o. through to s.o.; *ponerle una multa a alguien* fine s.o.; *pongamos que* let's suppose *o* assume that **2** *v/r* **ponerse** *ropa* put on; *ponte en el banco* go and sit on the bench; *se puso ahí* she stood over there; *dile que se ponga* tell her to come to the phone; *ponerse pálido* turn pale; *ponerse furioso* get angry; *ponerse enfermo* become *o* fall ill; *ponerse a* start to

pongo¹ *vb* → **poner**

pongo² *m Pe* indentured Indian laborer

poni *m* ZO pony

poniente *m* west

pontífice *m* pontiff; *sumo pontífice*

Pope

ponzoñoso *adj* poisonous

pop 1 *adj* pop; *música pop* pop music **2** *m* pop

popa *f* MAR stern

popular *adj* popular; *(del pueblo)* folk *atr*; *barrio* lower-class

popularidad *f* popularity

popularizar ⟨1f⟩ *v/t* popularize

póquer *m* poker

por *prp* ◇ *motivo* for, because of; *lo hizo por amor* she did it out of love; *luchó por sus ideales* he fought for his ideals ◇ *medio* by; *por avión* by air; *por correo* by mail, *Br tb* by post ◇ *tiempo: por un segundo* L.Am. for a second; *por la mañana* in the morning ◇ *movimiento: por la calle* down the street; *por un tunel* through a tunnel; *por aquí* this way ◇ *posición aproximada* around, about; *está por aquí* it's around here (somewhere) ◇ *cambio: por cincuenta pesos* for fifty pesos ◇ *otros usos: por hora* an *o* per hour; *dos por dos* two times two; *¿por qué?* why?; *el motivo por el cual o por el que ...* the reason why ...

porcelana *f* porcelain, china; *de porcelana* porcelain *atr*, china *atr*

porcentaje *m* percentage

porche *m* porch

porción *f* portion

pordiosero *m*, -a *f* beggar

porfiar ⟨1c⟩ *v/i* insist (*en* on)

pormenor *m* detail

porno 1 *adj* porn *atr* **2** *m* porn

pornografía *f* pornography

pornográfico *adj* pornographic

poro *m* pore

poroso *adj* porous

poroto *m Rpl, Chi* bean; *porotos verdes* L.Am. green beans

porque *conj* because; *porque sí* just because

porqué *m* reason

porquería *f (suciedad)* filth; F *cosa de poca calidad* piece of trash F

porra *f* baton; *(palo)* club; *¡vete a la porra!* F go to hell! F

porrazo *m: darle un porrazo a alguien* F hit s.o.; *darse o pegarse un porrazo* crash (*contra* into)

porro *m* F joint F

porrón *m* container from which wine is poured straight into the mouth

portaaviones *m inv* aircraft carrier

portada *f* TIP front page; *de revista* cover;

ARQUI front

portafolios *m inv* briefcase

portal *m* foyer; *(entrada)* doorway

portaligas *m inv Arg, Chi* garter belt, *Br* suspender belt

portarse ⟨1a⟩ *v/r* behave

portátil *adj* portable

portavoz *m/f* spokesman; *mujer* spokeswoman

portazo *m: dar un portazo* F slam the door

porte *m (aspecto)* appearance, air; *(gasto de correo)* postage

portento *m* wonder; *persona* genius

porteño *Arg* **1** *adj* of Buenos Aires, Buenos Aires *atr* **2** *m*, -a *f* native of Buenos Aires

portería *f* reception; *casa* superintendent's apartment, *Br* caretaker's flat; DEP goal

portero *m* doorman; *de edificio* superintendent, *Br* caretaker; DEP goalkeeper; *portero automático* intercom, *Br* entryphone

portón *m* large door

Portugal Portugal

portugués 1 *m/adj* Portuguese **2** *m*, -esa *f* persona Portuguese

porvenir *m* future

posada *f C.Am., Méx* Christmas party; *(fonda)* inn

posar ⟨1a⟩ **1** *v/t mano* lay, place (*sobre* on); *posar la mirada en* gaze at **2** *v/r* posarse *de ave, insecto*, AVIA land

posavasos *m inv* coaster

posdata *f* postscript

poseer ⟨2e⟩ *v/t* possess; *(ser dueño de)* own, possess

posesión *f* possession; *tomar posesión (de un cargo)* POL take up office

posguerra *f* postwar period

posibilidad *f* possibility

posibilitar ⟨1a⟩ *v/t* make possible

posible *adj* possible; *en lo posible* as far as possible; *hacer todo lo posible* do everything possible; *es posible que ...* perhaps ...

posición *f tb* MIL, *fig* position; *social* standing, status

positivo *adj* positive

posmoderno *adj* postmodern

poso *m* dregs *pl*

posología *f* dosage

posponer ⟨2r; *part* **pospuesto**⟩ *v/t* postpone

pospuesto *part* → **posponer**

posta *f: a posta* on purpose

postal 1 *adj* mail *atr*, postal **2** *f* postcard

poste *m* post

póster *m* poster

postergar ⟨1a⟩ *v/t* postpone

posteridad *f* posterity

posterior *adj* later, subsequent; *(trasero)* rear *atr*, back *atr*

postizo 1 *adj* false **2** *m* hairpiece

postor *m* bidder; *al mejor postor* to the highest bidder

postrar ⟨1a⟩ **1** *v/t*: *la gripe lo postró* he was laid up with flu **2** *v/r* **postrarse** prostrate o.s.

postre *m* dessert; *a la postre* in the end

postular ⟨1a⟩ *v/t hipótesis* put forward, advance

póstumo *adj* posthumous

postura *f tb fig* position

pos(t)venta *adj inv* after-sales *atr*

potable *adj* drinkable; *fig* F passable; *agua potable* drinking water

potaje *m* GASTR stew

potasio *m* potassium

potencia *f* power; *en potencia* potential

potencial *m/adj* potential

potenciar ⟨1b⟩ *v/t fig* foster, promote

potentado *m*, **-a** *f* tycoon

potente *adj* powerful

potestad *f* authority; *patria potestad* parental authority

potingue *m* F *desp* lotion, cream

potro *m* zo colt

pozo *m* well; MIN shaft; *Rpl* pothole; *un pozo sin fondo fig* a bottomless pit

pozol *m C.Am.* corn liquor

pozole *m Méx* corn stew

práctica *f* practice

practicar ⟨1g⟩ *v/t* practice, *Br* practise; *deporte* play; *practicar la equitación / la esgrima* ride / fence

práctico *adj* practical

pradera *f* prairie, grassland

prado *m* meadow

pragmático *adj* pragmatic

pragmatismo *m* pragmatism

pral. *abr* (= *principal*) first

preámbulo *m* preamble

prebenda *f* sinecure

precalentamiento *m* DEP warm-up

precario *adj* precarious

precaución *f* precaution; *tomar precauciones* take precautions

precavido *adj* cautious

precedente 1 *adj* previous **2** *m* precedent

preceder ⟨2a⟩ *v/t* precede

preceptivo *adj* compulsory, mandatory

preciado *adj* precious

preciarse ⟨1b⟩ *v/r*: *cualquier fontanero que se precie ...* any self-respecting plumber ...

precinto *m* seal

precio *m* price; *precio de venta al público* recommended retail price

preciosidad *f*: *esa casa / chica es una preciosidad* that house / girl is gorgeous o beautiful

precioso *adj (de valor)* precious; *(hermoso)* beautiful

preciosura *f L.Am.* F → *preciosidad*

precipicio *m* precipice

precipitación *f (prisa)* hurry, haste; *precipitaciones* rain *sg*

precipitado *adj* hasty, sudden

precipitarse ⟨1a⟩ *v/r* rush; *fig* be hasty

precisamente *adv* precisely

precisión *f* precision

preciso *adj* precise, accurate; *ser preciso* be necessary

preconcebido *adj* preconceived

precoz *adj* early; *niño* precocious

precursor *m*, **precursora** *f* precursor, forerunner

predecesor *m*, **predecesora** *f* predecessor

predecir ⟨3p; *part* **predicho** ⟩ *v/t* predict

predestinar ⟨1a⟩ *v/t* predestine

predicado *m* predicate

predicador *m*, **predicadora** *f* preacher

predicar ⟨1g⟩ *v/t* preach; *predicar con el ejemplo* F practice (*Br* practise) what one preaches

predicción *f* prediction, forecast

predicho *part* → **predecir**

predilecto *adj* favo(u)rite

predisponer ⟨2r⟩ *v/t* prejudice

predisposición *f tb* MED predisposition; *(tendencia)* tendency; *una predisposición en contra de* a prejudice against

predispuesto *adj* predisposed (*a* to)

predominante *adj* predominant

predominar ⟨1a⟩ *v/t* predominate

preeminente *adj* preeminent

preescolar *adj* preschool

preestreno *m* preview

preexistente *adj* pre-existing

prefabricado *adj* prefabricated

prefacio *m* preface, foreword

preferencia *f* preference

preferente *adj* preferential

preferible *adj* preferable (*a* to); *es preferible que ...* it's better if ...

preferido 1 *part* → **preferir 2** *adj* favo(u)rite

preferir ⟨3i⟩ *v/t* prefer

prefijo *m* prefix; TELEC area code, *Br* dialling code

pregonar ⟨1a⟩ *v/t* proclaim, make public

pregunta *f* question

preguntar ⟨1a⟩ **1** *v/t* ask **2** *v/i* ask; *preguntar por algo* ask about sth; *preguntar*

P

por alguien *paradero* ask for s.o.; *salud etc* ask about s.o. **3** *v/r* **preguntarse** wonder

prehistoria *f* prehistory

prehistórico *adj* prehistoric

prejuicio *m* prejudice

prelado *m* prelate

prelavado *m* prewash

preliminar 1 *adj* preliminary; DEP qualifying **2** *m* L.Am. qualifier

preludio *m* prelude

premamá *adj* maternity *atr*

prematrimonial *adj* premarital

prematuro 1 *adj* premature **2** *m*, *-a f* premature baby

premeditado *adj* premeditated

premeditación *f* premeditation; **con premeditación** deliberately

premiado 1 *adj* prizewinning **2** *m*, *-a f* prizewinner

premiar ⟨1b⟩ *v/t* award a prize to

premio *m* prize

premisa *f* premise

premonición *f* premonition

premura *f* haste

prenatal *adj* prenatal

prenda *f* item of clothing, garment; *garantía* security; *en juegos* forfeit; **no soltar prenda** not say a word (**sobre** about)

prender ⟨2a; *part* **preso**⟩ **1** *v/t a fugitivo* capture; *sujetar* pin up; L.Am. *fuego* light; L.Am. *luz* switch on, turn on; **prender fuego a** set fire to **2** *v/i de planta* take; *(empezar a arder)* catch; *de moda* catch on

prendería *f Esp* pawnbroker's, pawn shop

prensa *f* press; **prensa amarilla** gutter press

prensar ⟨1a⟩ *v/t* press

preñado *adj* pregnant

preocupación *f* worry, concern

preocupado *adj* worried (**por** about), concerned (**por** about)

preocupante *adj* worrying

preocupar ⟨1a⟩ **1** *v/t* worry, concern **2** *v/r* **preocuparse** worry (**por** about); **preocuparse de** *(encargarse)* look after, take care of

preparación *f* preparation; *(educación)* education; *para trabajo* training

preparado *adj* ready, prepared

preparador *m*, **preparadora** *f*: **preparador físico** trainer

preparar ⟨1a⟩ **1** *v/t* prepare, get ready **2** *v/r* **prepararse** get ready (**para** for), prepare o.s. (**para** for); *de tormenta, crisis* be brewing

preparativos *mpl* preparations

preponderante *adj* predominant

preposición *f* preposition

prepotente *adj* arrogant

prerrogativa *f* prerogative

presa *f* *(dique)* dam; *(embalse)* reservoir; *(víctima)* prey; L.Am. **para comer** bite to eat

presagio *m* omen, sign; *(premonición)* premonition

prescindir ⟨3a⟩ *v/i*: **prescindir de** *(privarse de)* do without; *(omitir)* leave out, dispense with; *(no tener en cuenta)* disregard

prescribir ⟨3a; *part* **prescrito**⟩ *v/i* JUR prescribe

prescrito *part* → **prescribir**

presencia *f* presence; **buena presencia** smart appearance

presenciar ⟨1b⟩ *v/t* witness; *(estar presente a)* attend, be present at

presentación *f* presentation; COM launch; *entre personas* introduction

presentador *m*, **presentadora** *f* TV presenter

presentar ⟨1a⟩ **1** *v/t* present; *a alguien* introduce; *producto* launch; *solicitud* submit **2** *v/r* **presentarse** *en sitio* show up; *(darse a conocer)* introduce o.s.; *a examen* take; *de problema, dificultad* arise; *a elecciones* run

presente 1 *adj* present; **tener algo presente** bear sth in mind; **¡presente!** here! **2** *m tiempo* present **3** *m/fpl*: **los presentes** those present

presentimiento *m* premonition

presentir ⟨3i⟩ *v/t* foresee; **presiento que vendrá** I have a feeling he'll come

preservar ⟨1a⟩ *v/t* protect

preservativo *m* condom

presidencia *f* presidency; *de compañía* presidency, *Br* chairmanship; *de comité* chairmanship

presidencial *adj* presidential

presidente *m*, *-a f* president; *de gobierno* premier, prime minister; *de compañía* president, *Br* chairman, *Br mujer* chairwoman; *de comité* chair

presidiario *m*, *-a f* prisoner

presidir ⟨3a⟩ *v/t* be president of; *reunión* chair, preside over

presión *f* pressure; **presión sanguínea** blood pressure

presionar ⟨1a⟩ *v/t botón* press; *fig* put pressure on, pressure

preso 1 *part* → **prender 2** *m*, *-a f* prisoner

prestación *f* provision; **prestación social sustitutoria** MIL community service in lieu of military service

prestado *adj*: **dejar prestado algo** lend sth; **pedir prestado algo** borrow sth

problemático

prestamista *m/f* moneylender

préstamo *m* loan; *préstamo bancario* bank loan

prestar ⟨1a⟩ *v/t dinero* lend; *ayuda* give; *L.Am.* borrow; *prestar atención* pay attention

prestidigitador *m*, **prestidigitadora** *f* conjurer

prestigio *m* prestige

prestigioso *adj* prestigious

presumido *adj* conceited; (*coqueto*) vain

presumir ⟨3a⟩ **1** *v/t* presume **2** *v/i* show off; *presumir de algo* boast *o* brag about sth; *presume de listo* he thinks he's very clever

presuntamente *adv* allegedly

presunto *adj* alleged, suspected

presuntuoso *adj* conceited

presuponer ⟨2r, *part* **presupuesto**⟩ *v/t* assume

presupuesto 1 *part* → **presuponer 2** *m* POL budget

presuroso *adj* hurried

pretencioso *adj* pretentious

pretender ⟨2a⟩ *v/t*: *pretendía convencerlos* he was trying to persuade them

pretendiente *m de mujer* suitor

pretensión *f L.Am.* (*arrogancia*) vanity; *sin pretensiones* unpretentious

pretérito *m* GRAM preterite

pretextar ⟨1a⟩ *v/t* claim

pretexto *m* pretext

prevalecer ⟨2d⟩ *v/t* prevail (*sobre* over)

prevaricación *f* corruption

prevención *f* prevention

prevenido 1 *part* → **prevenir 2** *adj* well-prepared

prevenir ⟨3s⟩ *v/t* prevent; (*avisar*) warn (*contra* against)

preventivo *adj* preventive, preventative

prever ⟨2v; *part* **previsto**⟩ *v/t* foresee

previo *adj* previous; *sin previo aviso* without (prior) warning

previsible *adj* foreseeable

previsión *f* (*predicción*) forecast; (*preparación*) foresight

previsor *adj* farsighted

previsto 1 *part* → **prever 2** *adj* foreseen, expected; *tener previsto* have planned

prieto *adj L.Am.* dark-skinned

prima *f de seguro* premium; (*pago extra*) bonus

primacía *f* supremacy, primacy; (*prioridad*) priority

primario *adj* primary

primavera *f* spring; BOT primrose

primer *adj* first

primera *f* first class; AUTO first gear; *a la primera* first-time; *de primera* F first-class, first-rate

primerizo *adj* inexperienced, green F; *madre* new, first-time

primero 1 *adj* first; *primeros auxilios pl* first aid *sg* **2** *m*, **-a** *f* first (one) **3** *adv* first

primitivo *adj* primitive; (*original*) original

primo *m*, **-a** *f* cousin

primogénito 1 *adj* first **2** *m*, **-a** *f* first child

primordial *adj* fundamental

primoroso *adj* exquisite

princesa *f* princess

principal *adj* main, principal; *lo principal* the main *o* most important thing

príncipe *m* prince

principiante 1 *adj* inexperienced **2** *m/f* beginner

principio *m* principle; *en tiempo* beginning; *a principios de abril* at the beginning of April; *en principio* in principle

pringar ⟨1h⟩ **1** *v/t ensuciar* get greasy; *fig* F get involved (*en* in) **2** *v/r* **pringarse** get greasy; *fig* F get mixed up (*en* in)

pringoso *adj* greasy

prioridad *f* priority

prioritario *adj* priority *atr*

prisa *f* hurry, rush; *darse prisa* hurry (up); *tener prisa* be in a hurry *o* rush

prisión *f* prison, jail

prisionero 1 *adj* captive **2** *m*, **-a** *f* prisoner

prismáticos *mpl* binoculars

priva *f Esp* F booze F

privacidad *f* privacy

privación *f acción* deprivation; *sufrir privaciones* suffer privation(s) *o* hardship

privado 1 *part* → **privar 2** *adj* private

privar ⟨1a⟩ **1** *v/t*: *privar a alguien de algo* deprive s.o. of sth **2** *v/r* **privarse** deprive o.s.; *privarse de algo* deprive o.s. of sth, go without sth

privatización *f* privatization

privatizar ⟨1f⟩ *v/t* privatize

privilegiado *adj* privileged; (*excelente*) exceptional

privilegio *m* privilege

pro 1 *prp* for, in aid of; *en pro de* for **2** *m* pro; *los pros y los contras* the pros and cons

proa *f* MAR bow

probabilidad *f* probability

probable *adj* probable, likely; *es probable que venga* she'll probably come

probador *m* fitting room

probar ⟨1m⟩ **1** *v/t teoría* test, try out; (*comer un poco de*) taste, try; (*comer por primera vez*) try **2** *v/i* try; *probar a hacer* try doing **3** *v/r* **probarse** try on

probeta *f* test tube

problema *m* problem

problemático *adj* problematic

procedencia *f* origin, provenance

proceder ⟨2a⟩ **1** *v/i* come (**de** from); (*actuar*) proceed; (*ser conveniente*) be fitting; **proceder a** proceed to; **proceder contra alguien** initiate proceedings against s.o. **2** *m* conduct

procedimiento *m* procedure, method; JUR proceedings *pl*

procesado *m*, -a *f* accused, defendant

procesador *m* INFOR processor; **procesador de textos** word processor

procesamiento *m*: **procesamiento de textos** word processing

procesar ⟨1a⟩ *v/t* INFOR process; JUR prosecute

procesión *f* procession

proceso *m* process; JUR trial; **proceso de datos / textos** INFOR data / word processing

proclamar ⟨1a⟩ *v/t* proclaim

proclive *adj* given (**a** to)

procrear ⟨1a⟩ *v/i* breed, procreate *fml*

procurar ⟨1a⟩ *v/t* try; **procura no llegar tarde** try not to be late

prodigar ⟨1h⟩ **1** *v/t* be generous with **2** *v/r* **prodigarse** (*aparecer*) be seen in public

prodigio *m* wonder, miracle; *persona* prodigy

prodigioso *adj* prodigious

pródigo *adj* (*generoso*) generous; (*derrochador*) extravagant

producción *f* production

producir ⟨3o⟩ **1** *v/t* produce; (*causar*) cause **2** *v/r* **producirse** happen, occur; **se produjo un ruido tremendo** there was a tremendous noise

productividad *f* productivity

productivo *adj* productive; *empresa* profitable

producto *m* product; **producto interior bruto** gross domestic product; **producto nacional bruto** gross national product

productor *m*, **productora** *f* producer

produjo *vb* → **producir**

produzco *vb* → **producir**

proeza *f* feat, exploit

profana *f* laywoman

profanar ⟨1a⟩ *v/t* defile, desecrate

profano **1** *adj fig* lay *atr* **2** *m* layman

profecía *f* prophecy

profesar ⟨1a⟩ *v/t* REL profess; *fig* feel, have

profesión *f* profession

profesional *m/f & adj* professional

profesor *m*, **profesora** *f* teacher; *de universidad* professor, *Br* lecturer

profesorado *m* faculty, *Br* staff *pl*

profeta *m* prophet

profetizar ⟨1f⟩ *v/t* prophesy

profiláctico **1** *adj* preventive, prophylactic *fml* **2** *m* condom

prófugo *m*, -a *f* JUR fugitive

profundidad *f* depth

profundizar ⟨1f⟩ *v/i*: **profundizar en algo** go into sth in depth

profundo *adj* deep; *pensamiento, persona* profound

profuso *adj* abundant, plentiful

programa *m* program, *Br* programme; INFOR program; EDU syllabus; **programa de estudios** curriculum

programación *f* RAD, TV programs *pl*, *Br* programmes; INFOR programming

programador *m*, **programadora** *f* programmer

programar ⟨1a⟩ *v/t aparato* program, *Br* programme; INFOR program; (*planear*) schedule

progresar ⟨1a⟩ *v/i* progress, make progress

progresista *m/f & adj* progressive

progresivo *adj* progressive

progreso *m* progress

prohibición *f* ban (**de** on)

prohibido *adj* forbidden

prohibir ⟨3a⟩ *v/t* forbid; *oficialmente* ban

prohibitivo *adj precio* prohibitive

prójimo *m* fellow human being

prole *f* offspring

proletario **1** *adj* proletarian **2** *m*, -a *f* proletarian

proliferación *f* proliferation

proliferar ⟨1a⟩ *v/t* proliferate

prolífico *adj* prolific

prolijo *adj* long-winded; (*minucioso*) detailed

prólogo *m* preface

prolongado *adj* prolonged, lengthy

prolongar ⟨1h⟩ **1** *v/t* extend, prolong **2** *v/r* **prolongarse** go *o* carry on; *en espacio* extend

promedio *m* average

promesa *f* promise

prometedor *adj* bright, promising

prometer ⟨2a⟩ **1** *v/t* promise **2** *v/r* **prometerse** get engaged

prometida *f* fiancée

prometido **1** *part* → **prometer 2** *adj* engaged **3** *m* fiancé

prominente *adj* prominent

promiscuidad *f* promiscuity

promiscuo *adj* promiscuous

promoción *f* promotion; EDU year

promocionar ⟨1a⟩ *v/t* promote

promotor *m*, **promotora** *f* promoter; **promotor inmobiliario** developer

promover ⟨2h⟩ *v/t* promote; (*causar*) provoke, cause

promulgar ⟨1h⟩ v/t ley promulgate
pronombre m GRAM pronoun
pronosticar ⟨1g⟩ v/t forecast
pronóstico m MED prognosis; **pronóstico del tiempo** weather forecast
pronto 1 adj prompt **2** adv (dentro de poco) soon; (temprano) early; **de pronto** suddenly; **tan pronto como** as soon as
pronunciación f pronunciation
pronunciar ⟨1b⟩ v/t pronounce; (decir) say; **pronunciar un discurso** give a speech
propaganda f advertising; POL propaganda
propagar ⟨1h⟩ **1** v/t spread **2** v/r **propagarse** spread
propano m propane
propasarse ⟨1a⟩ v/r go too far
propenso adj prone (**a** to); **ser propenso a hacer** be prone to do, have a tendency to do
propiciar ⟨1b⟩ v/t (favorecer) promote; (causar) bring about
propicio adj favo(u)rable
propiedad f property
propietario m, **-a** f owner
propina f tip
propinar ⟨1a⟩ v/t golpe, paliza give
propio adj own; (característico) characteristic (**de**), typical (**de** of); (adecuado) suitable (**para** for); **la -a directora** the director herself
proponer ⟨2r; part **propuesto**⟩ v/t propose, suggest
proporción f proportion
proporcional adj proportional
proporcionar ⟨1a⟩ v/t provide, supply; satisfacción give
proposición f proposal, suggestion
propósito m (intención) intention; (objetivo) purpose; **a propósito** on purpose, (por cierto) by the way
propuesto part → **proponer**
propuesta f proposal
propugnar ⟨1a⟩ v/t advocate
propulsar ⟨1a⟩ v/t TÉC propel; fig promote
propulsor m (motor) engine
prórroga f DEP overtime, Br extra time
prorrogar ⟨1h⟩ v/t plazo extend
prorrumpir ⟨3a⟩ v/i burst (**en** into)
prosa f prose
prosaico adj mundane, prosaic
proseguir ⟨3d & 3l⟩ **1** v/t carry on, continue **2** v/i continue (**con** with)
proselitismo m proselytism
prospecto m directions for use pl; de propaganda leaflet
prosperar ⟨1a⟩ v/i prosper, thrive
prosperidad f prosperity

próspero adj prosperous, thriving
próstata f prostate
prostíbulo m brothel
prostitución f prostitution
prostituirse ⟨3g⟩ v/r prostitute o.s.
prostituta f prostitute
prostituto m male prostitute
protagonista m/f personaje main character; actor, actriz star; de una hazaña hero; mujer heroine
protagonizar ⟨1f⟩ v/t star in, play the lead in; incidente play a leading role in
protección f protection
proteger ⟨2c⟩ v/t protect (**de** from)
proteína f protein
protésico m, **-a** f: **protésico dental** dental technician
prótesis f prosthesis
protesta f protest
protestante m/f Protestant
protestar ⟨1a⟩ **1** v/t protest **2** v/i (quejarse) complain (**por, de** about); (expresar oposición) protest (**contra, por** about, against)
protocolo m protocol
prototipo m TÉC prototype
protuberancia f protuberance
prov. abr (= **provincia**) province
provecho m benefit; **¡buen provecho!** enjoy (your meal); **sacar provecho de** benefit from
proveedor m, **proveedora** f supplier; **proveedor de (acceso a) Internet** Internet Service Provider, ISP
proveer ⟨2e; part **provisto**⟩ v/t supply; **proveer a alguien de algo** supply s.o. with sth
provenir ⟨3s⟩ v/i come (**de** from)
proverbio m proverb
providencia f providence
provincia f province
provincial adj provincial
provinciano 1 adj provincial **2** m, **-a** f provincial
provisional adj provisional
provisiones fpl provisions
provisto 1 part → **proveer 2** adj: **provisto de** equipped with
provocación f provocation
provocador adj provocative
provocar ⟨1g⟩ v/t cause; al enfado provoke; sexualmente lead on; **¿te provoca un café?** S. Am. how about a coffee?
provocativo adj provocative
proxeneta m pimp
proxenetismo m procuring
proximidad f proximity
próximo adj (siguiente) next; (cercano) near, close

P

proyección f MAT, PSI projection; *de película* showing

proyectar ⟨1a⟩ v/t project; *(planear)* plan; *película* show; *sombra* cast

proyectil m missile

proyecto m plan; *trabajo* project; *proyecto de ley* bill; *tenir en proyecto hacer algo* plan to do sth

proyector m projector

prudencia f caution, prudence

prudente adj careful, cautious

prueba f tb TIP proof; JUR piece of evidence; DEP event; EDU test; *a prueba de bala* bulletproof; *poner algo a prueba* put sth to the test

P.S. abr (= *postscriptum* (*posdata*)) PS (= postscript)

pseudo... pref pseudo-

pseudónimo m pseudonym

psicoanálisis f (psycho)analysis

psicoanalista m/f (psycho)analyst

psicodélico adj psychedelic

psicología f psychology

psicológico adj psychological

psicólogo m, -a f psychologist

psicópata m/f psychopath

psicosis f inv psychosis

psicoterapia f psychotherapy

psiquiatra m/f psychiatrist

psiquiatría f psychiatry

psiquiátrico adj psychiatric

psíquico adj psychic

pta abr (= *peseta*) peseta

ptas abr (= *pesetas*) pesetas

púa f ZO spine, quill; MÚS plectrum, pick

pub m bar

pubertad f puberty

publicación f publication

publicar ⟨1g⟩ 1 v/t publish 2 v/r publicarse come out, be published

publicidad f *(divulgación)* publicity; COM advertising; *(anuncios)* advertisements pl

publicista m/f advertising executive

publicitario 1 adj advertising atr 2 m, -a f advertising executive

público 1 adj public; *escuela* public, Br state 2 m public; TEA audience; DEP spectators pl, crowd

pucho m S. Am. P cigarette butt, Br fag end F; *no valer un pucho* be completely worthless

pude vb → *poder*

púdico adj modest

pudín m pudding

pudo vb → *poder*

pudor m modesty

pudrir ⟨3a⟩ 1 v/t rot 2 v/r pudrirse rot; *pudrirse de envidia* be green with envy

pueblerino m, -a f hick desp

pueblero m, -a f L.Am. villager; *de pueblo más grande* townsman; *mujer* townswoman

pueblo m village; *más grande* town

puedo vb → *poder*

puente m bridge; *hacer puente* have a day off between a weekend and a public holiday

puenting m bungee jumping

puerco 1 adj dirty; *fig* filthy F **2** m ZO pig; *puerco espín* porcupine

puericultura f childcare

puerro m BOT leek

puerta f door; *en valla* gate; DEP goal; *puerta de embarque* gate

puerto m MAR port; GEOG pass

Puerto Rico Puerto Rico

puertorriqueño 1 adj Puerto Rican **2** m, -a f Puerto Rican

pues conj well; *fml (porque)* as, since; *pues bien* well; *¡pues sí!* of course!

puesta f: *puesta a punto* tune-up; *puesta de sol* sunset

puestero m, -a f L.Am. stall holder

puesto 1 part → *poner* **2** m *lugar* place; *en mercado* stand, stall; MIL post; *puesto (de trabajo)* job **3** conj: *puesto que* since, given that

pugnar ⟨1a⟩ v/i fight *(por* for; *por hacer* to do)

puja f *(lucha)* struggle; *en subasta* bid

pujar ⟨1a⟩ v/i *(luchar)* struggle; *en subasta* bid

pulcro adj immaculate

pulga f ZO flea; *tener malas pulgas* fig F be bad-tempered

pulgada f inch

pulgar m thumb

pulimentar ⟨1a⟩ v/t polish

pulir ⟨3a⟩ v/t polish

pulla f gibe

pulmón m lung

pulmonía f MED pneumonia

pulpa f pulp

pulpería f L.Am. mom-and-pop store, Br corner shop

pulpero m, -a f S. Am. storekeeper, shopkeeper

púlpito m pulpit

pulpo m ZO octopus

pulque m Méx pulque *(alcoholic drink made from cactus)*

pulquería f Méx pulque bar

pulsación f beat; *al escribir a máquina* key stroke

pulsar ⟨1a⟩ v/t botón, tecla press

pulsera f bracelet

pulso m pulse; *fig* steady hand; *tomar el pulso a alguien* take s.o.'s pulse; *tomar*

el pulso a algo *fig* take the pulse of sth
pulular ⟨1a⟩ *v/i* mill around
pulverizador *m* spray
pulverizar ⟨1f⟩ *v/t* spray; (*convertir en polvo*) pulverize, crush
puma *m* zo puma, mountain lion
puna *f L.Am.* GEOG high Andean plateau; MED altitude sickness
pundonor *m* pride
punitivo *adj* punitive
punta *f* tip; (*extremo*) end; *de lápiz*, GEOG point; *L.Am.* (*grupo*) group; **sacar punta a** sharpen
puntada *f* stitch
puntapié *m* kick
puntera *f* toe
puntería *f* aim
puntero 1 *adj* leading **2** *m* pointer
puntiagudo *adj* pointed, sharp
puntilla *f*: **de puntillas** on tippy-toe, *Br* on tiptoe
puntilloso *adj* particular, punctilious *fml*
punto *m* point; *señal* dot; *signo de puntuación* period, *Br* full stop; *en costura, sutura* stitch; **dos puntos** colon; **punto muerto** AUTO neutral; **punto de vista** point of view; **punto y coma** semicolon; **a punto** (*listo*) ready; (*a tiempo*) in time; **de punto** knitted; **en punto** on the dot; **estar a punto de** be about to; **hacer punto** knit; **hasta cierto punto** up to a point; **empresa** *f* **punto.com** dot.com (company)
puntuación *f* punctuation; DEP score; EDU grade, mark
puntual *adj* punctual
puntualidad *f* punctuality
puntualizar ⟨1f⟩ *v/t* (*señalar*) point out; (*aclarar*) clarify
punzada *f* sharp *o* stabbing pain
punzante *adj* stinging
puñado *m* handful
puñal *m* dagger
puñalada *f* stab wound
puñeta *f*: **¡puñeta(s)!** F for heaven's sake! F; **hacer la puñeta a alguien** F give s.o. a

hard time F
puñetazo *m* punch; **dar un puñetazo** punch
puño *m* fist; *de camisa* cuff; *de bastón, paraguas* handle
pupa *f* *en labio* cold sore; **hacerse pupa** *lenguaje infantil* hurt o.s.
pupila *f* pupil
pupitre *m* desk
pupusa *f L.Am.* filled dumpling
purasangre *m* thoroughbred
puré *m* purée; *sopa* cream; **puré de patatas** *or* **papas** *L.Am.* mashed potatoes
pureza *f* purity
purga *f* POL purge
purgante *m/adj* laxative, purgative
purgar ⟨1h⟩ *v/t* purge
purgatorio *m* REL purgatory
purificación *f* purification
purificar ⟨1g⟩ *v/t* purify
purista *m/f* purist
puritano 1 *adj* puritanical **2** *m*, **-a** *f* puritan
puro 1 *adj* pure; *casualidad, coincidencia* sheer; *Méx* (*único*) sole, only; **la -a verdad** the honest truth; **te sirven la -a comida** *Méx* they just serve food **2** *m* cigar
púrpura *f* purple
pus *m* pus
puse *vb* → **poder**
pusilánime *adj* fainthearted
puso *vb* → **poder**
puta *f* P whore P
putada *f* P dirty trick; **¡qué putada!** shit! P
putear ⟨1a⟩ *v/t L.Am.* P swear at; **putear alguien** *Esp* give s.o. a hard time, make life difficult for s.o.
puto *adj* P goddamn F, *Br* bloody F; **de puta madre** P great F, fantastic F
putrefacción *f* putrefaction
puzzle *m* jigsaw (puzzle)
PVC *abr* (= *cloruro de polivinilo*) PVC (= polyvinyl chloride)
P.V.P. *abr* (= *precio de venta al público*) RRP (= recommended retail price)
pza. *abr* (= *plaza*) sq (= square)

P

Q

q.e.p. d. *abr* (= *que en paz descanse*) RIP (= requiescat in pace)

que 1 *pron rel sujeto*: *persona* who, that; *cosa* which, that; *complemento*: *persona* that, whom *fml*; *cosa* that; which; *el coche que ves* the car that you can see, the car that *o* which you can see; *el que* the one that **2** *conj* that; *lo mismo que tú* the same as you; *¡que entre!* tell him to come in; *¡que descanses!* sleep well; *¡que sí!* I said yes; *¡que no!* I said no; *es que ...* the thing is ...; *yo que tú* if I were you

qué 1 *adj & pron interr* what; *¿qué pasó?* what happened?; *¿qué día es?* what day is it?; *¿qué vestido prefieres?* which dress do you prefer? **2** *adj & pron int*: *¡qué moto!* what a motorbike!; *¡qué de flores!* what a lot of flowers! **3** *adv*: *¡qué alto es!* he's so tall!; *¡qué bien!* great!

quebrada *f L.Am.* stream

quebradero *m*: *quebraderos de cabeza* F headaches

quebradizo *adj* brittle

quebrado 1 *adj* broken **2** *m* MAT fraction

quebrantahuesos *m inv* ZO lammergeier

quebrantar ⟨1a⟩ *v/t ley, contrato* break

quebrar ⟨1k⟩ **1** *v/t* break **2** *v/i* COM go bankrupt **3** *v/r* **quebrarse** break

quedar ⟨1a⟩ **1** *v/i* (*permanecer*) stay; *en un estado* be; (*sobrar*) be left; *quedó sin resolver* it remained unresolved, it wasn't sorted out; *te queda bien / mal de estilo* it suits you / doesn't suit you; *de talla* it fits you / doesn't fit you; *quedar cerca* be nearby; *quedar con alguien* F arrange to meet (with) s.o.; *quedar en algo* agree to sth; *¿queda mucho tiempo?* is there much time left? **2** *v/r* stay; *quedarse ciego* go blind; *quedarse con algo* keep sth; *me quedé sin comer* I ended up not eating

quehaceres *mpl* tasks

queja *f* complaint

quejarse ⟨1a⟩ *v/r* complain (*a* to; *de* about)

quejica *adj* F whining F

quejido *m* moan, groan

quejumbroso *adj* moaning

quemado *adj* burnt; *Méx* (*desvirtuado*) discredited; *quemado por el sol* sunburnt; *oler a quemado* smell of burning

quemadura *f* burn

quemar ⟨1a⟩ **1** *v/t* burn; *con agua* scald; F *recursos* use up; F *dinero* blow F **2** *v/i* be very hot **3** *v/r* **quemarse** burn o.s.; *de tostada, papeles* burn; *fig* burn o.s. out; *Méx* (*desvirtuarse*) become discredited

quena *f S. Am.* Indian flute

quepo *vb* → *caber*

queque *m L.Am.* cake

querella *f* JUR lawsuit

querellarse ⟨1a⟩ *v/r* JUR bring a lawsuit (*contra* against)

querer ⟨2u⟩ *v/t* (*desear*) want; (*amar*) love; *querer decir* mean; *sin querer* unintentionally; *quisiera ...* I would like ...

querido 1 *part* → *querer* **2** *adj* dear **3** *m*, *-a f* darling

queroseno *m* kerosene

querrá *vb* → *querer*

querría *vb* → *querer*

quesadilla *f* quesadilla (*folded tortilla*)

queso *m* cheese; *queso para untar* cheese spread; *queso rallado* grated cheese

quicio *m*: *sacar de quicio a alguien* F drive s.o. crazy F

quid *m*: *el quid de la cuestión* the nub of the question

quiebra *f* COM bankruptcy

quien *pron rel sujeto* who, that; *objeto* who, whom *fml*; that; *no soy quien para hacerlo* I'm not the right person to do it

quién *pron* who; *¿quién es?* who is it?; *¿de quién es este libro?* whose is this book?, who does this book belong to?

quienquiera *pron* whoever

quiero *vb* → *querer*

quieto *adj* still; *¡estáte quieto!* keep still!

quijotesco *adj* quixotic

quilate *m* carat

quilla *f* keel

quimera *f* pipe dream

química *f* chemistry

químico 1 *adj* chemical **2** *m*, *-a f* chemist

quimioterapia *f* MED chemotherapy

quimono *m* kimono

quincalla *f* junk

quince *adj* fifteen

quincena *f* two weeks, *Br* fortnight

quiniela *f* lottery where the winners are decided by soccer results

quinientos *adj* five hundred

quinina *f* quinine

quinquenio *m* five-year period

quinta f MIL draft, Br call-up; **es de mi quinta** he's my age
quinteto m MÚS quintet
quinto 1 adj fifth **2** m MIL conscript
quiosco m kiosk; **quiosco de prensa** newsstand, Br newsagent's
quiosquero m, -a f newspaper vendor
quirófano m operating room, Br operating theatre
quiromancia, quiromancía f palmistry
quirúrgico adj surgical
quise vb → **querer**
quisiera vb → **querer**
quiso vb → **querer**
quisque F: **todo quisque** everyone and his brother F, Br the world and his wife F

quisquilla f ZO shrimp
quisquilloso adj touchy
quiste m MED cyst
quitaesmalte m nail varnish remover
quitamanchas m inv stain remover
quitar ⟨1a⟩ **1** v/t ropa take off, remove; obstáculos remove; **quitar algo a alguien** take sth (away) from s.o.; **quitar la mesa** clear the table **2** v/i: **¡quita!** get out of the way! **3** v/r **quitarse** ropa, gafas take off; (apartarse) get out of the way; **quitarse algo/a alguien de encima** get rid of s.o./sth; **¡quítate de en medio!** F get out of the way!
quizá(s) adv perhaps, maybe
quórum m quorum

R

rabadilla f ANAT coccyx
rábano m BOT radish; **me importa un rábano** F I don't give a damn F
rabia f MED rabies sg; **dar rabia a alguien** make s.o. mad; **tener rabia a alguien** have it in for s.o.
rabiar ⟨1b⟩ v/i: **rabiar de dolor** be in agony; **hacer rabiar a alguien** fig F jerk s.o.'s chain F, pull s.o.'s leg F; **rabiar por** be dying for
rabieta f tantrum
rabino m rabbi
rabioso adj MED rabid; fig furious
rabo m tail
rabón adj L.Am. animal short-tailed
rácano adj F stingy F, mean
racha f spell
racial adj racial
racimo m bunch
ración f share; (porción) serving, portion
racional adj rational
racionalizar ⟨1f⟩ v/t rationalize
racionamiento m rationing
racionar ⟨1a⟩ v/t ration
racismo m racism
racista m/f & adj racist
radar m radar
radiación f radiation
radiactividad f radioactivity
radiactivo adj radioactive
radiador m radiator
radiante adj radiant
radiar ⟨1b⟩ v/t radiate

radical m/f & adj radical
radicalismo m radicalism
radicar ⟨1g⟩ v/i stem (**en** from), lie (**en** in)
radio 1 m MAT radius; QUÍM radium; L.Am. radio; **en un radio de** within a radius of; **radio de acción** range **2** f radio; **radio despertador** clock radio
radioaficionado m radio ham
radiocasete m radio cassette player
radiodifusión f broadcasting
radiofónico adj radio atr
radiografía f X-ray
radiografiar ⟨1c⟩ v/t X-ray
radiología f radiology
radiólogo m, -a f radiologist
radiotaxi m radio taxi
radiotelegrafista m/f radio operator
radioyente m/f listener
ráfaga f gust; de balas burst
rafia f raffia
rafting m rafting
ragú m GASTR ragout
raído adj threadbare
rail, raíl m rail
raíz f root; **raíz cuadrada / cúbica** MAT square / cube root; **a raíz de** as a result of; **echar raíces** de persona put down roots
raja f (rodaja) slice; (corte) cut; (grieta) crack
rajar ⟨1a⟩ **1** v/t fruta cut, slice; cerámica crack; neumático slash **2** v/i F gossip **3** v/r **rajarse** fig F back out F

rajatabla: *a rajatabla* strictly, to the letter

ralentí *m*: *al ralentí* AUTO idling; FOT in slow motion

ralentizar ⟨1f⟩ *v/t* slow down

rallador *m* grater

rallar ⟨1a⟩ *v/t* GASTR grate

rally(e) *m* rally

rama *f* branch; POL wing; *andarse por las ramas* beat about the bush

ramificación *f* ramification

ramo *m* COM sector; *ramo de flores* bunch of flowers

rampa *f* ramp; *rampa de lanzamiento* launch pad

ramplón *adj* vulgar

rana *f* ZO frog

ranchera *f typical Mexican song*

ranchero 1 *adj*: *canción -a* romantic ballad; *música -a* music of northern Mexico 2 *m L.Am.* rancher

rancho *m Méx* small farm; *L.Am.* (*barrio de chabolas*) shanty town

rancio *adj* rancid; *fig* ancient

rango *m* rank; *de alto rango* high-ranking

ranking *m* ranking

ranura *f* slot

rapapolvo *m* F telling-off F

rapar ⟨1a⟩ *v/t pelo* crop

rapaz 1 *adj* predatory; *ave rapaz* bird of prey 2 *m*, *-a f* F kid F

rape *m pescado* anglerfish; *al rape pelo* cropped

rapidez *f* speed, rapidity

rápido 1 *adj* quick, fast 2 *m* rapids *pl*

rapiña *f* pillage

raptar ⟨1a⟩ *v/t* kidnap

rapto *m* kidnap

raptor *m*, *raptora f* kidnapper

raqueta *f* racket

raquítico *adj fig* rickety

rareza *f* scarcity, rarity

raro *adj* rare

ras *m*: *a ras de tierra* at ground level

rasante *adj vuelo* low

rasca *f L.Am.*: *pegarse una rasca* F get plastered F

rascacielos *m inv* skyscraper

rascado *adj L.Am.* F plastered F

rascar ⟨1g⟩ *v/t* scratch; *superficie* scrape, scratch

rasero *m*: *medir por el mismo rasero* treat equally

rasgado *adj boca* wide; *ojos rasgados* almond-shaped eyes

rasgar ⟨1h⟩ *v/t* tear (up)

rasgo *m* feature; *a grandes rasgos* broadly speaking

rasguño *m* MED scratch

raso 1 *adj* flat, level; *soldado raso* priv.

vate 2 *m material* satin; *al raso* in the open air

raspa *f* fishbone; *L.Am.* F (*reprimanda*) telling-off

raspado *m Méx* water ice

raspadura *f* scrape

raspar ⟨1a⟩ 1 *v/t* scrape; *con lija* sand 2 *v/i* be rough

rastra *f*: *entrar a rastras* drag o.s. in, crawl in

rastreador *adj*: *perro rastreador* tracker dog

rastrear ⟨1a⟩ 1 *v/t persona* track; *bosque, zona comb* 2 *v/i* rake

rastrero *adj* mean, low

rastrillo *m* rake

rastro *m* flea market; (*huella*) trace; *desaparecer sin dejar rastro* vanish without trace

rastrojo *m* stubble

rasurar ⟨1a⟩ *v/t* shave

rata *f* ZO rat

ratero *m*, *-a f* petty thief

raticida *m* rat poison

ratificar ⟨1g⟩ *v/t* POL ratify

rato *m* time, while; *ratos libres* spare time *sg*; *al poco rato* after a short time *o* while; *todo el rato* all the time; *un buen rato* a good while, a pretty long time; *pasar el rato* pass the time; *he pasado un buen / mal rato* I've had a great / an awful time

ratón *m* ZO, INFOR mouse

ratonera *f* mouse trap

raudal *m*: *tienen dinero a raudales* they've got loads of money F

raudo *adj* swift

raya *f* GRAM dash; ZO ray; *de pelo* part, *Br* parting; *a o de rayas* striped; *pasarse de la raya* overstep the mark, go too far

rayado *adj disco, superficie* scratched

rayano *adj* bordering (*en* on)

rayar ⟨1a⟩ 1 *v/t* scratch; (*tachar*) cross out 2 *v/i* border (*en* on), verge (*en* on)

rayo *m* FÍS ray; METEO (bolt of) lightning; *rayo láser* laser beam; *rayo X* X-ray; *rayos ultravioleta* ultraviolet rays

raza *f* race; *de animal* breed

razón *f* reason; *a razón de precio* at; *dar la razón a alguien* admit that s.o. is right; *entrar en razón* see sense; *perder la razón* lose one's mind; *tener razón* be right

razonable *adj precio* reasonable

razonamiento *m* reasoning

razonar ⟨1a⟩ *v/i* reason

RDSI *abr* (= *Red Digital de Servicios Integrados*) ISDN (= Integrated Services Digital Network)

reacción f reaction (*a* to); *avión a reacción* jet (aircraft)
reaccionar ⟨1a⟩ v/i react (*a* to)
reaccionario 1 adj reactionary **2** m, -a f reactionary
reacio adj reluctant (*a* to)
reactivación f COM revival, upturn
reactivar ⟨1a⟩ v/t COM revive
reactor m reactor; (*motor*) jet engine
reafirmar ⟨1a⟩ v/t reaffirm **2** v/r reafirmarse: *reafirmarse en idea* reassert
reajuste m adjustment; *reajuste ministerial* POL cabinet reshuffle
real adj (*regio*) royal; (*verdadero*) real
realeza f royalty
realidad f reality; *en realidad* in fact, in reality
realismo m realism
realista 1 adj realistic **2** m/f realist
realización f fulfil(l)ment; RAD, TV production
realizador m, **realizadora** f de película director; RAD, TV producer
realizar ⟨1f⟩ **1** v/t tarea carry out; RAD, TV produce; RAD, TV realize **2** v/r realizarse de persona fulfil(l) o.s.
realquilar ⟨1a⟩ v/t sublet
realzar ⟨1f⟩ v/t highlight
reanimación f revival
reanimar ⟨1a⟩ v/t revive
reanudación f resumption
reanudar ⟨1a⟩ v/t resume
reaparecer ⟨2d⟩ v/i reappear
reaparición f reappearance
reaseguro m reinsurance
rebaja f reduction; *rebajas de verano / invierno* summer / winter sale
rebajar ⟨1a⟩ **1** v/t precio lower, reduce; *mercancías* reduce **2** v/r rebajarse lower o.s., humble o.s.
rebanada f slice
rebanar ⟨1a⟩ v/t slice
rebañar ⟨1a⟩ v/t: *rebañar algo* wipe sth clean
rebaño m flock
rebasar ⟨1a⟩ v/t Méx AUTO pass, Br overtake
rebatir ⟨3a⟩ v/t razones rebut, refute
rebeca f cardigan
rebeco m ZO chamois
rebelarse ⟨1a⟩ v/r rebel
rebelde 1 adj rebel atr **2** m/f rebel
rebeldía f rebelliousness
rebelión f rebellion
reblandecer ⟨2d⟩ v/t soften
rebobinar ⟨1a⟩ v/t rewind
rebosar ⟨1a⟩ v/i overflow
rebotar ⟨1a⟩ **1** v/t bounce; (*disgustar*) annoy **2** v/i bounce, rebound

rebote m bounce; *de rebote* on the rebound
rebozar ⟨1f⟩ v/t GASTR coat
rebuscado adj over-elaborate
rebuznar ⟨1a⟩ v/i bray
recado m errand; *Rpl* (*arnés*) harness; *dejar un recado* leave a message
recaída f MED relapse
recalar ⟨1a⟩ v/i MAR put in (*en* at), call (*en* at)
recalcar ⟨1g⟩ v/t stress, emphasize
recalcitrante adj recalcitrant
recalentar ⟨1k⟩ v/t comida warm *o* heat up
recámara f de arma de fuego chamber; *L.Am.* (*dormitorio*) bedroom
recambio m COM spare part
recapacitar ⟨1a⟩ v/t think over, reflect on
recapitular ⟨1a⟩ v/t recap
recargar ⟨1h⟩ v/t batería recharge; *recipiente* refill; *recargar un 5%* charge 5% extra
recargo m surcharge
recatado adj modest; (*cauto*) cautious
recato m modesty; (*prudencia*) caution
recauchutar ⟨1a⟩ v/t neumáticos retread
recaudación f acción collection; cantidad takings pl
recaudar ⟨1a⟩ v/t impuestos, dinero collect
recaudo m: *poner a buen recaudo* put in a safe place
recelo m mistrust
recepción f en hotel reception
recepcionista m/f receptionist
receptivo adj receptive
receptor m receiver
recesión f recession
receta f GASTR recipe; *receta médica* prescription
recetar ⟨1a⟩ v/t MED prescribe
recetario m recipe book
rechazar ⟨1f⟩ v/t reject; MIL repel
rechazo m rejection
rechinar ⟨1a⟩ v/i creak, squeak
rechistar ⟨1a⟩ v/i protest; *sin rechistar* F without a murmur, without complaining
rechoncho adj F dumpy F
rechupete: *de rechupete* F delicious
recibidor m entrance hall
recibimiento m reception
recibir ⟨3a⟩ v/t receive
recibo m (sales) receipt
reciclable adj recyclable
reciclado, reciclaje m recycling
reciclar ⟨1a⟩ v/t recycle
recién adv newly; *L.Am.* (*hace poco*) just; *recién casados* newly-weds; *recién nacido* newborn; *recién pintado* wet

paint; **recién llegamos** we've only just
arrived
reciente *adj* recent
recinto *m* premises *pl*; *área* grounds *pl*
recio *adj* sturdy, tough
recipiente *m* container
recíproco *adj* reciprocal
recital *m* recital
recitar ⟨1a⟩ *v/t* recite
reclamación *f* complaint; POL claim, demand
reclamar ⟨1a⟩ **1** *v/t* claim, demand **2** *v/i*
complain
reclame *m* L.Am. advertisement
reclamo *m* lure
reclinable *adj*: **asiento reclinable** reclin-
ing seat
reclinar ⟨1a⟩ **1** *v/t* rest **2** *v/r* **reclinarse**
lean, recline (**contra** against)
recluir ⟨3g⟩ *v/t* imprison, confine
reclusión *f* JUR imprisonment, confinement
recluso *m*, **-a** *f* prisoner
recluta *m/f* recruit
reclutar ⟨1a⟩ *v/t tb* COM recruit
recobrar ⟨1a⟩ **1** *v/t* recover **2** *v/r* **recobrar-
se** recover (**de** from)
recogedor *m* dustpan
recogepelotas *m/f inv* ball boy; *niña* ball
girl
recoger ⟨2c⟩ **1** *v/t* pick up, collect; *habitación* tidy up; AGR harvest; (*mostrar*)
show **2** *v/r* **recogerse** go home
recogida *f* collection; **recogida de basuras** garbage collection, Br refuse collection; **recogida de equipajes** baggage re-
claim
recolectar ⟨1a⟩ *v/t* AGR harvest, bring in
recomendación *f* recommendation
recomendar ⟨1k⟩ *v/t* recommend
recompensa *f* reward
recompensar ⟨1a⟩ *v/t* reward
recomponer ⟨2r; *part* **recompuesto** ⟩ *v/t*
mend
reconciliación *f* reconciliation
reconciliar ⟨1b⟩ **1** *v/t* reconcile **2** *v/r* **reconciliarse** make up (**con** with), be reconciled (**con** with)
recóndito *adj* remote
reconfortar ⟨1a⟩ *v/t* comfort
reconocer ⟨2d⟩ *v/t* recognize; *errores* admit, acknowledge; *area* reconnoiter, Br
reconnoitre; MED examine
reconocimiento *m* recognition; *de error*
acknowledge(m)ent; MED examination,
check-up; MIL reconnaissance
reconquista *f* reconquest
reconquistar ⟨1a⟩ *v/t* reconquer
reconsiderar ⟨1a⟩ *v/t* reconsider

reconstrucción *f* reconstruction
reconstruir ⟨3g⟩ *v/t fig* reconstruct
reconvenir ⟨3s⟩ *v/i* JUR counterclaim
reconversión *f* COM restructuring
recopilación *f* compilation
recopilar ⟨1a⟩ *v/t* compile
récord 1 *adj* record(-breaking) **2** *m* record
recordar ⟨1m⟩ *v/t* remember, recall; **recordar algo a alguien** remind s.o. of sth
recordatorio *m* reminder
recorrer ⟨2a⟩ *v/t distancia* cover, do; *a pie*
walk; *territorio, país* go around, travel
around; *camino* go along, travel along
recorrido *m* route; DEP round
recortar ⟨1a⟩ *v/t* cut out; *fig* cut
recorte *m fig* cutback; **recorte de periódico** cutting, clipping; **recorte salarial**
salary cut
recostarse ⟨1m⟩ *v/r* lie down
recoveco *m* nook, cranny; *en camino*
bend
recrearse ⟨1a⟩ *v/r* amuse o.s.
recreativo *adj* recreational; **juegos recreativos** amusements
recreo *m* recreation; EDU recess, Br break
recriminar ⟨1a⟩ *v/t* reproach
recrudecerse ⟨2d⟩ *v/r* intensify
recta *f* DEP straight; **recta final** *tb fig* home
straight
rectángulo *m* rectangle
rectificar ⟨1g⟩ *v/t* correct, rectify; *camino*
straighten
rectitud *f* rectitude, probity
recto *adj* straight; (*honesto*) honest
rector *m* rector, Br vice-chancellor
rectorado *m* rector's office, Br vice-chancellor's office
recuadro *m* TIP inset, box
recubierto *part* → **recubrir**
recubrir ⟨3a; *part* **recubierto** ⟩ *v/t* cover
(**de** with)
recuento *m* count; **recuento de votos** re-
count
recuerdo *m* memory; **da recuerdos a
Luís** give my regards to Luís
recuperación *f tb fig* recovery
recuperar ⟨1a⟩ **1** *v/t tiempo* make up; *algo
perdido* recover **2** *v/r* **recuperarse** recover (**de** from)
recurrir ⟨3a⟩ **1** *v/t* JUR appeal against **2** *v/i*:
recurrir a resort to, turn to
recurso *m* JUR appeal; *material* resource;
recursos humanos human resources;
recursos naturales natural resources
red *f* net; INFOR, *fig* network; **caer en las
redes de** *fig* fall into the clutches of; **Red
Digital de Servicios Integrados** Integrated Services Digital Network
redacción *f* writing; *de editorial* editorial

department; EDU essay
redactar ⟨1a⟩ v/t write, compose
redactor m, **redactora** f COM editor
redada f raid
redentor m, **redentora** f COM redeemer; **el Redentor** REL the Savio(u)r
redoble m MÚS (drum)roll
redomado adj F total, out-and-out
redonda f: **a la redonda** around, round about
redondear ⟨1a⟩ v/t para más round up; para menos round down; (rematar) round off
redondo adj round; negocio excellent; **caer redondo** flop down
reducción f reduction; MED setting
reducido adj precio reduced; espacio small, confined
reducir ⟨3o⟩ 1 v/t reduce (a to); MIL overcome 2 v/r **reducirse** come down (a to)
reducto m redoubt
redujo vb → **reducir**
redundancia f tautology
redundar ⟨1a⟩ v/i have an impact (en on)
reeditar ⟨1a⟩ v/t republish, reissue
reelegir ⟨3c & 3l⟩ v/t re-elect
reembolsar ⟨1a⟩ v/t refund
reembolso m refund; **contra reembolso** collect on delivery, Br cash on delivery, COD
reemplazar ⟨1f⟩ v/t replace
reencarnación f REL reincarnation
reestructurar ⟨1a⟩ v/t restructure
refacción f L.Am. de edificio refurbishment; AUTO spare part
referencia f reference; **hacer referencia a** refer to, make reference to, **referencias** COM references
referéndum m referendum
referente adj: **referente a** referring to, relating to
referirse ⟨3i⟩ v/r refer (a to)
refilón m: **mirar de refilón** glance at
refinado adj tb fig refined
refinar ⟨1a⟩ v/t TÉC refine
refinería f TÉC refinery
reflector m reflector; EL spotlight
reflejar ⟨1a⟩ v/t tb fig reflect 2 v/r **reflejarse** be reflected
reflejo m reflex; imagen reflection
reflexión f fig reflection, thought
reflexionar ⟨1a⟩ v/t reflect on, ponder
reflexivo adj GRAM reflexive
reflotar ⟨1a⟩ v/t COM refloat
reforestar ⟨1a⟩ v/t reforest
reforma f reform; **reformas** pl (obras) refurbishment sg; (reparaciones) repairs
reformador m, **reformadora** f reformer
reformar ⟨1a⟩ 1 v/t reform; edificio refur-

bish; (reparar) repair 2 v/r **reformarse** mend one's ways, reform
reformatorio m reform school, reformatory
reformista 1 adj reformist, reform atr 2 m/f reformer
reforzar ⟨1f & 1m⟩ v/t reinforce; vigilancia increase, step up
refrán m saying
refrenar ⟨1a⟩ v/t restrain, contain
refrescante adj refreshing
refrescar ⟨1g⟩ 1 v/t tb fig refresh; conocimientos brush up 2 v/i cool down 3 v/r **refrescarse** cool down
refresco m soda, Br soft drink
refriega f MIL clash, skirmish
refrigerador m refrigerator
refrigerar ⟨1a⟩ v/t refrigerate
refrigerio m snack
refuerzo m reinforcement; **refuerzos** MIL reinforcements
refugiado m, -a f refugee
refugiarse ⟨1b⟩ v/r take refuge
refugio m refuge
refulgente adj dazzling
refunfuñar ⟨1a⟩ v/i grumble
refutar ⟨1a⟩ v/t refute
regadera f watering can; Méx (ducha) shower; **estar como una regadera** F be nuts F
regadío m: **tierra de regadío** irrigated land
regalar ⟨1a⟩ v/t: **regalar algo a alguien** give sth to s.o., give s.o. sth
regaliz m BOT licorice, Br liquorice
regalo m gift, present
regañadientes: **a regañadientes** reluctantly
regañar ⟨1a⟩ 1 v/t tell off 2 v/i quarrel
regaña f F telling off
regar ⟨1h & 1k⟩ v/t water; AGR irrigate
regata f regatta
regatear ⟨1a⟩ v/t DEP get past, dodge; **no regatear esfuerzos** spare no effort
regazo m lap
regenerar ⟨1a⟩ v/t regenerate
regente m/f regent
regidor 1 adj governing, ruling 2 m, **regidora** f TEA stage manager
régimen m POL regime; MED diet; **estar a régimen** be on a diet
regimiento m MIL regiment
regio adj regal, majestic; S. Am. F (estupendo) great F, fantastic F
región f region
regional adj regional
regionalismo m regionalism
regir ⟨3l & 3c⟩ 1 v/t rule, govern 2 v/i apply, be in force 3 v/r **regirse** be guided

R

(*por* by)

registrar ⟨1a⟩ **1** *v/t* register; *casa* search **2** *v/r* **registrarse** be recorded; *se registró un máximo de 45 °C* a high of 45°C was recorded

registro *m* register; *de casa* search; **registro civil** register of births, marriages and deaths

regla *f* (*norma*) rule; *para medir* ruler; MED period; **por regla general** as a rule

reglamentar ⟨1a⟩ *v/t* regulate

reglamentario *adj* regulation *atr*

reglamento *m* regulation

regocijarse ⟨1a⟩ *v/r* rejoice (*de* at), take delight (*de* in)

regocijo *m* delight

regodearse ⟨1a⟩ *v/r* gloat (*con* over), delight (*en* in)

regresar ⟨1a⟩ **1** *v/i* return **2** *v/t* *Méx* return, give back **3** *v/r* **regresarse** *L.Am.* return

regreso *m* return

regüeldo *m* F belch

reguero *m* trail; **como un reguero de pólvora** *fig* like wildfire

regulación *f* regulation; *de temperatura* control

regular 1 *adj sin variar* regular; (*común*) ordinary; (*habitual*) regular, normal; (*no muy bien*) so-so **2** ⟨1a⟩ *v/t* TÉC regulate; *temperatura* control

regularidad *f* regularity

regularizar ⟨1f⟩ *v/t* regularize

regusto *m* aftertaste

rehabilitación *f* MED, *fig* rehabilitation; ARQUI restoration

rehabilitar ⟨1a⟩ *v/t* ARQUI restore

rehacer ⟨2s; *part* **rehecho** ⟩ *v/t película, ropa, cama* remake; *trabajo, ejercicio* redo; *casa, vida* rebuild

rehén *m* hostage

rehice *vb* → **rehacer**

rehizo *vb* → **rehacer**

rehogar ⟨1h⟩ *v/t* GASTR fry

rehuir ⟨3g⟩ *v/t* shy away from

rehusar ⟨1a⟩ *v/t* refuse, decline

reimprimir ⟨3a⟩ *v/t* reprint

reina *f* queen

reinado *m* reign

reinante *adj tb fig* reigning

reinar ⟨1a⟩ *v/i tb fig* reign

reincidente 1 *adj* repeat **2** *m/f* repeat offender

reincidir ⟨3a⟩ *v/i* reoffend

reincorporarse ⟨1a⟩ *v/r* return (*a* to)

reino *m tb fig* kingdom; **el Reino Unido** the United Kingdom

reinserción *f*: **reinserción social** social rehabilitation

reinsertar ⟨1a⟩ *v/t* rehabilitate

reinstaurar ⟨1a⟩ *v/t* bring back

reintegrarse ⟨1a⟩ *v/r* return (*a* to)

reintegro *m* (*en lotería*) prize in the form of a refund of the stake money

reír ⟨3m⟩ **1** *v/i* laugh **2** *v/r* **reírse** laugh (*de* at)

reiterar ⟨1a⟩ *v/t* repeat, reiterate

reivindicación *f* claim

reivindicar ⟨1g⟩ *v/t* claim; **reivindicar un atentado** claim responsibility for an attack

reja *f* AGR plowshare, *Br* ploughshare; (*barrote*) bar, railing; **meter entre rejas** *fig* F put behind bars

rejilla *f* FERR luggage rack

rejuvenecer ⟨2d⟩ *v/t* rejuvenate

relación *f* relationship; **relaciones públicas** *pl* public relations, PR *sg*

relacionado *adj* related (*con* to)

relacionarse ⟨1a⟩ *v/r* be connected (*con* to), be related (*con* to)

relajación *f* relaxation

relajante *adj* relaxing

relajar ⟨1a⟩ **1** *v/t* relax **2** *v/r* **relajarse** relax

relajo *m* *C.Am., Méx* uproar

relamerse ⟨2a⟩ *v/r* lick one's lips

relámpago *m* flash of lightning; **viaje relámpago** flying visit

relatar ⟨1a⟩ *v/t* tell, relate

relatividad *f* relativity

relativo *adj* relative; **relativo a** regarding, about

relato *m* short story

relax *m* relaxation

releer ⟨2e⟩ *v/t* reread

relegar ⟨1h⟩ *v/t* relegate

relevante *adj* relevant

relevar ⟨1a⟩ *v/t* MIL relieve; **relevar a alguien de algo** relieve s.o. of sth

relevo *m* MIL change; (*sustituto*) relief, replacement; **carrera de relevos** relay (race); **tomar el relevo de alguien** take over from s.o., relieve s.o.

relicario *m* shrine

relieve *m* relief; **poner de relieve** highlight

religión *f* religion

religiosa *f* nun

religioso 1 *adj* religious **2** *m* monk

relinchar ⟨1a⟩ *v/i* neigh

reliquia *f* relic

rellano *m* landing

rellenar ⟨1a⟩ *v/t* fill; GASTR *pollo, pimientos* stuff; *formulario* fill out, fill in

relleno 1 *adj* GASTR *pollo, pimientos* stuffed; *pastel* filled **2** *m tb en cojín* stuffing; *en pastel* filling

reloj *m* clock; *de pulsera* watch, wristwatch; **reloj de pared** wall clock; **reloj de sol** sundial

relojería f watchmaker's

relojero m, **-a** f watchmaker

reluciente adj sparkling, glittering

remanso m backwater; **remanso de paz** fig haven of peace

remar ⟨1a⟩ v/i row

remarcar ⟨1g⟩ v/t stress, emphasize

rematar ⟨1a⟩ **1** v/t finish off; L.Am. COM auction **2** v/i en fútbol shoot

remate m L.Am. COM auction, sale; en fútbol shot; **ser tonto de remate** be a complete idiot

remediar ⟨1b⟩ v/t remedy; **no puedo remediarlo** I can't do anything about it

remedio m remedy; **sin remedio** hopeless; **no hay más remedio que ...** there's no alternative but to ...

rememorar ⟨1a⟩ v/t remember

remendar ⟨1k⟩ v/t con parche patch; (zurcir) darn

remesa f (envío) shipment, consignment; L.Am. dinero remittance

remezón m L.Am. earth tremor

remiendo m (parche) patch; (zurcido) darn

remilgado adj fussy, finicky

reminiscencia f reminiscence

remiso adj reluctant (a to)

remite m en carta return address

remitente m/f sender

remitir ⟨3a⟩ **1** v/t send, ship; en texto refer (a to) **2** v/i MED go into remission; de crisis ease (off)

remo m pala oar; deporte rowing

remodelar ⟨1a⟩ v/t redesign, remodel

remojar ⟨1a⟩ v/t soak; L.Am. F acontecimiento celebrate

remojo m: **poner a o en remojo** leave to soak

remojón m drenching, soaking; **darse un remojón** go for a dip

remolacha f beet, Br beetroot; **remolacha azucarera** sugar beet

remolcador m tug

remolcar ⟨1g⟩ v/t AUTO, MAR tow

remolino m de aire eddy; de agua whirlpool

remolón m, **-ona** f F slacker; **hacerse el remolón** slack (off)

remolque m AUTO trailer

remontarse ⟨1a⟩ v/r en el tiempo go back (a to)

remonte m ski lift

remorder ⟨2h⟩ v/t: **me remuerde la conciencia** I have a guilty conscience

remordimiento m remorse

remoto adj remote; **no tengo ni la más -a idea** I haven't the faintest idea

remover ⟨2h⟩ v/t (agitar) stir; L.Am. (destituir) dismiss; C.Am., Méx (quitar) remove

remplazar v/t → **reemplazar**

remuneración f remuneration

remunerar ⟨1a⟩ v/t pay

renacentista adj Renaissance atr

renacer ⟨2d⟩ v/i fig be reborn

Renacimiento m Renaissance

renacuajo m zo tadpole; F persona shrimp F

renal adj ANAT renal, kidney atr

rencilla f fight, argument

rencor m resentment; **guardar rencor a alguien** bear s.o. a grudge

rencoroso adj resentful

rendición f surrender

rendija f crack; (hueco) gap

rendimiento m performance; FIN yield; (producción) output

rendir ⟨3l⟩ **1** v/t honores pay, do; beneficio produce, yield **2** v/i perform **3** v/r rendirse surrender

renegado 1 adj renegade atr **2** m renegade

renegar ⟨1h & 1k⟩ v/i: **renegar de alguien** disown s.o.; **renegar de algo** renounce sth

renegrido adj blackened

RENFE abr (= Red Nacional de Ferrocarriles Españoles) Spanish rail operator

renglón m line; **a renglón seguido** immediately after

rengo adj CSur lame

renguear ⟨1a⟩ v/i CSur limp, walk with a limp

reno m zo reindeer

renombre m: **de renombre** famous, renowned

renovación f renewal

renovador adj: **las fuerzas renovadoras** the forces of renewal

renovar ⟨1m⟩ v/t renew

renta f income; de casa rent; **renta per cápita** income per capita

rentabilidad f profitability

rentable adj profitable

rentar ⟨1a⟩ v/t (arrendar) rent out, (alquiler) rent; carro hire

renuente adj reluctant, unwilling

renunciar ⟨1b⟩ v/i: **renunciar a** tabaco, alcohol etc give up; puesto resign; demanda drop

reñir ⟨3h & 3l⟩ **1** v/t tell off **2** v/i quarrel, fight F

reo m, **-a** f accused

reojo: **de reojo** out of the corner of one's eye

repantigarse ⟨1h⟩ v/r lounge, sprawl
reparación f repair; fig reparation
reparar ⟨1a⟩ **1** v/t repair **2** v/i: **reparar en algo** notice sth
reparo m: **poner reparos a** find problems with; **no tener reparos en** have no reservations about
repartición f S. Am. department
repartidor m delivery man
repartir ⟨3a⟩ v/t (dividir) share out, divide up; productos deliver
reparto m (división) share-out, distribution; TEA cast; **reparto a domicilio** home delivery
repasar ⟨1a⟩ v/t trabajo go over again; EDU revise
repecho m steep slope
repelente adj fig repellent, repulsive; F niño horrible **2** m repellent
repelús m: **dar repelús a alguien** F give s.o. the creeps F
repente: **de repente** suddenly
repentino adj sudden
repercusión f fig repercussion
repercutir ⟨3a⟩ v/i have repercussions (**en** on)
repertorio m TEA, MÚS repertoire
repetición f repetition
repetido adj repeated
repetir ⟨3l⟩ **1** v/t repeat **2** v/i de comida repeat **3** v/r **repetirse** happen again
repetitivo adj repetitive
repipi adj F (afectado) affected; **es tan repipi** niño he's such a know-it-all F
repisa f shelf
replantear ⟨1a⟩ v/t pregunta, problema bring up again
replegarse ⟨1h & 1k⟩ v/r MIL withdraw
repleto adj full (**de** of)
réplica f replica
replicar ⟨1g⟩ v/t reply
repoblar ⟨1m⟩ v/t repopulate
repollo m BOT cabbage
reponerse ⟨2r; part **repuesto**⟩ v/r recover (**de** from)
reportaje m story, report
reportero m, **-a** f reporter; **reportero gráfico** press photographer
reposacabezas m inv AUTO headrest
reposar ⟨1a⟩ v/i rest; de vino settle
reposera f L.Am. lounger
reposición f TEA revival; TV repeat
reposo m rest
repostar ⟨1a⟩ v/i refuel
repostería f pastries pl
reprender ⟨2a⟩ v/t scold, tell off
represa f dam; (embalse) reservoir
represalia f reprisal
representación f representation; TEA per-

formance; **en representación de** on behalf of
representante m/f tb COM representative
representar ⟨1a⟩ v/t represent; obra put on, perform; papel play; **representar menos años** look younger
represión f repression
reprimenda f reprimand
reprimir ⟨3a⟩ v/t tb PSI repress
reprobar ⟨1m⟩ v/t condemn; L.Am. EDU fail
reprochar ⟨1a⟩ v/t reproach
reproche m reproach
reproducción f BIO reproduction
reproducir ⟨3o⟩ **1** v/t reproduce **2** v/r **reproducirse** BIO reproduce, breed
reptil m ZO reptile
república f republic
republicano 1 adj republican **2** m, **-a** f republican
repudiar ⟨1b⟩ v/t fml repudiate; herencia renounce
repuesto 1 part → **reponerse 2** m spare part, replacement; **de repuesto** spare
repugnancia f disgust, repugnance
repugnante adj disgusting, repugnant
repugnar ⟨1a⟩ v/t disgust, repel
repulsión f repulsion
repulsivo adj repulsive
repuse vb → **reponerse**
reputación f reputation
requerir ⟨3i⟩ v/t require; JUR summons
requesón m cottage cheese
requetebién adv F really well, brilliantly F
réquiem m requiem
requisar ⟨1a⟩ v/t Arg, Chi MIL requisition
requisito m requirement
res f L.Am. bull; **carne f de res** beef; **reses** pl cattle pl
resaca f MAR undertow, undercurrent; de beber hangover
resaltar ⟨1a⟩ **1** v/t highlight, stress **2** v/i ARQUI jut out; fig stand out
resarcirse ⟨3b⟩ v/r make up (**de** for)
resbaladizo adj slippery; fig tricky
resbalar ⟨1a⟩ v/i slide; fig slip (up)
resbalón m slip; fig F slip-up
resbaloso adj L.Am. slippery
rescatar ⟨1a⟩ v/t persona, animal rescue, save; bienes save
rescate m de peligro rescue; en secuestro ransom
rescindir ⟨3a⟩ v/t cancel; contrato terminate
rescisión f cancellation; de contrato termination
reseco adj (seco) parched; (flaco) skinny
resentimiento m resentment
resentirse ⟨3i⟩ v/r get upset; de rendi-

miento, calidad suffer; *resentirse de algo* suffer from the effects of sth

reseña *f de libro etc* review

reseñar ⟨1a⟩ *v/t* review

reserva 1 *f* reservation; *reserva natural* nature reserve; *sin reservas* without reservation **2** *m/f* DEP reserve

reservar ⟨1a⟩ **1** *v/t (guardar)* set aside, put by; *billete* reserve **2** *v/r* **reservarse** save o.s. (*para* for)

resfriado 1 *adj:* **estar resfriado** have a cold **2** *m* cold

resfriarse ⟨1c⟩ *v/r* catch cold

resfrío *m L.Am.* cold

resguardar ⟨1a⟩ **1** *v/t* protect (*de* from) **2** *v/r* **resguardarse** protect o.s. (*de* from)

resguardo *m* COM counterfoil

residencia *f* residence; *residencia de ancianos* or *para la tercera edad* retirement home

residencial 1 *adj* residential **2** *f Arg, Chi* boarding house

residente 1 *adj* resident **2** *m/f* resident

residir ⟨3a⟩ *v/i* reside; *residir en fig* lie in

residual *adj* residual; *(de desecho)* waste *atr*

residuo *m* residue; *residuos* waste *sg*

resignación *f* actitud resignation

resignarse ⟨1a⟩ *v/r* resign o.s. (*a* to)

resina *f* resin

resistencia *f* resistance; EL, TÉC resistor

resistir ⟨3a⟩ **1** *v/i* resist; *(aguantar)* hold out **2** *v/t* tentación resist; *frío, dolor etc* stand, bear **3** *v/r* **resistirse** be reluctant (*a* to)

resolución *f* actitud determination, decisiveness; *de problema* solution (*de* to); JUR ruling

resolver ⟨2h; *part* **resuelto**⟩ **1** *v/t* problema solve **2** *v/r* **resolverse** decide (*a* to; *por* on)

resonar ⟨1m⟩ *v/i* echo

resoplar ⟨1a⟩ *v/i* snort

resorte *m* spring

respaldar ⟨1a⟩ *v/t* back, support

respaldo *m de silla* back; *fig* backing, support

respectar ⟨1a⟩ *v/i:* **por lo que respecta a ...** as regards ..., as far as ... is concerned

respectivo *adj* respective

respecto *m:* **al respecto** on the matter; **con respecto a** regarding, as regards

respetable *adj* respectable

respetar ⟨1a⟩ *v/t* respect

respeto *m* respect

respetuoso *adj* respectful

respiración *f* breathing; *estar con respiración asistida* MED be on a respirator

respirar ⟨1a⟩ *v/t & v/i* breathe

respiratorio *adj* respiratory

respiro *m fig* breather, break

resplandeciente *adj* shining

resplandor *m* shine, gleam

responder ⟨2a⟩ **1** *v/t* answer **2** *v/i:* **responder a** answer, reply to; MED respond to; *descripción* fit, match; *(ser debido a)* be due to

responsabilidad *f* responsibility

responsabilizarse ⟨1f⟩ *v/r* take responsibility (*de* for)

responsable 1 *adj* responsible (*de* for) **2** *m/f* person responsible (*de* for); *los responsables del crimen* those responsible for the crime

respuesta *f (contestación)* reply, answer; *fig* response

resquebrajar ⟨1a⟩ **1** *v/t* crack **2** *v/r* **resquebrajarse** crack

resquicio *m* gap

resta *f* MAT subtraction

restablecer ⟨2d⟩ **1** *v/t* re-establish **2** *v/r* **restablecerse** recover

restablecimiento *m* re-establishment; *de enfermo* recovery

restante 1 *adj* remaining **2** *m/fpl:* **los / las restantes** *pl* the rest *pl*, the remainder *pl*

restar ⟨1a⟩ **1** *v/t* subtract; *restar importancia a* play down the importance of **2** *v/i* remain, be left

restauración *f* restoration

restaurante *m* restaurant

restaurar ⟨1a⟩ *v/t* restore

restituir ⟨3g⟩ *v/t* restore; *en cargo* reinstate

resto *m* rest, remainder; *los restos mortales* the (mortal) remains

restregar ⟨1h & 1k⟩ *v/t* scrub

restricción *f* restriction

restringir ⟨3c⟩ *v/t* restrict, limit

resucitar ⟨1a⟩ **1** *v/t* resuscitate; *fig* revive **2** *v/i de persona* rise from o come back from the dead

resuello *m* puffing, heavy breathing

resuelto 1 *part* → **resolver 2** *adj* decisive, resolute

resultado *m* result; *sin resultado* without success

resultar ⟨1a⟩ *v/i* turn out; *resultar caro* prove expensive, turn out to be expensive; *resulta que ...* it turns out that ...

resumen *m* summary; *en resumen* in short

resumir ⟨3a⟩ *v/t* summarize

resurgir ⟨3d⟩ *v/i* reappear, come back

resurrección *f* REL resurrection

retaguardia *f* MIL rearguard

retahíla *f* string

retar ⟨1a⟩ *v/t* challenge; *Rpl (regañar)*

R

scold, tell off
retardar ⟨1a⟩ v/t delay
retazo m fig snippet, fragment
retención f MED retention; de persona detention; **retención fiscal** tax deduction
retener ⟨2l⟩ v/t dinero etc withhold, deduct; persona detain, hold
reticencia f reticence
reticente adj reticent
retintín m: **con retintín** F sarcastically
retirada f MIL retreat, withdrawal
retirado adj (jubilado) retired; (alejado) remote, out-of-the-way
retirar ⟨1a⟩ 1 v/t take away, remove; acusación, dinero withdraw 2 v/r retirarse MIL withdraw
retiro m lugar retreat
reto m challenge; Rpl (regañina) scolding, telling-off
retobado adj L.Am. unruly
retocar ⟨1g⟩ v/t FOT retouch, touch up; (acabar) put the finishing touches to
retomar ⟨1a⟩ v/t: **retomar algo** fig take sth up again
retoque m FOT touching-up; (acabado) finishing touch
retorcer ⟨2b & 2h⟩ v/t twist
retorcido adj fig twisted
retorcijón m stomach cramp
retórica f rhetoric
retornar ⟨1a⟩ v/i return
retorno m return
retortijón m cramps pl, Br stomach cramp
retozar ⟨1f⟩ v/i frolic, romp
retractar ⟨1a⟩ v/t retract, withdraw
retraer ⟨2p; part retraído⟩ 1 v/t retract 2 v/r retraerse withdraw
retraído 1 part → **retraer 2** adj withdrawn
retransmisión f RAD, TV transmission, broadcast
retransmitir ⟨3a⟩ v/t transmit, broadcast
retrasado 1 part → **retrasar 2** adj tren, entrega late; con trabajo, pagos behind; **está retrasado en clase** he's lagging behind in class; **retrasado mental** mentally handicapped
retrasar ⟨1a⟩ 1 v/t hold up; reloj put back; reunión postpone, put back 2 v/i reloj lose time; en los estudios be behind 3 v/r retrasarse (atrasarse) be late; de reloj lose time; con trabajo, pagos get behind
retraso m delay; **ir con retraso** be late
retratar ⟨1a⟩ v/t FOT take a picture of; fig depict
retrato m picture; **retrato-robot** composite photo, E-Fit®
retrete m bathroom
retribución f salary
retroactivo adj retroactive

retroceder ⟨2a⟩ v/i go back, move back; fig back down
retroceso m fig backward step
retrógrado adj retrograde
retroproyector m overhead projector
retrospectiva f retrospective
retrovisor m AUTO rear-view mirror; **retrovisor exterior** wing mirror
retumbar ⟨1a⟩ v/i boom
retuve vb → **retener**
reuma, reúma m MED rheumatism
reunificación f POL reunification
reunión f meeting; de amigos get-together
reunir ⟨3a⟩ 1 v/t personas bring together; requisitos meet, fulfil(l); datos gather (together) 2 v/r reunirse meet up, get together; COM meet
reutilizar ⟨1f⟩ v/t re-use
revalorizar ⟨1f⟩ 1 v/t revalue 2 v/r revalorizarse appreciate (**en** by), increase in value (**en** by)
revaluar vb → **revalorizar**
revancha f revenge
revelación f revelation
revelado m development
revelar ⟨1a⟩ v/t FOT develop
reventa f resale
reventar ⟨1k⟩ 1 v/i burst; **lleno a reventar** full to bursting 2 v/t puerta etc break down 3 v/r reventarse burst; **se reventó a trabajar** fig he worked his butt off F
reventón m AUTO blowout
reverberar ⟨1a⟩ v/i de sonido reverberate
reverencia f reverence; saludo: de hombre bow; de mujer curtsy
reverendo m REL reverend
reversible adj ropa reversible
reverso m reverse, back
revés m setback; tenis backhand; **al o del revés** back to front; **con el interior fuera** inside out
revestir ⟨3l⟩ v/t TÉC cover (**de** with); **revestir gravedad** be serious
revisación f L.Am. check-up
revisada f L.Am. → **revisión**
revisar ⟨1a⟩ v/t check, inspect
revisión f check, inspection; AUTO service; **revisión técnica** roadworthiness test, Br MOT (test); **revisión médica** check-up
revisor m, revisora f FERR (ticket) inspector
revista f magazine; **pasar revista a** MIL inspect, review; fig review
revivir ⟨3a⟩ 1 v/i revive 2 v/t relive
revocar ⟨1g & 1m⟩ v/t pared render; JUR revoke
revolcarse ⟨1g & 1m⟩ v/r roll around
revolcón m tumble; F de amantes roll in the hay F

revolotear ⟨1a⟩ v/t flutter
revoltijo, revoltillo m mess, jumble
revoltoso adj niño naughty
revolución f revolution
revolucionario 1 adj revolutionary **2** m, -a f revolutionary
revólver m revolver
revolver ⟨2h; part **revuelto** ⟩ **1** v/t GASTR stir; estómago turn; (desordenar) mess up **2** v/i rummage (en in) **3** v/r revolverse del tiempo worsen
revuelo m stir
revuelto 1 part → **revolver 2** adj mar rough; gente restless
rey m king
reyerta f fight
rezagarse ⟨1h⟩ v/r drop back, fall behind
rezar ⟨1f⟩ **1** v/t oración say **2** v/i pray; de texto say
rezo m prayer
rezongar ⟨1h⟩ v/i grumble
rezumar ⟨1a⟩ v/t & v/i ooze
ría f → **reír 2** f estuary
riachuelo m stream
riada f flood
ribera f shore, bank
riberano L.Am. **1** adj L.Am. coastal; de río riverside atr **2** m, -a f person who lives by the sea / river
ribereño de bordering (on)
rica f rich woman
rico 1 adj rich; comida delicious; F niño cute, sweet; **rico en vitaminas** rich in vitamins **2** m rich man; **nuevo rico** nouveau riche
ridiculizar ⟨1f⟩ v/t ridicule
ridículo 1 adj ridiculous **2** m ridicule; **hacer el ridículo, quedar en ridículo** make a fool of o.s.
ríe vb → **reír**
riego 1 vb → **regar 2** m AGR irrigation; **riego sanguíneo** blood flow
rien vb → **reír**
rienda f rein; **dar rienda suelta a** give free rein to
riesgo m risk; **a riesgo de** at the risk of; **correr el riesgo** run the risk (**de** of)
riesgoso adj L.Am. risky
rifa f raffle
rifar ⟨1a⟩ **1** v/t raffle **2** v/r rifarse fig fight over
rifle m rifle
rige vb → **regir**
rigidez f rigidity; de carácter inflexibility; fig strictness
rígido adj rigid; carácter inflexible; fig strict
rigor m rigo(u)r
riguroso adj rigorous, harsh

rima f rhyme
rimar ⟨1a⟩ v/i rhyme (**con** with)
rimbombante adj ostentatious
rímel m mascara
rincón m corner
rinde vb → **rendir**
rinoceronte m ZO rhino, rhinoceros
riña f quarrel, fight
riñe vb → **reñir**
riñón m ANAT kidney; **costar un riñón** F cost an arm and a leg F
riñonera f fanny pack, Br bum bag
río 1 m river; **río abajo / arriba** up / down river; **el Río de la Plata** the River Plate **2** vb → **reír**
rioplatense adj of / from the River Plate area, River Plate atr
riqueza f wealth
risa f laugh; **risas** pl laughter sg; **dar risa** be funny; **morirse de risa** kill o.s. laughing; **tomar algo a risa** treat sth as a joke
ristra f string
risueño adj cheerful
rítmico adj rhythmic(al)
ritmo m rhythm; de desarrollo rate, pace
rito m rite
ritual m/adj ritual
rival m/f rival
rivalidad f rivalry
rivalizar ⟨1f⟩ v/i: **rivalizar con** rival
rizado adj curly
rizar ⟨1f⟩ **1** v/t curl **2** rizarse v/r curl
robar ⟨1a⟩ v/t persona, banco rob; objeto steal; naipe take, pick up
roble m BOT oak
robo m robbery, en casa burglary
robot m robot; **robot de cocina** food processor
robótica f robotics
robustecer ⟨2d⟩ **1** v/t strengthen **2** v/r robustecerse become stronger
robusto adj robust, sturdy
roca f rock
roce m fig friction, **tener roces con** come into conflict with
rociar ⟨1c⟩ v/t spray
rocín m F nag
rocío m dew
rock m MÚS rock
rococó adj rococo
rocódromo m climbing wall
rocoto m S. Am. hot red pepper
rodaballo m ZO turbot
rodaja f slice
rodaje m de película shooting, filming; AUTO breaking in, Br running in
rodapié m baseboard, Br skirting board
rodar ⟨1m⟩ **1** v/i roll; de coche go, travel (**a**

R

at); *sin rumbo fijo* wander **2** *v/t película* shoot; AUTO break in, *Br* run in

rodear ⟨1a⟩ **1** *v/t* surround **2** *v/r* **rodearse** surround o.s. (*de* with)

rodeo *m* detour; *con caballos y vaqueros etc* rodeo; *andarse con rodeos* beat about the bush; *hablar sin rodeos* speak plainly, not beat about the bush

rodilla *f* knee; *de rodillas* kneeling, on one's knees; *hincarse or ponerse de rodillas* kneel (down)

rodillo *m* rolling pin; TÉC roller

rododendro *m* BOT rhododendron

roedor *m* rodent

roer ⟨2za⟩ *v/t* gnaw; *fig* eat into

rogar ⟨1h & 1m⟩ *v/t* ask for; (*implorar*) beg for, plead for; *hacerse de rogar* play hard to get

rojizo *adj* reddish

rojo 1 *adj* red; *al rojo vivo* red hot **2** *m* color red **3** *m*, -*a f* POL red, commie F

rol *m* role

rollizo *adj* F chubby

rollo *m* FOT roll; *fig* F drag F; *buen / mal rollo* F good / bad atmosphere; *¡qué rollo!* F what a drag! F

Roma Rome

romance *m* romance

románico *m/adj* Romanesque

romano 1 *adj* Roman **2** *m*, -*a f* Roman

romántico 1 *adj* romantic **2** *m*, -*a f* romantic

rombo *m* rhombus

romero *m* BOT rosemary

rompecabezas *m* puzzle

rompehielos *m inv* icebreaker

romper ⟨2a; *part* **roto**⟩ **1** *v/t* break; (*hacer añicos*) smash; *tela, papel* tear **2** *v/i* break; *romper a* start to; *romper con alguien* break up with s.o. **3** *v/r* **romperse** break

rompopo *m* C.Am., *Méx bebida* eggnog

ron *m* rum

roncar ⟨1g⟩ *v/i* snore

roncha *f* MED bump, swelling

ronco *adj* hoarse; *quedarse ronco* go hoarse

ronda *f* round

rondar ⟨1a⟩ **1** *v/t* patrol; *me ronda una idea* I have an idea going around in my head **2** *v/i* F hang around

ronquido *m* snore; *ronquidos pl* snoring *sg*

ronronear ⟨1a⟩ *v/i de gato* purr

roña *f* grime

roñoso *adj* grimy, grubby

ropa *f* clothes *pl*; *ropa de cama* bedclothes *pl*; *ropa interior* underwear; *ropa íntima* L.Am. underwear

ropero *m* closet, *Br* wardrobe

rosa 1 *adj* pink **2** *f* BOT rose; *fresco como una rosa* fresh as a daisy; *ver algo de color de rosa* see sth through rose-col-o(u)red glasses

rosado 1 *adj* pink; *vino* rosé **2** *m* rosé

rosal *m* rosebush

rosario *m* REL rosary; *fig* string

rosbif *m* GASTR roast beef

rosca *f* TÉC thread; GASTR F *pastry similar to a donut*

rosco *m* GASTR *pastry similar to a donut*; *no comerse un rosco* P not get anywhere

roscón *m* GASTR *large ring-shaped cake*

rosquilla *f pastry similar to a donut*

rosticería *f* L.Am. *type of deli that sells roast chicken*

rostro *m* face

rotación *f* rotation

rotisería *f* L.Am. deli, delicatessen

roto 1 *part* → **romper 2** *adj pierna etc* broken; (*hecho añicos*) smashed; *tela, papel* torn **3** *m*, -*a f* Chi one of the urban poor

rotonda *f* traffic circle, *Br* roundabout

rotoso *adj* Rpl F scruffy

rotulador *m* fiber-tip, *Br* fibre-tip, felt-tip

rótulo *m* sign

rotundo *adj fig* categorical

rotura *f* breakage; *una rotura de cadera* MED a broken hip

rozadura *f* chafing, rubbing

rozagante *adj* healthy

rozar ⟨1f⟩ **1** *v/t* rub; (*tocar ligeramente*) brush; *fig* touch on **2** *v/i* rub **3** *v/r* **rozarse** rub; (*desgastarse*) wear

rte. *abr* (= *remitente*) sender

ruana *f Ecuad* poncho

rubeola, rubéola *f* MED German measles *sg*

rubí *m* ruby

rubicundo *adj* ruddy

rubio *adj* blond; *tabaco rubio* Virginia tobacco

ruborizarse ⟨1f⟩ *v/r* go red, blush

rúbrica *f* heading; *de firma* flourish

rubro *m* L.Am. category, heading

rudeza *f* roughness

rudimentario *adj* rudimentary

rudo *adj* rough

rueda *f* wheel; *rueda dentada* cogwheel; *rueda de prensa* press conference; *rueda de recambio* spare wheel

ruedo *m* TAUR bullring

ruego 1 *vb* → **rogar 2** *m* request

rufián *m* rogue

rugby *m* rugby

rugido *m* roar

rugir ⟨3c⟩ *v/i* roar

rugoso *adj superficie* rough
ruido *m* noise; **hacer ruido** make a noise; **mucho ruido y pocas nueces** all talk and no action
ruidoso *adj* noisy
ruin *adj* despicable, mean; (*tacaño*) mean, miserly
ruina *f* ruin; **llevar a alguien a la ruina** *fig* bankrupt s.o.
ruiseñor *m* zo nightingale
ruleta *f* roulette
ruletero *m* Méx cab *o* taxi driver
rulo *m* roller
rumbeador *m* Rpl tracker
rumbear ⟨1a⟩ *v/i* L.Am. head (**para** for)
rumbo *m* course; **tomar rumbo a** head for; **perder el rumbo** *fig* lose one's way

rumboso *adj* lavish
rumiar ⟨1b⟩ *v/t fig* ponder
rumor *m* rumo(u)r
rumorearse ⟨1a⟩ *v/r* be rumo(u)red
rupestre *adj*: **pintura rupestre** cave painting
ruptura *f* de relaciones breaking off; **de pareja** break-up
rural 1 *adj* rural **2** *m* Rpl station wagon, Br estate car; **rurales** Méx (rural) police
Rusia Russia
ruso 1 *adj* Russian **2** *m*, **-a** *f* Russian
rústico *adj* rustic
ruta *f* route
rutina *f* routine
rutinario *adj* routine *atr*

S

S *abr* (= **sur**) S (= South(ern))
S.A. *abr* (= **sociedad anónima**) inc (= incorporated), Br plc (= public limited company)
sábado *m* Saturday
sábana *f* sheet; **sábana ajustable** fitted sheet
sabana *f* savanna(h)
sabandija *f* bug, creepy-crawly
sabañón *m* chilblain
sabelotodo *m* F know-it-all F, Br know-all F
saber ⟨2n⟩ **1** *v/t* know (**de** about); **saber hacer algo** know how to do sth, be able to do sth; **no lo supe hasta más tarde** I didn't find out till later; **hacer saber algo a alguien** let s.o. know sth; **¡qué sé yo!** who knows?; **que yo sepa** as far as I know; **sabérselas todas** F know every trick in the book **2** *v/i* taste (**a** of); **me sabe a quemado** it tastes burnt to me; **me sabe mal** *fig* it upsets me **3** *m* knowledge, learning
sabiduría *f* wisdom; (*conocimientos*) knowledge
sabiendas *fpl*: **a sabiendas** knowingly; **a sabiendas que** knowing full well that
sabio 1 *adj* wise; (*sensato*) sensible **2** *m*, **-a** *f* wise person; (*experto*) expert
sabiondo *m*, **-a** *f* know- it-all F, Br know-all F
sablazo *m*: **dar un sablazo a alguien** F

scrounge money off s.o.
sable *m* saber, Br sabre
sablear ⟨1a⟩ *v/t & v/i* L.Am. F scrounge (**a** from)
sabor *m* flavo(u)r, taste; **dejar mal sabor de boca** *fig* leave a bad taste in the mouth
saborear ⟨1a⟩ *v/t* savo(u)r; *fig* relish
sabotaje *m* sabotage
saboteador *m*, **saboteadora** *f* saboteur
sabotear ⟨1a⟩ *v/t* sabotage
sabroso *adj* tasty; *fig* juicy; L.Am. (*agradable*) nice, pleasant
sabrosura *f* L.Am. tasty dish
sabueso *m fig* sleuth
sacacorchos *m inv* corkscrew
sacamuelas *m inv desp* F dentist
sacapuntas *m inv* pencil sharpener
sacar ⟨1g⟩ **1** *v/t* take out; *mancha* take out, remove; *información* get; *disco, libro* bring out; *fotocopias* make; **sacar a alguien a bailar** ask s.o. to dance; **sacar algo en claro** (*entender*) make sense of sth; **sacar de paseo** take for a walk **2** *v/r* **sacarse** L.Am. *ropa* take off
sacarina *f* saccharin(e)
sacerdote *m* priest
sacerdotisa *f* priestess
saciar ⟨1b⟩ *v/t fig* satisfy, fulfill
saciedad *f*: **repetir algo hasta la saciedad** *fig* repeat sth time and again, repeat sth ad nauseam

S

saco *m* sack; *L.Am.* jacket; **saco de dormir** sleeping bag; **entrar a saco en** F burst into, barge into F

sacramento *m* sacrament

sacrificar ⟨1g⟩ **1** *v/t* sacrifice; (*matar*) slaughter **2** *v/r* **sacrificarse** make sacrifices (**por** for)

sacrificio *m* sacrifice

sacrilegio *m* sacrilege

sacristán *m* sexton

sacristía *f* vestry

sacudida *f* shake, jolt; EL shock

sacudir ⟨3a⟩ **1** *v/t tb fig* shake; F *niño* beat, wallop F **2** *v/r* **sacudirse** shake off, shrug off; **sacudirse alguien** (**de encima**) get rid of s.o.

sádico 1 *adj* sadistic **2** *m*, **-a** *f* sadist

sadismo *m* sadism

safari *m* safari; **safari fotográfico** photographic safari

sagaz *adj* shrewd, sharp

Sagitario *m/f inv* ASTR Sagittarius

sagrado *adj* sacred, holy

sagrario *m* tabernacle

Sahara Sahara

sainete *m* TEA short farce, one-act play

sal 1 *f* salt; **sal común** cooking salt; **sal marina** sea salt **2** *vb* → **salir**

sala *f* room, hall; *de cine* screen; JUR court room; **sala de embarque** AVIA departure lounge; **sala de espera** waiting room; **sala de estar** living room; **sala de fiestas** night club; **sala de sesiones** *or* **de juntas** boardroom

saladero *m L.Am.* meat / fish salting factory

salado *adj* salted; (*con demasiada sal*) salty; (*no dulce*) savo(u)ry; *fig* funny, witty; *C.Am., Chi, Rpl* F pric(e)y F

salamandra *f* ZO salamander

salamanquesa *f* ZO gecko

salami *m* salami

salar ⟨1a⟩ **1** *v/t* add salt to; salt; *para conservar* salt **2** *m Arg* salt mine

salarial *adj* salary *atr*

salario *m* salary; **salario base** basic wage; **salario mínimo** minimum wage

salazón *f* salted fish / meat; **en salazón** salt *atr*

salchicha *f* sausage

salchichón *m type of spiced sausage*

saldar ⟨1a⟩ *v/t disputa* settle; *deuda* settle, pay; *géneros* sell off

saldo *m* COM balance; (*resultado*) result; **saldo acreedor** credit balance; **saldo deudor** debit balance; **de saldo** reduced, on sale

saldré *vb* → **salir**

salero *m* salt cellar; *fig* wit

saleroso *adj* funny, witty

salga *vb* → **salir**

salgo *vb* → **salir**

salida *f* exit, way out; TRANSP departure; *de carrera* start; **salida de emergencia** emergency exit; **salida de tono** ill-judged remark

saliente *adj* projecting, protruding; *presidente* retiring, outgoing

salir ⟨3r⟩ **1** *v/i* leave, go out; (*aparecer*) appear, come out; **salir de** (*ir fuera de*) leave, go out of; (*venir fuera de*) leave, come out of; **salir a alguien** take after s.o.; **salir a 1000 pesetas** cost 1000 pesetas; **salir bien / mal** turn out well / badly; **el dibujo no me sale** FI can't get this drawing right; **no me salió el trabajo** I didn't get the job; **salir con alguien** date s.o., go out with s.o.; **salir perdiendo** end up losing **2** *v/r* **salirse** *de líquido* overflow; (*dejar*) leave; **salirse de la carretera** leave the road, go off the road; **salirse con la suya** get what one wants

salitre *m* saltpeter, *Br* saltpetre

saliva *f* saliva; **tragar saliva** hold one's tongue

salmo *m* psalm

salmón *m* ZO salmon; **color salmón** salmon

salmonete *m* ZO red mullet

salmuera *f* pickle, brine

salobre *adj* salt; (*con demasiada sal*) salty

salomónico *adj* just, fair

salón *m* living room; **salón de actos** auditorium, hall; **salón de baile** dance hall; **salón de belleza** beauty parlo(u)r, beautician's

salpicadera *f Méx* AUTO fender, *Br* mudguard

salpicadero *m* AUTO dash(board)

salpicadura *f* stain

salpicar ⟨1g⟩ *v/t* splash, spatter (**con** with); *fig* sprinkle, pepper

salpicón *m* GASTR vegetable salad with chopped meat or fish

salpimentar ⟨1k⟩ *v/t* season (with salt and pepper)

salsa *f* GASTR sauce; *baile* salsa; **en su salsa** *fig* in one's element

salsera *f* sauce boat

saltamontes *m inv* ZO grasshopper

saltar ⟨1a⟩ **1** *v/i* jump, leap; **saltar a la vista** *fig* be obvious, be clear; **saltar sobre** pounce on; **saltar a la comba** jump rope, *Br* skip **2** *v/t valla* jump **3** *v/r* **saltarse** (*omitir*) miss, skip

saltear ⟨1a⟩ *v/t* GASTR sauté

saltimbanqui *m* acrobat

salto *m* leap, jump; **salto de agua** waterfall; **salto de altura** high jump; **salto de longitud** long jump; **salto mortal** somersault

saltón adj: **ojos saltones** bulging eyes

salubridad f L.Am. health; **Salubridad** L.Am. Department of Health

salud f health; **¡(a tu) salud!** cheers!

saludable adj healthy

saludar ⟨1a⟩ v/t say hello to, greet; MIL salute

saludo m greeting; MIL salute; **saludos en carta** best wishes

salva f: **salva de aplausos** round of applause

salvación f REL salvation

salvado m bran

salvador m REL savio(u)r

salvadoreño 1 adj Salvador(e)an 2 m, -a f Salvador(e)an

salvaguardar ⟨1a⟩ v/t safeguard, protect

salvajada f atrocity, act of savagery; **decir una salvajada** say something outrageous

salvaje 1 adj wild; (bruto) brutal 2 m/f savage

salvajismo m savagery

salvamanteles m inv table mat

salvamento m rescue; **buque de salvamento** life boat

salvapantallas m inv INFOR screensaver

salvar ⟨1a⟩ 1 v/t save; obstáculo get round, get over 2 v/r **salvarse** escape, get out

salvavidas m inv life belt

salvedad f (excepción) exception

salvo 1 adj: **estar a salvo** be safe (and sound); **ponerse a salvo** reach safety 2 adv & prp except, save; **salvo error u omisión** errors and omissions excepted

sambenito m: **le han colgado el sambenito de vago** F they've got him down as idle F

sambumbia f L.Am. watery drink

San adj Saint

sanar ⟨1a⟩ 1 v/t cure 2 v/i de persona get well, recover; de herida heal

sanatorio m sanitarium, clinic

sanción f JUR penalty, sanction

sancionar ⟨1a⟩ v/t penalize; (multar) fine

sancocho m W.I. type of stew

sandalia f sandal

sándalo m BOT sandalwood

sandez f nonsense; **decir sandeces** talk nonsense

sandía f watermelon

sandunga f F wit

sandunguero adj L.Am. F witty

sandwich m tostado toasted sandwich;

L.Am. sin tostar sandwich

saneamiento m cleaning up; COM restructuring, rationalization

sanear ⟨1a⟩ v/t clean up; COM restructure, rationalize

sangrar ⟨1a⟩ 1 v/t **sangrar a alguien** fig F sponge off s.o. 2 v/i bleed

sangre f blood; **sangre fría** fig calmness, coolness; **a sangre fría** fig in cold blood; **no llegará la sangre al río** it won't come to that, it won't be that bad

sangría f GASTR sangria

sangriento adj bloody

sangrigordo adj Méx tedious, boring

sanguijuela f ZO, fig leech

sanguinario adj bloodthirsty

sanidad f health

sanitario adj (public) health atr

sanitarios mpl bathroom fittings

sano adj healthy; **sano y salvo** safe and well; **cortar por lo sano** take drastic measures

sanseacabó: y sanseacabó F and that's that F

santa f Saint

santiamén m: **en un santiamén** F in an instant

santidad f: **Su Santidad** His Holiness

santiguarse ⟨1i⟩ v/r cross o.s., make the sign of the cross

santo 1 adj holy 2 m saint; **santo y seña** F password; **¿a santo de qué?** F what on earth for? F; **no es santo de mi devoción** F I don't like him very much

santuario m fig sanctuary

santurrón m, -ona f sanctimonious person

saña f viciousness

sapo m ZO toad; **echar sapos y culebras** fig curse and swear

saque m en tenis serve; **saque de banda** en fútbol throw-in; **saque de esquina** corner (kick); **tener buen saque** F have a big appetite

saquear ⟨1a⟩ v/t sack, ransack

sarampión m MED measles

sarao m party

sarape m Méx poncho, blanket

sarcasmo m sarcasm

sarcástico adj sarcastic

sarcófago m sarcophagus

sardina f sardine; **como sardinas en lata** like sardines

sargento m sergeant

sarna f MED scabies

sarnoso adj scabby

sarpullido m MED rash

sarro m tartar

sarta f string, series

sartén f frying pan; **tener la sartén por el mango** fig be the boss, be in the driving seat

sastra f tailor(ess)

sastre m tailor

satán, satanás m Satan

satánico adj satanic

satélite m satellite; **ciudad satélite** satellite town

satén, satín m satin

sátira f satire

satírico adj satirical

satirizar ⟨1f⟩ v/t satirize

satisfacción f satisfaction

satisfacer ⟨2s; part **satisfecho** ⟩ v/t satisfy; requisito, exigencia meet, fulfil(l); deuda settle, pay off

satisfactorio adj satisfactory

satisfecho 1 part → **satisfacer 2** adj satisfied; (lleno) full; **darse por satisfecho** be satisfied (**con** with)

saturar ⟨1a⟩ v/t saturate

sauce m BOT willow; **sauce llorón** weeping willow

saúco m BOT elder

saudí m/f & adj Saudi

saudita m/f Saudi

sauna f sauna

savia f sap

saxofón, saxófono m saxophone, sax F

sazón f: **a la sazón** at that time

sazonar ⟨1a⟩ v/t GASTR season

scooter m motor scooter

se ◇ pron complemento indirecto: a él (to) him; a ella (to) her; a usted, ustedes (to) you; a ellos (to) them; **se lo daré** I will give it to him / her / you / them
◇ reflexivo: con él himself; con ella herself; cosa itself; con usted yourself; con ustedes yourselves; con ellos themselves; **se vistió** he got dressed, he dressed himself; **se lavó las manos** she washed her hands; **se abrazaron** they hugged each other
◇ oración impersonal: **se cree** it is thought; **se habla español** Spanish spoken

sé vb → **saber**

sea vb → **ser**

sebo m grease, fat

secador m: **secador (de pelo)** hair dryer

secadora f dryer

secar ⟨1g⟩ **1** v/t dry **2** v/r **secarse** dry

sección f section

secesión f POL secession

seco adj dry; fig persona curt, brusque; **parar en seco** stop dead

secreción f secretion

secretaria f secretary; **secretaria de dirección** executive secretary

secretaría f secretary's office; de organización secretariat

secretario m tb POL secretary

secreter m mueble writing desk

secretismo m secrecy

secreto 1 adj secret **2** m secret; **un secreto a voces** an open secret; **en secreto** in secret

secta f sect

sectario adj sectarian

sectarismo m sectarianism

sector m sector

secuaz m/f follower

secuela f MED after-effect

secuencia f sequence

secuencial adj INFOR sequential

secuestrador m, **secuestradora** f kidnapper

secuestrar ⟨1a⟩ v/t barco, avión hijack; persona abduct, kidnap

secuestro m de barco, avión hijacking; de persona abduction, kidnapping; **secuestro aéreo** hijacking

secundar ⟨1a⟩ v/t support, back

secundario adj secondary

sed f tb fig thirst; **tener sed** be thirsty

seda f silk; **como una seda** F as smooth as silk

sedal m fishing line

sedante m sedative

sede f de organización headquarters; de acontecimiento site; **sede social** head office

sedentario adj sedentary

sedición f sedition

sediento adj thirsty; **estar sediento de** fig thirst for

sedimentar ⟨1a⟩ v/t deposit

sedimento m sediment

sedoso adj silky

seducción f seduction; (atracción) attraction

seducir ⟨3o⟩ v/t seduce; (atraer) attract; (cautivar) captivate, charm

seductor 1 adj seductive; (atractivo) attractive; oferta tempting **2** m seducer

seductora f seductress

segadora f reaper, harvester

segar ⟨1h & 1k⟩ v/t reap, harvest

seglar adj secular, lay atr

segmento m segment

segregación f segregation; **segregación racial** racial segregation

segregar ⟨1h⟩ v/t segregate

seguida f: **en seguida** at once, immediately

seguido 1 adj consecutive, successive; **ir todo seguido** go straight on **2** adv

L.Am. often, frequently

seguidor *m*, **seguidora** *f* follower, supporter

seguimiento *m* monitoring

seguir ⟨3l & 3d⟩ **1** *v/t* follow; *seguir a alguien* follow s.o. **2** *v/i* continue, carry on; *sigue enfadado conmigo* he's still angry with me; *seguir haciendo algo* go on doing sth, continue to do sth

según 1 *prp* according to; *según él* according to him **2** *adv* it depends

segunda *f*: *de segunda fig* second-rate

segundero *m* second hand

segundo *m/adj* second

seguridad *f* safety; *contra crimen* security; *(certeza)* certainty; *Seguridad Social Esp* Social Security

seguro 1 *adj* safe; *(estable)* steady; *(cierto)* sure; *es seguro (cierto)* it's a certainty; *seguro de sí mismo* self-confident, sure of o.s. **2** *adv* for sure **3** *m* COM insurance; *de puerta, coche* lock; *L.Am. (imperdible)* safety pin; *poner el seguro* lock the door; *ir sobre seguro* be on the safe side

seis *adj* six

seiscientos *adj* six hundred

seísmo *m* earthquake

selección *f* selection; *selección nacional* DEP national team

seleccionador *m*, **seleccionadora** *f* DEP: *seleccionador nacional* national team manager

seleccionar ⟨1a⟩ *v/t* choose, select

selectividad *f* *en España* university entrance exam

selecto *adj* select, exclusive

sellar ⟨1a⟩ *v/t* seal

sello *m* stamp; *fig* hallmark; *sello discográfico* record label

selva *f* *(bosque)* forest; *(jungla)* jungle

semáforo *m* traffic light

semana *f* week; *Semana Santa* Holy Week, Easter

semanal *adj* weekly

semanario *m* weekly

semblante *m* face

sembrado *m* sown field

sembrar ⟨1k⟩ *v/t* sow; *fig: pánico, inquietud etc* spread

semejante 1 *adj* similar; *jamás he oído semejante tontería* I've never heard such nonsense **2** *m* fellow human being, fellow creature

semejanza *f* similarity

semejarse ⟨1a⟩ *v/r* look alike, resemble each other

semen *m* BIO semen

semental *m toro* stud bull; *caballo* stallion

semestre *m* six-month period; EDU semester

semicírculo *m* semicircle

semiconductor *m* EL semiconductor

semifinal *f* DEP semifinal

semilla *f* seed

seminario *m* seminary

seminarista *m* seminarian

semítico *adj* Semitic

sémola *f* semolina

senado *m* senate

senador *m*, **senadora** *f* senator

sencillez *f* simplicity

sencillo 1 *adj* simple **2** *m L.Am.* small change

senda *f* path, track

senderismo *m* trekking, hiking

sendecrista *m/f* walker, hiker

sendero *m* path, track

sendos, -as *adj pl*: *les entregó sendos diplomas* he presented each of them with a diploma

senil *adj* senile

seno *m tb fig* bosom; *senos* breasts

sensación *f* feeling, sensation; *causar sensación fig* cause a sensation

sensacional *adj* sensational

sensacionalista *adj* sensationalist

sensatez *f* good sense

sensato *adj* sensible

sensibilidad *f* feeling; *(emotividad)* sensitivity

sensibilizar ⟨1f⟩ *v/t* make aware (*sobre* of)

sensible *adj* sensitive; *(apreciable)* appreciable, noticeable

sensiblero *adj* sentimental, schmaltzy F

sensor *m* sensor

sensorial *adj* sensory

sensual *adj* sensual

sensualidad *f* sensuality

sentada *f* sit-down

sentado *adj* sitting, seated; *dar por sentado fig* take for granted, assume

sentar ⟨1k⟩ *v/t fig* establish, create; *sentar las bases* lay the foundations, pave the way **2** *v/i*: *sentar bien a alguien de comida* agree with s.o.; *le sienta bien esa chaqueta* that jacket suits her, she looks good in that jacket **3** *v/r* sentarse sit down

sentencia *f* JUR sentence

sentenciar ⟨1b⟩ *v/t* JUR sentence

sentido *m* sense; *(significado)* meaning; *sentido común* common sense; *sentido del humor* sense of humo(u)r; *perder / recobrar el sentido* lose / regain consciousness

sentimental *adj* emotional; *ser senti-*

mental be sentimental
sentimentalismo *m* sentiment
sentimiento *m* feeling; *lo acompaño en el sentimiento* my condolences
sentir 1 *m* feeling, opinion **2** ⟨3i⟩ *v/t* feel; (*percibir*) sense; *lo siento* I'm sorry **3** *v/r* **sentirse** feel; *L.Am.* (*ofenderse*) take offense, *Br* take offence
seña *f* gesture, sign; *me hizo una seña para que entrara* he gestured to me to go in; *señas pl* address *sg*; *hacer señas* wave
señal *f* signal; *fig* sign, trace; COM deposit, down payment; *en señal de* as a token of, as a mark of
señalado *adj* special
señalar ⟨1a⟩ *v/t* indicate, point out
señalizar ⟨1f⟩ *v/t* signpost
Señor *m* Lord
señor *m* gentleman, man; *trato* sir; *escrito* Mr; *el señor López* Mr López; *los señores López* Mr and Mrs López
señora *f* lady, woman; *trato* ma'am, *Br* madam; *escrito* Mrs, Ms; *la señora López* Mrs López; *mi señora* my wife; *señoras y señores* ladies and gentlemen
señoría *f*: *su señoría* your Hono(u)r
señorial *adj* lordly, noble
señorita *f* young lady, young woman; *tratamiento* miss; *escrito* Miss; *la señorita López* Ms López, Miss López
señuelo *m* decoy
sepa *vb* → **saber**
separación *f* separation; *separación de bienes* JUR division of property
separado *adj* separated; *por separado* separately
separar ⟨1a⟩ **1** *v/t* separate **2** *v/r* **separarse** separate, split up F
separatismo *m* separatism
separatista *m/f* & *adj* separatist
sepia *f* ZO cuttlefish
sept.ᵉ *abr* (= *septiembre*) Sept. (= September)
septentrional *adj* northern
septiembre *m* September
séptimo *adj* seventh
sepulcro *m* tomb
sepultar ⟨1a⟩ *v/t* bury
sepultura *f* burial; (*tumba*) tomb; *dar sepultura a alguien* bury s.o.
sequedad *f fig* curtness
sequía *f* drought
séquito *m* retinue, entourage
ser ⟨2w; *part* **sido**⟩ **1** *v/i* be: *ser de Sevilla* be from Seville; *ser de madera / plata* be made of wood / silver; *es de Juan* it's Juan's, it belongs to Juan; *ser para* be for; *a no ser que* unless;

¡eso es! exactly!, that's right!; *es que ...* the thing is ...; *es de esperar* it's to be hoped; *¿cuánto es?* how much is it?; *¿qué es de ti?* how's life?, how're things?; *o sea* in other words **2** *m* being
Serbia Serbia
serenarse ⟨1a⟩ *v/r* calm down; *del tiempo* clear up
serenata *f* MÚS serenade
serenidad *f* calmness, serenity
sereno 1 *m*: *dormir al sereno* sleep outdoors **2** *adj* calm, serene
serial *m* TV, RAD series
serie *f* series; *fuera de serie* out of this world, extraordinary
seriedad *f* seriousness
serio *adj* serious; (*responsable*) reliable; *en serio* seriously
sermón *m* sermon
sermonear ⟨1a⟩ *v/i* preach
seropositivo *adj* MED HIV positive
serpentina *f* streamer
serpiente *f* ZO snake; *serpiente de cascabel* rattlesnake
serranía *f* mountainous region
serrar ⟨1k⟩ *v/t* saw
serrín *m* sawdust
serrucho *m* handsaw
servicial *adj* obliging, helpful
servicio *m* service; *servicios pl* restroom *sg*, *Br* toilets; *servicio doméstico* domestic service; *servicio militar* military service; *servicio pos(t)venta* after-sales service; *servicio de atención al cliente* customer service; *estar de servicio* be on duty
servidor *m* INFOR server
servil *adj* servile
servilismo *m* servility
servilleta *f* napkin, serviette
servilletero *m* napkin ring
servir ⟨3l⟩ **1** *v/t* serve **2** *v/i* be of use; *¿para qué sirve esto?* what is this (used) for?; *no servir de nada* be no use at all **3** *v/r* **servirse** help o.s.; *comida* help oneself to
servodirección power steering
sésamo *m* sesame
sesenta *adj* sixty
sesgar ⟨1h⟩ *v/t* slant, skew
sesión *f* session; *en cine, teatro* show, performance
sesionar ⟨1a⟩ *v/i L.Am.* be in session
seso *m* ANAT brain; *fig* brains *pl*, sense; *sesos* GASTR brains
set *m tenis* set
seta *f* BOT mushroom; *venenosa* toadstool
setecientos *adj* seven hundred
setenta *adj* seventy

seto *m* hedge

s.e.u.o. *abr* (= *salvo error u omisión*) E & OE (= errors and omissions excepted)

seudónimo *m* pseudonym

severo *adj* severe

sevillanas *fpl* folk dance from Seville

sexismo *m* sexism

sexista *m/f* & *adj* sexist

sexo *m* sex

sexto *adj* sixth

sexual *adj* sexual

sexualidad *f* sexuality

sexy *adj inv* sexy

shock *m* MED shock

si *conj* if; *si no* if not; *como si* as if; *por si* in case; *me pregunto si vendrá* I wonder whether he'll come

sí **1** *adv* yes **2** *pron tercera persona: singular masculino* himself; *femenino* herself; *cosa, animal* itself; *plural* themselves; *usted* yourself; *ustedes* yourselves; *por sí solo* by himself / itself, on his / its own

siamés *adj* Siamese

sibarita *m* bon vivant, epicure

Siberia Siberia

sicario *m* hired assassin

Sicilia Sicily

SIDA *abr* (= *síndrome de inmunidad deficiente adquirida*) Aids (= acquired immune-deficiency syndrome)

sidecar *m* sidecar

sideral *adj viajes* space *atr*; *espacio sideral* outer space

siderurgia *f* iron and steel making

sido *part* → *ser*

sidra *f* cider

siembra *f* sowing

siempre *adv* always; *siempre que* providing that, as long as; *lo de siempre* the same old story, *para siempre* for ever

sien *f* ANAT temple

siendo *vb* → *ser*

siento *vb* → *sentir*

sierra *f* saw; GEOG mountain range

siesta *f* siesta, nap; *dormir la siesta* have a siesta o nap

siete *adj* seven

sífilis *f* MED syphilis

siga *vb* → *seguir*

sigilo *m* secrecy, stealth

sigiloso *adj* stealthy

sigla *f* abbreviation, acronym

siglo *m* century; *hace siglos or un siglo que no le veo fig* I haven't seen him in a long long time

signatario *m*, -a *f* signatory

significado *m* meaning

significar ⟨1g⟩ *v/t* mean, signify

significativo *adj* meaningful, significant

signo *m* sign; *signo de admiración* exclamation mark; *signo de interrogación* question mark; *signo de puntuación* punctuation mark

sigo *vb* → *seguir*

siguiente **1** *adj* next, following **2** *pron* next (one)

sílaba *f* syllable

silbar ⟨1a⟩ *v/i* & *v/t* whistle

silbato *m* whistle

silbido *m* whistle

silenciador *m* AUTO muffler, *Br* silencer

silencio *m* silence; *en silencio* in silence, silently

silencioso *adj* silent

silicio *m* QUÍM silicon

silicona *f* silicone

silla *f* chair; *silla de montar* saddle; *silla de ruedas* wheelchair

sillín *m* saddle

sillón *m* armchair, easy chair

silueta *f* silhouette

silvestre *adj* wild

silvicultura *f* forestry

simbiosis *f* symbiosis

simbolismo *m* symbolism

simbolizar ⟨1f⟩ *v/t* symbolize

símbolo *m* symbol

simétrico *adj* symmetrical

similar *adj* similar

similitud *f* similarity

simio *m* ZO ape

simpatía *f* warmth, friendliness

simpático *adj* nice, like(e)able

simpatizante *m/f* sympathizer, supporter

simpatizar ⟨1f⟩ *v/i* sympathize

simple **1** *adj* simple, (*mero*) ordinary **2** *m* simpleton

simplicidad *f* simplicity

simplificar ⟨1g⟩ *v/t* simplify

simplista *adj* simplistic

simposio *m* symposium

simulación *f* simulation

simulacro *m* (*cosa falsa*) pretense, *Br* pretence, sham; (*simulación*) simulation; *simulacro de incendio* fire drill

simulador *m* simulator

simular ⟨1a⟩ *v/t* simulate

simultanear ⟨1a⟩ *v/t*: *simultanear dos cargos* hold two positions at the same time

simultáneo *adj* simultaneous

sin *prp* without; *sin que* without; *sin preguntar* without asking

sinagoga *f* synagogue

sinceridad *f* sincerity

sincero *adj* sincere

síncope *m* MED blackout

sincronizar ⟨1f⟩ *v/t* synchronize

S

sindical *adj* (labor, *Br* trade) union *atr*

sindicalismo *m* (labor, *Br* trade) union movement

sindicalista *m/f* (labor, *Br* trade) union member

sindicato *m* (labor, *Br* trade) union

síndrome *m* syndrome

sinfín *m*: **un sinfín de ...** no end of ...

sinfonía *f* MÚS symphony

singular 1 *adj* singular; *fig* outstanding, extraordinary **2** *m* GRAM singular

siniestro 1 *adj* sinister **2** *m* accident; (*catástrofe*) disaster

sinnúmero *m*: **un sinnúmero de** no end of

sino 1 *m* fate **2** *conj* but; (*salvo*) except; **no cena en casa, sino en el bar** he doesn't have dinner at home, he has it in the bar

sinónimo 1 *adj* synonymous **2** *m* synonym

sinopsis *f inv* synopsis

sinsentido *m* nonsense

sintaxis *f* syntax

síntesis *f inv* synthesis; (*resumen*) summary

sintético *adj* synthetic

sintetizador *m* MÚS synthesizer

síntoma *m* symptom

sintonía *f melodía* theme tune, signature tune; RAD tuning, reception; **estar en la sintonía de** RAD be tuned to

sintonizar ⟨1f⟩ **1** *v/t radio* tune in **2** *v/i fig* be in tune (**con** with)

sinuoso *adj* winding

sinusitis *f* MED sinusitis

sinvergüenza *m/f* swine; **¡qué sinvergüenza!** (*descarado*) what a nerve!

siquiera *adv*: **ni siquiera** not even; **siquiera bebe algo** *L.Am.* at least have a drink

sirena *f* siren; MYTH mermaid

Siria Syria

sirve *vb* → **servir**

sirvienta *f* maid

sirviente *m* servant

sisar ⟨1a⟩ *v/t* F pilfer

sísmico *adj* seismic

sistema *m* system; **sistema operativo** operating system

sistemático *adj* systematic

sitiar ⟨1b⟩ *v/t* surround, lay siege to

sitio *m* place; (*espacio*) room; **hacer sitio** make room; **en ningún sitio** nowhere; **sitio web** web site

situación *f* situation

situar ⟨1e⟩ **1** *v/t* place, put **2** *v/r* **situarse** be

S.L. *abr* (= **sociedad limitada**) Ltd (= limited)

slip *m* underpants *pl*

s/n *abr* (= **sin número**) not numbered

sobaco *m* armpit

sobar ⟨1a⟩ *v/t* handle, finger; F *sexualmente* grope F

soberanía *f* sovereignty

soberano *m*, **-a** *f* sovereign

soberbia *f* pride, arrogance

soberbio *adj* proud, arrogant; *fig* superb

sobornar ⟨1a⟩ *v/t* bribe

soborno *m* bribe

sobra *f* surplus, excess; **hay de sobra** there's more than enough; **sobras** leftovers

sobradamente *adv conocido* well

sobrar ⟨1a⟩ *v/t*: **sobra comida** there's food left over; **me sobró pintura** I had some paint left over; **sobraba uno** there was one left

sobre 1 *m* envelope **2** *prp* on; **sobre esto** about this; **sobre las tres** about three o'clock; **sobre todo** above all, especially

sobrecargar ⟨1h⟩ *v/t* overload

sobrecargo *m* AVIA chief flight attendant; MAR purser

sobrecoger ⟨2c⟩ *v/t* (*asustar*) strike fear into; (*impresionar*) have an effect on

sobredosis *f inv* overdose

sobrehumano *adj* superhuman

sobremesa *f*: **de sobremesa** afternoon *atr*

sobrenatural *adj* supernatural

sobrenombre *m* nickname

sobrentenderse ⟨2g⟩ *v/r*: **se sobrentiende de que ...** needless to say, ...

sobrepasar ⟨1a⟩ **1** *v/t* exceed, surpass; **me sobrepasa en altura** he is taller than me **2** *v/r* **sobrepasarse** go too far

sobrepeso *m* excess weight

sobreponerse ⟨2r; *part* **sobrepuesto** ⟩ *v/r*: **sobreponerse a** overcome, get over

sobrepuesto *part* → **sobreponerse**

sobresaliente *adj* outstanding, excellent

sobresalir ⟨3r⟩ *v/t* stick out, protrude; *fig* excel; **sobresalir entre** stand out among

sobresaltar ⟨1a⟩ **1** *v/t* startle **2** *v/r* **sobresaltarse** jump, start

sobresalto *m* jump, start

sobreseer ⟨2e⟩ *v/t* JUR dismiss

sobrestimar ⟨1a⟩ *v/t* overestimate

sobresueldo *m* bonus

sobrevalorar ⟨1a⟩ *v/t* overrate

sobrevenir ⟨3s⟩ *v/i* happen; **de guerra** break out

sobrevivir ⟨3a⟩ *v/i* survive

sobrevolar ⟨1m⟩ *v/t* fly over

sobriedad *f* soberness; **de comida**, **decoración** simplicity; (*moderación*) restraint

sobrina *f* niece

sobrino *m* nephew

sobrio *adj* sober; *comida, decoración* simple; *(moderado)* restrained

socarrón *adj* sarcastic, snide F

socavar ⟨1a⟩ *v/t tb fig* undermine

socavón *m* hollow

sociable *adj* sociable

social *adj* social

socialismo *m* socialism

socialista *m/f & adj* socialist

sociedad *f* society; ***sociedad anónima*** public corporation, *Br* public limited company; ***sociedad de consumo*** consumer society

socio *m*, **-a** *f de club, asociación etc* member; COM partner

sociología *f* sociology

socorrer ⟨2a⟩ *v/t* help, assist

socorrista *m/f* life guard

socorro *m* help, assistance; **¡socorro!** help!

soda *f* soda (water)

sodio *m* sodium

sofá *m* sofa

sofisticación *f* sophistication

sofisticado *adj* sophisticated

sofocante *adj* suffocating

sofocar ⟨1g⟩ **1** *v/t* suffocate; *incendio* put out **2** *v/r* **sofocarse** *fig* get embarrassed; *(irritarse)* get angry

sofoco *m fig* embarrassment

sofreír ⟨3m⟩ *v/t* sauté

sofrito *m* GASTR mixture of fried onions, peppers etc

software *m* INFOR software

soga *f* rope; **estar con la soga al cuello** F be in big trouble F

sois *vb* → **ser**

soja *f* soy, *Br* soya

sol *m* sun; **hace sol** it's sunny; **tomar el sol** sunbathe

solamente *adv* only

solapa *f* lapel

solar *m* vacant lot

solariego *adj:* **casa -a** family seat

solario, solárium *m* solarium

soldado *m/f* soldier

soldador *m* welder

soldadura *f* welding, soldering

soldar ⟨1m⟩ *v/t* weld, solder

soleado *adj* sunny

soledad *f* solitude, loneliness

solemne *adj* solemn

soler ⟨2h⟩ *v/i:* **soler hacer algo** usually do sth; **suele venir temprano** he usually comes early; **solía visitarme** he used to visit me

solera *f* traditional character

solfeo *m* (tonic) sol-fa

solicitante *m/f* applicant

solicitar ⟨1a⟩ *v/t* request; *empleo, beca* apply for

solícito *adj* attentive

solicitud *f* application, request

solidaridad *f* solidarity

solidario *adj* supportive, understanding

solidarizarse ⟨1f⟩ *v/r:* **solidarizarse con alguien** support s.o., back s.o.

solidez *f* solidity; *fig* strength

sólido *adj* solid; *fig* sound

solista *m/f* soloist

solitaria *f* zo tapeworm

solitario 1 *adj* solitary; *lugar* lonely **2** *m* solitaire, *Br* patience; **actuó en solitario** he acted alone

soliviantar ⟨1a⟩ **1** *v/t* incite, stir up **2** *v/r* **soliviantarse** *v/r* rise up, rebel

sollozar ⟨1f⟩ *v/i* sob

sollozo *m* sob

solo *adj* single; **estar solo** be alone; **sentirse solo** feel lonely; **un solo día** a single day; **a solas** alone, by o.s.; **por sí solo** by o.s.

sólo *adv* only, just

solomillo *m* GASTR sirloin

solsticio *m* solstice

soltar ⟨1m⟩ **1** *v/t* let go of; *(librar)* release, let go; *olor* give off **2** *v/r* **soltarse** free o.s.; **soltarse a andar / hablar** begin *o* start to walk / talk

soltera *f* single *o* unmarried woman

soltero 1 *adj* single, not married **2** *m* bachelor, unmarried man

solterona *f desp* old maid

soltura *f* fluency, ease

soluble *adj* soluble

solución *f* solution

solucionar ⟨1a⟩ *v/t* solve

solventar ⟨1a⟩ *v/t* resolve, settle

solvente *adj* solvent

somanta *f* F beating

sombra *f* shadow; **a la sombra de un árbol** in the shade of a tree; **a la sombra de** *fig* under the protection of; **sombra de ojos** eye shadow

sombrero *m* hat; **sombrero de copa** top hat

sombrilla *f* sunshade, beach umbrella

sombrío *adj fig* somber, *Br* sombre

someter ⟨2a⟩ **1** *v/t* subject; **someter algo a votación** put sth to the vote **2** *v/r* **someterse** yield (*a* to); *al ley* comply (*a* with); *(rendirse)* give in (*a* to); **someterse a tratamiento** undergo treatment

somier *m* bed base

somnífero *m* sleeping pill

somnolencia *f* sleepiness, drowsiness

somnoliento *adj* sleepy, drowsy

somos *vb* → **ser**

son[1] *m* sound; **al son de** to the sound of; **en son de paz** in peace

son[2] *vb* → **ser**

sonado *adj* F famous, well-known

sonajero *m* rattle

sonámbulo *m* sleep-walker

sonar ⟨1m⟩ **1** *v/i* ring out; **sonar a** sound like; **me suena esa voz** I know that voice, that voice sounds familiar **2** *v/r* **sonarse: sonarse (la nariz)** blow one's nose

sonata *f* MÚS sonata

sonda *f* MED catheter; **sonda espacial** space probe

sondaje *m* L.Am. poll, survey

sondear ⟨1a⟩ *v/t* fig survey, poll

sondeo *m*: **sondeo (de opinión)** survey, (opinion) poll

soneto *m* sonnet

sonido *m* sound

soniquete *m* droning

sonreír ⟨3m⟩ *v/i* smile

sonriente *adj* smiling

sonrisa *f* smile

sonrojar ⟨1a⟩ **1** *v/t*: **sonrojar a alguien** make s.o. blush **2** *v/r* **sonrojarse** blush

sonrojo *m* blush

sonsacar ⟨1g⟩ *v/t*: **sonsacar algo** worm sth out (**a** of), wheedle sth out (**a** of)

sonso *adj* L.Am. F silly

soñador **1** *adj* dreamy **2** *m* dreamer

soñar ⟨1m⟩ *v/t* dream (**con** about) **2** *v/i* dream; **¡ni soñarlo!** dream on! F

soñolencia *f* → **somnolencia**

soñoliento *adj* → **somnoliento**

sopa *f* soup; **estar hecho una sopa** F be sopping wet; **hasta en la sopa** F all over the place F

sopapo *m* F smack, slap

sopera *f* soup tureen

sopesar ⟨1a⟩ *v/t* fig weigh up

sopetón *m*: **de sopetón** unexpectedly

soplar ⟨1a⟩ **1** *v/i* del viento blow **2** *v/t* vela blow out; polvo blow away; **soplar algo a la policía** tip the police off about sth

soplete *m* welding torch

soplo *m*: **en un soplo** F in an instant

soplón *m* F informer, stool pigeon F

soponcio *m*: **le dio un soponcio** F he passed out

sopor *m* drowsiness, sleepiness

soporífero *adj* soporific

soportal *m* porch

soportar ⟨1a⟩ *v/t* fig put up with, bear; **no puedo soportar a José** I can't stand José

soporte *m* support, stand; **soporte lógico** INFOR software; **soporte físico** INFOR hardware

soprano MÚS **1** *m* soprano **2** *m/f* soprano

sorber ⟨2a⟩ *v/t* sip

sorbete *m* sorbet; C.Am. ice cream

sorbetería *f* C.Am. ice-cream parlo(u)r

sorbo *m* sip

sordera *f* deafness

sórdido *adj* sordid

sordo **1** *adj* deaf **2** *m*, -a *f* deaf person; **hacerse el sordo** turn a deaf ear

sordomudo **1** *adj* deaf and dumb **2** *m*, -a *f* deaf-mute

sorna *f* sarcasm; **con sorna** sarcastically, mockingly

sorocharse ⟨1a⟩ *v/r* Pe, Bol get altitude sickness

soroche *m* Pe, Bol altitude sickness

sorprendente *adj* surprising

sorprender ⟨2a⟩ *v/t* surprise

sorpresa *f* surprise; **de** or **por sorpresa** by surprise

sortear ⟨1a⟩ *v/t* draw lots for; obstáculo get round

sorteo *m* (lotería) lottery, (prize) draw

sortija *f* ring

sortilegio *m* spell, charm

SOS *m* SOS

sosa *f* QUÍM: **sosa cáustica** caustic soda

sosegado *adj* calm

sosegarse ⟨1h & 1k⟩ *v/r* calm down

sosería *f* insipidity, dullness

sosiego *m* calm, quiet

soslayar *adj*: **de soslayo** sideways

soslayo **1** *adj* tasteless, insipid; fig dull **2** *m*, -a *f* stick-in-the-mud F

sospecha *f* suspicion

sospechar ⟨1a⟩ **1** *v/t* suspect **2** *v/i* be suspicious; **sospechar de alguien** suspect someone

sospechoso **1** *adj* suspicious **2** *m*, -a *f* suspect

sostén *m* brassiere, bra; fig pillar, mainstay

sostener ⟨2l⟩ **1** *v/t* familia support; opinión hold **2** *v/r* **sostenerse** support o.s.; de pie stand up; **en el poder** stay, remain

sota *f* naipes jack

sotana *f* REL cassock

sótano *m* basement, Br cellar

soterrar ⟨1k⟩ *v/t* bury

soviético *adj* Soviet

soy *vb* → **ser**

soya *f* L.Am. soy, Br soya

spot *m* TV commercial

spray *m* spray

sprint *m* sprint

squash *m* DEP squash

Sr. *abr* (= **señor**) Mr

Sra. *abr* (= **señora**) Mrs

Sres. *abr* (= **Señores**) Messrs (= Messieurs)

Srta. *abr* (= **Señorita**) Miss

stand *m* COM stand

stock *m* stock; **tener en stock** have in stock

su, sus *adj pos*: de él his; de ella her; de cosa its; de usted, ustedes your; de ellos their; de uno one's

suave *adj* soft, smooth; *sabor, licor* mild

suavidad *f* softness, smoothness; *de sabor, licor* mildness

suavizante *m de pelo, ropa* conditioner

suavizar ⟨1f⟩ *v/t tb fig* soften

subacuático *adj* underwater

subalterno 1 *adj* subordinate **2** *m*, -a *f* subordinate

subasta *f* auction; **sacar a subasta** put up for auction

subastar ⟨1a⟩ *v/t* auction (off)

subcampeón *m* DEP runner-up

subconsciente *m/adj* subconscious

subcontrata(ción) *f* subcontracting

subdesarrollado *adj* underdeveloped

subdesarrollo *m* underdevelopment

subdirector *m*, **subdirectora** *f* deputy manager

súbdito *m* subject

subestimar ⟨1a⟩ *v/t* underestimate

subida *f* rise, ascent; **subida de los precios** rise in prices

subido 1 *part* → **subir 2** *adj*: **subido de tono** *fig* risqué, racy

subir ⟨3a⟩ **1** *v/t cuesta, escalera* go up, climb; *montaña* climb; *objeto* raise, lift; *intereses, precio* raise **2** *v/i para indicar acercamiento* come up; *para indicar alejamiento* go up; *de precio* rise, go up; *a un tren, autobús* get on; *a un coche* get in **3** *v/r* **subirse** go up; *a un árbol* climb

súbito *adj*: **de súbito** suddenly, all of a sudden

subjetivo *adj* subjective

subjuntivo *m* GRAM subjunctive

sublevar ⟨1a⟩ **1** *v/t* incite to revolt; *fig* infuriate, get angry **2** *v/r* **sublevarse** rise up, revolt

sublimación *f fig* sublimation

sublime *adj* sublime, lofty

subliminal *adj* subliminal

submarinismo *m* scuba diving

submarinista *m/f* scuba diver

submarino 1 *adj* underwater **2** *m* submarine

subnormal *adj* subnormal

subordinado 1 *adj* subordinate **2** *m*, -a *f* subordinate

subproducto *m* by-product

subrayar ⟨1a⟩ *v/t* underline; *fig* underline, emphasize

subrepticio *adj* surreptitious

subsanar ⟨1a⟩ *v/t* put right, rectify

subsidiario *adj* subsidiary

subsidio *m* welfare; *Br* benefit; **subsidio de paro** *or* **desempleo** unemployment compensation (*Br* benefit)

subsistencia *f* subsistence, survival; *de pobreza, tradición* persistence

subsistir ⟨3a⟩ *v/i* live, survive; *de pobreza, tradición* live on, persist

subte *m Rpl* subway, *Br* underground

subterfugio *m* subterfuge

subterráneo 1 *adj* underground **2** *m L.Am* subway, *Br* underground

subtítulo *m* subtitle

suburbio *m* slum area

subvención *f* subsidy

subvencionar ⟨1a⟩ *v/t* subsidize

subversivo *adj* subversive

subyacente *adj* underlying

subyugar ⟨1h⟩ *v/t* subjugate

succionar ⟨1a⟩ *v/t* suck

sucedáneo *m* substitute

suceder ⟨2a⟩ *v/i* happen, occur; **suceder a** follow; **¿qué sucede?** what's going on?

sucesión *f* succession; **sucesión al trono** succession to the throne

sucesivo *adj* successive; **en lo sucesivo** from now on

suceso *m* event

sucesor *m*, **sucesora** *f* successor

suciedad *f* dirt

sucio *adj tb fig* dirty

suculento *adj* succulent

sucumbir ⟨3a⟩ *v/i* succumb, give in

sucursal *f* COM branch

sudaca *m/f desp* South American

sudadera *f* sweatshirt

Sudáfrica South Africa

sudafricano 1 *adj* South African **2** *m*, -a *f* South African

Sudamérica South America

sudamericano 1 *adj* South American **2** *m*, -a *f* South American

sudar ⟨1a⟩ *v/i* sweat

sudario *m* REL shroud

sudeste *m* southeast

sudoeste *m* southwest

sudor *m* sweat

sudoración *f* perspiration

sudoroso *adj* sweaty

Suecia Sweden

sueco 1 *adj* Swedish **2** *m*, -a *f* Swede; **hacerse el sueco** F pretend not to hear, act dumb F

suegra *f* mother-in-law

suegro *m* father-in-law

suela *f de zapato* sole

sueldo *m* salary

suelo *m en casa* floor; *en el exterior* earth, ground; AGR soil; *estar por los suelos* F be at rock bottom F

suelto 1 *adj* loose, free; *un pendiente suelto* a single earring; *andar suelto* be at large **2** *m* loose change

sueño *m (estado de dormir)* sleep; *(fantasía, imagen mental)* dream; *tener sueño* be sleepy

suero *m* MED saline solution; *sanguíneo* blood serum

suerte *f* luck; *por suerte* luckily; *echar a suertes* toss for, draw lots for; *probar suerte* try one's luck

suertero *m*, **-a** *f L.Am.*, **suertudo** *m*, **-a** *f L.Am.* F lucky devil F

suéter *m* sweater

suficiente 1 *adj* enough, sufficient **2** *m* EDU pass

sufragar ⟨1h⟩ *v/t* COM meet, pay

sufragio *m*: *sufragio universal* universal suffrage

sufrimiento *m* suffering

sufrir ⟨3a⟩ **1** *v/t fig* suffer, put up with **2** *v/i* suffer *(de* from)

sugerencia *f* suggestion

sugerir ⟨3i⟩ *v/t* suggest

sugestionar ⟨1a⟩ *v/t* influence

sugestivo *adj* suggestive

suicida 1 *adj* suicidal **2** *m/f* suicide victim

suicidarse ⟨1a⟩ *v/r* commit suicide

suicidio *m* suicide

suite *f* suite

Suiza Switzerland

suizo 1 *adj* Swiss **2** *m*, **-a** *f* Swiss **3** *m* GASTR *sugar topped bun*

sujetador *m* brassiere, bra

sujetapapeles *m inv* paperclip

sujetar ⟨1a⟩ *v/t* hold (down), keep in place; *(sostener)* support

sujeto 1 *adj* secure **2** *m* individual; GRAM subject

sulfurarse ⟨1a⟩ *v/r fig* F blow one's top F

suma *f* sum; *en suma* in short

sumamente *adv* extremely, highly

sumar ⟨1a⟩ **1** *v/t* add; *5 y 6 suman 11* 5 and 6 make 11 **2** *v/i* add up **3** *v/r* *sumarse*: *sumarse a* join

sumario *m* summary; JUR indictment

sumergir ⟨3c⟩ *v/t* submerge, immerse **2** *v/r* *sumergirse fig* immerse o.s. (*en* in), throw o.s. (*en* into)

sumidero *m* drain

suministrar ⟨1a⟩ *v/t* supply, provide

suministro *m* supply

sumir ⟨3a⟩ **1** *v/t fig* plunge, throw (*en* in-

to) **2** *v/r* *sumirse fig* sink (*en* into)

sumisión *f* submission

sumiso *adj* submissive

sumo *adj* supreme; *con sumo cuidado* with the utmost care; *a lo sumo* at the most

suntuoso *adj* sumptuous

supe *vb* → *saber*

supedítar ⟨1a⟩ *v/t* make conditional (*a* upon)

súper *adj* F super F, great F

superable *adj* surmountable

superación *f* overcoming, surmounting

superar ⟨1a⟩ **1** *v/t persona* beat; *límite* go beyond, exceed; *obstáculo* overcome, surmount **2** *v/r* *superarse* surpass o.s., excel o.s.

superávit *m* surplus

superchería *f* trick, swindle

superdotado *adj* gifted

superficial *adj* superficial, shallow

superficialidad *f* superficiality, shallowness

superficie *f* surface

superfluo *adj* superfluous

superior 1 *adj* upper; *en jerarquía* superior; *ser superior a* be superior to **2** *m* superior

superiora *f* REL Mother Superior

superioridad *f* superiority

superlativo *adj* superlative

supermercado *m* supermarket

superpoblación *f* overpopulation

superponer ⟨2r⟩ *v/t* superimpose

superpotencia *f* POL superpower

superpuesto *adj* superimposed

supersónico *adj* supersonic

superstición *f* superstition

supersticioso *adj* superstitious

supervisar ⟨1a⟩ *v/t* supervise

supervisor *m*, **supervisora** *f* supervisor

supervivencia *f* survival

superviviente 1 *adj* surviving **2** *m/f* survivor

suplantar ⟨1a⟩ *v/t* replace, take the place of

suplementario *adj* supplementary

suplemento *m* supplement

suplente *m/f* substitute, stand-in

súplica *f* plea

suplicar ⟨1g⟩ *v/t cosa* plead for, beg for; *persona* beg

suplicio *m fig* torment, ordeal

suplir ⟨3a⟩ *v/t carencia* make up for; *(sustituir)* substitute

supo *vb* → *saber*

suponer ⟨2r; *part* *supuesto* ⟩ *v/t* suppose, assume

suposición *f* supposition

supositorio *m* MED suppository
supremacía *f* supremacy
supremo *adj* supreme
supresión *f* suppression; *de impuesto, ley* abolition; *de restricción* lifting; *de servicio* withdrawal
suprimir ⟨3a⟩ *v/t* suppress; *ley, impuesto* abolish; *restricción* lift; *servicio* withdraw; *puesto de trabajo* cut
supuesto 1 *part* → **suponer 2** *adj* supposed, alleged; *por supuesto* of course **3** *m* assumption
sur *m* south
surco *m* AGR furrow
sureño *adj* southern
surf(ing) *m* surfing
surfista *m/f* surfer
surgir ⟨3c⟩ *v/i fig* emerge; *de problema* come up; *de agua* spout
surrealismo *m* surrealism
surtido 1 *adj* assorted; *bien surtido* COM well stocked **2** *m* assortment, range
surtidor *m*: *surtidor de gasolina* or *de nafta* gas pump, *Br* petrol pump
surtir ⟨3a⟩ **1** *v/t* supply; *surtir efecto* have the desired effect **2** *v/i* spout **3** *v/r* surtirse stock up (*de* with)
susceptible *adj* touchy; *ser susceptible de mejora* leave room for improvement
suscitar ⟨1a⟩ *v/t* arouse; *polémica* generate; *escándalo* provoke
suscribir ⟨3a; *part* suscrito⟩ **1** *v/t* subscribe to **2** *v/r* suscribirse subscribe
suscripción *f* subscription
suscriptor *m*, **suscriptora** *f* subscriber
suscrito *part* → *suscribir*
suspender ⟨2a⟩ **1** *v/t empleado, alumno* suspend; *objeto* hang; *reunión* adjourn;

examen fail **2** *v/i* EDU fail
suspense *m fig* suspense
suspensión *f* suspension
suspenso 1 *adj alumnos suspensos* students who have failed; *en suspenso* suspended **2** *m* fail
suspensores *mpl* L.Am. suspenders, *Br* braces
suspicacia *f* suspicion
suspicaz *adj* suspicious
suspirar ⟨1a⟩ *v/i* sigh; *suspirar por algo* yearn for sth, long for sth
suspiro *m* sigh
sustancia *f* substance
sustancial *adj* substantial
sustantivo *m* GRAM noun
sustentar ⟨1a⟩ *v/t* sustain; *familia* support; *opinión* maintain
sustento *m* means of support
sustitución *f* substitution
sustituir ⟨3g⟩ *v/t*: *sustituir X por Y* replace X with Y, substitute Y for X
sustituto *m* substitute
susto *m* fright, scare; *dar* or *pegar un susto a alguien* give s.o. a fright
sustraer ⟨2p; *part* sustraído⟩ *v/t* subtract, take away; (*robar*) steal
sustraído *part* → *sustraer*
susurrar ⟨1a⟩ *v/t* whisper
susurro *m* whisper
sutil *adj fig* subtle
sutileza *f fig* subtlety
suyo, suya *pron pos*: *de él* his; *de ella* hers; *de usted, ustedes* yours; *de ellos* theirs; *los suyos* his / her etc folks, his / her etc family, *hacer de las -as* get up to one's old tricks; *salirse con la -a* get one's own way

T

tabaco *m* tobacco
tábano *m* ZO horsefly
tabarra *f*: *dar la tabarra a alguien* F bug s.o. F
taberna *f* bar
tabernero *m* bar owner, *Br* landlord; (*camarero*) bartender
tabique *m* partition, partition wall
tabla *f de madera* board, plank; PINT panel; (*cuadro*) table; *tabla de multiplicar* multiplication table; *tabla de planchar*

ironing board; *tabla de surf* surf board; *acabar* or *quedar en tablas* end in a tie
tablero *m* board, plank; *de juego* board; *tablero de mandos* or *de instrumentos* AUTO dashboard
tableta *f*: *tableta de chocolate* chocolate bar
tablón *m* plank; *tablón de anuncios* bulletin board, *Br* notice board
tabú *m* taboo
tabulador *m tb* INFOR tab key

taburete *m* stool
tacañería *f* F miserliness, stinginess F
tacaño 1 *adj* F miserly, stingy F **2** *m*, **-a** *f* F miser, tightwad F
tacha *f* flaw, blemish; **sin tacha** beyond reproach
tachadura *f* crossing-out
tachar ⟨1a⟩ *v/t* cross out
tacho *m* Rpl (*papelera*) wastepaper basket; *en la calle* garbage can, Br litter basket
tachón *m* crossing-out
tachuela *f* thumbtack, Br drawing pin
tácito *adj* tacit
taciturno *adj* taciturn
taco *m* F (*palabrota*) swear word; *L.Am.* heel; GASTR taco (*filled tortilla*)
tacón *m de zapato* heel; **zapatos de tacón** high-heeled shoes
táctica *f* tactics *pl*
táctico *adj* tactical
tacto *m* (sense of) touch; *fig* tact, discretion
TAE *abr* (= **tasa anual efectiva**) APR (= annual percentage rate)
tahona *f* bakery
tahúr *m* gambler, card-sharp F
taita *m S. Am.* F dad, pop F; *S. Am.* (*abuelo*) grandfather
tajada *f* GASTR slice; **agarrar una tajada** F get drunk; **sacar tajada** take a cut F
tajamar *m S. Am.* (*dique*) dike
tajante *adj* categorical
tajo *m* cut
tal 1 *adj* such; **no dije tal cosa** I said no such thing; **el gerente era un tal Lucas** the manager was someone called Lucas **2** *adv*: **tal como** so as; **dejó la habitación tal cual la encontró** she left the room just as she found it; **tal para cual** two of a kind; **tal vez** maybe, perhaps; **¿qué tal?** how's it going?; **¿que tal la película?** what was the movie like?; **con tal de que** + *subj* as long as, provided that
tala *f de árboles* felling
taladrar ⟨1a⟩ *v/t* drill
taladro *m* drill
talante *m* (*genio, humor*) mood; *un talante bonachón* a kindly nature; *de mal talante* in a bad mood
talar ⟨1a⟩ *v/t árbol* fell, cut down
talco *m* talc, talcum; *polvos de talco* talcum powder
talego *m* P 1000 pesetas
talento *m* talent
talismán *m* talisman
talla *f* size; (*estatura*) height; *C.Am.* F (*mentira*) lie; *dar la talla* fig make the grade

tallar ⟨1a⟩ *v/t* carve; *piedra preciosa* cut
tallarín *m* noodle
taller *m* workshop; *taller mecánico* AUTO repair shop; *taller de reparaciones* repair shop
tallo *m* BOT stalk, stem
talón *m* ANAT heel; COM stub; *talón de Aquiles* fig Achilles' heel; *pisar los talones a alguien* be hot on s.o.'s heels
talonario *m*: *talonario de cheques* check book, Br cheque book
tamal *m Méx, C.Am.* tamale (*meat wrapped in a leaf and steamed*)
tamaño 1 *adj*: *tamaño fallo / problema* such a great mistake / problem **2** *m* size
tambalearse ⟨1a⟩ *v/r* stagger, lurch; *de coche* sway
tambarria *f C.Am., Pe, Bol* F party
también *adv* also, too, as well; *yo también* me too; *él también dice que ...* he also says that ...
tambo *m Rpl* dairy farm; *Méx* type of large container
tambor *m* drum; *persona* drummer
tamborilear ⟨1a⟩ *v/i* drum with one's fingers
tamiz *m* sieve
tampoco *adv* neither; *él tampoco va* he's not going either
tampón *m* tampon; *de tinta* ink-pad
tan *adv* so; *tan ... como ...* as ... as ...; *tan sólo* merely
tanatorio *m* funeral parlo(u)r
tanda *f series, batch; (*turno*) shift; *L.Am.* (commercial) break; *tanda de penaltis* DEP penalty shootout
tanga *m* tanga
tangente *f* MAT tangent; *salir or irse por la tangente* F sidestep the issue, duck the question F
tangible *adj* fig tangible
tango *m* tango
tanque *m tb* MIL tank
tantear ⟨1a⟩ *v/t* feel; (*calcular a ojo*) work out roughly; *situación* size up; *persona* sound out; (*probar*) try out; *tantear el terreno* fig see how the land lies
tantito *adv Méx* a little
tanto 1 *pron* so much; *igual cantidad* as much; *un tanto* a little; *tantos pl* so many *pl*; *igual número* as many; *tienes tanto* you have so much; *no hay tantos como ayer* there aren't as many as yesterday; *a las -as de la noche* in the small hours **2** *adv* so much; *igual cantidad* as much; *periodo* so long; *tardó tanto como él* he took as long as him; *tanto mejor* so much the better; *no es para tanto*

it's not such a big deal; *estar al tanto* be informed (*de* about); *por lo tanto* therefore, so 3 *m* point; *tanto por ciento* percentage

tapa *f* lid; *tapa dura* hardback

tapacubos *m inv* AUTO hub cap

tapadera *f* lid; *fig* front

tapadillo *m*: *de tapadillo* on the sly

tapado *m Arg, Chi* coat

tapar ⟨1a⟩ **1** *v/t* cover; *recipiente* put the lid on **2** *v/r taparse* wrap up; *taparse los ojos* cover one's eyes

taparrabo *m* loincloth

tapete *m* tablecloth; *poner algo sobre el tapete* bring sth up for discussion

tapia *f* wall; *más sordo que una tapia* as deaf as a post

tapicería *f* upholstery

tapicero *m*, *-a f* upholsterer

tapioca *f* tapioca

tapir *m* tapir

tapiz *m* tapestry

tapizar ⟨1f⟩ *v/t* upholster

tapón *m* top, cap; *de baño* plug; *de tráfico* traffic jam

taponar ⟨1a⟩ *v/t* block; *herida* swab

tapujo *m*: *sin tapujos* openly

taquicardia *f* MED tachycardia

taquigrafía *f* shorthand

taquilla *f* ticket office; TEA box-office; *C.Am.* (*bar*) small bar

taquillero 1 *adj cantante* popular; *una película -a* a hit movie, a box-office hit **2** *m*, *-a f* ticket clerk

tara *f* defect

tarado *adj* F stupid, dumb F

tarántula *f* ZO tarantula

tararear ⟨1a⟩ *v/t* hum

tardar ⟨1a⟩ *v/i* take a long time; *tardamos dos horas* we were two hours overdue o late; *¡no tardes!* don't be late; *a más tardar* at the latest; *¿cuánto se tarda …?* how long does it take to …?

tarde 1 *adv* late; *tarde o temprano* sooner or later **2** *f hasta las 5 ó 6* afternoon; *desde las 5 ó 6* evening; *¡buenas tardes!* good afternoon / evening; *por la tarde* in the afternoon / evening; *de tarde en tarde* from time to time

tardón *adj* F slow; (*impuntual*) late

tarea *f* task, job; *tareas pl domésticas* housework *sg*

tarifa *f* rate; *de tren* fare; *tarifa plana* flat rate

tarima *f* platform; *suelo de tarima* wooden floor

tarjeta *f* card; *tarjeta amarilla* DEP yellow card; *tarjeta de crédito* credit card; *tarjeta de embarque* AVIA boarding card;

tarjeta de sonido INFOR sound card; *tarjeta de visita* (business) card; *tarjeta gráfica* INFOR graphics card; *tarjeta inteligente* smart card; *tarjeta monedero* electronic purse; *tarjeta postal* postcard; *tarjeta roja* DEP red card; *tarjeta telefónica* phone card

tarro *m* jar; P (*cabeza*) head

tarta *f* cake; *plana* tart; *tarta helada* ice-cream cake

tartamudear ⟨1a⟩ *v/i* stutter, stammer

tartamudez *f* stuttering, stammering

tartamudo 1 *adj* stuttering, stammering; *ser tartamudo* stutter, stammer **2** *m*, *-a f* stutterer, stammerer

tartera *f* lunch box

tarugo *m* F blockhead

tarumba F crazy F; *volverse tarumba* go crazy

tasa *f* rate; (*impuesto*) tax; *tasa de desempleo* or *paro* unemployment rate

tasar ⟨1a⟩ *v/t* fix a price for; (*valorar*) assess

tasca *f* F bar

tata *m L.Am.* F (*abuelo*) grandpa F

tatarabuela *f* great-great-grandmother

tatarabuelo *m* great-great-grandfather

tataranieta *f* great-great-granddaughter

tataranieto *m* great-great-grandson

tate *int* F (*ahora caigo*) oh I see; (*cuidado*) look out!

tatuaje *m* tattoo

taurino *adj* bullfighting *atr*

Tauro *m/f inv* ASTR Taurus

tauromaquia *f* bullfighting

taxi *m* cab, taxi

taxista *m/f* cab o taxi driver

taza *f* cup; *del váter* bowl

tazón *m* bowl

te *pron directo* you; *indirecto* (to) you; *reflexivo* yourself

té *m* tea

teatral *adj fig* theatrical

teatro *m tb fig* theater, *Br* theatre

tebeo *m* children's comic

techar ⟨1a⟩ *v/t* roof

techo *m* ceiling; (*tejado*) roof; *techo solar* AUTO sun-roof; *los sin techo* the homeless; *tocar techo* fig peak

tecla *f* key

teclado *m* MÚS, INFOR keyboard

teclear ⟨1a⟩ *v/t* key

técnica *f* technique

técnico 1 *adj* technical **2** *m/f* technician; *de televisor, lavadora etc* repairman

tecnología *f* technology; *alta tecnología* hi-tech; *tecnología punta* state-of-the-art technology, leading-edge technology

tecolote *m Méx, C.Am.* (*búho*) owl

T

tedio *m* tedium
tedioso *adj* tedious
teja *f* roof tile; *a toca teja* in hard cash
tejado *m* roof
tejanos *mpl* jeans
tejemanejes *mpl* F scheming *sg*, plotting *sg*
tejer ⟨2a⟩ **1** *v/t* weave; *(hacer punto)* knit; F *intriga* devise **2** *v/i* *L.Am.* F plot, scheme
tejido *m* fabric; ANAT tissue
tejo *m* BOT yew; *tirar a alguien los tejos* F hit on s.o. F, come on to s.o. F
tejón *m* ZO badger
Tel. *abr* (= *teléfono*) Tel. (= telephone)
tela *f* fabric, material; *tela de araña* spiderweb; *poner en tela de juicio* call into question; *hay tela para rato* F there's a lot to be done
telar *m* loom
telaraña *f* spiderweb
tele *f* F TV, *Br* telly F
telearrastre *m* drag lift
telebanca *f* telephone banking
telecabina *f* cable car
telecomedia *f* sitcom
telecompra *f* home shopping
telecomunicaciones *fpl* telecommunications
telediario *m* TV (television) news *sg*
teledirigido *adj* remote-controlled
teléf. *abr* (= *teléfono*) tel. (= telephone)
teleférico *m* cable car
telefilm(e) *m* TV movie
telefonear ⟨1a⟩ *v/t & v/i* call, phone
telefonema *m* *L.Am.* (phone) message
telefónico *adj* (tele)phone *atr*
teléfono *m* (tele)phone; *teléfono inalámbrico* cordless (phone); *teléfono móvil* cellphone, *Br* mobile (phone)
telégrafo *m* telegraph
telegrama *m* telegram
telemando *m* remote control
telemática *f* data comms
telenovela *f* soap (opera)
teleobjetivo *m* FOT telephoto lens
telepatía *f* telepathy
telescópico *adj* telescopic
telescopio *m* telescope
teleserie *f* (television) series
telesilla *f* chair lift
telespectador *m*, **telespectadora** *f* (television) viewer
telesquí *m* drag lift
teletexto *m* teletext
teletienda *f* home shopping
teletrabajo *m* teleworking
teletrabajador *m*, **teletrabajadora** *f* teleworker

televidente *m/f* (television) viewer
televisar ⟨1a⟩ *v/t* televise
televisión *f* television; *televisión por cable* cable (television); *televisión digital* digital television; *televisión de pago* pay-per-view television; *televisión vía satélite* satellite television
televisivo *adj* television *atr*
televisor *m* TV, television (set); *televisor en color* color TV
télex *m* telex
telón *m* TEA curtain; *el telón de acero* POL the Iron Curtain; *telón de fondo* *fig* backdrop, background
telonero *m*, **-a** *f* supporting artist
tema *m* subject, topic; MÚS, *de novela* theme
temario *m* syllabus
temático *adj* thematic
temblar ⟨1k⟩ *v/i* tremble, shake; *de frío* shiver
temblor *m* trembling, shaking; *de frío* shivering; *L.Am.* (*terremoto*) earthquake; *temblor de tierra* earth tremor
tembloroso *adj* trembling, shaking; *de frío* shivering
temer ⟨2a⟩ **1** *v/t* be afraid of **2** *v/r* **temerse** be afraid; *me temo que no podrá venir* I'm afraid he won't be able to come; *temerse lo peor* fear the worst
temerario *adj* rash, reckless
temeridad *f* rashness, recklessness
temible *adj* terrifying
temor *m* fear
témpano *m* ice floe
temperamento *m* temperament
temperante *adj* *Méx* teetotal
temperatura *f* temperature
tempestad *f* storm
tempestuoso *adj* *tb fig* stormy
templado *adj* warm; *clima* temperate; *fig* moderate, restrained
templanza *f* restraint
templar ⟨1a⟩ *v/t ira, nervios etc* calm
templo *m* temple
temporada *f* season; *una temporada* a time, some time
temporal 1 *adj* temporary **2** *m* storm
temporizador *m* timer
tempranear ⟨1a⟩ *v/i L.Am.* get up early
temprano *adj & adv* early
ten *vb* → *tener*
tenacidad *f* tenacity
tenaz *adj* determined, tenacious
tenaza *f* pincer, claw; *tenazas* pincers; *para las uñas* pliers
tendedero *m* clotheshorse, airer
tendencia *f* tendency; (*corriente*) trend
tendencioso *adj* tendentious

tender ⟨2g⟩ **1** v/t ropa hang out; cable lay; **le tendió la mano** he held out his hand to her **2** v/i: **tender a** tend to **3** v/r **tenderse** lie down

tenderete m stall

tendero m, -a f storekeeper, shopkeeper

tendido m EL: **tendido eléctrico** power lines pl

tendón m ANAT tendon; **tendón de Aquiles** Achilles' tendon

tenebroso adj dark, gloomy

tenedor m fork

tener ⟨2l⟩ **1** v/t have; **tener 10 años** be 10 (years old); **tener un metro de ancho / largo** be one metre (Br meter) wide / long; **tener por** consider to be; **tengo que madrugar** I must get up early, I have to o I've got to get up early; **conque ¿esas tenemos?** so that's how it is, eh? **2** v/r **tenerse** stand up; fig stand firm; **se tiene por atractivo** he thinks he's attractive

tenga vb → **tener**

tengo vb → **tener**

tenia f ZO tapeworm

teniente m/f MIL lieutenant

tenis m tennis; **tenis de mesa** table tennis

tenista m/f tennis player

tenor m MÚS tenor; **a tenor de** along the lines of

tenorio m lady-killer

tensar ⟨1a⟩ v/t tighten; músculo tense, tighten

tensión f tension; EL voltage; MED blood pressure

tenso adj tense; cuerda, cable taut

tentación f temptation

tentáculo m ZO, fig tentacle

tentador adj tempting

tentar ⟨1k⟩ v/t tempt, entice

tentativa f attempt

tentempié m F snack

tenue adj faint

teñir ⟨3h & 3l⟩ v/t dye; fig tinge

teología f theology

teorema m theorem

teoría f theory; **en teoría** in theory

tequila m tequila

terapeuta m/f therapist

terapéutico adj therapeutic

terapia f therapy

tercer adj third; **Tercer Mundo** Third World

tercermundista adj Third-World atr

tercero m/adj third

terciarse ⟨1b⟩ v/r de oportunidad come up

tercio m third

terciopelo m velvet

terco adj stubborn

tergiversar ⟨1a⟩ v/t distort, twist

termas fpl hot springs

térmico adj heat atr

terminación f GRAM ending

terminal **1** m INFOR terminal **2** f AVIA terminal; **terminal de autobuses** bus station

terminante adj categorical

terminar ⟨1a⟩ **1** v/t end, finish **2** v/i end, finish; (parar) stop **3** v/r **terminarse** run out; (finalizar) come to an end; **se ha terminado la leche** we've run out of milk, the milk's all gone

término m end, conclusion; (palabra) term; **término municipal** municipal area; **por término medio** on average; **poner término a algo** put an end to sth

terminología f terminology

termita f ZO termite

termo m thermos® (flask)

termómetro m thermometer

termostato m thermostat

ternera f calf; GASTR veal

ternero m calf

terno m CSur suit

ternura f tenderness

terracota f terracotta

terraplén m embankment

terrateniente m/f landowner

terraza f terrace; (balcón) balcony; (café) sidewalk café

terremoto m earthquake

terrenal adj earthly, worldly

terreno m land; fig field; **un terreno** a plot o piece of land; **terreno de juego** DEP field

terrestre adj animal land atr; transporte surface atr; **la atmósfera terrestre** the earth's atmosphere

terrible adj terrible, awful

territorial adj territorial

territorio m territory

terrón m lump, clod; **terrón de azúcar** sugar lump

terror m terror

terrorífico adj terrifying

terrorismo m terrorism

terrorista **1** adj terrorist atr **2** m/f terrorist

terso adj smooth

tertulia f TV debate, round table discussion

tertuliar ⟨1b⟩ v/i L.Am. get together for a discussion

tesina f dissertation

tesis f inv thesis

tesitura f situation

tesón m tenacity, determination

tesorero m, -a f treasurer

tesoro *m* treasure; ***tesoro público*** treasury

test *m* test

testa *f* head

testaferro *m* front man

testamento *m* JUR will

testarudez *f* stubbornness

testarudo *adj* stubborn

testículo *m* ANAT testicle

testificar ⟨1g⟩ 1 *v/t* (*probar, mostrar*) be proof of; ***testificar que*** JUR testify that, give evidence that 2 *v/i* testify, give evidence

testigo 1 *m/f* JUR witness; ***testigo de cargo*** witness for the prosecution; ***testigo ocular*** *or* ***presencial*** eye witness 2 *m* DEP baton

testimonio *m* testimony, evidence

teta *f* F boob F; ZO teat, nipple

tétanos *m* MED tetanus

tetera *f* teapot

tetilla *f de hombre* nipple

tetina *f de biberón* teat

tetrabrik® *m* carton

tétrico *adj* gloomy

textil 1 *adj* textile *atr* 2 *mpl:* ***textiles*** textiles

texto *m* text

textual *adj* textual

textura *f* texture

tez *f* complexion

ti *pron* you; *reflexivo* yourself; ***¿y a ti qué te importa?*** so what?, what's it to you?

tía *f* aunt; F (*chica*) girl, chick F; ***¡tía buena!*** F hey gorgeous! F

tianguis *m* Méx, C.Am. market

tibio *adj* tb F lukewarm

tiburón *m* ZO, *fig* F shark

tic *m* MED tic

ticket *m* (*sales*) receipt

tictac *m* tick-tock

tiempo *m* time; (*clima*) weather; GRAM tense; ***tiempo libre*** spare time, free time; ***tiempo real*** INFOR real time; *a **tiempo*** in time; *a un tiempo, al mismo tiempo* at the same time; *antes de tiempo llegar* ahead of time, early; *celebrar victoria* too soon; ***con tiempo*** in good time, early; ***desde hace mucho tiempo*** for a long time; ***hace buen*** / ***mal tiempo*** the weather's fine / bad; ***hace mucho tiempo*** a long time ago

tienda *f* store, shop; ***tienda de campaña*** tent; ***ir de tiendas*** go shopping

tiene *vb* → **tener**

tientas *fpl:* ***andar a tientas*** *fig* feel one's way

tiento *m:* ***con tiento*** *fig* carefully

tierno *adj* soft; *carne* tender; *pan* fresh; *persona* tender-hearted

tierra *f* land; *materia* soil, earth; (*patria*) native land, homeland; ***la Tierra*** the earth; ***tierra firme*** dry land, terra firma; ***echar por tierra*** ruin, wreck

tieso *adj* stiff, rigid

tiesto *m* flower pot

tifón *m* typhoon

tifus *m* MED typhus

tigre *m* ZO tiger; *L.Am.* puma; *L.Am.* (*leopardo*) jaguar

tigresa *f* tigress

tijeras *fpl* scissors

tila *f* lime blossom tea

tildar ⟨1a⟩ *v/t:* ***tildar a alguien de*** *fig* brand s.o. as

tilde *f* accent; *en ñ* tilde

tilín *m:* ***me hizo tilín*** F I took an immediate liking to her

timador *m*, **timadora** *f* cheat

timar ⟨1a⟩ *v/t* cheat

timba *f* F gambling den

timbal *m* MÚS kettle drum

timbre *m de puerta* bell; *Méx* (*postage*) stamp

timidez *f* shyness, timidity

tímido *adj* shy, timid

timo *m* confidence trick, swindle

timón *m* MAR, AVIA rudder

tímpano *m* ANAT eardrum

tina *f* large jar; *L.Am.* (*bañera*) (bath)tub

tinglado *m fig* F mess

tinieblas *fpl* darkness *sg*

tino *m* aim, marksmanship; (*sensatez*) judg(e)ment; ***con mucho tino*** wisely, sensibly

tinta *f* ink; ***de buena tinta*** *fig* on good authority; ***medias tintas*** *fig* half measures

tinte *m* dye; *fig* veneer, gloss

tinterillo *m L.Am.* F shyster F

tintero *m* inkwell; ***dejarse algo en el tintero*** leave sth unsaid

tintin(e)ar ⟨1a⟩ *v/t* jingle

tinto *adj:* ***vino tinto*** red wine

tintorería *f* dry cleaner's

tío *m* uncle; F (*tipo*) guy F; F *apelativo* pal F

tiovivo *m* carousel, merry-go-round

típico *adj* typical (*de* of)

tipo *m* type, kind; F *persona* guy F; COM rate; ***tipo de cambio*** exchange rate; ***tipo de interés*** interest rate; ***tener buen tipo*** be well built; *de mujer* have a good figure

tipográfico *adj* typographic(al)

tíquet, tiquete *m L.Am.* receipt

tiquismiquis *m/f* F fuss-budget F, *Br* fusspot F

tira *f* strip; ***la tira de*** F loads of F, masses of F; ***tira y afloja*** *fig* give and take

tonelada

tirabuzón *m* curl; (*sacacorchos*) corkscrew

tirachinas *m inv* slingshot, *Br* catapult

tirada *f* TIP print run; *de una tirada* in one go

tiradero *m Méx* dump

tirado *adj* P (*barato*) dirt-cheap F; *estar tirado* (*fácil*) be a walkover F *o* a piece of cake F

tiradores *mpl Arg* suspenders, *Br* braces

tiranía *f* tyranny

tirano 1 *adj* tyrannical **2** *m*, **-a** *f* tyrant

tirante 1 *adj* taut; *fig* tense **2** *m* strap; *tirantes* suspenders, *Br* braces

tirantez *f fig* tension

tirar ⟨1a⟩ **1** *v/t* throw; *edificio, persona* knock down; (*volcar*) knock over; *basura* throw away; *dinero* waste, throw away F; TIP print; F *en examen* fail **2** *v/i* pull, attract; (*disparar*) shoot; *tirar a* tend toward; *tirar a conservador* have conservative tendencies; *tirar de algo* pull sth; *ir tirando* F get by, manage **3** *v/r* *tirarse* throw o.s.; F *tiempo* spend; *tirarse a alguien* P screw s.o. P

tirita *f* MED Bandaid®, *Br* plaster

tiritar ⟨1a⟩ *v/i* shiver

tiro *m* shot; *tiro al blanco* target practice; *al tiro* CSur F at once, right away; *de tiros largos* F dressed up; *ni a tiros* F for love nor money; *le salió el tiro por la culata* F it backfired on him; *le sentó como un tiro* F he needed it like a hole in the head F

tirón *m* tug, jerk; *de un tirón* at a stretch, without a break

tiroteo *m* shooting

tirria *f*: *tener tirria a alguien* F have it in for s.o. F

tisana *f* herbal tea

títere *m tb fig* puppet; *no dejar títere con cabeza* F spare no-one

titiritero *m*, *-a* *f* acrobat

titubear ⟨1a⟩ *v/i* waver, hesitate

titubeo *m* wavering, hesitation

titular *m de periódico* headline

titularse ⟨1a⟩ *v/r* be entitled

título *m* title; *universitario* degree; JUR title; COM bond; *tener muchos títulos* be highly qualified; *a título de* as; *títulos de crédito* credits

tiza *f* chalk

tiznar ⟨1a⟩ *v/t* blacken

tizón *m* ember

tlapalería *f Méx* hardware store

TLC *abr* (= *Tratado de Libre Comercio*) NAFTA (= North American Free Trade Agreement)

toalla *f* towel; *tirar or arrojar la toalla fig*

throw in the towel

toallero *m* towel rail

tobillo *m* ankle

tobogán *m* slide

tocadiscos *m inv* record player

tocado *adj*: *estar tocado fig* F be crazy F

tocador *m* dressing-table

tocante: *en lo tocante a …* with regard to …

tocar ⟨1g⟩ **1** *v/t* touch; MÚS play **2** *v/i* *L.Am. a la puerta* knock (on the door); *L.Am.* (*sonar la campanita*) ring the doorbell; *te toca jugar* it's your turn **3** *v/r* *tocarse* touch

tocateja: *a tocateja* in hard cash

tocayo *m*, *-a* *f* namesake

tocino *m* bacon

tocólogo *m*, *-a* *f* obstetrician

todavía *adv* still; yet; *todavía no ha llegado* he still hasn't come, he hasn't come yet; *todavía no* not yet

todo 1 *adj* all; *todos los domingos* every Sunday; *-a la clase* the whole *o* the entire class **2** *adv* all; *estaba todo sucio* it was all dirty; *con todo* all the same; *del todo* entirely, absolutely **3** *pron* all, everything; *pl* everybody, everyone; *ir a por -as* go all out

todoterreno *m* AUTO off-road *o* all-terrain vehicle

toldo *m* awning; *L.Am.* Indian hut

tolerancia *f* tolerance

tolerar ⟨1a⟩ *v/t* tolerate

toma *f* FOT shot, take; *toma de conciencia* realization; *toma de corriente* outlet, socket; *toma de posesión* POL taking office

tomado *adj Méx* F (*borracho*) drunk

tomadura *f*: *tomadura de pelo* F joke

tomar ⟨1a⟩ **1** *v/t* take; *decisión* make, take; *bebida, comida* have, *tomarla con alguien* F have it in for s.o. F; *tomar el sol* sunbathe; *¡toma!* here (you are); *toma y daca* give and take **2** *v/i* *L.Am.* drink; *tomar por la derecha* turn right **3** *v/r* *tomarse* take; *comida, bebida* have; *se lo tomó a pecho* he took it to heart

tomate *m* tomato

tomavistas *m inv* movie camera, cine camera

tomillo *m* BOT thyme

tomo *m* volume; tome; *un timador de tomo y lomo* F an out-and-out conman

ton *m*: *sin ton ni son* for no particular reason

tonada *f* song

tonalidad *f* tonality

tonel *m* barrel, cask

tonelada *f peso* ton

tónica *f* tonic

tónico *m* MED tonic

tonificar ⟨1g⟩ *v/t* tone up

tono *m* MÚS, MED, PINT tone

tontería *f fig* stupid *o* dumb F thing; **tonterías** *pl* nonsense *sg*

tonto 1 *adj* silly, foolish 2 *m*, -a *f* fool, idiot; **hacer el tonto** play the fool; **hacerse el tonto** act dumb F

top *m prenda* top

topacio *m* MIN topaz

toparse ⟨1a⟩ *v/r*: **toparse con alguien** bump into s.o., run into s.o.

tope *m* limit; *pieza* stop; *Méx* en la calle speed bump; **pasarlo a tope** F have a great time; **estar hasta los topes** F be bursting at the seams F

tópico *m* cliché, platitude

topo *m* ZO mole

toque *m*: **toque de queda** MIL, *fig* curfew; **dar los últimos toques** put the finishing touches (*a* to)

toquilla *f* shawl

tórax *m* ANAT thorax

torbellino *m* whirlwind

torcer ⟨2b & 2h⟩ 1 *v/t* twist; (*doblar*) bend; (*girar*) turn 2 *v/i* turn; **torcer a la derecha** turn right 3 *v/r* **torcerse** twist, bend; *fig* go wrong; **torcerse un pie** sprain one's ankle

torcido *adj* twisted, bent

toreador *m esp* L.Am. bullfighter

torear ⟨1a⟩ 1 *v/i* fight bulls 2 *v/t* fight; *fig* dodge, sidestep

toreo *m* bullfighting

torera *f*: **saltarse algo a la torera** F flout sth, disregard sth

torero *m* bullfighter

tormenta *f* storm

tormento *m* torture

tornado *m* tornado, twister F

tornarse ⟨1a⟩ *v/r* triste, difícil etc become

torneo *m* competition, tournament

tornillo *m* screw; *con tuerca* bolt; **le falta un tornillo** F he's got a screw loose F

torniquete *m* turnstile; MED tourniquet

torno *m de alfarería* wheel; **en torno a** around, about

toro *m* bull; **ir a los toros** go to a bullfight; **coger el toro por los cuernos** take the bull by the horns

toronja *f* L.Am. grapefruit

torpe *adj* clumsy; (*tonto*) dense, dim

torpedo *m* MIL torpedo

torpeza *f* clumsiness; (*necedad*) stupidity

torre *f* tower; **torre de control** AVIA control tower

torrencial *adj* torrential

torrente *m fig* avalanche, flood

torrezno *m* GASTR fried rasher of bacon

tórrido *adj* torrid

torrija *f* GASTR French toast

torta *f* cake; *plana* tart; F slap

tortazo *m* F crash; (*bofetada*) punch

tortícolis *m* MED crick in the neck

tortilla *f* omelette; L.Am. tortilla

tortillera *f* V dyke F, lesbian

tortuga *f* ZO tortoise; *marina* turtle; **a paso de tortuga** *fig* at a snail's pace

tortuoso *adj fig* tortuous

tortura *f tb fig* torture

torturar ⟨1a⟩ *v/t* torture

tos *f* cough

tosco *adj fig* rough, coarse

toser ⟨2a⟩ *v/i* cough

tostada *f* piece of toast

tostado *adj* (*moreno*) brown, tanned

tostador *m* toaster

tostar ⟨1m⟩ 1 *v/t* toast; *café* roast; **al sol** tan 2 *v/r* **tostarse** tan, get brown

tostón *m* F bore

total 1 *adj* total, complete; **en total** altogether, in total 2 *m* whole; **un total de 50 personas** a total of 50 people

totalidad *f* totality

totalitario *adj* totalitarian

tóxico *adj* toxic

toxicómano *m*, -a *f* drug addict

toxina *f* toxin

tozudo *adj* obstinate

trabajador 1 *adj* hard-working 2 *m*, trabajadora *f* worker; **trabajador eventual** casual worker

trabajar ⟨1a⟩ 1 *v/i* work 2 *v/t* work; *tema, músculos* work on

trabajo *m* work; **trabajo en equipo** team work; **trabajo temporal** temporary work; **trabajo a tiempo parcial** part-time work

trabajoso *adj* hard, laborious

trabalenguas *m inv* tongue twister

trabar ⟨1a⟩ 1 *v/t* conversación, amistad strike up 2 *v/r* **trabarse** get tangled up

trabucarse ⟨1g⟩ *v/r* get all mixed up

tracción *f* TÉC traction; **tracción delantera/trasera** front / rear-wheel drive

tractor *m* tractor

tradición *f* tradition

tradicional *adj* traditional

traducción *f* translation

traducir ⟨3o⟩ *v/t* translate

traductor *m*, traductora *f* translator

traer ⟨2p; *part* traído⟩ 1 *v/t* bring; **traer consigo** involve, entail; **este periódico la trae en portada** this newspaper carries it on the front page 2 *v/r* **traerse: este asunto se las trae** F it's a very tricky

matter
traficante *m* dealer
traficar ⟨1g⟩ *v/i* deal (**en** in)
tráfico *m* traffic; **tráfico de drogas** drug trafficking, drug dealing
tragaperras *f inv* slot machine
tragar ⟨1h⟩ **1** *v/t* swallow; **no lo trago** I can't stand him *o* bear him **2** *v/r* **tragarse** *tb* fig F swallow
tragedia *f* tragedy
trágico *adj* tragic
tragicomedia *f* tragicomedy
trago *m* mouthful; F *bebida* drink; **de un trago** in one gulp; **pasar un mal trago** *fig* have a hard time
tragón *adj* greedy
traición *f* treachery, betrayal
traicionar ⟨1a⟩ *v/t* betray
traidor **1** *adj* treacherous **2** *m*, **traidora** *f* traitor
traido *part* → **traer**
traigo *vb* → **traer**
tráiler *m* trailer
traje **1** *m* suit; **traje de baño** swimsuit **2** *vb* → **traer**
trajín *m* hustle and bustle
trajo *vb* → **traer**
trama *f* (*tema*) plot
tramar ⟨1a⟩ *v/t complot* hatch
tramitar ⟨1a⟩ *v/t documento: de persona* apply for; *de banco etc* process
trámite *m* formality
tramo *m* section, stretch; *de escaleras* flight
trampa *f* trap; (*truco*) scam F, trick; **hacer trampas** cheat
trampilla *f* trapdoor
trampolín *m* diving board
tramposo *m*, **-a** *f* cheat, crook
tranca *f*: **llevaba una tranca increíble** F he was wasted F *o* smashed F; **a trancas y barrancas** with great difficulty
trancazo *m* F dose of flu
trance *m* (*momento difícil*) tough time; **en trance** in a trance
tranquilidad *f* calm, quietness
tranquilizante *m* tranquilizer, *Br* tranquillizer
tranquilizar ⟨1f⟩ *v/t*: **tranquilizar a alguien** calm s.o. down
tranquillo *m*: **coger el tranquillo de algo** F get the hang of sth F
tranquilo *adj* calm, quiet; **¡tranquilo!** don't worry; **déjame tranquilo** leave me alone
transacción *f* COM deal, transaction;
transar ⟨1a⟩ *v/i L.Am.* (*ser vendido*) sell out
transatlántico **1** *adj* transatlantic **2** *m* lin-

er
transbordador *m* ferry; **transbordador espacial** space shuttle
transbordo *m*: **hacer transbordo** TRANSP transfer, change
transcendental *adj fig* momentous
transcurrir ⟨3a⟩ *v/i de tiempo* pass, go by
transcurso *m* course; *de tiempo* passing
transeúnte *m/f* passer-by
transexual *m/f* transsexual
transferencia *f* COM transfer
transformación *f* transformation
transformador *m* EL transformer
transformar ⟨1a⟩ *v/t* transform
transfronterizo *adj* cross-border
tránsfuga *m/f* POL defector
transfusión *f*: **transfusión de sangre** blood transfusion
transgénico *adj* genetically modified
transgredir ⟨3a⟩ *v/t* infringe
transición *f* transition
transigir ⟨3c⟩ *v/i* compromise, make concessions
transistor *m* transistor
transitivo *adj* GRAM transitive
tránsito *m* COM transit; *L.Am.* (*circulación*) traffic
translúcido *adj* translucent
transmisión *f* transmission; **transmisión de datos** data transmission; **enfermedad de transmisión sexual** sexually transmitted disease
transmitir ⟨3a⟩ *v/t* spread; RAD, TV broadcast, transmit
transparencia *f para proyectar* transparency, slide
transparente *adj* transparent
transpiración *f* perspiration
transpirar ⟨1a⟩ *v/i* perspire
transplantar ⟨1a⟩ *v/t* transplant
transportar ⟨1a⟩ *v/t* transport
transporte *m* transport
tranvía *m* streetcar, *Br* tram
trapecio *m* trapeze
trapecista *m/f* trapeze artist(e)
trapiche *m C.Sur* sugar mill *o* press
trapicheo *m* F shady deal F
trapo *m viejo* rag; *para limpiar* cloth; **trapos** F clothes
trapujear ⟨1a⟩ *v/t & v/i C.Am.* smuggle
tráquea *f* ANAT windpipe, trachea
traqueteo *m* rattle, clatter
tras *prp en el espacio* behind; *en el tiempo* after
trasero **1** *adj* rear *atr*, back *atr* **2** *m* F butt F, *Br* rear end F
trasiego *m fig* bustle
trasladar ⟨1a⟩ **1** *v/t* move; *trabajador* transfer **2** *v/r* **trasladarse** move (**a** to);

se traslada *Méx: en negocio* under new management

traslado *m* move; *de trabajador* transfer; **traslado al aeropuerto** airport transfer

trasluz *m*: **al trasluz** against the light

trasnochar ⟨1a⟩ *v/i (acostarse tarde)* go to bed late, stay up late; *(no dormir)* stay up all night; *L.Am.* stay overnight, spend the night

traspapelar ⟨1a⟩ *v/t* mislay

traspasar ⟨1a⟩ *v/t (atravesar)* go through; COM transfer

traspié *m* trip, stumble; **dar un traspié** *fig* slip up, blunder

trasplantar ⟨1a⟩ *v/t* AGR, MED transplant

trasplante *m* AGR, MED transplant

trastada *f* F prank, trick; **hacer trastadas** get up to mischief

traste *m*: **irse al traste** F fall through, go down the tubes F

trastero *m* lumber room

trasto *m* *desp* piece of junk; *persona* good-for-nothing

trastornar ⟨1a⟩ *v/t* upset; *(molestar)* inconvenience

trastorno *m* inconvenience; MED disorder

tratado *m* *esp* POL treaty; **Tratado de Libre Comercio** North American Free Trade Agreement

tratamiento *m* treatment; **tratamiento de datos / textos** INFOR data / word processing

tratar ⟨1a⟩ **1** *v/t* treat; *(manejar)* handle; *(dirigirse a)* address (**de** as); *gente* come into contact with; *tema* deal with **2** *v/i*: **tratar con alguien** deal with s.o.; **tratar de** *(intentar)* try to **3** *v/r* **tratarse**: **¿de qué se trata?** what's it about?

trato *m* *de prisionero, animal* treatment; COM deal; **malos tratos** *pl* ill treatment *sg*, abuse *sg*; **tener trato con alguien** have dealings with s.o.; **¡trato hecho!** it's a deal

trauma *m* trauma

traumatizar ⟨1f⟩ *v/t* traumatize

traumatólogo *m*, **-a** *f* trauma specialist, traumatologist

través *m*: **a través de** through

travesaño *m en fútbol* crossbar

travesía *f* crossing

travesti *m* transvestite, drag artist

travesura *f* bit of mischief, prank

travieso *adj niño* mischievous

trayecto *m* journey; **10 dólares por trayecto** 10 dollars each way

trayectoria *f* *fig* course, path

trazar ⟨1f⟩ *v/t (dibujar)* draw; *ruta* plot, trace; *(describir)* outline, describe

trazo *m* line

trébol *m* BOT clover

trece *adj* thirteen; **mantenerse** *or* **seguir en sus trece** stand firm, not budge

trecho *m* stretch, distance

tregua *f* truce, cease-fire; **sin tregua** relentlessly

treinta *adj* thirty

tremebundo *adj* horrendous, frightening

tremendo *adj* awful, dreadful; *éxito, alegría* tremendous

tren *m* FERR train; **tren de alta velocidad** high speed train; **tren de lavado** car wash; **vivir a todo tren** F live in style; **estar como un tren** F be absolutely gorgeous

trenca *f* duffel coat

trenza *f* plait

trepa *m* F *socialmente* social climber; *en el trabajo* careerist

trepar ⟨1a⟩ *v/i* climb (**a** up), scale (**a** sth)

trepidante *adj* *fig* frenetic

tres *adj* three

trescientos *adj* three hundred

tresillo *m* living-room suite, *Br* three-piece suite

treta *f* trick, ploy

triángulo *m* triangle

tribu *f* tribe

tribuna *f* grandstand

tribunal *m* court; **Tribunal Supremo** Supreme Court

tributo *m* tribute; *(impuesto)* tax

triciclo *m* tricycle

tricotar ⟨1a⟩ *v/i* knit

trifulca *f* F brawl, punch-up F

trigo *m* wheat

trillado *adj* *fig* hackneyed, clichéd

trillar ⟨1a⟩ *v/t* AGR thresh

trillizos *mpl* triplets

trillón *m* quintillion, *Br* trillion

trimestral *adj* quarterly

trimestre *m* quarter; *escolar* semester, *Br* term

trinar ⟨1a⟩ *v/i* trill, warble; **está que trina** *fig* F he's fuming F, he's hopping mad F

trincar ⟨1g⟩ *v/t* F *criminal* catch

trinchera *f* MIL trench

trineo *m* sled, sleigh

trino *m* trill, warble

trío *m* trio

tripa *f* F belly F, gut F; **hacer de tripas corazón** *fig* pluck up courage

triple *m*: **el triple que el año pasado** three times as much as last year

triplicar ⟨1g⟩ *v/t* triple, treble

trípode *m* tripod

tripulación *f* AVIA, MAR crew

tripular ⟨1a⟩ *v/t* man

triquiñuela *f* F dodge F, trick

tris *m*: **estuvo en un tris de caerse** F she came within an inch of falling

triste *adj* sad

tristeza *f* sadness

triturar ⟨1a⟩ *v/t* grind

triunfar **1** *adj* winning **2** *m*, triunfadora *f* winner, victor

triunfar ⟨1a⟩ *v/i* triumph, win

triunfo *m* triumph, victory; **en naipes** trump

trivial *adj* trivial

triza *f*: **hacer trizas** F jarrón smash to bits; papel, vestido tear to shreds

trocear ⟨1a⟩ *v/t* cut into pieces, cut up

troche: **había errores a troche y moche** F there were mistakes galore F

trofeo *m* trophy

troglodita *m/f* cave-dweller

troj(e) *f Arg* granary

trola *f* F fib

trolebús *m* trolley bus

tromba *f*: **tromba de agua** downpour

trombón *m* MÚS trombone

trombosis *f* MED thrombosis

trompa **1** *adj* F wasted F **2** *f* MÚS horn; ZO trunk

trompazo *m L.Am.* F whack F; **darse un trompazo con algo** F bang into sth

trompearse ⟨1a⟩ *L.Am.* F fight, lay into each other F

trompeta *f* MÚS trumpet

trompetista *m/f* MÚS trumpeter

trompicón *m*: **a trompicones** in fits and starts

trompo *m* spinning top

trona *f* high chair

tronar ⟨1m⟩ *v/i* thunder

troncha *f S. Am.* slice, piece

tronchante *adj* F sidesplitting

troncharse ⟨1a⟩ *v/r*: **troncharse de risa** F split one's sides laughing

tronco *m* trunk; cortado log; **dormir como un tronco** sleep like a log

trono *m* throne

tropa *f* MIL (soldado raso) ordinary soldier; **tropas** troops

tropel *m*: **en tropel** in a mad rush; **salir en tropel** pour out

tropezar ⟨1f & 1k⟩ *v/i* trip, stumble

tropical *adj* tropical

trópico *m* tropic

tropiezo *m* fig setback

tropilla *f L.Am.* herd

trotar ⟨1a⟩ *v/i* fig gad around

trote *m* trot; **ya no estoy para esos trotes** I'm not up to it any more

trozo *m* piece

trucha *f* ZO trout

truco *m* trick; **coger el truco a algo** F get the hang of sth F

truculento *adj* horrifying

trueno *m* thunder

trueque *m* barter

trufa *f* BOT truffle

truhán *m* rogue

Tte. *abr* (= **Teniente**) Lieut. (= Lieutenant)

tú *pron sg* you; **tratar de tú** address as 'tu'

tu, tus *adj pos* your

tuberculosis *f* MED TB, tuberculosis

tubería *f* pipe

tubo *m* tube; **tubo de escape** AUTO exhaust (pipe); **por un tubo** F an enormous amount

tucán *m* ZO toucan

tuerca *f* TÉC nut

tulipán *m* BOT tulip

tullido *m* cripple

tumba *f* tomb, grave

tumbar ⟨1a⟩ **1** *v/t* knock down **2** *v/r* tumbarse lie down

tumbo *m* tumble; **ir dando tumbos** stagger along

tumbona *f* (sun) lounger

tumor *m* MED tumo(u)r

tumulto *m* uproar

tuna *f Méx fruta* prickly pear

tunda *f* F beating

tundra *f* GEOG tundra

túnel *m* tunnel; **túnel de lavado** car wash

Túnez Tunisia

túnica *f* tunic

tuntún: **decir algo al buen tuntún** say sth off the top of one's head

tupé *m* F quiff

tupido *adj* pelo thick; vegetación denso, thick

turbante *m* turban

turbar ⟨1a⟩ **1** *v/t* (emocionar) upset; paz, tranquilidad disturb; (avergonzar) embarrass **2** *v/r* turbarse (emocionarse) get upset; de paz, tranquilidad be disturbed; (avergonzarse) get embarrassed

turbina *f* turbine

turbio *adj* cloudy, murky; fig shady, murky

turbo *m* turbo

turbulencia *f* turbulence

turbulento *adj* turbulent

turco **1** *adj* Turkish **2** *m*, -a *f* Turk

turismo *m* tourism; automóvil sedan, Br saloon (car); **turismo rural** tourism in rural areas

turista *m/f* tourist

turístico *adj* tourist atr

turnarse ⟨1a⟩ *v/r* take it in turns

turno *m* turn; **turno de noche** night shift; **por turnos** in turns

turquesa *f piedra preciosa* turquoise; *azul turquesa* turquoise
Turquía Turkey
turrón *m* nougat
turulato *adj* F stunned, dazed
tute *m*: *darse un tute* F work like a dog F, slave F
tutear ⟨1a⟩ *v/t* address as 'tu'

tutiplén: *había comida a tutiplén* F there was loads *o* masses to eat F
tutor *m*, **tutora** *f* EDU tutor
tuve *vb* → **tener**
tuvo *vb* → **tener**
tuyo, tuya *pron pos* yours; *los tuyos* your folks, your family
TV *abr* (= **televisión**) TV (= television)

U

u *conj* (*instead of* **o** *before words starting with* o) or
ubicación *f L.Am.* location; (*localización*) finding
ubicado *adj* located, situated
ubicar ⟨1g⟩ **1** *v/t L.Am.* place, put; (*localizar*) locate **2** *v/r* **ubicarse** be located, be situated; *en un empleo* get a job
ubicuo *adj* ubiquitous
ubre *f* udder
UCI *abr* (= **Unidad de Cuidados Intensivos**) ICU (= Intensive Care Unit)
Ud. *pron* → **usted**
Uds. *pron* → **usted**
UE *abr* (= **Unión Europea**) EU (= European Union)
ufano *adj* conceited; (*contento*) proud
ujier *m* usher
úlcera *f* MED ulcer
ulcerarse ⟨1a⟩ *v/r* MED become ulcerous, ulcerate
ulterior *adj* subsequent
últimamente *adv* lately
ultimar ⟨1a⟩ *v/t* finalize; *L.Am.* (*rematar*) finish off
ultimátum *m* ultimatum
último *adj* last; (*más reciente*) latest; *piso* top *atr*; *-as noticias* latest news *sg*; *por último* finally; *está en las -as* he doesn't have long (to live)
ultra *m* POL right-wing extremist
ultraderecha *f* POL extreme right
ultrajante ⟨1a⟩ *adj* outrageous; *palabras* insulting
ultrajar ⟨1a⟩ *v/t* outrage; (*insultar*) insult
ultraje *m* outrage; (*insulto*) insult
ultraligero *m* AVIA microlight
ultramarinos *mpl* groceries; *tienda de ultramarinos* grocery store, *Br* grocer's (shop)
ultramoderno *adj* ultramodern

ultranza: *a ultranza* for all one is worth; *un defensor a ultranza de algo* an ardent defender of sth
ultrasónico *adj* ultrasonic
ultrasonido *m* ultrasound
ultratumba *f*: *la vida de ultratumba* life beyond the grave
ultravioleta *adj* ultraviolet
ulular ⟨1a⟩ *v/i de viento* howl; *de búho* hoot
umbilical *adj* ANAT umbilical
umbral *m fig* threshold; *en el umbral de fig* on the threshold of
umbrío *adj* shady
un, una *art a*; *antes de vocal y h muda* an; *unos coches / pájaros* some cars / birds
unánime *adj* unanimous
unanimidad *f* unanimity; *por unanimidad* unanimously
unción *f fig* unction
undécimo *adj* eleventh
ungir ⟨3c⟩ *v/t* REL anoint
ungüento *m* ointment
únicamente *adv* only
único *adj* only; (*sin par*) unique; *es único* it's unique; *hijo único* only child; *lo único que ...* the only thing that ...
unicornio *m* MYTH unicorn
unidad *f* MIL, MAT unit; (*cohesión*) unity; *unidad de cuidados intensivos*, *unidad de vigilancia intensiva* MED intensive care unit; *unidad de disco* INFOR disk drive; *unidad monetaria* monetary unity
unido *adj* united; *una familia -a* a close-knit family
unificación *f* unification
unificar ⟨1g⟩ *v/t* unify
uniformar ⟨1a⟩ *v/t fig* standardize
uniforme 1 *adj* uniform; *superficie* even **2** *m* uniform

unilateral *adj* unilateral

unión *f* union; ***Unión Europea*** European Union

unir ⟨3a⟩ **1** *v/t* join; *personas* unite; *características* combine (**con** with); *ciudades* link **2** *v/r* **unirse** join together; ***unirse a*** join

unisex *adj* unisex

unísono *adj*: ***al unísono*** in unison

unitario *adj* unitary; ***precio unitario*** unit price

universal *adj* universal

universidad *f* university; ***universidad a distancia*** university correspondence school, *Br* Open University

universitario 1 *adj* university *atr* **2** *m*, -a *f* (*estudiante*) university student

universo *m* universe

uno 1 *pron* one; ***es la -a*** it's one o'clock; ***me lo dijo uno*** someone *o* somebody told me; ***una a uno, uno por uno, de uno en uno*** one by one; ***no dar ni -a*** F not get anything right; ***unos cuantos*** a few, some; ***unos niños*** some children; ***-as mil pesetas*** about a thousand pesetas **2** *m* one; ***el uno de enero*** January first, the first of January

untar ⟨1a⟩ *v/t* spread; ***untar a alguien*** F (*sobornar*) grease s.o.'s palm

untuoso *adj fig* oily

uña *f* ANAT nail; ZO claw; ***defenderse con uñas y dientes*** *fig* F fight tooth and nail; ***ser uña y carne*** *personas* be extremely close

uperisado *adj*: ***leche -a*** UHT milk

uranio *m* uranium

urbanidad *f* civility

urbanismo *m* city planning, *Br* town planning

urbanización *f* (urban) development; (*colonia*) housing development, *Br* housing estate

urbanizar ⟨1f⟩ *v/t terreno* develop

urbano *adj* urban; (*cortés*) courteous; ***guardia urbano*** local police officer

urbe *f* city

urdir ⟨3a⟩ *v/t complot* hatch

urea *f* urea

uretra *f* ANAT urethra

urgencia *f* urgency; (*prisa*) haste; MED emergency; ***urgencias*** *pl* emergency room *sg*, *Br* casualty *sg*

urgente *adj* urgent

urgir ⟨3c⟩ *v/i* be urgent

urinario *m* urinal

urna *f* urn; ***urna electoral*** ballot box

urólogo *m* MED urologist

urraca *f* ZO magpie

URSS *abr* (= ***Unión de las Repúblicas Socialistas Soviéticas***) USSR (= Union of Soviet Socialist Republics)

urticaria *f* MED hives

Uruguay Uruguay

uruguayo 1 *adj* Uruguayan **2** *m*, -a *f* Uruguayan

usado *adj* (*gastado*) worn; (*de segunda mano*) second hand

usar ⟨1a⟩ **1** *v/t* use; *ropa, gafas* wear **2** *v/i*: ***listo para usar*** ready to use **3** *v/r* **usarse** be used

uso *m* use; (*costumbre*) custom; ***obligatorio el uso de casco*** helmets must be worn; ***en buen uso*** still in use

usted *pron* you; ***tratar de usted*** address as 'usted'; ***ustedes*** *pl* you; ***de usted / ustedes*** your; ***es de usted / ustedes*** it's yours

usual *adj* common, usual

usuario *m*, -a *f* INFOR user

usufructo *m* JUR usufruct

usura *f* usury

usurero *m*, -a *f* usurer

usurpar ⟨1a⟩ *v/t* usurp

utensilio *m* tool; *de cocina* utensil; ***utensilios*** *pl* equipment *sg*; ***utensilios*** *pl* ***de pesca*** fishing tackle *sg*

útero *m* ANAT uterus

útil 1 *adj* useful **2** *m* tool; ***útiles*** *pl* ***de pesca*** fishing tackle *sg*

utilidad *f* usefulness

utilitario 1 *adj* functional, utilitarian **2** *m* AUTO compact

utilitarismo *m* utilitarianism

utilización *f* use

utilizar ⟨1f⟩ *v/t* use

utopía *f* utopia

utópico *adj* utopian

uva *f* BOT grape; ***estar de mala uva*** F be in a foul mood; ***tener mala uva*** F be a nasty piece of work F

UVI *abr* (= ***Unidad de Vigilancia Intensiva***) ICU (= Intensive Care Unit)

úvula *f* ANAT uvula

U

V

va *vb* → **ir**

vaca *f* cow; GASTR beef; **vaca lechera** dairy cow; **vaca marina** manatee, sea cow; **mal** *or* **enfermedad de las vacas locas** F mad cow disease F

vacaciones *fpl* vacation *sg*, *Br* holiday *sg*; **de vacaciones** on vacation, *Br* on holiday

vacante 1 *adj* vacant, empty **2** *f* job opening, position, *Br* vacancy; **cubrir una vacante** fill a position

vaciar ⟨1b⟩ **1** *v/t* empty **2** *v/r* **vaciarse** empty

vacilación *f* hesitation

vacilante *adj* unsteady; (*dubitativo*) hesitant

vacilar ⟨1a⟩ **1** *v/i* hesitate; *de fe, resolución* waver; *de objeto* wobble, rock; *de persona* stagger; *Méx* F (*divertirse*) have fun **2** *v/t* F make fun of

vacío 1 *adj* empty **2** *m* FÍS vacuum; *fig espacio* void; **vacío de poder** power vacuum; **vacío legal** loophole; **dejar un vacío** *fig* leave a gap; **envasado al vacío** vacuum packed; **hacer el vacío a alguien** *fig* ostracize s.o.

vacuna *f* vaccine

vacunación *f* vaccination

vacunar ⟨1a⟩ *v/t* vaccinate

vacuno *adj* bovine; **ganado vacuno** cattle *pl*

vacuo *adj fig* vacuous

vadear ⟨1a⟩ *v/t río* ford; *dificultad* get around

vado *m* ford; **en la calle** entrance ramp; **vado permanente** *letrero* keep clear

vagabundear ⟨1a⟩ *v/i* drift around

vagabundo 1 *adj perro* stray **2** *m*, -a *f* hobo, *Br* tramp

vagancia *f* laziness, idleness

vagar ⟨1h⟩ *v/i* wander

vagido *m de bebe* cry

vagina *f* ANAT vagina

vago *adj* (*holgazán*) lazy; (*indefinido*) vague; **hacer el vago** laze around

vagón *m de carga* wagon; *de pasajeros* car, *Br* coach; **vagón restaurante** dining car, *Br tb* restaurant car

vaguear ⟨1a⟩ *v/i* laze around

vaguedad *f* vagueness

vahído *m* MED dizzy spell

vaho *m* (*aliento*) breath; (*vapor*) steam

vaina *f* BOT pod; *S. Am.* F drag F

vainilla *f* vanilla

vais *vb* → **ir**

vaivén *m* to-and-fro, swinging; **vaivenes** *fig* ups and downs

vajilla *f* dishes *pl*; *juego* dinner service, set of dishes

vale *m* voucher, coupon

valedero *adj* valid

valentía *f* bravery

valer ⟨2q⟩ **1** *v/t* be worth; (*costar*) cost **2** *v/i de billete, carné* be valid; (*estar permitido*) be allowed; (*tener valor*) be worth; (*servir*) be of use; **no valer para algo** be no good at sth; **vale más caro** it's more expensive; **sus consejos me valieron de mucho** his advice was very useful to me; **más vale ...** it's better to ...; **más te vale ...** you'd better ...; **¡vale!** okay, sure **3** *v/r* **valerse** manage (by o.s.); **valerse de** make use of

valeriana *f* BOT valerian

valeroso *adj* valiant

valga *vb* → **valer**

valgo *vb* → **valer**

valía *f* worth

validar ⟨1a⟩ *v/t* validate

validez *f* validity

válido *adj* valid

valiente *adj* brave; *irón* fine

valija *f* (*maleta*) bag, suitcase, *Br tb* case; **valija diplomática** diplomatic bag

valioso *adj* valuable

valla *f* fence; DEP, *fig* hurdle; **valla publicitaria** billboard, *Br* hoarding; **carrera de vallas** DEP hurdles

vallado *m* fence

vallar ⟨1a⟩ *v/t* fence in

valle *m* valley

valor *m* value; (*valentía*) courage; **valor añadido**, *L.Am.* **valor agregado** value added; **valor nominal** *de acción* nominal value; *de título* par value; **objetos de valor** valuables; **valores** COM securities

valoración *f* (*tasación*) valuation

valorar ⟨1a⟩ *v/t* value (**en** at); (*estimar*) appreciate, value

vals *m* waltz

valuar ⟨1e⟩ *v/t* value

válvula *f* ANAT, EL valve; **válvula de escape** *fig* safety valve

vampiro *m fig* vampire

van *vb* → **ir**

vanagloriarse ⟨1b⟩ *v/r* boast (**de** about), brag (**de** about)

vandálico *adj* destructive

vandalismo *m* vandalism

vándalo *m*, **-a** *f* vandal

vanguardia *f* MIL vanguard; **de vanguardia** *fig* avant-garde

vanidad *f* vanity

vanidoso *adj* conceited, vain

vano *adj* futile, vain; **en vano** in vain

vapor *m* vapo(u)r; *de agua* steam; **cocinar al vapor** steam

vaporizar ⟨1f⟩ **1** *v/t* vaporize **2** *v/r* **vaporizarse** vaporize

vaporoso *adj* vaporous; *fig: vestido* gauzy, filmy

vapulear ⟨1a⟩ *v/t* beat up

vapuleo *m* beating

vaquería *f* dairy

vaquero 1 *adj tela* denim; **pantalones vaqueros** jeans **2** *m* cowboy, cowhand

vaquilla *f* heifer

vara *f* stick; TÉC rod; *(bastón de mando)* staff

varapalo *m* F *(contratiempo)* hitch F, setback

variable *adj* variable; *tiempo* changeable

variación *f* variation

variado *adj* varied

variar ⟨1c⟩ **1** *v/t* vary; *(cambiar)* change **2** *v/i* vary; *(cambiar)* change; **para variar** for a change

varice *f* MED varicose vein

varicela *f* MED chickenpox

variedad *f* variety; **variedades** *pl* vaudeville *sg*, *Br* variety *sg*

variopinto *adj* varied, diverse

varios *adj* several

varita *f*: **varita mágica** magic wand

variz *f* varicose vein

varón *m* man, male

varonil *adj* manly, virile

vas *vb* → **ir**

vasallo *m* vassal

vasco 1 *adj* Basque; **País Vasco** Basque country **2** *m idioma* Basque **3** *m*, **-a** *f* Basque

Vascongadas *fpl* Basque country *sg*

vascuence *m* Basque

vascular *adj* ANAT vascular

vasectomía *f* MED vasectomy

vaselina *f* Vaseline®

vasija *f* container, vessel

vaso *m* glass; ANAT vessel

vasto *adj* vast

Vaticano *m* Vatican

vaticinar ⟨1a⟩ *v/t* predict, forecast

vaticinio *m* prediction, forecast

vatio *m* EL watt

vaya 1 *vb* → **ir 2** *int* well!

V.° B.° *abr* (= **visto bueno**) approved, OK

Vd. *pron* → **usted**

Vds. *pron* → **usted**

ve *vb* → **ir**, **ver**

vea *vb* → **ver**

vecindad *f Méx* poor area

vecindario *m* neighbo(u)rhood

vecino 1 *adj* neighbo(u)ring **2** *m*, **-a** *f* neighbo(u)r

vedado *m*: **vedado de caza** game reserve

vedar ⟨1a⟩ *v/t* ban, prohibit

vedette *f* star

vegetación *f* vegetation

vegetal 1 *adj* vegetable, plant *atr* **2** *m* vegetable

vegetar ⟨1a⟩ *v/i fig* vegetate

vegetariano 1 *adj* vegetarian **2** *m*, **-a** *f* vegetarian

vehemente *adj* vehement

vehículo *m tb fig* vehicle; MED carrier

veinte *m/adj* twenty

veintena *f* twenty; *aproximadamente* about twenty

vejación *f* humiliation

vejar ⟨1a⟩ *v/t* humiliate

vejestorio *m* F old fossil F, old relic F

vejez *f* old age

vejiga *f* ANAT bladder

vela *f para alumbrar* candle; DEP sailing; *de barco* sail; **a toda vela** F flat out F, all out F; **estar a dos velas** F be broke F; **pasar la noche en vela** stay up all night

velada *f* evening

velador *m L.Am. lámpara* bedlamp, *Br* bedside light; *Chi mueble* nightstand, *Br* bedside table

velar ⟨1a⟩ *v/i*. **velar por algo** look after sth

velatorio *m* wake

velcro® *m* Velcro

veleidad *f* fickleness

velero *m* MAR sailing ship

veleta 1 *f* weathervane **2** *m/f fig* weathercock

vello *m* (body) hair

velo *m* veil

velocidad *f* speed; *(marcha)* gear

velódromo *m* velodrome

veloz *adj* fast, speedy

ven *vb* → **venir**

vena *f* ANAT vein; **le dio la vena y lo hizo** F she just upped and did it F; **estar en vena** F be on form

venado *m* ZO deer

vencedor 1 *adj* winning **2** *m*, **vencedora** *f* winner

vencejo *m* ZO swift

vencer ⟨2b⟩ **1** *v/t* defeat; *fig (superar)* overcome **2** *v/i* win; COM *de plazo etc* expire

vencido adj: **darse por vencido** admit defeat, give in; **a la tercera va la -a** third time lucky

vencimiento m expiration, Br expiry; **de bono** maturity

venda f bandage

vendaje m MED dressing

vendar ⟨1a⟩ v/t MED bandage, dress; **vendar los ojos a alguien** blindfold s.o.

vendaval m gale

vendedor m, **vendedora** f seller

vender ⟨2a⟩ **1** v/t sell; fig (traicionar) betray **2** v/r **venderse** sell o.s.; **venderse al enemigo** sell out to the enemy

vendimia f grape harvest

vendimiar ⟨1b⟩ v/t uvas harvest, pick

vendré vb → **venir**

veneno m poison

venenoso adj poisonous

venerable adj venerable

venerar ⟨1a⟩ v/t venerate, worship

venéreo adj MED venereal

venezolano 1 adj Venezuelan **2** m, -a f Venezuelan

Venezuela Venezuela

venga vb → **venir**

venganza f vengeance, revenge

vengar ⟨1h⟩ **1** v/t avenge **2** v/r **vengarse** take revenge (**de** on; **por** for)

vengativo adj vengeful

vengo vb → **venir**

venir ⟨3s⟩ **1** v/i come; **venir de España** come from Spain; **venir bien** be convenient; **venir mal** be inconvenient; **le vino una idea** an idea occurred to him; **viene a ser lo mismo** it comes down to the same thing; **el año que viene** next year; **¡venga!** come on; **¿a qué viene eso?** why do you say that? **2** v/r **venirse: venirse abajo** collapse; fig: de persona fall apart, go to pieces

venta f sale; **venta por correo** or **por catálogo** mail order; **venta al detalle** or **al por menor** retail; **en venta** for sale

ventaja f advantage; DEP **en carrera, partido** lead; **ventaja fiscal** tax advantage

ventajoso adj advantageous

ventana f window; **ventana de la nariz** nostril

ventanilla f AVIA, AUTO, FERR window; MAR porthole

ventilación f ventilation

ventilador m fan

ventilar ⟨1a⟩ v/t air; fig: problema talk over; opiniones air

ventisca f blizzard

ventosa f ZO sucker

ventosidad f wind, flatulence

ventrílocuo m ventriloquist

veo vb → **ver**

ver ⟨2v; part **visto**⟩ **1** v/t see; televisión watch; JUR pleito hear; L.Am. (mirar) look at; **está por ver** it remains to be seen; **no puede verla** fig he can't stand the sight of her; **no tiene nada que ver con** it doesn't have anything to do with; **¡a ver!** let's see; **¡hay que ver!** would you believe it!; **ya veremos** we'll see **2** v/i L.Am. (mirar) look; **ve aquí dentro** L.Am. look in here **3** v/r **verse** see o.s.; (encontrarse) see one another; **¡habráse visto!** would you believe it!; **¡se las verá conmigo!** F he'll have me to deal with!

veranear ⟨1a⟩ v/i spend the summer vacation o Br holidays

veraniego adj summer atr

verano m summer

veras f: **de veras** really, truly

verbal adj GRAM verbal

verbena f (fiesta) party

verbo m GRAM verb

verborrea f desp verbosity

verdad f truth; **a decir verdad** to tell the truth; **de verdad** real, proper; **no te gusta, ¿verdad?** you don't like it, do you?; **vas a venir, ¿verdad?** you're coming, aren't you?; **es verdad** it's true, it's the truth

verdadero adj true; (cierto) real

verde 1 adj green; fruta unripe; F chiste blue, dirty; **viejo verde** dirty old man; **poner verde a alguien** F criticize s.o. **2** m green; **los verdes** POL the Greens

verdoso adj greenish

verdugo m executioner

verdulería f fruit and vegetable store, Br greengrocer's

verdura f: **verdura(s)** (hortalizas) greens pl, (green) vegetables pl

vereda f S. Am. sidewalk, Br pavement; **meter alguien en vereda** fig put s.o. back on the straight and narrow, bring s.o. into line

veredicto m JUR, fig verdict

verga f rod

vergel m orchard

vergonzoso adj disgraceful, shameful; (tímido) shy

vergüenza f shame; (escándalo) disgrace; **me da vergüenza** I'm embarrassed; **es una vergüenza** it's a disgrace; **no sé cómo no se te cae la cara de vergüenza** you should be ashamed (of yourself)

vericuetos mpl fig twists and turns

verídico adj true

verificar ⟨1g⟩ v/t verify

verja f railing; (puerta) iron gate

vermú, vermut *m* vermouth

verosímil *adj* realistic; (*creíble*) plausible

verruga *f* wart

versado *adj* well-versed (**en** in)

versar ⟨1a⟩ *v/i*: **versar sobre** deal with, be about

versátil *adj* fickle; *artista* versatile

versículo *m* verse

versión *f* version; **en versión original película** original language version

verso *m* verse

vértebra *f* ANAT vertebra

vertedero *m* dump, tip

verter ⟨2g⟩ *v/t* dump; (*derramar*) spill; *fig*: *opinión* voice

vertical *adj* vertical

vertido *m* dumping; **vertidos** *pl* waste *sg*

vertiente *f* L.Am. (*cuesta*) slope; (*lado*) side

vertiginoso *adj* dizzy; (*rápido*) frantic

vértigo *m* MED vertigo; **darle a alguien vértigo** make s.o. dizzy

vesícula *f* blister; **vesícula biliar** ANAT gall-bladder

vespa® *f* motorscooter

vestíbulo *m* de casa hall; *de edificio público* lobby

vestido *m* dress; *L.Am. de hombre* suit

vestigio *m* vestige, trace

vestir ⟨3l⟩ **1** *v/t* dress; (*llevar puesto*) wear **2** *v/i* dress; **vestir de negro** wear black, dress in black; **vestir de uniforme** wear a uniform **3** *v/r* **vestirse** get dressed; **vestirse de algo** dress up; **vestirse de algo** wear sth

vestuario *m* DEP locker room; TEA wardrobe

veta *f* MIN vein

vetar ⟨1a⟩ *v/t* POL veto

veterano **1** *adj* veteran; (*experimentado*) experienced **2** *m*, **-a** *f* veteran

veterinario **1** *adj* veterinary **2** *m*, **-a** *f* veterinarian, vet

veto *m* veto

vetusto *adj* ancient

vez *f* time; **a la vez** at the same time; **a su vez** for his / her part; **cada vez que** every time that; **de vez en cuando** from time to time; **en vez de** instead of; **érase una vez** once upon a time, there was; **otra vez** again; **tal vez** perhaps, maybe; **una vez** once; **a veces** sometimes; **muchas veces** (*con frecuencia*) often; **hacer las veces de** objeto serve as; **de persona** act as

vi *vb* → **ver**

vía **1** *f* FERR track; **vía estrecha** FERR narrow gauge; **darle vía libre a alguien** give s.o. a free hand; **por vía aérea** by air; **en**

vías de *fig* in the process of **2** *prp* via

viable *adj* plan, *solución* viable, feasible

viaducto *m* viaduct

viajante *m/f* sales rep

viajar ⟨1a⟩ *v/i* travel

viaje *m* trip, journey; **viaje organizado** package tour; **viaje de ida** outward journey; **viaje de ida y vuelta** round trip; **viaje de novios** honeymoon; **viaje de vuelta** return journey

viajero *m*, **-a** *f* travel(l)er

viario *adj* road *atr*; **educación -a** instruction in road safety

víbora *f* tb *fig* viper

vibración *f* vibration

vibrante *adj* fig exciting

vibrar ⟨1a⟩ *v/t* vibrate

vicaría *f* pastor's house, vicarage; **pasar por la vicaría** F get married in church

vicecónsul *m* vice-consul

vicepresidente *m*, **-a** *f* POL vice-president; COM vice-president, *Br* deputy chairman

vicerrector *m* vice-rector

viceversa *adv*: **y viceversa** and vice versa

viciado *adj* aire stuffy

viciarse ⟨1b⟩ *v/r* fall into bad habits

vicio *m* vice; **pasarlo de vicio** F have a great time F

vicioso *adj* vicious; (*corrompido*) depraved

vicisitudes *fpl* ups and downs

víctima *f* victim

victimar ⟨1a⟩ *v/t* L.Am. kill

victoria *f* victory; **cantar victoria** claim victory

victorioso *adj* victorious

vicuña *f* ZO vicuna

vid *f* vine

vida *f* life; *esp* TÉC life span; **de por vida** for life; **en mi vida** never (in my life); **ganarse la vida** earn a living; **hacer la vida imposible a alguien** make s.o.'s life impossible; **vida mía** my love

vidente *m/f* seer, clairvoyant

vídeo *m* video

videocámara *f* video camera

videocas(s)et(t)e *m* video cassette

videoclip *m* pop video

videoconferencia *f* video conference

videojuego *m* video game

videotex(to) *m* videotext

vidriera *f* L.Am. shop window

vidrio *m* L.Am. glass; (*ventana*) window

vieira *f* ZO scallop

vieja *f* old woman

viejo **1** *adj* old **2** *m* old man; **mis viejos** F my folks F

viendo *vb* → **ver**

viene *vb* → **venir**

V

viento *m* wind; **viento en popa** *fig* F splendidly; **contra viento y marea** *fig* come what may; **hacer viento** be windy; **proclamar a los cuatro vientos** *fig* shout from the rooftops

vientre *m* belly

viernes *m inv* Friday; **Viernes Santo** Good Friday

Vietnam Vietnam

vietnamita *adj & m/f* Vietnamese

viga *f* beam, girder

vigente *adj legislación* in force

vigésimo *adj* twentieth

vigilante 1 *adj* watchful, vigilant **2** *m* *L.Am.* policeman; **vigilante nocturno** night watchman; **vigilante jurado** security guard

vigilar ⟨1a⟩ **1** *v/i* keep watch **2** *v/t* watch; *a un preso* guard

vigor *m* vigo(u)r; **en vigor** in force

vigoroso *adj* vigorous

vil *adj* vile, despicable

vilipendiar ⟨1b⟩ *v/t* insult, vilify *fml*; *(despreciar)* revile

villa *f* town

villancico *m* Christmas carol

villano 1 *adj* villainous **2** *m*, **-a** *f* villain

vilo: **en vilo** in the air; *fig* in suspense, on tenterhooks; **levantar en vilo** lift off the ground; **tener a alguien en vilo** *fig* keep s.o. in suspense *o* on tenterhooks

vinagre *m* vinegar

vinagrera *f* vinegar bottle; *S. Am.* *(indigestión)* indigestion; **vinagreras** *pl* cruet *sg*

vinagreta *f* vinaigrette

vincha *f* *S. Am.* hairband

vinculante *adj* binding

vincular ⟨1a⟩ *v/t* link (**a** to); *(comprometer)* bind

vínculo *m* link; *fig (relación)* tie, bond

vindicar ⟨1g⟩ *v/t* vindicate

vine *vb* → **venir**

vinícola *adj región, país* wine-growing *atr*; *industria* wine-making *atr*

viniendo *vb* → **venir**

vinicultura *f* wine-growing

vino 1 *m* wine; **vino blanco** white wine; **vino de mesa** table wine; **vino tinto** red wine **2** *vb* → **venir**

viña *f* vineyard

viñatero *m*, **-a** *f* *S. Am.* wine grower

viñedo *m* vineyard

viñeta *f* TIP vignette

vio *vb* → **ver**

viola *f* MÚS viola

violación *f* rape; *de derechos* violation

violador *m*, **violadora** *f* rapist

violar ⟨1a⟩ *v/t* rape

violencia *f* violence

violentar ⟨1a⟩ *v/t* *puerta* force; *(incomodar)* embarrass

violento *adj* violent; *(embarazoso)* embarrassing; *persona* embarrassed

violeta 1 *f* BOT violet **2** *m/adj* violet

violín *m* violin

violinista *m/f* violinist

violonc(h)elo *m* cello

VIP *m* VIP

viperino *adj* malicious; **lengua -a** sharp tongue

viral *adj* viral

virar ⟨1a⟩ *v/t* MAR, AVIA turn

virgen 1 *adj* virgin; *cinta* blank; **lana virgen** pure new wool **2** *f* virgin

virginidad *f* virginity

Virgo *m/f inv* ASTR Virgo

virguería *f*: **hace virguerías** P he's a whizz F

vírico *adj* viral

viril *adj* virile, manly

virtual *adj* virtual

virtud *f* virtue; **en virtud de** by virtue of

virtuoso 1 *adj* virtuous **2** *m*, **-a** *f* virtuoso

viruela *f* MED smallpox

virulento *adj* MED, *fig* virulent

virus *m inv* MED virus; **virus informático** computer virus

viruta *f* shaving

visa *f* *L.Am.* visa

visado *m* visa

vísceras *fpl* guts, entrails

visceral *adj fig* gut *atr*, visceral

viscoso *adj* viscous

visera *f de gorra* peak; *de casco* visor

visibilidad *f* visibility

visible *adj* visible; *fig* evident, obvious

visillo *m* sheer; *Br* net curtain

visión *f* vision, sight; *fig* vision; *(opinión)* view; **tener visión de futuro** be forward looking

visita *f* visit; **visita a domicilio** house call; **visita guiada** guided tour; **hacer una visita a alguien** visit s.o.

visitante 1 *adj* visiting; DEP away **2** *m/f* visitor

visitar ⟨1a⟩ *v/t* visit

vislumbrar ⟨1a⟩ *v/t* glimpse

visos *mpl*: **tener visos de** show signs of

visón *m* ZO mink

víspera *f* eve; **en vísperas de** on the eve of

vista *f* (eye)sight; JUR hearing; **vista cansada** MED tired eyes; **a la vista** COM at sight, on demand; **a primera vista** at first sight; **con vistas a** with a view to; **en vista de** in view of; **hasta la vista** bye!, see you!; **hacer la vista gorda** *fig* F turn a blind eye; **tener vista para algo** *fig* have a good eye for sth; **volver la vista atrás** *tb fig* look back

vistazo *m* look; **echar un vistazo a** take a (quick) look at

viste *vb* → **ver, vestir**

visto 1 *part* → **ver 2** *adj*: **está bien visto** it's the done thing; **está mal visto** it's not done, it's not the done thing; **está visto que** it's obvious that; **estar muy visto** be old hat, not be original; **por lo visto** apparently **3** *m* check(mark), *Br* tick; **dar el visto bueno** give one's approval

vistoso *adj* eye-catching

visual *adj* visual

visualizar ⟨1f⟩ *v/t* visualize; **en pantalla** display

vital *adj* vital; **persona** lively

vitalicio *adj* life *atr*, for life; **renta -a** life annuity

vitalidad *f* vitality, liveliness

vitamina *f* vitamin

viticultor *m*, **viticultora** *f* wine grower

vítores *mpl* cheers, acclaim *sg*

vitorear ⟨1a⟩ *v/t* cheer

vítreo *adj* vitreous

vitrificar ⟨1g⟩ *v/t* vitrify

vitrina *f* display cabinet; *L.Am.* shop window

vitrocerámica *f* ceramic hob

vituperar ⟨1a⟩ *v/t* condemn

viuda *f* widow

viudedad *f* widowhood; **pensión de viudedad** widow's pension

viudo 1 *adj* widowed **2** *m* widower; **quedarse viudo** be widowed

viva *int* hurrah!; **¡viva el rey!** long live the king!

vivaz *adj* bright, sharp

vivencia *f* experience

víveres *mpl* provisions

vívido *adj* vivid

vivienda *f* housing; (*casa*) house

vivir ⟨3a⟩ **1** *v/t* live through, experience **2** *v/i* live; **vivir de algo** live on sth

vivo *adj* alive; *color* bright; *ritmo* lively; *fig* F sharp, smart

vocabulario *m* vocabulary

vocación *f* vocation

vocal 1 *m/f* member **2** *f* vowel

vocalista *m/f* vocalist

vocalizar ⟨1f⟩ *v/i* vocalize

voceador *m*, **voceadora** *f* *Méx* newspaper vendor

vocerío *m* uproar

vocero *m*, **-a** *f* esp *L.Am.* spokesperson

vociferar ⟨1a⟩ *v/i* shout

vodka *m* vodka

volador *adj* flying

volandas: **en volandas** *fig* in the air

volante 1 *adj* flying **2** *m* AUTO steering wheel; *de vestido* flounce; MED referral (slip)

volar ⟨1m⟩ **1** *v/i* fly; *fig* vanish **2** *v/t* fly; *edificio* blow up

volátil *adj tb fig* volatile

volatilizarse ⟨1f⟩ *v/r fig* vanish into thin air

volcán *m* volcano

volcánico *adj* volcanic

volcar ⟨1g & 1m⟩ **1** *v/t* knock over; (*vaciar*) empty; *barco, coche* overturn **2** *v/i de coche, barco* overturn **3** *v/r* volcarse tip over; **volcarse por alguien** F bend over backwards for s.o., go out of one's way for s.o.; **volcarse en algo** throw o.s. into sth

volea *f tenis* volley

voleibol *m* volleyball

voleo *m*: **a voleo** at random

voley-playa *m* beach volleyball

voltaje *m* EL voltage

voltear ⟨1a⟩ **1** *v/t L.Am.* (*invertir*) turn over; *Rpl* (*tumbar*) knock over; **voltear el jersey** turn the sweater inside out; **voltear la cabeza** turn one's head **2** *v/i* roll over; *de campanas* ring out

voltereta *f* somersault

voltio *m* EL volt

voluble *adj* erratic, unpredictable

volumen *m* TIP, MÚS, RAD volume; **volumen de negocios** COM turnover

voluntad *f* will; **buena / mala voluntad** good / ill will

voluntario 1 *adj* volunteer **2** *m*, **-a** *f* volunteer

voluntarioso *adj* willing, enthusiastic

voluptuoso *adj* voluptuous

volver ⟨2h; *part* **vuelto**⟩ **1** *v/t página, mirada etc* turn (*a* to; *hacia* toward); **volver loco** drive crazy **2** *v/i* return; **volver a hacer algo** do sth again **3** *v/r* volverse turn round; **volverse loco** go crazy

vomitar ⟨1a⟩ **1** *v/t* throw up; *lava* hurl, throw out **2** *v/i* throw up, be sick; **tengo ganas de vomitar** I feel nauseous, *Br* I feel sick

vómito *m* MED vomit

vorágine *f* (*remolino*) whirlpool; *fig* whirl

voraz *adj* voracious; *incendio* fierce

vos *pron pers sg Rpl, C.Am., Ven* you

vosotros, vosotras *pron pers pl* you

votación *f* vote, ballot

votar ⟨1a⟩ **1** *v/t* (*aprobar*) vote **2** *v/i* vote

voto *m* POL vote; **voto en blanco** spoiled ballot paper

voy *vb* → **ir**

voz *f* voice; *fig* rumo(u)r; **voz activa / pa-**

siva GRAM active / passive voice; *a media voz* in a hushed voice, in a low voice; *a voz en grito* at the top of one's voice; *en voz alta* aloud; *en voz baja* in a low voice; *correr la voz* spread the word; *llevar la voz cantante* fig call the tune, call the shots; *no tener voz ni voto* fig not have a say; *voz en off* voice-over

vuelco 1 *vb* → *volcar* **2** *m*: *dar un vuelco* fig F take a dramatic turn; *me dio un vuelco el corazón* my heart missed a beat

vuelo 1 *vb* → *volar* **2** *m* flight; *vuelo chárter* charter flight; *vuelo nacional* domestic flight; *al vuelo* coger, cazar in mid-air; *una falda con vuelo* a full skirt

vuelta *f* return; *en carrera* lap; *vuelta de carnero* L.Am. half-somersault; *vuelta al mundo* round-the- world trip; *a la vuelta* on the way back; *a la vuelta de la esquina* fig just around the corner; *dar la vuelta* llave etc turn; *dar media vuelta* turn round; *dar una vuelta* go for a walk; *dar cien vueltas a alguien* F be a hundred times better than s.o. F

vuelto 1 *part* → *volver* **2** *m* L.Am. change

vuelvo *vb* → *volver*

vuestro 1 *adj pos* your **2** *pron* yours

vulgar *adj* vulgar, common; *abundante* common

vulgaridad *f* vulgarity

vulgo *m* lower classes *pl*

vulnerable *adj* vulnerable

W

w. *abr* (= *watio*) w (= watt)
walkman *m* personal stereo
wáter *m* bathroom, toilet
waterpolo *m* DEP water polo

WC *abr* WC
whisky *m* whiskey, *Br* whisky
windsurf(ing) *m* wind-surfing
windsurfista *m/f* windsurfer

X, Y

xenofobia *f* xenophobia
xilófono *m* MÚS xylophone
y *conj* and
ya *adv* already; (*ahora mismo*) now; *¡ya!* incredulidad oh, yeah!, sure!; *comprensión* I know, I understand; *asenso* OK, sure; *al terminar* finished!, done!; *ya no vive aquí* he doesn't live here any more, he no longer lives here; *ya que* since, as; *ya lo sé* I know; *ya viene* she's coming now; *¿lo puede hacer? – ¡ya lo creo!* can she do it? - you bet!; *ya ... ya ... * either ... or ...
yacaré *m* L.Am. ZO cayman
yacer ⟨2y⟩ *v/i* lie
yacimiento *m* MIN deposit
yanqui *m/f* Yankee
yapa *f* L.Am. bit extra (for free); *Pe, Bol*

(propina) tip
yate *m* yacht
yaya *f* grandma
yayo *m* grandpa
yedra *f* BOT ivy
yegua *f* ZO mare
yema *f* yolk; *yema del dedo* fingertip
yendo *vb* → *ir*
yerba *f* L.Am. grass; *yerba mate* maté
yerbatero *m*, -a *f* Rpl herbalist
yerno *m* son-in-law
yeso *m* plaster
yo *pron* I; *soy yo* it's me; *yo que tú* if I were you
yodo *m* iodine
yoga *m* yoga
yogur *m* yog(h)urt
yonqui *m/f* F junkie

yuca f BOT yucca
yugo m yoke
Yugoslavia Yugoslavia
yugoslavo 1 adj Yugoslav(ian) 2 m, -a f
Yugoslav(ian)

yugular adj ANAT jugular
yute m jute
yuxtaposición f juxtaposition
yuyo m L.Am. weed

Z

zacatal m C.Am., Méx pasture
zacate m C.Am., Méx fodder
zafarse ⟨1a⟩ v/r get away (de from); (soltarse) come undone; zafarse de algo
(evitar) get out of sth
zafio adj coarse
zafiro m sapphire
zaga f: ir a la zaga bring up the rear
zalamero 1 adj flattering; empalagoso
syrupy, sugary 2 m, -a f flatterer, sweet
talker
zamba f Arg (baile) Argentinian folk-
dance
zambomba f MÚS type of drum
zambullirse ⟨3h⟩ v/r dive (en into); fig
throw o.s. (en into), immerse o.s. (en in)
zamparse ⟨1a⟩ v/r F wolf down F
zanahoria f carrot
zancada f stride
zancadilla f fig obstacle; poner or echar
la zancadilla a alguien trip s.o. up
zancudo m L.Am. mosquito
zángano m zo drone; fig F lazybones sg
zanja f ditch
zanjar ⟨1a⟩ v/t problemas settle; dificultades overcome
zapatería f shoe store, shoe shop
zapatero m, -a f shoemaker; zapatero re-
mendón shoe mender
zapatilla f slipper; de deporte sneaker, Br
trainer
Zapatista m/f Méx member or supporter
of the Zapatista National Liberation
Army
zapato m shoe
zapear ⟨1a⟩ v/i TV F channel hop
zapeo, zapping m TV F channel hopping
zarandear ⟨1a⟩ v/t shake violently, buffet;

zarandear a alguien fig give s.o. a hard
time
zarpa f paw
zarpar ⟨1a⟩ v/i MAR set sail (para for)
zarza f BOT bramble
zarzamora f BOT blackberry
zarzuela f MÚS type of operetta
zascandilear ⟨1a⟩ v/i mess around
zigzaguear ⟨1a⟩ v/i zigzag
zinc m zinc
zócalo m baseboard, Br skirting board
zodíaco, zodiaco m AST zodiac
zona f area, zone
zoncería f L.Am. F stupid thing
zonzo adj L.Am. F stupid
zoo m zoo
zoológico 1 adj zoological 2 m zoo
zoom m FOT zoom
zopilote m L.Am. zo turkey buzzard
zorra f zo vixen; P whore P
zorro 1 adj sly, crafty 2 m zo fox; fig old
fox
zozobrar ⟨1a⟩ v/i MAR overturn; fig go under
zueco m clog
zulo m hiding place
zumba f L.Am., Méx (paliza) beating
zumbar ⟨1a⟩ 1 v/i buzz; me zumban los
oídos my ears are ringing o buzzing 2 v/t
golpe, bofetada give
zumbido m buzzing
zumo m juice
zurcir ⟨3b⟩ v/t calcetines darn; chaqueta,
pantalones patch
zurdo 1 adj left-handed 2 m, f left-hander
zurrar ⟨1a⟩ v/t TÉC tan; zurrar a alguien F
tan s.o.'s hide F

Activity & Reference Section

The following section contains three parts, each of which will help you in your learning:

Games and puzzles to help you learn to use this dictionary and practice your Spanish-language skills. You'll learn about the different features of this dictionary and how to look something up effectively.

Basic words and expressions to reinforce your learning and help you master the basics.

A short grammar reference to help you use the language correctly.

Using Your Dictionary

Using a bilingual dictionary is important if you want to speak, read or write in a foreign language. Unfortunately, if you don't understand the symbols in your dictionary or the format of the entries, you'll make mistakes.

What kind of mistakes? Think of some of the words you know in English that sound or look alike. For example, think about the word *ring*. How many meanings can you think of for this word, *ring*? Try to list at least three.

a. _____

b. _____

c. _____

Now look up *ring* in the English side of the dictionary. There are nine Spanish words that correspond to the single English word *ring*. Some of these Spanish words are listed below in scrambled form.

Unscramble the jumbled Spanish words, then draw a line connecting each Spanish word with of the appropriate English meaning.

Spanish jumble	English meanings
1. ROSNA	a. a circle around something
2. LONAIL	b. the action of a bell or telephone (to ring)
3. ATSPI	c. jewelry worn on the finger
4. NOOT	d. the boxing venue
5. GNRI	e. one of the venues at a circus
6. LÍCCURO	f. the ring or tone of someone's voice

With so many Spanish words, each meaning something different, you must be careful to choose the right one. Using the wrong definition can obscure your meaning. Imagine the bizarre and misleading sentences you would make if you never looked beyond the first definition.

For example:

The boxer wearily entered the circle.

She always wore the circle left to her by her grandmother.

I was waiting for the phone circle when there was a knock at the door.

If you choose the wrong definition, you simply won't be understood. Mistakes like these are easy to avoid, once you know what to look for when using your dictionary. The following pages will review the structure of your bilingual dictionary and show you how to pick the right word when you use it. Read the tips and guidelines, then complete the puzzles and exercises to practice what you have learned.

Identifying Headwords

If you are looking for a single word in the dictionary, you simply look for that word's location in alphabetical order. However, if you are looking for a phrase, or an object that is described by several words, you will have to decide which word to look up.

Two-word terms are listed by their first word. If you are looking for the Spanish equivalent of *shooting star*, you will find it under *shooting*.

So-called phrasal verbs in English are found in a block under the main verb. The phrasal verbs *go ahead*, *go back*, *go off*, *go on*, *go out*, and *go up* are all found in a block after *go*.

Idiomatic expressions are found under the key word in the expression. The phrase *give someone a ring*, meaning to call someone, is found in the entry for *ring*.

Feminine headwords that are variants of a masculine headword and share a meaning with the masculine word will be found in alphabetical order with their masculine counterpart. In Spanish a male lawyer is called an **abogado** and a female lawyer is an **abogada**. Both of the words are found in alphabetical order under the masculine form, **abogado**.

Find the following words and phrases in your bilingual dictionary. Identify the headword under which you should look for each. Then, try to find all of the headwords in the word-search puzzle on the next page.

1. in the middle of	9. that's a relief
2. be in shock	10. take advantage of
3. break in	11. bailarín
4. dog	12. tan pronto como
5. bring up	13. sin duda
6. string someone along	14. colgar de un hilo
7. be in jeopardy	15. menos mal
8. get away with it	

z	h	r	u	o	v	ó	l	x	q	r	e	r	p	o	u	j	k
u	g	e	d	u	a	v	c	l	x	f	í	u	e	t	e	c	i
í	a	e	z	ó	v	c	d	e	ñ	u	i	a	j	l	j	k	u
m	e	q	t	b	a	h	g	l	w	a	o	ú	c	p	i	r	y
e	é	w	c	i	o	a	p	f	m	l	r	g	o	h	r	e	s
k	n	k	b	g	t	y	z	o	i	u	n	i	p	b	s	h	f
c	f	ñ	i	n	g	b	s	h	z	i	d	r	a	a	i	g	e
í	s	e	a	d	n	r	f	e	r	e	a	á	r	i	y	n	t
u	e	v	o	l	u	e	r	t	a	e	l	d	d	l	o	o	r
o	d	e	n	u	m	a	s	ó	m	s	e	z	y	a	e	t	y
a	h	d	s	o	i	k	b	r	i	n	g	w	o	r	l	m	s
ñ	e	o	d	q	m	i	d	d	l	e	j	d	l	í	r	a	q
b	d	g	c	o	r	g	l	e	y	d	n	i	o	n	u	l	l
e	z	g	n	k	z	w	a	c	s	u	n	s	e	i	e	a	f
l	w	y	u	f	v	ó	o	i	d	a	i	l	q	r	t	g	
c	é	f	g	i	r	a	m	l	o	a	c	e	d	u	i	á	a
a	n	r	y	t	e	i	s	e	g	p	r	o	n	t	o	a	w
u	ñ	a	c	a	s	n	e	l	e	h	s	e	s	g	r	d	ó

Alphabetization

The entries in a bilingual dictionary are in alphabetical order. They are ordered from A to Z for each language. If words begin with the same letter or letters, they are alphabetized from A to Z using the first unique letter in each word.

Practice alphabetizing the following words. Rewrite the words in alphabetical order, using the space provided below. Next to each word also write the number that is associated with it. Then follow that order to connect the dots on the next page. Not all of the dots will be used, only those whose numbers appear in the word list.

universo	1	fecha	48
sueño	2	hasta	57
ciudad	3	calle	59
escuela	4	repente	60
nos	7	hoy	62
aquí	8	bastante	65
entender	9	mágico	74
disfraz	10	mañana	75
cuchillo	15	vida	76
jamás	16	algo	77
lente	17	zapato	77
tiempo	20	marrón	79
boleta	21	pie	81
nadie	23	otro	82
dulce	27	miel	84
más	30	lavaplatos	86
corazón	41	gritar	87
piel	42	miedo	93
así	44	flor	95
silla	45	despacio	99
llover	46		

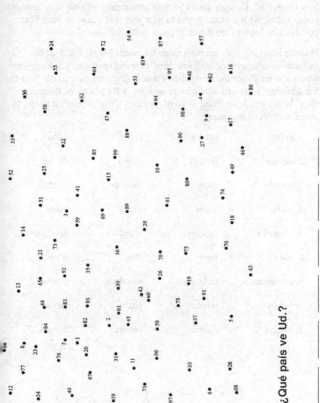

¿Qué país ve Ud.?

Spelling

Like any dictionary, a bilingual dictionary will tell you if you have spelled a word right. But how can you look up a word if you don't know how to spell it? Though it may be time consuming, the only way to check your spelling with a dictionary is to take your best guess, or your best guesses, and look to see which appears in the dictionary.

Practice checking your spelling using the words below. Each group includes one correct spelling and three incorrect spellings. Look up the words and cross out the misspelled versions (the ones you do not find in the dictionary). Rewrite the correct spelling in the blanks on the next page. When you have filled in all of the blanks, use the circled letters to reveal a mystery message.

1. esfara	esfera	esfira	esfura
2. devisa	deviza	divisa	diviza
3. mendir	mentir	mindir	mintir
4. viata	viota	viuda	viuta
5. abagado	apagedo	apagado	apadato
6. paor	peor	pior	pour
7. mammeca	manmeca	mandeca	manteca
8. jarbín	jardén	jardín	jartiín
9. corana	corena	corona	coruna

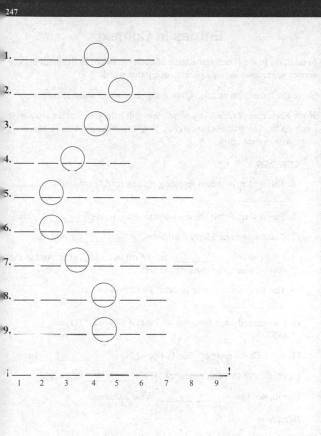

1. ___ ___ ___ ◯ ___ ___ ___ ___

2. ___ ___ ___ ___ ◯ ___

3. ___ ___ ___ ◯ ___ ___ ___

4. ___ ___ ◯ ___

5. ___ ◯ ___ ___ ___ ___ ___ ___

6. ___ ◯ ___ ___

7. ___ ___ ◯ ___ ___ ___

8. ___ ___ ___ ◯ ___ ___ ___

9. ___ ___ ___ ◯ ___ ___

i ___ ___ ___ ___ ___ ___ ___ ___ ___ !
　1　2　3　4　5　6　7　8　9

Entries in Context

In addition to the literal translation of each headword in the dictionary, entries sometimes include phrases using that word.

Solve the crossword puzzle below using the correct word in context.

Hint: Each clue contains key words that will help you find the answer. Look up the key words in each clue. You'll find the answers in expressions within each entry.

ACROSS

4. The sticker in the no smoking section read "**prohibido** _____."

5. The students read the story aloud. They read en _____ alta.

7. They wished us Merry Christmas, or _____ **Navidad**.

8. **En primer** _____, he got off to a rough start. And in the second place, the competition was stiff.

9. The food was vacuum packed. **Fue envasado al** _____.

11. I wondered what time it was; I asked a friend, "¿Qué _____ es?"

12. Hey! That's none of your business! No es _____ tuyo.

16. ¿Gracias? Oh, don't mention it. No _____ de qué.

17. Oh, no! Qué _____. What a shame!

DOWN

1. She had lost her lighter, so she asked her friend for a light, "¿**Tienes** _____?"

2. It's pouring rain! **Está lloviendo a** _____.

3. He plans to be in the lead soon. **Va a estar en** _____.

5. Do you dine out once in a while? Sure, de _____ en cuando.

6. Tonight she will pick out her clothes and pack her bags (**hacer la** _____). Tomorrow she is leaving on vacation.

10. They have open-air seating on the patio, if you'd prefer to dine **al** _____ **libre**.

11. _____ **en día** (nowadays), many women have careers. This may not have been the case for previous generations.

13. The weather is nice. It's sunny out. **Hace** _____.

14. Good night. ¡**Buenas** _____! See you again tomorrow.

15. You wonder if it is worth all the trouble? I think so. **En mi opinion, vale la** _____.

Word Families

Some English words have several related meanings that are represented by different words in Spanish. These related meanings belong to the same word family and are grouped together under a single English headword. Other words, while they look the same, do not belong to the same word family. These words are written under a separate headword.

Think back to our first example, *ring*. The translations **círculo, anillo,** and **pista** all refer to related meanings of *ring* in English. They are all circular things, though in different contexts. **Timbrazo, dar un telefonazo a alguien,** and **sonar,** however, refer to a totally different meaning of *ring* in English: the sound a bell or phone makes.

The word family for circles, with all of its nuanced Spanish translations, is grouped together under *ring¹*. The word family for sounds is grouped together under *ring²*.

Study the lists of words below. Each group includes three Spanish translations belonging to one word family, and one Spanish translation of an identical-looking but unrelated English word. Eliminate the translation that is not in the same word family as the others. Then rewrite the misfit word in the corresponding blanks. When you have filled in all of the blanks, use the circled letters to reveal a bonus message.

Hint: Look up the Spanish words to find out what they mean. Then look up those words in the English-Spanish side of your dictionary to find the word family that contains the Spanish words.

1. encender	iluminar	ligero	luz
2. atasco	aprieto	embutir	mermelada
3. a juego	fósforo	igualar	partida
4. estampilla	patear	sello	timbre
5. anillo	cuadrilátero	pista	timbrazo

1. __ __ ◯ __ __ __ __

2. __ __ __ __ ◯ __ __ __ __ __

3. __ __ ◯ __ __ __ __

4. __ __ ◯ __ __ __ __ __

5. __ __ __ __ __ __ __ __ ◯ __

__ __ __ __ __
1   2   3   4   5

Regional variation

Spanish is a world language with several regional variants. Historical change and influence have produced diverse vocabularies across the Spanish-speaking world.

This dictionary leaves universal words unmarked. Words specific to a particular country or region are marked with abbreviations for that location. For example, words used only in Central America are marked in the dictionary with **C.Am**. Vocabulary used only in Mexico is marked with the abbreviation **Méx**, and so forth. A full list of these abbreviations is found on pages 10–11.

Look up the following words and indicate the regional or country affiliation in each box.

carro	majada	tuna	pelazón	abarrotes
afanar	papa	rebasar	terno	abalear
choclo	ñapa	corotos	chichera	chompa
chicha	frutilla	huachafo	egreso	okupa
plática	vecindad	hilachos	mañero	guanaco

If this puzzle were a BINGO card, which country or region would win?

_____

Running Heads

Running heads are the words printed in blue at the top of each page. The running head on the left tells you the first headword on the left-hand page. The running head on the right tells you the last headword on the right-hand page. All the words that fall in alphabetical order between the two running heads appear on those two dictionary pages.

Look up the running head on the page where each headword appears, and write it in the space provided. Then unscramble the jumbled running heads and match them with what you wrote.

Headword	Running head	Jumbled running head
1. apenas	APAGAR	FOLOCNÓ
2. bombilla		CILIMO
3. cómodo		ÍTFICNOPE
4. famoso		SUTOJ
5. joven		MOOSS
6. magia		RAAGAP
7. minuto		OOPCA
8. oreja		CEHILBO
9. polvo		DARALSATR
10. sorna		NEIVE
11. transición		GIAAM
12. vetusto		CAHFAAD

Parts of Speech

In Spanish and English, words are categorized into different *parts of speech*. These labels tell us what function a word performs in a sentence. In this dictionary, the part of speech is given before a word's definition.

Nouns are things. *Verbs* describe actions. *Adjectives* describe nouns in sentences. For example, the adjective *pretty* tells you about the noun *girl* in the phrase *a pretty girl*. *Adverbs* also describe, but they modify verbs, adjectives, and other adverbs. The adverb *quickly* tells you more about how the action is carried out in the phrase *ran quickly*.

Prepositions specify relationships in time and space. They are words such as *in*, *on*, *before*, or *with*. *Articles* are words that accompany nouns. Words like *the* and *a* or *an* modify the noun, marking it as specific or general, and known or unknown.

Conjunctions are words like *and*, *but*, and *if* that join phrases and sentences together. *Pronouns* take the place of nouns in a sentence.

The following activity uses words from the dictionary in a Sudoku-style puzzle. In Sudoku puzzles, the numbers 1 to 9 are used to fill in grids. All digits 1 to 9 must appear, but cannot be repeated, in each square, row, and column.

In the following puzzles, you are given a set of words for each part of the grid. Look up each word to find out its part of speech. Then arrange the words within the square so that, in the whole puzzle, you do not repeat any part of speech within a column or row.

Hint: If one of the words given in the puzzle is a noun, then you know that no other nouns can be put in that row or column of the grid. Use the process of elimination to figure out where the other parts of speech can go.

Let's try a small puzzle first. You will use the categories noun *n*, verb *v*, adjective *adj*, and preposition *prp* to solve this puzzle. The sections are numbered from top left to bottom right.

Part 1

a, beber, cocina, **correcto**

Part 2

de, **donación**, escapar, espartano

Part 3

en, huelga, inferior, jugar

Part 4

lotería, **montar**, móvil, para

	correcto		
			donación
		montar	
en			

Now try a larger puzzle. For this puzzle, you will use the categories noun *n*, verb *v*, adjective *adj*, preposition *prp*, article *art*, and pronoun *pron*. The sections are numbered from top left to bottom right.

Part 1

antiguo, **ascensor**, **batir**, la, él, en

Part 2

charla, dócil, **educar**, ella, entre, los

Part 3

cierto, con, cola, **descansar**, **nosotros**, una

Part 4

cultura, **exclusivo**, ellos, leer, sin, un

Part 5

a, diferente, ejercer, ejemplo, **las**, yo

Part 6

de, el, familia, mantener, marinero, **Usted**

		batir	charla		
ascensor					educar
	descansar			cultura	
una	nosotros			exclusivo	
a		las			Usted
		yo	de		

Gender

Spanish nouns belong to one of two groups: feminine or masculine. A noun's gender is indicated in an entry after the headword or pronunciation with **m** for masculine, **f** for feminine, and **m/f** if the same form of the word can be used for a man or a woman.

In some cases, the masculine and feminine forms of one word mean two different things. For example, the masculine **un partido** means *a political party*. The feminine **una partida** means *a game or match*. The gender associated with each meaning follows the headword in the dictionary entry.

Look up the words in the grids below. Circle the feminine words. Put an **X** through the masculine words.

pie	persona	mano
distrito	huracán	computadora
lengua	jamón	disco

naranja	saco	manzana
estrella	mesa	objeto
miel	miedo	tren

gorro	océano	estación
escalera	onda	sirena
sabor	policía	lobo

Think of these as tic-tac-toe grids. Does masculine or feminine win more matches?

Adjectives

Adjectives in Spanish change form to agree in gender and number with the noun they modify. In many cases, the feminine form ends in −a, and the masculine form ends in −o. An −s is added to make the plural for either gender. Some adjectives have irregular forms, in this case, the irregular forms are written out after the headword.

Use the dictionary to determine whether the nouns in the following phrases are masculine or feminine, singular or plural. Then write in the correct inflected form of the adjective. Check your answers against the word search. The correct forms are found in the puzzle.

1. a difficult exam   un examen _____

2. a tall woman   una mujer _____

3. an important message   un mensaje _____

4. secondary school   la escuela _____

5. the red cars   los carros _____

6. an unforgettable picnic   un picnic _____

7. a beautiful girl   una chica _____

8. a romantic song   una canción _____

9. the first time   la _____ vez

10. two Peruvian monuments   dos monumentos _____

11. a heavy backpack   una mochila _____

t	r	v	g	m	l	u	o	b	p	o	á	o	a	e	l	é	ó
f	e	á	í	f	í	n	l	ú	b	i	s	ú	t	u	é	n	i
k	p	a	i	c	o	b	v	m	h	e	a	i	l	ú	q	a	r
p	r	c	b	ú	g	m	s	i	t	p	e	r	u	a	n	o	s
g	i	b	o	u	m	c	é	a	ñ	e	ú	w	e	k	s	g	u
q	m	i	n	r	d	e	c	y	o	d	i	g	í	f	k	e	é
á	e	s	i	d	o	i	e	á	c	z	i	b	e	m	f	o	b
n	r	á	t	á	t	s	i	e	u	e	ú	f	i	o	n	d	e
n	a	ó	a	n	u	é	i	a	ú	ú	p	l	í	n	t	i	ó
u	s	e	á	p	í	j	e	a	c	r	v	m	c	c	o	u	í
í	é	m	o	p	e	s	a	d	a	e	l	j	e	é	i	à	d
p	o	c	i	t	s	e	c	u	n	d	a	r	i	a	u	l	v
r	u	o	a	b	e	a	l	t	a	é	a	o	g	h	g	é	e
r	o	v	á	p	k	s	x	p	h	a	r	w	g	a	h	g	a
é	w	ó	ì	d	o	u	e	i	m	p	o	r	t	a	n	t	e
é	s	u	z	j	e	v	c	g	u	o	á	ú	o	i	é	v	u
v	o	n	o	i	e	n	i	z	é	e	i	v	u	h	o	k	í
p	z	r	i	n	o	l	v	i	d	a	b	l	e	b	p	l	t
i	s	c	f	a	i	p	e	t	k	ó	i	f	é	e	a	g	u
é	e	e	d	i	v	c	i	o	s	é	h	s	r	r	f	z	é

Verbs

Verbs are listed in the dictionary in their infinitive form. To use the verb in a sentence, you must conjugate it and use the form that agrees with the sentence's subject.

Most verbs fall into categories with other verbs that are conjugated in the same way. In the verb appendix of this dictionary, you will find an example of each category, along with conjugations of common irregular verbs.

For this puzzle, conjugate the given verbs in the present tense. Use the context and the subject pronoun to determine the person and number of the form you need. The correct answer fits in the crossword spaces provided.

Hint: The verb class code given in the verb's dictionary entry tells you which model conjugation to follow.

ACROSS

2. Los jugadores _____ Cubanos, de la Habana. **ser**

4. Yo _____ el periódico por la mañana. **leer**

5. Los sábados, yo _____ con mi familia. **descansar**

8. Yo tengo un gato, y él _____ un perro. **tener**

9. Tú _____ a la fiesta ¿verdad? **ir**

11. Nosotros _____ al cine. **ir**

13. Mis hijos _____ mucho la televisión. **mirar**

14. Yo _____ siempre las llaves. **perder**

15. Carlos _____ la maleta antes de ir de vacaciones. **hacer**

16. Tú _____ visitar Machu Picchu? **querer**

17. ¿Ustedes _____ una palabra en el diccionario? **buscar**

18. Machu Picchu _____ en el Perú. **estar**

DOWN

1. Nosotros _____ cuando habla el profesor. **comprender**

3. Los amigos _____ algo en la cafetería antes de comer. **beber**

6. Los alumnos _____ de la clase a las tres. **salir**

7. Yo _____ por lo menos ocho horas por noche. **dormir**

9. Nosotros siempre _____ a Sudamérica. **viajar**

10. El equipo argentino _____ el partido. **ganar**

12. Ella _____ la puerta cuando llega a casa. **cerrar**

When you are reading Spanish, you face a different challenge. You see a conjugated verb in context and need to determine what its infinitive is in order to understand its meaning.

For the next puzzle, you will see conjugated verbs in the sentences. Figure out which verb the conjugated form represents, and write the infinitive (the headword form) in the puzzle.

ACROSS

3. Martín y Anita **llegaron** a las ocho.

5. ¿Por qué no **viene** a la fiesta tu novio?

7. ¡**Ganamos**!

10. Quiero que Ustedes **hagan** la tarea.

11. Las hojas **caen** en el otoño.

13. El chico **esconde** los caramelos.

15. No entiendo lo que **dices**.

16. Rita **cumple** diez años mañana.

18. Sofía **compartió** su bocadillo con sus amigos.

19. ¿Qué te **parece** el libro?

DOWN

1. No **volvimos** a casa.

2. Los alumnos **dieron** el examen.

4. A los niños les **gustan** mucho los videojuegos.

6. Ellos **hablaban** siempre con los amigos.

8. Las mujeres **prepararon** la cena.

9. Que yo **sepa**, está bien.

12. **Tomas** el sol en la playa.

14. El gato **se duerme** en el sillón.

16. Los abuelos **comieron** en casa.

17. El se **murió**.

Riddles

Solve the following riddles in English. Give the Spanish word for the riddle's solution.

1. This cold season is followed by spring.

$\overline{\hspace{0.5em}}\ \overline{\hspace{0.5em}}\ \overline{\hspace{0.5em}}\ \overline{\hspace{0.5em}}\ \overline{\hspace{0.5em}}\ \overline{\hspace{0.5em}}\ \overline{\hspace{0.5em}}\ \overline{\hspace{0.5em}}$
15 27 25 15   5   6 27 16

2. You don't want to forget this type of clothing when you go to the beach.

1   6   9 20   5   13   5   28   9   7 16

3. This thing protects you from the rain, but it's bad luck to open it indoors!

17   9   6   9 11 14   9 10

4. This adjective is the opposite of "difficult."

12   29   24   15   18

5. This is the number that follows three and precedes five.

24   14   9   1   6   16

6. If you are injured or very ill, you should go to this place.

2   16 10 17 15   1   9 18

7. This mode of transportation has only two wheels. It is also good exercise!

28 15 24 15 24 18   5   1   5

8. This large mammal lives in the ocean.

28	9	18	18	5	27	9

9. This person is your mother's mother.

9	28	14	9	18	9

10. There are twelve of these in a year.

26	5	10

11. Wearing this in the car is a safety precaution.

24	15	27	1	14	6	30	27	13	5

10	5	11	14	6	15	13	9	13

12. Snow White bit into this red fruit and fell into a long slumber.

26	9	27	22	9	27	9

13. This professional brings letters and packages to your door.

24	9	6	1	5	6	16

14. This midday meal falls between breakfast and dinner.

9	18	26	14	5	6	22	16

15. A very young dog is referred to as this.

24	9	24	2	16	6	6	16

Cryptogram

Use the number-to-letter correspondence from the riddles to fill in the hidden message. When you are done, translate the Spanish message into English. What does it say?

14	27		26	16	13	15	10	26	16		5	27
5	10	17	9	7	16	18		13	15	24	5	
:		5	27		28	16	24	9				
	24	5	6	6	9	13	9		,		27	16
5	27	1	6	9	27		26	16	10	24	9	10

Translation:

_____ _____ _____ _____ _____ :

_____ _____ _____ , ____

_____ _____ .

Answer Key

Using Your Dictionary

a–c. Answers will vary

1. sonar, b
2. anillo, c
3. pista, e

4. tono, f
5. ring, d
6. círculo, a

Identifying Headwords

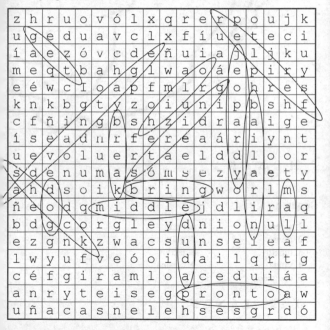

Alphabetization

algo, aquí, así, bastante, boleta, calle, ciudad, corazón, cuchillo,
despacio, disfraz, dulce, entender, escuela, fecha, flor, gritar, hasta,
hoy, jamás, lavaplatos, lente, llover, mágico, mañana, marrón, más,
miedo, miel, nadie, nos, otro, pie, piel, repente, silla, sueño, tiempo,
universo, vida, zapato

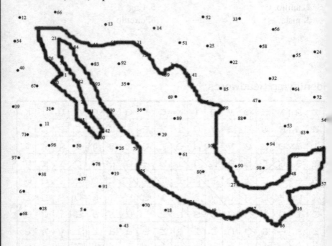

<u>M</u> <u>E</u> <u>X</u> <u>I</u> <u>K</u> <u>O</u>

Spelling

1. esfera
2. divisa
3. mentir
4. viuda
5. apagado
6. peor
7. manteca
8. jardín
9. corona

¡<u>E</u> <u>S</u> <u>T</u> <u>U</u> <u>P</u> <u>E</u> <u>N</u> <u>D</u> <u>O</u>!

Entries in Context

Word Families

1. ligero
2. mermelada
3. fósforo

4. patear
5. timbrazo

¡<u>G</u> <u>E</u> <u>S</u> <u>T</u> <u>O</u>!

Regional Variation

L. Am. carro (○)	CSur majada	Mex tuna	C. Am. pelazón	L. Am. abarrotes
C. Am. afanar	L. Am. papa (○)	Mex rebasar	CSur terno	S. Am. abalear
Rpl choclo	S. Am. ñapa	L. Am. corotos (○)	C. Am. chichera	S. Am. chompa
L. Am. chicha	S. Am. frutilla	Pe huachafo	L. Am. egreso (○)	Esp okupa
Mex plática	Mex vecindad	Mex hilachos	Rpl mañero	L. Am. guanaco (○)

Latin America

Running Heads

Headword	Running head	Jumbled running head
1. apenas	<u>APAGAR</u>	FOLOCNÓ
2. bombilla	<u>BOLICHE</u>	CILIMO
3. cómodo	<u>COLOFÓN</u>	ÍTFICNOPE
4. famoso	<u>FACHADA</u>	SUTOJ
5. joven	<u>JUSTO</u>	MOOSS
6. magia	<u>MAGIA</u>	RAAGAP
7. minuto	<u>MILICO</u>	OOPCA
8. oreja	<u>OPACO</u>	CEHILBO
9. polvo	<u>PONTÍFICE</u>	DARALSATR
10. sorna	<u>SOMOS</u>	NEIVE
11. transición	<u>TRASLADAR</u>	GIAAM
12. vetusto	<u>VIENE</u>	CAHFAAD

Parts of Speech

cocina	**correcto**	de	escapar
beber	a	espartano	**donación**
inferior	huelga	**montar**	para
en	jugar	lotería	móvil

él	la	**batir**	charla	entre	dócil
ascensor	en	antiguo	los	ella	**educar**
cierto	**descansar**	con	ellos	**cultura**	un
una	**nosotros**	cola	leer	**exclusivo**	sin
a	ejemplo	**las**	marinero	mantener	**Usted**
ejercer	diferente	**yo**	**de**	el	familia

Gender

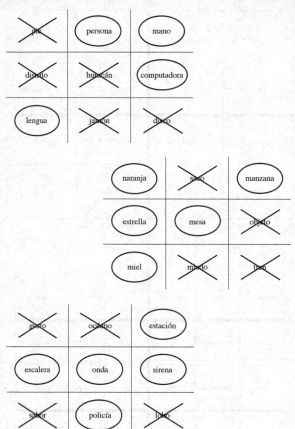

~~pie~~	persona	mano
~~distrito~~	~~huracán~~	computadora
lengua	~~jabón~~	~~disco~~

naranja	~~saco~~	manzana
estrella	mesa	~~objeto~~
miel	~~miedo~~	~~tren~~

~~gorro~~	~~océano~~	estación
escalera	onda	sirena
~~sabor~~	policía	~~lobo~~

Feminine wins the most matches.

Adjectives

1. un examen **difícil**
2. una mujer **alta**
3. un mensaje **importante**
4. la escuela **secundaria**
5. los carros **rojos**
6. un picnic **inolvidable**
7. una chica **bonita**
8. una canción **romántica**
9. la **primera** vez
10. dos monumentos **peruanos**
11. una mochila **pesada**

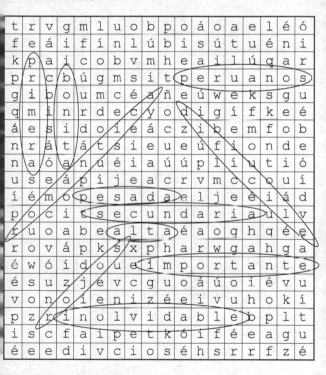

t	r	v	g	m	l	u	o	b	p	o	á	o	a	e	l	é	ó
f	e	á	i	f	í	n	l	ú	b	i	s	ú	t	u	é	n	i
k	p	a	i	c	o	b	v	m	h	e	a	i	l	ú	g	a	r
p	r	c	b	ú	g	m	s	i	t	p	e	r	u	a	n	o	s
g	i	b	o	u	m	c	é	a	ñ	e	ú	w	e	k	s	g	u
q	m	i	n	r	d	e	c	y	o	d	i	g	í	f	k	e	é
á	e	s	i	d	o	i	é	á	c	z	i	b	e	m	f	o	b
n	r	á	t	á	t	s	i	e	u	e	ú	f	i	o	n	d	e
n	a	ó	a	n	ú	é	i	a	ú	ú	p	l	í	u	t	i	ó
u	s	e	á	p	í	j	e	a	c	r	v	m	c	c	o	u	í
í	é	m	o	p	e	s	a	d	a	e	l	j	e	é	i	á	d
p	o	c	i	t	s	e	c	u	n	d	a	r	i	a	u	l	v
r	u	o	a	b	e	a	l	t	a	é	a	o	q	h	q	é	e
r	o	v	á	p	k	s	x	p	h	a	r	w	g	a	h	g	a
é	w	ó	i	d	o	u	e	l	m	p	o	r	t	a	n	t	e
é	s	u	z	j	é	v	c	g	u	o	á	ú	o	i	é	v	u
v	o	n	o	l	e	n	i	z	é	e	i	v	u	h	o	k	í
p	z	r	i	n	o	l	v	i	d	a	b	l	e	b	p	l	t
i	s	c	f	a	i	p	e	t	k	ó	i	f	é	e	a	g	u
é	e	e	d	i	v	c	i	o	s	é	h	s	r	r	f	z	é

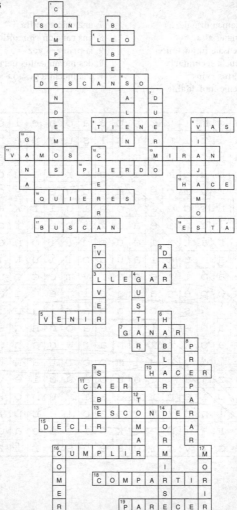

Verbs

Riddles

1. invierno
2. traje de baño
3. paraguas
4. fácil
5. cuatro
6. hospital
7. bicicleta
8. ballena
9. abuela
10. mes
11. cinturón de seguridad
12. manzana
13. cartero
14. almuerzo
15. cachorro

Cryptogram

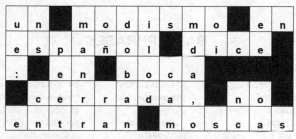

u	n		m	o	d	i	s	m	o		e	n
e	s	p	a	ñ	o	l		d	i	c	e	
:		e	n		b	o	c	a				
	c	e	r	r	a	d	a	,		n	o	
e	n	t	r	a	n		m	o	s	c	a	s

A Spanish proverb says: into a closed mouth, no flies enter.

BASIC SPANISH PHRASES & GRAMMAR

Pronunciation

In this section we have used a simplified phonetic system to represent the sounds of Spanish. Simply read the pronunciation as if it were English.

Stress

The acute accent (´) is used in Spanish to indicate a syllable is stressed, e.g. **río** (reeo). Since some words have more than one meaning, the accent mark is also used to distinguish between them, e.g.: **él** (*he*) and **el** (*the*); **sí** (*yes*) and **si** (*if*).

BASIC PHRASES

Essential

Good afternoon!	**¡Buenas tardes!**	bweh-nahs tahrdehs
Good evening!	**¡Buenas noches!**	bweh-nahs nochehs
Goodbye!	**¡Adiós!**	ah-deeyos
..., please!	**..., por favor.**	por fahbor
Thank you!	**¡Gracias!**	grah-seeyahs
Yes.	**Sí.**	see
No.	**No.**	no
Sorry!	**¡Lo siento!**	lo seeyehn-to
Where are the restrooms?	**¿Dónde están los baños?**	dondeh ehstahn los bahnyos
When?	**¿Cuándo?**	kwahn-doh
What?	**¿Qué?**	keh
Where?	**¿Dónde?**	dondeh
Here.	**Aquí.**	ahkee
There.	**Allí.**	ahyee
On the right.	**A la derecha.**	ah lah dehrehchah
On the left.	**A la izquierda.**	ah lah eeskeeyehr-dah
Do you have ...?	**¿Tiene ...?**	teeyeh-neh
I'd like ...	**Quisiera ...**	keeseeyeh-rah
How much is that?	**¿Cuánto cuesta?**	kwahn-to kwehs-tah

| Where is …? | ¿Dónde está …? | dondeh ehstah |
| Where can I get …? | ¿Dónde puedo encontrar …? | dondeh pweh-doh ehnkontrahr |

Communication Difficulties

Do you speak English?	¿Habla inglés?	ah-blah een-glehs
Does anyone here speak English?	¿Hay alguien aquí que hable inglés?	eye ahl-geeyehn ah-keeh keh ah-bleh een-glehs
Did you understand that?	¿Ha entendido?	ah ehntehn-dee-doh
I understand.	Entiendo.	ehntiehn-doh
I didn't understand that.	No lo he entendido.	no lo eh ehntehn-dee-doh
Could you speak a bit more slowly, please?	¿Podría hablar un poco más despacio, por favor?	podree-ah ah-blahr oon poko mahs despah-seeyo por fahbor
Could you please repeat that?	¿Podría repetirlo, por favor?	podree-ah rehpeh-teer-lo por fahbor
What does … mean?	¿Qué significa …?	keh seegnee-fee-kah
Could you write it down for me, please?	¿Podría escribírmelo, por favor?	podree-ah ehskree-beer-mehlo por fahbor

Greetings

Good morning!	¡Buenos días!	bwehnos dee-ahs
Good afternoon!	¡Buenas tardes!	bwehnahs tahrdehs
Good evening/night!	¡Buenas noches!	bwehnahs nocheh
Hello!	¡Hola!	Olah
How are you?	¿Cómo está?	komo ehstah
How are things?	¿Qué tal?	keh tahl
Fine, thanks. And you?	Bien, gracias. ¿Y usted?	beeyehn grah-seeyahs ee oostehd
I'm afraid I have to go now.	Lo siento, pero me tengo que ir.	lo seeyehn-toh pehro meh tehngo keh eer
Goodbye!	¡Adiós!	ah-deeyos
See you soon / tomorrow!	¡Hasta pronto / mañana!	ahstah pronto / mah-nyah-nah

| It was nice meeting you. | **Me alegro de haberle conocido.** | meh ahleh-gro deh ah-behrleh kono-see-doh |
| Have a good trip! | **¡Buen viaje!** | bwehn beeyah-kheh |

Meeting People

What's your name?	**¿Cómo se llama / te llamas?**	komo seh yahmah / teh yahmahs
My name is …	**Me llamo …**	meh yahmo
Where are you from?	**¿De dónde es / eres?**	deh dohndeh ehs / ehrehs
I'm from …	**Soy de …**	soy deh
– the US. –	**los Estados Unidos.**	los ehstah-dos oonee-dos
– Canada.	**Canadá.**	kah-nahdah
– the UK. –	**Gran Bretaña.**	grahn brehtah-nyah

Expressing Likes and Dislikes

Very good!	**¡Muy bien!**	mwee beeyehn
I'm very happy.	**Estoy muy contento (m)/contenta (f).**	ehs-toy mwee kon-tehnto/kon-tehn-tah
I like that.	**Me gusta.**	meh goos-tah
What a shame!	**¡Qué pena!**	keh pehnah
I'd rather …	**Preferiría …**	prehfehree-reeah
I don't like it.	**No me gusta.**	no meh goos-tah
I'd rather not.	**No me apetece.**	no meh ahpehteh-seh
Certainly not.	**¡De ninguna manera!**	deh neengoo-nah mahneh-rah

Expressing Requests and Thanks

Thank you very much.	**Muchas gracias.**	moochahs grah-seeyahs
Thanks, you too.	**Gracias, igualmente.**	grah-seeyahs eeg-wahl-mehnteh
May I?	**¿Puedo?**	pwehdoh

Please, …	**Por favor …**	por fahbor
No, thank you.	**No, gracias.**	no grah-seeyahs
Could you help me?	**¿Podría ayudarme?**	podree-ah ahy-oodahr-meh
That's very nice of you.	**Muy amable de su parte.**	mwee ahmah-bleh deh soo pahrteh
Thank you very much for all your trouble / help.	**Le agradezco las molestias / la ayuda.**	leh ahgrah-dehsko lahs molehs-teeyahs / lah ahyoodah
You're welcome.	**De nada.**	deh nahdah

Apologies

Sorry!	**¡Perdón!**	pehrdon
Excuse me!	**¡Perdone!**	pehr-doneh
I'm sorry about that.	**Lo siento.**	lo seeyehn-toh
Don't worry about it!	**¡No importa!**	no importah
How embarrassing!	**Esto me resulta muy desagradable.**	ehsto meh reh-sooltah mwee deh-sahgrah-dahbleh
It was a misunderstanding.	**Ha sido un malentendido.**	ah seedo oon mahlehn-tehndee-doh

GRAMMAR

Regular Verbs and Their Tenses

There are three verb types which follow a regular pattern, their infinitives ending in **-ar**, **-er**, and **-ir**, e.g. *to speak* **hablar**, *to eat* **comer**, *to live* **vivir**. Here are the most commonly used forms. The **vosotros** forms are only used in Spain. In Latin America **ustedes** is used to address more than one person formally or informally.

	Present	*Past*	*Future*
yo *I*	hablo	hablé	hablaré
tú *you (informal)*	hablas	hablaste	hablarás

él/ella/Ud. *he/she/* *you (form.)*	habla	habló	hablará
nosotros *we*	hablamos	hablamos	hablaremos
vosotros *you* *(pl. inform.) [Spain]*	habláis	hablasteis	hablaréis
ellos/ellas/Uds. *they/you (form.)*	hablan	hablaron	hablarán

yo *I*	como	comí	comeré
tú *you (inform.)*	comes	comiste	comerás
él/ella/Ud. *he/she/* *you (form.)*	come	comió	comerá
nosotros *we*	comemos	comimos	comeremos
vosotros *you* *(pl. inform.) [Spain]*	coméis	comisteis	comeréis
ellos/ellas/Uds. *they/you (form.)*	comen	comieron	comerán

yo *I*	vivo	viví	viviré
tú *you (inform.)*	vives	viviste	vivirás
él/ella/Ud. *he/she/* *you (form.)*	vive	vivió	vivirá
nosotros *we*	vivimos	vivimos	viviremos
vosotros *you* *(pl. inform.) [Spain]*	vivís	vivisteis	viviréis
ellos/ellas/Uds. *they/you (form.)*	viven	vivieron	vivirán

Very often, people omit the pronoun, using only the verb form.

Examples: Vivo en Madrid. *I live in Madrid.*
¿Habla español? *Do you speak Spanish?*

There are many irregular verbs whose forms differ considerably.

To be – ser and estar

Spanish has two verbs for *to be*, ser and estar. Their usage is complex. Here are some general guidelines:

Ser is used to identify people or objects, to describe their basic and natural characteristics, also to tell time and dates.

Examples:	¡Es caro! *That is expensive!*
	Somos médicos. *We're doctors.*
	Son las dos. *It's 2 o'clock.*

Estar is used when the state of a person or object is changeable and to indicate locations.

Examples:	Estoy cansado. *I'm tired.*
	¿Dónde estuvo? *Where was he?*
	Estarán en Roma. *They'll be in Rome.*

	Present	**Past**	**Future**
yo	soy/estoy	fui/estuve	seré/estaré
tú	eres/estás	fuiste/estuviste	serás/estarás
él/ella/Ud.	es/está	fue/estuvo	será/estará
nosotros	somos/ estamos	fuimos/estuvimos	seremos/ estaremos
vosotros *[Spain]*	sois/estáis	fuisteis/estuvisteis	seréis/estaréis
ellos/ellas/Uds.	son/están	fueron/estuvieron	serán/estarán

Nouns and Articles

Generally nouns ending in -o are masculine, and those ending in -a are feminine. Their definite articles—meaning *the*—are el (m) and la (f). In the plural, the article is los (m) and las (f). Plural nouns end in -s, or -es when the singular form ends with a consonant.

Examples: Singular el tren *the train* Plural los trenes *the trains*
la mesa *the table* las mesas *the tables*

The definite articles also change according to gender: un (m), una (f), unos (m/pl), unas (f/pl).

Examples: Singular un libro *a book* Plural unos libros *books*
una casa *a house* unas casas *houses*

Possessive articles relate to the gender of the noun that follows:

Examples:	¿Dónde está su billete? *Where is your ticket?*
	Vuestro tren sale a las 8. *Your train leaves at 8.*
	Busco mis maletas. *I'm looking for my suitcases.*

	Singular	**Plural**
my	mi	mis
your (inform.)	tu	tus
his/her/its/your (form.)	su	sus
our	nuestro/a	nuestros/as
your (pl. inform.)[Spain]	vuestro/a	vuestros/as
their/your (pl. form.)	su	sus

Word Order

The conjugated verb comes after the subject.

Examples: **Yo trabajo en Madrid.** *I work in Madrid.*

Questions are formed by reversing the order of subject and verb, changing the intonation of the affirmative sentence, or using key question words like *when? ¿cuándo?*.

Examples: **¿Tiene Ud. mapas?** *Do you have maps?*
¿Cuándo cerrará el banco? *When will the bank close?*

Negations

Negative sentences are formed by adding *no* (*not*) to that part of the sentence which is to be negated.

Examples: **No fumamos.** *We don't smoke.*
No es nuevo. *It's not new.*
El autobús no llegó. *The bus didn't arrive.*
¿Por qué no escuchas? *Why don't you listen?*

Imperatives (Command Form)

Imperative sentences are formed by using the stem of the verb with the appropriate ending.

Examples:

tú *you (inform.)*	¡Habla! *Speak!*	[no hables]
Ud. *you (form.)*	¡Hable! *Speak!*	
nosotros *we*	¡Hablemos! *Let's speak!*	
vosotros *you (inform. pl.)*	¡Hablad! *Speak!*	[no habléis]
[Spain]		
Uds. *you (form. pl.)*	¡Hablen! *Speak!*	

Comparative and Superlative

Comparative and superlative are formed by adding **más** (*more*), **lo más** (*the most*), **menos** (*less*) or **lo menos** (*the least*) before the adjective or noun.

Adjective	Comparative	Superlative
grande	más grande	lo más grande
big, large	*bigger*	*the biggest*
costoso	menos costoso	lo menos costoso
expensive	*less expensive*	*the least expensive*

Examples: Estas postales son las más baratas. *These postcards are the cheapest.*
Pepe tiene menos dinero que Juan. *Pepe has less money than Juan.*

Possessive Pronouns

Pronouns serve as substitutes and relate to the gender.

	Singular	Plural
mine	mío/a	míos/as
yours (inform. sing.)	tuyo/a	tuyos/as
yours (form.)	suyo/a	suyos/as
his/her/its	suyo/a	suyos/as
ours	nuestro/a	nuestros/as
yours (pl. inform.)	vuestro/a	vuestros/as
[Spain]		
theirs	suyo/a	suyos/as

Examples: Sus hijos y los míos. *Your children and mine.*
¿Es tuyo este café? *Is this coffee yours?*

Adjectives

Adjectives describe nouns. They agree with the noun in gender and number. Masculine forms end in -o, feminine forms in -a. In general, adjectives come after the noun. The feminine form is generally the same if the masculine form ends in -e or with a consonant.

Examples: **Tenemos un coche viejo.** *We have an old car.*
Mi jefa es simpática. *My boss is nice.*
El mar/La flor es azul. *The ocean / flower is blue.*

Most adjectives form their plurals the same way as nouns:

Examples: **una casa roja** *a red house*
unas casas rojas *red houses*

Adverbs and Adverbial Expressions

Adverbs describe verbs. They are formed by adding **-mente** to the feminine form of the adjective if it differs from the masculine. Otherwise add **-mente** to the masculine form.

Examples: **María conduce lentamente.** *Maria drives very slowly.*
Roberto conduce rápidamente. *Robert drives fast.*
Ud. habla español bien. *You speak Spanish well.*

Some common adverbial time expressions:

actualmente *presently*
todavía *still*
todavía no *not yet*
ya no *not anymore*

Part 2

English-Spanish
Dictionary

A

a [ə] *stressed* [eɪ] *art* un(a); *$50 a ride* 50 dólares por viaje

a·back [əˈbæk] *adv: taken aback* desconcertado (*by* por)

a·ban·don [əˈbændən] *v/t* abandonar

a·bashed [əˈbæʃt] *adj* avergonzado

a·bate [əˈbeɪt] *v/i of storm, flood* amainar

ab·at·toir [ˈæbətwɑːr] matadero *m*

ab·bey [ˈæbɪ] abadía *f*

ab·bre·vi·ate [əˈbriːvɪeɪt] *v/t* abreviar

ab·bre·vi·a·tion [əbriːvɪˈeɪʃn] abreviatura *f*

ab·di·cate [ˈæbdɪkeɪt] *v/i* abdicar

ab·di·ca·tion [æbdɪˈkeɪʃn] abdicación *f*

ab·do·men [ˈæbdəmən] abdomen *m*

ab·dom·i·nal [æbˈdɒmɪnl] *adj* abdominal

ab·duct [əbˈdʌkt] *v/t* raptar, secuestrar

ab·duc·tion [əbˈdʌkʃn] rapto *m*, secuestro *m*

◆ **a·bide by** [əˈbaɪd] *v/t* atenerse a

a·bil·i·ty [əˈbɪlətɪ] capacidad *f*, habilidad *f*

a·blaze [əˈbleɪz] *adj* en llamas

a·ble [ˈeɪbl] *adj (skillful)* capaz, hábil; *be able to* poder; *I wasn't able to see / hear* no conseguí *or* pude ver / escuchar

a·ble-bod·ied [eɪblˈbɑːdiːd] *adj* sano

ab·nor·mal [æbˈnɔːrml] *adj* anormal

ab·nor·mal·ly [æbˈnɔːrməlɪ] *adv* anormalmente; *behave* de manera anormal

a·board [əˈbɔːrd] **1** *prep* a bordo de **2** *adv* a bordo; *be aboard* estar a bordo; *go aboard* subir a bordo

ab·ol·ish [əˈbɑːlɪʃ] *v/t* abolir

ab·o·li·tion [æbəˈlɪʃn] abolición *f*

a·bort [əˈbɔːrt] *v/t mission, launch* suspender, cancelar; COMPUT cancelar

a·bor·tion [əˈbɔːrʃn] aborto *m (provocado)*; *have an abortion* abortar

a·bor·tive [əˈbɔːrtɪv] *adj* fallido

a·bout [əˈbaʊt] **1** *prep (concerning)* acerca de, sobre; *what's it about? of book, movie* ¿de qué trata? **2** *adv (roughly)* más o menos; *be about to* … *(be going to)* estar a punto de …; *be about (somewhere near)* estar por ahí; *there are a lot of people about* hay un montón de gente por ahí

a·bove [əˈbʌv] **1** *prep* por encima de; *500 m above sea level* 500 m sobre el nivel del mar; *above all* por encima de todo, sobre todo **2** *adv: on the floor above* en el piso de arriba

a·bove-men·tioned [əbʌvˈmenʃnd] *adj* arriba mencionado

ab·ra·sion [əˈbreɪʒn] abrasión *f*

ab·ra·sive [əˈbreɪsɪv] *adj personality* abrasivo

a·breast [əˈbrest] *adv* de frente, en fondo; *keep abreast of* mantenerse al tanto de

a·bridge [əˈbrɪdʒ] *v/t* abreviar, condensar

a·broad [əˈbrɔːd] *adv live* en el extranjero; *go* al extranjero

a·brupt [əˈbrʌpt] *adj departure* brusco, repentino; *manner* brusco, rudo

a·brupt·ly [əˈbrʌptlɪ] *adv (suddenly)* repentinamente; *(curtly)* bruscamente

ab·scess [ˈæbsɪs] absceso *m*

ab·sence [ˈæbsəns] *of person* ausencia *f*; *(lack)* falta *f*

ab·sent [ˈæbsənt] *adj* ausente

ab·sen·tee [æbsənˈtiː] *n* ausente *m/f*

ab·sen·tee·ism [æbsənˈtiːɪzm] absentismo *m*

ab·sent-mind·ed [æbsəntˈmaɪndɪd] *adj* despistado, distraído

ab·sent-mind·ed·ly [æbsəntˈmaɪndɪdlɪ] *adv* distraídamente

ab·so·lute [ˈæbsəluːt] *adj power* absoluto; *idiot* completo; *mess* total

ab·so·lute·ly [ˈæbsəluːtlɪ] *adv (completely)* absolutamente, completamente; *absolutely not!* ¡en absoluto!; *do you agree? - absolutely!* ¿estás de acuerdo? - ¡completamente!

ab·so·lu·tion [æbsəˈluːʃn] REL absolución *f*

ab·solve [əbˈzɑːlv] *v/t* absolver

ab·sorb [əbˈsɔːrb] *v/t* absorber, *absorbed in* … absorto en …

ab·sorb·en·cy [əbˈsɔːrbənsɪ] absorbencia *f*

ab·sorb·ent [əbˈsɔːrbənt] *adj* absorbente

ab·sorb·ent 'cot·ton algodón *m* hidrófilo

ab·sorb·ing [əbˈsɔːrbɪŋ] *adj* absorbente

ab·stain [əbˈsteɪn] *v/i from voting* abstenerse

ab·sten·tion [əbˈstenʃn] *in voting* abstención *f*

ab·stract [ˈæbstrækt] *adj* abstracto

ab·struse [əbˈstruːs] *adj* abstruso

ab·surd [əbˈsɜːrd] *adj* absurdo

ab·surd·i·ty [əbˈsɜːrdətɪ] lo absurdo

a·bun·dance [əˈbʌndəns] abundancia *f*

a·bun·dant [əˈbʌndənt] *adj* abundante

a·buse[1] [əˈbjuːs] *n (insults)* insultos *mpl*; *of thing* maltrato *m*; *he shouted abuse at me* me insultó; *(child) abuse physical* malos tratos *mpl* a menores; *sexual* agresión f sexual a menores

a·buse² [ə'bju:z] v/t (physically) abusar de; (verbally) insultar

a·bu·sive [ə'bju:sɪv] adj language insultante, injurioso; **become abusive** ponerse a insultar

a·bys·mal [ə'bɪzml] adj F (very bad) desastroso F

a·byss [ə'bɪs] abismo m

AC ['eɪsi:] abbr (= **alternating current**) CA (= corriente f alterna)

ac·a·dem·ic [ækə'demɪk] **1** n académico(-a) m(f), profesor(a) m(f) **2** adj académico

a·cad·e·my [ə'kædəmɪ] academia f

ac·cede [ək'si:d] v/i accede; **accede to** acceder a

ac·cel·e·rate [ək'seləreɪt] v/t & v/i acelerar

ac·cel·e·ra·tion [əkselə'reɪʃn] aceleración f

ac·cel·e·ra·tor [ək'seləreɪtər] of car acelerador m

ac·cent ['æksənt] when speaking acento m; (emphasis) énfasis m

ac·cen·tu·a·te [ək'sentueɪt] v/t acentuar

ac·cept [ək'sept] v/t & v/i aceptar

ac·cep·ta·ble [ək'septəbl] adj aceptable

ac·cept·ance [ək'septəns] aceptación f

ac·cess ['ækses] **1** n acceso m; **have access to** computer tener acceso a; child tener derecho a visitar **2** v/t also COMPUT acceder a

'ac·cess code COMPUT código m de acceso

ac·ces·si·ble [ək'sesəbl] adj accesible

ac·ces·sion [ək'seʃn] acceso m

ac·ces·so·ry [ək'sesərɪ] for wearing accesorio m, complemento m; LAW cómplice m/f

'ac·cess road carretera f de acceso

'ac·cess time COMPUT tiempo m de acceso

ac·ci·dent ['æksɪdənt] accidente m; **by accident** por casualidad

ac·ci·den·tal [æksɪ'dentl] adj accidental

ac·ci·den·tal·ly [æksɪ'dentlɪ] adv sin querer

ac·claim [ə'kleɪm] **1** n alabanza f, aclamación f; **meet with acclaim** ser alabado or aclamado **2** v/t alabar, aclamar

ac·cla·ma·tion [əklə'meɪʃn] aclamación f

ac·cli·mate, ac·cli·ma·tize [ə'klaɪmət, ə'klaɪmətaɪz] v/t aclimatarse

ac·com·mo·date [ə'kɑːmədeɪt] v/t alojar; requirements satisfacer, hacer frente a

ac·com·mo·da·tions [əkɑːmə'deɪʃnz] npl alojamiento m

ac·com·pa·ni·ment [ə'kʌmpənɪmənt] MUS acompañamiento m

ac·com·pa·nist [ə'kʌmpənɪst] MUS acompañante m/f

ac·com·pa·ny [ə'kʌmpənɪ] v/t (pret & pp **accompanied**) also MUS acompañar

ac·com·plice [ə'kʌmplɪs] cómplice m/f

ac·com·plish [ə'kʌmplɪʃ] v/t task realizar; goal conseguir, lograr

ac·com·plished [ə'kʌmplɪʃt] adj consumado

ac·com·plish·ment [ə'kʌmplɪʃmənt] of a task realización f; (talent) habilidad f; (achievement) logro m

accord [ə'kɔːrd] acuerdo m; **of one's own accord** de motu propio

ac·cord·ance [ə'kɔːrdəns]: **in accordance with** de acuerdo con

ac·cord·ing [ə'kɔːrdɪŋ] adv: **according to** según

ac·cord·ing·ly [ə'kɔːrdɪŋlɪ] adv (consequently) por consiguiente; (appropriately) como corresponde

ac·cor·di·on [ə'kɔːrdɪən] acordeón m

ac·cor·di·on·ist [ə'kɔːrdɪənɪst] acordeonista m/f

ac·count [ə'kaʊnt] financial cuenta f; (report, description) relato m, descripción f; **give an account of** relatar, describir; **on no account** de ninguna manera, bajo ningún concepto; **on account of** a causa de; **take sth into account, take account of sth** tener algo en cuenta, tener en cuenta algo

◆ **account for** v/t (explain) explicar; (make up, constitute) suponer, constituir

ac·count·abil·i·ty [əkaʊntə'bɪlətɪ] responsabilidad f

ac·coun·ta·ble [ə'kaʊntəbl] adj responsable (to ante); **be held accountable** ser considerado responsable

ac·coun·tant [ə'kaʊntənt] contable m/f, L.Am. contador(a) m(f)

ac'count hold·er titular m/f de una cuenta

ac'count num·ber número m de cuenta

ac·counts [ə'kaʊnts] npl contabilidad f

ac·cu·mu·late [ə'kjuːmjuleɪt] **1** v/t acumular **2** v/i acumularse

ac·cu·mu·la·tion [əkjuːmjuˈleɪʃn] acumulación f

ac·cu·ra·cy ['ækjurəsɪ] precisión f

ac·cu·rate ['ækjurət] adj preciso

ac·cu·rate·ly ['ækjurətlɪ] adv con precisión

ac·cu·sa·tion [ækjuːˈzeɪʃn] acusación f

ac·cuse [ə'kjuːz] v/t: **accuse s.o. of sth** acusar a alguien de algo; **be accused of** LAW ser acusado de

ac·cused [ə'kjuːzd] n LAW acusado(-a) m(f)

ac·cus·ing [əˈkjuːzɪŋ] *adj* acusador

ac·cus·ing·ly [əˈkjuːzɪŋlɪ] *adv* say en tono acusador; *he looked at me accusingly* me lanzó una mirada acusadora

ac·cus·tom [əˈkʌstəm] *v/t* acostumbrar; *get accustomed to* acostumbrarse a; *be accustomed to* estar acostumbrado a

ace [eɪs] *in cards* as *m*; *(in tennis: shot)* ace *m*

ache [eɪk] **1** *n* dolor *m* **2** *v/i* doler

a·chieve [əˈtʃiːv] *v/t* conseguir, lograr

a·chieve·ment [əˈtʃiːvmənt] *of ambition* consecución *f*, logro *m*; *(thing achieved)* logro *m*

ac·id [ˈæsɪd] *n* ácido *m*

a·cid·i·ty [əˈsɪdətɪ] acidez *f*; *fig* sarcasmo *m*

ac·id 'rain lluvia *f* ácida

'ac·id test *fig* prueba *f* de fuego

ac·knowl·edge [əkˈnɑːlɪdʒ] *v/t* reconocer; *acknowledge receipt of a letter* acusar recibo de una carta

ac·knowl·edg(e)·ment [əkˈnɑːlɪdʒmənt] reconocimiento *m*; *of a letter* acuse *f* de recibo

ac·ne [ˈækni] MED acné *m*, acne *m*

a·corn [ˈeɪkɔːrn] BOT bellota *f*

a·cous·tics [əˈkuːstɪks] acústica *f*

ac·quaint [əˈkweɪnt] *v/t fml*: *be acquainted with* conocer

ac·quaint·ance [əˈkweɪntəns] *person* conocido(-a) *m(f)*

ac·qui·esce [ækwɪˈes] *v/i fml* acceder

ac·qui·es·cence [ækwɪˈesns] *fml* aquiescencia *f*

ac·quire [əˈkwaɪr] *v/t* adquirir

ac·qui·si·tion [ækwɪˈzɪʃn] adquisición *f*

ac·quis·i·tive [əˈkwɪzətɪv] *adj* consumista

ac·quit [əˈkwɪt] *v/t* LAW absolver

ac·quit·tal [əˈkwɪtl] LAW absolución *f*

a·cre [ˈeɪkər] acre *m* (4.047m2)

a·cre·age [ˈeɪkərɪdʒ] superficie *f* en acres

ac·ri·mo·ni·ous [ækrɪˈmoʊniəs] *adj* áspero, agrio

ac·ro·bat [ˈækrəbæt] acróbata *m/f*

ac·ro·bat·ic [ækrəˈbætɪk] *adj* acrobático

ac·ro·bat·ics [ækrəˈbætɪks] *npl* acrobacias *fpl*

ac·ro·nym [ˈækrənɪm] acrónimo *m*

a·cross [əˈkrɑːs] **1** *prep* al otro lado de; *she lives across the street* vive al otro lado de la calle; *sail across the Atlantic* cruzar el Atlántico navegando **2** *adv* de un lado a otro; *it's too far to swim across* está demasiado lejos como para cruzar a nado; *once you're across* cuando hayas llegado al otro lado; *10 m across* 10 m de ancho

a·cryl·ic [əˈkrɪlɪk] *adj* acrílico

act [ækt] **1** *v/i* THEA actuar; *(pretend)* hacer teatro; *act as* actuar *or* hacer de **2** *n (deed)*, *of play* acto *m*; *in vaudeville* número *m*; *(law)* ley *f*; *it's just an act (pretense)* es puro teatro; *act of God* caso *m* fortuito

act·ing [ˈæktɪŋ] **1** *n in a play* interpretación *f*; *as profession* teatro *m* **2** *adj (temporary)* en funciones

ac·tion [ˈækʃn] acción *f*; *out of action machine* sin funcionar; *person* fuera de combate; *take action* actuar; *bring an action against* LAW demandar a

ac·tion 're·play TV repetición *f* (de la jugada)

ac·tive [ˈæktɪv] *adj also* GRAM activo; *party member* en activo

ac·tiv·ist [ˈæktɪvɪst] POL activista *m/f*

ac·tiv·i·ty [ækˈtɪvətɪ] actividad *f*

ac·tor [ˈæktər] actor *m*

ac·tress [ˈæktrɪs] actriz *f*

ac·tu·al [ˈæktʃʊəl] *adj* verdadero, real

ac·tu·al·ly [ˈæktʃʊəlɪ] *adv (in fact, to tell the truth)* en realidad; *did you actually see her?* ¿de verdad llegaste a verla?; *he actually did it!* ¡aunque parezca mentira lo hizo!; *actually, I do know him (stressing converse)* pues sí, de hecho lo conozco; *actually, it's not finished yet* el caso es que todavía no está terminado

ac·u·punc·ture [ˈækjəpʌŋktʃər] acupuntura *f*

a·cute [əˈkjuːt] *adj pain* agudo; *sense* muy fino

a·cute·ly [əˈkjuːtlɪ] *adv (extremely)* extremadamente; *acutely aware* plenamente consciente

ad [æd] → *advertisement*

ad·a·mant [ˈædəmənt] *adj* firme

ad·a·mant·ly [ˈædəməntlɪ] *adv* firmemente

Ad·am's ap·ple [ædəmzˈæpəl] nuez *f*

a·dapt [əˈdæpt] **1** *v/t* adaptar **2** *v/i of person* adaptarse

a·dapt·a·bil·i·ty [ədæptəˈbɪlətɪ] adaptabilidad *f*

a·dapt·a·ble [əˈdæptəbl] *adj* adaptable

a·dap·ta·tion [ædæpˈteɪʃn] *of play etc* adaptación *f*

a·dapt·er [əˈdæptər] *electrical* adaptador *m*

add [æd] **1** *v/t* añadir; MATH sumar **2** *v/i of person* sumar

◆ **add on** *v/t 15% etc* sumar

◆ **add up 1** *v/t* sumar **2** *v/i fig* cuadrar

ad·der [ˈædər] víbora *f*

ad·dict [ˈædɪkt] adicto(-a) *m(f)*; *drug addict* drogadicto(-a) *m(f)*

ad·dic·ted [ə'dɪktɪd] *adj* adicto; *be addicted to* ser adicto a

ad·dic·tion [ə'dɪkʃn] adicción *f*

ad·dic·tive [ə'dɪktɪv] *adj* adictivo

ad·di·tion [ə'dɪʃn] MATH suma *f*; *to list, company etc* incorporación *f*; *of new drive etc* instalación *f*; *in addition* además; *in addition to* además de

ad·di·tion·al [ə'dɪʃnl] *adj* adicional

ad·di·tive ['ædɪtɪv] aditivo *m*

add-on ['ædɒn] extra *m*, accesorio *m*

ad·dress [ə'dres] 1 *n* dirección *f*; *form of address* tratamiento *m* 2 *v/t letter* dirigir; *audience* dirigirse a; *how do you address the judge?* ¿qué tratamiento se le da al juez?

ad'dress book agenda *f* de direcciones

ad·dress·ee [ædre'siː] destinatario(-a) *m(f)*

ad·ept ['ædept] *adj* experto; *be adept at* ser un experto en

ad·e·quate ['ædɪkwət] *adj* suficiente; *(satisfactory)* aceptable

ad·e·quate·ly ['ædɪkwətlɪ] *adv* suficientemente; *(satisfactorily)* aceptablemente

ad·here [əd'hɪr] *v/i* adherirse
◆ **adhere to** *v/t surface* adherirse a; *rules* cumplir

ad·he·sive [əd'hiːsɪv] *n* adhesivo *m*

ad·he·sive 'plas·ter esparadrapo *m*

ad·he·sive 'tape cinta *f* adhesiva

ad·ja·cent [ə'dʒeɪsnt] *adj* adyacente

ad·jec·tive ['ædʒɪktɪv] adjetivo *m*

ad·join [ə'dʒɔɪn] *v/t* lindar con

ad·join·ing [ə'dʒɔɪnɪŋ] *adj* contiguo

ad·journ [ə'dʒɜːrn] *v/i of court, meeting* aplazar

ad·journ·ment [ə'dʒɜːrnmənt] aplazamiento *m*

ad·just [ə'dʒʌst] *v/t* ajustar, regular

ad·just·a·ble [ə'dʒʌstəbl] *adj* ajustable, regulable

ad·just·ment [ə'dʒʌstmənt] ajuste *m*; *psychological* adaptación *f*

ad lib [æd'lɪb] 1 *adj* improvisado 2 *adv* improvisadamente 3 *v/i (pret & pp adbed)* improvisar

ad·min·is·ter [əd'mɪnɪstər] *v/t* administrar

ad·min·is·tra·tion [ədmɪnɪ'streɪʃn] administración *f*

ad·min·is·tra·tive [ədmɪnɪ'strətɪv] *adj* administrativo

ad·min·is·tra·tor [əd'mɪnɪstreɪtər] administrador(a) *m(f)*

ad·mi·ra·ble ['ædmərəbl] *adj* admirable

ad·mi·ra·bly ['ædmərəblɪ] *adv* admirablemente

ad·mi·ral ['ædmərəl] almirante *m*

ad·mi·ra·tion [ædmə'reɪʃn] admiración *f*

ad·mire [əd'maɪr] *v/t* admirar

ad·mir·er [əd'maɪrər] admirador(a) *m(f)*

ad·mir·ing [əd'maɪrɪŋ] *adj* de admiración

ad·mir·ing·ly [əd'maɪrɪŋlɪ] *adv* con admiración

ad·mis·si·ble [əd'mɪsəbl] *adj* admisible

ad·mis·sion [əd'mɪʃn] *(confession)* confesión *f*; *admission free* entrada gratis

ad·mit [əd'mɪt] *v/t (pret & pp admitted) to a place* dejar entrar; *to school, organization* admitir; *to hospital* ingresar; *(confess)* confesar; *(accept)* admitir

ad·mit·tance [əd'mɪtəns] admisión *f*; *no admittance* prohibido el paso

ad·mit·ted·ly [əd'mɪtedlɪ] *adv*: *he didn't use those exact words, admittedly* es verdad que no utilizó exactamente esas palabras

ad·mon·ish [əd'mɑːnɪʃ] *v/t fml* reprender

a·do [ə'duː]: *without further ado* sin más dilación

ad·o·les·cence [ædə'lesns] adolescencia *f*

ad·o·les·cent [ædə'lesnt] 1 *n* adolescente *m/f* 2 *adj* de adolescente

a·dopt [ə'dɑːpt] *v/t child, plan* adoptar

a·dop·tion [ə'dɑːpʃn] *of child* adopción *f*

a·dop·tive 'par·ents [ədɑːptɪv] *npl* padres *mpl* adoptivos

a·dor·a·ble [ə'dɔːrəbl] *adj* encantador

ad·o·ra·tion [ædə'reɪʃn] adoración *f*

a·dore [ə'dɔːr] *v/t* adorar; *I adore chocolate* me encanta el chocolate

a·dor·ing [ə'dɔːrɪŋ] *adj expression* lleno de adoración; *his adoring fans* sus entregados fans

ad·ren·al·in [ə'drenəlɪn] adrenalina *f*

a·drift [ə'drɪft] *adj* a la deriva; *fig* perdido

ad·u·la·tion [ædu'leɪʃn] adulación *f*

a·dult ['ædʌlt] 1 *n* adulto(-a) *m(f)* 2 *adj* adulto

a·dult ed·u'ca·tion educación *f* para adultos

a·dul·ter·ous [ə'dʌltərəs] *adj relationship* adúltero

a·dul·ter·y [ə'dʌltərɪ] adulterio *m*

'a·dult film *euph* película *f* para adultos

ad·vance [əd'væns] 1 *n money* adelanto *m*; *in science,* MIL avance *m*; *in advance* con antelación; *get money* por adelantado; *48 hours in advance* con 48 horas de antelación; *make advances (progress)* avanzar, progresar; *sexually* insinuarse 2 *v/i* MIL avanzar; *(make progress)* avanzar, progresar 3 *v/t theory* presentar; *sum of money* adelantar; *human knowledge, a cause* hacer avanzar

ad·vance 'book·ing reserva *f* (anticipada)

ad·vanced [ədˈvænst] *adj country, level, learner* avanzado

ad·vance 'no·tice aviso *m* previo

ad·vance 'pay·ment pago *m* por adelantado

ad·van·tage [ədˈvæntɪdʒ] ventaja *f*; *there's no advantage to be gained* no se gana nada; *it's to your advantage* te conviene; *take advantage of* aprovecharse de

ad·van·ta·geous [ædvənˈteɪdʒəs] *adj* ventajoso

ad·vent [ˈædvent] *fig* llegada *f*

'ad·vent cal·en·dar calendario *m* de Adviento

ad·ven·ture [ədˈventʃər] aventura *f*

ad·ven·tur·ous [ədˈventʃərəs] *adj person* aventurero; *investment* arriesgado

ad·verb [ˈædvɜːrb] adverbio *m*

ad·ver·sa·ry [ˈædvərserɪ] adversario(-a) *m(f)*

ad·verse [ˈædvɜːrs] *adj* adverso

ad·vert [ˈædvɜːrt] → *advertisement*

ad·ver·tise [ˈædvərtaɪz] **1** *v/t* anunciar **2** *v/i* anunciarse, poner un anuncio

ad·ver·tise·ment [ædvɜːrˈtaɪsmənt] anuncio *m*

ad·ver·tis·er [ˈædvərtaɪzər] anunciante *m/f*

ad·ver·tis·ing [ˈædvərtaɪzɪŋ] publicidad *f*

'ad·ver·tis·ing a·gen·cy agencia *f* de publicidad

'ad·ver·tis·ing budg·et presupuesto *m* para publicidad

'ad·ver·tis·ing cam·paign campaña *f* publicitaria

'ad·ver·tis·ing rev·e·nue ingresos *mpl* por publicidad

ad·vice [ədˈvaɪs] consejo *m*; *he gave me some advice* me dio un consejo; *take s.o.'s advice* seguir el consejo de alguien

ad·vis·a·ble [ədˈvaɪzəbl] *adj* aconsejable

ad·vise [ədˈvaɪz] *v/t person, caution* aconsejar; *government* asesorar; *I advise you to leave* te aconsejo que te vayas

ad·vis·er [ədˈvaɪzər] asesor(a) *m(f)*

ad·vo·cate [ˈædvəkeɪt] *v/t* abogar por

aer·i·al [ˈerɪəl] *n* antena *f*

aer·i·al 'pho·to·graph fotografía *f* aérea

aer·o·bics [eˈroʊbɪks] *nsg* aerobic *m*

aer·o·dy·nam·ic [eroʊdaɪˈnæmɪk] *adj* aerodinámico

aer·o·nau·ti·cal [eroʊˈnɔːtɪkl] *adj* aeronáutico

aer·o·plane [ˈeroʊpleɪn] *Br* avión *m*

aer·o·sol [ˈerəsɑːl] aerosol *m*

aer·o·space in·dus·try [ˈerəspeɪs] industria *f* aeroespacial

aes·thet·ic *etc Br* → *esthetic etc*

af·fa·ble [ˈæfəbl] *adj* afable

af·fair [əˈfer] *(matter, business)* asunto *m*; *(love affair)* aventura *f*, lío *m*; *foreign affairs* asuntos *mpl* exteriores; *have an affair with* tener una aventura *o* lío con

affect [əˈfekt] *v/t also* MED afectar

af·fec·tion [əˈfekʃn] afecto *m*, cariño

af·fec·tion·ate [əˈfekʃnət] *adj* afectuoso, cariñoso

af·fec·tion·ate·ly [əˈfekʃnətlɪ] *adv* con afecto, cariñosamente

af·fin·i·ty [əˈfɪnətɪ] afinidad *f*

af·fir·ma·tive [əˈfɜːrmətɪv] *adj* afirmativo; *answer in the affirmative* responder afirmativamente

af·flu·ence [ˈæfluəns] prosperidad *f*, riqueza *f*

af·flu·ent [ˈæfluənt] *adj* próspero, acomodado; *affluent society* sociedad *f* opulenta

af·ford [əˈfɔːrd] *v/t* permitirse; *be able to afford sth financially* poder permitirse algo; *I can't afford the time* no tengo tiempo; *it's a risk we can't afford to take* es un riesgo que no podemos permitirnos tomar

af·ford·a·ble [əˈfɔːrdəbl] *adj* asequible

a·float [əˈfloʊt] *adj boat* a flote; *keep the company afloat* mantener la compañía a flote

a·fraid [əˈfreɪd] *adj*: *be afraid* tener miedo; *be afraid of* tener miedo de; *I'm afraid of cats* tengo miedo a los gatos; *he's afraid of the dark* le da miedo la oscuridad; *I'm afraid of annoying him* me da miedo enfadarle; *I'm afraid expressing regret* me temo; *he's very ill, I'm afraid* me temo que está muy enfermo; *I'm afraid so* (me) temo que sí; *I'm afraid not* (me) temo que no

a·fresh [əˈfreʃ] *adv* de nuevo

Af·ri·ca [ˈæfrɪkə] África

Af·ri·can [ˈæfrɪkən] **1** *adj* africano **2** *n* africano(-a) *m(f)*

af·ter [ˈæftər] **1** *prep* después de; *after all* después de todo; *after that* después de eso; *it's ten after two* son las dos y diez **2** *adv* después; *the day after* el día siguiente

af·ter·math [ˈæftərmæθ] *time* periodo *m* posterior *(of* a); *state of affairs* repercusiones *fpl*

af·ter·noon [æftərˈnuːn] tarde *f*; *in the afternoon* por la tarde; *this afternoon* esta tarde; *good afternoon* buenas tardes

'af·ter sales serv·ice servicio *m* posventa

'af·ter·shave loción *f* para después del afeitado, after shave *m*

'af·ter·taste regusto *m*
af·ter·ward ['æftərwərd] *adv* después
a·gain [ə'geɪn] *adv* otra vez; *I never saw him again* no lo volví a ver
a·gainst [ə'genst] *prep lean* contra; *the USA against Brazil* SP Estados Unidos contra *Brasil*; *I'm against the idea* estoy en contra de la idea; *what do you have against her?* ¿que tienes en contra de ella?; *against the law* ilegal
age [eɪdʒ] **1** *n* of person, object edad *f*; (*era*) era *f*; *at the age of ten* a los diez años; *under age* menor de edad; *she's five years of age* tiene cinco años; *I've been waiting for ages* llevo siglos esperando F; *I haven't seen him for ages* hace siglos que no lo veo F **2** *v/i* envejecer
aged¹ [eɪdʒd] *adj*: *aged 16* con 16 años de edad
a·ged² ['eɪdʒɪd] **1** *adj*: *her aged parents* sus ancianos padres **2** *n*: *the aged* los ancianos
'age group grupo *m* de edades
'age lim·it límite *m* de edad
a·gen·cy ['eɪdʒənsɪ] agencia *f*
a·gen·da [ə'dʒendə] orden *m* del día; *on the agenda* en el orden del día
a·gent ['eɪdʒənt] agente *m/f*, representante *m/f*
ag·gra·vate ['ægrəveɪt] *v/t* agravar; (*annoy*) molestar
ag·gre·gate ['ægrɪgət] *n* SP: *win on aggregate* ganar en el total de la eliminatoria
ag·gres·sion [ə'greʃn] agresividad *f*
ag·gres·sive [ə'gresɪv] *adj* agresivo; (*dynamic*) agresivo, enérgico
ag·gres·sive·ly [ə'gresɪvlɪ] *adv* agresivamente
a·ghast [ə'gæst] *adj* horrorizado
ag·ile ['ædʒəl] *adj* ágil
a·gil·i·ty [ə'dʒɪlətɪ] agilidad *f*
ag·i·tate ['ædʒɪteɪt] *v/i: agitate for* hacer campaña a favor de
ag·i·tat·ed ['ædʒɪteɪtɪd] *adj* agitado
ag·i·ta·tion [ædʒɪ'teɪʃn] agitación *f*
ag·i·ta·tor [ædʒɪ'teɪtər] agitador(a) *m(f)*
AGM [eɪdʒiː'em] *abbr* (= *annual general meeting*) junta *f* general annual
ag·nos·tic [æg'nɑːstɪk] *n* agnóstico(-a) *m(f)*
a·go [ə'goʊ] *adv: 2 days ago* hace dos días; *long ago* hace mucho tiempo; *how long ago?* ¿hace cuánto tiempo?; *how long ago did he leave?* ¿hace cuánto se marchó?
a·gog [ə'gɑːg] *adj: be agog at sth* estar emocionado con algo
ag·o·nize ['ægənaɪz] *v/i* atormentarse

(*over* por), angustiarse (*over* por)
ag·o·niz·ing ['ægənaɪzɪŋ] *adj* pain atroz; wait angustioso
ag·o·ny ['ægənɪ] agonía *f*
a·gree [ə'griː] **1** *v/i* estar de acuerdo; *of figures* coincidir; (*reach agreement*) ponerse de acuerdo; *I agree* estoy de acuerdo; *it doesn't agree with me* of food no me sienta bien **2** *v/t price* acordar; *agree that sth should be done* acordar que hay que hacer algo
a·gree·a·ble [ə'griːəbl] *adj* (*pleasant*) agradable; *be agreeable fml* (*in agreement*) estar de acuerdo
a·gree·ment [ə'griːmənt] (*consent, contract*) acuerdo *m*; *reach agreement on* llegar a un acuerdo sobre
ag·ri·cul·tur·al [ægrɪ'kʌltʃərəl] *adj* agrícola
ag·ri·cul·ture ['ægrɪkʌltʃər] agricultura *f*
a·head [ə'hed] *adv position* delante; *movement* adelante; *in race* por delante, en cabeza; *be ahead of* estar por delante de; *plan / think ahead* planear con antelación / pensar con anticipación
aid [eɪd] **1** *n* ayuda *f*; *come to s.o.'s aid* acudir a ayudar a alguien **2** *v/t* ayudar
aide [eɪd] asistente *m/f*
Aids [eɪdz] sida *m*
ail·ing ['eɪlɪŋ] *adj economy* débil, frágil
ail·ment ['eɪlmənt] achaque *m*
aim [eɪm] **1** *n in shooting* puntería *f*; (*objective*) objetivo *m* **2** *v/i in shooting* apuntar; *aim at doing sth, aim to do sth* tener como intención hacer algo **3** *v/t remark* dirigir; *he aimed the gun at me* me apuntó con la pistola; *be aimed at* of remark etc estar dirigido a; of gun estar apuntando a
aim·less ['eɪmlɪs] *adj* sin objetivos
air [er] **1** *n* aire *m*; *by air travel* en avión; *send mail* por correo aéreo; *in the open air* al aire libre; *on the air* RAD, TV en el aire **2** *v/t room* airear; fig: views airear, ventilar
'air·bag airbag *m*, bolsa *f* de aire
'air·base base *f* aérea
'air-con·di·tioned *adj* con aire acondicionado, climatizado
'air-con·di·tion·ing *m* aire acondicionado
'air·craft avión *m*, aeronave *f*
'air·craft car·ri·er portaaviones *m inv*
'air fare (precio *m* del) Span billete *m* or L.Am. boleto *m* de avión
'air·field aeródromo *m*, campo *m* de aviación
'air force fuerza *f* aérea
'air host·ess azafata *f*, L.Am. aeromoza *f*
'air let·ter aerograma *m*

'air·lift 1 *n* puente *m* aéreo **2** *v/t* transportar mediante puente aéreo

'air·line línea *f* aérea

'air·lin·er avión *m* de pasajeros

'air·mail: by airmail por correo aéreo

'air·plane avión *m*

'air·pock·et bolsa *f* de aire

'air pol·lu·tion contaminación *f* del aire

'air·port aeropuerto *m*

'air·sick: get airsick marearse (*en avión*)

'air·space espacio *m* aéreo

'air ter·mi·nal terminal *f* aérea

'air·tight *adj container* hermético

'air traf·fic tráfico *m* aéreo

'air-traf·fic con·trol control *m* del tráfico aéreo

'air-traf·fic con·trol·ler controlador(a) *m(f)* del tráfico aéreo

air·y ['erɪ] *adj room* aireado; *attitude* despreocupado, ligero

aisle [aɪl] pasillo *m*

'aisle seat asiento *m* de pasillo

a·jar [ə'dʒɑːr] *adj*: **be ajar** estar entreabierto

a·lac·ri·ty [ə'lækrətɪ] presteza *f*

a·larm [ə'lɑːrm] **1** *n* alarma *f*; **raise the alarm** dar la alarma **2** *v/t* alarmar

a'larm clock reloj *m* despertador

a·larm·ing [ə'lɑːrmɪŋ] *adj* alarmante

a·larm·ing·ly [ə'lɑːrmɪŋlɪ] *adv* de forma alarmante

al·bum ['ælbəm] *for photographs, (record)* álbum *m*

al·co·hol ['ælkəhɑːl] alcohol *m*

al·co·hol·ic [ælkə'hɑːlɪk] **1** *n* alcohólico(-a) *m(f)* **2** *adj* alcohólico

a·lert [ə'lɜːrt] **1** *n signal* alerta *f*; **be on the alert** estar alerta **2** *v/t* alertar **3** *adj* alerta

al·ge·bra ['ældʒɪbrə] álgebra *f*

a·li·bi ['ælɪbaɪ] coartada *f*

a·li·en ['eɪlɪən] **1** *n* (*foreigner*) extranjero(-a) *m(f)*; *from space* extraterrestre *m/f* **2** *adj* extraño; **be alien to s.o.** ser ajeno a alguien

a·li·en·ate ['eɪlɪəneɪt] *v/t* alienar, provocar el distanciamiento de

a·light [ə'laɪt] *adj* en llamas

a·lign [ə'laɪn] *v/t* alinear

a·like [ə'laɪk] **1** *adj*: **be alike** parecerse **2** *adv* igual; **old and young alike** viejos y jóvenes sin distinción

al·i·mo·ny ['ælɪmənɪ] pensión *f* alimenticia

a·live [ə'laɪv] *adj*: **be alive** estar vivo

all [ɔːl] **1** *adj* todo(s) **2** *pron* todo; **all of us / them** todos nosotros / ellos; **he ate all of it** se lo comió todo; **that's all, thanks** eso es todo, gracias; **for all I care** para lo que me importa; **for all I know**

por lo que sé; **all at once** (*suddenly*) de repente; (*at the same time*) a la vez; **all but** (*except*) todos menos; (*nearly*) casi; **all the better** mucho mejor; **all the time** desde el principio; **they're not at all alike** no se parecen en nada; **not at all!** ¡en absoluto!; **two all** SP empate a dos; **all right → alright**

al·lay [ə'leɪ] *v/t* apaciguar

al·le·ga·tion [ælɪ'geɪʃn] acusación *f*

al·lege [ə'ledʒ] *v/t* alegar

al·leged [ə'ledʒd] *adj* presunto

al·leg·ed·ly [ə'ledʒɪdlɪ] *adv* presuntamente, supuestamente

al·le·giance [ə'liːdʒəns] lealtad *f*

al·ler·gic [ə'lɜːrdʒɪk] *adj* alérgico; **be allergic to** ser alérgico a

al·ler·gy ['ælərdʒɪ] alergia *f*

al·le·vi·ate [ə'liːvɪeɪt] *v/t* aliviar

al·ley ['ælɪ] callejón *m*

al·li·ance [ə'laɪəns] alianza *f*

al·lo·cate ['æləkeɪt] *v/t* asignar

al·lo·ca·tion [ælə'keɪʃn] asignación *f*

al·lot [ə'lɑːt] *v/t* (*pret & pp* **allotted**) asignar

al·low [ə'laʊ] *v/t* (*permit*) permitir; (*calculate for*) calcular; **they don't allow smoking** no está permitido fumar, está prohibido fumar; **it's not allowed** no está permitido; **he allowed us to leave** nos permitió salir

◆ **allow for** *v/t* tener en cuenta

al·low·ance [ə'laʊəns] (*money*) asignación *f*; (*pocket money*) paga *f*; **make allowances** *for weather etc* tener en cuenta; *for person* disculpar

al·loy ['ælɔɪ] aleación *f*

'all-pur·pose *adj* multiuso

'all-round *adj* completo

'all-time: be at an all-time low haber alcanzado un mínimo histórico

◆ **al·lude to** [ə'luːd] *v/t* aludir a

al·lur·ing [ə'lʊrɪŋ] *adj* atractivo, seductor

all-wheel 'drive *adj* con tracción a las cuatro ruedas

al·ly ['ælaɪ] *n* aliado(-a) *m(f)*

Al·might·y [ɔːl'maɪtɪ]: **the Almighty** el Todopoderoso

al·mond ['ɑːmənd] almendra *f*

al·most ['ɔːlmoʊst] *adv* casi

a·lone [ə'loʊn] *adj* solo

a·long [ə'lɒŋ] **1** *prep* (*situated beside*) a lo largo de; **the shop is halfway along Baker Street** la tienda está a mitad de Baker Street; **walk along this path** sigue por esta calle **2** *adv*: **would you like to come along?** ¿te gustaría venir con nosotros?; **he always brings the dog along** siempre trae al perro; **along with** junto con; **all**

along (*all the time*) todo el tiempo; desde el principio

a·long·side [əlɔːŋ'saɪd] *prep* (*in co-operation with*) junto a; (*parallel to*) al lado de

a·loof [ə'luːf] *adj* distante, reservado

a·loud [ə'laud] *adv* en voz alta

al·pha·bet ['ælfəbet] alfabeto *m*

al·pha·bet·i·cal [ælfə'betɪkl] *adj* alfabético

al·read·y [ɔːl'redi] *adv* ya

al·right [ɔːl'raɪt] *adj* (*not hurt, in working order*) bien; *is it alright to leave now?* (*permitted*) ¿puedo irme ahora?; *is it alright to take these out of the country?* ¿se pueden sacar éstos del país?; *is it alright with you if I ...?* ¿te importa si ...?; *alright, you can have one!* de acuerdo, ¡puedes tomar uno!; *alright, I heard you!* vale, ¡te he oído!; *everything is alright now between them* vuelven a estar bien; *that's alright* (*don't mention it*) de nada; (*I don't mind*) no importa

al·so ['ɔːlsou] *adv* también

al·tar ['ɔːltər] altar *m*

al·ter ['ɔːltər] *v/t* alterar

al·ter·a·tion [ɔːltə'reɪʃn] alteración *f*

al·ter·nate 1 *v/i* ['ɔːltərneɪt] alternar 2 *adj* ['ɔːltərnət] alterno

al·ter·nat·ing cur·rent ['ɔːltərneɪtɪŋ] corriente *f* alterna

al·ter·na·tive [ɔːl'tɜːrnətɪv] 1 *n* alternativa *f* 2 *adj* alternativo

al·ter·na·tive·ly [ɔːl'tɜːrnətɪvlɪ] *adv* como alternativa

al·though [ɔːl'ðou] *conj* aunque, si bien

al·ti·tude ['æltɪtuːd] *of plane, city* altitud *f*; *of mountain* altura *f*

al·to·geth·er [ɔːltə'geðər] *adv* (*completely*) completamente; (*in all*) en total

al·tru·ism ['æltruːɪzm] altruismo *m*

al·tru·is·tic [æltru'ɪstɪk] *adj* altruista

a·lu·min·i·um [æljuː'mɪnɪəm] *Br*, **a·lu·mi·num** [ə'luːmənəm] aluminio *m*

al·ways ['ɔːlweɪz] *adv* siempre

a. m. ['eɪem] *abbr* (= *ante meridiem*) a. m.; *at 11 a.m* a las 11 de la mañana

a·mal·gam·ate [ə'mælgəmeɪt] *v/i of companies* fusionarse

a·mass [ə'mæs] *v/t* acumular

am·a·teur ['æmətʃur] *n unskilled* aficionado(-a) *m(f)*; *SP* amateur *m/f*

am·a·teur·ish ['æmətʃurɪʃ] *adj pej* chapucero

a·maze [ə'meɪz] *v/t* asombrar

a·mazed [ə'meɪzd] *adj* asombrado; *we were amazed to hear ...* nos asombró oír ...

a·maze·ment [ə'meɪzmənt] asombro *m*

a·maz·ing [ə'meɪzɪŋ] *adj* (*surprising*) asombroso; F (*very good*) alucinante F

a·maz·ing·ly [ə'meɪzɪŋlɪ] *adv* increíblemente

Am·a·zon ['æmæzən] *n*: *the Amazon* el Amazonas

Am·a·zo·ni·an [æmə'zouniən] *adj* amazónico

am·bas·sa·dor [æm'bæsədər] embajador(a) *m(f)*

am·ber ['æmbər] *adj* ámbar; *at amber* en ámbar

am·bi·dex·trous [æmbɪ'dekstrəs] *adj* ambidiestro

am·bi·ence ['æmbɪəns] ambiente *m*

am·bi·gu·i·ty [æmbɪ'gjuːətɪ] ambigüedad *f*

am·big·u·ous [æm'bɪgjuəs] *adj* ambiguo

am·bi·tion [æm'bɪʃn] *also pej* ambición *f*

am·bi·tious [æm'bɪʃəs] *adj* ambicioso

am·biv·a·lent [æm'bɪvələnt] *adj* ambivalente

am·ble ['æmbl] *v/i* deambular

am·bu·lance ['æmbjuləns] ambulancia *f*

am·bush ['æmbuʃ] 1 *n* emboscada *f* 2 *v/t* tender una emboscada a

a·mend [ə'mend] *v/t* enmendar

a·mend·ment [ə'mendmənt] enmienda *f*

a·mends [ə'mendz] *npl*: *make amends for* compensar

a·men·i·ties [ə'miːnətɪz] *npl* servicios *mpl*

A·mer·i·ca [ə'merɪkə] *continent* América; *USA* Estados *mpl* Unidos

A·mer·i·can [ə'merɪkən] 1 *n North American* estadounidense *m/f* 2 *adj North American* estadounidense

A'mer·i·can plan pensión *f* completa

a·mi·a·ble ['eɪmɪəbl] *adj* afable, amable

a·mi·ca·ble ['æmɪkəbl] *adj* amistoso

a·mi·ca·bly ['æmɪkəblɪ] *adv* amistosamente

am·mu·ni·tion [æmju'nɪʃn] munición *f*; *fig* argumentos *mpl*

am·ne·sia [æm'niːzɪə] amnesia *f*

am·nes·ty ['æmnəstɪ] amnistía *f*

a·mong(st) [ə'mʌŋ(st)] *prep* entre

a·mor·al [eɪ'mɔːrəl] *adj* amoral

a·mount [ə'maunt] cantidad *f*; (*sum of money*) cantidad *f*, suma *f*

◆ **amount to** *v/t* ascender a; *his contribution didn't amount to much* su contribución no fue gran cosa

am·phib·i·an [æm'fɪbɪən] anfibio *m*

am·phib·i·ous [æm'fɪbɪəs] *adj animal, vehicle* anfibio

am·phi·the·a·ter, *Br* **am·phi·the·a·tre** ['æmfɪθɪətər] anfiteatro *m*

am·ple ['æmpl] *adj* abundante; *$4 will be ample* 4 dólares serán más que suficientes

am·pli·fi·er ['æmplɪfaɪr] amplificador *m*

am·pli·fy ['æmplɪfaɪ] *v/t* (*pret & pp* **amplified**) *sound* amplificar

am·pu·tate ['æmpjuteɪt] *v/t* amputar

am·pu·ta·tion [æmpjʊ'teɪʃn] amputación *f*

a·muse [ə'mjuːz] *v/t* (*make laugh etc*) divertir; (*entertain*) entretener

a·muse·ment [ə'mjuːzmənt] (*merriment*) diversión *f*; (*entertainment*) entretenimiento *m*; *amusements* (*games*) juegos *mpl*; *what do you do for amusement?* ¿qué haces para entretenerte?; *to our great amusement* para nuestro regocijo

a·muse·ment ar·cade [ɑːr'keɪd] salón *m* de juegos recreativos

a·muse·ment park parque *m* de atracciones

a·mus·ing [ə'mjuːzɪŋ] *adj* divertido

an·a·bol·ic ster·oid [ænə'bɑːlɪk] esteroide *m* anabolizante

a·nae·mi·a *etc Br* → **anemia** *etc*

an·aes·thet·ic *etc Br* → **anesthetic** *etc*

an·a·log ['ænəlɑːg] *adj* COMPUT analógico

a·nal·o·gy [ə'nælədʒɪ] analogía *f*

a·nal·y·sis [ə'næləsɪs] (*pl analyses* [ə'næləsiːz]) análisis *m inv*; (*psychoanalysis*) psicoanálisis *m inv*

an·a·lyst ['ænəlɪst] analista *m/f*; PSYCH psicoanalista *m/f*

an·a·lyt·i·cal [ænə'lɪtɪkl] *adj* analítico

an·a·lyze ['ænəlaɪz] *v/t* analizar; (*psychoanalyse*) psicoanalizar

an·arch·y ['ænərkɪ] anarquía *f*

a·nat·o·my [ə'nætəmɪ] anatomía *f*

an·ces·tor ['ænsestɔr] antepasado(-a) *m(f)*

an·chor ['æŋkər] **1** *n* NAUT ancla *f*; TV presentador(-a) *m(f)* **2** *v/i* NAUT anclar

an·cient ['eɪnʃənt] *adj* antiguo

an·cil·lar·y [æn'sɪlərɪ] *adj staff* auxiliar

and [ənd] *stressed* [ænd] *conj* y

An·de·an ['ændiən] *adj* andino

An·des ['ændiːz] *npl: the Andes* los Andes

an·ec·dote ['ænɪkdoʊt] anécdota *f*

a·ne·mi·a [ə'niːmɪə] anemia *f*

a·ne·mic [ə'niːmɪk] *adj* anémico

an·es·thet·ic [ænəs'θetɪk] *n* anestesia *f*

an·es·the·tist [ə'niːsθətɪst] anestesista *m/f*

an·gel ['eɪndʒl] REL ángel *m*; *fig* ángel *m*, cielo *m*

an·ger ['æŋgər] **1** *n* enfado *m*, enojo *m* **2** *v/t* enfadar, enojar

an·gi·na [æn'dʒaɪnə] angina *f* (de pecho)

an·gle ['æŋgl] *n* ángulo *m*

An·glo-Sax·on [æŋgloʊ'sæksn] **1** *adj* an-

glosajón **2** *n person* anglosajón(-ona) *m(f)*

an·gry ['æŋgrɪ] *adj* enfadado, enojado; *be angry with s.o.* estar enfadado *or* enojado con alguien

an·guish ['æŋgwɪʃ] angustia *f*

an·gu·lar ['æŋgjʊlər] *adj* anguloso

an·i·mal ['ænɪml] animal *m*

an·i·mat·ed ['ænɪmeɪtɪd] *adj* animado

an·i·ma·ted car·toon dibujos *mpl* animados

an·i·ma·tion [ænɪ'meɪʃn] (*liveliness*), *of cartoon* animación *f*

an·i·mos·i·ty [ænɪ'mɑːsətɪ] animosidad *f*

an·kle ['æŋkl] tobillo *m*

an·nex ['æneks] **1** *n building* edificio *m* anexo **2** *v/t state* anexionar

an·nexe ['æneks] *n Br building* edificio *m* anexo

an·ni·hi·late [ə'naɪəleɪt] *v/t* aniquilar

an·ni·hi·la·tion [ənaɪə'leɪʃn] aniquilación *f*

an·ni·ver·sa·ry [ænɪ'vɜːrsərɪ] (*wedding anniversary*) aniversario *m*

an·no·tate ['ænəteɪt] *v/t report* anotar

an·nounce [ə'naʊns] *v/t* anunciar

an·nounce·ment [ə'naʊnsmənt] anuncio *m*

an·nounc·er [ə'naʊnsər] TV, RAD presentador(a) *m(f)*

an·noy [ə'nɔɪ] *v/t* molestar, irritar; *be annoyed* estar molesto *or* irritado

an·noy·ance [ə'nɔɪəns] (*anger*) irritación *f*; (*nuisance*) molestia *f*

an·noy·ing [ə'nɔɪɪŋ] *adj* molesto, irritante

an·nu·al ['ænʊəl] *adj* anual

an·nu·al gen·er·al 'meet·ing junta *f* general anual

an·nu·i·ty [ə'nuːətɪ] anualidad *f*

an·nul [ə'nʌl] *v/t* (*pret & pp annulled*) *marriage* anular

an·nul·ment [ə'nʌlmənt] anulación *f*

a·non·y·mous [ə'nɑːnɪməs] *adj* anónimo

an·o·rak ['ænəræk] *Br* anorak *m*

an·o·rex·i·a [ænə'reksɪə] anorexia *f*

an·o·rex·ic [ænə'reksɪk] *adj* anoréxico

an·oth·er [ə'nʌðər] **1** *adj* otro **2** *pron* otro(-a) *m(f)*; *they helped one another* se ayudaron (el uno al otro); *do they know one another?* ¿se conocen?

ans·wer ['ænsər] **1** *n to letter, person, question* respuesta *f*, contestación *f*; *to problem* solución *f* **2** *v/t letter, person, question* responder, contestar; *answer the door* abrir la puerta; *answer the telephone* responder *or Span* coger al teléfo-

♦ **answer back** *v/t & v/i* contestar, replicar

♦ **answer for** *v/t* responder de

an·swer·ing ma·chine ['ænsərɪŋ] TELEC contestador *m* (automático)

ans·wer·phone ['ænsərfoun] TELEC contestador *m* (automático)

ant [ænt] hormiga *f*

an·tag·o·nism [æn'tægənɪzm] antagonismo *m*

an·tag·o·nis·tic [æntægə'nɪstɪk] *adj* hostil

an·tag·o·nize [æn'tægənaɪz] *v/t* antagonizar, enfadar

Ant·arc·tic [ænt'ɑːrktɪk] *n*: *the Antarctic* el Antártico

an·te·na·tal [æntɪ'neɪtl] *adj* prenatal

an·ten·na [æn'tenə] *of insect, for* TV antena *f*

an·thol·o·gy [æn'θɑːlədʒɪ] antología *f*

an·thro·pol·o·gy [ænθrə'pɑːlədʒɪ] antropología *f*

an·ti·bi·ot·ic [æntɪbaɪ'ɑːtɪk] *n* antibiótico *m*

an·ti·bod·y ['æntɪbɑːdɪ] anticuerpo *m*

an·tic·i·pate [æn'tɪsɪpeɪt] *v/t* esperar, prever

an·tic·i·pa·tion [æntɪsɪ'peɪʃn] expectativa *f*, previsión *f*

an·ti·clock·wise ['æntɪklɑːkwaɪz] *adv* Br en dirección contraria a las agujas del reloj

an·tics ['æntɪks] *npl* payasadas *fpl*

an·ti·dote ['æntɪdout] antídoto *m*

an·ti·freeze ['æntɪfriːz] anticongelante *m*

an·tip·a·thy [æn'tɪpəθɪ] antipatía *f*

an·ti·quat·ed ['æntɪkweɪtɪd] *adj* anticuado

an·tique [æn'tiːk] *n* antigüedad *f*

an'tique dealer anticuario(-a) *m(f)*

an·tiq·ui·ty [æn'tɪkwɑːtɪ] antigüedad *f*

an·ti·sep·tic [æntɪ'septɪk] **1** *adj* antiséptico **2** *n* antiséptico *m*

an·ti·so·cial [æntɪ'souʃl] *adj* antisocial, poco sociable

an·ti·vi·rus pro·gram [æntɪ'vaɪrəs] COMPUT (programa *m*) antivirus *m inv*

anx·i·e·ty [æŋ'zaɪətɪ] ansiedad *f*

anx·ious ['æŋkʃəs] *adj* preocupado; *(eager)* ansioso; *be anxious for* for news etc esperar ansiosamente

an·y ['enɪ] **1** *adj*: *are there any diskettes / glasses?* ¿hay disquetes / vasos?; *is there any bread / improvement?* ¿hay algo de pan / alguna mejora?; *there aren't any diskettes / glasses* no hay disquetes / vasos; *there isn't any bread / improvement* no hay pan / ninguna mejora; *have you any idea at all?* ¿tienes alguna idea?; *any one of them could win* cualquiera de ellos podría ganar **2** *pron* alguno(-a); *do you*

have any? ¿tienes alguno(s)?; *there aren't any left* no queda ninguno; *there isn't any left* no queda; *any of them could be guilty* cualquiera de ellos podría ser culpable **3** *adv*: *is that any better / easier?* ¿es mejor / más fácil así?; *don't like it any more* ya no me gusta

an·y·bod·y ['enɪbɑːdɪ] *pron* alguien; *there wasn't anybody there* no había nadie allí

an·y·how ['enɪhau] *adv* en todo caso, de todos modos; *if I can help you anyhow, please let me know* si puedo ayudarte de alguna manera, por favor dímelo

an·y·one ['enɪwʌn] → *anybody*

an·y·thing ['enɪθɪŋ] *pron* algo; *with negatives* nada; *I didn't hear anything* no oí nada; *anything but* todo menos; *anything else?* ¿algo más?

an·y·way ['enɪweɪ] → *anyhow*

an·y·where ['enɪwer] *adv* en alguna parte; *is Peter anywhere around?* ¿está Peter por ahí?; *he never goes anywhere* nunca va a ninguna parte; *I can't find it anywhere* no lo encuentro por ninguna parte

a·part [ə'pɑːrt] *adv* aparte; *the two cities are 250 miles apart* las dos ciudades están a 250 millas la una de la otra; *live apart* of people vivir separado; *apart from* aparte de

a·part·ment [ə'pɑːrtmənt] apartamento *m*, *Span* piso *m*, *Am* departamento *m*

a'part·ment block bloque *m* de apartamentos *or* Span pisos

ap·a·thet·ic [æpə'θetɪk] *adj* apático

ap·a·thy ['æpəθɪ] apatía *f*

ape [eɪp] simio *m*

a·pe·ri·tif [ə'perɪtiːf] aperitivo *m*

ap·er·ture ['æpərtʃər] PHOT apertura *f*

a·piece [ə'piːs] *adv* cada uno

a·pol·o·get·ic [əpɑːlə'dʒetɪk] *adj letter* de disculpa; *he was very apologetic* por ... pedía constantes disculpas por ...

a·pol·o·gize [ə'pɑːlədʒaɪz] *v/i* disculparse, pedir perdón

a·pol·o·gy [ə'pɑːlədʒɪ] disculpa *f*

a·pos·tle [ə'pɑːsl] REL apóstol *m*

a·pos·tro·phe [ə'pɑːstrəfɪ] GRAM apóstrofo *m*

ap·pall [ə'pɒːl] *v/t* horrorizar, espantar

ap·pal·ling [ə'pɒːlɪŋ] *adj* horroroso

ap·pa·ra·tus [æpə'reɪtəs] aparatos *mpl*

ap·par·ent [ə'pærənt] *adj* aparente, evidente; *become apparent that ...* hacerse evidente que ...

ap·par·ent·ly [ə'pærəntlɪ] *adv* al parecer, por lo visto

ap·pa·ri·tion [æpə'rɪʃn] *(ghost)* aparición

f

ap·peal [ə'pi:l] **1** *n* (*charm*) atractivo *m*; *for funds etc* llamamiento *m*; LAW apelación *f* **2** *v/i* LAW apelar
◆ **appeal to** *v/t* (*be attractive to*) atraer a
◆ **appeal for** *v/t* solicitar

ap·peal·ing [ə'pi:lɪŋ] *adj idea, offer* atractivo; *glance* suplicante

ap·pear [ə'pɪr] *v/i* aparecer; *in court* comparecer; (*look, seem*) parecer; *it appears that ...* parece que ...

ap·pear·ance [ə'pɪrəns] aparición *f*; *in court* comparecencia *f*; (*look*) apariencia *f*, aspecto *m*; *put in an appearance* hacer acto de presencia

ap·pease [ə'pi:z] *v/t* apaciguar

ap·pen·di·ci·tis [əpendɪ'saɪtɪs] apendicitis *m*

ap·pen·dix [ə'pendɪks] MED, *of book etc* apéndice *m*

ap·pe·tite ['æpɪtaɪt] *also fig* apetito *m*

ap·pe·tiz·er ['æpɪtaɪzər] aperitivo *m*

ap·pe·tiz·ing ['æpɪtaɪzɪŋ] *adj* apetitoso

ap·plaud [ə'plɔːd] **1** *v/i* aplaudir **2** *v/t also fig* aplaudir

ap·plause [ə'plɔːz] aplauso *m*

ap·ple ['æpl] manzana *f*

ap·ple 'pie tarta *f* de manzana

ap·ple 'sauce compota *f* de manzana

ap·pli·ance [ə'plaɪəns] aparato *m*; *household* electrodoméstico *m*

ap·plic·a·ble [ə'plɪkəbl] *adj* aplicable; *it's not applicable to foreigners* no se aplica a extranjeros

ap·pli·cant ['æplɪkənt] solicitante *m/f*

ap·pli·ca·tion [æplɪ'keɪʃn] *for job, passport etc* solicitud *f*; *for university* solicitud *f* (de admisión)

ap·pli·ca·tion form *for passport* impreso *m* de solicitud; *for university* impreso *m* de solicitud de admisión

ap·ply [ə'plaɪ] **1** *v/t* (*pret & pp* **applied**) *rules, solution, ointment* aplicar **2** *v/i* (*pret & pp* **applied**) *of rule, law* aplicarse
◆ **apply for** *v/t job, passport* solicitar; *university* solicitar el ingreso en
◆ **apply to** *v/t* (*contact*) dirigirse a; (*affect*) aplicarse a

ap·point [ə'pɔɪnt] *v/t to position* nombrar, designar

ap·point·ment [ə'pɔɪntmənt] *to position* nombramiento *m*, designación *f*; *meeting* cita *f*; *make an appointment with the doctor* pedir hora con el doctor

ap·point·ments *diary* agenda *f* de citas

ap·prais·al [ə'preɪz(ə)l] evaluación *f*

ap·pre·cia·ble [ə'pri:ʃəbl] *adj* apreciable

ap·pre·ci·ate [ə'pri:ʃɪeɪt] **1** *v/t* (*value*) apreciar; (*be grateful for*) agradecer;

(*acknowledge*) ser consciente de; *thanks, I appreciate it* te lo agradezco **2** *v/i* FIN revalorizarse

ap·pre·ci·a·tion [əpri:ʃɪ'eɪʃn] *of kindness etc* agradecimiento *m*; *of music etc* aprecio *m*

ap·pre·ci·a·tive [ə'pri:ʃətɪv] *adj* agradecido

ap·pre·hen·sive [æprɪ'hensɪv] *adj* aprensivo, temeroso

ap·pren·tice [ə'prentɪs] aprendiz(a) *m(f)*

ap·proach [ə'proʊtʃ] **1** *n* aproximación *f*; (*proposal*) propuesta *f*; *to problem* enfoque *m* **2** *v/t* (*get near to*) aproximarse a; (*contact*) ponerse en contacto con; *problem* enfocar

ap·proach·a·ble [ə'proʊtʃəbl] *adj person* accesible

ap·pro·pri·ate¹ [ə'proʊprɪət] *adj* apropiado, adecuado

ap·pro·pri·ate² [ə'proʊprɪeɪt] *v/t* apropiarse de; (*euph: steal*) apropiarse de

ap·prov·al [ə'pru:vl] aprobación *f*

ap·prove [ə'pru:v] **1** *v/i*: *my parents don't approve* a mis padres no les parece bien **2** *v/t* aprobar
◆ **approve of** *v/t* aprobar; *her parents don't approve of me* no les gusto a sus padres

ap·prox·i·mate [ə'prɑːksɪmət] *adj* aproximado

ap·prox·i·mate·ly [ə'prɑːksɪmətlɪ] *adv* aproximadamente

ap·prox·i·ma·tion [əprɑːksɪ'meɪʃn] aproximación *f*

APR [eɪpi:'ɑː] *abbr* (= *annual percentage rate*) TAE *f* (= *tasa f anual equivalente*)

a·pri·cot ['æprɪkɑːt] albaricoque *m*, *L.Am.* damasco *m*

A·pril ['eɪprəl] abril *m*

apt [æpt] *adj remark* oportuno; *be apt to ...* ser propenso a ...

ap·ti·tude ['æptɪtuːd] aptitud *f*; *he has a natural aptitude for ...* tiene aptitudes naturales para ...

'ap·ti·tude test prueba *f* de aptitud

aq·ua·lung ['ækwəlʌŋ] escafandra *f* autónoma

a·quar·i·um [ə'kweriəm] acuario *m*

A·quar·i·us [ə'kweriəs] ASTR Acuario *m/f inv*

a·quat·ic [ə'kwætɪk] *adj* acuático

Ar·ab ['ærəb] **1** *adj* árabe **2** *n* árabe *m/f*

Ar·a·bic ['ærəbɪk] **1** *adj* árabe **2** *n* árabe *m*

ar·a·ble ['ærəbl] *adj* arable, cultivable

ar·bi·tra·ry ['ɑːrbɪtrerɪ] *adj* arbitrario

ar·bi·trate ['ɑːrbɪtreɪt] *v/i* arbitrar

ar·bi·tra·tion [ɑːrbɪ'treɪʃn] arbitraje *m*

ar·bi·tra·tor [ˈɑːrbɪˈtreɪtər] árbitro(-a) *m(f)*

arch [ɑːrtʃ] *n* arco *m*

ar·chae·ol·o·gy *etc Br →* **archeology** *etc*

ar·cha·ic [ɑːrˈkeɪɪk] *adj* arcaico

ar·che·o·log·i·cal [ɑːrkɪəˈlɑːdʒɪkl] *adj* arqueológico

ar·che·ol·o·gist [ɑːrkɪˈɑːlədʒɪst] arqueólogo(-a) *m(f)*

ar·che·ol·o·gy [ɑːrkɪˈɑːlədʒɪ] arqueología *f*

ar·cher [ˈɑːrtʃər] arquero(-a) *m(f)*

ar·chi·tec·t [ˈɑːrkɪtekt] arquitecto(-a) *m(f)*

ar·chi·tec·tur·al [ɑːrkɪˈtektʃərəl] *adj* arquitectónico

ar·chi·tec·ture [ˈɑːrkɪtektʃər] arquitectura *f*

ar·chives [ˈɑːrkaɪvz] *npl* archivos *mpl*

arch·way [ˈɑːrtʃweɪ] arco *m*

Arc·tic [ˈɑːrktɪk] *n:* **the Arctic** el Ártico

ar·dent [ˈɑːrdənt] *adj* ardiente, ferviente

ar·du·ous [ˈɑːrdjʊəs] *adj* arduo

ar·e·a [ˈerɪə] área *f,* zona *f; of activity, study etc* área *f,* ámbito *m*

ˈar·e·a code TELEC prefijo *m*

a·re·na [əˈriːnə] SP estadio *m*

Ar·gen·ti·na [ɑːrdʒənˈtiːnə] Argentina

Ar·gen·tin·i·an [ɑːrdʒənˈtɪnɪən] **1** *adj* argentino **2** *n* argentino(-a) *m(f)*

ar·gu·a·bly [ˈɑːrgjʊəblɪ] *adv* posiblemente

ar·gue [ˈɑːrgjuː] **1** *v/i (quarrel)* discutir; *(reason)* argumentar **2** *v/t:* **argue that ...** argumentar que ...

ar·gu·ment [ˈɑːrgjʊmənt] *(quarrel)* discusión *m; (reasoning)* argumento *m*

ar·gu·ment·a·tive [ɑːrgjʊˈmentətɪv] *adj* discutidor

a·ri·a [ˈɑːrɪə] MUS aria *f*

ar·id [ˈærɪd] *adj land* árido

Ar·i·es [ˈeriːz] ASTR Aries *m/f inv*

a·rise [əˈraɪz] *v/i (pret arose, pp arisen) of situation, problem* surgir

a·ris·en [əˈrɪzn] *pp →* **arise**

a·ris·toc·ra·cy [ærɪˈstɑːkrəsɪ] aristocracia *f*

a·ris·to·crat [əˈrɪstəkræt] aristócrata *m/f*

a·ris·to·crat·ic [ærɪstəˈkrætɪk] *adj* aristocrático

a·rith·me·tic [əˈrɪθmətɪk] aritmética *f*

arm[1] [ɑːrm] *n of person, chair* brazo *m*

arm[2] [ɑːrm] *v/t* armar

ar·ma·ments [ˈɑːrməmənts] *npl* armamento *m*

arm·chair [ˈɑːrmtʃer] sillón *m*

armed [ɑːrmd] *adj* armado

armed ˈforc·es *npl* fuerzas *fpl* armadas

armed ˈrob·ber·y atraco *m* a mano armada

ar·mor, *Br* **ar·mour** [ˈɑːrmər] armadura *f*

ar·mored ˈve·hi·cle, *Br* **ar·moured ˈve·hi·cle** [ˈɑːrmərd] vehículo *m* blindado

arm·pit [ˈɑːrmpɪt] sobaco *m*

arms [ɑːrmz] *npl (weapons)* armas *fpl*

ar·my [ˈɑːrmɪ] ejército *m*

a·ro·ma [əˈroʊmə] aroma *m*

a·rose [əˈroʊz] *pret →* **arise**

a·round [əˈraʊnd] **1** *prep (enclosing)* alrededor de; **it's around the corner** está a la vuelta de la esquina **2** *adv (in the area)* por ahí; *(encircling)* alrededor; *(roughly)* alrededor de, aproximadamente; *(with expressions of time)* en torno a; **he lives around here** vive por aquí; **walk around** pasear; **she has been around** *(has traveled, is experienced)* tiene mucho mundo; **he's still around** F *(alive)* todavía está rondando por ahí F

a·rouse [əˈraʊz] *v/t* despertar; *sexually* excitar

ar·range [əˈreɪndʒ] *v/t (put in order)* ordenar; *furniture* ordenar, disponer; *flowers, music* arreglar; *meeting, party etc* organizar; *time and place* acordar; **I've arranged to meet her** he quedado con ella

◆ **arrange for** *v/t:* **I arranged for Jack to collect it** quedé para que Jack lo recogiera

ar·range·ment [əˈreɪndʒmənt] *(plan)* plan *m,* preparativo *m; (agreement)* acuerdo *m; (layout: of furniture etc)* orden *m,* disposición *f; of flowers, music* arreglo *m;* **I've made arrangements for the neighbors to water my plants** he quedado con los vecinos para que rieguen mis plantas

ar·rears [əˈrɪərz] *npl* atrasos *mpl;* **be in arrears** *of person* ir atrasado

ar·rest [əˈrest] **1** *n* detención *f,* arresto *m;* **be under arrest** estar detenido *or* arrestado **2** *v/t* detener, arrestar

ar·riv·al [əˈraɪvl] llegada *f;* **on your arrival** al llegar; **arrivals** *at airport* llegadas *fsg*

ar·rive [əˈraɪv] *v/i* llegar

◆ **arrive at** *v/t place, decision etc* llegar a

ar·ro·gance [ˈærəgəns] arrogancia *f*

ar·ro·gant [ˈærəgənt] *adj* arrogante

ar·ro·gant·ly [ˈærəgəntlɪ] *adv* con arrogancia

ar·row [ˈæroʊ] flecha *f*

arse [ɑːrs] *Br* P culom P

ar·se·nic [ˈɑːrsənɪk] arsénico *m*

ar·son [ˈɑːrsn] incendio *m* provocado

ar·son·ist [ˈɑːrsənɪst] pirómano(-a) *m(f)*

art [ɑːrt] arte *m;* **the arts** las artes

ar·te·ry [ˈɑːrtərɪ] MED arteria *f*

'art gal·ler·y *public* museo *m*; *private* galería *f* de arte

ar·thri·tis [ɑːrˈθraɪtɪs] artritis *f*

ar·ti·choke [ˈɑːrtɪʃouk] alcachofa *f*, *L.Am.* alcaucil *m*

ar·ti·cle [ˈɑːrtɪkl] artículo *m*

ar·tic·u·late [ɑːrˈtɪkjulət] *adj person* elocuente

ar·ti·fi·cial [ɑːrtɪˈfɪʃl] *adj* artificial

ar·ti·fi·cial in'tel·li·gence inteligencia *f* artificial

ar·til·le·ry [ɑːrˈtɪlərɪ] artillería *f*

ar·ti·san [ˈɑːrtɪzæn] artesano(-a) *m(f)*

ar·tist [ˈɑːrtɪst] *(painter, artistic person)* artista *m/f*

ar·tis·tic [ɑːrˈtɪstɪk] *adj* artístico

'arts de·gree licenciatura *f* en letras

as [æz] **1** *conj (while, when)* cuando; *(because, like)* como; *as if* como si; *as usual* como de costumbre; *as necessary* como sea necesario **2** *adv* como; *as high / pretty as …* tan alto / guapa como …; *as much as that?* ¿tanto? **3** *prep* como; *work as a team* trabajar en equipo; *as a child / schoolgirl* cuando era un niño / una colegiala; *work as a teacher / translator* trabajar como profesor / traductor; *as for* por lo que respecta a; *as Hamlet* en el papel del Hamlet

asap [ˈeɪzæp] *abbr (= as soon as possible)* cuanto antes

as·bes·tos [æzˈbestəs] amianto *m*, asbesto *m*

As·cen·sion [əˈsenʃn] REL Ascensión *f*

ash [æʃ] ceniza *f*; *ashes of person* cenizas *fpl*

a·shamed [əˈʃeɪmd] *adj* avergonzado, *L.Am.* apenado; *be ashamed of* estar avergonzado *or L.Am.* apenado de; *you should be ashamed of yourself* debería darte vergüenza *or L.Am.* pena; *it's nothing to be ashamed of* no tienes por qué avergonzarte *or L.Am.* apenarte

'ash bin, 'ash can cubo *m* de la basura

a·shore [əˈʃɔːr] *adv* en tierra; *go ashore* desembarcar

ash·tray [ˈæʃtreɪ] cenicero *m*

A·sia [ˈeɪʃə] Asia

A·sian [ˈeɪʃən] **1** *adj* asiático **2** *n* asiático(-a) *m(f)*

a·side [əˈsaɪd] *adv* a un lado; *move aside please* apártense, por favor; *he took me aside* me llevó aparte; *aside from* aparte de

ask [æsk] **1** *v/t person, question* preguntar; *question* hacer; *(invite)* invitar; *favor* pedir; *can I ask you something?* ¿puedo hacerte una pregunta?; *ask s.o. for sth* pedir algo a alguien; *he asked me*

to leave me pidió que me fuera; *ask s.o. about sth* preguntar por algo a alguien **2** *v/i*: *all you need to do is ask* no tienes más que pedirlo

◆ *ask after* *v/t person* preguntar por

◆ *ask for* *v/t person; drink* pedir

◆ *ask out* *v/t for a drink, night out* invitar a salir

ask·ing price [ˈæskɪŋ] precio *m* de salida

a·sleep [əˈsliːp] *adj* dormido; *be (fast) asleep* estar (profundamente) dormido; *fall asleep* dormirse, quedarse dormido

as·par·a·gus [əˈspærəgəs] espárragos *mpl*

as·pect [ˈæspekt] aspecto *m*

as·phalt [ˈæsfælt] *n* asfalto *m*

as·phyx·i·ate [æˈsfɪksɪeɪt] *v/t* asfixiar

as·phyx·i·a·tion [æsfɪksɪˈeɪʃn] asfixia *f*

as·pi·ra·tion [æspəˈreɪʃn] aspiración *f*

as·pi·rin [ˈæsprɪn] aspirina *f*

ass¹ [æs] *(idiot)* burro(-a) *m(f)*

ass² [æs] P *(backside)* culo P; *(sex)* sexo *m*

as·sai·lant [əˈseɪlənt] asaltante *m/f*

as·sas·sin [əˈsæsɪn] asesino(-a) *m(f)*

as·sas·sin·ate [əˈsæsɪneɪt] *v/t* asesinar

as·sas·sin·a·tion [əsæsɪˈneɪʃn] asesinato *m*

as·sault [əˈsɔːlt] **1** *n* agresión *f*; *(attack)* ataque *m* **2** *v/t* atacar, agredir

as·sem·ble [əˈsembl] **1** *v/t parts* montar **2** *v/i of people* reunirse

as·sem·bly [əˈsemblɪ] *of parts* montaje *m*; POL asamblea *f*

as·sem·bly line cadena *f* de montaje

as·sem·bly plant planta *f* de montaje

as·sent [əˈsent] *v/i* asentir, dar el consentimiento

as·sert [əˈsɜːrt] *v/t* afirmar, hacer valer; *assert o.s.* mostrarse firme

as·ser·tive [əˈsɜːrtɪv] *adj person* seguro y firme

as·sess [əˈses] *v/t situation* evaluar; *value* valorar

as·sess·ment [əˈsesmənt] evaluación *f*

as·set [ˈæset] FIN activo *m*; *fig* ventaja *f*; *she's an asset to the company* es de gran valor para la compañía

ass·hole [ˈæshoul] V *(idiot)* gilipollas *m/f inv* V, *L.Am.* pendejo(-a) *m(f)* V

as·sign [əˈsaɪn] *v/t person, thing* asignar

as·sign·ment [əˈsaɪnmənt] *(task, study)* trabajo *m*

as·sim·i·late [əˈsɪmɪleɪt] *v/t information* asimilar; *person into group* integrar

as·sist [əˈsɪst] *v/t* ayudar

as·sis·tance [əˈsɪstəns] ayuda *f*, asistencia *f*

as·sis·tant [əˈsɪstənt] ayudante *m/f*; *Br in*

store dependiente(-a) *m(f)*

as·sis·tant di'rec·tor director(a) *m(f)* adjunto

as·sis·tant 'man·ag·er *of business* subdirector(a) *m(f)*; *of hotel, restaurant, store* subdirector(a) *m(f)*, subgerente *m/f*

as·so·ci·ate 1 *v/t* [ə'souʃɪeɪt] asociar; **he has long been associated with the Royal Ballet** ha estado vinculado al Royal Ballet durante mucho tiempo **2** *v/i* [ə'souʃɪeɪt]: **associate with** relacionarse con **3** [ə'souʃɪət] colega *m/f*

as·so·ci·ate pro'fes·sor profesor(a) *m(f)* adjunto(a)

as·so·ci·a·tion [əsousɪ'eɪʃn] asociación *f*; **in association with** conjuntamente con

as·sort·ed [ə'sɔːrtɪd] *adj* surtido, diverso

as·sort·ment [ə'sɔːrtmənt] *of food* surtido *m*; *of people* diversidad *f*

as·sume [ə'suːm] *v/t* (*suppose*) suponer

as·sump·tion [ə'sʌmpʃn] suposición *f*

as·sur·ance [ə'ʃurəns] garantía *f*; (*confidence*) seguridad *f*

as·sure [ə'ʃur] *v/t* (*reassure*) asegurar

as·sured [ə'ʃurd] *adj* (*confident*) seguro

as·ter·isk ['æstərɪsk] asterisco *m*

asth·ma ['æsmə] asma *f*

asth·mat·ic [æs'mætɪk] *adj* asmático

as·ton·ish [ə'stɑːnɪʃ] *v/t* asombrar, sorprender; **be astonished** estar asombrado *or* sorprendido

as·ton·ish·ing [ə'stɑːnɪʃɪŋ] *adj* asombroso, sorprendente

as·ton·ish·ing·ly [ə'stɑːnɪʃɪŋlɪ] *adv* asombrosamente

as·ton·ish·ment [ə'stɑːnɪʃmənt] asombro *m*, sorpresa *f*

as·tound [ə'staund] *v/t* pasmar

as·tound·ing [ə'staundɪŋ] *adj* pasmoso

a·stray [ə'streɪ] *adv*: **go astray** extraviarse; *morally* descarriarse

a·stride [ə'straɪd] **1** *adv* a horcajadas **2** *prep* a horcajadas sobre

as·trol·o·ger [ə'strɑːlədʒər] astrólogo(-a) *m(f)*

as·trol·o·gy [ə'strɑːlədʒɪ] astrología *f*

as·tro·naut ['æstrənɔːt] astronauta *m/f*

as·tron·o·mer [ə'strɑːnəmər] astrónomo(-a) *m(f)*

as·tro·nom·i·cal [æstrə'nɑːmɪkl] *adj price etc* astronómico

as·tron·o·my [ə'strɑːnəmɪ] astronomía *f*

as·tute [ə'stuːt] *adj* astuto, sagaz

a·sy·lum [ə'saɪləm] (*mental asylum*) manicomio *m*; *political* asilo *m*

at [ət] *stressed* [æt] *prep with places* en; **at Joe's** *house* en casa de Joe; *bar* en el bar de Joe; **at the door** a la puerta; **at 10 dollars** a 10 dólares; **at the age of 18** a los 18

años; **at 5 o'clock** a las 5; **at 150 km/h** a 150 km./h.; **be good / bad at sth** ser bueno / malo haciendo algo

ate [eɪt] *pret* → **eat**

a·the·ism ['eɪθɪɪzm] ateísmo *m*

a·the·ist ['eɪθɪɪst] ateo(-a) *m(f)*

ath·lete ['æθliːt] atleta *m/f*

ath·let·ic [æθ'letɪk] *adj* atlético

ath·let·ics [æθ'letɪks] atletismo *m*

At·lan·tic [ət'læntɪk] *n*: **the Atlantic** el Atlántico

at·las ['ætləs] atlas *m inv*

ATM [eɪtiː'em] *abbr* (= **automatic teller machine**) cajero *m* automático

at·mos·phere ['ætməsfɪr] *of earth* atmósfera *f*; (*ambiance*) ambiente *m*

at·mos·pher·ic pol'lu·tion [ætməs'ferɪk] contaminación *f* atmosférica

at·om ['ætəm] átomo *m*

'at·om bomb bomba *f* atómica

a·tom·ic [ə'tɑːmɪk] *adj* atómico

a·tom·ic 'en·er·gy energía *f* atómica *or* nuclear

a·tom·ic 'waste desechos *mpl* radiactivos

a·tom·iz·er ['ætəmaɪzər] atomizador *m*

a·tone [ə'toun] *v/i*: **atone for** expiar

a·tro·cious [ə'trouʃəs] *adj* atroz, terrible

a·troc·i·ty [ə'trɑːsətɪ] atrocidad *f*

at·tach [ə'tætʃ] *v/t* sujetar, fijar; *importance* atribuir; **be attached to** (*fond of*) tener cariño a

at·tach·ment [ə'tætʃmənt] (*fondness*) cariño *m* (**to** *to*)

at·tack [ə'tæk] **1** *n* ataque *m* **2** *v/t* atacar

at·tempt [ə'tempt] **1** *n* intento *m*; **an attempt on the world record** un intento de batir el récord del mundo **2** *v/t* intentar

at·tend [ə'tend] *v/t* acudir a

◆ **attend to** *v/t* ocuparse de; *customer* atender

at·tend·ance [ə'tendəns] asistencia *f*

at·tend·ant [ə'tendənt] *in museum etc* vigilante *m/f*

at·ten·tion [ə'tenʃn] atención *f*; **bring sth to s.o.'s attention** informar a alguien de algo; **your attention please** atención, por favor; **pay attention** prestar atención

at·ten·tive [ə'tentɪv] *adj listener* atento

at·tic ['ætɪk] ático *m*

at·ti·tude ['ætɪtuːd] actitud *f*

attn *abbr* (= **for the attention of**) atn (= a la atención de)

at·tor·ney [ə'tɜːrnɪ] abogado(-a) *m(f)*; **power of attorney** poder *m* (notarial)

at·tract [ə'trækt] *v/t* atraer; **attract attention** llamar la atención; **attract s.o.'s attention** atraer la atención de alguien; **be**

attracted to s.o. sentirse atraído por alguien

at·trac·tion [əˈtrækʃn] atracción *f*, atractivo *m*; *romantic* atracción *f*

at·trac·tive [əˈtræktɪv] *adj* atractivo

at·trib·ute¹ [əˈtrɪbjuːt] *v/t* atribuir; *attribute sth to ...* atribuir algo a ...

at·trib·ute² [ˈætrɪbjuːt] *n* atributo *m*

au·ber·gine [ˈoʊbərʒiːn] *Br* berenjena *f*

auc·tion [ˈɔːkʃn] **1** *n* subasta *f*, *L.Am.* remate *m* **2** *v/t* subastar, *L.Am.* rematar

◆ **auction off** *v/t* subastar, *L.Am.* rematar

auc·tio·neer [ɔːkʃəˈnɪr] subastador(a) *m(f)*, *L.Am.* rematador(a) *m(f)*

au·da·cious [ɔːˈdeɪʃəs] *adj plan* audaz

au·dac·i·ty [ɔːˈdæsətɪ] audacia *f*

au·di·ble [ˈɔːdəbl] *adj* audible

au·di·ence [ˈɔːdɪəns] *in theater, at show* público *m*, espectadores *mpl*; TV audiencia *f*

Au·di·o [ˈɔːdɪoʊ] *adj* de audio

au·di·o·vi·su·al [ɔːdɪoʊˈvɪʒʊəl] *adj* audiovisual

au·dit [ˈɔːdɪt] **1** *n* auditoría *f* **2** *v/t* auditar; *course* asistir de oyente a

au·di·tion [ɔːˈdɪʃn] **1** *n* audición *f* **2** *v/i* hacer una prueba

au·di·tor [ˈɔːdɪtər] auditor(a) *m(f)*

au·di·to·ri·um [ɔːdɪˈtɔːrɪəm] *of theater etc* auditorio *m*

Au·gust [ˈɔːɡəst] agosto *m*

aunt [ænt] tía *f*

au pair [oʊˈper] au pair *m/f*

au·ra [ˈɔːrə] aura *f*

aus·pic·es [ˈɔːspɪsɪz] *npl* auspicios *mpl*; *under the auspices of* bajo los auspicios de

aus·pi·cious [ɔːˈspɪʃəs] *adj* propicio

aus·tere [ɔːˈstɪr] *adj interior* austero

aus·ter·i·ty [ɔːsˈterətɪ] *economic* austeridad *f*

Aus·tral·i·a [ɔːˈstreɪlɪə] Australia

Aus·tral·i·an [ɔːˈstreɪlɪən] **1** *adj* australiano **2** *n* australiano(-a) *m(f)*

Aus·tri·a [ˈɔːstrɪə] Austria

Aus·tri·an [ˈɔːstrɪən] **1** *adj* austriaco **2** *n* austriaco(-a) *m(f)*

au·then·tic [ɔːˈθentɪk] *adj* auténtico

au·then·tic·i·ty [ɔːθenˈtɪsətɪ] autenticidad *f*

au·thor [ˈɔːθər] *of story, novel* escritor(a) *m(f)*; *of text* autor(a) *m(f)*

au·thor·i·tar·i·an [əθɔːrɪˈterɪən] *adj* autoritario

au·thor·i·ta·tive [ɔːˈθɔːrɪtətɪv] *adj* autorizado

au·thor·i·ty [əˈθɔːrətɪ] autoridad *f*; *(permission)* autorización *f*; *be an authority on* ser una autoridad en; *the authorities* las autoridades

au·thor·i·za·tion [ɔːθəraɪˈzeɪʃn] autorización *f*

au·thor·ize [ˈɔːθəraɪz] *v/t* autorizar; *be authorized to ...* estar autorizado para ...

au·tis·tic [ɔːˈtɪstɪk] *adj* autista

au·to·bi·og·ra·phy [ɔːtəbaɪˈɑːɡrəfɪ] autobiografía *f*

au·to·crat·ic [ɔːtəˈkrætɪk] *adj* autocrático

au·to·graph [ˈɔːtəɡræf] autógrafo *m*

au·to·mate [ˈɔːtəmeɪt] *v/t* automatizar

au·to·mat·ic [ɔːtəˈmætɪk] **1** *adj* automático **2** *n car* (coche *m*) automático *m*; *gun* pistola *f* automática; *washing machine* lavadora *f* automática

au·to·mat·i·cal·ly [ɔːtəˈmætɪklɪ] *adv* automáticamente

au·to·ma·tion [ɔːtəˈmeɪʃn] automatización *f*

au·to·mo·bile [ˈɔːtəmoʊbiːl] automóvil *m*, coche *m*, *L.Am.* carro *m*, *Rpl* auto *m*

'au·to·mo·bile in·dus·try industria *f* automovilística

au·ton·o·mous [ɔːˈtɑːnəməs] *adj* autónomo

au·ton·o·my [ɔːˈtɑːnəmɪ] autonomía *f*

au·to·pi·lot [ˈɔːtoʊpaɪlət] piloto *m* automático

au·top·sy [ˈɔːtɑːpsɪ] autopsia *f*

au·tumn [ˈɔːtəm] *Br* otoño *m*

aux·il·ia·ry [ɔːɡˈzɪljərɪ] *adj* auxiliar

a·vail [əˈveɪl] **1** *n: to no avail* en vano **2** *v/t: avail o.s. of* aprovechar

a·vai·la·ble [əˈveɪləbl] *adj* disponible

av·a·lanche [ˈævəlænʃ] avalancha *f*, alud *m*

av·a·rice [ˈævərɪs] avaricia *f*

av·e·nue [ˈævənjuː] avenida *f*; *fig* camino *m*

av·e·rage [ˈævərɪdʒ] **1** *adj* medio; *(of mediocre quality)* regular **2** *n* promedio *m*, media *f*; *above / below average* por encima / por debajo del promedio; *on average* como promedio, de media **3** *v/t: I average six hours of sleep a night* duermo seis horas cada noche como promedio *or* de media

◆ **average out** *v/t* calcular el promedio *or* la media de

◆ **average out at** *v/t* salir a

a·verse [əˈvɜːrs] *adj: not be averse to* no ser reacio a

a·ver·sion [əˈvɜːrʃn] aversión *f*; *have an aversion to* tener aversión a

a·vert [əˈvɜːrt] *v/t one's eyes* apartar; *crisis* evitar

a·vi·a·tion [eɪvɪˈeɪʃn] aviación *f*

av·id [ˈævɪd] *adj* ávido

av·o·ca·do [ɑːvəˈkɑːdou] aguacate *m*, *S. Am.* palta *f*

a·void [əˈvɔid] *v/t* evitar; *you've been avoiding me* has estado huyendo de mí

a·void·a·ble [əˈvɔidəbl] *adj* evitable

a·wait [əˈweit] *v/t* aguardar, esperar

a·wake [əˈweik] *adj* despierto; *it kept me awake* no me dejó dormir

a·ward [əˈwɔːrd] **1** *n (prize)* premio *m* **2** *v/t prize, damages* conceder

a·ware [əˈwer] *adj*: *be aware of sth* ser consciente de algo; *become aware of sth* darse cuenta de algo

a·ware·ness [əˈwernis] conciencia *f*

a·way [əˈwei] *adv*: *look away* mirar hacia otra parte; *I'll be away until ... traveling* voy a estar fuera hasta ...; *sick* no voy a ir hasta ...; *it's 2 miles away* está a 2 millas;

Christmas is still six weeks away todavía quedan seis semanas para Navidad; *take sth away from s.o.* quitar algo a alguien; *put sth away* guardar algo

a·way match SP partido *m* fuera de casa

awe·some [ˈɒːsəm] *adj* F *(terrific)* alucinante F

aw·ful [ˈɒːfəl] *adj* horrible, espantoso; *I feel awful* me siento fatal

aw·ful·ly [ˈɒːfəli] *adv* F *(very)* tremendamente; *awfully bad* malísimo

awk·ward [ˈɒːkwərd] *adj (clumsy)* torpe; *(difficult)* difícil; *(embarrassing)* embarazoso; *feel awkward* sentirse incómodo

awn·ing [ˈɒːnɪŋ] toldo *m*

ax, *Br* **axe** [æks] **1** *n* hacha *f* **2** *v/t project etc* suprimir; *budget, job* recortar

ax·le [ˈæksl] eje *m*

B

BA [biːˈei] *abbr* (= *Bachelor of Arts*) Licenciatura *f* en Filosofía y Letras

ba·by [ˈbeibi] *n* bebé *m*

'**ba·by boom** explosión *f* demográfica

'**ba·by car·riage** [ˈkærɪdʒ] cochecito *m* de bebé

ba·by·ish [ˈbeibiɪʃ] *adj* infantil

'**ba·by-sit** *v/i (pret & pp baby-sat)* hacer de *Span* canguro *or L.Am.* babysitter

'**ba·by-sit·ter** [ˈsitər] *Span* canguro *m/f*, *L.Am.* babysitter *m/f*

bach·e·lor [ˈbætʃələr] soltero *m*

back [bæk] **1** *n of person, clothes* espalda *f; of car, bus, house* parte *f* trasera *or* de atrás; *of paper, book* dorso *m; of drawer* fondo *m; of chair* respaldo *m;* SP defensa *m/f; in back in store* en la trastienda; *in the back (of the car)* atrás (del coche); *at the back of the bus* en la parte trasera *or* de atrás del autobús; *back to front* del revés; *at the back of beyond* en el quinto pino **2** *adj* trasero; *back road* carretera *f* secundaria **3** *adv* atrás; *please stand back* póngase más para atrás **2** *meters back from the edge* a 2 metros del borde; *back in 1935* allá por el año 1935; *give sth back to s.o.* devolver algo a alguien; *she'll be back tomorrow* volverá mañana; *when are you coming back?* ¿cuándo volverás?; *take sth back to the store because unsatisfactory*

devolver alguien a la tienda; *they wrote / phoned back* contestaron a la carta/a la llamada; *he hit me back* me devolvió el golpe **4** *v/t (support)* apoyar, respaldar; *horse* apostar por **5** *v/i he backed into the garage* entró en el garaje marcha atrás

◆ **back away** *v/i* alejarse (hacia atrás)

◆ **back down** *v/i* echarse atrás

◆ **back off** *v/i* echarse atrás

◆ **back onto** *v/t* dar por la parte de atrás a

◆ **back out** *v/i of commitment* echarse atrás

◆ **back up 1** *v/t (support)* respaldar; *file* hacer una copia de seguridad de; *traffic was backed up all the way to ...* el atasco llegaba hasta ... **2** *v/i in car* dar marcha atrás; *of drains* atascarse

'**back·ache** dolor *m* de espalda

'**back·bit·ing** cotilleo *m*, chismorreo *m*

'**back·bone** ANAT columna *f* vertebral, espina *f* dorsal; *(fig: courage)* agallas *fpl*; *(fig: mainstay)* columna *f* vertebral

'**back·break·ing** *adj* extenuante, deslomador

back 'burn·er: *put sth on the back burner* aparcar algo

'**back·date** *v/t*: *a salary increase backdated to 1st January* una subida salarial con efecto retroactivo a partir del 1 de enero 'back·door puerta *f* trasera

back·er ['bækər]: *the backers of the movie financially* las personas que financiaron la película

'back·fire *v/i fig: it backfired on us* nos salió el tiro por la culata

'back·ground *n* fondo *m*; *of person* origen *m*, historia *f* personal; *of situation* contexto *m*; *she prefers to stay in the background* prefiere permanecer en un segundo plano

'back·hand *n in tennis* revés *m*

back·ing ['bækɪŋ] *n (support)* apoyo *m*, respaldo *m*; MUS acompañamiento *m*

'back·ing group MUS grupo *m* de acompañamiento

'back·lash reacción *f* violenta

'back·log acumulación *f*

'back·pack **1** *n* mochila *f* **2** *v/i* viajar con la mochila a cuestas

'back·pack·er mochilero(-a) *m(f)*

'back·pack·ing viajes *mpl* con la mochila a cuestas

'back·ped·al *v/i fig* echarse atrás, dar marcha atrás

'back seat *of car* asiento *m* trasero *or* de atrás

back-seat 'driv·er: *he's a terrible back-seat driver* va siempre incordiando al conductor con sus comentarios

'back·space (key) (tecla *f* de) retroceso *m*

'back·stairs *npl* escalera *f* de servicio

'back street *npl* callejuela *f*

'back streets *npl* callejuelas *fpl*; *poorer, dirtier part of a city* zonas *fpl* deprimidas

'back·stroke SP espalda *f*

'back·track *v/i* volver atrás, retroceder

'back·up *(support)* apoyo *m*, respaldo *m*; *for police* refuerzos *mpl*; COMPUT copia *f* de seguridad; *take a backup* COMPUT haz una copia de seguridad

'back·up disk COMPUT disquete *m* con la copia de seguridad

back·ward ['bækwərd] **1** *adj child* retrasado; *society* atrasado; *glance* hacia atrás **2** *adv* hacia atrás

'back·yard jardín *m* trasero; *in s.o.'s backyard fig* en la misma puerta de alguien

ba·con ['beɪkn] tocino *m*, *Span* bacon *m*

bac·te·ri·a [bæk'tɪrɪə] *npl* bacterias *fpl*

bad [bæd] *adj* malo; *before singular masculine noun* mal; *cold, headache* grave; *mistake, accident* grave; *I've had a bad day* he tenido un mal día; *smoking is bad for you* fumar es malo; *it's not bad* no está mal; *that's really too bad (shame)* es una verdadera pena; *feel bad about (guilty)* sentirse mal por; *I'm*

bad at math se me dan mal las matemáticas; *Friday's bad, how about Thursday?* el viernes me viene mal, ¿qué tal el jueves?

bad 'debt deuda *f* incobrable

badge [bædʒ] insignia *f*, chapa *f*; *of policeman* placa *f*

bad·ger ['bædʒər] *v/t* acosar, importunar

bad 'lan·guage palabrotas *fpl*

bad·ly ['bædlɪ] *adv injured* gravemente; *damaged* seriamente; *work* mal; *I did really badly in the exam* el examen me salió fatal; *he hasn't done badly in life, business etc* no le ha ido mal, *you're badly in need of a haircut* necesitas urgentemente un corte de pelo; *he is badly off poor* anda mal de dinero

bad-man·nered [bæd'mænərd] *adj: be bad-mannered* tener malos modales

bad·min·ton ['bædmɪntən] bádminton *m*

bad-tem·pered [bæd'tempərd] *adj* malhumorado

baf·fle ['bæfl] *v/t* confundir, desconcertar; *be baffled* estar confundido *or* desconcertado; *I'm baffled why she left* no consigo entender por qué se fue

baf·fling ['bæflɪŋ] *adj mystery, software* desconcertante, incomprensible

bag [bæg] bolsa *f*; *for school* cartera *f*; *(purse)* bolso *m*, *S. Am.* cartera *f*, *Mex* bolsa *f*

bag·gage ['bægɪdʒ] equipaje *m*

'bag·gage car RAIL vagón *m* de equipajes

'bag·gage check consigna *f*

'bag·gage re·claim ['riːkleɪm] recogida *f* de equipajes

bag·gy ['bægɪ] *adj* ancho, holgado

'bag·pipes *npl* gaita *f*

bail [beɪl] *n* LAW libertad *f* bajo fianza; *(money)* fianza *f*; *on bail* bajo fianza

◆ **bail out 1** *v/t* LAW pagar la fianza de **2** *v/i of airplane* tirarse en paracaídas

bait [beɪt] *n* cebo *m*

bake [beɪk] *v/t* hornear, cocer al horno

baked 'beans [beɪkt] *npl* alubias con salsa de tomate

baked po·ta·to *Span* patata *f* *or* *L.Am.* papa *f* asada (con piel)

bak·er ['beɪkər] panadero(-a) *m(f)*

bak·er·y ['beɪkərɪ] panadería *f*

bak·ing pow·der ['beɪkɪŋ] levadura *f*

bal·ance ['bæləns] **1** *n* equilibrio *m*; *(remainder)* resto *m*; *of bank account* saldo *m* **2** *v/t* poner en equilibrio; *balance the books* cuadrar las cuentas **3** *v/i* mantenerse en equilibrio; *of accounts* cuadrar

bal·anced ['bælənst] *adj (fair)* objetivo; *diet, personality* equilibrado

bal·ance of 'pay·ments balanza *f* de pagos

bal·ance of 'trade balanza *f* comercial

'bal·ance sheet balance *m*

bal·co·ny ['bælkənɪ] *of house* balcón *m*; *in theater* anfiteatro *m*

bald [bɔːld] *adj* calvo; *he's going bald* se está quedando calvo; *bald spot* calva *f*

bald·ing ['bɔːldɪŋ] *adj* medio calvo

Bal·kan ['bɔːlkən] *adj* balcánico

Bal·kans ['bɔːlkənz] *npl: the Balkans* los Balcanes

ball [bɔːl] *tennis-ball size* pelota *f*; *football size* balón *m*, pelota *f*; *billiard-ball size* bola *f*; *on the ball* despierto; *play ball fig* cooperar; *the ball's in his court* le toca actuar a él, la pelota está en su tejado

bal·lad ['bæləd] balada *f*

ball 'bear·ing rodamiento *m* de bolas

bal·le·ri·na [bælə'riːnə] bailarina *f*

bal·let ['bæleɪ] ballet *m*

'bal·let danc·er bailarín (-ina) *m(f)*

'ball game (*baseball*) partido *m* de béisbol; *that's a different ball game* F esa es otra cuestión F

bal·lis·tic mis·sile [bə'lɪstɪk] misil *m* balístico

bal·loon [bə'luːn] globo *m*

bal·loon·ist [bə'luːnɪst] piloto *m* de globo aerostático

bal·lot ['bælət] **1** *n* voto *m* **2** *v/t members* consultar por votación

'bal·lot box urna *f*

'bal·lot pa·per papeleta *f*

'ball·park (*baseball*) campo *m* de béisbol; *you're in the right ballpark* F no vas descaminado

'ball·park fig·ure F cifra *f* aproximada

'ball·point (pen) bolígrafo *m*, *Mex* pluma *f*, *Rpl* birome *m*

balls [bɔːlz] *npl* V huevos *mpl* V; (*courage*) huevos *mpl* V; (*nonsense*) tonterías *fpl*, paridas *fpl* F

bam·boo [bæm'buː] *n* bambú *m*

ban [bæn] **1** *n* prohibición *f* **2** *v/t* (*pret & pp banned*) prohibir; *ban s.o. from doing sth* prohibir a alguien que haga algo

ba·nal [bə'næl] *adj* banal

ba·na·na [bə'nænə] plátano *m*, *Rpl* banana *f*

band [bænd] banda *f*; *pop* grupo *m*

ban·dage ['bændɪdʒ] **1** *n* vendaje *m* **2** *v/t* vendar

'Band-Aid® *Span* tirita *f*, *L.Am.* curita *f*

B&B [biːn'biː] *abbr* (= *bed and breakfast*) hostal *m* familiar

ban·dit ['bændɪt] bandido *m*

'band·wag·on: jump on the bandwagon

subirse al carro

ban·dy ['bændɪ] *adj legs* arqueado

bang [bæŋ] **1** *n noise* estruendo *m*, estrépito *m*; (*blow*) golpe *m*; *the door closed with a bang* la puerta se cerró de un portazo **2** *v/t door* cerrar de un portazo; (*hit*) golpear; *bang o.s. on the head* golpearse la cabeza **3** *v/i* dar golpes; *the door banged shut* la puerta se cerró de un portazo

ban·gle ['bæŋgl] brazalete *m*, pulsera *f*

bangs [bæŋz] flequillo *m*

ban·is·ters ['bænɪstərz] *npl* barandilla *f*

ban·jo ['bændʒoʊ] banjo *m*

bank¹ [bæŋk] *of river* orilla *f*

bank² [bæŋk] **1** *n* FIN banco *m* **2** *v/i: I bank with ...* mi banco es el ... **3** *v/t money* ingresar, depositar

◆ **bank on** *v/t* contar con; *don't bank on it* no cuentes con ello

'bank ac·count cuenta *f* (bancaria)

'bank bal·ance saldo *m* bancario

'bank bill billete *m*

bank·er ['bæŋkər] banquero *m*

'bank·er's card tarjeta *f* bancaria

bank·ing ['bæŋkɪŋ] banca *f*

'bank loan préstamo *m* bancario

'bank man·ag·er director(a) *m(f)* de banco

'bank rate tipo *m* de interés bancario

'bank·roll *v/t* financiar

bank·rupt ['bæŋkrʌpt] **1** *adj* en bancarrota *or* quiebra; *go bankrupt* quebrar, ir a la quiebra; *of person* arruinarse **2** *v/t* llevar a la quiebra

bank·rupt·cy ['bæŋkrʌpsɪ] *of person, company* quiebra *f*, bancarrota *f*

'bank state·ment extracto *m* bancario

ban·ner ['bænər] pancarta *f*

banns [bænz] *npl* amonestaciones *fpl*

ban·quet ['bæŋkwɪt] *n* banquete *m*

ban·ter ['bæntər] *n* bromas *fpl*

bap·tism ['bæptɪzm] bautismo *m*

bap·tize [bæp'taɪz] *v/t* bautizar

bar¹ [bɑːr] *n of iron* barra *f*; *of chocolate* tableta *f*; *for drinks* bar *m*; (*counter*) barra *f*; *a bar of soap* una pastilla de jabón; *be behind bars* (*in prison*) estar entre barrotes

bar² [bɑːr] *v/t* (*pret & pp barred*) *from premises* prohibir la entrada a; *bar s.o. from doing sth* prohibir a alguien que haga algo

bar³ [bɑːr] *prep* (*except*) excepto

bar·bar·i·an [bɑːr'berɪən] bárbaro(-a) *m(f)*

bar·bar·ic [bɑːr'bærɪk] *adj* brutal, inhumano

bar·be·cue ['bɑːrbɪkjuː] **1** *n* barbacoa *f* **2**

v/t cocinar en la barbacoa

barbed 'wire [bɑːbd] alambre *f* de espino

bar·ber ['bɑːrbər] barbero *m*

bar·bi·tu·rate [bɑːr'bɪtjərət] barbitúrico *m*

'**bar code** código *m* de barras

bare [ber] *adj* (*naked*) desnudo; (*empty: room*) vacío; (*mountainside*) pelado, raso; *floor* descubierto; *in one's bare feet* descalzo

'**bare·foot** *adj* descalzo

bare·head·ed [ber'hedɪd] *adj* sin sombrero

'**bare·ly** ['berlɪ] *adv* apenas; *he's barely five* acaba de cumplir cinco años

bar·gain ['bɑːrgɪn] **1** *n* (*deal*) trato *m*; (*good buy*) ganga *f*; *into the bargain* además *2 v/i* regatear, negociar

◆ **bargain for** *v/t* (*expect*) imaginarse, esperar

barge [bɑːrdʒ] *n* NAUT barcaza *f*

◆ **barge into** *v/t person* tropezarse con; *room* irrumpir en

bar·i·tone ['bærɪtoun] *n* barítono *m*

bark[1] [bɑːrk] **1** *n of dog* ladrido *m* **2** *v/i* ladrar

bark[2] [bɑːrk] *of tree* corteza *f*

bar·ley ['bɑːrlɪ] cebada *f*

'**bar·maid** *Br* camarera *f*, *L.Am.* mesera *f*, *Rpl* moza *f*

'**bar·man** camarero *m*, *L.Am.* mesero *m*, *Rpl* mozo *m*

barn [bɑːrn] granero *m*

ba·rom·e·ter [bə'rɑːmɪtər] *also fig* barómetro *m*

Ba·roque [bə'rɑːk] *adj* barroco

bar·racks ['bærəks] *npl* MIL cuartel *m*

bar·rage [bə'rɑːʒ] MIL barrera *f* (de fuego); *fig* aluvión *m*

bar·rel ['bærəl] (*container*) tonel *m*, barril *m*

bar·ren ['bærən] *adj land* yermo, árido

bar·ri·cade ['bærɪkeɪd] *n* barricada *f*

bar·ri·er ['bærɪər] *also fig* barrera *f*; *language barrier* barrera *f* lingüística

bar·ring ['bɑːrɪŋ] *prep* salvo, excepto; *barring accidents* salvo imprevistos

bar·ris·ter ['bærɪstər] *Br* abogado(-a) *m(f)* (*que aparece en tribunales*)

bar·row ['bærou] carretilla *f*

'**bar ten·der** camarero(-a) *m(f)*, *L.Am.* mesero(-a) *m(f)*, *Rpl* mozo(-a) *m(f)*

bar·ter ['bɑːrtər] **1** *n* trueque *m* **2** *v/t* cambiar, trocar (*for* por)

base [beɪs] **1** *n bottom, center* base *f*; *base camp* campamento *m* base **2** *v/t* basar (*on* en); *be based in* *of soldier* estar destinado en; *of company* tener su sede en

'**base·ball** *ball* pelota *f* de béisbol; *game* béisbol *m*

'**base·ball bat** bate *m* de béisbol

'**base·ball cap** gorra *f* de béisbol

'**base·ball play·er** jugador(a) *m(f)* de béisbol, *L.Am.* pelotero(-a) *m(f)*

'**base·board** rodapié *m*

base·less ['beɪslɪs] *adj* infundado

base·ment ['beɪsmənt] *of house, store* sótano *m*

'**base rate** FIN tipo *m* de interés básico

bash [bæʃ] **1** *n* F porrazo *m* F **2** *v/t* dar un porrazo a F

ba·sic ['beɪsɪk] *adj* (*rudimentary*) básico; *room* modesto, sencillo; *language skills* elemental; (*fundamental*) fundamental; *basic salary* sueldo *m* base

ba·sic·al·ly ['beɪsɪklɪ] *adv* básicamente

ba·sics ['beɪsɪks] *npl*: *the basics* lo básico, los fundamentos; *get down to basics* centrarse en lo esencial

bas·il ['bæzɪl] albahaca *f*

ba·sil·i·ca [bə'zɪlɪkə] basílica *f*

ba·sin ['beɪsn] *for washing* barreño *m*; *in bathroom* lavabo *m*

ba·sis ['beɪsɪs] (*pl bases* ['beɪsiːz]) base *f*; *on the basis of what you've told me* de acuerdo con lo que me has dicho

bask [bæsk] *v/i* tomar el sol

bas·ket ['bæskɪt] cesta *f*; *in basketball* canasta *f*

'**bas·ket·ball** *game* baloncesto *m*, *L.Am.* básquetbol *m*; *ball* balón *m* o pelota *f* de baloncesto; *basketball player* baloncestista *m/f*, *L.Am.* basquebolista *m/f*

Basque [bæsk] **1** *adj* vasco **2** *n person* vasco(-a) *m(f)*; *language* vasco *m*

bass [beɪs] **1** *n part, singer* bajo *m*; *instrument* contrabajo *m* **2** *adj* bajo

bas·tard ['bæstərd] ilegítimo(-a) *m(f)*, bastardo(-a) *m(f)*; P cabrón(-ona) *m(f)* P; *poor bastard* pobre desgraciado; *stupid bastard* desgraciado

bat[1] [bæt] **1** *n for baseball* bate *m*; *for table tennis* pala *f* **2** *v/i* (*pret & pp batted*) *in baseball* batear

bat[2] [bæt] *v/t* (*pret & pp batted*): *he didn't bat an eyelid* no se inmutó

bat[3] [bæt] (*animal*) murciélago *m*

batch [bætʃ] *n of students* tanda *f*; *of data* conjunto *m*; *of bread* hornada *f*; *of products* lote *m*

ba·ted ['beɪtɪd] *adj*: *with bated breath* con la respiración contenida

bath [bæθ] baño *m*; *have a bath, take a bath* darse *o* tomar un baño

bathe [beɪð] *v/i* (*swim, have a bath*) bañarse

bath·ing cost·ume, bathing suit ['beɪðɪŋ] bañador *m*, traje *m* de baño

B

'bath mat alfombra f de baño
'bath·robe albornoz m
'bath·room for bath, washing hands, cuarto m de baño; (toilet) servicio m, L.Am. baño m
'bath tow·el toalla f de baño
'bath·tub bañera f
bat·on [bəˈtɑːn] of conductor batuta f
bat·tal·i·on [bəˈtæliən] MIL batallón m
bat·ter ['bætər] n masa f; in baseball bateador(a) m(f)
bat·tered ['bætərd] adj maltratado
bat·ter·y ['bætəri] in watch, flashlight pila f; in computer, car batería f
'bat·ter·y charg·er ['tʃɑːrdʒər] cargador m de pilas / baterías
bat·ter·y-op·e·rat·ed [bætəriˈɑːpəreɪtɪd] adj que funciona con pilas
bat·tle ['bætl] 1 n also fig batalla f 2 v/i against illness etc luchar
'bat·tle·field, 'bat·tle·ground campo m de batalla
'bat·tle·ship acorazado m
bawd·y ['bɔːdɪ] adj picante, subido de tono
bawl [bɔːl] v/i (shout) gritar, vociferar; (weep) berrear
◆ bawl out v/t F echar la bronca a F
bay [beɪ] (inlet) bahía f
bay·o·net ['beɪənet] n bayoneta f
bay 'win·dow ventana f en saliente
BC [biːˈsiː] abbr (= before Christ) a.C. (= antes de Cristo)
be [biː] ◇ v/i (pret was / were, pp been) permanent characteristics, profession, nationality ser; position, temporary condition estar; was she there? ¿estaba allí?; it's me soy yo; how much is / are...? ¿cuánto es / son ...?; there is, there are hay; be careful ten cuidado; don't be sad no estés triste
◇ has the mailman been? ¿ha venido el cartero?; I've never been to Japan no he estado en Japón; I've been here for hours he estado aquí horas
◇ tags: that's right, isn't it? eso es, ¿no?; she's Chinese, isn't she? es china, ¿verdad?
◇ v/aux: I am thinking estoy pensando; he was running corría; you're being stupid estás siendo un estúpido
◇ obligation: you are to do what I tell you harás lo que yo te diga; I was to help him escape se suponía que se iba a ayudar a escaparse; you are not to tell anyone no debes decírselo a nadie
◇ passive: he was arrested fue detenido, lo detuvieron; they have been sold se han vendido

◆ be in for v/t: he's in for a big disappointment se va a llevar una gran desilusión
beach [biːtʃ] n playa f
'beach ball pelota f de playa
'beach·wear ropa f playera
beads [biːdz] npl cuentas fpl
beak [biːk] pico m
'be-all: the be-all and end-all lo más importante del mundo
beam [biːm] 1 n in ceiling etc viga f 2 v/i (smile) sonreír de oreja a oreja 3 v/t (transmit) emitir
bean [biːn] judía f, alubia f, L.Am. frijol m, S. Am. poroto m; green beans judías fpl verdes, Mex ejotes mpl, S. Am. porotos mpl verdes; coffee beans granos mpl de café; be full of beans F estar lleno de vitalidad
'bean·bag cojín relleno de bolitas
bear¹ [ber] animal oso(-a) m(f)
bear² [ber] 1 v/t (pret bore, pp borne) weight resistir; costs correr con; (tolerate) aguantar, soportar; child dar a luz; she bore him six children le dio seis hijos 2 v/i (pret bore, pp borne): bring pressure to bear on ejercer presión sobre
◆ bear out v/t (confirm) confirmar
bear·a·ble ['berəbl] adj soportable
beard [bɪrd] barba f
beard·ed ['bɪrdɪd] adj con barba
bear·ing ['berɪŋ] in machine rodamiento m, cojinete m; that has no bearing on the case eso no tiene nada que ver con el caso
'bear mar·ket FIN mercado m a la baja
beast [biːst] animal bestia f; person bestia m/f
beat [biːt] 1 n of heart latido m; of music ritmo m 2 v/i (pret beat, pp beaten) of heart latir; of rain golpear; beat about the bush andarse por las ramas 3 v/t (pret beat, pp beaten) in competition derrotar, ganar a; (hit) pegar a; (pound) golpear; beat it! F ¡lárgate! F; it beats me no logro entender
◆ beat up v/t dar una paliza a
beat·en ['biːtən] adj: off the beaten track retirado 2 pp → beat
beat·ing ['biːtɪŋ] (physical) paliza f
beat-up adj F destartalado F
beau·ti·cian [bjuːˈtɪʃn] esteticista m/f
beau·ti·ful ['bjuːtəfəl] adj woman, house, day, story, movie bonito, precioso, L.Am. lindo; smell, taste, meal delicioso, L.Am. rico; vacation estupendo; thanks, that's just beautiful! ¡muchísimas gracias, está maravilloso!
beau·ti·ful·ly ['bjuːtɪfəlɪ] adv cooked, do-

ne perfectamente, maravillosamente

beaut·y ['bju:tɪ] *of woman, sunset* belleza *f*

'beaut·y par·lor ['pɑːrlər] salón *m* de belleza

◆ **bea·ver away** *v/i* F trabajar como un burro F

be·came [bɪ'keɪm] *pret* → **become**

be·cause [bɪ'kɑːz] *conj* porque; *because it was too expensive* porque era demasiado caro; *because of* debido a, a causa de; *because of you, we don't go* gracias a ti, no podemos ir

beck·on ['bekn] *v/i* hacer señas

be·come [bɪ'kʌm] *v/i* (*pret* **became**, *pp* **become**) hacerse, volverse; *it became clear that ...* quedó claro que ...; *he became a priest* se hizo sacerdote; *she's becoming very forgetful* cada vez es más olvidadiza; *what's become of her?* ¿qué fue de ella?

be·com·ing [bɪ'kʌmɪŋ] *adj* favorecedor, apropiado

bed [bed] *n* cama *f*; *of flowers* macizo; *of sea* fondo *m*; *of river* cauce *m*, lecho *m*; *go to bed* ir a la cama; *he's still in bed* aún está en la cama; *go to bed with s.o.* irse a la cama *or* acostarse con alguien

'bed·clothes *npl* ropa *f* de cama

bed·ding ['bedɪŋ] ropa *f* de cama

bed·lam ['bedləm] F locura *f*, jaleo *m*

bed·rid·den ['bedrɪdən] *adj*: *be bedridden* estar postrado en cama

'bed·room dormitorio *m*, *L.Am.* cuarto *m*

'bed·side; *be at the bedside of* estar junto a la cama de

'bed·spread colcha *f*

'bed·time hora *f* de irse a la cama

bee [biː] abeja *f*

booch [bl:ʧ] haya *f*

beef [biːf] *n* carne *f* de vaca *or* vacuna; F (*complaint*) queja *f* 2 *v/i* F (*complain*) quejarse

◆ **boof up** *v/t* reforzar, fortalecer

'beef·bur·ger hamburguesa *f*

'bee·hlve colmena *f*

'bee·line; *make a beeline for* ir directamente a

been [bɪn] *pp* → **be**

beep [biːp] 1 *n* pitido *m* 2 *v/i* pitar 3 *v/t* (*call on pager*) llamar con el buscapersonas

beep·er ['biːpər] buscapersonas *m inv*, *Span* busca *m*

beer [bɪr] cerveza *f*

beet [biːt] remolacha *f*

bee·tle ['biːtl] escarabajo *m*

be·fore [bɪ'fɔːr] 1 *prep* (*time*) antes de; (*space, order*) antes de, delante de 2

adv antes; *I've seen this movie before* ya he visto esta película; *have you been to Japan before?* ¿habías estado antes *or* ya en Japón?; *the week / day before* la semana / el día anterior 3 *conj* antes de que

be·fore·hand *adv* de antemano

be·friend [bɪ'frend] *v/t* hacerse amigo de

beg [beg] 1 *v/i* (*pret & pp* **begged**) mendigar, pedir 2 *v/t* (*pret & pp* **begged**): *beg s.o. to sth* rogar *or* suplicar a alguien que haga algo

began [bɪ'gæn] *pret* → **begin**

beg·gar ['begər] *n* mendigo(-a) *m(f)*

be·gin [bɪ'gɪn] 1 *v/i* (*pret* **began**, *pp* **begun**) empezar, comenzar; *to begin with* (*at first*) en un primer momento, al principio; (*in the first place*) para empezar 2 *v/t* (*pret* **began**, *pp* **begun**) empezar, comenzar; *begin to do sth, begin doing sth* empezar *or* comenzar a hacer algo

be·gin·ner [bɪ'gɪnər] principiante *m/f*

be·gin·ning [bɪ'gɪnɪŋ] principio *m*, comienzo *m*; (*origin*) origen *m*

be·grudge [bɪ'grʌdʒ] *v/t* (*envy*) envidiar; (*give reluctantly*) dar a regañadientes

be·gun [bɪ'gʌn] *pp* → **begin**

be·half [bɪ'hɑːf]: *on behalf of, in behalf of* en nombre de; *on my / his behalf* en nombre mío / suyo

be·have [bɪ'heɪv] *v/i* comportarse, portarse; *be·have (o.s.)* comportarse *or* portarse bien; *behave (yourself)*! ¡pórtate bien!

be·hav·ior [bɪ'heɪvɪər] comportamiento *m*, conducta *f*

be·hind [bɪ'haɪnd] 1 *prep in position, order* detrás de; *in progress* por detrás de; *be behind ...* (*responsible for*) estar detrás de ...; (*support*) respaldar ... 2 *adv* (*at the back*) detrás; *be behind in match* ir perdiendo; *be behind with sth* estar atrasado con algo; *leave sth behind* dejarse algo

bcige [beɪʒ] *adj* beige, *Span* beis

be·ing ['biːɪŋ] *existence, creature* ser *m*

be·lat·ed [bɪ'leɪtɪd] *adj* tardío

belch [belʧ] 1 *n* eructo *m* 2 *v/i* eructar

Bel·gian ['beldʒən] 1 *adj* belga 2 *n* belga *m/f*

Bel·gium ['beldʒəm] Bélgica *f*

be·lief [bɪ'liːf] creencia *f*; *it's my belief that* creo que ...

be·lieve [bɪ'liːv] *v/t* creer

◆ **believe in** *v/t* creer en

be·liev·er [bɪ'liːvər] REL creyente *m/f*; *fig* partidario(a) *m(f)* (*in* de)

be·lit·tle [bɪ'lɪtl] *v/t* menospreciar

Be·lize [be'liːz] *n* Belice

bell [bel] *of bike, door, school* timbre *m*; *of church* campana *f*

'bell·hop botones *m inv*

bel·lig·er·ent [bɪ'lɪdʒərənt] *adj* beligerante

bel·low ['beloʊ] **1** *n* bramido *m* **2** *v/i* bramar

bel·ly ['belɪ] *of person* estómago *m*, barriga *f*; (*fat stomach*) barriga *f*, tripa *f*; *of animal* panza *f*

'bel·ly·ache *v/i* F refunfuñar

be·long [bɪ'lɒŋ] *v/i*: *where does this belong?* ¿dónde va esto?; *I don't belong here* no encajo aquí

◆ **belong to** *v/t of object, money* pertenecer a; *club* pertenecer a, ser socio de

be·long·ings [bɪ'lɒŋɪŋz] *npl* pertenencias *fpl*

be·loved [bɪ'lʌvɪd] *adj* querido

be·low [bɪ'loʊ] **1** *prep* debajo de; *in amount, rate, level* por debajo de **2** *adv* abajo; *in text* más abajo; *see below* véase más abajo; *10 degrees below* 10 grados bajo cero

belt [belt] *n* cinturón *m*; *tighten one's belt* fig apretarse el cinturón

bench *seat* banco *m*; (*workbench*) mesa *f* de trabajo

'bench·mark punto *m* de referencia

bend [bend] **1** *n* curva *f* **2** *v/t* (*pret & pp bent*) doblar **3** *v/i* (*pret & pp bent*) torcer, girar; *of person* flexionarse

◆ **bend down** *v/i* agacharse

bend·er ['bendər] F parranda *f* F

be·neath [bɪ'niːθ] **1** *prep* debajo de; *she thinks a job like that is beneath her* cree que un trabajo como ése le supondría rebajarse **2** *adv* abajo

ben·e·fac·tor ['benɪfæktər] benefactor(a) *m(f)*

ben·e·fi·cial [benɪ'fɪʃl] *adj* beneficioso

ben·e·fi·ci·a·ry [benɪ'fɪʃərɪ] beneficiario(-a) *m(f)*

ben·e·fit ['benɪfɪt] **1** *n* beneficio *m*, ventaja *f* **2** *v/t* beneficiar **3** *v/i* beneficiarse

be·nev·o·lence [bɪ'nevələns] benevolencia *f*

be·nev·o·lent [bɪ'nevələnt] *adj* benevolente

be·nign [bɪ'naɪn] *adj* agradable; MED benigno

bent [bent] *pret & pp* → **bend**

be·queath [bɪ'kwiːð] *v/t also fig* legar

be·quest [bɪ'kwest] legado *m*

be·reaved [bɪ'riːvd] **1** *adj*: *the bereaved parents* los padres del difunto **2** *n*: *the bereaved* los familiares del difunto

be·ret ['bereɪ] boina *f*

ber·ry ['berɪ] baya *f*

ber·serk [bər'sɜːrk] *adv*: *go berserk* F volverse loco

berth [bɜːrθ] *on ship* litera *f*; *on train* camarote *m*; *for ship* amarradero *m*; *give s.o. a wide berth* evitar a alguien

be·seech [bɪ'siːtʃ] *v/t*: *beseech s.o. to do sth* suplicar a alguien que haga algo

be·side [bɪ'saɪd] *prep* al lado de, junto a; *be beside o.s.* estar fuera de sí; *that's beside the point* eso no tiene nada que ver

be·sides [bɪ'saɪdz] **1** *adv* además **2** *prep* (*apart from*) aparte de, además de

be·siege [bɪ'siːdʒ] *v/t fig* asediar, cercar

best [best] **1** *adj* mejor **2** *adv* mejor; *which did you like best?* ¿cuál te gustó más?; *it would be best if ...* sería mejor si ...; *I like her best* ella es la que más me gusta **3** *n*: *do one's best* hacer todo lo posible; *I did my best to convince her* hice todo lo posible por convencerla; *the best person, thing* el / la mejor; *we insist on the best* insistimos en lo mejor; *we'll just have to make the best of it* tendremos que arreglárnoslas; *all the best!* ¡buena suerte!, ¡que te vaya bien!

best be'fore date fecha *f* de caducidad

best 'man *at wedding* padrino *m*

'best-sell·er éxito *m* de ventas, best-seller *m*

bet [bet] **1** *n* apuesta *f*; *place a bet* hacer una apuesta **2** *v/i/a also fig* apostar; *I bet he doesn't come* apuesto a que no viene; *you bet!* ¡ya lo creo!

be·tray [bɪ'treɪ] *v/t* traicionar; *husband, wife* engañar

be·tray·al [bɪ'treɪəl] traición *f*; *of husband, wife* engaño *m*

bet·ter ['betər] **1** *adj* mejor; *get better in skills, health* mejorar; *he's better in health* está mejor **2** *adv* mejor; *you'd better ask permission* sería mejor que pidieras permiso; *I'd really better not* mejor no; *all the better for us* tanto mejor para nosotros; *I like her better* me gusta más ella

bet·ter 'off *adj* (*wealthier*) más rico

be·tween [bɪ'twiːn] *prep* entre; *between you and me* entre tú y yo

bev·er·age ['bevərɪdʒ] *fml* bebida *f*

be·ware [bɪ'wer] *v/t*: *beware of* tener cuidado con

be·wil·der [bɪ'wɪldər] *v/t* desconcertar

be·wil·der·ment [bɪ'wɪldərmənt] desconcierto *m*

be·yond [bɪ'jɑːnd] **1** *prep in space* más allá de; *she has changed beyond recognition* ha cambiado tanto que es difícil reconocerla; **it's beyond me** (*don't understand*) no logro entender; (*can't do it*) me es imposible **2** *adv* más allá

bi·as ['baɪəs] *n against* prejuicio *m*; *in favor of* favoritismo *m*

bi·as(s)ed [baɪəst] *adj* parcial

bib [bɪb] *for baby* babero *m*

Bi·ble ['baɪbl] Biblia *f*

bib·li·cal ['bɪblɪkl] *adj* bíblico

bib·li·og·ra·phy [bɪblɪ'ɑːɡrəfɪ] bibliografía *f*

bi·car·bon·ate of so·da [baɪ'kɑːrbəneɪt] bicarbonato *m* sódico

bi·cen·ten·ni·al [baɪsen'tenɪəl] bicentenario *m*

bi·ceps ['baɪseps] *npl* bíceps *mpl*

bick·er ['bɪkər] *v/i* reñir, discutir

bi·cy·cle ['baɪsɪkl] bicicleta *f*

bid [bɪd] **1** *n at auction* puja *f*; (*attempt*) intento *m* **2** *v/i* (*pret & pp* **bid**) *at auction* pujar

bid·der ['bɪdər] postor(a) *m(f)*; **the highest bidder** el mejor postor

bi·en·ni·al [baɪ'enɪəl] *adj* bienal

bi·fo·cals [baɪ'foukəlz] *npl* gafas *fpl* or *L.Am.* lentes *mpl* bifocales

big [bɪɡ] **1** *adj* grande; *before singular nouns* gran; *my big brother / sister* mi hermano / hermana mayor; *big name* nombre *m* importante **2** *adv*: *talk big* alardear, fanfarronear

big·a·mist ['bɪɡəmɪst] bígamo(-a) *m(f)*

big·a·mous ['bɪɡəməs] *adj* bígamo

big·a·my ['bɪɡəmɪ] bigamia *f*

'big·head F creído(-a) *m(f)* F

big·head·ed [bɪɡ'hedɪd] *adj* F creído F

big·ot ['bɪɡət] fanático(-a) *m(f)*, intolerante *m/f*

hike [haɪk] **1** *n* F bici f F; *motorbike* moto *f* **2** *v/i* ir en bici

bik·er ['baɪkər] motero(-a) *m(f)*

bi·ki·ni [bɪ'kiːnɪ] biquini *m*

bi·lat·er·al [baɪ'lætərəl] *adj* bilateral

bi·lin·gual [baɪ'lɪŋɡwəl] *adj* bilingüe

bill [bɪl] **1** *n for gas, electricity* factura *f*, recibo *m*; *Br in hotel, restaurant* cuenta *f*; (*money*) billete *m*; POL proyecto *m* de ley; (*poster*) cartel *m* **2** *v/t* (*invoice*) enviar la factura a

'bill·board valla *f* publicitaria

'bill·fold cartera *f*, billetera *f*

bil·li·ards ['bɪljərdz] *nsg* billar *m*

bil·li·on ['bɪljən] mil millones *mpl*, millardo *m*

bill of ex'change FIN letra *f* de cambio

bill of 'sale escritura *f* de compraventa

bin [bɪn] *n* cubo *m*

bi·na·ry ['baɪnərɪ] *adj* binario

bind [baɪnd] *v/t* (*pret & pp* **bound**) (*con-*

nect) unir; (*tie*) atar; (LAW: *oblige*) obligar

bind·ing ['baɪndɪŋ] **1** *adj agreement, promise* vinculante **2** *n of book* tapa *f*

bi·noc·u·lars [bɪ'nɑːkjulərz] *npl* prismáticos *mpl*

bi·o·chem·ist [baɪoʊ'kemɪst] bioquímico(-a) *m(f)*

bi·o·chem·is·try [baɪoʊ'kemɪstrɪ] bioquímica *f*

bi·o·de·gra·da·ble [baɪoʊdɪ'ɡreɪdəbl] *adj* biodegradable

bi·og·ra·pher [baɪ'ɑːɡrəfər] biógrafo(-a) *m(f)*

bi·og·ra·phy [baɪ'ɑːɡrəfɪ] biografía *f*

bi·o·log·i·cal [baɪoʊ'lɑːdʒɪkl] *adj* biológico; *biological parents* padres *mpl* biológicos; *biological detergent* detergente *m* biológico

bi·ol·o·gist [baɪ'ɑːlədʒɪst] biólogo(-a) *m(f)*

bi·ol·o·gy [baɪ'ɑːlədʒɪ] biología *f*

bi·o·tech·nol·o·gy [baɪoʊtek'nɑːlədʒɪ] biotecnología *f*

bird [bɜːrd] ave *f*, pájaro *m*

'bird·cage jaula *f* para pájaros

bird of 'prey ave *f* rapaz

'bird sanc·tu·a·ry reserva *f* de aves

bird's eye 'view vista *f* panorámica; *get a bird's eye view of sth* ver algo a vista de pájaro

bi·ro® ['baɪroʊ] *Br* bolígrafo *m*, *Mex* pluma *f*, *Rpl* birome *m*

birth [bɜːrθ] *also fig* nacimiento *m*; (*labor*) parto *m*; *give birth to child* dar a luz; *of animal* parir; *date of birth* fecha *f* de nacimiento; *the land of my birth* mi tierra natal

'birth cer·tif·i·cate partida *f* de nacimiento

'birth con·trol control *m* de natalidad

'birth·day cumpleaños *m inv*; *happy birthday!* ¡feliz cumpleaños!

'birth·day cake tarta *f* de cumpleaños

'birth·mark marca *f* de nacimiento, antojo *m*

'birth·place lugar *m* de nacimiento

'birth·rate tasa *f* de natalidad

bis·cuit ['bɪskɪt] bollo *m*, panecillo *m*; *Br* galleta *f*

bi·sex·u·al ['baɪsekʃuəl] **1** *adj* bisexual **2** *n* bisexual *m/f*

bish·op ['bɪʃəp] obispo *m*

bit [bɪt] *n* (*piece*) trozo *m*; (*part*) parte *f*; *of puzzle* pieza *f*; COMPUT bit *m*; *a bit* (*a little*) un poco; *let's sit down for a bit* sentémonos un rato; *you haven't changed a bit* no has cambiado nada; *a bit of* (*a little*) un poco de; *a bit of news* una noticia; *a bit of advice* un consejo; *bit by*

bit poco a poco; *I'll be there in a bit* estaré allí dentro de un rato

bit² [bɪt] *pret* → **bite**

bitch [bɪtʃ] **1** *n dog* perra *f*; F *woman* zorra *f* F **2** *v/i* F (*complain*) quejarse

bitch·y ['bɪtʃɪ] *adj* F *person* malicioso; *remark* a mala leche F

bite [baɪt] **1** *n of dog* mordisco *m*; *of spider, mosquito* picadura *f*; *of snake* mordedura *f*, picadura *f*; *of food* bocado *m*; *let's have a bite (to eat)* vamos a comer algo **2** *v/t* (*pret* **bit**, *pp* **bitten**) *of dog* morder; *of mosquito, flea* picar; *of snake* picar, morder; *bite one's nails* morderse las uñas **3** *v/i* (*pret* **bit**, *pp* **bitten**) *of dog* morder; *of mosquito, flea* picar; *of snake* morder, picar; *of fish* picar

bit·ten ['bɪtn] *pp* → **bite**

bit·ter ['bɪtər] *adj taste* amargo; *person* resentido; *weather* helador; *argument* agrio

bit·ter·ly ['bɪtərlɪ] *adv resent* amargamente; *it's bitterly cold* hace un frío helador

bi·zarre [bɪ'zɑːr] *adj* extraño, peculiar

blab [blæb] *v/i* (*pret & pp* **blabbed**) F irse de la lengua F

blab·ber·mouth ['blæbərmaʊθ] F bocazas *m/f inv* F

black [blæk] **1** *adj* negro; *coffee* solo; *tea* sin leche; *fig* negro, aciago **2** *n* (*color*) negro *m*; (*person*) negro(-a) *m(f)*; *be in the black* FIN no estar en números rojos; *in black and white* en blanco y negro; *in writing* por escrito

◆ **black out** *v/i* perder el conocimiento

'black·ber·ry mora *f*

'black·bird mirlo *m*

'black·board pizarra *f*, encerado *m*

black 'box caja *f* negra

black 'cof·fee café *m* solo

black e'con·o·my economía *f* sumergida

black·en ['blækn] *v/t fig: person's name* manchar

black 'eye ojo *m* morado

'black·head espinilla *f*, punto *m* negro

black 'ice *Br* placas *fpl* de hielo

'black·list 1 *n* lista *f* negra **2** *v/t* poner en la lista negra

'black·mail 1 *n* chantaje *m*; *emotional blackmail* chantaje *m* emocional **2** *v/t* chantajear

'black·mail·er chantajista *m/f*

black 'mar·ket mercado *m* negro

'black·ness ['blæknɪs] oscuridad *f*

'black·out ELEC apagón *m*; MED desmayo *m*; *have a blackout* desmayarse

'black·smith herrero *m*

blad·der ['blædər] vejiga *f*

blade [bleɪd] *of knife, sword* hoja *f*; *of propeller* pala *f*; *of grass* brizna *f*

blame [bleɪm] **1** *n* culpa *f*; *I got the blame for it* me echaron la culpa **2** *v/t* culpar; *blame s.o. for sth* culpar a alguien de algo

bland [blænd] *adj smile* insulso; *food* insípido, soso

blank [blæŋk] **1** *adj* (*not written on*) en blanco; *tape* virgen; *look* inexpresivo **2** *n* (*empty space*) espacio *m* en blanco; *my mind's a blank* tengo la mente en blanco

blank 'check, *Br* **blank 'cheque** cheque *m* en blanco

blan·ket ['blæŋkɪt] *n* manta *f*, *L.Am.* frazada *f*; *a blanket of snow* un manto de nieve

blare [bler] *v/i* retumbar

◆ **blare out 1** *v/i* retumbar **2** *v/t* emitir a todo volumen

blas·pheme [blæs'fiːm] *v/i* blasfemar

blas·phe·my ['blæsfəmɪ] blasfemia *f*

blast [blæst] **1** *n* (*explosion*) explosión *f*; (*gust*) ráfaga *f* **2** *v/t tunnel* abrir (*con explosivos*); *rock* volar; *blast!* F ¡mecachis!

◆ **blast off** *v/i of rocket* despegar

'blast fur·nace alto horno *m*

'blast-off despegue *m*

bla·tant ['bleɪtənt] *adj* descarado

blaze [bleɪz] **1** *n* (*fire*) incendio *m*; *a blaze of color* una explosión de color **2** *v/i of fire* arder

◆ **blaze away** *v/i with gun* disparar sin parar

blaz·er ['bleɪzər] americana *f*

bleach [bliːtʃ] **1** *n for clothes* lejía *f*; *for hair* decolorante *m* **2** *v/t hair* aclarar, desteñir

bleak [bliːk] *adj countryside* inhóspito; *weather* desapacible; *future* desolador

blear·y-eyed ['blɪrɪaɪd] *adj* con ojos de sueño

bleat [bliːt] *v/i of sheep* balar

bled [bled] *pret & pp* → **bleed**

bleed [bliːd] **1** *v/i* (*pret & pp* **bled**) sangrar; *he's bleeding internally* tiene una hemorragia interna; *bleed to death* desangrarse **2** *v/t* (*pret & pp* **bled**) *fig* sangrar

bleed·ing ['bliːdɪŋ] *n* hemorragia *f*

bleep [bliːp] **1** *n* pitido *m* **2** *v/i* pitar **3** *v/t* (*call on pager*) llamar con el buscapersonas

bleep·er ['bliːpər] buscapersonas *m inv*, *Span* busca *m*

blem·ish ['blemɪʃ] **1** *n* imperfección *f* **2** *v/t* *reputation* manchar

blend [blend] **1** *n of coffee etc* mezcla *f*; *fig* combinación *f* **2** *v/t* mezclar

◆ **blend in 1** *v/i of person in environment* pasar desapercibido; *of animal with surroundings etc* confundirse; *of furniture etc* combinar **2** *v/t in cooking* añadir

blend·er ['blendər] *machine* licuadora *f*

bless [bles] *v/t* bendecir; (***God***) ***bless you!*** ¡que Dios te bendiga!; *in response to sneeze* ¡Jesús!; *be blessed with* tener la suerte de

bless·ing ['blesɪŋ] *also fig* bendición *f*

blew [blu:] *pret* → **blow²**

blind [blaɪnd] **1** *adj* ciego; *corner* sin visibilidad; *be blind to sth fig* no ver algo **2** *npl: the blind* los ciegos, los invidentes **3** *v/t of sun* cegar; *she was blinded in an accident* se quedó ciega a raíz de un accidente; *love blinded her to his faults* el amor le impedía ver sus defectos

blind 'al·ley callejón *m* sin salida

blind 'date cita *f* a ciegas

'blind·fold 1 *n* venda *f* **2** *v/t* vendar los ojos a **3** *adv* con los ojos cerrados

blind·ing ['blaɪndɪŋ] *adj light* cegador; *headache* terrible

blind·ly ['blaɪndlɪ] *adv* a ciegas; *fig* ciegamente

'blind spot *in road* punto *m* sin visibilidad; *in driving mirror* ángulo *m* muerto; *(ability that is lacking)* punto *m* flaco

blink [blɪŋk] *v/i* parpadear

blink·ered ['blɪŋkərd] *adj fig* cerrado

blip [blɪp] *on radar screen* señal *f*, luz *f*; *it's just a blip fig* es algo momentáneo

bliss [blɪs] felicidad *f*; *it was bliss* fue fantástico

blis·ter ['blɪstər] **1** *n* ampolla *f* **2** *v/i* ampollarse; *of paint* hacer burbujas

bliz·zard ['blɪzərd] ventisca *f*

bloat·ed ['bloutɪd] *adj* hinchado

blob [blɑ:b] *of liquid* goterón *m*

bloc [blɑ:k] POL bloque *m*

block [blɑ:k] **1** *n* bloque *m*; *buildings* manzana *f*, *L.Am.* cuadra *f*; *of shares* paquete *m*; *(blockage)* bloqueo *m* **2** *v/t* bloquear; *sink* atascar

◆ **block in** *v/t with vehicle* bloquear el paso a

◆ **block out** *v/t light* impedir el paso de

◆ **block up** *v/t sink etc* atascar

block·ade [blɑ:'keɪd] **1** *n* bloqueo *m* **2** *v/t* bloquear

block·age ['blɑ:kɪdʒ] obstrucción *f*

block·bust·er ['blɑ:kbʌstər] gran éxito *m*

block 'let·ters *npl* letras *fpl* mayúsculas

blond [blɑ:nd] *adj* rubio

blonde [blɑ:nd] *n woman* rubia *f*

blood [blʌd] sangre *f*; *in cold blood* a sangre fría

'blood al·co·hol lev·el nivel *m* de alcohol en sangre

'blood bank banco *m* de sangre

'blood bath baño *m* de sangre

'blood do·nor donante *m/f* de sangre

'blood group grupo *m* sanguíneo

blood·less ['blʌdlɪs] *adj coup* incruento, pacífico

'blood poi·son·ing septicemia *f*

'blood pres·sure tensión *f* (arterial), presión *f* sanguínea

'blood re·la·tion: she's not a blood relation of mine no nos unen lazos de sangre

'blood sam·ple muestra *f* de sangre

'blood·shed derramamiento *m* de sangre

'blood·shot *adj* enrojecido

'blood·stain mancha *f* de sangre

'blood·stained *adj* ensangrentado, manchado de sangre

'blood·stream flujo *m* sanguíneo

'blood test análisis *m inv* de sangre

'blood·thirst·y *adj* sanguinario; *movie* macabro

'blood trans·fu·sion transfusión *f* sanguínea

'blood ves·sel vaso *m* sanguíneo

blood·y ['blʌdɪ] *adj hands etc* ensangrentado; *battle* sangriento; *Br* F maldito F, *Span* puñetero F; *bloody hell!* ¡ostras! F

bloom [blu:m] **1** *n* flor *f*; *in bloom* en flor **2** *v/i also fig* florecer

blos·som ['blɑ:səm] **1** *n* flores *fpl* **2** *v/i also fig* florecer

blot [blɑ:t] **1** *n* mancha *f*, borrón *m*; *be a blot on the landscape* estropear el paisaje **2** *v/t* (*pret & pp* **blotted**) (*dry*) secar

◆ **blot out** *v/t* borrar; *sun, view* ocultar

blotch [blɑ:tʃ] *on skin* erupción *f*, mancha *f*

blotch·y ['blɑ:tʃɪ] *adj: blotchy skin* piel con erupciones

blouse [blauz] blusa *f*

blow¹ [blou] *n* golpe *m*

blow² [blou] *v/t* (*pret* **blew**, *pp* **blown**) *smoke* exhalar; *whistle* tocar; F (*spend*) fundir F; *opportunity* perder, desaprovechar; *blow one's nose* sonarse (la nariz) **2** *v/i* (*pret* **blew**, *pp* **blown**) *of wind, person* soplar; *of whistle* sonar; *of fuse* fundirse; *of tire* reventarse

◆ **blow off 1** *v/t* llevarse **2** *v/i* salir volando

◆ **blow out 1** *v/t candle* apagar **2** *v/i of candle* apagarse

◆ **blow over 1** *v/t* derribar, hacer caer **2** *v/i* caerse, derrumbarse; *of storm* amainar; *of argument* calmarse

◆ **blow up 1** *v/t with explosives* volar; *ba-*

lloon hinchar; *photograph* ampliar **2** *v/i*
explotar; F (*become angry*) ponerse furioso
'blow-dry *v/t* (*pret & pp* **blow-dried**) secar (*con secador*)
'blow-job V mamada *f* V
'blow-out *of tire* reventón *m*; F (*big meal*)
comilona *f* F
'blow-up *of photo* ampliación *f*
blown [bloʊn] *pp* → **blow²**
blue [bluː] **1** *adj* azul; F *movie* porno *inv* F
2 *n* azul *m*
'blue-ber-ry arándano *m*
blue 'chip *adj* puntero, de primera fila
blue-'col-lar work-er trabajador(a) *m(f)*
manual
'blue-print plano *m*; (*fig: plan*) proyecto
m, plan *m*
blues [bluːz] *npl* MUS blues *m inv*; **have
the blues** estar deprimido
'blues sing-er cantante *m/f* de blues
bluff [blʌf] **1** *n* (*deception*) farol *m* **2** *v/i* ir
de farol
blun-der ['blʌndər] **1** *n* error *m* de bulto,
metedura *f* de pata **2** *v/i* cometer un error
de bulto, meter la pata
blunt [blʌnt] *adj pencil* sin punta; *knife*
desafilado; *person* franco
blunt-ly ['blʌntlɪ] *adv speak* francamente
blur [blɜːr] **1** *n* imagen *f* desenfocada;
everything is a blur todo está desenfocado **2** *v/t* (*pret & pp* **blurred**) desdibujar
blurb [blɜːrb] *on book* nota *f* promocional
◆ blurt out [blɜːrt] *v/t* soltar
blush [blʌʃ] **1** *n* rubor *m*, sonrojo *m* **2** *v/i*
ruborizarse, sonrojarse
blush-er ['blʌʃər] *cosmetic* colorete *m*
blus-ter ['blʌstər] *v/i* protestar encolerizadamente
blus-ter-y ['blʌstərɪ] *adj* tempestuoso
BO [biː'oʊ] *abbr* (= **body odor**) olor *m*
corporal
board [bɔːrd] **1** *n* tablón *m*, tabla *f*; *for game* tablero *m*; *for notices* tablón *m*;
board (of directors) consejo *m* de administración; **on board** *on plane, boat,
train* a bordo; **take on board** *comments
etc* aceptar, tener en cuenta; (*fully realize
truth of*) asumir; **across the board** de
forma general **2** *v/t airplane etc* embarcar; *train* subir a **3** *v/i of passengers* embarcar; **board with** *as lodger* hospedarse
con
◆ board up *v/t* cubrir con tablas
board-er ['bɔːrdər] huésped *m/f*
'board game juego *m* de mesa
'board-ing card tarjeta *f* de embarque
'board-ing house hostal *m*, pensión *f*
'board-ing pass tarjeta *f* de embarque

'board-ing school internado *m*
'board meet-ing reunión *m* del consejo
de administración
'board room sala *f* de reuniones *or* juntas
'board-walk paseo *m* marítimo con tablas
boast [boʊst] **1** *n* presunción *f*, jactancia *f*
2 *v/i* presumir, alardear (**about** de)
boat [boʊt] barco *m*; *small, for leisure* barca *f*; **go by boat** ir en barco
bob¹ [bɑːb] *haircut* corte *m* a lo chico
bob² [bɑːb] *v/i* (*pret & pp* **bobbed**) *of
boat etc* mecerse
◆ bob up *v/i* aparecer
'bob-sleigh, 'bob-sled bobsleigh *m*
bod-ice ['bɑːdɪs] cuerpo *m*
bod-i-ly ['bɑːdɪlɪ] **1** *adj* corporal; *needs* físico; *function* fisiológico **2** *adv eject* en
volandas
bod-y ['bɑːdɪ] cuerpo *m*; *dead* cadáver *m*;
body of water masa *f* de agua
'body-guard guardaespaldas *m/f inv*
'body lan-guage lenguaje *m* corporal
'bod-y o-dor olor *m* corporal
'bod-y pierc-ing piercing *m*, perforaciones *fpl* corporales
'body-shop MOT taller *m* de carrocería
'bod-y stock-ing malla *f*
'bod-y suit body *m* 'body-work MOT carrocería *f*
bog-gle ['bɑːgl] *v/i*: **the mind boggles!**
¡no quiero ni pensarlo!
bo-gus ['boʊgəs] *adj* falso
boil¹ [bɔɪl] *n* (*swelling*) forúnculo
boil² [bɔɪl] **1** *v/t liquid* hervir; *egg, vegetables* cocer **2** *v/i* hervir
◆ boil down to *v/t* reducirse a
◆ boil over *v/i of milk etc* salirse
boil-er ['bɔɪlər] caldera *f*
'boil-ing point ['bɔɪlɪŋ] *of liquid* punto *m*
de ebullición; **reach boiling point** *fig*
perder la paciencia
bois-ter-ous ['bɔɪstərəs] *adj* escandaloso
bold [boʊld] **1** *adj* valiente, audaz; *text* en
negrita **2** *n* (*print*) negrita *f*; **in bold** en
negrita
Bo-liv-i-a [bə'lɪvɪə] *n* Bolivia
Bo-liv-i-an [bə'lɪvɪən] **1** *adj* boliviano **2** *n*
boliviano(-a) *m(f)*
bol-ster ['boʊlstər] *v/t confidence* reforzar
bolt [boʊlt] **1** *n on door* cerrojo *m*, pestillo
m; *with nut* perno *m*; *of lightning* rayo *m*;
like a bolt from the blue de forma inesperada **2** *adv*: **bolt upright** erguido **3** *v/t*
(*fix with bolts*) atornillar; *close* cerrar
con cerrojo *or* pestillo **4** *v/i* (*run off*) fugarse, escaparse
bomb [bɑːm] **1** *n* bomba *f* **2** *v/t* MIL bombardear; *of terrorist* poner una bomba en

bom·bard [bɑːm'bɑːrd] v/t (attack) bombardear; **bombard s.o. with questions** bombardear alguien con preguntas

'**bomb attack** atentado m con bomba

bomb·er ['bɑːmər] airplane bombardero m; terrorist terrorista m/f (que pone bombas)

'**bomb·er jack·et** cazadora f de aviador

'**bomb·proof** adj a prueba de bombas

'**bomb scare** amenaza f de bomba

'**bomb·shell** (fig: news) bomba f

bond [bɑːnd] **1** n (tie) unión f; FIN bono m **2** v/i of glue adherirse

bone [boʊn] **1** n hueso m; of fish espina f **2** v/t meat deshuesar; fish quitar las espinas a

bon·fire ['bɑːnfaɪr] hoguera f

bon·net ['bɑːnɪt] Br of car capó m

bo·nus ['boʊnəs] money plus m, bonificación f; (something extra) ventaja f adicional; **a Christmas bonus** un plus por Navidad

boo [buː] **1** n abucheo m **2** v/t & v/i abuchear

boob [buːb] n P (breast) teta f P

boo·boo ['buːbuː] n F metedura f de pata

book [bʊk] **1** n libro m; of matches caja f (de solapa) **2** v/t (reserve) reservar; of policeman multar **3** v/i (reserve) reservar, hacer una reserva

'**book·case** estantería f, librería f

booked up [bʊkt'ʌp] adj lleno, completo; person ocupado

book·ie ['bʊkɪ] F corredor(a) m(f) de apuestas

book·ing ['bʊkɪŋ] (reservation) reserva f

'**book·ing clerk** taquillero(-a) m(f)

'**book·keep·er** tenedor(a) m(f) de libros

'**book·keep·ing** contabilidad f

book·let ['bʊklɪt] folleto m

'**book·mak·er** corredor(a) m(f) de apuestas

books [bʊks] npl (accounts) contabilidad f; **do the books** llevar la contabilidad; **cook the books** falsificar las cuentas

'**book·sell·er** librero(-a) m(f)

'**book·shelf** estante m

'**book·store** librería f

'**book·stall** puesto m de venta de libros

'**book to·ken** vale m para comprar libros

boom[1] [buːm] **1** n boom m **2** v/i of business desarrollarse, experimentar un boom

boom[2] [buːm] n noise estruendo m

boon·ies ['buːnɪz] npl F: **they live out in the boonies** viven en el quinto pino F

boor [bʊr] basto m, grosero m

boor·ish ['bʊrɪʃ] adj basto, grosero

boost [buːst] **1** n to sales, economy impul-

so m; **your confidence needs a boost** necesitas algo que te dé más confianza **2** v/t production, prices estimular; morale levantar

boot [buːt] n bota f; Br of car maletero m, C.Am., Mex cajuela f, Rpl baúl m

◆ **boot out** v/t F echar

◆ **boot up** v/t & v/i COMPUT arrancar

booth [buːð] at market, fair cabina f; (in restaurant) mesa rodeada por bancos fijos

booze [buːz] n F bebida f, Span priva f F

bor·der ['bɔːrdər] **1** n between countries frontera f; (edge) borde m; on clothing ribete m **2** v/t country limitar con; river bordear

◆ **border on** limitar con; (be almost) rayar en

'**bor·der·line** adj: **a borderline case** un caso dudoso

bore[1] [bɔːr] **1** v/t hole taladrar; **bore a hole in sth** taladrar algo

bore[2] [bɔːr] **1** n (person) pesado(-a) m(f), pelma m/f inv F; **it's such a bore** ¡qué pesadez or Span lata! **2** v/t aburrir

bore[3] [bɔːr] pret → **bear**[2]

bored [bɔːrd] adj aburrido; **I'm bored** me aburro, estoy aburrido

bore·dom ['bɔːrdəm] aburrimiento m

bor·ing ['bɔːrɪŋ] adj aburrido; **be boring** ser aburrido

born [bɔːrn] adj: **be born** nacer; **where were you born?** ¿dónde naciste?; **a born teacher** haber nacido para ser profesor

borne [bɔːrn] pp → **bear**[2]

bor·row ['bɑːroʊ] v/t tomar prestado

bos·om ['bʊzm] of woman pecho m

boss [bɑːs] jefe(-a) m(f)

◆ **boss about** v/t dar órdenes a

boss·y ['bɑːsɪ] adj mandón

bo·tan·i·cal [bə'tænɪkl] adj botánico

bo·tan·ic·(·al) gar·dens npl jardín m botánico

bot·a·nist ['bɑːtənɪst] botánico(-a) m(f)

bot·a·ny ['bɑːtənɪ] botánica f

botch [bɑːtʃ] v/t arruinar, estropear

both [boʊθ] **1** adj & pron ambos, los dos; **I know both (of the) brothers** conozco a ambos hermanos, conozco a los dos hermanos; **both of them** ambos, los dos **2** adv: **both my mother and I** tanto mi madre como yo; **he's both handsome and intelligent** es guapo y además inteligente; **is it business or pleasure?** – **both** ¿es de negocios o de placer? – las dos cosas

both·er ['bɑːðər] **1** n molestias fpl; **it's no bother** no es ninguna molestia **2** v/t (dis-

turb) molestar; *(worry)* preocupar **3** *v/i* preocuparse; **don't bother!** *(you needn't do it)* ¡no te preocupes!; **you needn't have bothered** no deberías haberte molestado

bot·tle ['bɑːtl] **1** *n* botella *f*; *for baby* biberón *m* **2** *v/t* embotellar

◆ bottle up *v/t feelings* reprimir, contener

'bot·tle bank contenedor *m* de vidrio

bot·tled wa·ter ['bɑːtld] agua *f* embotellada

'bot·tle·neck *n in road* embotellamiento *m*, atasco *m*; *in production* cuello *m* de botella

'bot·tle-o·pen·er abrebotellas *m inv*

bot·tom ['bɑːtəm] **1** *adj* inferior, de abajo **2** *n of drawer, case, pan* fondo *m*; *of hill, page* pie *m*; *of pile* parte *f* inferior; *(underside)* parte *f* de abajo; *of street* final *m*; *of garden* fondo *m*; *(buttocks)* trasero *m*; **at the bottom of the screen** en la parte inferior de la pantalla

◆ bottom out *v/i* tocar fondo

bot·tom 'line *(fig: financial outcome)* saldo *m* final; *(real issue)* realidad *f*

bought [bɔːt] *pret & pp →* **buy**

boul·der ['bouldər] roca *f* redondeada

bounce [bauns] **1** *v/t ball* botar **2** *v/i of ball* botar, rebotar; *on sofa etc* saltar; *of rain* rebotar; *of check* ser rechazado

bounc·er ['baunsər] portero *m*, gorila *m*

bounc·y ['baunsɪ] *adj ball* que bota bien; *cushion, chair* mullido

bound¹ [baund] *adj*: **be bound to do sth** *(obliged to)* estar obligado a hacer algo; **she's bound to call an election soon** *(sure to)* seguro que convoca elecciones pronto

bound² [baund] *adj*: **be bound for** *of ship* llevar destino a

bound³ [baund] **1** *n (jump)* salto *m* **2** *v/i* saltar

bound⁴ [baund] *pret & pp →* **bind**

bound·a·ry ['baundərɪ] límite *m*; *between countries* frontera *f*

bound·less ['baundlɪs] *adj* ilimitado, infinito

bou·quet [bu'keɪ] *(flowers)* ramo *m*

bour·bon ['bɜːrbən] bourbon *m*

bout [baut] MED ataque *m*; *in boxing* combate *m*

bou·tique [buːˈtiːk] boutique *f*

bow¹ [bau] **1** *n as greeting* reverencia *f* **2** *v/i* saludar con la cabeza **3** *v/t head* inclinar

bow² [bou] *(knot)* lazo *m*; MUS, *for archery* arco *m*

bow³ [bau] *of ship* proa *f*

bow·els ['bauəlz] *npl* entrañas *fpl*

bowl¹ [boul] *for rice, cereals etc* cuenco *m*; *for soup* plato *m* sopero; *for salad* ensaladera *f*; *for washing* barreño *m*, palangana *f*

bowl² [boul] **1** *n (ball)* bola *f* **2** *v/i in bowling* lanzar la bola

◆ bowl over *v/t (fig: astonish)* impresionar, maravillar

bowl·ing ['boulɪŋ] bolos *mpl*

'bowl·ing al·ley bolera *f*

bow 'tie [bou] pajarita *f*

box¹ [bɑːks] *n container* caja *f*; *on form* casilla *f*

box² [bɑːks] *v/i* boxear

box·er ['bɑːksər] boxeador(a) *m(f)*

'box·er shorts *npl* calzoncillos *mpl*, boxers *mpl*

box·ing ['bɑːksɪŋ] boxeo *m*

'box·ing glove guante *m* de boxeo

'box·ing match combate *m* de boxeo

'box·ing ring cuadrilátero *m*, ring *m*

'box num·ber *at post office* apartado *m* de correos

'box of·fice taquilla *f*, *L.Am.* boletería *f*

boy [bɔɪ] niño *m*, chico *m*; *(son)* hijo *m*

boy·cott ['bɔɪkɑːt] **1** *n* boicot *m* **2** *v/t* boicotear

'boy·friend novio *m*

boy·ish ['bɔɪɪʃ] *adj* varonil

boy'scout boy scout *m*

bra [brɑː] *Br* sujetador *m*, sostén *m*

brace [breɪs] *on teeth* aparato *m*

brace·let ['breɪslɪt] pulsera *f*

brack·et ['brækɪt] *for shelf* escuadra *f*; **(square) bracket** *in text* corchete *m*

brag [bræg] *v/i (pret & pp* bragged*)* presumir, fanfarronear

braid [breɪd] *n in hair* trenza *f*; *trimming* trenzado *m*

braille [breɪl] braille *m*

brain [breɪn] cerebro *m*; **use your brain** utiliza la cabeza

'brain dead *adj* MED clínicamente muerto

brain·less ['breɪnlɪs] *adj* F estúpido

brains [breɪnz] *npl (intelligence)* inteligencia *f*; **the brains of the operation** el cerebro de la operación

'brain·storm idea *f* genial

brain·storm·ing ['breɪnstɔːrmɪŋ] tormenta *f* de ideas

'brain sur·geon neurocirujano(-a) *m(f)*

'brain sur·ger·y neurocirugía *f*

'brain tu·mor tumor *m* cerebral

'brain·wash *v/t* lavar el cerebro a

'brain·wave *(brilliant idea)* idea *f* genial

brain·y ['breɪnɪ] *adj* F: **be brainy** tener mucho coco F, ser una lumbrera

brake [breɪk] **1** *n* freno *m*; **act as a brake on** frenar **2** *v/i* frenar '**brake flu·id** MOT líquido *m* de frenos

'**brake light** MOT luz *f* de frenado

'**brake ped·al** MOT pedal *m* del freno

branch [bræntʃ] *n* of tree rama *f*; of bank, company sucursal *f*

◆ **branch off** v/i of road bifurcarse

◆ **branch out** v/i diversificarse; **they've branched out into furniture** han empezado a trabajar también con muebles

brand [brænd] **1** *n* marca *f* **2** v/t: **be branded a liar** ser tildado de mentiroso

brand 'im·age imagen *f* de marca

bran·dish ['brændɪʃ] v/t blandir

brand 'lead·er marca *f* líder del mercado

brand 'loy·al·ty lealtad *f* a una marca

'**brand name** nombre *m* comercial

brand-'new *adj* nuevo, flamante

bran·dy ['brændɪ] brandy *m*, coñac *m*

brass [bræs] *alloy* latón *m*; **the brass** MUS los metales

brass 'band banda *f* de música

bras·siere [brə'zɪr] sujetador *m*, sostén *m*

brat [bræt] *pej* niñato(-a) *m(f)*

bra·va·do [brə'vɑːdoʊ] bravuconería *f*

brave [breɪv] *adj* valiente, valeroso

brave·ly ['breɪvlɪ] *adv* valientemente, valerosamente

brav·er·y ['breɪvərɪ] valentía *f*, valor *m*

brawl [brɔːl] **1** *n* pelea *f* **2** v/i pelearse

brawn·y ['brɔːnɪ] *adj* fuerte, musculoso

Bra·zil [brə'zɪl] Brasil

Bra·zil·ian [brə'zɪlɪən] **1** *adj* brasileño **2** *n* brasileño(-a) *m(f)*

breach [briːtʃ] *n* (*violation*) infracción *f*, incumplimiento; *in party* ruptura *f*

breach of 'con·tract LAW incumplimiento *m* de contrato

bread [bred] *n* pan *m*

'**bread·crumbs** *npl for cooking* pan *m* rallado; *for birds* migas *fpl*

'**bread knife** cuchillo *m* del pan

breadth [bredθ] *of road* ancho *m*; *of knowledge* amplitud *f*

'**bread·win·ner**: **be the breadwinner** ser el que gana el pan

break [breɪk] **1** *n in bone etc* fractura *f*, rotura *f*; (*rest*) descanso *m*; *in relationship* separación *f* temporal; **give s.o. a break** F (*opportunity*) ofrecer una oportunidad a alguien; **take a break** descansar; **without a break** *work, travel* sin descanso **2** v/t (*pret* **broke**, *pp* **broken**) *machine, device* romper, estropear; *stick* romper, partir; *arm, leg* fracturar, romper; *glass, egg* romper; *rules, law* violar, incumplir; *promise* romper; *news* dar; *record* batir **3** v/i (*pret* **broke**, *pp* **broken**) *of machine, device* romperse, estropearse; *of glass, egg* romperse; *of stick* partirse, rom-

perse; *of news* saltar; *of storm* estallar, comenzar; *of boy's voice* cambiar

◆ **break away** v/i (*escape*) escaparse; *from family* separarse; *from organization* escindirse; *from tradition* romper (**from** con)

◆ **break down 1** v/i *of vehicle* averiarse, estropearse; *of machine* estropearse; *of talks* romperse; *in tears* romper a llorar; *mentally* venirse abajo **2** v/t *of door* derribar; *figures* detallar, desglosar

◆ **break even** v/i COM cubrir gastos

◆ **break in** v/i (*interrupt*) interrumpir; *of burglar* entrar

◆ **break off 1** v/t partir; *relationship* romper; **they've broken it off** han roto **2** v/i (*stop talking*) interrumpirse

◆ **break out** v/i (*start up*) comenzar; *of fighting* estallar; *of disease* desatarse; *of prisoners* escaparse, darse a la fuga; **he broke out in a rash** le salió un sarpullido

◆ **break up 1** v/t *into component parts* descomponer; *fight* poner fin a **2** v/i *of ice* romperse; *of couple* terminar, separarse; *of band* separarse; *of meeting* terminar

break·a·ble ['breɪkəbl] *adj* rompible, frágil

break·age ['breɪkɪdʒ] rotura *f*

'**break·down** *of vehicle, machine* avería *f*; *of talks* ruptura *f*; (*nervous breakdown*) crisis *f inv* nerviosa; *of figures* desglose *m*

break-'e·ven point punto *m* de equilibrio

break·fast ['brekfəst] *n* desayuno *m*; **have breakfast** desayunar

'**break·fast tel·e·vi·sion** televisión *f* matinal

'**break-in** entrada *f* (*mediante la fuerza*); *robbery* robo *m*; **we've had a break-in** han entrado a robar

'**break·through** *in plan, negotiations* paso *m* adelante; *of science, technology* avance *m*

'**break-up** *of marriage, partnership* ruptura *f*, separación *f*

breast [brest] *of woman* pecho *m*

'**breast-feed** v/t (*pret* & *pp* **breastfed**) amamantar

'**breast-stroke** braza *f*

breath [breθ] respiración *f*; **get your breath back** recuperar el aliento; **be out of breath** estar sin respiración; **take a deep breath** respira hondo

Breath·a·lyz·er® ['breθəlaɪzər] alcoholímetro *m*

breathe [briːð] **1** v/i respirar **2** v/t (*inhale*) aspirar, respirar; (*exhale*) exhalar, espirar

◆ **breathe in** v/t & v/i aspirar, inspirar

◆ **breathe out** v/t & v/i espirar

breath·ing ['briːðɪŋ] *n* respiración *f*

breath·less ['breθlɪs] *adj*: *arrive breath-less* llegar sin respiración, llegar jadeando

breath·less·ness ['breθlɪsnɪs] dificultad *f* para respirar

breath·tak·ing ['breθteɪkɪŋ] *adj* impresionante, sorprendente

bred [bred] *pret & pp* → **breed**

breed [briːd] **1** *n* raza *f* **2** *v/t* (*pret & pp* **bred**) criar; *plants* cultivar; *fig* causar, generar **3** *v/i* (*pret & pp* **bred**) *of animals* reproducirse

breed·er ['briːdər] *of animals* criador(a) *m(f)*; *of plants* cultivador(a) *m(f)*

breed·ing ['briːdɪŋ] *of animals* cría *f*; *of plants* cultivo *m*; *of person* educación *f*

breed·ing ground *fig* caldo *m* de cultivo

breeze [briːz] brisa *f*

breez·i·ly ['briːzɪlɪ] *adv fig* jovialmente, tranquilamente

breez·y ['briːzɪ] *adj* ventoso; *fig* jovial, tranquilo

brew [bruː] **1** *v/t beer* elaborar; *tea* preparar, hacer **2** *v/i of storm* avecinarse; *of trouble* fraguarse

brew·er ['bruːər] fabricante *m/f* de cerveza

brew·er·y ['bruːərɪ] fábrica *f* de cerveza

bribe [braɪb] **1** *n* soborno *m*, *Mex* mordida *f*, *S. Am.* coima *f* **2** *v/t* sobornar

brib·er·y ['braɪbərɪ] soborno *m*, *Mex* mordida *f*, *S. Am.* coima *f*

brick [brɪk] ladrillo *m*

'brick·lay·er albañil *m/f*

brid·al suite ['braɪdl] suite *f* nupcial

bride [braɪd] novia *f* (*en boda*)

'bride·groom novio *m* (*en boda*)

'brides·maid dama *f* de honor

bridge¹ [brɪdʒ] **1** *n also* NAUT puente *m*; *of nose* caballete *m* **2** *v/t gap* superar, salvar

bridge² [brɪdʒ] *card game* bridge *m*

bri·dle ['braɪdl] brida *f*

brief¹ ['briːf] *adj* breve, corto

brief² [briːf] **1** *n* (*mission*) misión *f* **2** *v/t*: *brief s.o. on sth* informar a alguien de algo

'brief·case maletín *m*

brief·ing ['briːfɪŋ] reunión *f* informativa

brief·ly ['briːflɪ] *adv* (*for a short period of time*) brevemente; (*in a few words*) en pocas palabras; (*to sum up*) en resumen

briefs [briːfs] *npl for women* bragas *fpl*; *for men* calzoncillos *mpl*

bright [braɪt] *adj color* vivo; *smile* radiante; *future* brillante, prometedor; (*sunny*) soleado, luminoso; (*intelligent*) inteligente

◆ **bright·en up** ['braɪtn] **1** *v/t* alegrar **2** *v/i of weather* aclararse; *of face, person* ale-grarse, animarse

bright·ly ['braɪtlɪ] *adv shine* intensamente, fuerte; *smile* alegremente

bright·ness ['braɪtnɪs] *of light* brillo *m*; *of weather* luminosidad *f*; *of smile* alegría *f*; (*intelligence*) inteligencia *f*

bril·liance ['brɪljəns] *of person* genialidad *f*; *of color* resplandor *m*

bril·liant ['brɪljənt] *adj sunshine etc* resplandeciente, radiante; (*very good*) genial; (*very intelligent*) brillante

brim [brɪm] *of container* borde *m*; *of hat* ala *f*

brim·ful ['brɪmfəl] *adj* rebosante

bring [brɪŋ] *v/t* (*pret & pp* **brought**) traer; *bring it here, will you* tráelo aquí, por favor; *can I bring a friend?* ¿puedo traer a un amigo?, puedo venir con un amigo?

◆ **bring about** *v/t* ocasionar; *bring about peace* traer la paz

◆ **bring around** *v/t from a faint* hacer volver en sí; (*persuade*) convencer, persuadir

◆ **bring back** *v/t* (*return*) devolver; (*re-introduce*) reinstaurar; *memories* traer

◆ **bring down** *v/t fence, tree* tirar, echar abajo; *government* derrocar; *bird, airplane* derribar; *rates, inflation, price* reducir

◆ **bring in** *v/t interest, income* generar; *legislation* introducir; *verdict* pronunciar

◆ **bring on** *v/t illness* provocar

◆ **bring out** *v/t book, video, new product* sacar

◆ **bring to** *v/t from a faint* hacer volver en sí

◆ **bring up** *v/t child* criar, educar; *subject* mencionar, sacar a colación; (*vomit*) vomitar

brink [brɪŋk] borde *m*; *be on the brink of sth fig* estar a punto de hacer algo

brisk [brɪsk] *adj person, voice* enérgico; *walk* rápido; *trade* animado

bris·tle ['brɪsl] *v/i*: *the streets are bristling with policemen* las calles están atestadas de policías

brist·les ['brɪslz] *npl on chin* pelos *mpl*; *of brush* cerdas *fpl*

Brit [brɪt] F británico(-a) *m(f)*

Brit·ain ['brɪtn] Gran Bretaña

Brit·ish ['brɪtɪʃ] **1** *adj* británico **2** *n*: *the British* los británicos

Brit·on ['brɪtn] británico(-a) *m(f)*

brit·tle ['brɪtl] *adj* frágil, quebradizo

broach [brəʊtʃ] *v/t subject* sacar a colación

broad [brɔːd] **1** *adj smile, range* amplio; (*general*) general; *in broad daylight* a plena luz del día; *in broad terms* en líneas generales **2** *n* F (*woman*) tía *f* F

'broad·cast 1 *n* emisión *f*; *a live broad-*

B

'cast una retransmisión en directo **2** *v/t* emitir, retransmitir

'broad·cast·er presentador(a) *m(f)*

'broad·cast·ing televisión *f*

broad·en ['brɔːdn] **1** *v/t* ensancharse, ampliarse **2** *v/t* ensanchar; **broaden one's horizons** ampliar los horizontes

'broad·jump salto *m* de longitud

broad·ly ['brɔːdlɪ] *adv* en general; **broadly speaking** en términos generales

broad·mind·ed [brɔːd'maɪndɪd] *adj* tolerante, abierto

broad·mind·ed·ness [brɔːd'maɪndɪdnɪs] mentalidad *f* abierta

broc·co·li ['brɑːkəlɪ] brécol *m*, brócoli *m*

bro·chure ['broʊʃər] folleto *m*

broil [brɔɪl] *v/t* asar a la parrilla

broil·er ['brɔɪlər] *on stove* parrilla *f*; *chicken* pollo *m* (para asar)

broke [broʊk] **1** *adj* F: **be broke** *temporarily* estar sin blanca F; *long term* estar arruinado; **go broke** (*go bankrupt*) arruinarse **2** *pret* → **break**

bro·ken ['broʊkn] **1** *adj* roto; *home* deshecho; **they talk in broken English** chapurrean el inglés **2** *pp* → **break**

bro·ken-heart·ed [broʊkn'hɑːrtɪd] *adj* desconsolado, destrozado

bro·ker ['broʊkər] corredor(a) *m(f)*, agente *m/f*

bron·chi·tis [brɑːŋ'kaɪtɪs] bronquitis *f*

bronze [brɑːnz] *n* bronce *m*

brooch [broʊtʃ] broche *m*

brood [bruːd] *v/i of person* darle vueltas a las cosas; **brood about sth** darle vueltas a algo

broom [bruːm] escoba *f*

broth [brɑːθ] *soup* sopa *f*; *stock* caldo *m*

broth·el ['brɑːθl] burdel *m*

broth·er ['brʌðər] hermano *m*

'broth·er-in-law (*pl* **brothers-in-law**) cuñado *m*

broth·er·ly ['brʌðərlɪ] *adj* fraternal

brought [brɔːt] *pret & pp* → **bring**

brow [braʊ] (*forehead*) frente *f*; *of hill* cima *f*

brown [braʊn] **1** *n* marrón *m*, *L.Am.* color *m* café **2** *adj* marrón; *eyes, hair* castaño; (*tanned*) moreno **3** *v/t in cooking* dorar **4** *v/i in cooking* dorarse

'brown-bag *v/t* (*pret & pp* **brown-bagged**) F: **brownbag it** llevar la comida al trabajo

Brown·ie ['braʊnɪ] escultista *f*

'Brown·ie points *npl* tantos *mpl*; **earn Brownie points** anotarse tantos

brown·ie ['braʊnɪ] (*cake*) pastel *m* de chocolate y nueces

'brown-nose *v/t* P lamer el culo a P

brown 'pa·per papel *m* de estraza

brown pa·per 'bag bolsa *f* de cartón

brown 'sug·ar azúcar *m or f* moreno(-a)

browse [braʊz] *v/i in store* echar una ojeada; **browse through a book** hojear un libro

brows·er ['braʊzər] COMPUT navegador *m*

bruise [bruːz] **1** *n* magulladura *f*, cardenal *f*; *on fruit* maca *f* **2** *v/t arm, fruit* magullar; (*emotionally*) herir **3** *v/i of person* hacerse cardenales; *of fruit* macarse

bruis·ing ['bruːzɪŋ] *adj* fig doloroso

brunch [brʌntʃ] combinación de desayuno y almuerzo

bru·nette [bruː'net] *n* morena *f*

brunt [brʌnt]: **this area bore the brunt of the flooding** esta zona fue la más castigada por la inundación; **we bore the brunt of the layoffs** fuimos los más perjudicados por los despidos

brush [brʌʃ] **1** *n* cepillo *m*; *conflict* roce *m* **2** *v/t* cepillar; (*touch lightly*) rozar; (*move away*) quitar

◆ **brush against** *v/t* rozar

◆ **brush aside** *v/t* hacer caso omiso a, no hacer caso a

◆ **brush off** *v/t* sacudir; *criticism* no hacer caso a

◆ **brush up** *v/t* repasar

'brush·work PAINT pincelada *f*

brusque [brʊsk] *adj* brusco

Brus·sels ['brʌslz] Bruselas

Brus·sels sprouts *npl* coles *fpl* de Bruselas

bru·tal ['bruːtl] *adj* brutal

bru·tal·i·ty [bruː'tælətɪ] brutalidad *f*

bru·tal·ly ['bruːtəlɪ] *adv* brutalmente; **be brutally frank** ser de una sinceridad aplastante

brute [bruːt] bestia *m/f*

brute 'force fuerza *f* bruta

bub·ble ['bʌbl] *n* burbuja *f*

'bub·ble bath baño *m* de espuma

'bub·ble gum chicle *m*

'bub·ble wrap *n* plástico *m* para embalar (*con burbujas*)

bub·bly ['bʌblɪ] *n* F (*champagne*) champán *m*

buck[1] [bʌk] *n* F (*dollar*) dólar *m*

buck[2] [bʌk] *v/i of horse* corcovear

buck[3] [bʌk] *n*: **pass the buck** escurrir el bulto

buck·et ['bʌkɪt] *n* cubo *m*

buck·le[1] ['bʌkl] **1** *n* hebilla *f* **2** *v/t belt* abrochar

buck·le[2] ['bʌkl] *v/i of wood, metal* combarse

◆ **buckle down** *v/i* ponerse a trabajar

bud [bʌd] n BOT capullo m, brote m

bud·dy ['bʌdɪ] F amigo(-a) m(f), Span colega m/f F; form of address Span colega m/f F, L.Am. compadre m/f F

budge [bʌdʒ] 1 v/t mover; (make reconsider) hacer cambiar de opinión 2 v/i moverse; (change one's mind) cambiar de opinión

bud·ger·i·gar ['bʌdʒərɪgɑːr] periquito m

bud·get ['bʌdʒɪt] 1 n presupuesto m; be on a budget tener un presupuesto limitado 2 v/i administrarse

◆ budget for v/t contemplar en el presupuesto

bud·gie ['bʌdʒɪ] F periquito m

buff¹ [bʌf] adj color marrón claro

buff² [bʌf] n aficionado(-a) m(f); a movie buff un cinéfilo

buf·fa·lo ['bʌfəlou] búfalo m

buff·er ['bʌfər] RAIL tope m; COMPUT búfer m; fig barrera f

buf·fet¹ ['bufeɪ] n (meal) bufé m

buf·fet² ['bʌfɪt] v/t of wind sacudir

bug [bʌg] 1 n insect bicho m; virus virus m inv; (spying device) micrófono m oculto; COMPUT error m 2 v/t (pret & pp bugged) room colocar un micrófono en; F (annoy) fastidiar F, jorobar F

bug·gy ['bʌgɪ] for baby silla f de paseo

bu·gle ['bjuːgl] corneta f, clarín m

build [bɪld] 1 n of person constitución f, complexión f 2 v/t (pret & pp built) construir, edificar

◆ build up 1 v/t strength aumentar; relationship fortalecer; collection acumular 2 v/i of dirt acumularse; of pressure, excitement aumentar

'build·er ['bɪldər] albañil m/f; company constructora f

'build·ing ['bɪldɪŋ] edificio m; activity construcción f

'build·ing blocks npl for child piezas fpl de construcción

'build·ing site obra f

'build·ing so·ci·e·ty Br caja f de ahorros

'build·ing trade industria f de la construcción

'build-up (accumulation) accumulación f; after all the build-up publicity después de tantas expectativas

built [bɪlt] pret & pp → build

built-in ['bɪltɪn] adj cupboard empotrado; flash incorporado

built-up 'ar·e·a zona f urbanizada

bulb [bʌlb] BOT bulbo m; (light bulb) bombilla f, L.Am. foco m

bulge [bʌldʒ] 1 n bulto m, abultamiento m 2 v/i of eyes salirse de las órbitas; of wall abombarse

bu·lim·i·a [buˈlɪmɪə] bulimia f

bulk [bʌlk]: the bulk of el grueso or la mayor parte de; in bulk a granel

bulk·y ['bʌlkɪ] adj voluminoso

bull [bul] animal toro m

bull·doze ['buldouz] v/t (demolish) demoler, derribar; bulldoze s.o. into sth fig obligar a alguien a hacer algo

bull·doz·er ['buldouzər] bulldozer m

bul·let ['bulɪt] bala f

bul·le·tin ['bulɪtɪn] boletín m

bul·le·tin board on wall tablón m de anuncios; COMPUT tablón m de anuncios, BBS f

'bul·let-proof adj antibalas inv

'bull fight corrida f de toros

'bull fight·er torero(-a) m(f)

'bull fight·ing tauromaquia f, los toros

'bull mar·ket FIN mercado m al alza

'bull ring plaza f de toros

'bull's-eye diana f, blanco m; hit the bull's-eye dar en el blanco

'bull·shit 1 n V Span gilipollez f V, L.Am. pendejada f V 2 v/i (pret & pp bullshitted) V decir Span gilipolleces V or L.Am. pendejadas V

bul·ly ['bulɪ] 1 n matón(-ona) m(f); child abusón(-ona) m(f) 2 v/t (pret & pp bullied) intimidar

bul·ly·ing ['bulɪɪŋ] n intimidación f

bum [bʌm] 1 n F (tramp) vagabundo(-a) m(f); (worthless person) inútil m/f 2 adj F (useless) inútil 3 v/t (pret & pp bummed) F cigarette etc gorronear

◆ bum around, bum about v/t F (travel) vagabundear (in por); (be lazy) vaguear

bum·ble·bee ['bʌmblbiː] abejorro m

bump [bʌmp] 1 n (swelling) chichón m; on road bache m; get a bump on the head darse un golpe en la cabeza 2 v/t golpear

◆ bump into v/t table chocar con; (meet) encontrarse con

◆ bump off v/t F (murder) cargarse a F

◆ bump up v/t F (prices) aumentar

bump·er ['bʌmpər] 1 n MOT parachoques m inv; the traffic was bumper to bumper el tráfico estaba colapsado 2 adj (extremely good) excepcional, extraordinario

'bump-start v/t car arrancar un coche empujándolo; fig: economy reanimar

bump·y ['bʌmpɪ] adj con baches; flight movido

bun [bʌn] hairstyle moño m; for eating bollo m

bunch [bʌntʃ] of people grupo m; of keys manojo m; of flowers ramo m; of grapes racimo m; thanks a bunch ironic no sabes lo que te lo agradezco

bun·dle ['bʌndl] *of clothes* fardo *m*; *of wood* haz *m*
◆ **bundle up** *v/t* liar; (*dress warmly*) abrigar

bung [bʌŋ] *v/t Br* F echar

bun·gee jump·ing ['bʌndʒɪdʒʌmpɪŋ] puenting *m*

bun·gle ['bʌŋgl] *v/t* echar a perder

bunk [bʌŋk] litera *f*

bunk beds *npl* literas *fpl*

buoy [bɔɪ] *n NAUT* boya *f*

buoy·ant ['bɔɪənt] *adj* animado, optimista; *economy* boyante

bur·den ['bɜːrdn] **1** *n also fig* carga *f* **2** *v/t*: **burden s.o. with sth** *fig* cargar a alguien con algo

bu·reau ['bjʊroʊ] (*chest of drawers*) cómoda *f*; (*office*) departamento *m*, oficina *f*; *a translation bureau* una agencia de traducción

bu·reauc·ra·cy [bjʊ'rɑːkrəsɪ] burocracia *f*

bu·reau·crat ['bjʊrəkræt] burócrata *m/f*

bu·reau·crat·ic [bjʊrə'krætɪk] *adj* burocrático

burg·er ['bɜːrgər] hamburguesa *f*

bur·glar ['bɜːrglər] ladrón(-ona) *m(f)*

'bur·glar a·larm alarma *f* antirrobo

bur·glar·ize ['bɜːrgləraɪz] *v/t* robar

bur·glar·y ['bɜːrglərɪ] robo *m*

bur·gle ['bɜːrgl] *v/t Br* robar

bur·i·al ['berɪəl] entierro *m*

bur·ly ['bɜːrlɪ] *adj* corpulento, fornido

burn [bɜːrn] **1** *n* quemadura *f* **2** *v/t* (*pret & pp burnt*) quemar; **be burned to death** morir abrasado **3** *v/i* (*pret & pp burnt*) *of wood, meat, in sun* quemarse
◆ **burn down 1** *v/t* incendiar **2** *v/i* incendiarse
◆ **burn out** *v/t*: **burn o.s. out** quemarse; *a burned-out car* un coche carbonizado

'burn·out F (*exhaustion*) agotamiento *m*

burnt [bɜːrnt] *pret & pp → burn*

burp [bɜːrp] **1** *n* eructo *m* **2** *v/i* eructar **3** *v/t*: *baby* hacer eructar a

burst [bɜːrst] **1** *n in water pipe* rotura *f*; *of gunfire* ráfaga *f*; *in a burst of energy* en un arrebato de energía **2** *adj tire* reventado **3** *v/t* (*pret & pp burst*) *balloon* reventar **4** *v/i* (*pret & pp burst*) *of balloon, tire* reventar; **burst into a room** irrumpir en una habitación; **burst into tears** echarse a llorar; **burst out laughing** echarse a reír

bur·y ['berɪ] *v/t* (*pret & pp buried*) enterrar; **be buried under** (*covered by*) estar sepultado por; **bury o.s. in work** meterse de lleno en el trabajo

bus [bʌs] **1** *n local* autobús *m*, *Mex* ca-

mión *m*, *Arg* colectivo *m*, *C.Am.* guagua *f*; *long distance* autobús *m*, *Span* autocar *m*; *school bus* autobús *m* escolar **2** *v/t* (*pret & pp bussed*) llevar en autobús

'bus·boy ayudante *m* de camarero

'bus driv·er conductor(a) *m(f)* de autobús

bush [bʊʃ] *plant* arbusto *m*; *type of countryside* monte *m*

bushed [bʊʃt] *adj* F (*tired*) molido F

bush·y ['bʊʃɪ] *adj beard* espeso

busi·ness ['bɪznɪs] negocios *mpl*; (*company*) empresa *f*; (*sector*) sector *m*; (*affair, matter*) asunto *m*; *as subject of study* empresariales *fpl*; *on business* de negocios; *that's none of your business!* ¡no es asunto tuyo!; *mind your own business!* ¡no te metas en lo que no te importa!

'busi·ness card tarjeta *f* de visita

'busi·ness class clase *f* ejecutiva

'busi·ness hours *npl* horario *m* de oficina

busi·ness·like ['bɪznɪslaɪk] *adj* eficiente

'busi·ness lunch almuerzo *m* de negocios

'busi·ness·man hombre *m* de negocios, ejecutivo *m*

'busi·ness meet·ing reunión *f* de negocios

'busi·ness school escuela *f* de negocios

'busi·ness stud·ies *nsg course* empresariales *mpl*

'busi·ness trip viaje *m* de negocios

'busi·ness·wom·an mujer *f* de negocios, ejecutiva *f*

'bus lane carril *m* bus

'bus shel·ter marquesina *f*

'bus sta·tion estación *f* de autobuses

'bus stop parada *f* de autobús

'bus tick·et billete *m or L.Am.* boleto *m* de autobús

bust¹ [bʌst] *n of woman* busto *m*

bust² [bʌst] **1** *adj* F (*broken*) escacharrado F: *go bust* quebrar **2** *v/t* F escacharrar F
◆ **bus·tle about** ['bʌsl] *v/i* trajinar

'bust-up F corte *m*

bust·y ['bʌstɪ] *adj* pechugona

bus·y ['bɪzɪ] **1** *adj also* TELEC ocupado; *full of people* abarrotado; *of restaurant etc*: *making money* ajetreado; *the line was busy* estaba ocupado, *Span* comunicaba; *she leads a very busy life* lleva una vida muy ajetreada; *be busy doing sth* estar ocupado *or* atareado haciendo algo **2** *v/t* (*pret & pp busied*): *busy o.s. with* entretenerse con algo

'bus·y·bod·y metomentodo *m/f*, entro-

C

metido(-a) *m(f)*

'**bus·y sig·nal** señal *f* de ocupado *or Span* comunicando

but [bʌt] *unstressed* [bət] **1** *conj* pero; *it's not me but my father you want* no me quieres a mí sino a mi padre; *but then (again)* pero **2** *prep*: *all but him* todos excepto él; *the last but one* el penúltimo; *the next but one* el próximo no, el otro; *the next page but one* la página siguiente a la próxima; *but for you* si no hubiera sido por ti; *nothing but the best* sólo lo mejor

butch·er ['butʃər] carnicero(-a) *m(f)*; *murderer* asesino(-a) *m(f)*

butt [bʌt] **1** *n of cigarette* colilla *f*; *of joke* blanco *m*; F (*buttocks*) trasero *m* F **2** *v/t* dar un cabezazo a; *of goat, bull* embestir
◆ **butt in** *v/i* inmiscuirse, entrometerse

but·ter ['bʌtər] **1** *n* mantequilla *f* **2** *v/t* untar de mantequilla
◆ **butter up** *v/t* F hacer la pelota a F

'**but·ter·fly** *insect* mariposa *f*

but·tocks ['bʌtəks] *npl* nalgas *fpl*

but·ton ['bʌtn] **1** *n on shirt, machine* botón *m*; (*badge*) chapa *f* **2** *v/t* abotonar
◆ **button up** *v/t* abotonar

'**but·ton·hole 1** *n in suit* ojal *m* **2** *v/t* acorralar

but·tress ['bʌtrəs] contrafuerte *m*

bux·om ['bʌksəm] *adj* de amplios senos

buy [baɪ] **1** *n* compra *f*, adquisición *f* **2** *v/t* (*pret & pp* **bought**) comprar; *can I buy you a drink?* ¿quieres tomar algo?; *$5 doesn't buy much* con 5 dólares no se puede hacer gran cosa
◆ **buy off** *v/t* (*bribe*) sobornar
◆ **buy out** *v/t* COM comprar la parte de
◆ **buy up** *v/t* acaparar

buy·er [baɪr] comprador(a) *m(f)*

buzz [bʌz] **1** *n* zumbido *m*; *she gets a real buzz out of it* F (*thrill*) le vuelve loca, le entusiasma **2** *v/i of insect* zumbar; *with buzzer* llamar por el interfono **3** *v/t with buzzer* llamar por el interfono a
◆ **buzz off** *v/i* F largarse F, *Span* pirarse F

buz·zard ['bʌzərd] ratonero *m*

buzz·er ['bʌzər] timbre *m*

'**buzz·word** palabra *f* de moda

by [baɪ] **1** *prep to show agent by*: (*near, next to*) al lado de, junto a; (*no later than*) no más tarde de; *mode of transport* en; *she rushed by me* pasó rápidamente por mi lado; *as we drove by the church* cuando pasábamos por la iglesia; *side by side* uno junto al otro; *by day / night* de día / noche; *by bus / train* en autobús / tren; *by the dozen* por docenas; *by the hour / ton* por hora / por tonelada; *by my watch* en mi reloj; *by nature* por naturaleza; *a play by …* una obra de …; *by o.s. without company* solo; *I did it by myself* lo hice yo solito; *by a couple of minutes* por un par de minutos; **2** *measurement* 2 por 4; *by this time tomorrow* mañana a esta hora; *by this time next year* el año que viene por estas fechas; *go by, pass by* pasar **2** *adv*: *by and by* (*soon*) dentro de poco

bye(-bye) [baɪ] adiós

by·gones ['baɪgɑːnz]: *let bygones be bygones* lo pasado, pasado está

'**by·pass 1** *n road* circunvalación *f*; MED bypass *m* **2** *v/t* sortear

'**by·prod·uct** subproducto *m*

'**by·stand·er** ['baɪstændər] transeúnte *m/f*

byte [baɪt] byte *m*

'**by·word**: *be a byword for* ser sinónimo de

C

cab [kæb] (*taxi*) taxi *m*; *of truck* cabina *f*; *cab driver* taxista *m/f*

cab·a·ret ['kæbəreɪ] cabaret *m*

cab·bage ['kæbɪdʒ] col *f*, repollo *m*

cab·in ['kæbɪn] *of plane* cabina *f*; *of ship* camarote *m*

'**cab·in at·tend·ant** auxiliar *m/f* de vuelo

'**cab·in crew** personal *m* de a bordo

cab·i·net ['kæbɪnɪt] armario *m*; POL gabinete *m*; *drinks cabinet* mueble *m* bar; *medicine cabinet* botiquín *m*; *display cabinet* vitrina *f*

'**cab·i·net mak·er** ebanista *m/f*

ca·ble ['keɪbl] cable *m*; *cable (TV)* televisión *f* por cable

'**ca·ble car** teleférico *m*

'**ca·ble tel·e·vi·sion** televisión *f* por cable

'**cab rank**, '**cab stand** parada *f* de taxis

323   **camper**

cac·tus ['kæktəs] cactus *m inv*
ca·dav·er [kə'dævər] cadáver *m*
CAD [kæd] *abbr* (= *computer assisted design*) CAD *m* (= diseño asistido por *Span* ordenador *or L.Am.* computadora)
cad·die ['kædɪ] **1** *n in golf* caddie *m/f* **2** *v/i* hacer de caddie
ca·det [kə'det] cadete *m*
cadge [kædʒ] *v/t* F: **cadge sth from s.o.** gorronear algo a alguien
Cae·sar·e·an *Br* → **Cesarean**
caf·é ['kæfeɪ] café *m*, cafetería *f*
caf·e·te·ri·a [kæfɪ'tɪrɪə] cafetería *f*, cantina *f*
caf·feine ['kæfiːn] cafeína *f*
cage [keɪdʒ] jaula *f*
ca·gey ['keɪdʒɪ] *adj* cauteloso, reservado; **he's cagey about how old he is** es muy reservado con respecto a su edad
ca·hoots [kə'huːts] *npl* F: **be in cahoots with** estar conchabado con
ca·jole [kə'dʒoʊl] *v/t* engatusar, persuadir
cake [keɪk] **1** *n big* tarta *f*; *small* pastel *m*; **be a piece of cake** F estar chupado F **2** *v/i* endurecerse
ca·lam·i·ty [kə'læmətɪ] calamidad *f*
cal·ci·um ['kælsɪəm] calcio *m*
cal·cu·late ['kælkjuleɪt] *v/t* calcular
cal·cu·lat·ing ['kælkjuleɪtɪŋ] *adj* calculador
cal·cu·la·tion [kælkju'leɪʃn] cálculo *m*
cal·cu·la·tor ['kælkjuleɪtər] calculadora *f*
cal·en·dar ['kælɪndər] calendario *m*
calf¹ [kæf] (*pl* **calves** [kævz]) (*young cow*) ternero(-a) *m(f)*, becerro(-a) *m(f)*
calf² [kæf] (*pl* **calves** [kævz]) *of leg* pantorrilla *f*
'calf·skin *n* piel *f* de becerro
cal·i·ber, *Br* cal·i·bre ['kælɪbər] *of gun* calibre *m*; **a man of his calibre** un hombre de su calibre
Cal·i·for·ni·an [kælɪ'fɔːnɪən] **1** *adj* californiano(-a) *m(f)*
call [kɔːl] **1** *n* llamada *f*; (*demand*) llamamiento *m*; **there's a call for you** tienes una llamada, te llaman; **I'll give you a call tomorrow** te llamaré mañana; **make a call** hacer una llamada; **a call for help** una llamada de socorro; **be on call** estar de guardia **2** *v/t also* TELEC llamar; *meeting* convocar; **he called him a liar** le llamó mentiroso; **what have they called the baby?** ¿qué nombre le han puesto al bebé?; **but we call him Tom** pero le llamamos Tom; **call s.o. names** insultar a alguien; **I called him his name** lo llamé **3** *v/i also* TELEC llamar; (*visit*) pasarse; **can I tell him who's calling?** ¿quién le llama?; **call for help** pedir

ayuda a gritos
◆ **call at** *v/t* (*stop at*) pasarse por; *of train* hacer parada en
◆ **call back 1** *v/t* (*phone again*) volver a llamar; (*return call*) devolver la llamada; (*summon*) hacer volver **2** *v/i on phone* volver a llamar; (*make another visit*) volver a pasar
◆ **call for** *v/t* (*collect*) pasar a recoger; (*demand*) pedir, exigir; (*require*) requerir
◆ **call in 1** *v/t* (*summon*) llamar **2** *v/i* (*phone*) llamar; **he called in sick** llamó para decir que estaba enfermo
◆ **call off** *v/t* (*cancel*) cancelar; *strike* desconvocar
◆ **call on** *v/t* (*urge*) instar; (*visit*) visitar
◆ **call out** *v/t* (*shout*) gritar; (*summon*) llamar
◆ **call up** *v/t* (*on phone*) llamar; COMPUT abrir, visualizar
'call cen·ter centro *m* de atención telefónica
call·er ['kɔːlər] *on phone* persona *f* que llama; (*visitor*) visitante *m/f*
'call girl prostituta *f* (*que concierta sus citas por teléfono*)
cal·lous ['kæləs] *adj* cruel, desalmado
cal·lous·ly ['kæləslɪ] *adv* cruelmente
cal·lous·ness ['kæləsnɪs] crueldad *f*
calm [kɑːm] **1** *adj sea* tranquilo; *weather* apacible; *person* tranquilo, sosegado; **please keep calm** por favor mantengan la calma **2** *n* calma *f*; **call for calm** pedir calma
◆ **calm down 1** *v/t* calmar, tranquilizar **2** *v/i of sea, weather* calmarse; *of person* calmarse, tranquilizarse
calm·ly ['kɑːmlɪ] *adv* con calma, tranquilamente
cal·o·rie ['kælərɪ] caloría *f*
cam·cor·der ['kæmkɔːrdər] videocámara *f*
came [keɪm] *pret* → **come**
cam·e·ra ['kæmərə] cámara *f*
'cam·e·ra·man *n* camarógrafo *m*, camarógrafo *m*
cam·i·sole ['kæmɪsoʊl] camisola *f*
cam·ou·flage ['kæməflɑːʒ] **1** *n* camuflaje *m* **2** *v/t* camuflar
camp [kæmp] **1** *n* campamento *m*; **make camp** acampar; **refugee camp** campo *m* de refugiados **2** *v/i* acampar
cam·paign [kæm'peɪn] **1** *n* campaña *f* **2** *v/i* hacer campaña (*for* a favor de)
cam·paign·er [kæm'peɪnər] defensor(a) *m(f)* (*for* de); **a campaigner against racism** una persona que hace campaña contra el racismo
camp·er ['kæmpər] *person* campista *m/f*; *vehicle* autocaravana *f*

camp·ing ['kæmpɪŋ] acampada *f*; *on campsite* camping *m*; **go camping** ir de acampada *or* camping

'**camp·site** camping *m*

cam·pus ['kæmpəs] campus *m*

can¹ [kæn] *unstressed* [kən] *v/aux* (*pret* **could**) ◇ (*ability*) poder; **can you swim?** ¿sabes nadar?; **can you hear me?** ¿me oyes?; **I can't see** no veo; **can you speak French?** ¿hablas francés?; **can he call me back?** ¿me podría devolver la llamada?; **as fast / well as you can** tan rápido / bien como puedas; **I can't go any further - you can and you will!** ¡no puedo más - ¡ya lo creo que puedes!

◇ (*permission*) poder; **can I help you?** ¿te puedo ayudar?; **can you help me?** ¿me puedes ayudar?; **can I have a beer / coffee?** ¿me pones una cerveza / un café?; **that can't be right** debe haber un error

can² [kæn] **1** *n for drinks etc* lata *f* **2** *v/t* (*pret & pp* **canned**) enlatar

Can·a·da ['kænədə] Canadá

Ca·na·di·an [kə'neɪdɪən] **1** *adj* canadiense **2** *n* canadiense *m/f*

ca·nal [kə'næl] *waterway* canal *m*

ca·nar·y [kə'nerɪ] canario *m*

can·cel ['kænsl] *v/t* cancelar

can·cel·la·tion [kænsə'leɪʃn] cancelación *f*

can·cel·la·tion fee tarifa *f* de cancelación de reserva

can·cer ['kænsər] cáncer *m*

Can·cer ['kænsər] ASTR Cáncer *m/f inv*

can·cer·ous ['kænsərəs] *adj* canceroso

c & f *abbr* (= *cost and freight*) C&F (= costo y flete)

can·did ['kændɪd] *adj* sincero, franco

can·di·da·cy ['kændɪdəsɪ] candidatura *f*

can·di·date ['kændɪdət] *for position* candidato(-a) *m(f)*; *in exam* candidato(-a) *m(f)*, examinando(-a) *m(f)*

can·did·ly ['kændɪdlɪ] *adv* sinceramente, francamente

can·died ['kændiːd] *adj* confitado

can·dle ['kændl] vela *f*

'**can·dle·stick** candelero *m*; *short* palmatoria *f*

can·dor, *Br* **can·dour** ['kændər] sinceridad *f*, franqueza *f*

can·dy ['kændɪ] (*sweet*) caramelo *m*; (*sweets*) dulces *mpl*; **a box of candy** una caja de caramelos *or* dulces

cane [keɪn] caña *f*; *for walking* bastón *m*

can·is·ter ['kænɪstər] bote *m*

can·na·bis ['kænəbɪs] cannabis *m*, hachís *m*

canned [kænd] *adj fruit, tomatoes* enlatado, en lata; (*recorded*) grabado

can·ni·bal·ize ['kænɪbəlaɪz] *v/t* canibalizar

can·not ['kænɑːt] → **can¹**

can·ny ['kænɪ] *adj* (*astute*) astuto

ca·noe [kə'nuː] canoa *f*, piragua *f*

'**can o·pen·er** abrelatas *m inv*

can't [kænt] → **can¹**

can·tan·ker·ous [kæn'tæŋkərəs] *adj* arisco, cascarrabias

can·teen [kæn'tiːn] *in plant* cantina *f*, cafetería *f*

can·vas ['kænvəs] *for painting* lienzo *m*; *material* lona *f*

can·vass ['kænvəs] **1** *v/t* (*seek opinion of*) preguntar **2** *v/i* POL hacer campaña (**for** en favor de)

can·yon ['kænjən] cañón *m*

cap [kæp] *n hat* gorro *m*; *with peak* gorra *f*; *of bottle, jar* tapón *m*; *of pen, of lens* tapa *f*

ca·pa·bil·i·ty [keɪpə'bɪlətɪ] capacidad *f*; **it's beyond my capabilities** no entra dentro de mis posibilidades

ca·pa·ble ['keɪpəbl] *adj* (*efficient*) capaz, competente; **be capable of** ser capaz de

ca·pac·i·ty [kə'pæsətɪ] capacidad *f*; *of car engine* cilindrada *f*; **a capacity crowd** un lleno absoluto; **the job is well within your capacity** el trabajo está dentro de tus posibilidades; **in my capacity as ...** en mi calidad de ...

cap·i·tal ['kæpɪtl] *n of country* capital *f*; (*capital letter*) mayúscula *f*; *money* capital *m*

cap·i·tal ex'pend·i·ture inversión *f* en activo fijo

cap·i·tal 'gains tax impuesto *m* sobre las plusvalías

cap·i·tal 'growth crecimiento *m* del capital

cap·i·tal·ism ['kæpɪtəlɪzm] capitalismo *m*

'**cap·i·tal·ist** ['kæpɪtəlɪst] **1** *adj* capitalista **2** *n* capitalista *m/f*

◆ **cap·i·tal·ize on** ['kæpɪtəlaɪz] *v/t* aprovecharse de

cap·i·tal 'let·ter letra *f* mayúscula

cap·i·tal 'pun·ish·ment pena *f* capital, pena *f* de muerte

ca·pit·u·late [kə'pɪtʊleɪt] *v/i* capitular

ca·pit·u·la·tion [kæpɪtʊ'leɪʃn] capitulación *f*

Cap·ri·corn ['kæprɪkɔːrn] ASTR Capricornio *m/f inv*

cap·size [kæp'saɪz] **1** *v/i* volcar **2** *v/t* hacer volcar

cap·sule ['kæpsʊl] *of medicine* cápsula *f*; (*space capsule*) cápsula *f* espacial

cap·tain ['kæptɪn] *n of ship, team,* MIL capitán(-ana) *m(f); of aircraft* comandante *m/f*

cap·tion ['kæpʃn] *n* pie *m* de foto

cap·ti·vate ['kæptɪveɪt] *v/t* cautivar, fascinar

cap·tive ['kæptɪv] **1** *adj* prisionero **2** *n* prisionero(-a) *m(f)*

cap·tive 'mar·ket mercado *m* cautivo

cap·tiv·i·ty [kæp'tɪvətɪ] cautividad *f*

cap·ture ['kæptʃər] **1** *n of city* toma *f; of criminal, animal* captura *f* **2** *v/t person, animal* capturar; *city, building* tomar; *market share* ganar; *(portray)* captar

car [kɑːr] *coche m, L.Am.* carro *m, Rpl* auto *m; of train* vagón *m; by car* en coche

ca·rafe [kə'ræf] garrafa *f,* jarra *f*

car·at ['kærət] quilate *m*

car·bo·hy·drate [kɑːrbou'haɪdreɪt] carbohidrato *m*

'car bomb coche *m* bomba

car·bon mon·ox·ide [kɑːrbənmən'ɑːksaɪd] monóxido *m* de carbono

car·bu·ret·er, car·bu·ret·or [kɑːrbə'retər] carburador *m*

car·cass ['kɑːrkəs] cadáver *m*

car·cin·o·gen [kɑːr'sɪnədʒen] agente *m* cancerígeno *or* carcinógeno

car·cin·o·gen·ic [kɑːrsɪnə'dʒenɪk] *adj* cancerígeno, carcinógeno

card [kɑːrd] *to mark occasion,* COMPUT, *business* tarjeta *f; (postcard)* (tarjeta *f)* postal *f; (playing card)* carta *f,* naipe *m; game of cards* partida *f* de cartas

'card·board cartón *m*

'card·board 'box caja *f* de cartón

car·di·ac ['kɑːrdɪæk] *adj* cardíaco

car·di·ac ar'rest paro *m* cardíaco

car·di·gan ['kɑːrdɪɡən] cárdigan *m*

car·di·nal ['kɑːrdɪnl] *n* REL cardenal *m*

'card in·dex fichero *m*

'card key llave *f* tarjeta

'card phone tarjeta *f* telefónica

care [ker] **1** *n* cuidado *m; (medical care)* asistencia *f* médica; *(worry)* preocupación *f; care of → c/o; take care (be cautious)* tener cuidado; *take care (of yourself)! (goodbye)* ¡cuídate!; *take care of dog, tool, house, garden* cuidar; *baby* cuidar (de); *(deal with)* ocuparse de; *I'll take care of the bill* yo pago la cuenta; *(handle)* **with care!** *on label* frágil **2** *v/i* preocuparse; *I don't care!* ¡me da igual!; *I couldn't care less* ¡me importa un pimiento!; *if you really cared ...* si de verdad te importara ...

◆ **care about** *v/t* preocuparse por

◆ **care for** *v/t (look after: person)* cuidar (de); *(look after: plant)* cuidar; *he*

doesn't care for me the way he used to ya no le gusto como antes; *would you care for a drink?* ¿le apetece tomar algo?

ca·reer [kə'rɪr] carrera *f; career prospects* perspectivas *fpl* profesionales

ca'reers of·fi·cer asesor(a) *m(f)* de orientación profesional

'care·free *adj* despreocupado

care·ful ['kerfəl] *adj (cautious, thorough)* cuidadoso; *be careful* tener cuidado; *(be) careful!* ¡(ten) cuidado!

care·ful·ly ['kerfəlɪ] *adv (with caution)* con cuidado; *worded etc* cuidadosamente

care·less ['kerlɪs] *adj* descuidado; *you are so careless!* ¡qué descuidado eres!

care·less·ly ['kerlɪslɪ] *adv* descuidadamente

car·er ['kerər] persona que cuida de un familiar o enfermo

ca·ress [kə'res] **1** *n* caricia *f* **2** *v/t* acariciar

care·tak·er ['kerteɪkər] conserje *m*

'care·worn *adj* agobiado

'car fer·ry ferry *m,* transbordador *m*

car·go ['kɑːrɡou] cargamento *m*

'car hire alquiler *m* de coches *or* automóviles

'car hire com·pa·ny empresa *f* de alquiler de coches *or* automóviles

car·i·ca·ture ['kærɪkətʃər] *n* caricatura *f*

car·ing ['kerɪŋ] *adj person* afectuoso, bondadoso; *society* solidario

'car me·chan·ic mecánico(-a) *m(f)* de coches *or* automóviles

car·nage ['kɑːrnɪdʒ] matanza *f,* carnicería *f*

car·na·tion [kɑːr'neɪʃn] clavel *m*

car·ni·val ['kɑːrnɪvl] feria *f*

car·ol ['kærəl] *n* villancico *m*

car·ou·sel [kærə'sel] *at airport* cinta *f* transportadora de equipajes; *for slide projector* carro *m; (merry-go-round)* tiovivo *m*

'car park *Br* estacionamiento *m, Span* aparcamiento *m*

car·pen·ter ['kɑːrpɪntər] carpintero(-a) *m(f)*

car·pet ['kɑːrpɪt] alfombra *f*

'car phone teléfono *m* de coche

'car·pool *n* acuerdo para compartir el vehículo entre varias personas que trabajan en el mismo sitio

'car port estacionamiento *m* con techo

'car ra·di·o autorradio *m*

car·ri·er ['kærɪər] *company* transportista *m; airline* línea *f* aérea; *of disease* portador(a) *m(f)*

car·rot ['kærət] zanahoria *f*

car·ry ['kærɪ] **1** *v/t (pret & pp carried) of*

C

person llevar; *disease* ser portador de; *of ship, plane, bus etc* transportar; *proposal* aprobar; **be carrying a child** *of pregnant woman* estar embarazada; **get carried away** dejarse llevar por la emoción, emocionarse **2** *v/i* (*pret & pp* **carried**) *of sound* oírse

◆ **carry on 1** *v/i* (*continue*) seguir, continuar; (*make a fuss*) organizar un escándalo; (*have an affair*) tener un lío **2** *v/t* (*conduct*) mantener; *business* efectuar

◆ **carry out** *survey etc* llevar a cabo

'**car seat** *for child* asiento *m* para niño

cart [kɑːrt] carro *m*

car·tel [kɑːr'tel] cartel *m*

car·ton ['kɑːrtn] *for storage, transport* caja *f* de cartón; *for milk etc* cartón *m*, tetrabrik *m®*; *for eggs, of cigarettes* cartón *m*

car·toon [kɑːr'tuːn] *in newspaper, magazine* tira *f* cómica; *on* tv, *movie* dibujos *mpl* animados

car·toon·ist [kɑːr'tuːnɪst] dibujante *m/f* de chistes

car·tridge ['kɑːrtrɪdʒ] *for gun* cartucho *m*

carve [kɑːrv] *v/t meat* trinchar; *wood* tallar

carv·ing ['kɑːrvɪŋ] *figure* talla *f*

'**car wash** lavado *m* de automóviles

case¹ [keɪs] *container* funda *f*; *of scotch, wine* caja *f*; (*suitcase*) maleta *f*

case² [keɪs] *n instance, criminal,* MED caso *m*; LAW causa *f*; **I think there's a case for dismissing him** creo que hay razones fundadas para despedirlo; **the case for the prosecution** (los argumentos jurídicos de) la acusación; **make a case for sth** defender algo; **in case ...** por si ...; **in case of emergency** en caso de emergencia; **in any case** en cualquier caso; **in that case** en ese caso

'**case his·to·ry** MED *historial m médico*

'**case·load** número *m* de casos

cash [kæʃ] **1** *n* (*dinero m en*) efectivo *m*; **I'm a bit short of cash** no tengo mucho dinero; **cash down** al contado; **pay (in) cash** pagar en efectivo; **cash on delivery** → **COD 2** *v/t check* hacer efectivo

◆ **cash in on** *v/t* sacar provecho de

'**cash cow** fuente *f* de ingresos

'**cash desk** caja *f*

cash 'dis·count descuento *m* por pago al contado

'**cash di·spens·er** *Br* cajero *m* automático

'**cash flow** flujo *m* de caja, cash-flow *m*; **cash flow problems** problemas *fpl* de liquidez

cash·ier [kæ'ʃɪr] *n in store etc* cajero(-a) *m(f)*

cash·mere ['kæʃmɪr] *adj* cachemir *m*

'**cash·point** cajero *m* automático

'**cash re·gis·ter** caja *f* registradora

ca·si·no [kə'siːnou] casino *m*

cas·ket ['kæskɪt] (*coffin*) ataúd *m*

cas·se·role ['kæsəroul] *n meal* guiso *m*: *container* cacerola *f*, cazuela *f*

cas·sette [kə'set] cinta *f*, casete *f*

cas'sette play·er, cas'sette re·cord·er casete *m*

cast [kæst] **1** *n of play* reparto *m*; (*mold*) molde *m* **2** *v/t* (*pret & pp* **cast**) *doubt, suspicion* proyectar; *metal* fundir; *play* seleccionar el reparto de; **they cast Alan as ...** le dieron a Alan el papel de ...

◆ **cast off** *v/i of ship* soltar amarras

caste [kæst] casta *f*

cast·er ['kæstər] *on chair etc* ruedecita *f*

Cas·til·ian [kæs'tɪljən] **1** *adj* castellano **2** *n person* castellano(-a) *m(f)*; *language* castellano *m*

cast 'i·ron *n* hierro *m* fundido

cast-'i·ron *adj* de hierro fundido

cas·tle ['kæsl] castillo *m*

'**cast-or** ['kæstər] → **caster**

cas·trate [kæ'streɪt] *v/t* castrar

cas·tra·tion [kæ'streɪʃn] castración *f*

cas·u·al ['kæʒuəl] *adj* (*by chance*) casual; (*offhand*) despreocupado; (*not formal*) informal; (*not permanent*) eventual; **it was just a casual remark** no era más que un comentario hecho de pasada; **he was very casual about the whole thing** parecía no darle mucha importancia al asunto; **casual sex** relaciones *fpl* sexuales (con parejas) ocasionales

cas·u·al·ly ['kæʒuəlɪ] *adv dressed* de manera informal; *say* a la ligera

cas·u·al·ty ['kæʒuəltɪ] víctima *f*

'**cas·u·al wear** ropa *f* informal

cat [kæt] gato *m*

Cat·a·lan ['kætəlæn] **1** *adj* catalán **2** *n person* catalán(-ana) *m(f)*; *language* catalán *m*

cat·a·log, *Br* **cat·a·logue** ['kætələɡ] *n* catálogo *m*

cat·a·lyst ['kætəlɪst] catalizador *m*

cat·a·lyt·ic con·vert·er [kætə'lɪtɪk] catalizador *m*

cat·a·pult ['kætəpʌlt] **1** *v/t fig to fame, stardom* catapultar, lanzar **2** *n* catapulta *f*; *toy* tirachinas *m inv*

cat·a·ract ['kætərækt] MED catarata *f*

ca·tas·tro·phe [kə'tæstrəfɪ] catástrofe *f*

cat·a·stroph·ic [kætə'strɑːfɪk] *adj* catastrófico

catch [kætʃ] **1** *n* parada *f* (*sin que la pelota toque el suelo*); *of fish* captura *f*, pesca *f*; (*locking device*) cierre *m*; (*problem*) pega f; **there has to be a catch** tiene que haber una trampa **2** v/t (pret & pp **caught**) ball agarrar, Span coger; animal atrapar; escaped prisoner capturar; (get on: bus, train) tomar, Span coger; (not miss: bus, train) alcanzar, Span coger; fish pescar; in order to speak to alcanzar, pillar; (hear) oír; illness agarrar, Span coger; **catch (a) cold** agarrar or Span coger un resfriado, resfriarse; **catch s.o.'s eye** of person, object llamar la atención de alguien; **catch sight of, catch a glimpse of** ver; **catch s.o. doing sth** atrapar or Span coger a alguien haciendo algo

◆ **catch on** v/i (become popular) cuajar, ponerse de moda, (understand) darse cuenta

◆ **catch up** v/i: **catch up with s.o.** alcanzar a alguien; **he's having to work hard to catch up** tiene que trabajar muy duro para ponerse al día

◆ **catch up on** v/t: **catch up on one's sleep** recuperar sueño; **there's a lot of work to catch up on** hay mucho trabajo atrasado

catch-22 [kætʃtwentiˈtuː]: **it's a catch-22 situation** es como la pescadilla que se muerde la cola

catch·er [ˈkætʃər] in baseball cácher, cátcher m

catch·ing [ˈkætʃɪŋ] adj also fig contagioso

catch·y [ˈkætʃɪ] adj tune pegadizo

cat·e·gor·ic [kætəˈɡɔːrɪk] adj categórico

cat·e·gor·i·cal·ly [kætəˈɡɔːrɪklɪ] adv categóricamente

cat·e·go·ry [ˈkætəɡɔːrɪ] categoría f

◆ **ca·ter for** [ˈkeɪtər] v/t (meet the needs of) cubrir las necesidades de; (provide food for) organizar la comida para

ca·ter·er [ˈkeɪtərər] hostelero(-a) m(f)

ca·ter·pil·lar [ˈkætərpɪlər] oruga f

ca·the·dral [kəˈθiːdrəl] catedral f

Cath·o·lic [ˈkæθəlɪk] **1** adj católico **2** n católico(-a) m(f)

Ca·thol·i·cism [kəˈθɑːlɪsɪzm] catolicismo m

'cat·nap **1** n cabezada f **2** v/i (pret & pp **catnapped**) echarse una cabezada f

'cat's eyes on road captafaros mpl (en el centro de la calzada)

cat·sup [ˈkætsʌp] ketchup m, catchup m

cat·tle [ˈkætl] npl ganado m

cat·ty [ˈkætɪ] adj malintencionado

'cat·walk pasarela f

caught [kɒːt] pret & pp → **catch**

cau·li·flow·er [ˈkɒːlɪflaʊər] coliflor f

cause [kɒːz] **1** n causa f; (grounds) motivo m, razón f **2** v/t causar, provocar

caus·tic [ˈkɒːstɪk] adj fig cáustico

cau·tion [ˈkɒːʃn] **1** n (carefulness) precaución f, prudencia f; **caution is advised** se recomienda prudencia **2** v/t (warn) prevenir (**against** contra)

cau·tious [ˈkɒːʃəs] adj cauto, prudente

cau·tious·ly [ˈkɒːʃəslɪ] adv cautelosamente, con prudencia

cav·al·ry [ˈkævəlrɪ] caballería f

cave [keɪv] cueva f

◆ **cave in** v/i of roof hundirse

cav·i·ar [ˈkævɪɑːr] caviar m

cav·i·ty [ˈkævətɪ] caries f inv

cc¹ [siːˈsiː] **1** abbr (= **carbon copy**) copia f **2** v/t memo enviar una copia de; person enviar una copia a

cc² [siːˈsiː] abbr (= **cubic centimeters**) cc (centimetros mpl cúbicos); mot cilindrada f

CD [siːˈdiː] abbr (= **compact disc**) CD m (= disco m compacto)

CD play·er (reproductor m de) CD m

CD-ROM [siːdiːˈrɑːm] CD-ROM m

CD-ROM drive lector m de CD-ROM

cease [siːs] **1** v/i cesar **2** v/t suspender; **cease doing sth** dejar de hacer algo

'cease-fire alto m el fuego

ceil·ing [ˈsiːlɪŋ] of room techo m; (limit) tope m, límite m

cel·e·brate [ˈselɪbreɪt] **1** v/i: **let's celebrate with a bottle of champagne** celebrémoslo con una botella de champán **2** v/t celebrar, festejar; (observe) celebrar

cel·e·brat·ed [ˈselɪbreɪtɪd] adj célebre; **be celebrated for** ser célebre por

cel·e·bra·tion [selɪˈbreɪʃn] celebración f

ce·leb·ri·ty [sɪˈlebrətɪ] celebridad f

cel·e·ry [ˈselərɪ] apio m

cel·i·ba·cy [ˈselɪbəsɪ] celibato m

cel·i·bate [ˈselɪbət] adj célibe

cell [sel] for prisoner, in spreadsheet celda f; bio célula f

cel·lar [ˈselər] of house sótano m; for wine bodega f

cel·list [ˈtʃelɪst] violonchelista m/f

cel·lo [ˈtʃelou] violonchelo m

cel·lo·phane [ˈseləfeɪn] celofán m

'cell phone, cel·lu·lar phone [ˈseljələr] (teléfono m) móvil m, L.Am. (teléfono m) celular m

cel·lu·lite [ˈseljulaɪt] celulitis f

ce·ment [sɪˈment] **1** n cemento m **2** v/t colocar con cemento; friendship consolidar

cem·e·tery [ˈsemətərɪ] cementerio m

cen·sor [ˈsensər] v/t censor(a) m(f)

cen·sus [ˈsensəs] censo m

cent [sent] céntimo m

cen·te·na·ry [senˈtiːnərɪ] centenario m

cen·ter [ˈsentər] **1** n centro m; **in the cen-**

center on

ter of en el centro de **2** *v/t* centrar

◆ **center on** *v/t* centrarse en

cen·ter of 'grav·i·ty centro *m* de gravedad

cen·ti·grade ['sentɪɡreɪd] *adj* centígrado; **10 degrees centigrade** 10 grados centígrados

cen·ti·me·ter, *Br* **cen·ti·me·tre** ['sentɪmiːtər] centímetro *m*

cen·tral ['sentrəl] *adj* central; *location, apartment* céntrico; **central Chicago** el centro de Chicago; **be central to sth** ser el eje de algo

Cen·tral A'mer·i·ca *n* Centroamérica, América Central

Cen·tral A'mer·i·can 1 *adj* centroamericano, de (la) América *f* Central **2** *n* centroamericano(-a) *m(f)*

cen·tral 'heat·ing calefacción *f* central

cen·tral·ize ['sentrəlaɪz] *v/t* centralizar

cen·tral 'lock·ing MOT cierre *m* centralizado

cen·tral 'pro·ces·sing u·nit unidad *f* central de proceso

cen·tre *Br* → **center**

cen·tu·ry ['sentʃərɪ] siglo *m*

CEO [siːiː'oʊ] *abbr* (= **Chief Executive Officer**) consejero(-a) *m(f)* delegado

ce·ram·ic [sɪ'ræmɪk] *adj* de cerámica

ce·ram·ics [sɪ'ræmɪks] (*pl: objects*) objetos *mpl* de cerámica; (*sing: art*) cerámica *f*

ce·re·al ['sɪrɪəl] (*grain*) cereal *m*; (*breakfast cereal*) cereales *mpl*

cer·e·mo·ni·al [serɪ'moʊnɪəl] **1** *adj* ceremonial **2** *n* ceremonial *m*

cer·e·mo·ny ['serɪmənɪ] (*event, ritual*) ceremonia *f*

cer·tain ['sɜːrtn] *adj* (*sure*) seguro; (*particular*) cierto; **I'm certain** estoy seguro; **it's certain that ...** es seguro que ...; **a certain Mr S.** un cierto Sr. S.; **make certain** asegurarse; **know / say for certain** saber / decir con certeza

cer·tain·ly ['sɜːrtnlɪ] *adv* (*definitely*) claramente; (*of course*) por supuesto; **certainly not!** ¡por supuesto que no!

cer·tain·ty ['sɜːrtntɪ] (*confidence*) certeza *f*, certidumbre *f*; (*inevitability*) seguridad *f*; **it's a certainty** es seguro; **he's a certainty for the gold medal** va a ganar seguro la medalla de oro

cer·tif·i·cate [sər'tɪfɪkət] (*qualification*) título *m*; (*official paper*) certificado *m*

cer·ti·fied pub·lic ac·count·ant ['sɜːrtɪfaɪd] censor(a) *m(f)* jurado de cuentas

cer·ti·fy ['sɜːrtɪfaɪ] *v/t* (*pret & pp* **certified**) certificar

Ce·sar·e·an [sɪ'zerɪən] *n* cesárea *f*

ces·sa·tion [se'seɪʃn] cese *m*

c/f *abbr* (= **cost and freight**) CF (= costo y flete)

CFC [siːef'siː] *abbr* (= **chlorofluorocarbon**) CFC *m* (= clorofluorocarbono *m*)

chain [tʃeɪn] **1** *n also of hotels etc* cadena *f* **2** *v/t* encadenar: **chain sth. to sth** encadenar algo/a alguien a algo

chain re'ac·tion reacción *f* en cadena

'chain-smoke *v/i* fumar un cigarrillo tras otro, fumar como un carretero

'chain-smok·er *persona que fuma un cigarrillo tras otro*

'chain store *store* tienda *f* (de una cadena); *company* cadena *f* de tiendas

chair [tʃer] **1** *n* silla *f*; (*armchair*) sillón *m*; *at university* cátedra *f*; **the chair** (*electric chair*) la silla eléctrica; *at meeting* la presidencia; **go to the chair** ser ejecutado en la silla eléctrica; **take the chair** ocupar la presidencia **2** *v/t meeting* presidir

'chair lift telesilla *f*

'chair·man presidente *m*

chair·man·ship ['tʃermənʃɪp] presidencia *f*

'chair·per·son presidente(-a) *m(f)*

'chair·wom·an presidenta *f*

cha·let ['ʃæleɪ] chalet *m*, chalé *m*

chal·ice ['tʃælɪs] REL cáliz *m*

chalk [tʃɔːk] *for writing* tiza *f*; *in soil* creta *f*

chal·lenge ['tʃælɪndʒ] **1** *n* (*difficulty*) desafío *m*, reto *m*; *in race, competition* ataque *m* **2** *v/t* desafiar, retar; (*call into question*) cuestionar

chal·leng·er ['tʃælɪndʒər] aspirante *m/f*

chal·leng·ing ['tʃælɪndʒɪŋ] *adj job, undertaking* estimulante

cham·ber·maid ['tʃeɪmbərmeɪd] camarera *f* (de hotel)

'cham·ber mu·sic música *f* de cámara

Cham·ber of 'Com·merce Cámara *f* de Comercio

cham·ois (leath·er) ['ʃæmɪ] ante *m*

cham·pagne [ʃæm'peɪn] champán *m*

cham·pi·on ['tʃæmpɪən] **1** *n* SP campeón(-ona) *m(f)*; *of cause* abanderado(-a) *m(f)* **2** *v/t* (*cause*) abanderar

cham·pi·on·ship ['tʃæmpɪənʃɪp] campeonato *m*

chance [tʃæns] (*possibility*) posibilidad *f*; (*opportunity*) oportunidad *f*; (*risk*) riesgo *m*; (*luck*) casualidad *f*, suerte *f*; **there's not much chance of that happening** no es probable que ocurra; **leave nothing to chance** no dejar nada a la improvisación; **by chance** por casualidad; **take a chance** correr el riesgo; **I'm not taking any chances** no voy a correr ningún riesgo

Chan·cel·lor ['tʃænsələr] *in Germany* canciller *m*; **Chancellor (of the Exchequer)** in Britain Ministro(-a) *m(f)* de Hacienda

chan·de·lier [ʃændə'lɪr] araña *f* (de luces)

change [tʃeɪndʒ] **1** *n* cambio *m*; (*small coins*) suelta *f*; *from purchase* cambio *m*, *Span* vuelta *f*, *L.Am.* vuelto *m*; *a change is as good as a rest* a veces cambiar es lo mejor; *that makes a nice change* eso es una novedad bienvenida; *for a change* para variar; *a change of clothes* una muda **2** *v/t* cambiar; *change trains* hacer transbordo; *change one's clothes* cambiarse de ropa **3** *v/i* cambiar; (*put on different clothes*) cambiarse; (*take different train / bus*) hacer transbordo; *the lights changed to green* el semáforo se puso verde

change·a·ble ['tʃeɪndʒəbl] *adj* variable, cambiante

'**change·o·ver** transición *f* (**to** a); *in relay race* relevo *m*

chang·ing room ['tʃeɪndʒɪŋ] SP vestuario *m*; *in shop* probador *m*

chan·nel ['tʃænl] *on* TV, *at sea* canal *m*

chant [tʃænt] **1** *n* REL canto *m*; *of fans* cántico *m*; *of demonstrators* consigna *f* **2** *v/i* gritar **3** *v/t* corear

cha·os ['keɪɑːs] caos *m*; *it was chaos at the airport* la situación en el aeropuerto era caótica

cha·ot·ic [keɪ'ɑːtɪk] *adj* caótico

chap [tʃæp] *n Br* F tipo *m* F, *Span* tío *m* F

chap·el ['tʃæpl] capilla *f*

chapped [tʃæpt] *adj lips* cortados; *hands* agrietado

chap·ter ['tʃæptər] *of book* capítulo *m*; *of organization* sección *f*

char·ac·ter ['kærɪktər] *nature, personality, in printing* carácter *m*; *person, in book, play* personaje *m*; *he's a real character* es todo un personaje

char·ac·ter·is·tic [kærɪktə'rɪstɪk] **1** *n* característica *f* **2** *adj* característico

char·ac·ter·is·ti·cal·ly [kærɪktə'rɪstɪklɪ] *adv* de modo característico; *he was characteristically rude* fue grosero como de costumbre

char·ac·ter·ize ['kærɪktəraɪz] *v/t (be typical of)* caracterizar; (*describe*) describir, clasificar

cha·rade [ʃə'rɑːd] *fig* farsa *f*

char·broiled ['tʃɑːrbrɔɪld] *adj* a la brasa

char·coal ['tʃɑːrkəʊl] *for barbecue* carbón *m* vegetal; *for drawing* carboncillo *m*

charge [tʃɑːrdʒ] **1** *n (fee)* tarifa *f*; LAW cargo *m*, acusación *f*; *free of charge* gratis; *bank charges* comisiones *fpl* bancarias; *will that be cash or charge?* ¿pagará en efectivo o con tarjeta?; *be in charge* es-

tar a cargo; *take charge* hacerse cargo **2** *v/t sum of money* cobrar; (*put on account*) pagar con tarjeta; LAW acusar (**with** de); *battery* cargar; *please charge it to my account* cárguelo a mi cuenta **3** *v/i (attack)* cargar

'**charge ac·count** cuenta *f* de crédito

'**charge card** tarjeta *f* de compra

cha·ris·ma [kə'rɪzmə] carisma *m*

char·is·mat·ic [kærɪz'mætɪk] *adj* carismático

char·i·ta·ble ['tʃærɪtəbl] *adj institution, donation* de caridad; *person* caritativo

char·i·ty ['tʃærətɪ] *assistance* caridad *f*; *organization* entidad *f* benéfica

char·la·tan ['ʃɑːrlətən] charlatán(-ana) *m(f)*

charm [tʃɑːrm] **1** *n (appealing quality)* encanto *m*; *on bracelet etc* colgante *m* **2** *v/t* (*delight*) encantar

charm·ing ['tʃɑːrmɪŋ] *adj* encantador

charred [tʃɑːrd] *adj* carbonizado

chart [tʃɑːrt] (*diagram*) gráfico *m*; (*map*) carta *f* de navegación; *the charts* MUS las listas de éxitos

'**char·ter flight** vuelo *m* chárter

chase [tʃeɪs] **1** *n* persecución *f* **2** *v/t* perseguir

♦ **chase away** *v/t* ahuyentar

chas·sis ['ʃæsɪ] *of car* chasis *m inv*

chat [tʃæt] **1** *n* charla *f*, *Mex* plática *f* **2** *v/i* (*pret & pp chatted*) charlar, *Mex* platicar

'**chat show** tertulia *f* televisiva

'**chat show host** presentador(a) *m(f)* de tertulia televisiva

chat·ter ['tʃætər] **1** *n* cháchara *f* **2** *v/i talk* parlotear; *of teeth* castañetear

'**chat·ter·box** charlatán(-ana) *m(f)*

chat·ty ['tʃætɪ] *adj person* hablador

chauf·feur ['ʃəʊfər] *n* chófer *m*, *L.Am.* chofer *m*

'**chauf·feur-driv·en** *adj* con chófer *or L.Am.* chofer

chau·vin·ist ['ʃəʊvɪnɪst] *n (male chauvinist)* machista *m*

chau·vin·is·tic [ʃəʊvɪ'nɪstɪk] *adj* chovinista; (*sexist*) machista

cheap [tʃiːp] *adj (inexpensive)* barato; (*nasty*) chabacano; (*mean*) tacaño

cheat [tʃiːt] **1** *n (person)* tramposo(-a) *m(f)* **2** *v/t* engañar; *cheat s.o. out of sth* estafar algo a alguien **3** *v/i in exam* copiar; *in cards etc* hacer trampa; *cheat on one's wife* engañar a la esposa

check[1] [tʃek] **1** *adj shirt* a cuadros **2** *n* cuadro *m*

check[2] [tʃek] FIN cheque *m*; *in restaurant etc* cuenta *f*; *the check please* la cuenta, por favor

check³ [tʃek] **1** *n* to verify sth comprobación *f*; *keep in check, hold in check* mantener bajo control; *keep a check on* llevar el control de **2** *v/t* (*verify*) comprobar; *machinery* inspeccionar; (*restrain, stop*) contener, controlar; *with a checkmark* poner un tic en; *coat* dejar en el guardarropa; *package* dejar en consigna **3** *v/i* comprobar; *check for* comprobar
◆ **check in** *v/i* at airport facturar; at hotel registrarse
◆ **check off** *v/t* marcar (*como comprobada*)
◆ **check on** *v/t* vigilar
◆ **check out 1** *v/i* of hotel dejar el hotel **2** *v/t* (*look into*) investigar; *club, restaurant etc* probar
◆ **check up on** *v/t* hacer averiguaciones sobre, investigar
◆ **check with** *v/t* of person hablar con; (*tally: of information*) concordar con
'**check·book** talonario *m* de cheques, *L.Am.* chequera *f*
checked [tʃekt] *adj material* a cuadros
'**check·er·board** ['tʃekərbɔːrd] tablero *m* de ajedrez
check·ered ['tʃekərd] *adj pattern* a cuadros; *career* accidentado
'**check·ers** ['tʃekərz] *nsg* damas *fpl*
'**check-in** (**coun·ter**) mostrador *m* de facturación
'**check·ing ac·count** ['tʃekɪŋ] cuenta *f* corriente
'**check-in time** hora *f* de facturación
'**check·list** lista *f* de verificación
'**check mark** tic *m*
'**check·mate** *n* jaque *m* mate
'**check-out** caja *f*
'**check-out time** from hotel hora *f* de salida
'**check·point** control *m*
'**check·room** for coats guardarropa *m*; for baggage consigna *f*
'**check·up** medical chequeo *m* (médico), revisión *f* (médica); dental revisión *f* (en el dentista)
cheek [tʃiːk] ANAT mejilla *f*
'**cheek·bone** pómulo *m*
cheer [tʃɪr] **1** *n* ovación *f*; **cheers!** toast ¡salud!; **the cheers of the fans** los vítores de los aficionados **2** *v/t* ovacionar, vitorear **3** *v/t* LANZAR vítores
◆ **cheer on** *v/t* animar
◆ **cheer up 1** *v/i* animarse; **cheer up!** ¡ánimate! **2** *v/t* animar
cheer·ful ['tʃɪrfəl] *adj* alegre, contento
cheer·ing ['tʃɪrɪŋ] *n* vítores *mpl*
cheer·i·o ['tʃɪri'oʊ] *Br* F ¡chao! F

'**cheer·lead·er** animadora *f*
cheese [tʃiːz] queso *m*
'**cheese·burg·er** hamburguesa *f* de queso
'**cheese·cake** tarta *f* de queso
chef [ʃef] chef *m*, jefe *m* de cocina
chem·i·cal ['kemɪkl] **1** *adj* químico **2** *n* producto *m* químico
chem·i·cal 'war·fare guerra *f* química
chem·ist ['kemɪst] in laboratory químico(-a) *m(f)*; *Br* dispensing farmacéutico(-a) *m(f)*
chem·is·try ['kemɪstri] química *f*; *fig* sintonía *f*, química *f*
chem·o·ther·a·py [kiːmoʊ'θerəpɪ] quimioterapia *f*
cheque [tʃek] *Br* → **check²**
cher·ish ['tʃerɪʃ] *v/t photo etc* apreciar mucho, tener mucho cariño a; *person* querer mucho; *hope* albergar
cher·ry ['tʃeri] fruit cereza *f*; tree cerezo *m*
cher·ub ['tʃerəb] in painting, sculpture querubín *m*
chess [tʃes] ajedrez *m*
'**chess·board** tablero *m* de ajedrez
'**chess·man, '**chess·piece** pieza *f* de ajedrez
chest [tʃest] of person pecho *m*; box cofre *m*; **get sth off one's chest** desahogarse
chest·nut ['tʃesnʌt] castaña *f*; tree castaño *m*
chest of 'draw·ers cómoda *f*
chew [tʃuː] *v/t* mascar, masticar; of dog, rats mordisquear
◆ **chew out** *v/t* F echar una bronca a F
chew·ing gum ['tʃuːɪŋ] chicle *m*
chic [ʃiːk] *adj* chic, elegante
chick [tʃɪk] young chicken pollito *m*; young bird polluelo *m*; F girl nena *f* F
chick·en ['tʃɪkɪn] **1** *n* gallina *f*; food pollo *m*; F (coward) gallina *f* F **2** *adj* F (cowardly) cobarde; **be chicken** ser un(a) gallina F
◆ **chicken out** *v/i* F acobardarse
'**chick·en·feed** F calderilla *f*
chief [tʃiːf] **1** *n* jefe(-a) *m(f)* **2** *adj* principal
chief ex·ec·u·tive 'of·fi·cer consejero(-a) *m(f)* delegado
chief·ly ['tʃiːflɪ] *adv* principalmente
chil·blain ['tʃɪlbleɪn] sabañón *m*
child [tʃaɪld] (pl **children** ['tʃɪldrən]) niño(-a) *m(f)*; son hijo *m*; daughter hija *f*; pej niño(-a) *m(f)*, crío(-a) *m(f)*
'**child a·buse** malos tratos *mpl* a menores
'**child·birth** parto *m*
'**child·hood** ['tʃaɪldhʊd] infancia *f*
child·ish ['tʃaɪldɪʃ] *adj pej* infantil
child·ish·ness ['tʃaɪldɪʃnɪs] *pej* infantilismo *m*

child·ish·ly ['tʃaɪldɪʃlɪ] *adv pej* de manera infantil

child·less ['tʃaɪldlɪs] *adj* sin hijos

child·like ['tʃaɪldlaɪk] *adj* infantil

'**child·mind·er** niñero(-a) *m(f)*

'**child·ren** ['tʃɪldrən] *pl* → **child**

Chil·e ['tʃɪlɪ] *n* Chile

Chil·e·an ['tʃɪlɪən] **1** *adj* chileno **2** *n* chileno(-a) *m(f)*

chill [tʃɪl] **1** *n illness* resfriado *m*; *there's a chill in the air* hace bastante fresco **2** *v/t wine* poner a enfriar

◆ **chill out** *v/i* P tranquilizarse

chil·(l)i (**pep·per**) ['tʃɪlɪ] chile *m*, *Span* guindilla *f*

chill·y ['tʃɪlɪ] *adj weather, welcome* fresco; *I'm feeling a bit chilly* tengo fresco

chime [tʃaɪm] *v/i* campanada *f*

chim·ney ['tʃɪmnɪ] chimenea *f*

chim·pan·zee [tʃɪm'pænziː] chimpancé *m*

chin [tʃɪn] barbilla *f*

Chi·na ['tʃaɪnə] China

chi·na ['tʃaɪnə] porcelana *f*

Chi·nese [tʃaɪ'niːz] **1** *adj* chino **2** *n* (*language*) chino *m*; (*person*) chino(-a) *m(f)*

chink [tʃɪŋk] *gap* resquicio *m*; *sound* tintineo *m*

chip [tʃɪp] **1** *n of wood* viruta *f*; *of stone* lasca *f*; *damage* mella *f*; *in gambling* ficha *f*; *chips* patatas *fpl* fritas **2** *v/t* (*pret & pp* **chipped**) (*damage*) mellar

◆ **chip in** *v/i* (*interrupt*) interrumpir; *with money* poner dinero

chip·munk ['tʃɪpmʌŋk] ardilla *f* listada

chi·ro·prac·tor ['kaɪroʊpræktər] quiropráctico(-a) *m(f)*

chirp [tʃɜːrp] *v/i* piar

chis·el ['tʃɪzl] *n for stone* cincel *m*; *for wood* formón *m*

chit·chat ['tʃɪtʃæt] charla *f*

chiv·al·rous ['ʃɪvlrəs] *adj* caballeroso

chive [tʃaɪv] cebollino *m*

chlo·rine ['klɔːriːn] cloro *m*

chlor·o·form ['klɔːrəfɔːrm] *n* cloroformo *m*

choc·a·hol·ic [tʃɑːkə'hɔːlɪk] *n* F adicto(-a) al chocolate

chock-a-block [tʃɑːkə'blɑːk] *adj* F abarrotado F

chock-full [tʃɑːk'fʊl] *adj* F de bote en bote F

choc·o·late ['tʃɑːkələt] chocolate *m*; *a box of chocolates* una caja de bombones; *hot chocolate* chocolate *m* caliente

'**choc·o·late cake** pastel *m* de chocolate

choice [tʃɔɪs] **1** *n* elección *f*; (*selection*) selección *f*; *you have a choice of rice or potatoes* puedes elegir entre arroz y pa-

tatas; *the choice is yours* tú eliges; *I had no choice* no tuve alternativa **2** *adj* (*top quality*) selecto

choir [kwaɪr] coro *m*

'**choir·boy** niño *m* de coro

choke [tʃoʊk] **1** *n* MOT estárter *m* **2** *v/i* ahogarse; *choke on sth* atragantarse con algo **3** *v/t* estrangular; *screams* ahogar

cho·les·te·rol [kə'lestəroʊl] colesterol *m*

choose [tʃuːz] *v/t & v/i* (*pret* **chose**, *pp* **chosen**) elegir, escoger

choos·ey ['tʃuːzɪ] *adj* F exigente

chop [tʃɑːp] **1** *n meat* chuleta *f*; *with one chop of the ax* con un hachazo **2** *v/t* (*pret & pp* **chopped**) *wood* cortar; *meat* trocear; *vegetables* picar

◆ **chop down** *v/t tree* talar

chop·per ['tʃɑːpər] F (*helicopter*) helicóptero *m*

'**chop·sticks** *npl* palillos *mpl* (chinos)

cho·ral ['kɔːrəl] *adj* coral

chord [kɔːrd] MUS acorde *m*

chore [tʃɔːr] tarea *f*

chor·e·o·graph ['kɔːrɪəgræf] *v/t* coreografiar

chor·e·og·ra·pher [kɔːrɪ'ɑːgrəfər] coreógrafo(-a) *m(f)*

chor·e·og·ra·phy [kɔːrɪ'ɑːgrəfɪ] coreografía *f*

cho·rus ['kɔːrəs] *singers* coro *m*; *of song* estribillo *m*

chose [tʃoʊz] *pret* → **choose**

cho·sen ['tʃoʊzn] *pp* → **choose**

Christ [kraɪst] Cristo; *Christ!* ¡Dios mío!

chris·ten ['krɪsn] *v/t* bautizar

chris·ten·ing ['krɪsnɪŋ] bautizo *m*

Chris·tian ['krɪstʃən] **1** *n* cristiano(-a) *m(f)* **2** *adj* cristiano

Chris·ti·an·i·ty [krɪstɪ'ænətɪ] cristianismo *m*

'**Chris·tian name** nombre *m* de pila

Christ·mas ['krɪsməs] Navidad(es) *f(pl)*; *at Christmas* en Navidad(es); *Merry Christmas!* ¡Feliz Navidad!

'**Christ·mas card** crismas *m inv*, tarjeta *f* de Navidad

Christ·mas 'Day día *f* de Navidad

Christ·mas 'Eve Nochebuena *f*

'**Christ·mas present** regalo *m* de Navidad

'**Christ·mas tree** árbol *m* de Navidad

chrome, **chro·mi·um** [kroʊm, 'kroʊmɪəm] cromo *m*

chro·mo·some ['kroʊməsoʊm] cromosoma *m*

chron·ic ['krɑːnɪk] *adj* crónico

chron·o·log·i·cal [krɑːnə'lɑːdʒɪkl] *adj* cronológico; *in chronological order* en orden cronológico

chrys·an·the·mum [krɪ'sænθəməm] crisantemo *m*

chub·by ['ʧʌbɪ] *adj* rechoncho

chuck [ʧʌk] *v/t* F tirar

◆ **chuck out** *v/t* F *object* tirar; *person* echar

chuck·le ['ʧʌkl] **1** *n* risita *f* **2** *v/i* reírse por lo bajo

chum [ʧʌm] amigo(-a) *m(f)*

chum·my ['ʧʌmɪ] *adj* F: **be chummy with** ser amiguete de F

chunk [ʧʌŋk] trozo *m*

chunk·y ['ʧʌŋkɪ] *adj sweater* grueso; *person, build* cuadrado, fornido

church [ʧɜːʧ] iglesia *f*

church 'hall *sala parroquial empleada para diferentes actividades*

church 'serv·ice oficio *m* religioso

'church·yard cementerio *m* (al lado de iglesia)

churl·ish ['ʧɜːrlɪʃ] *adj* maleducado, grosero

chute [ʃuːt] rampa *f*; *for garbage* colector *m* de basura

CIA [siːaɪ'eɪ] *abbr* (= *Central Intelligence Agency*) CIA *f* (= Agencia *f* Central de Inteligencia)

ci·der ['saɪdər] sidra *f*

CIF [siːaɪ'ef] *abbr* (= *cost, insurance, freight*) CIF (= costo, seguro y flete)

ci·gar [sɪ'gɑːr] (cigarro *m*) puro *m*

cig·a·rette [sɪgə'ret] cigarrillo *m*

cig·a·rette end colilla *f*

cig·a·rette light·er encendedor *m*, mechero *m*

cig·a·rette pa·per papel *m* de fumar

cin·e·ma ['sɪnɪmə] cine *m*

cin·na·mon ['sɪnəmən] canela *f*

cir·cle ['sɜːkl] **1** *n* círculo *m*; *sit in a circle* sentarse en círculo **2** *v/t* (*draw circle around*) poner un círculo alrededor de; *his name was circled in red* su nombre tenía un círculo rojo alrededor **3** *v/i* of *plane, bird* volar en círculo

cir·cuit ['sɜːkɪt] circuito *m*; (*lap*) vuelta *f*

'cir·cuit board COMPUT placa *f* or tarjeta *f* de circuitos

'cir·cuit break·er ELEC cortacircuitos *m inv*

'cir·cuit train·ing SP: *do circuit training* hacer circuitos de entrenamiento

cir·cu·lar ['sɜːrkjʊlər] **1** *n giving information* circular *f* **2** *adj* circular

cir·cu·late ['sɜːrkjʊleɪt] **1** *v/i* circular **2** *v/t memo* hacer circular

cir·cu·la·tion [sɜːrkjʊ'leɪʃn] circulación *f*; *of newspaper, magazine* tirada *f*

cir·cum·fer·ence [sər'kʌmfərəns] circunferencia *f*

cir·cum·stances ['sɜːrkəmstənsɪz] *npl* circunstancias *fpl*; *financial* situación *f* económica; *under no circumstances* en ningún caso, de ninguna manera; *under the circumstances* dadas las circunstancias

cir·cus ['sɜːrkəs] circo *m*

cir·rho·sis (of the liv·er) [sɪ'rousɪs] cirrosis *f* (hepática)

cis·tern ['sɪstɜːrn] cisterna *f*

cite [saɪt] *v/t* citar

cit·i·zen ['sɪtɪzn] ciudadano(-a) *m(f)*

cit·i·zen·ship ['sɪtɪznʃɪp] ciudadanía *f*

citr·us ['sɪtrəs] *adj* cítrico; *citrus fruit* cítrico *m*

cit·y ['sɪtɪ] ciudad *f*

city 'cen·ter centro *m* de la ciudad

city 'hall ayuntamiento *m*

civ·ic ['sɪvɪk] *adj* cívico

civ·il ['ʃɪvl] *adj* civil; (*polite*) cortés

civ·il en·gi·neer ingeniero(-a) *m(f)* civil

ci·vil·i·an [sɪ'vɪljən] **1** *n* civil *m/f* **2** *adj clothes* de civil

ci·vil·i·ty [sɪ'vɪlɪtɪ] cortesía *f*

civ·i·li·za·tion [sɪvəlar'zeɪʃn] civilización *f*

civ·i·lize ['sɪvəlaɪz] *v/t person* civilizar

civ·il 'rights *npl* derechos *mpl* civiles

civ·il 'ser·vant funcionario(-a) *m(f)*

civ·il 'ser·vice administración *f* pública

civ·il 'war guerra *f* civil

claim [kleɪm] **1** *n* (*request*) reclamación *f* (*for* de); (*right*) derecho *m*; (*assertion*) afirmación *f* **2** *v/t* (*ask for as a right*) reclamar; (*assert*) afirmar; *lost property* reclamar; *they have claimed responsibility for the attack* se han atribuido la responsabilidad del ataque

claim·ant ['kleɪmənt] reclamante *m/f*

clair·voy·ant [kler'vɔɪənt] *n* clarividente *m/f*, vidente *m/f*

clam [klæm] almeja *f*

◆ **clam up** *v/i* (*pret & pp clammed*) F cerrarse, callarse

clam·ber ['klæmbər] *v/i* trepar (*over* por)

clam·my ['klæmɪ] *adj* húmedo

clam·or, *Br* **clam·our** ['klæmər] *noise* griterío *m*; *outcry* clamor *m*

◆ **clamor for** *v/t justice* clamar por; *ice cream* pedir a gritos

clamp [klæmp] **1** *n fastener* abrazadera *f*, mordaza *f* **2** *v/t fasten* sujetar con abrazadera; *car* poner un cepo a

◆ **clamp down** *v/i* actuar contundentemente

◆ **clamp down on** *v/t* actuar contundentemente contra

clan [klæn] clan *m*

clan·des·tine [klæn'destɪn] *adj* clandesti-

climate

no

clang [klæŋ] **1** *n* sonido *m* metálico **2** *v/i* resonar; *the metal door clanged shut* la puerta metálica se cerró con gran estrépito

clap [klæp] *v/t & v/i* (*pret & pp clapped*) (*applaud*) aplaudir

clar·et ['klærɪt] *wine* burdeos *m inv*

clar·i·fi·ca·tion [klærɪfɪ'keɪʃn] aclaración *f*

clar·i·fy ['klærɪfaɪ] *v/t* (*pret & pp clarified*) aclarar

clar·i·net [klærɪ'net] clarinete *m*

clar·i·ty ['klærətɪ] claridad *f*

clash [klæʃ] **1** *n* choque *m*, enfrentamiento *m*; *of personalities* choque *m* **2** *v/i* chocar, enfrentarse; *of colors* desentonar; *of events* coincidir

clasp [klæsp] **1** *n* broche *m*, cierre *m* **2** *v/t in hand* estrechar; *he clasped the precious documents to him* agarró firmemente los valiosos documentos

class [klæs] **1** *n lesson, students* clase *f*; *social class* clase *f* social **2** *v/t* clasificar (*as* como)

clas·sic ['klæsɪk] **1** *adj* clásico **2** *n* clásico *m*

clas·si·cal ['klæsɪkl] *adj music* clásico

clas·si·fi·ca·tion [klæsɪfɪ'keɪʃn] clasificación *f*

clas·si·fied ['klæsɪfaɪd] *adj information* reservado

'clas·si·fied ad·(ver·tise·ment) anuncio *m* por palabras

clas·si·fy ['klæsɪfaɪ] *v/t* (*pret & pp classified*) clasificar

'class·mate compañero(-a) *m(f)* de clase

'class·room clase *f*, aula *f*

'class war·fare lucha *f* de clases

class·y ['klæsɪ] *adj* F con clase

clat·ter ['klætər] **1** *n* estrépito *m* **2** *v/i* hacer ruido

clause [klɔːz] *in agreement* cláusula *f*; GRAM cláusula *f*, oración *f*

claus·tro·pho·bi·a [klɔːstrə'foʊbɪə] claustrofobia *f*

claw [klɔː] **1** *n also fig* garra *f*; *of lobster* pinza *f* **2** *v/t* (*scratch*) arañar

clay [kleɪ] arcilla *f*

clean [kliːn] **1** *adj* limpio **2** *adv* F (*completely*) completamente **3** *v/t* limpiar; *clean one's teeth* limpiarse los dientes; *I must have my coat cleaned* tengo que llevar el abrigo a la tintorería

◆ **clean out** *v/t closet, closet* limpiar por completo; *fig* desplumar

◆ **clean up 1** *v/t also fig* limpiar; *papers* recoger **2** *v/i* limpiar; (*wash*) lavarse; *on stock market etc* ganar mucho dinero

clean·er ['kliːnər] *person* limpiador(a) *m(f)*; (*dry*) *cleaner* tintorería *f*

clean·ing wom·an ['kliːnɪŋ] señora *f* de la limpieza

cleanse [klenz] *v/t skin* limpiar

cleans·er ['klenzər] *for skin* loción *f* limpiadora

cleans·ing cream ['klenzɪŋ] crema *f* limpiadora

clear [klɪr] **1** *adj* claro; *weather, sky* despejado; *water* transparente; *conscience* limpio; *I'm not clear about it* no lo tengo claro; *I didn't make myself clear* no me expliqué claramente **2** *adv* *stand clear of the doors* apartarse de las puertas; *steer clear of* evitar **3** *v/t roads etc* despejar; (*acquit*) absolver; (*authorize*) autorizar; (*earn*) ganar, sacar; *the guards cleared everybody out of the room* los guardias sacaron a todo el mundo de la habitación; *you're cleared for takeoff* tiene autorización *or* permiso para despegar; *clear one's throat* carraspear **4** *v/i of sky, mist* despejarse; *of face* alegrarse

◆ **clear away** *v/t* quitar

◆ **clear off** *v/i* F largarse F

◆ **clear out 1** *v/t closet* ordenar, limpiar **2** *v/i* marcharse

◆ **clear up 1** *v/i* ordenar; *of weather* despejarse; *of illness, rash* desaparecer **2** *v/t* (*tidy*) ordenar; *mystery, problem* aclarar

clear·ance ['klɪrəns] *space* espacio *m*; (*authorization*) autorización *f*

clear·ance sale liquidación *f*

clear·ing ['klɪrɪŋ] claro *m*

clear·ly ['klɪrlɪ] *adv* claramente, *she is clearly upset* está claro que está disgustada

cleav·age ['kliːvɪdʒ] escote *m*

cleav·er ['kliːvər] cuchillo *m* de carnicero

clem·en·cy ['klemənsɪ] clemencia *f*

clench [klentʃ] *v/t teeth, fist* apretar

cler·gy ['klɜːrdʒɪ] clero *m*

cler·gy·man ['klɜːrdʒɪmæn] clérigo *m*

clerk [klɜːrk] *administrative* oficinista *m/f*; *in store* dependiente(-a) *m/f*

clev·er ['klevər] *adj person, animal* listo; *idea, gadget* ingenioso

clev·er·ly ['klevərlɪ] *adv designed* ingeniosamente

cli·ché ['kliːʃeɪ] tópico *m*, cliché *m*

cli·chéd ['kliːʃeɪd] *adj* estereotipado

click [klɪk] **1** *n* COMPUT clic *m* **2** *v/i* hacer clic

◆ **click on** *v/t* COMPUT hacer clic en

cli·ent ['klaɪənt] cliente *m/f*

cli·en·tele [kliːən'tel] clientela *f*

cli·mate ['klaɪmət] *also fig* clima *m*

'cli·mate change cambio *m* climático

cli·mat·ic [klaɪ'mætɪk] *adj* climático

cli·max ['klaɪmæks] *n* clímax *m*, punto *m* culminante

climb [klaɪm] **1** *n up mountain* ascensión *f*, escalada *f* **2** *v/t hill, ladder* subir; *mountain* subir, escalar; *tree* trepar a **3** *v/i* subir (*into* a); *up mountain* subir, escalar; *of inflation etc* subir

◆ **climb down** *v/i from ladder etc* bajar

climb·er ['klaɪmər] *person* escalador(a) *m(f)*, alpinista *m/f*, *L.Am.* andinista *m/f*

climb·ing ['klaɪmɪŋ] escalada *f*, alpinismo *m*, *L.Am.* andinismo *m*

'climb·ing wall rocódromo *m*

clinch [klɪntʃ] *v/t deal* cerrar; *that clinches it* ¡ahora sí que está claro!

cling [klɪŋ] *v/i* (*pret & pp* **clung**) *of clothes* pegarse al cuerpo

◆ **cling to** *v/t person, idea* aferrarse a

'cling·film plástico *m* transparente (para alimentos)

cling·y ['klɪŋɪ] *adj child, boyfriend* pegajoso

clin·ic ['klɪnɪk] clínica *f*

clin·i·cal ['klɪnɪkl] *adj* clínico

clink [klɪŋk] **1** *n noise* tintineo *m* **2** *v/i* tintinear

clip¹ [klɪp] **1** *n fastener* clip *m* **2** *v/t* (*pret & pp* **clipped**): *clip sth to sth* sujetar algo a algo

clip² [klɪp] **1** *n extract* fragmento *m* **2** *v/t* (*pret & pp* **clipped**) *hair, grass* cortar; *hedge* podar

clip·pers ['klɪpərz] *npl for hair* maquinilla *f*; *for nails* cortaúñas *m inv*; *for gardening* tijeras *fpl* de podar

clip·ping ['klɪpɪŋ] *from newspaper* recorte *m*

clique [kliːk] camarilla *f*

cloak *n* capa *f*

'cloak·room *Br* guardarropa *m*

clock [klɑːk] reloj *m*

'clock·wise *adv* en el sentido de las agujas del reloj

'clock·work: *it went like clockwork* salió a la perfección

◆ **clog up** [klɑːg] **1** *v/i* (*pret & pp* **clogged**) bloquearse **2** *v/t* (*pret & pp* **clogged**) bloquear

clone [kloʊn] **1** *n* clon *m* **2** *v/t* clonar

close¹ [kloʊs] **1** *adj family* cercano; *friend* íntimo; *bear a close resemblance to* parecerse mucho a; *the closest town* la ciudad más cercana; *be close to s.o. emotionally* estar muy unido a alguien **2** *adv* cerca; *close to the school* cerca del colegio; *close at hand* a mano;

close by cerca

close² [kloʊz] **1** *v/t* cerrar **2** *v/i of door, shop* cerrar; *of eyes* cerrarse

◆ **close down** *v/t & v/i* cerrar

◆ **close in** *v/i of fog* echarse encima; *of troops* aproximarse, acercarse

◆ **close up 1** *v/t building* cerrar **2** *v/i* (*move closer*) juntarse

closed [kloʊzd] *adj store, eyes* cerrado

closed-cir·cuit 'tel·e·vi·sion circuito *m* cerrado de televisión

'close-knit *adj* muy unido

close·ly ['kloʊslɪ] *adv listen, watch* atentamente; *cooperate* de cerca

clos·et ['klɑːzɪt] armario *m*

close-up ['kloʊsʌp] primer plano *m*

clos·ing date ['kloʊzɪŋ] fecha *f* límite

'clos·ing time hora *f* de cierre

clo·sure ['kloʊʒər] cierre *m*

clot [klɑːt] **1** *n of blood* coágulo *m* **2** *v/i* (*pret & pp* **clotted**) *of blood* coagularse

cloth [klɑːθ] (*fabric*) tela *f*, tejido *m*; *for cleaning* trapo *m*

clothes [kloʊðz] *npl* ropa *f*

'clothes brush cepillo *m* para la ropa

'clothes hang·er percha *f*

'clothes·horse tendedero *m* plegable

'clothes-line cuerda *f* de tender la ropa

'clothes peg, 'clothes·pin pinza *f* (de la ropa)

cloth·ing ['kloʊðɪŋ] ropa *f*

cloud [klaʊd] *n* nube *f*; *a cloud of dust* una nube de polvo

◆ **cloud over** *v/i of sky* nublarse

'cloud·burst chaparrón *m*

cloud·less ['klaʊdlɪs] *adj sky* despejado

cloud·y ['klaʊdɪ] *adj* nublado

clout [klaʊt] (*fig: influence*) influencia *f*

clove of 'gar·lic [kloʊv] diente *m* de ajo

clown [klaʊn] *also fig* payaso *m*

club [klʌb] *n weapon* palo *m*, garrote *m*; *in golf* palo *m*; *organization* club *m*; *clubs in cards* tréboles

clue [kluː] pista *f*; *I haven't a clue* F (*don't know*) no tengo idea F; *he hasn't a clue* F (*is useless*) no tiene ni idea F

clued-up [kluːd'ʌp] *adj* F puesto F; *be clued-up on sth* F estar puesto sobre algo F

clump [klʌmp] *n of earth* terrón *m*; *of flowers etc* grupo *m*

clum·si·ness ['klʌmzɪnɪs] torpeza *f*

clum·sy ['klʌmzɪ] *adj person* torpe

clung [klʌŋ] *pret & pp* → **cling**

clus·ter ['klʌstər] **1** *n* grupo *m* **2** *v/i of people* apiñarse; *of houses* agruparse

clutch [klʌtʃ] **1** *n* MOT embrague *m* **2** *v/t* agarrar

◆ **clutch at** *v/t*: *clutch at sth* agarrarse a

algo

clut·ter ['klʌtər] **1** *n* desorden *m*; *all the clutter on my desk* la cantidad de cosas que hay encima de mi mesa **2** *v/t* (*also: clutter up*) abarrotar

Co. *abbr* (= *Company*) Cía. (= Compañía *f*)

c/o *abbr* (= *care of*) en el domicilio de

coach [kəʊtʃ] **1** *n* (*trainer*) entrenador(a) *m(f)*; *of singer, actor* profesor(a) *m(f)*; *on train* vagón *m*; *Br* (*bus*) autobús *m* **2** *v/t footballer* entrenar; *singer* preparar

coach·ing ['kəʊtʃɪŋ] entrenamiento *m*

co·ag·u·late [kəʊ'ægjʊleɪt] *v/i of blood* coagularse

coal [kəʊl] carbón *m*

'coal·mine mina *f* de carbón

coarse [kɔːrs] *adj* áspero; *hair* basto; (*vulgar*) basto, grosero

coarse·ly ['kɔːrslɪ] *adv* (*vulgarly*) de manera grosera; *coarsely ground coffee* café molido grueso

coast [kəʊst] *n* costa *f*; *at the coast* en la costa

coast·al ['kəʊstl] *adj* costero

coast·er ['kəʊstər] posavasos *m inv*

'coast·guard *organization* servicio *m* de guardacostas; *person* guardacostas *m/f inv*

'coast·line litoral *m*, costa *f*

coat [kəʊt] **1** *n* chaqueta *f*, *L.Am.* saco *m*; (*overcoat*) abrigo *m*; *of animal* pelaje *m*; *of paint etc* capa *f*, mano *f* **2** *v/t* (*cover*) cubrir (*with* de)

'coat·hang·er percha *f*

coat·ing ['kəʊtɪŋ] capa *f*

co·au·thor ['kəʊɔ:θər] **1** *n* coautor(a) *m(f)* **2** *v/t*: *co-author a book* escribir un libro conjuntamente

coax [kəʊks] *v/t* persuadir; *coax sth out of s.o.* sonsacar algo a alguien

cob·bled ['kɑːbld] *adj* adoquinado

cob·ble·stone ['kɑːblstəʊn] adoquín *m*

cob·web ['kɑːbweb] telaraña *f*

co·caine [kə'keɪn] cocaína *f*

cock [kɑːk] *n* (*chicken*) gallo *m*; (*any male bird*) macho *m*

cock-eyed [kɑːk'aɪd] *adj* F *idea etc* ridículo

'cock·pit *of plane* cabina *f*

cock·roach ['kɑːkrəʊtʃ] cucaracha *f*

'cock·tail cóctel *m* (bebida)

'cock·tail par·ty cóctel *m* (fiesta)

'cock·tail shak·er coctelera *f*

cock·y ['kɑːkɪ] *adj* F creído, chulo

co·coa ['kəʊkəʊ] *drink* cacao *m*

co·co·nut ['kəʊkənʌt] coco *m*

'co·co·nut palm cocotero *m*

COD [siːoʊ'diː] *abbr* (= *collect on delivery*) entrega *f* contra reembolso

cod·dle ['kɑːdl] *v/t sick person* cuidar; *child* mimar

code [kəʊd] *n* código *m*; *in code* cifrado

co·ed·u·ca·tion·al [kəʊedʊ'keɪʃnl] *adj* mixto

co·erce [kəʊ'ɜːrs] *v/t* coaccionar

co·ex·ist [kəʊɪg'zɪst] *v/i* coexistir

co·ex·ist·ence [kəʊɪg'zɪstəns] coexistencia *f*

cof·fee ['kɑːfɪ] café *m*; *a cup of coffee* un café

'cof·fee bean grano *m* de café

'cof·fee break pausa *f* para el café

'cof·fee cup taza *f* de café

'cof·fee grind·er ['graɪndər] molinillo *m* de café

'cof·fee mak·er cafetera *f* (para preparar)

'cof·fee pot cafetera *f* (para servir)

'cof·fee shop café *m*, cafetería *f*

'cof·fee ta·ble mesa *f* de centro

cof·fin ['kɑːfɪn] féretro *m*, ataúd *m*

cog [kɑːg] diente *m*

co·gnac ['kɑːnjæk] coñac *m*

'cog·wheel rueda *f* dentada

co·hab·it [kəʊ'hæbɪt] *v/i* cohabitar

co·her·ent [kəʊ'hɪrənt] *adj* coherente

coil [kɔɪl] **1** *n of rope* rollo *m*; *of smoke* espiral *f*; *of snake* anillo *m* **2** *v/t*: *coil (up)* enrollar

coin [kɔɪn] *n* moneda *f*

co·in·cide [kəʊɪn'saɪd] *v/i* coincidir

co·in·ci·dence [kəʊ'ɪnsɪdəns] coincidencia *f*

coke [kəʊk] P (*cocaine*) coca *f*

Coke® [kəʊk] Coca-Cola® *f*

cold [kəʊld] **1** *adj also fig* frío; *I'm (feeling) cold* tengo frío; *it's cold of weather* hace frío; *in cold blood* a sangre fría; *get cold feet* F ponerse nervioso **2** *n* frío *m*; MED resfriado *m*; *I have a cold* estoy resfriado, tengo un resfriado

cold-blood·ed [kəʊld'blʌdɪd] *adj* de sangre fría; *fig: murder* a sangre fría

cold call·ing ['kɔːlɪŋ] COM visitas o llamadas comerciales hechas sin cita previa

'cold cuts *npl* fiambres *mpl*

cold·ly ['kəʊldlɪ] *adv* fríamente, con frialdad

cold·ness ['kəʊldnɪs] frialdad *f*

'cold sore calentura *f*

cole·slaw ['kəʊlslɔː] ensalada de col, cebolla, zanahoria y mayonesa

col·ic ['kɑːlɪk] cólico *m*

col·lab·o·rate [kə'læbəreɪt] *v/i* colaborar (*on* en)

col·lab·o·ra·tion [kəlæbə'reɪʃn] colaboración *f*

col·lab·o·ra·tor [kəˈlæbəreɪtər] colaborador(a) *m(f)*; *with enemy* colaboracionista *m/f*

col·lapse [kəˈlæps] *v/i of roof, building* hundirse, desplomarse; *of person* desplomarse

col·lap·si·ble [kəˈlæpsəbl] *adj* plegable

col·lar [ˈkɑːlər] cuello *m*; *for dog* collar *m*

'col·lar·bone clavícula *f*

col·league [ˈkɑːliːg] colega *m/f*

col·lect [kəˈlekt] **1** *v/t* recoger; *as hobby* coleccionar **2** *v/i (gather together)* reunirse **3** *adv:* **call collect** llamar a cobro revertido

col·lect call llamada *f* a cobro revertido

col·lect·ed [kəˈlektɪd] *adj works, poems etc* completo; *person* sereno

col·lec·tion [kəˈlekʃn] colección *f*; *in church* colecta *f*

col·lec·tive [kəˈlektɪv] *adj* colectivo

col·lec·tive 'bar·gain·ing negociación *f* colectiva

col·lec·tor [kəˈlektər] coleccionista *m/f*

col·lege [ˈkɑːlɪdʒ] universidad *f*

col·lide [kəˈlaɪd] *v/i* chocar, colisionar (*with* con *or* contra)

col·li·sion [kəˈlɪʒn] choque *m*, colisión *f*

col·lo·qui·al [kəˈloʊkwɪəl] *adj* coloquial

Co·lom·bi·a [kəˈlʌmbɪə] Colombia

Co·lom·bi·an [kəˈlʌmbɪən] **1** *adj* colombiano **2** *n* colombiano(-a) *m(f)*

co·lon [ˈkoʊlən] *punctuation)* dos puntos *mpl*; ANAT colon *m*

colo·nel [ˈkɜːrnl] coronel *m*

co·lo·ni·al [kəˈloʊnɪəl] *adj* colonial

co·lo·nize [ˈkɑːlənaɪz] *v/t country* colonizar

co·lo·ny [ˈkɑːlənɪ] colonia *f*

col·or [ˈkʌlər] **1** *n* color *m*; *in color movie etc* en color; **colors** MIL bandera *f* **2** *v/t one's hair* teñir **3** *v/i (blush)* ruborizarse

'col·or-blind *adj* daltónico

col·ored [ˈkʌlərd] *adj person* de color

'col·or fast *adj* que no destiñe

col·or·ful [ˈkʌlərfəl] *adj* lleno de colores; *account* colorido

col·or·ing [ˈkʌlərɪŋ] color *m*

'col·or pho·to·graph fotografía *f* en color

'col·or scheme combinación *f* de colores

'col·or TV televisión *f* en color

co·los·sal [kəˈlɑːsl] *adj* colosal

col·our *etc Br* → **color** *etc*

colt [koʊlt] potro *m*

Co·lum·bus [kəˈlʌmbəs] Colón *m*

col·umn [ˈkɑːləm] *architectural, of text* columna *f*

col·umn·ist [ˈkɑːləmɪst] columnista *m/f*

co·ma [ˈkoʊmə] coma *m*; **be in a coma** estar en coma

comb [koʊm] **1** *n* peine *m* **2** *v/t hair, area* peinar; **comb one's hair** peinarse

com·bat [ˈkɑːmbæt] **1** *n* combate *m* **2** *v/t* combatir

com·bi·na·tion [kɑːmbɪˈneɪʃn] combinación *f*

com·bine [kəmˈbaɪn] **1** *v/t* combinar; *ingredients* mezclar **2** *v/i* combinarse

com·bine har·vest·er [kɑːmbaɪnˈhɑːrvɪstər] cosechadora *f*

com·bus·ti·ble [kəmˈbʌstɪbl] *adj* combustible

com·bus·tion [kəmˈbʌstʃn] combustión *f*

come [kʌm] *v/i (pret came, pp come) toward speaker* venir; *toward listener* ir; *of train, bus* llegar, venir; **don't come too close** no te acerques demasiado; **you'll come to like it** llegará a gustarte; **how come?** F ¿y eso?; **how come you've stopped going to the club?** ¿cómo es que has dejado de ir al club?

◆ **come about** *v/i (happen)* pasar, suceder

◆ **come across 1** *v/t (find)* encontrar **2** *v/i: his humor comes across as ...* su humor da la impresión de ser ...; **she comes across as ...** da la impresión de ser ...

◆ **come along** *v/i (come too)* venir; *(turn up)* aparecer; *(progress)* marchar; **why don't you come along?** ¿por qué no te vienes con nosotros?

◆ **come apart** *v/i* desmontarse; *(break)* romperse

◆ **come around** *v/i to s.o.'s home* venir, pasarse; *(regain consciousness)* volver en sí

◆ **come away** *v/i (leave)* salir; *of button etc* caerse

◆ **come back** *v/i* volver; **it came back to me** lo recordé

◆ **come by 1** *v/i* pasarse **2** *v/t (acquire)* conseguir; **how did you come by that bruise?** ¿cómo te has dado ese golpe?

◆ **come down** *v/i* bajar; *of rain, snow* caer **2** *v/t: he came down the stairs* bajó las escaleras

◆ **come for** *v/t (attack)* atacar; *(collect thing)* venir a por; *(collect person)* venir a buscar a

◆ **come forward** *v/i (present o.s.)* presentarse

◆ **come from** *v/t (travel somewhere)* venir de; *(originate from)* ser de

◆ **come in** *v/i* entrar; *of train* llegar; *of tide* subir; **come in!** ¡entre!, ¡adelante!

◆ **come in for** *v/t* recibir; **come in for criticism** recibir críticas

◆ **come in on** *v/t:* **come in on a deal** participar en un negocio

◆ **come off** v/i *of handle etc* soltarse, caerse; *of paint etc* quitarse

◆ **come on** v/i (*progress*) marchar, progresar; **come on!** ¡vamos!; **oh come on, you're exaggerating** ¡vamos, hombre!, estás exagerando

◆ **come out** v/i salir; *of book* publicarse; *of stain* irse, quitarse; *of gay* declararse homosexual públicamente

◆ **come to 1** v/t *place* llegar a; *of hair, dress, water* llegar hasta; **that comes to $70** eso suma 70 dólares **2** v/i (*regain consciousness*) volver en sí

◆ **come up** v/i subir; *of sun* salir; **something has come up** ha surgido algo

◆ **come up with** v/t *solution* encontrar; **John came up with a great idea** a John se le ocurrió una idea estupenda

'**come·back** regreso m; **make a come·back** regresar

co·me·di·an [kə'miːdɪən] humorista m/f; *pej* payaso(-a) m(f)

'**come·down** gran decepción f

com·e·dy ['kɑːmədɪ] comedia f

com·et ['kɑːmɪt] cometa m

come·up·pance [kʌm'ʌpəns] n F: **he'll get his comeuppance** tendrá su merecido

com·fort ['kʌmfərt] **1** n comodidad f, confort m; (*consolation*) consuelo m **2** v/t consolar

com·for·ta·ble ['kʌmfərtəbl] adj *chair* cómodo; *house, room* cómodo, confortable; **be comfortable** *of person* estar cómodo; *financially* estar en una situación holgada

com·ic ['kɑːmɪk] **1** n *to read* cómic m; (*comedian*) cómico(-a) m(f) **2** adj cómico

com·i·cal ['kɑːmɪkl] adj cómico

'**com·ic book** cómic m

'**com·ics** ['kɑːmɪks] npl tiras fpl cómicas

'**com·ic strip** tira f cómica

com·ma ['kɑːmə] coma f

com·mand [kə'mænd] **1** n orden f **2** v/t ordenar, mandar

com·man·deer [kɑːmən'dɪr] v/t requisar

com·man·der [kə'mændər] comandante m/f

com·man·der·in·'chief comandante m/f en jefe

com·mand·ing of·fi·cer [kə'mændɪŋ] oficial m/f al mando

com·mand·ment [kə'mændmənt] mandamiento m; **the Ten Commandments** REL los Diez Mandamientos

com·mem·o·rate [kə'meməreɪt] v/t conmemorar m: *in*

com·mem·o·ra·tion [kəmemə'reɪʃn] *in*

commemoration of en conmemoración de

com·mence [kə'mens] v/t & v/i comenzar

com·mend [kə'mend] v/t encomiar, elogiar

com·mend·a·ble [kə'mendəbl] adj encomiable

com·men·da·tion [kəmen'deɪʃn] *for bravery* mención f

com·men·su·rate [kə'menʃərət] adj: **commensurate with** acorde con

com·ment ['kɑːment] **1** n comentario m; **no comment!** ¡sin comentarios! **2** v/i hacer comentarios (**on** sobre)

com·men·ta·ry ['kɑːmənterɪ] comentarios mpl

com·men·tate ['kɑːmənteɪt] v/i hacer de comentarista

com·men·ta·tor ['kɑːmənteɪtər] comentarista m/f

com·merce ['kɑːmɜːrs] comercio m

com·mer·cial [kə'mɜːrʃl] **1** adj comercial **2** n (*advert*) anuncio m (publicitario)

com·mer·cial 'break pausa f publicitaria

com·mer·cial·ize [kə'mɜːrʃlaɪz] v/t *Christmas* comercializar

com·mer·cial 'trav·el·er viajante m/f de comercio

com·mis·e·rate [kə'mɪzəreɪt] v/i: **she commiserated with me on my failure to get the job** me dijo cuánto sentía que no hubiera conseguido el trabajo

com·mis·sion [kə'mɪʃn] **1** n (*payment, committee*) comisión f; (*job*) encargo m **2** v/t: **she has been commissioned ...** se le ha encargado ...

com·mit [kə'mɪt] v/t (*pret & pp committed*) *crime* cometer; *money* comprometer; **commit o.s.** comprometerse

com·mit·ment [kə'mɪtmənt] compromiso m (**to** con); **he's afraid of commitment** tiene miedo de comprometerse

com·mit·tee [kə'mɪtɪ] comité m

com·mod·i·ty [kə'mɑːdətɪ] *raw material* producto m básico; *product* bien m de consumo

com·mon ['kɑːmən] adj común, *in common* al igual (**with** que); **have sth in common with s.o.** tener algo en común con alguien

com·mon 'law wife esposa f de hecho

com·mon·ly ['kɑːmənlɪ] adv comúnmente

Com·mon 'Mar·ket Mercado m Común

'**com·mon·place** adj común

Com·mons ['kɑːmənz] npl: **the Commons** *in Britain* la Cámara de los Co-

munes
com·mon 'sense sentido *m* común
com·mo·tion [kə'mouʃn] alboroto *m*
com·mu·nal [kə'mjuːnl] *adj* comunal
com·mu·nal·ly [kəm'juːnəlɪ] *adv* en comunidad
com·mu·ni·cate [kə'mjuːnɪkeɪt] **1** *v/i* comunicarse **2** *v/t* comunicar
com·mu·ni·ca·tion [kəmjuːnɪ'keɪʃn] comunicación *f*
com·mu·ni·ca·tions *npl* comunicaciones *fpl*
com·mu·ni·ca·tions sat·el·lite satélite *m* de telecomunicaciones
com·mu·ni·ca·tive [kə'mjuːnɪkətɪv] *adj person* comunicativo
Com·mu·nion [kə'mjuːnjən] REL comunión *f*
com·mu·ni·qué [kə'mjuːnɪkeɪ] comunicado *m*
Com·mu·nism ['kɑːmjʊnɪzəm] comunismo *m*
Com·mu·nist ['kɑːmjʊnɪst] **1** *adj* comunista **2** *n* comunista *m/f*
com·mu·ni·ty [kə'mjuːnətɪ] comunidad *f*
com·mu·ni·ty cen·ter centro *m* comunitario
com·mu·ni·ty serv·ice servicios *mpl* a la comunidad (como pena)
com·mute [kə'mjuːt] **1** *v/i* viajar al trabajo; *commute to work* viajar al trabajo **2** *v/t* LAW conmutar
com·mut·er [kə'mjuːtər] persona que viaja al trabajo
com·mut·er traf·fic *tráfico generado por los que se desplazan al trabajo*
com·mut·er train *tren de cercanías que utilizan los que se desplazan al trabajo*
com·pact **1** *adj* [kəm'pækt] compacto **2** *n* ['kɑːmpækt] MOT utilitario *m*
com·pact 'disc (disco *m*) compacto *m*
com·pan·ion [kəm'pænjən] compañero(-a) *m(f)*
com·pan·ion·ship [kəm'pænjənʃɪp] compañía *f*
com·pa·ny ['kʌmpənɪ] COM empresa *f*, compañía *f*; (*companionship, guests*) compañía *f*; *keep s.o. company* hacer compañía a alguien
com·pa·ny 'car coche *m* de empresa
com·pa·ny 'law derecho *m* de sociedades
com·pa·ra·ble ['kɑːmpərəbl] *adj* comparable
com·par·a·tive [kəm'pærətɪv] **1** *adj* (*relative*) relativo; *study* comparado; GRAM comparativo; *comparative form* GRAM comparativo *m* **2** *n* GRAM comparativo *m*
com·par·a·tive·ly [kəm'pærətɪvlɪ] *adv* relativamente

com·pare [kəm'per] **1** *v/t* comparar; *compared with ...* comparado con ...; *you can't compare them* no se pueden comparar **2** *v/i* compararse
com·pa·ri·son [kəm'pærɪsn] comparación *f*; *there's no comparison* no hay punto de comparación
com·part·ment [kəm'pɑːrtmənt] compartimento *m*
com·pass ['kʌmpəs] brújula *f*; (*a pair of*) *compasses* GEOM un compás
com·pas·sion [kəm'pæʃn] compasión *f*
com·pas·sion·ate [kəm'pæʃənət] *adj* compasivo
com·pas·sion·ate 'leave *permiso laboral por muerte o enfermedad grave de un familiar*
com·pat·i·bil·i·ty [kəmpætə'bɪlɪtɪ] compatibilidad *f*
com·pat·i·ble [kəm'pætəbl] *adj* compatible; *we're not compatible* no somos compatibles
com·pel [kəm'pel] *v/t* (*pret & pp compelled*) obligar
com·pel·ling [kəm'pelɪŋ] *adj argument* poderoso; *movie, book* fascinante
com·pen·sate ['kɑːmpənseɪt] **1** *v/t with money* compensar **2** *v/i* *compensate for* compensar
com·pen·sa·tion [kɑːmpən'seɪʃn] (*money*) indemnización *f*; (*reward, comfort*) compensación *f*
com·pete [kəm'piːt] *v/i* competir (*for* por)
com·pe·tence ['kɑːmpɪtəns] competencia *f*
com·pe·tent ['kɑːmpɪtənt] *adj* competente; *I'm not competent to judge* no estoy capacitado para juzgar
com·pe·tent·ly ['kɑːmpɪtəntlɪ] *adv* competentemente
com·pe·ti·tion [kɑːmpə'tɪʃn] (*contest*) concurso *m*; SP competición *f*; (*competitors*) competencia *f*; *the government wants to encourage competition* el gobierno quiere fomentar la competencia
com·pet·i·tive [kəm'petətɪv] *adj* competitivo
com·pet·i·tive·ly [kəm'petətɪvlɪ] *adv* competitivamente; *competitively priced* con un precio muy competitivo
com·pet·i·tive·ness [kəm'petɪtɪvnɪs] COM competitividad *f*; *of person* espíritu *m* competitivo
com·pet·i·tor [kəm'petɪtər] *in contest* concursante *m/f*; SP competidor(a) *m(f)*, contrincante *m/f*; COM competidor(a) *m(f)*
com·pile [kəm'paɪl] *v/t* compilar

com·pla·cen·cy [kəm'pleɪsənsɪ] complacencia f

com·pla·cent [kəm'pleɪsənt] adj complaciente

com·plain [kəm'pleɪn] v/i quejarse, protestar; *to shop, manager* quejarse; ***complain of*** MED estar aquejado de

com·plaint [kəm'pleɪnt] queja f, protesta f; MED dolencia f

com·ple·ment ['kɑːmplɪmənt] v/t complementar; ***they complement each other*** se complementan

com·ple·men·ta·ry [kɑːmplɪ'mentərɪ] adj complementario; ***the two are complementary*** los dos se complementan

com·plete [kəm'pliːt] 1 adj (*total*) absoluto, total; (*full*) completo; (*finished*) finalizado, terminado; ***I made a complete fool of myself*** quedé como un verdadero tonto 2 v/t *task, building etc* finalizar, terminar; *course* completar; *form* rellenar

com·plete·ly [kəm'pliːtlɪ] adv completamente

com·ple·tion [kəm'pliːʃn] finalización f, terminación f

com·plex ['kɑːmpleks] 1 adj complejo 2 n *also* PSYCH complejo m

com·plex·ion [kəm'plekʃn] *facial* tez f

com·plex·i·ty [kəm'pleksɪtɪ] complejidad f

com·pli·ance [kəm'plaɪəns] cumplimiento (**with** de)

com·pli·cate ['kɑːmplɪkeɪt] v/t complicar

com·pli·cat·ed ['kɑːmplɪkeɪtɪd] adj complicado

com·pli·ca·tion [kɑːmplɪ'keɪʃn] complicación f; ***complications*** MED complicaciones f/pl

com·pli·ment ['kɑːmplɪmənt] 1 n cumplido m 2 v/t hacer un cumplido a (**on** por)

com·pli·men·ta·ry [kɑːmplɪ'mentərɪ] adj elogioso; (*free*) de regalo, gratis

'com·pli·ments slip nota f de cortesía

com·ply [kəm'plaɪ] v/i (*pret & pp **complied***) cumplir; ***comply with*** cumplir

com·po·nent [kəm'pəʊnənt] pieza f, componente m

com·pose [kəm'pəʊz] v/t *also* MUS componer; ***be composed of*** estar compuesto de; ***compose o.s.*** serenarse

com·posed [kəm'pəʊzd] adj (*calm*) sereno

com·pos·er [kəm'pəʊzər] MUS compositor(a) m(f)

com·po·si·tion [kɑːmpə'zɪʃn] *also* MUS composición f; (*essay*) redacción f

com·po·sure [kəm'pəʊʒər] compostura f

com·pound ['kɑːmpaʊnd] n CHEM compuesto m

com·pound 'in·ter·est interés m compuesto *or* combinado

com·pre·hend [kɑːmprɪ'hend] v/t (*understand*) comprender

com·pre·hen·sion [kɑːmprɪ'henʃn] comprensión f

com·pre·hen·sive [kɑːmprɪ'hensɪv] adj detallado

com·pre·hen·sive in'sur·ance seguro m a todo riesgo

com·pre·hen·sive·ly [kɑːmprɪ'hensɪvlɪ] adv detalladamente

com·press 1 n ['kɑːmpres] MED compresa f 2 v/t [kəm'pres] *air, gas* comprimir; *information* condensar

com·prise [kəm'praɪz] v/t comprender; ***be comprised of*** constar de

com·pro·mise ['kɑːmprəmaɪz] 1 n solución f negociada; ***I've had to make compromises all my life*** toda mi vida he tenido que hacer concesiones 2 v/i transigir, efectuar concesiones 3 v/t *principles* traicionar; (*jeopardize*) poner en peligro; ***compromise o.s.*** ponerse en un compromiso

com·pul·sion [kəm'pʌlʃn] PSYCH compulsión f

com·pul·sive [kəm'pʌlsɪv] adj *behavior* compulsivo; *reading* absorbente

com·pul·so·ry [kəm'pʌlsərɪ] adj obligatorio

com·put·er [kəm'pjuːtər] *Span* ordenador m, *L.Am.* computadora f; ***have sth on computer*** tener algo en el *Span* ordenador *or L.Am.* computadora

com·put·er-aid·ed de'sign [kəmpjuːtər'eɪdɪd] diseño m asistido por *Span* ordenador *or L.Am.* computadora

com·put·er-aid·ed man·u'fac·ture fabricación f asistida por *Span* ordenador *or L.Am.* computadora

com·put·er-con'trolled adj controlado por *Span* ordenador *or L.Am.* computadora

com'put·er game juego m de *Span* ordenador *or L.Am.* computadora

com·put·er·ize [kəm'pjuːtəraɪz] v/t informatizar, *L.Am.* computarizar

com·put·er 'lit·er·ate adj con conocimientos de informática *or L.Am.* computación

com·put·er 'sci·ence informática f, *L.Am.* computación f

com·put·er 'sci·en·tist informático(-a) m(f)

com·put·ing [kəm'pjuːtɪŋ] n informática f, *L.Am.* computación f

com·rade ['kɑːmreɪd] (*friend*) compañero(-a) m(f); POL camarada m/f

com·rade·ship ['kɒ:mreɪdʃɪp] camaradería *f*

con [kɒn] **1** n F timo *m* F **2** *v/t* (*pret & pp* **conned**) F timar F

con·ceal [kən'siːl] *v/t* ocultar

con·ceal·ment [kən'siːlmənt] ocultación *f*

con·cede [kən'siːd] *v/t* (*admit*) admitir, reconocer; *goal* encajar

con·ceit [kən'siːt] engreimiento *m*, presunción *f*

con·ceit·ed [kən'siːtɪd] *adj* engreído, presuntuoso

con·cei·va·ble [kən'siːvəbl] *adj* concebible

con·ceive [kən'siːv] *v/i of woman* concebir; *conceive of* (*imagine*) imaginar; *I can't conceive of that happening* no puedo imaginar que eso vaya a pasar

con·cen·trate ['kɒ:nsəntreɪt] **1** *v/i* concentrarse **2** *v/t one's attention, energies* concentrar

con·cen·trat·ed ['kɒ:nsəntreɪtɪd] *adj juice etc* concentrado

con·cen·tra·tion [kɒ:nsən'treɪʃn] concentración *f*

con·cept ['kɒ:nsept] concepto *m*

con·cep·tion [kən'sepʃn] *of child* concepción *f*

con·cern [kən'sɜːrn] **1** n (*anxiety, care*) preocupación *f*; (*business*) asunto *m*; (*company*) empresa *f*; *it's none of your concern* no es asunto tuyo; *cause concern* preocupar, inquietar **2** *v/t* (*involve*) concernir, incumbir; (*worry*) preocupar, inquietar; *concern o.s. with* preocuparse de

con·cerned [kən'sɜːrnd] *adj* (*anxious*) preocupado, inquieto (*about* por); (*caring*) preocupado (*about* por); (*involved*) en cuestión; *as far as I'm concerned* por lo que a mí respecta

con·cern·ing [kən'sɜːrnɪŋ] *prep* en relación con, sobre

con·cert ['kɒ:nsərt] concierto *m*

con·cert·ed [kən'sɜːrtɪd] *adj* (*joint*) concertado, conjunto

'con·cert·mas·ter primer violín *m/f*

con·cer·to [kən'tʃertoʊ] concierto *m*

con·ces·sion [kən'seʃn] (*compromise*) concesión *f*

con·cil·i·a·to·ry [kənsɪlɪ'eɪtərɪ] *adj* conciliador

con·cise [kən'saɪs] *adj* conciso

con·clude [kən'kluːd] *v/t & v/i* (*deduce, end*) concluir (*from* de)

con·clu·sion [kən'kluːʒn] (*deduction*) conclusión *f*; (*end*) conclusión *f*; *in conclusion* en conclusión

con·clu·sive [kən'kluːsɪv] *adj* concluyente

con·coct [kən'kɒ:kt] *v/t meal, drink* preparar; *excuse, story* urdir

con·coc·tion [kən'kɒ:kʃn] *food* mejunje *m*; *drink* brebaje *m*, pócima *f*

con·crete ['kɒ:ŋkriːt] **1** *adj* concreto; *concrete jungle* jungla *f* de asfalto **2** n hormigón *m*, *L.Am.* concreto *m*

con·cur [kən'kɜːr] *v/i* (*pret & pp* **concurred**) coincidir

con·cus·sion [kən'kʌʃn] conmoción *f* cerebral

con·demn [kən'dem] *v/t* condenar; *building* declarar en ruina; *condemn s.o. to a life of poverty* condenar a alguien a vivir en la miseria

con·dem·na·tion [kɒ:ndəm'neɪʃn] *of action* condena *f*

con·den·sa·tion [kɒ:nden'seɪʃn] *on walls, windows* condensación *f*

con·dense [kən'dens] **1** *v/t* (*make shorter*) condensar **2** *v/i of steam* condensarse

con·densed 'milk [kən'densd] leche *f* condensada

con·de·scend [kɒ:ndɪ'send] *v/i: he condescended to speak to me* se dignó a hablarme

con·de·scend·ing [kɒ:ndɪ'sendɪŋ] *adj* (*patronizing*) condescendiente

con·di·tion [kən'dɪʃn] **1** n (*state*) condiciones *fpl*; *of health* estado *m*; *illness* enfermedad *f*; (*requirement, term*) condición *f*; *conditions* (*circumstances*) condiciones *fpl*; *on condition that ...* a condición de que ...; *you're in no condition to drive* no estás en condiciones de conducir **2** *v/t* PSYCH condicionar

con·di·tion·al [kən'dɪʃnl] **1** *adj* acceptance condicional **2** n GRAM condicional *m*

con·di·tion·er [kən'dɪʃnər] *for hair* suavizante *m*, acondicionador *m*; *for fabric* suavizante *m*

con·di·tion·ing [kən'dɪʃnɪŋ] PSYCH condicionamiento *m*

con·do ['kɒ:ndoʊ] F *apartment* apartamento *m*, *Span* piso *m*; *building* bloque de apartamentos

con·do·lences [kən'doʊlənsɪz] *npl* condolencias *fpl*

con·dom ['kɒ:ndəm] condón *m*, preservativo *m*

con·do·min·i·um [kɒ:ndə'mɪnɪəm] → *condo*

con·done [kən'doʊn] *v/t actions* justificar

con·du·cive [kən'duːsɪv] *adj: conducive to* propicio para

con·duct 1 n ['kɒ:ndʌkt] (*behavior*) conducta *f* **2** *v/t* ['kɒ:ndʌkt] (*carry out*) realizar, hacer; ELEC conducir; MUS dirigir; **conduct o.s.** comportarse

con·duct·ed 'tour [kən'dʌktɪd] visita f guiada

con·duc·tor [kən'dʌktər] MUS director(a) m(f) de orquesta; *on train* revisor(-a) m(f); PHYS conductor m

cone [kəʊn] GEOM, *on highway* cono m; *for ice cream* cucurucho m; *of pine tree* piña f

con·fec·tion·er [kən'fekʃənər] pastelero(-a) m(f)

con·fec·tion·ers' sug·ar azúcar m or f glas

con·fec·tion·e·ry [kən'fekʃənrɪ] *(candy)* dulces mpl

con·fed·e·ra·tion [kənfedə'reɪʃn] confederación f

con·fer [kən'fɜːr] **1** v/t *(pret & pp conferred) confer sth on s.o. (bestow)* conferir or otorgar algo a alguien **2** v/i *(pret & pp conferred) (discuss)* deliberar

con·fe·rence ['kɑːnfərəns] congreso m; *discussion* conferencia f

con·fe·rence room sala f de conferencias

con·fess [kən'fes] **1** v/t confesar; *I confess I don't know* confieso que no lo sé **2** v/i confesar; REL confesarse; *confess to a weakness for sth* confesar una debilidad por algo

con·fes·sion [kən'feʃn] confesión f; *I've a confession to make* tengo algo que confesar

con·fes·sion·al [kən'feʃnl] REL confesionario m

con·fes·sor [kən'fesər] REL confesor m

con·fide [kən'faɪd] v/t confiar **2** v/i: *confide in s.o.* confiarse a alguien

con·fi·dence ['kɑːnfɪdəns] confianza f; *(secret)* confidencia f; *in confidence* en confianza, confidencialmente

con·fi·dent ['kɑːnfɪdənt] adj *(self-assured)* seguro de sí mismo; *(convinced)* seguro

con·fi·den·tial [kɑːnfɪ'denʃl] adj confidencial, secreto

con·fi·den·tial·ly [kɑːnfɪ'denʃlɪ] adv confidencialmente

con·fi·dent·ly ['kɑːnfɪdəntlɪ] adv con seguridad

con·fine [kən'faɪn] v/t *(imprison)* confinar, recluir; *(restrict)* limitar; *be confined to one's bed* tener que guardar cama

con·fined [kən'faɪnd] adj *space* limitado

con·fine·ment [kən'faɪnmənt] *(imprisonment)* reclusión f; MED parto m

con·firm [kən'fɜːrm] v/t confirmar

con·fir·ma·tion [kɑːnfər'meɪʃn] confir-

mación f

con·firmed [kən'fɜːrmd] adj *(inveterate)* empedernido; *I'm a confirmed believer in ...* creo firmemente en ...

con·fis·cate ['kɑːnfɪskeɪt] v/t confiscar

con·flict 1 n ['kɑːnflɪkt] conflicto m **2** v/i [kən'flɪkt] *(clash)* chocar; *conflicting loyalties* lealtades fpl encontradas

con·form [kən'fɔːrm] v/i ser conformista; *conform to standards etc* ajustarse a

con·form·ist [kən'fɔːrmɪst] n conformista m/f

con·front [kən'frʌnt] v/t *(face)* hacer frente a, enfrentarse; *(tackle)* hacer frente a

con·fron·ta·tion [kɑːnfrən'teɪʃn] confrontación f, enfrentamiento m

con·fuse [kən'fjuːz] v/t confundir; *confuse s.o. with s.o.* confundir a alguien con alguien

con·fused [kən'fjuːzd] adj *person* confundido; *situation, piece of writing* confuso

con·fus·ing [kən'fjuːzɪŋ] adj confuso

con·fu·sion [kən'fjuːʒn] *(muddle, chaos)* confusión f

con·geal [kən'dʒiːl] v/i *of blood* coagularse; *of fat* solidificarse

con·gen·ial [kən'dʒiːnɪəl] adj *person* simpático, agradable; *occasion, place* agradable

con·gen·i·tal [kən'dʒenɪtl] adj MED congénito

con·gest·ed [kən'dʒestɪd] adj *roads* congestionado

con·ges·tion [kən'dʒestʃn] *also* MED congestión f; *traffic congestion* congestión f circulatoria

con·grat·u·late [kən'grætʃʊleɪt] v/t felicitar

con·grat·u·la·tions [kəngrætʃʊ'leɪʃnz] npl felicitaciones fpl; *congratulations on ...* felicidades por ...; *let me offer my congratulations* permita que le dé la enhorabuena

con·grat·u·la·to·ry [kəngrætʃʊ'leɪtərɪ] adj de felicitación

con·gre·gate ['kɑːngrɪgeɪt] v/i *(gather)* congregarse

con·gre·ga·tion [kɑːngrɪ'geɪʃn] REL congregación f

con·gress ['kɑːngres] *(conference)* congreso m; *Congress in US* Congreso m

Con·gres·sion·al [kən'greʃnl] adj del Congreso

Con·gress·man ['kɑːngresmən] congresista m

Con·gress·wo·man ['kɑːngreswʊmən] congresista f

C

con·ni·fer ['kɑːnɪfər] conífera f

con·jec·ture [kən'dʒektʃər] n (*speculation*) conjetura f

con·ju·gate ['kɑːndʒugeɪt] v/t GRAM conjugar

con·junc·tion [kən'dʒʌŋkʃn] GRAM conjunción f; **in conjunction with** junto con

con·junc·ti·tis [kəndʒʌŋktɪ'vaɪtɪs] conjuntivitis f

◆ con·jure up ['kɑːndʒər] v/t (*produce*) hacer aparecer; (*evoke*) evocar

con·jur·er, con·jur·or ['kʌndʒərər] (*magician*) prestidigitador(a) m(f)

con·jur·ing tricks ['kʌndʒərɪŋ] npl juegos mpl de manos

con man ['kɑːnmæn] F timador m F

con·nect [kə'nekt] v/t conectar; (*link*) relacionar, vincular; **to power supply** enchufar

con·nect·ed [kə'nektɪd] adj: **be well-connected** estar bien relacionado; **be connected with** estar relacionado con

con·nect·ing flight [kə'nektɪŋ] vuelo m de conexión

con·nec·tion [kə'nekʃn] conexión f; *when traveling* conexión f, enlace; (*personal contact*) contacto m; **in connection with** en relación con

con·nois·seur [kɑːnə'sɜːr] entendido(-a) m(f)

con·quer ['kɑːŋkər] v/t conquistar; *fig: fear etc* vencer

con·quer·or ['kɑːŋkərər] conquistador(a) m(f)

con·quest ['kɑːŋkwest] *of territory* conquista f

con·science ['kɑːnʃəns] conciencia f; **a guilty conscience** un sentimiento de culpa; **it was on my conscience** me remordía la conciencia

con·sci·en·tious [kɑːnʃɪ'enʃəs] adj concienzudo

con·sci·en·tious·ness [kɑːnʃɪ'enʃəsnəs] aplicación f

con·sci·en·tious ob·ject·or [kɑːnʃɪ'enʃəs] objetor(a) m(f) de conciencia

con·scious ['kɑːnʃəs] adj consciente; **be conscious of** ser consciente de

con·scious·ly ['kɑːnʃəslɪ] adv conscientemente

con·scious·ness ['kɑːnʃəsnɪs] (*awareness*) conciencia f; MED con(s)ciencia f; **lose / regain consciousness** quedar inconsciente / volver en sí

con·sec·u·tive [kən'sekjutɪv] adj consecutivo

con·sen·sus [kən'sensəs] consenso m

con·sent [kən'sent] **1** n consentimiento m **2** v/i consentir (**to** en)

con·se·quence ['kɑːnsɪkwəns] (*result*) consecuencia f; **as a consequence o** como consecuencia de

con·se·quent·ly ['kɑːnsɪkwəntlɪ] adv (*therefore*) por consiguiente

con·ser·va·tion [kɑːnsər'veɪʃn] (*preser vation*) conservación f, protección f

con·ser·va·tion·ist [kɑːnsər'veɪʃnɪst] ecologista m/f

con·ser·va·tive [kən'sɜːrvətɪv] **1** adj (*conventional*) conservador; *estimat* prudente **2** n Br POL **Conservative** Con servador(a) m(f)

con·ser·va·to·ry [kən'sɜːrvətɔːrɪ] MU conservatorio m

con·serve **1** n ['kɑːnsɜːrv] (*jam*) compota f **2** v/t [kən'sɜːrv] conservar

con·sid·er [kən'sɪdər] v/t (*regard*) consid erar; (*show regard for*) mostrar consider ación por; (*think about*) considerar; **it i considered to be ...** se considera que e ...

con·sid·e·ra·ble [kən'sɪdrəbl] adj consid erable

con·sid·e·ra·bly [kən'sɪdrəblɪ] adv con siderablemente

con·sid·er·ate [kən'sɪdərət] adj consider ado

con·sid·er·ate·ly [kən'sɪdərətlɪ] adv cor consideración

con·sid·e·ra·tion [kənsɪdə'reɪʃn] (*thoughtfulness, concern*) consideració f; (*factor*) factor m; **take sth into cons deration** tomar algo en consideración **after much consideration** tras mucha deliberaciones; **your proposal is unde consideration** su propuesta está siend estudiada

con·sign·ment [kən'saɪnmənt] COM envío m

◆ con·sist of [kən'sɪst] v/t consistir en

con·sis·ten·cy [kən'sɪstənsɪ] (*texture* consistencia f; (*unchangingness*) coher encia f, consecuencia f; *of player* regular idad f, constancia f

con·sis·tent [kən'sɪstənt] adj person co herente, consecuente; *improvement change* constante

con·sis·tent·ly [kən'sɪstəntlɪ] adv per form con regularidad or constancia; *im prove* continuamente; **he's consistently late** llega tarde sistemáticamente

con·so·la·tion [kɑːnsə'leɪʃn] consuelo m **if it's any consolation** si te sirve de con suelo

con·sole [kən'soul] v/t consolar

con·sol·i·date [kən'sɑːlɪdeɪt] v/t consoli dar

con·so·nant ['kɑːnsənənt] n GRAM consonante *f*

con·sor·ti·um [kənˈsɔːrtiəm] consorcio *m*

con·spic·u·ous [kənˈspɪkjuəs] *adj* llamativo; *he felt very conspicuous* sentía que estaba llamando la atención

con·spi·ra·cy [kənˈspɪrəsɪ] conspiración *f*

con·spi·ra·tor [kənˈspɪrətər] conspirador(a) *m(f)*

con·spire [kənˈspaɪr] *v/i* conspirar

con·stant [ˈkɑːnstənt] *adj* (*continuous*) constante

con·stant·ly [ˈkɑːnstəntlɪ] *adv* constantemente

con·ster·na·tion [kɑːnstərˈneɪʃn] consternación *f*

con·sti·pat·ed [ˈkɑːnstɪpeɪtɪd] *adj* estreñido

con·sti·pa·tion [kɑːnstɪˈpeɪʃn] estreñimiento *m*

con·sti·tu·ent [kənˈstɪtjuənt] *n* (*component*) elemento *m* constitutivo, componente *m*

con·sti·tute [ˈkɑːnstɪtuːt] *v/t* constituir

con·sti·tu·tion [kɑːnstɪˈtuːʃn] constitución *f*

con·sti·tu·tion·al [kɑːnstɪˈtuːʃənl] *adj* POL constitucional

con·straint [kənˈstreɪnt] (*restriction*) restricción *f*, límite *m*

con·struct [kənˈstrʌkt] *v/t building etc* construir

con·struc·tion [kənˈstrʌkʃn] construcción *f*; *under construction* en construcción

con'struc·tion in·dus·try sector *m* de la construcción

con'struc·tion site obra *f*

con'struc·tion work·er obrero(-a) *m(f)* de la construcción

con·struc·tive [kənˈstrʌktɪv] *adj* constructivo

con·sul [ˈkɑːnsl] cónsul *m/f*

con·su·late [ˈkɑːnsʊlət] consulado *m*

con·sult [kənˈsʌlt] *v/t* (*seek the advice of*) consultar

con·sul·tan·cy [kənˈsʌltənsɪ] *company* consultoría *f*, asesoría *f*; (*advice*) asesoramiento *m*

con·sul·tant [kənˈsʌltənt] *n* (*adviser*) asesor(a) *m(f)*, consultor(a) *m(f)*

con·sul·ta·tion [kɑːnslˈteɪʃn] consulta *f*; *have a consultation with* consultar con

con·sume [kənˈsuːm] *v/t* consumir

con·sum·er [kənˈsuːmər] (*purchaser*) consumidor(a) *m(f)*

con·sum·er 'con·fi·dence confianza *f* de los consumidores

con·sum·er goods *npl* bienes *mpl* de consumo

con·sum·er so·ci·e·ty sociedad *f* de consumo

con·sump·tion [kənˈsʌmpʃn] consumo *m*

con·tact [ˈkɑːntækt] **1** *n* contacto; *keep in contact with s.o.* mantenerse en contacto con alguien; *come into contact with s.o.* entrar en contacto con alguien **2** *v/t* contactar con, ponerse en contacto con

'con·tact lens lentes *fpl* de contacto, *Span* lentillas *fpl*

'con·tact num·ber número *m* de contacto

con·ta·gious [kənˈteɪdʒəs] *adj also fig* contagioso

con·tain [kənˈteɪn] *v/t* (*hold, hold back*) contener; *contain o.s.* contenerse

con·tain·er [kənˈteɪnər] (*recipient*) recipiente *m*; COM contenedor *m*

con'tain·er ship buque *m* de transporte de contenedores

con·tam·i·nate [kənˈtæmɪneɪt] *v/t* contaminar

con·tam·i·na·tion [kəntæmɪˈneɪʃn] contaminación *f*

con·tem·plate [ˈkɑːntəmpleɪt] *v/t* contemplar

con·tem·po·ra·ry [kənˈtempərərɪ] **1** *adj* contemporáneo **2** *n* contemporáneo(-a) *m(f)*

con·tempt [kənˈtempt] desprecio *m*, desdén *m*; *be beneath contempt* ser despreciable

con·temp·ti·ble [kənˈtemptəbl] *adj* despreciable

con·temp·tu·ous [kənˈtemptʃuəs] *adj* despectivo

con·tend [kənˈtend] *v/i*: *contend for ...* competir por ...; *contend with* enfrentarse a

con·tend·er [kənˈtendər] SP, POL contendiente *m/f*; *against champion* aspirante *m/f*

con·tent¹ [ˈkɑːntent] *n* contenido *m*

con·tent² [kənˈtent] **1** *adj* satisfecho; *I'm quite content to sit here* me contento con sentarme aquí **2** *v/t*: *content o.s. with* contentarse con

con·tent·ed [kənˈtentɪd] *adj* satisfecho

con·ten·tion [kənˈtenʃn] (*assertion*) argumento *m*; *be in contention for* tener posibilidades de ganar

con·ten·tious [kənˈtenʃəs] *adj* polémico

con·tent·ment [kənˈtentmənt] satisfacción *f*

con·tents [ˈkɑːntents] *npl of house, letter, bag etc* contenido *m*; *list: in book* tabla *f* de contenidos

con·test¹ [ˈkɑːntest] *n* (*competition*) concurso *m*; (*struggle, for power*) lucha *f*

con·test² [kən'test] v/t leadership etc presentarse como candidato a; decision, will impugnar

con·tes·tant [kən'testənt] concursante m/f; in competition competidor(a) m(f)

con·text ['kɑ:ntekst] contexto m; **look at sth in context / out of context** examinar algo en contexto / fuera de contexto

con·ti·nent ['kɑ:ntɪnənt] n continente m

con·ti·nen·tal [kɑ:ntɪ'nentl] adj continental

con·tin·gen·cy [kən'tɪndʒənsɪ] contingencia f, eventualidad f

con·tin·u·al [kən'tɪnjuəl] adj continuo

con·tin·u·al·ly [kən'tɪnjuəlɪ] adv continuamente

con·tin·u·a·tion [kəntɪnju'eɪʃn] continuación f

con·tin·ue [kən'tɪnju:] **1** v/t continuar; **to be continued** continuará; **he continued to drink** continuó bebiendo **2** v/i continuar

con·ti·nu·i·ty [kɑ:ntɪ'nju:ətɪ] continuidad f

con·tin·u·ous [kən'tɪnjuəs] adj continuo

con·tin·u·ous·ly [kən'tɪnjuəslɪ] adv continuamente, ininterrumpidamente

con·tort [kən'tɔ:rt] v/t face contraer; body contorsionar

con·tour ['kɑ:ntʊr] contorno m

con·tra·cep·tion [kɑ:ntrə'sepʃn] anticoncepción f

con·tra·cep·tive [kɑ:ntrə'septɪv] n (device, pill) anticonceptivo m

con·tract¹ ['kɑ:ntrækt] n contrato m

con·tract² [kən'trækt] **1** v/i (shrink) contraerse **2** v/t illness contraer

con·trac·tor [kən'træktər] contratista m/f; **building contractor** constructora f

con·trac·tu·al [kən'træktuəl] adj contractual

con·tra·dict [kɑ:ntrə'dɪkt] v/t statement desmentir; person contradecir

con·tra·dic·tion [kɑ:ntrə'dɪkʃn] contradicción f

con·tra·dic·to·ry [kɑ:ntrə'dɪktərɪ] adj account contradictorio

con·trap·tion [kən'træpʃn] F artilugio m F

con·trar·y¹ ['kɑ:ntrərɪ] **1** adj contrario; **contrary to** al contrario de **2** n: **on the contrary** al contrario

con·tra·ry² [kən'trerɪ] adj (perverse) difícil

con·trast 1 n ['kɑ:ntræst] contraste m; **by contrast** por contraste **2** v/t & v/i [kən'træst] contrastar

con·trast·ing [kən'træstɪŋ] adj opuesto

con·tra·vene [kɑ:ntrə'vi:n] v/t contravenir

con·trib·ute [kən'trɪbju:t] **1** v/i contribuir (**to** a) **2** v/t money, time, suggestion contribuir con, aportar

con·tri·bu·tion [kɑ:ntrɪ'bju:ʃn] money contribución f; to political party, church donación f; of time, effort, to debate contribución f, aportación f; to magazine colaboración f

con·trib·u·tor [kən'trɪbjutər] of money donante m/f; to magazine colaborador(a) m(f)

con·trol [kən'troul] **1** n control m; **take / lose control of** tomar / perder el control de; **lose control of o.s.** perder el control; **circumstances beyond our control** circunstancias ajenas a nuestra voluntad; **be in control of** controlar; **we're in control of the situation** tenemos la situación controlada or bajo control; **get out of control** descontrolarse; **under control** bajo control; **controls** of aircraft, vehicle controles mpl; (restrictions) controles mpl **2** v/t (pret & pp **controlled**) (govern) controlar, dominar; (restrict, regulate) controlar; **control o.s.** controlarse

con'trol cen·ter, Br **con'trol centre** centro m de control

con'trol freak F persona obsesionada con controlar todo

con·trolled 'sub·stance [kən'trould] estupefaciente m

con·trol·ling 'in·ter·est [kən'troulɪŋ] FIN participación f mayoritaria, interés m mayoritario

con'trol pan·el panel m de control

con'trol tow·er torre f de control

con·tro·ver·sial [kɑ:ntrə'vɜ:rʃl] adj polémico, controvertido

con·tro·ver·sy ['kɑ:ntrəvɜ:rsɪ] polémica f, controversia f

con·va·lesce [kɑ:nvə'les] v/i convalecer

con·va·les·cence [kɑ:nvə'lesns] convalecencia f

con·vene [kən'vi:n] v/t convocar

con·ve·ni·ence [kən'vi:nɪəns] conveniencia f; **at your / my convenience** a su / mi conveniencia; **all (modern) conveniences** todas las comodidades

con've·ni·ence food comida f preparada

con've·ni·ence store tienda f de barrio

con·ve·ni·ent [kən'vi:nɪənt] adj location, device conveniente; time, arrangement oportuno; **it's very convenient living so near the office** vivir cerca de la oficina es muy cómodo; **the apartment is convenient for the station** el apartamento está muy cerca de la estación; **I'm afraid Monday isn't convenient**

me temo que el lunes no me va bien

con·ve·ni·ent·ly [kən'viːnɪəntlɪ] *adv* convenientemente; **conveniently located for theaters** situado cerca de los teatros

con·vent ['kɑːnvənt] convento *m*

con·ven·tion [kən'venʃn] (*tradition*) convención *f*; (*conference*) congreso *m*

con·ven·tion·al [kən'venʃnl] *adj* convencional

con·ven·tion cen·ter palacio *m* de congresos

con·ven·tion·eer [kən'venʃnɪr] congresista *m/f*

◆ **con·verge on** [kən'vɜːrdʒ] *v/t* converger en

con·ver·sant [kən'vɜːrsənt] *adj*: **be conversant with** estar familiarizado con

con·ver·sa·tion [kɑːnvər'seɪʃn] conversación *f*; **make conversation** conversar; **have a conversation** mantener una conversación

con·ver·sa·tion·al [kɑːnvər'seɪʃnl] *adj* coloquial

con·verse ['kɑːnvɜːrs] *n* (*opposite*): **the converse** lo opuesto

con·verse·ly [kən'vɜːrslɪ] *adv* por el contrario

con·ver·sion [kən'vɜːrʃn] conversión *f*

con'ver·sion ta·ble tabla *f* de conversión

con·vert 1 *n* ['kɑːnvɜːrt] converso(-a) *m(f)* (**to** a) 2 *v/t* [kən'vɜːrt] convertir

con·ver·ti·ble [kən'vɜːrtəbl] *n car* descapotable *m*

con·vey [kən'veɪ] *v/t* (*transmit*) transmitir; (*carry*) transportar

con·vey·or belt [kən'veɪər] cinta *f* transportadora

con·vict 1 *n* ['kɑːnvɪkt] convicto(-a) *m(f)* 2 *v/t* [kən'vɪkt] *LAW*: **convict s.o. of sth** declarar a alguien culpable de algo

con·vic·tion [kən'vɪkʃn] *LAW* condena *f*; (*belief*) convicción *f*

con·vince [kən'vɪns] *v/t* convencer: **I'm convinced he's lying** estoy convencido de que miente

con·vinc·ing [kən'vɪnsɪŋ] *adj* convincente

con·viv·i·al [kən'vɪvɪəl] *adj* (*friendly*) agradable

con·voy ['kɑːnvɔɪ] *of ships, vehicles* convoy *m*

con·vul·sion [kən'vʌlʃn] *MED* convulsión *f*

cook [kʊk] 1 *n* cocinero(-a) *m(f)*; **I'm a good cook** soy un buen cocinero, cocino bien 2 *v/t* cocinar; **a cooked meal** una comida caliente; **cook the books** F falsificar las cuentas 3 *v/i* cocinar

'**cook·book** libro *m* de cocina

cook·e·ry ['kʊkərɪ] cocina *f*

cook·ie ['kʊkɪ] galleta *f*

cook·ing ['kʊkɪŋ] *food* cocina *f*

cool [kuːl] 1 *n*: **keep one's cool** F mantener la calma; **lose one's cool** F perder la calma 2 *adj weather, breeze* fresco; *drink* frío; (*calm*) tranquilo, sereno; (*unfriendly*) frío 3 *v/i of food, interest* enfriarse; *of tempers* calmarse 4 *v/t*: **cool it** F cálmate

◆ **cool down** 1 *v/i* enfriarse; *of weather* refrescar; *fig: of tempers* calmarse, tranquilizarse 2 *v/t food* enfriar; *fig* calmar, tranquilizar

cool·ing-'off pe·ri·od fase *f* de reflexión

co·op·e·rate [kouˈɑːpəreɪt] *v/i* cooperar

co·op·e·ra·tion [kouɑːpəˈreɪʃn] cooperación *f*

co·op·e·ra·tive [kouˈɑːpərətɪv] 1 *n* COM cooperativa *f* 2 *adj* COM conjunto; (*helpful*) cooperativo

co·or·di·nate [kouˈɔːrdɪneɪt] *v/t activities* coordinar

co·or·di·na·tion [kouɔːrdɪˈneɪʃn] coordinación *f*

cop [kɑːp] *n* F poli *m/f* F

cope [koʊp] *v/i* arreglárselas; **cope with** poder con

cop·i·er ['kɑːpɪər] *machine* fotocopiadora *f*

co·pi·lot ['koʊpaɪlət] copiloto *m/f*

co·pi·ous ['koʊpɪəs] *adj* copioso

cop·per ['kɑːpər] *n metal* cobre *m*

cop·y ['kɑːpɪ] 1 *n* copia *f*; *of book* ejemplar *m*; *of record, CD* copia *f*; (*written material*) texto *m*; **make a copy of a file** COMPUT hacer una copia de un archivo 2 *v/t* (*pret & pp* **copied**) copiar

'**cop·y·cat** F copión (-ona) *m(f)* F, copiota *m/f* F

'**cop·y·cat crime** delito *m* inspirado en otro

'**cop·y·right** *n* copyright *m*, derechos *mpl* de reproducción

'**cop·y·writ·er** *in advertising* creativo(-a) *m(f)* (*de publicidad*)

cor·al ['kɑːrəl] coral *m*

cord [kɔːrd] (*string*) cuerda *f*, cordel *m*; (*cable*) cable *m*

cor·di·al ['kɔːrdʒəl] *adj* cordial

cord·less 'phone ['kɔːrdlɪs] teléfono *m* inalámbrico

cor·don ['kɔːrdn] cordón *m*

◆ **cordon off** *v/t* acordonar

cords [kɔːrdz] *npl pants* pantalones *mpl* de pana

cor·du·roy ['kɔːrdərɔɪ] pana *f*

core [kɔːr] 1 *n of fruit* corazón *m*; *of problem* meollo *m*; *of organization, party* núcleo *m* 2 *v/t fruit* sacar el corazón a

3 *adj issue, meaning* central

co·ri·an·der ['kɒrɪændər] cilantro *m*

cork [kɔːrk] *in bottle* (tapón *m* de) corcho *m*; *material* corcho *m*

'cork·screw *n* sacacorchos *m inv*

corn [kɔːrn] *grain* maíz *m*

cor·ner ['kɔːrnər] **1** *n of page, street* esquina *f*; *of room* rincón *m*; *(bend: on road)* curva *f*; *in soccer* córner *m*, saque *m* de esquina; *in the corner* en el rincón; *I'll meet you on the corner* te veré en la esquina **2** *v/t person* arrinconar; *corner a market* monopolizar un mercado **3** *v/i of driver, car* girar

'cor·ner kick *in soccer* saque *m* de esquina, córner *m*

'corn·flakes *npl* copos *mpl* de maíz

'corn·starch harina *f* de maíz

corn·y ['kɔːrnɪ] *adj* F *(sentimental)* cursi F; *joke* manido

cor·o·na·ry ['kɒrənerɪ] **1** *adj* coronario **2** *n* infarto *m* de miocardio

cor·o·ner ['kɒrənər] *oficial encargado de investigar muertes sospechosas*

cor·po·ral ['kɔːrpərəl] *n* cabo *m/f*

cor·po·ral 'pun·ish·ment castigo *m* corporal

cor·po·rate ['kɔːrpərət] *adj* COM corporativo, de empresa; *corporate image* imagen *f* corporativa; *corporate loyalty* lealtad *f* a la empresa

cor·po·ra·tion [kɔːrpə'reɪʃn] *(business)* sociedad *f* anónima

corps [kɔːr] *nsg* cuerpo *m*

corpse [kɔːrps] cadáver *m*

cor·pu·lent ['kɔːrpjʊlənt] *adj* corpulento

cor·pus·cle ['kɔːrpʌsl] corpúsculo *m*

cor·ral [kə'ræl] *n* corral *m*

cor·rect [kə'rekt] **1** *adj* correcto; *time* exacto; *you are correct* tiene razón **2** *v/t* corregir

cor·rec·tion [kə'rekʃn] corrección *f*

cor·rect·ly [kə'rektlɪ] *adv* correctamente

cor·re·spond [kɑːrɪ'spɑːnd] *v/i (match)* corresponderse; *correspond to* corresponder a; *correspond with* corresponderse con; *(write letters)* mantener correspondencia con

cor·re·spon·dence [kɑːrɪ'spɑːndəns] *(matching)* correspondencia *f*, relación *f*; *(letters)* correspondencia *f*

cor·re·spon·dent [kɑːrɪ'spɑːndənt] *(letter writer)* correspondiente *m/f*; *(reporter)* corresponsal *m/f*

cor·re·spon·ding [kɑːrɪ'spɑːndɪŋ] *adj (equivalent)* correspondiente

cor·ri·dor ['kɔːrɪdər] *in building* pasillo *m*

cor·rob·o·rate [kə'rɑːbəreɪt] *v/t* corroborar

cor·rode [kə'roʊd] **1** *v/t* corroer **2** *v/i* corroerse

cor·ro·sion [kə'roʊʒn] corrosión *f*

cor·ru·gated 'card·board ['kɑːrəgeɪtɪd] cartón *m* ondulado

cor·ru·gated 'i·ron chapa *f* ondulada

cor·rupt [kə'rʌpt] **1** *adj* corrupto; COMPUT corrompido **2** *v/t* corromper; *(bribe)* sobornar

cor·rup·tion [kə'rʌpʃn] corrupción *f*

cos·met·ic [kɑːz'metɪk] *adj* cosmético; *fig* superficial

cos·met·ics [kɑːz'metɪks] *npl* cosméticos *mpl*

cos·met·ic 'sur·geon especialista *m/f* en cirugía estética

cos·met·ic 'sur·ger·y cirugía *f* estética

cos·mo·naut ['kɑːzmənɔːt] cosmonauta *m/f*

cos·mo·pol·i·tan [kɑːzmə'pɑːlɪtən] *adj city* cosmopolita

cost[1] [kɑːst] **1** *n also fig* costo *m*, *Span* coste *m*; *at all costs* cueste lo que cueste; *I've learnt to my cost* por desgracia he aprendido **2** *v/t (pret & pp cost) money, time* costar; *how much does it cost?* ¿cuánto cuesta?; *it cost me my health* me costó mi salud

cost[2] [kɑːst] *v/t (pret & pp costed)* FIN *proposal, project* estimar el costo de

cost and 'freight COM costo *or Span* coste y flete

Cos·ta Ri·ca ['kɑːstə'riːkə] *n* Costa Rica

Cos·ta Ri·can ['kɑːstə'riːkən] **1** *adj* costarricense **2** *n* costarricense *m/f*

'cost-con·scious *adj* consciente del costo *or Span* coste

'cost-ef·fec·tive *adj* rentable

'cost, in·sur·ance, freight COM costo *or Span* coste, seguro y flete

cost·ly ['kɑːstlɪ] *adj mistake* caro

cost of 'liv·ing costo *m or Span* coste *m* de la vida

cost 'price precio *m* de costo *or Span* coste

cos·tume ['kɑːstuːm] *for actor* traje *m*

cos·tume 'jew·el·ler·y *Br*, **costume 'jew·el·ry** bisutería *f*

'cos·y *Br* → **cozy**

cot [kɑːt] *(camp-bed)* catre *m*

cot·tage ['kɑːtɪdʒ] casa *f* de campo, casita *f*

cot·tage 'cheese queso *m* fresco

cot·ton ['kɑːtn] **1** *n* algodón *m* **2** *adj* de algodón

♦ **cotton on** *v/i* F darse cuenta

♦ **cotton on to** *v/t* F darse cuenta de

♦ **cotton to** *v/t* F: *I never cottoned to her* nunca me cayó bien cot·ton 'can·dy algodón *m* dulce

cot·ton 'wool *Br* algodón *m* (hidrófilo)

couch [kaʊtʃ] *n* sofá *m*

'couch po·ta·to F teleadicto(-a) *m(f)* F

cou·chette [kuːʃet] litera *f*

cough [kɑːf] **1** *n* tos *f*; *to get attention* carraspeo *m* **2** *v/i* toser; *to get attention* carraspear

◆ **cough up** *v/t blood etc* toser; F *money* soltar, *Span* apoquinar F **2** *v/i* F (*pay*) soltar dinero, *Span* apoquinar F

'cough med·i·cine, 'cough syr·up jarabe *m* para la tos

could [kʊd] **1** *v/aux.* **could I have my key?** ¿me podría dar la llave?; **could you help me?** ¿me podrías ayudar?; **this could be our bus** puede que éste sea nuestro autobús; **you could be right** puede que tengas razón; **I couldn't say for sure** no sabría decirlo con seguridad; **he could have got lost** a lo mejor se ha perdido; **you could have warned me!** ¡me podías haber avisado! **2** *pret* → **can¹**

coun·cil ['kaʊnsl] *n* (*assembly*) consejo *m*

'coun·cil·man concejal *m*

coun·cil·or ['kaʊnsələr] concejal(a) *m(f)*

coun·sel ['kaʊnsl] **1** *n* (*advice*) consejo *m*; (*lawyer*) abogado(-a) *m(f)* **2** *v/t course of action* aconsejar; *person* ofrecer apoyo psicológico

coun·sel·ing, *Br* coun·sel·ling ['kaʊnslɪŋ] apoyo *m* psicológico

coun·sel·or *Br*, coun·sel·or ['kaʊnslər] (*adviser*) consejero(-a) *m(f)*; *of student* orientador(a) *m(f)*; LAW abogado(-a) *m(f)*

count¹ [kaʊnt] **1** *n* (*number arrived at*) cuenta *f*; (*action of counting*) recuento *m*; *in baseball, boxing* cuenta *f*; **what is your count?** ¿cuántos has contado?; **keep count of** llevar la cuenta de; **lose count of** perder la cuenta de; **at the last count** en el último recuento **2** *v/i to ten etc* contar; (*be important*) contar; (*qualify*) contar, valer **3** *v/t* contar

◆ **count on** *v/t* contar con

count² [kaʊnt] *nobleman* conde *m*

'count·down cuenta *f* atrás

coun·te·nance ['kaʊntənəns] *v/t* tolerar

coun·ter¹ ['kaʊntər] *n in shop* mostrador *m*; *in café* barra *f*; *in game* ficha *f*

coun·ter² ['kaʊntər] **1** *v/t* contrarrestar **2** *v/i* (*retaliate*) responder

coun·ter³ ['kaʊntər] *adv*: **run counter to** estar en contra de

'coun·ter·act *v/t* contrarrestar

coun·ter·at'tack **1** *n* contraataque *m* **2** *v/i* contraatacar

'coun·ter·bal·ance **1** *n* contrapeso *m* **2** *v/t*

contrarrestar, contrapesar

coun·ter'clock·wise *adv* en sentido contrario al de las agujas del reloj

coun·ter·es·pi·o·nage contraespionaje *m*

coun·ter·feit ['kaʊntərfɪt] **1** *v/t* falsificar **2** *adj* falso

'coun·ter·part (*person*) homólogo(-a) *m(f)*

coun·ter·pro'duc·tive *adj* contraproducente

'coun·ter·sign *v/t* refrendar

coun·tess ['kaʊntɪs] condesa *f*

count·less ['kaʊntlɪs] *adj* incontables

coun·try ['kʌntrɪ] *n* (*nation*) país *m*; *as opposed to town* campo *m*; **in the country** en el campo

coun·try and 'west·ern MUS música *f* country

'coun·try·man (*fellow countryman*) compatriota *m*

'coun·try·side campo *m*

coun·ty ['kaʊntɪ] condado *m*

coup [kuː] POL golpe *m* (de Estado); *fig* golpe *m* de efecto

cou·ple ['kʌpl] *n* pareja *f*; **just a couple** un par; **a couple of** un par de

cou·pon ['kuːpɑːn] cupón *m*

cour·age ['kʌrɪdʒ] valor *m*, coraje *m*

cou·ra·geous [kəˈreɪdʒəs] *adj* valiente

cou·ra·geous·ly [kəˈreɪdʒəslɪ] *adv* valientemente

cou·ri·er ['kʊrɪr] (*messenger*) mensajero(-a) *m(f)*; *with tourist party* guía *m/f*

course [kɔːrs] *n* (*series of lessons*) curso *m*; (*part of meal*) plato *m*; *of ship, plane* rumbo *m*; *for horse race* circuito *m*; *for golf* campo *m*; *for skiing, marathon* recorrido *m*; **change course** *of ship, plane* cambiar de rumbo; **of course** (*certainly*) claro, por supuesto; (*naturally*) por supuesto; **of course not** claro que no; **course of action** táctica *f*; **course of treatment** tratamiento *m*; **in the course of ...** durante ...

court [kɔːrt] *n* LAW tribunal *m*; (*courthouse*) palacio *m* de justicia; SP pista *f*, cancha *f*; **take s.o. to court** llevar a alguien a juicio

'court case proceso *m*, causa *f*

cour·te·ous ['kɜːrtɪəs] *adj* cortés

cour·te·sy ['kɜːrtəsɪ] cortesía *f*

'court·house palacio *m* de justicia

court 'mar·tial **1** *n* consejo *m* de guerra **2** *v/t* formar un consejo de guerra a

'court or·der orden *f* judicial

'court·room sala *f* de juicios

'court·yard patio *m*

cous·in ['kʌzn] primo(-a) *m(f)*

cove [kouv] (*small bay*) cala f

cov·er ['kʌvər] **1** n *protective* funda f; *of book, magazine* portada f; (*insurance*) protección f; (*shelter*) protección f; **covers for bed** manta y sábanas fpl; **we took cover from the rain** nos pusimos a cubierto de la lluvia **2** v/t cubrir

◆ **cover up 1** v/t cubrir; *scandal* encubrir **2** v/i disimular; **cover up for s.o.** encubrir a alguien

cov·er·age ['kʌvərɪdʒ] *by media* cobertura f informativa

cov·er·ing let·ter ['kʌvərɪŋ] carta f

cov·ert [kou'vɜːrt] adj encubierto

'cov·er-up encubrimiento m

cow [kau] vaca f

cow·ard ['kauərd] cobarde m/f

cow·ard·ice ['kauərdɪs] cobardía f

cow·ard·ly ['kauərdlɪ] adj cobarde

'cow·boy vaquero m

cow·er ['kauər] v/i agacharse, amilanarse

co-work·er ['kouwɜːrkər] compañero(a) m(f) de trabajo

coy [kɔɪ] adj (*evasive*) evasivo; (*flirtatious*) coqueto

co·zy ['kouzɪ] adj *room* acogedor; *job* cómodo

CPU [siːpiːˈjuː] abbr (= **central processing unit**) CPU f (= unidad f central de proceso)

crab [kræb] n cangrejo m

crack [kræk] **1** n grieta f; *in cup, glass* raja f; (*joke*) chiste m (malo) **2** v/t *cup, glass* rajar; *nut* cascar; *code* descifrar; F (*solve*) resolver; **crack a joke** contar un chiste **3** v/i rajarse; **get cracking** F poner manos a la obra F

◆ **crack down on** v/t castigar severamente

◆ **crack up** v/i (*have breakdown*) sufrir una crisis nerviosa; F (*laugh*) desternillarse F

'crack-brained adj F chiflado F

'crack·down medidas fpl severas

cracked [krækt] adj *cup, glass* rajado; F (*crazy*) chiflado F

crack·er ['krækər] *to eat* galleta f salada

crack·le ['krækl] v/i *of fire* crepitar

cra·dle ['kreɪdl] n *for baby* cuna f

craft¹ [kræft] NAUT embarcación f

craft² [kræft] (*skill*) arte m; (*trade*) oficio m

crafts·man ['kræftsmən] artesano m

craft·y ['kræftɪ] adj astuto

crag [kræg] *rock* peñasco m, risco m

cram [kræm] v/t embutir

cramp [kræmp] n calambre m; **stomach cramp** retorcijón m

cramped [kræmpt] adj *room, apartment* pequeño

cramps [kræmps] npl calambre m; **stomach cramps** retorcijón m

cran·ber·ry ['krænberɪ] arándano m agrio

crane [kreɪn] **1** n *machine* grúa f **2** v/t: **crane one's neck** estirar el cuello

crank [kræŋk] n *person* maniático(-a) m(f), persona f rara

'crank·shaft cigüeñal m

crank·y ['kræŋkɪ] adj (*bad-tempered*) gruñón

crash [kræʃ] **1** n *noise* estruendo m, estrépito m; *accident* accidente m; COM quiebra f, crac m; COMPUT bloqueo m; **a crash of thunder** un trueno **2** v/i *of car, airplane* estrellarse (**into** con *or* contra); *of thunder* sonar; COM *of market* hundirse, desplomarse; COMPUT bloquearse, colgarse; F (*sleep*) dormir, Span sobar F; **the waves crashed onto the shore** las olas chocaban contra la orilla; **the vase crashed to the ground** el jarrón se cayó con estruendo **3** v/t car estrellar

◆ **crash out** v/i F (*fall asleep*) dormirse, Span quedarse sobado

'crash bar·ri·er quitamiedos m inv

'crash course curso m intensivo

'crash di·et dieta f drástica

'crash hel·met casco m protector

'crash-land v/i realizar un aterrizaje forzoso

'crash 'land·ing aterrizaje m forzoso

crate [kreɪt] (*packing case*) caja f

cra·ter ['kreɪtər] *of volcano* cráter m

crave [kreɪv] v/t ansiar

crav·ing ['kreɪvɪŋ] ansia f, deseo m; *of pregnant woman* antojo m; **I have a craving for ...** me apetece muchísimo ...

crawl [krɔːl] **1** n *in swimming* crol m; **at a crawl** (*very slowly*) muy lentamente **2** v/i *on floor* arrastrarse; *of baby* andar a gatas; (*move slowly*) avanzar lentamente

◆ **crawl with** v/t estar abarrotado de

cray·fish ['kreɪfɪʃ] *freshwater* cangrejo m de río; *saltwater* langosta f

cray·on ['kreɪɑːn] n lápiz m de color

craze [kreɪz] locura f (**for** de); **the latest craze** la última locura *o* moda

cra·zy ['kreɪzɪ] adj loco; **be crazy about** estar loco por

creak [kriːk] **1** n *of hinge, door* chirrido m; *of floor* crujido m **2** v/i *of hinge, door* chirriar; *of floor, shoes* crujir

creak·y ['kriːkɪ] adj *hinge, door* que chirria; *floor, shoes* que cruje

cream [kriːm] **1** n *for skin* crema f; *for coffee, cake* nata f; (*color*) crema m **2** adj crema

cream 'cheese queso m blanco para untar

cream·er ['kri:mər] (*pitcher*) jarra *f* para la nata; *for coffee* leche *f* en polvo

cream·y ['kri:mɪ] *adj* with lots of cream cremoso

crease [kri:s] **1** *n accidental* arruga *f*; *deliberate* raya *f* **2** *v/t accidentally* arrugar

cre·ate [kri:'eɪt] *v/t & v/i* crear

cre·a·tion [kri:'eɪʃn] creación *f*

cre·a·tive [kri:'eɪtɪv] *adj* creativo

cre·a·tor [kri:'eɪtər] creador(a) *m(f)*; (*founder*) fundador(a) *m(f)*; **the Creator** REL el Creador

crea·ture ['kri:tʃər] *animal, person* criatura *f*

crèche [kreʃ] *for children* guardería *f* (infantil); REL nacimiento *m*, belén *m*

cred·i·bil·i·ty [kredə'bɪlətɪ] credibilidad *f*

cred·i·ble ['kredəbl] *adj* creíble

cred·it ['kredɪt] **1** *n* FIN crédito *m*; (*honor*) crédito *m*, reconocimiento *m*; **be in cre·dit** tener un saldo positivo; **get the credit for sth** recibir reconocimiento por algo **2** *v/t* (*believe*) creer; **would you credit it!** ¡te lo puedes creer!; **credit an amount to an account** abonar una cantidad a una cuenta

cred·i·ta·ble ['kredɪtəbl] *adj* estimable, honorable

cred·it card tarjeta *f* de crédito

cred·it lim·it límite *m* de crédito

cred·i·tor ['kredɪtər] acreedor(a) *m(f)*

cred·it·wor·thy *adj* solvente

cred·u·lous ['kredʊləs] *adj* crédulo

creed [kri:d] (*beliefs*) credo *m*

creek [kri:k] (*stream*) arroyo *m*

creep [kri:p] **1** *n pej* asqueroso(-a) *m(f)* **2** *v/i* (*pret & pp* **crept**) moverse sigilosamente

creep·er ['kri:pər] BOT enredadera *f*

creeps [kri:ps] *npl* F: **the house / he gives me the creeps** la casa / él me pone la piel de gallina F

creep·y ['kri:pɪ] *adj* F espeluznante F

cre·mate [krɪ'meɪt] *v/t* incinerar

cre·ma·tion [krɪ'meɪʃn] incineración *f*

cre·ma·to·ri·um [kremə'tɔ:rɪəm] crematorio *m*

crept [krept] *pret & pp* → **creep**

cres·cent ['kresənt] *n shape* medialuna *f*; **crescent moon** cuarto *m* creciente

crest [krest] *of hill* cima *f*; *of bird* cresta *f*

crest·fal·len *adj* abatido

crev·ice ['krevɪs] grieta *f*

crew [kru:] *n of ship, airplane* tripulación *f*; *of repairmen etc* equipo *m*; (*crowd, group*) grupo *m*, pandilla *f*

'crew cut rapado *m*

'crew neck cuello *m* redondo

crib [krɪb] *n for baby* cuna *f*

crick [krɪk]: **have a crick in the neck** tener tortícolis

crick·et ['krɪkɪt] *insect* grillo *m*

crime [kraɪm] (*offense*) delito *m*; *serious, also fig* crimen *m*

crim·i·nal ['krɪmɪnl] **1** *n* delincuente *m/f*, criminal *m/f* **2** *adj* (*relating to crime*) criminal; (LAW: *not civil*) penal; (*shameful*) vergonzoso; *act* delictivo; **it's crimi·nal** (*shameful*) es un crimen

crim·son ['krɪmzn] *adj* carmesí

cringe [krɪndʒ] *v/i with embarrassment* sentir vergüenza ajena

crip·ple ['krɪpl] **1** *n* (*disabled person*) inválido(-a) *m(f)* **2** *v/t person* dejar inválido; *fig: country, industry* paralizar

cri·sis ['kraɪsɪs] (*pl crises* ['kraɪsi:z]) crisis *f inv*

crisp [krɪsp] *adj weather, air* fresco; *lettu·ce, apple, bacon* crujiente; *new shirt, bills* flamante

cri·te·ri·on [kraɪ'tɪrɪən] (*standard*) criterio *m*

crit·ic ['krɪtɪk] crítico(-a) *m(f)*

crit·i·cal ['krɪtɪkl] *adj* (*making criticisms, serious*) crítico; *moment etc* decisivo

crit·i·cal·ly ['krɪtɪklɪ] *adv speak etc* en tono de crítica; **critically ill** en estado crítico

crit·i·cism ['krɪtɪsɪzm] crítica *f*

crit·i·cize ['krɪtɪsaɪz] *v/t* criticar

croak [krouk] **1** *n of frog* croar *m* **2** *v/i of frog* croar

cro·chet ['krouʃeɪ] **1** *n* ganchillo *m* **2** *v/t* hacer a ganchillo

crock·e·ry ['krɑ:kərɪ] vajilla *f*

croc·o·dile ['krɑ:kədaɪl] cocodrilo *m*

cro·cus ['kroukəs] azafrán *m*

cro·ny ['krounɪ] F amiguete *m/f* F

crook [kruk] *n* ladrón (-ona) *m(f)*; *disho·nest trader* granuja *m/f*

crook·ed ['krukɪd] *adj* (*not straight*) torcido; (*dishonest*) deshonesto

crop [krɑ:p] **1** *n also fig* cosecha *f*; *plant grown* cultivo *m* **2** *v/t* (*pret & pp* **crop·ped**) *hair* cortar; *photo* recortar

◆ **crop up** *v/i* salir

cross [krɑ:s] **1** *adj* (*angry*) enfadado, enojado **2** *n cruz f* **3** *v/t* (*go across*) cruzar; **cross o.s.** REL santiguarse; **cross one's legs** cruzar las piernas; **keep one's fin·gers crossed** cruzar los dedos; **it never crossed my mind** no se me ocurrió **4** *v/i* (*go across*) cruzar; *of lines* cruzarse, cortarse

◆ **cross off, cross out** *v/t* tachar

'cross·bar *of goal* larguero *m*; *of bicycle* barra *f*; *in high jump* listón *m* 'cross·check 1 n comprobación f 2 v/t comprobar

cross-coun·try ('ski·ing) esquí m de fondo

crossed 'check, Br crossed 'cheque [krɑːst] cheque m cruzado

cross-ex·am·i'na·tion LAW interrogatorio m

cross-ex'am·ine v/t LAW interrogar

cross-'eyed adj bizco

cross·ing ['krɑːsɪŋ] NAUT travesía f

'cross·roads nsg also fig encrucijada f

'cross-sec·tion of people muestra f representativa

'cross·walk paso m de peatones

'cross·word (puz·zle) crucigrama m

crotch [krɑːtʃ] of person, pants entrepierna f

crouch [krautʃ] v/i agacharse

crow [krou] n bird corneja f; as the crow flies en línea recta

'crow·bar palanca f

crowd [kraud] n multitud f, muchedumbre f; at sports event público m

crowd·ed ['kraudɪd] adj abarrotado (with de)

crown [kraun] 1 n on head, tooth corona f 2 v/t tooth poner una corona a

cru·cial ['kruːʃl] adj crucial

cru·ci·fix ['kruːsɪfɪks] crucifijo m

cru·ci·fix·ion [kruːsɪ'fɪkʃn] crucifixión f

cru·ci·fy ['kruːsɪfaɪ] v/t (pret & pp crucified) also fig crucificar

crude [kruːd] 1 adj (vulgar) grosero; (unsophisticated) primitivo 2 n: crude (oil) crudo m

crude·ly ['kruːdlɪ] adv speak groseramente; made de manera primitiva

cru·el ['kruːəl] adj cruel (to con)

cru·el·ty ['kruːəltɪ] crueldad f (to con)

cruise [kruːz] 1 n crucero m; go on a cruise ir de crucero 2 v/i of people hacer un crucero; of car ir a la velocidad de crucero; of plane volar

'cruise lin·er transatlántico m

cruis·ing speed ['kruːzɪŋ] of vehicle velocidad f de crucero; fig: of project etc ritmo m normal

crumb [krʌm] miga f

crum·ble ['krʌmbl] 1 v/t desmigajar 2 v/i of bread desmigajarse; of stonework desmenuzarse; fig: of opposition etc desmoronarse

crum·bly ['krʌmblɪ] adj cookie que se desmigaja; stonework que se desmenuza

crum·ple ['krʌmpl] 1 v/t (crease) arrugar 2 v/i (collapse) desplomarse

crunch [krʌntʃ] 1 n: when it comes to the crunch a la hora de la verdad 2 v/i of

snow, gravel crujir

cru·sade [kruː'seɪd] n also fig cruzada f

crush [krʌʃ] 1 n (crowd) muchedumbre f; have a crush on estar loco por 2 v/t aplastar; (crease) arrugar; they were crushed to death murieron aplastado●

3 v/i (crease) arrugarse

crust [krʌst] on bread corteza f

crust·y ['krʌstɪ] adj bread crujiente

crutch [krʌtʃ] for injured person muleta f

cry [kraɪ] 1 n (call) grito m; have a cry● llorar 2 v/t (pret & pp cried) (call) grita●

3 v/i (pret & pp cried) (weep) llorar

◆ cry out v/t & v/i gritar

◆ cry out for v/t (need) pedir a gritos

cryp·tic ['krɪptɪk] adj críptico

crys·tal ['krɪstl] cristal m

crys·tal·lize ['krɪstəlaɪz] 1 v/t cristalizar 2●

v/i cristalizarse

cub [kʌb] cachorro m; of bear osezno m●

Cu·ba ['kjuːbə] Cuba

Cu·ban ['kjuːbən] 1 adj cubano 2 n cubano(-a) m(f)

cube [kjuːb] shape cubo m

cu·bic ['kjuːbɪk] adj cúbico

cu·bic ca'pac·i·ty TECH cilindrada f

cu·bi·cle ['kjuːbɪkl] (changing room) cu● bículo m

cu·cum·ber ['kjuːkʌmbər] pepino m

cud·dle ['kʌdl] 1 n abrazo 2 v/t abrazar

cud·dly ['kʌdlɪ] adj kitten etc tierno

cue [kjuː] n for actor etc pie m, entrada f● for pool taco m

cuff [kʌf] 1 n of shirt puño m; of pant● vuelta f; (blow) cachete m; off the cuf● improvisado 2 v/t (hit) dar un cachete a●

'cuff link gemelo m

cul-de-sac ['kʌldəsæk] callejón m sin sa● ida

cu·li·nar·y ['kʌlɪnərɪ] adj culinario

cul·mi·nate ['kʌlmɪneɪt] v/i culminar (i● en)

cul·mi·na·tion [kʌlmɪ'neɪʃn] culminación● f

cul·prit ['kʌlprɪt] culpable m/f

cult [kʌlt] (sect) secta f

cul·ti·vate ['kʌltɪveɪt] v/t also fig cultivar

cul·ti·vat·ed ['kʌltɪveɪtɪd] adj person cul● to

cul·ti·va·tion [kʌltɪ'veɪʃn] of land cultivo● m

cul·tur·al ['kʌltʃərəl] adj cultural

cul·ture ['kʌltʃər] artistic cultura f

cul·tured ['kʌltʃərd] adj (cultivated) culto

'cul·ture shock choque m cultural

cum·ber·some ['kʌmbərsəm] adj engorroso

cu·mu·la·tive ['kjuːmjʊlətɪv] adj acumulativo

cun·ning ['kʌnɪŋ] **1** n astucia f **2** adj astuto

cup [kʌp] n taza f; trophy copa f

cup·board ['kʌbərd] armario m

'cup fi·nal final f de (la) copa

cu·po·la ['kjuːpələ] cúpula f

cur·a·ble ['kjuərəbl] adj curable

cu·ra·tor [kju'reɪtər] conservador(a) m(f)

curb [kɜːrb] **1** n of street bordillo m; on powers etc freno f **2** v/t frenar

cur·dle ['kɜːrdl] v/i of milk cortarse

cure [kjur] **1** n MED cura f **2** v/t MED, meat curar

cur·few ['kɜːrfjuː] toque m de queda

cu·ri·os·i·ty [kjurɪ'ɑːsətɪ] (inquisitiveness) curiosidad f

cu·ri·ous ['kjurɪəs] adj (inquisitive, strange) curioso

cu·ri·ous·ly ['kjurɪəslɪ] adv (inquisitively) con curiosidad; (strangely) curiosamente; **curiously enough** curiosamente

curl [kɜːrl] **1** n in hair rizo m; of smoke voluta f **2** v/t hair rizar; (wind) enroscar **3** v/i of hair rizarse; of leaf, paper etc ondularse

◆ curl up v/i acurrucarse

curl·y ['kɜːrlɪ] adj hair rizado; tail enroscado

cur·rant ['kʌrənt] (dried fruit) pasa f de Corinto

cur·ren·cy ['kʌrənsɪ] money moneda f; **foreign currency** divisas fpl

cur·rent ['kʌrənt] **1** n in sea, ELEC corriente f **2** adj (present) actual

cur·rent af·fairs, cur·rent e'vents npl la actualidad

cur·rent af·fairs pro·gram programa m de actualidad

'cur·rent ac·count Br cuenta f corriente

cur·rent·ly ['kʌrəntlɪ] adv actualmente

cur·ric·u·lum [kə'rɪkjuləm] plan m de estudios

cur·ric·u·lum vi·tae ['viːtaɪ] Br currículum m vitae

cur·ry ['kʌrɪ] curry m

curse [kɜːrs] **1** n (spell) maldición f; (swearword) palabrota f **2** v/t maldecir; (swear at) insultar **3** v/i (swear) decir palabrotas

cur·sor ['kɜːrsər] COMPUT cursor m

cur·so·ry ['kɜːrsərɪ] adj rápido, superficial

curt [kɜːrt] adj brusco, seco

cur·tail [kɜːr'teɪl] v/t acortar

cur·tain ['kɜːrtn] cortina f; THEA telón m

curve [kɜːrv] **1** n curva f **2** v/i (bend) curvarse

cush·ion ['kuʃn] **1** n for couch etc cojín m **2** v/t blow, fall amortiguar

cus·tard ['kʌstərd] natillas fpl

cus·to·dy ['kʌstədɪ] of children custodia f; **in custody** LAW detenido

cus·tom ['kʌstəm] (tradition) costumbre f; COM clientela f; **it's the custom in France** es costumbre en Francia; **as was his custom** como era costumbre en él; **thank you for your custom** at shop gracias por comprar aquí

cus·tom·a·ry ['kʌstəmərɪ] adj acostumbrado, de costumbre; **it is customary to …** es costumbre …

cus·tom-'built adj hecho de encargo

cus·tom·er ['kʌstəmər] cliente(-a) m(f)

cus·tom-'made adj hecho de encargo

cus·tom·er re'la·tions npl relaciones fpl con los clientes

cus·tom·er 'serv·ice atención f al cliente

cus·toms ['kʌstəmz] npl aduana f

'cus·toms clear·ance despacho m de aduanas

'cus·toms in·spec·tion inspección f aduanera

'cus·toms of·fi·cer funcionario(-a) m(f) de aduanas

cut [kʌt] **1** n with knife etc, of garment corte m; (reduction) recorte (**in** de); **my hair needs a cut** necesito un corte de pelo **2** v/t (pret & pp cut) cortar; (reduce) recortar; hours acortar; **get one's hair cut** cortarse el pelo; **I've cut my finger** me he cortado el dedo

◆ cut back **1** v/i in costs recortar gastos **2** v/t staff numbers recortar

◆ cut down **1** v/t tree talar, cortar **2** v/i in expenses gastar menos; in smoking / drinking fumar / beber menos

◆ cut down on v/t: **cut down on the cigarettes** fumar menos; **cut down on chocolate** comer menos chocolate

◆ cut off v/t with knife, scissors etc cortar; (isolate) aislar; **I was cut off** se me ha cortado la comunicación

◆ cut out v/t with scissors recortar; (eliminate) eliminar; **cut that out!** F ¡ya está bien! F; **be cut out for sth** estar hecho para algo

◆ cut up v/t meat etc trocear

'cut·back recorte m

cute [kjuːt] adj (pretty) guapo, lindo; (sexually attractive) atractivo; (smart, clever) listo; **it looks really cute on you** eso te queda muy mono

cu·ti·cle ['kjuːtɪkl] cutícula f

'cut-off date fecha f límite

cut-'price adj goods rebajado; store de productos rebajados

'cut-throat adj competition despiadado

cut·ting ['kʌtɪŋ] **1** n from newspaper etc

recorte *m* **2** *adj remark* hiriente
cy·ber·space ['saɪbərspeɪs] ciberespacio *m*
cy·cle ['saɪkl] **1** *n* (*bicycle*) bicicleta *f*; (*series of events*) ciclo *m* **2** *v/i* ir en bicicleta
'cy·cle path vía *f* para bicicletas; *part of roadway* carril *m* bici
cy·cling ['saɪklɪŋ] ciclismo *m*
cy·clist ['saɪklɪst] ciclista *m/f*
cyl·in·der ['sɪlɪndər] cilindro *m*
cy·lin·dri·cal [sɪ'lɪndrɪkl] *adj* cilíndrico
cyn·ic ['sɪnɪk] escéptico(-a) *m/f*, suspi-

caz *m/f*
cyn·i·cal ['sɪnɪkl] *adj* escéptico, suspicaz
cyn·i·cal·ly ['sɪnɪklɪ] *adv smile, remark* con escepticismo *or* suspicacia
cyn·i·cism ['sɪnɪsɪzm] escepticismo *m*, suspicacia *f*
cy·press ['saɪprəs] ciprés *m*
cyst [sɪst] quiste *m*
Czech [tʃek] **1** *adj* checo; *the Czech Republic* la República Checa **2** *n person* checo(-a) *m(f)*; *language* checo *m*

D

DA *abbr* (= *district attorney*) fiscal *m/f* (del distrito)
dab [dæb] **1** *n small amount* pizca *f* **2** *v/t* (*pret & pp* **dabbed**) (*remove*) quitar; (*apply*) poner
◆ **dab·ble in** *v/t* ser aficionado a
dad [dæd] *talking to him* papá *m*; *talking about him* padre *m*
dad·dy ['dædɪ] *talking to him* papi *m*; *talking about him* padre *m*
daf·fo·dil ['dæfədɪl] narciso *m*
dag·ger ['dægər] daga *f*
dai·ly ['deɪlɪ] **1** *n* (*paper*) diario *m* **2** *adj* diario
dain·ty ['deɪntɪ] *adj* grácil, delicado
dair·y ['derɪ] *on farm* vaquería *f*
'dair·y prod·ucts *npl* productos *mpl* lácteos
dais ['deɪɪs] tarima *f*
dai·sy ['deɪzɪ] margarita *f*
dam [dæm] **1** *n for water* presa *f* **2** *v/t* (*pret & pp* **dammed**) *river* embalsar
dam·age ['dæmɪdʒ] **1** *n* daños *mpl*; *fig: to reputation etc* daño *m* **2** *v/t also fig* dañar; *you're damaging your health* estás perjudicando tu salud
dam·ages ['dæmɪdʒɪz] *npl* LAW daños *mpl* y perjuicios
dam·ag·ing ['dæmɪdʒɪŋ] *adj* perjudicial
dame [deɪm] F (*woman*) mujer *f*, *Span* tía *f* F
damn [dæm] **1** *interj* F ¡mecachis! F **2** *n* F: *I don't give a damn!* ¡me importa un pimiento! F **3** *adj* F maldito F **4** *adv* F muy; *a damn stupid thing* una tontería monumental **5** *v/t* (*condemn*) condenar; *damn it!* F ¡maldita sea! F; *I'm damned if ...* F ya

lo creo que ... F
damned [dæmd] → **damn** *adj, adv*
damn·ing ['dæmɪŋ] *adj evidence* condenatorio; *report* crítico
damp [dæmp] *adj* húmedo
damp·en ['dæmpən] *v/t* humedecer
dance [dæns] **1** *n* baile *m* **2** *v/i* bailar; *would you like to dance?* ¿le gustaría bailar?
danc·er ['dænsər] bailarín (-ina) *m(f)*
danc·ing ['dænsɪŋ] baile *m*
dan·de·lion ['dændɪlaɪən] diente *m* de león
dan·druff ['dændrʌf] caspa *f*
dan·druff sham'poo champú *m* anticaspa
Dane [deɪn] danés(-esa) *m(f)*
dan·ger ['deɪndʒər] peligro *m*; *be in danger* estar en peligro; *out of danger of patient* estar fuera de peligro; *be in no danger* no estar en peligro
dan·ger·ous ['deɪndʒərəs] *adj* peligroso
dan·ger·ous 'driv·ing conducción *f* peligrosa
dan·ger·ous·ly ['deɪndʒərəslɪ] *adv drive* peligrosamente; *dangerously ill* gravemente enfermo
dan·gle ['dæŋgl] **1** *v/t* balancear **2** *v/i* colgar
Da·nish ['deɪnɪʃ] **1** *adj* danés **2** *n language* danés *m*
'Da·nish (pas·try) pastel *m* de hojaldre (*dulce*)
dare [der] **1** *v/i* atreverse; *dare to do sth* atreverse a hacer algo; *how dare you!* ¡cómo te atreves! **2** *v/t*: *dare s.o. to do sth* desafiar a alguien para que haga algo
dare·dev·il ['derdevɪl] temerario(-a) *m(f)*

dar·ing ['deɪrɪŋ] *adj* atrevido

dark [dɑːrk] **1** *n* oscuridad *f*; *in the dark* en la oscuridad; *after dark* después de anochecer; *keep s.o. in the dark about sth fig* no revelar algo a alguien **2** *adj* oscuro; *hair* oscuro, moreno; *dark green / blue* verde / azul oscuro

dark·en ['dɑːrn] *v/i of sky* oscurecerse

dark 'glass·es *npl* gafas *fpl* oscuras, *L.Am.* lentes *fpl* oscuras

dark·ness ['dɑːrknɪs] oscuridad *f*; *in darkness* a oscuras

'dark·room PHOT cuarto *m* oscuro

dar·ling ['dɑːrlɪŋ] **1** *n* cielo *m*; *yes my darling* sí cariño **2** *adj* encantador; *darling Ann, how are you?* querida Ann, ¿cómo estás?

darn¹ [dɑːrn] **1** *n* (*mend*) zurcido *m* **2** *v/t* (*mend*) zurcir

darn², **darned** [dɑːrn, dɑːrnd] → *damn adj, adv*

dart [dɑːrt] **1** *n for throwing* dardo *m* **2** *v/i* lanzarse, precipitarse

darts [dɑːrts] *nsg* dardos *mpl*

'dart(s)·board diana *f*

dash [dæʃ] **1** *n punctuation* raya *f*; (*small amount*) chorrito *m*; (MOT: *dashboard*) salpicadero *m*; *make a dash for* correr hacia **2** *v/i* correr; *I must dash* tengo que darme prisa; *he dashed downstairs* bajó las escaleras corriendo **3** *v/t hopes* frustrar, truncar

♦ **dash off 1** *v/i* irse **2** *v/t* (*write quickly*) escribir rápidamente

'dash·board salpicadero *m*

da·ta ['deɪtə] datos *mpl*

'da·ta·base base *f* de datos

da·ta 'cap·ture captura *f* de datos

da·ta 'pro·cess·ing proceso *m* or tratamiento *m* de datos

da·ta pro'tec·tion protección *f* de datos

da·ta 'stor·age almacenamiento *m* de datos

date¹ [deɪt] *fruit* dátil *m*

date² [deɪt] **1** *n* fecha *f*; (*meeting*) cita *f*; (*person*) pareja *f*; *what's the date today?* ¿qué fecha es hoy?, ¿a qué fecha estamos?; *out of date clothes* pasado de moda; *passport* caducado; *up to date* al día **2** *v/t letter, check* fechar; (*go out with*) salir con; *that dates you* (*shows your age*) eso demuestra lo viejo que eres

dat·ed ['deɪtɪd] *adj* anticuado

daub [dɒːb] *v/t* embadurnar

daugh·ter ['dɒːtər] hija *f*

'daugh·ter-in-law (*pl* **daughters-in-law**) nuera *f*

daunt [dɒːnt] *v/t* acobardar, desalentar

daw·dle ['dɒːdl] *v/i* perder el tiempo

dawn [dɒːn] **1** *n* amanecer *m*, alba *f*; *fig: of new age* albores *mpl* **2** *v/i* amanecer; *it dawned on me that ...* me di cuenta de que ...

day [deɪ] día *m*; *what day is it today?* ¿qué día es hoy?, ¿a qué día estamos?; *day off* día *m* de vacaciones; *by day* durante el día; *day by day* día tras día; *the day after* el día siguiente; *the day after tomorrow* pasado mañana; *the day before* el día anterior; *the day before yesterday* anteayer; *day in day out* un día sí y otro también; *in those days* en aquellos tiempos; *one day* un día; *the other day* (*recently*) el otro día; *let's call it a day!* ¡dejémoslo!

'day·break amanecer *m*, alba *f*

'day care servicio *m* de guardería

'day·dream 1 *n* fantasía *f* **2** *v/i* soñar despierto

'day·dream·er soñador(a) *m(f)*

'day·light luz *f* del día

'day·light 'sav·ing time horario *m* de verano

'day·time: in the daytime durante el día

'day trip excursión *m* en el día

daze [deɪz] *n: in a daze* aturdido

dazed [deɪzd] *adj* aturdido

daz·zle ['dæzl] *v/t also fig* deslumbrar

DC [diː'siː] *abbr* (= **direct current**) corriente *f* continua; (= **District of Columbia**) Distrito *m* de Columbia

dead [ded] **1** *adj person, plant* muerto; *battery* agotado; *light bulb* fundido; F *place* muerto F; *the phone is dead* no hay línea **2** *adv* F (*very*) tela de F, la mar de F; *dead beat, dead tired* hecho polvo; *that's dead right* tienes toda la razón del mundo **3** *n: the dead* (*dead people*) los muertos; *in the dead of night* a altas horas de la madrugada

dead·en ['dedn] *v/t pain, sound* amortiguar

dead 'end (*street*) callejón *m* sin salida

dead-'end job trabajo *m* sin salidas

dead 'heat empate *m*

'dead·line fecha *f* tope; *for newspaper, magazine* hora *f* de cierre; *meet a deadline* cumplir un plazo

'dead·lock *n in talks* punto *m* muerto

dead·ly ['dedlɪ] *adj* (*fatal*) mortal; F (*boring*) mortal F

deaf [def] *adj* sordo

deaf-and-'dumb *adj* sordomudo

deaf·en ['defn] *v/t* ensordecer

deaf·en·ing ['defnɪŋ] *adj* ensordecedor

deaf·ness ['defnɪs] sordera *f*

deal [diːl] **1** *n* acuerdo *m*; *I thought we had a deal?* creía que habíamos hecho un trato; *it's a deal!* ¡trato hecho!; *a good deal* (*bargain*) una ocasión; *a good deal* (*a lot*) mucho; *a great deal of* (*lots*) mucho(s) 2 *v/t* (*pret & pp* **dealt**) *cards* repartir; *deal a blow to* asestar un golpe a

◆ **deal in** *v/t* (*trade in*) comerciar con; *deal in drugs* traficar con drogas

◆ **deal out** *v/t cards* repartir

◆ **deal with** *v/t* (*handle*) *situation* hacer frente a; *customer, applications* encargarse de; (*do business with*) hacer negocios con

deal·er ['di:lər] (*merchant*) comerciante *m/f*; (*drug dealer*) traficante *m/f*

deal·ing ['di:lɪŋ] (*drug dealing*) tráfico *m*

deal·ings ['di:lɪŋz] *npl* (*business*) tratos *mpl*

dealt [delt] *pret & pp* → **deal**

dean [di:n] *of college* decano(-a) *m(f)*

dear [dɪr] *adj* querido; (*expensive*) caro; *Dear Sir* Muy Sr. Mío; *Dear Richard / Margaret* Querido Richard / Querida Margaret; (*oh*) *dear!, dear me!* ¡oh, cielos!

dear·ly ['dɪrlɪ] *adv love* muchísimo

death [deθ] muerte *f*

death cer·tif·i·cate certificado *m* de defunción

death pen·al·ty pena *f* de muerte

death toll saldo *m* de víctimas mortales

de·ba·ta·ble [dɪ'beɪtəbl] *adj* discutible

de·bate [dɪ'beɪt] **1** *n also* POL debate *m* **2** *v/i* debatir; *I debated with myself whether to go* me debatía entre ir o no ir **3** *v/t* debatir

de·bauch·er·y [dɪ'bɔ:tʃərɪ] libertinaje *m*

deb·it ['debɪt] **1** *n* cargo *m* **2** *v/t account* cargar en; *amount* cargar

'deb·it card tarjeta *f* de débito

deb·ris ['debri:] *of building* escombros *mpl*; *of airplane, car* restos *mpl*

debt [det] deuda *f*; *be in debt financially* estar endeudado

debt·or ['detər] deudor(-a) *m(f)*

de·bug [di:'bʌɡ] *v/t* (*pret & pp* **debugged**) *room* limpiar de micrófonos; COMPUT depurar

dé·but ['deɪbju:] *n* debut *m*

dec·ade [dekeɪd] década *f*

dec·a·dence [dekədəns] decadencia *f*

dec·a·dent ['dekədənt] *adj* decadente

de·caf·fein·at·ed [di:'kæfɪneɪtɪd] *adj* descafeinado

de·cant·er [dɪ'kæntər] licorera *f*

de·cap·i·tate [dɪ'kæpɪteɪt] *v/t* decapitar

de·cay [dɪ'keɪ] **1** *n of wood, plant* putrefacción *f*; *of civilization* declive *m*; *in teeth* caries *f inv* **2** *v/i of wood, plant* pu-

drirse; *of civilization* decaer; *of teeth* cariarse

de·ceased [dɪ'si:st]: *the deceased* el difunto / la difunta

de·ceit [dɪ'si:t] engaño *m*, mentira *f*

de·ceit·ful [dɪ'si:tfəl] *adj* mentiroso

de·ceive [dɪ'si:v] *v/t* engañar

De·cem·ber [dɪ'sembər] diciembre *m*

de·cen·cy ['di:sənsı] decencia *f*; *he had the decency to ...* tuvo la delicadeza de ...

de·cent ['di:sənt] *adj* decente; (*adequately dressed*) presentable

de·cen·tral·ize [di:'sentrəlaɪz] *v/t* descentralizar

de·cep·tion [dɪ'sepʃn] engaño *m*

de·cep·tive [dɪ'septɪv] *adj* engañoso

de·cep·tive·ly [dɪ'septɪvlɪ] *adv*: *it looks deceptively simple* parece muy fácil

dec·i·bel ['desɪbel] decibelio *m*

de·cide [dɪ'saɪd] **1** *v/t* decidir **2** *v/i* decidir; *you decide* decide tú; *it's so hard to decide* es tan difícil decidirse

de·cid·ed [dɪ'saɪdɪd] *adj* (*definite*) tajante

de·cid·er [dɪ'saɪdər]: *this match will be the decider* este partido será el que decida

de·ci·sion [dɪ'sɪʒn] decisión *f*; *come to a decision* llegar a una decisión

de·ci·sion-mak·er [dɪ'saɪvsɪv]: *who's the decision-maker here?* ¿quién toma aquí las decisiones?

de·ci·sive [dɪ'saɪsɪv] *adj* decidido; (*crucial*) decisivo

deck [dek] *of ship* cubierta *f*; *of cards* baraja *f*

'deck·chair tumbona *f*

dec·la·ra·tion [deklə'reɪʃn] (*statement*) declaración *f*

de·clare [dɪ'kler] *v/t* (*state*) declarar

de·cline [dɪ'klaɪn] **1** *n* (*fall*) descenso *m*; *in standards* caída *f*; *in health* empeoramiento *m* **2** *v/t invitation* declinar; *decline to comment* declinar hacer declaraciones **3** *v/i* (*refuse*) rehusar; (*decrease*) declinar; *of health* empeorar

de·clutch [di:'klʌtʃ] *v/i* desembragar

de·code [di:'koud] *v/t* descodificar

de·com·pose [di:kəm'pouz] *v/i* descomponerse

dé·cor ['deɪkɔ:r] decoración *f*

dec·o·rate ['dekəreɪt] *v/t with paint* pintar; *with paper* empapelar; (*adorn*) dec-

defuse

orar; *soldier* condecorar

dec·o·ra·tion [dekəˈreɪʃn] *paint* pintado *m*; *paper* empapelado *m*; *(ornament)* decoración *f*

dec·o·ra·tive [ˈdekərətɪv] *adj* decorativo

dec·o·ra·tor [ˈdekəreɪtər] *(interior decorator)* decorador(a) *m(f)*; *with paint* pintor(a) *m(f)*; *with wallpaper* empapelador(a) *m(f)*

de·co·rum [dɪˈkɔːrəm] decoro *m*

de·coy [ˈdiːkɔɪ] *n* señuelo *m*

de·crease 1 *n* [ˈdiːkriːs] disminución *f*, reducción *f* (*in* de) **2** *v/t* [dɪˈkriːs] disminuir, reducir **3** *v/i* [dɪˈkriːs] disminuir, reducirse

de·crep·it [dɪˈkrepɪt] *adj car, coat, shoes* destartalado; *person* decrépito

ded·i·cate [ˈdedɪkeɪt] *v/t book etc* dedicar; *dedicate o.s. to* dedicarse a

ded·i·ca·ted [ˈdedɪkeɪtɪd] *adj* dedicado

ded·i·ca·tion [dedɪˈkeɪʃn] *in book* dedicatoria *f*; *to cause, work* dedicación *f*

de·duce [dɪˈduːs] *v/t* deducir

de·duct [dɪˈdʌkt] *v/t* descontar; *deduct sth from sth* descontar alguien de alguien

de·duc·tion [dɪˈdʌkʃn] *from salary, (conclusion)* deducción *f*

dee·jay [ˈdiːdʒeɪ] F disk jockey *m/f*, *Span* pincha *m/f* F

deed [diːd] *n (act)* acción *f*, obra *f*; LAW escritura *f*

deem [diːm] *v/t* estimar

deep [diːp] *adj* profundo; *color* intenso; *be in deep trouble* estar metido en serios apuros

deep·en [ˈdiːpn] **1** *v/t* profundizar **2** *v/i* hacerse más profundo, *of crisis, mystery* agudizarse

'**deep freeze** *n* congelador *m*

'**deep-froz·en food** comida *f* congelada

'**deep-fry** *v/t (pret & pp deep-fried)* freír (*en mucho aceite*)

deep 'fry·er freidora *f*

deer [dɪr] (*pl deer*) ciervo *m*

de·face [dɪˈfeɪs] *v/t* desfigurar, dañar

def·a·ma·tion [defəˈmeɪʃn] difamación *f*

de·fam·a·to·ry [dɪˈfæmətərɪ] *adj* difamatorio

de·fault [dɪˈfɔːlt] *adj* COMPUT por defecto

de·feat [dɪˈfiːt] **1** *n* derrota *f* **2** *v/t* derrotar; *of task, problem* derrotar, vencer

de·feat·ist [dɪˈfiːtɪst] *adj attitude* derrotista

de·fect [ˈdiːfekt] *n* defecto *m*

de·fec·tive [dɪˈfektɪv] *adj* defectuoso

de·fence *etc Br* → *defense etc*

de·fend [dɪˈfend] *v/t* defender

de·fend·ant [dɪˈfendənt] acusado(-a)

m(f); *in civil case* demandado(-a) *m(f)*

de·fense [dɪˈfens] defensa *f*; *come to s.o.'s defense* salir en defensa de alguien

de'fense budg·et POL presupuesto *m* de defensa

de'fense law·yer abogado(-a) *m(f)* defensor(a)

de·fense·less [dɪˈfenslɪs] *adj* indefenso

de'fense play·er defensa *m/f*

De'fense Sec·re·ta·ry POL ministro(-a) *m(f)* de Defensa; *in USA* secretario *m* de Defensa

de'fense wit·ness LAW testigo *m/f* de la defensa

de·fen·sive [dɪˈfensɪv] **1** *n: on the defensive* a la defensiva; *go on the defensive* ponerse a la defensiva **2** *adj weaponry* defensivo; *stop being so defensive!* ¡no hace falta que te pongas tan a la defensiva!

de·fen·sive·ly [dɪˈfensɪvlɪ] *adv* a la defensiva

de·fer [dɪˈfɜːr] *v/t (pret & pp deferred)* (*postpone*) aplazar, diferir

def·er·ence [ˈdefərəns] deferencia *f*

def·er·en·tial [defəˈrenʃl] *adj* deferente

de·fi·ance [dɪˈfaɪəns] desafío *m*; *in defiance of* desafiando

de·fi·ant [dɪˈfaɪənt] *adj* desafiante

de·fi·cien·cy [dɪˈfɪʃənsɪ] (*lack*) deficiencia *f*, carencia *f*

de·fi·cient [dɪˈfɪʃnt] *adj* deficiente, carente; *be deficient in ...* carecer de ...

def·i·cit [ˈdefɪsɪt] déficit *m*

de·fine [dɪˈfaɪn] *v/t word, objective* definir

def·i·nite [ˈdefɪnɪt] *adj date, time, answer* definitivo; *improvement* claro; (*certain*) seguro; *are you definite about that?* ¿estás seguro de eso?; *nothing definite has been arranged* no se ha acordado nada de forma definitiva

def·i·nite 'ar·ti·cle GRAM artículo *m* determinado *or* definido

def·i·nite·ly [ˈdefɪnɪtlɪ] *adv* con certeza, sin lugar a dudas

def·i·ni·tion [defɪˈnɪʃn] definición *f*

de·fin·i·tive [dɪˈfɪnətɪv] *adj* definitivo

de·flect [dɪˈflekt] *v/t* desviar; *criticism* distraer; *be deflected from* desviarse de

de·for·est·a·tion [dɪfɑːrɪsˈteɪʃn] deforestación *f*

de·form [dɪˈfɔːrm] *v/t* deformar

de·for·mi·ty [dɪˈfɔːrmɪtɪ] deformidad *f*

de·fraud [dɪˈfrɔːd] *v/t* defraudar

de·frost [diːˈfrɒst] *v/t food, fridge* descongelar

deft [deft] *adj* hábil, diestro

de·fuse [diːˈfjuːz] *v/t bomb* desactivar; *si-*

tuation calmar

de·fy [dɪˈfaɪ] *v/t* (*pret & pp* **defied**) desafiar

de·gen·e·rate [dɪˈdʒenəreɪt] *v/i* degenerar; **degenerate into** degenerar en

de·grade [dɪˈgreɪd] *v/t* degradar

de·grad·ing [dɪˈgreɪdɪŋ] *adj position, work* degradante

de·gree [dɪˈgriː] *from university* título *m*; *of temperature, angle, latitude* grado *m*; **there is a degree of truth in that** hay algo de verdad en eso; **a degree of compassion** algo de compasión; **by degrees** gradualmente; **get one's degree** graduarse, *L.Am.* egresar

de·hy·drat·ed [diːhaɪˈdreɪtɪd] *adj* deshidratado

de·ice [diːˈaɪs] *v/t* deshelar

de·ic·er [diːˈaɪsər] *spray* descongelador *m*, descongelante *m*

deign [deɪn] *v/i:* **deign to** dignarse a

de·i·ty [ˈdiːɪtɪ] deidad *f*

de·ject·ed [dɪˈdʒektɪd] *adj* abatido, desanimado

de·lay [dɪˈleɪ] **1** *n* retraso *m* **2** *v/t* retrasar; **be delayed** llevar retraso **3** *v/i* retrasarse

del·e·gate [ˈdelɪgət] **1** *n* delegado(-a) *m(f)* **2** [ˈdelɪgeɪt] *v/t task* delegar; *person* delegar en

del·e·ga·tion [delɪˈgeɪʃn] delegación *f*

de·lete [dɪˈliːt] *v/t* borrar; (*cross out*) tachar; **delete where not applicable** táchese donde no corresponda

de·le·tion [dɪˈliːʃn] *act* borrado *m*; *that deleted* supresión *f*

del·i [ˈdelɪ] → **delicatessen**

de·lib·e·rate 1 *adj* [dɪˈlɪbərət] deliberado, intencionado **2** *v/i* [dɪˈlɪbəreɪt] deliberar

de·lib·e·rate·ly [dɪˈlɪbərətlɪ] *adv* deliberadamente, a propósito

del·i·ca·cy [ˈdelɪkəsɪ] delicadeza *f*; *of health* fragilidad *f*; *food* exquisitez *f*, manjar *m*

del·i·cate [ˈdelɪkət] *adj fabric, problem* delicado; *health* frágil

del·i·ca·tes·sen [delɪkəˈtesn] tienda *f* de productos alimenticios de calidad

del·i·cious [dɪˈlɪʃəs] *adj* delicioso

de·light [dɪˈlaɪt] *n* placer *m*

de·light·ed [dɪˈlaɪtɪd] *adj* encantado; **I'd be delighted to come** me encantaría venir

de·light·ful [dɪˈlaɪtfəl] *adj* encantador

de·lim·it [diːˈlɪmɪt] *v/t* delimitar

de·lin·quen·cy [dɪˈlɪŋkwənsɪ] delincuencia *f*

de·lin·quent [dɪˈlɪŋkwənt] *n* delincuente *m/f*

de·lir·i·ous [dɪˈlɪrɪəs] *adj* MED delirante;

(*ecstatic*) entusiasmado; **she's delirious about the new job** está como loca con el nuevo trabajo

de·liv·er [dɪˈlɪvər] *v/t* entregar, repartir; *message* dar; *baby* dar a luz; *speech* pronunciar

de·liv·er·y [dɪˈlɪvərɪ] *of goods, mail* entrega *f*, reparto *m*; *of baby* parto *m*

de·liv·er·y charge gastos *mpl* de envío

de·liv·er·y date fecha *f* de entrega

de·liv·er·y man repartidor *m*

de·liv·er·y note nota *f* de entrega

de·liv·er·y serv·ice servicio *m* de reparto

de·liv·er·y van furgoneta *f* de reparto

de luxe [dəˈlʊks] *adj* de lujo

◆ delve into [delv] *v/t* rebuscar en

de·lude [dɪˈluːd] *v/t* engañar; **you're deluding yourself** te estás engañando a ti mismo

del·uge [ˈdeljuːdʒ] **1** *n* diluvio *m*; *fig* avalancha *f* **2** *v/t fig* inundar (**with**)

de·lu·sion [dɪˈluːʒn] engaño *m*; **you're under a delusion if you think ...** te engañas si piensas que ...

de·mand [dɪˈmænd] **1** *n* exigencia *f*; *by union* reivindicación *f*; COM demanda *f*; **in demand** solicitado **2** *v/t* exigir; (*require*) requerir

de·mand·ing [dɪˈmændɪŋ] *adj job* que exige mucho; *person* exigente

de·mean·ing [dɪˈmiːnɪŋ] *adj* degradante

de·ment·ed [dɪˈmentɪd] *adj* demente

de·mise [dɪˈmaɪz] fallecimiento *m*; *fig* desaparición *f*

dem·i·tasse [ˈdemɪtæs] taza *f* de café

dem·o [ˈdemoʊ] *protest* manifestación *f*; *of video etc* maqueta *f*

de·moc·ra·cy [dɪˈmɑːkrəsɪ] democracia *f*

dem·o·crat [ˈdeməkræt] demócrata *m/f*; **Democrat** POL Demócrata *m/f*

dem·o·crat·ic [deməˈkrætɪk] *adj* democrático

dem·o·crat·ic·al·ly [deməˈkrætɪklɪ] *adv* democráticamente

'dem·o disk disco *m* de demostración

de·mo·graph·ic [demoʊˈgræfɪk] *adj* demográfico

de·mol·ish [dɪˈmɑːlɪʃ] *v/t building* demoler; *argument* destruir, echar por tierra

dem·o·li·tion [deməˈlɪʃn] *of building* demolición *f*; *of argument* destrucción *f*

de·mon [ˈdiːmən] demonio *m*

dem·on·strate [ˈdemənstreɪt] **1** *v/t* mostrar **2** *v/i politically* manifestarse

dem·on·stra·tion [demənˈstreɪʃn] demostración *f*; *protest* manifestación *f*

de·mon·stra·tive [dɪˈmɑːnstrətɪv] *adj person* extrovertido, efusivo; GRAM demostrativo

de·mon·stra·tor ['demənstreɪtər] *protester* manifestante *m/f*

de·mor·al·ized [dɪ'mɔːrəlaɪzd] *adj* desmoralizado

de·mor·al·iz·ing [dɪ'mɔːrəlaɪzɪŋ] *adj* desmoralizador

de·mote [diː'moʊt] *v/t* degradar

de·mure [dɪ'mjʊər] *adj* solemne, recatado

den [den] (*study*) estudio *m*

de·ni·al [dɪ'naɪəl] *of rumor, accusation* negación *f*; *of request* denegación *f*

den·im ['denɪm] tela *f* vaquera

den·ims ['denɪmz] *npl* (*jeans*) vaqueros *mpl*

Den·mark ['denmɑːrk] Dinamarca

de·nom·i·na·tion [dɪnɑːmɪ'neɪʃn] *of money* valor *m*; *religious* confesión *f*

de·nounce [dɪ'naʊns] *v/t* denunciar

dense [dens] *adj smoke, fog* denso; *foliage* espeso; *crowd* compacto; F (*stupid*) corto

dense·ly ['densli] *adv:* **densely populated** densamente poblado

den·si·ty ['densɪtɪ] *of population* densidad *f*

dent [dent] **1** *n* abolladura *f* **2** *v/t* abollar

den·tal ['dentl] *adj* dental; **dental surgeon** odontólogo(-a) *m(f)*

den·ted ['dentɪd] *adj* abollado

den·tist ['dentɪst] dentista *m/f*

den·tist·ry ['dentɪstrɪ] odontología *f*

den·tures ['dentʃərz] *npl* dentadura *f* postiza

de·ny [dɪ'naɪ] *v/t* (*pret & pp* **denied**) *charge, rumor* negar; *right, request* denegar

de·o·do·rant [diː'oʊdərənt] desodorante *m*

de·part [dɪ'pɑːrt] *v/i* salir; **depart from** (*deviate from*) desviarse de

de·part·ment [dɪ'pɑːrtmənt] departamento *m*; *of government* ministerio *m*

De·part·ment of 'De·fense Ministerio *m* de Defensa

De·part·ment of the In·te·ri·or Ministerio *m* del Interior

De·part·ment of 'State Ministerio *m* de Asuntos Exteriores

de'part·ment store grandes almacenes *mpl*

de·par·ture [dɪ'pɑːrtʃər] salida *f*; *of person from job* marcha *f*; (*deviation*) desviación *f*; **a new departure** *for government, organization* una innovación; *for company* un cambio; *for actor, artist, writer* una nueva experiencia

de'par·ture lounge sala *f* de embarque

de'par·ture time hora *f* de salida

de·pend [dɪ'pend] *v/i* depender; **that depends** depende; **it depends on the**

weather depende del tiempo; **I depend on you** dependo de ti

de·pen·da·ble [dɪ'pendəbl] *adj* fiable

de·pen·dant [dɪ'pendənt] → **dependent**

de·pen·dence, de·pen·den·cy [dɪ'pendəns, dɪ'pendənsɪ] dependencia *f*

de·pen·dent [dɪ'pendənt] **1** *n* persona a cargo de otra; **how many dependents do you have?** ¿cuántas personas tiene a su cargo? **2** *adj* dependiente (**on** de)

de·pict [dɪ'pɪkt] *v/t* describir

de·plete [dɪ'pliːt] *v/t* agotar, mermar

de·plor·a·ble [dɪ'plɔːrəbl] *adj* deplorable

de·plore [dɪ'plɔːr] *v/t* deplorar

de·ploy [dɪ'plɔɪ] *v/t* (*use*) utilizar; (*position*) desplegar

de·pop·u·la·tion [diːpɑːpjə'leɪʃn] despoblación *f*

de·port [dɪ'pɔːrt] *v/t* deportar

de·por·ta·tion [diːpɔːr'teɪʃn] deportación *f*

de·por'ta·tion or·der orden *f* de deportación

de·pose [dɪ'poʊz] *v/t* deponer

de·pos·it [dɪ'pɑːzɪt] **1** *n in bank, of oil* depósito *m*; *of coal* yacimiento *m*; *on purchase* señal *f*, depósito *m* **2** *v/t money* depositar, *Span* ingresar; (*put down*) depositar

de'pos·it ac·count *Br* cuenta *f* de ahorro *or* de depósito

dep·o·si·tion [diːpoʊ'zɪʃn] LAW declaración *f*

dep·ot ['diːpoʊ] (*train station*) estación *f* de tren; (*bus station*) estación *f* de auto buses; *for storage* depósito *m*

de·praved [dɪ'preɪvd] *adj* depravado

de·pre·ci·ate [dɪ'priːʃieɪt] *v/i* FIN depreciarse

de·pre·ci·a·tion [dɪpriːʃɪ'eɪʃn] FIN depreciación *f*

de·press [dɪ'pres] *v/t person* deprimir

de·pressed [dɪ'prest] *adj person* deprimido

de·press·ing [dɪ'presɪŋ] *adj* deprimente

de·pres·sion [dɪ'preʃn] MED, *economic* depresión *f*; *meteorological* borrasca *f*

dep·ri·va·tion [deprɪ'veɪʃn] privación *f*

de·prive [dɪ'praɪv] *v/t* privar; **deprive s.o. of sth** privar a alguien de algo

de·prived [dɪ'praɪvd] *adj* desfavorecido

depth [depθ] profundidad *f*; *of color* intensidad *f*; **in depth** (*thoroughly*) en profundidad; **in the depths of winter** en pleno invierno; **be out of one's depth** *in water* no tocar el fondo; *fig: in discussion etc* saber muy poco

dep·u·ta·tion [depjʊ'teɪʃn] delegación *f*

◆ **dep·u·tize for** ['depjʊtaɪz] *v/t* sustituir

D

dep·u·ty ['depjʊtɪ] segundo(-a) *m(f)*

'dep·u·ty lead·er vicelíder *m/f*

de·rail [dɪ'reɪl] *v/t* hacer descarrilar; **be derailed** *of train* descarrilar

de·ranged [dɪ'reɪndʒd] *adj* perturbado, trastornado

de·reg·u·late [dɪ'regjʊleɪt] *v/t* liberalizar, desregular

de·reg·u·la·tion [dɪregjʊ'leɪʃn] liberalización *f*, desregulación *f*

der·e·lict ['derəlɪkt] *adj* en ruinas

de·ride [dɪ'raɪd] *v/t* ridiculizar, mofarse de

de·ri·sion [dɪ'rɪʒn] burla *f*, mofa *f*

de·ri·sive [dɪ'raɪsɪv] *adj* burlón

de·ri·sive·ly [dɪ'raɪsɪvlɪ] *adv* burlonamente

de·ri·so·ry [dɪ'raɪsərɪ] *adj amount, salary* irrisorio

de·riv·a·tive [dɪ'rɪvətɪv] *adj* (*not original*) poco original

de·rive [dɪ'raɪv] *v/t* obtener, encontrar; **be derived from** *of word* derivar(se) de

der·ma·tol·o·gist [dɜːrmə'tɑːlədʒɪst] dermatólogo(-a) *m(f)*

de·rog·a·to·ry [dɪ'rɑːgətɔːrɪ] *adj* despectivo

de·scend [dɪ'send] **1** *v/t* descender por; **be descended from** descender de **2** *v/i* descender; *of mood, darkness* caer

de·scen·dant [dɪ'sendənt] descendiente *m/f*

de·scent [dɪ'sent] descenso *m*; (*ancestry*) ascendencia *f*; **of Chinese descent** de ascendencia china

de·scribe [dɪ'skraɪb] *v/t* describir; **describe sth as sth** definir a algo como algo

de·scrip·tion [dɪ'skrɪpʃn] descripción *f*

des·e·crate ['desɪkreɪt] *v/t* profanar

des·e·cra·tion [desɪ'kreɪʃn] profanación *f*

de·seg·re·gate [diː'segrəgeɪt] *v/t* acabar con la segregación racial en

des·ert¹ ['dezərt] *n also fig* desierto *m*

de·sert² [dɪ'zɜːrt] **1** *v/t* (*abandon*) abandonar **2** *v/i of soldier* desertar

de·sert·ed [dɪ'zɜːrtɪd] *adj* desierto

de·sert·er [dɪ'zɜːrtər] MIL desertor(a) *m(f)*

de·ser·ti·fi·ca·tion [dɪzɜːrtɪfɪ'keɪʃn] desertización *f*

de·ser·tion [dɪ'zɜːrtn] (*abandonment*) abandono *m*; MIL deserción *f*

des·ert 'is·land isla *f* desierta

de·serve [dɪ'zɜːrv] *v/t* merecer

de·sign [dɪ'zaɪn] **1** *n* diseño *m*; (*pattern*) motivo *m* **2** *v/t* diseñar; **not designed for heavy use** no está diseñado para ser utilizado constantemente

des·ig·nate ['dezɪgneɪt] *v/t person* designar; *area* declarar

de·sign·er [dɪ'zaɪnər] diseñador(a) *m(f*

de'sign·er clothes *npl* ropa *f* de diseño

de'sign fault defecto *m* de diseño

de'sign school escuela *f* de diseño

de·sir·a·ble [dɪ'zaɪrəbl] *adj* deseable *house* apetecible, atractivo

de·sire [dɪ'zaɪr] *n* deseo *m*; **I have no de sire to see him** no me apetece verle

desk [desk] *in classroom* pupitre *m*; *in ho me, office* mesa *f*; *in hotel* recepción *f*

'desk clerk recepcionista *m/f*

'desk di·a·ry agenda *f*

'desk·top *also on screen* escritorio *m computer Span* ordenador *m* de escritor io, *L.Am.* computadora *f* de escritorio

desk·top 'pub·lish·ing autoedición *f*

des·o·late ['desələt] *adj place* desolado

de·spair [dɪ'sper] **1** *n* desesperación *f*; *i* **despair** desesperado **2** *v/i* desesperarse; **despair of finding something to wea** he perdido la esperanza de encontrar al go para ponerme

des·per·ate ['despərət] *adj* desesperado; **be desperate** estar desesperado; **b desperate for a drink/cigarette** neces itar una bebida / un cigarrillo desespera damente

des·per·a·tion [despə'reɪʃn] desespera ción *f*; **an act of desperation** un acto de sesperado

des·pic·a·ble [dɪs'pɪkəbl] *adj* despreci able

de·spise [dɪ'spaɪz] *v/t* despreciar

de·spite [dɪ'spaɪt] *prep* a pesar de

de·spon·dent [dɪ'spɑːndənt] *adj* abatido desanimado

des·pot ['despɑːt] déspota *m/f*

des·sert [dɪ'zɜːrt] postre *m*

des·ti·na·tion [destɪ'neɪʃn] destino *m*

des·tined ['destɪnd] *adj*: **be destined fo** *fig* estar destinado a

des·ti·ny ['destɪnɪ] destino *m*

des·ti·tute ['destɪtuːt] *adj* indigente; **b destitute** estar en la miseria

de·stroy [dɪ'strɔɪ] *v/t* destruir

de·stroy·er [dɪ'strɔɪr] NAUT destructor *m*

de·struc·tion [dɪ'strʌkʃn] destrucción *f*

de·struc·tive [dɪ'strʌktɪv] *adj* destructi vo; *child* revoltoso

de·tach [dɪ'tætʃ] *v/t* separar, soltar

de·tach·a·ble [dɪ'tætʃəbl] *adj* desmont able, separable

de·tached [dɪ'tætʃt] *adj* (*objective*) distan ciado

de·tach·ment [dɪ'tætʃmənt] (*objectivity*) distancia *f*

de·tail ['diːteɪl] *n* detalle *m*; **in detail** en detalle

de·tailed ['diːteɪld] *adj* detallado

de·tain [dɪˈteɪn] v/t (hold back) entretener; as prisoner detener

de·tain·ee [diːteɪnˈiː] detenido(-a) m(f)

de·tect [dɪˈtekt] v/t percibir; of device detectar

de·tec·tion [dɪˈtekʃn] of criminal, crime descubrimiento m; of smoke etc detección f

de·tec·tive [dɪˈtektɪv] detective m/f

de·tec·tive nov·el novela f policiaca or de detectives

de·tec·tor [dɪˈtektər] detector m

dé·tente [deɪtɑːnt] POL distensión f

de·ten·tion [dɪˈtenʃn] (imprisonment) detención f

de·ter [dɪˈtɜːr] v/t (pret & pp **deterred**) disuadir; **deter s.o. from doing sth** disuadir a alguien de hacer algo

de·ter·gent [dɪˈtɜːrdʒənt] detergente m

de·te·ri·o·rate [dɪˈtɪriəreɪt] v/i deteriorarse; of weather empeorar

de·te·ri·o·ra·tion [dɪtɪriəˈreɪʃn] deterioro m; of weather empeoramiento m

de·ter·mi·na·tion [dɪtɜːrmɪˈneɪʃn] (resolution) determinación f

de·ter·mine [dɪˈtɜːrmɪn] v/t (establish) determinar

de·ter·mined [dɪˈtɜːrmɪnd] adj resuelto, decidido; **I'm determined to succeed** estoy decidido a triunfar

de·ter·rent [dɪˈterənt] n elemento m disuasorio; **act as a deterrent** actuar como elemento disuasorio; **nuclear deterrent** disuasión f nuclear

de·test [dɪˈtest] v/t detestar

de·test·a·ble [dɪˈtestəbl] adj detestable

de·to·nate [ˈdetəneɪt] **1** v/t hacer detonar or explotar **2** v/i detonar, explotar

de·to·na·tion [detəˈneɪʃn] detonación f, explosión f

de·tour [ˈdiːtʊr] n rodeo m; (diversion) desvío m; **make a detour** dar un rodeo

♦ **de·tract from** [dɪˈtrækt] v/t achievement quitar méritos a; beauty quitar atractivo a; **the bad weather didn't detract from their enjoyment** el mal tiempo no impidió que disfrutaran

de·tri·ment [ˈdetrɪmənt]: **to the detriment of** en detrimento de

de·tri·men·tal [detrɪˈmentl] adj perjudicial (**to** para)

deuce [duːs] in tennis deuce m

de·val·u·a·tion [diːvæljuˈeɪʃn] of currency devaluación f

de·val·ue [diːˈvælju] v/t currency devaluar

dev·a·state [ˈdevəsteɪt] v/t crops, countryside, city devastar; fig: person asolar

dev·a·stat·ing [ˈdevəsteɪtɪŋ] adj devastador

de·vel·op [dɪˈveləp] **1** v/t film revelar; land, site urbanizar; activity, business desarrollar; (originate) desarrollar; (improve on) perfeccionar; illness, cold contraer **2** v/i (grow) desarrollarse; **develop into** convertirse en

de·vel·op·er [dɪˈveləpər] of property promotor(a) m(f) inmobiliario(-a)

de·vel·op·ing 'coun·try [dɪˈveləpɪŋ] país m en vías de desarrollo

de·vel·op·ment [dɪˈveləpmənt] of film revelado m; of land, site urbanización f; of business, country desarrollo m; (event) acontecimiento m; (origination) desarrollo m; (improving) perfeccionamiento m

de·vice [dɪˈvaɪs] tool aparato m, dispositivo m

dev·il [ˈdevl] also fig diablo m, demonio m

de·vi·ous [ˈdiːvɪəs] adj (sly) retorcido

de·vise [dɪˈvaɪz] v/t idear

de·void [dɪˈvɔɪd] adj: **be devoid of** estar desprovisto de

dev·o·lu·tion [diːvəˈluːʃn] POL traspaso m de competencias

de·vote [dɪˈvoʊt] v/t dedicar (**to** a)

de·vot·ed [dɪˈvoʊtɪd] adj son etc afectuoso; **be devoted to s.o.** tener mucho cariño a alguien

dev·o·tee [devoʊˈtiː] entusiasta m/f

de·vo·tion [dɪˈvoʊʃn] devoción f

de·vour [dɪˈvaʊər] v/t food, book devorar

de·vout [dɪˈvaʊt] adj devoto

dew [duː] rocío m

dex·ter·i·ty [dekˈsterətɪ] destreza f

di·a·be·tes [daɪəˈbiːtiːz] nsg diabetes f

di·a·bet·ic [daɪəˈbetɪk] **1** n diabético(-a) m(f) **2** adj diabético; foods para diabéticos

di·ag·nose [ˈdaɪəgnoʊz] v/t diagnosticar; **she has been diagnosed as having cancer** se le ha diagnosticado un cáncer

di·ag·no·sis [daɪəgˈnoʊsɪs] (pl **diagnoses** [daɪəgˈnoʊsiːz]) diagnóstico m

di·ag·o·nal [daɪˈægənl] adj diagonal

di·ag·o·nal·ly [daɪˈægənlɪ] adv diagonalmente, en diagonal

di·a·gram [ˈdaɪəgræm] diagrama m

di·al [ˈdaɪl] **1** n of clock esfera f; of instrument cuadrante m; TELEC disco m **2** v/t & v/i (pret & pp **dialed**, Br **dialled**) TELEC marcar

di·a·lect [ˈdaɪəlekt] dialecto m

di·al·ling tone Br → **dial tone**

di·a·log, Br **di·a·logue** [ˈdaɪəlɒg] diálogo m

di·a·log box COMPUT ventana f de diálogo

'di·al tone tono *m* de marcar

di·am·e·ter ['daɪ'æmɪtər] diámetro *m*; *a circle 6 cms in diameter* un círculo de 6 cms. de diámetro

di·a·met·ri·cal·ly [daɪə'metrɪkəlɪ] *adv*: *diametrically opposed* diametralmente opuesto

di·a·mond ['daɪmənd] *also in cards* diamante *m*; *shape* rombo *m*

di·a·per ['daɪpər] pañal *m*

di·a·phragm ['daɪəfræm] ANAT, *contraceptive* diafragma *m*

di·ar·rhe·a, *Br* **di·ar·rhoe·a** [daɪə'riːə] diarrea *f*

di·a·ry ['daɪrɪ] *for thoughts* diario *m*; *for appointments* agenda *f*

dice [daɪs] **1** *n* dado *m*; *pl* dados *mpl* **2** *v/t food* cortar en dados

di·chot·o·my [daɪ'kɑːtəmɪ] dicotomía *f*

dic·tate [dɪk'teɪt] *v/t* dictar

dic·ta·tion [dɪk'teɪʃn] dictado *m*

dic·ta·tor [dɪk'teɪtər] POL dictador(a) *m(f)*

dic·ta·to·ri·al [dɪktə'tɔːrɪəl] *adj* dictatorial

dic·ta·tor·ship [dɪk'teɪtərʃɪp] dictadura *f*

dic·tion·a·ry ['dɪkʃənerɪ] diccionario *m*

did [dɪd] *pret* → **do**

die [daɪ] *v/i* morir; *die of cancer* / *Aids* morir de cáncer / sida; *I'm dying to know* / *leave* me muero de ganas de saber / marchar

◆ **die away** *v/i of noise* desaparecer

◆ **die down** *v/i of noise* irse apagando; *of storm* amainar; *of fire* irse extinguiendo; *of excitement* calmarse

◆ **die out** *v/i of custom, species* desaparecer

die·sel ['diːzl] *fuel* gasoil *m*, gasóleo *m*

di·et ['daɪət] **1** *n* (*regular food*) dieta *f*; *for losing weight, for health reasons* dieta *f*, régimen *m* **2** *v/i to lose weight* hacer dieta *or* régimen

di·e·ti·tian [daɪə'tɪʃn] experto(-a) *m(f)* en dietética

dif·fer ['dɪfər] *v/i* (*be different*) ser distinto; (*disagree*) discrepar; *the male differs from the female in* ... el macho se diferencia de la hembra por ...

dif·fer·ence ['dɪfrəns] diferencia *f*; (*disagreement*) diferencia *f*, discrepancia *f*; *it doesn't make any difference* (*doesn't change anything*) no cambia nada; (*doesn't matter*) da lo mismo

dif·fer·ent ['dɪfrənt] *adj* diferente, distinto (*from, than* que)

dif·fer·en·ti·ate [dɪfə'renʃɪeɪt] *v/i* diferenciar, distinguir (*between* entre); *differentiate between treat differently* establecer diferencias entre

dif·fer·ent·ly ['dɪfrəntlɪ] *adv* de manera diferente

dif·fi·cult ['dɪfɪkəlt] *adj* difícil

dif·fi·cul·ty ['dɪfɪkəltɪ] dificultad *f*; *with difficulty* con dificultades

dif·fi·dence ['dɪfɪdəns] retraimiento *m*

dif·fi·dent ['dɪfɪdənt] *adj* retraído

dig [dɪg] *v/t & v/i* (*pret & pp* **dug**) cavar

◆ **dig out** *v/t* (*find*) encontrar

◆ **dig up** *v/t* levantar, cavar; *information* desenterrar

di·gest [daɪ'dʒest] *v/t also fig* digerir

di·gest·i·ble [daɪ'dʒestəbl] *adj food* digerible

di·ges·tion [daɪ'dʒestʃn] digestión *f*

di·ges·tive [daɪ'dʒestɪv] *adj* digestivo

dig·ger ['dɪgər] *machine* excavadora *f*

dig·it ['dɪdʒɪt] (*number*) dígito *m*; *a 4 digit number* un número de 4 dígitos

di·gi·tal ['dɪdʒɪtl] *adj* digital

dig·ni·fied ['dɪgnɪfaɪd] *adj* digno

dig·ni·ta·ry ['dɪgnɪterɪ] dignatario(-a) *m(f)*

dig·ni·ty ['dɪgnɪtɪ] dignidad *f*

di·gress [daɪ'gres] *v/i* divagar, apartarse del tema

di·gres·sion [daɪ'greʃn] digresión *f*

dike [daɪk] *wall* dique *m*

di·lap·i·dat·ed [dɪ'læpɪdeɪtɪd] *adj* destartalado

di·late [daɪ'leɪt] *v/i of pupils* dilatarse

di·lem·ma [dɪ'lemə] dilema *m*; *be in a dilemma* estar en un dilema

dil·et·tante [dɪle'tæntɪ] diletante *m/f*

dil·i·gent ['dɪlɪdʒənt] *adj* diligente

di·lute [daɪ'luːt] *v/t* diluir

dim [dɪm] **1** *adj room* oscuro; *light* tenue; *outline* borroso, confuso; (*stupid*) tonto; *prospects* remoto **2** *v/t* (*pret & pp* **dimmed**): *dim the headlights* poner las luces cortas **3** *v/i* (*pret & pp* **dimmed**) *of lights* atenuarse

dime [daɪm] moneda *f* de diez centavos

di·men·sion [daɪ'menʃn] (*measurement*) dimensión *f*

di·min·ish [dɪ'mɪnɪʃ] *v/t & v/i* disminuir

di·min·u·tive [dɪ'mɪnʊtɪv] **1** *n* diminutivo *m* **2** *adj* diminuto

dim·ple ['dɪmpl] hoyuelo *m*

din [dɪn] *n* estruendo *m*

dine [daɪn] *v/i fml* cenar

din·er ['daɪnər] *person* comensal *m/f*; *restaurant* restaurante *m* barato

din·ghy ['dɪŋgɪ] (*small yacht*) bote *m* de vela; (*rubber boat*) lancha *f* neumática

din·gy ['dɪndʒɪ] *adj* sórdido; (*dirty*) sucio

'din·ing car ['daɪnɪŋ] RAIL vagón *m* restaurante, coche *m* comedor

'din·ing room comedor *m*

'**din·ing ta·ble** mesa *f* de comedor

din·ner ['dɪnər] *in the evening* cena *f*; *at midday* comida *f*; *(formal gathering)* cena *f* de gala

'**din·ner guest** invitado(-a) *m(f)* a cenar

'**din·ner jack·et** esmoquin *m*

'**din·ner par·ty** cena *f*

'**din·ner serv·ice** vajilla *f*

di·no·saur ['daɪnəsɔːr] dinosaurio *m*

dip [dɪp] **1** *n (swim)* baño *m*, zambullida *f*; *for food* salsa *f*; *(slope)* inclinación *f*, pendiente *f*; *(depression)* hondonada *f* **2** *v/t (pret & pp **dipped**)* meter; ***dip the head·lights*** poner las luces cortas **3** *v/i (pret & pp **dipped**) of road* bajar

di·plo·ma [dɪ'ploʊmə] diploma *m*

di·plo·ma·cy [dɪ'ploʊməsɪ] *also fig* diplomacia *f*

dip·lo·mat ['dɪpləmæt] diplomático(-a) *m(f)*

dip·lo·mat·ic [dɪplə'mætɪk] *adj also fig* diplomático

dip·lo·mat·i·cal·ly [dɪplə'mætɪklɪ] *adv* de forma diplomática

dip·lo·mat·ic im·mu·ni·ty inmunidad *f* diplomática

dire [daɪr] *adj* terrible; ***be in dire need of*** necesitar acuciantemente

di·rect [daɪ'rekt] **1** *adj* directo **2** *v/t play, movie, attention* dirigir; ***can you direct me to the museum?*** ¿me podría indicar cómo se va al museo?

di·rect 'cur·rent ELEC corriente *f* continua

di·rec·tion [dɪ'rekʃn] dirección *f*; ***directions** to a place* indicaciones *fpl*; *(instructions)* instrucciones *fpl*; *for medicine* posología *f*; ***let's ask for directions*** preguntemos cómo se va; ***directions for use*** modo *m* de empleo

di·rec·tion in·di·ca·tor MOT intermitente *m*

di·rec·tive [dɪ'rektɪv] directiva *f*

di·rect·ly [dɪ'rektlɪ] **1** *adv (straight)* directamente; *(soon)* pronto; *(immediately)* ahora mismo **2** *conj* en cuanto

di·rec·tor [dɪ'rektər] director(a) *m(f)*

di·rec·to·ry [dɪ'rektərɪ] directorio *m*; TELEC guía *f* telefónica

dirt [dɜːrt] suciedad *f*

'**dirt cheap** *adj* F tirado F

dirt·y ['dɜːrtɪ] **1** *adj* sucio; *(pornographic)* pornográfico, obsceno **2** *v/t (pret & pp **dirtied**)* ensuciar

dirt·y 'trick jugarreta *f*; ***play a dirty trick on s.o.*** hacer una jugarreta a alguien

disc [dɪsk] *(CD)* compact *m* (disc)

dis·a·bil·i·ty [dɪsə'bɪlɪtɪ] discapacidad *f*, minusvalía *f*

dis·a·bled [dɪs'eɪbld] **1** *n*: ***the disabled*** los discapacitados *mpl* **2** *adj* discapacita-

---

do

dis·ad·van·tage [dɪsəd'væntɪdʒ] *(draw·back)* desventaja *f*; ***be at a disadvantage*** estar en desventaja

dis·ad·van·taged [dɪsəd'væntɪdʒd] *adj* desfavorecido

dis·ad·van·ta·geous [dɪsædvæn'teɪdʒəs] *adj* desventajoso, desfavorable

dis·a·gree [dɪsə'griː] *v/i of person* no estar de acuerdo, discrepar; ***let's agree to disagree*** aceptemos que no nos vamos a poner de acuerdo

◆ **disagree with** *v/t of person* no estar de acuerdo con, discrepar con; *of food* sentar mal; ***lobster disagrees with me*** la langosta me sienta mal

dis·a·gree·a·ble [dɪsə'griːəbl] *adj* desagradable

dis·a·gree·ment [dɪsə'griːmənt] desacuerdo *m*; *(argument)* discusión *f*

dis·ap·pear [dɪsə'pɪr] *v/i* desaparecer

dis·ap·pear·ance [dɪsə'pɪrəns] desaparición *f*

dis·ap·point [dɪsə'pɔɪnt] *v/t* desilusionar, decepcionar

dis·ap·point·ed [dɪsə'pɔɪntɪd] *adj* desilusionado, decepcionado

dis·ap·point·ing [dɪsə'pɔɪntɪŋ] *adj* decepcionante

dis·ap·point·ment [dɪsə'pɔɪntmənt] desilusión *f*, decepción *f*

dis·ap·prov·al [dɪsə'pruːvl] desaprobación *f*

dis·ap·prove [dɪsə'pruːv] *v/i* desaprobar, estar en contra; ***disapprove of*** desaprobar, estar en contra de

dis·ap·prov·ing [dɪsə'pruːvɪŋ] *adj* desaprobatorio, de desaprobación

dis·ap·prov·ing·ly [dɪsə'pruːvɪŋlɪ] *adv* con desaprobación

dis·arm [dɪs'ɑːrm] **1** *v/t* desarmar **2** *v/i* desarmarse

dis·ar·ma·ment [dɪs'ɑːrməmənt] desarme *m*

dis·arm·ing [dɪs'ɑːrmɪŋ] *adj* cautivador

dis·as·ter [dɪ'zæstər] desastre *m*

di'sas·ter ar·e·a zona *f* catastrófica; *(fig: person)* desastre *m*

di·sas·trous [dɪ'zæstrəs] *adj* desastroso

dis·band [dɪs'bænd] **1** *v/t* disolver **2** *v/i* disolverse

dis·be·lief [dɪsbə'liːf] incredulidad *f*; ***in disbelief*** con incredulidad

dis·card [dɪ'skɑːrd] *v/t* desechar; *boy·friend* deshacerse de

di·scern [dɪ'sɜːrn] *v/t* distinguir, percibir

di·scern·i·ble [dɪ'sɜːrnəbl] *adj* perceptible

di·scern·ing [dɪ'sɜːrnɪŋ] *adj* entendido, exigente

dis·charge 1 *n* ['dɪstʃɑːrdʒ] *from hospital* alta *f*; *from army* licencia *f* **2** *v/t* [dɪs-'tʃɑːrdʒ] *from hospital* dar el alta a; *from army* licenciar; *from job* despedir

di·sci·ple [dɪ'saɪpl] *religious* discípulo *m*

dis·ci·pli·nar·y [dɪsɪ'plɪnərɪ] *adj* disciplinario

dis·ci·pline ['dɪsɪplɪn] **1** *n* disciplina *f* **2** *v/t child, dog* castigar; *employee* sancionar

'disc jock·ey disc jockey *m/f*, *Span* pinchadiscos *m/f inv*

dis·claim [dɪs'kleɪm] *v/t* negar

dis·close [dɪs'kloʊs] *v/t* revelar

dis·clo·sure [dɪs'kloʊʒər] revelación *f*

dis·co ['dɪskoʊ] discoteca *f*

dis·col·or, *Br* **dis·col·our** [dɪs'kʌlər] *v/i* decolorar

dis·com·fort [dɪs'kʌmfərt] (*pain*) molestia *f*; (*embarrassment*) incomodidad *f*

dis·con·cert [dɪskən'sɜːrt] *v/t* desconcertar

dis·con·cert·ed [dɪskən'sɜːrtɪd] *adj* desconcertado

dis·con·nect [dɪskə'nekt] *v/t* desconectar

dis·con·so·late [dɪs'kɑːnsələt] *adj* desconsolado

dis·con·tent [dɪskən'tent] descontento *m*

dis·con·tent·ed [dɪskən'tentɪd] *adj* descontento

dis·con·tin·ue [dɪskən'tɪnjuː] *v/t product* dejar de producir; *bus, train service* suspender; *magazine* dejar de publicar

dis·cord ['dɪskɔːrd] MUS discordancia *f*; *in relations* discordia *f*

dis·co·theque ['dɪskətek] discoteca *f*

dis·count 1 *n* ['dɪskaʊnt] descuento *m* **2** *v/t* [dɪs'kaʊnt] *goods* descontar; *theory* descartar

dis·cour·age [dɪs'kʌrɪdʒ] *v/t* (*dissuade*) disuadir (**from** de); (*dishearten*) desanimar, desalentar

dis·cour·age·ment [dɪs'kʌrɪdʒmənt] disuasión *f*; (*being disheartened*) desánimo *m*, desaliento *m*

dis·cov·er [dɪ'skʌvər] *v/t* descubrir

dis·cov·er·er [dɪ'skʌvərər] descubridor(a) *m(f)*

dis·cov·er·y [dɪ'skʌvərɪ] descubrimiento *m*

dis·cred·it [dɪs'kredɪt] *v/t* desacreditar

di·screet [dɪ'skriːt] *adj* discreto

di·screet·ly [dɪ'skriːtlɪ] *adv* discretamente

di·screp·an·cy [dɪ'skrepənsɪ] discrepancia *f*

di·scre·tion [dɪ'skreʃn] discreción *f*; **at your discretion** a discreción; **use your**

discretion usa tu criterio

di·scrim·i·nate [dɪ'skrɪmɪneɪt] *v/i* discriminar (**against** contra); **discriminate between** (*distinguish*) distinguir entre

di·scrim·i·nat·ing [dɪ'skrɪmɪneɪtɪŋ] *adj* entendido, exigente

di·scrim·i·na·tion [dɪ'skrɪmɪneɪʃn] *sexual, racial etc* discriminación *f*

dis·cus ['dɪskəs] SP *object* disco *m*; *event* lanzamiento *m* de disco

di·scuss [dɪ'skʌs] *v/t* discutir; *of article* analizar

di·scus·sion [dɪ'skʌʃn] discusión *f*

'dis·cus throw·er lanzador(a) *m(f)* de disco

dis·dain [dɪs'deɪn] *n* desdén *m*

dis·ease [dɪ'ziːz] enfermedad *f*

dis·em·bark [dɪsəm'bɑːrk] *v/i* desembarcar

dis·en·chant·ed [dɪsən'tʃæntɪd] *adj*: **disenchanted with** desencantado con

dis·en·gage [dɪsən'geɪdʒ] *v/t* soltar

dis·en·tan·gle [dɪsən'tæŋgl] *v/t* desenredar

dis·fig·ure [dɪs'fɪgər] *v/t* desfigurar

dis·grace [dɪs'greɪs] **1** *n* vergüenza *f*; **it's a disgrace!** ¡qué vergüenza!; **in disgrace** desacreditada **2** *v/t* deshonrar

dis·grace·ful [dɪs'greɪsfəl] *adj behavior, situation* vergonzoso, lamentable

dis·grunt·led [dɪs'grʌntld] *adj* descontento

dis·guise [dɪs'gaɪz] **1** *n* disfraz *m*; **in disguise** disfrazado **2** *v/t voice, handwriting* cambiar; *fear, anxiety* disfrazar; **disguise o.s. as** disfrazarse de; **he was disguised as** iba disfrazado de

dis·gust [dɪs'gʌst] **1** *n* asco *m*, repugnancia *f*; **in disgust** asqueado **2** *v/t* dar asco, repugnar; **I'm disgusted by ...** me da asco *or* me repugna ...

dis·gust·ing [dɪs'gʌstɪŋ] *adj habit, smell, food* asqueroso, repugnante; **it is disgusting that ...** da asco que ..., es repugnante que ...

dish [dɪʃ] (*part of meal, container*) plato *m*

'dish·cloth paño *m* de cocina

dis·heart·en·ed [dɪs'hɑːrtnd] *adj* desalentado, descorazonado

dis·heart·en·ing [dɪs'hɑːrtnɪŋ] *adj* descorazonador

di·shev·eled [dɪ'ʃevld] *adj hair, clothes* desaliñado; *person* despeinado

dis·hon·est [dɪs'ɑːnɪst] *adj* deshonesto

dis·hon·es·ty [dɪs'ɑːnɪstɪ] deshonestidad *f*

dis·hon·or [dɪs'ɑːnər] *n* deshonra *f*; **bring dishonor on** deshonrar a

dis·hon·o·ra·ble [dɪsˈɑːnərəbl] *adj* deshonroso

dis·hon·our *etc Br* → **dishonor** *etc*

dish·wash·er *person* lavaplatos *m/f inv*; *machine* lavavajillas *m inv*, lavaplatos *m inv*

dish·wash·ing liq·uid lavavajillas *m inv*

dish·wa·ter agua *f* de lavar los platos

dis·il·lu·sion [dɪsɪˈluːʒn] *v/t* desilusionar

dis·il·lu·sion·ment [dɪsɪˈluːʒnmənt] desilusión *f*

dis·in·clined [dɪsɪnˈklaɪnd] *adj*: **she was disinclined to believe him** no estaba inclinada a creerle

dis·in·fect [dɪsɪnˈfekt] *v/t* desinfectar

dis·in·fec·tant [dɪsɪnˈfektənt] desinfectante *m*

dis·in·her·it [dɪsɪnˈherɪt] *v/t* desheredar

dis·in·te·grate [dɪsˈɪntəgreɪt] *v/i* desintegrarse; *of marriage* deshacerse

dis·in·terest·ed [dɪsˈɪntərestɪd] *adj (unbiased)* desinteresado

dis·joint·ed [dɪsˈdʒɔɪntɪd] *adj* deshilvanado

disk [dɪsk] *also* COMPUT disco *m*; **on disk** en disco

disk drive COMPUT unidad *f* de disco

disk·ette [dɪsˈket] disquete *m*

dis·like [dɪsˈlaɪk] **1** *n* antipatía *f* **2** *v/t*: **she dislikes being kept waiting** no le gusta que la hagan esperar; **I dislike him** no me gusta

dis·lo·cate [ˈdɪsləkeɪt] *v/t shoulder* dislocar

dis·lodge [dɪsˈlɑːdʒ] *v/t* desplazar, mover de su sitio

dis·loy·al [dɪsˈlɔɪəl] *adj* desleal

dis·loy·al·ty [dɪsˈlɔɪəltɪ] deslealtad *f*

dis·mal [ˈdɪzməl] *adj weather* horroroso, espantoso; *news, prospect* negro; *person (sad)* triste; *person (negative)* negativo; *failure* estrepitoso

dis·man·tle [dɪsˈmæntl] *v/t* desmantelar

dis·may [dɪsˈmeɪ] **1** *n (alarm)* consternación *f*; *(disappointment)* desánimo *m* **2** *v/t* consternar

dis·miss [dɪsˈmɪs] *v/t employee* despedir; *suggestion* rechazar; *idea, possibility* descartar

dis·miss·al [dɪsˈmɪsl] *of employee* despido *m*

dis·mount [dɪsˈmaʊnt] *v/i* desmontar

dis·o·be·di·ence [dɪsəˈbiːdɪəns] desobediencia *f*

dis·o·be·di·ent [dɪsəˈbiːdɪənt] *adj* desobediente

dis·o·bey [dɪsəˈbeɪ] *v/t* desobedecer

dis·or·der [dɪsˈɔːrdər] *(untidiness)* desorden *m*; *(unrest)* desórdenes *mpl*; MED dolencia *f*

dis·or·der·ly [dɪsˈɔːrdərlɪ] *adj room, desk* desordenado; *mob* alborotado

dis·or·gan·ized [dɪsˈɔːrgənaɪzd] *adj* desorganizado

dis·o·ri·ent·ed [dɪsˈɔːrɪəntɪd] *adj* desorientado

dis·own [dɪsˈoʊn] *v/t* repudiar, renegar de

di·spar·ag·ing [dɪˈspærɪdʒɪŋ] *adj* despreciativo

dis·par·i·ty [dɪˈspærətɪ] disparidad *f*

dis·pas·sion·ate [dɪˈspæʃənət] *adj (objective)* desapasionado

di·spatch [dɪˈspætʃ] *v/t (send)* enviar

di·spen·sa·ry [dɪˈspensərɪ] *in pharmacy* dispensario *m*

◆ **di·spense with** [dɪˈspens] *v/t* prescindir de

di·spense [dɪˈspens] *v/t* dispensar

di·sperse [dɪˈspɜːrs] **1** *v/t* dispersar **2** *v/i of crowd* dispersarse; *of mist* disiparse

di·spir·it·ed [dɪˈspɪrɪtɪd] *adj* desalentado, abatido

dis·place [dɪsˈpleɪs] *v/t (supplant)* sustituir

di·splay [dɪˈspleɪ] **1** *n* muestra *f*; *in store window* objetos *mpl* expuestos; COMPUT pantalla *f*; **be on display** estar expuesto **2** *v/t emotion* mostrar; *at exhibition, for sale* exponer; COMPUT visualizar

di·splay cab·i·net *in museum, shop* vitrina *f*

di·splease [dɪsˈpliːz] *v/t* desagradar, disgustar

dis·plea·sure [dɪsˈpleʒər] desagrado *m*, disgusto *m*

dis·po·sa·ble [dɪˈspoʊzəbl] *adj* desechable; **disposable income** ingreso(s) *m(pl)* disponible(s)

dis·pos·al [dɪˈspoʊzl] eliminación *f*; **I am at your disposal** estoy a su disposición; **put sth at s.o.'s disposal** poner algo a disposición de alguien

◆ **dis·pose of** [dɪˈspoʊz] *v/t (get rid of)* deshacerse de

dis·posed [dɪˈspoʊzd] *adj*: **be disposed to do sth** *(willing)* estar dispuesto a hacer algo; **be well disposed towards** estar bien dispuesto hacia

dis·po·si·tion [dɪspəˈzɪʃn] *(nature)* carácter *m*

dis·pro·por·tion·ate [dɪsprəˈpɔːrʃənət] *adj* desproporcionado

dis·prove [dɪsˈpruːv] *v/t* refutar

di·spute [dɪˈspjuːt] **1** *n* disputa *f*; *industrial* conflicto *m* laboral **2** *v/t* discutir; *(fight over)* disputarse; **I don't dispute that** eso no lo discuto

dis·qual·i·fi·ca·tion [dɪskwɑːlɪfɪˈkeɪʃn] descalificación *f*

dis·qual·i·fy [dɪs'kwɑːlɪfaɪ] v/t (pret & pp **disqualified**) descalificar

dis·re·gard [dɪsrə'gɑːrd] **1** n indiferencia f **2** v/t no tener en cuenta

dis·re·pair [dɪsrə'per]: *in a state of disrepair* deteriorado

dis·rep·u·ta·ble [dɪs'repjʊtəbl] adj poco respetable; *area* de mala reputación

dis·re·spect [dɪsrə'spekt] falta f de respeto

dis·re·spect·ful [dɪsrə'spektfəl] adj irrespetuoso

dis·rupt [dɪs'rʌpt] v/t train service trastornar, alterar; *meeting, class* interrumpir

dis·rup·tion [dɪs'rʌpʃn] of train service alteración f; of meeting, class interrupción f

dis·rup·tive [dɪs'rʌptɪv] adj perjudicial; *he's very disruptive in class* causa muchos problemas en clase

dis·sat·is·fac·tion [dɪssætɪs'fækʃn] insatisfacción f

dis·sat·is·fied [dɪs'sætɪsfaɪd] adj insatisfecho

dis·sen·sion [dɪ'senʃn] disensión f

dis·sent [dɪ'sent] **1** n discrepancia f **2** v/i: *dissent from* disentir de

dis·si·dent [ˈdɪsɪdənt] n disidente m/f

dis·sim·i·lar [dɪs'sɪmɪlər] adj distinto

dis·so·ci·ate [dɪ'soʊʃɪeɪt] v/t disociar; *dissociate o.s. from* disociarse de

dis·so·lute [ˈdɪsəluːt] adj disoluto

dis·so·lu·tion [ˈdɪsəluːʃn] POL disolución f

dis·solve [dɪ'zɑːlv] **1** v/t substance disolver **2** v/i of substance disolverse

dis·suade [dɪ'sweɪd] v/t disuadir; *dissuade s.o. from doing sth* disuadir a alguien de hacer algo

dis·tance [ˈdɪstəns] **1** n distancia f; *in the distance* en la lejanía **2** v/t distanciar; *distance o.s. from* distanciarse de

dis·tant [ˈdɪstənt] adj place, time, relative distante, lejano; *(fig: aloof)* distante

dis·taste [dɪs'teɪst] desagrado m

dis·taste·ful [dɪs'teɪstfəl] adj desagradable

dis·till·er·y [dɪs'tɪləri] destilería f

dis·tinct [dɪ'stɪŋkt] adj *(clear)* claro; *(different)* distinto; *as distinct from* a diferencia de

dis·tinc·tion [dɪ'stɪŋkʃn] *(differentiation)* distinción f; *hotel / product of distinction* un hotel / producto destacado

dis·tinc·tive [dɪ'stɪŋktɪv] adj característico

dis·tinct·ly [dɪ'stɪŋktlɪ] adv claramente, con claridad; *(decidedly)* verdaderamente

dis·tin·guish [dɪ'stɪŋgwɪʃ] v/t distinguir; *distinguish between X and Y* distinguir entre X e Y

dis·tin·guished [dɪ'stɪŋgwɪʃt] adj distinguido

dis·tort [dɪ'stɔːrt] v/t distorsionar

dis·tract [dɪ'strækt] v/t distraer

dis·trac·tion [dɪ'strækʃn] distracción f; *drive s.o. to distraction* sacar a alguien de quicio

dis·traught [dɪ'strɔːt] adj angustiado, consternado

dis·tress [dɪ'stres] **1** n sufrimiento m; *in distress* of ship, aircraft en peligro **2** v/t *(upset)* angustiar

dis·tress·ing [dɪ'stresɪŋ] adj angustiante

dis'tress sig·nal señal m de socorro

dis·trib·ute [dɪ'strɪbjuːt] v/t distribuir, repartir; COM distribuir

dis·tri·bu·tion [dɪstrɪ'bjuːʃn] distribución f

dis·tri'bu·tion ar·range·ment COM acuerdo m de distribución

dis·trib·u·tor [dɪ'strɪbjuːtər] COM distribuidor(a) m(f)

dis·trict [ˈdɪstrɪkt] *(area)* zona f; *(neighborhood)* barrio m

dis·trict at'tor·ney fiscal m/f del distrito

dis·trust [dɪs'trʌst] **1** n desconfianza f **2** v/t desconfiar de

dis·turb [dɪ'stɜːrb] v/t *(interrupt)* molestar; *(upset)* preocupar; *do not disturb* no molestar

dis·turb·ance [dɪ'stɜːrbəns] *(interruption)* molestia f; *disturbances (civil unrest)* disturbios mpl

dis·turbed [dɪ'stɜːrbd] adj *(concerned, worried)* preocupado, inquieto; *mentally* perturbado

dis·turb·ing [dɪ'stɜːrbɪŋ] adj *(worrying)* inquietante; *you may find some scenes disturbing* algunas de las escenas pueden herir la sensibilidad del espectador

dis·used [dɪs'juːzd] adj abandonado

ditch [dɪtʃ] **1** n zanja f **2** v/t F *(get rid of)* deshacerse de; *boyfriend* plantar F; *plan* abandonar

dith·er [ˈdɪðər] v/i vacilar

dive [daɪv] **1** n salto m de cabeza; *underwater* inmersión f; of plane descenso m en picado; F bar etc antro m F; *take a dive* F of dollar etc desplomarse **2** v/i *(pret also dove)* tirarse de cabeza; *underwater* bucear; of plane descender en picado

div·er [ˈdaɪvər] off board saltador(a) m(f) de trampolín; *underwater* buceador(a) m(f)

di·verge [daɪ'vɜːrdʒ] v/i bifurcarse

di·verse [daɪ'vɜːrs] adj diverso

di·ver·si·fi·ca·tion [daɪvɜːrsɪfɪ'keɪʃn] COM diversificación f

di·ver·si·fy [daɪ'vɜːrsɪfaɪ] v/i (pret & pp **diversified**) COM diversificarse

di·ver·sion [daɪ'vɜːrʃn] for traffic desvío f; to distract attention distracción f

di·ver·si·ty [daɪ'vɜːrsətɪ] diversidad f

di·vert [daɪ'vɜːrt] v/t traffic, attention desviar

di·vest [daɪ'vest] v/t: **divest s.o. of sth** despojar a alguien de algo

di·vide [dɪ'vaɪd] v/t also fig dividir; **divide 16 by 4** dividir 16 entre 4

div·i·dend ['dɪvɪdend] FIN dividendo m; **pay dividends** fig resultar beneficioso

di·vine [dɪ'vaɪn] adj also F divino

div·ing ['daɪvɪŋ] from board salto m de trampolín; (scuba diving) buceo m, submarinismo m

div·ing board trampolín m

di·vis·i·ble [dɪ'vɪzəbl] adj divisible

di·vi·sion [dɪ'vɪʒn] división f

di·vorce [dɪ'vɔːrs] 1 n divorcio m; **get a divorce** divorciarse 2 v/t divorciarse de; **get divorced** divorciarse 3 v/i divorciarse

di·vorced [dɪ'vɔːrst] adj divorciado

di·vor·cee [dɪvɔːr'siː] divorciado(-a) m(f)

di·vulge [daɪ'vʌldʒ] v/t divulgar, dar a conocer

DIY [diːaɪ'waɪ] abbr (= **do it yourself**) bricolaje m

DIY store tienda f de bricolaje

diz·zi·ness ['dɪzɪnɪs] mareo m

diz·zy ['dɪzɪ] adj mareado; **feel dizzy** estar mareado

DJ ['diːdʒeɪ] abbr (= **disc jockey**) disc jockey m/f, Span pinchadiscos m/f inv; (= **dinner jacket**) esmoquin m

DNA [diːen'eɪ] abbr (= **deoxyribonucleic acid**) AND m (= ácido m desoxirribonucleico)

do [duː] 1 v/t (pret **did**, pp **done**) hacer; **100 mph** etc ir a; **do one's hair** peinarse; **what are you doing tonight?** ¿qué vas a hacer esta noche?; **I don't know what to do** no sé qué hacer; **do it right now!** hazlo ahora mismo; **have one's hair done** arreglarse el pelo 2 v/i (pret **did**, pp **done**) (be suitable, enough): **that'll do nicely** eso bastará; **that will do!** ¡ya vale!; **do well** of business ir bien; **he's doing well** le van bien las cosas; **well done!** (congratulations!) ¡bien hecho!; **how do you do?** encantado de conocerle 3 v/aux: **do you know him?** ¿lo conoces?; **I don't know** no sé; **do be quick** date prisa, por favor; **do you like Des Moines?** -

yes I do ¿te gusta Des Moines? - sí; **he works hard, doesn't he?** trabaja mucho, ¿verdad?; **don't you believe me?** ¿no me crees?; **you do believe me, don't you?** me crees, ¿verdad?; **you don't know the answer, do you? - no I don't** no sabes la respuesta, ¿no es así? - no, no la sé

♦ **do away with** v/t (abolish) abolir

♦ **do in** v/t F (exhaust) machacar F; **I'm done in** estoy hecho polvo F

♦ **do out of** v/t: **do s.o. out of sth** timar alguien a algo F

♦ **do up** v/t (renovate) renovar; **buttons, coat** abrocharse; **laces** atarse

♦ **do with** v/t: **I could do with ...** no me vendría mal ...; **he won't have anything to do with it** (won't get involved) no quiere saber nada de ello

♦ **do without** 1 v/i: **you'll have to do without** te las tendrás que arreglar 2 v/t pasar sin

do·cile ['dousəl] adj dócil

dock[1] [dɑːk] 1 n NAUT muelle m 2 v/i of ship atracar; of spaceship acoplarse

dock[2] [dɑːk] n LAW banquillo m (de los acusados)

dock·yard Br astillero m

doc·tor ['dɑːktər] n MED médico m; form of address doctor m

doc·tor·ate ['dɑːktərət] doctorado m

doc·trine ['dɑːktrɪn] doctrina f

doc·u·dra·ma ['dɑːkjudrɑːmə] docudrama m

doc·u·ment ['dɑːkjumənt] n documento m

doc·u·men·ta·ry [dɑːkju'mentərɪ] n program documental m

doc·u·men·ta·tion [dɑːkjumen'teɪʃn] documentación f

dodge [dɑːdʒ] v/t blow, person esquivar; issue, question eludir

doe [dou] deer cierva f

dog [dɒːɡ] 1 n perro(-a) m(f) 2 v/t (pret & pp **dogged**) of bad luck perseguir

dog catch·er perrero(-a) m(f)

dog-eared ['dɒːɡɪrd] adj book sobado, con las esquinas dobladas

dog·ged ['dɒːɡɪd] adj tenaz

dog·gie ['dɒːɡɪ] in children's language perrito m

dog·gy bag ['dɒːɡɪbæɡ] bolsa para las sobras de la comida

dog·house: **be in the doghouse** F haber caído en desgracia

dog·ma ['dɒːɡmə] dogma m

dog·mat·ic [dɒːɡ'mætɪk] adj dogmático

do-good·er ['duːɡudər] pej buen(a) samaritano(-a) m(f)

'dog tag MIL chapa f de identificación

'dog-tired adj F hecho polvo F

do-it-your·self ['du:ɪtjər'self] bricolaje m

dol·drums ['dɒuldrəmz]: **be in the dol-drums** of economy estar en un bache; **doldrums** of person estar deprimido

◆ **dole out** v/t repartir

doll [dɑːl] toy muñeca f; F woman muñeca f F

◆ **doll up** v/t: **get dolled up** emperifollarse

dol·lar ['dɑːlər] dólar m

dol·lop ['dɑːləp] n F cucharada f

dol·phin ['dɑːlfɪn] delfín m

dome [dɒum] of building cúpula f

do·mes·tic [də'mestɪk] **1** adj chores doméstico, del hogar; news, policy nacional **2** n empleado(-a) m(f) del hogar

do·mes·tic 'an·i·mal animal m doméstico

do·mes·ti·cate [də'mestɪkeɪt] v/t animal domesticar; **be domesticated** of person estar domesticado

do'mes·tic flight vuelo m nacional

dom·i·nant ['dɑːmɪnənt] adj dominante

dom·i·nate ['dɑːmɪneɪt] v/t dominar

dom·i·na·tion [dɑːmɪ'neɪʃn] dominación f

dom·i·neer·ing [dɑːmɪ'nɪrɪŋ] adj dominante

dom·i·no ['dɑːmɪnou] ficha f de dominó; **play dominoes** jugar al dominó

do·nate [dou'neɪt] v/t donar

do·na·tion [dou'neɪʃn] donación f, donativo m; MED donación f

done [dʌn] pp → **do**

don·key ['dɑːŋkɪ] burro m

do·nor ['dounər] of money, MED donante m/f

do·nut ['dounʌt] dónut m

doo·dle ['du:dl] v/i garabatear

doom [du:m] n (fate) destino m; (ruin) fatalidad f

doomed [du:md] adj project condenado al fracaso; **we are doomed** (bound to fail) estamos condenados al fracaso; (going to die) vamos a morir

door [dɔːr] puerta f; **there's someone at the door** hay alguien en la puerta

'door·bell timbre m

'door·knob pomo m

'door·man portero m

'door·mat felpudo m

'door·step umbral m

'door·way puerta f

dope [doup] n **1** (drugs) droga f; F (idiot) lelo(-a) m(f); F (information) información f **2** v/t drogar

dor·mant ['dɔːrmənt] adj plant aletargado; volcano inactivo

dor·mi·to·ry ['dɔːrmɪtɔːrɪ] dormitorio m (colectivo); (hall of residence) residencia f de estudiantes

dos·age ['dousɪdʒ] dosis f inv

dose [dous] n dosis f inv

dot [dɑːt] n punto m; **on the dot** (exactly) en punto

◆ **dote on** [dout] v/t adorar a

dot.com (com·pany) [dɑːt'kɑːm] empresa f punto.com

dot·ing ['doutɪŋ] adj: **my doting aunt** mi tía, que tanto me adora

dot·ted line ['dɑːtɪd] línea f de puntos

dou·ble ['dʌbl] **1** n person doble m/f; room habitación f doble **2** adj inflation is now in double figures la inflación ha superado ya el 10% **3** adv: **they offered me double what the others did** me ofrecieron el doble que la otra gente **4** v/t doblar, duplicar **5** v/i doblarse, duplicarse; **it doubles as ...** hace también de ...

◆ **double back** v/i (go back) volver sobre sus pasos

◆ **double up** v/i in pain doblarse; (share) compartir habitación

dou·ble-'bass contrabajo m

dou·ble 'bed cama f de matrimonio

dou·ble-breast·ed [dʌbl'brestɪd] adj cruzado

dou·ble'check v/t & v/i volver a comprobar

dou·ble 'chin papada f

dou·ble'cross v/t engañar, traicionar

dou·ble 'glaz·ing doble acristalamiento m

dou·ble'park v/i aparcar en doble fila

'dou·ble-quick adj: **in double-quick time** muy rápidamente

'dou·ble room habitación f doble

dou·bles ['dʌblz] in tennis dobles mpl

doubt [daut] **1** n duda f; (uncertainty) dudas fpl; **be in doubt** ser incierto; **not be in doubt** estar claro; **no doubt** (probably) sin duda **2** v/t dudar; **we never doubted you** nunca dudamos de ti

doubt·ful ['dautfəl] adj remark, look dubitativo; **be doubtful** of person tener dudas; **it is doubtful whether ...** es dudoso que ...

doubt·ful·ly ['dautfəlɪ] adv lleno de dudas

doubt·less ['dautlɪs] adj sin duda, indudablemente

dough [dou] masa f; F (money) Span pasta f F, L.Am. plata f F

dough·nut ['dounʌt] dónut m

dove[1] [dʌv] also fig paloma f

dove[2] [douv] pret → **dive**

dow·dy ['daʊdɪ] *adj* poco elegante

Dow Jones Av·er·age [daʊdʒəʊnz'ævə-rɪdʒ] índice *m* Dow Jones

down¹ [daʊn] *n* (*feathers*) plumón *m*

down² [daʊn] **1** *adv* (*downward*) (hacia) abajo; *pull the blind down* baja la persiana; *put it down on the table* ponlo en la mesa; *when the leaves come down* cuando se caen las hojas; *cut down a tree* cortar un árbol; *she was down on her knees* estaba arrodillada; *the plane was shot down* el avión fue abatido; *down there* allá abajo; *fall down* caerse; *die down* amainar; *$200 down* (*as deposit*) una entrada de 200 dólares; *down south* hacia el sur; *be down of price, rate* haber bajado; *of numbers, amount* haber descendido; (*not working*) no funcionar; F (*depressed*) estar deprimido or con la depre F **2** *prep*: *run down the stairs* bajar las escaleras corriendo; *the lava rolled down the hill* la lava descendía por la colina; *walk down the street* andar por la calle; *down the corridor* por el pasillo **3** *v/t* (*swallow*) tragar; (*destroy*) derribar

'down-and-out *n* vagabundo(-a) *m(f)*

'down·cast *adj* (*dejected*) deprimido

'down·fall caída *f*; *of person* perdición *f*

'down·grade *v/t* degradar; *the hurricane has been downgraded to a storm* el huracán ha sido reducido a la categoría de tormenta

down·heart·ed [daʊn'hɑːrtɪd] *adj* abatido

down'hill *adv* cuesta abajo; *go downhill fig* ir cuesta abajo

'down·hill ski·ing descenso *m*

'down·load *v/t* COMPUT descargar, bajar

'down·mark·et *adj* barato

'down pay·ment entrada *f*; *make a down payment on sth* pagar la entrada de algo

'down·play *v/t* quitar importancia a

'down·pour chaparrón *m*, aguacero *m*

'down·right 1 *adj lie* evidente; *idiot* completo **2** *adv dangerous* extremadamente; *stupid* completamente

'down·side (*disadvantage*) desventaja *f*, inconveniente *m*

'down·size 1 *v/t car* reducir el tamaño de; *company* reajustar la plantilla de **2** *v/i of company* reajustar la plantilla

'down·stairs 1 *adj* del piso de abajo; *my downstairs neighbors* los vecinos de abajo **2** *adv*: *the kitchen is downstairs* la cocina está en el piso de abajo; *I ran downstairs* bajé corriendo

down-to-'earth *adj approach, person* práctico, realista

'down·town 1 *n* centro *m* **2** *adj* del centro **2** *adv*: *I'm going downtown* voy al centro; *he lives downtown* vive en el centro

'down·turn *in economy* bajón *m*

'down·ward ['daʊnwərd] **1** *adj* descendente **2** *adv* a la baja

doze [doʊz] **1** *n* cabezada *f*, sueño *m* **2** *v/i* echar una cabezada

◆ **doze off** *v/i* quedarse dormido

doz·en ['dʌzn] docena *f*; *dozens of* F montonadas de F

drab [dræb] *adj* gris

draft [dræft] **1** *n of air* corriente *f*; *of document* borrador *m*; MIL reclutamiento *m*; *draft* (*beer*), *beer on draft* cerveza *f* de barril **2** *v/t document* redactar un borrador de; MIL reclutar

'draft dodg·er prófugo(-a) *m(f)*

draft·ee [dræf'tiː] recluta *m/f*

drafts·man ['dræftsmən] delineante *m/f*

draft·y ['dræftɪ] *adj*: *it's drafty here* hace mucha corriente aquí

drag [dræg] **1** *n*: *it's a drag having to ...* es un latazo tener que ... F; *he's a drag* F es un peñazo F; *the main drag* F la calle principal; *in drag* vestido de mujer **2** *v/t* (*pret & pp* **dragged**) (*pull*) arrastrar; (*search*) dragar **3** *v/i* (*pret & pp* **dragged**) *of time* pasar despacio; *of show, movie* ser pesado; *drag s.o. into sth* (*involve*) meter a alguien en algo; *drag sth out of s.o.* (*get information from*) arrancar algo de alguien

◆ **drag away** *v/t*. *drag o.s. away from the TV* despegarse de la TV

◆ **drag in** *v/t into conversation* introducir

◆ **drag on** *v/i* (*last long time*) alargarse

◆ **drag out** *v/t* (*prolong*) alargar

◆ **drag up** *v/t* F (*mention*) sacar a relucir

drag·on ['drægn] dragón *m*; *fig* ogro *m*

drain [dreɪn] **1** *n pipe* sumidero *m*, desagüe *m*; *under street* alcantarilla *f*; *a drain on resources* una sangría en los recursos **2** *v/t water, vegetables* escurrir; *land* drenar; *glass, tank, oil* vaciar; *person* agotar **3** *v/i of dishes* escurrir

◆ **drain away** *v/i of liquid* irse

◆ **drain off** *v/t water* escurrir

drain·age ['dreɪnɪdʒ] (*drains*) desagües *mpl*; *of water from soil* drenaje *m*

'drain·pipe tubo *m* de desagüe

dra·ma ['drɑːmə] (*art form*) drama *m*, teatro *m*; (*excitement*) dramatismo *m*; (*play: on* TV) drama *m*, obra *f* de teatro

dra·mat·ic [drə'mætɪk] *adj* dramático; *scenery* espectacular

dra·mat·i·cal·ly [drə'mætɪklɪ] *adv say* con dramatismo, de manera dramática; *decline, rise, change etc* espectacularmente

dram·a·tist ['dræmətɪst] dramaturgo(-a) *m(f)*

dram·a·ti·za·tion [dræmətaɪ'zeɪʃn] *(play)* dramatización *f*

dram·a·tize ['dræmətaɪz] *v/t also fig* dramatizar

drank [dræŋk] *pret* → **drink**

drape [dreɪp] *v/t cloth* cubrir; **draped in** *(covered with)* cubierto con

drap·er·y ['dreɪpərɪ] ropajes *mpl*

drapes [dreɪps] *npl* cortinas *fpl*

dras·tic ['dræstɪk] *adj* drástico

draught *Br* → **draft**

draw [drɔː] **1** *n in match, competition* empate *m*; *in lottery* sorteo *m*; *(attraction)* atracción *f* **2** *v/t (pret* **drew**, *pp* **drawn)** *picture, map* dibujar; *cart* tirar de; *curtain* correr; *in lottery* sortear; *gun, knife* sacar; *(attract)* atraer; *(lead)* llevar; *from bank account* sacar, retirar **3** *v/i (pret* **drew**, *pp* **drawn)** dibujar; *in match, competition* empatar; **draw near** acercarse

◆ **draw back 1** *v/i (recoil)* echarse atrás **2** *v/t (pull back)* retirar

◆ **draw on 1** *v/i (approach)* aproximarse **2** *v/t (make use of)* utilizar

◆ **draw out** *v/t wallet, money from bank* sacar

◆ **draw up 1** *v/t document* redactar; *chair* acercar **2** *v/i of vehicle* parar

'**draw·back** desventaja *f*, inconveniente *m*

draw·er[1] [drɔːr] *of desk etc* cajón *m*

draw·er[2] [drɔːr] **she's a good drawer** dibuja muy bien

draw·ing ['drɔːɪŋ] dibujo *m*

'**draw·ing board** tablero *m* de dibujo; **go back to the drawing board** *fig* volver a empezar otra vez

'**draw·ing pin** *Br* chincheta *f*

drawl [drɔːl] *n* acento *m* arrastrado

drawn [drɔːn] *pp* → **draw**

dread [dred] *v/t* tener pavor a; **I dread him ever finding out** me da pavor pensar que lo pueda llegar a descubrir; **I dread going to the dentist** me da pánico ir al dentista

dread·ful ['dredfəl] *adj* horrible, espantoso; **it's a dreadful pity you won't be there** es una auténtica pena que no vayas a estar allí

dread·ful·ly ['dredfəlɪ] *adv* F *(extremely)* terriblemente, espantosamente F; *behave* fatal

dream [driːm] **1** *n* sueño *m* **2** *adj*: **win your dream house!** ¡gane la casa de sus sueños! **3** *v/t* soñar; *(daydream)* soñar (despierto) **4** *v/i* soñar; *(daydream)* soñar (despierto); **I dreamt about you last night** anoche soñé contigo

◆ **dream up** *v/t* inventar

dream·er ['driːmər] *(daydreamer)* soñador(a) *m(f)*

dream·y ['driːmɪ] *adj voice, look* soñador

drear·y ['drɪrɪ] *adj* triste, deprimente

dredge [dredʒ] *v/t harbor, canal* dragar

◆ **dredge up** *v/t fig* sacar a relucir

dregs [dregz] *npl of coffee* posos *mpl*; **the dregs of society** la escoria de la sociedad

drench [drentʃ] *v/t* empapar; **get drenched** empaparse

dress [dres] **1** *n for woman* vestido *m*; *(clothing)* traje *m*; **he has no dress sense** no sabe vestir(se); **the company has a dress code** la compañía tiene unas normas sobre la ropa que deben llevar los empleados **2** *v/t person* vestir; *wound* vendar; **get dressed** vestirse **3** *v/i (get dressed)* vestirse; **well, in black etc** vestir(se) (**in** de)

◆ **dress up** *v/i* arreglarse, vestirse elegante; *(wear a disguise)* disfrazarse (**as** de)

'**dress cir·cle** piso *m* principal

dress·er ['dresər] *(dressing table)* tocador *f*; *in kitchen* aparador *m*

dress·ing ['dresɪŋ] *for salad* aliño *m*, *Span* arreglo *m*; *for wound* vendaje *m*

dress·ing 'down regañar *m*; **give s.o. a dressing down** regañar a alguien

'**dress·ing room** *in theater* camerino *m*

'**dress·ing ta·ble** tocador *f*

'**dress·mak·er** modisto(-a) *m(f)*

'**dress re·hears·al** ensayo *m* general

dress·y ['dresɪ] *adj* F elegante

drew [druː] *pret* → **draw**

drib·ble ['drɪbl] *v/i of person, baby* babear; *of water* gotear; *SP* driblar

dried [draɪd] *adj fruit etc* seco

dri·er [draɪr] → **dryer**

drift [drɪft] **1** *n of snow* ventisquero *m* **2** *v/i of snow* amontonarse; *of ship* ir a la deriva; *(go off course)* desviarse del rumbo; *of person* vagar

◆ **drift apart** *v/i of couple* distanciarse

drift·er ['drɪftər] vagabundo(-a) *m(f)*

drill [drɪl] **1** *n tool* taladro *m*; *exercise* simulacro *m*; *MIL* instrucción *f* **2** *v/t hole* taladrar, perforar **3** *v/i for oil* hacer perforaciones; *MIL* entrenar

'**dril·ling rig** ['drɪlɪŋrɪg] *(platform)* plataforma *f* petrolífera

dri·ly ['draɪlɪ] *adv remark* secamente, lacónicamente

drink [drɪŋk] **1** *n* bebida *f*; **a drink of ...** un vaso de ...; **go for a drink** ir a tomar algo **2** *v/t (pret* **drank**, *pp* **drunk)** beber **3** *v/i (pret* **drank**, *pp* **drunk)** beber, *L.Am.*

tomar; **I don't drink** no bebo
◆ **drink up 1** v/i (*finish drink*) acabarse la bebida **2** v/t (*drink completely*) beberse todo
drink·a·ble ['drɪŋkəbl] *adj* potable
drink 'driv·ing conducción *f* bajo los efectos del alcohol
drink·er ['drɪŋkər] bebedor(a) *m(f)*
drink·ing ['drɪŋkɪŋ]: **I'm worried about his drinking** me preocupa que beba tanto; **a drinking problem** un problema con la bebida
drink·ing wa·ter agua *f* potable
drinks ma·chine máquina *f* expendedora de bebidas
drip [drɪp] **1** *n* gota *f*; MED gotero *m*, suero *m* **2** v/i (*pret & pp* **dripped**) gotear
drip-dry *adj* que no necesita planchado
drip·ping ['drɪpɪŋ] *adv*: **dripping wet** empapado
drive [draɪv] **1** *n* outing vuelta *f*, paseo *m* (en coche); (*energy*) energía *f*; COMPUT unidad *f*; (*campaign*) campaña *f*; **it's a short drive from the station** está a poca distancia en coche de la estación; **with left-/right-hand drive** MOT con el volante a la izquierda/a la derecha **2** v/t (*pret* **drove**, *pp* **driven**) *vehicle* conducir, *L.Am.* manejar; (*own*) tener; (*take in car*) llevar (en coche); TECH impulsar; **that noise/ he is driving me mad** ese ruido/él me está volviendo loco **3** v/i (*pret* **drove**, *pp* **driven**) conducir, *L.Am.* manejar; **don't drink and drive** si bebes, no conduzcas; **I drive to work** voy al trabajo en coche
◆ **drive at** v/t: **what are you driving at?** ¿qué insinúas?
◆ **drive away 1** v/t llevarse en un coche; (*chase off*) ahuyentar **2** v/i marcharse
◆ **drive in** v/t *nail* remachar
◆ **drive off** → **drive away**
drive-in *n* (*movie theater*) autocine *m*
driv·el ['drɪvl] *n* tonterías *fpl*
driv·en ['drɪvn] *pp* → **drive**
driv·er ['draɪvər] conductor(a) *m(f)*; Br *of train* maquinista *m/f*, COMPUT controlador *m*
driv·er's li·cense carné *m* de conducir
drive·thru ['draɪvθruː] *restaurante/banco etc* en el que se atiende al cliente sin que salga del coche
drive·way camino *m* de entrada
driv·ing ['draɪvɪŋ] **1** *n* conducción *f*; **his driving is appalling** conduce *or L.Am.* maneja fatal **2** *adj rain* torrencial
driv·ing 'force fuerza *f* motriz
driving in·struct·or profesor(a) *m(f)* de autoescuela

driv·ing les·son clase *f* de conducir
driv·ing li·cence Br carné *m* de conducir
driv·ing school autoescuela *f*
driv·ing test examen *m* de conducir *or L.Am.* manejar
driz·zle ['drɪzl] **1** *n* llovizna *f* **2** v/i lloviznar
drone [droun] *n noise* zumbido *m*
droop [druːp] v/i *of plant* marchitarse; **her shoulders drooped** se encorvó
drop [drɑːp] **1** *n* gota *f*; *in price, temperature* caída *f*; **could I have a drop more milk, please?** ¿me podría poner un poquitín más de leche, por favor? **2** v/t (*pret & pp* **dropped**) *object* dejar caer; *person from car* dejar; *person from team* excluir; (*stop seeing*) abandonar; *charges, demand etc* retirar; (*give up*) dejar; **drop a line to** mandar unas líneas a **3** v/i (*pret & pp* **dropped**) caer, caerse; (*decline*) caer; *of wind* amainar
◆ **drop in** v/i (*visit*) pasar a visitar
◆ **drop off 1** v/t *person* dejar; (*deliver*) llevar **2** v/i (*fall asleep*) dormirse; (*decline*) disminuir
◆ **drop out** v/i (*withdraw*) retirarse; **drop out of school** abandonar el colegio
drop·out (*from school*) alumno que ha abandonado los estudios; *from society* marginado(-a) *m(f)*
drops [drɑːps] *npl for eyes* gotas *fpl*
drought [draʊt] sequía *f*
drove [droʊv] *pret* → **drive**
drown [draʊn] **1** v/i ahogarse **2** v/t *person, sound* ahogar; **be drowned** ahogarse
drow·sy ['draʊzɪ] *adj* soñoliento(-a)
drudg·e·ry ['drʌdʒərɪ]: **the job is sheer drudgery** el trabajo es terriblemente pesado
drug [drʌg] **1** *n* MED, *illegal* droga *f*; **be on drugs** drogarse **2** v/t (*pret & pp* **drugged**) drogar
drug ad·dict drogadicto(-a) *m(f)*
drug deal·er traficante *m/f* de drogas
drug·gist ['drʌgɪst] farmacéutico(-a) *m(f)*
drug·store tienda *f* en la que se venden medicinas, cosméticos, periódicos y que a veces tiene un bar
drug traf·fick·ing tráfico *m* de drogas
drum [drʌm] *n* MUS tambor *m*; *container* barril *m*
◆ **drum into** v/t (*pret & pp* **drummed**): **drum sth into s.o.** meter algo en la cabeza de alguien
◆ **drum up** v/t: **drum up support** buscar apoyos
drum·mer ['drʌmər] tambor *m*, tamborilero(-a) *m(f)*
drum·stick MUS baqueta *f*; *of poultry*

D

muslo *m*

drunk [drʌŋk] **1** *n* borracho(-a) *m(f)* **2** *adj* borracho; **get drunk** emborracharse **3** *pp* → **drink**

drunk·en [drʌŋkn] *voices, laughter* borracho; *party* con mucho alcohol

dry [draɪ] **1** *adj* seco; *where alcohol is banned* donde está prohibido el consumo de alcohol **2** *v/t & v/i* (*pret & pp* **dried**) secar
◆ **dry out** *v/i* secarse; *of alcoholic* desintoxicarse
◆ **dry up** *v/i* of river secarse; F (*be quiet*) cerrar el pico F

'dry-clean *v/t* limpiar en seco

'dry clean·er tintorería *f*

'dry-clean·ing (*clothes*): **would you pick up my drycleaning for me?** ¿te importaría recogerme la ropa de la tintorería?

dry·er [draɪr] *machine* secadora *f*

DTP [diːtiːpiː] *abbr* (= **desk-top publishing**) autoedición *f*

du·al [duːəl] *adj* doble

dub [dʌb] *v/t* (*pret & pp* **dubbed**) *movie* doblar

du·bi·ous [duːbɪəs] *adj* dudoso; (*having doubts*) inseguro; **I'm still dubious about the idea** todavía tengo mis dudas sobre la idea

duch·ess [dʌtʃɪs] duquesa *f*

duck [dʌk] **1** *n* pato *m*, pata *f* **2** *v/i* agacharse **3** *v/t one's head* agachar; *question* eludir

dud [dʌd] *n* F (*false bill*) billete *m* falso

due [duː] *adj* (*proper*) debido; **the money due me** el dinero que se me debe; **payment is now due** el pago se debe hacer efectivo ahora; **is there a train due soon?** ¿va a pasar un tren pronto?; **when is the baby due?** ¿cuando está previsto que nazca el bebé?; **he's due to meet him next month** tiene previsto reunirse con él el próximo mes; **due to** (*because of*) debido a; **be due to** (*be caused by*) ser debido a; **in due course** en su debido momento

dues [duːz] *npl* cuota *f*

du·et [duːet] MUS dúo *m*

dug [dʌg] *pret & pp* → **dig**

duke [djuːk] duque *m*

dull [dʌl] *adj weather* gris; *sound, pain* sordo; (*boring*) aburrido, soso

du·ly [duːlɪ] *adv* (*as expected*) tal y como se esperaba; (*properly*) debidamente

dumb [dʌm] *adj* (*mute*) mudo; F (*stupid*) estúpido; **a pretty dumb thing to do** una tontería

dumb·found·ed [dʌmˈfaʊndɪd] *adj* boquiabierto

dum·my [dʌmɪ] *for clothes* maniquí *m*

dump [dʌmp] **1** *n for garbage* vertedero *m*, basurero *m*; (*unpleasant place*) lugar *m* de mala muerte **2** *v/t* (*deposit*) dejar; (*dispose of*) deshacerse de; *toxic waste, nuclear waste* verter

dump·ling [dʌmplɪŋ] *bola de masa dulce o salada*

dune [duːn] duna *f*

dung [dʌŋ] estiércol *m*

dun·ga·rees [dʌŋgəriːz] *npl* pantalone mpl de trabajo

dunk [dʌŋk] *v/t in coffee etc* mojar

du·o [duːoʊ] MUS dúo *m*

du·plex (**a·part·ment**) [duːpleks] dúplex *m*

du·pli·cate 1 *n* [duːplɪkət] duplicado *m* **in duplicate** por duplicado **2** *v/t* [duːplɪkeɪt] (*copy*) duplicar, hacer un duplicado de; (*repeat*) repetir

du·pli·cate 'key llave *f* duplicada

du·ra·ble [dʊrəbl] *adj material* duradero, durable; *relationship* duradero

du·ra·tion [dʊˈreɪʃn] duración *f*; **for the duration of her visit** mientras dure su visita

du·ress [dʊres]: **under duress** bajo coacción

dur·ing [dʊrɪŋ] *prep* durante

dusk [dʌsk] crepúsculo *m*, anochecer *m*

dust [dʌst] **1** *n* polvo *m* **2** *v/t* quitar el polvo a; **dust sth with sth** (*sprinkle*) espolvorear algo con algo

'dust cov·er *for book* sobrecubierta *f*

dust·er [dʌstər] (*cloth*) trapo *m* del polvo

'dust jack·et *of book* sobrecubierta *f*

'dust·pan recogedor *m*

dust·y [dʌstɪ] *adj* polvoriento

Dutch [dʌtʃ] **1** *adj* holandés; **go Dutch** F pagar a escote F **2** *n* (*language*) neerlandés *m*; **the Dutch** los holandeses

du·ty [duːtɪ] *n* deber *m*; (*task*) obligación *f*, tarea *f*; *on goods* impuesto *m*; **be on duty** estar de servicio; **be off duty** estar fuera de servicio

du·ty-'free 1 *adj* libre de impuestos **2** *n* productos *mpl* libres de impuestos

du·ty-'free shop tienda *f* libre de impuestos

dwarf [dwɔːrf] **1** *n* enano *m* **2** *v/t* empequeñecer

◆ **dwell on** [dwel] *v/t*: **dwell on the past** pensar en el pasado; **don't dwell on what he said** no des demasiada importancia a lo que ha dicho

dwin·dle [dwɪndl] *v/i* disminuir, menguar

dye [daɪ] **1** *n* tinte *m* **2** *v/t* teñir

dy·ing [daɪɪŋ] *adj person* moribundo; *industry, tradition* en vías de desaparición

dy·nam·ic [daɪˈnæmɪk] *adj person* diná

mico
dy·na·mism ['daɪnəmɪzm] dinamismo *m*
dy·na·mite ['daɪnəmaɪt] *n* dinamita *f*
dy·na·mo ['daɪnəmoʊ] TECH dinamo *f*, dínamo *f*

dy·nas·ty ['daɪnəstɪ] dinastía *f*
dys·lex·i·a [dɪs'leksɪə] dislexia *f*
dys·lex·ic [dɪs'leksɪk] **1** *adj* disléxico **2** *n* disléxico(-a) *m(f)*

E

each [iːtʃ] **1** *adj* cada **2** *adv*: *he gave us one each* nos dio uno a cada uno; *they're $1.50 each* valen 1.50 dólares cada uno **3** *pron* cada uno; *each other* el uno al otro; *we love each other* nos queremos
ea·ger ['iːgər] *adj* ansioso; *she's always eager to help* siempre está deseando ayudar
ea·ger·ly ['iːgərlɪ] *adv* ansiosamente
ea·ger·ness ['iːgərnɪs] entusiasmo *m*
ea·gle ['iːgl] águila *f*
ea·gle-eyed [iːgl'aɪd] *adj* con vista de lince
ear¹ [ɪr] *of person, animal* oreja *f*; *sense* oído *m*
ear² [ɪr] *of corn* espiga *f*
ear·ache dolor *m* de oídos
ear·drum tímpano *m*
ear·lobe lóbulo *m*
ear·ly ['ɜːrlɪ] **1** *adj (not late)* temprano; *(ahead of time)* anticipado; *(farther back in time)* primero; *(in the near future)* pronto; *music* antiguo; *let's have an early supper* cenemos temprano; *in early October* a principios de octubre; *in the early hours of the morning* a primeras horas de la madrugada; *an early Picasso* un Picasso de su primera época; *I'm an early riser* soy madrugador **2** *adv (not late)* pronto, temprano; *(ahead of time)* antes de tiempo; *it's too early to say* es demasiado pronto como para poder decir nada; *earlier than* antes que
ear·ly bird madrugador(a) *m(f)*
ear·mark ['ɪrmɑːrk] *v/t* destinar; *earmark sth for sth* destinar algo a algo
earn [ɜːrn] *v/t salary* ganar; *interest* devengar; *holiday, drink etc* ganarse; *earn one's living* ganarse la vida
ear·nest ['ɜːrnɪst] *adj* serio; *in earnest* en serio
earn·ings ['ɜːrnɪŋz] *npl* ganancias *fpl*

ear·phones *npl* auriculares *fpl*
ear-pierc·ing *adj* estrepitoso
ear·ring pendiente *m*
ear·shot: *within earshot* al alcance del oído; *out of earshot* fuera del alcance del oído
earth [ɜːrθ] *(soil)* tierra *f*; *(world, planet)* Tierra *f*; *where on earth ...?* F ¿dónde diablos ...? F
earth·en·ware ['ɜːrθnwer] *n* loza *mpl*
earth·ly ['ɜːrθlɪ] *adj* terrenal; *it's no earthly use* F no sirve para nada
earth·quake ['ɜːrθkweɪk] terremoto *m*
earth-shat·ter·ing ['ɜːrθʃætərɪŋ] *adj* extraordinario
ease [iːz] **1** *n* facilidad *f*; *be at (one's) ease, feel at ease* sentirse cómodo; *feel ill at ease* sentirse incómodo **2** *v/t (relieve)* aliviar **3** *v/i of pain* disminuir
♦ **ease off 1** *v/t (remove)* quitar con cuidado **2** *v/i of pain* disminuir; *of rain* amainar
ea·sel ['iːzl] caballete *m*
eas·i·ly ['iːzɪlɪ] *adv (with ease)* fácilmente; *(by far)* con diferencia
east [iːst] **1** *n* este *m* **2** *adj* oriental, este; *wind* del este **3** *adv travel* hacia el este
Eas·ter ['iːstər] Pascua *f*; *period* Semana *f* Santa
Eas·ter 'Day Domingo *m* de Resurrección
'Eas·ter egg huevo *m* de pascua
eas·ter·ly ['iːstərlɪ] *adj* del este
Eas·ter 'Mon·day Lunes *m* Santo
Eas·ter 'Sun·day Domingo *m* de Resurrección
east·ern ['iːstərn] *adj* del este; *(oriental)* oriental
east·er·ner ['iːstərnər] *habitante de la costa oeste* estadounidense
east·ward ['iːstwərd] *adv* hacia el este
eas·y ['iːzɪ] *adj* fácil; *(relaxed)* tranquilo; *take things easy (slow down)* tomarse las cosas con tranquilidad; *take it easy!*

(*calm down*) ¡tranquilízate!

'eas·y chair sillón *m*

eas·y-go·ing ['i:zɪgoʊɪŋ] *adj* tratable

eat [i:t] *v/t & v/i* (*pret* **ate**, *pp* **eaten**) comer

◆ **eat out** *v/i* comer fuera

◆ **eat up** *v/t* comerse; *fig: use up* acabar con

eat·a·ble ['i:təbl] *adj* comestible

eat·en ['i:tn] *pp* → **eat**

eau de Co·logne [oʊdəkə'loʊn] agua *f* de colonia

eaves [i:vz] *npl* alero *m*

eaves·drop ['i:vzdrɑːp] *v/i* (*pret & pp* **eavesdropped**) escuchar a escondidas (*on s.o.*) alguien)

ebb [eb] *v/i of tide* bajar

◆ **ebb away** *v/i fig of courage, strength* desvanecerse

ec·cen·tric [ɪk'sentrɪk] **1** *adj* excéntrico **2** *n* excéntrico(-a) *m(f)*

ec·cen·tric·i·ty [ɪksen'trɪsɪtɪ] excentricidad *f*

ech·o ['ekoʊ] **1** *n* eco *m* **2** *v/i* resonar **3** *v/t words* repetir; *views* mostrar acuerdo con

e·clipse [ɪ'klɪps] **1** *n* eclipse *m* **2** *v/t fig* eclipsar

e·co·lo·gi·cal [i:kə'lɑːdʒɪkl] *adj* ecológico

e·co·lo·gi·cal·ly [i:kə'lɑːdʒɪklɪ] *adv* ecológicamente

e·co·lo·gi·cal·ly 'friend·ly *adj* ecológico

e·col·o·gist [i:'kɑːlədʒɪst] ecologista *m/f*

e·col·o·gy [i:'kɑːlədʒɪ] ecología *f*

ec·o·nom·ic [i:kə'nɑːmɪk] *adj* económico

ec·o·nom·i·cal [i:kə'nɑːmɪkl] *adj (cheap)* económico; (*thrifty*) cuidadoso

ec·o·nom·i·cal·ly [i:kə'nɑːmɪklɪ] *adv (in terms of economics)* económicamente; (*thriftily*) de manera económica

ec·o·nom·ics [i:kə'nɑːmɪks] *nsg (science)* economía *f*; (*npl: financial aspects*) aspecto *m* económico

e·con·o·mist [ɪ'kɑːnəmɪst] economista *m/f*

e·con·o·mize [ɪ'kɑːnəmaɪz] *v/i* economizar, ahorrar

◆ **economize on** *v/t* economizar, ahorrar

e·con·o·my [ɪ'kɑːnəmɪ] *of a country* economía *f*; (*saving*) ahorro *m*

e'con·o·my class *f* turista

e'con·o·my drive intento *m* de ahorrar

e'con·o·my size tamaño *m* económico

e·co·sys·tem ['i:koʊsɪstm] ecosistema *m*

e·co·tour·ism ['i:koʊtʊrɪzm] ecoturismo *m*

ec·sta·sy ['ekstəsɪ] éxtasis *m*

ec·stat·ic [ɪk'stætɪk] *adj* muy emocionado, extasiado

Ec·ua·dor ['ekwədɔːr] *n* Ecuador

Ec·ua·dor·e·an [ekwə'dɔːrən] **1** *adj* ecuatoriano **2** *n* ecuatoriano(-a) *m(f)*

ec·ze·ma ['eksmə] eczema *f*

edge [edʒ] **1** *n of knife* filo *m*; *of table, seat, road, cliff* borde *m*; *in voice* irritación *f*; **on edge** tenso **2** *v/t* ribetear **3** *v/i (move slowly)* acercarse despacio

edge·wise ['edʒwaɪz] *adv* de lado; **couldn't get a word in edgewise** no me dejó decir una palabra

edg·y ['edʒɪ] *adj* tenso

ed·i·ble ['edɪbl] *adj* comestible

ed·it ['edɪt] *v/t text* corregir; *book* editar; *newspaper* dirigir; TV *program, movie* montar

e·di·tion [ɪ'dɪʃn] edición *f*

e·di·tor ['edɪtər] *of text, book* editor(a) *m(f)*; *of newspaper* director(a) *m(f)*; *of* TV *program, movie* montador(a) *m(f)* **sports / political editor** redactor(a) *m(f)* de deportes / política

ed·i·to·ri·al [edɪ'tɔːrɪəl] **1** *adj* editorial **2** *n in newspaper* editorial *m*

EDP [i:di:'pi:] *abbr* (= **electronic data processing**) procesamiento *m* electrónico de datos

ed·u·cate ['edʒəkeɪt] *v/t child* educar; *consumers* concienciar

ed·u·cat·ed ['edʒəkeɪtɪd] *adj person* culto

ed·u·ca·tion [edʒə'keɪʃn] educación *f*; **the education system** el sistema educativo

ed·u·ca·tion·al [edʒə'keɪʃnl] *adj* educativo; (*informative*) instructivo

eel [i:l] anguila *f*

ee·rie ['ɪrɪ] *adj* escalofriante

ef·fect [ɪ'fekt] efecto *m*; **take effect** *of medicine, drug* hacer efecto; **come into effect** *of law* entrar en vigor

ef·fec·tive [ɪ'fektɪv] *adj (efficient)* efectivo; (*striking*) impresionante; **effective May 1** a partir del 1 de mayo

ef·fem·i·nate [ɪ'femɪnət] *adj* afeminado

ef·fer·ves·cent [efər'vesnt] *adj* efervescente; *personality* chispeante

ef·fi·cien·cy [ɪ'fɪʃənsɪ] *of person* eficiencia *f*; *of machine* rendimiento *f*; *of system* eficacia *f*

ef·fi·cient [ɪ'fɪʃənt] *adj person* eficiente; *machine* de buen rendimiento; *method* eficaz

ef·fi·cient·ly [ɪ'fɪʃəntlɪ] *adv* eficientemente

ef·flu·ent ['efluənt] aguas *fpl* residuales

ef·fort ['efərt] (*struggle, attempt*) esfuerzo *m*; **make an effort to do sth** hacer un esfuerzo por hacer algo

ef·fort·less ['efərtlɪs] *adj* fácil

ef·fron·te·ry [ɪ'frʌntərɪ] desvergüenza *f*

ef·fu·sive [ɪ'fjuːsɪv] *adj* efusivo

e.g. [iː'dʒiː] p. ej.

e·gal·i·tar·i·an [ɪgælɪ'terɪən] *adj* igualitario

egg [eg] huevo *m*; *of woman* óvulo *m*
◆ **egg on** *v/t* incitar

egg·cup huevera *f*

egg·head F cerebrito(-a) *m(f)* F

egg·plant berenjena *f*

egg·shell cáscara *f* de huevo

egg tim·er reloj *m* de arena

e·go [ˈiːɡoʊ] PSYCH ego *m*; *(self-esteem)* amor *m* propio

e·go·cen·tric [iːɡoʊˈsentrɪk] *adj* egocéntrico

e·go·ism [ˈiːɡoʊɪzm] egoísmo *m*

e·go·ist [ˈiːɡoʊɪst] egoísta *m/f*

E·gypt [ˈiːdʒɪpt] Egipto

E·gyp·tian [ɪˈdʒɪpʃn] **1** *adj* egipcio **2** *n* egipcio(-a) *m(f)*

ei·der·down [ˈaɪdərdaʊn] *quilt* edredón *m*

eight [eɪt] ocho

eigh·teen [eɪˈtiːn] dieciocho

eigh·teenth [eɪˈtiːnθ] *n & adj* decimoctavo

eighth [eɪtθ] *n & adj* octavo

eigh·ti·eth [ˈeɪtɪɪθ] *n & adj* octogésimo

eigh·ty [ˈeɪtɪ] ochenta

ei·ther [ˈaɪðər] **1** *adj* cualquiera de los dos; *with negative constructions* ninguno de los dos; *(both)* cada, ambos; *he wouldn't accept either of the proposals* no quería aceptar ninguna de las dos propuestas **2** *pron* cualquiera de los dos; *with negative constructions* ninguno de los dos **3** *adv* tampoco; *I won't go either* yo tampoco iré **4** *conj*: *either ... or* choice o ... o; *with negative constructions* ni ... ni

e·ject [ɪˈdʒekt] **1** *v/t* expulsar **2** *v/i from plane* eyectarse

◆ **eke out** [iːk] *v/t (make last)* hacer durar

el [el] → *elevated railroad*

e·lab·o·rate **1** *adj* [ɪˈlæbərət] elaborado **2** *v/t* [ɪˈlæbəreɪt] elaborar **3** *v/i* [ɪˈlæbəreɪt] dar detalles

e·lab·o·rate·ly [ɪˈlæbəreɪtlɪ] *adv* elaboradamente

e·lapse [ɪˈlæps] *v/i* pasar

e·las·tic [ɪˈlæstɪk] **1** *adj* elástico **2** *n* elástico *m*

e·las·ti·ca·ted [ɪˈlæstɪkeɪtɪd] *adj* elástico

e·las·ti·ci·ty [ɪlæsˈtɪsətɪ] elasticidad *f*

e·las·ti·cized [ɪˈlæstɪsaɪzd] *adj* elástico

e·lat·ed [ɪˈleɪtɪd] *adj* eufórico

el·a·tion [ɪˈleɪʃn] euforia *f*

el·bow [ˈelboʊ] **1** *n* codo *m* **2** *v/t* dar un codazo a; *elbow out of the way* apartar a codazos

el·der [ˈeldər] **1** *adj* mayor **2** *n* mayor *m/f*;

she's two years my elder es dos años mayor que yo

el·der·ly [ˈeldərlɪ] **1** *adj* mayor **2** *n*: *the elderly* las personas mayores

el·dest [ˈeldəst] **1** *adj* mayor **2** *n* mayor *m/f*; *the eldest* el mayor

e·lect [ɪˈlekt] *v/t* elegir; *elect to do sth* decidir hacer algo

e·lect·ed [ɪˈlektɪd] *adj* elegido

e·lec·tion [ɪˈlekʃn] elección *f*; *call an election* convocar elecciones

e·lec·tion cam·paign campaña *f* electoral

e·lec·tion day día *m* de las elecciones

e·lec·tive [ɪˈlektɪv] *adj* opcional; *subject* optativo

e·lec·tor [ɪˈlektər] elector(a) *m(f)*, votante *m/f*

e·lec·to·ral sys·tem [ɪˈlektərəl] sistema *m* electoral

e·lec·to·rate [ɪˈlektərət] electorado *m*

e·lec·tric [ɪˈlektrɪk] *adj* eléctrico; *fig atmosphere* electrizado

e·lec·tri·cal [ɪˈlektrɪkl] *adj* eléctrico

e·lec·tri·cal en·gi·neer ingeniero(-a) *m(f)* electrónico

e·lec·tri·cal en·gi·neer·ing ingeniería *f* electrónica

e·lec·tric 'blan·ket manta *f or L.Am.* cobija *f* eléctrica

e·lec·tric 'chair silla *f* eléctrica

e·lec·tri·cian [ɪlekˈtrɪʃn] electricista *m/f*

e·lec·tri·ci·ty [ɪlekˈtrɪsətɪ] electricidad *f*

e·lec·tric 'ra·zor maquinilla *f* eléctrica

e·lec·tric 'shock descarga *f* eléctrica

e·lec·tri·fy [ɪˈlektrɪfaɪ] *v/t (pret & pp electrified)* electrificar; *fig* electrizar

e·lec·tro·cute [ɪˈlektrəkjuːt] *v/t* electrocutar

e·lec·trode [ɪˈlektroʊd] electrodo *m*

e·lec·tron [ɪˈlektrɑːn] electrón *m*

e·lec·tron·ic [ɪlekˈtrɑːnɪk] *adj* electrónico

e·lec·tron·ic da·ta 'pro·ces·sing procesamiento *m* electrónico de datos

e·lec·tron·ic 'mail correo *m* electrónico

e·lec·tron·ics [ɪlekˈtrɑːnɪks] electrónica *f*

el·e·gance [ˈelɪɡəns] elegancia *f*

el·e·gant [ˈelɪɡənt] *adj* elegante

el·e·gant·ly [ˈelɪɡəntlɪ] *adv* elegantemente

el·e·ment [ˈelɪmənt] *also* CHEM elemento *m*

el·e·men·ta·ry [elɪˈmentərɪ] *adj (rudimentary)* elemental

el·e·men·ta·ry school escuela *f* primaria

el·e·men·ta·ry teacher maestro(-a) *m(f)*

el·e·phant [ˈelɪfənt] elefante *m*

el·e·vate [ˈelɪveɪt] *v/t* elevar

el·e·vat·ed 'rail·road [ˈelɪveɪtɪd] ferrocarril *m* elevado el·e·va·tion [elɪ'veɪʃn] (*altitude*) altura *f*

el·e·va·tor ['elɪveɪtər] ascensor *m*

el·e·ven [ɪ'levn] once

el·e·venth [ɪ'levnθ] *n & adj* undécimo; *at the eleventh hour* justo en el último minuto

el·i·gi·ble ['elɪdʒəbl] *adj* que reúne los requisitos; *eligible to vote* con derecho al voto; *be eligible to do sth* tener derecho a hacer algo

el·i·gi·ble 'bach·e·lor buen partido *m*

e·lim·i·nate [ɪ'lɪmɪneɪt] *v/t* eliminar; *poverty* acabar con; (*rule out*) descartar

e·lim·i·na·tion [ɪ'lɪmɪneɪʃn] eliminación *f*

e·lite [eɪ'liːt] **1** *n* élite *f* **2** *adj* de élite

elk [elk] ciervo *m* canadiense

e·lipse [ɪ'lɪps] elipse *f*

elm [elm] olmo *m*

e·lope [ɪ'loup] *v/i* fugarse con un amante

el·o·quence ['eləkwəns] elocuencia *f*

el·o·quent ['eləkwənt] *adj* elocuente

el·o·quent·ly ['eləkwəntlɪ] *adv* elocuentemente

El Sal·va·dor [el'sælvədɔːr] *n* El Salvador

else [els] *adv*: *anything else?* ¿algo más?; *if you've got nothing else to do* si no tienes nada más que hacer; *no one else* nadie más; *everyone else is going* todos (los demás) van, va todo el mundo; *who else was there?* ¿quién más estaba allí?; *someone else* otra persona; *something else* algo más; *let's go somewhere else* vamos a otro sitio; *or else* si no

else·where ['elswer] *adv* en otro sitio

e·lude [ɪ'luːd] *v/t* (*escape from*) escapar de; (*avoid*) evitar; *the name eludes me* no me acuerdo del nombre

e·lu·sive [ɪ'luːsɪv] *adj* evasivo

e·ma·ci·at·ed [ɪ'meɪsɪeɪtɪd] *adj* demacrado

e-mail ['iːmeɪl] **1** *n* correo *m* electrónico **2** *v/t person* mandar un correo electrónico a

'e-mail ad·dress dirección *f* de correo electrónico, dirección *f* electrónica

e·man·ci·pat·ed [ɪ'mænsɪpeɪtɪd] *adj* emancipado

e·man·ci·pa·tion [ɪmænsɪ'peɪʃn] emancipación *f*

em·balm [ɪm'baːm] *v/t* embalsamar

em·bank·ment [ɪm'bæŋkmənt] *of river* dique *m*; RAIL terraplén *m*

em·bar·go [em'baːrgou] embargo *m*

em·bark [ɪm'baːrk] *v/i* embarcar

♦ embark on *v/t* embarcarse en

em·bar·rass [ɪm'bærəs] *v/t* avergonzar; *he embarrassed me in front of everyone* me hizo pasar vergüenza delante de todos

em·bar·rassed [ɪm'bærəst] *adj* avergonzado; *I was embarrassed to ask* me daba vergüenza preguntar

em·bar·rass·ing [ɪm'bærəsɪŋ] *adj* embarazoso

em·bar·rass·ment [ɪm'bærəsmənt] embarazo *m*, apuro *m*

em·bas·sy ['embəsɪ] embajada *f*

em·bel·lish [ɪm'belɪʃ] *v/t* adornar; *story* exagerar

em·bers ['embərz] *npl* ascuas *fpl*

em·bez·zle [ɪm'bezl] *v/t* malversar

em·bez·zle·ment [ɪm'bezlmənt] malversación *f*

em·bez·zler [ɪm'bezlər] malversador(a) *m(f)*

em·bit·ter [ɪm'bɪtər] *v/t* amargar

em·blem ['embləm] emblema *m*

em·bod·i·ment [ɪm'baːdɪmənt] personificación *f*

em·bod·y [ɪm'baːdɪ] *v/t (pret & pp embodied)* personificar

em·bo·lism ['embəlɪzm] embolia *f*

em·boss [ɪm'baːs] *v/t metal* repujar; *paper* grabar en relieve

em·brace [ɪm'breɪs] **1** *n* abrazo *m* **2** *v/t* (*hug*) abrazar; (*take in*) abarcar **3** *v/i* of *two people* abrazarse

em·broi·der [ɪm'brɔɪdər] *v/t* bordar; *fig* adornar

em·broi·der·y [ɪm'brɔɪdərɪ] bordado *m*

em·bry·o ['embrɪou] embrión *m*

em·bry·on·ic [embrɪ'aːnɪk] *adj fig* embrionario

em·e·rald ['emərəld] esmeralda *f*

e·merge [ɪ'mɜːrdʒ] *v/i* (*appear*) emerger, salir; *of truth* aflorar; *it has emerged that* se ha descubierto que

e·mer·gen·cy [ɪ'mɜːrdʒənsɪ] emergencia *f*; *in an emergency* en caso de emergencia

emer·gen·cy 'ex·it salida *f* de emergencia

e·mer·gen·cy 'land·ing aterrizaje *m* forzoso

e·mer·gen·cy serv·ices *npl* servicios *mpl* de urgencia

em·er·y board ['emərɪ] lima *f* de uñas

em·i·grant ['emɪgrənt] emigrante *m/f*

em·i·grate ['emɪgreɪt] *v/i* emigrar

em·i·gra·tion [emɪ'greɪʃn] emigración *f*

Em·i·nence ['emɪnəns] REL: *His Eminence* Su Eminencia

em·i·nent ['emɪnənt] *adj* eminente

em·i·nent·ly ['emɪnəntlɪ] *adv* sumamente

e·mis·sion [ɪ'mɪʃn] *of gases* emisión *f*

e·mit [ɪ'mɪt] *v/t (pret & pp emitted)* emitir; *heat, odor* desprender

e·mo·tion [ɪ'mouʃn] emoción *f*

e·mo·tion·al [ɪˈmouʃənl] *adj problems, development* sentimental; *(full of emotion)* emotivo

em·pa·thize [ˈempəθaɪz] *v/i:* **empathize with** identificarse con

em·pe·ror [ˈempərər] emperador *m*

em·pha·sis [ˈemfəsɪs] *in word* acento *m; fig* énfasis *m*

em·pha·size [ˈemfəsaɪz] *v/t syllable* acentuar; *fig* hacer hincapié en

em·phat·ic [ɪmˈfætɪk] *adj* enfático

em·pire [ˈempaɪr] imperio *m*

em·ploy [ɪmˈplɔɪ] *v/t* emplear; **he's employed as a ...** trabaja de ...

em·ploy·ee [emplɔɪˈiː] empleado(-a) *m(f)*

em·ploy·er [emˈplɔɪər] empresario(-a) *m(f)*

em·ploy·ment [emˈplɔɪmənt] empleo *m; (work)* trabajo *m;* **be looking for employment** buscar trabajo

em·ploy·ment a·gen·cy agencia *f* de colocaciones

em·press [ˈemprɪs] emperatriz *f*

emp·ti·ness [ˈemptɪnɪs] vacío *m*

emp·ty [ˈemptɪ] **1** *adj* vacío; *promise* vana **2** *v/t (pret & pp **emptied**) drawer, pockets* vaciar; *glass, bottle* acabar **3** *v/i (pret & pp **emptied**) of room, street* vaciarse

em·u·late [ˈemjuleɪt] *v/t* emular

e·mul·sion [ɪˈmʌlʃn] *paint* emulsión *f*

en·a·ble [ɪˈneɪbl] *v/t* permitir; **enable s.o. to do sth** permitir a alguien hacer algo

en·act [ɪˈnækt] *v/t law* promulgar; THEA representar

e·nam·el [ɪˈnæml] *n* esmalte *m*

enc *abbr (= **enclosure(s)**)* documento(s) *m(pl)* adjunto(s)

en·chant [ɪnˈtʃænt] *v/t (delight)* encantar

en·chant·ing [ɪnˈtʃæntɪŋ] *adj* encantador

en·cir·cle [ɪnˈsɜːrkl] *v/t* rodear

encl *abbr (= **en·clo·sure(s)**)* documento(s) *m(pl)* adjunto(s)

en·close [ɪnˈklouz] *v/t Br in letter* adjuntar; *area* rodear; **please find enclosed ...** remito adjunto ...

en·clo·sure [ɪnˈklouʒər] *with letter* documento *m* adjunto

en·core [ˈɑːŋkɔːr] bis *m*

en·coun·ter [ɪnˈkauntər] **1** *n* encuentro *m* **2** *v/t person* encontrarse con; *problem, resistance* tropezar con

en·cour·age [ɪnˈkʌrɪdʒ] *v/t* animar; *violence* fomentar

en·cour·age·ment [ɪnˈkʌrɪdʒmənt] ánimo *m*

en·cour·ag·ing [ɪnˈkʌrɪdʒɪŋ] *adj* alentador

◆ **en·croach on** [ɪnˈkroutʃ] *v/t land* inva-

dir; *rights* usurpar; *time* quitar

en·cy·clo·pe·di·a [ɪnsaɪkləˈpiːdɪə] enciclopedia *f*

end [end] **1** *n of journey, month* final *m; (extremity)* extremo *m; (bottom)* fondo *m; (conclusion, purpose)* fin *m;* **at the other end of town** al otro lado de la ciudad; **in the end** al final; **for hours on end** durante horas y horas; **stand sth on end** poner de pie algo; **at the end of July** a finales de julio; **in the end** al final; **put an end to** poner fin a **2** *v/t* terminar, finalizar **3** *v/i* terminar

◆ **end up** *v/i* acabar

en·dan·ger [ɪnˈdeɪndʒər] *v/t* poner en peligro

en·dan·gered spe·cies especie *f* en peligro de extinción

en·dear·ing [ɪnˈdɪrɪŋ] *adj* simpático

en·deav·or [ɪnˈdevər] **1** *n* esfuerzo *m* **2** *v/t* procurar

en·dem·ic [ɪnˈdemɪk] *adj* endémico

end·ing [ˈendɪŋ] *final m;* GRAM terminación *f*

end·less [ˈendlɪs] *adj* interminable

en·dorse [ɪnˈdɔːrs] *v/t check* endosar; *candidacy* apoyar; *product* representar

en·dorse·ment [ɪnˈdɔːrsmənt] *of check* endoso *m; of candidacy* apoyo *m; of product* representación *f*

end prod·uct producto *m* final

end re·sult resultado *m* final

en·dur·ance [ɪnˈdʊrəns] resistencia *f*

en·dure [ɪnˈdʊər] **1** *v/t* resistir **2** *v/i (last)* durar

en·dur·ing [ɪnˈdʊrɪŋ] *adj* duradero

end-'us·er usuario(-a) *m(f)* final

en·e·my [ˈenəmɪ] enemigo(-a) *m(f)*

en·er·get·ic [enərˈdʒetɪk] *adj* enérgico

en·er·get·i·cal·ly [enərˈdʒetɪklɪ] *adv* enérgicamente

en·er·gy [ˈenərdʒɪ] energía *f*

'en·er·gy-sav·ing *adj device* que ahorra energía

'e·ner·gy sup·ply suministro *m* de energía

en·force [ɪnˈfɔːrs] *v/t* hacer cumplir

en·gage [ɪnˈgeɪdʒ] **1** *v/t (hire)* contratar **2** *v/i* TECH engranar

◆ **engage in** *v/t* dedicarse a

en·gaged [ɪnˈgeɪdʒd] *adj to be married* prometido; **get engaged** prometerse

en·gaged tone *Br* TELEC señal *f* de ocupado *or Span* comunicando

en·gage·ment [ɪnˈgeɪdʒmənt] *(appointment, to be married)* compromiso *m;* MIL combate *m*

en·gage·ment ring anillo *m* de compromiso

en·gag·ing [ɪnˈgeɪdʒɪŋ] *adj smile, person* atractivo

en·gine [ˈendʒɪn] motor *m*

en·gi·neer [endʒɪˈnɪr] **1** *n* ingeniero(-a) *m(f)*; NAUT, RAIL maquinista *m/f* **2** *v/t fig: meeting etc* tramar

en·gi·neer·ing [endʒɪˈnɪrɪŋ] ingeniería *f*

Eng·land [ˈɪŋglənd] Inglaterra *f*

Eng·lish [ˈɪŋglɪʃ] **1** *adj* inglés(-esa) **2** *n language* inglés *m*; **the English** los ingleses

Eng·lish 'Chan·nel Canal *m* de la Mancha

'Eng·lish·man inglés *m*

'Eng·lish·wom·an inglesa *f*

en·grave [ɪnˈgreɪv] *v/t* grabar

en·grav·ing [ɪnˈgreɪvɪŋ] grabado *m*

en·grossed [ɪnˈgroust] *adj* absorto (*in* en)

en·gulf [ɪnˈgʌlf] *v/t* devorar

en·hance [ɪnˈhæns] *v/t* realzar

e·nig·ma [ɪˈnɪgmə] enigma *m*

en·ig·mat·ic [enɪgˈmætɪk] *adj* enigmático

en·joy [ɪnˈdʒɔɪ] *v/t* disfrutar; **enjoy o.s.** divertirse; **enjoy (your meal)!** ¡que aproveche!

en·joy·a·ble [ɪnˈdʒɔɪəbl] *adj* agradable

en·joy·ment [ɪnˈdʒɔɪmənt] diversión *f*

en·large [ɪnˈlɑːrdʒ] *v/t* ampliar

en·large·ment [ɪnˈlɑːrdʒmənt] ampliación *f*

en·light·en [ɪnˈlaɪtn] *v/t* educar

en·list [ɪnˈlɪst] **1** *v/i* MIL alistarse **2** *v/t*: **I enlisted his help** conseguí que me ayudara

en·liv·en [ɪnˈlaɪvn] *v/t* animar

en·mi·ty [ˈenmətɪ] enemistad *f*

e·nor·mi·ty [ɪˈnɔːrmətɪ] magnitud *f*

e·nor·mous [ɪˈnɔːrməs] *adj* enorme; *satisfaction, patience* inmenso

e·nor·mous·ly [ɪˈnɔːrməslɪ] *adv* enormemente

e·nough [ɪˈnʌf] **1** *adj pron* suficiente, bastante; **will $50 be enough?** ¿llegará con 50 dólares?; **I've had enough!** ¡estoy harto!; **that's enough, calm down!** ¡ya basta, tranquilízate! **2** *adv* suficientemente, bastante; **the bag isn't big enough** la bolsa no es lo suficientemente or bastante grande; **strangely enough** curiosamente

en·quire [ɪnˈkwaɪr] → **inquire**

en·raged [ɪnˈreɪdʒd] *adj* enfurecido

en·rich [ɪnˈrɪtʃ] *v/t* enriquecer

en·roll [ɪnˈroul] *v/i* matricularse

en·roll·ment [ɪnˈroulmənt] matrícula *f*

en·sue [ɪnˈsuː] *v/i* sucederse

en suite [ˈɑːnswiːt] *adj*: **en suite bathroom** baño *m* privado

en·sure [ɪnˈʃʊər] *v/t* asegurar

en·tail [ɪnˈteɪl] *v/t* conllevar

en·tan·gle [ɪnˈtæŋgl] *v/t: in rope* enredar; **become entangled in** enredarse en; **become entangled with** *in love affair* liarse con

en·ter [ˈentər] **1** *v/t room, house* entrar en; *competition* participar en; *person, horse in race* inscribir; *(write down)* anotar; COMPUT introducir **2** *v/i* entrar; THEA entrar en escena; *in competition* inscribirse **3** *n* COMPUT intro *m*

en·ter·prise [ˈentərpraɪz] *(initiative)* iniciativa *f*; *(venture)* empresa *f*

en·ter·pris·ing [ˈentərpraɪzɪŋ] *adj* con iniciativa

en·ter·tain [entərˈteɪn] **1** *v/t (amuse)* entretener; *(consider: idea)* considerar **2** *v/i (have guests)*: **we entertain a lot** recibimos a mucha gente

en·ter·tain·er [entərˈteɪnər] artista *m/f*

en·ter·tain·ing [entərˈteɪnɪŋ] *adj* entretenido

en·ter·tain·ment [entərˈteɪnmənt] entretenimiento *m*

en·thrall [ɪnˈθrɔːl] *v/t* cautivar

en·thu·si·as·m [ɪnˈθuːzɪæzm] entusiasmo *m*

en·thu·si·ast [ɪnˈθuːzɪæst] entusiasta *m/f*

en·thu·si·as·tic [ɪnθuːzɪˈæstɪk] *adj* entusiasta; **be enthusiastic about sth** estar entusiasmado con algo

en·thu·si·as·tic·al·ly [ɪnθuːzɪˈæstɪklɪ] *adv* con entusiasmo

en·tice [ɪnˈtaɪs] *v/t* atraer

en·tire [ɪnˈtaɪr] *adj* entero; **the entire school is going** va al ir todo el colegio

en·tire·ly [ɪnˈtaɪrlɪ] *adv* completamente

en·ti·tle [ɪnˈtaɪtl] *v/t: entitle s.o. to sth** dar derecho a alguien a algo; **be entitled to** tener derecho a

en·ti·tled [ɪnˈtaɪtld] *adj book* titulado

en·trance [ˈentrəns] entrada *f*; THEA entrada *f* en escena

en·tranced [ɪnˈtrænst] *adj* encantado

'en·trance ex·am(·i·na·tion) examen *m* de acceso

'en·trance fee (cuota *f* de) entrada *f*

en·trant [ˈentrənt] participante *m/f*

en·treat [ɪnˈtriːt] *v/t* suplicar; **entreat s.o. to do sth** suplicar a alguien que haga algo

en·trenched [ɪnˈtrentʃt] *adj attitudes* arraigado

en·tre·pre·neur [ɑːntrəprəˈnɜːr] empresario(-a) *m(f)*

en·tre·pre·neur·i·al [ɑːntrəprəˈnɜːrɪəl] *adj* empresarial

en·trust [ɪnˈtrʌst] *v/t* confiar; **entrust s.o.**

with sth, entrust sth to s.o. confiar algo a alguien

en·try ['entrɪ] entrada f; *for competition* inscripción f; *in diary etc* entrada f; **no entry** prohibida la entrada; **the winning entry was painted by …** el cuadro ganador fue pintado por …

en·try form impreso m de inscripción

en·try·phone portero m automático

en·try vi·sa visado m

e·nu·me·rate ['nuːmərert] v/t enumerar

en·vel·op [ɪn'veləp] v/t cubrir

en·ve·lope ['envəloup] sobre m

en·vi·a·ble ['envɪəbl] adj envidiable

en·vi·ous ['envɪəs] adj envidioso; **be envious of s.o.** tener envidia de alguien

en·vi·ron·ment [ɪn'vaɪrənmənt] (nature) medio m ambiente; (surroundings) entorno m, ambiente m

en·vi·ron·men·tal [ɪnvaɪrən'mentl] adj medioambiental

en·vi·ron·men·tal·ist [ɪnvaɪrən'mentəlɪst] ecologista m/f

en·vi·ron·men·tal·ly 'friend·ly [ɪnvaɪrən'mentəlɪ] adj ecológico, que no daña el medio ambiente

en·vi·ron·men·tal pol·lu·tion contaminación f medioambiental

en·vi·ron·men·tal pro·tec·tion protección f medioambiental

en·vi·rons [ɪn'vaɪrənz] npl alrededores mpl

en·vis·age [ɪn'vɪzɪdʒ] v/t imaginar

en·voy ['envɔɪ] enviado(-a) m(f)

en·vy ['envɪ] 1 n envidia f; **be the envy of** ser la envidia de 2 v/t (pret & pp envied) envidiar; **envy s.o. sth** envidiar a alguien algo

e·phem·er·al [ɪ'femərəl] adj efímero

ep·ic ['epɪk] 1 n epopeya f 2 adj journey épico; **a task of epic proportions** una tarea monumental

ep·i·cen·ter ['epɪsentr] epicentro m

ep·i·dem·ic [epɪ'demɪk] epidemia f

ep·i·lep·sy ['epɪlepsɪ] epilepsia f

ep·i·lep·tic [epɪ'leptɪk] epiléptico(-a) m(f)

ep·i·lep·tic 'fit ataque m epiléptico

ep·i·log, Br **ep·i·logue** ['epɪlɔːg] epílogo m

ep·i·sode ['epɪsoud] of story, soap opera episodio m, capítulo m; (happening) episodio m; **let's forget the whole episode** olvidemos lo sucedido

ep·i·taph ['epɪtæf] epitafio m

e·poch ['iːpɔk] era f

e·poch-mak·ing ['iːpɔːkmeɪkɪŋ] adj que hace época

e·qual ['iːkwl] 1 adj igual; **equal amounts of milk and water** la misma cantidad de leche y de agua; **equal opportunities** igualdad f de oportunidades; **be equal to** a task estar capacitado para 2 n igual m/f 3 v/t (pret & pp equaled, Br equalled) (with numbers) equivaler; (be as good as) igualar; **four times twelve equals 48** cuatro por doce, (igual a) cuarenta y ocho

e·qual·i·ty [ɪ'kwɑːlətɪ] igualdad f

e·qual·ize ['iːkwəlaɪz] 1 v/t igualar 2 v/i Br sp empatar

e·qual·iz·er ['iːkwəlaɪzər] Br sp gol m del empate

e·qual·ly ['iːkwəlɪ] adv igualmente; share, divide en partes iguales; **equally, …** igualmente, …

e·qual 'rights npl igualdad f de derechos

e·quate [ɪ'kweɪt] v/t equiparar; **equate sth with sth** equiparar algo con algo

e·qua·tion [ɪ'kweɪʒn] MATH ecuación f

e·qua·tor [ɪ'kweɪtər] ecuador m

e·qui·lib·ri·um [iːkwɪ'lɪbrɪəm] equilibrio m

e·qui·nox ['iːkwɪnɑːks] equinoccio m

e·quip [ɪ'kwɪp] v/t (pret & pp equipped) equipar; **he's not equipped to handle it** fig no está preparado para llevarlo

e·quip·ment [ɪ'kwɪpmənt] equipo m

eq·ui·ty ['ekwətɪ] FIN acciones fpl ordinarias

e·quiv·a·lent [ɪ'kwɪvələnt] 1 adj equivalente; **be equivalent to** equivaler a 2 n equivalente m

e·ra ['ɪrə] era f

e·rad·i·cate [ɪ'rædɪkeɪt] v/t erradicar

e·rase [ɪ'reɪz] v/t borrar

e·ras·er [ɪ'reɪzər] for pencil goma f (de borrar); for chalk borrador m

e·rect [ɪ'rekt] 1 adj erguido 2 v/t levantar, erigir

e·rec·tion [ɪ'rekʃn] of building etc construcción f; of penis erección f

er·go·nom·ic [ɜːrgoʊ'nɑːmɪk] adj furniture ergonómico

e·rode [ɪ'roud] v/t also fig erosionar

e·ro·sion [ɪ'rouʒn] also fig erosión f

e·rot·ic [ɪ'rɑːtɪk] adj erótico

e·rot·i·cism [ɪ'rɑːtɪsɪzm] erotismo m

er·rand ['erənd] recado m; **run errands** hacer recados

er·rat·ic [ɪ'rætɪk] adj irregular; course errático

er·ror ['erər] error m

'er·ror mes·sage COMPUT mensaje m de error

e·rupt [ɪ'rʌpt] v/i of volcano entrar en erupción; of violence brotar; of person explotar

E

e·rup·tion [ɪ'rʌpʃn] *of volcano* erupción *f*;
of violence brote *f*

es·ca·late ['eskəleɪt] *v/i* intensificarse

es·ca·la·tion [eskə'leɪʃn] intensificación *f*

es·ca·la·tor ['eskəleɪtər] escalera *f*
mecánica

es·cape [ɪ'skeɪp] **1** *n of prisoner, animal*
fuga *f*; *of gas* escape *m*, fuga *f*; **have a
narrow escape** escaparse por los pelos
2 *v/i of prisoner, animal, gas* escaparse
3 *v/t: the word escapes me* no consigo
recordar la palabra

es·cape chute AVIA tobogán *m* de emergencia

es·cort 1 *n* ['eskɔːrt] acompañante *m/f*;
guard escolta *m/f*; *under escort* escoltado **2** *v/t* [ɪ'skɔːrt] escoltar; *socially* acompañar

es·pe·cial [ɪ'speʃl] → *special*

es·pe·cial·ly [ɪ'speʃlɪ] *adv* especialmente

es·pi·o·nage ['espɪənɑːʒ] espionaje *m*

es·pres·so (*cof·fee*) [es'presou] café *m*
exprés

es·say ['eseɪ] *n creative* redacción *f*; *factual* trabajo *m*

es·sen·tial [ɪ'senʃl] *adj* esencial; *the essential thing is ...* lo esencial es ...

es·sen·tial·ly [ɪ'senʃlɪ] *adv* esencialmente; fundamentalmente

es·tab·lish [ɪ'stæblɪʃ] *v/t company* fundar; (*create, determine*) establecer; *establish o.s. as* establecerse como

es·tab·lish·ment [ɪ'stæblɪʃmənt] *firm,
shop etc* establecimiento *m*; *the Establishment* el orden establecido

es·tate [ɪ'steɪt] (*area of land*) finca *f*;
(*possessions of dead person*) patrimonio
m

es·tate a·gen·cy *Br* agencia *f* inmobiliaria

es·thet·ic [ɪs'θetɪk] *adj* estético

es·ti·mate ['estɪmət] **1** *n* estimación *f*; *for
job* presupuesto *m* **2** *v/t* estimar; *estimated time of arrival* hora *f* estimada de llegada

es·ti·ma·tion [estɪ'meɪʃn] estima *f*; *he
has gone up / down in my estimation*
le tengo en más / menos estima; *in my
estimation* (*opinion*) a mi parecer

es·tranged [ɪs'treɪndʒd] *adj wife, husband* separado

es·tu·a·ry ['estʃəwerɪ] estuario *m*

ETA [iːtiː'eɪ] *abbr* (= *estimated time of
arrival*) hora *f* estimada de llegada

etc [et'setrə] *abbr* (= *et cetera*) etc (= etcétera)

etch·ing ['etʃɪŋ] aguafuerte *m*

e·ter·nal [ɪ'tɜːrnl] *adj* eterno

e·ter·ni·ty [ɪ'tɜːrnətɪ] eternidad *f*

eth·i·cal ['eθɪkl] *adj* ético

eth·ics ['eθɪks] ética *f*; *code of ethics* código *m* ético

eth·nic ['eθnɪk] *adj* étnico

eth·nic 'group grupo *m* étnico

eth·nic mi'nor·i·ty minoría *f* étnica

EU [iː'juː] *abbr* (= *European Union*) UE
(=Unión *f* Europea)

eu·phe·mism ['juːfəmɪzm] eufemismo *m*

eu·pho·ri·a [juː'fɔːrɪə] euforia *f*

eu·ro ['jʊrou] euro *m*

Eu·rope ['jʊrəp] Europa

Eu·ro·pe·an [jʊrə'pɪən] **1** *adj* europeo **2**
europeo(-a) *m(f)*

Eu·ro·pe·an Com'mis·sion Comisión
Europea

Eu·ro·pe·an 'Par·lia·ment Parlamento *m*
Europeo

Eu·ro·pe·an plan media pensión *f*

Eu·ro·pe·an 'Un·ion Unión *f* Europea

eu·tha·na·si·a [juːθə'neɪzɪə] eutanasia *f*

e·vac·u·ate [ɪ'vækjueɪt] *v/t* evacuar

e·vade [ɪ'veɪd] *v/t* evadir

e·val·u·ate [ɪ'væljueɪt] *v/t* evaluar

e·val·u·a·tion [ɪvælju'eɪʃn] evaluación *f*

e·van·gel·ist [ɪ'vændʒəlɪst] evangelista
m/f

e·vap·o·rate [ɪ'væpəreɪt] *v/i of water*
evaporarse; *of confidence* desvanecerse

e·vap·o·ra·tion [ɪvæpə'reɪʃn] *of water*
evaporación *f*

e·va·sion [ɪ'veɪʒn] evasión *f*

e·va·sive [ɪ'veɪsɪv] *adj* evasivo

eve [iːv] víspera *f*

e·ven ['iːvn] **1** *adj* (*regular*) regular; (*level*) llano; *number* par; *distribution* igualado; *I'll get even with him* me las pagará
2 *adv* incluso; *even bigger / better* incluso *or* aún mayor / mejor; *not even* ni siquiera; *even so* aun así; *even if* aunque
even if he begged me aunque me lo suplicara **3** *v/t: even the score* empatar,
igualar el marcador

eve·ning ['iːvnɪŋ] tarde *f*; *after dark*
noche *f*; *in the evening* por la tarde /
noche; *this evening* esta tarde / noche;
yesterday evening anoche *f*; *good evening* buenas *fpl* noches

'eve·ning class clase *f* nocturna

'eve·ning dress *for woman* traje *f* de
noche; *for man* traje *f* de etiqueta

eve·ning 'pa·per periódico *m* de la tarde
or vespertino

e·ven·ly ['iːvnlɪ] *adv* (*regularly*) regularmente

e·vent [ɪ'vent] acontecimiento *m*; SP prueba *f*; *at all events* en cualquier caso

e·vent·ful [ɪ'ventfəl] *adj* agitado, lleno de
incidentes

e·ven·tu·al [ɪˈventʃʊəl] *adj* final
e·ven·tu·al·ly [ɪˈventʃʊəlɪ] *adv* finalmente
ev·er [ˈevər] *adv*: *if I ever hear you ...* como te oiga ...; *have you ever been to Japan?* ¿has estado alguna vez en Japón?; *for ever* siempre; *ever since* desde entonces; *ever since she found out about it* desde que se enteró de ello; *ever since I've known him* desde que lo conozco
ev·er·green [ˈevərgriːn] *n* árbol *m* de hoja perenne
ev·er·last·ing [evərˈlæstɪŋ] *adj love* eterno
ev·ery [ˈevrɪ] *adj* cada; *I see him every day* le veo todos los días; *you have every reason to ...* tienes toda la razón para ...; *one in every ten* uno de cada diez; *every other day* cada dos días; *every now and then* de vez en cuando
ev·ery·bod·y [ˈevrɪbɑːdɪ] → *everyone*
ev·ery·day [ˈevrɪdeɪ] *adj* cotidiano
ev·ery·one [ˈevrɪwʌn] *pron* todo el mundo
ev·ery·thing [ˈevrɪθɪŋ] *pron* todo
ev·ery·where [ˈevrɪwer] *adv* en *or* por todos sitios; (*wherever*) dondequiera que
e·vict [ɪˈvɪkt] *v/t* desahuciar
ev·i·dence [ˈevɪdəns] *also* LAW prueba(s) *f*(*pl*); *give evidence* prestar declaración
ev·i·dent [ˈevɪdənt] *adj* evidente
ev·i·dent·ly [ˈevɪdəntlɪ] *adv* (*clearly*) evidentemente; (*apparently*) aparentemente, al parecer
e·vil [ˈiːvl] **1** *adj* malo **2** *n* mal *m*
e·voke [ɪˈvouk] *v/t image* evocar
ev·o·lu·tion [iːvəˈluːʃn] evolución *f*
e·volve [ɪˈvɑːlv] *v/i* evolucionar
ewe [juː] oveja *f*
ex- [eks-] *pref* ex-
ex [eks] F (*former wife, husband*) ex *m/f* F
ex·act [ɪgˈzækt] *adj* exacto
ex·act·ing [ɪgˈzæktɪŋ] *adj* exigente; *task* duro
ex·act·ly [ɪgˈzæktlɪ] *adv* exactamente; *exactly!* ¡exactamente!
ex·ag·ge·rate [ɪgˈzædʒəreɪt] *v/t & v/i* exagerar
ex·ag·ge·ra·tion [ɪgzædʒəˈreɪʃn] exageración *f*
ex·am [ɪgˈzæm] examen *m*; *take an exam* hacer un examen; *pass / fail an exam* aprobar/ suspender un examen
ex·am·i·na·tion [ɪgzæmɪˈneɪʃn] examen *m*; *of patient* reconocimiento *m*
ex·am·ine [ɪgˈzæmɪn] *v/t* examinar; *patient* reconocer
ex·am·in·er [ɪgˈzæmɪnər] EDU examinador(a) *m(f)*

ex·am·ple [ɪgˈzæmpl] ejemplo *m*; *for example* por ejemplo; *set a good / bad example* dar buen / mal ejemplo
ex·as·pe·rat·ed [ɪgˈzæspəreɪtɪd] *adj* exasperado
ex·as·pe·rat·ing [ɪgˈzæspəreɪtɪŋ] *adj* exasperante
ex·ca·vate [ˈekskəveɪt] *v/t* excavar
ex·ca·va·tion [ekskəˈveɪʃn] excavación *f*
ex·ca·va·tor [ˈekskəveɪtər] excavadora *f*
ex·ceed [ɪkˈsiːd] *v/t* (*be more than*) exceder; (*go beyond*) sobrepasar
ex·ceed·ing·ly [ɪkˈsiːdɪŋlɪ] *adj* sumamente
ex·cel [ɪkˈsel] **1** *v/i* (*pret & pp* **excelled**) sobresalir (*at* en) **2** *v/t* (*pret & pp* **excelled**): *excel o.s.* superarse a sí mismo
ex·cel·lence [ˈeksələns] excelencia *f*
ex·cel·lent [ˈeksələnt] *adj* excelente
ex·cept [ɪkˈsept] *prep* excepto; *except for* a excepción de; *except that* sólo que
ex·cep·tion [ɪkˈsepʃn] excepción *f*; *with the exception of* a excepción de; *take exception to* molestarse por
ex·cep·tion·al [ɪkˈsepʃnl] *adj* excepcional
ex·cep·tion·al·ly [ɪkˈsepʃnlɪ] *adv* (*extremely*) excepcionalmente
ex·cerpt [ˈeksɜːrpt] extracto *m*
ex·cess [ɪkˈses] **1** *n* exceso *m*; *eat / drink to excess* comer / beber en exceso; *in excess of* superior a **2** *adj* excedente
ex·cess 'bag·gage exceso *m* de equipaje
ex·cess 'fare suplemento *m*
ex·ces·sive [ɪkˈsesɪv] *adj* excesivo
ex·change [ɪksˈtʃeɪndʒ] **1** *n* intercambio *m*; *in exchange* a cambio (*for* de) **2** *v/t* cambiar
ex'change rate FIN tipo *m* de cambio
ex·ci·ta·ble [ɪkˈsaɪtəbl] *adj* excitable
ex·cite [ɪkˈsaɪt] *v/t* (*make enthusiastic*) entusiasmar
ex·cit·ed [ɪkˈsaɪtɪd] *adj* emocionado, excitado; *sexually* excitado; *get excited* emocionarse; *get excited about* emocionarse *or* excitarse con
ex·cite·ment [ɪkˈsaɪtmənt] emoción *f*, excitación *f*
ex·cit·ing [ɪkˈsaɪtɪŋ] *adj* emocionante
ex·claim [ɪkˈskleɪm] *v/t* exclamar
ex·cla·ma·tion [ekskləˈmeɪʃn] exclamación *f*
ex·cla'ma·tion point signo *m* de admiración
ex·clude [ɪkˈskluːd] *v/t* excluir; *possibility* descartar
ex·clud·ing [ɪkˈskluːdɪŋ] *prep* excluyendo
ex·clu·sive [ɪkˈskluːsɪv] *adj* exclusivo
ex·com·mu·ni·cate [ekskəˈmjuːnɪkeɪt]

E

v/t REL excomulgar

ex·cru·ci·a·ting [ɪkˈskruːʃɪeɪtɪŋ] *adj* pain terrible

ex·cur·sion [ɪkˈskɜːrʃn] excursión *f*

ex·cuse 1 *n* [ɪkˈskjuːs] excusa *f* **2** *v/t* [ɪkˈskjuːz] (*forgive*) excusar, perdonar; (*allow to leave*) disculpar; **excuse s.o. from sth** dispensar a alguien de algo; **excuse me to get past, interrupting** perdone, disculpe; *to get attention* perdone, oiga

e·x·e·cute [ˈeksɪkjuːt] *v/t criminal, plan* ejecutar

ex·e·cu·tion [eksɪˈkjuːʃn] *of criminal, plan* ejecución *f*

ex·e·cu·tion·er [eksɪˈkjuːʃnər] verdugo *m*

ex·ec·u·tive [ɪɡˈzekjutɪv] ejecutivo(-a) *m(f)*

ex·ec·u·tive 'brief·case maletín *m* de ejecutivo

ex·ec·u·tive 'wash·room baño *m* para ejecutivos

ex·em·pla·ry [ɪgˈzemplərɪ] *adj* ejemplar

ex·empt [ɪgˈzempt] *adj* exento; **be exempt from** estar exento de

ex·er·cise [ˈeksərsaɪz] **1** *n* ejercicio *m*; *take exercise* hacer ejercicio **2** *v/t muscle* ejercitar; *dog* pasear; *caution* proceder con; *exercise restraint* controlarse **3** *v/i* hacer ejercicio

'ex·er·cise bike bicicleta *f* estática

'ex·er·cise book EDU cuaderno de ejercicios

ex·ert [ɪgˈzɜːrt] *v/t authority* ejercer; **exert o.s.** esforzarse

ex·er·tion [ɪgˈzɜːrʃn] esfuerzo *m*

ex·hale [eksˈheɪl] *v/t* exhalar

ex·haust [ɪgˈzɔːst] **1** *n fumes* gases *mpl* de la combustión; *pipe* tubo *m* de escape **2** *v/t* (*tire*) cansar; (*use up*) agotar

ex·haust·ed [ɪgˈzɔːstɪd] *adj* (*tired*) agotado

ex'haust fumes *npl* gases *mpl* de la combustión

ex·haust·ing [ɪgˈzɔːstɪŋ] *adj* agotador

ex·haus·tion [ɪgˈzɔːstʃn] agotamiento *m*

ex·haus·tive [ɪgˈzɔːstɪv] *adj* exhaustivo

ex'haust pipe tubo *m* de escape

ex·hib·it [ɪgˈzɪbɪt] **1** *n in exhibition* objeto *m* expuesto **2** *v/t of gallery* exhibir; *of artist* exponer; (*give evidence of*) mostrar

ex·hi·bi·tion [eksɪˈbɪʃn] exposición *f*; *of bad behavior, skill* exhibición *f*

ex·hi·bi·tion·ist [eksɪˈbɪʃnɪst] exhibicionista *m/f*

ex·hil·a·rat·ing [ɪgˈzɪləreɪtɪŋ] *adj* estimulante

ex·ile [ˈeksaɪl] **1** *n* exilio *m*; *person* exilia-

do(-a) *m(f)* **2** *v/t* exiliar

ex·ist [ɪgˈzɪst] *v/i* existir; **exist on** subsistir a base de

ex·ist·ence [ɪgˈzɪstəns] existencia *f*; **be in existence** existir; **come into existence** crearse, nacer

ex·ist·ing [ɪgˈzɪstɪŋ] *adj* existente

ex·it [ˈeksɪt] **1** *n* salida *f*; THEA salida *f*, mutis *m* **2** *v/i* COMPUT salir

ex·on·e·rate [ɪgˈzɑːnəreɪt] *v/t* exonerar de

ex·or·bi·tant [ɪgˈzɔːrbɪtənt] *adj* exorbitante

ex·ot·ic [ɪgˈzɑːtɪk] *adj* exótico

ex·pand [ɪkˈspænd] **1** *v/t* expandir **2** *v/i* expandirse; *of metal* dilatarse

♦ **expand on** *v/t* desarrollar

ex·panse [ɪkˈspæns] extensión *f*

ex·pan·sion [ɪkˈspænʃn] expansión *f*; *o, metal* dilatación *f*

ex·pat·ri·ate [eksˈpætrɪət] **1** *adj* expatriado **2** *n* expatriado(-a) *m(f)*

ex·pect [ɪkˈspekt] **1** *v/t* esperar; (*suppose*, suponer, imaginar(se); (*demand*) exigir **2** *v/i*: **be expecting** (*be pregnant*) estar en estado; *I expect so* eso espero, creo que sí

ex·pec·tant [ɪkˈspektənt] *adj crowd* expectante

ex·pec·tant 'moth·er futura madre *f*

ex·pec·ta·tion [ekspekˈteɪʃn] expectativa *f*; *live up to people's expectations o you* (*demands*) estar a la altura de lo que se espera de uno

ex·pe·di·ent [ɪkˈspiːdɪənt] *adj* oportuno, conveniente

ex·pe·di·tion [ekspɪˈdɪʃn] expedición *f*

ex·pel [ɪkˈspel] *v/t* (*pret & pp expelled*) *person* expulsar

ex·pend [ɪkˈspend] *v/t energy* gastar

ex·pend·a·ble [ɪkˈspendəbl] *adj person* prescindible

ex·pen·di·ture [ɪkˈspendɪtʃər] gasto *m*

ex·pense [ɪkˈspens] gasto *m*; *at great expense* gastando mucho dinero; *at the company's expense* a cargo de la empresa; *a joke at my expense* una broma a costa mía; *at the expense of his health* a costa de su salud

ex'pense ac·count cuenta *f* de gastos

ex·pens·es [ɪkˈspensɪz] *npl* gastos *mpl*

ex·pen·sive [ɪkˈspensɪv] *adj* caro

ex·pe·ri·ence [ɪkˈspɪrɪəns] **1** *n* experiencia *f* **2** *v/t* experimentar

ex·pe·ri·enced [ɪkˈspɪrɪənst] *adj* experimentado

ex·per·i·ment [ɪkˈsperɪmənt] **1** *n* experimento *m* **2** *v/i* experimentar; *experiment on animals* experimentar con; *experiment with* (*try out*) probar

ex·per·i·men·tal [ɪkspɛrɪ'mentl] adj experimental

ex·pert ['ekspɜːrt] **1** adj experto **2** n experto(-a) m(f)

ex·pert ad'vice la opinión de un experto

ex·pert·ise [ekspɜːr'tiːz] destreza f, pericia f

ex·pire [ɪk'spaɪr] v/i caducar

ex·pi·ry [ɪk'spaɪrɪ] of lease, contract vencimiento m; of passport caducidad f

ex'pi·ry date of food, passport fecha f de caducidad; **be past its expiry date** haber caducado

ex·plain [ɪk'spleɪn] **1** v/t explicar **2** v/i explicarse

ex·pla·na·tion [eksplə'neɪʃn] explicación f

ex·plan·a·tor·y [ɪk'splænətɔːrɪ] adj explicativo

ex·plic·it [ɪk'splɪsɪt] adj instructions explícito

ex·plic·it·ly [ɪk'splɪsɪtlɪ] adv state explícitamente; forbid terminantemente

ex·plode [ɪk'sploʊd] **1** v/i of bomb explotar **2** v/t bomb hacer explotar

ex·ploit[1] ['eksplɔɪt] n hazaña f

ex·ploit[2] [ɪk'splɔɪt] v/t person, resources explotar

ex·ploi·ta·tion [eksplɔɪ'teɪʃn] of person explotación f

ex·plo·ra·tion [eksplə'reɪʃn] exploración f

ex·plor·a·to·ry [ɪk'splɔːrətərɪ] adj surgery exploratorio

ex·plore [ɪk'splɔːr] v/t country etc explorar; possibility estudiar

ex·plor·er [ɪk'splɔːrər] explorador(a) m(f)

ex·plo·sion [ɪk'sploʊʒn] of bomb, in population explosión f

ex·plo·sive [ɪk'sploʊsɪv] n explosivo m

ex·port ['ekspɔːrt] **1** n action exportación f; item producto m de exportación; **exports** npl exportaciones fpl **2** v/t also COMPUT exportar

'ex·port cam·paign campaña f de exportación

ex·port·er ['ekspɔːrtər] exportador(a) m(f)

ex·pose [ɪk'spoʊz] v/t (uncover) exponer; scandal sacar a la luz; **he's been exposed as a liar** ha quedado como un mentiroso; **expose sth to sth** exponer algo a algo

ex·po·sure [ɪk'spoʊʒər] exposición f; PHOT foto(grafía) f

ex·press [ɪk'spres] **1** adj (fast) rápido; (explicit) expreso **2** n train expreso m; bus autobús m directo **3** v/t expresar; **ex-press o.s. well / clearly** expresarse bien / con claridad

ex·press el·e·va·tor ascensor rápido que sólo para en algunos pisos

ex·pres·sion [ɪk'spreʃn] voiced muestra f; phrase, on face expresión f; **read with expression** leer con sentimiento

ex·pres·sive [ɪk'spresɪv] adj expresivo

ex·press·ly [ɪk'spreslɪ] adv state expresamente; forbid terminantemente

ex·press·way [ɪk'spresweɪ] autopista f

ex·pul·sion [ɪk'spʌlʃn] from school, of diplomat expulsión f

ex·qui·site [ek'skwɪzɪt] adj (beautiful) exquisito

ex·tend [ɪk'stend] **1** v/t house, investigation ampliar; (make wider) ensanchar; (make bigger) agrandar; runway, path alargar; contract, visa prorrogar; thanks, congratulations extender **2** v/i of garden etc llegar

ex·ten·sion [ɪk'stenʃn] to house ampliación f; of contract, visa prórroga f; TELEC extensión f

ex·ten·sion ca·ble cable m de extensión

ex·ten·sive [ɪk'stensɪv] adj damage cuantioso; knowledge considerable; search extenso, amplio

ex·tent [ɪk'stent] alcance m; **to such an extent that** hasta el punto de que; **to a certain extent** hasta cierto punto

ex·ten·u·at·ing cir·cum·stances [ɪk'stenjueɪtɪŋ] npl circunstancias fpl atenuantes

ex·te·ri·or [ɪk'stɪrɪər] **1** adj exterior **2** n exterior m

ex·ter·mi·nate [ɪk'stɜːrmɪneɪt] v/t exterminar

ex·ter·nal [ɪk'stɜːrnl] adj (outside) exterior, externo

ex·tinct [ɪk'stɪŋkt] adj species extinguido

ex·tinc·tion [ɪk'stɪŋkʃn] of species extinción f

ex·tin·guish [ɪk'stɪŋgwɪʃ] v/t fire extinguir, apagar; cigarette apagar

ex·tin·guish·er [ɪk'stɪŋgwɪʃər] extintor m

ex·tort [ɪk'stɔːrt] v/t obtener mediante extorsión; **extort money from** extorsionar a

ex·tor·tion [ɪk'stɔːrʃn] extorsión f

ex·tor·tion·ate [ɪk'stɔːrʃənət] adj prices desorbitado

ex·tra ['ekstrə] **1** n extra m; in movie extra m/f **2** adj extra; **meals are extra** las comidas se pagan aparte; **that's $1 extra** cuesta 1 dólar más **3** adv super; **extra strong** extrafuerte; **extra special** muy especial

E

ex·tra 'charge recargo *m*
ex·tract¹ ['ekstrækt] *n* extracto *m*
ex·tract² [ɪk'strækt] *v/t* sacar; *coal, oil, tooth* extraer; *information* sonsacar
ex·trac·tion [ɪk'strækʃn] *of oil, coal, tooth* extracción *f*
ex·tra·dite ['ekstrədaɪt] *v/t* extraditar
ex·tra·di·tion [ekstrə'dɪʃn] extradición *f*
ex·tra·di·tion trea·ty tratado *m* de extradición
ex·tra·mar·i·tal [ekstrə'mærɪtl] *adj* extramarital
ex·tra·or·di·nar·i·ly [ekstrɔː'rdɪn'erɪli] *adv* extraordinariamente
ex·tra·or·di·na·ry [ɪk'strɔːrdɪnerɪ] *adj* extraordinario
ex·trav·a·gance [ɪk'strævəgəns] *with money* despilfarro *m*; *of claim etc* extravagancia *f*
ex·trav·a·gant [ɪk'strævəgənt] *adj with money* despilfarrador; *claim* extravagante
ex·treme [ɪk'striːm] **1** *n* extremo *m* **2** *adj* extremo; *views* extremista
ex·treme·ly [ɪk'striːmlɪ] *adv* extremada-

mente, sumamente
ex·trem·ist [ɪk'striːmɪst] extremista *m/f*
ex·tri·cate ['ekstrɪkeɪt] *v/t* liberar
ex·tro·vert ['ekstrəvɜːrt] **1** *adj* extrovertido **2** *n* extrovertido(-a) *m(f)*
ex·u·be·rant [ɪg'zuːbərənt] *adj* exuberante
ex·ult [ɪg'zʌlt] *v/i* exultar
eye [aɪ] **1** *n of person, needle* ojo *m*; **keep an eye on** (*look after*) estar pendiente de; (*monitor*) estar pendiente de, vigilar **2** *v/t* mirar
'eye·ball globo *m* ocular
'eye·brow ceja *f*
'eye-catch·ing *adj* llamativo
'eye·glass·es *npl* gafas *fpl*, *L.Am.* anteojos *mpl*, *L.Am.* lentes *mpl*
'eye·lash pestaña *f*
'eye·lid párpado *m*
'eye·lin·er lápiz *m* de ojos
'eye-sha·dow sombra *f* de ojos
'eye·sight vista *f*
'eye·sore engendro *m*, monstruosidad *f*
'eye strain vista *f* cansada
'eye·wit·ness testigo *m/f* ocular

F

F *abbr* (= **Fahrenheit**) F
fab·ric ['fæbrɪk] (*material*) tejido *m*
fab·u·lous ['fæbjʊləs] *adj* fabuloso, estupendo
fab·u·lous·ly ['fæbjʊləslɪ] *adv* rich tremendamente; *beautiful* increíblemente
fa·çade [fə'sɑːd] *of building, person* fachada *f*
face [feɪs] **1** *n* cara *f*; **face to face** cara a cara; **lose face** padecer una *humillación* **2** *v/t* (*be opposite*) estar enfrente de; (*confront*) enfrentarse a
◆ **face up to** *v/t* hacer frente a
'face-cloth toallita *f*
'face-lift lifting *m*, estiramiento *m* de piel
'face pack mascarilla *f* (*facial*)
face 'val·ue: **take sth at face value** tomarse algo literalmente
fa·cial ['feɪʃl] *n* limpieza *f* de cutis
fa·cil·i·tate [fə'sɪlɪteɪt] *v/t* facilitar
fa·cil·i·ties [fə'sɪlətɪz] *npl* instalaciones *fpl*
fact [fækt] hecho *m*; **in fact, as a matter of fact** de hecho

fac·tion ['fækʃn] facción *f*
fac·tor ['fæktər] factor *m*
fac·to·ry ['fæktərɪ] fábrica *f*
fac·ul·ty ['fækəltɪ] (*hearing etc*), *at university* facultad *f*
fad [fæd] moda *f*
fade [feɪd] *v/i of colors* desteñirse, perder color; *of memories* desvanecerse
fad·ed ['feɪdɪd] *adj color, jeans* desteñido, descolorido
fag¹ [fæg] F (*homosexual*) maricón *m* F
fag² [fæg] *Br* F (*cigarette*) pitillo *m* F
Fahr·en·heit ['færənhaɪt] *adj* Fahrenheit
fail [feɪl] **1** *v/i* fracasar; *of plan* fracasar, fallar **2** *n*: **without fail** sin falta
fail·ing ['feɪlɪŋ] *n* fallo *m*
fail·ure ['feɪljər] fracaso *m*; *in exam* suspenso *m*; **I feel such a failure** me siento un fracasado
faint [feɪnt] **1** *adj line, smile* tenue; *smell, noise* casi imperceptible **2** *v/i* desmayarse
faint·ly ['feɪntlɪ] *adv smile, smell* levemente
fair¹ [fer] *n* COM feria *f*

fair² [fer] *adj* hair rubio; *complexion* claro; *(just)* justo

fair·ly ['ferli] *adv treat* justamente, con justicia; *(quite)* bastante

fair·ness ['fernis] *of treatment* imparcialidad *f*

fai·ry ['feri] hada *f*

'fai·ry tale cuento *m* de hadas

faith [feiθ] fe *f*, confianza *f*; REL fe *f*

faith·ful ['feiθfəl] *adj* fiel; **be faithful to one's partner** ser fiel a la pareja

faith·ful·ly ['feiθfəli] *adv* religiosamente

Falk·land Is·lands ['fɔːlklənd] *npl:* **the Falkland Islands** las Islas Malvinas

fake [feik] **1** *n* falsificación *f* **2** *adj* falso **3** *v/t (forge)* falsificar; *(feign)* fingir

fall¹ [fɔːl] *n season* otoño *m*

fall² [fɔːl] **1** *v/i (pret fell, pp fallen) of person* caerse; *of government, prices, temperature, night* caer; **it falls on a Tuesday** cae en martes; **fall ill** enfermar, caer enfermo; **I fell off the wall** me caí del muro **2** *n* caída *f*

◆ **fall back on** *v/t* recurrir a

◆ **fall behind** *v/i with work, studies* retrasarse

◆ **fall down** *v/i* caerse

◆ **fall for** *v/t person* enamorarse de; *(be deceived by)* dejarse engañar por; **I'm amazed you fell for it** me sorprende mucho que picaras

◆ **fall out** *v/i of hair* caerse; *(argue)* pelearse

◆ **fall over** *v/i* caerse

◆ **fall through** *v/i of plans* venirse abajo

fal·len ['fɔːlən] *pp* → **fall²**

fal·li·ble ['fæləbl] *adj* falible

'fall-out lluvia *f* radiactiva

false [fɔːls] *adj* falso

false a'larm falsa alarma *f*

false·ly ['fɔːlsli] *adv:* **be falsely accused of sth** ser acusado falsamente de algo

false 'start *in race* salida *f* nula

false 'teeth *npl* dentadura *f* postiza

fal·si·fy ['fɔːlsifai] *v/t (pret & pp falsified)* falsificar

fame [feim] fama *f*

fa·mil·i·ar [fə'miljər] *adj* familiar; **get familiar** *(intimate)* tomarse demasiadas confianzas; **be familiar with sth** estar familiarizado con algo; **that looks familiar** eso me resulta familiar; **that sounds familiar** me suena

fa·mil·i·ar·i·ty [fəmili'ærɪti] *with subject etc* familiaridad *f*

fa·mil·i·ar·ize [fə'miljəraiz] *v/t:* **familiarize o.s. with ...** familiarizarse con ...

fam·i·ly ['fæməli] familia *f*

fam·i·ly 'doc·tor médico *m/f* de familia

fam·i·ly name apellido *m*

fam·i·ly 'plan·ning planificación *f* familiar

fam·i·ly 'plan·ning clin·ic clínica *f* de planificación familiar

fam·i·ly 'tree árbol *m* genealógico

fam·ine ['fæmin] hambruna *f*

fam·ished ['fæmiʃt] *adj* F: **I'm famished** estoy muerto de hambre F

fa·mous ['feiməs] *adj* famoso; **be famous for ...** ser famoso por ...

fan¹ [fæn] *n (supporter)* seguidor(a) *m(f)*; *of singer, band* admirador(a) *m(f)*, fan *m/f*

fan² [fæn] **1** *n electric* ventilador *m*; *hand-held* abanico *m* **2** *v/t (pret & pp fanned)* abanicar; **fan o.s.** abanicarse

fa·nat·ic [fə'nætik] *n* fanático(-a) *m(f)*

fa·nat·i·cal [fə'nætikl] *adj* fanático

fa·nat·i·cism [fə'nætisizm] fanatismo *m*

'fan belt MOT correa *f* del ventilador

fan·cy ['fænsi] **1** *adj (luxurious)* de lujo; *(complicated)* sofisticado **2** *n:* **as the fancy takes you** como te apetezca; **take a fancy to s.o.** encapricharse de alguien **3** *v/t (pret & pp fancied):* **do you fancy an ice cream?** ¿te apetece un helado?

fan·cy 'dress disfraz *m*

fan·cy-'dress par·ty fiesta *f* de disfraces

fang [fæŋ] colmillo *m*

'fan mail cartas *fpl* de los fans

fan·ta·size ['fæntəsaiz] *v/i* fantasear *(about* sobre*)*

fan·tas·tic [fæn'tæstik] *adj (very good)* fantástico, excelente; *(very big)* inmenso

fan·tas·ti·cal·ly [fæn'tæstikli] *adv (extremely)* sumamente, increíblemente

fan·ta·sy ['fæntəsi] fantasía *f*

far [fɑːr] *adv* lejos; *(much)* mucho; **far bigger / faster** mucho más grande / rápido; **far away** lejos; **how far is it to ...?** ¿a cuánto está ...?; **as far as the corner / hotel** hasta la esquina / el hotel; **as far as I can see** tal y como lo veo yo; **as far as I know** que yo sepa; **you've gone too far** *in behavior* te has pasado; **so far so good** por ahora muy bien

farce [fɑːrs] farsa *f*

fare [fer] *n price* tarifa *f*; *actual money* dinero *m*

Far 'East Lejano Oriente *m*

fare·well [fer'wel] *n* despedida *f*

fare·well par·ty fiesta *f* de despedida

far-fetched [fɑːr'fetʃt] *adj* inverosímil, exagerado

farm [fɑːrm] *n* granja *f*

farm·er ['fɑːrmər] granjero(-a) *m(f)*

'farm·house granja *f*, alquería *f*

farm·ing ['fɑːrmɪŋ] *n* agricultura *f*

'**farm·work·er** trabajador(a) *m(f)* del campo

'**farm·yard** corral *m*

far·off *adj* lejano

far·sight·ed [fɑːr'saɪtɪd] *adj* previsor; *optically* hipermétrope

fart [fɑːrt] **1** *n* F pedo *m* F **2** *v/i* F tirarse un pedo F

far·ther ['fɑːðər] *adv* más lejos; *farther away* más allá, más lejos

far·thest ['fɑːðəst] *adv travel etc* más lejos

fas·ci·nate ['fæsɪneɪt] *v/t* fascinar; *be fascinated by …* estar fascinado por …

fas·ci·nat·ing ['fæsɪneɪtɪŋ] *adj* fascinante

fas·ci·na·tion [fæsɪ'neɪʃn] fascinación *f*

fas·cism ['fæʃɪzm] fascismo *m*

fas·cist ['fæʃɪst] **1** *n* fascista *m/f* **2** *adj* fascista

fash·ion ['fæʃn] *n* moda *f*; (*manner*) modo *m*, manera *f*; *in fashion* de moda; *out of fashion* pasado de moda

fash·ion·a·ble ['fæʃnəbl] *adj* de moda

fash·ion·a·bly ['fæʃnəblɪ] *adv dressed* a la moda

'**fash·ion-con·scious** *adj* que sigue la moda

'**fash·ion de·sign·er** modisto(-a) *m(f)*

'**fash·ion mag·a·zine** revista *f* de modas

'**fash·ion show** desfile *f* de moda, pase *m* de modelos

fast[1] [fæst] **1** *adj* rápido; *be fast of clock* ir adelantado **2** *adv* rápido; *stuck fast* atascado; *fast asleep* profundamente dormido

fast[2] [fæst] *n not eating* ayuno *m*

fas·ten ['fæsn] **1** *v/t window, lid* cerrar (*poniendo el cierre*); *dress* abrochar; *fasten sth onto sth* asegurar algo a algo **2** *v/i of dress etc* abrocharse

fas·ten·er ['fæsnər] *for dress, lid* cierre *f*

fast '**food** comida *f* rápida

fast-food '**res·tau·rant** restaurante *f* de comida rápida

fast '**for·ward 1** *n on video etc* avance *m* rápido **2** *v/i* avanzar

'**fast lane** *on road* carril *f* rápido; *in the fast lane fig: of life* con un tren de vida acelerado

'**fast train** (tren *m*) rápido *m*

fat [fæt] **1** *adj* gordo **2** *n on meat, for baking* grasa *f*

fa·tal ['feɪtl] *adj illness* mortal; *error* fatal

fa·tal·i·ty [fə'tælətɪ] víctima *f* mortal

fa·tal·ly ['feɪtəlɪ] *adv* mortalmente; *fatally injured* herido mortalmente

fate [feɪt] *n* destino *m*

fat·ed ['feɪtɪd] *adj*: *be fated to do sth* estar predestinado a hacer algo

fat-free *adj* sin grasas

fa·ther ['fɑːðər] *n* padre *m*; *Father Martin* REL el Padre Martin

Fa·ther '**Christ·mas** *Br* Papá *m* Noel

fa·ther·hood ['fɑːðərhʊd] paternidad *f*

'**fa·ther-in-law** (*pl* **fathers-in-law**) suegro *m*

fa·ther·ly ['fɑːðəlɪ] *adj* paternal

fath·om ['fæðəm] *n* NAUT braza *f*

◆ **fathom out** *v/t fig* entender

fa·tigue [fə'tiːɡ] *n* cansancio *m*, fatiga *f*

fat·so ['fætsoʊ] F gordinflón (-ona) *m(f)* F

fat·ten ['fætn] *v/t animal* engordar

fat·ty ['fætɪ] **1** *adj* graso **2** *n* F (*person*) gordinflón (-ona) *m(f)* F

fau·cet ['fɔːsɪt] *Span* grifo *m*, *L.Am.* llave *f*

fault [fɔːlt] *n* (*defect*) fallo *m*; *it's your / my fault* es culpa tuya / mía; *find fault with …* encontrar defectos a …

fault·less ['fɔːltlɪs] *adj* impecable

fault·y ['fɔːltɪ] *adj goods* defectuoso

fa·vor ['feɪvər] **1** *n* favor *m*; *do s.o. a favor* hacer un favor a alguien; *do me a favor!* (*don't be stupid*) ¡haz el favor!; *in favor of …* a favor de …; *be in favor of …* estar a favor de … **2** *v/t* (*prefer*) preferir

fa·vo·ra·ble ['feɪvərəbl] *adj reply etc* favorable

fa·vo·rite ['feɪvərɪt] **1** *n* favorito(-a) *m(f)*; *food* comida *f* favorita **2** *adj* favorito

fa·vor·it·ism ['feɪvrɪtɪzm] favoritismo *m*

fa·vour *etc Br* → **favor** *etc*

fax [fæks] **1** *n* fax *m*; *send sth by fax* enviar algo por fax **2** *v/t* enviar por fax: *fax sth to s.o.* enviar algo por fax a alguien

FBI [efbiː'aɪ] *abbr* (= **Federal Bureau of Investigation**) FBI *m*

fear [fɪr] **1** *n* miedo *m*, temor *m* **2** *v/t* temer, tener miedo a

fear·less ['fɪrlɪs] *adj* valiente, audaz

fear·less·ly ['fɪrlɪslɪ] *adv* sin miedo

fea·si·bil·i·ty stud·y [fiːzə'bɪlətɪ] estudio *m* de viabilidad

fea·si·ble ['fiːzəbl] *adj* factible, viable

feast [fiːst] *n* banquete *m*, festín *m*

feat [fiːt] hazaña *f*, proeza *f*

feath·er ['feðər] pluma *f*

fea·ture ['fiːtʃər] **1** *n on face* rasgo *m*, facción *f*; *of city, building, plan, style* característica *f*; *article in paper* reportaje *m*; *movie* largometraje *f*; *make a feature of …* destacar … **2** *v/t movie featuring …* una película en la que aparece …

'**fea·ture film** largometraje *m*

Feb·ru·a·ry ['februerɪ] febrero *m*

fed [fed] *pret & pp* → **feed**

ed·e·ral ['fedərəl] *adj* federal

ed·e·ra·tion [fedə'reɪʃn] federación *f*

ed 'up *adj* F harto, hasta las narices F; **be fed up with ...** estar harto *or* hasta las narices de ...

ee [fiː] *of lawyer, doctor, consultant* honorarios *mpl; for entrance* entrada *f; for membership* cuota *f*

ee·ble ['fiːbl] *adj person, laugh* débil; *attempt* flojo; *excuse* pobre

'eed [fiːd] *v/t (pret & pp* fed*)* alimentar, dar de comer a

'feed·back *n* reacción *f*; **we'll give you some feedback as soon as possible** le daremos nuestra opinión *or* nuestras reacciones lo antes posible

'eel [fiːl] 1 *v/t (pret & pp* felt*) (touch)* tocar; *(sense)* sentir; *(think)* creer, pensar; **you can feel the difference** se nota la diferencia 2 *v/i (pret & pp* felt*)*: **it feels like silk / cotton** tiene la textura de la seda / algodón; **your hand feels hot** tienes la mano caliente; **I feel hungry** tengo hambre; **I feel tired** estoy cansado; **how are you feeling today?** ¿cómo te encuentras hoy?; **how does it feel to be rich?** ¿qué se siente siendo rico?; **do you feel like a drink / meal?** ¿te apetece una bebida / comida?; **I feel like going / staying** me apetece ir / quedarme; **I don't feel like it** no me apetece

◆ feel up to *v/t* sentirse con fuerzas para

'eel·er ['fiːlər] *of insect* antena *f*

'feel-good fac·tor sensación *f* positiva

'eel·ing ['fiːlɪŋ] sentimiento *m; (sensation)* sensación *f*; **what are your feelings about it?** ¿qué piensas sobre ello?; **I have mixed feelings about him** me inspira sentimientos contradictorios; **I have this feeling that ...** tengo el presentimiento de que ...

'eet [fiːt] *pl* → foot

'e·line ['fiːlaɪn] *adj* felino

ell [fel] *pret* → fall²

'el·low ['feloʊ] *n (man)* tipo *m*

'fel·low 'cit·i·zen conciudadano(-a) *m(f)*

'fel·low 'coun·try·man compatriota *m/f*

'fel·low 'man prójimo *m*

'el·o·ny ['felənɪ] delito *m* grave

felt [felt] 1 *n* fieltro *m* 2 *pret & pp* → feel

'felt 'tip, felt-tip 'pen rotulador *m*

fe·male ['fiːmeɪl] 1 *adj animal, plant* hembra; *relating to people* femenino 2 *n of animals, plants* hembra *f; person* mujer *f*

fem·i·nine ['femɪnɪn] 1 *adj also* GRAM femenino 2 *n* GRAM femenino *m*

fem·i·nism ['femɪnɪzm] feminismo *m*

fem·i·nist ['femɪnɪst] 1 *n* feminista *m/f* 2 *adj* feminista

fence [fens] *n around garden etc* cerca *f*, valla *f*; F *criminal* perista *m/f*; **sit on the fence** nadar entre dos aguas

◆ fence in *v/t land* cercar, vallar

fenc·ing ['fensɪŋ] SP esgrima *f*

fend [fend] *v/i*: **fend for o.s.** valerse por sí mismo

fend·er ['fendər] MOT aleta *f*

fer·ment¹ [fə'ment] *v/i of liquid* fermentar

fer·ment² ['fɜːrment] *n (unrest)* agitación *f*

fer·men·ta·tion [fɜːrmen'teɪʃn] fermentación *f*

fern [fɜːrn] *n* helecho *m*

fe·ro·cious [fə'roʊʃəs] *adj* feroz

fer·ry ['ferɪ] *n* ferry *m*, transbordador *m*

fer·tile ['fɜːrtəl] *adj* fértil

fer·til·i·ty [fɜːr'tɪlətɪ] fertilidad *f*

fer·til·i·ty drug medicamento *m* para el tratamiento de la infertilidad

fer·ti·lize ['fɜːrtəlaɪz] *v/t* fertilizar

fer·ti·liz·er ['fɜːrtəlaɪzər] *for soil* fertilizante *m*

fer·vent ['fɜːrvənt] *adj admirer* ferviente

fer·vent·ly ['fɜːrvəntlɪ] *adv* fervientemente

fes·ter ['festər] *v/i of wound* enconarse

fes·ti·val ['festɪvl] festival *m*

fes·tive ['festɪv] *adj* festivo; **the festive season** la época navideña, las Navidades

fes·tiv·i·ties [fe'stɪvətɪz] *npl* celebraciones *fpl*

fe·tal ['fiːtl] *adj* fetal

fetch [fetʃ] *v/t person* recoger; *thing* traer, ir a buscar; *price* alcanzar

fe·tus ['fiːtəs] feto *m*

feud [fjuːd] 1 *n* enemistad *f* 2 *v/i* estar enemistado

fe·ver ['fiːvər] fiebre *f*

fe·ver·ish ['fiːvərɪʃ] *adj* con fiebre; *fig: excitement* febril

few [fjuː] 1 *adj (not many)* pocos; **a few things** unos pocos; **quite a few, a good few** (*a lot*) bastantes 2 *pron (not many)* pocos(-as); **a few** *(some)* unos pocos; **quite a few, a good few** *(a lot)* bastantes; **few of them could speak English** de ellos muy pocos hablaban inglés

fewer ['fjuːər] *adj* menos; **fewer than** menos que ...; *with numbers* menos de ...

fi·an·cé [fɪ'ɑːnseɪ] prometido *m*, novio *m*

fi·an·cée [fɪ'ɑːnseɪ] prometida *f*, novia *f*

fi·as·co [fɪ'æskoʊ] fiasco *m*

fib [fɪb] *n* F bola *f*

fi·ber ['faɪbər] *n* fibra *f*

'fi·ber·glass *n* fibra *f* de vidrio

fi·ber 'op·tic de fibra óptica

fi·ber 'op·tics fibra f óptica

fi·bre Br → **fiber**

fick·le ['fɪkl] adj inconstante, mudable

fic·tion ['fɪkʃn] n (novels) literatura f de ficción; (made-up story) ficción f

fic·tion·al ['fɪkʃnl] adj de ficción

fic·ti·tious [fɪk'tɪʃəs] adj ficticio

fid·dle ['fɪdl] 1 n (violin) violín m; *it's a fiddle* F (cheat) es un amaño 2 v/t: *fiddle around with* enredar con; *fiddle around with* enredar con 3 v/t accounts, result amañar

fi·del·i·ty [fɪ'delətɪ] fidelidad f

fid·get ['fɪdʒɪt] v/i moverse; *stop fidgeting!* ¡estáte quieto!

fid·get·y ['fɪdʒɪtɪ] adj inquieto

field [fiːld] also of research etc campo m; for sport campo m, L.Am. cancha f; (competitors in race) participantes mpl; *that's not my field* no es mi campo

field·er ['fiːldər] in baseball fildeador(-a) m(f)

'field e·vents npl pruebas fpl de salto y lanzamiento

fierce [fɪrs] adj animal feroz; wind, storm violento

fierce·ly ['fɪrslɪ] adv ferozmente

fi·er·y ['faɪrɪ] adj fogoso, ardiente

fif·teen [fɪf'tiːn] quince

fif·teenth [fɪf'tiːnθ] n & adj decimoquinto

fifth [fɪfθ] n & adj quinto

fif·ti·eth ['fɪftɪɪθ] n & adj quincuagésimo

fif·ty ['fɪftɪ] cincuenta

fif·ty-'fif·ty adv a medias

fig [fɪg] higo m

fight [faɪt] 1 n lucha f, pelea f; (argument) pelea f; fig: for survival, championship etc lucha f; in boxing combate m; *have a fight* (argue) pelearse 2 v/t (pret & pp **fought**) enemy, person luchar contra, pelear contra; in boxing pelear contra; disease, injustice luchar contra, combatir 3 v/i (pret & pp **fought**) luchar, pelear; (argue) pelearse

◆ **fight for** v/t one's rights, a cause luchar por

fight·er ['faɪtər] combatiente m/f; airplane caza m; (boxer) púgil m; *she's a fighter* tiene espíritu combativo

fight·ing ['faɪtɪŋ] n physical, verbal peleas fpl; MIL luchas fpl, combates mpl

fig·u·ra·tive ['fɪgjərətɪv] adj figurado

fig·ure ['fɪgər] 1 n figura f; (digit) cifra f 2 v/t F (think) imaginarse, pensar

◆ **figure on** v/t F (plan) pensar

◆ **figure out** v/t (understand) entender; calculation resolver

'fig·ure skat·er patinador(a) m(f) artístico(-a)

'fig·ure skat·ing patinaje m artístico

file[1] [faɪl] 1 n of documents expediente m; COMPUT archivo m, fichero m 2 v/t documents archivar

◆ **file away** v/t documents archivar

file[2] [faɪl] n for wood, fingernails lima f

'file cab·i·net archivador m

'file man·ag·er COMPUT administrador m de archivos

fi·li·al ['fɪlɪəl] adj filial

fill [fɪl] 1 v/t llenar; tooth empastar, L.Am. emplomar 2 n: *eat one's fill* hincharse

◆ **fill in** v/t form, hole rellenar; *fill s.o. in* poner a alguien al tanto

◆ **fill in for** v/t sustituir a

◆ **fill out 1** v/t form rellenar 2 v/i (get fatter) engordar

◆ **fill up 1** v/t llenar (hasta arriba) 2 v/i of stadium, theater llenarse

fil·let ['fɪlɪt] n filete m

fill·ing ['fɪlɪŋ] 1 n in sandwich relleno m; in tooth empaste m, L.Am. emplomadura f 2 adj: *be filling* of food llenar mucho

'fill·ing sta·tion estación f de servicio, gasolinera f

film [fɪlm] 1 n for camera carrete m; (movie) película f 2 v/t person, event filmar

'film-mak·er cineasta m/f

'film star estrella f de cine

fil·ter ['fɪltər] 1 n filtro m 2 v/t coffee, liquid filtrar

◆ **filter through** v/i of news reports filtrarse

'fil·ter pa·per papel m de filtro

'fil·ter tip (cigarette) cigarrillo m con filtro

filth [fɪlθ] suciedad f, mugre f

filth·y ['fɪlθɪ] adj sucio, mugriento; language etc obsceno

fin [fɪn] of fish aleta f

fi·nal ['faɪnl] 1 adj (last) último; decision final, definitivo 2 n SP final f

fi·na·le [fɪ'nælɪ] final m

fi·nal·ist ['faɪnəlɪst] finalista m/f

fi·nal·ize ['faɪnəlaɪz] v/t plans, design ultimar

fi·nal·ly ['faɪnəlɪ] adv finalmente, por último; (at last) finalmente, por fin

fi·nance ['faɪnæns] 1 n finanzas fpl 2 v/t financiar

fi·nan·ces ['faɪnænsɪz] npl finanzas fpl

fi·nan·cial [faɪ'nænʃl] adj financiero

fi·nan·cial·ly [faɪ'nænʃəlɪ] adv económicamente

fi·nan·cial 'year Br ejercicio m económico

fi·nan·cier [faɪ'nænsɪr] financiero(-a) m(f)

find [faɪnd] v/t (pret & pp **found**) encon-

trar, hallar; *if you find it too hot / cold* si
te parece demasiado frío / caliente; *find
s.o. innocent / guilty* LAW declarar a alguien inocente / culpable; *I find it strange that ...* me sorprende que ...; *how did
you find the hotel?* ¿qué te pareció el
hotel?

♦ **find out 1** *v/t* descubrir, averiguar **2** *v/i*
(*discover*) descubrir; *can you try to find
out?* ¿podrías enterarte?

'find·ings ['faɪndɪŋz] *npl of report* conclusiones *fpl*

'ine[1] [faɪn] *adj day, weather* bueno; *wine,
performance, city* excelente; *distinction,
line* fino; *how's that? - that's fine*
¿qué tal está? - bien; *that's fine by me*
por mí no hay ningún problema; *how
are you? - fine* ¿cómo estás? - bien

'ine[2] [faɪn] **1** *n* multa *f* **2** *v/t* multar, poner
una multa a

'ine-'tooth comb: *go through sth with a
fine-tooth comb* revisar algo minuciosamente

'ine-'tune *v/t engine, fig* afinar, hacer los
últimos ajustes a

'in·ger ['fɪŋgər] **1** *n* dedo *m* **2** *v/t* tocar

'fin·ger·nail *n* uña *f*

'fin·ger·print *n* huella *f* digital *or* dactilar **2** *v/t* tomar las huellas digitales *or*
dactilares a

'fin·ger·tip *n* punta *f* del dedo; *have sth at
one's fingertips* saberse algo al dedillo

'fin·i·cky ['fɪnɪki] *adj person* quisquilloso;
design enrevesado

'fin·ish ['fɪnɪʃ] **1** *v/t* acabar, terminar; *finish doing sth* acabar *or* terminar de
hacer algo **2** *v/i* acabar, terminar **3** *n of
product* acabado *m*; *of race* final *f*

♦ **finish off** *v/t* acabar, terminar

♦ **finish up** *v/t food* acabar, terminar; *he
finished up liking it* acabó gustándole

♦ **finish with** *v/t boyfriend etc* cortar con

'fin·ish·ing line ['fɪnɪʃɪŋ] línea *f* de meta

Fin·land ['fɪnlənd] Finlandia

Finn [fɪn] finlandés (-esa) *m(f)*

Finn·ish ['fɪnɪʃ] **1** *adj* finlandés **2** *n language* finés *m*

fir [fɜːr] abeto *m*

fire [faɪr] **1** *n* fuego *m*; *electric, gas* estufa *f*;
(*blaze*) incendio *m*; (*bonfire, campfire
etc*) hoguera *f*; *be on fire* estar ardiendo;
catch fire prender; *set sth on fire, set
fire to sth* prender fuego a algo **2** *v/i
(shoot)* disparar; (*on / at* sobre/a) **3** *v/t* F
(*dismiss*) despedir

'fire a·larm alarma *f* contra incendios

'fire·arm arma *f* de fuego

'fire·crack·er petardo *m*

'fire de·part·ment (cuerpo *m* de) bomb-

eros *mpl*

'fire door puerta *f* contra incendios

'fire drill simulacro *m* de incendio; *Br* 'fire
en·gine coche *m* de bomberos

'fire es·cape salida *f* de incendios

'fire ex·tin·guish·er extintor *m*

'fire fight·er bombero (-a) *m(f)*

'fire·guard pantalla *f*, parachispas *m inv*;
Br 'fire·man bombero *m*

'fire·place chimenea *f*, hogar *m*

'fire sta·tion parque *m* de bomberos

'fire truck coche *m* de bomberos

'fire·wood leña *f*

'fire·works *npl* fuegos *mpl* artificiales

firm[1] [fɜːrm] *adj* firme; *a firm deal* un
acuerdo en firme

firm[2] [fɜːrm] *n* COM empresa *f*

first [fɜːrst] **1** *adj* primero; *who's first
please?* ¿quién es el primero, por favor?
2 *n* primero(-a) *m(f)* **3** *adv* primero; *first
of all (for one reason)* en primer lugar; *at
first* al principio

first aid primeros *mpl* auxilios

first-'aid box, first-'aid kit botiquín *m* de
primeros auxilios

'first-born *adj* primogénito

first class 1 *adj ticket, seat* de primera
(clase); (*very good*) excelente **2** *adv travel*
en primera (clase)

first 'floor planta *f* baja, *Br* primer piso *m*

first'hand *adj* de primera mano

First 'La·dy *of US* primera dama *f*

first·ly ['fɜːrstli] *adv* en primer lugar

first 'name nombre *m* (de pila)

first 'night estreno *m*

first of'fend·er delincuente *m/f* sin antecedentes

first of'fense primer delito *m*

first-'rate *adj* excelente

fis·cal ['fɪskl] *adj* fiscal

fis·cal 'year año *m* fiscal

fish [fɪʃ] **1** *n (pl fish)* **1** *n* pez *m*; *to eat* pescado *m*; *drink like a fish* F beber como un
cosaco F; *feel like a fish out of water*
sentirse fuera de lugar **2** *v/i* pescar

'fish·bone espina *f* (de pescado)

fish·er·man ['fɪʃərmən] pescador *m*

fish·ing ['fɪʃɪŋ] pesca *f*

'fish·ing boat (barco *m*) pesquero *m*

'fish·ing line sedal *m*

'fish·ing rod caña *f* de pescar

'fish stick palito *m* de pescado

fish·y ['fɪʃi] *adj* F (*suspicious*) sospechoso

fist [fɪst] puño *m*

fit[1] [fɪt] *n* MED ataque *m*; *a fit of rage / jealousy* un arrebato de cólera / un ataque
de celos

fit[2] [fɪt] *adj physically* en forma; *morally*
adecuado; *he's not fit to be President*

fit

no está en condiciones ser Presidente;
keep fit mantenerse en forma

fit³ [fɪt] **1** *v/t (attach)* colocar; **these pants
don't fit me any more** estos pantalones
ya no me entran; **it fits you perfectly** te
queda perfectamente **2** *v/i (pret & pp fitted) of clothes* quedar bien; *of piece of
furniture* caber **3** *n*: **it's a good fit**
of jacket etc queda bien; *of piece of furniture* cabe bien; **it's a tight fit** no hay
mucho espacio

◆ **fit in** *v/i of person in group* encajar; **it
fits in with our plans** encaja con nuestros planes **2** *v/t*: **fit s.o. into** schedule
etc hacer un hueco a alguien

fit·ful ['fɪtfəl] *adj sleep* intermitente

fit·ness ['fɪtnɪs] *physical* buena forma *f*

'fit·ness cen·ter, *Br* **'fit·ness cen·tre**
gimnasio *m*

fit·ted 'kitch·en ['fɪtɪd] cocina *f* a medida

fit·ted 'sheet sábana *f* ajustable

fit·ter ['fɪtər] *n* técnico(-a) *m(f)*

fit·ting ['fɪtɪŋ] *adj* apropiado

fit·tings ['fɪtɪŋz] *npl* equipamiento *m*

five [faɪv] cinco

fix [fɪks] **1** *n (solution)* solución *f*; **be in a
fix** F estar en un lío F **2** *v/t (attach)* fijar;
(repair) arreglar, reparar; *(arrange: meeting etc)* organizar; *lunch* preparar; *dis-
honestly: match etc* amañar; **fix sth onto
sth** fijar algo a algo; **I'll fix you a drink** te
preparé una bebida

◆ **fix up** *v/t meeting* organizar; **it's all fixed up** está todo organizado

fixed [fɪkst] *adj* fijo

fix·ings ['fɪkɪŋz] *npl* guarnición *f*

fix·ture ['fɪkstʃər] *(in room)* parte fija del
mobiliario o la decoración de una habitación

◆ **fizz·le out** ['fɪzl] *v/i* F quedarse en nada

fiz·zy ['fɪzɪ] *adj drink* con gas

flab [flæb] *on body* grasa *f*

flab·ber·gast ['flæbərgæst] *v/t* F: **be flab-
bergasted** quedarse estupefacto *or Span*
alucinado F

flab·by ['flæbɪ] *adj muscles etc* fofo

flag¹ [flæg] *n* bandera *f*

flag² [flæg] *v/i (pret & pp flagged) (tire)*
desfallecer

'flag·pole asta *f* (de bandera)

fla·grant ['fleɪgrənt] *adj* flagrante

'flag·ship *fig* estandarte *m*

'flag·staff asta *f* (de bandera)

'flag·stone losa *f*

flair [fler] *n (talent)* don *m*; **have a natural
flair for** tener dotes para

flake [fleɪk] *n of snow* copo *m*; *of skin* escama *f*; *of plaster* desconchón *m*

◆ **flake off** *v/i of skin* descamarse; *of plas-*

ter, paint desconcharse

flak·y ['fleɪkɪ] *adj skin* con escamas; *pair.*
desconchado

flak·y 'pas·try hojaldre *m*

flam·boy·ant [flæm'bɔɪənt] *adj personality* extravagante

flam·boy·ant·ly [flæm'bɔɪəntlɪ] *adv dressed* extravagantemente

flame [fleɪm] *n* llama *f*; **go up in flames**
ser pasto de las llamas

fla·men·co [flə'meŋkou] flamenco *m*

fla'men·co danc·er bailaor(a) *m(f)*

flam·ma·ble ['flæməbl] *adj* inflamable

flan [flæn] tarta *f*

flank [flæŋk] **1** *n of horse etc* costado *m*,
MIL flanco *m* **2** *v/t* flanquear; **be flanked
by** estar flanqueado por

flap [flæp] **1** *n of envelope, pocket* solapa
f; *of table* hoja *f*; **be in a flap** F estar histérico F **2** *v/t (pret & pp flapped)* wings,
batir **3** *v/i (pret & pp flapped) of flag etc*
ondear

flare [fler] **1** *n (distress signal)* bengala *f*;
in dress vuelo *m* **2** *v/t*: **flare one's nostrils** hinchar las narices resoplando

◆ **flare up** *v/i of violence* estallar; *of illness, rash* exacerbarse, empeorar; *of fire*
llamear; *(get very angry)* estallar

flash [flæʃ] **1** *n of light* destello *m*; PHOT
flash *m*; **in a flash** F en un abrir y cerrar
de ojos; **have a flash of inspiration** tener
una inspiración repentina; **a flash of
lightning** un relámpago **2** *v/i of light* destellar **3** *v/t* **flash one's headlights** echar
las luces

'flash·back *in movie* flash-back *m*, escena
f retrospectiva

flash·er ['flæʃər] MOT intermitente *m*

'flash·light linterna *f*; PHOT flash *m*

flash·y ['flæʃɪ] *adj pej* ostentoso, chillón

flask [flæsk] *(hip flask)* petaca *f*

flat¹ [flæt] **1** *adj surface, land* llano, plano
beer sin gas; *battery* descargado; *tire* de-
sinflado; *shoes* bajo; MUS bemol; **and
that's flat** F y sanseacabó F **2** *adv* MUS demasiado bajo; **flat out** work, run, drive a
tope; **the factory is producing flat out**
la fábrica está al máximo de su capacidad
productiva **3** *n Br (flat tire)* pinchazo *m*

flat² [flæt] *n Br* apartamento *m*, *Span* piso
m

flat-chest·ed [flæt'tʃestɪd] *adj* plana de
pecho

flat·ly ['flætlɪ] *adv refuse, deny* rotundamente

'flat rate tarifa *f* única

flat·ten ['flætn] *v/t land, road* allanar,
aplanar; *by bombing, demolition* arrasar

flat·ter ['flætər] *v/t* halagar, adular

flat·ter·er ['flætərər] adulador(a) *m(f)*

flat·ter·ing ['flætərɪŋ] *adj comments* halagador; *color, clothes* favorecedor

flat·ter·y ['flætərɪ] halagos *mpl*, adulación *f*

flat·u·lence ['flætjʊləns] flatulencia *f*

'**flat·ware** (*cutlery*) cubertería *f*

flaunt [flɔːnt] *v/t* hacer ostentación de, alardear de

flau·tist ['flɔːtɪst] flautista *m/f*

fla·vor ['fleɪvər] **1** *n* sabor *m* **2** *v/t food* condimentar

fla·vor·ing ['fleɪvərɪŋ] *n* aromatizante *m*

fla·vour *etc Br → flavor etc*

flaw [flɔː] *n* defecto *m*, fallo *m*

flaw·less ['flɔːlɪs] *adj* impecable

flea [fliː] *n* pulga *f*

fleck [flek] mota *f*

fled [fled] *pret & pp → flee*

flee [fliː] *v/i* (*pret & pp fled*) escapar, huir

fleece [fliːs] *v/t* F desplumar F

fleet [fliːt] *n* NAUT, *of vehicles* flota *f*

fleet·ing ['fliːtɪŋ] *adj visit etc* fugaz; **catch a fleeting glimpse of** vislumbrar fugazmente a

flesh [fleʃ] *n* carne *f*; *of fruit* pulpa *f*; **meet / see s.o. in the flesh** conocer / ver a alguien en persona

flex [fleks] *v/t muscles* flexionar

flex·i·bil·i·ty [fleksə'bɪlətɪ] flexibilidad *f*

flex·i·ble ['fleksəbl] *adj* flexible; **I'm quite flexible** *about arrangements, timing* soy bastante flexible

'**flex·time** ['flekstaɪm] horario *m* flexible

flew [fluː] *pret → fly³*

flick [flɪk] *v/t tail* sacudir; **he flicked a fly off his hand** espantó una mosca que tenía en la mano; **she flicked her hair out of her eyes** se apartó el pelo de los ojos

◆ **flick through** *v/t book, magazine* hojear

flick·er ['flɪkər] *v/i of light, screen* parpadear

fli·er [flaɪr] (*circular*) folleto *m*

flies [flaɪz] *npl Br on pants* bragueta *f*

flight [flaɪt] *n in airplane* vuelo *m*; (*fleeing*) huida *f*; **not capable of flight** incapaz de volar; **flight (of stairs)** tramo *m* (de escaleras)

'**flight at·tend·ant** auxiliar *m/f* de vuelo

'**flight crew** tripulación *f*

'**flight deck** AVIA cabina *f* del piloto

'**flight num·ber** número *m* de vuelo

'**flight path** ruta *f* de vuelo

'**flight re·cord·er** caja *f* negra

'**flight time** *departure* hora *f* del vuelo; *duration* duración *f* del vuelo

flight·y ['flaɪtɪ] *adj* inconstante

flim·sy ['flɪmzɪ] *adj structure, furniture*

en·deble; *dress, material* débil; *excuse* pobre

flinch [flɪntʃ] *v/i* encogerse

fling [flɪŋ] **1** *v/t* (*pret & pp flung*) arrojar, lanzar; **fling o.s. into a chair** dejarse caer en una silla **2** *n* F (*affair*) aventura *f*

◆ **flip over** [flɪp] *v/i* volcar

◆ **flip through** *v/t* (*pret & pp flipped*) *magazine* hojear

flip·per ['flɪpər] *for swimming* aleta *f*

flirt [flɜːrt] **1** *v/i* flirtear, coquetear **2** *n* ligón (-ona) *m(f)*

flir·ta·tious [flɜːr'teɪʃəs] *adj* coqueto

float [flout] *v/i also* FIN flotar

float·ing vot·er ['floutɪŋ] votante *m/f* indeciso(-a)

flock [flɑːk] **1** *n of sheep* rebaño *m* **2** *v/i* acudir en masa

flog [flɑːg] *v/t* (*pret & pp flogged*) (*whip*) azotar

flood [flʌd] **1** *n* inundación *f* **2** *v/t of river* inundar

◆ **flood in** *v/i* llegar en grandes cantidades

'**flood·ing** ['flʌdɪŋ] inundaciones *fpl*

'**flood·light** *n* foco *m*

'**flood·lit** ['flʌdlɪt] *adj match* con luz artificial

'**flood wa·ters** *npl* crecida *f*

floor [flɔːr] *n* suelo *m*; (*story*) piso *m*

'**floor·board** *n* tabla *f* del suelo

'**floor cloth** trapo *m* del suelo

'**floor lamp** lámpara *f* de pie

flop [flɑːp] **1** *v/i* (*pret & pp flopped*) dejarse caer; *v/i* (*fail*) pinchar F **2** *n* F (*failure*) pinchazo *m* F

flop·py ['flɑːpɪ] *adj ears* caído; *hat* blando; (*weak*) flojo

flop·py ('**disk**) disquete *m*

flor·ist ['flɔːrɪst] florista *m/f*

floss [flɑːs] **1** *n for teeth* hilo *m* dental **2** *v/t*: **floss one's teeth** limpiarse los dientes con hilo dental

flour [flaʊr] harina *f*

flour·ish ['flʌrɪʃ] *v/i of plant* crecer rápidamente; *of business, civilization* florecer, prosperar

flour·ish·ing ['flʌrɪʃɪŋ] *adj business, trade* floreciente, próspero

flow [flou] **1** *v/i* fluir **2** *n* flujo *m*

'**flow·chart** diagrama *m* de flujo

flow·er [flaʊr] **1** *n* flor *f* **2** *v/i* florecer

'**flow·er·bed** parterre *m*

'**flow·er·pot** tiesto *m*, maceta *f*

'**flow·er show** exposición *f* floral

flow·er·y ['flaʊrɪ] *adj pattern* floreado; *style of writing* florido

flown [floun] *pp → fly³*

flu [fluː] gripe *f*

fluc·tu·ate ['flʌktjʊeɪt] v/i fluctuar

fluc·tu·a·tion [flʌktjʊ'eɪʃn] fluctuación f

flu·en·cy ['fluːənsɪ] in a language fluidez f

flu·ent ['fluːənt] adj: **he speaks fluent Spanish** habla español con soltura

flu·ent·ly ['fluːəntlɪ] adv speak, write con soltura

fluff [flʌf] material pelusa f

fluff·y ['flʌfɪ] adj esponjoso; **fluffy toy** juguete m de peluche

fluid ['fluːɪd] n fluido m

flung [flʌŋ] pret & pp → **fling**

flunk [flʌŋk] v/t F subject suspender, Span catear F

flu·o·res·cent [flʊ'resnt] adj light fluorescente

flur·ry ['flʌrɪ] of snow torbellino m

flush [flʌʃ] **1** v/t **flush the toilet** tirar de la cadena; **flush sth down the toilet** tirar algo por el retrete **2** v/i (go red in the face) ruborizarse; **the toilet won't flush** la cisterna no funciona **3** adj (level): **be flush with ...** estar a la misma altura que ...
◆ **flush away** v/t: **flush sth away** down toilet tirar algo por el retrete
◆ **flush out** v/t rebels etc hacer salir

flus·ter ['flʌstər] v/t: **get flustered** ponerse nervioso

flute [fluːt] MUS flauta f; glass copa f de champán

flut·ist ['fluːtɪst] flautista m/f

flut·ter ['flʌtər] v/i of bird, wings aletear; of flag ondear; of heart latir con fuerza

fly[1] [flaɪ] n insect mosca f

fly[2] [flaɪ] n pants bragueta f

fly[3] [flaɪ] **1** v/i (pret **flew**, pp **flown**) of bird, airplane volar; in airplane volar, ir en avión; of flag ondear; **fly into a rage** enfurecerse; **she flew out of the room** salió a toda prisa de la habitación **2** v/t (pret **flew**, pp **flown**) airplane pilotar; airline volar con; (transport by air) enviar por avión
◆ **fly away** v/i of bird salir volando; of airplane alejarse
◆ **fly back** v/i (travel back) volver en avión
◆ **fly in 1** v/i of airplane, passengers llegar en avión **2** v/t supplies etc transportar en avión
◆ **fly off** v/i of hat etc salir volando
◆ **fly out** v/i irse (en avión); **when do you fly out?** ¿cuándo os vais?
◆ **fly past** v/i in formation pasar volando en formación; of time volar

fly·ing ['flaɪɪŋ] n volar m

fly·ing 'sau·cer platillo m volante

foam [foʊm] n on liquid espuma f

foam 'rub·ber gomaespuma f

FOB [efoʊ'biː] abbr (= **free on board**) franco a bordo

fo·cus ['foʊkəs] **1** n of attention, PHOT foco m; **be in focus / out of focus** PHOT estar enfocado / desenfocado **2** v/t: **focus one's attention on** concentrar la atención en **3** v/i enfocar
◆ **focus on** v/t problem, issue concentrarse en; PHOT enfocar

fod·der ['fɑːdər] forraje m

fog [fɑːg] niebla f
◆ **fog up** v/i (pret & pp **fogged**) empañarse

'fog·bound adj paralizado por la niebla

fog·gy ['fɑːgɪ] adj neblinoso, con niebla; **it's foggy** hay niebla; **I haven't the foggiest idea** no tengo la más remota idea

foi·ble ['fɔɪbl] manía f

foil[1] [fɔɪl] n papel m de aluminio

foil[2] [fɔɪl] v/t (thwart) frustrar

fold[1] [foʊld] **1** v/t paper etc doblar; **fold one's arms** cruzarse de brazos **2** v/i of business quebrar **3** n in cloth etc pliegue m
◆ **fold up 1** v/t plegar **2** v/i of chair, table plegarse

fold[2] [foʊld] n for sheep etc redil m

fold·er ['foʊldər] for documents, COMPUT carpeta f

fold·ing ['foʊldɪŋ] adj plegable; **folding chair** silla f plegable

fo·li·age ['foʊlɪɪdʒ] follaje m

folk [foʊk] (people) gente f; **my folks** (family) mi familia; **evening folks** F buenas noches, gente F

'folk dance baile m popular

'folk mu·sic música f folk or popular

'folk sing·er cantante m/f de folk

'folk song canción m/f folk or popular

fol·low ['fɑːloʊ] **1** v/t seguir; (understand) entender; **follow me** sígueme **2** v/i logically deducirse; **it follows from this that ...** de esto se deduce que ...; **you go first and I'll follow** tú ve primero que yo te sigo; **the requirements are as follows** los requisitos son los siguientes
◆ **follow up** v/t letter, inquiry hacer el seguimiento de

fol·low·er ['fɑːloʊər] seguidor(a) m(f)

fol·low·ing ['fɑːloʊɪŋ] **1** adj siguiente **2** n people seguidores(-as) mpl (fpl); **the following** lo siguiente

'fol·low-up meet·ing reunión m de seguimiento

'fol·low-up vis·it to doctor etc visita f de seguimiento

fol·ly ['fɑːlɪ] (madness) locura f

fond [fɑːnd] adj (loving) cariñoso; memory entrañable; **he's fond of travel /**

music le gusta viajar / la música; **I'm very fond of him** le tengo mucho cariño

fon·dle ['fɑːndl] v/t acariciar

fond·ness ['fɑːndnɪs] *for s.o.* cariño *m* (**for** por); *for wine, food* afición *f* (**for** por)

font [fɑːnt] *for printing* tipo *m*; *in church* pila *f* bautismal

food [fuːd] comida *f*

'**food chain** cadena *f* alimentaria

food·ie ['fuːdɪ] *F* gourmet *m/f*

'**food mix·er** robot *m* de cocina

food poi·son·ing ['fuːdpɔɪznɪŋ] intoxicación *f* alimentaria

fool [fuːl] **1** *n* tonto(-a) *m(f)*, idiota *m/f*; **you stupid fool!** ¡estúpido!; **make a fool of o.s.** ponerse en ridículo **2** v/t engañar
◆ **fool about, fool around** v/i hacer el tonto; *sexually* tener un lío
◆ **fool around with** v/t *knife, drill etc* enredar con algo; *sexually* tener un lío con

'**fool·har·dy** *adj* temerario

fool·ish ['fuːlɪʃ] *adj* tonto

fool·ish·ly ['fuːlɪʃlɪ] *adv*: **I foolishly ...** cometí la tontería de ...

'**fool·proof** *adj* infalible

foot [fut] *(pl **feet** [fiːt]) also measurement* pie *m*; *of animal* pata *f*; **on foot** a pie, caminando, andando; **I've been on my feet all day** llevo todo el día de pie; **be back on one's feet** estar recuperado; **at the foot of the page / hill** al pie de la página / de la colina; **put one's foot in it** *F* meter la pata F

foot·age ['futɪdʒ] secuencias *fpl*, imágenes *fpl*

'**foot·ball** *Br (soccer)* fútbol *m*; *American style* fútbol *m* americano; *ball* balón *m* or pelota *f* (de fútbol)

'**foot·ball play·er** *American style* jugador(a) *m(f)* de fútbol americano; *Br in soccer* jugador(a) *m(f)* de fútbol, futbolista *m/f*

'**foot·bridge** puente *m* peatonal

foot·er ['futər] *in document* pie *m* de página

foot·hills ['futhɪlz] *npl* estribaciones *fpl*

'**foot·hold** *n in climbing* punto *m* de apoyo; **gain a foothold** *fig* introducirse

foot·ing ['futɪŋ] *(basis)*: **put the business back on a secure footing** volver a afianzar la empresa; **lose one's footing** perder el equilibrio; **be on the same / a different footing** estar en / no estar en igualdad de condiciones; **be on a friendly footing with ...** tener relaciones de amistad con ...

foot·lights ['futlaɪts] *npl* candilejas *fpl*

'**foot·mark** pisada *f*

'**foot·note** nota *f* a pie de página

'**foot·path** sendero *m*

'**foot·print** pisada *f*

'**foot·step** paso *m*; **follow in s.o.'s footsteps** seguir los pasos de alguien

'**foot·stool** escabel *m*

'**foot·wear** calzado *m*

for [fər, fɔːr] *prep* ◇ *purpose, destination etc* para; **a train for ...** un tren para *or* hacia ...; **clothes for children** ropa para niños; **it's too big / small for you** te queda demasiado grande / pequeño; **here's a letter for you** hay una carta para ti; **this is for you** esto es para ti; **what's for lunch?** ¿qué hay para comer?; **the steak is for me** el filete es para mí; **what is this for?** ¿para qué sirve esto?; **what for?** ¿para qué?
◇ *time* durante; **for three days / two hours** durante tres días / dos horas; **it lasts for two hours** dura dos horas; **please get it done for Monday** por favor tenlo listo para el lunes
◇ *distance*: **I walked for a mile** caminé una milla; **it stretches for 100 miles** se extiende 100 millas
◇ *(in favor of)*: **I am for the idea** estoy a favor de la idea
◇ *(instead of, in behalf of)*: **let me do that for you** déjame que te lo haga; **we are agents for ...** somos representantes de ...
◇ *(in exchange for)* por; **I bought it for $25** lo compré por 25 dólares: **how much did you sell it for?** ¿por cuánto lo vendiste?

for·bade [fər'bæd] *pret* → **torbid**

for·bid [fər'bɪd] v/t *(pret* **forbade**, *pp* **forbidden**) prohibir; **forbid s.o. to do sth** prohibir a alguien hacer algo

for·bid·den [fər'bɪdn] **1** *adj* prohibido; **smoking / parking forbidden** prohibido fumar / aparcar **2** *pp* → **torbid**

for·bid·ding [fər'bɪdɪŋ] *adj person, tone, look* amenazador; *rockface* imponente; *prospect* intimidador

force [fɔːrs] **1** *n* fuerza *f*; **come into force** *of law etc* entrar en vigor; **the forces** MIL las fuerzas **2** v/t *door, lock* forzar; **force s.o. to do sth** forzar a alguien a hacer algo; **force sth open** forzar algo
◆ **force back** v/t *tears* contener

forced [fɔːrst] *adj* forzado

forced 'land·ing aterrizaje *m* forzoso

force·ful ['fɔːrsfəl] *adj argument* poderoso; *speaker* vigoroso; *character* enérgico

force·ful·ly ['fɔːrsfəlɪ] *adv* de manera convincente

for·ceps ['fɔːrseps] *npl* MED fórceps *m inv*

for·ci·ble ['fɔːrsəbl] *adj entry* por la fuerza

for·ci·bly ['fɔːrsəbli] *adv* por la fuerza

ford [fɔːrd] *n* vado *m*

fore [fɔːr] *n*: **come to the fore** salir a la palestra

'**fore·arm** antebrazo *m*

fore·bears ['fɔːrberz] *npl* antepasados *mpl*

fore·bod·ing [fɔːr'boʊdɪŋ] premonición *f*

'**fore·cast 1** *n* pronóstico *m*; *of weather* pronóstico *m* (del tiempo) **2** *v/t* (*pret & pp* **forecast**) pronosticar

'**fore·court** (*of garage*) explanada en la parte de delante

'**fore·fa·thers** ['fɔːrfɑːðərz] *npl* ancestros *mpl*

'**fore·fin·ger** (dedo *m*) índice *m*

'**fore·front**: **be in the forefront of** estar a la vanguardia de

'**fore·gone** *adj*: **that's a foregone conclusion** eso ya se sabe de antemano

'**fore·ground** primer plano *m*

'**fore·hand** *in tennis* derecha *f*

'**fore·head** frente *f*

for·eign ['fɑːrən] *adj* extranjero; **a foreign holiday** unas vacaciones en el extranjero

for·eign af'fairs *npl* asuntos *mpl* exteriores

for·eign 'aid ayuda *f* al exterior

for·eign 'bod·y cuerpo *m* extraño

for·eign 'cur·ren·cy divisa *f* extranjera

for·eign·er ['fɑːrənər] extranjero(-a) *m(f)*

for·eign ex'change divisas *fpl*

for·eign 'lan·guage idioma *m* extranjero

'**For·eign Of·fice** *in UK* Ministerio *m* de Asuntos Exteriores

for·eign 'pol·i·cy política *f* exterior

For·eign 'Sec·re·ta·ry *in UK* Ministro(-a) *m(f)* de Asuntos Exteriores

'**fore·man** capataz *m*

'**fore·most** *adv* principal; **what was foremost in my mind was the worry that ...** mi principal preocupación era que ...

fo·ren·sic 'medi·cine [fə'rensɪk] medicina *f* forense

fo·ren·sic 'scien·tist forense *m/f*

'**fore·run·ner** predecesor(a) *m(f)*

fore'see *v/t* (*pret* **foresaw**, *pp* **foreseen**) prever

fore·see·a·ble [fər'siːəbl] *adj* previsible; **in the foreseeable future** en un futuro próximo

fore'seen *pp* → **foresee**

'**fore·sight** previsión *f*

for·est ['fɑːrɪst] bosque *m*

for·est·ry ['fɑːrɪstrɪ] silvicultura

'**fore·taste** anticipo *m*

fore'tell *v/t* (*pret & pp* **foretold**) predecir

for·ev·er [fə'revər] *adv* siempre; **it is forever raining here** aquí llueve constantemente; **I will remember this day forever** no me olvidaré nunca de ese día

'**fore·word** ['fɔːrwɜːrd] prólogo *m*

for·feit ['fɔːrfət] *v/t* (*lose*) perder; (*give up*) renunciar a

for·gave [fər'geɪv] *pret* → **forgive**

forge [fɔːrdʒ] *v/t* falsificar

◆ **forge ahead** *v/i* progresar rápidamente

forg·er ['fɔːrdʒər] falsificador(a) *m(f)*

forg·er·y ['fɔːrdʒərɪ] falsificación *f*

for·get [fər'get] *v/t* (*pret* **forgot**, *pp* **forgotten**) olvidar; **I forgot his name** se me olvidó su nombre; **forget to do sth** olvidarse de hacer algo

for·get·ful [fər'getfəl] *adj* olvidadizo

for'get-me-not *flower* nomeolvides *m inv*

for·give [fər'gɪv] *v/t & v/i* (*pret* **forgave**, *pp* **forgiven**) perdonar

for·gi·ven [fər'gɪvn] *pp* → **forgive**

for·give·ness [fər'gɪvnɪs] perdón *m*

for·got [fər'gɑːt] *pret* → **forget**

for·got·ten [fər'gɑːtn] *pp* → **forget**

fork [fɔːrk] *n for eating* tenedor *m*; *for garden* horca *f*; *in road* bifurcación *f*

◆ **fork out** *v/t & v/i* F (*pay*) apoquinar F

forked *adj tongue* bífido; *stick* bifurcado

fork·lift 'truck carretilla *f* elevadora

form [fɔːrm] **1** *n shape* forma *f*; (*document*) formulario *m*, impreso *m*; **be on / off form** estar / no estar en forma **2** *v/t in clay etc* moldear; *friendship* establecer; *opinion* formarse; *past tense etc* formar; (*constitute*) formar, constituir **3** *v/i* (*take shape, develop*) formarse

form·al ['fɔːrml] *adj* formal; *recognition etc* oficial; *dress* de etiqueta

for·mal·i·ty [fər'mælətɪ] formalidad *f*; **it's just a formality** sólo es una formalidad; **the formalities** las formalidades

for·mal·ly ['fɔːrməlɪ] *adv speak, behave* formalmente; *accepted, recognized* oficialmente

for·mat ['fɔːrmæt] **1** *v/t* (*pret & pp* **formatted**) *diskette, document* formatear **2** *n of paper, program etc* formato *m*

for·ma·tion [fɔːr'meɪʃn] formación *f*; **formation flying** vuelo *m* en formación

for·ma·tive ['fɔːrmətɪv] *adj* formativo; **in his formative years** en sus años de formación

for·mer ['fɔːrmər] *adj* antiguo; **the former** el primero; **the former arrangement** la situación de antes

for·mer·ly ['fɔːrmərlɪ] *adv* antiguamente

for·mi·da·ble ['fɔːrmɪdəbl] *adj* persona-

F

lity formidable; *opponent, task* terrible

or·mu·la ['fɔːrmjʊlə] MATH, CHEM, *fig* fórmula *f*

or·mu·late ['fɔːrmjʊleɪt] *v/t* (*express*) formular

or·ni·cate ['fɔːrnɪkeɪt] *v/i fml* fornicar

or·ni·ca·tion [fɔːrnɪ'keɪʃn] *fml* fornicación *f*

ort [fɔːrt] MIL fuerte *m*

orth [fɔːrθ] *adv*: **back and forth** de un lado para otro; **and so forth** y así sucesivamente; **from that day forth** desde ese día en adelante

orth·com·ing ['fɔːrθkʌmɪŋ] *adj* (*future*) próximo; *personality* comunicativo

forth·right *adj* directo

or·ti·eth ['fɔːrtɪɪθ] *n & adj* cuadragésimo

ort·night ['fɔːrtnaɪt] *Br* quincena *f*

or·tress ['fɔːrtrɪs] MIL fortaleza *f*

or·tu·nate ['fɔːrtʃnət] *adj* afortunado

or·tu·nate·ly ['fɔːrtʃnətlɪ] *adv* afortunadamente

or·tune ['fɔːrtʃən] (*fate, money*) fortuna *f*; (*luck*) fortuna *f*, suerte *f*; **tell s.o.'s fortune** decir a alguien la buenaventura

for·tune-tell·er adivino(-a) *m(f)*

or·ty ['fɔːrtɪ] cuarenta; **have forty winks** F echarse una siestecilla F

o·rum ['fɔːrəm] *fig* foro *m*

or·ward ['fɔːrwərd] **1** *adv* hacia delante **2** *adj pej: person* atrevido **3** *n* SP delantero(-a) *m(f)* **4** *v/t letter* reexpedir

for·ward·ing ad·dress ['fɔːrwərdɪŋ] dirección a la que reexpedir correspondencia

for·ward·ing a·gent COM transitario(-a) *m(f)*

for·ward-look·ing *adj* con visión de futuro, moderno

os·sil ['fɑːsəl] fósil *m*

os·sil·ized ['fɑːsəlaɪzd] *adj* fosilizado

os·ter ['fɑːstər] *v/t child* acoger, adoptar (temporalmente); *attitude, belief* fomentar

fos·ter child niño(-a) *m(f)* en régimen de acogida

fos·ter home hogar *m* de acogida

fos·ter par·ents *npl* familia *f* de acogida

oul [faʊl] **1** *n* SP falta *f* **2** *adj smell, taste* asqueroso; *weather* terrible **3** *v/t* SP hacer (una) falta a

ound[1] [faʊnd] *v/t school etc* fundar

ound[2] [faʊnd] *pret & pp* → **find**

oun·da·tion [faʊn'deɪʃn] *of theory etc* fundamento *m*; (*organization*) fundación *f*

oun·da·tions [faʊn'deɪʃnz] *npl of building* cimientos *mpl*

found·er ['faʊndər] *n* fundador(a) *m(f)*

found·ing ['faʊndɪŋ] *n* fundación *f*

foun·dry ['faʊndrɪ] fundición *f*

foun·tain ['faʊntɪn] fuente *f*

'foun·tain pen pluma *f* (estilográfica)

four [fɔːr] cuatro; **on all fours** a gatas, a cuatro patas

four-let·ter 'word palabrota *f*

four-post·er (**'bed**) cama *f* de dosel

'four-star *adj hotel etc* de cuatro estrellas

four·teen [fɔːr'tiːn] catorce

four·teenth [fɔːr'tiːnθ] *n & adj* decimocuarto

fourth [fɔːrθ] *n & adj* cuarto

four-wheel 'drive MOT vehículo *m* con tracción a las cuatro ruedas; *type of drive* tracción *f* a las cuatro ruedas

fowl [faʊl] ave *f* de corral

fox [fɑːks] **1** *n* zorro *m* **2** *v/t* (*puzzle*) dejar perplejo

foy·er ['fɔɪər] vestíbulo *m*

frac·tion ['frækʃn] fracción *f*; MATH fracción *f*, quebrado *m*

frac·tion·al·ly ['frækʃnəlɪ] *adv* ligeramente

frac·ture ['fræktʃər] **1** *n* fractura *f* **2** *v/t* fracturar; **he fractured his arm** se fracturó el brazo

fra·gile ['frædʒəl] *adj* frágil

frag·ment ['frægmənt] *n* fragmento *m*

frag·men·ta·ry ['frægməntərɪ] *adj* fragmentario

fra·grance ['freɪgrəns] fragancia *f*

fra·grant ['freɪgrənt] *adj* fragante

frail [freɪl] *adj* frágil, delicado

frame [freɪm] **1** *n of picture, window* marco *m*; *of eyeglasses* montura *f*; *of bicycle* cuadro *m*; **frame of mind** estado *m* de ánimo **2** *v/t picture* enmarcar; F *person* tender una trampa a

'frame-up F trampa *f*

'frame·work estructura *f*; *for agreement* marco *m*

France [fræns] Francia *f*

fran·chise ['fræntʃaɪz] *n for business* franquicia *f*

frank [fræŋk] *adj* franco

frank·furt·er ['fræŋkfɜːrtər] salchicha *f* de Fráncfort

frank·ly ['fræŋklɪ] *adv* francamente; **frankly, it's not worth it** francamente *or* la verdad, no vale la pena

frank·ness ['fræŋknɪs] franqueza *f*

fran·tic ['fræntɪk] *adj* frenético

fran·ti·cal·ly ['fræntɪklɪ] *adv* frenéticamente

fra·ter·nal [frə'tɜːrnl] *adj* fraternal

fraud [frɔːd] fraude *m*; *person* impostor(a) *m(f)*

fraud·u·lent ['frɔːdjʊlənt] adj fraudulento

fraud·u·lent·ly ['frɔːdjʊləntlɪ] adv frau-
dulentamente

frayed [freɪd] adj cuffs deshilachado

freak [friːk] **1** n unusual event fenómeno
m anormal; two-headed person, animal
etc monstruo m, monstruosidad f; F
strange person bicho m raro F; movie /
jazz freak F un fanático del cine / jazz F
2 adj wind, storm etc anormal

freck·le ['frekl] peca f

free [friː] **1** adj libre; no cost gratis, gratuito; are you free this afternoon? ¿estás
libre esta tarde?; free and easy relajado;
for free travel, get sth gratis **2** v/t prisi-
oners liberar

free·bie ['friːbɪ] F regalo m; as a freebie
de regalo

free·dom ['friːdəm] libertad f

free·dom of 'speech libertad f de expresión

free·dom of the 'press libertad f de prensa

free 'en·ter·prise empresa f libre

free 'kick in soccer falta f, golpe m franco

free·lance ['friːlæns] **1** adj autónomo,
free-lance **2** adv: work freelance trabajar como autónomo or free-lance

free·lanc·er ['friːlænsər] autónomo(-a)
m(f), free-lance m/f

free·load·er ['friːloʊdər] F gorrón (-ona)
m(f)

free·ly ['friːlɪ] adv admit libremente

free mar·ket e'con·o·my economía f de
libre mercado

free-range 'chick·en pollo m de corral

free-range 'eggs npl huevos mpl de corral

free 'sam·ple muestra f gratuita

free 'speech libertad f de expresión

'free·way autopista f

free·wheel v/i on bicycle ir sin pedalear

free 'will libre albedrío m; he did it of his
own free will lo hizo por propia iniciativa

freeze [friːz] **1** v/t (pret froze, pp frozen)
food, wages, video congelar; river congelar, helar **2** v/i (pret froze, pp frozen) of
water congelarse, helarse

♦ **freeze over** v/i of river helarse

'freeze-dried adj liofilizado

freez·er ['friːzər] congelador m

freez·ing ['friːzɪŋ] **1** adj muy frío; it's
freezing (cold) of weather hace mucho
frío; of water está muy frío; I'm freezing
(cold) tengo mucho frío **2** n: 10 below
freezing diez grados bajo cero

'freez·ing com·part·ment congelador m

'freez·ing point punto m de congelació

freight [freɪt] n transporte; costs flete m

'freight car on train vagón m de merca
cías

freight·er ['freɪtər] ship carguero m; ai
plane avión m de carga

'freight train tren m de mercancías

French [frentʃ] **1** adj francés **2** n languag
francés m; the French los franceses

French 'bread pan m de barra

French 'doors npl puerta f cristalera

'French fries npl Span patatas fpl c
L.Am. papas fpl fritas

'French·man francés m

'French·wom·an francesa f

fren·zied ['frenzɪd] adj attack, activity fre
nético; mob desenfrenado

fren·zy ['frenzɪ] frenesí m; whip s.o. int
a frenzy poner a alguien frenético

fre·quen·cy ['friːkwənsɪ] also RAD fre
cuencia f

fre·quent¹ ['friːkwənt] adj frecuente
how frequent are the trains? ¿co
qué frecuencia pasan trenes?

fre·quent² [frɪ'kwent] v/t bar frecuenta

fre·quent·ly ['friːkwentlɪ] adv con fre
cuencia

fres·co ['freskoʊ] fresco m

fresh [freʃ] adj fresco; start nuevo; don
you get fresh with your mother! ¡n
seas descarado con tu madre!

fresh 'air aire m fresco

fresh·en ['freʃn] v/i of wind refrescar

♦ **freshen up 1** v/i refrescarse **2** v/t room
paintwork renovar, revivir

fresh·ly ['freʃlɪ] adv recién

'fresh·man estudiante m/f de primer añ

fresh·ness ['freʃnɪs] frescura f

'fresh·wa·ter adj de agua dulce

fret [fret] v/i (pret & pp fretted) poners
nervioso, inquietarse

Freud·i·an ['frɔɪdɪən] adj freudiano

fric·tion ['frɪkʃn] PHYS rozamiento m; be
ween people fricción f

'fric·tion tape cinta f aislante

Fri·day ['fraɪdeɪ] viernes m inv

fridge [frɪdʒ] nevera f, frigorífico m

fried 'egg [fraɪd] huevo m frito

fried po'ta·toes npl Span patatas fpl o
L.Am. papas fpl fritas

friend [frend] amigo(-a) m(f); mak
friends of one person hacer amigos; o
two people hacerse amigos; mak
friends with s.o. hacerse amigo de al
guien

friend·li·ness ['frendlɪnɪs] simpatía f

friend·ly ['frendlɪ] adj atmosphere agrad
able; person agradable, simpático; (eas
to use) fácil de usar; argument, match, re

lations amistoso; **be friendly with s.o.**
(*be friends*) ser amigo de alguien

friend-ship ['frendʃɪp] amistad *f*

ries [fraɪz] *npl Span* patatas *fpl* or *L.Am.*
papas *fpl* fritas

right [fraɪt] susto *m*; **give s.o. a fright** dar
un susto a alguien, asustar a alguien;
scream with fright gritar asustado

right-en ['fraɪtn] *v/t* asustar; **be frighte-**
ned estar asustado, tener miedo; **don't**
be frightened no te asustes, no tengas
miedo; **be frightened of** tener miedo de

♦ frighten away *v/t* ahuyentar, espantar

right-en-ing ['fraɪtnɪŋ] *adj noise*, *event*,
prospect aterrador, espantoso

ri-gid ['frɪdʒɪd] *adj sexually* frígido

rill [frɪl] *on dress etc* volante *m*; (*fancy ex-*
tra) extra *m*

rill-y ['frɪlɪ] *adj* de volantes

ringe [frɪndʒ] *on dress*, *curtains etc* flecos
mpl; *Br in hair* flequillo *m*; (*edge*) margen *m*

ringe ben-e-fits *npl* ventajas *fpl* adicio-
nales

risk [frɪsk] *v/t* cachear

risk-y ['frɪskɪ] *adj puppy etc* juguetón

♦ frit-ter away ['frɪtər] *v/t time* desperdiciar; *fortune* despilfarrar

ri-vol-i-ty [frɪ'vɑːlətɪ] frivolidad *f*

riv-o-lous ['frɪvələs] *adj* frívolo

rizz-y ['frɪzɪ] *adj hair* crespo

rog [frɑːg] rana *f*

frog-man hombre *m* rana

rom [frɑːm] *prep* ◇ *in time* desde, **from**
9 to 5 (o'clock) de 9 a 5; **from the 18th**
century desde el siglo XVIII; **from to-**
day on a partir de hoy; **from next Tues-**
day a partir del próximo martes
◇ *in space* de, desde: **from here to the-**
re de aquí hasta allí; **we drove he-**
re from Paris vinimos en coche desde
París
◇ *origin* de; **a letter from Jo** una carta
de Jo; **a gift from the management** un
regalo de la dirección; **it doesn't say**
who it's from no dice de quién es; **I**
am from New Jersey soy de Nueva Jersey; **made from bananas** hecho con
plátanos
◇ (*because of*): **tired from the journey**
cansado del viaje; **it's from overeating**
es por comer demasiado

ront [frʌnt] **1** *n of building*, *book* portada
f; (*cover organization*) tapadera *f*; MIL, *of*
weather frente *m*; *in front* delante; *in a*
race en cabeza; **the car in front** el coche
de delante; **in front of** delante de; **at the**
front of en la parte de delante de **2** *adj*
wheel, *seat* delantero **3** *v/t* TV *program*

presentar

front 'cov-er portada *f*

front 'door puerta *f* principal

front 'en-trance entrada *f* principal

fron-tier ['frʌntɪr] frontera *f*; *fig: of know-*
ledge, *science* límite *m*

front 'line MIL línea *f* del frente

front 'page *of newspaper* portada *f*, primera *f* plana

front page 'news *nsg* noticia *f* de portada
or de primera plana

front 'row primera fila *f*

front seat 'pas-sen-ger *in car* pasaje-
ro(-a) *m(f)* de delante

front-wheel 'drive tracción *f* delantera

frost [frɑːst] *n* escarcha *f*; **there was a**
frost last night anoche cayó una helada

'frost-bite congelación *f*

'frost-bit-ten *adj* congelado

frost-ed glass ['frɑːstɪd] vidrio *m* esmerilado

frost-ing ['frɑːstɪŋ] *on cake* glaseado *m*

frost-y ['frɑːstɪ] *adj weather* gélido; *fig:*
welcome glacial

froth [frɑːθ] *n* espuma *f*

froth-y ['frɑːθɪ] *adj cream etc* espumoso

frown [fraʊn] **1** *n*: **what's that frown for?**
¿por qué frunces el ceño? **2** *v/i* fruncir el
ceño

froze [froʊz] *pret* → **freeze**

fro-zen ['froʊzn] **1** *adj ground*, *food* congelado; *wastes* helado; **I'm frozen** F estoy
helado *or* congelado Γ **2** *pp* → **freeze**

fro-zen 'food comida *f* congelada

fruit [fruːt] fruta *f*

'fruit cake bizcocho *m* de frutas

fruit-ful ['fruːtfəl] *adj discussions etc* fructífero

'fruit juice *Span* zumo *m* or *L.Am.* jugo *m*
de fruta

fruit 'sal-ad macedonia *f*

frus-trate [frʌ'streɪt] *v/t person*, *plans*
frustrar

frus-trat-ed [frʌ'streɪtɪd] *adj* frustrado

frus-trat-ing [frʌ'streɪtɪŋ] *adj* frustrante

frus-tra-tion [frʌ'streɪʃn] frustración *f*;
sexual frustration frustración *f* sexual;
the frustrations of modern life las frus-
traciones de la vida moderna

fry [fraɪ] *v/t* (*pret & pp* **fried**) freír

'fry-pan sartén *f*

fuck [fʌk] *v/t* V *Span* follar con V, *L.Am.*
coger V; **fuck!** ¡joder! V; **fuck him!** ¡que
se joda! V

♦ fuck off *v/i* V: **fuck off!** ¡vete a la mierda! V

fuck-ing ['fʌkɪŋ] **1** *adj* puto V **2** *adv* V:
it's fucking crazy es un estupidez
¡coño!; **it was fucking brilliant!** ¡estuvo

de puta madre! V

fu·el ['fjʊəl] **1** n combustible m **2** v/t fig avivar

fu·gi·tive ['fjuːdʒətɪv] n fugitivo(-a) m(f)

ful·fil Br, **ful·fill** [fʊl'fɪl] v/t dream cumplir, realizar; task realizar; contract cumplir; **feel fulfilled** in job, life sentirse realizado

ful·fill·ing [fʊl'fɪlɪŋ] adj: **I have a fulfilling job** mi trabajo me llena

ful·fil·ment Br, **ful·fill·ment** [fʊl'fɪlmənt] of contract etc cumplimiento m; moral, spiritual satisfacción f

full [fʊl] adj lleno; account, schedule completo; life pleno; **full of** of water etc lleno de; **full up** hotel etc, with food lleno; **pay in full** pagar al contado

full 'board Br pensión f completa

'**full-grown** adj completamente desarrollado

'**full-length** adj dress de cuerpo entero; **full-length movie** largometraje m

full '**moon** luna f llena

full '**stop** Br punto m

full '**time** n full worker, job a tiempo completo **2** adv work a tiempo completo

ful·ly ['fʊlɪ] adv completamente; describe en detalle

fum·ble ['fʌmbl] v/t ball dejar caer
♦ **fumble about** v/i rebuscar

fume [fjuːm] v/i: **be fuming** F with anger echar humo F

fumes [fjuːmz] npl humos mpl

fun [fʌn] diversión f; **it was great fun** fue muy divertido; **bye, have fun!** ¡adiós, que lo paséis bien!; **for fun** para divertirse; **make fun of** burlarse de

func·tion ['fʌŋkʃn] **1** n (purpose) función f; (reception etc) acto m **2** v/i funcionar; **function as** hacer de

func·tion·al ['fʌŋkʃnl] adj funcional

fund [fʌnd] **1** n fondo m **2** v/t project etc financiar

fun·da·men·tal [fʌndə'mentl] adj fundamental; (crucial) esencial

fun·da·men·tal·ist [fʌndə'mentlɪst] n fundamentalista m/f

fun·da·men·tal·ly [fʌndə'mentlɪ] adv fundamentalmente

fund·ing ['fʌndɪŋ] (money) fondos mpl, financiación f

fu·ne·ral ['fjuːnərəl] funeral m

'**fu·ne·ral di·rec·tor** encargado(-a) m(f) de una funeraria

'**fu·ne·ral home** funeraria f

fun·gus ['fʌŋgəs] hongos mpl

fu·nic·u·lar ('rail·way) [fjuː'nɪkjʊlər] funicular m

fun·nel ['fʌnl] n of ship chimenea f

fun·nies ['fʌnɪz] npl F sección de humo

fun·ni·ly ['fʌnɪlɪ] adv (oddly) de modo ex traño; (comically) de forma divertida **funnily enough** curiosamente

fun·ny ['fʌnɪ] adj (comical) divertido, gra cioso; (odd) curioso, raro; **that's no funny** eso no tiene gracia

'**fun·ny bone** hueso m de la risa

fur [fɜːr] piel f

fu·ri·ous ['fjʊrɪəs] adj (angry) furioso (intense) furioso, feroz; effort febril; **a furious pace** a un ritmo vertiginoso

fur·nace ['fɜːrnɪs] horno m

fur·nish ['fɜːrnɪʃ] v/t room amueblar (supply) suministrar

fur·ni·ture ['fɜːrnɪtʃər] mobiliario m muebles mpl; **a piece of furniture** u mueble

fur·ry ['fɜːrɪ] adj animal peludo

fur·ther ['fɜːrðər] **1** adj (additional) ad cional; (more distant) más lejano; **there been a further development** ha pasad algo nuevo; **until further notice** hast nuevo aviso; **have you anything furthe to say?** ¿tiene algo más que añadir? **2** adv walk, drive más lejos; **further, I wan to say ...** además, quiero decir ...; **tw miles further (on)** dos millas más ade lante **3** v/t cause etc promover

fur·ther·more adv es más

fur·thest ['fɜːrðɪst] **1** adj: **the furthes point north** el punto más al norte; **th furthest stars** las estrellas más lejana **2** adv más lejos; **this is the furthes north I've ever been** nunca había estad tan al norte

fur·tive ['fɜːrtɪv] adj glance furtivo

fur·tive·ly ['fɜːrtɪvlɪ] adv furtivamente

fu·ry ['fjʊrɪ] (anger) furia f, ira f

fuse [fjuːz] **1** n ELEC fusible m **2** v/i ELE fundirse; **the lights have fused** se ha fundido los plomos **3** v/t ELEC fundir

'**fuse-box** caja f de fusibles

fu·se·lage ['fjuːzəlɑːʒ] fuselaje m

'**fuse wire** fusible m (hilo)

fu·sion ['fjuːʒn] fusión f

fuss [fʌs] n escándalo m; **make a fuss** (complain) armar un escándalo; (behav in exaggerated way) armar un escándalo **make a fuss of** (be very attentive to) de shacerse en atenciones con

fuss·y ['fʌsɪ] adj person quisquilloso; de sign etc recargado; **be a fussy eater** se un quisquilloso a la hora de comer

fu·tile ['fjuːtl] adj inútil, vano

fu·til·i·ty [fjuː'tɪlətɪ] inutilidad f

fu·ture ['fjuːtʃər] **1** n also GRAM futuro m **in future** en el futuro **2** adj futuro

fu·tures ['fjuːtʃərz] npl FIN futuros mpl

'fu·tures mar·ket FIN mercado *m* de futuros

fu·tur·is·tic [fju:tʃəˈrɪstɪk] *adj design* futurista

fuze [fju:z] → *fuse*

fuzz·y [ˈfʌzɪ] *adj hair* crespo; (*out of focus*) borroso

G

ga·la [ˈgɑːlə] gala *f*

gab [gæb] *n:* **have the gift of the gab** F tener labia F

gab·ble [ˈgæbl] *v/i* farfullar

◆ **gad about** [gæd] *v/i* (*pret & pp* **gadded**) pendonear

gad·get [ˈgædʒɪt] artilugio *m*, chisme *m*

gaffe [gæf] metedura *f* de pata

gag [gæg] **1** *n over mouth* mordaza *f*; (*joke*) chiste *m* **2** *v/t* (*pret & pp* **gagged**) *also fig* amordazar

gain [geɪn] *v/t* (*acquire*) ganar; *victory* obtener; **gain speed** cobrar velocidad; **gain 10 pounds** engordar 10 libras

gal·a [ˈgɑːlə] gala *f*

gal·ax·y [ˈgæləksɪ] AST galaxia *f*

gale [geɪl] vendaval *m*

gal·lant [ˈgælənt] *adj* galante

gall blad·der [ˈgɔːlblædər] vesícula *f* biliar

gal·le·ry [ˈgælərɪ] *for art* museo *m*; *in theater* galería *f*

gal·ley [ˈgælɪ] *on ship* cocina *f*

◆ **gal·li·vant around** [ˈgælɪvænt] *v/i* pendonear

gal·lon [ˈgælən] galón *m* (*en EE.UU. 3,785 litros, en GB 4,546*); **gallons of tea** F toneladas de té F

gal·lop [ˈgæləp] *v/i* galopar

gal·lows [ˈgæləʊz] *npl* horca *f*

gall·stone [ˈgɔːlstəʊn] cálculo *m* biliar

ga·lore [gəˈlɔːr] *adj: apples / novels galore* manzanas / novelas a montones

gal·va·nize [ˈgælvənaɪz] *v/t* TECH galvanizar; **galvanize s.o. into activity** hacer que alguien se vuelva más activo

gam·ble [ˈgæmbl] *v/i* jugar

gam·bler [ˈgæmblər] jugador(a) *m(f)*

gam·bling [ˈgæmblɪŋ] *n* juego *m*

game [geɪm] *n* (*sport*) partido *m*; *children's* juego *m*; *in tennis* juego *m*

'game re·serve coto *m* de caza

gang [gæŋ] *of friends* cuadrilla *f*, pandilla *f*; *of criminals* banda *f*

◆ **gang up on** *v/t* compincharse contra

'gang rape 1 *n* violación *f* colectiva **2** *v/t*
violar colectivamente

gan·grene [ˈgæŋgriːn] MED gangrena *f*

'gang war·fare lucha *f* entre bandas

'gang·way pasarela *f*

gaol [dʒeɪl] → *jail*

gap [gæp] *in wall* hueco *m*; *for parking, in figures* espacio *m*; *in time* intervalo *m*; *in conversation* interrupción *f*; *between two people's characters* diferencia *f*

gape [geɪp] *v/i of person* mirar boquiabierto

◆ **gape at** *v/t* mirar boquiabierto a

gap·ing [ˈgeɪpɪŋ] *adj hole* enorme

gar·age [gəˈrɑːʒ] *n for parking* garaje *m*; *for gas* gasolinera *f*; *for repairs* taller *m*

gar·bage [ˈgɑːrbɪdʒ] basura *f*; (*fig: nonsense*) tonterías *fpl*

'gar·bage bag bolsa *f* de la basura

'gar·bage can cubo *m* de la basura

'gar·bage truck camión *m* de la basura

gar·bled [ˈgɑːrbld] *adj message* confuso

gar·den [ˈgɑːrdn] jardín *m*

'gar·den cen·ter, *Br* **'gar·den cen·tre** vivero *m*, centro *m* de jardinería

gar·den·er [ˈgɑːrdnər] aficionado(-a) *m(f)* a la jardinería; *professional* jardinero(-a) *m(f)*

gar·den·ing [ˈgɑːrdnɪŋ] jardinería *f*

gar·gle [ˈgɑːrgl] *v/i* hacer gárgaras

gar·goyle [ˈgɑːrgɔɪl] ARCHI gárgola *f*

gar·ish [ˈgerɪʃ] *adj color* chillón; *design* estridente

gar·land [ˈgɑːrlənd] *n* guirnalda *f*

gar·lic [ˈgɑːrlɪk] ajo *m*

gar·lic 'bread pan *m* con ajo

gar·ment [ˈgɑːrmənt] prenda *f* (de vestir)

gar·nish [ˈgɑːrnɪʃ] *v/t* guarnecer (*with* con)

gar·ret [ˈgærɪt] buhardilla *f*

gar·ri·son [ˈgærɪsn] *n place* plaza *f*; *troops* guarnición *f*

gar·ter [ˈgɑːrtər] liga *f*

gas [gæs] *n* gas *m*; (*gasoline*) gasolina *f*, *Rpl* nafta *f*

gash [gæʃ] n corte m profundo

gas·ket ['gæskɪt] junta f

gas·o·line ['gæsəliːn] gasolina f, Rpl nafta f

gasp [gæsp] **1** n grito m apagado **2** v/i lanzar un grito apagado; ***gasp for breath*** luchar por respirar

'**gas ped·al** acelerador m

'**gas pipe·line** gasoducto m

'**gas pump** surtidor m (de gasolina)

'**gas sta·tion** cocina f de gas '**gas station** gasolinera f, S. Am. bomba f

gas·tric ['gæstrɪk] adj MED gástrico

gas·tric 'flu MED gripe f gastrointestinal

gas·tric 'juices npl jugos mpl gástricos

gas·tric 'ul·cer MED úlcera f gástrica

gate [geɪt] of house, at airport puerta f; made of iron verja f

'**gate·crash** v/t: ***gatecrash a party*** colarse en una fiesta

'**gate·way** also fig entrada f

gath·er ['gæðər] **1** v/t facts, information reunir; ***am I to gather that …?*** ¿debo entender que …?; ***gather speed*** ganar velocidad **2** v/i of crowd reunirse

◆ **gather up** v/t possessions recoger

gath·er·ing ['gæðərɪŋ] n (group of people) grupo m de personas

gau·dy ['gɔːdɪ] adj chillón, llamativo

gauge [geɪdʒ] **1** n indicador m **2** v/t pressure medir, calcular; opinion estimar, evaluar

gaunt [gɔːnt] adj demacrado

gauze [gɔːz] gasa f

gave [geɪv] pret → **give**

gaw·ky ['gɔːkɪ] adj desgarbado

gawp [gɔːp] v/i F mirar boquiabierto; ***don't just stand there gawping!*** ¡no te quedes ahí boquiabierto!

gay [geɪ] **1** n (homosexual) homosexual m, gay m **2** adj homosexual, gay

gaze [geɪz] **1** n mirada f **2** v/i mirar fijamente

◆ **gaze at** v/t mirar fijamente

GB [dʒiː'biː] abbr (= **Great Britain**) GB (= Gran Bretaña)

GDP [dʒiːdiː'piː] abbr (= **gross domestic product**) PIB m (= producto m interior bruto)

gear [gɪr] n equipment equipo m; in vehicles marcha f

'**gear·box** MOT caja f de cambios

'**gear le·ver**, '**gear shift** MOT palanca f de cambios

geese [giːs] pl → **goose**

gel [dʒel] for hair gomina f; for shower gel m

gel·a·tine ['dʒelətiːn] gelatina f

gel·ig·nite ['dʒelɪgnaɪt] gelignita f

gem [dʒem] gema f; (fig: book etc) joya f (person) cielo m

Gem·i·ni ['dʒemɪnaɪ] ASTR Géminis m/ inv

gen·der ['dʒendər] género m

gene [dʒiːn] gen m; ***it's in his genes*** lo lleva en los genes

gen·e·ral ['dʒenrəl] **1** n MIL general m; ***in general*** en general, por lo general **2** adj general

gen·e·ral e'lec·tion elecciones fpl generales

gen·er·al·i·za·tion [dʒenrəlaɪ'zeɪʃn] generalización f; ***that's a generalization*** eso es generalizar

gen·er·al·ize ['dʒenrəlaɪz] v/i generalizar

gen·er·al·ly ['dʒenrəlɪ] adv generalmente por lo general; ***generally speaking*** en términos generales

gen·er·al prac·ti·tion·er médico(-a) m(f) de cabecera or de familia

gen·er·ate ['dʒenəreɪt] v/t generar; a feeling provocar

gen·e·ra·tion [dʒenə'reɪʃn] generación f

gen·e·ra·tion gap conflicto m generacional

gen·e·ra·tor ['dʒenəreɪtər] generador m

ge·ner·ic drug [dʒə'nerɪk] MED medicamento m genérico

gen·e·ros·i·ty [dʒenə'rɑːsətɪ] generosidad f

gen·e·rous ['dʒenərəs] adj generoso

ge·net·ic [dʒɪ'netɪk] adj genético

ge·net·i·cal·ly [dʒɪ'netɪklɪ] adv genéticamente; ***genetically modified crops*** transgénico; ***be genetically modified*** estar modificado genéticamente

ge·net·ic 'code código m genético

ge·net·ic en·gi·neer·ing ingeniería f genética

ge·net·ic 'fin·ger·print identificación f genética

ge·net·i·cist [dʒɪ'netɪsɪst] genetista m/f especialista m/f en genética

ge·net·ics [dʒɪ'netɪks] genética f

ge·ni·al ['dʒiːnjəl] adj afable, cordial

ge·ni·us ['dʒiːnjəs] genio m

gen·o·cide ['dʒenəsaɪd] genocidio m

gen·tle ['dʒentl] adj person tierno, delicado; touch, detergent suave; breeze suave, ligero; slope poco inclinado; ***be gentle with it, it's fragile*** ten mucho cuidado con él, es frágil

gen·tle·man ['dʒentlmən] caballero m; ***he's a real gentleman*** es todo un caballero

gen·tle·ness ['dʒentlnɪs] of person ternura f, delicadeza; of touch, detergent, *breeze* suavidad *f*; *of slope* poca inclinación *f*

gen·tly ['dʒentlɪ] *adv* con delicadeza, poco a poco; *a breeze blew gently* sopla una ligera *or* suave brisa

gents [dʒents] *nsg Br toilet* servicio *m* de caballeros

gen·u·ine ['dʒenʊɪn] *adj antique* genuino, auténtico; *(sincere)* sincero

gen·u·ine·ly ['dʒenʊɪnlɪ] *adv* realmente, de verdad

ge·o·graph·i·cal [dʒɪə'græfɪkl] *adj features* geográfico

ge·og·ra·phy [dʒɪ'ɑːɡrəfɪ] geografía *f*

ge·o·log·i·cal [dʒɪə'lɑːdʒɪkl] *adj* geológico

ge·ol·o·gist [dʒɪ'ɑːlədʒɪst] geólogo(-a) *m(f)*

ge·ol·o·gy [dʒɪ'ɑːlədʒɪ] geología *f*

ge·o·met·ric, ge·o·met·ri·cal [dʒɪə'metrɪk(l)] *adj* geométrico

ge·om·e·try [dʒɪ'ɑːmətrɪ] geometría *f*

ge·ra·ni·um [dʒə'reɪnɪəm] geranio *m*

ger·i·at·ric [dʒerɪ'ætrɪk] **1** *adj* geriátrico **2** *n* anciano(-a) *m(f)*

germ [dʒɜːrm] *also fig* germen *m*

Ger·man ['dʒɜːrmən] **1** *adj* alemán **2** *n person* alemán (-ana) *m(f)*; *language* alemán *m*

Ger·man 'mea·sles *nsg* rubeola *f*

Ger·man 'shep·herd pastor *m* alemán

Germany ['dʒɜːrmənɪ] Alemania *f*

ger·mi·nate ['dʒɜːrmɪneɪt] *v/i of seed* germinar

germ 'war·fare guerra *f* bacteriológica

ges·tic·u·late [dʒe'stɪkjʊleɪt] *v/i* gesticular

ges·ture ['dʒestʃər] *n also fig* gesto *m*

get [ɡet] *v/t (pret got, pp got, gotten) (obtain)* conseguir; *(fetch)* traer; *(receive: letter, knowledge, respect)* recibir; *(catch: bus, train etc)* tomar, *Span* coger; *(arrive)* llegar; *(understand)* entender; *you can get them at the corner shop* los puedes comprar en la tienda de la esquina; *can I get you something to drink?* ¿quieres tomar algo?; *get tired* cansarse; *get drunk* emborracharse; *I'm getting old* me estoy haciendo mayor; *get the TV fixed* hacer que arreglen la televisión; *get s.o. to do sth* hacer que alguien haga algo; *get to do sth (have opportunity)* llegar a hacer algo; *get one's hair cut* cortarse el pelo; *get sth ready* preparar algo; *get going (leave)* marcharse, irse; *have got* tener; *he's got a lot of money* tiene mucho dinero; *I have got to study / see him* tengo que estudiar / verlo; *I don't want to, but I've got to* no

quiero, pero tengo que hacerlo; *get to know* llegar a conocer

◆ **get about** *v/i (travel)* viajar; *(be mobile)* desplazarse

◆ **get along** *v/i (come to party etc)* ir; *with s.o.* llevarse bien; *how are you getting along at school?* ¿cómo te van las cosas en el colegio?; *the patient is getting along nicely* el paciente está progresando satisfactoriamente

◆ **get at** *v/t (criticize)* meterse con; *(imply, mean)* querer decir

◆ **get away 1** *v/i (leave)* marcharse, irse **2** *v/t: get sth away from s.o.* quitar algo a alguien

◆ **get away with** *v/t* salir impune de; *get away with it* salirse con la suya; *she lets him get away with anything* le permite todo; *I'll let you get away with it this time* por esta vez te perdonaré

◆ **get back 1** *v/i (return)* volver; *I'll get back to you on that tomorrow* le responderé a eso mañana **2** *v/t (obtain again)* recuperar

◆ **get by** *v/i (pass)* pasar; *financially* arreglárselas

◆ **get down 1** *v/i from ladder etc* bajarse *(from* de); *(duck etc)* agacharse **2** *v/t (depress)* desanimar, deprimir

◆ **get down to** *v/t (start: work)* ponerse a; *get down to the facts* ir a los hechos

◆ **get in 1** *v/i (arrive)* llegar; *to car* subir(se), meterse; *how did they get in? of thieves, mice etc* ¿cómo entraron? **2** *v/t to suitcase etc* meter

◆ **get into** *v/t house* entrar en, meterse en; *car* subir(se) a, meterse en; *computer system* introducirse en

◆ **get off 1** *v/i from bus etc* bajarse; *(finish work)* salir; *(not be punished)* librarse **2** *v/t (remove)* quitar; *clothes, hat, footgear* quitarse; *get off my bike!* ¡bájate de mi bici!; *get off the grass!* ¡no pises la hierba!

◆ **get off with** *v/t: get off with a small fine* tener que pagar sólo una pequeña multa

◆ **get on 1** *v/i to bike, bus, train* montarse, subirse; *(be friendly)* llevarse bien; *(advance: of time)* hacerse tarde; *(become old)* hacerse mayor; *(make progress)* progresar; *how are you getting on with the new subjects?* ¿cómo te va con las nuevas asignaturas?; *it's getting on getting late* se está haciendo tarde; *he's getting on* se está haciendo mayor; *he's getting on for 50* está a punto de cumplir 50 **2** *v/t: get on the bus / one's bike* montarse en el autobús / la bici; *get one's shoes on* ponerse los zapatos; *I can't get these pants on* estos pantalones no me entran

◆ **get out** 1 *v/i of car, prison etc* salir; *get out!* ¡vete!, ¡fuera de aquí!; *let's get out of here* ¡salgamos de aquí!; *I don't get out much these days* últimamente no salgo mucho 2 *v/t nail, something jammed* sacar, extraer; *stain* quitar; *gun, pen* sacar

◆ **get over** *v/t fence etc* franquear; *disappointment* superar; *lover etc* olvidar

◆ **get over with** *v/t* terminar con; *let's get it over with* quitémonoslo de encima

◆ **get through** *v/i on telephone* conectarse; *obviously I'm just not getting through* está claro que no me estoy haciendo entender; *get through to s.o.* (*make self understood*) comunicarse con alguien

◆ **get up** 1 *v/i* levantarse 2 *v/t* (*climb*) subir

'get·a·way *from robbery* fuga *f*, huida *f*
'get·a·way car coche *m* utilizado en la fuga

'get-to·geth·er reunión *f*
ghast·ly ['gæstlɪ] *adj* terrible
gher·kin ['gɜːrkɪn] pepinillo *m*
ghet·to ['getoʊ] gueto *m*
ghost [goʊst] fantasma *m*
ghost·ly ['goʊstlɪ] *adj* fantasmal
'ghost town ciudad *f* fantasma
ghoul [guːl] macabro(-a) *m(f)*, morboso(-a) *m(f)*
ghoul·ish ['guːlɪʃ] *adj* macabro, morboso
gi·ant ['dʒaɪənt] 1 *n* gigante *m* 2 *adj* gigantesco, gigante
gib·ber·ish ['dʒɪbərɪʃ] F memeces *fpl* F, majaderías *fpl* F
gibe [dʒaɪb] *n* pulla *f*
gib·lets ['dʒɪblɪts] *npl* menudillos *mpl*
gid·di·ness ['gɪdɪnɪs] mareo *m*
gid·dy ['gɪdɪ] *adj* mareado; *feel giddy* estar mareado
gift [gɪft] regalo *m*
gift cer·tif·i·cate vale *m* de regalo
gift·ed ['gɪftɪd] *adj* con talento
'gift-wrap 1 *n* papel *m* de regalo 2 *v/t* (*pret & pp giftwrapped*) envolver para regalo
gig [gɪg] F concierto *m*, actuación *f*
gi·ga·byte ['gɪgəbaɪt] COMPUT gigabyte *m*
gi·gan·tic [dʒaɪ'gæntɪk] *adj* gigantesco
gig·gle ['gɪgl] 1 *v/i* soltar risitas 2 *n* risita *f*
gig·gly ['gɪglɪ] *adj* que suelta risitas
gill [gɪl] *of fish* branquia *f*
gilt [gɪlt] *n* dorado *m*; *gilts* FIN valores *mpl* del Estado
gim·mick ['gɪmɪk] truco *m*, reclamo *m*
gim·mick·y ['gɪmɪkɪ] *adj* superficial, artificioso

gin [dʒɪn] ginebra *f*; *gin and tonic* gin-tonic *m*
gin·ger ['dʒɪndʒər] 1 *n spice* jengibre *m* 2 *adj cat* color fuego; *he has ginger hair* es pelirrojo
gin·ger 'beer refresco con sabor a jengibre
'gin·ger·bread pan *m* de jengibre
gin·ger·ly ['dʒɪndʒərlɪ] *adv* cuidadosamente, delicadamente
gip·sy ['dʒɪpsɪ] gitano(-a) *m(f)*
gi·raffe [dʒɪ'ræf] jirafa *f*
gir·der ['gɜːrdər] *n* viga *f*
girl [gɜːrl] chica *f*; *young girl* niña *f*, chica *f*
'girl·friend *of boy* novia *f*; *of girl* amiga *f*
girl·ie mag·a·zine ['gɜːrlɪ] revista *f* porno
girl·ish ['gɜːrlɪʃ] *adj* de niñas
girl 'scout escultista *f*, scout *f*
gist [dʒɪst] esencia *f*
give [gɪv] *v/t* (*pret gave, pp given*) dar; *as present* regalar; (*supply: electricity etc*) proporcionar; *talk, lecture* dar, pronunciar; *cry, groan* soltar; *give her my love* dale recuerdos (de mi parte); *give s.o. a present* hacer un regalo a alguien

◆ **give away** *v/t as present* regalar; (*betray*) traicionar; *give o.s. away* descubrirse, traicionarse

◆ **give back** *v/t* devolver

◆ **give in** 1 *v/i* (*surrender*) rendirse 2 *v/t* (*hand in*) entregar

◆ **give off** *v/t smell, fumes* emitir, despedir

◆ **give onto** *v/t* (*open onto*) dar a

◆ **give out** 1 *v/t leaflets etc* repartir 2 *v/i supplies, strength* agotarse

◆ **give up** 1 *v/t smoking etc* dejar de; *give o.s. up to the police* entregarse a la policía 2 *v/i* (*stop making effort*) rendirse; *I find it hard to give up* me cuesta mucho dejarlo

◆ **give way** *v/i of bridge etc* hundirse
give-and-'take toma *m* y daca
giv·en ['gɪvn] *pp* → *give*
'giv·en name nombre *m* de pila
gla·ci·er ['gleɪʃər] glaciar *m*
glad [glæd] *adj* contento, alegre; *I was glad to see you* me alegré de verte
glad·ly ['glædlɪ] *adv* con mucho gusto
glam·or ['glæmər] atractivo *m*, glamour *m*
glam·or·ize ['glæməraɪz] *v/t* hacer atractivo, ensalzar
glam·or·ous ['glæmərəs] *adj* atractivo, glamoroso
glam·our *Br* → *glamor*
glance [glæns] 1 *n* ojeada *f*, vistazo *m* 2 *v/i* echar una ojeada *or* vistazo

◆ **glance at** *v/t* echar una ojeada *or* vistazo a

gland [glænd] glándula *f*

glan·du·lar 'fe·ver ['glændʒələr] mononucleosis *f inv* infecciosa

glare [gler] **1** *n of sun, headlights* resplandor *m* **2** *v/i of headlights* resplandecer

◆ **glare at** *v/t* mirar con furia a

glar·ing ['glerɪŋ] *adj mistake* garrafal

glar·ing·ly ['glerɪŋlɪ] *adv*: **it's glaringly obvious** está clarísimo

glass [glæs] *material* vidrio *m*; *for drink* vaso *m*

glass 'case vitrina *f*

glass·es *npl* gafas *fpl*, *L.Am.* lentes *mpl*, *L.Am.* anteojos *mpl*

'glass·house invernadero *m*

glaze [gleɪz] *n* vidriado *m*

◆ **glaze over** *v/i of eyes* vidriarse

glazed [gleɪzd] *adj expression* vidrioso

gla·zi·er ['gleɪzɪr] cristalero(-a) *m(f)*, vidriero(-a) *m(f)*

glaz·ing ['gleɪzɪŋ] cristales *mpl*, vidrios *mpl*

gleam [gli:m] **1** *n* resplandor *m*, brillo *m* **2** *v/i* resplandecer, brillar

glee [gli:] júbilo *m*, regocijo *m*

glee·ful ['gli:fəl] *adj* jubiloso

glib [glɪb] *adj* fácil

glib·ly ['glɪblɪ] *adv* con labia

glide [glaɪd] *v/i of bird, plane* planear; *of piece of furniture* deslizarse

glid·er ['glaɪdər] planeador *m*

glid·ing ['glaɪdɪŋ] *n sport* vuelo *m* sin motor

glim·mer ['glɪmər] **1** *n of light* brillo *m* tenue; **glimmer of hope** rayo *m* de esperanza **2** *v/i* brillar tenuemente

glimpse [glɪmps] **1** *n* vistazo *m*; **catch a glimpse of** vislumbrar **2** *v/t* vislumbrar

glint [glɪnt] **1** *n* destello *m*; *in eyes* centelleo *m* **2** *v/i of light* destellar; *of eyes* centellear

glis·ten ['glɪsn] *v/i* relucir, centellear

glit·ter ['glɪtər] *v/i* resplandecer, destellar

glit·ter·ati [glɪtər'ɑːtɪ] famosos *mpl*

gloat [gloʊt] *v/i* regodearse

◆ **gloat over** *v/t* regodearse de

glo·bal ['gloʊbl] *adj* global

glo·bal e'con·o·my economía *f* global

glo·bal 'mar·ket mercado *m* global

glo·bal 'war·ming calentamiento *m* global

globe [gloʊb] *(the earth)* globo *m*; *(model of earth)* globo *m* terráqueo

gloom [glu:m] *(darkness)* tinieblas *fpl*, oscuridad *f*; *mood* abatimiento *m*, melancolía *f*

gloom·i·ly ['glu:mɪlɪ] *adv* con abatimiento, melancólicamente

gloom·y ['glu:mɪ] *adj room* tenebroso, oscuro; *mood, person* abatido, melancólico

glo·ri·ous ['glɔːrɪəs] *adj weather, day* espléndido, maravilloso; *victory* glorioso

glo·ry ['glɔːrɪ] *n* gloria *f*

gloss [glɑːs] *n (shine)* lustre *m*, brillo *m*; *(general explanation)* glosa *f*

◆ **gloss over** *v/t* pasar por alto

glos·sa·ry ['glɑːsərɪ] glosario *m*

'gloss paint pintura *f* brillante

gloss·y ['glɑːsɪ] **1** *adj paper* cuché, satinado **2** *n magazine* revista *f* en color (en papel cuché *or* satinado)

glove [glʌv] guante *m*

'glove com·part·ment *in car* guantera *f*

'glove pup·pet marioneta *f* de guiñol (de guante)

glow [gloʊ] **1** *n of light, fire* resplandor *m*, brillo *m*; *in cheeks* rubor *m* **2** *v/i of light, fire* resplandecer, brillar; *of cheeks* ruborizarse

glow·er ['glaʊr] *v/i* fruncir el ceño

glow·ing ['gloʊɪŋ] *adj description* entusiasta

glu·cose ['glu:koʊs] glucosa *f*

glue [glu:] **1** *n* pegamento *m*, cola *f* **2** *v/t* pegar, encolar; **glue sth to sth** pegar *or* encolar algo a algo; **be glued to the radio / TV** F estar pegado a la radio / televisión F

glum [glʌm] *adj* sombrío, triste

glum·ly ['glʌmlɪ] *adv* con tristeza

glut [glʌt] *n* exceso *m*, superabundancia *f*

glut·ton ['glʌtn] glotón(-ona) *m(f)*

glut·ton·y ['glʌtənɪ] gula *f*, glotonería *f*

GMT [dʒiːemˈtiː] *abbr (= Greenwich Mean Time)* hora *f* del meridiano de Greenwich

gnarled [nɑːrld] *adj* nudoso

gnat [næt] *tipo de mosquito*

gnaw [nɒː] *v/t bone* roer

GNP [dʒiːenˈpiː] *abbr (= gross national product)* PNB *m* (= producto *m* nacional bruto)

go [goʊ] **1** *n (try)* intento *m*; **it's my go** me toca a mí; **have a go at sth** *(try)* intentar algo; *(complain about)* protestar contra algo; **on the go** en marcha; **in one go** *drink, write etc* de un tirón **2** *v/i (pret went, pp gone)* ir *(to* a*)*; *(leave)* irse, marcharse; *(work, function)* funcionar; *(come out: of stain etc)* irse; *(cease: of pain etc)* pasarse; *(match: of colors etc)* ir bien, pegar; **go shopping / jogging** ir de compras/a hacer footing; **I must be going** me tengo que ir; **let's go!** ¡vamos!; **go for a walk** ir a pasear *or* a dar un paseo; **go to bed** ir(se) a la cama; **go to school** ir al colegio; **how's the work**

going? ¿cómo va el trabajo?; **they're going for $50** (*being sold at*) se venden por 50 dólares; **hamburger to go** hamburguesa para llevar; **be all gone** (*finished*) haberse acabado; **go green** ponerse verde; **be going to do sth** ir a hacer algo

◆ **go ahead** *v/i and do sth* seguir adelante; **can I?** - **sure, go ahead** ¿puedo? - por supuesto, adelante

◆ **go ahead with** *v/t plans etc* seguir adelante con

◆ **go along with** *v/t suggestion* aceptar

◆ **go at** *v/t* (*attack*) atacar

◆ **go away** *v/i of person* irse, marcharse; *of rain, pain, clouds* desaparecer

◆ **go back** *v/i* (*return*) volver; (*date back*) remontarse; **we go back a long way** nos conocemos desde hace tiempo; **go back to sleep** volver a dormirse

◆ **go by** *v/i of car, time* pasar

◆ **go down** *v/i* bajar; *of sun* ponerse; *of ship* hundirse; **go down well / badly** *of suggestion etc* sentar bien / mal

◆ **go for** *v/t* (*attack*) atacar; **I don't much go for gin** no me va mucho la ginebra

◆ **go in** *v/i to room, house* entrar; *of sun* ocultarse; (*fit: of part etc*) ir, encajar

◆ **go in for** *v/t competition, race* tomar parte en; **I used to go in for badminton quite a lot** antes jugaba mucho al bádminton

◆ **go off 1** *v/i* (*leave*) marcharse; *of bomb* explotar, estallar; *of gun* dispararse; *of alarm* saltar; *of milk etc* echarse a perder **2** *v/t*: **I've gone off whisky** ya no me gusta el whisky

◆ **go on** *v/i* (*continue*) continuar; (*happen*) ocurrir, pasar; **go on, do it!** (*encouraging*) ¡venga, hazlo!; **what's going on?** ¿qué pasa?

◆ **go on at** *v/t* (*nag*) meterse con

◆ **go out** *v/i of person* salir; *of light, fire* apagarse

◆ **go out with** *v/t romantically* salir con

◆ **go over** *v/t* (*check*) examinar; (*do again*) repasar

◆ **go through** *v/t illness, hard times* atravesar; (*check*) revisar, examinar; (*read through*) estudiar

◆ **go under** *v/i* (*sink*) hundirse; *of company* ir a la quiebra

◆ **go up** *v/i* subir

◆ **go without 1** *v/t food etc* pasar sin **2** *v/i* pasar privaciones

goad [goʊd] *v/t* pinchar; **goad s.o. into doing sth** pinchar a alguien para que haga algo

'**go-a·head 1** *n* luz *f* verde; **when we get the go-ahead** cuando nos den la luz

verde **2** *adj* (*enterprising, dynamic*) dinámico

goal [goʊl] SP *target* portería *f*, *L.Am.* arco *m*; SP *point* gol *m*; (*objective*) objetivo *m*, meta *f*

goal·ie ['goʊlɪ] F portero(-a) *m(f)*, *L.Am.* arquero(-a) *m(f)*

'**goal·keep·er** portero(-a) *m(f)*, guardameta *m/f*, *Am* arquero(-a) *m(f)*

'**goal kick** saque *m* de puerta

'**goal·mouth** portería *f*

'**goal·post** poste *m*

goat [goʊt] cabra *f*

gob·ble ['gɑːbl] *v/t* engullir

◆ **gobble up** *v/t* engullir

gob·ble·dy·gook ['gɑːbldɪguːk] F jerigonza *f* F

'**go-be·tween** intermediario(-a) *m(f)*

god [gɑːd] dios *m*; **thank God!** ¡gracias a Dios!; **oh God!** ¡Dios mío!

'**god·child** ahijado(-a) *m(f)*

'**god·daugh·ter** ahijada *f*

'**god·dess** ['gɑːdɪs] diosa *f*

'**god·fa·ther** *also in mafia* padrino *m*

god·for·sak·en ['gɑːdfərseɪkən] *adj place* dejado de la mano de Dios

'**god·moth·er** madrina *f*

'**god·pa·rent** *man* padrino *m*; *woman* madrina *f*

'**god·send** regalo *m* del cielo

'**god·son** ahijado *m*

go·fer ['goʊfər] F recadero(-a) *m(f)*

gog·gles ['gɑːglz] *npl* gafas *fpl*

go·ing ['goʊɪŋ] *adj price etc* vigente; **going concern** empresa *f* en marcha

go·ings-on [goʊɪŋz'ɑːn] *npl* actividades *fpl*

gold [goʊld] **1** *n* oro *m* **2** *adj* de oro

gold·en ['goʊldn] *adj sky, hair* dorado

gold·en 'hand·shake gratificación entregada tras la marcha de un directivo

gold·en 'wed·ding (an·ni·ver·sa·ry) bodas *fpl* de oro

'**gold·fish** pez *m* de colores

'**gold mine** *fig* mina *f*

'**gold·smith** orfebre *m/f*

golf [gɑːlf] golf *m*

'**golf ball** pelota *f* de golf

'**golf club** *organization* club *m* de golf; *stick* palo *m* de golf

'**golf course** campo *m* de golf

golf·er ['gɑːlfər] golfista *m/f*

gone [gɑːn] *pp* → **go**

gong [gɑːŋ] gong *m*

good [gʊd] *adj* bueno; *food* bueno, rico; **a good many** muchos; **he's good at chess** se le da muy bien el ajedrez; **be good for s.o.** ser bueno para alguien

good·bye [gʊd'baɪ] adiós *m*, despedida *f*;

say goodbye to s.o., wish s.o. goodbye decir adiós a alguien, despedirse de alguien

'good-for-no·thing n inútil m/f

Good 'Fri·day Viernes m inv Santo

good-hu·mored, Br good-hu·moured [gʊd'hjuːmərd] adj jovial, afable

good-'look·ing [gʊd'lʊkɪŋ] adj woman, man guapo

good-na·tured [gʊd'neɪtʃərd] bondadoso

good·ness ['gʊdnɪs] adj moral bondad f; of fruit etc propiedades fpl, valor m nutritivo; thank goodness! ¡gracias a Dios!

goods [gʊdz] npl COM mercancías fpl, productos mpl

good·will buena voluntad f

good·y-good·y ['gʊdɪgʊdɪ] n F: she's a real goody-goody es demasiado buenaza F

goo·ey ['guːɪ] adj pegajoso

goof [guːf] v/i F meter la pata F

goose [guːs] (pl geese [giːs]) ganso m, oca f

goose·ber·ry ['gʊzberɪ] grosella f

'goose bumps npl carne f de gallina

'goose pim·ples npl carne f de gallina

gorge [gɔːrdʒ] 1 n garganta f, desfiladero m 2 v/t: gorge o.s. on sth comer algo hasta hartarse

gor·geous ['gɔːrdʒəs] adj weather maravilloso; dress, hair precioso; woman, man buenísimo; smell estupendo

go·ril·la [gə'rɪlə] gorila m

gosh [gɑːʃ] int ¡caramba!, ¡vaya!

go·'slow huelga f de celo

gos·pel ['gɑːspl] in Bible evangelio m; it's the gospel truth es la pura verdad

gos·sip ['gɑːsɪp] 1 n cotilleo m; person cotilla m/f 2 v/i cotillear

'gos·sip col·umn ecos mpl de sociedad

'gos·sip col·um·nist escritor(a) m(f) de los ecos de sociedad

gos·sip·y ['gɑːsɪpɪ] adj letter lleno de cotilleos

got [gɑːt] pret & pp → get

got·ten ['gɑːtn] pp → get

gour·met ['gʊrmeɪ] n gastrónomo(-a) m(f), gourmet m/f

gov·ern ['gʌvərn] v/t country gobernar

gov·ern·ment ['gʌvərnmənt] gobierno m

gov·er·nor ['gʌvənər] gobernador(a) m(f)

gown [gaʊn] long dress vestido m; wedding dress traje m; of academic, judge toga f; of surgeon bata f

grab [græb] v/t (pret & pp grabbed) agarrar; food tomar; grab some sleep dormir

grace [greɪs] of dancer etc gracia f, elegancia f; say grace bendecir la mesa

grace·ful ['greɪsfəl] adj elegante

grace·ful·ly ['greɪsfəlɪ] adv move con gracia or elegancia

gra·cious ['greɪʃəs] adj person amable; style, living elegante; good gracious! ¡Dios mío!

grade [greɪd] 1 n quality grado m; EDU curso m; (mark) nota f 2 v/t clasificar

'grade cross·ing paso m a nivel

'grade school escuela f primaria

gra·di·ent ['greɪdɪənt] pendiente f

grad·u·al ['grædʒuəl] adj gradual

grad·u·al·ly ['grædʒuəlɪ] adv gradualmente, poco a poco

grad·u·ate ['grædʒuət] 1 n licenciado (-a) m(f); from high school bachiller m/f 2 v/i from university licenciarse, L.Am. egresarse; from high school sacar el bachillerato

grad·u·a·tion [grædʒu'eɪʃn] graduación f

graf·fi·ti [grə'fiːtiː] graffiti m

graft [græft] 1 n BOT, MED injerto m; corruption corrupción f 2 v/t BOT, MED injertar

grain [greɪn] grano m; in wood veta f; go against the grain ir contra la naturaleza de alguien

gram [græm] gramo m

gram·mar ['græmər] gramática f

gram·mat·i·cal [grə'mætɪkl] adj gramatical

gram·mat·i·cal·ly adv gramaticalmente

grand [grænd] 1 adj grandioso; F (very good) estupendo, genial 2 n F ($1000) mil dólares

gran·dad ['grændæd] abuelito m

'grand·child nieto(a) m(f)

'grand·daugh·ter nieta f

gran·deur ['grændʒər] grandiosidad f

'grand·fa·ther abuelo m

'grand·fa·ther clock reloj m de pie

gran·di·ose ['grændɪoʊs] adj grandioso

grand 'jur·y jurado m de acusación, gran jurado

'grand·ma F abuelita f, yaya f F

'grand·moth·er abuela f

'grand·pa F abuelito m, yayo m F

'grand·par·ents npl abuelos mpl

grand pi'an·o piano m de cola

grand 'slam gran slam m

'grand·son nieto m

'grand·stand tribuna f

gran·ite ['grænɪt] granito m

gran·ny ['grænɪ] F abuelita f, yaya f F

grant [grænt] 1 n money subvención f 2 v/t conceder; take sth for granted dar algo por sentado; take s.o. for granted no apreciar a alguien lo suficiente

gran·u·lat·ed sug·ar ['grænʊleɪtɪd] azúcar *m or f* granulado(-a)

gran·ule ['grænjuːl] gránulo *m*

grape [greɪp] uva *f*

'grape·fruit pomelo *m*, *L.Am.* toronja *f*

'grape·fruit juice *Span* zumo *m* de pomelo, *L.Am.* jugo *m* de toronja

'grape·vine: *I've heard on the grapevine that …* me ha contado un pajarito que …

graph [græf] gráfico *m*, gráfica *f*

graph·ic ['græfɪk] **1** *adj* (*vivid*) gráfico **2** *n* COMPUT gráfico *m*

graph·ic·al·ly ['græfɪklɪ] *adv describe* gráficamente

graph·ic de·sign·er diseñador(a) *m(f)* gráfico(-a)

◆ **grap·ple with** ['græpl] *v/t attacker* forcejear con; *problem etc* enfrentarse a

grasp [græsp] **1** *n physical* asimiento *m*; *mental* comprensión *m* **2** *v/t physically* agarrar; (*understand*) comprender

grass [græs] *n* hierba *f*

'grass·hop·per saltamontes *m inv*

grass 'roots *npl people* bases *fpl*

grass 'wid·ow mujer cuyo marido está a menudo ausente durante largos periodos de tiempo

grass 'wid·ow·er hombre cuya mujer está a menudo ausente durante largos periodos de tiempo

gras·sy ['græsɪ] *adj* lleno de hierba

grate¹ [greɪt] *n metal* parrilla *f*, reja *f*

grate² [greɪt] **1** *v/t in cooking* rallar **2** *v/i of sound* rechinar

grate·ful ['greɪtfəl] *adj* agradecido; *we are grateful for your help* (le) agradecemos su ayuda; *I'm grateful to him* estoy agradecido

grate·ful·ly ['greɪtfəlɪ] *adv* con agradecimiento

grat·er ['greɪtər] rallador *m*

grat·i·fy ['grætɪfaɪ] *v/t (pret & pp grati·fied)* satisfacer, complacer

grat·ing ['greɪtɪŋ] **1** *n* reja *f* **2** *adj sound, voice* chirriante

grat·i·tude ['grætɪtuːd] gratitud *f*

gra·tu·i·tous [grəˈtuːɪtəs] *adj* gratuito

gra·tu·i·ty [grəˈtuːətɪ] propina *f*, gratificación *f*

grave¹ [greɪv] *n* tumba *f*, sepultura *f*

grave² [greɪv] *adj* grave

grav·el ['grævl] *n* gravilla *f*

'grave·stone lápida *f*

'grave·yard cementerio *m*

◆ **grav·i·tate toward** ['grævɪteɪt] *v/t* verse atraído por

grav·i·ty ['grævətɪ] PHYS gravedad *f*

gra·vy ['greɪvɪ] jugo *m* (de la carne)

gray [greɪ] *adj* gris; *be going gray* encanecer

gray-haired [greɪˈherd] *adj* canoso

'grey·hound galgo *m*

graze¹ [greɪz] *v/i of cow etc* pastar, pacer

graze² [greɪz] **1** *v/t arm etc* rozar, arañar **2** *n* rozadura *f*, arañazo *m*

grease [griːs] *n* grasa *f*

grease·proof 'pa·per papel *m* de cera *or* parafinado

greas·y ['griːsɪ] *adj food, hands, plate* grasiento; *hair, skin* graso

great [greɪt] *adj* grande, *before singular noun* gran; F (*very good*) estupendo, genial; *how was it? - great!* ¿cómo fue? - ¡estupendo *or* genial!; *great to see you again!* ¡me alegro de volver a verte!

Great 'Brit·ain Gran *Bret*aña *f*

great-'grand·child bisnieto(-a) *m(f)*

great-'grand·daugh·ter bisnieta *f*

great-'grand·fa·ther bisabuelo *m*

great-'grand·moth·er bisabuela *f*

great-'grand·par·ents *npl* bisabuelos *mpl*

great-'grand·son bisnieto *m*

great·ly ['greɪtlɪ] *adv* muy

great·ness ['greɪtnɪs] grandeza *f*

Greece [griːs] Grecia

greed [griːd] *for money* codicia *f*; *for food* gula *f*, glotonería *f*

greed·i·ly ['griːdɪlɪ] *adv* con codicia; *eat* con gula *or* glotonería

greed·y ['griːdɪ] *adj for food* glotón; *for money* codicioso

Greek [griːk] **1** *adj* griego **2** *n person* griego(-a) *m(f)*; *language* griego *m*

green [griːn] *adj* verde; *environmentally* ecologista, verde

green 'beans *npl* judías *fpl* verdes, *L.Am.* porotos *mpl* verdes, *Mex* ejotes *mpl*

'green card (*work permit*) permiso *m* de trabajo

'green·field site terreno *m* edificable en el campo

'green·horn F novato(-a) *m(f)* F

'green·house invernadero *m*

'green·house ef·fect efecto *m* invernadero

'green·house gas gas *m* invernadero

greens [griːnz] *npl* verduras *f*

green 'thumb: *have a green thumb* tener buena mano con la jardinería

greet [griːt] *v/t* saludar

greet·ing ['griːtɪŋ] saludo *m*

'greet·ing card tarjeta *f* de felicitación

gre·gar·i·ous [grɪˈgerɪəs] *adj person* sociable

gre·nade [grɪˈneɪd] granada *f*

grew [gru:] pret → **grow**

grey Br → **gray**

grid [grɪd] reja f, rejilla f

'grid·iron SP campo de fútbol americano

'grid·lock in traffic paralización m del tráfico

grief [gri:f] dolor m, aflicción f

grief-strick·en ['gri:fstrɪkn] adj afligido

griev·ance ['gri:vəns] queja f

grieve [gri:v] v/i sufrir; **grieve for s.o.** llorar por alguien

grill [grɪl] **1** n on window reja f **2** v/t (interrogate) interrogar

grille [grɪl] reja f

grim [grɪm] adj face severo; prospects desolador; surroundings lúgubre

gri·mace ['grɪməs] n gesto m, mueca f

grime [graɪm] mugre f

grim·ly ['grɪmlɪ] adv speak en tono grave

grim·y ['graɪmɪ] adj mugriento

grin [grɪn] **1** n sonrisa f (amplia) **2** v/i (pret & pp **grinned**) sonreír abiertamente

grind [graɪnd] v/t (pret & pp **ground**) coffee moler; meat picar; **grind one's teeth** hacer rechinar los dientes

grip [grɪp] **1** n: he lost his grip on the rope se le escapó la cuerda; **be losing one's grip** (losing one's skills) estar perdiendo el control **2** v/t (pret & pp **gripped**) agarrar

gripe [graɪp] **1** n F queja f **2** v/i F quejarse

grip·ping ['grɪpɪŋ] adj apasionante

gris·tle ['grɪsl] cartílago m

grit [grɪt] **1** n (dirt) arenilla f; for roads gravilla f **2** v/t (pret & pp **gritted**): **grit one's teeth** apretar los dientes

grit·ty ['grɪtɪ] adj F book, movie etc duro F, descarnado

groan [groʊn] **1** n gemido m **2** v/i gemir

gro·cer ['groʊsər] tendero(-a) m(f)

gro·cer·ies ['groʊsərɪz] npl comestibles mpl

gro·cer·y store ['groʊsərɪ] tienda f de comestibles or Mex abarrotes

grog·gy ['grɑ:gɪ] adj F grogui F

groin [grɔɪn] ANAT ingle f

groom [gru:m] **1** n for bride novio m; for horse mozo m de cuadra **2** v/t horse almohazar; (train, prepare) preparar; **well groomed** in appearance bien arreglado

groove [gru:v] ranura f

grope [groʊp] **1** v/i in the dark caminar a tientas **2** v/t sexually manosear

◆ **grope for** v/t door handle, the right word intentar encontrar

gross [groʊs] adj (coarse, vulgar) grosero; exaggeration tremendo; error craso; FIN bruto

gross do·mes·tic 'prod·uct producto m interior bruto

gross na·tion·al 'prod·uct producto m nacional bruto

ground¹ [graʊnd] **1** n suelo m, tierra f; (reason) motivo m; ELEC tierra f; **on the ground** en el suelo **2** v/t ELEC conectar a tierra

ground² [graʊnd] pret & pp → **grind**

'ground con·trol control m de tierra

'ground crew personal m de tierra

ground·ing ['graʊndɪŋ] in subject fundamento m; he's had a good grounding in electronics tiene buenos fundamentos de electrónica

ground·less ['graʊndlɪs] adj infundado

ground 'meat carne f picada

'ground·nut cacahuete m, L.Am. maní m, Mex cacahuate m

'ground plan plano m

'ground staff SP personal m de mantenimiento; at airport personal m de tierra

'ground·work trabajos mpl preliminares

group [gru:p] **1** n grupo m **2** v/t agrupar

group·ie ['gru:pɪ] F grupi f F

group 'ther·a·py terapia f de grupo

grouse [graʊs] **1** n F queja f **2** v/i F quejarse, refunfuñar

grov·el ['grɑ:vl] v/i fig arrastrarse

grow [groʊ] v/i (pret **grew**, pp **grown**) crecer; of number, amount crecer, incrementarse; **grow old / tired** envejecer / cansarse **2** v/t (pret **grew**, pp **grown**) flowers cultivar

◆ **grow up** v/i of person, city crecer; **grow up!** ¡no seas crío!

growl [graʊl] **1** n gruñido m **2** v/i gruñir

grown [groʊn] pp → **grow**

grown-up ['groʊnʌp] **1** n adulto(-a) m(f) **2** adj maduro

growth [groʊθ] of person, economy crecimiento m; (increase) incremento m; MED bulto m

grub [grʌb] of insect larva f, gusano

grub·by ['grʌbɪ] adj mugriento m

grudge [grʌdʒ] **1** n rencor m; **bear s.o. a grudge** guardar rencor a alguien **2** v/t: **grudge s.o. sth** feel envy envidiar algo a alguien

grudg·ing ['grʌdʒɪŋ] adj rencoroso

grudg·ing·ly ['grʌdʒɪŋlɪ] adv de mala gana

gru·el·ing, Br **gru·el·ling** ['gru:əlɪŋ] adj agotador

gruff [grʌf] adj seco, brusco

grum·ble ['grʌmbl] v/i murmurar, refunfuñar

grum·bler ['grʌmblər] quejica m/f

grump·y ['grʌmpɪ] adj cascarrabias

grunt [grʌnt] **1** n gruñido m **2** v/i gruñir

G

guar·an·tee [gærən'tiː] **1** n garantía f; **guarantee period** periodo m de garantía **2** v/t garantizar

guar·an·tor [gærən'tɔːr] garante m/f

guard [gɑːrd] **1** n (security guard) guardia m/f, guarda m/f; MIL guardia f; in prison guardián (-ana) m(f); **be on one's guard against** estar en guardia contra **2** v/t guardar, proteger

◆ guard against v/t evitar

'guard dog perro m guardián

guard·ed ['gɑːrdɪd] adj reply cauteloso

guard·i·an ['gɑːrdɪən] LAW tutor(a) m(f)

guard·i·an 'an·gel ángel m de la guardia

Gua·te·ma·la [gwætə'mɑːlə] n Guatemala

Gua·te·ma·lan [gwætə'mɑːlən] **1** adj guatemalteco **2** n guatemalteco(-a) m(f)

guer·ril·la [gə'rɪlə] guerrillero(-a) m(f)

guer·ril·la 'war·fare guerra f de guerrillas

guess [ges] **1** n conjetura f, suposición f **2** v/t the answer adivinar; **I guess so** me imagino or supongo que sí; **I guess not** me imagino or supongo que no **3** v/i adivinar

'guess·work conjeturas fpl

guest [gest] invitado(-a) m(f)

'guest·house casa f de huéspedes

'guest·room habitación f para invitados

guf·faw [gʌ'fɔː] **1** n carcajada f, risotada f **2** v/i carcajearse

guid·ance ['gaɪdəns] orientación f, consejo m

guide [gaɪd] **1** n person guía m/f; book guía f **2** v/t guiar

'guide·book guía f

guid·ed mis·sile ['gaɪdɪd] misil m teledirigido

'guide dog Br perro m lazarillo

guid·ed 'tour visita f guiada

'guide·lines ['gaɪdlaɪnz] npl directrices fpl, normas fpl generales

guilt [gɪlt] culpa f, culpabilidad f; LAW culpabilidad f

guilt·y ['gɪltɪ] adj also LAW culpable; **be guilty of sth** ser culpable de algo; **have a guilty conscience** tener remordimientos de conciencia

guin·ea pig ['gɪnɪpɪg] conejillo m de Indias, cobaya f; fig conejillo m de Indias

guise [gaɪz] apariencia f; **under the guise of** bajo la apariencia de

gui·tar [gɪ'tɑːr] guitarra f

gui·tar case estuche m de guitarra

gui·tar·ist [gɪ'tɑːrɪst] guitarrista m/f

gui·tar play·er guitarrista m/f

gulf [gʌlf] golfo m; fig abismo m; **the Gulf** el Golfo

Gulf of 'Mex·i·co Golfo m de México

gull [gʌl] bird gaviota f

gul·let ['gʌlɪt] ANAT esófago m

gul·li·ble ['gʌlɪbl] adj crédulo, ingenuo

gulp [gʌlp] **1** n of water etc trago m **2** v/i in surprise tragar saliva

◆ gulp down v/t drink tragar; food engullir

gum¹ [gʌm] in mouth encía f

gum² [gʌm] n (glue) pegamento m, cola f; (chewing gum) chicle m

gump·tion ['gʌmpʃn] sentido m común

gun [gʌn] pistol, revolver pistola f; rifle rifle m; cannon cañón m

◆ gun down v/t (pret & pp gunned) matar a tiros

'gun·fire disparos mpl

'gun·man hombre m armado

'gun·point: **at gunpoint** a punta de pistola

'gun·shot disparo m, tiro m

'gun·shot wound herida f de bala

gur·gle ['gɜːrgl] v/i of baby gorjear; of drain gorgotear

gu·ru ['guru] fig gurú m

gush [gʌʃ] v/i of liquid manar, salir a chorros

gush·y ['gʌʃɪ] adj F (enthusiastic) efusivo, exagerado

gust [gʌst] ráfaga f

gus·to ['gʌstou] entusiasmo m; **with gusto** con entusiasmo

gust·y ['gʌstɪ] adj weather ventoso, con viento racheado; **gusty wind** viento m racheado

gut [gʌt] **1** n intestino m; F (stomach) tripa f F **2** v/t (pret & pp gutted) (destroy) destruir

guts [gʌts] npl F (courage) agallas fpl F

guts·y ['gʌtsɪ] adj F (brave) valiente, con muchas agallas F

gut·ter ['gʌtər] on sidewalk cuneta f; on roof canal m, canalón m

guy [gaɪ] F tipo m F, Span tío m F; **hey, you guys** eh, gente

guz·zle ['gʌzl] v/t tragar, engullir

gym [dʒɪm] gimnasio m

gym·na·si·um [dʒɪm'neɪzɪəm] gimnasio m

gym·nast ['dʒɪmnæst] gimnasta m/f

gym·nas·tics [dʒɪm'næstɪks] gimnasia f

'gym shoes npl zapatillas fpl de gimnasia

gy·nae·col·o·gy etc Br → gynecology etc

gy·ne·col·o·gy [gaɪnɪ'kɑːlədʒɪ] ginecología f

gy·ne·col·o·gist [gaɪnɪ'kɑːlədʒɪst] ginecólogo(-a) m(f)

gyp·sy ['dʒɪpsɪ] gitano(-a) m(f)

H

hab·it ['hæbɪt] hábito m, costumbre m; **get into the habit of doing sth** adquirir el hábito de hacer algo

hab·it·a·ble ['hæbɪtəbl] adj habitable

hab·i·tat ['hæbɪtæt] hábitat m

ha·bit·u·al [hə'bɪtʊəl] adj habitual

hack [hæk] n poor writer gacetillero(-a) m(f)

hack·er ['hækər] COMPUT pirata m/f informático(-a)

hack·neyed ['hæknɪd] adj manido

had [hæd] pret & pp → **have**

had·dock ['hædək] eglefino m

hag·gard ['hægərd] adj demacrado

hag·gle ['hægl] v/i regatear; **haggle over sth** regatear algo

hail [heɪl] n granizo m

'hail·stone piedra f de granizo

'hail·storm granizada f

hair [her] pelo m, cabello m; single pelo m; (body hair) vello m; **have short / long hair** tener el pelo corto / largo

'hair·brush cepillo m

'hair·cut corte m de pelo; **have a haircut** cortarse el pelo

'hair·do F peinado m

'hair·dress·er peluquero(-a) m(f); **at the hairdresser** en la peluquería

'hair·dri·er, 'hair·dry·er secador m (de pelo)

hair·less ['herlɪs] adj sin pelo

'hair·pin horquilla f

hair·pin 'bend curva f muy cerrada

hair-rais·ing ['herreɪzɪŋ] adj espeluznante

hair re·mov·er [herrɪ'muːvər] depilatorio m

'hair's breadth fig: **by a hair's breadth** por un pelo

hair-split·ting ['hersplɪtɪŋ] n sutilezas fpl

'hair spray laca f

'hair·style peinado m

'hair·styl·ist estilista m/f, peluquero(-a) m(f)

hair·y ['herɪ] adj arm, animal peludo; F (frightening) espeluznante

half [hæf] **1** n (pl halves [hævz]) mitad f; **half past ten** las diez y media; **half after ten** las diez y media; **half an hour** media hora; **half a pound** media libra; **go halves with s.o. on sth** ir a medias con alguien en algo **2** adj medio; **at half price** a mitad de precio **3** adv a medias; **half finished** a medio acabar

half 'board Br media pensión f

half-heart·ed [hæf'hɑːrtɪd] adj desganado

half 'time **1** n SP descanso m **2** adj: **half time job** trabajo m a tiempo parcial; **half time score** marcador m en el descanso

half'way **1** adj stage, point intermedio **2** adv a mitad de camino

hall [hɔːl] large room sala f; (hallway in house) vestíbulo m

Hal·low·e·en [hælou'wiːn] víspera de Todos los Santos

halo ['heɪlou] halo m

halt [hɔːlt] **1** v/i detenerse **2** v/t detener **3** n alto m; **come to a halt** detenerse

halve [hæv] v/t input, costs, effort reducir a la mitad; apple partir por la mitad

ham [hæm] jamón m

ham·burg·er ['hæmbɜːrgər] hamburguesa f

ham·mer ['hæmər] **1** n martillo m **2** v/i: **hammer at the door** golpear la puerta

ham·mock ['hæmək] hamaca f

ham·per¹ ['hæmpər] n for food cesta f

ham·per² v/t (obstruct) estorbar, obstaculizar

ham·ster ['hæmstər] hámster m

hand [hænd] n mano m; of clock manecilla f; (worker) brazo m; **at hand, to hand** a mano; **at first hand** de primera mano, directamente; **by hand** a mano; **on the one hand ..., on the other hand** por una parte ..., por otra parte; **the work is in hand** se está llevando a cabo; **on your right hand** a mano derecha; **hands off!** ¡fuera las manos!; **hands up!** ¡arriba las manos!; **change hands** cambiar de manos; **give s.o. a hand** echar un a mano a alguien

◆ hand down v/t transmitir

◆ hand in v/t entregar

◆ hand on v/t pasar

◆ hand out v/t repartir

◆ hand over v/t entregar

'hand·bag Br bolso m, L.Am. cartera f

'hand·book manual m

'hand·cuff v/t esposar

hand·cuffs ['hæn(d)kʌfs] npl esposas fpl

hand·i·cap ['hændɪkæp] n desventaja f

hand·i·capped ['hændɪkæpt] adj physically minusválido, disminuido; **handicapped by lack of funds** en desventaja por carecer de fondos

hand·i·craft ['hændɪkræft] artesanía f

hand·i·work ['hændɪwɜːrk] manualidades *fpl*

hand·ker·chief ['hæŋkərtʃɪf] pañuelo *m*

han·dle ['hændl] **1** *n of door* manilla *f; of suitcase* asa *f; of pan, knife* mango *m* **2** *v/t goods, difficult person* manejar; *case, deal* llevar, encargarse de; *let me handle this* deja que me ocupe yo de esto

han·dle·bars ['hændlbɑːrz] *npl* manillar *m*, *L.Am.* manubrio *m*

'**hand lug·gage** equipaje *m* de mano

hand·made [hæn(d)'meɪd] *adj* hecho a mano

'**hand·rail** barandilla *f*

'**hand·shake** apretón *m* de manos

hands-off [hændz'ɑːf] *adj* no intervencionista

hand·some ['hænsəm] *adj* guapo, atractivo

hands-on [hændz'ɑːn] *adj* práctico; *he has a hands-on style of management* le gusta implicarse en todos los aspectos de la gestión

'**hand·writ·ing** caligrafía *f*

hand·writ·ten ['hændrɪtn] *adj* escrito a mano

hand·y ['hændɪ] *adj tool, device* práctico; *it's handy for the shops* está muy cerca de las tiendas; *it might come in handy* nos puede venir muy bien

hang [hæŋ] **1** *v/t (pret & pp hung)* *picture* colgar; *person* colgar, ahorcar *(pret & pp hanged)* **2** *v/i (pret & pp hung)* colgar; *of dress, hair* caer, colgar **3** *n*: *get the hang of sth* F agarrarle el tranquillo a algo F

◆ **hang about** *v/i*: *he's always hanging about on the street corner* siempre está rondando por la esquina; *hang about a minute!* F ¡un momento!

◆ **hang on** *v/i (wait)* esperar

◆ **hang on to** *v/t (keep)* conservar; *do you mind if I hang on to it for a while?* ¿te importa si me lo quedo durante un tiempo?

◆ **hang up** *v/i* TELEC colgar

han·gar ['hæŋər] hangar *m*

hang·er ['hæŋər] *for clothes* percha *f*

hang glid·er ['hæŋglaɪdər] *person* piloto *m* de ala delta; *device* ala *f* delta

hang glid·ing ['hæŋglaɪdɪŋ] ala *f* delta

'**hang·o·ver** resaca *f*

◆ **han·ker after** ['hæŋkər] *v/t* anhelar

han·kie, han·ky ['hæŋkɪ] F pañuelo *m*

hap·haz·ard [hæp'hæzərd] *adj* descuidado

hap·pen ['hæpn] *v/i* ocurrir, pasar, suceder; *if you happen to see him* si por casualidad lo vieras; *what has happened to you?* ¿qué te ha pasado?

◆ **happen across** *v/t* encontrar por casualidad

hap·pen·ing ['hæpnɪŋ] suceso *m*

hap·pi·ly ['hæpɪlɪ] *adv* alegremente; *(luckily)* afortunadamente

hap·pi·ness ['hæpɪnɪs] felicidad *f*

hap·py ['hæpɪ] *adj* feliz, contento; *coincidence* afortunado

hap·py-go-'luck·y *adj* despreocupado

'**hap·py hour** franja horaria en la que las bebidas son más baratas en los bares

har·ass [hə'ræs] *v/t* acosar; *enemy* asediar, hostigar

har·assed [hər'æst] *adj* agobiado

har·ass·ment [hə'ræsmənt] acoso *m*; *sexual harassment* acoso *m* sexual

har·bor, *Br* **har·bour** ['hɑːrbər] **1** *n* puerto *m* **2** *v/t criminal* proteger; *grudge* albergar

hard [hɑːrd] *adj* duro; *(difficult)* difícil; *facts, evidence* real; *hard of hearing* duro de oído

'**hard·back** *n* libro *m* de tapas duras

hard-boiled [hɑːrd'bɔɪld] *adj egg* duro

'**hard cop·y** copia *f* impresa

'**hard core** *n (pornography)* porno *m* duro

hard 'cur·ren·cy divisa *f* fuerte

hard 'disk disco *m* duro

hard·en ['hɑːrdn] **1** *v/t* endurecer **2** *v/i of glue, attitude* endurecerse

'**hard hat** casco *m; (construction worker)* obrero(-a) *m(f)* (de la construcción)

hard-head·ed [hɑːrd'hedɪd] *adj* pragmático

hard-heart·ed [hɑːrd'hɑːrtɪd] *adj* insensible

'**hard line** línea *f* dura; *take a hard line on* adoptar una línea dura en cuanto a

hard 'lin·er partidario(-a) *m(f)* de la línea dura

hard·ly ['hɑːrdlɪ] *adv* apenas; *did you agree? - hardly!* ¿estuviste de acuerdo? - ¡en absoluto!

hard·ness ['hɑːrdnɪs] dureza *f*; *(difficulty)* dificultad *f*

hard 'sell venta *f* agresiva

hard·ship ['hɑːrdʃɪp] penuria *f*, privación *f*

hard 'up *adj*: *be hard up* andar mal de dinero

'**hard·ware** ferretería *f*; COMPUT hardware *m*

'**hard·ware store** ferretería *f*

hard-work·ing [hɑːrd'wɜːrkɪŋ] *adj* trabajador

har·dy ['hɑːrdɪ] *adj* resistente

hare [her] liebre *f*

hare-brained ['herbreɪnd] *adj* alocado

harm [hɑːrm] **1** *n* daño *m; it wouldn't do*

any harm to buy two por comprar dos no pasa nada **2** v/t hacer daño a, dañar
harm·ful ['hɑːrmfəl] adj dañino, perjudicial
harm·less ['hɑːrmlɪs] adj inofensivo; *fun* inocente
har·mo·ni·ous [hɑːr'moʊnɪəs] adj armonioso
har·mo·nize ['hɑːrmənaɪz] v/i armonizar
har·mo·ny ['hɑːrmənɪ] MUS, *fig* armonía f
harp [hɑːrp] n arpa f
◆ **harp on about** v/t F dar la lata con F
har·poon [hɑːr'puːn] n arpón m
harsh [hɑːrʃ] adj *criticism, words* duro, severo; *color* chillón; *light* potente
harsh·ly ['hɑːrʃlɪ] adv con dureza *or* severidad
har·vest ['hɑːrvɪst] n cosecha f
hash [hæʃ] F: **make a hash of** fastidiar
hash browns npl Span patatas fpl or *L.Am.* papas fpl fritas
hash·ish ['hæʃiːʃ] n hachís m
'**hash mark** almohadilla f, el signo '#'
haste [heɪst] n prisa f
has·ten ['heɪsn] v/i: **hasten to do sth** apresurarse en hacer algo
hast·i·ly ['heɪstɪlɪ] adv precipitadamente
hast·y ['heɪstɪ] adj precipitado
hat [hæt] n sombrero m
hatch [hætʃ] n *for serving food* trampilla f; *on ship* escotilla f
◆ **hatch out** v/i *of eggs* romperse; *of chicks* salir del cascarón
hatch·et ['hætʃɪt] n hacha f; **bury the hatchet** enterrar el hacha de guerra
hate [heɪt] **1** n odio m **2** v/t odiar
ha·tred ['heɪtrɪd] n odio m
haugh·ty ['hɔːtɪ] adj altanero
haul [hɔːl] **1** n *of fish* captura f; *of robbery* botín m **2** v/t *(pull)* arrastrar
haul·age ['hɔːlɪdʒ] transporte m
'**haul·age com·pa·ny** empresa f de transporte
haul·i·er ['hɔːlɪr] transportista m
haunch [hɔːntʃ] *of person* trasero m; *of animal* pierna f
haunt [hɔːnt] **1** v/t: **this place is haunted** en este lugar hay fantasmas **2** n lugar m favorito
have [hæv] **1** v/t *(pret & pp had) (own)* tener ◇ *breakfast, lunch* tomar
◇ **I don't have a TV** no tengo televisión; **can I have a coffee?** ¿me da un café?; **can I have more time?** ¿me puede dar más tiempo?; **do you have ...?** ¿tiene ...?
◇ *must:* **have (got) to** tener que

◇ *causative:* **I'll have it faxed to you** te lo mandaré por fax; **I'll have it repaired** haré que lo arreglen; **I had my hair cut** me corté el pelo
◇ *v/aux:* **I have eaten** he comido; **have you seen her?** ¿la has visto?
◆ **have back** v/t: **when can I have it back?** ¿cuándo me lo devolverá?
◆ **have on** v/t *(wear)* llevar puesto; **do you have anything on tonight?** *(have planned)* ¿tenéis algo planeado para esta noche?
ha·ven ['heɪvn] *fig* refugio m
hav·oc ['hævək] estragos mpl; **play havoc with** hacer estragos en
hawk [hɔːk] *also fig* halcón m
hay [heɪ] heno m
'**hay fe·ver** fiebre f del heno
haz·ard ['hæzərd] n riesgo m, peligro m
'**haz·ard lights** npl MOT luces fpl de emergencia
haz·ard·ous ['hæzərdəs] adj peligroso, arriesgado; **hazardous waste** residuos mpl peligrosos
haze [heɪz] neblina f
ha·zel ['heɪzl] n *tree* avellano m
'**ha·zel·nut** avellana f
ha·zy ['heɪzɪ] adj *image, memories* confuso, vago; **I'm a bit hazy about it** no lo tengo muy claro
he [hiː] pron él; **he is French/a doctor** es francés / médico; **you're funny, he's not** tú tienes gracia, él no
head [hed] **1** n cabeza f; *(boss, leader)* jefe(-a) m(f); *of school* director(a) m(f); *on beer* espuma f; *of nail, line* cabeza f; **$15 a head** 15 dólares por cabeza; **heads or tails?** ¿cara o cruz?; **at the head of the list** encabezando la lista; **head over heels** *fall* rodando; *fall in love* locamente; **lose one's head** *(go crazy)* perder la cabeza **2** v/t *(lead)* estar a la cabeza de; *ball* cabecear
◆ **head for** v/t dirigirse a *or* hacia
'**head·ache** dolor m de cabeza
'**head·band** cinta f para la cabeza
head·er ['hedər] *in soccer* cabezazo m; *in document* encabezamiento m
'**head·hunt** v/t COM buscar, captar
'**head·hunt·er** COM cazatalentos m/f inv
head·ing ['hedɪŋ] *in list* encabezamiento m
'**head·lamp** faro m
'**head·light** faro m
'**head·line** n *in newspaper* titular m; **make the headlines** saltar a los titulares
'**head·long** adv *fall* de cabeza
'**head·mas·ter** director m
'**head·mis·tress** directora f

H

head 'of·fice *of company* central *f*

head-'on **1** *adv* crash de frente **2** *adj* crash frontal

'head·phones *npl* auriculares *mpl*

'head·quar·ters *npl of party, organization* sede *f; of army* cuartel *m* general

'head·rest reposacabezas *f inv*

'head·room *under bridge* gálibo *m; in car* espacio *m* vertical

'head·scarf pañuelo *m* (para la cabeza)

'head·strong *adj* cabezudo, testarudo

head 'teach·er director(a) *m(f)*

head 'wait·er maître *m*

'head·wind viento *m* contrario

head·y ['hedɪ] *adj drink, wine etc* que se sube a la cabeza

heal [hiːl] *v/t* curar

◆ heal up *v/i* curarse

health [helθ] salud *f; your health!* ¡a tu salud!

'health club gimnasio *m* (*con piscina, pista de tenis, sauna etc*)

'health food comida *f* integral

'health food store tienda *f* de comida integral

'health in·su·rance seguro *m* de enfermedad

'health re·sort centro *m* de reposo

health·y ['helθɪ] *adj person* sano; *food, lifestyle* saludable; *economy* saneado

heap [hiːp] *n* montón *m*

◆ heap up *v/t* amontonar

hear [hɪr] *v/t & v/i (prêt & pp* **heard**) oír

◆ hear about *v/t*: **have you heard about Mike?** ¿te has enterado de lo de Mike?; **they're bound to hear about it sooner or later** se van a enterar tarde o temprano

◆ hear from *v/t (have news from)* tener noticias de

hear·ing ['hɪrɪŋ] oído *m;* LAW vista *f; his hearing is not so good now* ahora ya no oye tan bien; **she was within hearing / out of hearing** estaba / no estaba lo suficientemente cerca como para oírlo

'hear·ing aid audífono *m*

'hear·say rumores *mpl;* **by hearsay** de oídas

hearse [hɜːrs] coche *m* fúnebre

heart [hɑːrt] *also fig* corazón *m; of problem* meollo *m;* **know sth by heart** saber algo de memoria; **hearts** *in cards* corazones *mpl*

'heart at·tack infarto *m*

'heart·beat latido *m*

'heart·break·ing ['hɑːrtbreɪkɪŋ] *adj* desgarrador

'heart·brok·en *adj* descorazonado

'heart·burn acidez *f* (de estómago)

'heart fail·ure paro *m* cardíaco

heart·felt ['hɑːrtfelt] *adj sympathy* sincero

hearth [hɑːrθ] chimenea *f*

heart·less ['hɑːrtlɪs] *adj* despiadado

heart-rend·ing ['hɑːrtrendɪŋ] *adj plea, sight* desgarrador

'heart throb F ídolo *m*

'heart trans·plant transplante *m* de corazón

heart·y ['hɑːrtɪ] *adj appetite* voraz; *meal* copioso; *person* cordial, campechano

heat [hiːt] *n* calor *m*

◆ heat up *v/t* calentar

heat·ed ['hiːtɪd] *adj swimming pool* climatizado; *discussion* acalorado

heat·er ['hiːtər] *in room* estufa *f;* **turn on the heater** *in car* enciende la calefacción

hea·then ['hiːðn] *n* pagano(-a) *m(f)*

heath·er ['heðər] brezo *m*

heat·ing ['hiːtɪŋ] calefacción *f*

'heat·proof, 'heat-re·sis·tant *adj* resistente al calor

'heat·stroke insolación *f*

'heat·wave ola *f* de calor

heave [hiːv] *v/t (lift)* subir

heav·en ['hevn] cielo *m;* **good heavens!** ¡Dios mío!

heav·en·ly ['hevnlɪ] *adj* F divino F

heav·y ['hevɪ] *adj* heavy; *cold, rain, accent, loss* fuerte; *smoker, drinker* empedernido; *loss of life* grande; *bleeding* abundante; **there's heavy traffic** hay mucho tráfico

heav·y·'du·ty *adj* resistente

'heav·y·weight *adj* SP de los pesos pesados

heck·le ['hekl] *v/t* interrumpir (*molestando*)

hec·tic ['hektɪk] *adj* vertiginoso, frenético

hedge [hedʒ] *n* seto *m*

hedge·hog ['hedʒhɑːg] erizo *m*

hedge·row ['hedʒroʊ] seto *m*

heed [hiːd] *v/t:* **pay heed to ...** hacer caso de ...

heel [hiːl] *of foot* talón *m; of shoe* tacón *m*

'heel bar zapatería *f*

hef·ty ['heftɪ] *adj weight, suitcase* pesado; *person* robusto

height [haɪt] altura *f;* **at the height of the season** en plena temporada

height·en ['haɪtn] *v/t effect, tension* intensificar

heir [er] heredero *m*

heir·ess ['erɪs] heredera *f*

held [held] *pret & pp* → **hold**

hel·i·cop·ter ['helɪkɑːptər] helicóptero *m*

hell [hel] infierno *m;* **what the hell are you doing / do you want?** F ¿qué demonios estás haciendo / quieres? F: **go to hell!** F ¡vete a paseo! F; **a hell of a lot** un montonazo F; **one hell of a nice guy** un tipo muy simpático or Span legal F

hel·lo [hə'loʊ] hola; TELEC ¿sí?, Span ¿diga?, Am ¿aló?, Rpl ¿oigo?, Mex ¿bueno?; **say hello to s.o.** saludar a alguien

helm [helm] NAUT timón m

hel·met ['helmɪt] casco m

help [help] **1** n ayuda f; **help!** ¡socorro! **2** v/t ayudar; **just help yourself** to food toma lo que quieras; **I can't help it** no puedo evitarlo; **I couldn't help laughing** no pude evitar reírme

help·er ['helpər] ayudante m/f

help·ful ['helpfəl] adj advice útil; person servicial

help·ing ['helpɪŋ] of food ración f

help·less ['helplɪs] adj (unable to cope) indefenso; (powerless) impotente

help·less·ly ['helplɪslɪ] adv impotentemente

help·less·ness ['helplɪsnɪs] impotencia f

'help screen COMPUT pantalla f de ayuda

hem [hem] n of dress etc dobladillo m

hem·i·sphere ['hemɪsfɪr] hemisferio m

'hem·line bajo m

hem·or·rhage ['hemərɪdʒ] **1** n hemorragia f **2** v/i sangrar

hen [hen] gallina f

hench·man ['henʧmən] pej sicario m

'hen par·ty despedida f de soltera

hen·pecked ['henpekt] adj: **henpecked husband** calzonazos mpl

hep·a·ti·tis [hepə'taɪtɪs] hepatitis f

her [hɜːr] **1** adj su; **her ticket** su entrada; **her books** sus libros **2** pron direct object la; indirect object le; after prep ella; **I know her** la conozco; **I gave her the keys** le di las llaves; **I sold it to her** se lo vendí; **this is for her** esto es para ella; **who do you mean? - her** ¿a quién te refieres? - a ella

herb [ɜːrb] hierba f

herb(al) ['tea ['ɜːrb(ə)l] infusión f

herd [hɜːrd] n rebaño m; of elephants manada f

here [hɪr] adv aquí; **over here** aquí; **here's to you!** as toast ¡a tu salud!; **here you are** giving sth ¡aquí tienes!; **here we are!** finding sth ¡aquí está!

he·red·i·ta·ry [hə'redɪterɪ] adj disease hereditario

he·red·i·ty [hə'redɪtɪ] herencia f

her·i·tage ['herɪtɪdʒ] patrimonio m

her·mit ['hɜːrmɪt] ermitaño(-a) m(f)

her·ni·a ['hɜːrnɪə] MED hernia f

he·ro ['hɪroʊ] héroe m

he·ro·ic [hɪ'roʊɪk] adj heroico

he·ro·i·cal·ly [hɪ'roʊɪklɪ] adv heroicamente

her·o·in ['heroʊɪn] heroína f

'her·o·in ad·dict heroinómano(-a) m(f)

her·o·ine ['heroʊɪn] heroína f

her·o·ism ['heroʊɪzm] heroísmo m

her·on ['herən] garza f

her·pes ['hɜːrpiːz] MED herpes m

her·ring ['herɪŋ] arenque m

hers [hɜːrz] pron el suyo, la suya; **hers are red** los suyos son rojos; **that book is hers** ese libro es suyo; **a cousin of hers** un primo suyo

her·self [hɜːr'self] pron reflexive se; emphatic ella misma; **she hurt herself** se hizo daño; **when she saw herself in the mirror** cuando se vio en el espejo; **he saw it herself** lo vio ella misma; **by herself** (alone) sola; (without help) ella sola, ella misma

hes·i·tant ['hezɪtənt] adj indeciso

hes·i·tant·ly ['hezɪtəntlɪ] adv con indecisión

hes·i·tate ['hezɪteɪt] v/i dudar, vacilar

hes·i·ta·tion [hezɪ'teɪʃn] vacilación f

het·er·o·sex·u·al [hetəroʊ'sekʃʊəl] adj heterosexual

hey·day ['heɪdeɪ] apogeo m

hi [haɪ] int ¡hola!

hi·ber·nate ['haɪbərneɪt] v/i hibernar

hic·cup ['hɪkʌp] n hipo m; (minor problem) tropiezo m, traspié m; **have the hiccups** tener hipo

hick [hɪk] pej F palurdo(-a) m(f) F, pueblerino(-a) m(f) F

'hick town pej F ciudad f provinciana

hid [hɪd] pret → **hide¹**

hid·den ['hɪdn] **1** adj meaning, treasure oculto **2** pp → **hide¹**

hid·den a·gen·da fig objetivo m secreto

hide¹ [haɪd] **1** v/t (pret hid, pp hidden) esconder **2** v/i (pret hid, pp hidden) esconderse

hide² n of animal escondrijo m

hide-and-'seek escondite m

'hide·a·way escondite m

hid·e·ous ['hɪdɪəs] adj espantoso, horrendo; person repugnante

hid·ing¹ ['haɪdɪŋ] (beating) paliza f

hid·ing² ['haɪdɪŋ]: **be in hiding** estar escondido; **go into hiding** esconderse

'hid·ing place escondite m

hi·er·ar·chy ['haɪərɑːrkɪ] jerarquía f

hi-fi ['haɪfaɪ] equipo m de alta fidelidad

high [haɪ] **1** adj alto; wind fuerte; (on drugs) colocado P; **have a very high opinion of** tener muy buena opinión de; **high in the sky** en lo alto; **it is high time you understood** ya va siendo hora de que entiendas **2** n MOT directa f; *in statistics* máximo m; EDU escuela f secundaria, *Span* instituto m **3** adv: *that's as high as we can go* eso es lo máximo que podemos ofrecer

'high·brow adj intelectual

'high·chair trona f

high-'class adj de categoría

High 'Court Tribunal m Supremo

high 'div·ing salto m de trampolín

high-'fre·quen·cy adj de alta frecuencia

high-'grade adj de calidad superior

high-hand·ed [haɪˈhændɪd] adj despótico

high-'heeled [haɪˈhiːld] adj de tacón alto

'high jump salto m de altura

high-'lev·el adj de alto nivel

'high life buena vida f

'high·light **1** n (*main event*) momento m cumbre; *in hair* reflejo m **2** v/t *with pen* resaltar; COMPUT seleccionar, resaltar

'high·light·er *pen* fluorescente m

high·ly ['haɪlɪ] adv *desirable, likely* muy; *be highly paid* estar muy bien pagado; *think highly of s.o.* tener una buena opinión de alguien

high·ly 'strung adj muy nervioso

high per'form·ance adj *drill, battery* de alto rendimiento

high-pitched [haɪˈpɪtʃt] adj agudo

'high point *of life, career* punto m culminante

high-pow·ered [haɪˈpaʊərd] adj *engine* potente; *intellectual* de alto(s) vuelo(s); *salesman* enérgico

high 'pres·sure **1** n *weather* altas presiones fpl **2** adj TECH a gran presión; *salesman* agresivo; *job, lifestyle* muy estresante

high 'priest sumo sacerdote m

'high school escuela f secundaria, *Span* instituto m

high so'ci·e·ty alta sociedad f

high-speed 'train tren m de alta velocidad

high 'tech **1** n alta f tecnología **2** adj de alta tecnología

high 'tide marea f alta

high 'wa·ter: *at high water* con la marea alta

'high·way autopista f

'high wire *in circus* cuerda f floja

hi·jack ['haɪdʒæk] **1** v/t *plane, bus* secuestrar **2** n *of plane, bus* secuestro m

hi·jack·er ['haɪdʒækər] *of plane, bus* secuestrador(a) m(f)

hike¹ [haɪk] **1** n caminata f **2** v/i caminar

hike² [haɪk] n *in prices* subida f

hik·er ['haɪkər] senderista m/f

hik·ing ['haɪkɪŋ] senderismo m

'hik·ing boots npl botas fpl de senderismo

hi·lar·i·ous [hɪˈleriəs] adj divertidísimo, graciosísimo

hill [hɪl] colina f; (*slope*) cuesta f

hill·bil·ly ['hɪlbɪlɪ] F rústico montañés

hill·side ['hɪlsaɪd] ladera f

hill·top ['hɪltɑːp] cumbre f

hill·y ['hɪlɪ] adj con colinas

hilt [hɪlt] puño m

him [hɪm] pron direct object lo; indirect object le; after prep él; *I know him* lo conozco; *I gave him the keys* le di las llaves; *I sold it to him* se lo vendí; *this is for him* esto es para él; *who do you mean? - him* ¿a quién te refieres? - a él

him·self [hɪmˈself] pron reflexive se; emphatic él mismo; *he hurt himself* se hizo daño; *when he saw himself in the mirror* cuando se vio en el espejo; *he saw it himself* lo vio él mismo; *by himself* (*alone*) solo; (*without help*) él solo, él mismo

hind [haɪnd] adj trasero

hin·der ['hɪndər] v/t obstaculizar, entorpecer

hin·drance ['hɪndrəns] estorbo m, obstáculo m

hind·sight ['haɪndsaɪt]: *with hindsight* a posteriori

hinge [hɪndʒ] n bisagra f

♦ hinge on v/t depender de

hint [hɪnt] n (*clue*) pista f; (*piece of advice*) consejo m; (*implied suggestion*) indirecta f; *of red, sadness etc* rastro m

hip [hɪp] n cadera f

hip 'pock·et bolsillo m trasero

hip·po·pot·a·mus [hɪpəˈpɑːtəməs] hipopótamo m

hire [haɪr] v/t alquilar

his [hɪz] **1** adj su; *his ticket* su entrada, la suya; *his books* sus libros **2** pron el suyo, la suya; *his are red* los suyos son rojos; *that ticket is his* esa entrada es suya; *a cousin of his* un primo suyo

His·pan·ic [hɪˈspænɪk] **1** n hispano(-a) m(f) **2** adj hispano, hispánico

hiss [hɪs] v/i *of snake, audience* silbar

his·to·ri·an [hɪˈstɔːriən] historiador(a) m(f)

his·tor·ic [hɪˈstɑːrɪk] adj histórico

his·tor·i·cal [hɪˈstɑːrɪkl] adj histórico

his·to·ry ['hɪstərɪ] historia f

hit [hɪt] **1** v/t (*pret & pp hit*) golpear; (*collide with*) chocar contra; *he was hit by a bullet* le alcanzó una bala; *it suddenly hit me* (*I realized*) de repente me di cuenta; *hit town* (*arrive*) llegar a la ciudad **2** n (*blow*) golpe m; MUS, (*success*) éxito *m*

◆ **hit back** *v/i physically* devolver el golpe; *verbally*, *with actions* responder
◆ **hit on** *v/t idea* dar con
◆ **hit out** *v/t* (*criticize*) atacar

hit-and-run *adj*: **hit-and-run accident** accidente en el que el vehículo causante se da a la fuga

hitch [hɪtʃ] **1** *n* (*problem*) contratiempo *m*; *without a hitch* sin ningún contratiempo **2** *v/t* enganchar; *hitch sth to sth* enganchar algo a algo; *hitch a ride* hacer autoestop **3** *v/i* (*hitchhike*) hacer autoestop
◆ **hitch up** *v/t wagon, trailer* enganchar

'hitch·hike *v/i* hacer autoestop
'hitch·hik·er autoestopista *m/f*
'hitch·hik·ing autoestop *m*

hi-'tech 1 *n* alta tecnología *f* **2** *adj* de alta tecnología
'hit-list lista *f* de blancos
'hit-man asesino *m* a sueldo
hit-or-'miss *adj* a la buena ventura
'hit squad grupo *m* de intervención especial

HIV [eɪtʃaɪ'viː] *abbr* (= **human immuno-deficiency virus**) VIH *m* (= virus *m inv* de la inmunodeficiencia *humana*)
hive [haɪv] *for bees* colmena *f*
◆ **hive off** *v/t* (COM: *separate off*) desprenderse de

HIV-'pos·i·tive *adj* seropositivo
hoard [hɔːrd] **1** *n* reserva *f* **2** *v/t* hacer acopio de; *money* acumular
hoard·er ['hɔːrdər] acaparador(a) *m(f)*
hoarse [hɔːrs] *adj* ronco
hoax [hoʊks] *n* bulo *m*, engaño *m*; *bomb hoax* amenaza *f* falsa de bomba
hob [haːb] *on cooker* placa *f*
hob·ble ['haːbl] *v/i* cojear
hob·by ['haːbɪ] hobby *m*, afición *f*
ho·bo ['hoʊboʊ] F vagabundo(-a) *m(f)*
hock·ey ['haːkɪ] (*ice hockey*) hockey *m* sobre hielo
hog [haːg] *n* (*pig*) cerdo *m*, *L.Am.* chancho *m*
hoist [hɔɪst] **1** *n* montacargas *m inv*; *manual* elevador *m* **2** *v/t* (*lift*) levantar, subir; *flag* izar; *they hoisted the winner up onto their shoulders* subieron al ganador a hombros
ho·kum ['hoʊkəm] F (*nonsense*) tonterías *fpl*; (*sentimental stuff*) cursilería *f*
hold [hoʊld] **1** *v/t* (*pret & pp held*) *in hand* llevar; (*support, keep in place*) sostener; *passport, license* tener; *prisoner, suspect* retener; (*contain*) contener; *job, post* ocupar; *course* mantener; *hold my hand* dame la mano; *hold one's breath* aguantar la respiración; *he can hold*

his drink sabe beber; *hold s.o. responsible* hacer a alguien responsable; *hold that ...* (*believe, maintain*) mantener que ...; *hold the line, please* TELEC espere, por favor **2** *n in ship, plane* bodega *f*; *take hold of sth* agarrar algo; *lose one's hold on sth on rope* soltar algo; *on reality* perder el contacto con algo
◆ **hold against** *v/t*: *hold sth against s.o.* tener algo contra alguien
◆ **hold back 1** *v/t crowds* contener; *facts, information* guardar **2** *v/i* (*not tell all*): *I'm sure he's holding back* estoy seguro de que no dice todo lo que sabe
◆ **hold on** *v/i* (*wait*) esperar; *now hold on a minute!* ¡un momento!
◆ **hold on to** *v/t* (*keep*) guardar; *belief* aferrarse a
◆ **hold out 1** *v/t hand* tender; *prospect* ofrecer **2** *v/i of supplies* durar; (*survive*) resistir, aguantar
◆ **hold up 1** *v/t hand* levantar; *bank etc* atracar; (*make late*) retrasar; *I was held up by the traffic* he llegado tarde por culpa del tráfico; *hold sth up as an example* poner a alguien como ejemplo
◆ **hold with** *v/t* (*approve of*): *I don't hold with that sort of behavior* no me parece bien ese tipo de comportamiento

'hold·all *Br* bolsa *f*
hold·er ['hoʊldər] (*container*) receptáculo *m*; *of passport, ticket etc* titular *m/f*; *of record* poseedor(a) *m(f)*
'hold·ing com·pa·ny holding *m*
'hold·up (*robbery*) atraco *m*; (*delay*) retraso *m*
hole [hoʊl] *in sleeve, wood, bag* agujero *m*; *in ground* hoyo *m*
hol·i·day ['haːlədeɪ] *single day* día *f* de fiesta; *period* vacaciones *fpl*; *take a holiday* tomarse vacaciones
Hol·land ['haːlənd] Holanda *f*
hol·low ['haːloʊ] *adj object* hueco; *cheeks* hundido; *promise* vacío
hol·ly ['haːlɪ] acebo *m*
hol·o·caust ['haːləkɔːst] holocausto *m*
hol·o·gram ['haːləgræm] holograma *m*
hol·ster ['hoʊlstər] pistolera *f*
ho·ly ['hoʊlɪ] *adj* santo
Ho·ly 'Spir·it Espíritu *m* Santo
'Ho·ly Week Semana *f* Santa
home [hoʊm] **1** *n* casa *f*; (*native country*) tierra *f*; *for old people* residencia *f*; *New York is my home* Nueva York es mi hogar; *at home* (*in house*) en casa; (*in country*) en mi / su / nuestra tierra; *make yourself at home* ponte cómodo; *at home and abroad* en el país y en el extranjero; *at home* SP en casa; *work from ho-*

me trabajar desde casa **2** *adv* a casa; *go home* ir a casa; *to country* ir a mi / tu / su tierra; *to town, part of country* ir a mi / tu / su ciudad

'home ad·dress domicilio *m*

'home 'bank·ing telebanca *f*, banca *f* electrónica

'home·com·ing vuelta *f* a casa

home com'put·er *Span* ordenador *m*, *L.Am.* computadora *f* doméstica

home·less ['houmlis] *adj* sin casa; *the homeless* los sin casa

'home·lov·ing *adj* hogareño

home·ly ['houmli] *adj* (*homeloving*) hogareño; (*not good-looking*) feúcho

'home'made *adj* casero

'home match partido *m* en casa

'home 'mov·ie película *f* casera

ho·me·op·a·thy [houmi'ɑːpəθi] homeopatía *f*

'home page *web site* página *f* personal; *on web site* página *f* inicial

'home·sick *adj* nostálgico; *be homesick* tener morriña

'home town ciudad *f* natal

home·ward ['houmwərd] *adv to own house* a casa; *to own country* a mi país

'home·work EDU deberes *mpl*

'home·work·ing COM teletrabajo *m*

hom·i·cide ['hɑːmisaid] *crime* homicidio *m*; *police department* brigada *f* de homicidios

hom·o·graph ['hɑːməgræf] homógrafo *m*

ho·mo·pho·bi·a [hɑːmə'foubiə] homofobia *f*

ho·mo·sex·u·al [hɑːmə'sekʃuəl] **1** *adj* homosexual **2** *n* homosexual *m/f*

Hon·du·ras [hɑːn'dʊrəs] *n* Honduras

Hon·du·ran [hɑːn'dʊrən] **1** *adj* hondureño **2** *n* hondureño(-a) *m(f)*

hon·est ['ɑːnist] *adj* honrado

hon·est·ly ['ɑːnistli] *adv* honradamente; *honestly!* ¡desde luego!

hon·es·ty ['ɑːnisti] honradez *f*

hon·ey ['hʌni] miel *f*; F (*darling*) cariño *m*, vida *f* mía

'hon·ey·comb panal *m*

'hon·ey·moon *n* luna *f* de miel

honk [hɑːŋk] *v/t horn* tocar

hon·or ['ɑːnər] **1** *n* honor *m* **2** *v/t* honrar

hon·or·a·ble ['ɑːnrəbl] *adj* honorable

hon·our *etc Br* → **honor** *etc*

hood [hʊd] *over head* capucha *f*; *over cooker* campana *f* extractora; MOT capó *m*; F (*gangster*) matón(-ona) *m(f)*

hood·lum ['huːdləm] matón(-ona) *m(f)*

hoof [huːf] casco *m*

hook [hʊk] gancho *m*; *to hang clothes on* colgador *m*; *for fishing* anzuelo *m*; *off*

the hook TELEC descolgado

hooked [hʊkt] *adj* enganchado; *be hooked on sth on drugs, fig* estar enganchado a algo

hook·er® ['hʊkər] F fulana *f* F

hook·ey ['hʊki] F: *play hookey* hacer novillos, *Mex* irse de pinta, *S. Am.* hacerse la rabona

hoo·li·gan ['huːligən] gamberro(-a) *m(f)*

hoo·li·gan·ism ['huːligənizm] gamberrismo *m*

hoop [huːp] aro *m*

hoot [huːt] **1** *v/t horn* tocar **2** *v/i of car* dar bocinazos; *of owl* ulular

hoo·ver® ['huːvər] **1** *n* aspirador *m*, aspiradora *f* **2** *v/t carpets, room* pasar el aspirador por, aspirar

hop¹ [hɑːp] *n plant* lúpulo *m*

hop² [hɑːp] *v/i* (*pret & pp* **hopped**) saltar

hope [houp] **1** *n* esperanza *f*; *there's no hope of that* no hay esperanza de eso **2** *v/i* esperar; *hope for sth* esperar algo; *we all hope for peace* todos ansiamos la paz **3** *v/t: I hope you like it* espero que te guste; *I hope so* eso espero; *I hope not* espero que no

hope·ful ['houpfəl] *adj* prometedor; *I'm hopeful that ...* espero que ...

hope·ful·ly ['houpfəli] *adv say, wait* esperanzadamente; *hopefully he hasn't forgotten* esperemos que no se haya olvidado

hope·less ['houplis] *adj position, prospect* desesperado; (*useless: person*) inútil

ho·ri·zon [hə'raizn] horizonte *m*

hor·i·zon·tal [hɑːri'zɑːntl] *adj* horizontal

hor·mone ['hɔːrmoun] hormona *f*

horn [hɔːrn] *of animal* cuerno *m*; MOT bocina *f*, claxon *m*

hor·net ['hɔːrnit] avispón *m*

horn-rimmed 'spec·ta·cles ['hɔːrnrimd] *npl* gafas *fpl* de concha

horn·y ['hɔːrni] *adj* F *sexually* cachondo F

hor·o·scope ['hɑːrəskoup] horóscopo *m*

hor·ri·ble ['hɑːribl] *adj* horrible; *person* muy antipático

hor·ri·fy ['hɑːrifai] *v/t* (*pret & pp* **horrified**) horrorizar; *I was horrified* me quedé horrorizado

hor·ri·fy·ing ['hɑːrifaiiŋ] *adj* horroroso

hor·ror ['hɑːrər] horror *m*

'hor·ror mov·ie película *f* de terror

hors d'oeu·vre [ɔːr'dɜːrv] entremés *m*

horse [hɔːrs] caballo *m*

'horse·back: *on horseback* a caballo

horse 'chest·nut castaño *m* de Indias

'horse·pow·er caballo *m* (de vapor)

'horse race carrera *f* de caballos

'horse·shoe herradura *f*

hor·ti·cul·ture ['hɔːrtɪkʌltʃər] horticultura f

hose [houz] n manguera f

hos·pice ['hɑːspɪs] hospital m para enfermos terminales

hos·pi·ta·ble [hɑːˈspɪtəbl] adj hospitalario

hos·pi·tal ['hɑːspɪtl] hospital m; **go into the hospital** ir al hospital

hos·pi·tal·i·ty [hɑːspɪˈtælətɪ] hospitalidad f

host [houst] n at party, reception anfitrión m; of TV program presentador(a) m(f)

hos·tage ['hɑːstɪdʒ] rehén m; **take s.o. hostage** tomar a alguien como rehén

'hos·tage tak·er persona que toma rehenes

hos·tel ['hɑːstl] for students residencia f; (youth hostel) albergue m

hos·tess ['houstɪs] at party, reception anfitriona f; on airplane azafata f; in bar cabaretera f

hos·tile ['hɑːstl] adj hostil

hos·til·i·ty [hɑːˈstɪlətɪ] of attitude hostilidad f; **hostilities** hostilidades fpl

hot [hɑːt] adj weather caluroso; object, water, food caliente; (spicy) picante; **it's hot** of weather hace calor; **I'm hot** tengo calor; **she's pretty hot at math** F (good) es una fenómena con las matemáticas F

'hot dog perrito m caliente

ho·tel [houˈtel] hotel m

'hot·plate placa f

'hot spot military, political punto m caliente

hour [aur] hora f

hour·ly ['aurlɪ] adj: **at hourly intervals** a intervalos de una hora; **an hourly bus** un autobús que pasa cada hora

house [haus] n casa f; **at your house** en tu casa

'house·boat barco-vivienda f

'house·break·ing allanamiento m de morada

'house·hold hogar m

house·hold 'name nombre m conocido

'house hus·band amo m de casa

'house·keep·er ama f de llaves

'house·keep·ing activity tareas fpl domésticas; money dinero m para gastos domésticos

House of Rep·re·sen·ta·tives npl Cámara f de Representantes

house·warm·ing (par·ty) ['hauswɔːrmɪŋ] fiesta f de estreno de una casa

'house·wife ama f de casa

'house·work tareas fpl domésticas

hous·ing ['hauzɪŋ] vivienda f; TECH cubierta f

'hous·ing con·di·tions npl condiciones fpl de la vivienda

hov·el ['hɑːvl] chabola f

hov·er ['hɑːvər] v/i of bird cernerse; of helicopter permanecer inmóvil en el aire

'hov·er·craft aerodeslizador m, hovercraft m

how [hau] adv cómo; **how are you?** ¿cómo estás?; **how about ...?** ¿qué te parece ...?; **how about a drink?** ¿te apetece tomar algo?; **how much?** ¿cuánto?; **how much is it?** of cost ¿cuánto vale or cuesta?; **how many?** ¿cuántos?; **how often?** ¿con qué frecuencia?; **how funny / sad!** ¡qué divertido / triste!

how·ev·er adv sin embargo; **however big / rich / small they are** independientemente de lo grandes / ricos / pequeños que sean

howl [haul] v/i of dog aullido m; of person in pain alarido m; with laughter risotada f

howl·er ['haulər] (mistake) error m garrafal

hub [hʌb] of wheel cubo m

'hub·cap tapacubos m inv

◆ hud·dle to·geth·er ['hʌdl] v/i apiñarse, acurrucarse

hue [hjuː] tonalidad f

huff [hʌf]: **be in a huff** estar enfurruñado

hug [hʌg] v/t (pret & pp hugged) abrazar

huge [hjuːdʒ] adj enorme

hull [hʌl] casco m

hul·la·ba·loo [hʌləbəˈluː] alboroto m

hum [hʌm] 1 v/t (pret & pp hummed) song, tune tararear 2 v/i (pret & pp hummed) of person tararear; of machine zumbar

hu·man ['hjuːmən] 1 n humano m 2 adj humano; **human error** error m or fallo m humano

hu·man 'be·ing scr m humano

hu·mane [hjuːˈmeɪn] adj humano

hu·man·i·tar·i·an [hjuːmænɪˈterɪən] adj humanitario

hu·man·i·ty [hjuːˈmænətɪ] humanidad f

hu·man 'race raza f humana

hu·man re'sourc·es npl recursos mpl humanos

hum·ble ['hʌmbl] adj humilde

hum·drum ['hʌmdrʌm] adj monótono, anodino

hu·mid ['hjuːmɪd] adj húmedo

hu·mid·i·fi·er [hjuːˈmɪdɪfaɪr] humidificador m

hu·mid·i·ty [hjuːˈmɪdətɪ] humedad f

hu·mil·i·ate [hjuːˈmɪlɪeɪt] v/t humillar

hu·mil·i·at·ing [hjuːˈmɪlɪeɪtɪŋ] adj humillante

H

hu·mil·i·a·tion [hjuːmɪlɪˈeɪʃn] humillación f

hu·mil·i·ty [hjuːˈmɪlətɪ] humildad f

hu·mor [ˈhjuːmər] humor m; **sense of humor** sentido m del humor

hu·mor·ous [ˈhjuːmərəs] adj gracioso

hu·mour Br → **humor**

hump [hʌmp] 1 n of camel, person joroba f; on road bache m 2 v/t F (carry) acarrear

hunch [hʌntʃ] n (idea) presentimiento m, corazonada f

hun·dred [ˈhʌndrəd] cien m; **a hundred dollars** cien dólares; **hundreds of birds** cientos or centenares de aves; **a hundred and one** ciento uno; **two hundred** doscientos

hun·dredth [ˈhʌndrədθ] n & adj centésimo

'hun·dred·weight 43 kilogramos

hung [hʌŋ] pret & pp → **hang**

Hun·gar·i·an [hʌŋˈgerɪən] 1 adj húngaro 2 n person húngaro(-a) m(f); language húngaro m

Hun·ga·ry [ˈhʌŋgərɪ] Hungría

hun·ger [ˈhʌŋgər] n hambre f

hung·'o·ver adj: **be hung-over** tener resaca

hun·gry [ˈhʌŋgrɪ] adj hambriento; **I'm hungry** tengo hambre

hunk [hʌŋk] n cacho m, pedazo m; F man cachas m inv F

hun·ky-dor·y [hʌŋkɪˈdɔːrɪ] adj F: **everything's hunky-dory** todo va de perlas

hunt [hʌnt] 1 n caza f, búsqueda f 2 v/t animal cazar

◆ **hunt for** v/t buscar

hunt·er [ˈhʌntər] cazador(a) m(f)

hunt·ing [ˈhʌntɪŋ] caza f

hur·dle [ˈhɜːrdl] sp valla f; (fig: obstacle) obstáculo m

hur·dler [ˈhɜːrdlər] sp vallista m/f

hur·dles npl sp vallas fpl

hurl [hɜːrl] v/t lanzar

hur·ray [huˈreɪ] int ¡hurra!

hur·ri·cane [ˈhʌrɪkən] huracán m

hur·ried [ˈhʌrɪd] adj apresurado

hur·ry [ˈhʌrɪ] 1 n prisa f; **be in a hurry** tener prisa 2 v/i (pret & pp **hurried**) darse prisa

◆ **hurry up** v/i darse prisa; **hurry up!** ¡date prisa! 2 v/t meter prisa a

hurt [hɜːrt] 1 v/i (pret & pp **hurt**) doler; **does it hurt?** ¿te duele? 2 v/t (pret & pp **hurt**) physically hacer daño a; emotionally herir; **I've hurt my hand** me he hecho daño en la mano; **did he hurt you?** ¿te hizo daño?

hus·band [ˈhʌzbənd] marido m

hush [hʌʃ] n silencio m; **hush!** ¡silencio!

◆ **hush up** v/t scandal etc acallar

husk [hʌsk] of peanuts etc cáscara f

hus·ky [ˈhʌskɪ] adj voice áspero

hus·tle [ˈhʌsl] 1 n agitación f; **hustle and bustle** ajetreo m 2 v/t person empujar

hut [hʌt] cabaña f, refugio m; workman's cobertizo m

hy·a·cinth [ˈhaɪəsɪnθ] jacinto m

hy·brid [ˈhaɪbrɪd] n híbrido m

hy·drant [ˈhaɪdrənt] boca f de riego or de incendios

hy·drau·lic [haɪˈdrɔːlɪk] adj hidráulico

hy·dro·e·lec·tric [haɪdroʊɪˈlektrɪk] adj hidroeléctrico

'hy·dro·foil [ˈhaɪdrəfɔɪl] boat hidroplaneador m

hy·dro·gen [ˈhaɪdrədʒən] hidrógeno m

'hy·dro·gen bomb bomba f de hidrógeno

hy·giene [ˈhaɪdʒiːn] higiene f

hy·gien·ic [haɪˈdʒiːnɪk] adj higiénico

hymn [hɪm] himno m

hype [haɪp] n bombo m

hy·per·ac·tive [haɪpərˈæktɪv] adj hiperactivo

hy·per·sen·si·tive [haɪpərˈsensɪtɪv] adj hipersensible

hy·per·ten·sion [haɪpərˈtenʃn] hipertensión f

hy·per·text [ˈhaɪpərtekst] comput hipertexto m

hy·phen [ˈhaɪfn] guión m

hyp·no·sis [hɪpˈnoʊsɪs] hipnosis f

hyp·no·ther·a·py [hɪpnoʊˈθerəpɪ] hipnoterapia f

hyp·no·tize [ˈhɪpnətaɪz] v/t hipnotizar

hy·po·chon·dri·ac [haɪpəˈkɑːndrɪæk] n hipocondríaco(-a) m(f)

hy·poc·ri·sy [hɪˈpɑːkrəsɪ] hipocresía f

hyp·o·crite [ˈhɪpəkrɪt] hipócrita m/f

hyp·o·crit·i·cal [hɪpəˈkrɪtɪkl] adj hipócrita

hy·po·ther·mi·a [haɪpoʊˈθɜːrmɪə] hipotermia f

hy·poth·e·sis [haɪˈpɑːθəsɪs] (pl **hypotheses** [haɪˈpɑːθəsiːz]) hipótesis f inv

hy·po·thet·i·cal [haɪpəˈθetɪkl] adj hipotético

hys·ter·ec·to·my [hɪstəˈrektəmɪ] histerectomía f

hys·te·ri·a [hɪˈstɪrɪə] histeria f

hys·ter·i·cal [hɪˈsterɪkl] adj person, laugh histérico; F (very funny) tronchante F; **become hysterical** ponerse histérico

hys·ter·ics [hɪˈsterɪks] npl ataque f de histeria; (laughter) ataque f de risa

I

I [aɪ] *pron* yo; *I am English/a student* soy inglés / estudiante; *you're crazy, I'm not* tú estás loco, yo no

ice [aɪs] *in drink, on road* hielo *m*; *break the ice fig* romper el hielo

◆ **ice up** *v/i of engine, wings* helarse

ice·berg ['aɪsbɜːrg] iceberg *m*

'ice-box nevera *f*, *Rpl* heladera *f*

'ice-break·er *ship* rompehielos *m inv*

'ice cream helado *m*

'ice cream par·lor heladería *f*

'ice cube cubito *m* de hielo

iced [aɪst] *drink* helado

iced 'cof·fee café *m* helado

'ice hock·ey hockey *m* sobre hielo

'ice rink pista *f* de hielo

'ice skate patín *m* de cuchilla

'ice skat·ing patinaje *m* sobre hielo

i·ci·cle ['aɪsɪkl] carámbano *m*

i·con ['aɪkɑːn] *also* COMPUT icono *m*

i·cy ['aɪsɪ] *adj road* con hielo; *surface* helado; *welcome* frío

ID [aɪ'diː] *abbr* (= *identity*) documentación *f*; *have you got any ID on you?* ¿lleva algún tipo de documentación?

i·dea [aɪ'diːə] idea *f*; *good idea!* ¡buena idea!; *I have no idea* no tengo ni idea; *it's not a good idea to ...* no es buena idea ...

i·deal [aɪ'diːəl] *adj (perfect)* ideal

i·deal·is·tic [aɪdɪə'lɪstɪk] *adj* idealista

i·deal·ly [aɪ'diːəlɪ] *adv*: *ideally situated* en una posición ideal; *ideally, we would do it like this* lo ideal sería que lo hiciéramos así

i·den·ti·cal [aɪ'dentɪkl] *adj* idéntico; *identical twins* gemelos(-as) *mpl (fpl)* idénticos(-as)

i·den·ti·fi·ca·tion [aɪdentɪfɪ'keɪʃn] identificación *f*; *papers etc* documentación *f*

i·den·ti·fy [aɪ'dentɪfaɪ] *v/t (pret & pp identified)* identificar

i·den·ti·ty [aɪ'dentɪtɪ] identidad *f*; *identity card* carné *m* de identidad

i·de·o·log·i·cal [aɪdɪə'lɑːdʒɪkl] *adj* ideológico

i·de·ol·o·gy [aɪdɪ'ɑːlədʒɪ] ideología *f*

id·i·om ['ɪdɪəm] *(saying)* modismo *m*

id·i·o·mat·ic [ɪdɪə'mætɪk] *adj natural* natural

id·i·o·syn·cra·sy [ɪdɪə'sɪŋkrəsɪ] peculiaridad *f*, rareza *f*

id·i·ot ['ɪdɪət] idiota *m/f*, estúpido(-a) *m/f*

id·i·ot·ic [ɪdɪ'ɑːtɪk] *adj* idiota, estúpido

i·dle ['aɪdl] **1** *adj not working* desocupado; *(lazy)* vago; *threat* vano; *machinery* inactivo; *in an idle moment* en un momento libre **2** *v/i of engine* funcionar al ralentí

◆ **idle away** *v/t the time etc* pasar ociosamente

i·dol ['aɪdl] ídolo *m*

i·dol·ize ['aɪdəlaɪz] *v/t* idolatrar

i·dyl·lic [ɪ'dɪlɪk] *adj* idílico

if [ɪf] *conj* si; *if only I hadn't shouted at her* ojalá no le hubiera gritado

ig·nite [ɪg'naɪt] *v/t* inflamar

ig·ni·tion [ɪg'nɪʃn] *in car* encendido *m*; *ignition key* llave *m* de contacto

ig·no·rance ['ɪgnərəns] ignorancia *f*

ig·no·rant ['ɪgnərənt] *adj* ignorante; *(rude)* maleducado; *be ignorant of sth* desconocer *or* ignorar algo

ig·nore [ɪg'nɔːr] *v/t* ignorar; COMPUT omitir

ill [ɪl] *adj* enfermo; *fall ill, be taken ill* caer enfermo; *feel ill at ease* no sentirse a gusto, sentirse incómodo

il·le·gal [ɪ'liːgl] *adj* ilegal

il·le·gi·ble [ɪ'ledʒəbl] *adj* ilegible

il·le·git·i·mate [ɪlɪ'dʒɪtɪmət] *adj child* ilegítimo

ill-fat·ed [ɪl'feɪtɪd] *adj* infortunado

il·lic·it [ɪ'lɪsɪt] *adj* ilícito

il·lit·e·rate [ɪ'lɪtərət] *adj* analfabeto

ill-man·nered [ɪl'mænərd] *adj* maleducado

ill-na·tured [ɪl'neɪtʃərd] *adj* malhumorado

ill·ness ['ɪlnɪs] enfermedad *f*

il·log·i·cal [ɪ'lɑːdʒɪkl] *adj* ilógico

ill-tem·pered [ɪl'tempərd] *adj* malhumorado

ill'treat *v/t* maltratar

il·lu·mi·nate [ɪ'luːmɪneɪt] *v/t building etc* iluminar

il·lu·mi·nat·ing [ɪ'luːmɪneɪtɪŋ] *adj remarks etc* iluminador, esclarecedor

il·lu·sion [ɪ'luːʒn] ilusión *f*

il·lus·trate ['ɪləstreɪt] *v/t* ilustrar

il·lus·tra·tion [ɪlə'streɪʃn] ilustración *f*

il·lus·tra·tor [ɪlə'streɪtər] ilustrador(a) *m(f)*

ill 'will rencor *m*

im·age ['ɪmɪdʒ] imagen *f*; *he's the image of his father* es la viva imagen de su padre

'im·age-con·scious *adj* preocupado por la imagen

i·ma·gi·na·ble [ɪ'mædʒɪnəbl] *adj* imaginable; *the biggest / smallest size imaginable* la talla más grande / más pequeña que se pueda imaginar

i·ma·gi·na·ry [ɪ'mædʒɪnərɪ] *adj* imaginario

i·ma·gi·na·tion [ɪmædʒɪ'neɪʃn] imaginación *f*; *it's all in your imagination* son imaginaciones tuyas

i·ma·gi·na·tive [ɪ'mædʒɪnətɪv] *adj* imaginativo

i·ma·gine [ɪ'mædʒɪn] *v/t* imaginar, imaginarse; *I can just imagine it* me lo imagino; *you're imagining things* son imaginaciones tuyas

im·be·cile ['ɪmbəsiːl] imbécil *m/f*

IMF [aɪem'ef] *abbr* (= *International Monetary Fund*) FMI *m* (= Fondo *m* Monetario Internacional)

im·i·tate ['ɪmɪteɪt] *v/t* imitar

im·i·ta·tion [ɪmɪ'teɪʃn] imitación *f*; *learn by imitation* aprender imitando

im·mac·u·late [ɪ'mækjʊlət] *adj* inmaculado

im·ma·te·ri·al [ɪmə'tɪrɪəl] *adj* (*not relevant*) irrelevante

im·ma·ture [ɪmə'tʃʊər] *adj* inmaduro

im·me·di·ate [ɪ'miːdɪət] *adj* inmediato; *the immediate family* los familiares más cercanos; *in the immediate neighborhood* en las inmediaciones

im·me·di·ate·ly [ɪ'miːdɪətlɪ] *adv* inmediatamente; *immediately after the bank / church* justo después del banco / la iglesia

im·mense [ɪ'mens] *adj* inmenso

im·merse [ɪ'mɜːrs] *v/t* sumergir; *immerse o.s. in* sumergirse en

im·mer·sion heat·er [ɪ'mɜːrʃn] calentador *m* de agua eléctrico

im·mi·grant ['ɪmɪɡrənt] *n* inmigrante *m/f*

im·mi·grate ['ɪmɪɡreɪt] *v/i* inmigrar

im·mi·gra·tion [ɪmɪ'ɡreɪʃn] inmigración *f*; *Immigration government department* (Departamento *m* de) Inmigración *f*

im·mi·nent ['ɪmɪnənt] *adj* inminente

im·mo·bi·lize [ɪ'moʊbɪlaɪz] *v/t factory* paralizar; *person, car* inmovilizar

im·mo·bi·liz·er [ɪ'moʊbɪlaɪzər] *on car* inmovilizador *m*

im·mod·e·rate [ɪ'mɑːdərət] *adj* desmedido, exagerado

im·mor·al [ɪ'mɔːrəl] *adj* inmoral

im·mor·al·i·ty [ɪmɔː'rælɪtɪ] inmoralidad *f*

im·mor·tal [ɪ'mɔːrtl] *adj* inmortal

im·mor·tal·i·ty [ɪmɔːr'tælɪtɪ] inmortalidad *f*

im·mune [ɪ'mjuːn] *adj to illness, infection* inmune; *from ruling, requirement* con inmunidad

im·mune sys·tem MED sistema *m* inmunológico

im·mu·ni·ty [ɪ'mjuːnətɪ] inmunidad *f*; *diplomatic immunity* inmunidad *f* diplomática

im·pact ['ɪmpækt] *n* impacto *m*; *the warning had no impact on him* el aviso no le hizo cambiar lo más mínimo

im·pair [ɪm'per] *v/t* dañar

im·paired [ɪm'perd] *adj*: *with impaired hearing / sight* con problemas auditivos / visuales

im·par·tial [ɪm'pɑːrʃl] *adj* imparcial

im·pass·a·ble [ɪm'pæsəbl] *adj road* intransitable

im·passe ['ɪmpæs] *in negotiations etc* punto *m* muerto

im·pas·sioned [ɪm'pæʃnd] *adj speech, plea* apasionado

im·pas·sive [ɪm'pæsɪv] *adj* impasible

im·pa·tience [ɪm'peɪʃəns] impaciencia *f*

im·pa·tient [ɪm'peɪʃənt] *adj* impaciente

im·pa·tient·ly [ɪm'peɪʃəntlɪ] *adv* impacientemente

im·peach [ɪm'piːtʃ] *v/t President* iniciar un proceso de destitución contra

im·pec·ca·ble [ɪm'pekəbl] *adj* impecable

im·pec·ca·bly [ɪm'pekəblɪ] *adv* impecablemente

im·pede [ɪm'piːd] *v/t* dificultar

im·ped·i·ment [ɪm'pedɪmənt] *in speech* defecto *m* del habla

im·pend·ing [ɪm'pendɪŋ] *adj* inminente

im·pen·e·tra·ble [ɪm'penɪtrəbl] *adj* impenetrable

im·per·a·tive [ɪm'perətɪv] **1** *adj* imprescindible **2** *n* GRAM imperativo *m*

im·per·cep·ti·ble [ɪmpər'septɪbl] *adj* imperceptible

im·per·fect [ɪm'pɜːrfekt] **1** *adj* imperfecto **2** *n* GRAM imperfecto *m*

im·pe·ri·al [ɪm'pɪrɪəl] *adj* imperial

im·per·son·al [ɪm'pɜːrsənl] *adj* impersonal

im·per·so·nate [ɪm'pɜːrsəneɪt] *v/t as a joke* imitar; *illegally* hacerse pasar por

im·per·ti·nence [ɪm'pɜːrtɪnəns] impertinencia *f*

im·per·ti·nent [ɪm'pɜːrtɪnənt] *adj* impertinente

im·per·tur·ba·ble [ɪmpər'tɜːrbəbl] *adj* imperturbable

im·per·vi·ous [ɪm'pɜːrvɪəs] *adj*: *impervious to* inmune a

im·pe·tu·ous [ɪm'petʃʊəs] *adj* impetuoso

im·pe·tus ['ɪmpɪtəs] *of campaign etc* ímpetu *m*

im·ple·ment **1** *n* ['ɪmplɪmənt] utensilio *m* **2** *v/t* ['ɪmplɪment] *measures etc* poner en práctica

im·pli·cate ['ɪmplɪkeɪt] *v/t* implicar; *implicate s.o. in sth* implicar a alguien en algo

im·pli·ca·tion [ɪmplɪ'keɪʃn] consecuencia *f*; *the implication is that ...* implica que ...

im·plic·it [ɪm'plɪsɪt] *adj* implícito; *trust* inquebrantable

im·plore [ɪm'plɔːr] *v/t* implorar

im·ply [ɪm'plaɪ] *v/i* (*pret & pp implied*) implicar; *are you implying I lied?* ¿insinúas que mentí?

im·po·lite [ɪmpə'laɪt] *adj* maleducado

im·port ['ɪmpɔːrt] **1** *n* importación *f* **2** *v/t* importar

im·por·tance [ɪm'pɔːrtəns] importancia *f*

im·por·tant [ɪm'pɔːrtənt] *adj* importante

im·por·ter [ɪm'pɔːrtər] importador(a) *m(f)*

im·pose [ɪm'pouz] *v/t tax* imponer; *impose o.s. on s.o.* molestar a alguien

im·pos·ing [ɪm'pouzɪŋ] *adj* imponente

im·pos·si·bil·i·ty [ɪmpɑːsɪ'bɪlɪtɪ] imposibilidad *f*

im·pos·si·ble [ɪm'pɑːsɪbəl] *adj* imposible

im·pos·tor [ɪm'pɑːstər] impostor(a) *m(f)*

im·po·tence ['ɪmpətəns] impotencia *f*

im·po·tent ['ɪmpətənt] *adj* impotente

im·pov·er·ished [ɪm'pɑːvərɪʃt] *adj* empobrecido

im·prac·ti·cal [ɪm'præktɪkəl] *adj* poco práctico

im·press [ɪm'pres] *v/t* impresionar; *be impressed by s.o./sth* quedar impresionado por alguien / algo; *I'm not impressed* no me parece nada extraordinario

im·pres·sion [ɪm'preʃn] impresión *f*; (*impersonation*) imitación *f*; *make a good / bad impression on s.o.* causar a alguien buena / mala impresión; *I get the impression that ...* me da la impresión de que ...

im·pres·sion·a·ble [ɪm'preʃənəbl] *adj* influenciable

im·pres·sive [ɪm'presɪv] *adj* impresionante

im·print ['ɪmprɪnt] *n of credit card* impresión *f*

im·pris·on [ɪm'prɪzn] *v/t* encarcelar

im·pris·on·ment [ɪm'prɪznmənt] encarcelamiento *m*

im·prob·a·ble [ɪm'prɑːbəbəl] *adj* improbable

im·prop·er [ɪm'prɑːpər] *adj behavior* incorrecto

im·prove [ɪm'pruːv] *v/t & v/i* mejorar

im·prove·ment [ɪm'pruːvmənt] mejora *f*, mejoría *f*

im·pro·vise ['ɪmprəvaɪz] *v/i* improvisar

im·pu·dent ['ɪmpjudənt] *adj* insolente, desvergonzado

im·pulse ['ɪmpʌls] impulso *m*; *do sth on an impulse* hacer algo impulsivamente

'impulse buy compra *f* impulsiva

im·pul·sive [ɪm'pʌlsɪv] *adj* impulsivo

im·pu·ni·ty [ɪm'pjuːnətɪ] impunidad *f*; *with impunity* impunemente

im·pure [ɪm'pjur] *adj* impuro

in [ɪn] **1** *prep* ◇ en; *in Washington / Milan* en Washington / Milán; *in the street* en la calle; *in the box* en la caja; *put it in your pocket* métetelo en el bolsillo; *wounded in the leg / arm* herido en la pierna / el brazo

◇ *in 1999* en 1999; *in two hours from now* dentro de dos horas

◇ (*over period of*) en; *in the morning* por la mañana; *in the summer* en verano; *in August* en agosto

◇ *in English / Spanish* en inglés / español; *in a loud voice* en voz alta; *in his style* en su estilo; *in yellow* de amarillo

◇ *in crossing the road* (*while*) al cruzar la calle; *in agreeing to this* (*by virtue of*) al expresar acuerdo con esto

◇ *in his novel* en su novela; *in Faulkner* en Faulkner

◇ *three in all* tres en total; *one in ten* uno de cada diez **2** *adv*: *is he in?* *at home* ¿está en casa?; *is the express in yet?* ¿ha llegado ya el expreso?; *when the diskette is in* cuando el disquete está dentro; *in here* aquí dentro **3** *adj* (*fashionable, popular*) de moda; *be in* estar de moda

in·a·bil·i·ty [ɪnə'bɪlɪtɪ] incapacidad *f*

in·ac·ces·si·ble [ɪnək'sesɪbl] *adj* inaccesible

in·ac·cu·rate [ɪn'ækjurət] *adj* inexacto

in·ac·tive [ɪn'æktɪv] *adj* inactivo

in·ad·e·quate [ɪn'ædɪkwət] *adj* insuficiente

in·ad·vis·a·ble [ɪnəd'vaɪzəbl] *adj* poco aconsejable

in·an·i·mate [ɪn'ænɪmət] *adj* inanimado

in·ap·pro·pri·ate [ɪnə'prouprɪət] *adj remark, thing to do* inadecuado, improcedente; *choice* inapropiado

in·ar·tic·u·late [ɪnɑːr'tɪkjulət] *adj*: *be inarticulate* expresarse mal

in·au·di·ble [ɪn'ɔːdəbl] *adj* inaudible

in·au·gu·ral [ɪ'nɔːgjurəl] *adj speech* inaugural

in·au·gu·rate [ɪ'nɔːgjureɪt] *v/t* inaugurar

in·born ['ɪnbɔːrn] *adj* innato

in·breed·ing ['ɪnbriːdɪŋ] endogamia *f*

inc. *abbr* (= *incorporated*) S.A. (= sociedad *f* anónima)

in·cal·cu·la·ble [ɪnˈkælkjʊləbl] *adj damage* incalculable

in·ca·pa·ble [ɪnˈkeɪpəbl] *adj* incapaz; *be incapable of doing sth* ser incapaz de hacer algo

in·cen·di·a·ry de·vice [ɪnˈsendɪrɪ] artefacto *m* incendiario

in·cense¹ [ˈɪnsens] *n* incienso *m*

in·cense² [ɪnˈsens] *v/t* encolerizar

in·cen·tive [ɪnˈsentɪv] incentivo *m*

in·ces·sant [ɪnˈsesnt] *adj* incesante

in·ces·sant·ly [ɪnˈsesntlɪ] *adv* incesantemente

in·cest [ˈɪnsest] incesto *m*

inch [ɪntʃ] *n* pulgada *f*

in·ci·dent [ˈɪnsɪdənt] incidente *m*

in·ci·den·tal [ɪnsɪˈdentl] *adj* sin importancia; *incidental expenses* gastos *mpl* varios

in·ci·den·tal·ly [ɪnsɪˈdentlɪ] *adv* a propósito

in·cin·e·ra·tor [ɪnˈsɪnəreɪtər] incinerador *m*

in·ci·sion [ɪnˈsɪʒn] incisión *f*

in·ci·sive [ɪnˈsaɪsɪv] *adj* incisivo

in·cite [ɪnˈsaɪt] *v/t* incitar; *incite s.o. to do sth* incitar a alguien a que haga algo

in·cle·ment [ɪnˈklemənt] *adj* inclemente

in·cli·na·tion [ɪnklɪˈneɪʃn] *(tendency, liking)* inclinación *f*

in·cline [ɪnˈklaɪn] *v/t: be inclined to do sth* tender a hacer algo

in·close, in·clos·ure → **enclose, enclosure**

in·clude [ɪnˈkluːd] *v/t* incluir

in·clud·ing [ɪnˈkluːdɪŋ] *prep* incluyendo

in·clu·sive [ɪnˈkluːsɪv] **1** *adj price* total, global **2** *prep: inclusive of* incluyendo, incluido **3** *adv: from Monday to Thursday inclusive* de lunes al jueves, ambos inclusive; *it costs $1000 inclusive* cuesta 1.000 dólares todo incluido

in·co·her·ent *adj* incoherente

in·come [ˈɪnkəm] ingresos *mpl*

'in·come tax impuesto *m* sobre la renta

in·com·ing [ˈɪnkʌmɪŋ] *adj tide* que sube; *incoming flight* vuelo *m* que llega; *incoming mail* correo *m* recibido; *incoming calls* llamadas *fpl* recibidas

in·com·pa·ra·ble [ɪnˈkɑːmpərəbl] *adj* incomparable

in·com·pat·i·bil·i·ty [ɪnkəmpætɪˈbɪlɪtɪ] incompatibilidad *f*

in·com·pat·i·ble [ɪnkəmˈpætɪbl] *adj* incompatible

in·com·pe·tence [ɪnˈkɑːmpɪtəns] incompetencia *f*

in·com·pe·tent [ɪnˈkɑːmpɪtənt] *adj* incompetente

in·com·plete [ɪnkəmˈpliːt] *adj* incompleto

in·com·pre·hen·si·ble [ɪnkəmprɪˈhensɪbl] *adj* incomprensible

in·con·cei·va·ble [ɪnkənˈsiːvəbl] *adj* inconcebible

in·con·clu·sive [ɪnkənˈkluːsɪv] *adj* no concluyente

in·con·gru·ous [ɪnˈkɑːŋɡrʊəs] *adj* incongruente

in·con·sid·er·ate [ɪnkənˈsɪdərət] *adj* desconsiderado

in·con·sis·tent [ɪnkənˈsɪstənt] *adj argument, behavior* incoherente, inconsecuente; *player* irregular; *be inconsistent with sth* no ser consecuente con algo

in·con·so·la·ble [ɪnkənˈsoʊləbl] *adj* inconsolable, desconsolado

in·con·spic·u·ous [ɪnkənˈspɪkjʊəs] *adj* discreto

in·con·ve·ni·ence [ɪnkənˈviːnɪəns] *n* inconveniencia *f*

in·con·ve·ni·ent [ɪnkənˈviːnɪənt] *adj* inconveniente, inoportuno

in·cor·po·rate [ɪnˈkɔːrpəreɪt] *v/t* incorporar

in·cor·po·rat·ed [ɪnˈkɔːrpəreɪtɪd] *adj* COM: *ABC Incorporated* ABC, sociedad *f* anónima

in·cor·rect [ɪnkəˈrekt] *adj* incorrecto

in·cor·rect·ly [ɪnkəˈrektlɪ] *adv* incorrectamente

in·cor·ri·gi·ble [ɪnˈkɑːrɪdʒəbl] *adj* incorregible

in·crease 1 *v/t & v/i* [ɪnˈkriːs] aumentar **2** *n* [ˈɪnkriːs] aumento *m*

in·creas·ing [ɪnˈkriːsɪŋ] *adj* creciente

in·creas·ing·ly [ɪnˈkriːsɪŋlɪ] *adv* cada vez más; *we're getting increasingly concerned* cada vez estamos más preocupados

in·cred·i·ble [ɪnˈkredɪbl] *adj (amazing, very good)* increíble

in·crim·i·nate [ɪnˈkrɪmɪneɪt] *v/t* incriminar; *incriminate o.s.* incriminarse

in·cu·ba·tor [ˈɪnkjʊbeɪtər] incubadora *f*

in·cur [ɪnˈkɜːr] *v/t (pret & pp incurred) costs* incurrir en; *debts* contraer; *s.o's anger* provocar

in·cur·a·ble [ɪnˈkjʊrəbl] *adj* incurable

in·debt·ed [ɪnˈdetɪd] *adj: be indebted to s.o.* estar en deuda con alguien

in·de·cent [ɪnˈdiːsnt] *adj* indecente

in·de·ci·sive [ɪndɪˈsaɪsɪv] *adj* indeciso

in·de·ci·sive·ness [ɪndɪˈsaɪsɪvnɪs] indecisión *f*

in·deed [ɪnˈdiːd] *adv (in fact)* ciertamente,

efectivamente; *yes, agreeing* ciertamente, en efecto; *very much indeed* muchísimo; *thank you very much indeed* muchísimas gracias

in·de·fi·na·ble [ɪndɪˈfaɪnəbl] *adj* indefinible

in·def·i·nite [ɪnˈdefɪnɪt] *adj* indefinido; *indefinite article* GRAM artículo *m* indefinido

in·def·i·nite·ly [ɪnˈdefɪnɪtlɪ] *adv* indefinidamente

in·del·i·cate [ɪnˈdelɪkət] *adj* poco delicado

in·dent 1 *n* [ˈɪndent] *in text* sangrado *m* **2** *v/t* [ɪnˈdent] *line* sangrar

in·de·pen·dence [ɪndɪˈpendəns] independencia *f*

In·de·pen·dence Day Día *m* de la Independencia

in·de·pen·dent [ɪndɪˈpendənt] *adj* independiente

in·de·pen·dent·ly [ɪndɪˈpendəntlɪ] *adv* *deal with* por separado; *independently of* al margen de

in·de·scri·ba·ble [ɪndɪˈskraɪbəbl] *adj* indescriptible

in·de·scrib·a·bly [ɪndɪˈskraɪbəblɪ] *adv* indescriptiblemente

in·de·struc·ti·ble [ɪndɪˈstrʌktəbl] *adj* indestructible

in·de·ter·mi·nate [ɪndɪˈtɜːrmɪnət] *adj* indeterminado

in·dex [ˈɪndeks] *n for book* índice *m*

ˈin·dex card ficha *f*

ˈin·dex fin·ger (dedo *m*) índice *m*

in·dex-·linked *adj* indexado

In·di·a [ˈɪndɪə] (la) India

In·di·an [ˈɪndɪən] **1** *adj* indio **2** *n from India* indio(-a) *m(f)*, hindú *m/f*; *American* indio(-a) *m(f)*

In·di·an ˈsum·mer *in northern hemisphere* veranillo *m* de San Martín; *in southern hemisphere* veranillo *m* de San Juan

in·di·cate [ˈɪndɪkeɪt] **1** *v/t* indicar **2** *v/i* *when driving* poner el intermitente

in·di·ca·tion [ɪndɪˈkeɪʃn] indicio *m*

in·di·ca·tor [ˈɪndɪkeɪtər] *on car* intermitente *m*

in·dict [ɪnˈdaɪt] *v/t* acusar

in·dif·fer·ence [ɪnˈdɪfrəns] indiferencia *f*

in·dif·fer·ent [ɪnˈdɪfrənt] *adj* indiferente; *(mediocre)* mediocre; *are you totally indifferent to the way I feel?* ¿no te importa lo más mínimo lo que sienta yo?

in·di·ges·ti·ble [ɪndɪˈdʒestɪbl] *adj* indigesto

in·di·ges·tion [ɪndɪˈdʒestʃn] indigestión *f*

in·dig·nant [ɪnˈdɪgnənt] *adj* indignado

in·dig·na·tion [ɪndɪgˈneɪʃn] indignación *f*

in·di·rect [ɪndɪˈrekt] *adj* indirecto

in·di·rect·ly [ɪndɪˈrektlɪ] *adv* indirectamente

in·dis·creet [ɪndɪˈskriːt] *adj* indiscreto

in·dis·cre·tion [ɪndɪˈskreʃn] indiscreción *f*

in·dis·crim·i·nate [ɪndɪˈskrɪmɪnət] *adj* indiscriminada

in·dis·pen·sa·ble [ɪndɪˈspensəbl] *adj* indispensable, imprescindible

in·dis·posed [ɪndɪˈspouzd] *adj* (*not well*) indispuesto; *be indisposed* hallarse indispuesto

in·dis·pu·ta·ble [ɪndɪˈspjuːtəbl] *adj* indiscutible

in·dis·pu·ta·bly [ɪndɪˈspjuːtəblɪ] *adv* indiscutiblemente

in·dis·tinct [ɪndɪˈstɪŋkt] *adj* indistinto, impreciso

in·dis·tin·guish·a·ble [ɪndɪˈstɪŋgwɪʃəbl] *adj* indistinguible

in·di·vid·u·al [ɪndɪˈvɪdʒʊəl] **1** *n* individuo *m* **2** *adj* individual

in·di·vid·u·a·list [ɪndɪˈvɪdʒʊəlɪst] *adj* individualista

in·di·vid·u·al·ly [ɪndɪˈvɪdʒʊəlɪ] *adv* individualmente

in·di·vis·i·ble [ɪndɪˈvɪzɪbl] *adj* indivisible

in·doc·tri·nate [ɪnˈdɑːktrɪneɪt] *v/t* adoctrinar

in·do·lence [ˈɪndələns] indolencia *f*

in·do·lent [ˈɪndələnt] *adj* indolente

In·do·ne·sia [ɪndəˈniːʒə] Indonesia

In·do·ne·sian [ɪndəˈniːʒən] **1** *adj* indonesio **2** *n person* indonesio(-a) *m(f)*

in·door [ˈɪndɔːr] *adj* *activities* de interior; *sport* de pista cubierta; *arena* cubierto; *athletics* en pista cubierta

in·doors [ɪnˈdɔːrz] *adv* dentro

in·dorse → *endorse*

in·dulge [ɪnˈdʌldʒ] **1** *v/t o.s., one's tastes* satisfacer **2** *v/i: indulge in a pleasure* entregarse a un placer; *if I might indulge in a little joke* si se me permite contar un chiste

in·dul·gent [ɪnˈdʌldʒənt] *adj* indulgente

in·dus·tri·al [ɪnˈdʌstrɪəl] *adj* industrial; *industrial action* acciones *fpl* reivindicativas

in·dus·tri·al dis·pute conflicto *m* laboral

in·dus·tri·al·ist [ɪnˈdʌstrɪəlɪst] industrial *m/f*

in·dus·tri·al·ize [ɪnˈdʌstrɪəlaɪz] **1** *v/t* industrializar **2** *v/i* industrializarse

in·dus·tri·al ˈwaste residuos *mpl* industriales

in·dus·tri·ous [ɪnˈdʌstrɪəs] *adj* trabajador, aplicado

in·dus·try [ˈɪndəstrɪ] industria *f*

in·ef·fec·tive [ɪnɪˈfektɪv] adj ineficaz

in·ef·fec·tu·al [ɪnɪˈfektʃʊəl] adj person inepto, incapaz

in·ef·fi·cient [ɪnɪˈfɪʃənt] adj ineficiente

in·el·i·gi·ble [ɪnˈelɪdʒɪbl] adj: be ineligible no reunir las condiciones

in·ept [ɪˈnept] adj inepto

in·e·qual·i·ty [ɪnɪˈkwɑːlɪtɪ] desigualdad f

in·es·ca·pa·ble [ɪnɪˈskeɪpəbl] adj inevitable

in·es·ti·ma·ble [ɪnˈestɪməbl] adj inestimable

in·ev·i·ta·ble [ɪnˈevɪtəbl] adj inevitable

in·ev·i·ta·bly [ɪnˈevɪtəblɪ] adv inevitablemente

in·ex·cu·sa·ble [ɪnɪkˈskjuːzəbl] adj inexcusable, injustificable

in·ex·haus·ti·ble [ɪnɪɡˈzɔːstəbl] adj supply inagotable

in·ex·pen·sive [ɪnɪkˈspensɪv] adj barato, económico

in·ex·pe·ri·enced [ɪnɪkˈspɪrɪənst] adj inexperto

in·ex·plic·a·ble [ɪnɪkˈsplɪkəbl] adj inexplicable

in·ex·pres·si·ble [ɪnɪkˈspresɪbl] adj joy indescriptible

in·fal·li·ble [ɪnˈfælɪbl] adj infalible

in·fa·mous [ˈɪnfəməs] adj infame

in·fan·cy [ˈɪnfənsɪ] infancia f

in·fant [ˈɪnfənt] bebé m

in·fan·tile [ˈɪnfəntaɪl] adj pej infantil, pueril

in·fan·try [ˈɪnfəntrɪ] infantería f

in·fan·try 'sol·dier soldado m/f de infantería, infante m/f

'in·fant school colegio m de párvulos

in·fat·u·at·ed [ɪnˈfætʃʊeɪtɪd] adj: be infatuated with s.o. estar encaprichado de alguien

in·fect [ɪnˈfekt] v/t infectar; he infected everyone with his cold contagió el resfriado a todo el mundo; become infected of wound infectarse; of person contagiarse

in·fec·tion [ɪnˈfekʃn] infección f

in·fec·tious [ɪnˈfekʃəs] adj disease infeccioso; laughter contagioso

in·fer [ɪnˈfɜːr] v/t (pret & pp inferred) inferir, deducir (from de)

in·fe·ri·or [ɪnˈfɪrɪər] adj inferior (to a)

in·fe·ri·or·i·ty [ɪnfɪrɪˈɑːrətɪ] in quality inferioridad f

in·fe·ri·or·i·ty com·plex complejo m de inferioridad

in·fer·tile [ɪnˈfɜːrtl] adj woman, plant estéril; soil estéril, yermo

in·fer·til·i·ty [ɪnfərˈtɪlɪtɪ] esterilidad f

in·fi·del·i·ty [ɪnfɪˈdelɪtɪ] infidelidad f

in·fil·trate [ˈɪnfɪltreɪt] v/t infiltrarse en

in·fi·nite [ˈɪnfɪnət] adj infinito

in·fin·i·tive [ɪnˈfɪnətɪv] infinitivo m

in·fin·i·ty [ɪnˈfɪnətɪ] infinidad f

in·firm [ɪnˈfɜːrm] adj enfermo, achacoso

in·fir·ma·ry [ɪnˈfɜːrmərɪ] enfermería f

in·fir·mi·ty [ɪnˈfɜːrmətɪ] debilidad f

in·flame [ɪnˈfleɪm] v/t despertar

in·flam·ma·ble [ɪnˈflæməbl] adj inflamable

in·flam·ma·tion [ɪnfləˈmeɪʃn] MED inflamación f

in·flat·a·ble [ɪnˈfleɪtəbl] adj dinghy hinchable, inflable

in·flate [ɪnˈfleɪt] v/t tire, dinghy hinchar, inflar; economy inflar

in·fla·tion [ɪnˈfleɪʃn] inflación f

in·fla·tion·a·ry [ɪnˈfleɪʃənərɪ] adj inflacionario, inflacionista

in·flec·tion [ɪnˈflekʃn] inflexión f

in·flex·i·ble [ɪnˈfleksɪbl] adj inflexible

in·flict [ɪnˈflɪkt] v/t infligir; inflict sth on s.o. infligir algo a alguien

'in-flight adj: in-flight entertainment entretenimiento m durante el vuelo

in·flu·ence [ˈɪnfluəns] 1 n influencia f; be a good / bad influence on s.o. tener una buena / mala influencia en alguien 2 v/t influir en, influenciar

in·flu·en·tial [ɪnfluˈenʃl] adj influyente

in·flu·en·za [ɪnfluˈenzə] gripe f

in·form [ɪnˈfɔːrm] 1 v/t informar; inform s.o. about sth informar a alguien de algo; please keep me informed por favor manténme informado 2 v/i: inform on s.o. delatar a alguien

in·for·mal [ɪnˈfɔːrməl] adj informal

in·for·mal·i·ty [ɪnfɔːrˈmælɪtɪ] informalidad f

in·form·ant [ɪnˈfɔːrmənt] confidente m/f

in·for·ma·tion [ɪnfərˈmeɪʃn] información f; a piece of information una información

in·for·ma·tion 'sci·ence informática f

in·for·ma·tion 'sci·en·tist informático(-a) m(f)

in·for·ma·tion tech'nol·o·gy tecnologías fpl de la información

in·for·ma·tive [ɪnˈfɔːrmətɪv] adj informativo; you're not being very informative no estás dando mucha información

in·form·er [ɪnˈfɔːrmər] confidente m/f

in·fra·red [ɪnfrəˈred] adj infrarrojo

in·fra·struc·ture [ˈɪnfrəstrʌktʃər] infraestructura f

in·fre·quent [ɪnˈfriːkwənt] adj poco frecuente

in·fu·ri·ate [ɪnˈfjʊrɪeɪt] v/t enfurecer, exasperar

in·fu·ri·at·ing [ɪnˈfjʊrɪeɪtɪŋ] *adj* exasperante

in·fuse [ɪnˈfjuːz] *v/i of tea* infundir

in·fu·sion [ɪnˈfjuːʒn] *(herb tea)* infusión *f*

in·ge·ni·ous [ɪnˈdʒiːnɪəs] *adj* ingenioso

in·ge·nu·i·ty [ɪndʒɪˈnuːətɪ] lo ingenioso

in·got [ˈɪŋɡət] lingote *m*

in·gra·ti·ate [ɪnˈɡreɪʃɪeɪt] *v/t*: *ingratiate o.s. with s.o.* congraciarse con alguien

in·grat·i·tude [ɪnˈɡrætɪtuːd] ingratitud *f*

in·gre·di·ent [ɪnˈɡriːdɪənt] *also fig* ingrediente *m*

in·hab·it [ɪnˈhæbɪt] *v/t* habitar

in·hab·it·a·ble [ɪnˈhæbɪtəbl] *adj* habitable

in·hab·i·tant [ɪnˈhæbɪtənt] habitante *m/f*

in·hale [ɪnˈheɪl] **1** *v/t* inhalar **2** *v/i when smoking* tragarse el humo

in·ha·ler [ɪnˈheɪlər] inhalador *m*

in·her·it [ɪnˈherɪt] *v/t* heredar

in·her·i·tance [ɪnˈherɪtəns] herencia *f*

in·hib·it [ɪnˈhɪbɪt] *v/t growth* impedir; *conversation* inhibir, cohibir

in·hib·it·ed [ɪnˈhɪbɪtɪd] *adj* inhibido, cohibido

in·hi·bi·tion [ɪnhɪˈbɪʃn] inhibición *f*

in·hos·pi·ta·ble [ɪnhaːˈspɪtəbl] *adj person* inhospitalario; *city, climate* inhóspito

in-house 1 *adj facilities* en el lugar de trabajo; *in-house team* equipo *m* en plantilla **2** *adv work* en la empresa

in·hu·man [ɪnˈhjuːmən] *adj* inhumano

i·ni·tial [ɪˈnɪʃl] **1** *adj* inicial **2** *n* inicial *f* *v/t (write initials on)* poner las iniciales en

i·ni·tial·ly [ɪˈnɪʃlɪ] *adv* inicialmente, al principio

i·ni·ti·ate [ɪˈnɪʃɪeɪt] *v/t* iniciar

i·ni·ti·a·tion [ɪnɪʃɪˈeɪʃn] iniciación *f*, inicio *m*

i·ni·tla·tive [ɪˈnɪʃətɪv] iniciativa *f*; *do sth on one's own initiative* hacer algo por iniciativa propia

in·ject [ɪnˈdʒekt] *v/t drug, fuel, capital* inyectar

in·jec·tion [ɪnˈdʒekʃn] *of drug, fuel, capital* inyección *f*

'in-joke: *it's an in-joke* es un chiste que entendemos nosotros

in·jure [ˈɪndʒər] *v/t* lesionar; *he injured his leg* se lesionó la pierna

in·jured [ˈɪndʒərd] **1** *adj leg* lesionado; *feelings* herido **2** *npl*: *the injured* los heridos

in·ju·ry [ˈɪndʒərɪ] lesión *f*; *wound* herida *f*

'in·jury time SP tiempo *m* de descuento

in·jus·tice [ɪnˈdʒʌstɪs] injusticia *f*

ink [ɪŋk] tinta *f*

ink·jet (**'prin·ter**) impresora *f* de chorro de tinta

in·land [ˈɪnlənd] *adj* interior; *mail* nacional

in-laws [ˈɪnlɔːz] *npl* familia *f* política

in·lay [ˈɪnleɪ] *n* incrustación *f*

in·let [ˈɪnlet] *of sea* ensenada *f*; *in machine* entrada *f*

in·mate [ˈɪnmeɪt] *of prison* recluso(-a) *m(f)*; *of mental hospital* paciente *m/f*

inn [ɪn] posada *f*, mesón *m*

in·nate [ɪˈneɪt] *adj* innato

in·ner [ˈɪnər] *adj* interior; *the inner ear* el oído interno

in·ner 'cit·y barrios degradados del centro de la ciudad; *inner city decay* degradación *m* del centro de la ciudad

'in·ner·most *adj feelings* más íntimo; *recess* más recóndito

in·ner 'tube cámara *f* (de aire)

in·no·cence [ˈɪnəsəns] inocencia *f*

in·no·cent [ˈɪnəsənt] *adj* inocente

in·no·cu·ous [ɪˈnaːkjʊəs] *adj* inocuo

in·no·va·tion [ɪnəˈveɪʃn] innovación *f*

in·no·va·tive [ɪnəˈveɪtɪv] *adj* innovador

in·no·va·tor [ˈɪnəveɪtər] innovador(a) *m(f)*

in·nu·me·ra·ble [ɪˈnuːmərəbl] *adj* innumerable

i·noc·u·late [ɪˈnaːkjuleɪt] *v/t* inocular

i·noc·u·la·tion [ɪˈnaːkjuˈleɪʃn] inoculación *f*

in·of·fen·sive [ɪnəˈfensɪv] *adj* inofensivo

in·or·gan·ic [ɪnɔːrˈɡænɪk] *adj* inorgánico

'in-pa·tient paciente *m/f* interno(-a)

in·put [ˈɪnput] **1** *n into project etc* contribución *f*, aportación *f*; COMPUT entrada *f* **2** *v/t (pret & pp* **inputted** *or* **input**) *into project* contribuir, aportar; COMPUT introducir

in·quest [ˈɪnkwest] investigación *f* (*Into* sobre)

in·quire [ɪnˈkwaɪr] *v/i* preguntar; *inquire Into sth* investigar algo

in·quir·y [ɪnˈkwaɪrɪ] consulta *f*, pregunta *f*; *into rail crash etc* investigación *f*

in·quis·i·tive [ɪnˈkwɪzətɪv] *adj* curioso, inquisitivo

in·sane [ɪnˈseɪn] *adj person* loco, demente; *idea* descabellado

in·san·i·ta·ry [ɪnˈsænɪterɪ] *adj* antihigiénico

in·san·i·ty [ɪnˈsænɪtɪ] locura *f*, demencia *f*

in·sa·tia·ble [ɪnˈseɪʃəbl] *adj* insaciable

in·scrip·tion [ɪnˈskrɪpʃn] inscripción *f*

in·scru·ta·ble [ɪnˈskruːtəbl] *adj* inescrutable

in·sect [ˈɪnsekt] insecto *m*

in·sec·ti·cide [ɪnˈsektɪsaɪd] insecticida *f*

'in·sect re·pel·lent repelente *m* contra insectos

in·se·cure [ɪnsɪˈkjʊr] *adj* inseguro

in·se·cu·ri·ty [ɪnsɪˈkjʊrɪtɪ] inseguridad *f*

in·sen·si·tive [ɪnˈsensɪtɪv] *adj* insensible

in·sen·si·tiv·i·ty [ɪnsensɪˈtɪvɪtɪ] insensibilidad *f*

in·sep·a·ra·ble [ɪnˈseprəbl] *adj* inseparable

in·sert 1 *n* [ˈɪnsɜːrt] *in magazine etc* encarte *m* **2** *v/t* [ɪnˈsɜːrt] *coin, finger, diskette* introducir, meter; *extra text* insertar; *insert sth into sth* introducir *or* meter algo en algo

in·ser·tion [ɪnˈsɜːrʃn] *act* introducción *f*, inserción *f*; *of text* inserción *f*

in·side [ɪnˈsaɪd] **1** *n of house, box* interior *m*; *somebody on the inside* alguien de dentro; *inside out* del revés; *turn sth inside out* dar la vuelta a algo (*de dentro a fuera*); *know sth inside out* saberse algo al dedillo **2** *prep* dentro de; *inside the house* dentro de la casa; *inside of 2 hours* dentro de 2 horas **3** *adv stay, remain* dentro; *go, carry* adentro; *we went inside* entramos **4** *adj*: *inside information* información *f* confidencial; *inside lane* SP calle *f* de dentro; *on road* carril *m* de la derecha; *inside pocket* bolsillo *m* interior

in·sid·er [ɪnˈsaɪdər] persona con acceso a información confidencial

in·sid·er 'deal·ing FIN uso *m* de información privilegiada

in·sides [ɪnˈsaɪdz] *npl* tripas *mpl*

in·sid·i·ous [ɪnˈsɪdɪəs] *adj* insidioso

in·sight [ˈɪnsaɪt]: *this film offers an insight into local customs* esta película permite hacerse una idea de las costumbres locales; *full of insight* muy perspicaz

in·sig·nif·i·cant [ɪnsɪɡˈnɪfɪkənt] *adj* insignificante

in·sin·cere [ɪnsɪnˈsɪr] *adj* poco sincero, falso

in·sin·cer·i·ty [ɪnsɪnˈserɪtɪ] falta *f* de sinceridad

in·sin·u·ate [ɪnˈsɪnʊeɪt] *v/t (imply)* insinuar

in·sist [ɪnˈsɪst] *v/i* insistir; *please keep it, I insist* por favor, insisto en que te lo quedes

◆ **insist on** *v/t* insistir en

in·sis·tent [ɪnˈsɪstənt] *adj* insistente

in·so·lent [ˈɪnsələnt] *adj* insolente

in·sol·u·ble [ɪnˈsɑːljʊbl] *adj problem* irresoluble; *substance* insoluble

in·sol·vent [ɪnˈsɑːlvənt] *adj* insolvente

in·som·ni·a [ɪnˈsɑːmnɪə] insomnio *m*

in·spect [ɪnˈspekt] *v/t* inspeccionar

in·spec·tion [ɪnˈspekʃn] inspección *f*

in·spec·tor [ɪnˈspektər] *in factory, of police* inspector(a) *m(f)*; *on buses* revisor(a) *m(f)*

in·spi·ra·tion [ɪnspəˈreɪʃn] inspiración *f*

in·spire [ɪnˈspaɪr] *v/t respect etc* inspirar; *be inspired by s.o./sth* estar inspirado por alguien / algo

in·sta·bil·i·ty [ɪnstəˈbɪlɪtɪ] *of character, economy* inestabilidad *f*

in·stall [ɪnˈstɔːl] *v/t* instalar

in·stal·la·tion [ɪnstəˈleɪʃn] instalación *f*; *military installation* instalación *f* militar

in·stal·ment *Br*, **in·stall·ment** [ɪnˈstɔːlmənt] *of story,* TV *drama etc* episodio *m*; *payment* plazo *m*

in'stall·ment plan compra *f* a plazos

in·stance [ˈɪnstəns] *(example)* ejemplo *m*; *for instance* por ejemplo

in·stant [ˈɪnstənt] **1** *adj* instantáneo **2** *n* instante *m*; *in an instant* en un instante

in·stan·ta·ne·ous [ɪnstənˈteɪnɪəs] *adj* instantáneo

in·stant 'cof·fee café *m* instantáneo

in·stant·ly [ˈɪnstəntlɪ] *adv* al instante

in·stead [ɪnˈsted] *adv*: *I'll take that one instead* me llevaré aquel en vez de otro; *would you like coffee instead?* ¿preferiría mejor café?; *I'll have coffee instead of tea* tomaré té en vez de café; *he went instead of me* fue en mi lugar

in·step [ˈɪnstep] empeine *m*

in·stinct [ˈɪnstɪŋkt] instinto *m*

in·stinc·tive [ɪnˈstɪŋktɪv] *adj* instintivo

in·sti·tute [ˈɪnstɪtuːt] **1** *n* instituto *m*; *for elderly* residencia *f* de ancianos; *for mentally ill* psiquiátrico *m* **2** *v/t new law* establecer; *inquiry* iniciar

in·sti·tu·tion [ɪnstɪˈtuːʃn] institución *f*; *(setting up)* iniciación *f*

in·struct [ɪnˈstrʌkt] *v/t (order)* dar instrucciones a; *(teach)* instruir; *instruct s.o. to do sth (order)* ordenar a alguien que haga algo

in·struc·tion [ɪnˈstrʌkʃn] instrucción *f*; *instructions for use* instrucciones *fpl* de uso

in·struc·tion man·u·al manual *m* de instrucciones

in·struc·tive [ɪnˈstrʌktɪv] *adj* instructivo

in·struc·tor [ɪnˈstrʌktər] instructor(a) *m(f)*

in·stru·ment [ˈɪnstrəmənt] MUS, *tool* instrumento *m*

in·sub·or·di·nate [ɪnsəˈbɔːrdɪnət] *adj* insubordinado

in·suf·fi·cient [ɪnsəˈfɪʃnt] *adj* insuficiente

in·su·late [ˈɪnsəleɪt] *v/t also* ELEC aislar

in·su·la·tion [ɪnsəˈleɪʃn] ELEC aislamiento *m*; *against cold* aislamiento *m* (térmico)

in·su·lin ['ɪnsəlɪn] insulina f

in·sult 1 n ['ɪnsʌlt] insulto m 2 v/t [ɪn'sʌlt] insultar

in·sur·ance [ɪn'ʃʊrəns] seguro m

in·sur·ance com·pa·ny compañía f de seguros, aseguradora f

in·sur·ance pol·i·cy póliza f de seguros

in·sur·ance pre·mi·um prima f (del seguro)

in·sure [ɪn'ʃʊr] v/t asegurar

in·sured [ɪn'ʃʊrd] 1 adj asegurado; **be insured** estar asegurado 2 n: **the insured** el asegurado, la asegurada

in·sur·moun·ta·ble [ɪnsər'maʊntəbl] adj insuperable

in·tact [ɪn'tækt] adj (not damaged) intacto

in·take ['ɪnteɪk] of college etc remesa f; **we have an annual intake of 300 students** cada año admitimos a 300 alumnos

in·te·grate ['ɪntɪgreɪt] v/t integrar (**into** en)

in·te·grat·ed 'cir·cuit ['ɪntɪgreɪtɪd] circuito m integrado

in·teg·ri·ty [ɪn'tegrətɪ] (honesty) integridad f; **a man of integrity** un hombre íntegro

in·tel·lect ['ɪntəlekt] intelecto m

in·tel·lec·tual [ɪntə'lektʃʊəl] 1 adj intelectual 2 n intelectual m/f

in·tel·li·gence [ɪn'telɪdʒəns] inteligencia f; (information) información f secreta

in·tel·li·gence of·fi·cer agente m/f del servicio de inteligencia

in·tel·li·gence ser·vice servicio m de inteligencia

in·tel·li·gent [ɪn'telɪdʒənt] adj inteligente

in·tel·li·gi·ble [ɪn'telɪdʒəbl] adj inteligible

in·tend [ɪn'tend] v/i: **intend to do sth** tener la intención de hacer algo; **that's not what I intended** no era mi intención

in·tense [ɪn'tens] adj sensation, pleasure, heat, pressure intenso; personality serio

in·ten·si·fy [ɪn'tensɪfaɪ] 1 v/t (pret & pp **intensified**) effect, pressure intensificar 2 v/i (pret & pp **intensified**) intensificarse

in·ten·si·ty [ɪn'tensətɪ] intensidad f

in·ten·sive [ɪn'tensɪv] adj study, training, treatment intensivo

in·ten·sive 'care (u·nit) MED (unidad f de) cuidados mpl intensivos

in·ten·sive 'course of language study curso m intensivo

in·tent [ɪn'tent] adj: **be intent on doing sth** (determined to do) estar decidido a hacer algo; (concentrating on) estar concentrado haciendo algo

in·ten·tion [ɪn'tenʃn] intención f; **I have no intention of ...** (refuse to) no tengo intención de ...

in·ten·tion·al [ɪn'tenʃənl] adj intencionado

in·ten·tion·al·ly [ɪn'tenʃnlɪ] adv a propósito, adrede

in·ter·ac·tion [ɪntər'ækʃn] interacción f

in·ter·ac·tive [ɪntər'æktɪv] adj interactivo

in·ter·cede [ɪntər'siːd] v/i interceder

in·ter·cept [ɪntər'sept] v/t interceptar

in·ter·change ['ɪntərtʃeɪndʒ] n of highways nudo m vial

in·ter·change·a·ble [ɪntər'tʃeɪndʒəbl] adj intercambiable

in·ter·com ['ɪntərkɑːm] in office, ship interfono m; for front door portero m automático

in·ter·course ['ɪntərkɔːrs] sexual coito m

in·ter·de·pend·ent [ɪntərdɪ'pendənt] adj interdependiente

in·ter·est ['ɪntrəst] 1 n also FIN interés m; **take an interest in sth** interesarse por algo 2 v/t interesar; **does that offer interest you?** ¿te interesa esa oferta?

in·terest·ed ['ɪntrəstɪd] adj interesado; **be interested in sth** estar interesado en algo; **thanks, but I'm not interested** gracias, pero no me interesa

in·terest-free 'loan préstamo m sin intereses

in·terest·ing ['ɪntrəstɪŋ] adj interesante

'in·terest rate tipo m de interés

interface ['ɪntərfeɪs] 1 n interface m, interfaz f 2 v/i relacionarse

in·ter·fere [ɪntər'fɪr] v/i interferir, entrometerse

♦ **interfere with** v/t afectar a; **the lock had been interfered with** alguien había manipulado la cerradura

in·ter·fer·ence [ɪntər'fɪrəns] intromisión f; on radio interferencia f

in·te·ri·or [ɪn'tɪrɪər] 1 adj interior 2 n interior m; **Department of the Interior** Ministerio m del Interior

in·te·ri·or 'dec·o·ra·tor interiorista m/f, decorador(a) m(f) de interiores

in·te·ri·or de'sign interiorismo m

in·te·ri·or de'sign·er interiorista m/f

in·ter·lude ['ɪntərluːd] at theater entreacto m, intermedio m; at concert intermedio m; (period) intervalo m

in·ter·mar·ry [ɪntər'mærɪ] v/i (pret & pp **intermarried**) casarse (con miembros de otra raza, religión o grupo); **the two tribes intermarried** los dos tribus se casaron entre sí

in·ter·me·di·ar·y [ɪntər'miːdɪərɪ] n intermediario

in·ter·me·di·ate [ɪntər'miːdɪət] *adj* intermedio *m*

in·ter·mis·sion [ɪntər'mɪʃn] *in theater* entreacto *m*, intermedio *m*; *in movie theater* intermedio *m*, descanso *m*

in·tern [ɪn'tɜːrn] *v/t* recluir

in·ter·nal [ɪn'tɜːrnl] *adj* interno

in·ter·nal com'bus·tion en·gine motor *m* de combustión interna

in·ter·nal·ly [ɪn'tɜːrnəlɪ] *adv* internamente

In·ter·nal 'Rev·e·nue (Ser·vice) Hacienda *f*, Span Agencia *f* Tributaria

in·ter·na·tion·al [ɪntər'næʃnl] **1** *adj* internacional **2** *in match* partido *m* internacional; *player* internacional *m/f*

In·ter·na·tion·al Court of 'Jus·tice Tribunal *m* Internacional de Justicia

in·ter·na·tion·al·ly [ɪntər'næʃnəlɪ] *adv* internacionalmente

In·ter·na·tion·al 'Mon·e·tar·y Fund Fondo *m* Monetario Internacional

In·ter·net ['ɪntərnet] Internet *f*; *on the Internet* en Internet

in·ter·nist [ɪn'tɜːrnɪst] internista *m/f*

in·ter·pret [ɪn'tɜːrprɪt] *v/t & v/i* interpretar

in·ter·pre·ta·tion [ɪntɜːrprɪ'teɪʃn] interpretación *f*

in·ter·pret·er [ɪn'tɜːrprɪtər] intérprete *m/f*

in·ter·re·lat·ed [ɪntərɪ'leɪtɪd] *adj facts* interrelacionado

in·ter·ro·gate [ɪn'terəgeɪt] *v/t* interrogar

in·ter·ro·ga·tion [ɪnterə'geɪʃn] interrogatorio *m*

in·ter·rog·a·tive [ɪntər'rɑːgətɪv] *n* GRAM (forma *f*) interrogativa *f*

in·ter·ro·ga·tor [ɪntərə'geɪtər] interrogador(a) *m(f)*

in·ter·rupt [ɪntər'rʌpt] **1** *v/t speaker* interrumpir **2** *v/i* interrumpir

in·ter·rup·tion [ɪntər'rʌpʃn] interrupción *f*

in·ter·sect [ɪntər'sekt] **1** *v/t* cruzar **2** *v/i* cruzarse

in·ter·sec·tion ['ɪntərsekʃn] *(crossroads)* intersección *f*

in·ter·state ['ɪntərsteɪt] *n* autopista *f* interestatal

in·ter·val ['ɪntərvl] intervalo *m*; *in theater* entreacto *m*, intermedio *m*; *at concert* intermedio *m*

in·ter·vene [ɪntər'viːn] *v/i of person, police etc* intervenir

in·ter·ven·tion [ɪntər'venʃn] intervención *f*

in·ter·view ['ɪntərvjuː] **1** *n* entrevista *f* **2** *v/t* entrevistar

in·ter·view·ee [ɪntərvjuː'iː] *on TV* entrevistado(-a) *m(f)*; *for job* candidato(-a) *m(f)*

in·ter·view·er ['ɪntərvjuːər] entrevistador(a) *m(f)*

in·tes·tine [ɪn'testɪn] intestino *m*

in·ti·ma·cy ['ɪntɪməsɪ] *of friendship* intimidad *f*; *sexual* relaciones *fpl* íntimas

in·ti·mate ['ɪntɪmət] *adj* íntimo

in·tim·i·date [ɪn'tɪmɪdeɪt] *v/t* intimidar

in·tim·i·da·tion [ɪntɪmɪ'deɪʃn] intimidación *f*

in·to ['ɪntʊ] *prep* en; *he put it into his suitcase* lo puso en su maleta; *translate into English* traducir al inglés; *he's into classical music* F *(likes)* le gusta *or* Span le va mucho la música clásica; *he's into local politics* F *(is involved with)* está muy metido en el mundillo de la política local; *when you're into the job* cuando te hayas metido en el trabajo

in·tol·e·ra·ble [ɪn'tɑːlərəbl] *adj* intolerable

in·tol·e·rant [ɪn'tɑːlərənt] *adj* intolerante

in·tox·i·cat·ed [ɪn'tɑːksɪkeɪtɪd] *adj* ebrio, embriagado

in·tran·si·tive [ɪn'trænsɪtɪv] *adj* intransitivo

in·tra·ve·nous [ɪntrə'viːnəs] *adj* intravenoso

in·trep·id [ɪn'trepɪd] *adj* intrépido

in·tri·cate ['ɪntrɪkət] *adj* intrincado, complicado

in·trigue 1 *n* ['ɪntriːg] intriga *f* **2** *v/t* [ɪn-'triːg] intrigar; *I would be intrigued to know* ... tendría curiosidad por saber ...

in·trigu·ing [ɪn'triːgɪn] *adj* intrigante

in·tro·duce [ɪntrə'duːs] *v/t* presentar; *new technique etc* introducir; *may I introduce ...?* permítame presentarle a ...; *he introduced me to his wife* me presentó a su esposa; *introduce s.o. to a new sport* iniciar a alguien en un deporte nuevo

in·tro·duc·tion [ɪntrə'dʌkʃn] *to person* presentación *f*; *to a new food, sport etc* iniciación *f*; *in book, of new techniques et* introducción *f*

in·tro·vert ['ɪntrəvɜːrt] *n* introvertido(-a) *m(f)*

in·trude [ɪn'truːd] *v/i* molestar

in·trud·er [ɪn'truːdər] intruso(-a) *m(f)*

in·tru·sion [ɪn'truːʒn] intromisión *f*

in·tu·i·tion [ɪntuː'ɪʃn] intuición *f*

in·vade [ɪn'veɪd] *v/t* invadir

in·val·id¹ [ɪn'vælɪd] *adj* nulo

in·va·lid² ['ɪnvəlɪd] *n* MED minusválido(-a) *m(f)*

in·val·i·date [ɪnˈvælɪdeɪt] *v/t claim, theory* invalidar

in·val·u·a·ble [ɪnˈvæljʊbl] *adj help, contributor* inestimable

in·var·i·a·bly [ɪnˈveɪrɪəblɪ] *adv (always)* invariablemente, siempre

in·va·sion [ɪnˈveɪʒn] invasión *f*

in·vent [ɪnˈvent] *v/t* inventar

in·ven·tion [ɪnˈvenʃn] *action* invención *f*; *thing invented* invento *m*

in·ven·tive [ɪnˈventɪv] *adj* inventivo, imaginativo

in·ven·tor [ɪnˈventər] inventor(-a) *m(f)*

in·ven·to·ry [ˈɪnvəntɔːrɪ] inventario *m*

in·verse [ɪnˈvɜːrs] *adj order* inverso

in·vert [ɪnˈvɜːrt] *v/t* invertir

in·vert·ed 'com·mas [ɪnˈvɜːrtɪd] *npl* comillas *fpl*

in·ver·te·brate [ɪnˈvɜːrtɪbrət] *n* invertebrado *m*

invest [ɪnˈvest] **1** *v/t* invertir **2** *v/i* invertir (*in* en)

in·ves·ti·gate [ɪnˈvestɪgeɪt] *v/t* investigar

in·ves·ti·ga·tion [ɪnvestɪˈgeɪʃn] investigación *f*

in·ves·ti·ga·tive 'jour·nal·ism [ɪnˈvestɪgətɪv] periodismo *m* de investigación

in·vest·ment [ɪnˈvestmənt] inversión *f*

in'vest·ment bank banco *m* de inversiones

in·ves·tor [ɪnˈvestər] inversor(a) *m(f)*

in·vig·or·at·ing [ɪnˈvɪgəreɪtɪŋ] *adj climate* vigorizante

in·vin·ci·ble [ɪnˈvɪnsəbl] *adj* invencible

in·vis·i·ble [ɪnˈvɪzɪbl] *adj* invisible

in·vi·ta·tion [ɪnvɪˈteɪʃn] invitación *f*

in·vite [ɪnˈvaɪt] *v/t* invitar; *he invited me out for a meal* me invitó a comer

◆ **invite in** *v/t*: *invite s.o. in* invitar a alguien a que entre

in·voice [ˈɪnvɔɪs] **1** *n* factura *f* **2** *v/t customer* enviar la factura a

in·vol·un·ta·ry [ɪnˈvɑːlənterɪ] *adj* involuntario

in·volve [ɪnˈvɑːlv] *v/t hard work, expense* involucrar, entrañar; *it would involve emigrating* supondría emigrar; *this doesn't involve you* esto no tiene nada que ver contigo; *what does it involve?* ¿en qué consiste?; *get involved with sth* involucrarse *or* meterse en algo; *the police didn't want to get involved* la policía no quería intervenir; *get involved with s.o. emotionally, romantically* tener una relación sentimental con alguien

in·volved [ɪnˈvɑːlvd] *adj (complex)* complicado

in·volve·ment [ɪnˈvɑːlvmənt] *in a project,*

crime etc participación *f*, intervención *f*

in·vul·ne·ra·ble [ɪnˈvʌlnərəbl] *adj* invulnerable

in·ward [ˈɪnwərd] **1** *adj feeling, smile* interior **2** *adv* hacia dentro

in·ward·ly [ˈɪnwərdlɪ] *adv* por dentro

i·o·dine [ˈaɪoʊdiːn] yodo *m*

IOU [aɪoʊˈjuː] *abbr (= I owe you)* pagaré *m*

IQ [aɪˈkjuː] *abbr (= intelligence quotient)* cociente *m* intelectual

I·ran [ɪˈrɑːn] Irán

I·ra·ni·an [ɪˈreɪnɪən] **1** *adj* iraní **2** *n* iraní *m/f*

I·raq [ɪˈrɑːk] Iraq, Irak

I·ra·qi [ɪˈrɑːkɪ] **1** *adj* iraquí **2** *n* iraquí *m/f*

Ire·land [ˈaɪrlənd] Irlanda

i·ris [ˈaɪrɪs] *of eye* iris *m inv*; *flower* lirio *m*

I·rish [ˈaɪrɪʃ] *adj* irlandés

'I·rish·man irlandés *m*

'I·rish·wom·an irlandesa *f*

i·ron [ˈaɪərn] **1** *n substance* hierro *m*; *for clothes* plancha *f* **2** *v/t shirts etc* planchar

i·ron·ic(al) [aɪˈrɑːnɪk(l)] *adj* irónico

i·ron·ing [ˈaɪərnɪŋ] planchado *m*; *do the ironing* planchar

'i·ron·ing board tabla *f* de planchar

'i·ron·works fundición *f*

i·ron·y [ˈaɪrənɪ] ironía *f*; *the irony of it all is that ...* lo irónico del tema es que ...

ir·ra·tion·al [ɪˈræʃənl] *adj* irracional

ir·rec·on·ci·la·ble [ɪrekənˈsaɪləbl] *adj* irreconciliable

ir·re·cov·e·ra·ble [ɪrɪˈkʌvərəbl] *adj* irrecuperable

ir·re·gu·lar [ɪˈregjʊlər] *adj* irregular

ir·rel·e·vant [ɪˈreləvənt] *adj* irrelevante

ir·rep·a·ra·ble [ɪˈrepərəbl] *adj* irreparable

ir·re·place·a·ble [ɪrɪˈpleɪsəbl] *adj object, person* irreemplazable

ir·re·pres·si·ble [ɪrɪˈpresəbl] *adj sense of humor* incontenible; *person* irreprimible

ir·re·proa·cha·ble [ɪrɪˈproʊtʃəbl] *adj* irreprochable

ir·re·sis·ti·ble [ɪrɪˈzɪstəbl] *adj* irresistible

ir·re·spec·tive [ɪrɪˈspektɪv] *adv*: *irrespective of* independientemente de

ir·re·spon·si·ble [ɪrɪˈspɑːnsəbl] *adj* irresponsable

ir·re·trie·va·ble [ɪrɪˈtriːvəbl] *adj* irrecuperable

ir·rev·e·rent [ɪˈrevərənt] *adj* irreverente

ir·re·vo·ca·ble [ɪˈrevəkəbl] *adj* irrevocable

ir·ri·gate [ˈɪrɪgeɪt] *v/t* regar

ir·ri·ga·tion [ɪrɪˈgeɪʃn] riego *m*

ir·ri·ga·tion ca·nal acequia *f*

ir·ri·ta·ble [ˈɪrɪtəbl] *adj* irritable

ir·ri·tate [ˈɪrɪteɪt] *v/t* irritar

ir·ri·tat·ing [ˈɪrɪteɪtɪŋ] *adj* irritante

ir·ri·ta·tion [ɪrɪˈteɪʃn] irritación *f*

Is·lam [ˈɪzlɑːm] (el) Islam

Is·lam·ic [ɪzˈlæmɪk] *adj* islámico

is·land [ˈaɪlənd] isla *f*; **(traffic) island** isleta *f*

is·land·er [ˈaɪləndər] isleño(-a) *m(f)*

i·so·late [ˈaɪsəleɪt] *v/t* aislar

i·so·lat·ed [ˈaɪsəleɪtɪd] *adj* aislado

i·so·la·tion [aɪsəˈleɪʃn] *of a region* aislamiento *m*; **in isolation** aisladamente

i·so·la·tion ward pabellón *m* de enfermedades infecciosas

ISP [aɪesˈpiː] *abbr* (= **Internet service provider**) proveedor *m* de (acceso a) Internet

Is·rael [ˈɪzreɪl] Israel

Is·rae·li [ɪzˈreɪlɪ] **1** *adj* israelí **2** *n person* israelí *m/f*

is·sue [ˈɪʃuː] **1** *n (matter)* tema *m*, asunto *m*; *of magazine* número *m*; **the point at issue** el tema que se debate; **take issue with s.o./sth** discrepar de algo / alguien **2** *v/t coins* emitir; *passports, visa* expedir; *warning* dar; **issue s.o. with sth** entregar algo a alguien

IT [aɪˈtiː] *abbr* (= **information technology**) tecnologías *fpl* de la información; **IT department** departamento de informática

it [ɪt] *pron as object* lo *m*, la *f*; **what color is it? - it is red** ¿de qué color es? - es rojo; **it's raining** llueve; **it's me / him** soy yo / es él; **it's Charlie here** TELEC soy Charlie; **it's your turn** te toca; **that's it!** *(that's right)* ¡eso sí!; *(finished)* ¡ya está!

I·tal·i·an [ɪˈtæljən] **1** *adj* italiano **2** *n person* italiano(-a) *m(f)*; *language* italiano *m*

I·ta·ly [ˈɪtəlɪ] Italia

itch [ɪtʃ] **1** *n* picor *m* **2** *v/i* picar

i·tem [ˈaɪtəm] *in list, accounts, (article)* artículo *m*; *on agenda* punto *m*; *of news* noticia *f*

i·tem·ize [ˈaɪtəmaɪz] *v/t invoice* detallar

i·tin·e·ra·ry [aɪˈtɪnərerɪ] itinerario *m*

its [ɪts] *poss adj* su; **where is its box?** ¿dónde está su caja?; **the dog has hurt its leg** el perro se ha hecho daño en la pata

it's [ɪts] → **it is, it has**

it·self [ɪtˈself] *pron reflexive* se; **the dog hurt itself** el perro se hizo daño; **the hotel itself is fine** el hotel en sí (mismo) está bien; **by itself** *(alone)* aislado, solo; *(automatically)* solo

i·vo·ry [ˈaɪvərɪ] marfil *m*

i·vy [ˈaɪvɪ] hiedra *f*

J

jab [dʒæb] *v/t* (*pret & pp jabbed*) clavar; **he jabbed his elbow into my ribs** me clavó el codo en las costillas

jab·ber [ˈdʒæbər] *v/i* parlotear

jack [dʒæk] MOT gato *m*; *in cards* jota *f*
♦ jack up *v/t* MOT levantar con el gato

jack·et [ˈdʒækɪt] *(coat)* chaqueta *f*; *of book* sobrecubierta *f*

jack·et po·ta·to *Span* patata *f* or *L.Am.* papa *f* asada *(con piel)*

'jack-knife 1 *n* navaja *f* **2** *v/i* derrapar *(por la parte del remolque)*

'jack·pot gordo *m*; **he hit the jackpot** le tocó el gordo

ja·cuz·zi [dʒəˈkuːzɪ] jacuzzi *m*

jade [dʒeɪd] *n* jade *m*

jad·ed [ˈdʒeɪdɪd] *adj* harto; *appetite* hastiado

jag·ged [ˈdʒægɪd] *adj* accidentado

jag·u·ar [ˈdʒægʊər] jaguar *m*

jail [dʒeɪl] *n* cárcel *f*; **he's in jail** está en la cárcel

jam¹ [dʒæm] *n for bread* mermelada *f*

jam² [dʒæm] **1** *n* MOT atasco *m*; F *(difficulty)* aprieto *m*; **be in a jam** estar en un aprieto **2** *v/t* (*pret & pp jammed*) *(ram)* meter, embutir; *(cause to stick)* atascar; *broadcast* provocar interferencias en; **be jammed** *of roads* estar colapsado; *of door, window* estar atascado; **jam on the brakes** dar un frenazo **3** *v/i* (*pret & pp jammed*) *(stick)* atascarse; **all ten of us managed to jam into the car** nos las arreglamos para meternos los diez en el coche

jam-'packed *adj* F abarrotado *(with de)*

jan·i·tor [ˈdʒænɪtər] portero(-a) *m(f)*

Jan·u·a·ry [ˈdʒænʊerɪ] enero *m*

Ja·pan [dʒəˈpæn] Japón

Jap·a·nese [dʒæpəˈniːz] **1** *adj* japonés **2** *n person* japonés(-esa) *m(f); language* japonés *m*; **the Japanese** los japoneses

jar¹ [dʒɑːr] *n container* tarro *m*

jar² [dʒɑːr] *v/i (pret & pp jarred) of noise* rechinar; **jar on** rechinar en

jar·gon [ˈdʒɑːrgən] jerga *f*

jaun·dice [ˈdʒɔːndɪs] *n* ictericia *f*

jaun·diced [ˈdʒɔːndɪst] *adj fig* resentido

jaunt [dʒɔːnt] *n* excursión *f*; **go on a jaunt** ir de excursión

jaun·ty [ˈdʒɔːntɪ] *adj* desenfadado

jav·e·lin [ˈdʒævlɪn] *(spear)* jabalina *f*; *event* (lanzamiento *m* de) jabalina *f*

jaw [dʒɔː] *n* mandíbula *f*

jay·walk·er [ˈdʒeɪwɔːkər] peatón(-ona) *m(f)* imprudente

ˈjay·walk·ing cruzar la calle de manera imprudente

jazz [dʒæz] *n* jazz *m*
♦ **jazz up** *v/t* F animar

jeal·ous [ˈdʒeləs] *adj* celoso; **be jealous of** *in love* tener celos de; *of riches etc* tener envidia de

jeal·ous·ly [ˈdʒeləslɪ] *adv* celosamente; *relating to possessions* con envidia

jeal·ous·y [ˈdʒeləsɪ] celos *mpl; of possessions* envidia *f*

jeans [dʒiːnz] *npl* vaqueros *mpl*, jeans *mpl*

jeep [dʒiːp] jeep *m*

jeer [dʒɪr] **1** *n* abucheo *m* **2** *v/i* abuchear; **jeer at** burlarse de

Jel·lo® [ˈdʒelou] gelatina *f*

jel·ly [ˈdʒelɪ] mermelada *f*

ˈjel·ly bean gominola *f*

ˈjel·ly·fish medusa *f*

jeop·ar·dize [ˈdʒepərdaɪz] *v/t* poner en peligro

jeop·ar·dy [ˈdʒepərdɪ]: **be in jeopardy** estar en peligro

jerk¹ [dʒɜːrk] **1** *n* sacudida *f* **2** *v/t* dar un tirón a

jerk² [dʒɜːrk] *n* F imbécil *m/f*, *Span* gilipollas *m/f inv* F

jerk·y [ˈdʒɜːrkɪ] *adj movement* brusco

jer·sey [ˈdʒɜːrzɪ] *(sweater)* suéter *m*, *Span* jersey *m*

jest [dʒest] **1** *n* broma *f*; **in jest** en broma **2** *v/i* bromear

Je·sus [ˈdʒiːzəs] Jesús

jet [dʒet] **1** *n of water* chorro *m*; *(nozzle)* boquilla *f*; *(airplane)* reactor *m*, avión *m* a reacción **2** *v/i (pret & pp jetted) travel* viajar en avión

jet-ˈblack *adj* azabache

ˈjet en·gine reactor *m*

ˈjet·lag desfase *m* horario, jet lag *m*

jet·ti·son [ˈdʒetɪsn] *v/t also fig* tirar por la borda

jet·ty [ˈdʒetɪ] malecón *m*

Jew [dʒuː] judío(-a) *m(f)*

jew·el [ˈdʒuːəl] joya *f*, alhaja *f*; *fig: person* joya *f*

jew·el·er, *Br* **jew·el·ler** [ˈdʒuːlər] joyero(-a) *m(f)*

jew·el·lery, *Br* **jew·el·ry** [ˈdʒuːlrɪ] joyas *fpl*, alhajas *fpl*

Jew·ish [ˈdʒuːɪʃ] *adj* judío

jif·fy [ˈdʒɪfɪ] F: **in a jiffy** en un periquete F

jig·saw (puzzle) [ˈdʒɪgsɔː] rompecabezas *m inv*, puzzle *m*

jilt [dʒɪlt] *v/t* dejar plantado

jin·gle [ˈdʒɪŋgl] **1** *n (song)* melodía *f* publicitaria **2** *v/i of keys, coins* tintinear

jinx [dʒɪŋks] *n* gafe *m*; **there's a jinx on this project** este proyecto está gafado

jit·ters [ˈdʒɪtərz] *npl* F: **I got the jitters** me entró el pánico or *Span* canguelo F

jit·ter·y [ˈdʒɪtərɪ] *adj* F nervioso

job [dʒɑːb] *(employment)* trabajo *m*, empleo *m; (task)* tarea *f*, trabajo *m*; **it's not my job to answer the phone** no me corresponde a mí contestar el teléfono; **I've got a few jobs to do around the house** tengo que hacer unas cuantas cosas en la casa; **out of a job** sin trabajo or empleo; **it's a good job you warned me** menos mal que me avisaste; **you'll have a job** *(it'll be difficult)* te va a costar Dios y ayuda

ˈjob de·scrip·tion (descripción *f* de las) responsabilidades *fpl* del puesto

ˈjob hunt *v/i*: **be job hunting** buscar trabajo

job·less [ˈdʒɑːblɪs] *adj* desempleado, *Span* parado

ˈjob sat·is·fac·tion satisfacción *f* con el trabajo

jock·ey [ˈdʒɑːkɪ] *n* jockey *m/f*

jog [dʒɑːg] **1** *n*: **go for a jog** ir a hacer jogging or footing **2** *v/i (pret & pp jogged) as exercise* hacer jogging or footing **3** *v/t (pret & pp jogged)* **jog s.o.'s memory** refrescar la memoria de alguien; **somebody jogged my elbow** alguien me dio en el codo
♦ **jog along** *v/i* F ir tirando P

jog·ger [ˈdʒɑːgər] *person* persona *f* que hace jogging or footing; *shoe* zapatilla *f* de jogging or footing

jog·ging [ˈdʒɑːgɪn] jogging *m*, footing *m*; **go jogging** ir a hacer jogging or footing

ˈjog·ging suit chándal *m*

john [dʒɑːn] P *(toilet)* baño *m*, váter *m*

join [dʒɔɪn] **1** *n* juntura *f* **2** *v/i of roads, rivers* juntarse; *(become a member)* ha-

J

cerse socio **3** v/t (*connect*) unir; *person* unirse a; *club* hacerse socio de; (*go to work for*) entrar en; *of road* desembocar en; *I'll join you at the theater* me reuniré contigo en el teatro

◆ **join in** v/i participar

◆ **join up** v/i MIL alistarse

join·er ['dʒɔɪnər] carpintero(-a) m(f)

joint [dʒɔɪnt] **1** n ANAT articulación f; *in woodwork* junta f; *of meat* pieza f; F (*place*) garito m F; *of cannabis* porro m F, canuto m F **2** adj (*shared*) conjunto

joint ac'count cuenta f conjunta

joint 'ven·ture empresa f conjunta

joke [dʒɔʊk] **1** n story chiste m; (*practical joke*) broma f; *play a joke on* gastar una broma a; *it's no joke* no tiene ninguna gracia F; **2** v/i bromear

jok·er ['dʒɔʊkər] *person* bromista m/f; F pej payaso(-a) m(f); *in cards* comodín m

jok·ing ['dʒɔʊkɪŋ]: *joking apart* bromas aparte

jok·ing·ly ['dʒɔʊkɪŋlɪ] adv en broma

jol·ly ['dʒɑːlɪ] adj alegre

jolt [dʒɔʊlt] **1** n (*jerk*) sacudida f **2** v/t (*push*) *somebody jolted my elbow* alguien me dio en el codo

jos·tle ['dʒɑːsl] v/t empujar

◆ **jot down** [dʒɑːt] v/t (*pret* & *pp* **jotted**) apuntar, anotar

jour·nal ['dʒɜːrnl] (*magazine*) revista f; (*diary*) diario m

jour·nal·ism ['dʒɜːrnəlɪzm] periodismo m

jour·nal·ist ['dʒɜːrnəlɪst] periodista m/f

jour·ney ['dʒɜːrnɪ] n viaje m

jo·vi·al ['dʒɔʊvɪəl] adj jovial

joy [dʒɔɪ] alegría f, gozo m

'joy·stick COMPUT joystick m

ju·bi·lant ['dʒuːbɪlənt] adj jubiloso

ju·bi·la·tion [dʒuːbɪ'leɪʃn] júbilo m

judge [dʒʌdʒ] **1** n LAW juez m/f, jueza f; *in competition* juez m/f, miembro m del jurado **2** v/t juzgar; (*estimate*) calcular **3** v/i juzgar; *judge for yourself* júzgalo por ti mismo

judg·ment ['dʒʌdʒmənt] LAW fallo m; (*opinion*) juicio m; *an error of judgment* una equivocación; *he showed good judgment* mostró tener criterio; *against my better judgment* a pesar de no estar convencido; *the Last Judgment* REL el Juicio Final

'Judg(e)·ment Day Día m del Juicio Final

ju·di·cial [dʒuː'dɪʃl] adj judicial

ju·di·cious [dʒuː'dɪʃəs] adj juicioso

ju·do ['dʒuːdɔʊ] m

jug·gle [dʒʌgl] v/t also fig hacer malabarismos con

jug·gler ['dʒʌglər] malabarista m/f

juice [dʒuːs] n Span zumo m, L.Am. jugo m

juic·y ['dʒuːsɪ] adj jugoso; *news, gossip* jugoso, sabroso

juke·box ['dʒuːkbɑːks] máquina f de discos

Ju·ly [dʒʊ'laɪ] julio m

jum·ble ['dʒʌmbl] n revoltijo m

◆ **jumble up** v/t revolver

jum·bo (jet) ['dʒʌmbɔʊ] jumbo m

'jum·bo(-sized) adj gigante

jump [dʒʌmp] **1** n salto m; (*increase*) incremento m, subida f; *give a jump of surprise* dar un salto **2** v/i saltar; (*increase*) dispararse; *you made me jump!* ¡me diste un susto!; *jump to one's feet* ponerse de pie de un salto; *jump to conclusions* sacar conclusiones precipitadas **3** v/t *fence etc* saltar; F (*attack*) asaltar; *jump the lights* saltarse un semáforo, pasarse un semáforo en rojo

◆ **jump at** v/t *opportunity* no dejar escapar

jump·er[1] ['dʒʌmpər] *dress* pichi m

jump·er[2] ['dʒʌmpər] SP saltador(a) m(f); *horse* caballo m de saltos

jump·y ['dʒʌmpɪ] adj nervioso; *get jumpy* ponerse nervioso

junc·tion ['dʒʌŋkʃn] *of roads* cruce m

junc·ture ['dʒʌŋktʃər] fml: *at this juncture* en esta coyuntura

June [dʒuːn] junio m

jun·gle ['dʒʌŋgl] selva f, jungla f

ju·ni·or ['dʒuːnjər] **1** adj subordinate de rango inferior; *younger* más joven **2** n *in rank* subalterno(-a) m(f); *she is ten years my junior* es diez años más joven que yo

ju·ni·or 'high escuela f secundaria (*para alumnos de entre 12 y 14 años*)

junk [dʒʌŋk] n trastos mpl

'junk food comida f basura

junk·ie ['dʒʌŋkɪ] F drogata m/f F

'junk mail propaganda f postal

'junk shop cacharrería f

'junk·yard depósito m de chatarra

ju·ris·dic·tion [dʒʊrɪs'dɪkʃn] LAW jurisdicción f

ju·ror ['dʒʊrər] miembro m del jurado

ju·ry ['dʒʊrɪ] jurado m

just [dʒʌst] **1** adj law, cause justo **2** adv (*barely*) justo; (*exactly*) justo, justamente; (*only*) sólo, solamente; *have just done sth* acabar de hacer algo; *I've just seen her* la acabo de ver; *just about* (*almost*) casi; *I was just about to leave when …* estaba a punto de salir cuando …; *just like that* (*abruptly*) de repente;

just now (*at the moment*) ahora mismo; *I saw her just now* (*a few moments ago*) la acabo de ver; *just you wait!* ¡ya verás!; *just be quiet!* ¡cállate de una vez!

jus·tice ['dʒʌstɪs] justicia *f*

jus·ti·fi·a·ble [dʒʌstɪ'faɪəbl] *adj* justificable

jus·ti·fia·bly [dʒʌstɪ'faɪəblɪ] *adv* justificadamente

jus·ti·fi·ca·tion [dʒʌstɪfɪ'keɪʃn] justificación *f*; *there's no justification for behavior like that* ese comportamiento es injustificable *or* no tiene justificación

jus·ti·fy ['dʒʌstɪfaɪ] *v/t* (*pret & pp justi-fied*) *also text* justificar

just·ly ['dʒʌstlɪ] *adv* (*fairly*) con justicia; (*rightly*) con razón

◆ **jut out** [dʒʌt] *v/i* (*pret & pp jutted*) sobresalir

ju·ve·nile ['dʒuːvənl] **1** *adj crime* juvenil; *court* de menores; *pej* infantil **2** *n fml* menor *m/f*

ju·ve·nile de·lin·quen·cy delincuencia *f* juvenil

ju·ve·nile de·lin·quent delincuente *m/f* juvenil

K

k [keɪ] *abbr* (= *kilobyte*) k (= kilobyte *m*); (= *thousand*) mil

kan·ga·roo [kæŋgə'ruː] canguro *m*

ka·ra·te [kə'rɑːtɪ] kárate *m*

ka'ra·te chop golpe *m* de kárate

ke·bab [kɪ'bæb] pincho *m*, brocheta *f*

keel [kiːl] NAUT quilla *f*

◆ **keel over** *v/i of structure* desplomarse; *of person* desmayarse

keen [kiːn] *adj* entusiasta, interesado; *interest* gran; *competition* reñido; *she's keen to learn* tiene mucho interés en aprender; *he's keen on football / her* le gusta el fútbol / ella; *I'm not keen on the idea* no me entusiasma la idea; *be keen to do sth* estar muy interesado en hacer algo

keep [kiːp] **1** *n* (*maintenance*) manutención *f*; *for keeps* F para siempre **2** *v/t* (*pret & pp kept*) guardar; (*not lose*) conservar; (*detain*) entretener; *family* mantener; *animals* tener, criar; *you can keep it* (*it's for you*) te lo puedes quedar; *keep trying!* ¡sigue intentándolo!; *don't keep interrupting!* ¡deja de interrumpirme!; *keep a promise* cumplir una promesa; *keep s.o. company* hacer compañía a alguien; *keep s.o. waiting* hacer esperar a alguien; *he can't keep anything to himself* no sabe guardar un secreto; *I kept the news of the accident to myself* no dije nada sobre el accidente; *keep sth from s.o.* ocultar algo a alguien; *we kept the news from him* no le contamos la noticia **3** *v/i* (*pret & pp kept*) *of food, milk* aguantar, conser-

varse; *keep calm!* ¡tranquilízate!; *keep quiet!* ¡cállate!

◆ **keep away 1** *v/i: keep away from that building* no te acerques a ese edificio **2** *v/t: keep the children away from the stove* no dejes que los niños se acerquen a la cocina

◆ **keep back** *v/t* (*hold in check*) contener; *information* ocultar

◆ **keep down** *v/t voice* bajar; *costs, inflation etc* reducir; *food* retener; *keep your voices down in the library* hablen en voz baja en la biblioteca; *tell the kids to keep the noise down* diles a los niños que no hagan tanto ruido; *I can't keep anything down* devuelvo todo lo que como

◆ **keep in** *v/t in school* castigar (*a quedarse en clase*); *the hospital's keeping her in* la tienen en observación

◆ **keep off 1** *v/t* (*avoid*) evitar; *keep off the grass!* ¡prohibido pisar el césped! **2** *v/i: if the rain keeps off* si no llueve

◆ **keep on 1** *v/i* continuar; *if you keep on interrupting me* si no dejas de interrumpirme; *keep on trying* sigue intentándolo **2** *v/t: the company kept them on* la empresa los mantuvo en el puesto; *keep your coat on!* *item of clothing* ¡no te quites el abrigo!

◆ **keep on at** *v/t* (*nag*): *my parents keep on at me to get a job* mis padres no dejan de decirme que busque un trabajo

◆ **keep out 1** *v/t: it keeps the cold out* protege del frío; *they must be kept out* no pueden entrar **2** *v/i: I told you*

to keep out! of a place ¡te dije que no entraras!; **I would keep out of it if I were you** yo en tu lugar no me metería; **keep out** as sign prohibida la entrada, prohibido el paso

◆ **keep to** v/t path seguir; rules cumplir, respetar

◆ **keep up 1** v/i when walking, running etc seguir or mantener el ritmo (**with** de); **keep up with s.o.** (stay in touch with) mantener contacto con alguien **2** v/t pace seguir, mantener; payments estar al corriente de; bridge, pants sujetar

keep·ing ['ki:pɪŋ] n: **be in keeping with** decor combinar con; **in keeping with** promises de acuerdo con

'**keep·sake** recuerdo m

keg [keg] barril m

ken·nel ['kenl] n caseta f del perro

ken·nels ['kenlz] npl residencia f canina

kept [kept] pret & pp → **keep**

ker·nel ['kɜːrnl] almendra f

ker·o·sene ['kerəsiːn] queroseno m

ketch·up ['ketʃʌp] ketchup m

ket·tle ['ketl] hervidor m

key [kiː] **1** n to door, drawer llave f; on keyboard, piano tecla f; of piece of music clave f; on map leyenda f **2** adj (vital) clave, crucial **3** v/t & v/i COMPUT teclear

◆ **key in** v/t datos introducir, teclear

'**key·board** COMPUT, MUS teclado m

'**key·board·er** COMPUT operador(a) m(f), persona que introduce datos en el ordenador

'**key·card** tarjeta f (de hotel)

keyed-up [kiːd'ʌp] adj nervioso

'**key·hole** ojo m de la cerradura

'**key·note** 'speech discurso m central

'**key·ring** llavero m

kha·ki ['kæki] adj caqui

kick [kɪk] **1** n patada f; **he got a kick out of watching them suffer** disfrutó viéndoles sufrir; (**just**) **for kicks** F por diversión **2** v/t dar una patada a; F habit dejar; **I kicked him in the shins** le di una patada en la espinilla **3** v/i of person patalear; of horse, mule cocear

◆ **kick around** v/t ball dar patadas a; F (discuss) comentar

◆ **kick in** v/t P money apoquinar F

◆ **kick off** v/i comenzar, sacar de centro; F (start) empezar

◆ **kick out** v/t of bar, company echar; of country, organization expulsar

◆ **kick up** v/t: **kick up a fuss** montar un numerito

'**kick·back** F (bribe) soborno m

'**kick·off** SP saque m

kid [kɪd] **1** n F (child) crío m F, niño m;

when I was a kid cuando era pequeño; **kid brother** hermano m pequeño; **kid sister** hermana f pequeña **2** v/t (pret & pp **kidded**) F tomar el pelo a **3** v/i (pret & pp **kidded**) F bromear; **I was only kidding** estaba bromeando

kid·der ['kɪdər] F vacilón m F

kid 'gloves: handle s.o. with kid gloves tratar a alguien con guante de seda

kid·nap ['kɪdnæp] v/t (pret & pp **kidnapped**) secuestrar

kid·nap·(p)er ['kɪdnæpər] secuestrador m

'**kid·nap·(p)ing** ['kɪdnæpɪŋ] secuestro m

kid·ney ['kɪdnɪ] ANAT riñón m; in cooking riñones mpl

'**kid·ney bean** alubia f roja de riñón

'**kid·ney ma·chine** MED riñón m artificial, máquina f de diálisis

kill [kɪl] v/t matar; **the drought killed all the plants** las plantas murieron como resultado de la sequía; **I had six hours to kill** tenía seis horas sin nada que hacer; **be killed in an accident** matarse en un accidente, morirse en un accidente; **kill o.s.** suicidarse; **kill o.s. laughing** F morirse de risa F

kil·ler ['kɪlər] (murderer) asesino m; **be a killer** of disease ser mortal

kil·ling ['kɪlɪŋ] n asesinato m; **make a killing** F (lots of money) forrarse F

kil·ling·ly ['kɪlɪŋlɪ] adv F: **killingly funny** para morirse de risa

kiln [kɪln] horno m

ki·lo ['kiːloʊ] kilo m

ki·lo·byte ['kɪloʊbaɪt] COMPUT kilobyte m

ki·lo·gram ['kɪloʊgræm] kilogramo m

ki·lo·me·ter, Br **ki·lo·me·tre** [kɪ'lɑːmɪtər] kilómetro m

kind¹ [kaɪnd] adj agradable, amable

kind² [kaɪnd] n (sort) tipo m; (make, brand) marca f; **all kinds of people** toda clase de personas; **I did nothing of the kind!** ¡no hice nada parecido!; **kind of ... sad, lonely, etc** un poco ...; **that's very kind of you** gracias por tu amabilidad

kin·der·gar·ten ['kɪndərgɑːrtn] guardería f, jardín m de infancia

kind-heart·ed [kaɪnd'hɑːrtɪd] adj agradable, amable

kind·ly ['kaɪndlɪ] **1** adj amable, agradable **2** adv con amabilidad; **kindly don't interrupt** por favor, no me interrumpa; **kindly lower your voice** ¿le importaría hablar más bajo?

kind·ness ['kaɪndnɪs] amabilidad f

king [kɪŋ] rey m

king·dom ['kɪŋdəm] reino m

'**king-size(d)** adj F cigarettes extralargo; **king-size(d) bed** cama f de matrimonio grande

kink [kıŋk] *n in hose etc* doblez *f*

kink·y ['kıŋkı] *adj* F vicioso

kiosk ['kiːɒsk] quiosco *m*

kiss [kıs] **1** *n* beso *m* **2** *v/t* besar **3** *v/i* besarse

kiss of 'life boca *m* a boca, respiración *f* artificial; **give s.o. the kiss of life** hacer a alguien el boca a boca

kit [kıt] (*equipment*) equipo *m*; **first aid kit** botiquín *m*; **tool kit** caja *f* de herramientas

kitch·en ['kıtʃın] cocina *f*

kitch·en·ette [kıtʃı'net] cocina pequeña

kitch·en 'sink: you've got everything but the kitchen sink F llevas la casa a cuestas F

kite [kaıt] cometa *f*

kit·ten ['kıtn] gatito *m*

kit·ty ['kıtı] *money* fondo *m*

klutz [klʌts] F (*clumsy person*) manazas *m & f*

knack [næk] habilidad *f*; **he has a knack of upsetting people** tiene la habilidad de disgustar a la gente; **I soon got the knack of the new machine** le pillé el truco a la nueva máquina rápidamente

knead [niːd] *v/t dough* amasar

knee [niː] *n* rodilla *f*

'knee-cap *n* rótula *f*

kneel [niːl] *v/i* (*pret & pp knelt*) arrodillarse

'knee-length *adj* hasta la rodilla

knelt [nelt] *pret & pp → kneel*

knew [nuː] *pret → know*

knick-knacks ['nıknæks] *npl* F baratijas *fpl*

knife [naıf] **1** *n* (*pl knives* [naıvz]) *for food* cuchillo *m*; *carried outside* navaja *f* **2** *v/t* acuchillar, apuñalar

knight [naıt] *n* caballero *m*

knit [nıt] **1** *v/t* (*pret & pp knitted*) tejer **2** *v/i* (*pret & pp knitted*) tricotar

♦ **knit together** *v/i of broken bone* soldarse

knit·ting ['nıtıŋ] punto *m*

'knit·ting nee·dle aguja *f* para hacer punto

'knit·wear prendas *fpl* de punto

knob [nɒb] *on door* pomo *m*; *on drawer* tirador *m*; *of butter* nuez *f*, trocito *m*

knock [nɒk] **1** *n on door* golpe *m*; (*blow*) golpe *m*; **there was a knock on the door** llamaron a la puerta **2** *v/t* (*hit*) golpear; F (*criticize*) criticar, meterse con F; **he was knocked to the ground** le tiraron al su-

elo **3** *v/i on the door* llamar

♦ **knock around 1** *v/t* F (*beat*) pegar a **2** *v/i* F (*travel*) viajar

♦ **knock down** *v/t of car* atropellar; *building*; *object* tirar al suelo; F (*reduce the price of*) rebajar

♦ **knock off 1** *v/t* P (*steal*) mangar P **2** *v/i* F (*stop work for the day*) acabar, *Span* plegar F

♦ **knock out** *v/t* (*make unconscious*) dejar K.O.; *of medicine* dejar para el arrastre F; *power lines etc* destruir; (*eliminate*) eliminar

♦ **knock over** *v/t* tirar; *of car* atropellar

'knock-down *adj: at a knockdown price* tirado

knock-kneed [nɑːkˈniːd] *adj* patizambo

'knock-out *n in boxing* K.O. *m*

knot [nɑːt] **1** *n* nudo *m* **2** *v/t* (*pret & pp knotted*) anudar

'knot-ty ['nɑːtı] *adj problem* complicado

know [noʊ] **1** *v/t* (*pret knew*, *pp known*) *fact, language, how to do sth* saber; *person, place* conocer; (*recognize*) reconocer; **will you let him know that ...?** ¿puedes decirle que ...? **2** *v/i* (*pret knew*, *pp known*) saber; **I don't know** no (lo) sé; **yes, I know** sí, lo sé **3** *n: people in the know* los enterados

'know-how pericia *f*

know·ing ['noʊıŋ] *adj* cómplice

know·ing·ly ['noʊıŋlı] *adv* (*wittingly*) deliberadamente; *smile etc* con complicidad

'know-it-all F sabiondo F

knowl·edge ['nɑːlıdʒ] conocimiento *m*; **to the best of my knowledge** por lo que sé; **have a good knowledge of ...** tener buenos conocimientos de ...

knowl·edge·a·ble ['nɑːlıdʒəbl] *adj: she's very knowledgeable about music* sabe mucho de música

known [noʊn] *pp → know*

knuck·le ['nʌkl] nudillo *m*

♦ **knuckle down** *v/i* aplicarse F

♦ **knuckle under** *v/i* F pasar por el aro F

KO [keıˈoʊ] (*knockout*) K.O.

Ko·ran [kəˈræn] Corán *m*

Ko·re·a [kəˈriːə] Corea *f*

Ko·re·an [kəˈriːən] **1** *adj* coreano **2** *n* coreano(a) *m(f)*; *language* coreano *m*

ko·sher ['koʊʃər] *adj* REL kosher; F legal F

kow·tow ['kaʊtaʊ] *v/i* reverenciar

ku·dos ['kjuːdɑːs] reconocimiento *m*, prestigio *m*

K

L

lab [læb] laboratorio *m*

la·bel ['leɪbl] **1** *n* etiqueta *f* **2** *v/t baggage* etiquetar

la·bor ['leɪbər] *n* (*work*) trabajo *m*; *in pregnancy* parto *m*; **be in labor** estar de parto

la·bor·a·to·ry ['læbrətɔːrɪ] laboratorio *m*

la·bor·a·to·ry tech·ni·cian técnico(-a) *m(f)* de laboratorio

la·bo·ri·ous [lə'bɔːrɪəs] *adj* laborioso

la·bored ['leɪbərd] *adj style, speech* elaborado

la·bor·er ['leɪbərər] obrero(-a) *m(f)*

'la·bor u·ni·on sindicato *m*

'la·bor ward MED sala *f* de partos

la·bour *etc Br* → **labor** *etc*

lace [leɪs] *n material* encaje *m*; *for shoe* cordón *m*

◆ **lace up** *v/t shoes* atar

lack [læk] **1** *n* falta *f*, carencia *f* **2** *v/t* carecer de; *he lacks confidence* le falta confianza **3** *v/i*: *be lacking* faltar

lac·quer ['lækər] *n for hair* laca *f*

lad [læd] muchacho *m*, chico *m*

lad·der ['lædər] *n* escalera *f* (de mano)

la·den ['leɪdn] *adj* cargado (*with* de)

la·dies room ['leɪdiːz] servicio *m* de señoras

la·dle ['leɪdl] *n* cucharón *m*, cazo *m*

la·dy ['leɪdɪ] señora *f*

'la·dy·bug mariquita *f*

'la·dy·like *adj* femenino

lag [læg] *v/t* (*pret & pp lagged*) *pipes* revestir con aislante

◆ **lag behind** *v/i* quedarse atrás

la·ger ['lɑːgər] cerveza *f* rubia

la·goon [lə'guːn] laguna *f*

laid [leɪd] *pret & pp* → **lay¹**

laid-back [leɪd'bæk] *adj* tranquilo, despreocupado

lain [leɪn] *pp* → **lie²**

lake [leɪk] lago *m*

lamb [læm] *animal, meat* cordero *m*

lame [leɪm] *adj person* cojo; *excuse* pobre

la·ment [lə'ment] **1** *n* lamento *m* **2** *v/t* lamentar

lam·en·ta·ble ['læməntəbl] *adj* lamentable

lam·i·nat·ed ['læmɪneɪtɪd] *adj surface* laminado; *paper* plastificado

lam·i·nat·ed 'glass cristal *m* laminado

lamp [læmp] lámpara *f*

'lamp·post farola *f*

'lamp·shade pantalla *f* (de lámpara)

land [lænd] **1** *n* tierra *f*; *by land* por tierra; *on land* en tierra; *work on the land as farmer* trabajar la tierra **2** *v/t airplane* aterrizar; *job* conseguir **3** *v/i airplane* aterrizar; *of capsule on the moon* alunizar; *of ball, sth thrown* caer; *it landed right on top of his head* le cayó justo en la cabeza

land·ing ['lændɪŋ] *n of airplane* aterrizaje *m*; *on moon* alunizaje *m*; *of staircase* rellano *m*

'land·ing field pista *f* de aterrizaje

'land·ing gear tren *m* de aterrizaje

'land·ing strip pista *f* de aterrizaje

'land·la·dy *of bar* patrona *f*; *of hostel etc* dueña *f*; *of rented room* casera *f*

'land·lord *of bar* patrón *m*; *of hostel etc* dueño *m*; *of rented room* casero *m*

'land·mark punto *m* de referencia; *fig* hito *m*

'land own·er terrateniente *m/f*

land·scape ['lændskeɪp] **1** *n* (*also painting*) paisaje *m* **2** *adv print* en formato apaisado

'land·slide corrimiento *m* de tierras

land·slide 'vic·to·ry victoria *f* arrolladora

lane [leɪn] *in country* camino *m*, vereda *f*; (*alley*) callejón *m*; MOT carril *m*

lan·guage ['læŋgwɪdʒ] lenguaje *m*; *of nation* idioma *f*, lengua *f*

'lan·guage lab laboratorio *m* de idiomas

lank [læŋk] *adj hair* lacio

lank·y ['læŋkɪ] *adj person* larguirucho

lan·tern ['læntərn] farol *f*

lap¹ [læp] *n of track* vuelta *f*

lap² [læp] *n of water* chapoteo *m*

◆ **lap up** *v/t* (*pret & pp lapped*) *drink, milk* beber a lengüetadas; *flattery* deleitarse con

lap³ [læp] *n of person* regazo *m*

la·pel [lə'pel] solapa *f*

lapse [læps] **1** *n* (*mistake, slip*) desliz *m*; *of time* lapso *m*; *a lapse of attention* un momento de distracción; *a lapse of memory* un olvido **2** *v/i of membership* vencer; *lapse into silence / despair* sumirse en el silencio / la desesperación; *she lapsed into English* empezó a hablar en inglés

lap·top ['læptɑːp] COMPUT ordenador *m* portátil, *L.Am.* computadora *f* portátil

lar·ce·ny ['lɑːrsənɪ] latrocinio *m*

lard [lɑːrd] manteca *f* de cerdo

lar·der ['lɑːrdər] despensa *f*

large [lɑːrdʒ] *adj* grande; *be at large of criminal, wild animal* andar suelto

large·ly [ˈlɑːrdʒlɪ] *adv* (*mainly*) en gran parte, principalmente

lark [lɑːrk] *bird* alondra *f*

lar·va [ˈlɑːrvə] larva *f*

lar·yn·gi·tis [lærɪnˈdʒaɪtɪs] laringitis *f*

lar·ynx [ˈlærɪŋks] laringe *f*

la·ser [ˈleɪzər] láser *m*

'la·ser beam rayo *m* láser

'la·ser print·er impresora *f* láser

lash[1] [læʃ] *v/t with whip* azotar

◆ **lash down** *v/t with rope* amarrar

◆ **lash out** *v/i with fists, words* atacar (*at* a), arremeter (*at* contra)

lash[2] [læʃ] *n* (*eyelash*) pestaña *f*

lass [læs] muchacha *f*, chica *f*

last[1] [læst] 1 *adj in series* último; (*preceding*) anterior; *last Friday* el viernes pasado; *last but one* penúltimo; *last night* anoche; *last but not least* por último, pero no por ello menos importante 2 *adv at last* por fin, al fin

last[2] [læst] *v/i* durar

last·ing [ˈlæstɪŋ] *adj* duradero

last·ly [ˈlæstlɪ] *adv* por último, finalmente

latch [lætʃ] *n* pestillo *m*

late [leɪt] 1 *adj: the bus is late again* el autobús vuelve a llegar tarde; *it's late* es tarde; *it's getting late* se está haciendo tarde; *of late* últimamente, recientemente, *the late 19th/20th century* la última parte del siglo XIX / XX; *in the late 19th/20th century* a finales del siglo XIX / XX 2 *adv arrive, leave* tarde

late·ly [ˈleɪtlɪ] *adv* últimamente, recientemente

lat·er [ˈleɪtər] *adv* más tarde; *see you later!* ¡hasta luego!; *later on* más tarde

lat·est [ˈleɪtɪst] *adj news, girlfriend* último

lathe [leɪð] *n* torno *m*

la·ther [ˈlɑːðər] *n from soap* espuma *f*; *in a lather* (*sweaty*) empapado de sudor

Lat·in [ˈlætɪn] 1 *adj* latino 2 *n* latín *m*

Lat·in A·mer·i·ca Latinoamérica, América Latina

La·tin A·mer·i·can 1 *n* latinoamericano(-a) *m(f)* 2 *adj* latinoamericano

La·ti·no [læˈtiːnou] 1 *adj* latino 2 *n* latino(-a)

lat·i·tude [ˈlætɪtuːd] *geographical* latitud *f*; (*freedom to act*) libertad *f*

lat·ter [ˈlætər] *adj* último 2 *n: Mr Brown and Mr White, of whom the latter was …* el Señor Brown y el Señor White, de quien el segundo *or* este último era …

laugh [læf] 1 *n* risa *f*; *it was a laugh* F fue genial 2 *v/i* reírse

◆ **laugh at** *v/t* reírse de

'laugh·ing stock: make o.s. a laughing stock ponerse en ridículo; *become a laughing stock* ser el hazmerreír

laugh·ter [ˈlæftər] risas *fpl*

launch [lɔːntʃ] 1 *n small boat* lancha *f*; *of ship* botadura *f*; *of rocket, new product* lanzamiento *m* 2 *v/t rocket, new product* lanzar; *ship* botar

'launch cer·e·mo·ny ceremonia *f* de lanzamiento

'launch·(ing) pad plataforma *f* de lanzamiento

laun·der [ˈlɔːndər] *v/t clothes* lavar (y planchar); *money* blanquear

laun·dro·mat [ˈlɔːndrəmæt] lavandería *f*

laun·dry [ˈlɔːndrɪ] *place* lavadero *m*; *dirty clothes* ropa *f* sucia; *clean clothes* ropa *f* lavada; *do the laundry* lavar la ropa, *Span* hacer la colada

lau·rel [ˈlɑːrəl] laurel *m*

lav·a·to·ry [ˈlævətɔːrɪ] *place* cuarto *m* de baño, lavabo *m*; *equipment* retrete *m*

lav·en·der [ˈlævəndər] espliego *m*, lavanda *f*

lav·ish [ˈlævɪʃ] *adj* espléndido

law [lɔː] ley *f*; *subject* derecho *m*; *be against the law* estar prohibido, ser ilegal

'law court juzgado *m*

law·a·bid·ing [ˈlɔːəbaɪdɪŋ] *adj* respetuoso con la ley

law·ful [ˈlɔːfəl] *adj* legal; *wife* legítimo

law·less [ˈlɔːlɪs] *adj* sin ley

lawn [lɔːn] césped *m*

'lawn mow·er cortacésped *m*

'law·suit pleito *m*

law·yer [ˈlɔːjər] abogado(-a) *m(f)*

lax [læks] *adj* poco estricto

lax·a·tive [ˈlæksətɪv] *n* laxante *m*

lay[1] [leɪ] *v/t* (*pret & pp laid*) (*put down*) dejar, poner; *eggs* poner; V *sexually* tirarse a V

lay[2] [leɪ] *pret* → **lie**[2]

◆ **lay into** *v/t* (*attack*) arremeter contra

◆ **lay off** *v/t workers* despedir

◆ **lay on** *v/t* (*provide*) organizar

◆ **lay out** *v/t objects* colocar, disponer; *page* diseñar, maquetar

'lay·a·bout F gandul(a) *m(f)* F

'lay-by *on road* área *f* de descanso

lay·er [ˈleɪər] estrato *m*; *of soil, paint* capa *f*

'lay·man laico *m*

'lay-off despido *m*

◆ **laze around** [leɪz] *v/i* holgazanear

la·zy [ˈleɪzɪ] *adj person* holgazán, perezoso; *day* ocioso

lb *abbr* (= *pound*) libra *f* (de peso)

LCD [elsiːˈdiː] *abbr* (= *liquid crystal dis-*

play) LCD, pantalla *f* de cristal líquido

lead¹ [liːd] **1** *v/t* (*pret & pp* **led**) *procession, race* ir al frente de; *company, team* dirigir; (*guide, take*) conducir **2** *v/i* (*pret & pp* **led**) *in race, competition* ir en cabeza; (*provide leadership*) tener el mando; *a street leading off the square* una calle que sale de la plaza; *where is this leading?* ¿adónde nos lleva esto? **3** *n in race* ventaja *f*; *be in the lead* estar en cabeza; *take the lead* ponerse en cabeza; *lose the lead* perder la cabeza

◆ **lead on** *v/i* (*go in front*) ir delante

◆ **lead up to** *v/t* preceder a; *I wonder what she's leading up to* me pregunto a dónde quiere ir a parar

lead² [liːd] *for dog* correa *f*

lead³ [led] *substance* plomo *m*

lead-ed ['ledɪd] *adj gas* con plomo

lead-er ['liːdər] líder *m*

lead-er-ship ['liːdərʃɪp] *of party etc* liderazgo *m*; *under his leadership* bajo su liderazgo

'**lead-er-ship con-test** pugna *f* por el liderazgo

lead-free ['ledfriː] *adj gas* sin plomo

lead-ing ['liːdɪŋ] *adj runner* en cabeza; *company, product* puntero

'**lead-ing-edge** *adj company* en la vanguardia; *technology* de vanguardia

leaf [liːf] (*pl* **leaves** [liːvz]) hoja *f*

◆ **leaf through** *v/t* hojear

leaf-let ['liːflət] folleto *m*

league [liːg] liga *f*

leak [liːk] **1** *n in roof* gotera *f*; *in pipe* agujero *m*; *of air, gas* fuga *f*, escape *m*; *of information* filtración *f* **2** *v/i of boat* hacer agua; *of pipe* tener un agujero; *of liquid, gas* fugarse, escaparse

◆ **leak out** *v/i of air, gas* fugarse, escaparse; *of news* filtrarse

leak-y ['liːkɪ] *adj pipe* con agujeros; *boat* que hace agua

lean¹ [liːn] **1** *v/i* (*be at an angle*) estar inclinado; *lean against sth* apoyarse en algo **2** *v/t* apoyar; *lean sth against sth* apoyar algo contra algo

lean² [liːn] *adj meat* magro; *style, prose* pobre, escueto

leap [liːp] **1** *n* salto *m*; *a great leap forward* un gran salto adelante **2** *v/i* (*pret & pp* **leaped** *or* **leapt**) saltar; *he leapt over the fence* saltó la valla; *they leapt into the river* se tiraron al río

leapt [lept] *pret & pp* → **leap**

'**leap year** año *m* bisiesto

learn [lɜːrn] **1** *v/t* aprender; (*hear*) enterarse de; *learn how to do sth* aprender a hacer algo **2** *v/i* aprender

learn-er ['lɜːrnər] estudiante *m/f*

'**learn-er driv-er** conductor(a) *m(f)* en prácticas

learn-ing ['lɜːrnɪŋ] *n* (*knowledge*) conocimientos *mpl*; *act* aprendizaje *m*

'**learn-ing curve** curva *f* de aprendizaje; *be on the learning curve* tener que aprender cosas nuevas

lease [liːs] **1** *n* (contrato *m* de) arrendamiento *m* **2** *v/t apartment, equipment* arrendar

◆ **lease out** *v/t apartment, equipment* arrendar

lease 'pur-chase arrendamiento *m* con opción de compra

leash [liːʃ] *for dog* correa *f*

least [liːst] **1** *adj* (*slightest*) menor; *the least amount, money, baggage* menos; *there's not the least reason to ...* no hay la más mínima razón para que ... **2** *adv* menos **3** *n* lo menos; *he drank the least* fue el que menos bebió; *not in the least surprised* en absoluto sorprendido; *at least* por lo menos

leath-er ['leðər] **1** *n* piel *f*, cuero **2** *adj* de piel, de cuero

leave [liːv] **1** *n* (*vacation*) permiso *m*; *on leave* de permiso **2** *v/t* (*pret & pp* **left**) *city, place* marcharse de, irse de; *person, food, memory,* (*forget*) dejar; *let's leave things as they are* dejemos las cosas tal y como están; *how did you leave things with him?* ¿cómo quedaron las cosas con él?; *leave s.o./sth alone* (*not touch, not interfere with*) dejar a alguien / algo en paz; *be left* quedar; *there is nothing left* no queda nada; *I only have one left* sólo me queda uno **3** *v/i* (*pret & pp* **left**) *of person* marcharse, irse; *of plane, train, bus* salir

◆ **leave behind** *v/t intentionally* dejar; (*forget*) olvidarse

◆ **leave on** *v/t hat, coat* dejar puesto; TV, *computer* dejar encendido

◆ **leave out** *v/t word, figure* omitir; (*not put away*) no guardar; *leave me out of this* a mí no me metas en esto

'**leav-ing par-ty** fiesta *f* de despedida

lec-ture ['lektʃər] **1** *n clase f; to general public* conferencia *f* **2** *v/i at university* dar clases (*in* de); *to general public* dar una conferencia

'**lec-ture hall** sala *f* de conferencias

'**lec-tur-er** ['lektʃərər] profesor(a) *m(f)*

LED [eliː'diː] *abbr* (= *light-emitting diode*) LED *m* (= diodo *m* emisor de luz)

led [led] *pret & pp* → **lead**¹

ledge [ledʒ] *of window* alféizar *f*; *on rock face* saliente *m*

ledg·er ['ledʒər] COM libro *m* mayor

leek [li:k] puerro *m*

leer [lɪr] *n sexual* mirada *f* impúdica; *evil* mirada *f* maligna

left [left] **1** *adj* izquierdo **2** *n also* POL izquierda *f*; **on the left** a la izquierda; **on the left of sth** a la izquierda de algo; **to the left** *turn, look* a la izquierda **3** *adv turn, look* a la izquierda

left[2] [left] *pret & pp* → **leave**

'left-hand *adj* de la izquierda; **on your left-hand side** a tu izquierda; *bend* a la izquierda

left-hand 'drive: *this car is left-hand drive* este coche tiene el volante a la izquierda

left-'handed *adj* zurdo

left 'lug·gage (of·fice) *Br* consigna *f*

'left-overs *npl food* sobras *fpl*

'left-wing *adj* POL izquierdista, de izquierdas

leg [leg] *of person* pierna *f*; *of animal* pata *f*; **pull s.o.'s leg** tomar el pelo a alguien

leg·a·cy ['legəsɪ] legado *m*

le·gal ['li:gl] *adj* legal

le·gal ad·vis·er asesor(a) *m(f)* jurídico(-a)

le·gal·i·ty [lɪ'gælətɪ] legalidad *f*

le·gal·ize ['li:gəlaɪz] *v/t* legalizar

le·gend ['ledʒənd] leyenda *f*

le·gen·da·ry ['ledʒəndrɪ] *adj* legendario

le·gi·ble ['ledʒəbl] *adj* legible

le·gis·late ['ledʒɪsleɪt] *v/i* legislar

le·gis·la·tion [ledʒɪs'leɪʃn] legislación *f*

le·gis·la·tive ['ledʒɪslətɪv] *adj* legislativo

le·gis·la·ture ['ledʒɪsləʧʃər] POL legislativo *m*

le·git·i·mate [lɪ'dʒɪtɪmət] *adj* legítimo

leg room espacio *m* para las piernas

lei·sure ['li:ʒər] ocio *m*; **I look forward to having more leisure** estoy deseando tener más tiempo libre; **do it at your leisure** tómate tu tiempo para hacerlo

'lei·sure cen·ter, *Br* **'lei·sure cen·tre** centro *m* recreativo

lei·sure·ly ['li:ʒəlɪ] *adj pace, lifestyle* tranquilo, relajado

'lei·sure time tiempo *m* libre

le·mon ['lemən] limón *m*

le·mon·ade [lemə'neɪd] limonada *f*

'le·mon juice zumo *m* de limón, *L.Am.* jugo de limón

le·mon 'tea té *m* con limón

lend [lend] *v/t (pret & pp* lent*)* prestar

length [leŋθ] longitud *f*; *(piece: of material etc)* pedazo *m*; **at length** *describe, explain* detalladamente; *(finally)* finalmente

length·en ['leŋθən] *v/t* alargar

length·y ['leŋθɪ] *adj speech, stay* largo

le·ni·ent ['li:nɪənt] *adj* indulgente, poco severo

lens [lenz] *of camera* objetivo *m*, lente *f*; *of eyeglasses* cristal *m*; *of eye* cristalino *m*; *(contact lens)* lente *m* de contacto, *Span* lentilla *f*

'lens cov·er *of camera* tapa *f* del objetivo

Lent [lent] REL Cuaresma *f*

lent [lent] *pret & pp* → **lend**

len·til ['lentl] lenteja *f*

len·til 'soup sopa *f* de lentejas

Leo ['li:oʊ] Leo ASTR *m/f inv*

leop·ard ['lepərd] leopardo *m*

le·o·tard ['li:oʊtɑːrd] malla *f*

les·bi·an ['lezbɪən] **1** *n* lesbiana *f* **2** *adj* lésbico, lesbiano

less [les] *adv* menos; *eat / talk less* comer / hablar menos; *less interesting / serious* menos interesante / serio; *it costs less* cuesta menos; *less than $200* menos de 200 dólares

les·sen ['lesn] **1** *v/t* disminuir **2** *v/i* reducirse, disminuir

les·son ['lesn] lección *f*

let [let] *v/t (pret & pp* let*) (allow)* dejar, permitir; *let s.o. do sth* dejar a alguien hacer algo; *let me go!* ¡déjame!; *let him come in!* ¡déjale entrar!; *let's go / stay* vamos / quedémonos; *let's not argue* no discutamos; *let alone* mucho menos; *let go of sth* *rope, handle* soltar algo, *let go of me!* ¡suéltame!

◆ **let down** *v/t hair* soltarse; *blinds* bajar; *(disappoint)* decepcionar, defraudar; *dress, pants* alargar

◆ **let in** *v/t to house* dejar pasar

◆ **let off** *v/t (not punish)* perdonar; *from car* dejar; *the court let him off with a small fine* el tribunal sólo le impuso una pequeña multa

◆ **let out** *v/t of room, building* alquilar, *Mex* rentar; *jacket etc* agrandar; *groan, yell* soltar

◆ **let up** *v/i (stop)* amainar

le·thal ['li:θl] *adj* letal

le·thar·gic [lɪ'θɑːrdʒɪk] *adj* aletargado, apático

leth·ar·gy ['leθərdʒɪ] sopor *m*, apatía *f*

let·ter ['letər] *of alphabet* letra *f*; *in mail* carta *f*

'let·ter·box buzón *m*

'let·ter·head *(heading)* membrete *m*; *(headed paper)* papel *m* con membrete

let·ter of 'cred·it COM carta *f* de crédito

let·tuce ['letɪs] lechuga *f*

'let·up: without a letup sin interrupción

leu·ke·mia [luːˈkiːmɪə] leucemia *f*

lev·el ['levl] **1** *adj field, surface* nivelado,

L

llano; *in competition, scores* igualado; **draw level with s.o.** *in race* ponerse a la altura de alguien 2 *n on scale, in hierarchy,* (*amount*) nivel *m;* **on the level** F (*honest*) honrado

lev·el-head·ed [levl'hedɪd] *adj* ecuánime, sensato

le·ver ['liːvər] 1 *n* palanca *f* 2 *v/t:* **lever sth open** abrir algo haciendo palanca

lev·er·age ['liːvrɪdʒ] apalancamiento *m;* (*influence*) influencia *f*

lev·y ['levɪ] *v/t* (*pret & pp* **levied**) *taxes* imponer

lewd [luːd] *adj* obsceno

li·a·bil·i·ty [laɪə'bɪlətɪ] (*responsibility*) responsabilidad *f;* (*likeliness*) propensión *f* (**to** a)

li·a·ble ['laɪəbl] *adj* (*responsible*) responsable (**for** de); **be liable to** (*likely*) ser propenso a

◆ li·aise with [lɪ'eɪz] *v/t* actuar de enlace con

li·ai·son [lɪ'eɪzɑːn] (*contacts*) contacto *m,* enlace *m*

li·ar [laɪr] mentiroso(-a) *m(f)*

li·bel ['laɪbl] 1 *n* calumnia *f,* difamación *f* 2 *v/t* calumniar, difamar

lib·e·ral ['lɪbərəl] *adj* (*broad-minded*), POL liberal; (*generous: portion etc*) abundante

lib·e·rate ['lɪbəreɪt] *v/t* liberar

lib·e·rat·ed ['lɪbəreɪtɪd] *adj* liberado

lib·e·ra·tion [lɪbə'reɪʃn] liberación *f*

lib·er·ty ['lɪbərtɪ] libertad *f;* **at liberty** *of prisoner etc* en libertad; **be at liberty to do sth** tener libertad para hacer algo

Li·bra ['liːbrə] ASTR Libra *m/f inv*

li·brar·i·an [laɪ'brerɪən] bibliotecario(-a) *m(f)*

li·bra·ry ['laɪbrərɪ] biblioteca *f*

Lib·y·a ['lɪbɪə] Libia

Lib·y·an ['lɪbɪən] 1 *adj* libio 2 *n* libio(-a) *m(f)*

lice [laɪs] *pl* → **louse**

li·cence *Br* → **license 1** *n*

li·cense ['laɪsns] 1 *n* permiso *m,* licencia *f* 2 *v/t* autorizar; **be licensed** tener permiso *or* licencia

'li·cense num·ber (número *m* de) matrícula *f*

'li·cense plate *of car* (placa *f* de) matrícula *f*

lick [lɪk] 1 *n* lamedura *f* 2 *v/t* lamer; **lick one's lips** relamerse

lick·ing ['lɪkɪŋ] F (*defeat*): **we got a licking** nos dieron una paliza F

li·co·rice ['lɪkərɪs] regaliz *m*

lid [lɪd] (*top*) tapa *f*

lie¹ [laɪ] 1 *n* mentira *f* 2 *v/i* mentir

lie² [laɪ] *v/i* (*pret* **lay**, *pp* **lain**) *of person* estar tumbado; *of object* estar; (*be situated*) estar, encontrarse; **lie on your stomach** túmbate boca abajo

◆ **lie down** *v/i* tumbarse

lie-in: have a lie-in quedarse un rato más en la cama

lieu [luː]: **in lieu of** en lugar de

lieu·ten·ant [luː'tenənt] teniente *m/f*

life [laɪf] (*pl* **lives** [laɪvz]) vida *f; of machine* vida *f,* duración *f;* **all her life** toda su vida; **that's life!** ¡así es la vida!

'life belt salvavidas *m inv*

'life·boat *from ship* bote *m* salvavidas; *from land* lancha *f* de salvamento

'life ex·pect·an·cy esperanza *f* de vida

'life·guard socorrista *m/f*

'life his·to·ry historia *f* de la vida

'life im·pris·on·ment cadena *f* perpetua

'life jack·et chaleco *m* salvavidas

'life·less ['laɪflɪs] *adj* sin vida

'life·like ['laɪflaɪk] *adj* realista

'life·long de toda la vida

'life pre·serv·er salvavidas *m inv*

'life-sav·ing *adj medical equipment, drug* que salva vidas

'life-sized *adj* de tamaño natural

'life-threat·en·ing *adj* que puede ser mortal

'life·time *n;* **in my lifetime** durante mi vida

lift [lɪft] 1 *v/t* levantar 2 *v/i of fog* disiparse 3 *n* (*Br: elevator*) ascensor *m;* **give s.o. a lift** llevar a alguien (en coche)

◆ **lift off** *v/i of rocket* despegar

'lift-off *of rocket* despegue *m*

lig·a·ment ['lɪgəmənt] ligamento *m*

light¹ [laɪt] 1 *n* luz *f; in the light of* a la luz de; **have you got a light?** ¿tienes fuego? 2 *v/t* (*pret & pp* **lighted** *or* **lit**) *fire, cigarette* encender; (*illuminate*) iluminar 3 *adj color, sky* claro; *room* luminoso

light² [laɪt] 1 *adj* (*not heavy*) ligero 2 *adv:* **travel light** viajar ligero de equipaje

◆ **light up** 1 *v/t* (*illuminate*) iluminar 2 *v/i* (*start to smoke*) encender un cigarrillo

'light bulb bombilla *f*

light·en¹ ['laɪtn] *v/t color* aclarar

light·en² ['laɪtn] *v/t load* aligerar

◆ **lighten up** *v/i of person* alegrarse; **come on, lighten up** venga, no te tomes las cosas tan en serio

light·er ['laɪtər] *for cigarettes* encendedor *m, Span* mechero *m*

light-head·ed [laɪt'hedɪd] (*dizzy*) mareado

light·heart·ed [laɪt'hɑːrtɪd] *adj* alegre

'light·house faro *m*

light·ing ['laɪtɪŋ] iluminación *f*

light·ly ['laɪtlɪ] *adv touch* ligeramente; **get off lightly** salir bien parado

light·ness[1] ['laɪtnɪs] *of room, color* claridad *f*

light·ness[2] ['laɪtnɪs] *in weight* ligereza *f*

light·ning ['laɪtnɪŋ]: **a flash of lightning** un relámpago; **they were struck by lightning** les cayó un rayo

'light·ning con·duc·tor pararrayos *m inv*

'light pen lápiz *m* óptico

'light·weight *n in boxing* peso *m* ligero

'light year año *m* luz

like[1] [laɪk] **1** *prep* como; **be like s.o.** ser como alguien; **what is she like?** ¿cómo es?; **it's not like him** (*not his character*) no es su estilo **2** *conj* F (*as*) como; **like I said** como dije

like[2] [laɪk] *v/t*: **I like it / her** me gusta; **I would like ...** querría ...; **I would like to ...** me gustaría ...; **would you like ...?** ¿querrías ...?; **would you like to ...?** ¿querrías ...?; **she likes to swim** le gusta nadar; **if you like** si quieres

like·a·ble ['laɪkəbl] *adj* simpático

like·li·hood ['laɪklɪhʊd] probabilidad *f*; **in all likelihood** con toda probabilidad

like·ly ['laɪklɪ] *adj* (*probable*) probable; **not likely!** ¡ni hablar!

like·ness ['laɪknɪs] (*resemblance*) parecido *m*

'like·wise ['laɪkwaɪz] *adv* igualmente; **pleased to meet you - likewise!** encantado de conocerle - ¡lo mismo digo!

lik·ing ['laɪkɪŋ] afición *f* (**for** a); **to your liking** a su gusto; **take a liking to s.o.** tomar cariño a alguien

li·lac ['laɪlək] *flower* lila *f*; *color* lila *m*

lil·y ['lɪlɪ] lirio *m*

lil·y of the 'val·ley lirio *m* de los valles

limb [lɪm] miembro *m*

lime[1] [laɪm] *fruit, tree* lima *f*

lime[2] [laɪm] *substance* cal *f*

lime'green *adj* verde lima

'lime·light: **be in the limelight** estar en el candelero

lim·it ['lɪmɪt] **1** *n* límite *m*; **within limits** dentro de un límite; **be off limits** *of place* ser zona prohibida; **that's the limit!** F ¡es el colmo! F **2** *v/t* limitar

lim·i·ta·tion [lɪmɪ'teɪʃn] limitación *f*

lim·it·ed 'com·pa·ny sociedad *f* limitada

li·mo ['lɪmoʊ] F limusina *f*

lim·ou·sine ['lɪməzi:n] limusina *f*

limp[1] [lɪmp] *adj* flojo

limp[2] [lɪmp] *n*: **he has a limp** cojea

line[1] [laɪn] *n of text, on road,* TELEC línea *f*; *of trees* fila *f*, hilera *f*; *of people* fila *f*, cola *f*; *of business* especialidad *f*; **what line are you in?** ¿a qué te dedicas?; **the line**

is busy está ocupado, *Span* está comunicando; *Span* está comunicando; **hold the line** no cuelgue; **draw the line at sth** no estar dispuesto a hacer algo; **line of inquiry** línea *f* de investigación; **line of reasoning** argumentación *f*; **stand in line** hacer cola; **in line with ...** (*conforming with*) en las mismas líneas que

line[2] [laɪn] *v/t* forrar

◆ **line up** *v/i* hacer cola

lin·e·ar ['lɪnɪər] *adj* lineal

lin·en ['lɪnɪn] *material* lino *m*; (*sheets etc*) ropa *f* blanca

lin·er ['laɪnər] *ship* transatlántico *m*

lines·man ['laɪnzmən] SP juez *m* de línea, linier *m*

lin·ger ['lɪŋgər] *v/i of person* entretenerse; *of pain* persistir

lin·ge·rie ['læ̃ʒərɪ:] lencería *f*

lin·guist ['lɪŋgwɪst] lingüista *m/f*; **she's a good linguist** se le dan bien los idiomas

lin·guis·tic [lɪŋ'gwɪstɪk] *adj* lingüístico

lin·ing ['laɪnɪŋ] *of clothes* forro *m*; *of brakes, pipe* revestimiento *m*

link [lɪŋk] **1** *n* (*connection*) conexión *f*; *between countries* vínculo *m*; *in chain* eslabón *m* **2** *v/t* conectar

◆ **link up** *v/i* encontrarse; TV conectar

li·on ['laɪən] león *m*

lip [lɪp] labio *m*

'lip·read *v/i* (*pret & pp* **lipread** [red]) leer los labios

'lip·stick barra *f* de labios

li·queur [lɪ'kjʊr] licor *m*

liq·uid ['lɪkwɪd] **1** *n* líquido *m* **2** *adj* líquido

liq·ui·date ['lɪkwɪdeɪt] *v/t assets* liquidar; F (*kill*) cepillarse a F

liq·ui·da·tion [lɪkwɪ'deɪʃn] liquidación *f*; **go into liquidation** ir a la quiebra

liq·uid·i·ty [lɪ'kwɪdɪtɪ] FIN liquidez *f*

liq·uid·ize ['lɪkwɪdaɪz] *v/t* licuar

liq·uid·iz·er ['lɪkwɪdaɪzər] licuadora *f*

liq·uor ['lɪkər] bebida *f* alcohólica

'liq·uor store tienda *f* de bebidas alcohólicas

lisp [lɪsp] **1** *n* ceceo *m* **2** *v/i* cecear

list [lɪst] **1** *n* lista *f* **2** *v/t* enumerar; COMPUT listar

lis·ten ['lɪsn] *v/i* escuchar; **I tried to persuade him, but he wouldn't listen** intenté convencerle, pero no me hizo ningún caso

◆ **listen in** *v/i* escuchar

◆ **listen to** *v/t radio, person* escuchar

lis·ten·er ['lɪsnər] *to radio* oyente *m/f*; **he's a good listener** sabe escuchar

list·ings mag·a·zine ['lɪstɪŋz] guía *f* de espectáculos

list·less ['lɪstlɪs] adj apático, lánguido

lit [lɪt] pret & pp → **light¹**

li·ter ['liːtər] litro m

lit·e·ral ['lɪtərəl] adj literal

lit·e·ral·ly ['lɪtərəlɪ] adv literalmente

lit·e·ra·ry ['lɪtərerɪ] adj literario

lit·e·rate ['lɪtərət] adj culto; **be literate** saber leer y escribir

lit·e·ra·ture ['lɪtrətʃər] literatura f; **about a product** folletos mpl, prospectos mpl

li·tre Br → **liter**

lit·ter ['lɪtər] basura f; of animal camada f

'lit·ter bas·ket papelera f

'lit·ter bin cubo m de la basura

lit·tle ['lɪtl] **1** adj pequeño; **the little ones** los pequeños **2** n poco m; **the little I know** lo poco que sé; **a little** un poco; **a little bread / wine** un poco de pan / vino; **a little is better than nothing** más vale poco que nada **3** adv: poco; **little by little** poco a poco; **a little better / bigger** poco mejor / más grande; **a little before 6** un poco antes de las 6

live¹ [lɪv] v/i vivir

◆ **live on** v/t rice, bread sobrevivir a base de **2** v/i (continue living) sobrevivir, vivir

◆ **live up**: **live it up** pasarlo bien

◆ **live up to** v/t responder a

◆ **live with** v/t vivir con

live² [laɪv] adj broadcast en directo; **ammunition** real; **wire** con corriente

live·li·hood ['laɪvlɪhʊd] vida f, sustento m; **earn one's livelihood** ganarse la vida

live·li·ness ['laɪvlɪnɪs] of person, music vivacidad f; of debate lo animado

live·ly ['laɪvlɪ] adj animado

liv·er ['lɪvər] MED, food hígado m

live·stock ['laɪvstɑːk] ganado m

liv·id ['lɪvɪd] adj (angry) enfurecido, furioso

liv·ing ['lɪvɪŋ] **1** adj vivo **2** n vida f; **what do you do for a living?** ¿en qué trabajas?; **earn one's living** ganarse la vida; **standard of living** estándar m de vida

'liv·ing room sala f de estar, salón m

liz·ard ['lɪzərd] lagarto m

load [loʊd] **1** n also ELEC carga f; **loads of** F montones de F **2** v/t car, truck, gun cargar; camera poner el carrete a; COMPUT: software cargar (en memoria); **load sth onto sth** cargar algo en algo

load·ed ['loʊdɪd] adj F (very rich) forrado F; (drunk) como una cuba

loaf [loʊf] n (pl loaves [loʊvz]) pan m; **a loaf of bread** una barra de pan, un pan

◆ **loaf about** v/i F gandulear F

loaf·er ['loʊfər] shoe mocasín m

loan [loʊn] **1** n préstamo m; **on loan** prestado **2** v/t prestar; **loan s.o. sth** prestar

algo a alguien

loathe [loʊð] v/t detestar, aborrecer

loath·ing ['loʊðɪŋ] odio m, aborrecimiento m

lob·by ['lɑːbɪ] n in hotel, theater vestíbulo m; POL lobby m, grupo m de presión

lobe [loʊb] of ear lóbulo m

lob·ster ['lɑːbstər] langosta f

lo·cal ['loʊkl] **1** adj local; **the local people** la gente del lugar; **I'm not local** no soy de aquí **2** n: **the locals** los del lugar; **are you a local?** ¿eres de aquí?

'lo·cal call TELEC llamada f local

lo·cal e'lec·tions npl elecciones fpl municipales

lo·cal 'gov·ern·ment administración f municipal

lo·cal·i·ty [loʊ'kælətɪ] localidad f

lo·cal·ly ['loʊkəlɪ] adv live, work cerca, en la zona; **it's well known locally** es muy conocido en la zona; **they are grown locally** son cultivados en la región

lo·cal 'pro·duce productos mpl del lugar

'lo·cal time hora f local

lo·cate [loʊ'keɪt] v/t new factory etc emplazar, ubicar; (identify position of) situar; **be located** encontrarse

lo·ca·tion [loʊ'keɪʃn] (siting) emplazamiento m; (identifying position of) localización f; **on location** movie en exteriores

lock¹ [lɑːk] of hair mechón m

lock² [lɑːk] **1** n on door cerradura f **2** v/t door cerrar (con llave)

◆ **lock away** v/t guardar bajo llave

◆ **lock in** v/t person encerrar; **I locked myself in** me quedé encerrado

◆ **lock out** v/t of house dejar fuera

◆ **lock up** v/t in prison encerrar

lock·er ['lɑːkər] taquilla f

'lock·er room vestuario m

lock·et ['lɑːkɪt] guardapelo m

lock·smith ['lɑːksmɪθ] cerrajero(-a) m(f)

lo·cust ['loʊkəst] langosta f

lodge [lɑːdʒ] **1** v/t complaint presentar **2** v/i of bullet alojarse

lodg·er ['lɑːdʒər] huésped m/f

loft [lɑːft] buhardilla f, desván m

loft·y ['lɑːftɪ] adj heights, ideals elevado

log [lɑːg] n wood tronco m; written record registro m

◆ **log off** v/i (pret & pp **logged**) salir

◆ **log on** v/i entrar

◆ **log on to** v/t entrar a

'log·book captain's cuaderno m de bitácora; driver's documentación f del vehículo

log 'cab·in cabaña f

log·ger·heads ['lɑːgərhedz]: **be at log-**

gerheads estar enfrentado

lo·gic ['lɑːdʒɪk] lógica f
lo·gic·al ['lɑːdʒɪkl] adj lógico
lo·gic·al·ly ['lɑːdʒɪklɪ] adv lógicamente
lo·gis·tics [ləˈdʒɪstɪks] logística f
lo·go ['lougou] logotipo m
loi·ter ['lɔɪtər] v/i holgazanear
lol·li·pop ['lɑːlɪpɑːp] piruleta f
Lon·don ['lʌndən] Londres
lone·li·ness ['lounlɪnɪs] of person, place soledad f
lone·ly ['lounlɪ] adj person solo; place solitario
lon·er ['lounər] solitario(-a) m(f)
long[1] [lɔːŋ] 1 adj largo; it's a long way hay un largo camino; it's two feet long mide dos pies de largo; the movie is three hours long la película dura tres horas 2 adv mucho tiempo; don't be long no tardes mucho; 5 weeks is too long 5 semanas son mucho tiempo; will it take long? ¿llevará mucho tiempo?; that was long ago eso fue hace mucho tiempo; long before them mucho antes; before long al poco tiempo; we can't wait any longer no podemos esperar más tiempo; she no longer works here ya no trabaja aquí; so long as (provided) siempre que; so long! ¡hasta la vista!
long[2] [lɔːŋ] v/i: long for sth home estar en falta algo; change anhelar or desear algo; be longing to do sth anhelar or desear hacer algo
long·'dis·tance adj race de fondo; flight de larga distancia; a long-distance phone-call una llamada de larga distancia, una conferencia interurbana
lon·gev·i·ty [lɑːnˈdʒevɪtɪ] longevidad f
long·ing ['lɔːŋɪŋ] n anhelo m, deseo m
lon·gi·tude ['lɑːndʒɪtuːd] longitud f
'long jump Br salto m de longitud
'long-range missile de largo alcance; forecast a largo plazo
long-sight·ed [lɔːŋˈsaɪtɪd] adj hipermétrope
long-sleeved [lɔːŋˈsliːvd] adj de manga larga
long·'stand·ing adj antiguo
'long term adj a largo plazo
'long wave RAD onda f larga
'long-wind·ed [lɔːŋˈwɪndɪd] adj prolijo
look [lʊk] 1 n (appearance) aspecto m; (glance) mirada f; give s.o. a look mirar a alguien / mirar algo; have a look at sth (examine) echar un vistazo a algo; can I have a look? ¿puedo echarle un vistazo?; can I have a look around? in shop etc ¿puedo echar un vistazo?; looks (beauty) atractivo m, guapura f 2

v/i mirar; (search) buscar; (seem) parecer; you look tired / different pareces cansado / diferente; he looks about 25 aparenta 25 años; how do things look to you? ¿qué te parece cómo están las cosas?; that looks good tiene buena pinta

◆ **look after** v/t children cuidar (de); property, interests proteger
◆ **look ahead** v/i fig mirar hacia el futuro
◆ **look around** 1 v/i mirar 2 v/t museum, city dar una vuelta por
◆ **look at** v/t mirar; (examine) estudiar; (consider) considerar; it depends how you look at it depende de cómo lo mires
◆ **look back** v/i mirar atrás
◆ **look down on** v/t mirar por encima del hombro a
◆ **look for** v/t buscar
◆ **look forward to** v/t estar deseando; I'm looking forward to the vacation tengo muchas ganas de empezar las vacaciones
◆ **look in on** v/t (visit) hacer una visita a
◆ **look into** v/t (investigate) investigar
◆ **look on** 1 v/i (watch) quedarse mirando 2 v/t: look on s.o./sth as (consider) considerar a alguien / algo como
◆ **look onto** v/t garden, street dar a
◆ **look out** v/i through, from window etc mirar; (pay attention) tener cuidado; look out! ¡cuidado!
◆ **look out for** v/t buscar; (be on guard against) tener cuidado con
◆ **look out of** v/t window mirar por
◆ **look over** v/t translation revisar, repasar; house inspeccionar
◆ **look round** v/t museum, city dar una vuelta por
◆ **look through** v/t magazine, notes echar un vistazo a, hojear
◆ **look to** v/t (rely on): we look to you for help acudimos a usted en busca de ayuda
◆ **look up** 1 v/i from paper etc levantar la mirada; (improve) mejorar; things are looking up las cosas están mejorando 2 v/t word, phone number buscar; (visit) visitar
◆ **look up to** v/t (respect) admirar
'look-out person centinela m, vigía m; be on the lookout for estar buscando
◆ **loom up** [luːm] v/i aparecer (out of de entre)
loon·y ['luːnɪ] 1 n F chalado(-a) m(f) F 2 adj F chalado F
loop [luːp] n bucle m
'loop·hole in law etc resquicio m or vacío m legal
loose [luːs] adj connection, button suelto; clothes suelto, holgado; morals disoluto,

relajado; *wording* impreciso; **loose change** suelto *m*, *L.Am.* sencillo *m*; **loose ends** *of problem, discussion* cabos *mpl* sueltos

loose·ly ['luːslɪ] *adv worded* vagamente

loos·en ['luːsn] *v/t collar, knot* aflojar

loot [luːt] **1** *n* botín *m* **2** *v/i* saquear

loot·er ['luːtər] saqueador(a) *m(f)*

◆ **lop off** [lɑːp] *v/t (pret & pp lopped) branch* cortar; podar

lop-sid·ed [lɑːp'saɪdɪd] *adj* torcido; *balance of committee* desigual

Lord [lɔːrd] *(God)* Señor *m*

Lord's 'Prayer padrenuestro *m*

lor·ry ['lɒrɪ] *Br* camión *m*

lose [luːz] **1** *v/t (pret & pp lost) object, match* perder **2** *v/i (pret & pp lost)* *sp* perder; *of clock* retrasarse; **I'm lost** me he perdido; **get lost!** F ¡vete a paseo!

◆ **lose out** *v/i* salir perdiendo

los·er ['luːzər] perdedor(-a) *m(f)*; F *in life* fracasado(-a) *m(f)*

loss [lɑːs] pérdida *f*; **make a loss** tener pérdidas; **I'm at a loss what to say** no sé qué decir

lost [lɑːst] **1** *adj* perdido **2** *pret & pp* → **lose**

lost-and-'found, *Br* **lost 'prop·er·ty (office)** oficina *f* de objetos perdidos

lot [lɑːt]: **the lot** todo; **a lot (of), lots (of)** mucho, muchos; **a lot of books, lots of books** muchos libros; **a lot of butter, lots of butter** mucha mantequilla; **a lot better / easier** mucho mejor / más fácil

lo·tion ['loʊʃn] loción *f*

lot·te·ry ['lɑːtərɪ] lotería *f*

loud [laʊd] *adj voice, noise* fuerte; *music* fuerte, alto; *color* chillón

loud'speak·er altavoz *m*, *L.Am.* altoparlante *m*

lounge [laʊndʒ] *in house* salón *m*

◆ **lounge about** *v/i* holgazanear

'lounge suit traje *m* de calle

louse [laʊs] *(pl lice* [laɪs]) piojo *m*

lous·y ['laʊzɪ] *adj* F asqueroso F; **I feel lousy** me siento de pena F

lout [laʊt] gamberro *m*

lov·a·ble ['lʌvəbl] *adj* adorable, encantador

love [lʌv] **1** *n* amor *m*; *in tennis* nada *f*; **be in love** estar enamorado (**with** de); **I'm in love with you** estoy enamorado de ti; **fall in love** enamorarse (**with** de); **make love** hacer el amor; **make love to …** hacer el amor con; **yes, my love** sí, amor **2** *v/t person, country, wine* amar; **she loves to watch tennis** le encanta ver tenis

'love af·fair aventura *f* amorosa

'love-life vida *f* amorosa

'love let·ter carta *f* de amor

love·ly ['lʌvlɪ] *adj face, hair, color, tune* precioso, lindo; *person, character* encantador; *holiday, weather, meal* estupendo; **we had a lovely time** nos lo pasamos de maravilla

lov·er ['lʌvər] amante *m/f*

lov·ing ['lʌvɪŋ] *adj* cariñoso

lov·ing·ly ['lʌvɪŋlɪ] *adv* con cariño

low [loʊ] **1** *adj bridge, salary, price, voice, quality* bajo; **be feeling low** estar deprimido; **we're low on gas / tea** nos queda poca gasolina / té **2** *n in weather* zona *f* de bajas presiones, borrasca *f*; *in sales, statistics* mínimo *m*

low·brow ['loʊbraʊ] *adj* poco intelectual, popular

low-'cal·o·rie *adj* bajo en calorías

'low-cut *adj dress* escotado

low·er ['loʊər] *v/t to the ground, hemline, price* bajar; *flag* arriar; *pressure* reducir

'low-fat *adj de bajo* contenido graso

'low-key *adj* discreto, mesurado

'low·lands *npl* tierras *fpl* bajas

low-'pres·sure ar·e·a zona *f* de bajas presiones, borrasca *f*

'low sea·son temporada *f* baja

'low tide marea *f* baja

loy·al ['lɔɪəl] *adj* leal, fiel (**to** a)

loy·al·ly ['lɔɪəlɪ] *adv* lealmente, fielmente

loy·al·ty ['lɔɪəltɪ] lealtad *f* (**to** a)

loz·enge ['lɑːzɪndʒ] *shape* rombo *m*; *tablet* pastilla *f*

Ltd *abbr (= limited)* S.L. *(= sociedad f limitada)*

lu·bri·cant ['luːbrɪkənt] lubricante *m*

lu·bri·cate ['luːbrɪkeɪt] *v/t* lubricar

lu·bri·ca·tion [luːbrɪ'keɪʃn] lubricación *f*

lu·cid ['luːsɪd] *adj (clear, sane)* lúcido

luck [lʌk] suerte *f*; **bad luck** mala suerte; **hard luck!** ¡mala suerte!; **good luck!** ¡buena suerte!

◆ **luck out** *v/i* F tener mucha suerte

luck·i·ly ['lʌkɪlɪ] *adv* afortunadamente, por suerte

luck·y ['lʌkɪ] *adj person, coincidence* afortunado; *day, number* de la suerte; **you were lucky** tuviste suerte; **she's lucky to be alive** tiene suerte de estar con vida; **that's lucky!** ¡qué suerte!

lu·cra·tive ['luːkrətɪv] *adj* lucrativo

lu·di·crous ['luːdɪkrəs] *adj* ridículo

lug [lʌg] *v/t (pret & pp lugged)* arrastrar

lug·gage ['lʌgɪdʒ] equipaje *m*

luke·warm ['luːkwɔːrm] *adj water* tibio, templado; *reception* indiferente

lull [lʌl] **1** *n in storm, fighting* tregua *f*; *in conversation* pausa *f* **2** *v/t*: **lull s.o. into a**

false sense of security dar a alguien una falsa sensación de seguridad
lul·la·by ['lʌləbaɪ] canción *f* de cuna, nana *f*
lum·ba·go [lʌmˈbeɪɡoʊ] lumbago *m*
lum·ber ['lʌmbər] *n* (*timber*) madera *f*
lu·mi·nous ['luːmɪnəs] *adj* luminoso
lump [lʌmp] *n of sugar, earth* terrón *m*; (*swelling*) bulto *m*
◆ **lump together** *v/t* agrupar
lump 'sum pago *m* único
lump·y ['lʌmpɪ] *adj liquid, sauce* grumoso; *mattress* lleno de bultos
lu·na·cy ['luːnəsɪ] locura *f*
lu·nar ['luːnər] *adj* lunar
lu·na·tic ['luːnətɪk] *n* lunático(-a) *m(f)*, loco(-a) *m(f)*
lunch [lʌntʃ] *n* almuerzo *m*, comida *f*; **have lunch** almorzar, comer
'lunch box fiambrera *f*
'lunch break pausa *f* para el almuerzo
'lunch hour hora *f* del almuerzo
'lunch·time hora *f* del almuerzo

lung [lʌŋ] pulmón *m*
'lung can·cer cáncer *m* de pulmón
◆ **lunge at** [lʌndʒ] *v/t* arremeter contra
lurch [lɜːrtʃ] *v/i of drunk* tambalearse; *of ship* dar sacudidas
lure [lʊr] **1** *n* atractivo *m* **2** *v/t* atraer
lu·rid ['lʊrɪd] *adj color* chillón; *details* espeluznante
lurk [lɜːrk] *v/i of person* estar oculto, estar al acecho
lus·cious ['lʌʃəs] *adj fruit, dessert* jugoso, exquisito; F *woman, man* cautivador
lush [lʌʃ] *adj vegetation* exuberante
lust [lʌst] *n* lujuria *f*
lux·u·ri·ous [lʌɡˈʒʊrɪəs] *adj* lujoso
lux·u·ri·ous·ly [lʌɡˈʒʊrɪəslɪ] *adv* lujosamente
lux·u·ry ['lʌkʃərɪ] **1** *n* lujo *m* **2** *adj* de lujo
lymph gland ['lɪmfɡlænd] ganglio *m* linfático
lynch [lɪntʃ] *v/t* linchar
lyr·i·cist ['lɪrɪsɪst] letrista *m/f*
lyr·ics ['lɪrɪks] *npl* letra *f*

M

M [em] *abbr* (= **medium**) M (= talla *f* media)
MA [em'eɪ] *abbr* (= **Master of Arts**) Máster *m* en Humanidades
ma'am [mæm] señora *f*
mac [mæk] F (*mackintosh*) impermeable *m*
ma·chine [məˈʃiːn] **1** *n* máquina *f* **2** *v/t with sewing machine* coser a máquina; TECH trabajar a máquina
ma'chine gun *n* ametralladora *f*
ma·chine-'read·a·ble *adj* legible por *Span* el ordenador *or L.Am.* la computadora
ma·chin·e·ry [məˈʃiːnərɪ] (*machines*) maquinaria *f*
ma·chine trans'la·tion traducción *f* automática
ma·chis·mo [məˈkɪzmoʊ] machismo *m*
mach·o ['mætʃoʊ] *adj* macho
mack·in·tosh ['mækɪntɑːʃ] impermeable *m*
mac·ro ['mækroʊ] COMPUT macro *m*
mad [mæd] *adj* (*insane*) loco; F (*angry*) enfadado; *a mad idea* una idea disparatada; *be mad about* F estar loco por; *drive*

s.o. mad volver loco a alguien; *go mad* (*become insane*) volverse loco; F (*with enthusiasm*) volverse loco F; *like mad* F *run, work* como un loco F; *Pa got real mad when I told him* papá se puso hecho una furia cuando se lo conté
mad·den ['mædn] *v/t* (*infuriate*) sacar de quicio
mad·den·ing ['mædnɪs] *adj* exasperante
made [meɪd] *pret & pp* → **make**
'mad·house *fig* casa *f* de locos
mad·ly ['mædlɪ] *adv* como loco; *madly in love* locamente enamorado
'mad·man loco *m*
mad·ness ['mædnɪs] locura *f*
Ma·don·na [məˈdɑːnə] madona *f*
Ma·fi·a ['mɑːfɪə]: *the Mafia* la mafia
mag·a·zine [mæɡəˈziːn] (*printed*) revista *f*
mag·got ['mæɡət] gusano *m*
Ma·gi ['meɪdʒaɪ] REL: *the Magi* los Reyes Magos
ma·gic ['mædʒɪk] **1** *n* magia *f*; *as if by magic, like magic* como por arte de magia **2** *adj* mágico; *there's nothing magic about it* no tiene nada de mágico

mag·i·cal ['mædʒɪkl] *adj* mágico

ma·gi·cian [mə'dʒɪʃn] *performer* mago(-a) *m(f)*

ma·gic 'spell hechizo *m*

ma·gic 'trick truco *m* de magia

mag·ic 'wand varita *f* mágica

mag·nan·i·mous [mæg'nænɪməs] *adj* magnánimo

mag·net ['mægnɪt] imán *m*

mag·net·ic [mæg'netɪk] *adj* magnético; *fig: personality* cautivador

mag·net·ic 'stripe banda *f* magnética

mag·net·ism [mæg'netɪzm] *of person* magnetismo *m*

mag·nif·i·cence [mæg'nɪfɪsəns] magnificencia *f*

mag·nif·i·cent [mæg'nɪfɪsənt] *adj* magnífico

mag·ni·fy ['mægnɪfaɪ] *v/t (pret & pp **magnified**)* aumentar; *difficulties* magnificar

mag·ni·fy·ing glass lupa *f*

mag·ni·tude ['mægnɪtuːd] magnitud *f*

ma·hog·a·ny [mə'hɑːgənɪ] caoba *f*

maid [meɪd] *(servant)* criada *f*; *in hotel* camarera *f*

maid·en name ['meɪdn] apellido *m* de soltera

maid·en 'voy·age viaje *m* inaugural

mail [meɪl] **1** *n* correo *m*; *put sth in the mail* echar algo al correo **2** *v/t letter* enviar (por correo)

'mail·box *also* COMPUT buzón *m*

'mail·ing list lista *f* de direcciones

'mail·man cartero *m*

mail·'or·der cat·a·log, *Br* **mail·'or·der cat·a·logue** catálogo *m* de venta por correo

mail·'or·der firm empresa *f* de venta por correo

'mail·shot mailing *m*

maim [meɪm] *v/t* mutilar

main [meɪn] *adj* principal; *she's alive, that's the main thing* está viva, es lo principal

'main course plato *m* principal

main 'en·trance entrada *f* principal

'main·frame *Span* ordenador *m* central, *L.Am.* computadora *f* central

'main·land tierra *f* firme; *on the mainland* en el continente

main·ly ['meɪnlɪ] *adv* principalmente

main 'road carretera *f* general

'main street calle *f* principal

main·tain [meɪn'teɪn] *v/t* mantener

main·te·nance ['meɪntənəns] mantenimiento *m*; *pay maintenance* pagar una pensión alimenticia

'main·te·nance costs *npl* gastos *mpl* de mantenimiento

'main·te·nance staff personal *m* de mantenimiento

ma·jes·tic [mə'dʒestɪk] *adj* majestuoso

ma·jes·ty ['mædʒestɪ] majestuosidad *f*; *Her Majesty* Su Majestad

ma·jor ['meɪdʒər] **1** *adj (significant)* importante, principal; *in C major* MUS en C mayor **2** *n* MIL comandante *m*

◆ **major in** *v/t* especializarse en

ma·jor·i·ty [mə'dʒɑːrətɪ] *also* POL mayoría *f*; *be in the majority* ser mayoría

make [meɪk] **1** *n (brand)* marca *f* **2** *v/t (pret & pp made)* hacer; *cars* fabricar, producir; *movie* rodar; *speech* pronunciar; *(earn)* ganar; MATH hacer; *two and two make four* dos y dos son cuatro; *make s.o. do sth (force to)* obligar a alguien a hacer algo; *(cause to)* hacer que alguien haga algo; *you can't make me do it!* ¡no puedes obligarme a hacerlo!; *make s.o. happy / angry* hacer feliz/enfadar a alguien; *make a decision* tomar una decisión; *make a telephone call* hacer una llamada telefónica; *made in Japan* hecho en Japón; *make it (catch bus, train)* llegar a tiempo; *(come)* ir; *(succeed)* tener éxito; *(survive)* sobrevivir; *what time do you make it?* ¿qué hora llevas?; *make believe* imaginarse; *make do with* conformarse con; *what do you make of it?* ¿qué piensas?

◆ **make for** *v/t (go toward)* dirigirse hacia

◆ **make off** *v/i* escaparse

◆ **make off with** *v/t (steal)* llevarse

◆ **make out** *v/t list* hacer, elaborar; *check* extender; *(see)* distinguir; *(imply)* pretender

◆ **make over** ceder

◆ **make up 1** *v/i of woman, actor* maquillarse; *after quarrel* reconciliarse **2** *v/t story, excuse* inventar; *face* maquillar; *(constitute)* suponer, formar; *be made up of* estar compuesto de; *make up one's mind* decidirse; *make it up after quarrel* reconciliarse

◆ **make up for** *v/t* compensar por

'make-be·lieve *n* ficción *f*, fantasía *f*

mak·er ['meɪkər] *(manufacturer)* fabricante *m*

make·shift ['meɪkʃɪft] *adj* improvisado

make-up ['meɪkʌp] *(cosmetics)* maquillaje *m*

'make-up bag bolsa *f* del maquillaje

mal·ad·just·ed [mælə'dʒʌstɪd] *adj* inadaptado

male [meɪl] **1** *adj (masculine)* masculino; *animal, bird, fish* macho; *male bosses* los jefes varones; *a male teacher* un profesor **2** *n man* hombre *m*, varón *m*; ani-

mal, *bird*, *fish* macho *m*

male 'chau·vin·ism machismo *m*

male chau·vin·ist 'pig machista *m*

male 'nurse enfermero *m*

ma·lev·o·lent ['mɔ'levələnt] *adj* malévolo

mal·func·tion [mæl'fʌŋkʃn] **1** *n* fallo *m* (**in** de) **2** *v/i* fallar

mal·ice ['mælɪs] malicia *f*

ma·li·cious [mɔ'lɪʃəs] *adj* malicioso

ma·lig·nant [mɔ'lɪgnənt] *adj tumor* maligno

mall [mɔːl] (*shopping mall*) centro *m* comercial

mal·nu·tri·tion [mælnuː'trɪʃn] desnutrición *f*

mal·treat [mæl'triːt] *v/t* maltratar

mal·treat·ment [mæl'triːtmənt] maltrato *m*

mam·mal ['mæml] mamífero *m*

mam·moth ['mæməθ] *adj* (*enormous*) gigantesco

man [mæn] **1** *n* (*pl* **men** [men]) hombre *m*; (*humanity*) el hombre; *in checkers* ficha *f* **2** *v/t* (*pret & pp* **manned**) *telephones, front desk* atender; *spacecraft* tripular

man·age ['mænɪdʒ] **1** *v/t business* dirigir; *money* gestionar; *suitcase* poder con; *manage to ...* conseguir ... **2** *v/i* (*cope*) arreglárselas

man·age·a·ble ['mænɪdʒəbl] *adj* (*easy to handle*) manejable; (*feasible*) factible

man·age·ment ['mænɪdʒmənt] (*managing*) gestión *f*, administración *f*; (*managers*) dirección *f*; *under his management* bajo su gestión

man·age·ment 'buy·out compra de una empresa por sus directores

man·age·ment con'sult·ant consultor(a) *m(f)* en administración de empresas

'man·age·ment stud·ies estudios *mpl* de administración de empresas

'man·age·ment team equipo *m* directivo

man·ag·er ['mænɪdʒər] *of hotel, company* director(a) *m(f)*; *of shop, restaurant* encargado(a) *m(f)*

man·a·ge·ri·al [mænɪ'dʒɪriəl] *adj* de gestión; *a managerial post* un puesto directivo

man·ag·ing di'rec·tor director(a) *m(f)* gerente

man·da·rin (or·ange) [mændərɪn'(ɔːrɪndʒ)] mandarina *f*

man·date ['mændeɪt] (*authority*) mandato *m*; (*task*) tarea *f*

man·da·to·ry ['mændətɔːrɪ] *adj* obligatorio

mane [meɪn] *of horse* crines *fpl*

ma·neu·ver [mɔ'nuːvər] **1** *n* maniobra *f* **2** *v/t* maniobrar; *she maneuvered him in-*

to giving her the assignment consiguió convencerle para que le diera el trabajo

man·gle ['mæŋgl] *v/t* (*crush*) destrozar

man·han·dle ['mænhændl] *v/t* mover a la fuerza

man·hood ['mænhʊd] (*maturity*) madurez *f*; (*virility*) virilidad *f*

'man-hour hora-hombre *f*

'man·hunt persecución *f*

ma·ni·a ['meɪnɪə] (*craze*) pasión *f*

ma·ni·ac ['meɪnɪæk] F chiflado(-a) *m(f)* F

man·i·cure ['mænɪkjʊr] manicura *f*

man·i·fest ['mænɪfest] **1** *adj* manifiesto **2** *v/t* manifestar; *manifest itself* manifestarse

ma·nip·u·late [mɔ'nɪpjʊleɪt] *v/t person, bones* manipular

ma·nip·u·la·tion [mɔnɪpjʊ'leɪʃn] *of person, bones* manipulación *f*

ma·nip·u·la·tive [mɔ'nɪpjʊlətɪv] *adj* manipulador

man'kind la hum*anidad*

man·ly ['mænlɪ] *adj* (*brave*) de hombres; (*strong*) varonil

'man-made *adj fibers, materials* sintético; *crater, structure* artificial

man·ner ['mænər] *of doing sth* manera *f*, modo *m*; (*attitude*) actitud *f*

man·ners ['mænərz] *npl* modales *mpl*; *good / bad manners* buena / mala educación; *have no manners* ser un maleducado

ma·noeu·vre *Br* → **maneuver**

'man·pow·er (*workers*) mano *f* de obra; *for other tasks* recursos *mpl* humanos

man·sion ['mænʃn] mansión *f*

'man·slaugh·ter *Br* homicidio *m* sin premeditación

man·tel·piece ['mæntlpiːs] repisa *f* de chimenea

man·u·al ['mænjʊəl] **1** *adj* manual **2** *n* manual *m*

man·u·al·ly ['mænjʊəlɪ] *adv* a mano

man·u·fac·ture [mænjʊ'fæktʃər] **1** *n* fabricación *f* **2** *v/t equipment* fabricar

man·u·fac·tur·er [mænjʊ'fæktʃərər] fabricante *m*

man·u·fac·tur·ing [mænjʊ'fæktʃərɪŋ] *adj industry* manufacturero

ma·nure [mɔ'nʊr] estiércol *m*

man·u·script ['mænjʊskrɪpt] manuscrito *m*

man·y ['menɪ] **1** *adj* muchos; *take as many apples as you like* toma todas las manzanas que quieras; *many times* muchas veces; *not many people / taxis* no mucha gente / muchos taxis; *too many problems / beers* demasiados problemas / demasiadas cervezas **2** *pron*

M

muchos; *a great many, a good many*
muchos; *how many do you need?*
¿cuántos necesitas?; *as many as 200*
are still missing hay hasta 200 desapa-
recidos

'man-year año-hombre *m*

map [mæp] mapa *m*
◆ map out *v/t (pret & pp mapped)*
proyectar

ma·ple ['meɪpl] arce *m*

mar [mɑːr] *v/t (pret & pp marred)* empañar

mar·a·thon ['mærəθɑːn] *race* maratón *m*
or f

mar·ble ['mɑːrbl] FIN *material* mármol *m*

March [mɑːrtʃ] marzo *m*

march [mɑːrtʃ] **1** *n* marcha **2** *v/i* marchar

march·er ['mɑːrtʃər] manifestante *mf*

mare [mer] yegua *f*

mar·ga·rine [mɑːrdʒə'riːn] margarina *f*

mar·gin ['mɑːrdʒɪn] *also* COM margen *m*;
by a narrow margin por un estrecho
margen

mar·gin·al ['mɑːrdʒɪnl] *adj (slight)* marginal

mar·gin·al·ly ['mɑːrdʒɪnlɪ] *adv (slightly)*
ligeramente

mar·i·hua·na, mar·i·jua·na [mærɪ'hwɑː-
nə] marihuana *f*

ma·ri·na [mə'riːnə] puerto *m* deportivo

mar·i·nade [mærɪ'neɪd] *n* adobo *m*

mar·i·nate ['mærɪneɪt] *v/t* adobar, marinar

ma·rine [mə'riːn] **1** *adj* marino **2** *n* MIL marine *m/f*, infante *m/f* de marina

mar·i·tal ['mærɪtl] *adj* marital

mar·i·tal 'sta·tus estado *m* civil

mar·i·time ['mærɪtaɪm] *adj* marítimo

mar·jo·ram ['mɑːrdʒərəm] mejorana *f*

mark¹ [mɑːrk] FIN marco *m*

mark² [mɑːrk] **1** *n* señal *f*, marca *f*; *(stain)*
marca *f*, mancha *f*; *(sign, token)* signo *m*,
señal *f*; *(trace)* señal *f*; EDU nota *f*; *leave*
one's mark dejar huella **2** *v/t (stain)* manchar; EDU calificar; *(indicate, commemo-*
rate) marcar **3** *v/i* of fabric mancharse
◆ mark down *v/t goods* rebajar
◆ mark off *v/t with a line etc* marcar; *(fig:*
set apart) distinguir
◆ mark up *v/t price* subir; *goods* subir de
precio

marked [mɑːrkt] *adj (definite)* marcado,
notable

mark·er ['mɑːrkər] *(highlighter)* rotulador *m*

mar·ket ['mɑːrkɪt] **1** *n* mercado *m*; *(stock*
market) bolsa *f*; *on the market* en el mercado **2** *v/t* comercializar

mar·ket·a·ble ['mɑːrkɪtəbl] *adj* comercia-

lizable

mar·ket e'con·o·my economía *f* de mercado

'mar·ket for·ces *npl* fuerzas *fpl* del mercado

'mar·ket·ing ['mɑːrkɪtɪŋ] marketing *m*

'mar·ket·ing cam·paign campaña *f* de
marketing

'mar·ket·ing de·part·ment departamento
m de marketing

'mar·ket·ing mix marketing mix *m*, *el pro-*
ducto, el precio, la distribución y la pro-
moción

'mar·ket·ing strat·e·gy estrategia *f* de
marketing

'mar·ket·place *in town* plaza *f* del mercado; *for commodities* mercado *m*

mar·ket re'search investigación *f* de
mercado

mar·ket 'share cuota *f* de mercado

mark-up ['mɑːrkʌp] margen *m*

mar·ma·lade ['mɑːrməleɪd] mermelada *f*
de naranja

mar·quee [mɑːr'kiː] carpa *f*

mar·riage ['mærɪdʒ] matrimonio *m*; *event*
boda *f*

'mar·riage cer·tif·i·cate certificado *m* de
matrimonio

mar·riage 'guid·ance coun·se·lor conse-
jero(-a) *m(f)* matrimonial

mar·ried ['mærɪd] *adj* casado; *be married*
to ... estar casado con ...

mar·ried 'life vida *f* matrimonial

mar·ry ['mærɪ] *v/t (pret & pp married)* casarse con; *of priest* casar; *get married* casarse

marsh [mɑːrʃ] pantano *m*, ciénaga *f*

mar·shal ['mɑːrʃl] *n in police* jefe(-a)
m(f) de policía; *in security service* miembro *m* del servicio de seguridad

marsh·mal·low [mɑːrʃ'mælou] dulce de
consistencia blanda

marsh·y ['mɑːrʃɪ] *adj* pantanoso

mar·tial arts [mɑːrʃl'ɑːrts] *npl* artes *fpl*
marciales

mar·tial 'law ley *f* marcial

mar·tyr ['mɑːrtər] mártir *m/f*

mar·tyred ['mɑːrtərd] *adj fig* de mártir

mar·vel ['mɑːrvl] maravilla *f*
◆ marvel at *v/t* maravillarse de

mar·ve·lous, *Br* mar·vel·lous ['mɑːrvə-
ləs] *adj* maravilloso

Marx·ism ['mɑːrksɪzm] marxismo *m*

Marx·ist ['mɑːrksɪst] **1** *adj* marxista **2** *n*
marxista *m/f*

mar·zi·pan ['mɑːrzɪpæn] mazapán *m*

mas·ca·ra [mæ'skærə] rímel *m*

mas·cot ['mæskət] mascota *f*

mas·cu·line ['mæskjulın] *adj* masculino

mas·cu·lin·i·ty [mæskju'lınətı] (*virility*) masculinidad *f*

mash [mæʃ] *v/t* hacer puré de, majar

mashed po·ta·toes [mæʃt] *npl* puré *m* de patatas *or L.Am.* papas

mask [mæsk] **1** *n* máscara *f*; *to cover mouth, nose* mascarilla *f* **2** *v/t feelings* enmascarar

'mask·ing tape cinta *f* adhesiva de pintor

mas·och·ism ['mæsəkızm] masoquismo *m*

mas·och·ist ['mæsəkıst] masoquista *m/f*

ma·son ['meısn] cantero *m*

ma·son·ry ['meısnrı] albañilería *f*

mas·que·rade [mæskə'reıd] **1** *n fig* mascarada *f* **2** *v/i*: *masquerade as* hacerse pasar por

mass¹ [mæs] **1** *n* (*great amount*) gran cantidad *f*; (*body*) masa *f*; *the masses* las masas; *masses of* F un montón de F **2** *v/i* concentrarse

mass² [mæs] REL misa *f*

mas·sa·cre ['mæsəkər] **1** *n* masacre *f*, matanza *f*; F *in sport* paliza *f* **2** *v/t* masacrar; F *in sport* dar una paliza a

mas·sage ['mæsɑ:ʒ] **1** *n* masaje *m* **2** *v/t* dar un masaje en; *figures* maquillar

'mas·sage par·lor, *Br* **'mas·sage parlour** salón *m* de masajes

mas·seur [mæ'sɜːr] masajista *m*

mas·seuse [mæ'sɜːrz] masajista *f*

mas·sive ['mæsıv] *adj* enorme; *heart attack* muy grave

mass 'me·di·a *npl* medios *mpl* de comunicación

mass·pro'duce *v/t* fabricar en serie

mass pro'duc·tion fabricación *f* en serie

mast [mæst] *of ship* mástil *m*; *for radio signal* torre *f*

mas·ter ['mæstər] **1** *n of dog* dueño *m*, amo *m*; *of ship* patrón *m*; *be a master of* ser un maestro de **2** *v/t skill, language, situation* dominar

'mas·ter bed·room dormitorio *m* principal

'mas·ter key llave *f* maestra

mas·ter·ly ['mæstəlı] *adj* magistral

'mas·ter·mind 1 *n* cerebro *m* **2** *v/t* dirigir, organizar

Mas·ter of 'Arts Máster *m* en Humanidades

mas·ter of 'cer·e·mo·nies maestro *m* de ceremonias

'mas·ter·piece obra *f* maestra

'mas·ter's (de·gree) máster *m*

mas·ter·y ['mæstərı] dominio *m*

mas·tur·bate ['mæstərbeıt] *v/i* masturbarse

mat [mæt] *for floor* estera *f*; *for table* salvamanteles *m inv*

match¹ [mætʃ] *for cigarette* cerilla *f*, fósforo *m*

match² [mætʃ] **1** *n* SP partido *m*; *in chess* partida *f*; *be no match for s.o.* no estar a la altura de alguien; *meet one's match* encontrar la horma de su zapato **2** *v/t* (*be the same as*) coincidir con; (*be in harmony with*) hacer juego con; (*equal*) igualar **3** *v/i of colors, patterns* hacer juego

'match·box caja *f* de cerillas

match·ing ['mætʃıŋ] *adj* a juego

'match stick cerilla *f*, fósforo *m*

mate [meıt] **1** *n of animal* pareja *f*; NAUT oficial *m/f* **2** *v/i* aparearse; *these birds mate for life* estas aves viven con la misma pareja toda la vida

ma·te·ri·al [mə'tırıəl] **1** *n* (*fabric*) tejido *m*; (*substance*) material *m*; *materials* materiales *mpl* **2** *adj* material

ma·te·ri·al·ism [mə'tırıəlızm] materialismo *m*

ma·te·ri·al·ist [mətırıə'lıst] materialista *m/f*

ma·te·ri·al·is·tic [mətırıə'lıstık] *adj* materialista

ma·te·ri·al·ize [mə'tırıəlaız] *v/i* (*appear*) aparecer; (*come into existence*) hacerse realidad

ma·ter·nal [mə'tɜːrnl] *adj* maternal; *my maternal grandfather* mi abuelo materno

ma·ter·ni·ty [mə'tɜːrnətı] maternidad *f*

ma'ter·ni·ty dress vestido *m* premamá

ma'ter·ni·ty leave baja *f* por maternidad

ma'ter·ni·ty ward pabellón *m* de maternidad

math [mæθ] matemáticas *fpl*

math·e·mat·i·cal [mæθə'mætıkl] *adj* matemático

math·e·ma·ti·cian [mæθəmə'tıʃn] matemático(-a) *m(f)*

math·e·mat·ics [mæθ'mætıks] matemáticas *fpl*

maths *Br* → **math**

mat·i·née ['mætıneı] sesión *f* de tarde

ma·tri·arch ['meıtrıɑːrk] matriarca *f*

mat·ri·mo·ny ['mætrəmoʊnı] matrimonio *m*

matt [mæt] *adj* mate

mat·ter ['mætər] **1** *n* (*affair*) asunto *m*; PHYS materia *f*; *you're only making matters worse* sólo estás empeorando las cosas; *as a matter of course* automáticamente; *as a matter of fact* de hecho; *what's the matter?* ¿qué pasa?; *no matter what she says* diga lo que diga **2** *v/i* importar; *it doesn't matter* no importa

mat·ter-of-ʹfact *adj* tranquilo

mat·tress [ˈmætrɪs] colchón *m*

ma·ture [məˈtʃʊr] **1** *adj* maduro **2** *v/i* of person madurar; *of insurance policy etc* vencer

ma·tu·ri·ty [məˈtʃʊrətɪ] madurez *f*

maul [mɔːl] *v/t of lion, tiger* atacar; *of critics* destrozar

max·i·mize [ˈmæksɪmaɪz] *v/t* maximizar

max·i·mum [ˈmæksɪməm] **1** *adj* máximo; *it will cost $500 maximum* costará 500 dólares como máximo **2** *n* máximo *m*

May [meɪ] mayo *m*

may [meɪ] *v/aux◇ possibility: it may rain* puede que llueva; *you may be right* puede que tengas razón; *it may not happen* puede que no ocurra

◆

◆ *permission* poder; *may I help / smoke?* ¿puedo ayudar / fumar?

may·be [ˈmeɪbiː] *adv* quizás, tal vez

ʹMay Day el Primero de Mayo

may·o, may·on·naise [ˈmeɪoʊ, meɪəˈneɪz] mayonesa *f*

may·or [mer] alcalde *m*

maze [meɪz] laberinto *m*

MB *abbr* (= *megabyte*) MB (= megabyte *m*)

MBA [embiːˈeɪ] *abbr* (= *Master of Business Administration*) MBA *m* (= Máster *m* en Administración de Empresas)

MBO [embiːˈoʊ] *abbr* (= *management buyout*) compra de una empresa por sus directivos

MC [emˈsiː] *abbr* (= *master of ceremonies*) maestro *m* de ceremonias

MD [emˈdiː] *abbr* (= *Doctor of Medicine*) Doctor(a) *m(f)* en Medicina; (= *managing director*) director(a) *m(f)* gerente

me [miː] *pron direct & indirect object* me; *after prep inf; he knows me* me conoce; *he gave me the keys* me dio las llaves; *he sold it to me* me lo vendió; *this is for me* esto es para mí; *who do you mean? - me?* ¿a quién te refieres? - ¿a mí?; *with me* conmigo; *it's me* soy yo; *taller than me* más alto que yo

mead·ow [ˈmedoʊ] prado *m*

mea·ger, Br mea·gre [ˈmiːgər] *adj* escaso, exiguo

meal [miːl] comida *f*; *enjoy your meal* ¡que aproveche!

ʹmeal·time hora *f* de comer

mean¹ [miːn] *adj with money* tacaño; *(nasty)* malo, cruel; *that was a mean thing to say* ha estado fatal que dijeras eso

mean² [miːn] **1** *v/t (pret & pp meant) (intend to say)* querer decir; *(signify)* querer decir, significar; *you weren't meant to hear that* no era mi intención que oyeras eso; *mean to do sth* tener la intención de hacer algo; *be meant for* ser para; *of remark* ir dirigido a; *doesn't it mean anything to you?* ¿(doesn't it matter?) ¿no te importa para nada? **2** *v/i (pret & pp meant): mean well* tener buena intención

mean·ing [ˈmiːnɪŋ] *of word* significado *m*

mean·ing·ful [ˈmiːnɪŋfəl] *adj (comprehensible)* con sentido; *(constructive)*, glance significativo

mean·ing·less [ˈmiːnɪŋlɪs] *adj* sin sentido

means [miːnz] *npl financial* medios *mpl*; *(nsg: way)* medio *m*; *a means of transport* un medio de transporte; *by all means (certainly)* por supuesto; *by all means check my figures* comprueba mis cifras, faltaría más; *by no means rich / poor* ni mucho menos rico / pobre; *by means of* mediante

meant [ment] *pret & pp* → **mean²**

mean·time [ˈmiːntaɪm] **1** *adv* mientras tanto **2** *n: in the meantime* mientras tanto

mean·while [ˈmiːnwaɪl] **1** *adv* mientras tanto **2** *n: in the meanwhile* mientras tanto

mea·sles [ˈmiːzlz] *nsg* sarampión *m*

mea·sure [ˈmeʒər] **1** *n (step)* medida *f*; *we've had a measure of success (certain amount)* hemos tenido cierto éxito **2** *v/t* medir **3** *v/i* medir

◆ **measure out** *v/t area, drink, medicine* medir; *sugar, flour, ingredients* pesar

◆ **measure up** *v/i* estar a la altura (*to* de)

mea·sure·ment [ˈmeʒərmənt] medida *f*; *system of measurement* sistema *m* de medidas

meas·ur·ing jug [ˈmeʒərɪŋ] jarra *m* graduada

ʹmeas·ur·ing tape cinta *f* métrica

meat [miːt] carne *f*

ʹmeat·ball albóndiga *f*

ʹmeat·loaf masa de carne cocinada en forma de barra de pan que se come fría

me·chan·ic [mɪˈkænɪk] mecánico(-a) *m(f)*

me·chan·i·cal [mɪˈkænɪkl] *adj also fig* mecánico

me·chan·i·cal en·gi·neer ingeniero(-a) *m(f)* industrial

me·chan·i·cal en·gi·neer·ing ingeniería *f* industrial

me·chan·i·cal·ly [mɪˈkænɪklɪ] *adv also fig* mecánicamente

mech·a·nism ['mekənizm] mecanismo *m*

mech·a·nize ['mekənaiz] *v/t* mecanizar

med·al ['medl] medalla *f*

med·a·list, *Br* **med·al·list** ['medəlist] medallista *m/f*

med·dle ['medl] *v/i* entrometerse; **don't meddle with the TV** no enredes con la televisión

me·di·a ['mi:diə] *npl:* **the media** los medios de comunicación

'me·di·a cov·er·age cobertura *f* informativa

'me·di·a e·vent acontecimiento *m* informativo

me·di·a 'hype revuelo *m* informativo

'me·di·a stud·ies ciencias *fpl* de la información

me·di·an strip [mi:diən'strip] mediana *f*

me·di·ate ['mi:dieit] *v/i* mediar

me·di·a·tion [mi:di'eiʃn] mediación *f*

me·di·a·tor ['mi:dieitər] mediador(a) *m(f)*

med·i·cal ['medikl] **1** *adj* médico **2** *n* reconocimiento *m* médico

'med·i·cal cer·tif·i·cate certificado *m* médico

'med·i·cal ex·am·i·na·tion reconocimiento *m* médico

'med·i·cal his·to·ry historial *m* médico

'med·i·cal pro·fes·sion profesión *f* médica; *(doctors)* médicos *mpl*

'med·i·cal re·cord ficha *m* médica

Med·i·care ['medikeər] *seguro de enfermedad para los ancianos en Estados Unidos*

med·i·cat·ed ['medikeitid] *adj* medicinal

med·i·ca·tion [medi'keiʃn] medicamento *m*, medicina *f*; **are you on any medication?** ¿está tomando algún medicamento?

me·dic·i·nal [mi'disinl] *adj* medicinal

medi·cine ['medsin] *science* medicina *f*; *(medication)* medicina *f*, medicamento *m*

'med·i·cine cab·i·net botiquín *m*

me·di·e·val [medi'i:vl] *adj* medieval

me·di·o·cre [mi:di'oukər] *adj* mediocre

me·di·oc·ri·ty [mi:di'ɑ:krəti] *of work etc, person* mediocridad *f*

med·i·tate ['mediteit] *v/i* meditar

med·i·ta·tion [medi'teiʃn] meditación *f*

Med·i·ter·ra·ne·an [meditə'reiniən] **1** *adj* mediterráneo **2** *n:* **the Mediterranean** el Mediterráneo

me·di·um ['mi:diəm] **1** *adj (average)* medio; *steak* a punto **2** *n size* talla *f* media; *(means)* medio *m*; *(spiritualist)* médium *m/f*

me·di·um-sized ['mi:diəmsaizd] *adj* de tamaño medio

me·di·um 'term: *in the medium term* a medio plazo

'me·di·um wave RAD onda *f* media

med·ley ['medli] *(assortment)* mezcla *f*

meek [mi:k] *adj* manso, dócil

meet [mi:t] **1** *v/t (pret & pp* **met***) by appointment* encontrarse con, reunirse con; *by chance, of eyes* encontrarse con; *(get to know)* conocer; *(collect)* ir a buscar; *in competition* enfrentarse con; *(satisfy)* satisfacer; **meet a deadline** cumplir un plazo **2** *v/i (pret & pp* **met***)* encontrarse; *in competition* enfrentarse; *of committee etc* reunirse; **have you two met?** ¿os conocíais? **3** *n* SP reunión *f*

◆ **meet with** *v/t person, opposition, approval* encontrarse con; **my attempts met with failure** mis intentos fracasaron

meet·ing ['mi:tiŋ] *by chance* encuentro *m; of committee, in business* reunión *f*; **he's in a meeting** está reunido

'meet·ing place lugar *m* de encuentro

meg·a·byte ['megəbait] COMPUT megabyte *m*

mel·an·chol·y ['melənkəli] *adj* melancólico

mel·low ['melou] **1** *adj* suave **2** *v/i of person* suavizarse, sosegarse

me·lo·di·ous [mi'loudiəs] *adj* melodioso

mel·o·dra·mat·ic [melədrə'mætik] *adj* melodramático

mel·o·dy ['melədi] melodía *f*

mel·on ['melən] melón *m*

melt [melt] **1** *v/i* fundirse, derretirse **2** *v/t* fundir, derretir

◆ **melt away** *v/i fig* desvanecerse

◆ **melt down** *v/t metal* fundir

melt·ing pot ['meltiŋpɑt] *fig* crisol *m*

mem·ber ['membər] miembro *m*

Mem·ber of 'Con·gress diputado(-a) *m(f)*

Mem·ber of 'Par·lia·ment *Br* diputado(-a) *m(f)*

mem·ber·ship ['membərʃip] afiliación *f*; *(number of members)* número *m* de miembros; **he applied for membership of the club** solicitó ser admitido en el club

'mem·ber·ship card tarjeta *f* de socio

mem·brane ['membrein] membrana *f*

me·men·to [me'mentou] recuerdo *m*

mem·o ['memou] nota *f*

mem·oirs ['memwɑːrz] *npl* memorias *fpl*

'mem·o pad bloc *m* de notas

mem·o·ra·ble ['memərəbl] *adj* memorable

me·mo·ri·al [mi'mɔːriəl] **1** *adj* conmemorativo **2** *n* monumento *m* conmemorativo

Me·mo·ri·al Day Día f de los Caídos

mem·o·rize ['meməraɪz] v/t memorizar

mem·o·ry ['meməri] (*recollection*) recuerdo m; (*power of recollection*, COMPUT memoria f; **I have no memory of the accident** no recuerdo el accidente; **have a good / bad memory** tener buena / mala memoria; **in memory of** en memoria de

men [men] pl → **man**

men·ace ['menɪs] 1 n (*threat*) amenaza f; *person* peligro m 2 v/t amenazar

men·ac·ing ['menɪsɪŋ] amenazador

mend [mend] 1 v/t reparar; *clothes* coser, remendar; *shoes* remendar 2 n: **be on the mend** after illness estar recuperándose

me·ni·al ['miːnɪəl] adj ingrato, penoso

men·in·gi·tis [menɪn'dʒaɪtɪs] meningitis f

men·o·pause ['menəpɔːz] menopausia f

'men's room servicio m de caballeros

men·stru·ate ['menstrʊeɪt] v/i menstruar

men·stru·a·tion [menstrʊ'eɪʃn] menstruación f

men·tal ['mentl] adj mental; F (*crazy*) chiflado F, pirado F

men·tal a'rith·me·tic cálculo m mental

men·tal 'cru·el·ty crueldad f mental

'men·tal hos·pi·tal hospital m psiquiátrico

men·tal 'ill·ness enfermedad f mental

men·tal·i·ty [men'tælətɪ] mentalidad f

men·tal·ly ['mentəlɪ] adv (*inwardly*) mentalmente

men·tal·ly 'hand·i·capped adj con minusvalía psíquica

men·tal·ly 'ill adj: **be mentally ill** sufrir una enfermedad mental

men·tion ['menʃn] 1 n mención f; **she made no mention of it** no lo mencionó 2 v/t mencionar; **don't mention it** (*you're welcome*) no hay de qué

men·tor ['mentɔːr] mentor(a) m(f)

men·u ['menuː] *for food*, COMPUT menú m

mer·ce·na·ry ['mɜːrsɪnərɪ] 1 adj mercenario 2 n MIL mercenario(-a) m(f)

mer·chan·dise ['mɜːrtʃəndaɪz] mercancías fpl, L.Am. mercadería f

mer·chant ['mɜːrtʃənt] comerciante m/f

mer·chant 'bank Br banco m mercantil

mer·ci·ful ['mɜːrsɪfəl] adj compasivo, piadoso

mer·ci·ful·ly ['mɜːrsɪfəlɪ] adv (*thankfully*) afortunadamente

mer·ci·less ['mɜːrsɪlɪs] adj despiadado

mer·cu·ry ['mɜːrkjʊrɪ] mercurio m

mer·cy ['mɜːrsɪ] clemencia f, compasión f; **be at s.o.'s mercy** estar a merced de alguien

mere [mɪr] adj mero, simple

mere·ly ['mɪrlɪ] adv meramente, simplemente

merge [mɜːrdʒ] v/i *of two lines etc* juntarse, unirse; *of companies* fusionarse

merg·er ['mɜːrdʒər] COM fusión f

mer·it ['merɪt] 1 n (*worth*) mérito m; (*advantage*) ventaja f; **she got the job on merit** consiguió el trabajo por méritos propios 2 v/t merecer

mer·ry ['merɪ] adj alegre; **Merry Christmas!** ¡Feliz Navidad!

'mer·ry-go-round tiovivo m

mesh [meʃ] malla f

mess [mes] (*untidiness*) desorden m; (*trouble*) lío m; **I'm in a bit of a mess** estoy metido en un lío; **be a mess** *of room, desk* estar desordenado; *of hair* estar revuelto; *of situation, s.o.'s life* ser un desastre

◆ **mess about, mess around 1** v/i enredar 2 v/t *person* jugar con

◆ **mess around with** v/t enredar con; *s.o.'s wife* tener un lío con

◆ **mess up** v/t *room, papers* desordenar; *task* convertir en una chapuza; *plans, marriage* estropear, arruinar

mes·sage ['mesɪdʒ] *also of movie etc* mensaje m

mes·sen·ger ['mesɪndʒər] (*courier*) mensajero(-a) m(f)

mess·y ['mesɪ] adj *room, person* desordenado; *job* sucio; *divorce, situation* desagradable

met [met] *pret & pp* → **meet**

me·tab·o·lism [mətæ'bəlɪzm] metabolismo m

met·al ['metl] 1 adj metálico 2 n metal m

me·tal·lic [mɪ'tælɪk] adj metálico

met·a·phor ['metəfər] metáfora f

me·te·or ['miːtɪər] meteoro m

me·te·or·ic [miːtɪ'ɑːrɪk] adj fig meteórico

me·te·or·ite ['miːtɪəraɪt] meteorito m

me·te·or·o·log·i·cal [miːtɪrə'lɑːdʒɪkl] adj meteorológico

me·te·or·ol·o·gist [miːtɪə'rɑːlədʒɪst] meteorólogo(-a) m(f)

me·te·or·ol·o·gy [miːtɪə'rɑːlədʒɪ] meteorología f

me·ter[1] ['miːtər] *for gas, electricity* contador m; (*parking meter*) parquímetro m

me·ter[2] ['miːtər] *unit of length* metro m

'me·ter read·ing lectura f del contador

meth·od ['meθəd] método m

me·thod·i·cal [mɪ'θɑːdɪkl] adj metódico

me·thod·i·cal·ly [mɪ'θɑːdɪklɪ] adv metódicamente

me·tic·u·lous [mə'tɪkjʊləs] adj meticuloso, minucioso

me·tre Br → **meter[2]**

met·ric ['metrɪk] adj métrico

me·trop·o·lis [mɪ'trɑ:pəlɪs] metrópolis f

met·ro·pol·i·tan [metrə'pɑ:lɪtən] adj metropolitano

mew [mju:] → miaow

Mex·i·can ['meksɪkən] 1 adj mexicano, mejicano 2 n mexicano(-a) m(f), mejicano(-a) m(f)

Mex·i·co ['meksɪkəʊ] México, Méjico

Mex·i·co 'Cit·y n Ciudad f de México, Mex México, Mex el Distrito Federal, Mex el D.F.

mez·za·nine (floor) ['mezəni:n] entresuelo m

mi·aow [mɪaʊ] 1 n maullido m 2 v/i maullar

mice [maɪs] pl → mouse

mick·ey mouse [mɪkɪ'maʊs] adj P course, qualification de tres al cuarto P

mi·cro·bi·ol·o·gy [maɪkrəʊbaɪ'ɑ:lədʒɪ] microbiología f

'mi·cro·chip microchip m

'mi·cro·cli·mate microclima m

mi·cro·cosm ['maɪkrəʊkɒzm] microcosmos m inv

'mi·cro·e·lec·tron·ics microelectrónica f

'mi·cro·film microfilm m

'mi·cro·or·gan·ism microorganismo m

'mi·cro·phone micrófono m

'mi·cro·pro·ces·sor microprocesador m

'mi·cro·scope microscopio m

mi·cro·scop·ic [maɪkrə'skɒpɪk] adj microscópico

'mi·cro·wave oven microondas m inv

'mid-air [mɪd'er]: in midair en pleno vuelo

mid·day ['mɪddeɪ] mediodía m

mid·dle ['mɪdl] 1 adj del medio; the middle child of five el tercero de cinco hermanos 2 n medio m; it's the middle of the night! ¡estamos en plena noche!; in the middle of of floor, room en medio de; of period of time a mitad or mediados de; in the middle of winter en pleno invierno; be in the middle of doing sth estar ocupado haciendo algo

'mid·dle-aged adj de mediana edad

'Mid·dle Ages npl Edad f Media

mid·dle 'class adj de clase media; the middle class(es) las clases medias

Mid·dle 'East Oriente m Medio

'mid·dle·man intermediario m

mid·dle 'man·age·ment mandos mpl intermedios

mid·dle 'name segundo nombre m

'mid·dle·weight boxer peso m medio

mid·dling ['mɪdlɪŋ] adj regular

mid·field·er [mɪd'fi:ldər] centrocampista m/f

midge [mɪdʒ] mosquito m (pequeño)

midg·et ['mɪdʒɪt] adj en miniatura

'mid·night ['mɪdnaɪt] medianoche f; at midnight a medianoche

'mid·sum·mer pleno verano m

'mid·way adv: we'll stop for lunch midway pararemos para comer a mitad de camino; midway through the meeting a mitad de la reunión

'mid·week adv a mitad de semana

'Mid·west Medio Oeste m (de Estados Unidos)

'mid·wife comadrona f

'mid·win·ter pleno invierno m

might[1] [maɪt] v/aux poder, ser posible que; I might be late puede or es posible que llegue tarde; it might rain puede or es posible que llueva; it might never happen puede or es posible que no ocurra nunca; he might have left a lo mejor se ha ido; you might have told me! ¡me lo podías haber dicho!

might[2] [maɪt] (power) poder m, fuerza f

might·y ['maɪtɪ] 1 adj poderoso 2 adv F (extremely) muy, cantidad de F

mi·graine ['mi:greɪn] migraña f

mi·grant work·er ['maɪgrənt] trabajador(a) m(f) itinerante

mi·grate [maɪ'greɪt] v/i emigrar

mi·gra·tion [maɪ'greɪʃn] emigración f

mike [maɪk] F micro m F

mild [maɪld] adj weather, climate apacible; cheese, voice suave; curry no muy picante; person afable, apacible

mil·dew ['mɪldu:] moho m

mild·ly ['maɪldlɪ] adv say sth con suavidad; spicy ligeramente; to put it mildly por no decir algo peor

mild·ness ['maɪldnɪs] of weather, voice suavidad f; of person afabilidad f

mile [maɪl] milla f; be miles better / easier F ser mil veces mejor / más fácil F

mile·age ['maɪlɪdʒ] millas fpl recorridas; unlimited mileage kilometraje m ilimitado

'mile·stone fig hito m

mil·i·tant ['mɪlɪtənt] 1 adj militante 2 n militante m/f

mil·i·ta·ry ['mɪlɪterɪ] 1 adj militar 2 n: the military el ejército, las fuerzas armadas

mil·i·ta·ry a'cad·e·my academia f militar

mil·i·ta·ry po'lice policía f militar

mil·i·ta·ry 'serv·ice servicio m militar

mi·li·tia [mɪ'lɪʃə] milicia f

milk [mɪlk] 1 n leche f 2 v/t ordeñar

milk 'choc·o·late chocolate m con leche

'milk jug jarra f de leche

milk of mag·ne·sia leche f de magnesia

'milk·shake batido m

milk·y ['mɪlkɪ] *adj with lots of milk* con mucha leche; *made with milk* con leche

Milk·y Way Vía *f* Láctea

mill [mɪl] *for grain* molino *m*; *for textiles* fábrica *f* de tejidos

◆ **mill about, mill around** *v/i* pulular

mil·len·ni·um [mɪ'lenɪəm] milenio *m*

mil·li·gram, *Br* **mil·li·gramme** ['mɪli-græm] miligramo *m*

mil·li·me·ter, *Br* **mil·li·me·tre** ['mɪlimiː-tər] milímetro *m*

mil·lion ['mɪljən] millón *m*

mil·lion·aire [mɪljə'ner] millonario(-a) *m(f)*

mime [maɪm] *v/t* representar con gestos

mim·ic ['mɪmɪk] **1** *n* imitador(a) *m(f)* **2** *v/t* (*pret & pp* **mimicked**) imitar

mince [mɪns] *v/t* picar

'mince·meat carne *f* picada

mince 'pie empanada *f* de carne picada

mind [maɪnd] **1** *n* mente *f*; *it's uppermost in my mind* es lo que más me preocupa; *it's all in your mind* son imaginaciones tuyas; *be out of one's mind* haber perdido el juicio; *bear, keep sth in mind* recordar; *I've a good mind to ...* estoy considerando seriamente ...; *change one's mind* cambiar de opinión; *it didn't enter my mind* no se me ocurrió; *give s.o. a piece of one's mind* cantarle a alguien las cuarenta; *make up one's mind* decidirse; *have something on one's mind* tener algo en la cabeza; *keep one's mind on sth* concentrarse en algo **2** *v/t* (*look after*) cuidar (de); (*heed*) prestar atención a; *I don't mind what we do* no me importa lo que hagamos; *do you mind if I smoke?*, *do you mind my smoking?* ¿le importa que fume?; *would you mind opening the window?* ¿le importaría abrir la ventana?; *mind the step!* ¡cuidado con el escalón!; *mind your own business!* ¡métete en tus asuntos! **3** *v/i*: *mind!* ¡ten cuidado!; *never mind!* ¡no importa!; *I don't mind* no me importa, me da igual

mind-bog·gling ['maɪndbɑːglɪŋ] *adj* increíble

mind·less ['maɪndlɪs] *adj violence* gratuito

mine¹ [maɪn] *pron* el mío, la mía; *mine are red* los míos son rojos; *that book is mine* eso libro es mío; *a cousin of mine* un primo mío

mine² [maɪn] **1** *n for coal etc* mina *f* **2** *v/i*: *mine for* extraer

mine³ [maɪn] **1** *n* (*explosive*) mina *f* **2** *v/t* minar

'mine·field MIL campo *m* de minas; *fig* campo *m* minado

min·er ['maɪnər] minero(-a) *m(f)*

min·e·ral ['mɪnərəl] *n* mineral *m*

'min·e·ral wa·ter agua *f* mineral

'mine·sweep·er NAUT dragaminas *m inv*

min·gle ['mɪŋgl] *v/i of sounds, smells* mezclarse; *at party* alternar

mi·ni ['mɪnɪ] *skirt* minifalda *f*

min·i·a·ture ['mɪnɪtʃər] *adj* en miniatura

'min·i·bus microbús *m*

min·i·mal ['mɪnɪməl] *adj* mínimo

min·i·mal·ism ['mɪnɪməlɪzm] minimalismo *m*

min·i·mize ['mɪnɪmaɪz] *v/t risk, delay* minimizar, reducir al mínimo; (*downplay*) minimizar, quitar importancia a

min·i·mum ['mɪnɪməm] **1** *adj* mínimo **2** *n* mínimo *m*

min·i·mum 'wage salario *m* mínimo

min·ing ['maɪnɪŋ] minería *f*

'min·i·se·ries TV miniserie *f*

'min·i·skirt minifalda *f*

min·is·ter ['mɪnɪstər] POL ministro(-a) *m(f)*; REL ministro(-a) *m(f)*, pastor(a) *m(f)*

min·is·te·ri·al [mɪnɪ'stɪrɪəl] *adj* ministerial

min·is·try ['mɪnɪstrɪ] POL ministerio *m*

mink [mɪŋk] *animal, fur* visón *m*; *coat* abrigo *m* de visón

mi·nor ['maɪnər] **1** *adj problem, setback* menor, pequeño; *operation, argument* de poca importancia; *aches and pains* leve; *in D minor* MUS en D menor **2** *n* LAW menor *m/f* de edad

mi·nor·i·ty [maɪ'nɑːrətɪ] minoría *f*; *be in the minority* ser minoría

mint [mɪnt] *n herb* menta *f*; *chocolate* pastilla *f* de chocolate con sabor a menta; *hard candy* caramelo *m* de menta

mi·nus ['maɪnəs] **1** *n* (*minus sign*) (signo *m* de) menos *m* **2** *prep* menos; *temperatures of minus 18* temperaturas de 18 grados bajo cero

mi·nus·cule ['mɪnəskjuːl] *adj* minúsculo

min·ute¹ ['mɪnɪt] *of time* minuto *m*; *in a minute* (*soon*) en un momento; *just a minute* un momento

mi·nute² [maɪ'nuːt] *adj* (*tiny*) diminuto, minúsculo; (*detailed*) minucioso; *in minute detail* minuciosamente

'mi·nute hand ['mɪnɪt] minutero *m*

mi·nute·ly [maɪ'nuːtlɪ] *adv in detail* minuciosamente; (*very slightly*) mínimamente

min·utes ['mɪnɪts] *npl of meeting* acta(s) *f(pl)*

mir·a·cle ['mɪrəkl] milagro *m*

mi·rac·u·lous [mɪ'rækjələs] *adj* milagroso

mi·rac·u·lous·ly [mɪˈrækjʊləslɪ] *adv* milagrosamente

mi·rage [ˈmɪrɑːʒ] espejismo *m*

mir·ror [ˈmɪrər] **1** *n* espejo *m*; MOT (espejo *m*) retrovisor *m* **2** *v/t* reflejar

mis·an·thro·pist [mɪˈzænθrəpɪst] misántropo(-a) *m(f)*

mis·ap·pre·hen·sion [mɪsæprɪˈhenʃn]: *be under a misapprehension* estar equivocado

mis·be·have [mɪsbəˈheɪv] *v/i* portarse mal

mis·be·hav·ior, *Br* **mis·be·hav·iour** [mɪsbəˈheɪvɪər] mal comportamiento *m*

mis·cal·cu·late [mɪsˈkælkjʊleɪt] *v/t & v/i* calcular mal

mis·cal·cu·la·tion [mɪsˈkælkjʊleɪʃn] error *m* de cálculo

mis·car·riage [ˈmɪskærɪdʒ] MED aborto *m* (espontáneo); *miscarriage of justice* error *m* judicial

mis·car·ry [ˈmɪskærɪ] *v/i* (*pret & pp mis·carried*) *of plan* fracasar

mis·cel·la·ne·ous [mɪsəˈleɪnɪəs] *adj* diverso; *put it in the file marked "miscellaneous"* ponlo en la carpeta de "varios"

mis·chief [ˈmɪstʃɪf] (*naughtiness*) travesura *f*, trastada *f*

mis·chie·vous [ˈmɪstʃɪvəs] *adj* (*naughty*) travieso; (*malicious*) malicioso

mis·con·cep·tion [mɪskənˈsepʃn] idea *f* equivocada

mis·con·duct [mɪsˈkɑːndʌkt] mala conducta *f*

mis·con·strue [mɪskənˈstruː] *v/t* malinterpretar

mis·de·mea·nor, *Br* **mis·de·mea·nour** [mɪsdəˈmiːnər] falta *f*, delito *m* menor

mi·ser [ˈmaɪzər] avaro(-a) *m(f)*

mis·e·ra·ble [ˈmɪzrəbl] *adj* (*unhappy*) triste, infeliz; *weather, performance* horroroso

mi·ser·ly [ˈmaɪzərlɪ] *adj person* avaro; *a miserly $ 150* 150 míseros dólares

mis·e·ry [ˈmɪzərɪ] (*unhappiness*) tristeza *f*, infelicidad *f*; (*wretchedness*) miseria *f*

mis·fire [mɪsˈfaɪr] *v/i of joke, scheme* salir mal

mis·fit [ˈmɪsfɪt] *in society* inadaptado(-a) *m(f)*

mis·for·tune [mɪsˈfɔːrtʃən] desgracia *f*

mis·giv·ings [mɪsˈgɪvɪŋz] *npl* recelo *m*, duda *f*

mis·guid·ed [mɪsˈgaɪdɪd] *adj person* equivocado; *attempt, plan* desacertado

mis·han·dle [mɪsˈhændl] *v/t situation* llevar mal

mis·hap [ˈmɪshæp] contratiempo *m*

mis·in·form [mɪsɪnˈfɔːrm] *v/t* informar mal

mis·in·ter·pret [mɪsɪnˈtɜːrprɪt] *v/t* malinterpretar

mis·in·ter·pre·ta·tion [mɪsɪntɜːrprɪˈteɪʃn] mala interpretación *f*

mis·judge [mɪsˈdʒʌdʒ] *v/t person, situation* juzgar mal

mis·lay [mɪsˈleɪ] *v/t* (*pret & pp mislaid*) perder

mis·lead [mɪsˈliːd] *v/t* (*pret & pp misled*) engañar

mis·lead·ing [mɪsˈliːdɪŋ] *adj* engañoso

mis·man·age [mɪsˈmænɪdʒ] *v/t* gestionar mal

mis·man·age·ment [mɪsˈmænɪdʒmənt] mala gestión *f*

mis·match [ˈmɪsmætʃ]: *there's a mismatch between the two sets of figures* los dos grupos de cifras no se corresponden

mis·placed [ˈmɪspleɪst] *adj loyalty* inmerecido; *enthusiasm* inoportuno

mis·print [ˈmɪsprɪnt] errata *f*

mis·pro·nounce [mɪsprəˈnaʊns] *v/t* pronunciar mal

mis·pro·nun·ci·a·tion [mɪsprənʌnsɪˈeɪʃn] pronunciación *f* incorrecta

mis·read [mɪsˈriːd] *v/t* (*pret & pp misread* [red]) *word, figures* leer mal; *situation* malinterpretar

mis·rep·re·sent [mɪsreprɪˈzent] *v/t* deformar, tergiversar

miss¹ [mɪs]: *Miss Smith* la señorita Smith; *miss!* ¡señorita!

miss² [mɪs] **1** *n* SP fallo *m*; *give sth a miss meeting, party etc* no ir a algo **2** *v/t target* no dar en; *emotionally* echar de menos; *bus, train, airplane* perder; (*not notice*) pasar por alto; (*not be present at*) perderse; *I ducked and he missed me* me agaché y no me dio; *you just missed her* (*she's just left*) se acaba de marchar; *we must have missed the turnoff* nos hemos debido pasar el desvío; *you don't miss much!* ¡no se te escapa una!; *miss a class* faltar a una clase **3** *v/i* fallar

mis·shap·en [mɪsˈʃeɪpən] *adj* deforme

mis·sile [ˈmɪsəl] *arma f* arrojadiza; *weapon* misil *m*

miss·ing [ˈmɪsɪŋ] *adj* desaparecido; *be missing of person, plane* haber desaparecido; *the missing money* el dinero que falta

mis·sion [ˈmɪʃn] *task* misión *f*; *people* delegación *f*

mis·sion·a·ry [ˈmɪʃənrɪ] REL misionero(-a) *m(f)*

M

mis·spell [mɪs'spel] *v/t* escribir incorrectamente

mist [mɪst] neblina *f*

◆ **mist over** *v/i of eyes* empañarse

◆ **mist up** *v/i of mirror, window* empañarse

mis·take [mɪ'steɪk] **1** *n* error *m*, equivocación *f*; **make a mistake** cometer un error *or* una equivocación, equivocarse; **by mistake** por error *or* equivocación **2** *v/t* (*pret* **mistook**, *pp* **mistaken**) confundir; **mistake X for Y** confundir X con Y

mis·tak·en [mɪ'steɪkən] **1** *adj* erróneo, equivocado; **be mistaken** estar equivocado **2** *pp* → **mistake**

mis·ter ['mɪstər] → **Mr**

mis·took [mɪ'stʊk] *pret* → **mistake**

mis·tress ['mɪstrɪs] *lover* amante *f*, querida *f*; *of servant* ama *f*; *of dog* dueña *f*, ama *f*

mis·trust [mɪs'trʌst] **1** *n* desconfianza *f* (*of* en) **2** *v/t* desconfiar de

mist·y ['mɪstɪ] *adj weather* neblinoso; *eyes* empañado; *color* borroso

mis·un·der·stand [mɪsʌndər'stænd] *v/t* (*pret & pp* **misunderstood**) entender mal

mis·un·der·stand·ing [mɪsʌndər'stændɪŋ] (*mistake*) malentendido *m*; (*argument*) desacuerdo *m*

mis·use 1 *n* [mɪs'juːs] uso *m* indebido **2** *v/t* [mɪs'juːz] usar indebidamente

mit·i·gat·ing cir·cum·stanc·es ['mɪtɪgeɪtɪŋ] *npl* circunstancias *fpl* atenuantes

mitt [mɪt] *in baseball* guante *m* de béisbol

mit·ten ['mɪtən] mitón *f*

mix [mɪks] **1** *n* (*mixture*) mezcla *f*; *cooking: ready to use* preparado *m* **2** *v/t* mezclar; **mix the flour in well** mezclar la harina bien; *cement* preparar **3** *v/i socially* relacionarse

◆ **mix up** *v/t* (*confuse*) confundir (**with** con); (*put in wrong order*) revolver, desordenar; **be mixed up** *emotionally* tener problemas emocionales; *of figures* estar confundido; *of papers* estar revuelto *or* desordenado; **be mixed up in** estar metido en; **get mixed up with** verse liado con

◆ **mix with** *v/t* (*associate with*) relacionarse con

mixed [mɪkst] *adj feelings* contradictorio; *reactions, reviews* variado

mixed 'mar·riage matrimonio *m* mixto

mix·er ['mɪksər] *for food* batidora *f*; *drink* refresco *m* (*para mezclar con bebida alcohólica*); **she's a good mixer** es muy sociable

mix·ture ['mɪkstʃər] mezcla *f*; *medicine*

preparado *m*

mix-up ['mɪksʌp] confusión *f*

moan [moʊn] **1** *n of pain* gemido *m* **2** *v/i in pain* gemir

mob [mɑːb] **1** *n* muchedumbre *f* **2** *v/t* (*pret & pp* **mobbed**) asediar, acosar

mo·bile ['moʊbəl] **1** *adj person* con movilidad; (*that can be moved*) móvil; **she's a lot less mobile now** ahora tiene mucha menos movilidad **2** *n* móvil *m*

mo·bile 'home casa *f* caravana

mo·bile 'phone *Br* teléfono *m* móvil

mo·bil·i·ty [moʊ'bɪlətɪ] movilidad *f*

mob·ster ['mɑːbstər] gángster *m*

mock [mɑːk] **1** *adj* fingido, simulado; **mock-Tudor houses** casas de estilo Tudor simulado; **mock exams / elections** exámenes *mpl*/elecciones *fpl* de prueba **2** *v/t* burlarse de

mock·er·y ['mɑːkərɪ] (*derision*) burlas *fpl*; (*travesty*) farsa *f*

mock-up ['mɑːkʌp] (*model*) maqueta *f*, modelo *m*

mode [moʊd] (*form*), COMPUT modo *m*; **mode of transportation** medio *m* de transporte

mod·el ['mɑːdl] **1** *adj employee, husband* modélico, modelo; **model boat / plane** maqueta *f* de un barco / avión **2** *n miniature* maqueta *f*, modelo *m*; (*pattern*) modelo *m*; (*fashion model*) modelo *m/f*; **male model** modelo *m* **3** *v/t*: **model clothes** trabajar de modelo; **she models swimsuits** trabaja de modelo de bañadores **4** *v/i for designer* trabajar de modelo; *for artist, photographer* posar

mo·dem ['moʊdem] módem *m*

mod·e·rate 1 *adj* ['mɑːdərət] moderado **2** *n* ['mɑːdərət] POL moderado(-a) *m(f)* **3** *v/t* ['mɑːdəreɪt] moderar

mod·e·rate·ly ['mɑːdərətlɪ] *adv* medianamente, razonablemente

mod·e·ra·tion [mɑːdə'reɪʃn] (*restraint*) moderación *f*; **in moderation** con moderación

mod·ern ['mɑːdn] *adj* moderno; **in the modern world** en el mundo contemporáneo

mod·ern·i·za·tion [mɑːdənaɪ'zeɪʃn] modernización *f*

mod·ern·ize ['mɑːdənaɪz] **1** *v/t* modernizar **2** *v/i of business, country* modernizarse

mod·ern 'lan·guag·es *npl* lenguas *fpl* modernas

mod·est ['mɑːdɪst] *adj* modesto

mod·es·ty ['mɑːdɪstɪ] modestia *f*

mod·i·fi·ca·tion [mɑːdɪfɪ'keɪʃn] modificación *f*

mod·i·fy ['mɑːdɪfaɪ] v/t (pret & pp **modi-fied**) modificar

mod·u·lar ['mɑːdʊlər] adj furniture por módulos

mod·ule ['mɑːduːl] módulo m

moist [mɔɪst] adj húmedo

moist·en ['mɔɪsn] v/t humedecer

mois·ture ['mɔɪstʃər] humedad f

mois·tur·iz·er ['mɔɪstʃəraɪzər] for skin crema f hidratante

mo·lar ['moʊlər] muela f, molar m

mo·las·ses [mə'læsɪz] npl melaza f

mold¹ [moʊld] on food moho m

mold² [moʊld] **1** n molde m **2** v/t clay, character moldear

mold·y ['moʊldɪ] adj food mohoso

mole [moʊl] on skin lunar m

mo·lec·u·lar [mə'lekjʊlər] adj molecular

mol·e·cule ['mɑːlɪkjuːl] molécula f

mo·lest [mə'lest] v/t child, woman abusar sexualmente de

mol·ly·cod·dle ['mɑːlɪkɑːdl] v/t F mimar, consentir

mol·ten ['moʊltən] adj fundido

mom [mɑːm] F mamá f

mo·ment ['moʊmənt] momento m; **at the moment** en estos momentos, ahora mismo; **for the moment** por el momento, por ahora

mo·men·tar·i·ly [moʊmən'terɪlɪ] adv (for a moment) momentáneamente; (in a moment) de un momento a otro

mo·men·ta·ry ['moʊmənterɪ] adj momentáneo

mo·men·tous [moʊ'mentəs] adj trascendental, muy importante

mo·men·tum [mə'mentəm] cobrar / perder impulso

mon·arch ['mɑːnərk] monarca m/f

mon·ar·chy ['mɑːnərkɪ] monarquía f

mon·as·tery ['mɑːnəsterɪ] monasterio m

mo·nas·tic [mə'næstɪk] adj monástico

Mon·day ['mʌndeɪ] lunes m inv

mon·e·ta·ry ['mɑːnɪterɪ] adj monetario

mon·ey ['mʌnɪ] dinero m; **he's making a lot of money** está ganando mucho dinero

'mon·ey belt faltriquera f

'mon·ey-lend·er prestamista m/f

'mon·ey mar·ket mercado m monetario

'mon·ey or·der giro m postal

mon·grel ['mʌŋɡrəl] perro m cruzado

mon·i·tor ['mɑːnɪtər] **1** n COMPUT monitor m **2** v/t controlar

monk [mʌŋk] monje m

mon·key ['mʌŋkɪ] mono m; F child diablillo m F

♦ **monkey about with** v/t F enredar con

'mon·key wrench llave f inglesa

mon·o·gram ['mɑːnəɡræm] monograma m

mon·o·grammed ['mɑːnəɡræmd] con monograma

mon·o·log, Br mon·o·logue ['mɑːnəlɑːɡ] monólogo m

mo·nop·o·lize [mə'nɑːpəlaɪz] v/t monopolizar

mo·nop·o·ly [mə'nɑːpəlɪ] monopolio m

mo·not·o·nous [mə'nɑːtənəs] adj monótono

mo·not·o·ny [mə'nɑːtənɪ] monotonía f

mon·soon [mɑːn'suːn] monzón m

mon·ster ['mɑːnstər] n monstruo m

mon·stros·i·ty [mɑːn'strɑːsətɪ] monstruosidad f

mon·strous ['mɑːnstrəs] adj (frightening, huge) monstruoso; (shocking) escandaloso

month [mʌnθ] mes m; **how much do you pay a month?** ¿cuánto pagas al mes?

month·ly ['mʌnθlɪ] **1** adj mensual **2** adv mensualmente **3** n magazine revista f mensual

mon·u·ment ['mɑːnʊmənt] monumento m

mon·u·ment·al [mɑːnʊ'mentl] adj fig monumental

mood [muːd] (frame of mind) humor m; (bad mood) mal humor m; of meeting, country atmósfera f; **be in a good / bad mood** estar de buen / mal humor; **I'm in the mood for a pizza** me apetece una pizza

mood·y ['muːdɪ] adj temperamental; (bad-tempered) malhumorado

moon [muːn] n luna f

'moon·light **1** n luz f de luna **2** v/i F estar pluriempleado irregularmente; **he's moonlighting as a barman** tiene un segundo empleo de camarero

'moon·lit adj iluminado por la luna

moor [mʊr] v/t boat atracar

moor·ing ['mʊrɪŋ] atracadero m

moose [muːs] alce m americano

mop [mɑːp] **1** n for floor fregona f; for dishes estropajo m (con mango) **2** v/t (pret & pp **mopped**) floor fregar; eyes, face limpiar

♦ **mop up** v/t limpiar; MIL acabar con

mope [moʊp] v/i estar abatido

mor·al ['mɔːrəl] **1** adj moral; person, behavior moralista **2** n of story moraleja f; **morals** moral f, moralidad f

mo·rale [mə'ræl] moral f

mo·ral·i·ty [mə'rælətɪ] moralidad f

mor·bid ['mɔːrbɪd] adj morboso

more [mɔːr] **1** adj más; **there are no more eggs** no quedan huevos; **some more** tea? ¿más té?; *more and more students / time* cada vez más estudiantes / tiempo **2** *adv* más; *more important* más importante; *more often* más a menudo; *more and more* cada vez más; *more or less* más o menos; *once more* una vez más; *he paid more than $100 for it* pagó más de 100 dólares por él; *he earns more than I do* gana más que yo; *I don't live there any more* ya no vivo allí **3** *pron* más; *do you want some more?* ¿quieres más?; *a little more* un poco más

more·o·ver [mɔːˈrouvər] *adv* además, lo que es más

morgue [mɔːrg] depósito *m* de cadáveres

morn·ing [ˈmɔːrnɪŋ] mañana *f*; *in the morning* por la mañana; *this morning* esta mañana; *tomorrow morning* mañana por la mañana; *good morning* buenos días

morn·ing 'sick·ness náuseas *fpl* matutinas (*típicas del embarazo*)

mo·ron [ˈmɔːraɪn] F imbécil *m/f* F, subnormal *m/f* F

mo·rose [məˈrous] *adj* hosco, malhumorado

mor·phine [ˈmɔːrfiːn] morfina *f*

mor·sel [ˈmɔːrsl] pedacito *m*

mor·tal [ˈmɔːrtl] **1** *adj* mortal **2** *n* mortal *m/f*

mor·tal·i·ty [mɔːrˈtælətɪ] mortalidad *f*

mor·tar[1] [ˈmɔːrtər] MIL mortero *m*

mor·tar[2] [ˈmɔːrtər] (*cement*) mortero *m*, argamasa *f*

mort·gage [ˈmɔːrgɪdʒ] **1** *n* hipoteca *f*, préstamo *m* hipotecario **2** *v/t* hipotecar

mor·ti·cian [mɔːrˈtɪʃn] encargado(-a) *m(f)* de una funeraria

mor·tu·a·ry [ˈmɔːrtueɪ] depósito *m* de cadáveres

mo·sa·ic [mouˈzeɪɪk] mosaico *m*

Mos·cow [ˈmɑːskau] Moscú *m*

Mos·lem [ˈmʊzlɪm] **1** *adj* musulmán **2** *n* musulmán(-ana) *m(f)*

mosque [mɑːsk] mezquita *f*

mos·qui·to [mɑːsˈkiːtou] mosquito *m*

moss [mɑːs] musgo *m*

moss·y [ˈmɑːsɪ] *adj* cubierto de musgo

most [moust] **1** *adj* la mayoría de **2** *adv* (*very*) muy, sumamente; *the most beautiful / interesting* el más hermoso / interesante; *that's the one I like most* ése es el que más me gusta; *most of all* sobre todo **3** *pron* la mayoría de; *I've read most of her novels* he leído la mayoría de sus novelas; *at (the) most* como mucho; *make the most of* aprovechar al máximo

most·ly [ˈmoustlɪ] *adv* principalmente, sobre todo

mo·tel [mouˈtel] motel *m*

moth [mɑːθ] mariposa *f* nocturna; (*clothes moth*) polilla *f*

'moth·ball bola *f* de naftalina

moth·er [ˈmʌðər] **1** *n* madre *f* **2** *v/t* mimar

'moth·er·board COMPUT placa *f* madre

'moth·er·hood maternidad *f*

Moth·er·ing 'Sun·day → *Mother's Day*

'moth·er-in-law (*pl mothers-in-law*) suegra *f*

moth·er·ly [ˈmʌðərlɪ] *adj* maternal

moth·er-of-'pearl nácar *m*

'Moth·er's Day Día *f* de la Madre

'moth·er tongue lengua *f* materna

mo·tif [mouˈtiːf] motivo *m*

mo·tion [ˈmouʃn] **1** *n* (*movement*) movimiento *m*; (*proposal*) moción *f*; *put, set things in motion* poner las cosas en marcha **2** *v/t*: *he motioned me forward* me indicó con un gesto que avanzara

mo·tion·less [ˈmouʃnlɪs] *adj* inmóvil

mo·ti·vate [ˈmoutɪveɪt] *v/t person* motivar

mo·ti·va·tion [moutɪˈveɪʃn] motivación *f*

mo·tive [ˈmoutɪv] motivo *m*

mo·tor [ˈmoutər] motor *m*

'mo·tor·bike moto *f*

'mo·tor·boat lancha *f* motora

mo·tor·cade [ˈmoutərkeɪd] caravana *f*, desfile *m* de coches

'mo·tor·cy·cle motocicleta *f*

'mo·tor·cy·clist motociclista *m/f*

'mo·tor home autocaravana *f*

mo·tor·ist [ˈmoutərɪst] conductor(a) *m(f)*, automovilista *m/f*

'mo·tor me·chan·ic mecánico(-a) *m(f)* (de automóviles)

'mo·tor rac·ing carreras *fpl* de coches

'mo·tor·scoot·er vespa® *f*

'mo·tor ve·hi·cle vehículo *m* de motor

'mo·tor·way *Br* autopista *f*

mot·to [ˈmɑːtou] lema *f*

mould *etc Br* → *mold[2] etc*

mound [maund] montículo *m*

mount [maunt] **1** *n* (*mountain*) monte *m*; (*horse*) montura *f*; *Mount McKinley* el Monte McKinley **2** *v/t steps* subir; *horse, bicycle* montar en; *campaign, photo* montar **3** *v/i* aumentar, crecer

♦ **mount up** *v/i* acumularse

moun·tain [ˈmauntɪn] montaña *f*

'moun·tain bike bicicleta *f* de montaña

moun·tain·eer [mauntɪˈnɪr] montañero(-a) *m(f)*, alpinista *m/f*, *L.Am.* andinista *m/f*

moun·tain·eer·ing [mauntɪˈnɪrɪŋ] montañismo *m*, alpinismo *m*, *L.Am.* andinismo *m*

moun·tain·ous ['maʊntɪnəs] *adj* montañoso

mount·ed po'lice ['maʊntɪd] policía *f* montada

mourn [mɔːrn] **1** *v/t* llorar **2** *v/i*: **mourn for s.o.** llorar la muerte de alguien

mourn·er ['mɔːrnər] doliente *m/f*

mourn·ful ['mɔːrnfəl] *adj* voice, face triste

mourn·ing ['mɔːrnɪŋ] luto *m*, duelo *m*; **be in mourning** estar de luto; **wear mourning** vestir de luto

mouse [maʊs] (*pl* **mice** [maɪs]) *also* COMPUT ratón *m*

'**mouse mat** COMPUT alfombrilla *f*

mous·tache → **mustache**

mouth [maʊθ] *of person* boca *f*; *of river* desembocadura *f*

mouth·ful ['maʊθfəl] *of food* bocado *m*; *of drink* trago *m*

'**mouth·or·gan** armónica *f*

'**mouth·piece** *of instrument* boquilla *f*; (*spokesperson*) portavoz *m/f*

'**mouth·wash** enjuague *m* bucal, elixir *m* bucal

'**mouth·wa·ter·ing** *adj* apetitoso

move [muːv] **1** *n in chess, checkers* movimiento *m*; (*step, action*) paso *m*; (*change of house*) mudanza *f*; **make the first move** dar el primer paso; **get a move on!** F ¡espabílate! F; **don't make a move!** ¡ni te muevas! **2** *v/t* mover; (*transfer*) trasladar; *emotionally* conmover; **move those papers out of your way** aparta esos papeles; **move house** mudarse de casa **3** *v/i* moverse; (*transfer*) trasladarse

♦ **move around** *v/i in room* andar; *from place to place* trasladarse, mudarse

♦ **move away** *v/i* alejarse, apartarse; (*move house*) mudarse

♦ **move in** *v/i to house, neighborhood* mudarse; *to office* trasladarse

♦ **move on** *v/i to another town* mudarse; *to another job* cambiarse; *to another subject* pasar a hablar de

♦ **move out** *v/i of house* mudarse; *of area* marcharse

♦ **move up** *v/i in league* ascender, subir; (*make room*) correrse

move·ment ['muːvmənt] *also organization, MUS* movimiento *m*

mov·ers ['muːvərz] *npl firm* empresa *f* de mudanzas; (*men*) empleados *mpl* de una empresa de mudanzas

mov·ie ['muːvɪ] película *f*; **go to a movie, the movies** ir al cine

mov·ie·go·er ['muːvɪgoʊər] aficionado(a) *m/f* al cine

'**mov·ie thea·ter** cine *m*, sala *f* de cine

mov·ing ['muːvɪŋ] *adj which can move* movible; *emotionally* conmovedor

mow [moʊ] *v/t grass* cortar

♦ **mow down** *v/t* segar la vida de

mow·er ['moʊər] cortacésped *m*

MP [em'piː] *abbr* (= **Member of Parliament**) *Br* diputado(-a) *m(f)*; *abbr* (= **Military Policeman**) policía *m* militar

mph [empiː'eɪtʃ] *abbr* (= **miles per hour**) millas *fpl* por hora

Mr ['mɪstər] Sr.

Mrs ['mɪsɪz] Sra.

Ms [mɪz] Sra. (*casda o no casuda*)

Mt *abbr* (= **Mount**) Monte *m*

much [mʌtʃ] **1** *adj* mucho; **so much money** tanto dinero; **as much ... as ...** tanto ... como **2** *adv* mucho; **I don't like him much** no me gusta mucho; **he's much more intelligent than ...** es mucho más inteligente que ...; **the house is much too large for one person** la casa es demasiado grande para una sola persona; **very much** mucho; **thank you very much** muchas gracias; **I love you very much** te quiero muchísimo; **too much** demasiado; **as much as ...** tanto ... como; **it may cost as much as half a million dollars** puede que haya malversado hasta medio millón de dólares; **I thought as much** eso es lo que pensaba **3** *pron* mucho; **what did she say? - nothing much** ¿qué dijo? - no demasiado

muck [mʌk] (*dirt*) suciedad *f*

mu·cus ['mjuːkəs] mocos *mpl*, mucosidad *f*

mud [mʌd] barro *m*

mud·dle ['mʌdl] **1** *n* lío *m* **2** *v/t person* liar; **you've got the story all muddled** te has hecho un lío con la *historia*

♦ **muddle up** *v/t* desordenar; (*confuse*) liar

mud·dy ['mʌdɪ] *adj* embarrado

mues·li ['mjuːzlɪ] muesli *m*

muf·fin ['mʌfɪn] magdalena *f*

muf·fle ['mʌfl] *v/t* ahogar, amortiguar

♦ **muffle up** *v/i* abrigarse

muf·fler ['mʌflər] MOT silenciador *m*

mug[1] [mʌg] *for tea, coffee* taza *f*; F (*face*) jeta *f* F, *Span* careto *m* F

mug[2] [mʌg] *v/t* (*pret & pp* **mugged**) (*attack*) atracar

mug·ger ['mʌgər] atracador(a) *m(f)*

mug·ging ['mʌgɪŋ] atraco *m*

mug·gy ['mʌgɪ] *adj* bochornoso

mule [mjuːl] *animal* mulo(-a) *m(f)*; (*slipper*) pantufla *f*

♦ **mull over** [mʌl] *v/t* reflexionar sobre

mul·ti·lat·e·ral [mʌltɪ'lætərəl] *adj* POL multilateral

M

mul·ti·lin·gual [mʌltɪˈlɪŋgwəl] adj multilingüe

mul·ti·me·di·a [mʌltɪˈmiːdɪə] 1 n multimedia f 2 adj multimedia

mul·ti·na·tion·al [mʌltɪˈnæʃnl] 1 adj multinacional 2 n COM multinacional f

mul·ti·ple [ˈmʌltɪpl] adj múltiple

mul·ti·ple 'choice ques·tion pregunta f tipo test

mul·ti·ple scle·ro·sis [skleˈroʊsɪs] esclerosis f múltiple

mul·ti·pli·ca·tion [mʌltɪplɪˈkeɪʃn] multiplicación f

mul·ti·ply [ˈmʌltɪplaɪ] 1 v/t (pret & pp **multiplied**) multiplicar 2 v/i (pret & pp **multiplied**) multiplicarse

mum·my [ˈmʌmɪ] Br mamá f

mum·ble [ˈmʌmbl] 1 n murmullo m 2 v/t farfullar 3 v/i hablar entre dientes

mumps [mʌmps] nsg paperas fpl

munch [mʌntʃ] 1 v/t mascar 2 v/i mascar

mu·ni·ci·pal [mjuːˈnɪsɪpl] adj municipal

mu·ral [ˈmjʊərəl] mural m

mur·der [ˈmɜːrdər] 1 n asesinato m 2 v/t person asesinar, matar; song destrozar

mur·der·er [ˈmɜːrdərər] asesino(-a) m(f)

mur·der·ous [ˈmɜːrdrəs] adj rage, look asesino

murk·y [ˈmɜːrkɪ] adj water turbio, oscuro; fig turbio

mur·mur [ˈmɜːrmər] 1 n murmullo m 2 v/t murmurar

mus·cle [ˈmʌsl] músculo m

mus·cu·lar [ˈmʌskjʊlər] adj pain, strain muscular; person musculoso

muse [mjuːz] v/i meditar, reflexionar

mu·se·um [mjuːˈzɪəm] museo m

mush·room [ˈmʌʃrʊm] 1 n seta f, hongo m; (button mushroom) champiñón m 2 v/i crecer rápidamente

mu·sic [ˈmjuːzɪk] música f; in written form partitura f

mu·sic·al [ˈmjuːzɪkl] 1 adj musical; person con talento para la música 2 n musical m

'mu·sic(·al) box caja f de música

mu·sic·al 'in·stru·ment instrumento m musical

mu·si·cian [mjuːˈzɪʃn] músico(-a) m(f)

mus·sel [ˈmʌsl] mejillón m

must [mʌst] v/aux ◇ necessity tener que, deber; **I must be on time** tengo que or debo llegar a la hora; **do you have to leave now? yes, I must** ¿tienes que marcharte ahora? - sí, debo marcharme; **I mustn't be late** no tengo que llegar tarde, no debo llegar tarde
◇ probability deber de; **it must be about 6 o'clock** deben de ser las seis; **they must have arrived by now** ya deben de haber llegado

mus·tache [məˈstæʃ] bigote m

mus·tard [ˈmʌstərd] mostaza f

must·y [ˈmʌstɪ] adj room que huele a humedad; smell a humedad

mute [mjuːt] adj animal mudo

mut·ed [ˈmjuːtɪd] adj color apagado; criticism débil

mu·ti·late [ˈmjuːtɪleɪt] v/t mutilar

mu·ti·ny [ˈmjuːtɪnɪ] 1 n motín m 2 v/i (pret & pp **mutinied**) amotinarse

mut·ter [ˈmʌtər] v/t & v/i murmurar

mut·ton [ˈmʌtn] carnero m

mu·tu·al [ˈmjuːtʃʊəl] adj mutuo

muz·zle [ˈmʌzl] 1 n of animal hocico m; for dog bozal m 2 v/t poner un bozal a; **muzzle the press** amordazar a la prensa

my [maɪ] adj mi; **my house** mi casa; **my parents** mis padres

my·op·ic [maɪˈɑːpɪk] adj miope

my·self [maɪˈself] pron reflexive me; emphatic yo mismo(-a); **when I saw myself in the mirror** cuando me vi en el espejo; **I saw it myself** lo vi yo mismo; **by myself** (alone) solo; (without help) yo solo, yo mismo

mys·te·ri·ous [mɪˈstɪrɪəs] adj misterioso

mys·te·ri·ous·ly [mɪˈstɪrɪəslɪ] adv misteriosamente

mys·te·ry [ˈmɪstərɪ] misterio m; **mystery (story)** relato m de misterio

mys·ti·fy [ˈmɪstɪfaɪ] v/t (pret & pp **mystified**) dejar perplejo

myth [mɪθ] also fig mito m

myth·i·cal [ˈmɪθɪkl] adj mítico

my·thol·o·gy [mɪˈθɑːlədʒɪ] mitología f

N

nab [næb] *v/t (pret & pp* **nabbed***)* F *(take for o.s.)* pescar F, agarrar

nag [næg] **1** *v/i (pret & pp* **nagged***) of person* dar la lata **2** *v/t (pret & pp* **nagged***)*: **nag s.o. to do sth** dar la lata a alguien para que haga algo

nag·ging ['nægɪŋ] *adj person* quejica; *doubt* persistente; *pain* continuo

nail [neɪl] *for wood* clavo *m; on finger, toe* uña *f*

'**nail clip·pers** *npl* cortaúñas *m inv*

'**nail file** lima *f* de uñas

'**nail pol·ish** esmalte *m* de uñas

'**nail pol·ish re·mov·er** quitaesmaltes *m inv*

'**nail scis·sors** *npl* tijeras *fpl* de manicura

'**nail var·nish** esmalte *m* de uñas

na·ive [naɪˈiːv] *adj* ingenuo

naked ['neɪkɪd] *adj* desnudo; *to the naked eye* a simple vista

name [neɪm] **1** *n* nombre *m; what's your name?* ¿cómo te llamas?; *call s.o. names* insultar a alguien; *make a name for o.s.* hacerse un nombre **2** *v/t: they named him Ben* le llamaron Ben

♦ **name for** *v/t: name s.o. for s.o.* poner a alguien el nombre de alguien

name·ly ['neɪmlɪ] *adv* a saber

'**name·sake** tocayo(-a) *m(f);* homónimo(-a) *m(f)*

'**name·tag** *on clothing etc* etiqueta *f*

nan·ny ['nænɪ] niñera *f*

nap [næp] *n* cabezada *f; have a nap* echar una cabezada

nape [neɪp] *nape of the neck* nuca *f*

nap·kin ['næpkɪn] *(table napkin)* servilleta *f; (sanitary napkin)* compresa *f*

nar·cot·ic [nɑːrˈkɑːtɪk] *n* narcótico *m*, estupefaciente *m*

nar'cot·ics a·gent agente *m/f* de la brigada de estupefacientes

nar·rate [nəˈreɪt] *v/t* narrar

nar·ra·tion [nəˈreɪʃn] *(telling)* narración *f*

nar·ra·tive ['nærətɪv] **1** *n (story)* narración *f* **2** *adj poem, style* narrativo

nar·ra·tor [nəˈreɪtər] narrador(a) *m(f)*

nar·row ['nærou] *adj street, bed, victory* estrecho; *views, mind* cerrado

nar·row·ly ['nærouli] *adv win* por poco; *narrowly escape sth* escapar por poco de algo

nar·row-mind·ed [nærou'maɪndɪd] *adj* cerrado

na·sal ['neɪzl] *adj voice* nasal

nas·ty ['næstɪ] *adj person, smell* desagradable, asqueroso; *thing to say* malintencionado; *weather* horrible; *cut, wound* feo; *disease* serio

na·tion ['neɪʃn] nación *f*

na·tion·al ['næʃənl] **1** *adj* nacional **2** *n* ciudadano(-a) *m(f)*

na·tion·al 'an·them himno *m* nacional

na·tion·al 'debt deuda *f* pública

na·tion·al·ism ['næʃənəlɪzm] nacionalismo *m*

na·tion·al·i·ty [næʃəˈnælətɪ] nacionalidad *f*

na·tion·al·ize ['næʃənəlaɪz] *v/t industry etc* nacionalizar

na·tion·al 'park parque *m* nacional

na·tive ['neɪtɪv] **1** *adj* nativo; *native language* lengua *f* materna **2** *n* nativo(-a) *m(f),* natural *m/f; tribesman* nativo(-a) *m(f),* indígena *m/f; he's a native of New York* es natural de Nueva York

na·tive 'coun·try país *m* natal

na·tive 'speak·er hablante *m/f* nativo(-a)

NATO ['neɪtou] *abbr (= North Atlantic Treaty Organization)* OTAN *f (=* Organización *f* del Tratado del Atlántico Norte)

nat·u·ral ['nætʃrəl] *adj* natural; *a natural blonde* una rubia natural

nat·u·ral 'gas gas *m* natural

nat·u·ral·ist ['nætʃrəlɪst] naturalista *m/f*

nat·u·ral·ize ['nætʃrəlaɪz] *v/t: become naturalized* naturalizarse, nacionalizarse

nat·u·ral·ly ['nætʃərəlɪ] *adv (of course)* naturalmente; *behave, speak* con naturalidad; *(by nature)* por naturaleza

nat·u·ral 'sci·ence ciencias *fpl* naturales

nat·u·ral 'sci·en·tist experto(-a) *m(f)* en ciencias naturales

na·ture ['neɪtʃər] naturaleza *f*

na·ture re'serve reserva *f* natural

naugh·ty ['nɔːtɪ] *adj* travieso, malo; *photograph, word etc* picante

nau·se·a ['nɔːzɪə] náusea *f*

nau·se·ate ['nɔːzɪeɪt] *v/t (fig: disgust)* dar náuseas a

nau·se·at·ing ['nɔːzɪeɪtɪŋ] *adj smell, taste* nauseabundo; *person* repugnante

nau·seous ['nɔːʃəs] *adj* nauseabundo; *feel nauseous* tener náuseas

nau·ti·cal ['nɔːtɪkl] *adj* náutico

'**nau·ti·cal mile** milla *f* náutica

na·val ['neɪvl] *adj* naval

'**na·val base** base *f* naval

na·vel ['neɪvl] ombligo m

nav·i·ga·ble ['nævɪgəbl] *adj river* navegable

nav·i·gate ['nævɪgeɪt] *v/i in ship, airplane*, COMPUT navegar; *in car* hacer de copiloto

nav·i·ga·tion [nævɪ'geɪʃn] navegación f; *in car* direcciones fpl

nav·i·ga·tor ['nævɪgeɪtər] *on ship* oficial m de derrota; *in airplane* navegante m/f; *in car* copiloto m/f

na·vy ['neɪvɪ] armada f, marina f (de guerra)

na·vy 'blue 1 n azul m marino **2** adj azul marino

near [nɪr] **1** adv cerca; ***come a bit nearer*** acércate un poco más **2** prep cerca de; ***near the bank*** cerca del banco; ***do you go near the bank?*** ¿pasa cerca del banco? **3** adj cercano, próximo; ***the nearest bus stop*** la parada de autobús más cercana *or* próxima; ***in the near future*** en un futuro próximo

near·by [nɪr'baɪ] adv live cerca

near·ly ['nɪrlɪ] adv casi

near-sight·ed [nɪr'saɪtɪd] adj miope

neat [niːt] adj ordenado; *whisky* solo, seco; *solution* ingenioso; F (*terrific*) genial F, estupendo F

ne·ces·sar·i·ly ['nesəserɪlɪ] adv necesariamente

ne·ces·sa·ry ['nesəserɪ] adj necesario, preciso; ***it is necessary to ...*** es necesario ..., hay que ...

ne·ces·si·tate [nɪ'sesɪteɪt] v/t exigir, hacer necesario

ne·ces·si·ty [nɪ'sesɪtɪ] *(being necessary)* necesidad f; *(something necessary)* necesidad f, requisito m imprescindible

neck [nek] cuello m

neck·lace ['neklɪs] collar m

'neck·line *of dress* escote m

'neck·tie corbata f

née [neɪ] adj de soltera

need [niːd] **1** n necesidad f; ***if need be*** si fuera necesario; ***in need*** necesitado; ***be in need of sth*** necesitar algo; ***there's no need to be rude / upset*** no hace falta ser grosero /que te enfades **2** v/t necesitar; ***you'll need to buy one*** tendrás que comprar uno; ***you don't need to wait*** no hace falta que esperes; ***I need to talk to you*** tengo que *or* necesito hablar contigo; ***need I say more?*** ¿hace falta que añada algo?

nee·dle ['niːdl] *for sewing, injection, on dial* aguja f

'nee·dle·work costura f

need·y ['niːdɪ] adj necesitado

neg·a·tive ['negətɪv] adj negativo; ***answer in the negative*** dar una respuesta negativa

ne·glect [nɪ'glekt] **1** n abandono m, descuido m **2** v/t garden, one's health descuidar, desatender; ***neglect to do sth*** no hacer algo

ne·glect·ed [nɪ'glektɪd] adj gardens abandonado, descuidado; *author* olvidado; ***feel neglected*** sentirse abandonado

neg·li·gence ['neglɪdʒəns] negligencia f

neg·li·gent ['neglɪdʒənt] adj negligente

neg·li·gi·ble ['neglɪdʒəbl] adj quantity, amount insignificante

ne·go·ti·a·ble [nɪ'goʊʃəbl] adj salary, contract negociable

ne·go·ti·ate [nɪ'goʊʃɪeɪt] **1** v/i negociar **2** v/t deal, settlement negociar; obstacles franquear, salvar; bend in road tomar

ne·go·ti·a·tion [nɪgoʊʃɪ'eɪʃn] negociación f; ***be under negotiation*** estar siendo negociado

ne·go·ti·a·tor [nɪ'goʊʃɪeɪtər] negociador(a) m(f)

Ne·gro pej ['niːgroʊ] negro(-a) m(f)

neigh [neɪ] v/i relinchar

neigh·bor ['neɪbər] vecino(-a) m(f)

neigh·bor·hood ['neɪbərhʊd] *in town* vecindario m, barrio m; ***in the neighborhood of ...*** fig alrededor de ...

neigh·bor·ing ['neɪbərɪŋ] adj house, state vecino, colindante

neigh·bor·ly ['neɪbərlɪ] adj amable

neigh·bour etc Br → **neighbor** etc

nei·ther ['niːðər] **1** adj ninguno; ***neither applicant was any good*** ninguno de los candidatos era bueno **2** pron ninguno(-a) m(f) **3** adv: ***neither ... nor ...*** ni ... ni ... **4** conj: ***neither do I*** yo tampoco; ***neither can I*** yo tampoco

ne·on light ['niːɑːn] luz f de neón

neph·ew ['nefjuː] sobrino m

nerd [nɜːrd] F petardo(-a) m(f)

nerve [nɜːrv] nervio m; *(courage)* valor m; *(impudence)* descaro m; ***it's bad for my nerves*** me pone de los nervios; ***get on s.o.'s nerves*** sacar de quicio a alguien

nerve-rack·ing ['nɜːrvrækɪŋ] adj angustioso, exasperante

ner·vous ['nɜːrvəs] adj person nervioso, inquieto; *twitch* nervioso; ***I'm nervous about meeting them*** la reunión con ellos me pone muy nervioso

ner·vous 'break·down crisis f inv nerviosa

ner·vous 'en·er·gy energía f

ner·vous·ness ['nɜːrvəsnɪs] nerviosismo m

ner·vous 'wreck manojo m de nervios

nerv·y ['nɜːrvɪ] adj (fresh) descarado

nest [nest] n nido m

nes·tle ['nesl] v/i acomodarse

net¹ [net] for fishing, tennis red f

net² [net] adj price, weight neto

net 'cur·tain visillo m

net 'pro·fit beneficio m neto

net·tle ['netl] ortiga f

'net·work of contacts, cells, COMPUT red f

neu·rol·o·gist [nʊəˈrɑːlədʒɪst] neurólogo(-a) m(f)

neu·ro·sis [nʊˈrəʊsɪs] neurosis f inv

neu·rot·ic [nʊˈrɑːtɪk] adj neurótico

neu·ter ['nuːtər] v/t animal castrar

neu·tral ['nuːtrl] 1 adj country neutral; color neutro 2 n gear punto m muerto; in neutral en punto muerto

neu·tral·i·ty [nuːˈtrælətɪ] neutralidad f

neu·tral·ize ['nuːtrəlaɪz] v/t neutralizar

nev·er ['nevər] adv nunca; you're never going to believe this no te vas a creer esto; you never promised, did you? no lo llegaste a prometer, ¿verdad?

nev·er-'end·ing adj interminable

nev·er·the·less [nevərðəˈles] adv sin embargo, no obstante

new [nuː] adj nuevo; this system is still new to me todavía no me he hecho con este sistema; I'm new to the job soy nuevo en el trabajo; that's nothing new no es nada nuevo

'new·born adj recién nacido

new·com·er ['nuːkʌmər] recién llegado(-a) m(f)

new·ly ['nuːlɪ] adv (recently) recientemente, recién

new·ly·weds [wedz] npl recién casados mpl

new 'moon luna f nueva

news [nuːz] nsg noticias fpl; on TV noticias fpl, telediario m; on radio noticias fpl; that's news to me no sabía eso

'news a·gen·cy agencia f de noticias

'news·a·gent quiosquero(-a) m(f)

'news·cast TV noticias fpl, telediario m; on radio noticias fpl

'news·cast·er TV presentador(a) m(f) de informativos

'news flash flash m informativo, noticia f de última hora

'news·pa·per periódico m

'news·read·er TV etc presentador(a) m(f) de informativos

'news re·port reportaje m

'news·stand quiosco m

'news·ven·dor vendedor(a) m(f) de periódicos

'New Year año m nuevo; Happy New Year! ¡Feliz Año Nuevo!

New Year's 'Day Día m de Año Nuevo

New Year's 'Eve Nochevieja f

New York [jɔːrk] 1 adj neoyorquino 2 n: New York (City) Nueva York

New York·er ['jɔːrkər] n neoyorquino(-a) m(f)

New Zea·land ['ziːlənd] Nueva Zelanda

New Zea·land·er ['ziːləndər] neozelandés(-esa) m(f), neocelandés(-esa) m(f)

next [nekst] 1 adj in time próximo, siguiente; in space siguiente, de al lado; next week la próxima semana, la semana que viene; the next week he came back again volvió a la semana siguiente; who's next? ¿quién es el siguiente? 2 adv luego, después; next, we're going to study ... a continuación, vamos a estudiar ...; next to (beside) al lado de; (in comparison with) en comparación con

next 'door 1 adj neighbor de al lado 2 adv live al lado

next of 'kin pariente m más cercano

nib·ble ['nɪbl] v/t mordisquear

Nic·a·ra·gua [nɪkəˈrɑːɡwə] Nicaragua

Nic·a·ra·guan [nɪkəˈrɑːɡwən] 1 adj nicaragüense 2 n nicaragüense m/f

nice [naɪs] adj trip, house, hair bonito, L.Am. lindo; person agradable, simpático; weather bueno, agradable; meal, food bueno, rico; be nice to your sister! ¡trata bien a tu hermana!; that's very nice of you es muy amable de tu parte

nice·ly ['naɪslɪ] adv written, presented bien; (pleasantly) amablemente

nice·ties ['naɪsətɪz] npl sutilezas fpl; refinamientos mpl; social niceties cumplidos mpl

niche [niːʃ] in market hueco m, nicho m; (special position) hueco m

nick [nɪk] n (cut) muesca f, mella f; in the nick of time justo a tiempo

nick·el ['nɪkl] níquel m; (coin) moneda de cinco centavos

'nick·name n apodo m, mote m

niece [niːs] sobrina f

nig·gard·ly ['nɪɡərdlɪ] adj amount, person mísero

night [naɪt] noche f; tomorrow night mañana por la noche; 11 o'clock at night las 11 de la noche; travel by night viajar de noche; during the night por la noche; stay the night quedarse a dormir; a room for 2 nights una habitación para 2 noches; work nights trabajar de noche; good night buenas noches; in the middle of the night en mitad de la noche

'night·cap drink copa f (tomada antes de ir a dormir)

'night·club club m nocturno, discoteca f

N

'night·dress camisón *m*
'night·fall: *at nightfall* al anochecer
'night flight vuelo *m* nocturno
'night·gown camisón *m*
night·ie ['naɪtɪ] camisón *m*
nigh·tin·gale ['naɪtɪŋgeɪl] ruiseñor *m*
'night·life vida *f* nocturna
'night·ly ['naɪtlɪ] **1** *adj: a nightly event* algo que sucede todas las noches **2** *adv* todas las noches
'night·mare *also fig* pesadilla *f*
'night por·ter portero *m* de noche
'night school escuela *f* nocturna
'night shift turno *m* de noche
'night·shirt camisa *f* de dormir
'night·spot local *m* nocturno
'night·time: *at nighttime, in the nighttime* por la noche
nil [nɪl] *Br* cero
nim·ble ['nɪmbl] *adj* ágil
nine [naɪn] nueve
nine·teen [naɪn'tiːn] diecinueve
nine·teenth [naɪn'tiːnθ] *n & adj* decimonoveno
nine·ti·eth ['naɪntɪɪθ] *n & adj* nonagésimo
nine·ty ['naɪntɪ] noventa
ninth [naɪnθ] *n & adj* noveno
nip [nɪp] *n* (*pinch*) pellizco *m*; (*bite*) mordisco *m*
nip·ple ['nɪpl] pezón *m*
ni·tro·gen ['naɪtrədʒn] nitrógeno *m*
no [noʊ] **1** *adv* no **2** *adj: there's no coffee / tea left* no queda café / té; *I have no family / money* no tengo familia / dinero; *I'm no linguist / expert* no soy un lingüista / experto; *no smoking / parking* prohibido fumar / aparcar
no·bil·i·ty [noʊ'bɪlətɪ] nobleza *f*
no·ble ['noʊbl] *adj* noble
no·bod·y ['noʊbɑːdɪ] *pron* nadie; *nobody knows* nadie lo sabe; *there was nobody at home* no había nadie en casa
nod [nɑːd] **1** *n* movimiento *m* de la cabeza **2** *v/i* (*pret & pp nodded*) asentir con la cabeza
◆ nod off *v/i* (*fall asleep*) quedarse dormido
no-hop·er [noʊ'hoʊpər] F inútil *m/f* F
noise [nɔɪz] ruido *m*
nois·y ['nɔɪzɪ] *adj* ruidoso
nom·i·nal ['nɑːmɪnl] *adj amount* simbólico
nom·i·nate ['nɑːmɪneɪt] *v/t* (*appoint*) nombrar; *nominate s.o. for a post* (*propose*) proponer a alguien para un puesto
nom·i·na·tion [nɑːmɪ'neɪʃn] (*appointment*) nombramiento *m*; (*proposal*) nominación *f*; *who was your nomination?* ¿a quién propusiste?

nom·i·nee [nɑːmɪ'niː] candidato(-a) *m(f)*
non ... [nɑːn] no ...
non-al·co·hol·ic *adj* sin alcohol
non-a·ligned *adj* no alineado
non-cha·lant ['nɑːʃələnt] *adj* despreocupado
non-com·mis·sioned 'of·fi·cer suboficial *m/f*
non·com'mit·tal *adj person*, *response* evasivo
non-de·script ['nɑːndɪskrɪpt] *adj* anodino
none [nʌn] *pron: none of the students* ninguno de los estudiantes; *none of the water* nada del agua; *there are none left* no queda ninguno; *there is none left* no queda nada
non·en·ti·ty nulidad *f*
none·the·less [nʌnðə'les] *adv* sin embargo, no obstante
non·ex'ist·ent *adj* inexistente
non'fic·tion no ficción *f*
non-(in)'flam·ma·ble *adj* incombustible, no inflamable
non-in·ter'fer·ence, non·in·ter'ven·tion no intervención *f*
non-'i·ron *adj shirt* que no necesita plancha
'no-no: *that's a no-no* F de eso nada
no-'non·sense *approach* directo
non'payment impago *f*
non·pol'lut·ing *adj* que no contamina
non'res·i·dent *n* no residente *m/f*
non-re·turn·a·ble [nɑːnrɪ'tɜːrnəbl] *adj* no retornable
non·sense ['nɑːnsəns] disparate *m*, tontería *f*; *don't talk nonsense* no digas disparates *or* tonterías; *nonsense, it's easy!* tonterías, ¡es fácil!
non'skid *adj tires* antideslizante
non'slip *adj surface* antideslizante
non'smok·er *person* no fumador(a) *m(f)*
non'stand·ard *adj* no estándar
non'stick *adj pans* antiadherente
non'stop **1** *adj flight, train* directo, sin escalas; *chatter* ininterrumpido **2** *adv fly, travel* directamente; *chatter, argue* sin parar
non'swim·mer: *be a nonswimmer* no saber nadar
non'u·nion *adj* no sindicado
non'vi·o·lence no violencia *f*
non'vi·o·lent *adj* no violento
noo·dles ['nuːdlz] *npl* tallarines *mpl* (chinos)
nook [nʊk] rincón *m*
noon [nuːn] mediodía *m*; *at noon* al mediodía
noose [nuːs] lazo *m* corredizo

nor [nɔːr] *conj* ni; *nor do I* yo tampoco, ni yo

norm [nɔːrm] norma *f*

nor·mal ['nɔːrml] *adj* normal

nor·mal·i·ty [nɔːr'mælətɪ] normalidad *f*

nor·mal·ize ['nɔːrməlaɪz] *v/t relationships* normalizar

nor·mal·ly ['nɔːrməlɪ] *adv (usually)* normalmente; *(in a normal way)* normalmente, con normalidad

north [nɔːrθ] **1** *n* norte *m*; *to the north of* al norte de **2** *adj* norte **3** *adv travel* al norte, *north of* al norte de

North Am·er·i·ca América del Norte, Norteamérica

North Am·er·i·can 1 *n* norteamericano(-a) *m(f)* **2** *adj* norteamericano

north·east *n* noreste *m*, noreste *m*

nor·ther·ly ['nɔːrðəlɪ] *adj* norte, del norte

nor·thern ['nɔːrðən] norteño, del norte

nor·thern·er ['nɔːrðənər] norteño(-a) *m(f)*

North Ko·re·a Corea del Norte

North Ko·re·an 1 *adj* norcoreano **2** *n* norcoreano(-a) *m(f)*

North Pole Polo *m* Norte

north·ward ['nɔːrðwərd] *adv travel* hacia el norte

north·west [nɔːrð'west] *n* noroeste *m*

Nor·way ['nɔːrweɪ] Noruega

Nor·we·gian [nɔːr'wiːdʒn] **1** *adj* noruego **2** *n person* noruego(-a) *m(f)*; *language* noruego *m*

nose [nəʊz] nariz *m*; *of animal* hocico *m*; *it was right under my nose!* ¡lo tenía delante de mis narices!

◆ **nose about** *v/i* F husmear

nose·bleed: *have a nosebleed* sangrar por la nariz

nos·tal·gia [nɑːˈstældʒɪə] nostalgia *f*

nos·tal·gic [nɑːˈstældʒɪk] *adj* nostálgico

nos·tril ['nɑːstrəl] ventana *f* de la nariz

nos·y ['nəʊzɪ] *adj* F entrometido

not [nɑːt] *adv* no; *not this one, that one* éste no, ése; *not now* ahora no; *not there* no allí; *not like that* así no; *not before Tuesday / next week* no antes del martes / de la próxima semana; *not for me, thanks* para mí no, gracias; *not a lot* no mucho; *it's not ready / allowed* no está listo / permitido; *I don't know* no lo sé; *I am not American* no soy americano; *he didn't help* no ayudó

no·ta·ble ['nəʊtəbl] *adj* notable

no·ta·ry ['nəʊtərɪ] notario(-a) *m(f)*

notch [nɑːtʃ] muesca *f*, mella *f*

note [nəʊt] *n written*, MUS nota *f*; *take notes* tomar notas; *take note of sth* prestar atención a algo

◆ **note down** *v/t* anotar

note·book cuaderno *m*, libreta *f*; COMPUT *Span* ordenador *m* portátil, *L.Am.* computadora *f* portátil

not·ed ['nəʊtɪd] *adj* destacado

note·pad bloc *m* de notas

note·pa·per papel *m* de carta

noth·ing ['nʌθɪŋ] *pron* nada; *nothing but* sólo; *nothing much* no mucho; *for nothing (for free)* gratis; *(for no reason)* por nada; *I'd like nothing better* me encantaría

no·tice ['nəʊtɪs] **1** *n on bulletin board, in street* cartel *m*, letrero *m*; *(advance warning)* aviso *m*; *in newspaper* anuncio *m*; *at short notice* con poca antelación; *until further notice* hasta nuevo aviso; *give s.o. his / her notice to quit job* despedir a alguien; *to leave house* comunicar a alguien que tiene que abandonar la casa; *hand in one's notice to employer* presentar la dimisión; *four weeks' notice* cuatro semanas de preaviso; *take notice of sth* observar algo, prestar atención a algo; *take no notice of s.o./sth* no hacer caso de alguien / algo **2** *v/t* notar, fijarse en

no·tice·a·ble ['nəʊtɪsəbl] *adj* apreciable, evidente

no·ti·fy ['nəʊtɪfaɪ] *v/t (pret & pp notified)* notificar, informar

no·tion ['nəʊʃn] noción *f*, idea *f*

no·tions ['nəʊsnz] *npl* artículos *mpl* de costura

no·to·ri·ous [nəʊˈtɔːrɪəs] *adj* de mala fama

nou·gat ['nuːgət] *especie de turrón*

nought [nɔːt] cero *m*

noun [naʊn] nombre *m*, sustantivo *m*

nour·ish·ing ['nʌrɪʃɪŋ] *adj* nutritivo

nour·ish·ment ['nʌrɪʃmənt] alimento *m*, alimentación *f*

nov·el ['nɑːvl] *n* novela *f*

nov·el·ist ['nɑːvlɪst] novelista *m/f*

no·vel·ty ['nɑːvəltɪ] *(being new)* lo novedoso; *(something new)* novedad *f*

No·vem·ber [nəʊ'vembər] noviembre *m*

nov·ice ['nɑːvɪs] principiante *m/f*

now [naʊ] *adv* ahora; *now and again, now and then* de vez en cuando; *by now* ya; *from now on* de ahora en adelante; *right now* ahora mismo; *just now (at this moment)* en este momento; *(a little while ago)* hace un momento; *now, now!* ¡vamos!; *now, where did I put it?* ¿y ahora dónde lo he puesto?

now·a·days ['naʊədeɪz] *adv* hoy en día

no·where ['nəʊwer] *adv* en ningún lugar;

it's nowhere near finished no está acabado ni mucho menos; **he was nowhere to be seen** no se le veía en ninguna parte
noz·zle ['nɑːzl] boquilla *f*
nu·cle·ar ['nuːklɪər] *adj* nuclear
nu·cle·ar 'en·er·gy energía *f* nuclear
nu·cle·ar 'fis·sion fisión *f* nuclear
'nu·cle·ar-free *adj* desnuclearizado
nu·cle·ar 'phys·ics física *f* nuclear
nu·cle·ar 'pow·er energía *f* nuclear; POL potencia *f* nuclear
nu·cle·ar 'pow·er sta·tion central *f* nuclear
nu·cle·ar re'ac·tor reactor *m* nuclear
nu·cle·ar 'waste residuos *mpl* nucleares
nu·cle·ar 'weap·on arma *f* nuclear
nude [nuːd] **1** *adj* desnudo **2** *n painting* desnudo *m*; **in the nude** desnudo
nudge [nʌdʒ] *v/t* dar un toque con el codo a
nud·ist ['nuːdɪst] *n* nudista *m/f*
nui·sance ['nuːsns] incordio *m*, molestia *f*; **make a nuisance of o.s.** dar la lata; **what a nuisance!** ¡qué incordio!
nuke [nuːk] *v/t* F atacar con armas nucleares
null and 'void [nʌl] *adj* nulo y sin efecto
numb [nʌm] *adj* entumecido; *emotionally* insensible
num·ber ['nʌmbər] **1** *n* número *m*; **a number of people** un cierto número de personas **2** *v/t* (*put a number on*) numerar
numeral ['nuːmərəl] número *m*
nu·me·rate ['nuːmərət] *adj* que sabe sumar y restar
nu·me·rous ['nuːmərəs] *adj* numeroso
nun [nʌn] monja *f*
nurse [nɜːrs] enfermero(-a) *m(f)*
nur·se·ry ['nɜːrsərɪ] guardería *f*; *for plants* vivero *m*
'nur·se·ry rhyme canción *f* infantil
'nur·se·ry school parvulario *m*, jardín *m* de infancia
'nur·se·ry school teach·er profesor(a) *m(f)* de parvulario
nurs·ing ['nɜːrsɪŋ] enfermería *f*
'nurs·ing home *for old people* residencia *f*
nut [nʌt] nuez *f*; *for bolt* tuerca *f*; **nuts** (*testicles*) pelotas *fpl* F
'nut·crack·ers *npl* cascanueces *m inv*
nu·tri·ent ['nuːtrɪənt] *n* nutriente *m*
nu·tri·tion [nuːtrɪʃn] nutrición *f*
nu·tri·tious [nuːtrɪʃəs] *adj* nutritivo
nuts [nʌts] *adj* F (*crazy*) chalado F, pirado F; **be nuts about s.o.** estar coladito por alguien F
'nut·shell: **in a nutshell** en una palabra
nut·ty ['nʌtɪ] *adj* taste a nuez; F (*crazy*) chalado F, pirado F
ny·lon ['naɪlɑːn] **1** *n* nylon *m* **2** *adj* de nylon

O

oak [oʊk] *tree, wood* roble *m*
oar [ɔːr] remo *m*
o·a·sis [oʊˈeɪsɪs] (*pl* **oases** [oʊˈeɪsiːz]) *also fig* oasis *m inv*
oath [oʊθ] LAW, (*swearword*) juramento *m*; **on oath** bajo juramento
'oat·meal harina *f* de avena
oats [oʊts] *npl* copos *mpl* de avena
o·be·di·ence [oʊˈbiːdɪəns] obediencia *f*
o·be·di·ent [oʊˈbiːdɪənt] *adj* obediente
o·be·di·ent·ly [oʊˈbiːdɪəntlɪ] *adv* obedientemente
o·bese [oʊˈbiːs] *adj* obeso
o·bes·i·ty [oʊˈbiːsɪtɪ] obesidad *f*
o·bey [oʊˈbeɪ] *v/t* obedecer
o·bit·u·a·ry [əˈbɪtʊerɪ] *n* necrología *f*, obituario *m*
ob·ject[1] ['ɑːbdʒɪkt] *n* (*thing*) objeto *m*;

(*aim*) objetivo *m*; GRAM objeto *m*
ob·ject[2] [əbˈdʒekt] *v/i* oponerse
◆ object to *v/t* oponerse a
ob·jec·tion [əbˈdʒekʃn] objeción *f*
ob·jec·tio·na·ble [əbˈdʒekʃnəbl] *adj* (*unpleasant*) desagradable
ob·jec·tive [əbˈdʒektɪv] **1** *adj* objetivo **2** *n* objetivo *m*
ob·jec·tive·ly [əbˈdʒektɪvlɪ] *adv* objetivamente
ob·jec·tiv·i·ty [əbˈdʒektɪvətɪ] objetividad *f*
ob·li·ga·tion [ɑːblɪˈɡeɪʃn] obligación *f*; **be under an obligation to s.o.** tener una obligación para con alguien
ob·lig·a·to·ry [əˈblɪɡətɔːrɪ] *adj* obligatorio
o·blige [əˈblaɪdʒ] *v/t* obligar; **much o-**

bliged! muy agradecido

•blig·ing [əˈblaɪdʒɪŋ] *adj* atento, servicial

•blique [əˈbliːk] **1** *adj reference* indirecto **2** *n in punctuation* barra *f* inclinada

•blit·er·ate [əˈblɪtəreɪt] *v/t city* destruir, arrasar; *memory* borrar

•bliv·i·on [əˈblɪvɪən] olvido *m*; *fall into oblivion* caer en el olvido

•bliv·i·ous [əˈblɪvɪəs] *adj*: *be oblivious of sth* no ser consciente de algo

ob·long [ˈɑːblɒːŋ] *adj* rectangular

ob·nox·ious [əbˈnɑːkʃəs] *adj person* detestable, odioso; *smell* repugnante

ob·scene [əbˈsiːn] *adj* obsceno; *salary, poverty* escandaloso

ob·scen·i·ty [əbˈsenətɪ] obscenidad *f*

ob·scure [əbˈskjʊr] *adj* oscuro

ob·scu·ri·ty [əbˈskjʊrətɪ] oscuridad *f*

ob·ser·vance [əbˈzɜːrvəns] *of festival* práctica *f*

ob·ser·vant [əbˈzɜːrvənt] *adj* observador

ob·ser·va·tion [ɑːbzəˈveɪʃn] *of nature, stars* observación *f*; *(comment)* observación *f*, comentario *m*

ob·ser·va·to·ry [əbˈzɜːrvətɔːrɪ] observatorio *m*

ob·serve [əbˈzɜːrv] *v/t* observar

ob·serv·er [əbˈzɜːrvər] observador(a) *m(f)*

ob·sess [ɑːbˈses] *v/t* obsesionar; *be obsessed by / with* estar obsesionado con / por

ob·ses·sion [ɑːbˈseʃn] obsesión *f*

ob·ses·sive [ɑːbˈsesɪv] *adj* obsesivo

ob·so·lete [ˈɑːbsəliːt] *adj* obsoleto

ob·sta·cle [ˈɑːbstəkl] obstáculo *m*

ob·ste·tri·cian [ɑːbstəˈtrɪʃn] obstetra *m/f*, tocólogo(-a) *m(f)*

ob·stet·rics [ɑːbˈstetrɪks] obstetricia *f*, tocología *f*

ob·sti·na·cy [ˈɑːbstɪnəsɪ] obstinación *f*

ob·sti·nate [ˈɑːbstɪnət] *adj* obstinado

ob·sti·nate·ly [ˈɑːbstɪnətlɪ] *adv* obstinadamente

ob·struct [ɑːbˈstrʌkt] *v/t road* obstruir; *investigation, police* obstaculizar

ob·struc·tion [əbˈstrʌkʃn] *on road etc* obstrucción *f*

ob·struc·tive [əbˈstrʌktɪv] *adj behavior, tactics* obstruccionista

ob·tain [əbˈteɪn] *v/t* obtener, lograr

ob·tain·a·ble [əbˈteɪnəbl] *adj products* disponible

ob·tru·sive [əbˈtruːsɪv] *adj* molesto; *the plastic chairs are rather obtrusive* las sillas de plástico desentonan por completo

ob·tuse [əbˈtuːs] *adj fig* duro de mollera

ob·vi·ous [ˈɑːbvɪəs] *adj* obvio, evidente

ob·vi·ous·ly [ˈɑːbvɪəslɪ] *adv* obviamente; *obviously!* ¡por supuesto!

oc·ca·sion [əˈkeɪʒn] ocasión *f*

oc·ca·sion·al [əˈkeɪʒnl] *adj* ocasional, esporádico; *I like the occasional whisky* me gusta tomarme un whisky de vez en cuando

oc·ca·sion·al·ly [əˈkeɪʒnlɪ] *adv* ocasionalmente, de vez en cuando

oc·cult [əˈkʌlt] **1** *adj* oculto **2** *n*: *the occult* lo oculto

oc·cu·pant [ˈɑːkjʊpənt] ocupante *m/f*

oc·cu·pa·tion [ɑːkjʊˈpeɪʃn] ocupación *f*

oc·cu·pa·tion·al 'ther·a·pist [ɑːkjʊˈpeɪʃnl] terapeuta *m/f* ocupacional

oc·cu·pa·tion·al 'ther·a·py terapia *f* ocupacional

oc·cu·py [ˈɑːkjʊpaɪ] *v/t (pret & pp occupied)* ocupar

oc·cur [əˈkɜːr] *v/i (pret & pp occurred)* ocurrir, suceder; *it occurred to me that ...* se me ocurrió que ...

oc·cur·rence [əˈkʌrəns] acontecimiento *m*

o·cean [ˈoʊʃn] océano *m*

o·ce·a·nog·ra·phy [oʊʃnˈɑːgrəfɪ] oceanografía *f*

o'clock [əˈklɑːk]: *at five / six o'clock* a las cinco / seis

Oc·to·ber [ɑːkˈtoʊbər] octubre *m*

oc·to·pus [ˈɑːktəpəs] pulpo *m*

OD [oʊˈdiː] *v/i* F *OD on drug* tomar una sobredosis de

odd [ɑːd] *adj (strange)* raro, extraño; *(not even)* impar; *the odd one out* el bicho raro; *50 odd* cerca de 50

'odd·ball F bicho *m* raro F

odds [ɑːdz] *npl*: *be at odds with sth / s.o.* no concordar con algo / estar peleado con alguien; *the odds are 10 to one* las apuestas están en 10 a 1; *the odds are that ...* lo más probable es que ...; *against all the odds* contra lo que se esperaba

odds and 'ends *npl objects* cacharros *mpl*; *things to do* cosillas *fpl*

'odds-on *adj favorite* indiscutible

o·di·ous [ˈoʊdɪəs] *adj* odioso

o·dom·e·ter [oʊˈdɑːmətər] cuentakilómetros *m inv*

o·dor, *Br* **o·dour** [ˈoʊdər] olor *m*

of [ɑːv], [əv] *prep possession* de; *the name of the street / hotel* el nombre de la calle / del hotel; *the color of the car* el color del coche; *the works of Dickens* las obras de Dickens; *five / ten minutes of twelve* las doce menos cinco / diez; *die of cancer* morir de cáncer; *love of*

money / **adventure** amor por el dinero / la aventura; **of the three this is ...** de los tres éste es ...

off [ɑːf] **1** *prep*: **off the main road** (*away from*) apartado de la carretera principal; (*leading off*) saliendo de la carretera principal; **$20 off the price** una rebaja en el precio de 20 dólares; **he's off his food** no come nada, está desganado **2** *adv*: **be off** (*of light*, TV, *machine*) estar apagado; (*of brake, lid, top* no estar puesto; *not at work*) faltar; *on vacation* estar de vacaciones; (*canceled*) estar cancelado; **we're off tomorrow** (*leaving*) nos vamos mañana; **I'm off to New York** me voy a Nueva York; **with his pants / hat off** sin los pantalones / el sombrero; **take a day off** tomarse un día de fiesta or un día libre; **it's 3 miles off** está a tres millas de distancia; **it's a long way off** *in distance* está muy lejos; *in future* todavía queda mucho tiempo; **he got into his car and drove off** se subió al coche y se marchó; **off and on** de vez en cuando **3** *adj*: **the off switch** el interruptor de apagado

of·fence *Br* → **offense**

of·fend [əˈfend] *v/t* (*insult*) ofender

of·fend·er [əˈfendər] LAW delincuente *m/f*; **offenders will be prosecuted** se procesará a los infractores

of·fense [əˈfens] LAW delito *m*; **take offense at sth** ofenderse por algo

of·fen·sive [əˈfensɪv] **1** *adj behavior, remark* ofensivo; *smell* repugnante **2** *n* (MIL: *attack*) ofensiva *f*; **go on(to) the offensive** pasar a la ofensiva

of·fer [ˈɑːfər] **1** *n* oferta *f* **2** *v/t* ofrecer; **offer s.o. sth** ofrecer algo a alguien

off·hand *adj attitude* brusco

of·fice [ˈɑːfɪs] *building* oficina *f*; *room* oficina *f*, despacho *m*; *position* cargo *m*

of·fice block bloque *m* de oficinas

of·fice hours *npl* horas *fpl* de oficina

of·fi·cer [ˈɑːfɪsər] MIL oficial *m/f*; *in police* agente *m/f*

of·fi·cial [əˈfɪʃl] **1** *adj* oficial **2** *n* funcionario(-a) *m(f)*

of·fi·cial·ly [əˈfɪʃlɪ] *adv* oficialmente

of·fi·ci·ate [əˈfɪʃɪeɪt] *v/i*: **with X officiating** con X celebrando la ceremonia

of·fi·cious [əˈfɪʃəs] *adj* entrometido

off-line *adv work* fuera de línea; **be off-line** *of printer* estar desconectado; **go off-line** desconectarse

off-peak *adj rates* en horas valle, fuera de las horas punta; **offpeak electricity** electricidad *f* en horas valle *or* fuera de las horas punta

off-sea·son 1 *adj rates, vacation* de temporada baja **2** *n* temporada *f* baja

off-set *v/t* (*pret & pp* **offset**) *losses, disad vantage* compensar

off-shore *adj drilling rig* cercano a la cos ta; *investment* en el exterior

off-side 1 *adj wheel etc* del lado del con ductor **2** *adv* SP fuera de juego

off-spring *of person* vástagos *mpl*, hijo *mpl*; *of animal* crías *fpl*

off-the-ˈrec·ord *adj* confidencial

off-white *adj* blancuzco

of·ten [ˈɑːfn] *adv* a menudo, frecuente mente *m*

oil [ɔɪl] **1** *n for machine, food, skin* aceite *m*; *petroleum* petróleo *m* **2** *v/t hinges bearings* engrasar

oil change cambio *m* del aceite

oil com·pa·ny compañía *f* petrolera

oil·field yacimiento *m* petrolífero

oil-fired *adj central heating* de gasóleo o fuel

oil paint·ing óleo *m*

oil-pro·duc·ing coun·try país *m* produc tor de petróleo

oil re·fin·e·ry refinería *f* de petróleo

oil rig plataforma *f* petrolífera

oil·skins *npl* ropa *f* impermeable

oil slick marea *f* negra

oil tank·er petrolero *m*

oil well pozo *m* petrolífero

oil·y [ˈɔɪlɪ] *adj* grasiento

oint·ment [ˈɔɪntmənt] ungüento *m*, po mada *f*

ok [oʊˈkeɪ] *adj, adv* F **can I? - ok** ¿puedo - de acuerdo *or* Span vale; **is it ok with you if ...?** ¿te parecería bien si ...?; **does that look ok?** ¿queda bien?; **that's ok by me** por mí, ningún problema; **are you ok?** (*well, not hurt*) ¿estás bien?; **are you ok for Friday?** ¿te va bien e viernes?; **he's ok** (*is a good guy*) es buena persona; **is this bus ok for ...?** ¿este au tobús va a ...?

old [oʊld] *adj* viejo; (*previous*) anterior antiguo; **an old man / woman** un ancia no / una anciana, un viejo / una vieja **how old are you / is he?** ¿cuántos años tienes / tiene?; **he's getting old** está ha ciéndose mayor

old age vejez *f*

old-ˈfash·ioned *adj clothes, style, ideas* anticuado, pasado de moda; *word* anti cuado

ol·ive [ˈɑːlɪv] aceituna *f*, oliva *f*

ol·ive oil aceite *m* de oliva

O·lym·pic ˈGames [əˈlɪmpɪk] *npl* Juegos *mpl* Olímpicos

om·e·let, *Br* **om·e·lette** [ˈɑːmlɪt] tortilla *f* (francesa)

om·i·nous ['ɑ:mɪnəs] *adj* siniestro

o·mis·sion [ou'mɪʃn] omisión *f*

o·mit [ə'mɪt] *v/t* (*pret & pp omitted*) omitir; *omit to do sth* no hacer algo

om·nip·o·tent [ɑ:m'nɪpətənt] *adj* omnipotente

om·nis·ci·ent [ɑ:m'nɪsɪənt] *adj* omnisciente

on [ɑ:n] **1** *prep* en; *on the table / wall* en la mesa / la pared; *on the bus / train* en el autobús / el tren; *on TV / the radio* en la televisión / la radio; *on Sunday* el domingo; *on the 1st of …* el uno de …; *this is on me* (*I'm paying*) invito yo; *have you any money on you?* ¿llevas dinero encima?; *on his arrival / departure* cuando llegue / se marche; *on hearing this* al escuchar esto **2** *adv*: *be on* of *light*, TV, *computer etc* estar encendido *or* L.Am. prendido; *of brake, lid, top* estar puesto; *of meeting etc*: *be scheduled to happen* haber sido acordado; *it's on at 5 am* of TV *program* lo dan *or* Span ponen a las cinco; *what's on tonight?* on TV *etc* ¿qué dan *or* Span ponen esta noche?; (*what's planned?*) ¿qué planes hay para esta noche?; *with his hat on* con el sombrero puesto; *you're on* (*I accept your offer etc*) trato hecho; *that's not on* (*not allowed, not done*) eso no se hace; *on you go* (*go ahead*) adelante; *walk / talk on* seguir caminando / hablando; *and so on* etcétera; *on and on* talk *etc* sin parar **3** *adj*: *the on switch* el interruptor de encendido

once [wʌns] **1** *adv* (*one time, formerly*) una vez; *once again, once more* una vez más; *at once* (*immediately*) de inmediato, inmediatamente; *all at once* (*suddenly*) de repente; (*all*) al mismo tiempo; *once upon a time there was …* érase una vez …; *once in a while* de vez en cuando; *once and for all* de una vez por todas; *for once* por una vez **2** *conj* una vez que; *once you have finished* una vez que hayas acabado

one [wʌn] **1** *number* uno *m* **2** *adj* un(a); *one day* un día **3** *pron* uno(-a); *which one?* ¿cuál?; *one by one* enter, deal with uno por uno; *we help one another* nos ayudamos mutuamente; *what can one say / do?* ¿qué puede uno decir / hacer?; *the little ones* los pequeños; *I for one* yo personalmente

one-'off *n* (*unique event, person*) hecho *m* aislado; (*exception*) excepción *f*

one-par·ent 'fam·i·ly familia *f* monoparental

one'self *pron* uno(-a) mismo(-a) *m(f)*; *do*

sth by oneself hacer algo sin ayuda; *look after oneself* cuidarse; *be by oneself* estar solo

one-sid·ed [wʌn'saɪdɪd] *adj* discussion, fight desigual

'one-way street calle *f* de sentido único

'one-way tick·et billete *m* de ida

on·ion ['ʌnjən] cebolla *f*

'on-line *adv* en línea; *go on-line to* conectarse a

'on-line serv·ice COMPUT servicio *m* en línea

on·look·er ['ɑ:nlʊkər] espectador(a) *m(f)*, curioso(-a) *m(f)*

on·ly ['oʊnlɪ] **1** *adv* sólo, solamente; *he was here only yesterday* estuvo aquí ayer mismo; *not only … but also …* no sólo *or* solamente … sino también …; *only just* por poco **2** *adj* único; *only son* hijo único

'on-set comienzo *m*

'on-side *adv* SP en posición reglamentaria

on-the-job 'train·ing formación *f* continua

on·to ['ɑ:ntu:] *prep*: *put sth onto sth* poner algo encima de algo

on·ward ['ɑ:nwərd] *adv* hacia adelante; *from … onward* de … en adelante

ooze [u:z] **1** *v/i* of liquid, mud rezumar **2** *v/t* rezumar; *he oozes charm* rezuma *or* rebosa encanto

o·paque [oʊ'peɪk] *adj* glass opaco

OPEC ['oʊpek] *abbr* (= **Organization of Petroleum Exporting Countries**) OPEP *f* (= Organización *f* de Países Exportadores de Petróleo)

o·pen ['oʊpən] **1** *adj* (*also honest*) abierto; *in the open air* al aire libre **2** *v/t* abrir **3** *v/i* of door, shop abrir; of flower abrirse
◆ **open up** *v/i* of person abrirse

o·pen-'air *adj* meeting, concert al aire libre; pool descubierto

'o·pen day jornada *f* de puertas abiertas

o·pen-'end·ed *adj* contract etc abierto

o·pen·ing ['oʊpənɪŋ] in wall etc abertura *f*; (*beginning: of film, novel etc*) comienzo *m*; (*job*) puesto *m* vacante

'o·pen·ing hours *npl* horario *m* de apertura

o·pen·ly ['oʊpənlɪ] *adv* (*honestly, frankly*) abiertamente

o·pen-mind·ed [oʊpən'maɪndɪd] *adj* de mentalidad abierta

o·pen 'plan of·fice oficina *f* de planta abierta

'o·pen tick·et billete *m* abierto

op·e·ra ['ɑ:pərə] ópera *f*

'**op·e·ra glass·es** npl gemelos mpl, prismáticos mpl

'**op·e·ra house** (teatro m de la) ópera f

'**op·e·ra sing·er** cantante m/f de ópera

op·e·rate ['ɑːpəreɪt] **1** v/i of company operar, actuar; of airline, bus service, MED operar; of machine funcionar (**on** con) **2** v/t machine manejar

◆ **operate on** v/t MED operar; **they operated on his leg** le operaron de la pierna

'**op·e·rat·ing in·struc·tions** npl instrucciones fpl de funcionamiento

'**op·e·rat·ing room** MED quirófano m

'**op·e·rat·ing sys·tem** COMPUT sistema m operativo

op·e·ra·tion [ɑːpə'reɪʃn] MED operación f; of machine manejo m; **operations** of company operaciones fpl, actividades fpl; **have an operation** MED ser operado

op·e·ra·tor ['ɑːpəreɪtər] TELEC operador(a) m(f); of machine operario(-a) m(f); (tour operator) operador m turístico

oph·thal·mol·o·gist [ɑːfθæl'mɑːlədʒɪst] oftalmólogo(-a) m(f)

o·pin·ion [ə'pɪnjən] opinión f; **in my opinion** en mi opinión

o'pin·ion poll encuesta f de opinión

op·po·nent [ə'pounənt] oponente m/f, adversario(-a) m(f)

op·por·tune ['ɑːpərtuːn] adj fml oportuno

op·por·tun·ist [ɑːpər'tuːnɪst] oportunista m/f

op·por·tu·ni·ty [ɑːpər'tuːnətɪ] oportunidad f

op·pose [ə'pouz] v/t oponerse a; **be opposed to ...** estar en contra de ...; **John, as opposed to George ...** John, al contrario que George ...

op·po·site ['ɑːpəzɪt] **1** adj contrario; views, characters, meaning opuesto; **the opposite side of town** al otro lado de la ciudad / al otro extremo de la calle; **the opposite sex** el sexo opuesto **2** n: **the opposite of** lo contrario de

op·po·site 'num·ber homólogo(-a) m(f)

op·po·si·tion [ɑːpə'zɪʃn] to plan, POL oposición f; **meet with opposition** encontrar oposición

op·press [ə'pres] v/t the people oprimir

op·pres·sive [ə'presɪv] adj rule, dictator opresor; weather agobiante

opt [ɑːpt] v/t: **opt to do sth** optar por hacer algo

op·ti·cal il·lu·sion ['ɑːptɪkl] ilusión f óptica

op·ti·cian [ɑːp'tɪʃn] óptico(-a) m(f)

op·ti·mism ['ɑːptɪmɪzm] optimismo m

op·ti·mist ['ɑːptɪmɪst] optimista m/f

op·ti·mis·tic [ɑːptɪ'mɪstɪk] adj optimista

op·tim·is·tic·al·ly [ɑːptɪ'mɪstɪklɪ] adv con optimismo

optimum ['ɑːptɪməm] **1** adj óptimo **2** n: **the optimum** lo ideal

op·tion ['ɑːpʃn] opción f

op·tion·al ['ɑːpʃnl] adj optativo

op·tion·al 'ex·tras npl accesorios mpl opcionales

or [ɔːr] conj o; before a word beginning with the letter o u ; **or else!** ¡más vale que no llegues tarde, ¡de lo contrario!

o·ral ['ɔːrəl] adj exam, sex oral; hygiene bucal

or·ange ['ɔːrɪndʒ] **1** adj color naranja **2** n fruit naranja f; color naranja m

'**or·ange juice** Span zumo m or L.Am. jugo de naranja

or·ange 'squash naranjada f

or·a·tor ['ɔːrətər] orador(a) m(f)

or·bit ['ɔːrbɪt] **1** n of earth órbita f; **send sth into orbit** poner algo en órbita **2** v/t the earth girar alrededor de

or·chard ['ɔːrtʃərd] huerta f (de frutales)

or·ches·tra ['ɔːrkɪstrə] orquesta f

or·chid ['ɔːrkɪd] orquídea f

or·dain [ɔːr'deɪn] v/t ordenar

or·deal [ɔːr'diːl] calvario m, experiencia f penosa

or·der ['ɔːrdər] **1** n (command) orden f; (sequence, being well arranged) orden m; for goods pedido m; **take s.o.'s order** in restaurant preguntar a alguien lo que va a tomar; **in order to** para; **out of order** (not functioning) estropeado; (not in sequence) desordenado **2** v/t (put in sequence, proper layout) ordenar; goods pedir, encargar; meal pedir; **order s.o. to do sth** ordenar a alguien hacer algo or que haga algo **3** v/i in restaurant pedir

or·der·ly ['ɔːrdərlɪ] **1** adj lifestyle ordenado, metódico **2** n in hospital celador(a) m(f)

or·di·nal num·ber ['ɔːrdɪnl] (número m) ordinal m

or·di·nar·i·ly [ɔːrdɪ'nerɪlɪ] adv (as a rule) normalmente

or·di·nar·y ['ɔːrdɪnerɪ] adj común, normal

ore [ɔːr] mineral, mena f

or·gan ['ɔːrgən] ANAT, MUS órgano m

or·gan·ic [ɔːr'gænɪk] adj food ecológico, biológico; fertilizer orgánico

or·gan·i·cal·ly [ɔːr'gænɪklɪ] adv grown ecológicamente, biológicamente

or·gan·ism ['ɔːrgənɪzm] organismo m

or·gan·i·za·tion [ɔːrgənaɪ'zeɪʃn] organización f

or·gan·ize ['ɔːrgənaɪz] v/t organizar

or·gan·ized 'crime crimen *m* organizado

or·gan·iz·er ['ɔːrgənaɪzər] *person* organizador(a) *m(f)*

or·gas·m ['ɔːrgæzm] orgasmo *m*

O·ri·ent ['ɔːriənt] Oriente

O·ri·ent [ɔːri'entl] **1** *adj* oriental **2** *n* oriental *m/f*

o·ri·en·tate ['ɔːriənteɪt] v/t (direct) orientar; **orientate o.s.** (get bearings) orientarse

or·i·gin ['ɑːrɪdʒɪn] origen *m*; **idea / person of Chinese origin** una idea / una persona de origen chino

o·rig·i·nal [ə'rɪdʒənl] **1** *adj* (not copied, first) original **2** *n* painting etc original *m*

o·rig·i·nal·i·ty [ərɪdʒən'ælətɪ] originalidad *f*

o·rig·i·nal·ly [ə'rɪdʒənəlɪ] *adv* originalmente; (at first) originalmente, en un principio

o·rig·i·nate [ə'rɪdʒəneɪt] **1** v/t scheme, idea crear **2** v/i of idea, belief originarse; of family proceder

o·rig·i·na·tor [ə'rɪdʒəneɪtər] of scheme etc creador(a) *m(f)*; **he's not an originator** no es un creador nato

or·na·ment ['ɔːrnəmənt] adorno *m*

or·na·men·tal [ɔːrnə'mentl] *adj* ornamental

or·nate [ɔːr'neɪt] *adj* style, architecture recargado

or·phan ['ɔːrfn] *n* huérfano(-a) *m(f)*

or·phan·age ['ɔːrfənɪdʒ] orfanato *m*

or·tho·dox ['ɔːrθədɑːks] *adj* REL, fig ortodoxo

or·tho·pe·dic [ɔːrθə'piːdɪk] *adj* ortopédico

os·ten·si·bly [ɑː'stensəblɪ] *adv* aparentemente

os·ten·ta·tion [ɑːsten'teɪʃn] ostentación *f*

os·ten·ta·tious [ɑːsten'teɪʃəs] *adj* ostentoso

os·ten·ta·tious·ly [ɑːsten'teɪʃəslɪ] *adv* de forma ostentosa

os·tra·cize ['ɑːstrəsaɪz] v/t condenar al ostracismo

oth·er ['ʌðər] **1** *adj* otro; **other people might not agree** puede que otros no estén de acuerdo; **the other day** (recently) el otro día; **every other day / person** cada dos días / personas **2** *n*: **the other** el otro; **the others** los otros

oth·er·wise ['ʌðərwaɪz] *adv* de lo contrario, si no; (differently) de manera diferente

ot·ter ['ɑːtər] nutria *f*

ought [ɔːt] v/aux: **I / you ought to know** debo / debes saberlo; **he / they ought**

to know debe / deben saberlo; **you ought to have done it** deberías haberlo hecho

ounce [aʊns] onza *f*

our [aʊr] *adj* nuestro *m*, nuestra *f*; **our brother** nuestro hermano; **our books** nuestros libros

ours [aʊrz] *pron* el nuestro, la nuestra; **ours are red** los nuestros son rojos; **that book is ours** ese libro es nuestro; **a friend of ours** un amigo nuestro

our·selves [aʊr'selvz] *pron reflexive* nos; *emphatic* nosotros mismos *mpl*, nosotras mismas *fpl*; **wo hurt ourselves** nos hicimos daño; **when we saw ourselves in the mirror** cuando nos vimos en el espejo; **we saw it ourselves** lo vimos nosotros mismos; **by ourselves** (alone) solos; (without help) nosotros solos, nosotros mismos

oust [aʊst] v/t from office derrocar

out [aʊt] *adv*: **be out** of light, fire estar apagado; of flower estar en flor; (not at home, not in building), of sun haber salido; **when we saw ourselves in of calculations** estar equivocado; (be published) haber sido publicado; (no longer in competition) estar eliminado; (no longer in fashion) estar pasado de moda; **the secret is out** el secreto ha sido revelado; **out here in Dallas** aquí en Dallas; **he's out in the garden** está en el jardín; **(get) out!** ¡vete!; **(get) out of my room!** ¡fuera de mi habitación!; **that's out!** (out of the question) ¡eso es imposible!; **he's out to win** (fully intends to) va a por la victoria

out·board 'mo·tor motor *m* de fueraborda

'out·break of violence, war estallido *m*

'out·build·ing edificio *m* anexo

'out·burst emotional arrebato *m*, arranque *m*

'out·cast *n* paria *m/f*

'out·come resultado *m*

'out·cry protesta *f*

out'dat·ed *adj* anticuado

out'do v/t (pret **outdid**, pp **outdone**) superar

out'door *adj* toilet, activities, life al aire libre

out'doors *adv* fuera

out·er ['aʊtər] *adj* wall etc exterior

out·er 'space espacio *m* exterior

'out·fit clothes traje *m*, conjunto *m*; (company, organization) grupo *m*

'out·go·ing *adj* flight saliente; personality extrovertida

out'grow v/t (pret **outgrew**, pp **outgrown**) old ideas dejar atrás

out·ing ['aʊtɪŋ] (*trip*) excursión *f*

out'last *v/t* durar más que

'out·let *of pipe* desagüe *m*; *for sales* punto *m* de venta

'out·line 1 *n of person, building etc* perfil *m*, contorno *m*; *of plan, novel* resumen *m* **2** *v/t plans etc* resumir

out'live *v/t* sobrevivir a

'out·look (*prospects*) perspectivas *fpl*

'out·ly·ing *adj areas* periférico

out'num·ber *v/t* superar en número

out of *prep* ◇ *motion* fuera de; **run out of the house** salir corriendo de la casa; **it fell out of the window** se cayó por la ventana
◇ *position*: **20 miles out of of Detroit** a 20 millas de Detroit
◇ *cause* por; **out of jealousy / curiosity** por celos / curiosidad
◇ *without*: **we're out of gas / beer** no nos queda gasolina / cerveza
◇ *from a group* de cada; **5 out of 10** 5 de cada 10

out-of-'date *adj* anticuado, desfasado

out-of-the-'way *adj* apartado

'out·pa·tient paciente *m/f* externo(-a)

'out·pa·tients (**clin·ic**) clínica *f* ambulatoria

'out·per·form *v/t* superar a

'out·put 1 *n of factory* producción *f*; COMPUT salida *f* **2** *v/t* (*pret & pp* **outputted** *or* **output**) (*produce*) producir

'out·rage 1 *n feeling* indignación *f*; *act* ultraje *m*, atrocidad *f* **2** *v/t* indignar, ultrajar; **I was outraged to hear ...** me indigné escuchar que ...

out·ra·geous [aʊt'reɪdʒəs] *adj acts* atroz; *prices* escandaloso

'out·right 1 *adj winner* absoluto **2** *adv win* completamente; *kill* en el acto

out'run *v/t* (*pret* **outran**, *pp* **outrun**) correr más que

'out·set principio *m*, comienzo *m*; **from the outset** desde el principio *or* comienzo

out'shine *v/t* (*pret & pp* **outshone**) eclipsar

'out·side 1 *adj surface, wall* exterior; *lane* de fuera **2** *adv sit, go* fuera **3** *prep* fuera de; (*apart from*) aparte de **4** *n of building, case etc* exterior *m*; **at the outside** a lo sumo

out·side 'broad·cast emisión *f* desde exteriores

out·sid·er [aʊt'saɪdər] *in life* forastero(-a) *m(f)*; **be an outsider** *in election, race* no ser uno de los favoritos

'out·size *adj clothing* de talla especial

'out·skirts *npl* afueras *fpl*

out'smart → **outwit**

out'stand·ing *adj success, quality* destacado, sobresaliente; *writer, athlete* excepcional; FIN: *invoice, sums* pendiente

out·stretched ['aʊtstretʃt] *adj hands* extendido

out'vote *v/t*: **be outvoted** perder la votación

out·ward ['aʊtwərd] *adj appearance* externo; *outward journey* viaje *m* de ida

out·ward·ly ['aʊtwərdli] *adv* aparentemente

out'weigh *v/t* pesar más que

out'wit *v/t* (*pret & pp* **outwitted**) mostrarse más listo que

o·val ['oʊvl] *adj* oval, ovalado

o·va·ry ['oʊvəri] ovario *m*

o·va·tion [oʊ'veɪʃn] ovación *f*; **give s.o. a standing ovation** aplaudir a alguien de pie

ov·en ['ʌvn] horno *m*

'ov·en glove, 'ov·en mitt manopla *f* para el horno

'ov·en·proof *adj* refractario

'ov·en·read·y *adj* listo para el horno

o·ver ['oʊvər] **1** *prep* (*above*) sobre, encima de; (*across*) al otro lado de; (*more than*) más de; (*during*) durante; **she walked over the street** cruzó la calle; **travel all over Brazil** viajar por todo Brasil; **let's talk over a drink / meal** hablemos mientras tomamos una bebida / comemos; **we're over the worst** lo peor ya ha pasado; **over and above** además de **2** *adv*: **be over** (*finished*) haber acabado; **there were just 6 over** sólo quedaban seis; **over to you** (*your turn*) te toca a ti; **over in Japan** allá en Japón; **over here / there** por aquí / allá; **it hurts all over** me duele por todas partes; **painted white all over** pintado todo de blanco; **it's all over** se ha acabado; **over and over again** una y otra vez; **do sth over** (*again*) volver a hacer algo

o·ver·all ['oʊvərɔːl] **1** *adj length* total **2** *adv* (*in general*) en general; **it measures six feet overall** mide en total seis pies

o·ver·alls ['oʊvərɔːlz] *npl* Span mono *m*, *L.Am.* overol *m*

o·ver·awe *v/t* intimidar; **be overawed by s.o./sth** sentirse intimidado por alguien / algo

o·ver·bal·ance *v/i* perder el equilibrio

o·ver·bear·ing *adj* dominante, despótico

o·ver·board *adv* por la borda; **man overboard!** ¡hombre al agua!; **go overboard for s.o./sth** entusiasmarse muchísimo con alguien / algo

o·ver·cast *adj day* nublado; *sky* cubierto

o·ver'charge v/t customer cobrar de más a

'o·ver·coat abrigo m

o·ver'come v/t (pret **overcame**, pp **overcome**) difficulties, shyness superar, vencer; **be overcome by emotion** estar embargado por la emoción

o·ver'crowd·ed adj train atestado; city superpoblado

o·ver'do v/t (pret **overdid**, pp **overdone**) (exaggerate) exagerar; in cooking recocer, cocinar demasiado; **you're overdoing things** te estás excediendo

o·ver'done adj meat demasiado hecho

'o·ver·dose n sobredosis f inv

'o·ver·draft descubierto m; **have an overdraft** tener un descubierto

o·ver'draw v/t (pret **overdrew**, pp **overdrawn**) account dejar al descubierto; **be $800 overdrawn** tener un descubierto de 800 dólares

o·ver'dressed adj demasiado trajeado

'o·ver·drive MOT superdirecta f

o·ver'due adj: **his apology was long overdue** se debía haber disculpado hace tiempo; **an overdue alteration** un cambio que había que haber efectuado hace tiempo

o·ver·es·ti·mate v/t abilities, value sobreestimar

o·ver·ex'pose v/t photograph sobreexponer

'o·ver·flow¹ n pipe desagüe m, rebosadero m

o·ver'flow² v/i of water desbordarse

o·ver'grown adj garden abandonado, cubierto de vegetación, **he's an overgrown baby** es como un niño

o·ver'haul v/t engine, plans revisar

'o·ver·head 1 adj lights, railway elevado 2 n FIN gastos mpl generales

o·ver'hear v/t (pret & pp **overheard**) oír por casualidad

o·ver'heat·ed adj recalentado

o·ver'joyed [ouvər'dʒɔɪd] adj contentísimo, encantado

'o·ver·kill: **that's overkill** eso es exagerar

'o·ver·land 1 adj route terrestre 2 adv travel por tierra

o·ver'lap v/i (pret & pp **overlapped**) of tiles etc solaparse; of periods of time coincidir; of theories tener puntos en común

o·ver'leaf adv: **see overleaf** véase al dorso

o·ver'load v/t vehicle, ELEC sobrecargar

o·ver'look v/t of tall building etc dominar; (not see) pasar por alto

o·ver·ly ['ouvərlɪ] adv excesivamente, demasiado

'o·ver·night adv travel por la noche; **stay overnight** quedarse a pasar la noche

o·ver'night bag bolso m de viaje

o·ver'paid adj: **be overpaid** cobrar demasiado

'o·ver·pass paso m elevado

o·ver·pop·u·lat·ed [ouvə'paːpjuleɪtɪd] adj superpoblado

o·ver'pow·er v/t physically dominar

o·ver'pow·er·ing [ouvər'pauriŋ] adj smell fortísimo; sense of guilt insoportable

o·ver'priced [ouvər'praɪst] adj demasiado caro

o·ver·rat·ed [ouvə'reɪtɪd] adj sobrevalorado

o·ver're·act v/i reaccionar exageradamente

o·ver'ride v/t (pret **overrode**, pp **overridden**) anular

o·ver'rid·ing adj concern primordial

o·ver'rule v/t decision anular

o·ver'run v/t (pret **overran**, pp **overrun**) country invadir; time superar; **be overrun with** estar plagado de

o·ver'seas 1 adv live, work en el extranjero; go al extranjero 2 adj extranjero

o·ver'see v/t (pret **oversaw**, pp **overseen**) supervisar

o·ver'shad·ow v/t fig eclipsar

'o·ver·sight descuido m

o·ver·sim·pli·fi·ca·tion simplificación f excesiva

o·ver'sim·pli·fy v/t (pret & pp **oversimplified**) simplificar en exceso

o·ver'sleep v/i (pret & pp **overslept**) quedarse dormido

o·ver'state v/t exagerar

o·ver'state·ment exageración f

o·ver'step v/t (pret & pp **overstepped**) fig traspasar; **overstep the mark** propasarse, pasarse de la raya

o·ver'take v/t (pret **overtook**, pp **overtaken**) in work, development adelantarse a; Br MOT adelantar

o·ver'throw¹ v/t (pret **overthrew**, pp **overthrown**) derrocar

'o·ver·throw² n derrocamiento m

'o·ver·time 1 n SP: **in overtime** en la prórroga 2 adv: **work in overtime** hacer horas extras

'o·ver·ture ['ouvərtʃur] MUS obertura f; **make overtures to** establecer contactos con

o·ver'turn 1 v/t vehicle volcar; object dar la vuelta a; government derribar 2 v/i of vehicle volcar

'o·ver·view visión f general

o·ver'weight adj con sobrepeso; **be overweight** estar demasiado gordo o·ver'whelm [ouvər'welm] v/t *with work* abrumar, inundar; *with emotion* abrumar; *be overwhelmed by* by response estar abrumado por

o·ver'whelm·ing [ouvər'welmɪŋ] adj *feeling* abrumador; *majority* aplastante

o·ver'work **1** n exceso m de trabajo **2** v/i trabajar en exceso **3** v/t hacer trabajar en exceso

owe [ou] v/t deber; *owe s.o. $500* deber a alguien 500 dólares; *owe s.o. an apology* deber disculpas a alguien; *how much do I owe you?* ¿cuánto te debo?

ow·ing to ['ouɪŋ] prep debido a

owl [aul] búho m

own¹ [oun] v/t poseer; *who owns the restaurant?* ¿de quién es el restaurante?, ¿quién es el propietario del restaurante?

own² [oun] **1** adj propio **2** pron: *a car / an apartment of my own* mi propio coche/ apartamento; *on my / his own* yo / él solo

◆ own up v/i confesar

own·er ['ounər] dueño(-a) m(f), propietario(-a) m(f)

own·er·ship ['ounərʃɪp] propiedad f

ox [ɑːks] buey m

ox·ide ['ɑːksaɪd] óxido m

ox·y·gen ['ɑːksɪdʒən] oxígeno m

oy·ster ['ɔɪstər] ostra f

oz abbr (= *ounce(s)*) onza(s) f(pl)

o·zone ['ouzoun] ozono m

'o·zone lay·er capa f de ozono

P

PA [piː'eɪ] abbr (= *personal assistant*) secretario(-a) m(f) personal

pace [peɪs] **1** n (step) paso m; (speed) ritmo m **2** v/i: *pace up and down* pasear de un lado a otro

'pace·mak·er MED marcapasos m inv; SP liebre f

Pa·cif·ic [pə'sɪfɪk]: *the Pacific (Ocean)* el (Océano) Pacífico

pac·i·fi·er ['pæsɪfaɪər] chupete m

pac·i·fism ['pæsɪfɪzm] pacifismo m

pac·i·fist ['pæsɪfɪst] n pacifista m/f

pac·i·fy ['pæsɪfaɪ] v/t (pret & pp *pacified*) tranquilizar; *country* pacificar

pack [pæk] **1** n (backpack) mochila f; of *cereal, food, cigarettes* paquete m; of *cards* baraja f **2** v/t *item of clothing etc* meter en la maleta; *goods* empaquetar; *groceries* meter en una bolsa; *pack one's bag / suitcase* hacer la bolsa / la maleta **3** v/t hacer la maleta

pack·age ['pækɪdʒ] **1** n paquete m; *employment package* of *offers etc* condiciones fpl de empleo **2** v/t *in packs* embalar; *idea, project* presentar

'pack·age deal *for holiday* paquete m

'pack·age tour viaje m organizado

pack·ag·ing ['pækɪdʒɪŋ] of *product* embalaje m; of *idea, project* presentación f; *it's all packaging* fig es sólo imagen

pack·ed [pækt] adj (crowded) abarrotado

pack·et ['pækɪt] paquete m

pact [pækt] pacto m

pad¹ [pæd] **1** n *for protection* almohadilla f; *for absorbing liquid* compresa f; *for writing* bloc m **2** v/t (pret & pp *padded*) *with material* acolchar; *speech, report* meter paja en

pad² v/i (move quietly) caminar silenciosamente

pad·ded shoulders ['pædɪd] hombreras fpl

pad·ding ['pædɪŋ] *material* relleno m; *in speech etc* paja f

pad·dle ['pædəl] **1** n *for canoe* canalete m, remo m **2** v/i *in canoe* remar; *in water* chapotear

'pad·dling pool ['pædlɪŋ] piscina f para niños

'pad·dock ['pædək] potrero m

pad·lock ['pædlɑːk] **1** n candado m **2** v/t *gate* cerrar con candado; *I padlocked my bike to the railings* até mi bicicleta a la verja con candado

page¹ [peɪdʒ] n of *book etc* página f; *page number* número m de página

page² [peɪdʒ] v/t (call) llamar; *by PA* llamar por megafonía; *by beeper* llamar por el buscapersonas or Span busca

pag·er ['peɪdʒər] buscapersonas m inv, Span busca m

paid [peɪd] pret & pp → **pay**

paid em'ploy·ment empleo m remunerado

pail [peɪl] cubo *m*

pain [peɪn] dolor *m*; **be in pain** sentir dolor; **take pains to ...** tomarse muchas molestias por ...; **a pain in the neck** F una lata F, un tostón F

pain·ful ['peɪnfəl] *adj* doloroso; *blow, condition, subject* doloroso; (*laborious*) difícil; **my arm is still very painful** me sigue doliendo mucho el brazo

pain·ful·ly ['peɪnfəlɪ] *adv* (*extremely, acutely*) extremadamente

pain·kill·er ['peɪnkɪlər] analgésico *m*

pain·less ['peɪnlɪs] *adj* indoloro; **be completely painless** doler nada

pains·tak·ing ['peɪnzteɪkɪŋ] *adj* meticuloso

paint [peɪnt] **1** *n* pintura *f* **2** *v/t* pintar

paint·brush ['peɪntbrʌʃ] *large* brocha *f*; *small* pincel *m*

paint·er ['peɪntər] *decorator* pintor(a) *m(f)* (de brocha gorda); *artist* pintor(a) *m(f)*

paint·ing ['peɪntɪŋ] *activity* pintura *f*; *picture* cuadro *m*

paint·work ['peɪntwɜːrk] pintura *f*

pair [per] *of shoes, gloves, objects* par *m*; *of people, animals* pareja *f*

pa·ja·ma ['jacket camisa *f* de pijama

pa·ja·ma 'pants pantalón *m* de pijama

pa·ja·mas [pə'dʒɑːməz] *npl* pijama *m*

Pa·ki·stan [puːkɪ'stɑːn] Paquistán, Pakistán

Pa·ki·sta·ni [puːkɪ'stɑːnɪ] **1** *n* paquistaní *m/f*, pakistaní *m/f* **2** *adj* paquistaní, pakistaní

pal [pæl] F (*friend*) amigo(-a) *m(f)*; *Span* colega *m/f* F; **hey pal, got a light?** oye amigo *or Span* tío, ¿tienes fuego?

pal·ace ['pælɪs] palacio *m*

pal·ate ['pælət] paladar *m*

pa·la·tial [pə'leɪʃl] *adj* palaciego

pale [peɪl] *adj person* pálido; **she went pale** palideció; **pale pink / blue** rosa / azul claro

Pal·e·stine ['pæləstaɪn] Palestina

Pal·e·stin·i·an [pælə'stɪnɪən] **1** *n* palestino(-a) *m(f)* **2** *adj* palestino

pal·let ['pælɪt] palé *m*

pal·lor ['pælər] palidez *f*

palm [pɑːm] *of hand* palma *f*; *tree* palmera *f*

pal·pi·ta·tions [pælpɪ'teɪʃnz] *npl* MED palpitaciones *fpl*

pal·try ['pɒːltrɪ] *adj* miserable

pam·per ['pæmpər] *v/t* mimar

pam·phlet ['pæmflɪt] *for information* folleto *m*; *political* panfleto *m*

pan [pæn] **1** *n for cooking* cacerola *f*; *for frying* sartén *f* **2** *v/t* (*pret & pp* **panned**) F

(*criticize*) poner por los suelos F

◆ **pan out** *v/i* (*develop*) salir

Pan·a·ma ['pænəmɑː] *n* Panamá

Pan·a·ma Ca'nal *n:* **the Panama Canal** el Canal de Panamá

Pan·a·ma 'Cit·y *n* Ciudad *f* de Panamá

Pan·a·ma·ni·an [pænə'meɪnɪən] **1** *adj* panameño **2** *n* panameño(-a) *m(f)*

pan·cake ['pænkeɪk] crepe *m*, *L.Am.* panqueque *m*

pan·da ['pændə] (oso *m*) panda *m*

pan·de·mo·ni·um [pændɪ'məʊnɪəm] pandemónium *m*, pandemonio *m*

◆ **pan·der to** ['pændər] *v/t* complacer

pane [peɪn] *of glass* hoja *f*

pan·el ['pænl] *panel m*; *people* grupo *m*, panel *m*

pan·el·ing ['pænəlɪŋ] paneles *mpl*; *of ceiling* artesonado *m*

pang [pæŋ]: **pangs of hunger** retortijones *mpl*; **pangs of remorse** remordimientos *mpl*

'**pan·han·dle** *v/i* F mendigar

pan·ic ['pænɪk] **1** *n* pánico *m* **2** *v/i* (*pret & pp* **panicked**) ser presa del pánico; **don't panic!** ¡que no cunda el pánico!

'**pan·ic buy·ing** FIN compra *f* provocada por el pánico

'**pan·ic sel·ling** FIN venta *f* provocada por el pánico

'**pan·ic-strick·en** presa del pánico

pan·o·ra·ma [pænə'rɑːmə] panorama *m*

pa·no·ra·mic [pænə'ræmɪk] *adj view* panorámico

pan·sy ['pænzɪ] *flower* pensamiento *m*

pant [pænt] *v/i* jadear

pan·ties ['pæntɪz] *npl Span* bragas *fpl*, *L.Am.* calzones *mpl*

pantihose → **pantyhose**

pants [pænts] *npl* pantalones *mpl*

pan·ty·hose ['pæntɪhoʊz] medias *fpl*, pantis *mpl*

pa·pal ['peɪpəl] *adj* papal

pa·per ['peɪpər] **1** *n* papel *m*; (*newspaper*) periódico *m*; *academic* estudio *m*; *at conference* ponencia *f*; (*examination paper*) examen *m*; **papers** (*documents*) documentos *mpl*; *of vehicle* (*identity papers*) papeles *mpl*, documentación *f*; **a piece of paper** un trozo de papel **2** *adj* de papel **3** *v/t room, walls* empapelar

'**paperback** libro *m* en rústica

paper 'bag bolsa *f* de papel

'**paper boy** repartidor *m* de periódicos

'**paper clip** clip *m*

'**paper cup** vaso *m* de papel

'**paperwork** papeleo *m*

par [puːr] *in golf* par *m*; **be on a par with** ser comparable a; **feel below par** sentirse en baja forma

par·a·chute ['pærəʃuːt] **1** n paracaídas m inv **2** v/i saltar en paracaídas **3** v/t troops, supplies lanzar en paracaídas

par·a·chut·ist ['pærəʃuːtɪst] paracaidista m/f

pa·rade [pə'reɪd] **1** n procession desfile m **2** v/i desfilar; show about) pasearse **3** v/t knowledge, new car hacer ostentación de

par·a·dise ['pærədaɪs] paraíso m

par·a·dox ['pærədɑːks] paradoja f

par·a·dox·i·cal [pærə'dɑːksɪkl] adj paradójico

par·a·dox·i·cal·ly [pærə'dɑːksɪklɪ] adv paradójicamente

par·a·graph ['pærəgræf] párrafo m

Par·a·guay ['pærəgwaɪ] n Paraguay

Par·a·guay·an [pærə'gwaɪən] **1** adj paraguayo **2** n paraguayo(-a) m(f)

par·al·lel ['pærəlel] **1** n in geometry paralela f; GEOG paralelo m; fig paralelismo m; **draw a parallel** establecer un paralelismo; **do two things in parallel** hacer dos cosas al mismo tiempo **2** adj also fig paralelo **3** v/t (match) equipararse a

pa·ral·y·sis [pə'ræləsɪs] parálisis f

par·a·lyze ['pærəlaɪz] v/t also fig paralizar

par·a·med·ic [pærə'medɪk] n auxiliar m/f sanitario(a)

pa·ram·e·ter [pə'ræmɪtər] parámetro m

par·a·mil·i·ta·ry [pærə'mɪlɪterɪ] **1** adj paramilitar **2** n paramilitar m/f

par·a·mount ['pærəmaʊnt] adj supremo, extremo; **be paramount** ser de importancia capital

par·a·noi·a [pærə'nɔɪə] paranoia f

par·a·noid ['pærənɔɪd] adj paranoico

par·a·pher·na·li·a [pærəfər'neɪlɪə] parafernalia f

par·a·phrase ['pærəfreɪz] v/t parafrasear

par·a·pleg·ic [pærə'pliːdʒɪk] n parapléjico(-a) m(f)

par·a·site ['pærəsaɪt] also fig parásito m

par·a·sol ['pærəsɑːl] sombrilla f

par·a·troop·er ['pærətruːpər] paracaidista m/f (militar)

par·cel ['pɑːrsl] n paquete m

◆ **parcel up** v/t empaquetar

parch [pɑːrtʃ] v/t secar; **be parched** F of person estar muerto de sed F

par·don ['pɑːrdn] **1** n LAW indulto m; **I beg your pardon?** (what did you say?) ¿cómo ha dicho?; **I beg your pardon** (I'm sorry) discúlpeme **2** v/t perdonar; LAW indultar; **pardon me?** ¿perdón?; **pardon me?** ¿qué?

pare [per] v/t (peel) pelar

par·ent ['perənt] father padre m; mother madre f; **my parents** mis padres

pa·ren·tal [pə'rentl] adj de los padres

'par·ent company empresa f matriz

par·ent-'teach·er association asociación f de padres y profesores

pa·ren·the·sis [pə'renθəsɪs] (pl **parentheses** [pə'renθəsiːz]) paréntesis m inv

par·ish ['pærɪʃ] parroquia f

park¹ [pɑːrk] n parque m

park² v/t & v/i MOT estacionar, Span aparcar

par·ka ['pɑːrkə] parka f

park·ing ['pɑːrkɪŋ] MOT estacionamiento m, Span aparcamiento m; **no parking** prohibido aparcar

'park·ing disc disco m (de aparcamiento

'park·ing ga·rage párking m, Span aparcamiento m

'park·ing lot estacionamiento m, Span aparcamiento m (al aire libre)

'park·ing me·ter parquímetro m

'park·ing place (plaza f de) estacionamiento or Span aparcamiento, sitio m para estacionar or Span aparcar

'park·ing tick·et multa f de estacionamiento

par·lia·ment ['pɑːrləmənt] parlamento m

par·lia·men·ta·ry [pɑːrlə'mentərɪ] adj parlamentario

pa·role [pə'roʊl] **1** n libertad f condicional; **be on parole** estar en libertad condicional **2** v/t poner en libertad condicional; **be paroled** salir en libertad condicional

par·rot ['pærət] loro m

pars·ley ['pɑːrslɪ] perejil m

part [pɑːrt] **1** n (portion, area) parte f (episode) parte f, episodio m; of machine pieza f (de repuesto); in play, film pape. m; in hair raya f; **take part in** tomar parte en **2** adv (partly) en parte; **part American part Spanish** medio americano medio español; **part fact, part fiction** con una parte de realidad y una parte de ficción **3** v/i separarse **4** v/t: **part one's hair** hacerse la raya

◆ **part with** v/t desprenderse de

'part ex·change: take sth in part exchange llevarse algo como parte del pago

par·tial ['pɑːrʃl] adj (incomplete) parcial **be partial to** tener debilidad por

par·tial·ly ['pɑːrʃəlɪ] adv parcialmente

par·ti·ci·pant [pɑːr'tɪsɪpənt] participante m/f

par·ti·ci·pate [pɑːr'tɪsɪpeɪt] v/i participar

par·ti·ci·pa·tion [pɑːrtɪsɪ'peɪʃn] participación f

par·ti·cle ['pɑːrtɪkl] PHYS partícula f (small amount) pizca f

par·tic·u·lar [pərˈtɪkjələr] *adj* (*specific*) particular, concreto; (*demanding*) exigente; *about friends, employees* selectivo; *pej* especial, quisquilloso; *you know how particular she is* ya sabes lo especial que es; *this particular morning* precisamente esta mañana; *in particular* en particular; *it's a particular favorite of mine* es uno de mis preferidos

par·tic·u·lar·ly [pərˈtɪkjələrli] *adv* particularmente, especialmente

par·ti·tion [pɑːrˈtɪʃn] **1** *n* (*screen*) tabique *m*; *of country* partición *f*, división *f* **2** *v/t country* dividir

◆ **partition off** *v/t* dividir con tabiques

part·ly [ˈpɑːrtli] *adv* en parte

part·ner [ˈpɑːrtnər] COM socio(-a) *m(f)*; *in relationship* compañero(-a) *m(f)*; *in tennis, dancing* pareja *f*

part·ner·ship [ˈpɑːrtnərʃɪp] COM sociedad *f*; *in particular activity* colaboración *f*

part of 'speech parte *f* de la oración

'part own·er copropietario(-a) *m(f)*

'part-time 1 *adj* a tiempo parcial **2** *adv work* a tiempo parcial

part-'tim·er: *be a part-timer* trabajar a tiempo parcial

par·ty [ˈpɑːrti] **1** *n* (*celebration*) fiesta *f*; POL partido *m*; (*group of people*) grupo *m*; *be a party to* tomar parte en **2** *v/i* (*pret & pp partied*) F salir de marcha F

pass [pæs] **1** *n* for entry, SP pase *m*; *in mountains* desfiladero *m*; *make a pass at* tirarle los tejos a **2** *v/t* (*hand*) pasar; (*go past*) pasar por delante de; (*overtake*) adelantar; (*go beyond*) sobrepasar; (*approve*) aprobar; *pass an exam* aprobar un examen; *pass sentence* LAW dictar sentencia; *pass the time* pasar el tiempo **3** *v/i of time* pasar; *in exam* aprobar; (*go away*) pasarse

◆ **pass around** *v/t* repartir

◆ **pass away** *v/i euph* fallecer, pasar a mejor vida

◆ **pass by 1** *v/t* (*go past*) pasar por **2** *v/i* (*go past*) pasarse

pass on 1 *v/t information, book* pasar; *pass on the savings to ...* *of supermarket etc* revertir el ahorro en ... **2** *v/i* (*euph: die*) fallecer, pasar a mejor vida

◆ **pass out** *v/i* (*faint*) desmayarse

◆ **pass through** *v/t town* pasar por

◆ **pass up** *v/t opportunity* dejar pasar

pass·a·ble [ˈpæsəbl] *adj road* transitable; (*acceptable*) aceptable

pas·sage [ˈpæsɪdʒ] (*corridor*) pasillo *m*; *from poem, book* pasaje *m*; *of time* paso *m*

pas·sage·way [ˈpæsɪdʒweɪ] pasillo *m*

pas·sen·ger [ˈpæsɪndʒər] pasajero(-a) *m(f)*

'pas·sen·ger seat asiento *m* de pasajero

pas·ser-by [pæsərˈbaɪ] (*pl passers-by*) transeúnte *m/f*

pas·sion [ˈpæʃn] pasión *f*; *a crime of passion* un crimen pasional

pas·sion·ate [ˈpæʃnət] *adj lover* apasionado; (*fervent*) fervoroso

pas·sive [ˈpæsɪv] **1** *adj* pasivo **2** *n* GRAM (*voz f*) pasiva *f*; *in the passive* en pasiva

'pass mark EDU nota *f* mínima para aprobar

Pass·o·ver [ˈpæsouvər] REL Pascua *f* de los hebreos

pass·port [ˈpæspɔːrt] pasaporte *m*

'pass·port control control *m* de pasaportes

pass·word [ˈpæswɜːrd] contraseña *f*

past [pæst] **1** *adj* (*former*) pasado; *his past life* su pasado; *the past few days* los últimos días; *that's all past now* todo eso es agua pasada **2** *n* pasado; *in the past* antiguamente **3** *prep in position* después de; *it's half past two* son las dos y media; *it's past seven o'clock* pasan de las siete; *it's past your bedtime* hace rato que tenías que haberte ido a la cama **4** *adv*: *run / walk past* pasar

pas·ta [ˈpæstə] pasta *f*

paste [peɪst] **1** *n* (*adhesive*) cola *f* **2** *v/t* (*stick*) pegar

pas·tel [pæsˈtel] **1** *n color* pastel *m* **2** *adj* pastel

pas·time [ˈpæstaɪm] pasatiempo *m*

past par·ti·ci·ple GRAM participio *m* pasado

pas·tra·mi [pæˈstrɑːmi] pastrami *m*, *carne de vaca ahumada con especias*

pas·try [ˈpeɪstri] *for pie* masa *f*; *small cake* pastel *m*

'past tense GRAM (*tiempo m*) pasado *m*

pas·ty [ˈpeɪsti] *adj complexion* pálido

pat [pæt] **1** *n* palmadita *f*; *give s.o. a pat on the back* fig dar una palmadita a alguien en la espalda **2** *v/t* (*pret & pp patted*) dar palmaditas a

patch [pætʃ] **1** *n on clothing* parche *m*; (*area*) mancha *f*; *a bad patch* (*period of time*) un mal momento, una mala racha; *patches of fog* zonas de niebla; *not be a patch on* fig no tener ni punto de comparación con **2** *v/t clothing* remendar

◆ **patch up** *v/t* (*repair temporarily*) hacer un remiendo a, arreglar a medias; *quarrel* solucionar

patch·work [ˈpætʃwɜːrk] **1** *n needlework* labor *f* de retazo **2** *adj* hecho de remiendos

P

patch·y ['pætʃɪ] *quality* desigual; *work, performance* irregular

pâ·té [pɑː'teɪ] paté *m*

pa·tent ['peɪtnt] **1** *adj* patente, evidente **2** *n for invention* patente *f* **3** *v/t invention* patentar

pa·tent 'leath·er charol *m*

pa·tent·ly ['peɪtntlɪ] (*clearly*) evidentemente, claramente

pa·ter·nal [pə'tɜːrnl] *relative* paterno; *pride, love* paternal

pa·ter·nal·ism [pə'tɜːrnlɪzm] paternalismo *m*

pa·ter·nal·is·tic [pətɜːrnl'ɪstɪk] *adj* paternalista

pa·ter·ni·ty [pə'tɜːrnɪtɪ] paternidad *f*

path [pæθ] *also fig* camino *m*

pa·thet·ic [pə'θetɪk] *adj invoking pity* patético; F (*very bad*) lamentable F

path·o·log·i·cal [pæθə'lɑːdʒɪkl] *adj* patológico

pa·thol·o·gy [pə'θɑːlədʒɪ] patología *f*

pa·thol·o·gist [pə'θɑːlədʒɪst] patólogo(-a) *m(f)*

pa·tience ['peɪʃns] paciencia *f*

pa·tient ['peɪʃnt] **1** *n* paciente *m/f* **2** *adj* paciente; *just be patient!* ¡ten paciencia!

pa·tient·ly ['peɪʃntlɪ] *adv* pacientemente

pat·i·o ['pætɪoʊ] patio *m*

pat·ri·ot ['peɪtrɪət] patriota *m/f*

pat·ri·ot·ic [peɪtrɪ'ɑːtɪk] *adj* patriótico

pat·ri·ot·ism ['peɪtrɪətɪzm] patriotismo *m*

pa·trol [pə'troʊl] **1** *n* patrulla *f*; *be on patrol* estar de patrulla **2** *v/t* (*pret & pp patrolled*) *streets, border* patrullar

pa·trol car coche *m* patrulla

pa·trol·man policía *m*, patrullero *m*

pa·trol wag·on furgón *m* policial

pa·tron ['peɪtrən] *of store, movie theater* cliente *m/f*; *of artist, charity etc* patrocinador(a) *m(f)*

pa·tron·ize ['pætrənaɪz] *v/t store* ser cliente de; *person* tratar con condescendencia o como a un niño

pa·tron·iz·ing ['pætrənaɪzɪŋ] condescendiente

pa·tron 'saint santo(-a) *m(f)* patrón(-ona), patrón(-ona) *m*

pat·ter ['pætər] **1** *n of rain etc* repiqueteo *m*; F (*of salesman*) parloteo *m* F **2** *v/i* repiquetear

pat·tern ['pætərn] *n on wallpaper, fabric* estampado *m*; *for knitting, sewing* diseño *m*; (*model*) modelo *m*; *in behavior, events* pauta *f*

pat·terned ['pætərnd] *adj* estampado

paunch [pɔːntʃ] barriga *f*

pause [pɔːz] **1** *n* pausa *f* **2** *v/i* parar; *when speaking* hacer una pausa **3** *v/t tape* poner en pausa

pave [peɪv] *with concrete* pavimentar; *with slabs* adoquinar; *pave the way for fig* preparar el terreno para

pave·ment ['peɪvmənt] (*Am: roadway*) calzada *f*; (*Br: sidewalk*) acera *f*

pav·ing stone ['peɪvɪŋ] losa *f*

paw [pɔː] **1** *n of animal* pata *f*; F (*hand*) pezuña *f* F **2** *v/t* F sobar *f*

pawn[1] [pɔːn] *n in chess* peón *m*; *fig* títere *m*

pawn[2] [pɔːn] *v/t* empeñar

'pawn·bro·ker prestamista *m/f*

'pawn·shop casa *f* de empeños

pay [peɪ] **1** *n* paga *f*, sueldo *m*; *in the pay of* a sueldo de **2** *v/t* (*pret & pp paid*) *employee, sum, bill* pagar; *pay attention* prestar atención; *pay s.o. a compliment* hacer un cumplido a alguien **3** *v/i* (*pret & pp paid*) pagar; (*be profitable*) ser rentable; *it doesn't pay to …* no conviene …; *pay for purchase* pagar; *you'll pay for this! fig* ¡me las pagarás!

◆ **pay back** *v/t person* devolver el dinero a *loan* devolver

◆ **pay in** *v/t to bank* ingresar

◆ **pay off 1** *v/t debt* liquidar; (*bribe*) sobornar **2** *v/i* (*be profitable*) valer la pena

◆ **pay up** *v/i* pagar

pay·a·ble ['peɪəbl] *adj* pagadero

'pay check cheque *m* del sueldo

'pay·day día *m* de paga

pay·ee [peɪ'iː] beneficiario(-a) *m(f)*

'pay en·ve·lope sobre *m* con la paga

pay·er ['peɪər] pagador(a) *m(f)*; *they are good payers* pagan puntualmente

pay·ment ['peɪmənt] pago *m*

'pay phone teléfono *m* público

'pay·roll *money* salarios *mpl*; *employees* nómina *f*; *be on the payroll* estar en nómina

pay·slip ['peɪslɪp] nómina *f* (*papel*)

PC [piː'siː] *abbr* (= *personal computer*) PC *m*, *Span* ordenador *m* or *L.Am.* computadora personal; (= *politically correct*) políticamente correcto

pea [piː] *Span* guisante *m*, *L.Am.* arveja *f*, *Mex* chícharo *m*

peace [piːs] paz *f*; (*quietness*) tranquilidad

peace·a·ble ['piːsəbl] *adj person* pacífico

'Peace Corps organización gubernamental estadounidense de ayuda al desarrollo

peace·ful ['piːsfəl] *adj* tranquilo; *demonstration* pacífico

peace·ful·ly ['piːsfəlɪ] *adv* pacíficamente

peach [piːtʃ] *fruit* melocotón *m*, *L.Am.* durazno *m*; *tree* melocotonero *m*, *L.Am.* duraznero *m*

pea·cock ['pi:kɑ:k] pavo m real

peak [pi:k] **1** n of mountain cima f; mountain pico m; fig clímax m **2** v/i alcanzar el máximo

'peak hours npl horas fpl punta

pea·nut ['pi:nʌt] cacahuete m, L.Am. maní m, Mex cacahuate m; **get paid peanuts** F cobrar una miseria F; **that's peanuts to him** F eso es calderilla para él F

pea·nut 'but·ter crema f de cacahuete

pear [per] pera f

pearl [pɜːrl] perla f

peas·ant ['peznt] campesino(-a) m(f)

peb·ble ['pebl] guijarro m

pe·can ['pi:kən] pacana f

peck [pek] **1** n bite picotazo m; kiss besito m **2** v/t bite picotear; kiss dar un besito a

pe·cu·li·ar [pɪ'kju:ljər] adj (strange) raro; **peculiar to** (special) característico de

pe·cu·li·ar·i·ty [pɪkju:lɪ'ærətɪ] (strangeness) rareza f; (special feature) peculiaridad f, característica f

ped·al ['pedl] **1** n of bike pedal m **2** v/i (turn pedals) pedalear; (cycle) recorrer en bicicleta

pe·dan·tic [pɪ'dæntɪk] adj puntilloso

ped·dle ['pedl] v/t drugs traficar or trapichear con

ped·es·tal ['pedəstl] for statue pedestal m

pe·des·tri·an [pɪ'destrɪən] n peatón(-ona) m(f)

pe·des·tri·an 'cros·sing paso m de peatones

pe·di·at·ric [pi:dɪ'ætrɪk] adj pediátrico

pe·di·a·tri·cian [pi:dɪə'trɪʃn] pediatra m/f

pe·di·at·rics [pi:dɪ'ætrɪks] pediatría f

ped·i·cure ['pedɪkjʊr] pedicura f

ped·i·gree ['pedɪgri:] **1** n of animal pedigrí; of person linaje m **2** adj con pedigrí

pee [pi:] v/i F hacer pis F, mear F

peek [pi:k] **1** n ojeada f, vistazo m **2** v/i echar una ojeada or vistazo

peel [pi:l] **1** n piel f **2** v/t fruit, vegetables pelar **3** v/i of nose, shoulders pelarse; of paint levantarse

◆ **peel off 1** v/t wrapper etc quitar; jacket etc quitarse **2** v/i of wrapper quitarse

peep [pi:p] → **peek**

peep·hole ['pi:phoʊl] mirilla f

peer¹ [pɪr] n (equal) igual m

peer² [pɪr] v/i mirar; **peer through the mist** buscar con la mirada entre la niebla; **peer at** forzar la mirada para ver

peeved [pi:vd] F mosqueado F

peg [peg] n for hat, coat percha f; for tent clavija f; **off the peg** de confección

pe·jo·ra·tive [pɪ'dʒɔːrətɪv] adj peyorativo

pel·let ['pelɪt] pelotita f; (bullet) perdigón m

pelt [pelt] **1** v/t: **pelt s.o. with sth** tirar algo a alguien **2** v/i: **they pelted along the road** F fueron a toda mecha por la carretera F; **it's pelting down** F está diluviando F

pel·vis ['pelvɪs] pelvis f

pen¹ [pen] n (ballpoint pen) bolígrafo m; (fountain pen) pluma f (estilográfica)

pen² [pen] (enclosure) corral m

pen³ [pen] → **penitentiary**

pe·nal·ize ['pi:nəlaɪz] v/t penalizar

pen·al·ty ['penəltɪ] sanción f; SP penalti m; **take the penalty** in soccer lanzar el penalti

'pen·al·ty ar·e·a SP área f de castigo

'pen·al·ty clause LAW cláusula f de penalización

'pen·al·ty kick (lanzamiento m de) penalti m

pen·al·ty 'shoot-out tanda f de penalties

'pen·al·ty spot punto m de penalti

pen·cil ['pensɪl] lápiz m

pen·cil sharp·en·er sacapuntas m inv

pen·dant ['pendənt] (necklace) colgante m

pend·ing ['pendɪŋ] **1** prep en espera de **2** adj pendiente; **be pending** awaiting a decision estar pendiente; about to happen ser inminente

pen·e·trate ['penɪtreɪt] v/t (pierce) penetrar; market penetrar

pen·e·trat·ing ['penɪtreɪtɪŋ] adj stare, scream penetrante; analysis exhaustivo

pen·e·tra·tion [penɪ'treɪʃn] penetración f; of defences incursión f; of market entrada f

'pen friend amigo(-a) m(f) por correspondencia

pen·guin ['peŋgwɪn] pingüino m

pen·i·cil·lin [penɪ'sɪlɪn] penicilina f

pe·nin·su·la [pə'nɪnsʊlə] península f

pe·nis ['pi:nɪs] pene m

pen·i·tence ['penɪtəns] (remorse) arrepentimiento m

pen·i·tent ['penɪtənt] adj arrepentido

pen·i·ten·tia·ry [penɪ'tenʃərɪ] prisión f, cárcel f

pen·knife ['pennaɪf] navaja f

'pen name seudónimo m

pen·nant ['penənt] banderín f

pen·ni·less ['penɪlɪs] adj sin un centavo

pen·ny ['penɪ] penique m

'pen pal amigo(-a) m(f) por correspondencia

pen·sion ['penʃn] pensión f

◆ **pension off** v/t jubilar

'pen·sion fund fondo m de pensiones

'pen·sion scheme plan m de jubilación

pen·sive ['pensɪv] adj pensativo

Pen·ta·gon ['pentəgɑːn]: **the Pentagon** el Pentágono

pen·tath·lon [pen'tæθlən] pentatlón *m*

Pen·te·cost ['pentɪkɑːst] Pentecostés *m*

pent·house ['penthaʊs] ático *m* (*de lujo*)

pent-up ['pentʌp] *adj* reprimido

pe·nul·ti·mate [pe'nʌltɪmət] *adj* penúltimo

peo·ple ['piːpl] *npl* gente *f*; (*individuals*) personas *fpl*; (*nsg: race, tribe*) pueblo *m*; **the people** (*citizens*) el pueblo, los ciudadanos; **the Spanish people** los españoles; **a lot of people think ...** muchos piensan que ...; **people say ...** se dice que ..., dicen que ...

pep·per ['pepər] *spice* pimienta *f*; *vegetable* pimiento *m*

pep·per·mint *sweet* caramelo *m* de menta

pep talk ['peptɔːk]: **give a pep talk** decir unas palabras de aliento

per [pɜːr] *prep* por; **per annum** al año, por año

per·ceive [pər'siːv] *v/t with senses* percibir; (*view, interpret*) interpretar

per·cent [pər'sent] *adv* por cien

per·cen·tage [pər'sentɪdʒ] porcentaje *m*, tanto *m* por ciento

per·cep·ti·ble [pər'septəbl] *adj* perceptible

per·cep·ti·bly [pər'septəblɪ] *adv* visiblemente

per·cep·tion [pər'sepʃn] *through senses* percepción *f*; *of situation* apreciación *f*; (*insight*) perspicacia *f*

per·cep·tive [pər'septɪv] *adj* perceptivo

perch [pɜːtʃ] **1** *n for bird* percha *f* **2** *v/i of bird* posarse; *of person* sentarse

per·co·late ['pɜːrkəleɪt] *v/i of coffee* filtrarse

per·co·la·tor ['pɜːrkəleɪtər] cafetera *f* de filtro

per·cus·sion [pər'kʌʃn] percusión *f*

per·cus·sion in·stru·ment instrumento *m* de percusión

pe·ren·ni·al [pə'renɪəl] *n* BOT árbol *m* de hoja perenne

per·fect 1 *n* ['pɜːrfɪkt] GRAM pretérito *m* perfecto **2** *adj* perfecto **3** *v/t* [pər'fekt] perfeccionar

per·fec·tion [pər'fekʃn] perfección *f*; **do sth to perfection** hacer algo a la perfección

per·fec·tion·ist [pər'fekʃnɪst] perfeccionista *m/f*

per·fect·ly ['pɜːrfɪktlɪ] perfectamente; (*totally*) completamente

per·fo·rat·ed ['pɜːrfəreɪtɪd] *adj line* perforado

per·fo·ra·tions [pɜːrfə'reɪʃnz] *npl* perforaciones *fpl*

per·form [pər'fɔːrm] **1** *v/t* (*carry out*) realizar, llevar a cabo; *of actors, musician etc* interpretar, representar **2** *v/i of actor, musician, dancer* actuar; *of machine* funcionar

per·form·ance [pər'fɔːrməns] *by actor, musician etc* actuación *f*, interpretación *f*; *of play* representación *f*; *of employee* rendimiento *m*; *of official, company, in sport* actuación *f*; *of machine* rendimiento *m*

per·form·ance car coche *m* de gran rendimiento

per·form·er [pər'fɔːrmər] intérprete *m/f*

per·fume ['pɜːrfjuːm] perfume *m*

per·func·to·ry [pər'fʌŋktərɪ] *adj* superficial

per·haps [pər'hæps] *adv* quizá(s), tal vez; **perhaps it's not too late** puede que no sea demasiado tarde

per·il ['perəl] peligro *m*

per·il·ous ['perələs] *adj* peligroso

pe·rim·e·ter [pə'rɪmɪtər] perímetro *m*

pe·rim·e·ter fence cerca *f*

pe·ri·od ['pɪrɪəd] periodo *m*, período *m*; (*menstruation*) periodo, regla *f*; *punctuation mark* punto *m*; **I don't want to, period!** F ¡no me da la gana y punto! F

pe·ri·od·ic [pɪrɪ'ɑːdɪk] *adj* periódico

pe·ri·od·i·cal [pɪrɪ'ɑːdɪkl] *n* publicación *f* periódica

pe·ri·od·i·cal·ly [pɪrɪ'ɑːdɪklɪ] *adv* periódicamente, con periodicidad

pe·riph·e·ral [pə'rɪfərəl] **1** *adj* (*not crucial*) secundario **2** *n* COMPUT periférico *m*

pe·riph·e·ry [pə'rɪfərɪ] periferia *f*

per·ish ['perɪʃ] *v/i of rubber* estropearse, picarse; *of person* perecer

per·ish·a·ble ['perɪʃəbl] *adj food* perecedero

per·jure ['pɜːrdʒər] *v/t*: **perjure o.s.** perjurar

per·ju·ry ['pɜːrdʒərɪ] perjurio *m*

perk [pɜːrk] *n of job* ventaja *f*

◆ **perk up 1** *v/t* animar **2** *v/i* animarse

perk·y ['pɜːrkɪ] (*cheerful*) animado

perm [pɜːrm] **1** *n permanent* **2** *v/t* hacer la permanente; **she had her hair permed** se hizo la permanente

per·ma·nent ['pɜːrmənənt] *adj* permanente

per·ma·nent·ly ['pɜːrmənəntlɪ] *adv* permanentemente

per·me·a·ble ['pɜːrmɪəbl] *adj* permeable

per·me·ate ['pɜːrmɪeɪt] *v/t* impregnar

per·mis·si·ble [pər'mɪsəbl] *adj* permisible

per·mis·sion [pər'mɪʃn] permiso *m*; **ask**

s.o.'s permission to ... pedir permiso a alguien para ...

per·mis·sive [pərˈmɪsɪv] *adj* permisivo

per·mit [ˈpɜːrmɪt] **1** *n* licencia *f* **2** *v/t* (*pret & pp* **permitted**) [pərˈmɪt] permitir; **permit s.o. to do sth** permitir a alguien que haga algo

per·pen·dic·u·lar [pɜːrpənˈdɪkjələr] *adj* perpendicular

per·pet·u·al *adj* perpetuo; *interruptions* continuo

per·pet·u·al·ly [pərˈpetʃʊəlɪ] *adv* constantemente

per·pet·u·ate [pərˈpetʃʊeɪt] *v/t* perpetuar

per·plex [pərˈpleks] *v/t* dejar perplejo

per·plexed [pərˈplekst] *adj* perplejo

per·plex·i·ty [pərˈpleksɪtɪ] perplejidad *f*

per·se·cute [ˈpɜːrsɪkjuːt] *v/t* perseguir; (*hound*) acosar

per·se·cu·tion [pɜːrsɪˈkjuːʃn] persecución *f*; (*harassment*) acoso *m*

per·se·cu·tor [pɜːrsɪˈkjuːtər] perseguidor(a) *m(f)*

per·se·ver·ance [pɜːrsɪˈvɪrəns] perseverancia *f*

per·se·vere [pɜːrsɪˈvɪr] *v/i* perseverar

per·sist [pərˈsɪst] *v/i* persistir; **persist in** persistir en

per·sis·tence [pərˈsɪstəns] (*perseverance*) perseverancia *f*; (*continuation*) persistencia *f*

per·sis·tent [pərˈsɪstənt] *adj person, questions* perseverante; *rain, unemployment etc* persistente

per·sis·tent·ly [pərˈsɪstəntlɪ] *adv* (*continually*) constantemente

per·son [ˈpɜːrsn] persona *f*; **in person** en persona

per·son·al [ˈpɜːrsənl] *adj* (*private*) personal; *life* privado; **don't make personal remarks** no hagas comentarios personales

per·son·al as·sist·ant secretario(-a) *m(f)* personal

'per·son·al col·umn sección *f* de anuncios personales

per·son·al com'put·er *Span* ordenador *m* personal, *L.Am.* computadora *f* personal

per·son·al 'hy·giene higiene *f* personal

per·son·al·i·ty [pɜːrsəˈnælətɪ] personalidad *f*; (*celebrity*) personalidad *f*, personaje *m*

per·son·al·ly [ˈpɜːrsənəlɪ] *adv* (*for my part*) personalmente; (*in person*) en persona; **don't take it personally** no te lo tomes como algo personal

per·son·al 'or·gan·iz·er organizador *m* personal

sonal

per·son·al 'ster·e·o walkman *m* ®

per·son·i·fy [pɜːrˈsɑːnɪfaɪ] *v/t* (*pret & pp* **personified**) *of person* personificar

per·son·nel [pɜːrsəˈnel] *employees, department* personal *m*

per·son·nel man·a·ger director(a) *m(f)* de personal

per·spec·tive [pərˈspektɪv] PAINT perspectiva *f*; **get sth into perspective** poner algo en perspectiva

per·spi·ra·tion [pɜːrspɪˈreɪʃn] sudor *m*, transpiración *f*

per·spire [pɜːrˈspaɪr] *v/i* sudar, transpirar

per·suade [pərˈsweɪd] *v/t* persuadir; **persuade s.o. to do sth** persuadir a alguien para que haga algo

per·sua·sion [pərˈsweɪʒn] persuasión *f*

per·sua·sive [pərˈsweɪsɪv] persuasivo

per·ti·nent [ˈpɜːrtɪnənt] *adj fml* pertinente

per·turb [pərˈtɜːrb] *v/t* perturbar

per·turb·ing [pərˈtɜːrbɪŋ] *adj* perturbador

Pe·ru [pəˈruː] *n* Perú

pe·ruse [pəˈruːz] *v/t fml* leer atentamente

Pe·ru·vi·an [pəˈruːvɪən] **1** *adj* peruano **2** *n* peruano(-a) *m(f)*

per·va·sive [pərˈveɪsɪv] *adj influence, ideas* dominante

per·verse [pərˈvɜːrs] *adj* (*awkward*) terco; **just to be perverse** sólo para llevar la contraria

per·ver·sion [pərˈvɜːrʃn] *sexual* perversión *f*

per·vert [ˈpɜːrvɜːrt] *n sexual* pervertido(-a) *m(f)*

pes·si·mism [ˈpesɪmɪzm] pesimismo *m*

pes·si·mist [ˈpesɪmɪst] pesimista *m/f*

pes·si·mis·tic [pesɪˈmɪstɪk] *adj* pesimista

pest [pest] plaga *f*; F *person* tostón *m* ⊢

pes·ter [ˈpestər] *v/t* acosar; **pester s.o. to do sth** molestar *or* dar la lata a alguien para que haga algo

pes·ti·cide [ˈpestɪsaɪd] pesticida *f*

pet [pet] **1** *n animal* animal *m* doméstico *or* de compañía; (*favorite*) preferido(-a) *m(f)* **2** *adj* preferido, favorito **3** *v/t* (*pret & pp* **petted**) *animal* acariciar **4** *v/i* (*pret & pp* **petted**) *of couple* magrearse F

pet·al [ˈpetl] pétalo *m*

◆ **pe·ter out** [ˈpiːtər] *v/i of rain* amainar; *of rebellion* irse extinguiendo; *of path* ir desapareciendo

pe·tite [pəˈtiːt] *adj* chiquito(-a); *size* menudo

pe·ti·tion [pəˈtɪʃn] *n* petición *f*

'pet name nombre *m* cariñoso

pet·ri·fied [ˈpetrɪfaɪd] *adj person* petrificado; *scream*, *voice* aterrorizado

pet·ri·fy ['petrɪfaɪ] *v/t* (*pret & pp **petri-fied***) dejar petrificado

pet·ro·chem·i·cal [petrou'kemɪkl] *adj* petroquímico

pet·rol ['petrl] *Br* gasolina *f*, *Arg* nafta *f*

pe·tro·le·um [pɪ'trouliəm] petróleo *m*

pet·ting ['petɪŋ] magreo *m* F

pet·ty ['petɪ] *adj person, behavior* mezquino; *details, problem* sin importancia

pet·ty 'cash dinero *m* para gastos menores

pet·u·lant ['petʃələnt] *adj* caprichoso

pew [pjuː] banco *m* (*de iglesia*)

pew·ter ['pjuːtər] peltre *m*

phar·ma·ceu·ti·cal [fɑːrmə'suːtɪkl] *adj* farmacéutico

phar·ma·ceu·ti·cals [fɑːmə'suːtɪklz] *npl* fármacos *mpl*

phar·ma·cist ['fɑːrməsɪst] *in store* farmacéutico(-a) *m(f)*

phar·ma·cy ['fɑːrməsɪ] *store* farmacia *f*

phase [feɪz] fase *f*; *go through a difficult phase* atravesar una mala etapa

♦ **phase in** *v/t* introducir gradualmente

♦ **phase out** *v/t* eliminar gradualmente

PhD [piːeɪtʃ'diː] *abbr* (= *Doctor of Philosophy*) Doctorado *m*

phe·nom·e·nal [fɪ'nɑːmɪnl] *adj* fenomenal

phe·nom·e·nal·ly [fɪ'nɑːmɪnlɪ] *adv* extraordinariamente; *stupid* increíblemente

phe·nom·e·non [fɪ'nɑːmɪnɑːn] fenómeno *m*

phil·an·throp·ic [fɪlən'θrɑːpɪk] *adj* filantrópico

phi·lan·thro·pist [fɪ'lænθrəpɪst] filántropo(-a) *m(f)*

phi·lan·thro·py [fɪ'lænθrəpɪ] filantropía *f*

Phil·ip·pines ['fɪlɪpiːnz] *npl*: *the Philippines* las Filipinas

phil·is·tine ['fɪlɪstaɪn] *n* filisteo(-a) *m(f)*

phi·los·o·pher [fɪ'lɑːsəfər] filósofo(-a) *m(f)*

phil·o·soph·i·cal [fɪlə'sɑːfɪkl] *adj* filosófico

phi·los·o·phy [fɪ'lɑːsəfɪ] filosofía *f*

pho·bi·a ['foubɪə] fobia *f*

phone [foun] **1** *n* teléfono *m*; *be on the phone* have a phone tener teléfono; *be talking* estar hablando por teléfono **2** *v/t* llamar (por teléfono) a **3** *v/i* llamar (por teléfono)

'**phone book** guía *f* (de teléfonos)

'**phone booth** cabina *f* (de teléfonos)

'**phone call** llamada *f* (telefónica)

'**phone card** *Br* tarjeta *f* telefónica

'**phone num·ber** número *m* de teléfono

pho·net·ics [fə'netɪks] fonética *f*

pho·n(e)y ['founɪ] *adj* F falso

pho·to ['foutou] *n* foto *f*

'**pho·to al·bum** álbum *m* de fotos

'**pho·to·cop·i·er** fotocopiadora *f*

'**pho·to·cop·y 1** *n* fotocopia *f* **2** *v/t* (*pret & pp **photocopied***) fotocopiar

pho·to·gen·ic [foutou'dʒenɪk] *adj* fotogénico

pho·to·graph ['foutəgræf] **1** *n* fotografía *f* **2** *v/t* fotografiar

pho·tog·ra·pher [fə'tɑːgrəfər] fotógrafo(-a) *m(f)*

pho·tog·ra·phy [fə'tɑːgrəfɪ] fotografía *f*

phrase [freɪz] **1** *n* frase *f* **2** *v/t* expresar

'**phrase·book** guía *f* de conversación

phys·i·cal ['fɪzɪkl] **1** *adj* físico **2** *n* MED reconocimiento *m* médico

phys·i·cal 'hand·i·cap minusvalía *f* física

phys·i·cal·ly ['fɪzɪklɪ] *adv* físicamente

phys·i·cal·ly 'hand·i·cap·ped disminuido(-a) *m(f)* físico

phy·si·cian [fɪ'zɪʃn] médico(-a) *m(f)*

phys·i·cist ['fɪzɪsɪst] físico(-a) *m(f)*

phys·ics ['fɪzɪks] física *f*

phys·i·o·ther·a·pist [fɪziou'θerəpɪst] fisioterapeuta *m/f*

phys·i·o·ther·a·py [fɪziou'θerəpɪ] fisioterapia *f*

phy·sique [fɪ'ziːk] físico *m*

pi·a·nist ['pɪənɪst] pianista *m/f*

pi·an·o [pɪ'ænou] piano *m*

pick [pɪk] **1** *n*: *take your pick* elige el que prefieras **2** *v/t* (*choose*) elegir, elegir; *flowers, fruit* recoger; *pick one's nose* meterse el dedo en la nariz **3** *v/i*: *pick and choose* ser muy exigente

♦ **pick at** *v/t*: *pick at one's food* comer como un pajarito

♦ **pick on** *v/t* (*treat unfairly*) meterse con; (*select*) elegir

♦ **pick out** *v/t* (*identify*) identificar

♦ **pick up 1** *v/t object* recoger, *Span* coger; *habit* adquirir, *Span* coger; *illness* contraer, *Span* coger; *in car, from ground, from airport etc* recoger; *telephone* descolgar; *language, skill* aprender; (*buy*) comprar; *criminal* detener; *pick s.o. up sexually* ligar con alguien; *pick up the tab* F pagar **2** *v/i* (*improve*) mejorar

pick·et ['pɪkɪt] **1** *n of strikers* piquete *m* **2** *v/t* hacer piquete delante de

'**pick·et fence** valla *f* de estacas

'**pick·et line** piquete *m*

pick·le ['pɪkl] *v/t* encurtir; *fish* poner en escabeche; *meat* poner en adobo

pick·les ['pɪklz] *npl* (*dill pickles*) encurtidos *mpl*

'**pick·pock·et** carterista *m/f*

481 piss

pick-up (truck) ['pɪkʌp] camioneta f
pick-y ['pɪkɪ] adj F tiquismiquis F
pic-nic ['pɪknɪk] 1 n picnic m 2 v/i (pret &
pp picnicked) ir de picnic
pic-ture ['pɪktʃər] 1 n (photo) fotografía f;
(painting) cuadro m; (illustration) dibujo
m; (movie) película f; on TV imagen f;
keep s.o. in the picture mantener a alguien al día 2 v/t imaginar
'pic-ture book libro m ilustrado
'pic-ture ,post-card postal f
pic-tur-esque [pɪktʃə'resk] adj pintoresco
pie [paɪ] pastel m
piece [piːs] (fragment) fragmento m; component, of game pieza f; a piece of
pie / bread un trozo de pastel / una rebanada de pan; a piece of advice un consejo; go to pieces derrumbarse; take to
pieces desmontar
◆ piece together v/t broken plate recomponer; facts, evidence reconstruir
piece-meal ['piːsmiːl] adv poco a poco
piece-work ['piːswɜːrk] n trabajo m a destajo
pier [pɪr] at seaside malecón m
pierce [pɪrs] v/t (penetrate) perforar; ears
agujerear
pierc-ing ['pɪrsɪŋ] adj scream desgarrador; gaze penetrante; wind cortante
pig [pɪg] also fig cerdo m; greedy glo-
tón(-a) m(f)
pi-geon ['pɪdʒɪn] paloma f
pi-geon-hole ['pɪdʒɪnhoʊl] n casillero m 2 v/t person
encasillar; proposal archivar
'pig-gy-bank ['pɪgɪbæŋk] hucha f
pig-head-ed [pɪg'hedɪd] adj F cabezota F
'pig-pen also fig pocilga f
'pig-skin piel f de cerdo
'pig-tail coleta f
pile [paɪl] montón m, pila f; a pile of work
F un montón de trabajo F
◆ pile up v/i of work, bills acumularse 2
v/t amontonar
piles [paɪlz] nsg MED hemorroides fpl
'pile-up ['paɪlʌp] MOT choque m múltiple
pil-fer-ing ['pɪlfərɪŋ] hurtos mpl
pil-grim ['pɪlgrɪm] peregrino(-a) m(f)
pil-grim-age ['pɪlgrɪmɪdʒ] peregrinación f
pill [pɪl] pastilla f; be on the pill tomar la
píldora
pil-lar ['pɪlər] pilar m
pil-lion ['pɪljən] of motor bike asiento m
trasero
pil-low ['pɪloʊ] n almohada f
'pil-low-case, 'pil-low-slip funda f de almohada
pi-lot ['paɪlət] 1 n of airplane piloto m/f;
for ship práctico m 2 v/t airplane pilotar
'pi-lot scheme plan m piloto

pimp [pɪmp] n proxeneta m, Span chulo m
F
pim-ple ['pɪmpl] grano m
pin [pɪn] 1 n for sewing alfiler m; in bowling bolo m; (badge) pin m; ELEC clavija f;
safety pin imperdible m 2 v/t (pret & pp
pinned) (hold down) mantener; (attach)
sujetar
◆ pin down v/t: pin s.o. down to a date
forzar a alguien a concretar una fecha
◆ pin up v/t notice sujetar con chinchetas
PIN [pɪn] PIN m personal identification
number número m de identificación personal
pin-cers ['pɪnsərz] npl of crab pinzas fpl;
tool tenazas fpl; a pair of pincers unas
tenazas fpl
pinch [pɪntʃ] 1 n pellizco m; of salt, sugar
etc pizca f; at a pinch si no queda otro
remedio; at a pinch with numbers como
máximo 2 v/t pellizcar 3 v/i of shoes apretar
pine¹ [paɪn] n tree pino m; wood (madera f
de) pino m
pine² [paɪn] v/i: pine for echar de menos
pine-ap-ple ['paɪnæpl] piña f, L.Am.
ananá(s) f
ping [pɪŋ] 1 n sonido m metálico 2 v/i
hacer un sonido metálico
ping-pong ['pɪŋpɑːŋ] pimpón m, ping-
-pong m
pink [pɪŋk] adj rosa
pin-na-cle ['pɪnəkl] fig cima f
'pin-point determinar
pins and 'nee-dles hormigueo m
'pin-stripe adj a rayas
pint [paɪnt] pinta f, medida equivalente a
0,473 litros en Estados Unidos o a 0,568
litros en Gran Bretaña
'pin-up modelo m/f de revista
pi-o-neer [paɪə'nɪr] 1 n fig pionero(-a)
m(f) 2 v/t ser pionero en
pi-o-neer-ing [paɪə'nɪrɪŋ] adj work pionero
pi-ous ['paɪəs] piadoso
pip [pɪp] n of fruit pepita f
pipe [paɪp] 1 n for smoking pipa f; for water, gas, sewage tubería f 2 v/t conducir
por tuberías
◆ pipe down v/i F cerrar el pico F
piped mu-sic [paɪpt'mjuːzɪk] hilo m musical
pipe-line for oil oleoducto m; for gas gasoducto m; in the pipeline fig en trámite
pip-ing hot [paɪpɪŋ'hɑːt] adj muy caliente
pi-rate ['paɪrət] 1 n pirata m/f 2 v/t software piratear
Pis-ces ['paɪsiːz] ASTR Piscis m/f inv
piss [pɪs] 1 v/i P (urinate) mear P; take the

piss out of s.o. P cachondearse de alguien P **2** n P (*urine*) meada f P

◆ **piss off** v/i P largarse F; **piss off!** P ¡vete al cuerno! P

pissed [pɪst] adj F (*annoyed*) cabreado P; Br P (*drunk*) borracho, pedo F

pis·tol ['pɪstl] pistola f

pis·ton ['pɪstən] pistón m

pit [pɪt] n (*hole*) hoyo m; (*coal mine*) mina f

pitch[1] [pɪtʃ] n MUS tono m

pitch[2] [pɪtʃ] **1** v/i in baseball lanzar la pelota **2** v/t in tent montar; *ball* lanzar

'**pitch black** adj negro como el carbón

pitch·er[1] ['pɪtʃər] baseball player lanzador(a) m(f); pícher m/f

pitch·er[2] ['pɪtʃər] container jarra f

pit·e·ous ['pɪtɪəs] adj patético

pit·fall ['pɪtfɔːl] dificultad f

pith [pɪθ] of citrus fruit piel f blanca

pit·i·ful ['pɪtɪfəl] adj sight lastimoso; excuse, attempt lamentable

pit·i·less ['pɪtɪləs] adj despiadado

pits [pɪts] npl in motor racing boxes mpl

'**pit stop** in motor racing parada f en boxes

pit·tance ['pɪtns] miseria f

pit·y ['pɪtɪ] **1** n pena f, lástima f; **it's a pity that** es una pena or lástima que; **what a pity!** ¡qué pena!; **take pity on** compadecerse de **2** v/t (pret & pp **pitied**) person compadecerse de

piv·ot ['pɪvət] v/i pivotar

piz·za ['piːtsə] pizza f

plac·ard ['plækɑːrd] pancarta f

place [pleɪs] **1** n sitio m; in race, competition puesto m; (seat) sitio m, asiento; **I've lost my place** in book no sé por dónde iba; **at my / his place** en mi / su casa; **in place of** en lugar de; **feel out of place** sentirse fuera de lugar; **take place** tener lugar, llevarse a cabo; **in the first place** (firstly) en primer lugar; (in the beginning) en principio **2** v/t (put) poner, colocar; **I know you but I can't quite place you** te conozco pero no recuerdo de qué; **place an order** hacer un pedido

'**place mat** mantel m individual

plac·id ['plæsɪd] adj apacible

pla·gia·rism ['pleɪdʒərɪzm] plagio m

pla·gia·rize ['pleɪdʒəraɪz] v/t plagiar

plague [pleɪg] **1** n plaga f **2** v/t (bother) molestar

plain[1] [pleɪn] n llanura f

plain[2] [pleɪn] **1** adj (clear, obvious) claro; (not fancy) simple; (not pretty) feíllo; (not patterned) liso; (blunt) directo; **plain chocolate** chocolate amargo **2** adv verdaderamente; **it's plain crazy** es una verdadera locura

'**plain-clothes**: **in plain-clothes** de paisano

plain·ly ['pleɪnlɪ] adv (clearly) evidentemente; (bluntly) directamente; (simply) con sencillez; **he's plainly upset** está claro que está enfadado

plain 'spo·ken adj directo

plain·tiff ['pleɪntɪf] demandante m/f

plain·tive ['pleɪntɪv] adj quejumbroso

plan [plæn] **1** n (project, intention) plan m (drawing) plano m; **wedding plans** preparaciones fpl para la boda **2** v/t (pret & pp **planned**) (prepare) planear; (design) hacer los planos de; **plan to do sth, plan on doing sth** planear hacer algo **3** v/i (pret & pp **planned**) hacer planes

plane[1] [pleɪn] n (airplane) avión m

plane[2] [pleɪn] tool cepillo m

plan·et ['plænɪt] planeta f

plank [plæŋk] of wood tablón m; fig: o policy punto m

plan·ning ['plænɪŋ] planificación f; **at the planning stage** en fase de estudio

plant[1] [plænt] **1** n planta f **2** v/t plantar

plant[2] [plænt] n (factory) fábrica f, planta f; (equipment) maquinaria f

plan·ta·tion [plæn'teɪʃn] plantación f

plaque [plæk] on wall, teeth placa f

plas·ter ['plæstər] **1** n on wall, ceiling yeso m **2** v/t wall, ceiling enyesar; **be plastered with** estar recubierto de

plas·ter cast escayola f

plas·tic ['plæstɪk] **1** n plástico **2** adj (made of plastic) de plástico

plas·tic 'bag bolsa f de plástico

'**plas·tic (mon·ey)** plástico m, tarjetas fp de pago

plas·tic 'sur·geon cirujano(-a) m(f) plástico(-a)

plas·tic 'sur·ge·ry cirugía f estética

plate [pleɪt] n for food plato m; (sheet o metal) chapa f; F PHOT placa f

pla·teau ['plætəu] meseta f

plat·form ['plætfɔːrm] (stage) plataforma f; of railroad station andén m; fig: political programa f

plat·i·num ['plætɪnəm] **1** n platino m **2** adj de platino

plat·i·tude ['plætɪtuːd] tópico m

pla·ton·ic [plə'tɑːnɪk] adj relationship platónico

pla·toon [plə'tuːn] of soldiers sección f

plat·ter ['plætər] for meat, fish fuente f

plau·si·ble ['plɔːzəbl] adj plausible

play [pleɪ] **1** n in theater, on TV obra f (de teatro); of children, in match, TECH juego m **2** v/i jugar; of musician tocar **3** v/t musical instrument tocar; piece of music interpretar, tocar; *game* jugar; *tennis, football* jugar a; *opponent* jugar contra; *(perform: Macbeth etc)* representar; *particular role* interpretar, hacer el papel de; *play a joke on* gastar una broma a

◆ **play around** *v/i* F *(be unfaithful)* acostarse con otras personas

◆ **play down** *v/t* quitar importancia a

◆ **play up** *v/i of machine* dar problemas; *of child* dar guerra

play·act ['pleɪækt] *v/i (pretend)* fingir

play·boy ['pleɪbɔɪ] playboy *m*

play·er ['pleɪr] SP jugador(a) *m(f)*; *(musician)* intérprete *m/f*; *(actor)* actor *m*, actriz *f*

play·ful ['pleɪfəl] *adj punch etc* de broma

play·ground ['pleɪgraʊnd] zona *f* de juegos

'**play·group** guardería *f*

'**play·ing card** ['pleɪŋkɑːrd] carta *f*

'**play·ing field** ['pleɪŋfiːld] campo *m* de deportes

play·mate ['pleɪmeɪt] compañero(-a) *m(f)* de juego

play·wright ['pleɪraɪt] autor(a) *m(f)*

pla·za ['plɑːzə] *for shopping* centro *m* comercial

plc [piːel'siː] *abbr (= Br public limited company)* S.A. *f* (= sociedad *f* anónima)

plea [pliː] *n* súplica *f*

plead [pliːd] *v/i*: **plead for mercy** pedir clemencia; **plead guilty / not guilty** declararse culpable / inocente; **she pleaded with me not to** me suplicó que no fuera

pleas·ant ['pleznt] *adj* agradable

please [pliːz] **1** *adv* por favor; **more tea? - yes, please** ¿más té? - sí, por favor; **please do** claro que sí, por supuesto **2** *v/t* complacer; **please yourself!** ¡haz lo que quieras!

pleased [pliːzd] *adj* contento; *(satisfied)* satisfecho; **pleased to meet you** encantado de conocerle; **I'm very pleased to be here** estoy muy contento de estar aquí

pleas·ing ['pliːzɪŋ] *adj* agradable

pleas·ure ['pleʒər] *(happiness, satisfaction, delight)* satisfacción *f*; *as opposed to work* placer *m*; **it's a pleasure** *(you're welcome)* no hay de qué; **with pleasure** faltaría más

pleat [pliːt] *n in skirt* tabla *f*

pleat·ed skirt ['pliːtɪd] falda *f* de tablas

pledge [pledʒ] **1** *n (promise)* promesa *f*; *(guarantee)* compromiso *m*; *(money)* donación *f*; **Pledge of Allegiance** juramento de lealtad a la bandera estadounidense **2** *v/t (promise)* prometer; *(guarantee)* comprometerse; *money* donar

plen·ti·ful ['plentɪfəl] *adj* abundante

plen·ty ['plentɪ] *(abundance)* abundancia *f*; **plenty of books / food** muchos libros / mucha comida; **we've got plenty of room** tenemos espacio más que suficiente; **that's plenty** es suficiente; **there's plenty for everyone** hay (suficiente) para todos

pli·a·ble ['plaɪəbl] *adj* flexible

pli·ers ['plaɪərz] *npl* alicates *mpl*; **a pair of pliers** unos alicates

plight [plaɪt] situación *f* difícil

plod [plɑːd] *v/i (pret & pp plodded) (walk)* arrastrarse

◆ **plod on** *v/i with a job* avanzar laboriosamente

plod·der ['plɑːdər] *(at work, school)* persona no especialmente lista pero muy trabajadora

plot[1] [plɑːt] *n (land)* terreno *m*

plot[2] [plɑːt] **1** *n (conspiracy)* complot *m*; *of novel* argumento *m* **2** *v/t (pret & pp plotted)* tramar **3** *v/i (pret & pp plotted)* conspirar

plot·ter ['plɑːtər] conspirador(a) *m(f)*; COMPUT plóter *m*

plough *Br*, **plow** [plaʊ] **1** *n* arado *m* **2** *v/t & v/i* arar

◆ **plow back** *v/t profits* reinvertir

pluck [plʌk] *v/t eyebrows* depilar; *chicken* desplumar

◆ **pluck up** *v/t*: **pluck up courage to …** reunir el valor para …

plug [plʌg] **1** *n for sink, bath* tapón *m*; *electrical* enchufe *m*; *(spark plug)* bujía *f*; **give a book a plug** dar publicidad a un libro **2** *v/t (pret & pp plugged) hole* tapar; *new book etc* hacer publicidad de

◆ **plug away at** *v/t* F trabajar con esfuerzo en

◆ **plug in** *v/t* enchufar

plum [plʌm] **1** *n fruit* ciruela *f*; *tree* ciruelo *m* **2** *adj* F: **plum job** un chollo de trabajo

plum·age ['pluːmɪdʒ] plumaje *m*

plumb [plʌm] *adj* vertical

◆ **plumb in** *v/t washing machine* conectar a la red del agua

plumb·er ['plʌmər] *Span* fontanero(-a) *m(f)*, *L.Am.* plomero(-a) *m(f)*

plumb·ing ['plʌmɪŋ] *(pipes)* tuberías *fpl*

plume [pluːm] *n (feather)* pluma *f*; *of smoke* nube *f*

plum·met ['plʌmɪt] *v/i of airplane, prices* caer en picado

plump [plʌmp] *adj* rellenito

◆ **plump for** *v/t* decidirse por

plunge [plʌndʒ] **1** *n* salto *m*; *in prices* caída *f*; **take the plunge** dar el paso **2** *v/i* precipitarse; *of prices* caer en picado **3**

P

v/t hundir; (*into water*) sumergir; **the city was plunged into darkness** la ciudad quedó inmersa en la oscuridad; **the news plunged him into despair** la noticia lo hundió en la desesperación

plung·ing ['plʌndʒɪŋ] *adj neckline* escotado

plu·per·fect ['pluː'pɜːrfɪkt] *n* GRAM pluscuamperfecto *m*

plu·ral ['plʊərəl] **1** *n* plural *m* **2** *adj* plural

plus [plʌs] **1** *prep* más; **I want John plus two other volunteers ...** quiero a John y a otros dos voluntarios ...; **$500 plus** más de 500 dólares **3** *n symbol* signo *m* más; (*advantage*) ventaja *f* **4** *conj* (*moreover, in addition*) además

plush [plʌʃ] *adj* lujoso

'plus sign signo *m* más

ply·wood ['plaɪwʊd] madera *f* contrachapada

PM [piː'em] *Br abbr* (= **Prime Minister**) Primer(a) *m(f)* Ministro(-a)

p.m. [piː'em] *abbr* (= **post meridiem**) p.m.; **at 3 p.m** a las 3 de la tarde; **at 11 p.m** a las 11 de la noche

pneu·mat·ic [nuː'mætɪk] *adj* neumático

pneu·mat·ic 'drill martillo *m* neumático

pneu·mo·ni·a [nuː'moʊnɪə] pulmonía *f*, neumonía *f*

poach¹ [poʊtʃ] *v/t* (*cook*) hervir

poach² [poʊtʃ] *v/t & v/i* (*hunt*) cazar furtivamente; *fish* pescar furtivamente

poached 'egg [poʊtʃt'eg] huevo *m* escalfado

poach·er ['poʊtʃər] *of game* cazador(a) *m(f)* furtivo(a); *of fish* pescador(a) *m(f)* furtivo(a)

P.O. Box [piː'oʊbɑːks] apartado *m* de correos

pock·et ['pɑːkɪt] **1** *n* bolsillo *m*; **line one's pockets** llenarse los bolsillos; **be $10 out of pocket** salir perdiendo 10 dólares **2** *adj* radio, dictionary de bolsillo **3** *v/t* meter en el bolsillo

'pock·et·book (*handbag*) bolso *m*; (*wallet*) cartera *f*; (*book*) libro *m* de bolsillo

pock·et 'cal·cu·la·tor calculadora *f* de bolsillo

'pock·et·knife navaja *f*

po·di·um ['poʊdɪəm] podio *m*

po·em ['poʊɪm] poema *m*

po·et ['poʊɪt] poeta *m*; poeta *f*, poetisa *f*

po·et·ic [poʊ'etɪk] *adj* poético

po·et·ic 'jus·tice justicia *f* divina

po·et·ry ['poʊɪtrɪ] poesía *f*

poign·ant ['pɔɪnjənt] *adj* conmovedor

point [pɔɪnt] **1** *n of pencil, knife* punta *f*; *in competition, argument* punto *m*; (*purpose*) objetivo *m*; (*moment*) momento *m*;

in decimals coma *f*; **what's the point of telling him?** ¿qué se consigue diciéndoselo?; **the point I'm trying to make ...** lo que estoy intentando decir ...; **at one point** en un momento dado; **that's beside the point** eso no viene a cuento; **be on the point of** estar a punto de; **get to the point** ir al grano; **the point is ...** la cuestión es que ...; **there's no point in waiting / trying** no vale la pena esperar / intentarlo **2** *v/i* señalar con el dedo **3** *v/t*: **he pointed the gun at me** me apuntó con la pistola

◆ **point out** *v/t sights* indicar; *advantages etc* destacar

◆ **point to** *v/t with finger* señalar con el dedo; (*fig: indicate*) indicar

'point-blank 1 *adj refusal, denial* categórico; **at point-blank range** a quemarropa **2** *adv refuse, deny* categóricamente

point·ed ['pɔɪntɪd] *adj remark* mordaz

point·er ['pɔɪntər] *for teacher* puntero *m*; (*hint*) consejo *m*; (*sign, indication*) indicador *m*

point·less ['pɔɪntləs] *adj* inútil; **it's pointless trying** no sirve de nada intentarlo

'point of sale *place* punto *m* de venta; *promotional material* material *m* promocional

'point of view punto *m* de vista

poise [pɔɪz] confianza *f*

poised [pɔɪzd] *adj person* con aplomo

poi·son ['pɔɪzn] **1** *n* veneno *m* **2** *v/t* envenenar

poi·son·ous ['pɔɪznəs] *adj* venenoso

poke [poʊk] **1** *n* empujón *m* **2** *v/t* (*prod*) empujar; (*stick*) clavar; **he poked his head out of the window** asomó la cabeza por la ventana; **poke fun at** reírse de; **poke one's nose into** F meter las narices en F

◆ **poke around** *v/i* F husmear

pok·er ['poʊkər] *card game* póquer *m*

pok·y ['poʊkɪ] *adj* F (*cramped*) enano, minúsculo

Po·land ['poʊlənd] Polonia *f*

po·lar ['poʊlər] *adj* polar

po·lar bear oso *m* polar *or* blanco

po·lar·ize ['poʊləraɪz] *v/t* polarizar

Pole [poʊl] polaco(-a) *m(f)*

pole¹ [poʊl] *for support* poste *m*; *for tent, pushing things* palo *m*

pole² [poʊl] *of earth* polo *m*

'pole star estrella *f* polar

'pole·vault salto *m* con pértiga

'pole-vault·er saltador(a) *m(f)* de pértiga

po·lice [pə'liːs] *n* policía *f*

po'lice car coche *m* de policía

po'lice·man policía *m*

po·lice state estado *m* policial

po·lice sta·tion comisaría *f* (de policía)

po·lice·wo·man (mujer *f*) policía *f*

pol·i·cy¹ ['pɑ:lɪsɪ] política *f*

pol·i·cy² ['pɑ:lɪsɪ] (*insurance policy*) póliza *f*

po·li·o ['pouliou] polio *f*

Pol·ish ['poulɪʃ] **1** *adj* polaco **2** *n* polaco *m*

pol·ish ['pɑ:lɪʃ] **1** *n* abrillantador *m*; (*nail polish*) esmalte *m* de uñas **2** *v/t* dar brillo a; *speech* pulir

◆ **polish off** *v/t food* acabar, comerse

◆ **polish up** *v/t skill* perfeccionar

po·lished ['pɑ:lɪʃt] *adj performance* brillante

po·lite [pə'laɪt] *adj* educado

po·lite·ly [pə'laɪtlɪ] *adv* educadamente

po·lite·ness [pə'laɪtnɪs] educación *f*

po·lit·i·cal [pə'lɪtɪkl] *adj* político

po·lit·i·cal·ly cor·rect [pə'lɪtɪklɪ kə'rekt] políticamente correcto

pol·i·ti·cian [pɑ:lɪ'tɪʃn] político(-a) *m(f)*

pol·i·tics ['pɑ:lətɪks] política *f*; *I'm not interested in politics* no me interesa la política; *what are my politics?* ¿cuáles son sus ideas políticas?

poll [poul] **1** *n* (*survey*) encuesta *f*, sondeo *m*; *the polls* (*election*) las elecciones; *go to the polls* (*vote*) acudir a las urnas **2** *v/t people* sondear; *votes* obtener

pol·len ['pɑ:lən] polen *m*

'pol·len count concentración *f* de polen en el aire

'poll·ing booth ['poulɪŋ] cabina *f* electoral

'poll·ing day día *m* de las elecciones

poll·ster ['poulstər] encuestador(a) *m(f)*

pol·lu·tant [pə'lu:tənt] contaminante *m*

pol·lute [pə'lu:t] *v/t* contaminar

pol·lu·tion [pə'lu:ʃn] contaminación *f*

po·lo ['poulou] SP polo *m*

'po·lo neck *sweater* suéter *m* de cuello alto

'po·lo shirt polo *m*

pol·y·eth·yl·ene [pɑ:lɪ'eθɪli:n] polietileno *m*

pol·y·es·ter [pɑ:lɪ'estər] poliéster *m*

pol·y·sty·rene [pɑ:lɪ'staɪri:n] poliestireno *m*

pol·y·un·sat·u·rat·ed [pɑ:lɪʌn'sætʃəreɪtɪd] *adj* poliinsaturado

pom·pous ['pɑ:mpəs] *adj* pomposo

pond [pɑ:nd] estanque *m*

pon·der ['pɑ:ndər] *v/i* reflexionar

pon·tiff ['pɑ:ntɪf] pontífice *m*

po·ny ['pounɪ] poni *m*

'po·ny·tail coleta *f*

poo·dle ['pu:dl] caniche *m*

pool¹ [pu:l] (*swimming pool*) piscina *f*,

L.Am. pileta *f*, *Mex* alberca *f*; *of water, blood* charco *m*

pool² [pu:l] *game* billar *m* americano

pool³ [pu:l] **1** *n* (*common fund*) bote *m*, fondo *m* común **2** *v/t resources* juntar

'pool hall sala *f* de billares

'pool table mesa *f* de billar americano

poop·ed [pu:pt] *adj* F hecho polvo F

poor [pur] **1** *adj* pobre; (*not good*) mediocre, malo; *be in poor health* estar enfermo; *poor old Tony!* ¡pobre(cito) Tony! **2** *n*: *the poor* los pobres

poor·ly ['purlɪ] **1** *adv adj* F (*unwell*): *feel poorly* encontrarse mal

pop¹ [pɑ:p] **1** *n noise* pequeño *m* ruido **2** *v/i* (*pret & pp popped*) *of balloon etc* estallar **3** *v/t* (*pret & pp popped*) *cork* hacer saltar; *balloon* pinchar

pop² [pɑ:p] **1** *n* MUS pop *m* **2** *adj* pop

pop³ [pɑ:p] F (*father*) papá *m* F

pop⁴ [pɑ:p] F (*put*) meter

◆ **pop in** *v/i* F (*make a brief visit*) pasar un momento

◆ **pop out** *v/i* F (*go out for a short time*) salir un momento

◆ **pop up** *v/i* F (*appear suddenly*) aparecer

'pop con·cert concierto *m* (de música) pop

'pop·corn ['pɑ:pkɔ:rn] palomitas *fpl* de maíz

pope [poup] papa *m*

'pop group grupo *m* (de música) pop

pop·py ['pɑ:pɪ] amapola *f*

Pop·sicle® ['pɑ:psɪkl] polo *m* (helado)

'pop song canción *f* pop

pop·u·lar ['pɑ:pjulər] *adj* popular; *contrary to popular belief* contrariamente a lo que se piensa

pop·u·lar·i·ty [pɑ:pju'lærətɪ] popularidad *f*

pop·u·late ['pɑ:pjuleɪt] *v/t* poblar

pop·u·la·tion [pɑ:pju'leɪʃn] población *f*

por·ce·lain ['pɔ:rsəlɪn] **1** *n* porcelana *f* **2** *adj* de porcelana

porch [pɔ:rtʃ] porche *m*

por·cu·pine ['pɔ:rkjupaɪn] puercoespín *m*

pore [pɔ:r] *of skin* poro *m*

◆ **pore over** *v/t* estudiar detenidamente

pork [pɔ:rk] cerdo *m*

porn [pɔ:rn] *n* F porno *m*

porn(o) [pɔ:rn, 'pɔ:rnou] *adj* F porno F

por·no·graph·ic [pɔ:rnə'græfɪk] *adj* pornográfico

porn·og·ra·phy [pɔ:r'nɑ:grəfɪ] pornografía *f*

po·rous ['pɔ:rəs] *adj* poroso

port¹ [pɔ:rt] *n town, area* puerto *m*

port² [pɔ:rt] *adj* (*left-hand*) a babor

por·ta·ble ['pɔːrtəbl] **1** adj portátil **2** n COMPUT portátil m; TV televisión f portátil

por·ter ['pɔːrtər] mozo(-a) m(f)

port·hole ['pɔːrthoul] NAUT portilla f

por·tion ['pɔːrʃn] n parte f; of food ración f

por·trait ['pɔːrtreɪt] **1** n retrato m **2** adv print en formato vertical

por·tray [pɔːr'treɪ] of artist, photographer retratar; of actor interpretar; of author describir

por·tray·al [pɔːr'treɪəl] by actor interpretación f, representación f; by author descripción f

Por·tu·gal ['pɔːrtʃugl] Portugal

Por·tu·guese [pɔːrtʃu'giːz] **1** adj portugués **2** n person portugués(-esa) m(f); language portugués m

pose [pouz] **1** n (pretense) pose f; it's all a pose no es más que una pose **2** v/i for artist, photographer posar; pose as hacerse pasar por **3** v/t: pose a problem/a threat representar un problema / una amenaza

posh [pɑːʃ] adj Br elegante, pej pijo

po·si·tion [pə'zɪʃn] **1** n posición f; (stance, point of view) postura f; (job) puesto m, empleo m; (status) posición f (social) **2** v/t situar, colocar

pos·i·tive ['pɑːzətɪv] adj positivo; be positive (sure) estar seguro

pos·i·tive·ly ['pɑːzətɪvlɪ] adv (decidedly) verdaderamente, sin lugar a dudas; (definitely) claramente

pos·sess [pə'zes] v/t poseer

pos·ses·sion [pə'zeʃn] posesión f; possessions posesiones fpl

pos·ses·sive [pə'zesɪv] person, GRAM posesivo

pos·si·bil·i·ty [pɑːsə'bɪlətɪ] posibilidad f; there is a possibility that ... cabe la posibilidad de que ...

pos·si·ble ['pɑːsəbl] adj posible; the shortest / quickest route possible la ruta más corto / rápido posible; the best possible ... el mejor ...

pos·si·bly ['pɑːsəblɪ] adv (perhaps) puede ser, quizás; that can't possibly be right no puede ser cierto; they're doing everything they possibly can están haciendo todo lo que pueden; could you possibly tell me ...? ¿tendría la amabilidad de decirme ...?

post¹ [poust] **1** n of wood, metal poste m **2** v/t notice pegar; on notice board poner; profits presentar; keep s.o. posted mantener a alguien al corriente

post² [poust] **1** n (place of duty) puesto m **2** v/t soldier, employee destinar; guards apostar

post³ [poust] **1** n Br (mail) correo m **2** v/t Br letter echar al correo

post·age ['poustɪdʒ] franqueo m

post·age stamp fml sello m, L.Am. estampilla f, Mex timbre m

post·al ['poustl] adj postal

post·card (tarjeta f) postal f

post·code Br código m postal

post·date v/t posfechar

post·er ['poustər] póster m, L.Am. afiche m

pos·te·ri·or [pɑː'stɪrɪər] n (hum: buttocks) trasero m

pos·ter·i·ty [pɑː'sterɪtɪ] posteridad f; for posterity para la posteridad

post·grad·u·ate ['poustgrædʒuət] **1** n posgraduado(-a) m(f) **2** adj de posgrado

post·hu·mous ['pɑːstuməs] adj póstumo

post·hu·mous·ly ['pɑːstuməslɪ] adv póstumamente

post·ing ['poustɪŋ] (assignment) destino m

post·mark ['poustmɑːrk] matasellos m inv

post·mor·tem [poust'mɔːrtəm] autopsia f

post of·fice oficina f de correos

post·pone [poust'poun] v/t posponer, aplazar

post·pone·ment [poust'pounmənt] aplazamiento m

pos·ture ['pɑːstʃər] postura f

post·war adj de posguerra

pot¹ [pɑːt] for cooking olla f; for coffee cafetera f; for tea tetera f; for plant maceta f

pot² [pɑːt] F (marijuana) maría f F

po·ta·to [pə'teɪtou] Span patata f, L.Am. papa f

po·ta·to crisps, Br **po·ta·to crisps** npl Span patatas fpl fritas, L.Am. papas fpl fritas

pot·bel·ly ['pɑːtbelɪ] barriga f

po·tent ['poutənt] adj potente

po·ten·tial [pə'tenʃl] **1** adj potencial **2** n potencial m

po·ten·tial·ly [pə'tenʃəlɪ] adv potencialmente

pot·hole ['pɑːthoul] in road bache m

pot·ter ['pɑːtər] n alfarero(-a) m(f)

pot·ter·y ['pɑːtərɪ] n alfarería f

pot·ty ['pɑːtɪ] n for baby orinal m

pouch [pautʃ] (bag) bolsa f; for tobacco petaca f; for amunition cartuchera f; for mail saca m

poul·try ['poultrɪ] birds aves fpl de corral; meat carne f de ave

pounce [pauns] v/i of animal saltar; fig echarse encima

pound[1] [paund] *n weight* libra *f (453,6 gr)*

pound[2] [paund] *n for strays* perrera *f; for cars* depósito *m*

pound[3] [paund] *v/i of heart* palpitar con fuerza; **pound on** *(hammer on)* golpear en

pound 'ster·ling libra *f* esterlina

pour [pɔːr] **1** *v/t into a container* verter; *spill* derramar; **pour s.o. some coffee** servir café a alguien **2** *v/i*: **it's pouring (with rain)** está lloviendo a cántaros
♦ **pour out** *v/t liquid* servir; *troubles* contar

pout [paut] *v/i* hacer un mohín

pov·er·ty ['pɑːvərtɪ] pobreza *f*

pov·er·ty-strick·en ['pɑːvərtɪstrɪkn] depauperado

pow·der ['paudər] **1** *n* polvo *m; for face* polvos *m*, colorete *m* **2** *v/t face* empolvarse

pow·er ['pauər] **1** *n (strength)* fuerza *f; of engine* potencia; *(authority)* poder *m; (energy)* energía *f; (electricity)* electricidad *f; in power* POL en el poder; *fall from power* perder el poder **2** *v/t*: *be powered by* estar impulsado a

'pow·er·as·sist·ed steering dirección *f* asistida

'pow·er cut apagón *m*

'pow·er fail·ure apagón *m*

pow·er·ful ['pauərfəl] *adj* poderoso; *car* potente; *drug* fuerte

pow·er·less ['pauərlɪs] *adj* impotente; *be powerless to ...* ser incapaz de ...

'pow·er line línea *f* de conducción eléctrica

'pow·er out·age apagón *m*

'pow·er sta·tion central *f* eléctrica

'pow·er steer·ing dirección *f* asistida

'pow·er u·nit fuente *f* de alimentación

PR [piː'ɑːr] *abbr (= public relations)* relaciones *fpl* públicas

prac·ti·cal ['præktɪkl] *adj* práctico; *layout* funcional

prac·ti·cal 'joke broma *f (que se gasta)*

prac·tic·al·ly ['præktɪklɪ] *adv behave, think* de manera práctica; *(almost)* prácticamente, casi

prac·tice ['præktɪs] **1** *n* práctica *f; (rehearsal)* ensayo *m; (custom)* costumbre *f; in practice (in reality)* en la práctica; *be out of practice* estar desentrenado; *practice makes perfect* a base de práctica se aprende **2** *v/i* practicar; *of musician* ensayar; *of footballer* entrenarse **3** *v/t* practicar; *law, medicine* ejercer

prac·tise *Br* → **practice** *v/i & v/t*

prag·mat·ic [præg'mætɪk] *adj* pragmatis-

mo *m*

prai·rie ['prerɪ] pradera *f*

praise [preɪz] **1** *n* elogio *m*, alabanza *f* **2** *v/t* elogiar

'praise·wor·thy *adj* elogiable

prank [præŋk] *n* travesura *f*

prat·tle ['prætl] *v/i* F parlotear F

prawn [prɔːn] *n* gamba *f*

pray [preɪ] *v/i* rezar

prayer [prer] oración *f*

preach [priːtʃ] **1** *v/i in church* predicar; *(moralize)* sermonear **2** *v/t sermon* predicar

preach·er ['priːtʃər] predicador(a) *m(f)*

pre·am·ble [priː'æmbl] preámbulo *m*

pre·car·i·ous [prɪ'kerɪəs] *adj* precario

pre·car·i·ous·ly [prɪ'kerɪəslɪ] *adv* precariamente

pre·cau·tion [prɪ'kɒːʃn] precaución *f; as a precaution* como precaución

pre·cau·tion·a·ry [prɪ'kɒːʃnrɪ] *adj measure* preventivo

pre·cede [prɪ'siːd] *v/t in time* preceder; *(walk in front of)* ir delante de

pre·ce·dent ['presɪdənt] precedente *m*

pre·ce·ding [prɪ'siːdɪŋ] *adj week, chapter* anterior

pre·cinct ['priːsɪŋkt] *(district)* distrito *m*

pre·cious ['preʃəs] *adj* preciado; *gem* precioso

pre·cip·i·tate [prɪ'sɪpɪteɪt] *v/t crisis* precipitar

pré·cis ['preɪsiː] *n* resumen *m*

pre·cise [prɪ'saɪs] *adj* preciso

pre·cise·ly [prɪ'saɪslɪ] *adv* exactamente

pre·ci·sion [prɪ'sɪʒn] precisión *f*

pre·co·cious [prɪ'koʊʃəs] *adj child* precoz

pre·con·ceived ['priːkənsiːvd] *adj idea* preconcebido

pre·con·di·tion [priːkən'dɪʃn] condición *f* previa

pred·a·tor ['predətər] *animal* depredador(a) *m(f)*

pred·a·to·ry ['predətɔːrɪ] *adj* depredador

pre·de·ces·sor ['priːdɪsesər] *in job* predecesor(a) *m(f); machine* modelo *m* anterior

pre·des·ti·na·tion [priːdestɪ'neɪʃn] predestinación *f*

pre·des·tined [priː'destɪnd] *adj*: *be predestined to* estar *pre*destinado a

pre·dic·a·ment [prɪ'dɪkəmənt] apuro *m*

pre·dict [prɪ'dɪkt] *v/t* predecir, pronosticar

pre·dict·a·ble [prɪ'dɪktəbl] *adj* predecible

pre·dic·tion [prɪ'dɪkʃn] predicción *f*, pronóstico *m*

pre·dom·i·nant [prɪ'dɑːmɪnənt] *adj* pre-

P

dominante

pre·dom·i·nant·ly [prɪ'dɑːmɪnəntlɪ] *adv* predominantemente

pre·dom·i·nate [prɪ'dɑːmɪneɪt] *v/i* predominar

pre·fab·ri·cat·ed [priː'fæbrɪkeɪtɪd] *adj* prefabricado

pref·ace ['prefɪs] *n* prólogo *m*, prefacio *m*

pre·fer [prɪ'fɜːr] *v/t* (*pret & pp* **preferred**) preferir; *prefer X to Y* preferir X a Y; *prefer to do* preferir hacer

pref·e·ra·ble ['prefərəbl] *adj* preferible; *anywhere is preferable to this* cualquier sitio es mejor que éste

pref·e·ra·bly ['prefərəblɪ] *adv* preferentemente

pref·e·rence ['prefərəns] *n* preferencia *f*

pref·er·en·tial [prefə'renʃl] *adj* preferente

pre·fix ['priːfɪks] prefijo *m*

preg·nan·cy ['pregnənsɪ] embarazo *m*

preg·nant ['pregnənt] *adj woman* embarazada; *animal* preñada

pre·heat ['priːhiːt] *v/t oven* precalentar

pre·his·tor·ic [priːhɪs'tɑːrɪk] *adj* prehistórico

pre·judge [priː'dʒʌdʒ] *v/t* prejuzgar, juzgar de antemano

prej·u·dice ['predʒʊdɪs] **1** *n* prejuicio *m* **2** *v/t person* predisponer, influir; *chances* perjudicar

prej·u·diced ['predʒʊdɪst] *adj* parcial, predispuesto

pre·lim·i·na·ry [prɪ'lɪmɪnerɪ] *adj* preliminar

pre·mar·i·tal [priː'mærɪtl] *adj* prematrimonial

pre·ma·ture ['priːmətʊr] *adj* prematuro

pre·med·i·tat·ed [priː'medɪteɪtɪd] *adj* premeditado

prem·i·er ['premɪr] *n* (*Prime Minister*) primer(a) ministro(-a) *m(f)*

prem·i·ère ['premɪer] *n* estreno *m*

prem·is·es ['premɪsɪz] *npl* local *m*

pre·mi·um ['priːmɪəm] *n in insurance* prima *f*

pre·mo·ni·tion [premə'nɪʃn] premonición *f*, presentimiento *m*

pre·na·tal [priː'neɪtl] *adj* prenatal

pre·oc·cu·pied [prɪ'ɑːkjʊpaɪd] *adj* preocupado

prep·a·ra·tion [prepə'reɪʃn] preparación *f*; *in preparation for* como preparación a; *preparations* preparativos *mpl*

pre·pare [prɪ'per] **1** *v/t* preparar; *be prepared to do sth* (*willing*) estar dispuesto a hacer algo; *be prepared for sth* (*be expecting, ready*) estar preparado para algo **2** *v/i* prepararse

prep·o·si·tion [prepə'zɪʃn] preposición *f*

pre·pos·ter·ous [prɪ'pɑːstərəs] *adj* ridículo, absurdo

prep school ['prepskuːl] escuela *f* primaria privada

pre·req·ui·site [priː'rekwɪzɪt] requisito *m* previo

pre·scribe [prɪ'skraɪb] *v/t of doctor* recetar

pre·scrip·tion [prɪ'skrɪpʃn] MED receta *f*

pres·ence ['prezns] presencia *f*; *in the presence of* en presencia de, delante de; *presence of 'mind* presencia *f* de ánimo

pres·ent¹ ['preznt] **1** *adj* (*current*) actual; *be present* estar presente **2** *n: the present also* GRAM el presente; *at present* en este momento

pres·ent² ['preznt] *n* (*gift*) regalo *m*

pre·sent³ [prɪ'zent] *v/t* presentar; *award* entregar; *program* presentar; *present s.o. with sth, present sth to s.o.* entregar algo a alguien

pre·sen·ta·tion [prezn'teɪʃn] *to audience* presentación *f*

pres·ent-day [preznt'deɪ] *adj* actual

pre·sent·er [prɪ'zentər] presentador(a) *m(f)*

pres·ent·ly ['prezntlɪ] *adv* (*at the moment*) actualmente; (*soon*) pronto

'pres·ent tense tiempo *m* presente

pres·er·va·tion [prezər'veɪʃn] conservación *f*; *of standards, peace* mantenimiento *m*

pre·ser·va·tive [prɪ'zɜːrvətɪv] *n* conservante *m*

pre·serve [prɪ'zɜːrv] **1** *n* (*domain*) dominio *m* **2** *v/t standards, peace etc* mantener; *food, wood* conservar

pre·side [prɪ'zaɪd] *v/i at meeting* presidir; *preside over meeting* presidir

pres·i·den·cy ['prezɪdənsɪ] presidencia *f*

pres·i·dent ['prezɪdnt] POL, *of company* presidente(-a) *m(f)*

pres·i·den·tial [prezɪ'denʃl] *adj* presidencial

press [pres] **1** *n: the press* la prensa **2** *v/t button* pulsar, presionar; (*urge*) presionar; (*squeeze*) apretar; *clothes* planchar **3** *v/i: press for* presionar para obtener

'press a·gen·cy agencia *f* de prensa

'press con·fer·ence rueda *f* or conferencia *f* de prensa

press·ing ['presɪŋ] *adj* urgente

pres·sure ['preʃər] **1** *n* presión *f*; *be under pressure* estar sometido a presión; *he is under pressure to resign* lo están presionando para que dimita **2** *v/t* presionar

pres·tige [pre'stiːʒ] prestigio *m*

pres·ti·gious [pre'stɪdʒəs] *adj* prestigioso

pre·su·ma·bly [prɪ'zuːməblɪ] *adv* presumiblemente, probablemente

pre·sume [prɪ'zuːm] suponer; *they were presumed dead* los dieron por muertos; *presume to do sth* fml tomarse la libertad de hacer algo

pre·sump·tion [prɪ'zʌmpʃn] *of innocence, guilt* presunción f

pre·sump·tu·ous [prɪ'zʌmptʊəs] *adj* presuntuoso

pre·sup·pose [priːsə'poʊs] *v/t* presuponer

pre·tax [priː'tæks] *adj* antes de impuestos

pre·tence *Br* → **pretense**

pre·tend [prɪ'tend] **1** *v/t* fingir, hacer como si; *claim* pretender; *pretend to be s.o.* hacerse pasar por alguien; *the children are pretending to be spacemen* los niños están jugando a que son astronautas **2** *v/i* fingir

pre·tense [prɪ'tens] farsa f

pre·ten·tious [prɪ'tenʃəs] *adj* pretencioso

pre·text ['priːtekst] pretexto m

pret·ty ['prɪtɪ] **1** *adj village, house, fabric etc* bonito, lindo; *child, woman* guapo, lindo **2** *adv (quite)* bastante

pre·vail [prɪ'veɪl] *v/i (triumph)* prevalecer

pre·vail·ing [prɪ'veɪlɪŋ] *adj* predominante

pre·vent [prɪ'vent] *v/t* impedir, evitar; *prevent s.o. (from) doing sth* impedir que alguien haga algo

pre·ven·tion [prɪ'venʃn] prevención f

pre·ven·tive [prɪ'ventɪv] *adj* preventivo

pre·view ['priːvjuː] **1** *n of movie, exhibition* preestreno m **2** *v/t* hacer la presentación previa de

pre·vi·ous ['priːvɪəs] *adj* anterior, previo

pre·vi·ous·ly ['priːvɪəslɪ] *adv* anteriormente, antes

pre·war ['priːwɔːr] *adj* de preguerra, de antes de la guerra

prey [preɪ] *n* presa f; *prey to* presa de

◆ **prey on** *v/t* atacar; *fig: of con man etc* aprovecharse de

price [praɪs] **1** *n* precio m **2** *v/t* COM poner precio a

price·less ['praɪslɪs] *adj* que no tiene precio

price tag etiqueta f del precio

price war guerra f de precios

pric·ey ['praɪsɪ] *adj* F carillo F

prick¹ [prɪk] **1** *n pain* punzada f **2** *v/t (jab)* pinchar

prick² [prɪk] *n* V *(penis)* polla f V, carajo m V; V *person* Span gilipollas m inv V, *L.Am.* pendejo m V

◆ **prick up** *v/t: prick up one's ears* of dog aguzar las orejas; *of person* prestar atención

prick·le ['prɪkl] *on plant* espina f

prick·ly ['prɪklɪ] *adj beard, plant* que pincha; *(irritable)* irritable

pride [praɪd] **1** *n in person, achievement* orgullo m; *(self-respect)* amor m propio **2** *v/t: pride o.s. on* enorgullecerse de

priest [priːst] sacerdote m; *(parish priest)* cura m

pri·ma·ri·ly [praɪ'merɪlɪ] *adv* principalmente

pri·ma·ry ['praɪmərɪ] **1** *adj* principal **2** *n* POL elecciones fpl primarias

prime [praɪm] **1** *n: be in one's prime* estar en la flor de la vida **2** *adj example, reason* primordial; *of prime importance* de suprema importancia

prime min·is·ter primer(a) ministro(-a) m(f)

prime time *n* TV horario m de mayor audiencia

prim·i·tive ['prɪmɪtɪv] *adj* primitivo

prince [prɪns] príncipe m

prin·cess [prɪn'ses] princesa f

prin·ci·pal ['prɪnsəpl] **1** *adj* principal **2** *n of school* director(a) m(f); *of university* rector(a) m(f)

prin·ci·pal·ly ['prɪnsəplɪ] *adv* principalmente

prin·ci·ple ['prɪnsəpl] principio m; *on principle* por principios; *in principle* en principio

print [prɪnt] **1** *n in book, newspaper etc* letra f; *(photograph)* grabado m; *out of print* agotado **2** *v/t* imprimir; *use block capitals* escribir en mayúsculas

◆ **print out** *v/t* imprimir

print·ed mat·ter ['prɪntɪd] impresos mpl

print·er ['prɪntər] *person* impresor(a) m(f); *machine* impresora f; *company* imprenta f

print·ing press ['prɪntɪŋpres] imprenta f

print·out copia f impresa

pri·or ['praɪər] **1** *adj* antes **2** *prep: prior to* antes de

pri·or·i·tize [praɪ'ɒrətaɪz] *v/t (put in order of priority)* ordenar atendiendo a las prioridades; *(give priority to)* dar prioridad a

pri·or·i·ty [praɪ'ɒrətɪ] prioridad f; *have priority* tener prioridad

pris·on ['prɪzn] prisión f, cárcel f

pris·on·er ['prɪznər] prisionero(-a) m(f); *take s.o. prisoner* hacer a alguien prisionero

pris·on·er of 'war prisionero(-a) m(f) de guerra

pri·va·cy ['prɪvəsɪ] intimidad f

pri·vate ['praɪvət] **1** *adj* privado **2** *n* MIL soldado m/f raso; *in private* en privado

P

pri·vate·ly ['praɪvətlɪ] adv (in private) en privado; with one other a solas; (inwardly) para sí; **privately owned** en manos privadas

'pri·vate sec·tor m privado

pri·va·tize ['praɪvətaɪz] v/t Br privatizar

priv·i·lege ['prɪvəlɪdʒ] (special treatment) privilegio m; (honor) honor m

priv·i·leged ['prɪvəlɪdʒd] adj privilegiado

prize [praɪz] 1 n premio m 2 v/t apreciar, valorar

prize·win·ner ['praɪzwɪnər] premiado(-a) m(f)

prize·win·ning ['praɪzwɪnɪŋ] adj premiado

pro¹ [proʊ] n: **the pros and cons** los pros y los contras

pro² [proʊ] → **professional**

pro³ [proʊ]: **be pro ...** (in favor of) estar a favor de; **the pro Clinton Democrats** los demócratas partidarios de Clinton

prob·a·bil·i·ty [prɑːbəˈbɪlətɪ] probabilidad f

prob·a·ble ['prɑːbəbl] adj probable

prob·a·bly ['prɑːbəblɪ] adv probablemente

pro·ba·tion [prəˈbeɪʃn] in job período m de prueba; LAW libertad f condicional; **be given probation** ser puesto en libertad condicional

pro·'ba·tion of·fi·cer oficial encargado de la vigilancia de los que están en libertad condicional

pro·'ba·tion pe·ri·od in job período m de prueba

probe [proʊb] 1 n (investigation) investigación f; scientific sonda f 2 v/t examinar; (investigate) investigar

prob·lem ['prɑːbləm] problema f; **no problem!** ¡claro!

pro·ce·dure [prəˈsiːdʒər] procedimiento m

pro·ceed [prəˈsiːd] v/i (go: of people) dirigirse; of work etc proseguir, avanzar; **proceed to do sth** pasar a hacer algo

pro·ceed·ings [prəˈsiːdɪŋz] npl (events) actos mpl

pro·ceeds ['proʊsiːdz] npl recaudación f

pro·cess ['prɑːses] 1 n proceso m; **in the process** (while doing it) al hacerlo 2 v/t food tratar; raw materials, data procesar; application tramitar

pro·ces·sion [prəˈseʃn] desfile m; religious procesión f

pro·claim [prəˈkleɪm] v/t declarar, proclamar

prod [prɑːd] 1 n empujoncito m 2 v/t (pret & pp **prodded**) dar un empujoncito a; **with elbow** dar un codazo a

prod·i·gy ['prɑːdɪdʒɪ]: (infant) **prodigy** niño(-a) m(f) prodigio

prod·uce¹ ['prɑːduːs] n productos mpl de campo

pro·duce² [prəˈduːs] v/t producir; (manufacture) fabricar; (bring out) sacar

pro·duc·er [prəˈduːsər] productor(a) m(f); (manufacturer) fabricante m/f

prod·uct ['prɑːdʌkt] producto m

pro·duc·tion [prəˈdʌkʃn] producción f

pro·'duc·tion ca·pac·i·ty capacidad f de producción

pro·'duc·tion costs npl costos mpl de producción

pro·duc·tive [prəˈdʌktɪv] adj productivo

pro·duc·tiv·i·ty [prɑːdʌkˈtɪvətɪ] productividad f

pro·fane [prəˈfeɪn] adj language profano

pro·fess [prəˈfes] v/t manifestar

pro·fes·sion [prəˈfeʃn] profesión f; **what's your profession?** ¿a qué se dedica?

pro·fes·sion·al [prəˈfeʃnl] 1 adj profesional; **turn professional** hacerse profesional 2 n profesional m/f

pro·fes·sion·al·ly [prəˈfeʃnlɪ] adv play sport profesionalmente; (well, skillfully) con profesionalidad

pro·fes·sor [prəˈfesər] catedrático(-a) m(f)

pro·fi·cien·cy [prəˈfɪʃnsɪ] competencia f

pro·fi·cient [prəˈfɪʃnt] competente; (skillful) hábil

pro·file ['proʊfaɪl] of face perfil m

prof·it ['prɑːfɪt] 1 n beneficio m 2 v/i: **profit by, profit from** beneficiarse de

prof·it·a·bil·i·ty [prɑːfɪtəˈbɪlətɪ] rentabilidad f

prof·it·a·ble ['prɑːfɪtəbl] adj rentable

'prof·it mar·gin margen m de beneficios

pro·found [prəˈfaʊnd] adj profundo

pro·found·ly [prəˈfaʊndlɪ] adv profundamente, enormemente; thank, apologize efusivamente

prog·no·sis [prɑːgˈnoʊsɪs] pronóstico m

pro·gram, Br pro·gramme ['proʊgræm] 1 n programa m 2 v/t (pret & pp **grammed**) COMPUT programar

pro·gram·mer ['proʊgræmər] COMPUT programador(a) m(f)

pro·gress 1 n ['proʊgres] progreso m; **make progress** hacer progresos; **in progress** en curso 2 v/i [prəˈgres] (advance in time) avanzar; (move on) pasar; (make progress) progresar; **how is the work progressing?** ¿cómo avanza el trabajo?

pro·gres·sive [prəˈgresɪv] adj (enlightened) progresista; (which progresses) progresivo

pro·gres·sive·ly [prə'gresɪvlɪ] *adv* progresivamente

pro·hib·it [prə'hɪbɪt] *v/t* prohibir

pro·hi·bi·tion [prouhɪ'bɪʃn] prohibición *f*; **during Prohibition** durante la ley seca

pro·hib·i·tive [prə'hɪbɪtɪv] *adj prices* prohibitivo

proj·ect¹ ['prɑːdʒekt] *n (plan, undertaking)* proyecto *m*; EDU trabajo *m*; *housing area* barriada *f* de viviendas sociales

pro·ject² [prə'dʒekt] **1** *v/t movie* proyectar; *figures, sales* calcular **2** *v/i (stick out)* sobresalir

pro·jec·tion [prə'dʒekʃn] *(forecast)* previsión *f*

pro·jec·tor [prə'dʒektər] *for slides* proyector *m*

pro·lif·ic [prə'lɪfɪk] *adj writer, artist* prolífico

pro·log, *Br* **pro·logue** ['prouloːg] prólogo *m*

pro·long [prə'lɔːŋ] *v/t* prolongar

prom [prɑːm] *(school dance)* baile de fin de curso

prom·i·nent ['prɑːmɪnənt] *adj nose, chin* prominente; *(significant)* destacado

prom·is·cu·i·ty [prɑːmɪ'skjuːətɪ] promiscuidad *f*

pro·mis·cu·ous [prə'mɪskjuəs] *adj* promiscuo

prom·ise ['prɑːmɪs] **1** *n* promesa *f* **2** *v/t* prometer; *she promised to help* prometió ayudar; *promise sth to s.o.* prometer algo a alguien **3** *v/i*: *do you promise?* ¿lo prometes?

prom·is·ing ['prɑːmɪsɪŋ] *adj* prometedor

pro·mote [prə'mout] *v/t employee* ascender; *(encourage, foster)* promover; COM promocionar

pro·mot·er [prə'moutər] *of sports event* promotor(a) *m(f)*

pro·mo·tion [prə'mouʃn] *of employee* ascenso *m*; *of scheme, idea*, COM promoción *f*

prompt [prɑːmpt] **1** *adj (on time)* puntual; *(speedy)* rápido **2** *adv*: *at two o'clock prompt* a las dos en punto **3** *v/t (cause)* provocar; *actor* apuntar **4** *n* COMPUT mensaje *m*; *go to the c prompt* ir a c:\

prompt·ly ['prɑːmptlɪ] *adv (on time)* puntualmente; *(immediately)* inmediatamente

prone [proun] *adj*: *be prone to* ser propenso a

pro·noun ['prounaun] pronombre *m*

pro·nounce [prə'nauns] *v/t word* pronunciar; *(declare)* declarar

pro·nounced [prə'naunst] *adj accent* marcado; *views* fuerte

pron·to ['prɑːntou] *adv* F ya, en seguida

pro·nun·ci·a·tion [prənʌnsɪ'eɪʃn] pronunciación *f*

proof [pruːf] *n* prueba(s) *f(pl)*; *of book* prueba *f*

prop [prɑːp] **1** *v/t (pret & pp propped)* apoyar **2** *n* THEA accesorio *m*
◆ **prop up** *v/t* apoyar

prop·a·gan·da [prɑːpə'gændə] propaganda *f*

pro·pel [prə'pel] *v/t (pret & pp propelled)* propulsar

pro·pel·lant [prə'pelənt] *in aerosol* propelente *m*

pro·pel·ler [prə'pelər] *of boat* hélice *f*

prop·er ['prɑːpər] *adj (real)* de verdad; *(fitting)* adecuado; *it's not proper* no está bien; *put it back in its proper place* vuelve a ponerlo en su sitio

prop·er·ly ['prɑːpərlɪ] *adv (correctly)* bien; *(fittingly)* adecuadamente

prop·er·ty ['prɑːpərtɪ] propiedad *f*; *(land)* propiedad(es) *f(pl)*

prop·er·ty de·vel·op·er promotor(a) *m(f)* inmobiliario(a)

proph·e·cy ['prɑːfəsɪ] profecía *f*

proph·e·sy ['prɑːfəsaɪ] *v/t (pret & pp prophesied)* profetizar

pro·por·tion [prə'pɔːrʃn] proporción *f*; *a large proportion of North Americans* gran parte de los norteamericanos; *proportions (dimensions)* proporciones *fpl*

pro·por·tion·al [prə'pɔːrʃnl] *adj* proporcional

pro·por·tion·al rep·re·sen·ta·tion POL representación *f* proporcional

pro·pos·al [prə'pouzl] *(suggestion)* propuesta *f*; *of marriage* proposición *f*

pro·pose [prə'pouz] **1** *v/t (suggest)* sugerir, proponer; *(plan)* proponerse **2** *v/i (make offer of marriage)* pedir la mano

prop·o·si·tion [prɑːpə'zɪʃn] **1** *n* propuesta *f* **2** *v/t woman* hacer proposiciones a

pro·pri·e·tor [prə'praɪətər] propietario(-a) *m(f)*

pro·pri·e·tress [prə'praɪətrɪs] propietaria *f*

prose [prouz] prosa *f*

pros·e·cute ['prɑːsɪkjuːt] *v/t* LAW procesar

pros·e·cu·tion [prɑːsɪ'kjuːʃn] LAW procesamiento *m*; *lawyers* acusación *f*; *he's facing prosecution* lo van a procesar

pros·e·cu·tor → *public prosecutor* fiscal *m/f*

pros·pect ['prɑːspekt] **1** *n (chance, likelihood)* probabilidad *f*; *(thought of something in the future)* perspectiva *f*; *prospects* perspectivas *fpl* (de futuro)

P

2 v/i: *prospect for* gold buscar
pro·spec·tive [prə'spektıv] adj potencial
pros·per ['praːspər] v/i prosperar
pros·per·i·ty [praː'sperətı] prosperidad f
pros·per·ous ['praːspərəs] adj próspero
pros·ti·tute ['praːstıtuːt] n prostituta f;
male prostitute prostituto m
pros·ti·tu·tion [praːstı'tuːʃn] prostitución f
pros·trate ['praːstreıt] adj postrado; *be prostrate with grief* postrado por el dolor
pro·tect [prə'tekt] v/t proteger
pro·tec·tion [prə'tekʃn] protección f
pro·tec·tion mon·ey dinero pagado a delincuentes a cambio de obtener protección; *paid to terrorists* impuesto m revolucionario
pro·tec·tive [prə'tektıv] adj protector
pro·tec·tive 'cloth·ing ropa f protectora
pro·tec·tor [prə'tektər] protector(a) m(f)
pro·tein ['proutiːn] proteína f
pro·test **1** n ['proutest] protesta f **2** v/i [prə'test] protestar, quejarse de; *(object to)* protestar contra **3** v/i [prə'test] protestar
Prot·es·tant ['praːtıstənt] **1** n protestante m/f **2** adj protestante
pro·test·er [prə'testər] manifestante m/f
pro·to·col ['proutəkaːl] protocolo m
pro·to·type ['proutətaıp] prototipo m
pro·tract·ed [prə'træktıd] adj prolongado, largo
pro·trude [prə'truːd] v/i sobresalir
pro·trud·ing [prə'truːdıŋ] adj saliente; *ears, teeth* prominente
proud [praud] adj orgulloso; *be proud of* estar orgulloso de
proud·ly ['praudlı] adv con orgullo, orgullosamente
prove [pruːv] v/t demostrar, probar
prov·erb ['praːvɜːrb] proverbio m, refrán m
pro·vide [prə'vaıd] v/t proporcionar; *provide sth to s.o., provide s.o. with sth* proporcionar algo a alguien; *provided (that) (on condition that)* con la condición de que, siempre que
♦ **provide for** v/t family mantener; *of law etc* prever
prov·ince ['praːvıns] provincia f
pro·vin·cial [prə'vınʃl] adj city provincial; *pej: attitude* de pueblo, provinciano
pro·vi·sion [prə'vıʒn] *(supply)* suministro m; *of law, contract* disposición f
pro·vi·sion·al [prə'vıʒnl] adj provisional
pro·vi·so [prə'vaızou] condición f
prov·o·ca·tion [praːvə'keıʃn] provocación f

pro·voc·a·tive [prə'vaːkətıv] adj provocador; *sexually* provocativo
pro·voke [prə'vouk] v/t *(cause, annoy)* provocar
prow [prau] NAUT proa f
prow·ess ['prauıs] proezas fpl
prowl [praul] v/i of tiger, burglar merodear
prowl·er ['praulər] merodeador(a) m(f)
prox·im·i·ty [praːk'sımətı] proximidad f
prox·y ['praːksı] *(authority)* poder m; *person* apoderado(-a) m(f)
prude [pruːd] mojigato(-a) m(f)
pru·dence ['pruːdns] prudencia f
pru·dent ['pruːdnt] adj prudente
prud·ish ['pruːdıʃ] adj mojigato
prune¹ [pruːn] n ciruela f pasa
prune² [pruːn] v/t plant podar; fig reducir
pry [praı] v/i (pret & pp pried) entrometerse
♦ **pry into** v/t entrometerse en
PS ['piːes] abbr (= *postscript*) PD (= posdata f)
pseu·do·nym ['suːdənım] pseudónimo m
psy·chi·at·ric [saıkı'ætrık] adj psiquiátrico
psy·chi·a·trist [saı'kaıətrıst] psiquiatra m/f
psy·chi·a·try [saı'kaıətrı] psiquiatría f
psy·chic ['saıkık] adj research paranormal; *I'm not psychic* no soy vidente
psy·cho·a·nal·y·sis [saıkouən'æləsıs] psicoanálisis m
psy·cho·an·a·lyst [saıkou'ænəlıst] psicoanalista m/f
psy·cho·an·a·lyze [saıkou'ænəlaız] v/t psicoanalizar
psy·cho·log·i·cal [saıkə'laːdʒıkl] adj psicológico
psy·cho·log·i·cal·ly [saıkə'laːdʒıklı] adv psicológicamente
psy·chol·o·gist [saı'kaːlədʒıst] psicólogo(-a) m(f)
psy·chol·o·gy [saı'kaːlədʒı] psicología f
psy·cho·path ['saıkoupæθ] psicópata m/f
psy·cho·so·mat·ic [saıkousə'mætık] adj psicosomático
PTO [piːtiː'ou] abbr (= *please turn over*) véase al dorso
pub [pʌb] Br bar m
pu·ber·ty ['pjuːbərtı] pubertad f
pu·bic hair ['pjuːbık] vello m púbico
pub·lic ['pʌblık] **1** adj público **2** n: *the public* el público; *in public* en público
pub·li·ca·tion [pʌblı'keıʃn] publicación f
pub·lic 'hol·i·day día m festivo
pub·lic·i·ty [pʌb'lısətı] publicidad f
pub·li·cize ['pʌblısaız] v/t *(make known)* publicar, hacer público; COM dar publici-

dad a

pub·lic 'li·bra·ry biblioteca f pública
pub·lic·ly ['pʌblɪklɪ] adv públicamente
pub·lic 'pros·e·cu·tor fiscal m/f
pub·lic re'la·tions npl relaciones públicas fpl
'pub·lic school Br colegio m privado, Am colegio m público
'pub·lic sec·tor sector m público
pub·lish ['pʌblɪʃ] v/t publicar
pub·lish·er ['pʌblɪʃər] person editor(a) m(f); company editorial f
pub·lish·ing ['pʌblɪʃɪŋ] industria f editorial
'pub·lish·ing com·pa·ny editorial f
pud·ding ['pʊdɪŋ] Br dish pudín m; part of meal postre m
pud·dle ['pʌdl] charco m
Puer·to Ri·can [pwertoʊ'ri:kən] 1 adj portorriqueño, puertorriqueño 2 n portorriqueño(-a) m(f), puertorriqueño(-a) m(f)
Puer·to Ri·co [pwertoʊ'ri:koʊ] n Puerto Rico
puff [pʌf] 1 n of wind racha f; from cigarette calada f; of smoke bocanada f 2 v/i (pant) resoplar; **puff on a cigarette** dar una calada a un cigarrillo
puff·y ['pʌfɪ] adj eyes, face hinchado
puke [pjuːk] 1 n P substance vomitona f P 2 v/i P echar la pota P
pull [pʊl] 1 n on rope tirón m; F (appeal) gancho m F; F (influence) enchufe m F 2 v/t (drag) arrastrar; (tug) tirar de; tooth sacar; **pull a muscle** sufrir un tirón en un músculo 3 v/i tirar
◆ **pull ahead** v/i in race, competition adelantarse
◆ **pull apart** v/t (separate) separar
◆ **pull away** v/t apartar
◆ **pull down** v/t (lower) bajar; (demolish) derribar
◆ **pull in** v/i of bus, train llegar
◆ **pull off** v/t quitar; item of clothing quitarse; F conseguir
◆ **pull out 1** v/t sacar; troops retirar; 2 v/i of an agreement, of troops retirarse; of ship salir
◆ **pull over** v/i parar en el arcén
◆ **pull through** v/i from an illness recuperarse
◆ **pull together 1** v/i (cooperate) cooperar 2 v/t: **pull o.s. together** tranquilizarse
◆ **pull up 1** v/t (raise) subir; item of clothing subirse; plant, weeds arrancar 2 v/i of car etc parar
pul·ley ['pʊlɪ] polea f
pull-o·ver ['pʊloʊvər] suéter m, Span jersey m

pulp [pʌlp] of fruit pulpa f; for paper-making pasta f
pul·pit ['pʊlpɪt] púlpito m
pul·sate [pʌl'seɪt] v/i of heart, blood palpitar; of music vibrar
pulse [pʌls] pulso m
pul·ver·ize ['pʌlvəraɪz] v/t pulverizar
pump [pʌmp] 1 n bomba f; (gas pump) surtidor m 2 v/t bombear
◆ **pump up** v/t inflar
pump·kin ['pʌmpkɪn] calabaza f
pun [pʌn] juego m de palabras
punch [pʌntʃ] 1 n (blow) puñetazo m; implement perforadora f 2 v/t with fist dar un puñetazo a; hole, ticket agujerear
'punch line última frase de un chiste
punc·tu·al ['pʌŋktʃʊəl] adj puntual
punc·tu·al·i·ty [pʌŋktʃʊ'ælətɪ] puntualidad f
punc·tu·al·ly ['pʌŋktʃʊəlɪ] adv puntualmente
punc·tu·ate ['pʌŋktʃʊeɪt] v/t puntuar
punc·tu·a·tion [pʌŋktʃʊ'eɪʃn] puntuación f
punc·tu·a·tion mark signo m de puntuación
punc·ture ['pʌŋktʃər] 1 n perforación f 2 v/t perforar
pun·gent ['pʌndʒənt] adj fuerte
pun·ish ['pʌnɪʃ] v/t person castigar
pun·ish·ing ['pʌnɪʃɪŋ] adj schedule exigente; pace fuerte
pun·ish·ment ['pʌnɪʃmənt] castigo m
punk (rock) ['pʌŋk(rɑːk)] MUS (música f) punk m
pu·ny ['pjuːnɪ] adj person enclenque
pup [pʌp] cachorro m
pu·pil¹ ['pjuːpl] of eye pupila f
pu·pil² ['pjuːpl] (student) alumno(-a) m(f)
pup·pet ['pʌpɪt] also fig marioneta f
'pup·pet gov·ern·ment gobierno m títere
pup·py ['pʌpɪ] cachorro m
pur·chase¹ ['pɜːrtʃəs] 1 n adquisición f, compra f 2 v/t adquirir, comprar
pur·chase² ['pɜːrtʃəs] (grip) agarre m
pur·chas·er ['pɜːrtʃəsər] comprador(a) m(f)
pure [pjʊr] adj puro; **pure new wool** pura lana f virgen
pure·ly ['pjʊrlɪ] adv puramente
pur·ga·to·ry ['pɜːrgətɔːrɪ] purgatorio m
purge [pɜːrdʒ] 1 n of political party purga f 2 v/t purgar
pu·ri·fy ['pjʊrɪfaɪ] v/t (pret & pp **purified**) water depurar
pu·ri·tan ['pjʊrɪtən] puritano(-a) m(f)
pu·ri·tan·i·cal [pjʊrɪ'tænɪkl] adj puritano
pu·ri·ty ['pjʊrɪtɪ] pureza f

P

pur·ple ['pɜːrpl] *adj* morado

Pur·ple 'Heart MIL *medalla concedida a los soldados heridos en combate*

pur·pose ['pɜːrpəs] (*aim, object*) propósito *m*, objeto *m*; **on purpose** a propósito; **what is the purpose of your visit?** ¿cuál es el objeto de su visita?

pur·pose·ful ['pɜːrpəsfəl] *adj* decidido

pur·pose·ly ['pɜːrpəsli] *adv* decididamente

purr [pɜːr] *v/i of cat* ronronear

purse [pɜːrs] *n* (*pocket book*) bolso *m*; *Br: for money* monedero *m*

pur·sue [pər'suː] *v/t person* perseguir; *career* ejercer; *course of action* proseguir

pur·su·er [pər'suːər] perseguidor(a) *m(f)*

pur·suit [pər'suːt] (*chase*) persecución *f*; *of happiness* búsqueda *f*; (*activity*) actividad *f*; **those in pursuit** los perseguidores

pus [pʌs] pus *m*

push [pʊʃ] **1** *n* (*shove*) empujón *m*; **at the push of a button** apretando un botón **2** *v/t* (*shove*) empujar; *button* apretar, pulsar; (*pressurize*) presionar; F *drugs* pasar F, mercadear con; **be pushed for cash** F estar pelado F, estar sin un centavo; **be pushed for time** F ir mal de tiempo F; **be pushing 40** F rondar los 40 **3** *v/i* empujar

◆ **push ahead** *v/i* seguir adelante

◆ **push along** *v/t cart etc* empujar

◆ **push away** *v/t* apartar

◆ **push off 1** *v/t lid* destapar; **2** *v/i Br* F (*leave*) largarse F

◆ **push on** *v/i* (*continue*) continuar

◆ **push up** *v/t prices* hacer subir

push·er ['pʊʃər] F *of drugs* camello *m* F

push-up ['pʊʃʌp] flexión *f* (de brazos)

push·y ['pʊʃi] *adj* F avasallador, agresivo

puss, pus·sy (cat) [pʊs, 'pʊsi (kæt)] F minino *m* F

◆ **pussy foot about** ['pʊsifʊt] *v/i* F andarse con rodeos

put [pʊt] *v/t* (*pret & pp put*) poner; *question* hacer; **put the cost at …** estimar el costo en …

◆ **put across** *v/t idea etc* hacer llegar

◆ **put aside** *v/t money* apartar, ahorrar; *work* dejar a un lado

◆ **put away** *v/t in closet etc* guardar; *in institution* encerrar; F (*consume*) consumir, cepillarse F; *money* apartar, ahorrar;

animal sacrificar

◆ **put back** *v/t* (*replace*) volver a poner

◆ **put by** *v/t money* apartar, ahorrar

◆ **put down** *v/t* dejar; *deposit* entregar; *rebellion* reprimir; (*belittle*) dejar en mal lugar; **put down in writing** poner por escrito; **put one's foot down** *in car* apretar el acelerador; (*be firm*) plantarse; **put sth down to sth** (*attribute*) atribuir algo a algo

◆ **put forward** *v/t idea etc* proponer, presentar

◆ **put in** *v/t* meter; *time* dedicar; *request, claim* presentar

◆ **put in for** *v/t* (*apply for*) solicitar

◆ **put off** *v/t light, radio, TV* apagar; (*postpone*) posponer, aplazar; (*deter*) desalentar; (*repel*) desagradar; **I was put off by the smell** el olor me quitó las ganas; **that put me off shellfish for life** me quitó las ganas de volver a comer marisco

◆ **put on** *v/t light, radio, TV* encender, *L.Am.* prender; *tape, music* poner; *jacket, shoes, eye glasses* ponerse; (*perform*) representar; (*assume*) fingir; **put on make-up** maquillarse; **put on the brake** frenar; **put on weight** engordar; **she's just putting it on** está fingiendo

◆ **put out** *v/t hand* extender; *fire, light* apagar

◆ **put through** *v/t:* **put s.o. through to s.o.** *on phone* poner a alguien con alguien

◆ **put together** *v/t* (*assemble, organize*) montar

◆ **put up** *v/t hand* levantar; *person* alojar; (*erect*) levantar; *prices* subir; *poster, notice* colocar; *money* aportar; **put your hands up!** ¡arriba las manos!; **put up for sale** poner en venta

◆ **put up with** *v/t* (*tolerate*) aguantar

putt [pʌt] *v/i* SP golpear con el putter

put·ty ['pʌti] masilla *f*

puz·zle ['pʌzl] **1** *n* (*mystery*) enigma *m*; *game* pasatiempos *mpl*; (*jigsaw puzzle*) puzzle *m*; (*crossword puzzle*) crucigrama *m* **2** *v/t* desconcertar; **one thing puzzles me** hay algo que no acabo de entender

puz·zling ['pʌzlɪŋ] *adj* desconcertante

PVC [piːviːˈsiː] *abbr* (= *polyvinyl chloride*) PVC *m* (= cloruro *m* de polivinilo)

py·ja·mas *Br* → **pajamas**

py·lon ['paɪlən] torre *f* de alta tensión

Q

quack[1] [kwæk] **1** n of duck graznido m **2** v/i graznar

quack[2] [kwæk] n F (bad doctor) matasanos m/f inv F

quad·ran·gle ['kwɑːdræŋgl] figure cuadrángulo m; courtyard patio m

quad·ru·ped ['kwɑːdruped] cuadrúpedo m

quad·ru·ple ['kwɑːdrupl] v/i cuadruplicarse

quad·ru·plets ['kwɑːdruplɪts] npl cuatrillizos(-as) mpl (fpl)

quads [kwɑːdz] npl F cuatrillizos(-as) mpl f (fpl)

quag·mire ['kwɑːgmaɪr] fig atolladero m

quail [kweɪl] v/i temblar (at ante)

quaint [kweɪnt] adj cottage pintoresco; (slightly eccentric: ideas etc) extraño

quake [kweɪk] **1** n (earthquake) terremoto m **2** v/i of earth, with fear temblar

qual·i·fi·ca·tion [kwɑːlɪfɪ'keɪʃn] from university etc título m; **have the right qualifications for a job** estar bien cualificado para un trabajo

qual·i·fied ['kwɑːlɪfaɪd] adj doctor, engineer, plumber etc titulado; (restricted) limitado; **I am not qualified to judge** no estoy en condiciones de poder juzgar

qual·i·fy ['kwɑːlɪfaɪ] **1** v/t (pret & pp qualified) of degree, course etc habilitar; remark etc matizar **2** v/i (pret & pp qualified) (get degree etc) titularse, L.Am. egresar; in competition calificarse; **they qualified for the final** se clasificaron para la final; **that doesn't qualify as …** eso no cuenta como …

qual·i·ty ['kwɑːlətɪ] calidad f; (characteristic) cualidad f

qual·i·ty con'trol control m de calidad

qualm [kwɑːm] **have no qualms about …** no tener reparos en …

quan·da·ry ['kwɑːndərɪ] dilema m

quan·ti·fy ['kwɑːntɪfaɪ] v/t (pret & pp quantified) cuantificar

quan·ti·ty ['kwɑːntətɪ] cantidad f

quan·tum 'phys·ics ['kwɑːntəm] física f cuántica

quar·an·tine ['kwɑːrəntiːn] cuarentena f

quar·rel ['kwɑːrəl] **1** n pelea f **2** v/i (pret & pp quarreled, Br quarrelled) pelearse

quar·rel·some ['kwɑːrəlsʌm] adj peleón

quar·ry[1] ['kwɑːrɪ] in hunt presa f

quar·ry[2] ['kwɑːrɪ] for mining cantera f

quart [kwɔːrt] cuarto m de galón

quar·ter ['kwɔːrtər] cuarto m; **25 cents** cuarto m de dólar; part of town barrio m; **a quarter of an hour** un cuarto de hora; **a quarter of 5** las cinco menos cuarto; **a quarter after 5** las cinco y cuarto

'quar·ter·back SP quarterback m, en fútbol americano, jugador que dirige el juego de ataque

quar·ter·'fi·nal cuarto m de final

quar·ter·'fi·nal·ist cuartofinalista m/f

quar·ter·ly ['kwɔːrtəlɪ] **1** adj trimestral **2** adv trimestralmente

'quar·ter·note MUS negra f

quar·ters ['kwɔːrtəz] npl MIL alojamiento m

quar·tet [kwɔːr'tet] MUS cuarteto m

quartz [kwɔːrts] cuarzo m

quash [kwɑːʃ] v/t rebellion aplastar, sofocar; court decision revocar

qua·ver ['kweɪvər] **1** n in voice temblor m **2** v/i of voice temblar

quay [kiː] muelle m

'quay·side muelle m

quea·sy ['kwiːzɪ] adj mareado; **get queasy** marearse

queen [kwiːn] reina f

queen 'bee abeja f reina

queer [kwɪr] adj (peculiar) raro, extraño

queer·ly ['kwɪrlɪ] adv de manera extraña

quell [kwel] v/t protest, crowd acallar; riot aplastar, sofocar

quench [kwentʃ] v/t thirst apagar, saciar; flames apagar

que·ry ['kwɪrɪ] **1** n duda f, pregunta f **2** v/t (pret & pp queried) (express doubt about) cuestionar; (check) comprobar; **query sth with s.o.** preguntar algo a alguien

quest [kwest] busca f

ques·tion ['kwestʃn] **1** n pregunta f; (matter) cuestión f, asunto m; **in question** (being talked about) en cuestión; (in doubt) en duda; **it's a question of money/time** es una cuestión de dinero/tiempo; **that's out of the question** eso es imposible **2** v/t person preguntar a; LAW interrogar; (doubt) cuestionar, poner en duda

ques·tion·a·ble ['kwestʃnəbl] adj cuestionable, dudoso

ques·tion·ing ['kwestʃnɪŋ] **1** adj look, tone inquisitivo **2** n interrogatorio m

'ques·tion mark signo m de interrogación

ques·tion·naire [kwestʃəˈner] cuestionario *m*

queue [kjuː] *n Br* cola *f*

quib·ble [ˈkwɪbl] *v/i* discutir (*por algo insignificante*)

quick [kwɪk] *adj* rápido; *be quick!* ¡date prisa!; *let's have a quick drink* vamos a tomarnos algo rápidamente; *can I have a quick look?* ¿me dejas echarle un vistazo?; *that was quick!* ¡qué rápido!

quick·ie [ˈkwɪkɪ]: *have a quickie* F (*quick drink*) tomarse una copa rápida

quick·ly [ˈkwɪklɪ] *adv* rápidamente, rápido, deprisa

'quick·sand arenas *fpl* movedizas

'quick·sil·ver azogue *m*

quick·wit·ted [kwɪkˈwɪtɪd] *adj* agudo

qui·et [ˈkwaɪət] *adj* tranquilo; *engine* silencioso; *keep quiet about sth* guardar silencio sobre algo; *quiet!* ¡silencio!

◆ **qui·et·en down** [ˈkwaɪətn] **1** *v/t children, class* tranquilizar, hacer callar **2** *v/i of children* tranquilizarse, callarse; *of political situation* calmarse

quiet·ly [ˈkwaɪətlɪ] *adv* (*not loudly*) silenciosamente; (*without fuss*) discretamente; (*peacefully*) tranquilamente; *speak quietly* hablar en voz baja

quiet·ness [ˈkwaɪətnɪs] *n of voice* suavidad *f*; *of night, street* silencio *m*, calma *f*

quilt [kwɪlt] *on bed* edredón *m*

quilt·ed [ˈkwɪltɪd] *adj* acolchado

quin·ine [ˈkwɪniːn] quinina *f*

quin·tet [kwɪnˈtet] MUS quinteto *m*

quip [kwɪp] **1** *n joke* broma *f*; *remark* salida *f* **2** *v/i* (*pret & pp quipped*) bromear

quirk [kwɜːrk] peculiaridad *f*, rareza *f*

quirk·y [ˈkwɜːrkɪ] *adj* peculiar, raro

quit [kwɪt] **1** *v/t* (*pret & pp quit*) *job* dejar, abandonar; *quit doing sth* dejar de hacer algo **2** *v/i* (*pret & pp quit*) (*leave job*) dimitir; COMPUT salir; *get one's notice to quit* from landlord recibir la notificación de desalojo

quite [kwaɪt] *adv* (*fairly*) bastante; (*completely*) completamente; *not quite ready* no listo del todo; *I didn't quite understand* no entendí bien; *is that right?* - *not quite* ¿es verdad? - no exactamente; *quite!* ¡exactamente!; *quite a lot* bastante; *quite a few* bastantes; *it was quite a surprise / change* fue toda una sorpresa / un cambio

quits [kwɪts] *adj*: *be quits with s.o.* estar en paz con alguien

quit·ter [ˈkwɪtər] F *persona que abandona fácilmente*

quiv·er [ˈkwɪvər] *v/i* estremecerse

quiz [kwɪz] **1** *n* concurso *m* (*de preguntas y respuestas*) **2** *v/t* (*pret & pp quizzed*) interrogar (*about* sobre)

'quiz mas·ter presentador de un concurso de preguntas y respuestas

'quiz pro·gram, *Br* **'quiz pro·gramme** programa *m* concurso (*de preguntas y respuestas*)

quo·ta [ˈkwoʊtə] cuota *f*

quo·ta·tion [kwoʊˈteɪʃn] *from author* cita *f*; (*price*) presupuesto *m*

quo'ta·tion marks *npl* comillas *fpl*

quote [kwoʊt] **1** *n from author* cita *f*; (*price*) presupuesto *m*; (*quotation mark*) comilla *f*; *in quotes* entre comillas **2** *v/t text* citar; *price* dar **3** *v/i*: *quote from an author* citar de un autor

R

rab·bi [ˈræbaɪ] rabino *m*

rab·bit [ˈræbɪt] conejo *m*

rab·ble [ˈræbl] chusma *f*, multitud *f*

rab·ble-rous·er [ˈræblraʊzər] agitador(a) *m(f)*

ra·bies [ˈreɪbiːz] *nsg* rabia *f*

rac·coon [rəˈkuːn] mapache *m*

race¹ [reɪs] *n of people* raza *f*

race² [reɪs] **1** *n* SP carrera *f*; *the races* horse races las carreras **2** *v/i* (*run fast*) correr; *he raced through his meal / work* acabó su comida / trabajo a toda velocidad **3** *v/t* correr contra; *I'll race you* te echo una carrera

'race·course hipódromo *m*

'race·horse caballo *m* de carreras

race riot disturbios *mpl* raciales

'race·track circuito *m*; *for horses* hipódromo *m*

ra·cial [ˈreɪʃl] *adj* racial; *racial equality* igualdad *f* racial

rac·ing [ˈreɪsɪŋ] carreras *fpl*

rac·ism ['reɪsɪzm] racismo *m*

ra·cist ['reɪsɪst] **1** *n* racista *m/f* **2** *adj* racista

rack [ræk] **1** *n* (*for bikes*) barras para aparcar bicicletas; *for bags on train* portaequipajes *m inv*; *for CDs* mueble *m* **2** *v/t*: **rack one's brains** devanarse los sesos

rack·et[1] ['rækɪt] SP raqueta *f*

rack·et[2] ['rækɪt] (*noise*) jaleo *m*; (*criminal activity*) negocio *m* sucio

ra·dar ['reɪdɑːr] radar *m*

'ra·dar screen pantalla *f* de radar

'ra·dar trap control *m* de velocidad por radar

ra·di·al 'tire. *Br* **ra·di·al 'tyre** ['reɪdɪəl] neumático *m* radial

ra·di·ance ['reɪdɪəns] esplendor *m*, brillantez *f*

ra·di·ant ['reɪdɪənt] *adj smile, appearance* resplandeciente, brillante

ra·di·ate ['reɪdɪeɪt] *v/i of heat, light* irradiar

ra·di·a·tion [reɪdɪ'eɪʃn] PHYS radiación *f*

ra·di·a·tor ['reɪdɪeɪtər] *in room, car* radiador *m*

rad·i·cal ['rædɪkl] **1** *adj* radical **2** *n* POL radical *m/f*

rad·i·cal·ism ['rædɪkəlɪzm] POL radicalismo *m*

rad·i·cal·ly ['rædɪklɪ] *adv* radicalmente

ra·di·o ['reɪdɪoʊ] radio *f*; **on the radio** en la radio; **by radio** por radio

ra·di·o·ac·tive [reɪdɪoʊ'æktɪv] *adj* radiactivo

ra·di·o·ac·tive 'waste residuos *mpl* radiactivos

ra·di·o·ac·tiv·i·ty [reɪdɪoʊæk'tɪvətɪ] radiactividad *f*

ra·di·o a'larm radio *f* despertador

ra·di·og·ra·pher [reɪdɪ'ɑːgrəfər] técnico(-a) *m(f)* de rayos X

ra·di·og·ra·phy [reɪdɪ'ɑːgrəfɪ] radiografía *f*

'ra·di·o sta·tion emisora *f* de radio

'ra·di·o tax·i radiotaxi *m*

ra·di·o'ther·a·py radioterapia *f*

rad·ish ['rædɪʃ] rábano *m*

ra·di·us ['reɪdɪəs] radio *m*

raf·fle ['ræfl] *n* rifa *f*

raft [ræft] balsa *f*

raf·ter ['ræftər] viga *f*

rag [ræg] *n for cleaning etc* trapo *m*; **in rags** con harapos

rage [reɪdʒ] **1** *n* ira *f*, cólera *f*; **be in a rage** estar encolerizado; **be all the rage** F estar arrasando F **2** *v/i of storm* bramar

rag·ged ['rægɪd] *adj* andrajoso

raid [reɪd] **1** *n by troops* incursión *f*; *by police* redada *f*; *by robbers* atraco *m*; FIN ataque *m*, incursión *f* **2** *v/t of troops* realizar una incursión en; *of police* realizar una redada en; *of robbers* atracar; *fridge, orchard* saquear

raid·er ['reɪdər] *on bank etc* atracador(a) *m(f)*

rail [reɪl] *n on track* riel *m*, carril *m*; (*handrail*) pasamanos *m inv*, baranda *f*; *for towel* barra *f*; **by rail** en tren

rail·ings ['reɪlɪŋz] *npl around park etc* verja *f*

rail·road ['reɪlroʊd] ferrocarril *m*

'rail·road sta·tion estación *f* de ferrocarril *or* de tren

rail·way ['reɪlweɪ] *Br* ferrocarril *m*

rain [reɪn] **1** *n* lluvia *f*; **in the rain** bajo la lluvia **2** *v/i* llover; **it's raining** llueve

'rain·bow arco *m* iris

'rain·check: **can I take a raincheck on that?** F ¿lo podríamos aplazar para algún otro momento?

'rain·coat impermeable *m*

'rain·drop gota *f* de lluvia

'rain·fall pluviosidad *f*, precipitaciones *fpl*

'rain for·est selva *f*

'rain·proof *adj fabric* impermeable

'rain·storm tormenta *f*, aguacero *m*

rain·y ['reɪnɪ] *adj* lluvioso; **it's rainy** llueve mucho

'rain·y sea·son estación *f* de las lluvias

raise [reɪz] **1** *n in salary* aumento *m* de sueldo **2** *v/t shelf etc* levantar; *offer* incrementar; *children* criar; *question* plantear; *money* reunir

rai·sin ['reɪzn] pasa *f*

rake [reɪk] *n for garden* rastrillo *m*

♦ **rake up** *v/t leaves* rastrillar; *fig* sacar a la luz

ral·ly ['rælɪ] *n* (*meeting, reunion*) concentración *f*; *political* mitin *m*; MOT rally *m*; *in tennis* peloteo *m*

♦ **rally round** *v/i* (*pret & pp* **rallied**) acudir a ayudar **2** *v/t* (*pret & pp* **rallied**): **rally round s.o.** acudir a ayudar a alguien

ram [ræm] **1** *n* carnero *m* **2** *v/t* (*pret & pp* **rammed**) *ship, car* embestir

RAM [ræm] COMPUT *abbr* (= **random access memory**) RAM *f* (= memoria *f* de acceso aleatorio)

ram·ble ['ræmbl] **1** *n walk* caminata *f*, excursión *f* **2** *v/i walk* caminar; *in speaking* divagar; (*talk incoherently*) hablar sin decir nada coherente

ram·bler ['ræmblər] *walker* senderista *m/f*, excursionista *m/f*

ram·bling ['ræmblɪŋ] **1** *n walking* senderismo *m*; *in speech* divagaciones *fpl* **2** *adj speech* inconexo

R

ramp [ræmp] rampa *f; for raising vehicle* elevador *m*

ram·page ['ræmpeɪdʒ] **1** *v/i* pasar arrasando con todo **2** *n: go on the rampage* pasar arrasando con todo

ram·pant ['ræmpənt] *adj inflation* galopante

ram·part ['ræmpɑːrt] muralla *f*

ram·shack·le ['ræmʃækl] *adj* destartalado, desvencijado

ran [ræn] *pret* → **run**

ranch [ræntʃ] rancho *m*

ranch·er ['ræntʃər] ranchero(-a) *m(f)*

ran·cid ['rænsɪd] *adj* rancio

ran·cor ['ræŋkər] rencor *m*

R & D [ɑːrən'diː] *abbr* (= **research and development**) I+D *f* (= investigación *f* y desarrollo)

ran·dom ['rændəm] **1** *adj* al azar; *random sample* muestra *f* aleatoria **2** *n: at random* al azar

ran·dy ['rændɪ] *adj Br* F cachondo F; *it makes me randy* me pone cachondo

rang [ræŋ] *pret* → **ring²**

range [reɪndʒ] **1** *n of products* gama *f; of gun, airplane* alcance *m; of voice* registro *m; of mountains* cordillera *f; at close range* de cerca **2** *v/i: range from X to Y* ir desde X a Y

rang·er ['reɪndʒər] guardabosques *m/f inv*

rank [ræŋk] **1** *n* MIL, *in society* rango *m; the ranks* MIL la tropa **2** *v/t* clasificar
♦ **rank among** *v/t* figurar entre

ran·kle ['ræŋkl] *v/i* doler; *it still rankles (with him)* todavía lo duele

ran·sack ['rænsæk] *v/t* saquear

ran·som ['rænsəm] *n* rescate *m; hold s.o. to ransom* pedir un rescate por alguien

'**ran·som mon·ey** (dinero *m* del) rescate *m*

rant [rænt] *v/i: rant and rave* despotricar

rap [ræp] **1** *n at door etc* golpe *m;* MUS rap *m* **2** *v/t* (*pret & pp* **rapped**) *table etc* golpear
♦ **rap at** *v/t window etc* golpear

rape¹ [reɪp] **1** *n* violación *f* **2** *v/t* violar

rape² [reɪp] *n* BOT colza *f*

'**rape vic·tim** víctima *m/f* de una violación

rap·id ['ræpɪd] *adj* rápido

ra·pid·i·ty [rə'pɪdətɪ] rapidez *f*

rap·id·ly ['ræpɪdlɪ] *adv* rápidamente

rap·ids ['ræpɪdz] *npl* rápidos *mpl*

rap·ist ['reɪpɪst] violador(a) *m(f)*

rap·port [ræ'pɔːr] relación *f; we've got a good rapport* nos entendemos muy bien

rap·ture ['ræptʃər]: *go into raptures over* extasiarse con

rap·tur·ous ['ræptʃərəs] *adj* clamoroso

rare [rer] *adj* raro; *steak* poco hecho

rare·ly ['rerlɪ] *adv* raramente, raras veces

rar·i·ty ['rerətɪ] rareza *f*

ras·cal ['ræskl] pícaro(-a) *m(f)*

rash¹ [ræʃ] *n* MED sarpullido *m*, erupción *f* cutánea

rash² [ræʃ] *adj action, behavior* precipitado

rash·ly ['ræʃlɪ] *adv* precipitadamente

rasp·ber·ry ['ræzberɪ] frambuesa *f*

rat [ræt] *n* rata *f*

rate [reɪt] **1** *n of exchange* tipo *m; of pay* tarifa *f;* (*price*) tarifa *f*, precio *m;* (*speed*) ritmo *m; rate of interest* FIN tipo *m* de interés; *at this rate* (*at this speed*) a este ritmo; (*if we carry on like this*) si seguimos así; *at any rate* (*anyway*) en todo caso; (*at least*) por lo menos **2** *v/t: rate s.o. as ...* considerar a alguien (como) ...; *rate s.o. highly* tener buena opinión de alguien

rather ['ræðər] *adv* bastante; *I would rather stay here* preferiría quedarme aquí; *or would you rather ...?* ¿o preferiría ...?

rat·i·fi·ca·tion [rætɪfɪ'keɪʃn] ratificación *f*

rat·i·fy ['rætɪfaɪ] *v/t* (*pret & pp* **ratified**) ratificar

rat·ings ['reɪtɪŋz] *npl* índice *m* de audiencia

ra·ti·o ['reɪʃɪoʊ] proporción *f*

ra·tion ['ræʃn] **1** *n* ración *f* **2** *v/t supplies* racionar

ra·tion·al ['ræʃənl] *adj* racional

ra·tion·al·i·ty [ræʃə'nælɪtɪ] racionalidad *f*

ra·tion·al·i·za·tion [ræʃənəlaɪ'zeɪʃn] racionalización *f*

ra·tion·al·ize ['ræʃənəlaɪz] *v/t* racionalizar *v/i* buscar una explicación racional

ra·tion·al·ly ['ræʃənlɪ] *adv* racionalmente

'**rat race** la vida frenética y competitiva

rat·tle ['rætl] **1** *n noise* traqueteo *m*, golpeteo *m; toy* sonajero *m* **2** *v/t chains etc* entrechocar **3** *v/i of chains etc* entrechocarse; *of crates* traquetear
♦ **rattle off** *v/t poem, list of names* decir rápidamente
♦ **rattle through** *v/t* hacer rápidamente

'**rat·tle·snake** serpiente *f* de cascabel

rau·cous ['rɔːkəs] *adj laughter, party* estridente

rav·age ['rævɪdʒ] *n: the ravages of time* los estragos del tiempo **2** *v/t* arrasar; *ravaged by war* arrasado por la guerra

rave [reɪv] **1** *v/i* (*talk deliriously*) delirar; (*talk wildly*) desvariar; *rave about sth* (*be very enthusiastic*) estar muy entusiasmado con algo **2** *n party* fiesta *f* tecno

rave re'view crítica *f* muy entusiasta

ra·ven ['reɪvn] cuervo *m*

reassure

rav·e·nous ['rævənəs] *adj appetite* voraz; *have a ravenous appetite* tener un hambre canina

rav·e·nous·ly ['rævənəslɪ] *adv* con voracidad

ra·vine [rə'viːn] barranco *m*

rav·ing ['reɪvɪŋ] *adv: raving mad* chalado

rav·ish·ing ['rævɪʃɪŋ] *adj* encantador, cautivador

raw [rɔː] *adj meat, vegetable* crudo; *sugar* sin refinar; *iron* sin tratar

raw ma·te·ri·als *npl* materias *fpl* primas

ray [reɪ] rayo *m*; *a ray of hope* un rayo de esperanza

raze [reɪz] *v/t: raze to the ground* arrasar *or* asolar por completo

ra·zor ['reɪzər] maquinilla *f* de afeitar

'ra·zor blade cuchilla *f* de afeitar

re [riː] *prep* COM con referencia a

reach [riːtʃ] **1** *n: within reach* al alcance; *out of reach* fuera del alcance **2** *v/t* llegar a; *decision, agreement, conclusion* alcanzar, llegar a; *can you reach it?* ¿alcanzas?, ¿llegas?

◆ **reach out** *v/i* extender el brazo

re·act [rɪ'ækt] *v/i* reaccionar

re·ac·tion [rɪ'ækʃn] reacción *f*

re·ac·tion·ar·y [rɪ'ækʃnrɪ] **1** *n* POL reaccionario(-a) *m(f)* **2** *adj* POL reaccionario

re·ac·tor [rɪ'æktər] *nuclear* reactor *m*

read [riːd] **1** *v/t (pret & pp read* [red]) *also* COMPUT leer **2** *v/i (pret & pp read* [red]) leer; *read to s.o.* leer a alguien

◆ **read out** *v/t aloud* leer en voz alta

◆ **read up on** *v/t* leer mucho sobre, estudiar

rea·da·ble ['riːdəbl] *adj handwriting* legible; *book* ameno

read·er ['riːdər] *person* lector(a) *m(f)*

read·i·ly ['redɪlɪ] *adv admit, agree* de buena gana

read·i·ness ['redɪnɪs] *in a state of readiness* preparado para actuar; *their readiness to help* la facilidad con la que ayudaron

read·ing ['riːdɪŋ] *activity* lectura *f*; *take a reading from the meter* leer el contador

'read·ing mat·ter lectura *f*

re·ad·just [riːə'dʒʌst] **1** *v/t equipment, controls* reajustar **2** *v/i to conditions* volver a adaptarse

read-'on·ly file COMPUT archivo *m* sólo de lectura

read-'on·ly mem·o·ry COMPUT memoria *f* sólo de lectura

read·y ['redɪ] *adj (prepared)* listo, preparado; *(willing)* dispuesto; *get (o.s.) ready* prepararse; *get sth ready* preparar algo

read·y 'cash dinero *m* contante y sonante

read·y-made *adj stew etc* precocinado; *solution* ya hecho

read·y-to-wear *adj* de confección

real [riːl] *adj* real; *surprise, genius* auténtico; *he's a real idiot* es un auténtico idiota

'real es·tate bienes *mpl* inmuebles

'real es·tate a·gent agente *m/f* inmobiliario(-a)

re·al·ism ['rɪəlɪzəm] realismo *m*

re·a·list ['rɪəlɪst] realista *m/f*

re·a·lis·tic [rɪə'lɪstɪk] *adj* realista

re·a·lis·tic·al·ly [rɪə'lɪstɪklɪ] *adv* realísticamente

re·al·i·ty [rɪ'ælətɪ] realidad *f*

re·a·li·za·tion [rɪəlaɪ'zeɪʃn]: *the realization dawned on me that ...* me di cuenta de que ...

re·a·lize ['rɪəlaɪz] *v/t* darse cuenta de; FIN *(yield)* producir; *(sell)* realizar, liquidar; *I realize now that ...* ahora me doy cuenta de que ...

real·ly ['rɪəlɪ] *adv in truth* de verdad; *big, small* muy; *I am really really sorry* lo siento en el alma; *really?* ¿de verdad?; *not really* as reply la verdad es que no

real 'time *n* COMPUT tiempo *m* real

real-time *adj* COMPUT en tiempo real

re·al·tor ['rɪːltər] agente *m/f* inmobiliario(-a)

re·al·ty ['riːltɪ] bienes *mpl* inmuebles

reap [riːp] *v/t* cosechar

re·ap·pear [riːə'pɪr] *v/i* reaparecer

re·ap·pear·ance [riːə'pɪrəns] reaparición *f*

rear [rɪr] **1** *n* parte *f* de atrás *or* de atrás; *seats, wheels, lights* trasero

rear 'end **1** *n* F *of person* trasero *m* **2** *v/t* MOT F dar un golpe por atrás a

rear 'light *of car* luz *f* trasera

re·arm [riː'ɑːrm] **1** *v/t* rearmar **2** *v/i* rearmarse

'rear·most *adj* último

re·ar·range [riːə'reɪndʒ] *v/t flowers* volver a colocar; *furniture* reordenar; *schedule, meetings* cambiar

rear-view 'mir·ror espejo *m* retrovisor

rea·son ['riːzn] **1** *n faculty* razón *f*; *(cause)* razón *f*, motivo *m*; *see / listen to reason* atender a razones **2** *v/i: reason with s.o.* razonar con alguien

rea·so·na·ble ['riːznəbl] *adj person* razonable; *a reasonable number of people* un buen número de personas

rea·so·na·bly ['riːznəblɪ] *adv act, behave* razonablemente; *(quite)* bastante

rea·son·ing ['riːznɪŋ] razonamiento *m*

re·as·sure [riːə'ʃʊr] *v/t* tranquilizar; *she reassured us of her continued support* nos aseguró que continuábamos contan-

R

do con su apoyo

re·as·sur·ing [riːəˈʃʊrɪŋ] *adj* tranquilizador

re·bate [ˈriːbeɪt] *money back* reembolso *m*

reb·el[1] [ˈrebl] *n* rebelde *m/f*; ***rebel troops*** tropas *fpl* rebeldes

reb·el[2] [rɪˈbel] *v/i (pret & pp rebelled)* rebelarse

reb·el·lion [rɪˈbeljən] rebelión *f*

reb·el·lious [rɪˈbeljəs] *adj* rebelde

reb·el·lious·ly [rɪˈbeljəslɪ] *adv* con rebeldía

reb·el·lious·ness [rɪˈbeljəsnɪs] rebeldía *f*

re·bound [rɪˈbaʊnd] *v/i of ball etc* rebotar

re·buff [rɪˈbʌf] *n* desaire *m*, rechazo *m*

re·build [ˈriːbɪld] *v/t (pret & pp rebuilt)* reconstruir

re·buke [rɪˈbjuːk] *v/t* reprender

re·call [rɪˈkɔːl] *v/t goods* retirar del mercado; *(remember)* recordar

re·cap [ˈriːkæp] *v/i (pret & pp recapped)* recapitular

re·cap·ture [riːˈkæpʃər] *v/t* MIL reconquistar; *criminal* volver a detener

re·cede [rɪˈsiːd] *v/i of flood waters* retroceder

re·ced·ing [rɪˈsiːdɪŋ] *adj forehead, chin* hundido; ***have a receding hairline*** tener entradas

re·ceipt [rɪˈsiːt] *for purchase* recibo *m*; ***acknowledge receipt of sth*** acusar recibo de algo; ***receipts*** FIN ingresos *mpl*

re·ceive [rɪˈsiːv] *v/t* recibir

re·ceiv·er [rɪˈsiːvər] *of letter* destinatario(-a) *m(f)*; TELEC auricular *m*; *for radio* receptor *m*; *in tennis* jugador(a) *m(f)* al resto

re·ceiv·er·ship [rɪˈsiːvərʃɪp]: ***be in receivership*** estar en suspensión de pagos

re·cent [ˈriːsnt] *adj* reciente

re·cent·ly [ˈriːsntlɪ] *adv* recientemente

re·cep·tion [rɪˈsepʃn] recepción *f*; *(welcome)* recibimiento *m*

re·cep·tion desk recepción *f*

re·cep·tion·ist [rɪˈsepʃnɪst] recepcionista *m/f*

re·cep·tive [rɪˈseptɪv] *adj*: ***be receptive to sth*** ser receptivo a algo

re·cess [ˈriːses] *n in wall etc* hueco *m*; EDU recreo *m*; *of parliament* periodo *m* vacacional

re·ces·sion [rɪˈseʃn] *economic* recesión *f*

re·charge [riːˈtʃɑːrdʒ] *v/t battery* recargar

re·ci·pe [ˈresəpɪ] receta *f*

ˈre·ci·pe book libro *m* de cocina, recetario *m*

re·cip·i·ent [rɪˈsɪpɪənt] *of parcel etc* destinatario(-a) *m(f)*; *of payment* receptor(a)

m(f)

re·cip·ro·cal [rɪˈsɪprəkl] *adj* recíproco

re·cit·al [rɪˈsaɪtl] MUS recital *m*

re·cite [rɪˈsaɪt] *v/t poem* recitar; *details, facts* enumerar

reck·less [ˈreklɪs] *adj* imprudente; *driving* temerario

reck·less·ly [ˈreklɪslɪ] *adv* con imprudencia; *drive* con temeridad

reck·on [ˈrekən] *v/i (think, consider)* estimar, considerar; ***I reckon it won't happen*** creo que no va a pasar

♦ **reckon on** *v/t* contar con

♦ **reckon with** *v/t*: ***have s.o./sth to reckon with*** tener que vérselas con alguien / algo

reck·on·ing [ˈrekənɪŋ] estimaciones *fpl*, cálculos *mpl*; ***by my reckoning*** según mis cálculos

re·claim [rɪˈkleɪm] *v/t land from sea* ganar, recuperar; *lost property, rights* reclamar

re·cline [rɪˈklaɪn] *v/i* reclinarse

re·clin·er [rɪˈklaɪnər] *chair* sillón *m* reclinable

re·cluse [rɪˈkluːs] solitario(-a) *m(f)*

rec·og·ni·tion [rekəgˈnɪʃn] *of state, s.o.'s achievements* reconocimiento *m*; ***in recognition of*** en reconocimiento a; ***be changed beyond recognition*** estar irreconocible

rec·og·niz·a·ble [rekəgˈnaɪzəbl] *adj* reconocible

rec·og·nize [ˈrekəgnaɪz] *v/t* reconocer

re·coil [rɪˈkɔɪl] *v/i* echarse atrás, retroceder

rec·ol·lect [rekəˈlekt] *v/t* recordar

rec·ol·lec·tion [rekəˈlekʃn] recuerdo *m*; ***I have no recollection of the accident*** no me acuerdo del accidente

rec·om·mend [rekəˈmend] *v/t* recomendar

rec·om·men·da·tion [rekəmenˈdeɪʃn] recomendación *f*

rec·om·pense [ˈrekəmpens] *n* recompensa *f*

rec·on·cile [ˈrekənsaɪl] *v/t people* reconciliar; *differences, facts* conciliar; ***reconcile o.s. to ...*** hacerse a la idea de ...; ***be reconciled*** *of two people* haberse reconciliado

rec·on·cil·i·a·tion [rekənsɪlɪˈeɪʃn] *of people* reconciliación *f*; *of differences, facts* conciliación *f*

re·con·di·tion [riːkənˈdɪʃn] *v/t* reacondicionar

re·con·nais·sance [rɪˈkɑːnɪsns] MIL reconocimiento *m*

re·con·sid·er [riːkənˈsɪdər] **1** *v/t offer, one's position* reconsiderar **2** *v/i*: ***won't***

you please reconsider? ¿por qué no lo reconsideras, por favor?

re·con·struct [ri:kən'strʌkt] v/t reconstruir

rec·ord[1] ['rekɔːrd] n MUS disco m; SP etc récord m; written document etc registro m, documento m; in database registro m; **records** archivos mpl; **say sth off the record** decir algo oficiosamente; **have a criminal record** tener antecedentes penales; **have a good record for sth** tener un buen historial en materia de algo

re·cord[2] [rɪ'kɔːrd] v/t electronically grabar; in writing anotar

'rec·ord-break·ing adj récord

re·cor·der [rɪ'kɔːrdər] MUS flauta f dulce

'rec·ord hold·er plusmarquista m/f

re'cord·ing [rɪ'kɔːrdɪŋ] grabación f

re'cord·ing stu·di·o estudio m de grabación

'rec·ord play·er tocadiscos m inv

re·count [rɪ'kaʊnt] v/t (tell) relatar

re·count ['riːkaʊnt] 1 n of votes segundo recuento m 2 v/t (count again) volver a contar

re·coup [rɪ'kuːp] v/t financial losses resarcirse de

re·cov·er [rɪ'kʌvər] 1 v/t sth lost, stolen goods recuperar; composure recobrar 2 v/i from illness recuperarse

re·cov·er·y [rɪ'kʌvərɪ] recuperación f; **he has made a good recovery** se ha recuperado muy bien

rec·re·a·tion [rekrɪ'eɪʃn] ocio m

rec·re·a·tion·al [rekrɪ'eɪʃnl] adj done for pleasure recreativo

re·cruit [rɪ'kruːt] 1 n MIL recluta m/f; to company nuevo(-a) trabajador(a) 2 v/t new staff contratar

re·cruit·ment [rɪ'kruːtmənt] MIL reclutamiento m; to company contratación f

re'cruit·ment drive MIL campaña f de reclutamiento; to company campaña f de contratación

rec·tan·gle ['rektæŋgl] rectángulo m

rec·tan·gu·lar [rek'tæŋgjʊlər] adj rectangular

rec·ti·fy ['rektɪfaɪ] v/t (pret & pp **rectified**) rectificar

re·cu·pe·rate [rɪ'kuːpəreɪt] v/i recuperarse

re·cur [rɪ'kɜːr] v/i (pret & pp **recurred**) of error, event repetirse; of symptoms reaparecer

re·cur·rent [rɪ'kʌrənt] adj recurrente

re·cy·cla·ble [riː'saɪkləbl] adj reciclable

re·cy·cle [riː'saɪkl] v/t reciclar

re·cy·cling [riː'saɪklɪŋ] reciclado m

red [red] adj rojo; **in the red** FIN en números rojos

Red 'Cross Cruz f Roja

red·den ['redn] v/i (blush) ponerse colorado

re·dec·o·rate [riː'dekəreɪt] v/t with paint volver a pintar; with paper volver a empapelar

re·deem [rɪ'diːm] v/t debt amortizar; REL redimir

re·deem·ing feat·ure [rɪ'diːmɪŋ]: **his one redeeming feature is that ...** lo único que lo salva es que ...

re·demp·tion [rɪ'dempʃn] REL redención f

re·de·vel·op [riːdɪ'veləp] v/t part of town reedificar

red-hand·ed [red'hændɪd] adj: **catch s.o. red-handed** coger a alguien con las manos en la masa

'red·head pelirrojo(-a) m(f)

red-'hot adj al rojo vivo

red-'let·ter day día m señalado

red 'light at traffic light semáforo m (en) rojo

red 'light dis·trict zona f de prostitución

red 'meat carne f roja

'red·neck F individuo racista y reaccionario, normalmente de clase trabajadora

re·dou·ble [riː'dʌbl] v/t: **redouble one's efforts** redoblar los esfuerzos

red 'pep·per vegetable pimiento m rojo

red 'tape F burocracia f, papeleo m

re·duce [rɪ'duːs] v/t reducir; price rebajar

re·duc·tion [rɪ'dʌkʃn] reducción f; in price rebaja f

re·dun·dant [rɪ'dʌndənt] adj (unnecessary) innecesario; **be made redundant** Br at work ser despedido

reed [riːd] BOT junco m

reef [riːf] in sea arrecife m

'reef knot nudo m de rizos

reek [riːk] v/i apestar (**of** a)

reel [riːl] n of film rollo m; of thread carrete m

♦ reel off v/t soltar

♦ re·e·lect v/t reelegir

re·e·lec·tion reelección f

re·'en·try of spacecraft reentrada f

ref [ref] F árbitro(-a) m(f)

re·fer [rɪ'fɜːr] v/t (pret & pp **referred**): **refer a decision / problem to s.o.** remitir una decisión / un problema a alguien

♦ refer to v/t (allude to) referirse a; dictionary etc consultar

ref·er·ee [refə'riː] SP árbitro(-a) m(f); (for job) persona que pueda dar referencias

ref·er·ence ['refərəns] referencia f; **with reference to** con referencia a

'ref·er·ence book libro m de consulta

R

'**reference li·bra·ry** biblioteca f de consulta

'**ref·er·ence num·ber** número m de referencia

ref·e·ren·dum [refə'rendəm] referéndum m

re·fill ['ri:fɪl] v/t tank, glass volver a llenar

re·fine [rɪ'faɪn] v/t oil, sugar refinar; technique perfeccionar

re·fined [rɪ'faɪnd] adj manners, language refinado

re·fine·ment [rɪ'faɪnmənt] to process, machine mejora f

re·fin·e·ry [rɪ'faɪnərɪ] refinería f

re·fla·tion [rɪ'fleɪʃn] reflación f

reflect [rɪ'flekt] **1** v/t light reflejar; **be reflected in** reflejarse en **2** v/i (think) reflexionar

re·flec·tion [rɪ'flekʃn] in water, glass etc reflejo f; (consideration) reflexión f

re·flex ['ri:fleks] in body reflejo m

re·flex re'ac·tion acto m reflejo

re·form [rɪ'fɔ:rm] **1** n reforma f **2** v/t reformar

re·form·er [rɪ'fɔ:rmər] reformador(a) m(f)

re·frain[1] [rɪ'freɪn] v/i fml abstenerse; **please refrain from smoking** se ruega no fumar

re·frain[2] [rɪ'freɪn] n in song, poem estribillo m

re·fresh [rɪ'freʃ] v/t person refrescar; **feel refreshed** sentirse fresco

re·fresh·er course [rɪ'freʃər] curso m de actualización o reciclaje

re·fresh·ing [rɪ'freʃɪŋ] adj drink refrescante; experience reconfortante

re·fresh·ments [rɪ'freʃmənts] npl refrigerio m

re·fri·ge·rate [rɪ'frɪdʒəreɪt] v/t refrigerar; **keep refrigerated** conservar refrigerado

re·fri·ge·ra·tor [rɪ'frɪdʒəreɪtər] frigorífico m, refrigerador m

re·fu·el [ri:'fjuəl] **1** v/t airplane reabastecer de combustible a **2** v/i of airplane repostar

ref·uge ['refju:dʒ] refugio m; **take refuge from** storm etc refugiarse

ref·u·gee [refju'dʒi:] refugiado(-a) m(f)

ref·u'gee camp campo m de refugiados

re·fund ['ri:fʌnd] **1** n ['ri:fʌnd] reembolso m; **give s.o. a refund** devolver el dinero a alguien **2** v/t [rɪ'fʌnd] reembolsar

re·fus·al [rɪ'fju:zl] negativa f

re·fuse[1] [rɪ'fju:z] **1** v/i negarse **2** v/t help, food rechazar; **refuse s.o. sth** negar algo a alguien; **refuse to do sth** negarse a hacer algo

ref·use[2] ['refju:s] (garbage) basura f

'**ref·use col·lec·tion** recogida f de basuras

'**ref·use dump** vertedero m

re·gain [rɪ'geɪn] v/t recuperar

re·gal ['ri:gl] adj regio

re·gard [rɪ'gɑːrd] **1** n: **have great regard for s.o.** sentir gran estima por alguien; **in this regard** en este sentido; **with regard to** con respecto a; (**kind**) **regards** saludos; **give my regards to Paula** dale saludos o recuerdos a Paula de mi parte; **with no regard for** sin tener en cuenta **2** v/t: **regard s.o./sth as sth** considerar a alguien / algo como algo; **I regard it as an honor** para mí es un honor; **as regards** con respecto a

re·gard·ing [rɪ'gɑːrdɪŋ] prep con respecto a

re·gard·less [rɪ'gɑːrdlɪs] adv a pesar de todo; **regardless of** sin tener en cuenta

re·gime [reɪ'ʒiːm] (government) régimen m

re·gi·ment ['redʒɪmənt] n regimiento m

re·gion ['riːdʒən] región f; **in the region of** del orden de

re·gion·al ['riːdʒənl] adj regional

re·gis·ter ['redʒɪstər] **1** n registro m; at school lista f **2** v/t birth, death registrar; vehicle matricular; letter certificar; emotion mostrar; **send a letter registered** enviar una carta por correo certificado **3** v/i at university, for a course matricularse; with police registrarse

re·gis·tered let·ter ['redʒɪstərd] carta f certificada

re·gis·tra·tion [redʒɪ'streɪʃn] registro m; at university, for course matriculación f

re·gis'tra·tion num·ber Br MOT (número m de) matrícula f

re·gret [rɪ'gret] **1** v/t (pret & pp regretted) lamentar, sentir **2** n arrepentimiento m, pesar m

re·gret·ful [rɪ'gretfəl] adj arrepentido

re·gret·ful·ly [rɪ'gretfəlɪ] adv lamentablemente

re·gret·ta·ble [rɪ'gretəbl] adj lamentable

re·gret·ta·bly [rɪ'gretəblɪ] adv lamentablemente

reg·u·lar ['regjələr] **1** adj regular; (normal, ordinary) normal **2** n at bar etc habitual m/f

reg·u·lar·i·ty [regjʊ'lærətɪ] regularidad f

reg·u·lar·ly ['regjʊlərlɪ] adv regularmente

reg·u·late ['regʊleɪt] v/t regular

reg·u·la·tion [regʊ'leɪʃn] (rule) regla f, norma f

re·hab ['riːhæb] F rehabilitación f

re·ha·bil·i·tate [riːhə'bɪlɪteɪt] v/t ex-criminal rehabilitar

re·hears·al [rɪ'hɜːrsl] ensayo *m*
re·hearse [rɪ'hɜːrs] *v/t & v/i* ensayar
reign [reɪn] **1** *n* reinado *m* **2** *v/i* reinar
re·im·burse [riːɪm'bɜːrs] *v/t* reembolsar
rein [reɪn] rienda *f*
re·in·car·na·tion [riːɪnkɑːr'neɪʃn] reencarnación *f*
re·in·force [riːɪn'fɔːrs] *v/t structure* reforzar; *beliefs* reafirmar
re·in·forced con·crete [riːɪn'fɔːrst] hormigón *m* armado
re·in·force·ments [riːɪn'fɔːrsmənts] *npl* MIL refuerzos *mpl*
re·in·state [riːɪn'steɪt] *v/t person in office* reincorporar; *paragraph in text* volver a colocar
re·it·er·ate [riː'ɪtəreɪt] *v/t fml* reiterar
re·ject [rɪ'dʒekt] *v/t* rechazar
re·jec·tion [rɪ'dʒekʃn] rechazo *m*; *he felt a sense of rejection* se sintió rechazado
re·lapse ['riːlæps] *n* MED recaída *f*; *have a relapse* sufrir una recaída
re·late [rɪ'leɪt] **1** *v/t story* relatar, narrar; *relate sth to sth connect* relacionar algo con algo **2** *v/i:* *relate to be connected with* estar relacionado con; *he doesn't relate to people* no se relaciona fácilmente con la gente
re·lat·ed [rɪ'leɪtɪd] *adj by family* emparentado; *events, ideas etc* relacionado; *are you two related?* ¿sois parientes?
re·la·tion [rɪ'leɪʃn] *in family* pariente *m/f*; *(connection)* relación *f*; *business / diplomatic relations* relaciones *fpl* comerciales / diplomáticas
re·la·tion·ship [rɪ'leɪʃnʃɪp] relación *f*
rel·a·tive ['relətɪv] **1** *n* pariente *m/f* **2** *adj* relativo; *X is relative to Y* X está relacionado con Y
rel·a·tive·ly ['relətɪvlɪ] *adv* relativamente
re·lax [rɪ'læks] **1** *v/i* relajarse; *relax!, don't get angry* ¡tranquilízate!, no te enfades **2** *v/t muscle, pace* relajar
re·lax·a·tion [riːlæk'seɪʃn] relajación *f*; *what do you do for relaxation?* ¿qué haces para relajarte?
re·laxed [rɪ'lækst] *adj* relajado
re·lax·ing [rɪ'læksɪŋ] *adj* relajante
re·lay [riː'leɪ] **1** *v/t message* pasar; *radio, TV signals* retransmitir **2** *n:* *relay (race)* carrera *f* de relevos
re·lease [rɪ'liːs] **1** *n from prison* liberación *f*, puesta *f* en libertad; *of CD etc* lanzamiento *m*; *CD, record* trabajo *m* **2** *v/t prisoner* liberar, poner en libertad; *parking brake* soltar; *information* hacer público
rel·e·gate ['relɪgeɪt] *v/t* relegar
re·lent [rɪ'lent] *v/i* ablandarse, ceder
re·lent·less [rɪ'lentlɪs] *adj (determined)*

implacable; *rain etc* que no cesa
re·lent·less·ly [rɪ'lentlɪslɪ] *adv* implacablemente; *rain* sin cesar
rel·e·vance ['reləvəns] pertinencia *f*
rel·e·vant ['reləvənt] *adj* pertinente
re·li·a·bil·i·ty [rɪlaɪə'bɪlətɪ] fiabilidad *f*
re·li·a·ble [rɪ'laɪəbl] *adj* fiable; *information* fiable, fidedigna
re·li·a·bly [rɪ'laɪəblɪ] *adv:* *I am reliably informed that* sé de buena fuente que
re·li·ance [rɪ'laɪəns] confianza *f*, dependencia *f*; *reliance on s.o./sth* confianza en alguien / algo, dependencia de alguien / algo
re·li·ant [rɪ'laɪənt] *adj:* *be reliant on* depender de
rel·ic ['relɪk] reliquia *f*
re·lief [rɪ'liːf] alivio *m*; *that's a relief* qué alivio; *in relief in art* en relieve
re·lieve [rɪ'liːv] *v/t pressure, pain* aliviar; *(take over from)* relevar; *be relieved at news etc* sentirse aliviado
re·li·gion [rɪ'lɪdʒən] religión *f*
re·li·gious [rɪ'lɪdʒəs] *adj* religioso
re·li·gious·ly [rɪ'lɪdʒəslɪ] *adv (conscientiously)* religiosamente
re·lin·quish [rɪ'lɪŋkwɪʃ] *v/t* renunciar a
rel·ish ['relɪʃ] **1** *n sauce* salsa *f*; *(enjoyment)* goce *m* **2** *v/t idea, prospect* gozar con; *I don't relish the idea* la idea no me entusiasma
re·live [riː'lɪv] *v/t the past, an event* revivir
re·lo·cate [riːlə'keɪt] *v/i of business, employee* trasladarse
re·lo·ca·tion [riːlə'keɪʃn] *of business, employee* traslado *m*
re·luc·tance [rɪ'lʌktəns] reticencia *f*
re·luc·tant [rɪ'lʌktənt] *adj* reticente, reacio; *be reluctant to do sth* ser reacio a hacer algo
re·luc·tant·ly [rɪ'lʌktəntlɪ] *adv* con reticencia
♦ re·ly on [rɪ'laɪ] *v/t (pret & pp relied)* depender de; *rely on s.o. to do sth* contar con alguien para hacer algo
re·main [rɪ'meɪn] *v/i (be left)* quedar; MATH restar; *(stay)* permanecer
re·main·der [rɪ'meɪndər] **1** *n also* MATH resto *m* **2** *v/t* vender como saldo
re·main·ing [rɪ'meɪnɪŋ] *adj* restante
re·mains [rɪ'meɪnz] *npl of body* restos *mpl (mortales)*
re·make ['riːmeɪk] *n of movie* nueva versión *f*
re·mand [rɪ'mænd] **1** *v/t:* *remand s.o. in custody* poner a alguien en prisión preventiva **2** *n:* *be on remand in prison* estar en prisión preventiva; *on bail* estar en libertad bajo fianza

R

re·mark [rɪˈmɑːrk] **1** *n* comentario *m*, observación *f* **2** *v/t* comentar, observar

re·mar·ka·ble [rɪˈmɑːrkəbl] *adj* notable, extraordinario

re·mark·a·bly [rɪˈmɑːrkəblɪ] *adv* extraordinariamente

re·mar·ry [riːˈmærɪ] *v/i* (*pret & pp* **remarried**) volver a casarse

rem·e·dy [ˈremədɪ] *n* MED, *fig* remedio *m*

re·mem·ber [rɪˈmembər] **1** *v/t s.o., sth* recordar, acordarse de; **remember to lock the door** acuérdate de cerrar la puerta; **remember me to her** dale recuerdos de mi parte **2** *v/i* recordar, acordarse; **I don't remember** no recuerdo, no me acuerdo

re·mind [rɪˈmaɪnd] *v/t*; **remind s.o. of sth** recordar algo a uno; **remind s.o. of s.o.** recordar alguien a uno; **you remind me of your father** me recuerdas a tu padre

re·mind·er [rɪˈmaɪndər] recordatorio *m*; *for payment* recordatorio *m* de pago

rem·i·nisce [remɪˈnɪs] *v/i* contar recuerdos

rem·i·nis·cent [remɪˈnɪsənt] *adj*: **be reminiscent of sth** recordar a algo, tener reminiscencias de algo

re·miss [rɪˈmɪs] *adj fml* negligente, descuidado

re·mis·sion [rɪˈmɪʃn] remisión *f*; **go into remission** MED remitir

rem·nant [ˈremnənt] resto *m*

re·morse [rɪˈmɔːrs] remordimientos *mpl*

re·morse·less [rɪˈmɔːrsləs] *adj person* despiadado; *pace, demands* implacable

re·mote [rɪˈmoʊt] *adj village, possibility* remoto; *(aloof)* distante; *ancestor* lejano

re·mote 'ac·cess COMPUT acceso *m* remoto

re·mote con'trol control *m* remoto; *for TV* mando *m* a distancia

re·mote·ly [rɪˈmoʊtlɪ] *adv related, connected* remotamente; **it's just remotely possible** es una posibilidad muy remota

re·mote·ness [rɪˈmoʊtnəs]: **the remoteness of the house** la lejanía *or* lo aislado de la casa

re·mov·a·ble [rɪˈmuːvəbl] *adj* de quita y pon

re·mov·al [rɪˈmuːvl] eliminación *f*

re·move [rɪˈmuːv] *v/t* eliminar; *top, lid* quitar; *coat etc* quitarse; *doubt, suspicion* despejar; *growth, organ* extirpar

re·mu·ner·a·tion [rɪmjuːnəˈreɪʃn] remuneración *f*

re·mu·ner·a·tive [rɪˈmjuːnərətɪv] *adj* bien remunerado

re·name [riːˈneɪm] *v/t* cambiar el nombre a

ren·der [ˈrendər] *v/t service* prestar; **render s.o. helpless / unconscious** dejar a uno indefenso / inconsciente

ren·der·ing [ˈrendərɪŋ] *of piece of music* interpretación *f*

ren·dez·vous [ˈrɑːndeɪvuː] *romantic* cita *f*; MIL encuentro *m*

re·new [rɪˈnuː] *v/t contract, license* renovar; *discussions* reanudar; **feel renewed** sentirse como nuevo

re·new·al [rɪˈnuːəl] *of contract etc* renovación *f*; *of discussions* reanudación *f*

re·nounce [rɪˈnaʊns] *v/t title, rights* renunciar a

ren·o·vate [ˈrenəveɪt] *v/t* renovar

ren·o·va·tion [renəˈveɪʃn] renovación *f*

re·nown [rɪˈnaʊn] renombre *m*

re·nowned [rɪˈnaʊnd] *adj* renombrado; **be renowned for sth** ser célebre por algo

rent [rent] **1** *n* alquiler *m*; **for rent** se alquila **2** *v/t apartment, car, equipment* alquilar, *Mex* rentar

rent·al [ˈrentl] *for apartment, for TV* alquiler *m*, *Mex* renta *f*

'rent·al a·gree·ment acuerdo *m* de alquiler

'rent·al car coche *m* de alquiler

'rent-'free *adv* sin pagar alquiler

re·o·pen [riːˈoʊpn] **1** *v/t* reabrir; *negotiations* reanudar **2** *v/i of theater etc* volver a abrir

re·or·gan·i·za·tion [riːɔːrgənaɪˈzeɪʃn] reorganización *f*

re·or·gan·ize [riːˈɔːrgənaɪz] *v/t* reorganizar

rep [rep] COM representante *m/f*, comercial *m/f*

re·paint [riːˈpeɪnt] *v/t* repintar

re·pair [rɪˈper] **1** *v/t fence, TV* reparar; *shoes* arreglar **2** *n to fence, TV* reparación *f*; *of shoes* arreglo *m*; **in a good / bad state of repair** en buen / mal estado

re'pair·man técnico *m*

re·pa·tri·ate [riːˈpætrɪeɪt] *v/t* repatriar

re·pa·tri·a·tion [riːˈpætrɪˈeɪʃn] repatriación *f*

re·pay [riːˈpeɪ] *v/t* (*pret & pp* **repaid**) *money* devolver; *person* pagar

re·pay·ment [riːˈpeɪmənt] devolución *f*; *installment* plazo *m*

re·peal [rɪˈpiːl] *v/t law* revocar

re·peat [rɪˈpiːt] **1** *v/t* repetir; **am I repeating myself?** ¿me estoy repitiendo? **2** *n* TV *program etc* repetición *f*

re·peat 'busi·ness COM negocio *m* que se repite

re·peat·ed [rɪˈpiːtɪd] *adj* repetido

re·peat·ed·ly [rɪ'piːtɪdlɪ] *adv* repetidamente, repetidas veces

re·peat 'or·der COM pedido *m* repetido

re·pel [rɪ'pel] *v/t* (*pret* & *pp* **repelled**) *invaders, attack* rechazar; *insects* repeler, ahuyentar; (*disgust*) repeler, repugnar

re·pel·lent [rɪ'pelənt] **1** *n* (*insect repellent*) repelente *m* **2** *adj* repelente, repugnante

re·pent [rɪ'pent] *v/i* arrepentirse

re·per·cus·sions [riːpər'kʌʃnz] *npl* repercusiones *fpl*

rep·er·toire ['repərtwɑːr] repertorio *m*

rep·e·ti·tion [repɪ'tɪʃn] repetición *f*

re·pet·i·tive [rɪ'petɪtɪv] *adj* repetitivo

re·place [rɪ'pleɪs] *v/t* (*put back*) volver a poner; (*take the place of*) reemplazar, sustituir

re·place·ment [rɪ'pleɪsmənt] *n person* sustituto(-a) *m(f)*; *thing* recambio *m*, reemplazo *m*

re·place·ment 'part (pieza *f* de) recambio *m*

re·play ['riːpleɪ] **1** *n recording* repetición *f* (de la jugada); *match* repetición *f* (del partido) **2** *v/t match* repetir

re·plen·ish [rɪ'plenɪʃ] *v/t container* rellenar; *supplies* reaprovisionar

rep·li·ca ['replɪkə] réplica *f*

re·ply [rɪ'plaɪ] **1** *n* respuesta *f*, contestación *f* **2** *v/t* & *v/i* (*pret* & *pp* **replied**) responder, contestar

re·port [rɪ'pɔːrt] **1** *n* (*account*) informe *m*; *by journalist* reportaje *m* **2** *v/t facts* informar; *to authorities* informar de, dar parte de; *report a person to the police* denunciar a alguien a la policía; *he is reported to be in Washington* se dice que está en Washington **3** *v/i of journalist* informar; (*present o.s.*) presentarse (*to* ante)

◆ **report to** *v/t in business* trabajar a las órdenes de

re'port card boletín *m* de evaluación

re·port·er [rɪ'pɔːrtər] reportero(-a) *m(f)*

re·pos·sess [riːpə'zes] *v/t* COM embargar

rep·re·hen·si·ble [reprɪ'hensəbl] *adj* recriminable

rep·re·sent [reprɪ'zent] *v/t* representar

rep·re·sen·ta·tive [reprɪ'zentətɪv] **1** *n* representante *m/f*; POL representante *m/f*, diputado(-a) *m(f)* **2** *adj* (*typical*) representativo

re·press [rɪ'pres] *v/t revolt* reprimir; *feelings, laughter* reprimir, controlar

re·pres·sion [rɪ'preʃn] POL represión *f*

re·pres·sive [rɪ'presɪv] *adj* POL represivo

re·prieve [rɪ'priːv] **1** *n* LAW indulto *m*; *fig* aplazamiento *m* **2** *v/t prisoner* indultar

rep·ri·mand ['reprɪmænd] *v/t* reprender

re·print ['riːprɪnt] **1** *n* reimpresión *f* **2** *v/t* reimprimir

re·pri·sal [rɪ'praɪzl] represalia *f*; *take reprisals* tomar represalias; *in reprisal for* en represalia por

re·proach [rɪ'prəʊtʃ] **1** *n* reproche *m*; *be beyond reproach* ser irreprochable **2** *v/t*: *reproach s.o. for sth* reprochar algo a alguien

re·proach·ful [rɪ'prəʊtʃfəl] *adj* de reproche

re·proach·ful·ly [rɪ'prəʊtʃfəlɪ] *adv look* con una mirada de reproche; *say* con tono de reproche

re·pro·duce [riːprə'djuːs] **1** *v/t atmosphere, mood* reproducir **2** *v/i* BIO reproducirse

re·pro·duc·tion [riːprə'dʌkʃn] reproducción *f*

re·pro·duc·tive [riːprə'dʌktɪv] *adj* reproductivo

rep·tile ['reptaɪl] reptil *m*

re·pub·lic [rɪ'pʌblɪk] república *f*

re·pub·li·can [rɪ'pʌblɪkən] **1** *n* republicano(-a) *m(f)* **2** *adj* republicano

re·pu·di·ate [rɪ'pjuːdɪeɪt] *v/t* (*deny*) rechazar

re·pul·sive [rɪ'pʌlsɪv] *adj* repulsivo

rep·u·ta·ble ['repjʊtəbl] *adj* reputado, acreditado

rep·u·ta·tion [repjʊ'teɪʃn] reputación *f*; *have a good / bad reputation* tener una buena / mala reputación

re·put·ed [rɪ'pjuːtɪd] *adj*: *be reputed to be* tener fama de ser

re·put·ed·ly [rɪ'pjuːtɪdlɪ] *adv* según se dice

re·quest [rɪ'kwest] **1** *n* petición *f*, solicitud *f*; *on request* por encargo **2** *v/t* pedir, solicitar

re·quiem ['rekwɪəm] MUS réquiem *m*

re·quire [rɪ'kwaɪr] *v/t* (*need*) requerir, necesitar; *it requires great care* se requiere mucho cuidado; *as required by law* como estipula la ley; *guests are required to ...* se ruega a los los invitados que ...

re·quired [rɪ'kwaɪrd] *adj* (*necessary*) necesario

re·quire·ment [rɪ'kwaɪrmənt] (*need*) necesidad *f*; (*condition*) requisito *m*

req·ui·si·tion [rekwɪ'zɪʃn] *v/t* requisar

re·route [riː'ruːt] *v/t airplane etc* desviar

re·run ['riːrʌn] **1** *n of TV program* reposición *f* **2** *v/t* (*pret* **reran**, *pp* **rerun**) *tape* volver a poner

re·sched·ule [riː'ʃeduːl] *v/t* volver a programar

res·cue ['reskjuː] **1** *n* rescate *m*; *come to*

s.o.'s rescue acudir al rescate de alguien **2** *v/t* rescatar

'res·cue par·ty equipo *m* de rescate

re·search [rɪ'sɜːrtʃ] *n* investigación *f*
◆ **research into** *v/t* investigar

re·search and de'vel·op·ment investigación *f* y desarrollo

re'search as·sist·ant ayudante *m/f* de investigación

re·search·er [rɪ'sɜːrtʃər] investigador(a) *m(f)*

re'search proj·ect proyecto *m* de investigación

re·sem·blance [rɪ'zembləns] parecido *m*, semejanza *f*

re·sem·ble [rɪ'zembl] *v/t* parecerse a

re·sent [rɪ'zent] *v/t* estar molesto por

re·sent·ful [rɪ'zentfəl] *adj* resentido

re·sent·ful·ly [rɪ'zentfəlɪ] *adv* con resentimiento

re·sent·ment [rɪ'zentmənt] resentimiento *m*

res·er·va·tion [rezər'veɪʃn] reserva *f*; **I have a reservation** in hotel, restaurant tengo una reserva

re·serve [rɪ'zɜːrv] **1** *n* reserva *f*; SP reserva *m/f*; **reserves** FIN reservas *fpl*; **keep sth in reserve** tener algo en la reserva **2** *v/t* seat, table reservar; judgment reservarse

re·served [rɪ'zɜːrvd] *adj* table, manner reservado

res·er·voir ['rezərvwɑːr] for water embalse *m*, pantano *m*

re·shuf·fle ['riːˌʃʌfl] **1** *n* POL remodelación *f* **2** *v/t* POL remodelar

re·side [rɪ'zaɪd] *v/i* fml residir

res·i·dence ['rezɪdəns] (fml: house etc) residencia *f*; (stay) estancia *f*

'res·i·dence per·mit permiso *m* de residencia

'res·i·dent ['rezɪdənt] **1** *n* residente *m/f* **2** *adj* (living in a building) residente

res·i·den·tial [rezɪ'denʃl] *adj* district residencial

res·i·due ['rezɪduː] residuo *m*

re·sign [rɪ'zaɪn] **1** *v/t* position dimitir de; **resign o.s. to** resignarse a **2** *v/i* from job dimitir

res·ig·na·tion [rezɪg'neɪʃn] from job dimisión *f*; mental resignación *f*

re·signed [re'zaɪnd] *adj* resignado; **we have become resigned to the fact that ...** nos hemos resignado a aceptar que ...

re·sil·i·ent [rɪ'zɪlɪənt] *adj* personality fuerte; material resistente

res·in ['rezɪn] resina *f*

re·sist [rɪ'zɪst] **1** *v/t* resistir; new measures oponer resistencia a **2** *v/i* resistir

re·sist·ance [rɪ'zɪstəns] resistencia *f*

re·sis·tant [rɪ'zɪstənt] *adj* material resistente; **resistant to heat / rust** resistente al calor/a la oxidación

res·o·lute ['rezəluːt] *adj* resuelto

res·o·lu·tion [rezə'luːʃn] resolución *f*; made at New Year etc propósito *m*

re·solve [rɪ'zɑːlv] *v/t* problem, mystery resolver; **resolve to do sth** resolver hacer algo

re·sort [rɪ'zɔːrt] *n* place centro *m* turístico; **as a last resort** como último recurso
◆ **resort to** *v/t* violence, threats recurrir a
◆ **re·sound with** [rɪ'zaʊnd] *v/t* resonar con

re·sound·ing [rɪ'zaʊndɪŋ] *adj* success, victory clamoroso

re·source [rɪ'sɔːrs] recurso *m*; **leave s.o. to his own resources** dejar que alguien se las arregle solo

re·source·ful [rɪ'sɔːrsfəl] *adj* person lleno de recursos; attitude, approach ingenioso

re·spect [rɪ'spekt] **1** *n* respeto *m*; **show respect to** mostrar respeto hacia; **with respect to** con respecto a; **in this / that respect** en cuanto a esto / eso; **in many respects** en muchos aspectos; **pay one's last respects to s.o.** decir el último adiós a alguien **2** *v/t* respetar

re·spect·a·bil·i·ty [rɪspektə'bɪlətɪ] respetabilidad *f*

re·spec·ta·ble [rɪ'spektəbl] *adj* respetable

re·spec·ta·bly [rɪ'spektəblɪ] *adv* respetablemente

re·spect·ful [rɪ'spektfəl] *adj* respetuoso

re·spect·ful·ly [rɪ'spektfəlɪ] *adv* respetuosamente, con respeto

re·spec·tive [rɪ'spektɪv] *adj* respectivo

re·spec·tive·ly [rɪ'spektɪvlɪ] *adv* respectivamente

res·pi·ra·tion [respɪ'reɪʃn] respiración *f*

res·pi·ra·tor [respɪ'reɪtər] MED respirador *m*

re·spite ['respaɪt] respiro *m*; **without respite** sin respiro

re·spond [rɪ'spɑːnd] *v/i* responder

re·sponse [rɪ'spɑːns] respuesta *f*

re·spon·si·bil·i·ty [rɪspɑːnsɪ'bɪlətɪ] responsabilidad *f*; **accept responsibility for** aceptar responsabilidad de; **a job with more responsibility** un trabajo con más responsabilidad

re·spon·si·ble [rɪ'spɑːnsəbl] *adj* responsable (**for** de); job de responsabilidad

re·spon·sive [rɪ'spɑːnsɪv] *adj* brakes que responde bien; **a responsive audience** una audiencia que muestra interés

rest¹ [rest] **1** *n* descanso *m*; **he needs a rest** necesita descansar; **set s.o.'s mind**

at rest tranquilizar a alguien **2** v/i descansar; **rest on** of theory, box apoyarse en; **it all rests with him** todo depende de él **3** v/t (lean, balance) apoyar

rest[2] [rest]: **the rest** el resto

res·tau·rant ['restrɔːnt] restaurante m

'res·tau·rant car vagón m or coche m restaurante

'rest cure cura f de reposo or descanso

rest·ful ['restfəl] adj tranquilo, relajante

'rest home residencia f de ancianos

rest·less ['restlɪs] adj inquieto; **have a restless night** pasar la noche

rest·less·ly ['restlɪslɪ] adv sin descanso

res·to·ra·tion [restə'reɪʃn] restauración f

re·store [rɪ'stɔːr] v/t building etc restaurar; (bring back) devolver

re·strain [rɪ'streɪn] v/t contener; **restrain o.s.** contenerse

re·straint [rɪ'streɪnt] (moderation) moderación f, comedimiento m

re·strict [rɪ'strɪkt] v/t restringir, limitar; **I'll restrict myself to ...** me limitaré a ...

re·strict·ed [rɪ'strɪktɪd] adj view limitado

re·strict·ed 'ar·e·a MIL zona f de acceso restringido

re·stric·tion [rɪ'strɪkʃn] restricción f, limitación f; **place restrictions upon s.o.** imponer restricciones or limitaciones a alguien

'rest room Am aseo m, servicios mpl

re·sult [rɪ'zʌlt] n resultado m; **as a result of this** como resultado de esto

◆ **result from** v/t resultar de

◆ **result in** v/t tener como resultado

re·sume [rɪ'zjuːm] **1** v/t reanudar **2** v/i continuar

ré·su·mé ['rezumeɪ] currículum m (vitae)

re·sump·tion [rɪ'zʌmpʃn] reanudación f

re·sur·face [riː'sɜːfɪs] **1** v/t roads volver a asfaltar **2** v/i (reappear) reaparecer

res·ur·rec·tion [rezə'rekʃn] REL resurrección f

re·sus·ci·tate [rɪ'sʌsɪteɪt] v/t resucitar, revivir

re·sus·ci·ta·tion [rɪsʌsɪ'teɪʃn] resucitación f

re·tail ['riːteɪl] **1** adv: **sell sth retail** vender algo al por menor **2** v/i: **retail at ...** su precio de venta al público es de ...

re·tail·er ['riːteɪlər] minorista m/f

're·tail out·let punto m de venta

're·tail price precio m de venta al público

re·tain [rɪ'teɪn] v/t conservar; heat retener

re·tain·er [rɪ'teɪnər] FIN anticipo m

re·tal·i·ate [rɪ'tælieɪt] v/i tomar represalias

re·tal·i·a·tion [rɪtæli'eɪʃn] represalias fpl; **in retaliation for** como represalia por

re·tard·ed [rɪ'tɑːrdɪd] adj mentally retrasado mental

re·think [riː'θɪŋk] v/t (pret & pp **rethought**) replantear

re·ti·cence ['retɪsns] reserva f

re·ti·cent ['retɪsnt] adj reservado

re·tire [rɪ'taɪr] v/i from work jubilarse

re·tired [rɪ'taɪrd] adj jubilado

re·tire·ment [rɪ'taɪrmənt] jubilación f

re'tire·ment age edad f de jubilación

re·tir·ing [rɪ'taɪrɪŋ] adj retraído, reservado

re·tort [rɪ'tɔːrt] **1** n réplica f **2** v/t replicar

re·trace [rɪ'treɪs] v/t: **they retraced their footsteps** volvieron sobre sus pasos

re·tract [rɪ'trækt] v/t claws retraer; undercarriage replegar; statement retirar

re·train [riː'treɪn] v/i reciclarse

re·treat [rɪ'triːt] **1** v/i retirarse **2** n MIL retirada f; place retiro m

re·trieve [rɪ'triːv] v/t recuperar

re·triev·er [rɪ'triːvər] dog perro m cobrador

ret·ro·ac·tive [retrou'æktɪv] adj law etc retroactivo

ret·ro·ac·tive·ly [retrou'æktɪvlɪ] adv con retroactividad

ret·ro·grade ['retrougreɪd] adj move, decision retrógrado

ret·ro·spect ['retrəspekt]: **in retrospect** en retrospectiva

ret·ro·spec·tive [retrə'spektɪv] n retrospectiva f

re·turn [rɪ'tɜːrn] **1** n to a place vuelta f, regreso m; (giving back) devolución f; COMPUT retorno m; in tennis resto m; (profit) rendimiento m; Br ticket billete m or L.Am. boleto m de ida y vuelta; **by return (of post)** a vuelta de correo; **many happy returns (of the day)** feliz cumpleaños; **in return for** a cambio de **2** v/t devolver; (put back) volver a colocar **3** v/i (go back, come back) volver, regresar; of good times, doubts etc volver

re·turn 'flight vuelo m de vuelta

re·turn 'jour·ney viaje m de vuelta

re·u·ni·fi·ca·tion [riːjuːnɪfɪ'keɪʃn] reunificación f

re·un·ion [riː'juːnjən] reunión f

re·u·nite [riːjuː'naɪt] v/t reunir

re·us·a·ble [riː'juːzəbl] adj reutilizable

re·use [riː'juːz] v/t reutilizar

rev [rev] n revolución f; **revs per minute** revoluciones por minuto

◆ **rev up** v/t (pret & pp **revved**) engine revolucionar

re·val·u·a·tion [riːvæljʊ'eɪʃn] revaluación f

re·veal [rɪ'viːl] v/t (make visible) revelar;

R

(*make known*) revelar, desvelar

re·veal·ing [rɪ'viːlɪŋ] *adj remark* revelador; *dress* insinuante, atrevido

◆ rev·el in ['revl] *v/t* (*pret & pp* **reveled**, *Br* **revelled**) deleitarse con

rev·e·la·tion [revə'leɪʃn] *n* revelación *f*

re·venge [rɪ'vendʒ] *n* venganza *f*; **take one's revenge** vengarse; **in revenge for** como venganza por

rev·e·nue ['revənuː] *ingresos mpl*

re·ver·be·rate [rɪ'vɜːrbəreɪt] *v/i of sound* reverberar

re·vere [rɪ'vɪr] *v/t* reverenciar

rev·e·rence ['revərəns] reverencia *f*

Rev·e·rend ['revərənd] REL Reverendo *m*

rev·e·rent ['revərənt] *adj* reverente

re·verse [rɪ'vɜːrs] 1 *adj sequence* inverso; **in reverse order** en orden inverso 2 *n* (*back*) dorso *m*; MOT marcha *f* atrás; **the reverse** (*the opposite*) lo contrario 3 *v/t sequence* invertir; **reverse a vehicle** hacer marcha atrás con un vehículo 4 *v/i* MOT hacer marcha atrás

revert [rɪ'vɜːrt] *v/i*: **revert to** volver a

re·view [rɪ'vjuː] 1 *n of book, movie* reseña *f*, crítica *f*; *of troops* revista *f*; *of situation etc* revisión *f* 2 *v/t book, movie* reseñar, hacer una crítica de; *troops* pasar revista a; *situation etc* revisar; EDU repasar

re·view·er [rɪ'vjuːər] *of book, movie* crítico(-a) *m(f)*

re·vise [rɪ'vaɪz] *v/t opinion, text* revisar

re·vi·sion [rɪ'vɪʒn] *of opinion, text* revisión *f*

re·viv·al [rɪ'vaɪvl] *of custom, old style etc* resurgimiento *m*; *of patient* reanimación *f*

re·vive [rɪ'vaɪv] 1 *v/t custom, old style etc* hacer resurgir; *patient* reanimar 2 *v/i of business, exchange rate etc* reactivarse

re·voke [rɪ'voʊk] *v/t law* derogar; *license* revocar

re·volt [rɪ'voʊlt] 1 *n* rebelión *f* 2 *v/i* rebelarse

re·volt·ing [rɪ'voʊltɪŋ] *adj* (*disgusting*) repugnante

rev·o·lu·tion [revə'luːʃn] POL revolución *f*; (*turn*) vuelta *f*, revolución *f*

rev·o·lu·tion·ar·y [revə'luːʃn ərɪ] 1 *n* POL revolucionario(-a) *m(f)* 2 *adj* revolucionario

rev·o·lu·tion·ize [revə'luːʃnaɪz] *v/t* revolucionar

re·volve [rɪ'vaːlv] *v/i* girar (**around** en torno a)

re·volv·er [rɪ'vaːlvər] revólver *m*

re·volv·ing 'door [rɪ'vaːlvɪŋ] puerta *f* giratoria

re·vue [rɪ'vjuː] THEA revista *f*

re·vul·sion [rɪ'vʌlʃn] repugnancia *f*

re·ward [rɪ'wɔːrd] 1 *n* recompensa *f* 2 *v/t financially* recompensar

re·ward·ing [rɪ'wɔːrdɪŋ] *adj experience* gratificante

re·wind [riː'waɪnd] *v/t* (*pret & pp* **rewound**) *film, tape* rebobinar

re·write [riː'raɪt] *v/t* (*pret* **rewrote**, *pp* **rewritten**) reescribir

rhet·o·ric ['retərɪk] retórica *f*

rhe·tor·i·cal 'ques·tion [rɪ'taːrɪkl] pregunta *f* retórica

rheu·ma·tism ['ruːmətɪzm] reumatismo *m*

rhi·no·ce·ros [raɪ'naːsərəs] rinoceronte *m*

rhu·barb ['ruːbaːrb] ruibarbo *m*

rhyme [raɪm] 1 *n* rima *f* 2 *v/i* rimar

rhythm ['rɪðm] ritmo *m*

rib [rɪb] ANAT costilla *f*

rib·bon ['rɪbən] cinta *f*

rice [raɪs] arroz *m*

rich [rɪtʃ] 1 *adj* (*wealthy*) rico; *food* sabroso; **it's too rich** es muy pesado 2 *n*: **the rich** los ricos

rich·ly ['rɪtʃlɪ] *adv*: **be richly deserved** ser muy merecido

rick·et·y ['rɪkətɪ] *adj* desvencijado

ric·o·chet ['rɪkəʃeɪ] *v/i* rebotar

rid [rɪd]: **get rid of** deshacerse de

rid·dance ['rɪdns] F: **good riddance to her!** ¡espero no volver a verla nunca!

rid·den ['rɪdn] *pp* → **ride**

rid·dle ['rɪdl] 1 *n* acertijo *m* 2 *v/t*: **be riddled with** estar lleno de

ride [raɪd] 1 *n on horse, in vehicle* paseo *m*, vuelta *f*; (*journey*) viaje *m*; **do you want a ride into town?** ¿quieres que te lleve al centro? 2 *v/t* (*pret* **rode**, *pp* **ridden**) *horse* montar a; *bike* montar en 3 *v/i* (*pret* **rode**, *pp* **ridden**) *on horse* montar; **can you ride?** ¿sabes montar?; **those who were riding at the back of the bus** los que iban en la parte de atrás del autobús

rid·er ['raɪdər] *on horse* jinete *m*, amazona *f*; *on bicycle* ciclista *m/f*; *on motorbike* motorista *m/f*

ridge [rɪdʒ] *raised strip* borde *m*; *of mountain* cresta *f*; *of roof* caballete *m*

rid·i·cule ['rɪdɪkjuːl] 1 *n* burlas *fpl* 2 *v/t* ridiculizar, poner en ridículo

ri·dic·u·lous [rɪ'dɪkjələs] *adj* ridículo

ri·dic·u·lous·ly [rɪ'dɪkjələslɪ] *adv expensive, difficult* terriblemente; **it's ridiculously easy** es facilísimo

rid·ing ['raɪdɪŋ] *on horseback* equitación *f*

ri·fle ['raɪfl] *n* rifle *m*

rift [rɪft] *in earth* grieta *f*; *in party etc* escisión *f*

rig [rɪg] **1** *n* (*oil rig*) plataforma *f* petrolífera; (*truck*) camión *m* **2** *v/t* (*pret & pp* **rigged**) *elections* amañar

right [raɪt] **1** *adj* (*correct*) correcto; (*suitable*) adecuado, apropiado; (*not left*) derecho; *it's not right to treat people like that* no está bien tratar así a la gente; *it's the right thing to do* es lo que hay que hacer; *be right of answer* estar correcto; *of person* tener razón; *of clock* ir bien; *put things right* arreglar las cosas; *that's right!* ¡eso es!; *that's all right doesn't matter* no te preocupes; *after s.o. says thank you* de nada; *is quite good* está bastante bien; *I'm all right not hurt* estoy bien; *have got enough* no, gracias; *all right, that's enough!* ¡ahora sí que ya está bien! **2** *adv* (*directly*) justo; (*not left*) a la derecha; *he broke it right off* lo rompió por completo; *right back in 1982* allá en 1982; *right now* ahora mismo **3** *n civil, legal etc* derecho *m*; *not left*, POL derecha *f*; *on the right also* POL a la derecha; *turn to the right, take a right* gira a la derecha; *be in the right* tener razón; *know right from wrong* distinguir lo que está bien de lo que está mal

right-an-gle ángulo *m* recto; *at right-angles to* en *or* formando ángulo recto con

right-ful [ˈraɪtfəl] *adj heir, owner etc* legítimo

'right-hand *adj*: *on the right-hand side* a mano derecha

right-hand 'drive *n* MOT vehículo *m* con el volante a la derecha

right-hand-ed [raɪtˈhændɪd] *adj person* diestro

right-hand 'man mano *f* derecha

right of 'way *in traffic* preferencia *f*; *across land* derecho *m* de paso

right 'wing *n* POL la derecha *f*; SP la banda derecha

right-'wing *adj* POL de derechas

right-wing ex'trem-ism POL extremismo *m* de derechas

right-'wing-er POL derechista *m/f*

rig-id [ˈrɪdʒɪd] *adj* rígido

rig-or [ˈrɪgər] *of discipline* rigor *m*; *the rigors of the winter* los rigores del invierno

rig-or-ous [ˈrɪgərəs] *adj* riguroso

rig-or-ous-ly [ˈrɪgərəslɪ] *adv check, examine* rigurosamente

rig-our *Br* → **rigor**

rile [raɪl] *v/t* F fastidiar, *Span* mosquear F

rim [rɪm] *of wheel* llanta *f*; *of cup* borde *m*;

of eye glasses montura *f*

ring¹ [rɪŋ] *n* (*circle*) círculo *m*; *on finger* anillo *m*; *in boxing* cuadrilátero *m*, ring *m*; *at circus* pista *f*

ring² [rɪŋ] **1** *n of bell* timbrazo; *of voice* tono *m*; *give s.o. a ring* Br TELEC dar un telefonazo a alguien **2** *v/t* (*pret* **rang**, *pp* **rung**) *bell* hacer sonar **3** *v/i* (*pret* **rang**, *pp* **rung**) *of bell* sonar; *please ring for attention* toque el timbre para que lo atiendan

'ring-lead-er cabecilla *m/f*

'ring-pull anilla *f*

rink [rɪŋk] pista *f* de patinaje

rinse [rɪns] **1** *n for hair color* reflejo *m* **2** *v/t* aclarar

ri-ot [ˈraɪət] **1** *n* disturbio *m* **2** *v/i* causar disturbios

ri-ot-er [ˈraɪətər] alborotador(a) *m(f)*

'riot police policía *f* antidisturbios

rip [rɪp] **1** *n in cloth etc* rasgadura *f* **2** *v/t* (*pret & pp* **ripped**) *cloth etc* rasgar; *rip sth open* romper algo rasgándolo

◆ **rip off** *v/t* F *customers* robar F, clavar F; (*cheat*) timar

◆ **rip up** *v/t letter, sheet* hacer pedazos

ripe [raɪp] *adj fruit* maduro

rip-en [ˈraɪpn] *v/i of fruit* madurar

ripe-ness [ˈraɪpnɪs] *of fruit* madurez *f*

'rip-off *n* F robo *m* F

rip-ple [ˈrɪpl] *on water* onda *f*

rise [raɪz] **1** *v/i* (*pret* **rose**, *pp* **risen**) *from chair etc* levantarse; *of sun* salir; *of rocket* ascender, subir; *of price, temperature, water* subir **2** *n in price, temperature* subida *f*, aumento *m*; *in water level* subida *f*; *in salary* aumento *m*; *give rise to* dar pie a

ris-en [ˈrɪzn] *pp* → **rise**

ris-er [ˈraɪzər]: *be an early riser* ser un madrugador; *be a late riser* levantarse tarde

risk [rɪsk] **1** *n* riesgo *m*, peligro *m*; *take a risk* arriesgarse **2** *v/t* arriesgar; *let's risk it* arriesguémonos

risk-y [ˈrɪskɪ] *adj* arriesgado

ris-qué [rɪˈskeɪ] *adj* subido de tono

rit-u-al [ˈrɪtuəl] **1** *n* ritual *m* **2** *adj* ritual

ri-val [ˈraɪvl] **1** *n* rival *m/f* **2** *v/t* rivalizar con; *I can't rival that* no puedo rivalizar con eso

ri-val-ry [ˈraɪvlrɪ] rivalidad *f*

riv-er [ˈrɪvər] río *m*

'riv-er-bank ribera *f*

'riv-er-bed lecho *m*

Riv-er 'Plate *n*: *the River Plate* el Río de la Plata

'riv-er-side **1** *adj* a la orilla del río **2** *n* ribera *f*, orilla *f* del río

R

riv·et ['rɪvɪt] **1** *n* remache *m* **2** *v/t* remachar; *rivet sth to sth* unir algo a algo con remaches

riv·et·ing ['rɪvɪtɪŋ] *adj* fascinante

road [roud] *in country* carretera *f*; *in city* calle *f*; *it's just down the road* está muy cerca

'**road·block** control *m* de carretera

'**road hog** *conductor(a) temerario(-a)*

'**road-hold·ing** *of vehicle* adherencia *f*, agarre *m*

'**road map** mapa *m* de carreteras

road '**safe·ty** seguridad *f* vial

'**road·side**: *at the roadside* al borde de la carretera

'**road-sign** señal *f* de tráfico

'**road·way** calzada *f*

'**road·wor·thy** *adj* en condiciones de circular

roam [roum] *v/i* vagar

roar [rɔːr] **1** *n of traffic, engine* estruendo *m*; *of lion* rugido *m*; *of person* grito *m*, bramido *m* **2** *v/i of engine, lion* rugir; *of person* gritar, bramar; *roar with laughter* reírse a carcajadas

roast [roust] **1** *n of beef etc* asado *m* **2** *v/t* asar **3** *v/i of food* asarse; *we're roasting* nos estamos asando

roast '**beef** rosbif *m*

'**roast·ing tin** [roustɪŋ] fuente *f* para asar

roast '**pork** cerdo *m* asado

rob [rɑːb] *v/t* (*pret & pp robbed*) *person* robar a; *bank* atracar, robar; *I've been robbed* me han robado

rob·ber ['rɑːbər] atracador(a) *m(f)*

rob·ber·y ['rɑːbərɪ] atraco *m*, robo *m*

robe [roub] *of judge* toga *f*; *of priest* sotana *f*; (*bathrobe*) bata *f*

rob·in ['rɑːbɪn] petirrojo *m*

ro·bot ['roubɑːt] robot *m*

ro·bust [rou'bʌst] *adj person, structure* robusto; *material* resistente; *be in robust health* tener una salud de hierro

rock [rɑːk] **1** *n* roca *f*; MUS rock *m*; *on the rocks* *of drink* con hielo; *their marriage is on the rocks* su matrimonio está en crisis **2** *v/t baby* acunar; *cradle* mecer; (*surprise*) sorprender, impactar **3** *v/i on chair* mecerse; *of boat* balancearse

'**rock band** grupo *m* de rock

rock '**bot·tom**: *reach rock bottom* tocar fondo

'**rock-bot·tom** *adj prices* mínimo

'**rock climb·er** escalador(a) *m(f)*

'**rock climb·ing** escalada *f* (en roca)

rock·et ['rɑːkɪt] **1** *n* cohete *m* **2** *v/i of prices etc* dispararse

rock·ing chair ['rɑːkɪŋ] mecedora *f*

'**rock·ing horse** caballito *m* de juguete

rock 'n roll [rɑːkn'roul] rock and roll *m*

'**rock star** estrella *f* del rock

rock·y ['rɑːkɪ] *adj beach, path* pedregoso

rod [rɑːd] vara *f*; *for fishing* caña *f*

rode [roud] *pret → ride*

ro·dent ['roudnt] roedor *m*

rogue [roug] granuja *m/f*, bribón(-ona) *m(f)*

role [roul] papel *m*

'**role mod·el** ejemplo *m*

roll [roul] **1** *n* (*bread roll*) panecillo *m*; *of film* rollo *m*; *of thunder* retumbo *m*; (*list, register*) lista *f* **2** *v/i of ball etc* rodar; *of boat* balancearse **3** *v/t*: *roll sth into a ball* hacer una bola con algo; *roll sth along the ground* hacer rodar algo por el suelo

◆ **roll over 1** *v/i* darse la vuelta **2** *v/t person, object* dar la vuelta a; (*renew*) renovar; (*extend*) refinanciar

◆ **roll up 1** *v/t sleeves* remangar **2** *v/i* F (*arrive*) llegar

'**roll-call** lista *f*

roll·er ['roulər] *for hair* rulo *m*

'**roll·er blade**® *n* patín *m* en línea

'**roll·er blind** persiana *f*

'**roll·er coast·er** ['roulərkoustər] montaña *f* rusa

'**roll·er skate** *n* patín *m* (de ruedas)

roll·ing pin ['roulɪŋ] rodillo *m* de cocina

ROM [rɑːm] COMPUT *abbr* (= *read only memory*) ROM *f* (= memoria *f* de sólo lectura)

Ro·man ['roumən] **1** *adj* romano **2** *n* romano(-a) *m(f)*

Ro·man 'Cath·o·lic 1 *n* REL católico(-a) *m(f)* romano(-a) **2** *adj* católico romano

ro·mance [rə'mæns] (*affair*) aventura *f* (amorosa); *novel* novela *f* rosa; *movie* película *f* romántica

ro·man·tic [rou'mæntɪk] *adj* romántico

ro·man·tic·al·ly [rou'mæntɪklɪ] *adv*: *be romantically involved with s.o.* tener un romance con alguien

roof [ruːf] techo *m*, tejado *m*; *have a roof over one's head* tener un techo donde dormir

'**roof-rack** MOT baca *f*

rook·ie ['rukɪ] F novato(-a) *m(f)*

room [ruːm] habitación *f*; (*space*) espacio *m*, sitio *m*; *there's no room for …* no hay sitio para …, no cabe …

'**room clerk** recepcionista *m/f*

'**room·mate** *sharing room* compañero(-a) *m(f)* de habitación; *sharing apartment* compañero(-a) *m(f)* de apartamento

'**room ser·vice** servicio *m* de habitaciones

room 'tem·per·a·ture temperatura *f* ambiente

room·y ['ruːmɪ] *adj house, car etc* espacioso; *clothes* holgado

root [ruːt] *n* raíz *f*; *roots of person* raíces *fpl*

◆ **root for** *v/t* F apoyar

◆ **root out** *v/t* (*get rid of*) cortar de raíz; (*find*) encontrar

rope [rəʊp] cuerda *f*; *thick* soga *f*; *show s.o. the ropes* poner a alguien al tanto

◆ **rope off** *v/t* acordonar

ro·sa·ry ['rəʊzərɪ] REL rosario *m*

rose[1] [rəʊz] BOT rosa *f*

rose[2] [rəʊz] *pret* → **rise**

rose·ma·ry ['rəʊzmərɪ] romero *m*

ros·trum ['rɑːstrəm] estrado *m*

ros·y ['rəʊzɪ] *adj cheeks* sonrosado; *future* de color de rosa

rot [rɑːt] **1** *n in wood* putrefacción *f* **2** *v/i* (*pret & pp* **rotted**) *of food, wood* pudrirse; *of teeth* cariarse

ro·ta ['rəʊtə] turnos *mpl*; *actual document* calendario *m* con los turnos

ro·tate [rəʊ'teɪt] **1** *v/i of blades, earth* girar **2** *v/t hacer* girar; *crops* rotar

ro·ta·tion [rəʊ'teɪʃn] *around the sun etc* rotación *f*; *do sth in rotation* hacer algo por turnos rotatorios

rot·ten ['rɑːtn] *adj food, wood etc* podrido; *weather, luck* horrible; *that was a rotten trick* ¡qué mala idea!

rough [rʌf] **1** *adj surface, ground* accidentado; *hands, skin* áspero; *voice* ronco; (*violent*) bruto; *crossing* movido; *seas* bravo; (*approximate*) aproximado; *rough draft* borrador *m* **2** *adv*: *sleep rough* dormir a la intemperie **3** *n in golf* rough *m* **4** *v/t*: *rough it* apañárselas

◆ **rough up** *v/t* F dar una paliza a

rough·age ['rʌfɪdʒ] *in food* fibra *f*

rough·ly ['rʌflɪ] *adv* (*approximately*) aproximadamente; (*harshly*) brutalmente; *roughly speaking* aproximadamente

rou·lette [ruː'let] ruleta *f*

round [raʊnd] **1** *adj* redondo; *in round figures* en números redondos **2** *n of mailman, doctor, drinks, competition* ronda *f*; *of toast* rebanada *f*; *in boxing match* round *m*, asalto *m* **3** *v/t corner* doblar **4** *adv, prep* → **around**

◆ **round off** *v/t edges* redondear; *meeting, night out* concluir

◆ **round up** *v/t figure* redondear (hacia la cifra más alta); *suspects, criminals* detener

round·a·bout ['raʊndəbaʊt] **1** *adj route, way of saying sth* indirecto **2** *n Br on road* rotonda *f*, *Span* glorieta *f*

'**round-the-world** *adj* alrededor del mundo

round 'trip viaje *m* de ida y vuelta

round trip 'tick·et billete *m or L.Am.* boleto *m* de ida y vuelta

'**round-up** *of cattle* rodeo *m*; *of suspects, criminals* redada *f*; *of news* resumen *m*

rouse [raʊz] *v/t from sleep* despertar; *interest, emotions* excitar, provocar

rous·ing ['raʊzɪŋ] *adj speech, finale* emocionante

route [raʊt] *n* ruta *f*, recorrido *m*

rou·tine [ruː'tiːn] **1** *adj* habitual **2** *n* rutina *f*; *as a matter of routine* como rutina

row[1] [rəʊ] *n* (*line*) hilera *f*; *5 days in a row* 5 días seguidos

row[2] [rəʊ] **1** *v/t boat* llevar remando **2** *v/i* remar

row[3] [raʊ] *n* (*quarrel*) pelea *f*, discusión *f*; (*noise*) alboroto *m*

'**row·boat** ['rəʊbəʊt] bote *m* de remos

row·dy ['raʊdɪ] *adj* alborotador, *Span* follonero

roy·al ['rɔɪəl] *adj* real

roy·al·ty ['rɔɪəltɪ] *royal persons* realeza *f*; *on book, recording* derechos *mpl* de autor

rub [rʌb] *v/t* (*pret & pp* **rubbed**) frotar

◆ **rub down** *v/t to clean* lijar

◆ **rub in** *v/t cream, ointment* extender, frotar; *don't rub it in! fig* ¡no me lo restriegues por las narices!

◆ **rub off** *v/t dirt* limpiar frotando; *paint etc* borrar **2** *v/i*: *it rubs off on you* se te contagia

rub·ber ['rʌbər] **1** *n material* goma *f*, caucho *m*; P (*condom*) goma *f* P **2** *adj* de goma *or* caucho

rub·ber 'band goma *f* elástica

rub·ber 'gloves *npl* guantes *mpl* de goma

rub·bish ['rʌbɪʃ] basura *f*; *poor quality* basura *f*, porquería *f*; (*nonsense*) tonterías *fpl*; *this radio is rubbish* esta radio es una basura *or* porquería; *don't talk rubbish!* ¡no digas tonterías!

rub·ble ['rʌbl] escombros *mpl*

ru·by ['ruːbɪ] *jewel* rubí *m*

ruck·sack ['rʌksæk] mochila *f*

rud·der ['rʌdər] timón *m*

rud·dy ['rʌdɪ] *adj complexion* rubicundo

rude [ruːd] *adj person, behavior* maleducado; *language* grosero; *it is rude to …* es de mala educación …; *I didn't mean to be rude* no pretendía faltar al respeto

rude·ly ['ruːdlɪ] *adv* (*impolitely*) groseramente

rude·ness ['ruːdnɪs] mala *f* educación, grosería *f*

ru·di·men·ta·ry [ruːdɪ'mentərɪ] *adj* rudimentario

ru·di·ments ['ruːdɪmənts] *npl* rudimentos *mpl*

rue·ful ['ruːfəl] *adj* arrepentido, compungido

rue·ful·ly ['ruːfəlɪ] *adv* con arrepentimiento

ruf·fi·an ['rʌfɪən] rufián *m*

ruf·fle ['rʌfl] **1** *n* on dress volante *m* **2** *v/t* *hair* despeinar; *clothes* arrugar; *person* alterar, enfadar; **get ruffled** alterarse

rug [rʌg] alfombra *f*; (*blanket*) manta *f* (de viaje)

rug·by ['rʌgbɪ] rugby *m*

'**rug·by match** partido *m* de rugby

'**rug·by play·er** jugador(a) *m(f)* de rugby

rug·ged ['rʌgɪd] *adj* *scenery*, *cliffs* escabroso, accidentado; *face* de rasgos duros; *resistance* decidido

ru·in ['ruːɪn] **1** *n* ruina *f*; **ruins** ruinas *fpl*; **in ruins** *city*, *building* en ruinas; *of plans*, *marriage* arruinado **2** *v/t* arruinar; **be ruined** *financially* estar arruinado *or* en la ruina

rule [ruːl] **1** *n* of club, game regla *f*, norma *f*; *of monarch* reinado *m*; *for measuring* regla *f*; **as a rule** por regla general **2** *v/t* *country* gobernar; **the judge ruled that ...** el juez dictaminó que ... **3** *v/i* *of monarch* reinar

◆ **rule out** *v/t* descartar

rul·er ['ruːlər] *for measuring* regla *f*; *of state* gobernante *m/f*

rul·ing ['ruːlɪŋ] **1** *n* fallo *m*, decisión *f* **2** *adj* *party* gobernante, en el poder

rum [rʌm] *n* drink ron *m*

rum·ble ['rʌmbl] *v/i* of stomach gruñir; *of train in tunnel* retumbar

◆ **rum·mage around** ['rʌmɪdʒ] *v/i* buscar revolviendo

'**rum·mage sale** rastrillo *m* benéfico

ru·mor ['ruːmər] **1** *n* rumor *m* **2** *v/t*: **it is rumored that ...** se rumorea que ...

rump [rʌmp] *of animal* cuartos *mpl* traseros

rum·ple ['rʌmpl] *of clothes*, *paper* arrugar

'**rump·steak** filete *m* de lomo

run [rʌn] **1** *n* on foot carrera *f*; *in car* viaje *m*; *in tights* carrera *f*; THEA: *of play* temporada *f*; **it has had a three year run** *of play* lleva tres años en cartel; **go for a run** ir a correr; **go for a run in the car** ir a dar una vuelta en el coche; **make a run for it** salir corriendo; **a criminal on the run** un criminal fugado; **in the short / long run** a corto / largo plazo; **a run on the dollar** un movimiento especulativo contra el dólar **2** *v/i* (*pret* **ran**, *pp* **run**) *of person*, *animal* correr; *of river* correr, discurrir; *of paint*, *make-up* correrse; *of play* estar

en cartel; *of engine*, *machine*, *software* funcionar; *in election* presentarse; **run for President** presentarse a las elecciones presidenciales; **the trains run every ten minutes** pasan trenes cada diez minutos; **it doesn't run on Saturdays** *of bus*, *train* no funciona los sábados; **don't leave the tap running** no dejes el grifo abierto; **his nose is running** le moquea la nariz; **her eyes are running** le lloran los ojos **3** *v/t* (*pret* **ran**, *pp* **run**) *race* correr; *business*, *hotel*, *project etc* dirigir; *software* usar; (*start*) ejecutar; *car* tener; (*use*) usar; **can I run you to the station?** ¿te puedo llevar hasta la estación?; **he ran his eye down the page** echó una ojeada a la página

◆ **run across** *v/t* (*meet*) encontrarse con; (*find*) encontrar

◆ **run away** *v/i* salir corriendo, huir; *from home* escaparse

◆ **run down 1** *v/t* (*knock down*) atropellar; (*criticize*) criticar; *stocks* reducir **2** *v/i* *of battery* agotarse

◆ **run into** *v/t* (*meet*) encontrarse con; *difficulties* tropezar con

◆ **run off 1** *v/i* salir corriendo **2** *v/t* (*print off*) tirar

◆ **run out** *v/i* of contract vencer; *of supplies* agotarse; **time has run out** se ha acabado el tiempo

◆ **run out of** *v/t* time, supplies quedarse sin; **I ran out of gas** me quedé sin gasolina; **I'm running out of patience** se me está acabando la paciencia

◆ **run over 1** *v/t* (*knock down*) atropellar; **can we run over the details again?** ¿podríamos repasar los detalles otra vez? **2** *v/i* of water etc desbordarse

◆ **run through** *v/t* (*rehearse*, *go over*) repasar

◆ **run up** *v/t* debts, large bill acumular; *clothes* coser

run·a·way ['rʌnəweɪ] *n* persona que se ha fugado de casa

run·down *adj* person débil, apagado; *part of town*, *building* ruinoso

rung¹ [rʌŋ] *of ladder* peldaño *m*

rung² [rʌŋ] *pp* → **ring²**

run·ner ['rʌnər] *athlete* corredor(a) *m(f)*

run·ner 'beans *npl* judías *fpl* verdes, *L.Am.* porotos *mpl* verdes, *Mex* ejotes *mpl*

run·ner-'up subcampeón(-ona) *m(f)*

run·ning ['rʌnɪŋ] **1** *n* el correr; (*jogging*) footing *m*; *of business* gestión *f* **2** *adj*: **for two days running** durante dos días seguidos

run·ning 'wa·ter agua *f* corriente

run·ny ['rʌnɪ] *adj mixture* fluido, líquido; *nose* que moquea

'run-up SP carrerilla *f*; *in the run-up to* en el periodo previo a

'run·way pista *f* de aterrizaje / despegue

rup·ture ['rʌptʃər] **1** *n* ruptura *f* **2** *v/i of pipe etc* romperse

ru·ral ['rʊrəl] *adj* rural

ruse [ruːz] artimaña *f*

rush [rʌʃ] **1** *n* prisa *f*; *do sth in a rush* hacer algo con prisas; *be in a rush* tener prisa; *what's the big rush?* ¿qué prisa tenemos? **2** *v/t person* meter prisa a; *meal* comer a toda prisa; *rush s.o. to hospital* llevar a alguien al hospital a toda prisa **3** *v/i* darse prisa

'rush hour hora *f* punta

Rus·sia ['rʌʃə] Rusia

Rus·sian ['rʌʃən] **1** *adj* ruso **2** *n* ruso(-a) *m(f)*; *language* ruso *m*

rust [rʌst] **1** *n* óxido *m* **2** *v/i* oxidarse

rus·tle ['rʌsl] **1** *n of silk, leaves* susurro *m* **2** *v/i of silk, leaves* susurrar

'rust-proof *adj* inoxidable

rust re·mov·er ['rʌstrɪmuːvər] desoxidante *m*

rust·y ['rʌstɪ] *adj* oxidado; *my French is pretty rusty* tengo el francés muy abandonado; *I'm a little rusty* estoy un poco falto de forma

rut [rʌt] *in road* rodada *f*; *be in a rut fig* estar estancado

ruth·less ['ruːθlɪs] *adj* implacable, despiadado

ruth·less·ly ['ruːθlɪslɪ] *adv* sin compasión, despiadadamente

ruth·less·ness ['ruːθlɪsnɪs] falta *f* de compasión

rye [raɪ] centeno *m*

'rye bread pan *m* de centeno

S

sab·bat·i·cal [sə'bætɪkl] *n year* año *m* sabático; *a 6 month sabbatical* 6 meses de excedencia

sab·o·tage ['sæbətɑːʒ] **1** *n* sabotaje *m* **2** *v/t* sabotear

sab·o·teur [sæbə'tɜːr] saboteador(a) *m(f)*

sac·cha·rin ['sækərɪn] *n* sacarina *f*

sa·chet ['sæʃeɪ] *of shampoo, cream etc* sobrecito *m*

sack [sæk] **1** *n bag* saco *m*; *for groceries* bolsa *f*; *he got the sack* F lo echaron **2** *v/t* F echar

sa·cred ['seɪkrɪd] *adj* sagrado

sac·ri·fice ['sækrɪfaɪs] **1** *n* sacrificio *m*; *make sacrifices fig* hacer sacrificios **2** *v/t* sacrificar

sac·ri·lege ['sækrɪlɪdʒ] sacrilegio *m*

sad [sæd] *adj person, face, song* triste; *state of affairs* lamentable, desgraciado

sad·dle ['sædl] **1** *n* silla *f* de montar **2** *v/t horse* ensillar; *saddle s.o. with sth fig* endilgar algo a alguien

sa·dism ['seɪdɪzm] sadismo *m*

sa·dist ['seɪdɪst] sádico(-a) *m(f)*

sa·dis·tic [sə'dɪstɪk] *adj* sádico

sad·ly ['sædlɪ] *adv look, say etc* con tristeza; *(regrettably)* lamentablemente

sad·ness ['sædnɪs] tristeza *f*

safe [seɪf] **1** *adj* seguro; *driver* prudente; *(not in danger)* a salvo; *is it safe to walk here?* ¿se puede andar por aquí sin peligro? **2** *n* caja *f* fuerte

'safe·guard 1 *n* garantía *f*; *as a safeguard against* como garantía contra **2** *v/t* salvaguardar

safe·ly ['seɪflɪ] *adv arrive* sin percances; *(successfully)* sin problemas; *drive* prudentemente; *assume* con certeza

'safe keep·ing: *give sth to s.o. for safe keeping* dar algo a alguien para que lo custodie

safe·ty ['seɪftɪ] seguridad *f*

'safe·ty belt cinturón *m* de seguridad

'safe·ty-con·scious *adj*: *be safety-conscious* tener en cuenta la seguridad

safe·ty 'first prevención *f* de accidentes

'safe·ty pin imperdible *m*

sag [sæg] **1** *n in ceiling etc* combadura *f* **2** *v/i (pret & pp sagged) of ceiling* combarse; *of rope* destensarse; *of tempo* disminuir

sa·ga ['sɑːgə] saga *f*

sage [seɪdʒ] *n herb* salvia *f*

Sa·git·tar·i·us [sædʒɪ'terɪəs] ASTR Sagitario *m/f inv*

said [sed] *pret & pp* → **say**

sail [seɪl] **1** *n of boat* vela *f*; *trip* viaje *m* (en barco); **go for a sail** salir a navegar **2** v/t *yacht* manejar **3** v/i navegar; *(depart)* zarpar, hacerse a la mar

'**sail·board 1** n tabla f de windsurf **2** v/i hacer windsurf

'**sail·board·ing** windsurf m

'**sail·boat** barco m de vela, velero m

sail·ing ['seɪlɪŋ] sp vela f

'**sail·ing ship** barco m de vela, velero m

sail·or ['seɪlər] *in the navy* marino m/f; *in the merchant navy*, sp marinero(-a) m(f); *I'm a good / bad sailor* no me mareo / me mareo con facilidad

saint [seɪnt] santo m

sake [seɪk]: *for my sake* por mí; *for the sake of peace* por la paz

sal·ad ['sæləd] ensalada f

sal·ad 'dress·ing aliño m or aderezo m para ensalada

sal·a·ry ['sælərɪ] sueldo m, salario f

'**sal·a·ry scale** escala f salarial

sale [seɪl] venta f; *reduced prices* rebajas fpl; *for sale* sign se vende; *is this for sale?* ¿está a la venta?; *be on sale* estar a la venta; *at reduced prices* estar de rebajas

sales [seɪlz] npl *department* ventas fpl

'**sales clerk** *in store* vendedor(a) m(f), dependiente(-a) m(f)

'**sales fig·ures** npl cifras fpl de ventas

'**sales·man** vendedor m

sales 'man·ag·er jefe(-a) m(f) de ventas

'**sales meet·ing** reunión f del departamento de ventas

'**sales·wo·man** vendedora f

sa·li·ent ['seɪlɪənt] adj sobresaliente, destacado

sa·li·va [sə'laɪvə] saliva f

salm·on ['sæmən] *(pl salmon)* salmón m

sa·loon [sə'luːn] MOT turismo m; *(bar)* bar m

salt [sɒlt] **1** n sal f **2** v/t *food* salar

'**salt·cel·lar** salero m

salt 'wa·ter agua f salada

'**salt-wa·ter fish** pez m de agua salada

salt·y ['sɒltɪ] adj salado

sal·u·tar·y ['sæljʊtərɪ] adj *experience* beneficioso

sa·lute [sə'luːt] **1** n MIL saludo m; *take the salute* presidir un desfile **2** v/t saludar; *fig (hail)* elogiar **3** v/i MIL saludar

Sal·va·dor(e)·an [sælvə'dɔːrən] **1** adj salvadoreño **2** n salvadoreño(-a) m(f)

sal·vage ['sælvɪdʒ] v/t *from wreck* rescatar

sal·va·tion [sæl'veɪʃn] *also fig* salvación f

Sal·va·tion 'Ar·my Ejército m de Salvación

same [seɪm] **1** adj mismo **2** pron: *the same* lo mismo; *Happy New Year - the*

same to you Feliz Año Nuevo - igualmente; *he's not the same any more* ya no es el mismo; *life isn't the same without you* la vida es distinta sin ti; *all the same (even so)* aun así; *men are all the same* todos los hombres son iguales; *it's all the same to me* me da lo mismo, me da igual **3** adv: *the same* igual

sam·ple ['sæmpl] n muestra f

sanc·ti·mo·ni·ous [sæŋktɪ'mounɪəs] adj mojigato

sanc·tion ['sæŋkʃn] **1** n *(approval)* consentimiento m, aprobación f; *(penalty)* sanción f **2** v/t *(approve)* sancionar

sanc·ti·ty ['sæŋktɪtɪ] carácter m sagrado

sanc·tu·a·ry ['sæŋktʃʊerɪ] santuario m

sand [sænd] **1** n arena f **2** v/t *with sandpaper* lijar

san·dal ['sændl] sandalia f

'**sand·bag** saco m de arena

'**sand·blast** v/t arenar

'**sand dune** duna f

sand·er ['sændər] *tool* lijadora f

'**sand·pa·per 1** n lija f **2** v/t lijar

'**sand·stone** arenisca f

sand·wich ['sænwɪʧ] **1** n *Span* bocadillo m, *L.Am.* sandwich m **2** v/t: *be sandwiched between two ...* estar encajonado entre dos ...

sand·y ['sændɪ] adj *soil* arenoso; *feet, towel etc* lleno de arena; *hair* rubio oscuro; *sandy beach* playa f de arena

sane [seɪn] adj cuerdo

sang [sæŋ] pret → **sing**

san·i·tar·i·um [sænɪ'terɪəm] sanatorio m

san·i·ta·ry ['sænɪterɪ] adj *conditions* salubre, higiénico; *sanitary installations* instalaciones fpl sanitarias

'**san·i·ta·ry nap·kin** compresa f

san·i·ta·tion [sænɪ'teɪʃn] *(sanitary installations)* instalaciones fpl sanitarias; *(removal of waste)* saneamiento f

san·i·ta·tion de·part·ment servicio m de limpieza

san·i·ty ['sænɪtɪ] razón f, juicio m

sank [sæŋk] pret → **sink**

San·ta Claus ['sæntəklɔːz] Papá Noel m, Santa Claus m

sap [sæp] **1** n *in tree* savia f **2** v/t *(pret & pp sapped)* *s.o.'s energy* consumir

sap·phire ['sæfaɪr] n *jewel* zafiro m

sar·cas·m ['sɑːrkæzm] sarcasmo m

sar·cas·tic [sɑːr'kæstɪk] adj sarcástico

sar·cas·ti·cal·ly [sɑːr'kæstɪklɪ] adv sarcásticamente

sar·dine [sɑːr'diːn] sardina f

sar·don·ic [sɑːr'dɑːnɪk] adj sardónico

sar·don·i·cal·ly [sɑːr'dɑːnɪklɪ] adv sardó-

S

nicamente

sash [sæʃ] *on dress* faja *f*; *on uniform* fajín *m*

sat [sæt] *pret & pp* → **sit**

Sa·tan ['seɪtn] Satán, Satanás

satch·el ['sætʃl] *for schoolchild* cartera *f*

sat·el·lite ['sætəlaɪt] satélite *m*

'sat·el·lite dish antena *f* parabólica

sat·el·lite T·V televisión *f* por satélite

sat·in ['sætɪn] **1** *adj* satinado **2** *n* satén *m*

sat·ire ['sætaɪr] sátira *f*

sa·tir·i·cal [sə'tɪrɪkl] *adj* satírico

sat·i·rist ['sætərɪst] escritor(a) *m(f)* de sátiras

sat·i·rize ['sætəraɪz] *v/t* satirizar

sat·is·fac·tion [sætɪs'fækʃn] satisfacción *f*; *I get satisfaction out of my job* mi trabajo me produce satisfacción; *is that to your satisfaction madam?* *fml* ¿está al gusto de la señora?

sat·is·fac·to·ry [sætɪs'fæktərɪ] *adj* satisfactorio; (*just good enough*) suficiente

sat·is·fy ['sætɪsfaɪ] *v/t* (*pret & pp **satisfied***) satisfacer; *conditions* cumplir; *I am satisfied* (*had enough to eat*) estoy lleno; *I am satisfied that ...* (*convinced*) estoy convencido *or* satisfecho de que ...; *I hope you're satisfied!* ¡estarás contento!

Sat·ur·day ['sætərdeɪ] sábado *m*

sauce [sɔːs] salsa *f*

'sauce·pan cacerola *f*

sau·cer ['sɔːsər] plato *m* (*de taza*)

sauc·y ['sɔːsɪ] *adj person, dress* descarado

Sa·u·di A·ra·bi·a [saʊdɪə'reɪbɪə] Arabia Saudí *or* Saudita

Sa·u·di A·ra·bi·an [saʊdɪə'reɪbɪən] **1** *adj* saudita, saudí **2** *n* saudita *m/f*, saudí *m/f*

sau·na ['sɔːnə] sauna *f*

saun·ter ['sɔːntər] *v/i* andar sin prisas

saus·age ['sɔːsɪdʒ] salchicha *f*

sav·age ['sævɪdʒ] **1** *adj animal, attack* salvaje; *criticism* feroz **2** *n* salvaje *m/f*

sav·age·ry ['sævɪdʒrɪ] crueldad *f*

save [seɪv] **1** *v/t* (*rescue*) rescatar, salvar; *money, time, effort* ahorrar; (*collect*) guardar; COMPUT guardar; *goal* parar; REL salvar **2** *v/i* (*put money aside*) ahorrar; SP hacer una parada **3** *n* SP parada *f*

◆ **save up for** *v/t* ahorrar para

sav·er ['seɪvər] *person* ahorrador(a) *m(f)*

sav·ing ['seɪvɪŋ] *amount saved, activity* ahorro *m*

sav·ings ['seɪvɪŋz] *npl* ahorros *mpl*

'sav·ings ac·count cuenta *f* de ahorros

'sav·ings and 'loan caja *f* de ahorros

'sav·ings bank caja *f* de ahorros

sa·vior, *Br* **sa·viour** ['seɪvjər] REL salva-

dor *m*

sa·vor ['seɪvər] *v/t* saborear

sa·vor·y ['seɪvərɪ] *adj not sweet* salado

sa·vour *etc Br* → **savor** *etc*

saw[1] [sɔː] **1** *n tool* serrucho *m*, sierra *f* **2** *v/t* aserrar

saw[2] [sɔː] *pret* → **see**

◆ **saw off** *v/t* cortar (con un serrucho)

'saw·dust serrín *m*, aserrín *m*

sax·o·phone ['sæksəfoʊn] saxofón *m*

say [seɪ] **1** *v/t* (*pret & pp **said***) decir; *poem* recitar; *that is to say* es decir; *what do you say to that?* ¿qué opinas de eso?; *what does the note say?* ¿qué dice la nota?, ¿qué pone en la nota? **2** *n*: *have one's say* expresar una opinión

say·ing ['seɪɪŋ] dicho *m*

scab [skæb] *on skin* costra *f*

scaf·fold·ing ['skæfəldɪŋ] *on building* andamiaje *m*

scald [skɔːld] *v/t* escaldar

scale[1] [skeɪl] *on fish, reptile* escama *f*

scale[2] [skeɪl] **1** *n* (*size*) escala *f*, tamaño *m*; *on thermometer, map,* MUS escala *f*; *on a larger scale* a gran escala; *on a smaller scale* a pequeña escala **2** *v/t cliffs etc* escalar

◆ **scale down** *v/t* disminuir, reducir

scale 'draw·ing dibujo *m* a escala

scales [skeɪlz] *npl for weighing* báscula *f*, peso *m*

scal·lop ['skæləp] *n shellfish* vieira *f*

scalp [skælp] *n* cuero *m* cabelludo

scal·pel ['skælpl] bisturí *m*

scam [skæm] F chanchullo *m* F

scam·pi ['skæmpi] gambas *fpl* rebozadas

scan [skæn] **1** *v/t* (*pret & pp **scanned***) *horizon* otear; *page* ojear; COMPUT escanear **2** *n of brain* escáner *m*; *of fetus* ecografía *f*

◆ **scan in** *v/t* COMPUT escanear

scan·dal ['skændl] escándalo *m*

scan·dal·ize ['skændəlaɪz] *v/t* escandalizar

scan·dal·ous ['skændələs] *adj affair, prices* escandaloso

Scan·di·na·vi·a [skændɪ'neɪvɪə] Escandinavia

scan·ner ['skænər] MED, COMPUT escáner *m*; *for foetus* ecógrafo *m*

scant [skænt] *adj* escaso

scant·i·ly ['skæntɪlɪ] *adv*: *be scantily clad* andar ligero de ropa

scant·y ['skæntɪ] *adj skirt* cortísimo; *bikini* mínimo

scape·goat ['skeɪpgoʊt] cabeza *f* de turco, chivo *m* expiatorio

scar [skɑːr] **1** *n* cicatriz *f* **2** *v/t* (*pret & pp* *scarred*) cicatrizar

scarce [skers] *adj in short supply* escaso; **make o.s. scarce** desaparecer

scarce·ly ['skersli] *adv*: **he had scarcely said it when ...** apenas lo había dicho cuando ...; **there was scarcely anything left** no quedaba casi nada; **I scarcely know her** apenas la conozco

scar·ci·ty ['skersiti] escasez *f*

scare [sker] **1** *v/t* asustar, atemorizar; **be scared of** tener miedo de **2** *n* (*panic, alarm*) miedo *m*, temor *m*; **give s.o. a scare** dar a alguien un susto

◆ **scare away** *v/t* ahuyentar

'scare-crow espantapájaros *m inv*

scare·mon·ger ['skermʌŋgər] alarmista *m/f*

scarf [skɑːrf] *around neck, over head* pañuelo *m*; *woollen* bufanda *f*

scar·let ['skɑːrlət] *adj* escarlata

scar·let 'fe·ver escarlatina *f*

scar·y ['skeri] *adj sight* espeluznante; **scary music** música de miedo

scath·ing ['skeiðiŋ] *adj* feroz

scat·ter ['skætər] **1** *v/t leaflets* esparcir; *seeds* diseminar; **be scattered all over the room** estar esparcido por toda la habitación **2** *v/i of people* dispersarse

scat·ter·brained ['skætərbreind] *adj* despistado

scat·tered ['skætərd] *adj showers, family, villages* disperso

scav·enge ['skævindʒ] *v/i* rebuscar; **scavenge for sth** rebuscar en busca de algo

scav·eng·er ['skævindʒər] *animal, bird* carroñero *m*; (*person*) persona que busca comida entre la basura

sce·nar·i·o [sɪ'nɑːrɪou] situación *f*

scene [siːn] escena *f*; *of accident, crime etc* lugar *m*; (*argument*) escena *f*, número *m*; **make a scene** hacer una escena, montar un número; **scenes** THEA decorados *mpl*; **jazz / rock scene** mundo del jazz / rock; **behind the scenes** entre bastidores

sce·ne·ry ['siːnəri] THEA escenario *m*

scent [sent] *n* olor *m*; (*perfume*) perfume *m*, fragancia *m*

scep·tic *etc Br* → **skeptic** *etc*

sched·ule ['ʃedu:l] **1** *n of events, work* programa *m*; *of exams* calendario *m*; *for train, work, of lessons* horario *m*; **be on schedule** *of work* ir según lo previsto; *of train* ir a la hora prevista; **be behind schedule** *of work, train etc* ir con retraso **2** *v/t* (*put on schedule*) programar; **it's scheduled for completion next month** está previsto que se complete el próximo mes

sched·uled 'flight ['ʃedu:ld] vuelo *m* regular

scheme [skiːm] **1** *n* (*plan*) plan *m*, proyecto *m*; (*plot*) confabulación *f* **2** *v/i* (*plot*) confabularse

schem·ing ['skiːmiŋ] *adj* maquinador

schiz·o·phre·ni·a [skitsə'friːniə] esquizofrenia *f*

schiz·o·phren·ic [skitsə'frenik] **1** *n* esquizofrénico(-a) *m(f)* **2** *adj* esquizofrénico

schol·ar ['skɑːlər] erudito(-a) *m(f)*

schol·ar·ly ['skɑːlərli] *adj* erudito

schol·ar·ship ['skɑːlərʃɪp] *scholarly work* estudios *mpl*; *financial award* beca *f*

school [skuːl] escuela *f*, colegio *m*; (*university*) universidad *f*

'school bag (*satchel*) cartera *f*

'school·boy escolar *m*

'school·children *npl* escolares *mpl*

'school days *npl*; **do you remember your school days?** ¿te acuerdas de cuándo ibas al colegio?

'school·girl escolar *f*

'school·mate compañero *m* de colegio

'school·teach·er maestro(-a) *m(f)*, profesor(a) *m(f)*

sci·at·i·ca [sai'ætikə] ciática *f*

sci·ence ['saiəns] ciencia *f*

sci·ence 'fic·tion *npl* ciencia *f* ficción

sci·en·tif·ic [saiən'tifik] *adj* científico

sci·en·tist ['saiəntist] científico(-a) *m(f)*

scis·sors ['sizərz] *npl* tijeras *fpl*

scoff¹ [skɑːf] *v/t* (*eat fast*) zamparse F

scoff² [skɑːf] *v/i* (*mock*) burlarse, mofarse

◆ **scoff at** *v/t* burlarse de, mofarse de

scold [skould] *v/t child, husband* regañar

scoop [skuːp] **1** *n implement* cuchara *f*; *for mud* pala *f*; (*story*) exclusiva *f* **2** *v/t*: **scoop sth into sth** recoger algo para meterlo en algo

◆ **scoop up** *v/t* recoger

scoot·er ['skuːtər] *with motor* escúter *m*; *child's* patinete *m*

scope [skoup] alcance *m*; (*freedom, opportunity*) oportunidad *f*; **he wants more scope to do his own thing** quiere más libertad para hacer lo que quiere

scorch [skɔːrtʃ] *v/t* quemar

scorch·ing ['skɔːrtʃiŋ] *adj* abrasador

score [skɔːr] **1** *n* SP resultado *m*; *in competition* puntuación *f*; (*written music*) partitura *f*; *of movie etc* banda *f* sonora, música *f*; **what's the score?** ¿cómo van?; **have a score to settle with s.o.** tener una cuenta pendiente con alguien; **keep (the) score** llevar el tanteo **2** *v/t goal* marcar; *point* anotar; (*cut: line*) marcar **3** v/i marcar; (*keep the score*) llevar el tanteo; ***that's where he scores*** ése es su punto fuerte

'score-board marcador m

scor·er ['skɔːrər] *of goal* goleador(a) m(f); *of point* anotador(a) m(f); (*official score-keeper*) encargado del marcador

scorn [skɔːrn] **1** n desprecio m; ***pour scorn on sth*** despreciar algo, menospreciar algo **2** v/t *idea, suggestion* despreciar

scorn·ful ['skɔːrnfəl] *adj* despreciativo

scorn·ful·ly ['skɔːrnfəlɪ] *adv* con desprecio

Scor·pi·o ['skɔːrpɪoʊ] ASTR Escorpio m/f inv

Scot [skɑːt] escocés(-esa) m(f)

Scotch [skɑːtʃ] (*whisky*) whisky m escocés

Scotch 'tape® celo m, L.Am. Durex® m

scot-'free *adv*: ***get off scot-free*** salir impune

Scot·land ['skɑːtlənd] Escocia

Scots·man ['skɑːtsmən] escocés m

Scots·wom·an ['skɑːtswʊmən] escocesa f

Scot·tish ['skɑːtɪʃ] *adj* escocés

scoun·drel ['skaʊndrəl] canalla m/f

scour¹ [skaʊr] v/t (*search*) rastrear, peinar

scour² ['skaʊər] v/t *pans* fregar

scout [skaʊt] n (*boy scout*) boy-scout m

scowl [skaʊl] **1** n ceño m **2** v/i fruncir el ceño

scram [skræm] v/i (*pret & pp* **scrammed**) F largarse F; ***scram!*** ¡largo!

scram·ble ['skræmbl] **1** n (*rush*) prisa f **2** v/t *message* cifrar, codificar **3** v/i (*climb*) trepar; ***he scrambled to his feet*** se levantó de un salto

scram·bled 'eggs ['skræmbld] *npl* huevos *mpl* revueltos

scrap [skræp] **1** n *metal* chatarra f; (*fight*) pelea f; *of food* trocito m; *of evidence* indicio m; *of common sense* pizca f **2** v/t (*pret & pp* **scrapped**) *plan, project* abandonar; *paragraph* borrar

'scrap·book álbum m de recortes

scrape [skreɪp] **1** n *on paintwork etc* arañazo m **2** v/t *paintwork* rayar; ***scrape a living*** apañarse

♦ scrape through v/i *in exam* aprobar por los pelos

'scrap heap: ***be good for the scrap heap*** *of person* estar para el arrastre; *of object* estar para tirar

scrap 'met·al chatarra f

scrap 'pa·per papel m usado

scrap·py ['skræpɪ] *adj work, writing* desorganizado

scratch [skrætʃ] **1** n *mark* marca f; ***have a scratch*** *to stop itching* rascarse; ***start from scratch*** empezar desde cero; ***your work isn't up to scratch*** tu trabajo es insuficiente **2** v/t (*mark: skin*) arañar; (*mark: paint*) rayar; *because of itch* rascarse **3** v/i *of cat etc* arañar; *because of itch* rascarse

scrawl [skrɔːl] **1** n garabato m **2** v/t garabatear

scraw·ny ['skrɔːnɪ] *adj* escuálido

scream [skriːm] **1** n grito m; ***screams of laughter*** carcajadas *fpl* **2** v/i gritar

screech [skriːtʃ] **1** n *of tires* chirrido m; (*scream*) chillido m **2** v/i *of tires* chirriar; (*scream*) chillar

screen [skriːn] **1** n *in room, hospital* mampara f; *protective* cortina f; *in movie theater* pantalla f; COMPUT monitor m, pantalla f **2** v/t (*protect, hide*) ocultar; *movie* proyectar; *for security reasons* investigar

'screen·play guión m

'screen sav·er COMPUT salvapantallas m inv

'screen test *for movie* prueba f

screw [skruː] **1** n *tornillo m*; V (*sex*) polvo m V **2** v/t: ***screw sth to sth*** atornillar algo a algo; V (*have sex with*) echar un polvo con V; F (*cheat*) timar F

♦ screw up **1** v/t *eyes* cerrar; *piece of paper* arrugar; F (*make a mess of*) fastidiar F **2** v/i F (*make a bad mistake*) meter la pata F

'screw·driv·er destornillador m

screwed up [skruːd'ʌp] *adj* F *psychologically* acomplejado

'screw top *on bottle* tapón m de rosca

screw·y ['skruːɪ] *adj* F chiflado F; *idea, film* descabellado F

scrib·ble ['skrɪbl] **1** n garabato m **2** v/t & v/i garabatear

scrimp [skrɪmp] v/i: ***scrimp and scrape*** pasar apuros, pasar estrecheces

script [skrɪpt] *for movie, play* guión m; *form of writing* caligrafía f

scrip·ture ['skrɪptʃər] escritura f; ***the (Holy) Scriptures*** las Sagradas Escrituras

'script·writ·er guionista m/f

scroll [skroʊl] n (*manuscript*) manuscrito m

♦ scroll down v/i COMPUT avanzar

♦ scroll up v/i COMPUT retroceder

scrounge [skraʊndʒ] v/t gorronear

scroung·er ['skraʊndʒər] gorrón(-ona) m(f)

scrub [skrʌb] v/t (*pret & pp* **scrubbed**) *floors* fregar; *hands* frotar

scrub·bing brush ['skrʌbɪŋ] *for floor* cepillo *m* para fregar

scruff·y ['skrʌfɪ] *adj* andrajoso, desaliñado

scrum [skrʌm] *in rugby* melé *f*

◆ **scrunch up** [skrʌntʃ] *v/t plastic cup etc* estrujar

scru·ples ['skru:plz] *npl* escrúpulos *mpl*

scru·pu·lous ['skru:pjələs] *adj with moral principles* escrupuloso; (*thorough*) meticuloso; *attention to detail* minucioso

scru·pu·lous·ly ['skru:pjələslɪ] *adv* (*meticulously*) minuciosamente

scru·ti·nize ['skru:tɪnaɪz] *v/t* (*examine closely*) estudiar, examinar

scru·ti·ny ['skru:tɪnɪ] escrutinio *m*; **come under scrutiny** ser objeto de investigación

scu·ba div·ing ['sku:bə] submarinismo *m*

scuf·fle ['skʌfl] *n* riña *f*

sculp·tor ['skʌlptər] escultor(a) *m(f)*

sculp·ture ['skʌlptʃər] escultura *f*

scum [skʌm] *on liquid* película *f* de suciedad; (*pej: people*) escoria *f*

sea [si:] *n* mar *m*; **by the sea** junto al mar

'sea·bed fondo *m* marino

'sea·bird ave *f* marina

sea·far·ing ['si:ferɪŋ] *adj nation* marinero

'sea·food marisco *m*

'sea·front paseo *m* marítimo

'sea·go·ing *adj vessel* de altura

'sea·gull gaviota *f*

seal[1] [si:l] *n animal* foca *f*

seal[2] [si:l] **1** *n on document* sello *m*; TECH junta *f*, sello *m* **2** *v/t container* sellar

◆ **seal off** *v/t area* aislar

'sea lev·el: above sea level sobre el nivel del mar; **below sea level** bajo el nivel del mar

seam [si:m] *n on garment* costura *f*; *of ore* filón *m*

'sea·man marinero *m*

seam·stress ['si:mstrɪs] modista *f*

'sea·port puerto *m* marítimo

'sea pow·er *nation* potencia *f* marítima

search [sɜ:rtʃ] **1** *n* búsqueda *f*; **be in search of** estar en busca de **2** *v/t baggage, person* registrar; **search a place for s.o.** buscar a alguien en un lugar

◆ **search for** *v/t* buscar

search·ing ['sɜ:rtʃɪŋ] *adj look* escrutador; *question* difícil

'search·light reflector *m*

'search par·ty grupo *m* de rescate

'search war·rant orden *f* de registro

'sea·shore orilla *f*

'sea·sick *adj* mareado; **get seasick** marearse

'sea·side costa *f*, playa *f*; **seaside resort** centro *m* de veraneo costero

sea·son ['si:zn] *n* (*winter, spring etc*) estación *f*; *for tourism etc* temporada *f*; **plums aren't in season at the moment** ahora no es temporada de ciruelas

sea·son·al ['si:znl] *adj fruit, vegetables* del tiempo; *employment* temporal

sea·soned ['si:znd] *adj wood* seco; *traveler, campaigner* experimentado

sea·son·ing ['si:znɪŋ] condimento *m*

'sea·son tick·et abono *m*

seat [si:t] **1** *n in room, bus, plane* asiento; *in theater* butaca *f*; *of pants* culera *f*; **please take a seat** por favor, siéntese **2** *v/t* (*have seating for*): **the hall can seat 200 people** la sala tiene capacidad para 200 personas; **please remain seated** por favor, permanezcan sentados

'seat belt cinturón *m* de seguridad

'sea ur·chin erizo *m* de mar

'sea·weed alga(s) *f(pl)*

se·clud·ed [sɪ'klu:dɪd] *adj* apartado

se·clu·sion [sɪ'klu:ʒn] aislamiento *m*

sec·ond[1] ['sekənd] **1** *n of time* segundo *m* **2** *adj* segundo **3** *adv come in* en segundo lugar **4** *v/t motion* apoyar

se·cond[2] [sɪ'kɑ:nd] *v/t*: **be seconded to** ser asignado a

sec·ond·a·ry ['sekənderɪ] *adj* secundario; **of secondary importance** de menor importancia

sec·ond·a·ry ed·u·ca·tion educación *f* secundaria

se·cond 'best *adj*: **be second best** ser el segundo mejor; *inferior* ser un segundón; **the second best runner in the school** el segundo mejor corredor del colegio

sec·ond 'big·gest *adj*: **it is the second biggest company in the area** es la segunda empresa más grande de la zona

sec·ond 'class *adj ticket* de segunda clase

sec·ond 'floor tercer piso *m*, *Br* segundo piso *m*

'sec·ond hand *n on clock* segundero *m*

sec·ond-'hand **1** *adj* de segunda mano **2** *adv buy* de segunda mano

sec·ond·ly ['sekəndlɪ] *adv* en segundo lugar

sec·ond-'rate *adj* inferior

sec·ond 'thoughts: **I've had second thoughts** he cambiado de idea

se·cre·cy ['si:krəsɪ] secretismo *m*

se·cret ['si:krət] **1** *n* secreto *m*; **in secret** en secreto **2** *adj* secreto

se·cret 'a·gent agente *m/f* secreto

sec·re·tar·i·al [sekrə'terɪəl] *adj tasks, job* de secretario

sec·re·tar·y ['sekrətərɪ] secretario(-a) *m(f)*; POL ministro(-a) *m(f)*

Sec·re·tar·y of 'State *in USA* Secretario(-a) *m(f)* de Estado

se·crete [sɪˈkriːt] *v/t* (*give off*) segregar; (*hide away*) esconder

se·cre·tion [sɪˈkriːʃn] secreción *f*

se·cre·tive [ˈsiːkrətɪv] *adj* reservado

se·cret·ly [ˈsiːkrətlɪ] *adv* en secreto

se·cret po'lice policía *f* secreta

se·cret 'ser·vice servicio *m* secreto

sect [sekt] secta *f*

sec·tion [ˈsekʃn] *of book, company, text* sección *f*; *of building* zona *f*; *of apple* parte *f*

sec·tor [ˈsektər] sector *m*

sec·u·lar [ˈsekjələr] *adj* laico

se·cure [sɪˈkjʊr] **1** *adj shelf etc* seguro; *job, contract* fijo **2** *v/t shelf etc* asegurar; *s.o.'s help* conseguir

se·cu·ri·ty [sɪˈkjʊrətɪ] seguridad *f*; *for investment* garantía *f*

se'cu·ri·ties mar·ket FIN mercado *m* de valores

se'cu·ri·ty a·lert alerta *f*

se'cu·ri·ty check control *m* de seguridad

se'cu·ri·ty-con·scious *adj* consciente de la seguridad

se'cu·ri·ty forces *npl* fuerzas *fpl* de seguridad

se'cu·ri·ty guard guardia *m/f* de seguridad

se'cu·ri·ty risk *person* peligro *m* (para la seguridad)

se·dan [sɪˈdæn] turismo *m*

se·date [sɪˈdeɪt] *v/t* sedar

se·da·tion [sɪˈdeɪʃn]: **be under sedation** estar sedado

sed·a·tive [ˈsedətɪv] *n* sedante *m*

sed·en·ta·ry [ˈsedəntɛrɪ] *adj job* sedentario

sed·i·ment [ˈsedɪmənt] sedimento *m*

se·duce [sɪˈduːs] *v/t* seducir

se·duc·tion [sɪˈdʌkʃn] seducción *f*

se·duc·tive [sɪˈdʌktɪv] *adj dress* seductor; *offer* tentador

see [siː] *v/t* (*pret saw, pp seen*) ver; (*understand*) entender, ver; *romantically* ver, salir con; **I see** ya veo; **can I see the manager?** ¿puedo ver al encargado?; **you should see a doctor** deberías ir a que te viera un médico; **see s.o. home** acompañar a alguien a casa; **see you!** F ¡hasta la vista!, ¡chao! F

◆ **see about** *v/t* (*look into*) **I'll see about getting it repaired** me encargaré de que lo arreglen

◆ **see off** *v/t at airport etc* despedir; (*chase away*) espantar

◆ **see out** *v/t*: **see s.o. out** acompañar a alguien a la puerta

◆ **see to** *v/t*: **see to sth** ocuparse de algo; **see to it that sth gets done** asegurarse de que algo se haga

seed [siːd] semilla *f*; *in tennis* cabeza *f* de serie; **go to seed** *of person* descuidarse; *of district* empeorarse

seed·ling [ˈsiːdlɪŋ] planta *f* de semillero

seed·y [ˈsiːdɪ] *adj bar, district* de mala calaña

see·ing 'eye dog [ˈsiːɪŋ] perro *m* lazarillo

see·ing (that) [ˈsiːɪŋ] *conj* dado que, ya que

seek [siːk] *v/t* (*pret & pp sought*) buscar

seem [siːm] *v/i* parecer; **it seems that ...** parece que ...

seem·ing·ly [ˈsiːmɪŋlɪ] *adv* aparentemente

seen [siːn] *pp* → **see**

seep [siːp] *v/i of liquid* filtrarse

◆ **seep out** *v/i of liquid* filtrarse

see-saw [ˈsiːsɔː] *n* sube y baja *m*

seethe [siːð] *v/i*: **be seething with anger** estar a punto de estallar (de cólera)

seg·ment [ˈsegmənt] segmento *m*

seg·ment·ed [segˈmentɪd] *adj* segmentado, dividido

seg·re·gate [ˈsegrɪgeɪt] *v/t* segregar

seg·re·ga·tion [segrɪˈgeɪʃn] segregación *f*

seis·mol·o·gy [saɪzˈmɑːlədʒɪ] sismología *f*

seize [siːz] *v/t s.o., s.o.'s arm* agarrar; *opportunity* aprovechar; *of Customs, police etc* incautarse de

◆ **seize up** *v/i of engine* atascarse

sei·zure [ˈsiːʒər] MED ataque *m*; *of drugs etc* incautación *f*; *amount seized* alijo *m*

sel·dom [ˈseldəm] *adv* raramente, casi nunca

se·lect [sɪˈlekt] **1** *v/t* seleccionar **2** *adj* (*exclusive*) selecto

se·lec·tion [sɪˈlekʃn] selección *f*; (*choosing*) elección *f*

se·lec·tion pro·cess proceso *m* de selección

se·lec·tive [sɪˈlektɪv] *adj* selectivo

self [self] (*pl* **selves** [selvz]) ego *m*; **my other self** mi otro yo

self-ad·dressed 'en·ve·lope [selfəˈdrest]: **send us a self-addressed envelope** envíenos un sobre con sus datos

self-as'sur·ance confianza *f* en sí mismo

self-as'sured [selfəˈʃʊrd] *adj* seguro de sí mismo

self-ca·ter·ing a'part·ment [selfˈkeɪtərɪŋ] *Br* apartamento *m or Span* piso *m* sin servicio de comidas

self-'cen·tered, *Br* **self-'cen·tred** [self-

'sent·ard] adj egoísta
self-'clean·ing [selfˈkliːnɪŋ] con autolimpieza
self-con'fessed [selfkənˈfest] adj: **he's a self-confessed megalomaniac** se confiesa megalómano
self-'con·fi·dence confianza f en sí mismo
self-'con·fi·dent adj seguro de sí mismo
self-'con·scious adj tímido
self-'con·scious·ness timidez f
self-con·tained [selfkənˈteɪnd] adj *apartment* independiente
self con'trol autocontrol m
self-de'fence Br, self-de'fense autodefensa f; **in self-defence** en defensa propia
self-'dis·ci·pline autodisciplina f
self-'doubt inseguridad f
self-em·ployed [selfɪmˈplɔɪd] adj autónomo
self-e'steem autoestima f
self-ex'pres·sion autoexpresión f
self-'ev·i·dent adj obvio
self-'gov·ern·ment autogobierno m
self-'in·terest interés m propio
self·ish [ˈselfɪʃ] adj egoísta
self·less [ˈselflɪs] adj desinteresado
self-made 'man [self'meɪd] hombre m hecho a sí mismo
self-'pit·y autocompasión f
self-'por·trait autorretrato m
self-pos·sessed [selfpəˈzest] adj sereno
self-re'li·ant adj autosuficiente
self-re'spect amor m propio
self-right·eous [self'raɪtʃəs] adj pej santurrón, intolerante
self-sat·is·fied [self'sætɪsfaɪd] adj pej pagado de sí mismo
self-'ser·vice adj de autoservicio
self-ser·vice 'res·tau·rant (restaurante m) autoservicio m
self-taught [self'tɔːt] adj autodidacta
sell [sel] v/t & v/i (pret & pp **sold**) vender
◆ **sell out** v/i of product agotarse; **we've sold out** se nos ha(n) agotado
◆ **sell out of** v/t agotar las existencias de
◆ **sell up** v/i vender todo
'sell-by date fecha f límite de venta; **be past its sell-by date** haber pasado la fecha límite de venta
sell·er [ˈselər] vendedor(a) m(f)
sell·ing [ˈselɪŋ] n COM ventas fpl
'sell·ing point COM ventaja f
Sel·lo·tape® [ˈseləteɪp] Br celo m, L.Am. Durex® m
se·men [ˈsiːmən] semen m
se·mes·ter [sɪˈmestər] semestre m
sem·i [ˈsemɪ] n truck camión m semirremolque

'sem·i·cir·cle semicírculo m
sem·i·cir·cu·lar adj semicircular
semi-'co·lon punto m y coma
sem·i·con'duc·tor ELEC semiconductor m
semi'fi·nal semifinal f
semi'fi·nal·ist semifinalista m/f
sem·i·nar [ˈsemɪnɑːr] seminario m
sem·i'skilled adj semicualificado
sen·ate [ˈsenət] senado m
sen·a·tor [ˈsenətər] senador(a) m(f); **Senator George Schwarz** el Senador George Schwarz
send [send] v/t (pret & pp **sent**) enviar, mandar; **the doctor sent him to a specialist** el médico lo envió or mandó a un especialista; **send her my best wishes** dale recuerdos de mi parte
◆ **send back** v/t devolver
◆ **send for** v/t mandar buscar
◆ **send in** v/t troops, application enviar, mandar; next interviewee hacer pasar
◆ **send off** v/t letter, fax etc enviar, mandar
send·er [ˈsendər] of letter remitente m/f
se·nile [ˈsiːnaɪl] adj senil
se·nil·i·ty [sɪˈnɪlətɪ] senilidad f
se·ni·or [ˈsiːnjər] adj (older) mayor; in rank superior
se·ni·or 'cit·i·zen persona f de la tercera edad
se·ni·or·i·ty [siːnjˈɑːrətɪ] in job antigüedad f
sen·sa·tion [senˈseɪʃn] sensación f
sen·sa·tion·al [senˈseɪʃnl] adj news, discovery sensacional
sense [sens] 1 n (meaning, point, hearing etc) sentido m; (feeling) sentimiento m; (common sense) sentido m común, sensatez f; **in a sense** en cierto sentido; **talk sense, man!** ¡no digas tonterías!; **come to one's senses** entrar en razón; **it doesn't make sense** no tiene sentido; **there's no sense in waiting** no tiene sentido que esperemos 2 v/t s.o.'s presence sentir, notar; **I could sense that something was wrong** tenía la sensación de que algo no iba bien
sense·less [ˈsenslɪs] adj (pointless) absurdo
sen·si·ble [ˈsensəbl] adj sensato; clothes, shoes práctico, apropiado
sen·si·bly [ˈsensəblɪ] adv con sensatez; **she wasn't sensibly dressed** no llevaba ropa apropiada
sen·si·tive [ˈsensətɪv] adj skin, person sensible
sen·si·tiv·i·ty [sensəˈtɪvətɪ] of skin, person sensibilidad f
sen·sor [ˈsensər] sensor m

sen·su·al ['senʃuəl] *adj* sensual

sen·su·al·i·ty [senʃu'ælətɪ] sensualidad *f*

sen·su·ous ['senʃuəs] *adj* sensual

sent [sent] *pret & pp → send*

sen·tence ['sentəns] **1** *n* GRAM oración *f*; LAW sentencia *f* **2** *v/t* LAW sentenciar, condenar

sen·ti·ment ['sentɪmənt] (*sentimentality*) sentimentalismo *m*; (*opinion*) opinión *f*

sen·ti·men·tal [sentɪ'mentl] *adj* sentimental

sen·ti·men·tal·i·ty [sentɪmen'tælətɪ] sentimentalismo *m*

sen·try ['sentrɪ] centinela *m*

sep·a·rate[1] ['sepərət] *adj* separado; **keep sth separate from sth** guardar algo separado de algo

separate[2] ['sepəreɪt] **1** *v/t* separar; **separate sth from sth** separar algo de algo **2** *v/i of couple* separarse

sep·a·rat·ed ['sepəreɪtɪd] *adj couple* separado

sep·a·rate·ly ['sepərətlɪ] *adv pay, treat* por separado

sep·a·ra·tion [sepə'reɪʃn] separación *f*

Sep·tem·ber [sep'tembər] septiembre *m*

sep·tic ['septɪk] *adj* séptico; **go septic** *of wound* infectarse

se·quel ['siːkwəl] continuación *f*

se·quence ['siːkwəns] *n* secuencia *f*; **in sequence** en orden; **out of sequence** en desorden; **the sequence of events** la secuencia de hechos

se·rene [sɪ'riːn] *adj* sereno

ser·geant ['sɑːrdʒənt] sargento *m/f*

se·ri·al ['sɪrɪəl] *n* on TV, *radio* serie *f*, serial *m*; *in magazine* novela *f* por entregas

se·ri·al·ize ['sɪrɪəlaɪz] *v/t novel on* TV emitir en forma de serie; *in newspaper* publicar por entregas

'se·ri·al kill·er asesino(-a) *m(f)* en serie

'se·ri·al num·ber *of product* número *m* de serie

'se·ri·al port COMPUT puerto *m* (en) serie

se·ries ['sɪriːz] *nsg* serie *f*

se·ri·ous ['sɪrɪəs] *adj situation, damage, illness* grave; (*person: earnest*) serio; *company* serio; **I'm serious** lo digo en serio; **we'd better take a serious look at it** deberíamos examinarlo seriamente

se·ri·ous·ly ['sɪrɪəslɪ] *adv injured* gravemente; **seriously intend to ...** tener intenciones firmes de ...; **seriously?** ¿en serio?; **take s.o. seriously** tomar a alguien en serio

se·ri·ous·ness ['sɪrɪəsnɪs] *of person* seriedad *f*; *of situation* seriedad *f*, gravedad *f*; *of illness* gravedad *f*

ser·mon ['sɜːrmən] sermón *m*

ser·vant ['sɜːrvənt] sirviente(-a) *m(f)*

serve [sɜːrv] **1** *n in tennis* servicio *m*, saque *m* **2** *v/t food, meal* servir; *customer in shop* atender; *one's country, the people* servir a; **it serves you right** ¡te lo mereces! **3** *v/i* servir; *in tennis* servir, sacar
◆ **serve up** *v/t meal* servir

serv·er ['sɜːrvər] *in tennis* jugador(a) *m(f)* al servicio; COMPUT servidor *m*

ser·vice ['sɜːrvɪs] **1** *n to customers, community* servicio *m*; *for vehicle, machine* revisión *f*; *in tennis* servicio *m*, saque *m*; **services** (*service sector*) el sector servicios; **the services** MIL las fuerzas armadas **2** *v/t vehicle, machine* revisar

'ser·vice ar·e·a área *f* de servicio

'ser·vice charge *in restaurant* servicio *m* (*tarifa*)

'ser·vice in·dus·try industria *f* de servicios

'ser·vice·man MIL militar *m*

'ser·vice pro·vid·er COMPUT proveedor *m* de servicios

'ser·vice sec·tor sector *m* servicios

'ser·vice sta·tion estación *f* de servicio

ser·vi·ette [sɜːrvɪ'et] servilleta *f*

ser·vile ['sɜːrvəl] *adj pej* servil

serv·ing ['sɜːrvɪŋ] *n of food* ración *f*

ses·sion ['seʃn] sesión *f*; *with boss* reunión *f*

set [set] **1** *n of tools* juego *m*; *of books* colección *f*; (*group of people*) grupo *m*; MATH conjunto *m*; (THEA: *scenery*) decorado *m*; *where a movie is made* plató *m*; *in tennis* set *m*; **television set** televisor *m*, **a set of dishes** una vajilla; **a set of glasses** una cristalería **2** *v/t* (*pret & pp set*) (*place*) colocar; *movie, novel etc* ambientar; *date, time, limit* fijar; *mechanism, alarm* poner; *clock* poner en hora; *broken limb* recomponer; *jewel* engastar; (*typeset*) componer; **set the table** poner la mesa **3** *v/i* (*pret & pp set*) *of sun* ponerse; *of glue* solidificarse **4** *adj views, ideas* fijo; (*ready*) preparado; **be dead set on sth** estar empeñado en hacer algo; **be very set in one's ways** ser de ideas fijas; **set meal** menú *m* (del día)
◆ **set apart** *v/t* distinguir
◆ **set aside** *v/t material, food* apartar; *money* ahorrar
◆ **set back** *v/t in plans etc* retrasar; **it set me back $400** me salió por 400 dólares
◆ **set off 1** *v/i on journey* salir **2** *v/t explosion* provocar; *bomb* hacer explotar; *chain reaction* desencadenar; *alarm* activar
◆ **set out 1** *v/i on journey* salir (**for** hacia) **2** *v/t ideas, goods* exponer; **set out to do**

S

sth (*intend*) tener la intención de hacer algo

◆ **set to** *v/i* (*start on a task*) empezar a trabajar

◆ **set up 1** *v/t new company* establecer; *equipment, machine* instalar; *market stall* montar; *meeting* organizar; F (*frame*) tender una trampa a **2** *v/i in business* emprender un negocio

'**set·back** contratiempo *m*

set·tee [se'tiː] (*couch, sofa*) sofá *m*

set·ting ['setɪŋ] *n of novel etc* escenario *m*; *of house* ubicación *f*

set·tle ['setl] **1** *v/i of bird, dust* posarse; *of building* hundirse; *to live* establecerse **2** *v/t dispute, uncertainty* resolver, solucionar; *debts* saldar; *nerves, stomach* calmar; *that settles it!* ¡está decidido!

◆ **settle down** *v/i* (*stop being noisy*) tranquilizarse; (*stop wild living*) sentar la cabeza; *in an area* establecerse

◆ **settle for** *v/t* (*take, accept*) conformarse con

◆ **settle up** *v/i* (*pay*) ajustar cuentas con

set·tled ['setld] *adj weather* estable

set·tle·ment ['setlmənt] *of claim* resolución *f*; *of debt* liquidación *f*; *of dispute* acuerdo *m*; (*payment*) suma *f*; *of building* hundimiento *m*

set·tler ['setlər] *in new country* colono *m*

'**set·up** (*structure*) estructura *f*; (*relationship*) relación *f*; F (*frameup*) trampa *f*

sev·en ['sevn] siete

sev·en·teen [sevn'tiːn] diecisiete

sev·en·teenth [sevn'tiːnθ] *n & adj* décimoséptimo

sev·enth ['sevnθ] *n & adj* séptimo

sev·en·ti·eth ['sevntɪɪθ] *n & adj* septuagésimo

sev·en·ty ['sevntɪ] setenta

sev·er ['sevər] *v/t cortar; relations* romper

sev·er·al ['sevrl] **1** *adj* varios **2** *pron* varios(-as) *mpl (fpl)*

se·vere [sɪ'vɪr] *adj illness* grave; *penalty, winter, weather* severo; *teacher* estricto

se·vere·ly [sɪ'vɪrlɪ] *adv punish, speak* con severidad; *injured, disrupted* gravemente

se·ver·i·ty [sɪ'verətɪ] severidad *f*; *of illness* gravedad *f*

Se·ville [sə'vɪl] *n* Sevilla

sew [soʊ] *v/t & v/i* (*pret sewed, pp sewn*) coser

◆ **sew on** *v/t button* coser

sew·age ['suːɪdʒ] aguas *fpl* residuales

'**sew·age plant** planta *f* de tratamiento de aguas residuales, depuradora *f*

sew·er ['suːər] alcantarilla *f*, cloaca *f*

sew·ing ['soʊɪŋ] *skill* costura *f*; *that being sewn* labor *f*

'**sew·ing ma·chine** máquina *f* de coser

sewn [soʊn] *pp* → **sew**

sex [seks] (*act, gender*) sexo *m*; **have sex with** tener relaciones sexuales con, acostarse con

sex·ist ['seksɪst] **1** *adj* sexista **2** *n* sexista *m/f*

sex·u·al ['sekʃʊəl] *adj* sexual

sex·u·al as·sault agresión *f* sexual

sex·u·al ha·rass·ment acoso *m* sexual

sex·u·al 'in·ter·course relaciones *fpl* sexuales

sex·u·al·i·ty [sekʃʊ'ælətɪ] sexualidad *f*

sex·u·al·ly ['sekʃʊlɪ] *adv* sexualmente; *sexually transmitted disease* enfermedad *f* de transmisión sexual

sex·y ['seksɪ] *adj* sexy *inv*

shab·bi·ly ['ʃæbɪlɪ] *adv dressed* con desaliño; *treat* muy mal, de manera muy injusta

shab·by ['ʃæbɪ] *adj coat etc* desgastado, raído; *treatment* malo, muy injusto

shack [ʃæk] choza *f*

shade [ʃeɪd] **1** *n for lamp* pantalla *f*; *of color* tonalidad *f*; *on window* persiana *f*; *in the shade* a la sombra **2** *v/t from sun, light* proteger de la luz

shad·ow ['ʃædoʊ] *n* sombra *f*

shad·y ['ʃeɪdɪ] *adj spot* umbrío; *character, dealings* sospechoso

shaft [ʃæft] TECH eje *m*, árbol *m*; *of mine* pozo *m*

shag·gy ['ʃægɪ] *adj hair, dog* greñudo

shake [ʃeɪk] **1** *n* sacudida *f*; *give sth a good shake* agitar algo bien **2** *v/t* (*pret shook, pp shaken*) agitar; *emotionally* conmocionar; *he shook his head* negó con la cabeza; *shake hands* estrechar *or* darse la mano; *shake hands with s.o.* estrechar *or* dar la mano a alguien **3** *v/i* (*pret shook, pp shaken*) *of voice, building, person* temblar

shak·en ['ʃeɪkən] **1** *adj emotionally* conmocionado **2** *pp* → **shake**

'**shake-up** reestructuración *f*

'**shak·y** ['ʃeɪkɪ] *adj table etc* inestable; *after illness* débil; *after shock* conmocionado; *grasp of sth, grammar etc* flojo; *voice, hand* tembloroso

shall [ʃæl] *v/aux* ◇ *future: I shall do my best* haré todo lo que pueda; *I shan't see them* no los veré

◇ *suggesting: shall we go?* ¿nos vamos?

shal·low ['ʃæloʊ] *adj water* poco profundo; *person* superficial

sham·bles ['ʃæmblz] *nsg* caos *m*

shame [ʃeɪm] **1** *n* vergüenza *f*, Col, Mex, Ven pena *f*; *bring shame on* avergonzar or *Col, Mex, Ven* apenar a; **shame on you!** ¡debería darte vergüenza!; **what a shame!** ¡qué pena *or* lástima! **2** *v/t* avergonzar, *Col, Mex, Ven* apenar; **shame s.o. into doing sth** avergonzar a alguien para que haga algo

shame·ful ['ʃeɪmfəl] *adj* vergonzoso

shame·ful·ly ['ʃeɪmfəlɪ] *adv* vergonzosamente

shame·less ['ʃeɪmlɪs] *adj* desvergonzado

sham·poo [ʃæm'puː] **1** *n* champú *m* **2** *v/t customer* lavar la cabeza a; *hair* lavar

shan·ty town ['ʃæntɪ] *Span* barrio *m* de chabolas, *Am* barriada *f*

shape [ʃeɪp] **1** *n* forma *f* **2** *v/t clay* modelar; *person's life, character* determinar; *the future* dar forma a

shape·less ['ʃeɪplɪs] *adj dress etc* amorfo

shape·ly ['ʃeɪplɪ] *adj figure* esbelto

share [ʃer] **1** *n* parte *f*; FIN acción *f*; **I did my share of the work** hice la parte del trabajo que me correspondía **2** *v/t feelings, opinions* compartir **3** *v/i* compartir

◆ **share out** *v/t* repartir

'**share·hold·er** accionista *m/f*

shark [ʃɑːrk] *fish* tiburón *m*

sharp [ʃɑːrp] **1** *adj knife* afilado; *mind* vivo; *pain* agudo; *taste* ácido **2** *adv* MUS demasiado alto; **at 3 o'clock sharp** a las tres en punto

charp·en ['ʃɑːrpn] *v/t knife* afilar; *pencil* sacar punta a; *skills* perfeccionar

sharp 'prac·tice triquiñuelas *fpl*, tejemanejes *mpl*

shot [ʃɒt] *pret & pp → shit*

shat·ter ['ʃætər] **1** *v/t glass* hacer añicos; *illusions* destrozar **2** *v/i of glass* hacerse añicos

shat·tered ['ʃætərd] *adj* F *(exhausted)* destrozado F, hecho polvo F; *(very upset)* destrozado F

shat·ter·ing ['ʃætərɪŋ] *adj news, experience* demoledor, sorprendente

shave [ʃeɪv] **1** *v/t* afeitar **2** *v/i* afeitarse **3** *n* afeitado *m*; **have a shave** afeitarse; **that was a close shave** ¡le faltó un pelo!

◆ **shave off** *v/t beard* afeitar; *from piece of wood* rebajar

shav·en ['ʃeɪvn] *adj head* afeitado

shav·er ['ʃeɪvər] *electric* máquinilla *f* de afeitar (eléctrica)

shav·ing brush ['ʃeɪvɪŋ] brocha *f* de afeitar

'**shav·ing soap** jabón *m* de afeitar

shawl [ʃɔːl] chal *m*

she [ʃiː] *pron* ella; **she is German/a student** es alemana / estudiante; **you're funny, she's not** tú tienes gracia, ella no

shears [ʃɪrz] *npl for gardening* tijeras *fpl*

(de podar); for sewing tijeras *fpl (grandes)*

sheath [ʃiːθ] *n for knife* funda *f*; *contraceptive* condón *m*

shed[1] [ʃed] *v/t (pret & pp shed) blood, tears* derramar; *leaves* perder; **shed light on** *fig* arrojar luz sobre

shed[2] [ʃed] *n* cobertizo *m*

sheep [ʃiːp] *(pl sheep)* oveja *f*

'**sheep·dog** perro *m* pastor

sheep·herd·er ['ʃiːphɜːrdər] pastor *m*

sheep·ish ['ʃiːpɪʃ] *adj* avergonzado

'**sheep·skin** *adj* lining (de piel) de borrego

sheer [ʃɪr] *adj madness, luxury* puro, verdadero; *hell* verdadero; *drop, cliffs* escarpado

sheet [ʃiːt] *for bed* sábana *f*; *of paper* hoja *f*; *of metal* chapa *f*, plancha *f*; *of glass* hoja *f*, lámina *f*

shelf [ʃelf] *(pl shelves [ʃelvz])* estante *m*; **shelves** estanterías *fpl*

shell [ʃel] **1** *n of mussel etc* concha *f*; *of egg* cáscara *f*; *of tortoise* caparazón *m*; MIL proyectil *m*; **come out of one's shell** *fig* salir del caparazón **2** *v/t peas* pelar; MIL bombardear (con artillería)

'**shell·fire** fuego *m* de artillería

'**shell·fish** marisco *m*

shel·ter ['ʃeltər] **1** *n* refugio *m*; *(bus shelter)* marquesina *f* **2** *v/i from rain, bombing etc* refugiarse **3** *v/t (protect)* proteger

shel·tered ['ʃeltərd] *adj place* resguardado; **lead a sheltered life** llevar una vida protegida

shelve [ʃelv] *v/t fig* posponer

shep·herd ['ʃepərd] *n* pastor *m*

sher·iff ['ʃerɪf] sheriff *m/f*

sher·ry ['ʃerɪ] jerez *m*

shield [ʃiːld] **1** *n* escudo *m*; *sports trophy* trofeo *m (en forma de escudo)*; TECH placa *f* protectora; *of policeman* placa *f* **2** *v/t (protect)* proteger

shift [ʃɪft] **1** *n* cambio *m*; *(period of work)* turno *m* **2** *v/t (move)* mover; *stains etc* eliminar **3** *v/i (move)* moverse; *(change)* trasladarse, desplazarse; *of wind* cambiar; **he was shifting!** F iba a toda mecha F

'**shift key** COMPUT tecla *f* de mayúsculas

'**shift work** trabajo *m* por turnos

'**shift work·er** trabajador(a) *m(f)* por turnos

shift·y ['ʃɪftɪ] *adj pej* sospechoso

shil·ly-shal·ly ['ʃɪlɪʃælɪ] *v/i (pret & pp shilly-shallied)* F titubear

shim·mer ['ʃɪmər] *v/i* brillar; *of roads in heat* reverberar

S

shin [ʃɪn] *n* espinilla *f*

shine [ʃaɪn] **1** *v/i* (*pret & pp* **shone**) brillar; *fig: of student etc* destacar (**at** en) **2** *v/t* (*pret & pp* **shone**): *could you shine a light in here?* ¿podrías alumbrar aquí? **3** *n on shoes etc* brillo *m*

shin·gle [ˈʃɪŋgl] *on beach* guijarros *mpl*

shin·gles [ˈʃɪŋglz] *nsg* MED herpes *m*

shin·y [ˈʃaɪnɪ] *adj surface* brillante

ship [ʃɪp] **1** *n* barco *m*, buque *m* **2** *v/t* (*pret & pp* **shipped**) (*send*) enviar; *by sea* enviar por barco

ship·ment [ˈʃɪpmənt] (*consignment*) envío *m*

'**ship·own·er** naviero(-a) *m(f)*, armador(a) *m(f)*

ship·ping [ˈʃɪpɪŋ] *n* (*sea traffic*) navíos *mpl*, buques *mpl*; (*sending by sea*) envío *m*; (*sending by sea*) envío *m* por barco

'**ship·ping com·pa·ny** (compañía *f*) naviera *f*

'**ship·ping costs** *npl* gastos *mpl* de envío

'**ship·shape** *adj* ordenado, organizado

'**ship·wreck 1** *n* naufragio *m* **2** *v/t: be shipwrecked* naufragar

'**ship·yard** astillero *m*

shirk [ʃɜːrk] *v/t* eludir

shirk·er [ˈʃɜːrkər] vago(-a) *m(f)*

shirt [ʃɜːrt] camisa *f*; *in his shirt sleeves* en mangas de camisa

shit [ʃɪt] **1** *n* P mierda *f* P; *I need a shit* tengo que cagar P **2** *v/i* (*pret & pp* **shat**) P cagar P **3** *interj* P mierda P!

shit·ty [ˈʃɪtɪ] *adj* F asqueroso F; *I feel shitty* me encuentro de pena F

shiv·er [ˈʃɪvər] *v/i* tiritar

shock [ʃɑːk] **1** *n* shock *m*, impresión *f*; ELEC descarga *f*; *be in shock* MED estar en estado de shock **2** *v/t* impresionar, dejar boquiabierto; *I was shocked by the news* la noticia me impresionó *or* dejó boquiabierto; *an artist who tries to shock his public* un artista que intenta escandalizar a su público

'**shock ab·sorb·er** [əbˈsɔːrbər] MOT amortiguador *m*

shock·ing [ˈʃɑːkɪŋ] *adj behavior, poverty* impresionante, escandaloso; F *prices* escandaloso; F *weather, spelling* terrible

shock·ing·ly [ˈʃɑːkɪŋlɪ] *adv behave* escandalosamente

shod·dy [ˈʃɑːdɪ] *adj goods* de mala calidad; *behavior* vergonzoso

shoe [ʃuː] zapato *m*

'**shoe·horn** *n* calzador *m*

'**shoe·lace** cordón *m*

'**shoe·mak·er** zapatero(-a) *m(f)*

'**shoe mend·er** zapatero(-a) *m(f)* remendón(-ona)

'**shoe·store** zapatería *f*

'**shoe·string**: *do sth on a shoestring* hacer algo con cuatro duros

shone [ʃɑːn] *pret & pp → shine*

◆ **shoo away** [ʃuː] *v/t children, chicken* espantar

shook [ʃuːk] *pret → shake*

shoot [ʃuːt] **1** *n* BOT brote *m* **2** *v/t* (*pret & pp* **shot**) disparar; *and kill* matar de un tiro; *movie* rodar; *shoot s.o. in the leg* disparar a alguien en la pierna

◆ **shoot down** *v/t airplane* derribar; *fig: suggestion* echar por tierra

◆ **shoot off** *v/i* (*rush off*) irse deprisa

◆ **shoot up** *v/i of prices* dispararse; *of children* crecer mucho; *of new suburbs, buildings etc* aparecer de repente; F *drug addict* chutarse F

'**shoot·ing star** [ˈʃuːtɪŋ] estrella *f* fugaz

shop [ʃɑːp] **1** *n* tienda *f*; *talk shop* hablar del trabajo **2** *v/i* (*pret & pp* **shopped**) comprar; *go shopping* ir de compras

shop·keep·er [ˈʃɑːkiːpər] tendero(-a) *m(f)*

shop·lift·er [ˈʃɑːplɪftər] ladrón(-ona) *m(f)* (*en tienda*)

shop·lift·ing [ˈʃɑːplɪftɪŋ] *n* hurtos *mpl* (*en tiendas*)

shop·per [ˈʃɑːpər] *person* comprador(a) *m(f)*

shop·ping [ˈʃɑːpɪŋ] *items* compra *f*; *I hate shopping* odio hacer la compra; *do one's shopping* hacer la compra

'**shop·ping bag** bolsa *f* de la compra

'**shop·ping cen·ter**, *Br* '**shop·ping cen·tre** centro *m* comercial

'**shop·ping list** lista *f* de la compra

'**shop·ping mall** centro *m* comercial

shop 'stew·ard representante *m/f* sindical

shop 'win·dow escaparate *m*, *L.Am.* vidriera *f*, *Mex* aparador *m*

shore [ʃɔːr] orilla *f*; *on shore* (*not at sea*) en tierra

short [ʃɔːrt] **1** *adj* corto; *in height* bajo; *it's just a short walk* está a poca distancia a pie; *we're short of fuel* nos queda poco combustible; *he's not short of ideas* no le faltan ideas; *time is short* hay poco tiempo **2** *adv: cut short vacation, meeting* interrumpir; *stop a person short* hacer pararse a una persona; *go short of* pasar sin; *in short* en resumen

short·age [ˈʃɔːrtɪdʒ] escasez *f*, falta *f*

short 'cir·cuit *n* cortocircuito *m*

short·com·ing [ˈʃɔːrtkʌmɪŋ] defecto *m*

'**short cut** atajo *m*

short·en [ˈʃɔːrtn] *v/t dress, hair, vacation* acortar; *chapter, article* abreviar; *work*

shrimp

day reducir

short·en·ing ['ʃɔːrtnɪŋ] *n grasa utilizada para hacer masa de pastelería*

'**short·fall** déficit *m*

'**short·hand** *n* taquigrafía *f*

short-hand·ed [ʃɔːrt'hændɪd] *adj* falto de personal

short-lived ['ʃɔːrtlɪvd] *adj* efímero

short·ly ['ʃɔːrtlɪ] *adv (soon)* pronto; *shortly before / after* justo antes / después

short·ness ['ʃɔːrtnɪs] *of visit* brevedad *f*; *in height* baja *f* estatura

shorts [ʃɔːrts] *npl* pantalones *mpl* cortos, shorts *mpl*; *underwear* calzoncillos *mpl*

short·sight·ed [ʃɔːrt'saɪtɪd] *adj* miope; *fig* corto de miras

short-sleeved ['ʃɔːrtsliːvd] *adj* de manga corta

short-staffed [ʃɔːrt'stæft] *adj* falto de personal

short 'sto·ry relato *m or* cuento corto

short-tem·pered [ʃɔːrt'tempərd] *adj* irascible

'**short-term** *adj* a corto plazo

'**short time**: *be on short time of workers* trabajar a jornada reducida

'**short wave** onda *f* corta

shot¹ [ʃɑːt] *from gun* disparo *m*; *(photograph)* fotografía *f*; *(injection)* inyección *f*; *be a good / poor shot* tirar bien / mal; *he accepted like a shot* aceptó al instante; *he ran off like a shot* se fue como una bala

shot² [ʃɑːt] *pret & pp →* **shoot**

'**shot·gun** escopeta *f*

should [ʃʊd] *v/aux: what should I do?* ¿qué debería hacer?; *you shouldn't do that* no deberías hacer eso; *that should be long enough* debería ser lo suficientemente largo; *you should have heard him!* ¡tendrías que haberle oído!

shoul·der ['ʃoʊldər] *n ANAT* hombro *m*

'**shoul·der bag** bolso *m* (de bandolera)

'**shoul·der blade** omóplato *m*, omoplato

'**shoul·der strap** *of brassiere, dress* tirante *m*; *of bag* correa *f*

shout [ʃaʊt] **1** *n* grito *m* **2** *v/t & v/i* gritar

◆ **shout at** *v/t* gritar a

shout·ing ['ʃaʊtɪŋ] *n* griterío *m*

shove [ʃʌv] **1** *n* empujón *m* **2** *v/t & v/i* empujar

◆ **shove in** *v/i in line* meterse empujando

◆ **shove off** *v/i* F *(go away)* largarse F

shov·el ['ʃʌvl] **1** *n* pala *f* **2** *v/t: shovel snow off the path* retirar a paladas la nieve del camino

show [ʃoʊ] **1** *n* THEA espectáculo *m*; TV programa *m*; *of emotion* muestra *f*; *on*

show *at exhibition* expuesto, en exposición **2** *v/t (pret showed, pp shown) passport, ticket* enseñar, mostrar; *interest, emotion* mostrar; *at exhibition* exponer; *movie* proyectar; *show s.o. sth, show sth to s.o.* enseñar *or* mostrar algo a alguien **3** *v/i (pret showed, pp shown) (be visible)* verse; *what's showing at …?* de movie qué ponen en el …?

◆ **show around** *v/t* enseñar; *he showed us around* nos enseñó la casa / el edificio *etc*

◆ **show in** *v/t* hacer pasar a

◆ **show off 1** *v/t skills* mostrar **2** *v/i pej* presumir, alardear

◆ **show up 1** *v/t shortcomings etc* poner de manifiesto; *don't show me up in public (embarrass)* no me avergüences en público **2** *v/i (be visible)* verse; F *(arrive, turn up)* aparecer

'**show busi·ness** el mundo del espectáculo

'**show·case** *n* vitrina *f*; *fig* escaparate *m*

'**show·down** enfrentamiento *m*

show·er ['ʃaʊər] **1** *n of rain* chaparrón *m*, chubasco *m*; *to wash* ducha *f*, *Mex* regadera *f*; *(party)* fiesta con motivo de un bautizo, una boda etc., en la que los invitados llevan obsequios; *take a shower* ducharse **2** *v/i* ducharse **3** *v/t: shower s.o. with compliments / praise* colmar a alguien de cumplidos / alabanzas

'**show·er cap** gorro *m* de baño

'**show·er cur·tain** cortina *f* de ducha

'**show·er·proof** *adj* impermeable

'**show·jump·ing** concurso *m* de saltos

shown [ʃoʊn] *pp →* **show**

'**show-off** *n pej* fanfarrón(-ona) *m(f)*

'**show·room** sala *f* de exposición *f*; *in showroom condition* como nuevo

show·y ['ʃoʊɪ] *adj jacket, behavior* llamativo

shrank [ʃræŋk] *pret →* **shrink¹**

shred [ʃred] **1** *n of paper etc* trozo *m*; *of fabric* jirón *m*; *there isn't a shred of evidence* no hay prueba alguna **2** *v/t (pret & pp shredded) paper* hacer trizas; *in cooking* cortar en tiras

shred·der ['ʃredər] *for documents* trituradora *f* (de documentos)

shrewd [ʃruːd] *adj person* astuto; *judgment, investment* inteligente

shrewd·ness ['ʃruːdnɪs] *of person* astucia *f*; *of decision* inteligencia *f*

shriek [ʃriːk] **1** *n* alarido *m*, chillido *m* **2** *v/i* chillar

shrill [ʃrɪl] *adj* estridente, agudo

shrimp [ʃrɪmp] gamba *f*; *larger Span* langostino *m*, *L.Am.* camarón *m*

S

shrine [fraɪn] santuario m

shrink[1] [frɪŋk] v/i (pret **shrank**, pp **shrunk**) of material encoger(se); level of support etc reducirse

shrink[2] [frɪŋk] n F (psychiatrist) psiquiatra m/f

'**shrink-wrap** v/t (pret & pp **shrink-wrapped**) envolver en plástico adherente

'**shrink-wrap·ping** material plástico adherente para envolver

shriv·el ['frɪvl] v/i of skin arrugarse; of leaves marchitarse

Shrove 'Tues·day [frouv] martes m inv de Carnaval

shrub [frʌb] arbusto m

shrub·ber·y ['frʌbərɪ] arbustos mpl

shrug [frʌg] 1 n: ... he said with a shrug ... dijo encogiendo los hombros 2 v/i (pret & pp **shrugged**) encoger los hombros 3 v/t (pret & pp **shrugged**): **shrug one's shoulders** encoger los hombros

shrunk [frʌŋk] pp → **shrink**[1]

shud·der ['fʌdər] 1 n of fear, disgust escalofrío m; of earth, building temblor m 2 v/i with fear, disgust estremecerse; of earth, building temblar; **I shudder to think** me estremezco de pensar

shuf·fle ['fʌfl] 1 v/t cards barajar 2 v/i in walking arrastrar los pies

shun [fʌn] v/t (pret & pp **shunned**) rechazar

shut [fʌt] v/t & v/i (pret & pp **shut**) cerrar

◆ **shut down** 1 v/t business cerrar; computer apagar 2 v/i of business cerrarse; of computer apagarse

◆ **shut off** v/t cortar

◆ **shut up** v/i F (be quiet) callarse; **shut up!** ¡cállate!

shut·ter ['fʌtər] on window contraventana f; PHOT obturador m

'**shut·ter speed** PHOT tiempo m de exposición

shut·tle ['fʌtl] v/i: **shuttle between** of bus conectar; of airplane hacer el puente aéreo entre

'**shut·tle-bus** at airport autobús m de conexión

'**shut·tle-cock** SP volante m

'**shut·tle ser·vice** servicio m de conexión

shy [faɪ] adj tímido

shy·ness ['faɪnɪs] timidez f

Si·a·mese 'twins [saɪə'miːz] npl siameses mpl (fpl)

sick [sɪk] adj enfermo; sense of humor morboso, macabro; society enfermo; **be sick of** (fed up with) estar harto de

sick·en ['sɪkn] 1 v/t (disgust) poner enfermo 2 v/i: **be sickening for sth** estar incubando algo

sick·en·ing ['sɪknɪŋ] adj stench nauseabundo; behavior, crime repugnante

'**sick leave** baja f (por enfermedad); **be on sick leave** estar de baja

sick·ly ['sɪklɪ] adj person enfermizo; color pálido

sick·ness ['sɪknɪs] enfermedad f; (vomiting) vómitos mpl

side [saɪd] n of box, house, field lado m; of mountain ladera f, vertiente f; of person costado m; SP equipo m; **take sides** (favor one side) tomar partido (**with** por); **I'm on your side** estoy de parte tuya; **side by side** uno al lado del otro; **at the side of the road** al lado de la carretera; **on the big / small side** un poco grande / pequeño

◆ **side with** v/t tomar partido por

'**side·board** aparador m

'**side·burns** npl patillas fpl

'**side dish** plato m de acompañamiento

'**side ef·fect** efecto m secundario

'**side·light** MOT luz f de posición

'**side·line 1** n actividad f complementaria 2 v/t: **feel sidelined** sentirse marginado

'**side·step** v/t (pret & pp **sidestepped**) fig evadir

'**side street** bocacalle f

'**side·track** v/t distraer; **get sidetracked** distraerse

'**side·walk** acera f, Rpl vereda f, Mex banqueta f

side·walk 'caf·é terraza f

'**side·ways** ['saɪdweɪz] adv de lado

siege [siːdʒ] sitio m; **lay siege to** sitiar

sieve [sɪv] n tamiz m

sift [sɪft] v/t flour tamizar; data examinar a fondo

◆ **sift through** v/t details, data pasar por el tamiz

sigh [saɪ] 1 n suspiro m; **heave a sigh of relief** suspirar de alivio 2 v/i suspirar

sight [saɪt] n vista f; (power of seeing) vista f, visión f; **sights** of city lugares mpl de interés; **he can't stand the sight of blood** no aguanta ver sangre; **I caught sight of him just as ...** lo vi justo cuando ...; **know by sight** conocer de vista; **within sight of** a la vista de; **as soon as the car was out of sight** en cuanto se dejó de ver el coche; **what a sight you look!** ¡qué pintas llevas!; **lose sight of** objective etc olvidarse de

sight·see·ing ['saɪtsiːɪŋ] n: **we like sightseeing** nos gusta hacer turismo; **go sightseeing** hacer turismo

'**sight·see·ing tour** visita f turística

sight·seer ['saɪtsiːər] turista m/f

sign [saɪn] 1 n señal f; outside shop, on

building cartel *m*, letrero *m*; *it's a sign of the times* es un signo de los tiempos que corren **2** *v/t & v/i* firmar

◆ **sign in** *v/i* registrarse

◆ **sign up** *v/i (join the army)* alistarse

sig·nal ['sɪɡnl] **1** *n* señal *f*; *send out all the wrong signals* dar a una impresión equivocada **2** *v/i of driver* poner el intermitente

sig·na·to·ry ['sɪɡnətɔːrɪ] *n* signatario(-a) *m(f)*, firmante *m/f*

sig·na·ture ['sɪɡnətʃər] *n* firma *f*

sig·na·ture 'tune sintonía *f*

sig·net ring ['sɪɡnɪt] sello *m (anillo)*

sig·nif·i·cance [sɪɡ'nɪfɪkəns] importancia *f*, relevancia *f*

sig·nif·i·cant [sɪɡ'nɪfɪkənt] *adj event etc* importante, relevante; *(quite large)* considerable

sig·nif·i·cant·ly [sɪɡ'nɪfɪkəntlɪ] *adv larger, more expensive* considerablemente

sig·ni·fy ['sɪɡnɪfaɪ] *v/t (pret & pp signified)* significar, suponer

'sign lan·guage lenguaje *m* por señas

'sign·post señal *f*

si·lence ['saɪləns] **1** *n* silencio *m*; *in silence work, march* en silencio; *silence!* ¡silencio! **2** *v/t* hacer callar

si·lenc·er ['saɪlənsər] *on gun* silenciador *m*

si·lent ['saɪlənt] *adj* silencioso; *movie* mudo; *stay silent (not comment)* permanecer callado

sil·hou·ette [sɪluː'et] *n* silueta *f*

sil·i·con ['sɪlɪkən] silicio *m*

sil·i·con 'chip chip *m* de silicio

sil·i·cone ['sɪlɪkoʊn] silicona *f*

silk [sɪlk] **1** *n* seda *f* **2** *adj shirt etc* de seda

silk·y ['sɪlkɪ] *adj hair, texture* sedoso

sil·li·ness ['sɪlɪnɪs] tontería *f*, estupidez *f*

sil·ly ['sɪlɪ] *adj* tonto, estúpido

si·lo ['saɪloʊ] silo *m*

sil·ver ['sɪlvər] **1** *n metal, medal* plata *f*; *(silver objects)* (objetos *mpl* de) plata *f* **2** *adj ring* de plata; *hair* canoso

sil·ver·plat·ed [sɪlvər'pleɪtɪd] *adj* plateado

sil·ver·ware ['sɪlvərwer] plata *f*

sil·ver 'wed·ding bodas *fpl* de plata

sim·i·lar ['sɪmɪlər] *adj* parecido, similar; *be similar to* ser parecido a, parecerse a

sim·i·lar·i·ty [sɪmɪ'lærətɪ] parecido *m*, similitud *f*

sim·i·lar·ly ['sɪmɪlərlɪ] *adv* de la misma manera

sim·mer ['sɪmər] *v/i in cooking* cocer a fuego lento; *be simmering (with rage)* estar a punto de explotar

◆ **simmer down** *v/i* tranquilizarse

sim·ple ['sɪmpl] *adj (easy, not fancy)* sencillo; *person* simple

sim·ple-mind·ed [sɪmpl'maɪndɪd] *adj pej* simplón

sim·plic·i·ty [sɪm'plɪsətɪ] *of task, design* sencillez *f*, simplicidad *f*

sim·pli·fy ['sɪmplɪfaɪ] *v/t (pret & pp simplified)* simplificar

sim·plis·tic [sɪm'plɪstɪk] *adj* simplista

sim·ply ['sɪmplɪ] *adv* sencillamente; *it is simply the best* es sin lugar a dudas el mejor

sim·u·late ['sɪmjʊleɪt] *v/t* simular

sim·ul·ta·ne·ous [saɪml'teɪnɪəs] *adj* simultáneo

sim·ul·ta·ne·ous·ly [saɪml'teɪnɪəslɪ] *adv* simultáneamente

sin [sɪn] **1** *n* pecado *m* **2** *v/i (pret & pp sinned)* pecar

since [sɪns] **1** *prep* desde; *since last week* desde la semana pasada **2** *adv* desde entonces; *I haven't seen him since* no lo he visto desde entonces **3** *conj in expressions of time* desde que; *(seeing that)* ya que, dado que; *since you left* desde que te marchaste; *since I have been living here* desde que vivo aquí; *since you don't like it* ya que *o* dado que no te gusta

sin·cere [sɪn'sɪr] *adj* sincero

sin·cere·ly [sɪn'sɪrlɪ] *adv* sinceramente; *I sincerely hope he appreciates it* espero de verdad que lo aprecie; *Yours sincerely* atentamente

sin·cer·i·ty [sɪn'serətɪ] sinceridad *f*

sin·ful ['sɪnfəl] *adj person* pecador; *things* pecaminoso; *it is sinful to ...* es pecado ...

sing [sɪŋ] *v/t & v/i (pret sang, pp sung)* cantar

singe [sɪndʒ] *v/t* chamuscar

sing·er ['sɪŋər] cantante *m/f*

sin·gle ['sɪŋɡl] **1** *adj (sole)* único, solo; *(not double)* único; *(not married)* soltero *m*; *there wasn't a single mistake* no había ni un solo error; *in single file* en fila india; *single currency* moneda única *f* **2** *n* sencillo *m*; *(single room)* habitación *f* individual; *person* soltero(-a) *m(f)*; *Br ticket* billete *m* *o L.Am.* boleto *m* de ida; *holidays for singles* vacaciones para gente sin pareja; *singles in tennis* individuales *mpl*

◆ **single out** *v/t (choose)* seleccionar; *(distinguish)* distinguir

sin·gle-breast·ed [sɪŋɡl'brestɪd] *adj* recto, con una fila de botones

sin·gle-'hand·ed [sɪŋɡl'hændɪd] **1** *adj* en solitario **2** *adv* en solitario

sin·gle-mind·ed ['sɪŋgl'maɪndɪd] adj determinado, resuelto

Sin·gle 'Mar·ket Mercado m Único

sin·gle 'moth·er madre f soltera

sin·gle 'pa·rent padre m/madre f soltero(-a)

sin·gle pa·rent 'fam·i·ly familia f monoparental

sin·gle 'room habitación f individual

sin·gu·lar ['sɪŋgjʊlər] **1** adj GRAM singular **2** n GRAM singular m; **in the singular** en singular

sin·is·ter ['sɪnɪstər] adj siniestro; sky amenazador

sink [sɪŋk] **1** n in kitchen fregadero m; in bathroom lavabo m **2** v/i (pret **sank**, pp **sunk**) of ship, object hundirse; of sun ponerse; of interest rates, pressure etc descender, bajar; **he sank onto the bed** se tiró a la cama **3** v/t (pret **sank**, pp **sunk**) ship hundir; funds invertir

◆ **sink in** v/i of liquid penetrar; **it still hasn't really sunk in** of realization todavía no lo he asumido

sin·ner ['sɪnər] pecador(a) m(f)

si·nus ['saɪnəs] seno m (nasal)

si·nus·i·tis ['saɪnə'saɪtɪs] MED sinusitis f

sip [sɪp] **1** n sorbo m **2** v/t (pret & pp **sipped**) sorber

sir [sɜːr] señor m; **excuse me, sir** perdone, caballero

si·ren ['saɪrən] sirena f

sir·loin ['sɜːrlɔɪn] solomillo m

sis·ter ['sɪstər] hermana f

sis·ter-in-law (pl **sisters-in-law**) cuñada f

sit [sɪt] **1** v/i (pret & pp **sat**) estar sentado; (sit down) sentarse **2** v/t (pret & pp **sat**) exam presentarse a

◆ **sit down** v/i sentarse

◆ **sit up** v/i in bed incorporarse; (straighten back) sentarse derecho; (wait up at night) esperar levantado

sit·com ['sɪtkɑːm] telecomedia f, comedia f de situación

site [saɪt] **1** n emplazamiento m; of battle lugar m **2** v/t new offices etc situar

sit·ting ['sɪtɪŋ] n of committee, court, for artist sesión f; for meals turno m

'sit·ting room sala f de estar, salón m

sit·u·at·ed ['sɪtʊeɪtɪd] adj situado

sit·u·a·tion [sɪtʊ'eɪʃn] situación f

six [sɪks] seis

six·teen [sɪks'tiːn] dieciséis

six·teenth [sɪks'tiːnθ] n & adj decimosexto

sixth [sɪksθ] n & adj sexto

six·ti·eth ['sɪkstɪɪθ] n & adj sexagésimo

six·ty ['sɪkstɪ] sesenta

size [saɪz] tamaño m; of loan importe m; of jacket talla f; of shoes número m

◆ **size up** v/t evaluar, examinar

siz·a·ble ['saɪzəbl] adj house, order considerable; meal copioso

siz·zle ['sɪzl] v/i chisporrotear

skate [skeɪt] **1** n patín m **2** v/i patinar

skate·board ['skeɪtbɔːrd] n monopatín m

skate·board·er ['skeɪtbɔːrdər] persona que patina en monopatín

skate·board·ing ['skeɪtbɔːrdɪŋ] patinaje m en monopatín

skat·er ['skeɪtər] patinador(a) m(f)

skat·ing ['skeɪtɪŋ] n patinaje m

'skat·ing rink pista f de patinaje

skel·e·ton ['skelɪtn] esqueleto m

'skel·e·ton key llave f maestra

skep·tic ['skeptɪk] escéptico(-a) m(f)

skep·ti·cal ['skeptɪkl] adj escéptico

skep·ti·cism ['skeptɪsɪzm] escepticismo m

sketch [sketʃ] **1** n boceto m, esbozo m; THEA sketch m **2** v/t bosquejar

'sketch·book cuaderno m de dibujo

sketch·y ['sketʃɪ] adj knowledge etc básico, superficial

skew·er ['skjʊər] n brocheta f

ski [skiː] **1** n esquí m **2** v/i esquiar

'ski boots npl botas fpl de esquí

skid [skɪd] **1** n of car resbalón m; of person resbalón m **2** v/i (pret & pp **skidded**) of car patinar; of person resbalar

ski·er ['skiːər] esquiador(a) m(f)

ski·ing ['skiːɪŋ] esquí m

'ski in·struc·tor monitor(a) m(f) de esquí

skil·ful etc Br → **skillful** etc

'ski lift remonte m

skill [skɪl] destreza f, habilidad f

skilled [skɪld] adj capacitado, preparado

skilled 'work·er trabajador(a) m(f) cualificado

'skill·ful ['skɪlfʊl] adj hábil, habilidoso

skill·ful·ly ['skɪlfəlɪ] adv con habilidad or destreza

skim [skɪm] v/t (pret & pp **skimmed**) surface rozar; milk desnatar, descremar

◆ **skim off** v/t the best escoger

◆ **skim through** v/t text leer por encima

skimmed 'milk [skɪmd] leche f desnatada or descremada

skimp·y ['skɪmpɪ] adj account etc superficial; dress cortísimo; bikini mínimo

skin [skɪn] **1** n piel f **2** v/t (pret & pp **skinned**) despellejar, desollar

'skin div·ing buceo m (en bañador)

skin·flint ['skɪnflɪnt] F agarrado(a) m(f) F, roñoso(-a) m(f)

'skin graft injerto m de piel

skin·ny ['skɪnɪ] adj escuálido

skin-tight adj ajustado

skip [skɪp] **1** n (little jump) brinco m, saltito m **2** v/i (pret & pp **skipped**) brincar **3** v/t (pret & pp **skipped**) (omit) pasar por alto

ski pole bastón m de esquí

skip-per ['skɪpər] NAUT patrón(-ona) m(f), capitán (-ana) m(f); of team capitán(-ana) m(f)

ski re-sort estación f de esquí

skirt [skɜːrt] n falda f

ski run pista f de esquí

ski tow telesquí m

skull [skʌl] cráneo m

skunk [skʌŋk] mofeta f

sky [skaɪ] cielo m

sky-light claraboya f

sky-line horizonte m

sky-scrap-er ['skaɪskreɪpər] rascacielos m inv

slab [slæb] of stone losa f; of cake etc trozo m grande

slack [slæk] adj rope flojo; work descuidado; period tranquilo; *discipline is very slack* no hay disciplina

slack-en ['slækn] v/t rope, pace aflojar; pace

◆ **slacken off** v/i of trading, pace disminuir

slacks [slæks] npl pantalones mpl

slain [sleɪn] pp → **slay**

slam [slæm] **1** v/t (pret & pp **slammed**) door cerrar de un golpe **2** v/i (pret & pp **slammed**) of door cerrarse de golpe

◆ **slam down** v/t estampar

slan-der ['slændər] **1** n difamación f **2** v/t difamar

slan-der-ous ['slændərəs] adj difamatorio

slang [slæŋ] argot m, jerga f; of a specific group jerga f

slant [slænt] **1** v/i inclinarse **2** n inclinación f; given to a story enfoque m

slant-ing ['slæntɪŋ] adj roof inclinado; eyes rasgado

slap [slæp] **1** n (blow) bofetada f, cachete m **2** v/t (pret & pp **slapped**) dar una bofetada or un cachete a; *slap s.o. in the face* dar una bofetada a alguien

slap-dash adj chapucero

slash [slæʃ] **1** n (cut) corte m, raja f; in punctuation barra f **2** v/t skin etc cortar; prices, costs recortar drásticamente; *slash one's wrists* cortarse las venas

slate [sleɪt] n pizarra f

slaugh-ter ['slɔːtər] **1** n of animals sacrificio m; of people, troops matanza f **2** v/t animals sacrificar; people, troops masacrar

slaugh-ter-house for animals matadero m

Slav [slɑːv] adj eslavo

slave [sleɪv] n esclavo(-a) m(f)

slave-driv-er F negrero(-a) m(f) F

slay [sleɪ] v/t (pret slew, pp slain) asesinar

slay-ing ['sleɪɪŋ] (murder) asesinato m

sleaze [sliːz] POL corrupción f

slea-zy ['sliːzɪ] adj bar sórdido; person de mala calaña

sled, sledge [sled, sledʒ] n trineo m

sledge ham-mer mazo m

sleep [sliːp] **1** n sueño m; *go to sleep* dormirse; *I need a good sleep* necesito dormir bien; *I couldn't get to sleep* no pude dormirme **2** v/i (pret & pp slept) dormir

◆ **sleep in** v/i (have a long lie) dormir hasta tarde

◆ **sleep on** v/t: *sleep on sth* decision consultar algo con la almohada

◆ **sleep with** v/t (have sex with) acostarse con

sleep-i-ly ['sliːpɪlɪ] adv: *say sth sleepily* decir algo medio dormido

sleep-ing bag ['sliːpɪŋ] saco m de dormir

sleep-ing car RAIL coche m cama

sleep-ing pill somnífero m, pastilla f para dormir

sleep-less ['sliːplɪs] adj: *have a sleepless night* pasar la noche en blanco

sleep-walk-er sonámbulo(-a) m(f)

sleep-walk-ing sonambulismo m

sleep-y ['sliːpɪ] adj adormilado, somnoliento; town tranquilo; *I'm sleepy* tengo sueño

sleet [sliːt] n aguanieve f

sleeve [sliːv] of jacket etc manga f

sleeve-less ['sliːvlɪs] adj sin mangas

sleigh [sleɪ] n trineo m

sleight of 'hand [slaɪt] juegos mpl de manos

slen-der ['slendər] adj figure, arms esbelto; income, margin escaso; chance remoto

slept [slept] pret & pp → **sleep**

slew [sluː] pret → **slay**

slice [slaɪs] **1** n of bread rebanada f; of cake trozo m; of salami, cheese loncha f; fig: of profits etc parte f **2** v/t loaf etc cortar (en rebanadas)

sliced 'bread [slaɪst] pan m de molde en rebanadas; *the greatest thing since sliced bread* F lo mejor desde que se inventó la rueda F

slick [slɪk] **1** adj performance muy logrado; (pej: cunning) con mucha labia **2** n of oil marea f negra

slid [slɪd] pret & pp → **slide**

slide [slaɪd] **1** n for kids tobogán m; PHOT

diapositiva f **2** v/i (*pret & pp* **slid**) deslizarse; *of exchange rate etc* descender **3** v/t (*pret & pp* **slid**) deslizar

slid-ing 'door ['slaɪdɪŋ] puerta f corredera

slight [slaɪt] **1** *adj person, figure* menudo; (*small*) pequeño; *accent* ligero; **I have a slight headache** me duele un poco la cabeza; **no, not in the slightest** no, en absoluto

slight-ly ['slaɪtlɪ] *adv* un poco

slim [slɪm] **1** *adj* delgado; *chance* remoto **2** v/i (*pret & pp* **slimmed**): **I'm slimming** estoy a dieta

slime [slaɪm] (*mud*) lodo m; *of slug etc* baba f

slim-y ['slaɪmɪ] *adj liquid* viscoso; *river bed* lleno de lodo

sling [slɪŋ] **1** n *for arm* cabestrillo m **2** v/t (*pret & pp* **slung**) F (*throw*) tirar

slip [slɪp] **1** n *on ice etc* resbalón m; (*mistake*) desliz m; **a slip of paper** un trozo de papel; **a slip of the tongue** un lapsus; **give s.o. the slip** dar esquinazo a alguien **2** v/i (*pret & pp* **slipped**) *on ice etc* resbalar; *of quality etc* empeorar; **he slipped out of the room** se fue de la habitación sigilosamente **3** v/t (*pret & pp* **slipped**) (*put*): **he slipped it into his briefcase** lo metió en su maletín sigilosamente; **it slipped my mind** se me olvidó

◆ **slip away** v/i *of time* pasar; *of opportunity* esfumarse; (*die quietly*) morir tranquilamente

◆ **slip off** v/t *jacket etc* quitarse

◆ **slip on** v/t *jacket etc* ponerse

◆ **slip out** v/i (*go out*) salir (sigilosamente)

◆ **slip up** v/i equivocarse

slipped 'disc [slɪpt] hernia f discal

slip-per ['slɪpər] zapatilla f (*de estar por casa*)

slip-pery ['slɪpərɪ] *adj surface, road* resbaladizo; *fish* escurridizo

slip-shod ['slɪpʃɑːd] *adj* chapucero

'slip-up (*mistake*) error m

slit [slɪt] **1** n (*tear*) raja f; (*hole*) rendija f; *in skirt* corte m **2** v/t (*pret & pp* **slit**) abrir; **slit s.o.'s throat** degollar a alguien

slith-er ['slɪðər] v/i deslizarse

sliv-er ['slɪvər] trocito m; *of wood, glass* astilla f

slob [slɑːb] *pej* dejado(-a) m/f, guarro(-a) m/f

slob-ber ['slɑːbər] v/i babear

slog [slɑːg] n paliza f

slo-gan ['sloʊgən] eslogan m

slop [slɑːp] v/t (*pret & pp* **slopped**) derramar

slope [sloʊp] **1** n *of roof, handwriting* inclinación f; *of mountain* ladera f; **buil**|
on a slope construido en una pendiente **2** v/i inclinarse; **the road slopes down to the sea** la carretera baja hasta el mar

slop-py ['slɑːpɪ] *adj* descuidado; *too sentimental* sensiblero

slot [slɑːt] **1** n ranura f; *in schedule* hueco m

◆ **slot in 1** v/t (*pret & pp* **slotted**) introducir **2** v/i (*pret & pp* **slotted**) encajar

'slot ma-chine *for cigarettes, food* máquina f expendedora; *for gambling* máquina f tragaperras

slouch [slaʊtʃ] v/i: **don't slouch** ponte derecho

slov-en-ly ['slʌvnlɪ] *adj* descuidado

slow [sloʊ] *adj* lento; **be slow** *of clock* ir retrasado

◆ **slow down 1** v/t *work, progress* restrasar; *traffic, production* ralentizar **2** v/i *in walking, driving* reducir la velocidad; *of production etc* relantizarse; **you need to slow down** *in lifestyle* tienes que tomarte las cosas con calma

'slow-down *in production* ralentización f

slow-ly ['sloʊlɪ] *adv* despacio, lentamente

slow 'mo-tion: in slow motion a cámara lenta

slow-ness ['sloʊnɪs] lentitud f

'slow-poke F tortuga f F

slug [slʌg] n *animal* babosa f

slug-gish ['slʌgɪʃ] *adj* lento

slum [slʌm] n *suburbio m, arrabal*

slump [slʌmp] **1** n *in trade* desplome m **2** v/i *economically* desplomarse, hundirse; (*collapse: of person*) desplomarse

slung [slʌŋ] *pret & pp* → **sling**

slur [slɜːr] **1** n *on s.o.'s character* difamación f **2** v/t (*pret & pp* **slurred**) *words* arrastrar

slurp [slɜːrp] v/t sorber

slurred [slɜːrd] *adj*: **his speech was slurred** habló arrastrando las palabras

slush [slʌʃ] nieve f derretida; (*pej: sentimental stuff*) sensiblería f

'slush fund fondo m para corruptelas

slush-y ['slʌʃɪ] *adj snow* derretido; *movie, novel* sensiblero

slut [slʌt] *pej* fulana f

sly [slaɪ] *adj* ladino; **on the sly** a escondidas

smack [smæk] **1** n: **a smack on the bottom** un azote; **a smack in the face** una bofetada **2** v/t *child* pegar; *bottom* dar un azote en

small [smɔːl] *adj* pequeño, *L.Am.* chico

small 'change cambio m, suelto m,

L.Am. sencillo *m*

small 'hours *npl* madrugada *f*

small-pox ['smɔːlpɑːks] viruela *f*

'small print letra *f* pequeña

'small talk: make small talk hablar de banalidades *or* trivialidades

smart [smɑːrt] **1** *adj* (*elegant*) elegante; (*intelligent*) inteligente; *pace* rápido; **get smart with** hacerse el listillo con **2** *v/i* (*hurt*) escocer

'smart ass F sabelotodo *m/f* F

'smart card tarjeta *f* inteligente

◆ **smart-en up** ['smɑːrtn] *v/t appearance* mejorar; *room* arreglar

smart-ly ['smɑːrtlɪ] *adv dressed* con elegancia

smash [smæʃ] **1** *n noise* estruendo *m*; (*car crash*) choque *m*; *in tennis* smash *m*, mate *m* **2** *v/t break* hacer pedazos *or* añicos; **he smashed the toys against the wall** estrelló los juguetes contra la pared; **he smashed his fist on the table** dio un puñetazo en la mesa; **smash sth to pieces** hacer algo añicos **3** *v/i break* romperse; **the driver smashed into ...** el conductor se estrelló contra ...

◆ **smash up** *v/t place* destrozar

smash 'hit F exitazo *m* F

smat-ter-ing ['smætərɪŋ] *of a language* nociones *fpl*

smear [smɪr] **1** *n of ink* borrón *m*; *of paint* mancha *f*; MED citología *f*; *on character* difamación *f* **2** *v/t character* difamar; **smear X over Y** untar *or* embadurnar Y de X

'smear cam-paign campaña *f* de difamación

smell [smel] **1** *n* olor *m*; **it has no smell** no huele a nada; **sense of smell** sentido *m* del olfato **2** *v/t* oler **3** *v/i unpleasantly* oler (mal); (*sniff*) olfatear; **you smell of beer** hueles a cerveza; **it smells good** huele bien

smell-y ['smelɪ] *adj* apestoso; **she had smelly feet** se olían los pies; **it's so smelly in here!** ¡qué mal huele aquí!

smile [smaɪl] **1** *n* sonrisa *f* **2** *v/i* sonreír

◆ **smile at** *v/t* sonreír a

smirk [smɜːrk] **1** *n* sonrisa *f* maligna **2** *v/i* sonreír malignamente

smog [smɑːg] *n* niebla *f* tóxica

smoke [smouk] **1** *n* humo *m*; **have a smoke** fumarse un cigarrillo **2** *v/t cigarettes* fumar; *bacon* ahumar **3** *v/i of person* fumar

smok-er ['smoukər] *person* fumador(a) *m(a)*

smok-ing ['smoukɪŋ]: **smoking is bad for you** fumar es malo; **no smoking** *sign*

prohibido fumar

'smok-ing com-part-ment RAIL compartimento *m* de fumadores

smok-y ['smoukɪ] *adj room, air* lleno de humo

smooth [smuːð] **1** *adj surface, skin* liso, suave; *sea* en calma; (*peaceful*) tranquilo; *ride, drive* sin vibraciones; *transition* sin problemas; *pej: person* meloso **2** *v/t hair* alisar

◆ **smooth down** *v/t with sandpaper etc* alisar

◆ **smooth out** *v/t paper, cloth* alisar

◆ **smooth over** *v/t:* **smooth things over** suavizar las cosas

smooth-ly ['smuːðlɪ] *adv without any problems* sin incidentes

smoth-er ['smʌðər] *v/t flames* apagar, sofocar; *person* asfixiar; **smother s.o. with kisses** comerse a alguien a besos; **he smothered the bread with jam** cubrió *or* embadurnó el pan de mermelada

smol-der, *Br* **smoul-der** ['smouldər] *v/i of fire* arder (*los rescoldos*); *fig: with anger* arder de rabia; *fig: with desire* arder en deseos

smudge [smʌdʒ] **1** *n of paint* mancha *f*; *of ink* borrón *m* **2** *v/t ink* emborronar; *paint* difuminar

smug [smʌg] *adj* engreído

smug-gle ['smʌgl] *v/t* pasar de contrabando

smug-gler ['smʌglər] contrabandista *m/f*

smug-gling ['smʌglɪŋ] contrabando *m*

smug-ly ['smʌglɪ] *adv* con engreimiento *or* suticiencia

smut-ty ['smʌtɪ] *adj joke, sense of humor* obsceno

snack [snæk] *n* tentempié *m*, aperitivo *m*

'snack bar cafetería *f*

snag [snæg] *n* (*problem*) inconveniente *m*, pega *f*

snail [sneɪl] caracol *m*

snake [sneɪk] *n* serpiente *f*

snap [snæp] **1** *n* chasquido *m*; PHOT foto *f* **2** *v/t* (*pret & pp* **snapped**) *break* romper **3** *v/i* (*pret & pp* **snapped**) *break* romperse; **none of your business, she snapped** no es asunto tuyo, saltó **4** *adj decision, judgment* rápido, súbito

◆ **snap up** *v/t bargains* llevarse

snap fast-en-er ['snæpfæsnər] automático *m*, corchete *m*

snap-py ['snæpɪ] *adj person, mood* irascible; *decision, response* rápido; (*elegant*) elegante

'snap-shot foto *f*

snarl [snɑːrl] **1** *n of dog* gruñido *m* **2** *v/i* gruñir

snatch [snætʃ] **1** v/t arrebatar; (steal) robar; (kidnap) secuestrar; **snatch sth from s.o.** arrebatar algo a alguien **2** v/i: **don't snatch** no lo agarres
♦ **snatch at** v/t intentar agarrar

snaz·zy ['snæzɪ] adj F vistoso; Span chulo F

sneak [sni:k] **1** n (telltale) chivato(-a) m(f) **2** v/t (remove, steal) llevarse; **sneak a glance at** mirar con disimulo a **3** v/i (tell tales) chivarse; **sneak into the room** entrar a la habitación a hurtadillas

sneak·ers ['sni:kərz] npl zapatillas fpl de deporte

sneak·ing ['sni:kɪŋ] adj: **have a sneaking suspicion that …** sospechar que …

sneak·y ['sni:kɪ] adj F (crafty) ladino, cuco F

sneer [snɪr] **1** n mueca f desdeñosa **2** v/i burlarse (**at** de)

sneeze [sni:z] **1** n estornudo m **2** v/i estornudar

snick·er ['snɪkər] **1** n risita f **2** v/i reírse (en voz baja)

sniff [snɪf] **1** v/i to clear nose sorberse los mocos; of dog olfatear **2** v/t (smell) oler; of dog olfatear

snip [snɪp] n F (bargain) ganga f

snip·er ['snaɪpər] francotirador(a) m(f)

sniv·el ['snɪvl] v/i gimotear

snob [snɑːb] presuntuoso(-a) m(f)

snob·ber·y ['snɑːbərɪ] presuntuosidad f

snob·bish ['snɑːbɪʃ] adj presuntuoso

snoop [snuːp] n fisgón(-ona) m(f)
♦ **snoop around** v/i fisgonear

snoot·y ['snuːtɪ] adj presuntuoso

snooze [snuːz] **1** n cabezada f; **have a snooze** echar una cabezada **2** v/i echar una cabezada

snore [snɔːr] v/i roncar

snor·ing ['snɔːrɪŋ] n ronquidos mpl

snor·kel ['snɔːrkl] n snorkel m, tubo m para buceo

snort [snɔːrt] v/i of bull, person bufar, resoplar

snout [snaut] of pig, dog hocico m

snow [snou] **1** n nieve f **2** v/i nevar
♦ **snow under** v/i: **be snowed under** estar desbordado

'**snow·ball** bola f de nieve

'**snow·bound** adj aislado por la nieve

'**snow chains** npl MOT cadenas fpl para la nieve

'**snow·drift** nevero m

'**snow·drop** campanilla f de invierno

'**snow·flake** copo m de nieve

'**snow·man** muñeco m de nieve

'**snow·plow** quitanieves f inv

'**snow·storm** tormenta f de nieve

snow·y ['snouɪ] adj weather de nieve; roads, hills nevado

snub [snʌb] **1** n desaire **2** v/t (pret & pp **snubbed**) desairar

snub-nosed ['snʌbnouzd] adj con la nariz respingona

snug [snʌg] adj (tight-fitting) ajustado; **we are nice and snug in here** aquí se está muy a gusto
♦ **snug·gle down** ['snʌgl] v/i acurrucarse
♦ **snug·gle up to** v/t acurrucarse contra

so [sou] **1** adv tan; **it was so easy** fue tan fácil; **I'm so cold** tengo tanto frío; **that was so kind of you** fue muy amable de tu parte; **not so much** no tanto; **so much easier** mucho más fácil; **you shouldn't eat / drink so much** no deberías comer / beber tanto; **I miss you so** te echo tanto de menos; **so am I / do I** yo también; **so is she / does she** ella también; **and so on** etcétera **2** pron: **I hope / think** so eso espero / creo; **you didn't tell me - I did so** no me lo dijiste - sí que lo hice; **50 or so** unos 50 **3** conj for that reason así que; in order that para que; **I got up late and so I missed the train** me levanté tarde y por eso perdí el tren; **so (that) I could come too** para que yo también pudiera venir; **so what?** F ¿y qué? F

soak [souk] v/t (steep) poner en remojo; of water, rain empapar
♦ **soak up** v/t liquid absorber; **soak up the sun** tostarse al sol

soaked [soukt] adj empapado; **be soaked to the skin** estar calado hasta los huesos

soak·ing (wet) ['soukɪŋ] adj empapado

so-and-so ['souənsou] F (unknown person) fulanito m; (euph: annoying person) canalla m/f

soap [soup] for washing jabón m

'**soap (op·e·ra)** telenovela f

soap·y ['soupɪ] adj water jabonoso

soar [sɔːr] v/i of rocket etc elevarse; of prices dispararse

sob [sɑːb] **1** n sollozo m **2** v/i (pret & pp **sobbed**) sollozar

so·ber ['soubər] adj (not drunk) sobrio; (serious) serio
♦ **sober up** v/i: **he sobered up** se le pasó la borrachera

so-'called adj (referred to as) así llamado; (incorrectly referred to as) mal llamado

soc·cer ['sɑːkər] fútbol m

'**soc·cer hoo·li·gan** hincha m violento

so·cia·ble ['souʃəbl] adj sociable

so·cial ['souʃl] adj social

so·cial 'dem·o·crat socialdemócrata m/f

so·cial·ism ['souʃəlɪzm] socialismo *m*
so·cial·ist ['souʃəlɪst] **1** *adj* socialista **2** *n* socialista *m/f*
so·cial·ize ['souʃəlaɪz] *v/i* socializar (**with** con)
'**soc·ial life** vida *f* social
so·cial 'sci·ence ciencia *f* social
'**so·cial work** trabajo *m* social
'**so·cial work·er** asistente(-a) *m(f)* social
so·ci·e·ty [sə'saɪətɪ] sociedad *f*
so·ci·ol·o·gist [sousɪ'ɑːlədʒɪst] sociólogo(-a) *m(f)*
so·ci·ol·o·gy [sousɪ'ɑːlədʒɪ] sociología *f*
sock[1] [sɑːk] *for wearing* calcetín *m*
sock[2] [sɑːk] **1** *n* (*punch*) puñetazo *m* **2** *v/t* (*punch*) dar un puñetazo
sock·et ['sɑːkɪt] *for light bulb* casquillo *m*; *of arm* cavidad *f*; *of eye* cuenca *f*; *Br electrical* enchufe *m*
so·da ['soudə] (*soda water*) soda *f*; (*ice-cream soda*) refresco de soda con helado
sod·den ['sɑːdn] *adj* empapado
so·fa ['soufə] sofá *m*
'**so·fa-bed** sofá cama *m*
soft [sɑːft] *adj voice, light, color, skin* suave; *pillow, attitude* blando; **have a soft spot for** tener una debilidad por
'**soft drink** refresco *m*
'**soft drug** droga *f* blanda
soft·en ['sɑːfn] **1** *v/t position* ablandar; *impact, blow* amortiguar **2** *v/i of butter, ice cream* ablandarse, reblandecerse
soft·ly ['sɑːftlɪ] *adv* suavemente
soft 'toy peluche *m*
soft·ware ['sɑːftwer] software *m*
sog·gy ['sɑːgɪ] *adj* empapado
soil [sɔɪl] **1** *n* (*earth*) tierra *f* **2** *v/t* ensuciar
so·lar 'en·er·gy ['soulər] energía *f* solar
'**so·lar pan·el** panel *m* solar
'**so·lar system** sistema *m* solar
sold [sould] *pret & pp* → **sell**
sol·dier ['souldʒər] soldado *m*
♦ soldier on *v/i* seguir adelante; **we'll have to soldier on without her** nos las tendremos que arreglar sin ella
sole[1] [soul] *n of foot* planta *f*; *of shoe* suela *f*
sole[2] [soul] *adj* único
sole·ly ['soulɪ] *adv* únicamente
sol·emn ['sɑːləm] *adj* solemne
so·lem·ni·ty [sə'lemnətɪ] solemnidad *f*
sol·emn·ly ['sɑːləmlɪ] *adv* solemnemente
so·lic·it [sə'lɪsɪt] *v/i of prostitute* abordar clientes
so·lic·i·tor [sə'lɪsɪtər] *Br* abogado(-a) *m(f)* (*que no aparece en tribunales*)
sol·id ['sɑːlɪd] *adj* sólido; (*without holes*) compacto; *gold, silver* macizo; **a solid hour** una hora seguida

sol·i·dar·i·ty [sɑːlɪ'dærətɪ] solidaridad *f*
so·lid·i·fy [sə'lɪdɪfaɪ] *v/i* (*pret & pp* **solidified**) solidificarse
so·lid·ly ['sɑːlɪdlɪ] *adv built* sólidamente; *in favor of sth* unánimemente
sol·il·o·quy [sə'lɪləkwɪ] soliloquio *f*
sol·i·taire [sɑːlɪ'ter] *card game* solitario *m*
sol·i·ta·ry ['sɑːlɪterɪ] *adj life, activity* solitario; (*single*) único
sol·i·ta·ry con'fine·ment prisión *f* incomunicada
sol·i·tude ['sɑːlɪtuːd] soledad *f*
so·lo ['soulou] **1** *n* MUS solo *m* **2** *adj* en solitario
so·lo·ist ['soulouɪst] solista *m/f*
sol·u·ble ['sɑːljubl] *adj substance, problem* soluble
so·lu·tion [sə'luːʃn] solución *f* (**to** a); (*mixture*) solución *f*
solve [sɑːlv] *v/t problem* solucionar, resolver; *mystery* resolver; *crossword* resolver, sacar
sol·vent ['sɑːlvənt] *adj financially* solvente
som·ber, *Br* **som·bre** ['sɑːmbər] *adj* (*dark*) oscuro; (*serious*) sombrío
some [sʌm] **1** *adj*: **would you like some water / cookies?** ¿quieres agua / galletas?; **some countries** algunos países; **I gave him some money** le di (algo de) dinero; **some people say that ...** hay quien dice ... **2** *pron*: **some of the group** parte del grupo; **would you like some?** ¿quieres?; **milk? - no thanks, I've got some** ¿leche? - gracias, ya tengo **3** *adv* (*a bit*): **we'll have to wait some** tendremos que esperar algo *or* un poco
some·bod·y ['sʌmbədɪ] *pron* alguien
'**some·day** *adv* algún día
'**some·how** *adv* (*by one means or another*) de alguna manera; (*for some unknown reason*) por alguna razón; **I've never liked him somehow** por alguna razón u otra nunca me cayó bien
'**some·one** *pron* → **somebody**
'**some·place** *adv* → **somewhere**
som·er·sault ['sʌmərsɔːlt] **1** *n* salto mortal **2** *v/i* dar un salto mortal
'**some·thing** *pron* algo; **would you like something to drink / eat?** ¿te gustaría beber / comer algo?; **is something wrong?** ¿pasa algo?
'**some·time** *adv*: **let's have lunch sometime** quedemos para comer un día de éstos; **sometime last year** en algún momento del año pasado
some·times ['sʌmtaɪmz] *adv* a veces
'**some·what** *adv* un tanto
'**some·where 1** *adv* en alguna parte *or* al-

gún lugar **2** *pron*: **let's go to somewhere quiet** vamos a algún sitio tranquilo; **I was looking for somewhere to park** buscaba un sitio donde aparcar

son [sʌn] hijo *m*

so·na·ta [səˈnɑːtə] MUS sonata *f*

song [sɒŋ] canción *f*

'song·bird pájaro *m* cantor

'song·writ·er cantautor(a) *m(f)*

'son-in-law (*pl* **sons-in-law**) yerno *m*

'son·net [ˈsɑːnɪt] soneto *m*

soon [suːn] *adv* pronto; **how soon can you be ready to leave?** ¿cuándo estarás listo para salir?; **he left soon after I arrived** se marchó al poco de llegar yo; **can't you get here any sooner?** ¿no podrías llegar antes?; **as soon as** tan pronto como; **as soon as possible** lo antes posible; **sooner or later** tarde o temprano; **the sooner the better** cuanto antes mejor

soot [sʊt] hollín *m*

soothe [suːð] *v/t* calmar

so·phis·ti·cat·ed [səˈfɪstɪkeɪtɪd] *adj* sofisticado

so·phis·ti·ca·tion [səfɪstɪkeɪʃn] sofisticación *f*

soph·o·more [ˈsɑːfəmɔːr] estudiante *m/f* de segundo año

sop·py [ˈsɑːpɪ] *adj* F sensiblero

so·pra·no [səˈprænoʊ] *n singer* soprano *m/f*; *voice* voz *f* de soprano

sor·did [ˈsɔːrdɪd] *adj affair, business* sórdido

sore [sɔːr] **1** *adj* (*painful*) dolorido; F (*angry*) enojado, *Span* mosqueado F; **is it sore?** ¿duele?; **I'm sore all over me** duele todo el cuerpo **2** *n* llaga *f*

sor·row [ˈsɑːroʊ] *n* pena *f*

sor·ry [ˈsɑːrɪ] *adj* (*sad: day, sight*) triste; (*I'm*) **sorry!** *apologizing* ¡lo siento!; (*I'm*) **sorry that I didn't tell you sooner** lamento no habértelo dicho antes; **I was so sorry to hear of her death** me dio mucha pena oír lo de su muerte; (*I'm*) **sorry but I can't help** lo siento pero no puedo ayudar; **I won't be sorry to leave here** no me arrepentiré de irme de aquí; **I feel sorry for her** siento pena *or* lástima por ella; **be a sorry sight** ofrecer un espectáculo lamentable

sort [sɔːrt] **1** *n* clase *f*, tipo *m*; **sort of** F un poco, algo; **is it finished? – sort of** F ¿está acabado? – más o menos **2** *v/t* ordenar, clasificar; COMPUT ordenar

◆ **sort out** *v/t papers* ordenar, clasificar; *problem* resolver, arreglar

SOS [esoʊˈes] SOS *m*; *fig* llamada *f* de auxilio

so-'so *adv* F así así F

sought [sɔːt] *pret & pp* → **seek**

soul [soʊl] REL, *fig: of a nation etc* alma *f*; *character* personalidad *f*; **the poor soul** el pobrecillo

sound¹ [saʊnd] **1** *adj* (*sensible*) sensato; (*healthy*) sano; *sleep* profundo **2** *adv*: **be sound asleep** estar profundamente dormido

sound² [saʊnd] **1** *n* sonido *m*; (*noise*) ruido *m* **2** *v/t* (*pronounce*) pronunciar; MED auscultar; **sound one's horn** tocar la bocina **3** *v/i*: **that sounds interesting** parece interesante; **she sounded unhappy** parecía triste

◆ **sound out** *v/t* sondear; **I sounded her out about the idea** sondeé a ver qué le parecía la idea

'sound card COMPUT tarjeta *f* de sonido

'sound ef·fects *npl* efectos *mpl* sonoros

sound·ly [ˈsaʊndlɪ] *adv sleep* profundamente; *beaten* rotundamente

'sound·proof *adj* insonorizado

'sound·track banda *f* sonora

soup [suːp] sopa *f*

'soup bowl cuenco *m*

souped-up [suːptˈʌp] *adj* F trucado

'soup plate plato *m* sopero

'soup spoon cuchara *f* sopera

sour [saʊr] *adj apple, orange* ácido, agrio; *milk* cortado; *comment* agrio

source [sɔːrs] *n* fuente *f*; *of river* nacimiento *m*; (*person*) fuente *f*

'sour cream nata *f* agria

south [saʊθ] **1** *adj* del sur, del sur **2** *n* sur *m*; **to the south of** al sur de **3** *adv* al sur; **south of** al sur de

South 'Af·ri·ca Sudáfrica

South 'Af·ri·can 1 *adj* sudafricano **2** *n* sudafricano(-a) *m(f)*

South A'mer·i·ca Sudamérica, América del Sur

South A'mer·i·can 1 *adj* sudamericano **2** *n* sudamericano(-a) *m(f)*

south'east 1 *n* sudeste *m*, sureste *m* **2** *adj* sudeste, sureste **3** *adv* al sudeste *or* sureste; **southeast of** al sudeste de

south·'east·ern *adj* del sudeste

south·er·ly [ˈsʌðərlɪ] *adj wind* sur, del sur; *direction* sur

south·ern [ˈsʌðərn] *adj* sureño

south·ern·er [ˈsʌðərnər] sureño(-a) *m(f)*

south·ern·most [ˈsʌðərnmoʊst] *adj* más al sur

South 'Pole Polo *m* Sur

south·ward [ˈsaʊθwərd] *adv* hacia el sur

south·'west 1 *n* sudoeste *m*, suroeste *m* **2** *adj* sudoeste, suroeste **3** *adv* al sudeste *or* suroeste; **southwest of** al sudoeste *or*

suroeste de
south·west·ern *adj* del sudoeste *or* suroeste
sou·ve·nir [suːvəˈnɪr] *n* recuerdo *m*
sove·reign [ˈsɑːvrɪn] *adj state* soberano
sove·reign·ty [ˈsɑːvrɪntɪ] *of state* soberanía *f*
So·vi·et [ˈsouviət] *adj* soviético
So·vi·et 'U·nion Unión *f* Soviética
sow[1] [sau] *n (female pig)* cerda *f*, puerca *f*
sow[2] [sou] *v/t (pret sowed, pp sown) seeds* sembrar
sown [soun] *pp* → **sow**[2]
soy·bean [sɔɪ] semilla *f* de soja
soy 'sauce salsa *f* de soja
space [speɪs] *n* espacio *m*
♦ **space out** *v/t* espaciar
'space-bar COMPUT barra *f* espaciadora
'space·craft nave *f* espacial
'space·ship nave *f* espacial
'space shut·tle transbordador *m* espacial
'space sta·tion estación *f* espacial
'space·suit traje *m* espacial
spa·cious [ˈspeɪʃəs] *adj* espacioso
spade [speɪd] *for digging* pala *f*; **spades** *in card game* picas *fpl*
'spade·work *fig* trabajo *m* preliminar
spa·ghet·ti [spəˈgetɪ] *nsg* espaguetis *mpl*
Spain [speɪn] España
span [spæn] *v/t (pret & pp spanned)* abarcar; *of bridge* cruzar
Span·iard [ˈspænjərd] español(a) *m(f)*
Span·ish [ˈspænɪʃ] **1** *adj* español **2** *n language* español *m*; **the Spanish** los españoles
spank [spæŋk] *v/t* azotar
spank·ing [ˈspæŋkɪŋ] azotaina *f*
span·ner [ˈspænər] *Br* llave *f*
spare [speɪr] **1** *v/t*: **can you spare me $50?** ¿me podrías dejar 50 dólares?; **we can't spare a single employee** no podemos prescindir ni de un solo trabajador; **can you spare the time?** ¿tienes tiempo?; **I have time to spare** me sobra el tiempo; **there were 5 to spare** sobraban cinco **2** *adj pair of glasses, set of keys* de repuesto; **do you have any spare cash?** ¿no te sobrará algo de dinero? **3** *n* recambio *m*, repuesto *m*
spare 'part pieza *f* de recambio *or* repuesto
spare 'ribs *npl* costillas *fpl* de cerdo
spare 'room habitación *f* de invitados
spare 'time tiempo *m* libre
spare 'tire, *Br* **spare 'tyre** MOT rueda *f* de recambio *or* repuesto
spar·ing [ˈsperɪŋ] *adj* moderado; **be sparing with** no derrochar
spar·ing·ly [ˈsperɪŋlɪ] *adv* con moderación

ción
spark [spɑːrk] *n* chispa *f*
spar·kle [ˈspɑːrkl] *v/i* destellar
spar·kling 'wine [ˈspɑːrklɪŋ] vino *m* espumoso
'spark plug bujía *f*
spar·row [ˈspærou] gorrión *m*
sparse [spɑːrs] *adj vegetation* escaso
sparse·ly [ˈspɑːrslɪ] *adv*: **sparsely populated** poco poblado
spar·tan [ˈspɑːrtn] *adj room* espartano
spas·mod·ic [spæzˈmɑːdɪk] *adj* intermitente
spat [spæt] *pret & pp* → **spit**
spate [speɪt] *fig* oleada *f*
spa·tial [ˈspeɪʃl] *adj* espacial
spat·ter [ˈspætər] *v/t*: **the car spattered mud all over me** el coche me salpicó de barro
speak [spiːk] **1** *v/i (pret spoke, pp spoken)* hablar **(to** con); *(make a speech)* dar una charla; **we're not speaking (to each other)** *(we've quarreled)* no nos hablamos; **speaking** TELEC al habla **2** *v/t (pret spoke, pp spoken) foreign language* hablar; **she spoke her mind** dijo lo que pensaba
♦ **speak for** *v/t* hablar en nombre de
♦ **speak out** *v/i*: **speak out against injustice** denunciar la injusticia
♦ **speak up** *v/i (speak louder)* hablar más alto
speak·er [ˈspiːkər] *at conference* conferenciante *m/f*; *(orator)* orador(a) *m(f)*; *of sound system* altavoz *m*, *L.Am.* altoparlante *m*; *of language* hablante *m/f*
spear [spɪr] lanza *f*
spear·mint [ˈspɪrmɪnt] hierbabuena *f*
spe·cial [ˈspeʃl] *adj* especial; **be on special** estar de oferta
spe·cial ef·fects *npl* efectos *mpl* especiales
spe·cial·ist [ˈspeʃlɪst] especialista *m/f*
spe·cial·ize [ˈspeʃəlaɪz] *v/i* especializarse **(in** en)
spe·cial·ly [ˈspeʃlɪ] *adv* → **especially**
spe·cial·i·ty [speʃɪˈælɪtɪ] *Br*, **spe·cial·ty** [ˈspeʃəltɪ] especialidad *f*
spe·cies [ˈspiːʃiːz] *nsg* especie *f*
spe·cif·ic [spəˈsɪfɪk] *adj* específico
spe·cif·i·cal·ly [spəˈsɪfɪklɪ] *adv* específicamente
spec·i·fi·ca·tions [spesɪfɪˈkeɪʃnz] *npl of machine etc* especificaciones *fpl*
spe·ci·fy [ˈspesɪfaɪ] *v/t (pret & pp specified)* especificar
spe·ci·men [ˈspesɪmən] muestra *f*
speck [spek] *of dust, soot* mota *f*
specs [speks] *npl* F *(spectacles)* gafas *fpl*,

L.Am. lentes *mpl*

spec·ta·cle ['spektəkl] (*impressive sight*) espectáculo *m*; (*a pair of*) **spectacles** unas gafas, *L.Am.* unos lentes

spec·tac·u·lar [spek'tækjʊlər] *adj* espectacular

spec·ta·tor [spek'teɪtər] espectador(a) *m(f)*

spec·ta·tor sport deporte *m* espectáculo

spec·trum ['spektrəm] *fig* espectro *m*

spec·u·late ['spekjʊleɪt] *v/i also* FIN especular

spec·u·la·tion [spekjʊ'leɪʃn] *also* FIN especulación *f*

spec·u·la·tor ['spekjʊleɪtər] FIN especulador(a) *m(f)*

sped [sped] *pret & pp* → **speed**

speech [spiːtʃ] (*address*) discurso *m*; *in play* parlamento *m*; (*ability to speak*) habla *f*, dicción *f*; (*way of speaking*) forma *f* de hablar

'speech de·fect defecto *m* del habla

speech·less ['spiːtʃlɪs] *adj with shock, surprise* sin habla; *I was left speechless* me quedé sin habla

'speech ther·a·pist logopeda *m/f*

'speech ther·a·py logopedia *f*

'speech writ·er redactor(a) *m(f)* de discursos

speed [spiːd] **1** *n* velocidad *f*; (*promptness*) rapidez *f*; *at a speed of 150 mph* a una velocidad de 150 millas por hora **2** *v/i* (*pret & pp* **sped**) *run* correr; *drive too quickly* sobrepasar el límite de velocidad; *we were speeding along* íbamos a toda velocidad

◆ **speed by** *v/i* pasar a toda velocidad

◆ **speed up 1** *v/i of car, driver* acelerar; *when working* apresurarse **2** *v/t process* acelerar

'speed·boat motora *f*, planeadora *f*

'speed bump resalto *m* (*para reducir la velocidad del tráfico*), *Arg* despertador *m*, *Mex* tope *m*

speed·i·ly ['spiːdɪlɪ] *adv* con rapidez

speed·ing ['spiːdɪŋ] *n*: *fined for speeding* multado por exceso de velocidad

'speed·ing fine multa *f* por exceso de velocidad

'speed lim·it *on roads* límite *m* de velocidad

speed·om·e·ter [spiː'dɑːmɪtər] velocímetro *m*

'speed trap control *m* de velocidad por radar

speed·y ['spiːdɪ] *adj* rápido

spell¹ [spel] **1** *v/t word* deletrear *how do you spell ...?* ¿cómo se escribe ... ? **2** *v/i* deletrear

spell² [spel] *n* (*period of time*) periodo *m*, temporada; *I'll take a spell at the wheel* te relevaré un rato al volante

'spell·bound *adj* hechizado

'spell·check COMPUT: *do a spellcheck on* pasar el corrector ortográfico a

'spell·check·er COMPUT corrector *m* ortográfico

spell·ing ['spelɪŋ] ortografía *f*

spend [spend] *v/t* (*pret & pp* **spent**) *money* gastar; *time* pasar

'spend·thrift *n pej* derrochador(a) *m(f)*

spent [spent] *pret & pp* → **spend**

sperm [spɜːrm] espermatozoide *m*; (*semen*) esperma *f*

'sperm bank banco *m* de esperma

'sperm count recuento *m* espermático

sphere [sfɪr] *also fig* esfera *f*; *sphere of influence* ámbito *m* de influencia

spice [spaɪs] *n* (*seasoning*) especia *f*

spic·y ['spaɪsɪ] *adj food* con especias; (*hot*) picante

spi·der ['spaɪdər] araña *f*

'spi·der·web telaraña *f*, tela *f* de araña

spike [spaɪk] *n* pincho *m*; *on running shoe* clavo *m*

spill [spɪl] **1** *v/t* derramar **2** *v/i* derramarse **3** *n* derrame *m*

spin¹ [spɪn] **1** *n* (*turn*) giro *m* **2** *v/t* (*pret & pp* **spun**) *hacer girar* **3** *v/i* (*pret & pp* **spun**) *of wheel* girar, dar vueltas; *my head is spinning* me da vueltas la cabeza

spin² [spɪn] *v/t wool, cotton* hilar; *web* tejer

◆ **spin around** *v/i of person, car* darse la vuelta

◆ **spin out** *v/t* alargar

spin·ach ['spɪnɪdʒ] espinacas *fpl*

spin·al ['spaɪnl] *adj* de la columna vertebral

spin·al 'col·umn columna *f* vertebral

spin·al 'cord médula *f* espinal

'spin doc·tor F asesor *encargado de dar la mejor prensa posible a un político o asunto*

'spin-dry *v/t* centrifugar

spin-'dry·er centrifugadora *f*

spine [spaɪn] *of person, animal* columna *f* vertebral; *of book* lomo *m*; *on plant, hedgehog* espina *f*

spine·less ['spaɪnlɪs] *adj* (*cowardly*) débil

'spin-off producto *m* derivade

spin·ster ['spɪnstər] solterona *f*

spin·y ['spaɪnɪ] *adj* espinoso

spi·ral ['spaɪrəl] **1** *n* espiral **2** *v/i* (*rise quickly*) subir vertiginosamente

spi·ral 'stair·case escalera *f* de caracol

spire [spaɪr] aguja *f*

spir·it ['spɪrɪt] *n* espíritu *m*; (*courage*) valor *m*; **in a spirit of cooperation** con espíritu de cooperación

spir·it·ed ['spɪrɪtɪd] *adj (energetic)* enérgico

'**spir·it lev·el** nivel *m* de burbuja

spir·its[1] ['spɪrɪts] *npl (alcohol)* licores *mpl*

spirits[2] ['spɪrɪts] *npl (morale)* la moral; **be in good / poor spirits** tener la moral alta / baja

spir·i·tu·al ['spɪrɪtʃuəl] *adj* espiritual

spir·it·u·al·ism ['spɪrɪtʃəlɪzm] espiritismo *m*

spir·it·u·al·ist ['spɪrɪtʃəlɪst] *n* espiritista *m*

spit [spɪt] *v/i (pret & pp spat)* of person escupir; **it's spitting with rain** está chispeando

◆ **spit out** *v/t food, liquid* escupir

spite [spaɪt] *n* rencor *m*; **in spite of** a pesar de

spite·ful ['spaɪtfəl] *adj* malo, malicioso

spite·ful·ly ['spaɪtfəlɪ] *adv* con maldad *or* malicia

spit·ting im·age ['spɪtɪŋ]: **be the spitting image of s.o.** ser el vivo retrato de alguien

splash [splæʃ] **1** *n small amount of liquid* chorrito *m; of color* mancha *f* **2** *v/t person* salpicar; **the car splashed mud all over me** el coche me salpicó de barro **3** *v/i of water* salpicar

◆ **splash down** *v/i of spacecraft* amerizar

◆ **splash out** *v/i in spending* gastarse una fortuna

'**splash·down** amerizaje *m*

splen·did ['splendɪd] *adj* espléndido

splen·dor, *Br* **splen·dour** ['splendər] esplendor *m*

splint [splɪnt] *n* MED tablilla *f*

splin·ter ['splɪntər] **1** *n* astilla *f* **2** *v/i* astillarse

'**splin·ter group** grupo *m* escindido

split [splɪt] **1** *n damage* raja *f; (disagreement)* escisión *f; (division, share)* reparto *m* **2** *v/t (pret & pp split) damage* rajar; *logs* partir en dos; *(cause disagreement in)* escindir; *(share)* repartir **3** *v/i (pret & pp split) (tear)* rajarse; *(disagree)* escindirse

◆ **split up** *v/i of couple* separarse

split per·son·al·i·ty PSYCH doble personalidad *f*

split·ting ['splɪtɪŋ] *adj:* **splitting headache** dolor *m* de cabeza atroz

splut·ter ['splʌtər] *v/i* farfullar

spoil [spɔɪl] *v/t* estropear, arruinar

'**spoil·sport** F aguafiestas *m/f inv* F

spoilt [spɔɪlt] *adj child* consentido, mimado; **be spoilt for choice** tener mucho donde elegir

spoke[1] [spouk] *of wheel* radio *m*

spoke[2] [spouk] *pret* → **speak**

spo·ken ['spoukən] *pp* → **speak**

spokes·man ['spouksmən] portavoz *m*

spokes·per·son ['spoukspɜrsən] portavoz *m/f*

spokes·wom·an ['spoukswumən] portavoz *f*

sponge [spʌndʒ] *n* esponja *f*

◆ **sponge off, sponge on** *v/t* F vivir a costa de

'**sponge cake** bizcocho *m*

spong·er ['spʌndʒər] F gorrón(-ona) *m(f)* F

spon·sor ['spɑːnsər] **1** *n* patrocinador *m* **2** *v/t* patrocinar

spon·sor·ship ['spɑːnsərʃɪp] patrocinio *m*

spon·ta·ne·ous [spɑːn'teɪnɪəs] *adj* espontáneo

spon·ta·ne·ous·ly [spɑːn'teɪnɪəslɪ] *adv* espontáneamente

spook·y ['spuːkɪ] *adj* F espeluznante, terrorífico

spool [spuːl] *n* carrete *m*

spoon [spuːn] *n* cuchara *f*

'**spoon-feed** *v/t (pret & pp spoonfed) fig* dar todo mascado a

spoon·ful ['spuːnfʊl] cucharada *f*

spo·rad·ic [spə'rædɪk] *adj* esporádico

sport [spɔːrt] *n* deporte *m*

sport·ing ['spɔːrtɪŋ] *adj* deportivo; **a sporting gesture** un gesto deportivo

'**sports car** [spɔːrts] (coche *m*) deportivo *m*

'**sports·coat** chaqueta *f* de sport

sports jour·nal·ist periodista *m/f* deportivo(-a)

'**sports·man** deportista *m*

'**sports med·i·cine** medicina *f* deportiva

'**sports news** *nsg* noticias *fpl* deportivas

'**sports page** página *f* de deportes

'**sports·wear** ropa *f* de deporte

'**sports·wom·an** deportista *f*

sport·y ['spɔːrtɪ] *adj person* deportista; *clothes* deportivo

spot[1] [spɑːt] *(pimple etc)* grano *m; (part of pattern)* lunar *m;* **a spot of ...** *(a little)* algo de ..., un poco de ...

spot[2] [spɑːt] *(place)* lugar *m*, sitio *m;* **on the spot** *(in the place in question)* en el lugar; *(immediately)* en ese momento; **put s.o. on the spot** poner a alguien en un aprieto

spot[3] [spɑːt] *v/t (pret & pp spotted) (notice)* ver; *(identify)* ver, darse cuenta de

spot check *n* control *m* al azar; **carry out**

S

spot check checks llevar a cabo controles al azar

spot·less ['spɑːtlɪs] *adj* inmaculado, impecable

'**spot·light** *n* foco *m*

spot·ted ['spɑːtɪd] *adj fabric* de lunares

spot·ty ['spɑːtɪ] *adj with pimples* con granos

spouse [spaʊs] *fml* cónyuge *m/f*

spout [spaʊt] **1** *n* pitorro *m* **2** *v/i of liquid* chorrear **3** *v/t* F soltar F

sprain [spreɪn] **1** *n* esguince *m* **2** *v/t* hacerse un esguince en

sprang [spræŋ] *pret →* **spring³**

sprawl [sprɔːl] *v/i* despatarrarse; *of city* expandirse; **send s.o. sprawling** *of punch* derribar de un golpe

sprawl·ing ['sprɔːlɪŋ] *adj city, suburbs* en expansión

spray [spreɪ] **1** *n of sea water, from fountain* rociada *f*; *for hair* spray *m*; *container* aerosol *m*, spray *m* **2** *v/t* rociar; **spray sth with sth** rociar algo de algo

'**spray·gun** pistola *f* pulverizadora

spread [spred] **1** *n of disease, religion etc* propagación *f*; F *(big meal)* comilona *f* F **2** *v/t (pret & pp spread) (lay)* extender; *butter, jelly* untar; *news, rumor* difundir; *disease* propagar; *arms, legs* extender **3** *v/i (pret & pp spread) of disease, fire* propagarse; *of rumor, news* difundirse; *of butter* extenderse, untarse

'**spread·sheet** COMPUT hoja *f* de cálculo

spree [spriː] F: **go (out) on a spree** ir de juerga; **go a shopping spree** salir a comprar a lo loco

sprig [sprɪg] ramita *f*

spright·ly ['spraɪtlɪ] *adj* lleno de energía

spring¹ [sprɪŋ] *n (season)* primavera *f*

spring² [sprɪŋ] *n (device)* muelle *m*

spring³ [sprɪŋ] **1** *n (jump)* brinco *m*, salto *m*; *(stream)* manantial *m* **2** *v/i (pret sprang, pp sprung)* brincar, saltar; **spring from** proceder de; **he sprang to his feet** se levantó de un salto

'**spring·board** trampolín *m*

spring 'chick·en *hum*: **she's no spring chicken** no es ninguna niña

spring-'clean·ing limpieza *f* a fondo

'**spring·time** primavera *f*

spring·y ['sprɪŋɪ] *adj mattress, ground* mullido; *walk* ligero; *piece of elastic* elástico

sprin·kle ['sprɪŋkl] *v/t* espolvorear; **sprinkle sth with sth** espolvorear algo con algo

sprin·kler ['sprɪŋklər] *for garden* aspersor *m*; *in ceiling* rociador *m* contra incendios

sprint [sprɪnt] **1** *n* esprint *m*; SP carrera *f* de velocidad **2** *v/i (run fast)* correr a toda velocidad; *of runner* esprintar

sprint·er ['sprɪntər] SP esprínter *m/f*, velocista *m/f*

sprout [spraʊt] **1** *v/i of seed* brotar **2** *n*: *(Brussels) sprouts* coles *fpl* de Bruselas

spruce [spruːs] *adj* pulcro

sprung [sprʌŋ] *pp →* **spring³**

spry [spraɪ] *adj* lleno *m* de energía

spun [spʌn] *pret & pp →* **spin¹**

spur [spɜːr] *n* espuela *f*; *fig* incentivo; **on the spur of the moment** sin pararse a pensar

◆ **spur on** *v/t (pret & pp spurred) (encourage)* espolear

spurt [spɜːrt] **1** *n in race* arrancada *f*; **put on a spurt** acelerar **2** *v/i of liquid* chorrear

sput·ter ['spʌtər] *v/i of engine* chisporrotear

spy [spaɪ] **1** *n* espía *m/f* **2** *v/i (pret & pp spied)* espiar **3** *v/t (pret & pp spied) (see)* ver

◆ **spy on** *v/t* espiar

squab·ble ['skwɑːbl] **1** *n* riña *f* **2** *v/i* reñir

squal·id ['skwɑːlɪd] *adj* inmundo, miserable

squal·or ['skwɑːlər] inmundicia *f*

squan·der ['skwɑːndər] *v/t money* despilfarrar

square [skwer] **1** *adj in shape* cuadrado; **square miles** millas cuadradas **2** *n also* MATH cuadrado *m*; *in town* plaza *f*; *in board game* casilla *f*; **we're back to square one** volvemos al punto de partida

◆ **square up** *v/i* hacer cuentas

square 'root raíz *f* cuadrada

squash¹ [skwɑːʃ] *n vegetable* calabacera *f*

squash² [skwɑːʃ] *n game* squash *m*

squash³ [skwɑːʃ] *v/t (crush)* aplastar

squat [skwɑːt] **1** *adj person, build* chaparro; *figure, buildings* bajo **2** *v/i (pret & pp squatted) sit* agacharse; **squat in a building** ocupar ilegalmente un edificio

squat·ter ['skwɑːtər] ocupante *m/f* ilegal, *Span* okupa *m/f* F

squeak [skwiːk] **1** *n of mouse* chillido *m*; *of hinge* chirrido *m* **2** *v/i of mouse* chillar; *of hinge* chirriar; *of shoes* crujir

squeak·y ['skwiːkɪ] *adj hinge* chirriante; *shoes* que crujen; *voice* chillón

'**squeak·y clean** *adj* F bien limpio

squeal [skwiːl] **1** *n* chillido *m*; **there was a squeal of brakes** se oyó una frenada estruendosa **2** *v/i* chillar; *of brakes* armar un estruendo

squeam·ish ['skwiːmɪʃ] *adj* aprensivo

squeeze [skwiːz] **1** *n of hand, shoulder*

apretón *m* **2** *v/t* (*press*) apretar; (*remove juice from*) exprimir
◆ **squeeze in 2** *v/t* meterse a duras penas
◆ **squeeze up** *v/i* to make space apretarse

squid [skwɪd] calamar *m*

squint [skwɪnt] *n*: **she has a squint** es estrábica, tiene estrabismo

squirm [skwɜːrm] *v/i* retorcerse

squir·rel ['skwɪrl] *n* ardilla *f*

squirt [skwɜːrt] **1** *v/t* lanzar un chorro de **2** *n* F *pej* canijo(-a) *m(f)* F, mequetrefe *m/f* F

St *abbr* (= **saint**) Sto; Sta (= santo *m*; santa *f*); (= **street**) c/ (= calle *f*)

stab [stæb] **1** *n* F intento *m*; **have a stab at sth** intentar algo **2** *v/t* (*pret & pp stabbed*) *person* apuñalar

sta·bil·i·ty [stə'bɪlətɪ] estabilidad *f*

sta·bi·lize ['steɪbɪlaɪz] **1** *v/t prices, boat* estabilizar **2** *v/i of prices etc* estabilizarse

sta·ble¹ ['steɪbl] *n for horses* establo *m*

sta·ble² ['steɪbl] *adj* estable; *patient's condition* estacionario

stack [stæk] **1** *n* (*pile*) pila *f*; (*smokestack*) chimenea *f*; **stacks of** F montones de F **2** *v/t* apilar

sta·di·um ['steɪdɪəm] estadio *m*

staff [stæf] *npl* (*employees*) personal *m*; (*teachers'*) profesorado *m*; **staff are not allowed to …** los empleados no tienen permitido …

staf·fer ['stæfər] empleado(-a) *m(f)*

'staff-room *in school* sala *f* de profesores

stag [stæg] ciervo *m*

stage¹ [steɪdʒ] *n in life, project etc* etapa *f*

stage² [steɪdʒ] **1** *n in* THEA escenario *m*; **go on the stage** hacerse actor / actriz **2** *v/t play* escenificar, llevar a escena; *demonstration* llevar a cabo

stage 'door entrada *f* de artistas

'stage fright miedo *m* escénico

'stage hand tramoyista *m/f*

stag·ger ['stægər] **1** *v/i* tambalearse **2** *v/t* (*amaze*) dejar anonadado; *coffee breaks etc* escalonar

stag·ger·ing ['stægərɪŋ] *adj* asombroso

stag·nant ['stægnənt] *adj also fig* estancado

stag·nate [stæg'neɪt] *v/i fig* estancarse

stag·na·tion [stæg'neɪʃn] estancamiento *m*

'stag par·ty despedida *f* de soltero

stain [steɪn] **1** *n* (*dirty mark*) mancha *f*; *for wood* tinte *m* **2** *v/t* (*dirty*) manchar; *wood* teñir **3** *v/i of wine etc* manchar, dejar mancha; *of fabric* mancharse

stained-glass 'win·dow [steɪnd] vidriera *f*

stain·less 'steel ['steɪnlɪs] *n* acero *m* inoxidable

'stain re·mov·er [rɪ'muːvər] quitamanchas *m inv*

stair [ster] escalón *m*; **the stairs** la(s) escalera(s)

'stair·case escalera(s) *f(pl)*

stake [steɪk] **1** *n of wood* estaca *f*; *when gambling* apuesta *f*; (*investment*) participación *f*; **be at stake** estar en juego **2** *v/t tree* arrodrigar; *money* apostar; *reputation* jugarse; *person* ayudar (*económicamente*)

stale [steɪl] *adj bread* rancio; *air* viciado; *fig*: *news* viejo

'stale·mate *in chess* tablas *fpl* (*por rey ahogado*); *fig* punto *m* muerto

stalk¹ [stɔːk] *n of fruit, plant* tallo *m*

stalk² [stɔːk] *v/t* (*follow*) acechar; *person* seguir

stalk·er ['stɔːkər] persona que sigue a otra obsesivamente

stall¹ [stɔːl] *n at market* puesto *m*; *for cow, horse* casilla *f*

stall² [stɔːl] **1** *v/i of vehicle, engine* calarse; *of plane* entrar en pérdida; (*play for time*) intentar ganar tiempo **2** *v/t engine* calar; *person* retener

stal·li·on ['stæljən] semental *m*

stalls [stɔːlz] *npl* patio *m* de butacas

stal·wart ['stɔːlwərt] *adj support, supporter* incondicional

stam·i·na ['stæmɪnə] resistencia *f*

stam·mer ['stæmər] **1** *n* tartamudeo *m* **2** *v/i* tartamudear

stamp¹ [stæmp] **1** *n for letter* sello *m*, *L.Am.* estampilla *f*, *Mex* timbre *m*; *device* tampón *m*; *mark made with device* sello *m* **2** *v/t* sellar; **stamped addressed envelope** sobre *m* franqueado con la dirección

stamp² [stæmp] *v/t*: **stamp one's feet** patear

◆ **stamp out** *v/t* (*eradicate*) terminar con

'stamp col·lect·ing filatelia *f*

'stamp col·lec·tion colección *f* de sellos *or L.Am.* estampillas *or Mex* timbres

'stamp col·lec·tor coleccionista *m/f* de sellos *or L.Am.* estampillas *or Mex* timbres

stam·pede [stæm'piːd] **1** *n of cattle etc* estampida *f*; *of people* desbandada *f* **2** *v/i of cattle etc* salir de estampida; *of people* salir en desbandada

stance [stæns] (*position*) postura *f*

stand [stænd] **1** *n at exhibition* puesto *m*, stand *m*; (*witness stand*) estrado *m*; (*support, base*) soporte *m*; **take the stand** LAW subir al estrado **2** *v/i* (*pret & pp stood*) of

S

building encontrarse, hallarse; *as opposed to sit* estar de pie; *(rise)* ponerse de pie; *did you notice two men standing near the window?* ¿viste a dos hombres al lado de la ventana?; *there was a large box standing in the middle of the floor* había una caja muy grande en mitad del suelo; *the house stands at the corner of ...* la casa se encuentra en la esquina de ...; *stand still* quedarse quieto; *where do you stand with Liz?* ¿cual es tu situación con Liz? **3** *v/t (pret & pp* **stood**) *(tolerate)* aguantar, soportar; *(put)* colocar; *you don't stand a chance* no tienes ninguna posibilidad; *stand s.o. a drink* invitar a alguien a una copa; *stand one's ground* mantenerse firme

♦ **stand back** *v/i* echarse atrás

♦ **stand by 1** *v/i (not take action)* quedarse sin hacer nada; *(be ready)* estar preparado **2** *v/t person* apoyar; *decision* atenerse a

♦ **stand down** *v/i (withdraw)* retirarse

♦ **stand for** *v/t (tolerate)* aguantar; *(represent)* significar

♦ **stand in for** *v/t* sustituir

♦ **stand out** *v/i* destacar

♦ **stand up 1** *v/i* levantarse **2** *v/t* F plantar F

♦ **stand up for** *v/t* defender; *stand up for yourself!* ¡defiéndete!

♦ **stand up to** *v/t* hacer frente a

stan·dard ['stændərd] **1** *adj (usual)* habitual **2** *n (level of excellence)* nivel *m*; TECH estándar *m*; *be up to standard* cumplir el nivel exigido; *not be up to standard* estar por debajo del nivel exigido; *my parents set very high standards* mis padres exigen mucho

stan·dard·ize ['stændərdaɪz] *v/t* normalizar

stan·dard of 'liv·ing nivel *m* de vida

'stand·by 1 *n ticket* billete *m* stand-by; *be on standby* estar en stand-by *or* en lista de espera **2** *adv fly* con un billete stand-by

'stand·by pas·sen·ger pasajero(-a) *m(f)* en stand-by *or* en lista de espera

stand·ing ['stændɪŋ] *n in society etc* posición *f; (repute)* reputación *f; a musician / politician of some standing* un reputado músico / político; *a relationship of long standing* una relación establecida hace mucho tiempo

'stand·ing room: *standing room only* no quedan asientos

stand·off·ish [stænd'ɑːfɪʃ] *adj* distante

'stand·point punto *m* de vista

'stand·still: *be at a standstill* estar para-

lizado; *bring to a standstill* paralizar

stank [stæŋk] *pret →* **stink**

stan·za ['stænzə] estrofa *f*

sta·ple¹ ['steɪpl] *n foodstuff* alimento *m* básico

sta·ple² ['steɪpl] **1** *n (fastener)* grapa *f v/t* grapar

sta·ple 'di·et dieta *f* básica

'sta·ple gun grapadora *f* industrial

sta·pler ['steɪplər] grapadora *f*

star [stɑːr] **1** *n also person* estrella *f* **2** *v/t (pret & pp* **starred**) *of movie* estar protagonizado por **3** *v/i (pret & pp* **starred**) *in movie:* *Depardieu starred in ...* Depardieu protagonizó ...

'star·board *adj* de estribor

starch [stɑːrtʃ] *in foodstuff* fécula *f*

stare [ster] **1** *n* mirada *f* fija **2** *v/i* mirar fijamente; *stare at* mirar fijamente

'star·fish estrella *f* de mar

stark [stɑːrk] **1** *adj landscape* desolado; *reminder, picture etc* desolador; *in stark contrast to* en marcado contraste con **2** *adv:* *stark naked* completamente desnudo

star·ling ['stɑːrlɪŋ] estornino *m*

star·ry ['stɑːrɪ] *adj night* estrellado

star·ry-eyed [stɑːrɪ'aɪd]] *adj person* cándido, ingenuo

Stars and 'Stripes la bandera estadounidense

start [stɑːrt] **1** *n (beginning)* comienzo *m*, principio *m; of race* salida *f; get off to a good / bad start* empezar bien / mal; *from the start* desde el principio; *well, it's a start!* bueno, ¡algo es algo! **2** *v/i* empezar, comenzar; *of engine, car* arrancar; *starting from tomorrow* a partir de mañana **3** *v/t* empezar, comenzar; *engine, car* arrancar; *business* montar; *start to do sth, start doing sth* empezar *or* comenzar a hacer algo; *he started to cry* se puso a llorar

start·er ['stɑːrtər] *(part of meal)* entrada *m*, entrante *m; of car* motor *m* de arranque

'start·ing point punto *m* de partida

'start·ing sal·a·ry sueldo *m* inicial

star·tle ['stɑːrtl] *v/t* sobresaltar

start·ling ['stɑːrtlɪŋ] *adj* sorprendente, asombroso

starv·a·tion [stɑːr'veɪʃn] inanición *f*, hambre *f*

starve [stɑːrv] *v/i* pasar hambre; *starve to death* morir de inanición *or* hambre; *I'm starving* F me muero de hambre F

state¹ [steɪt] **1** *n (condition, country)* estado *m; the States* (los) Estados Unidos **2** *adj capital etc* estatal, del estado; *ban-*

quet etc de estado
state² [steɪt] v/t declarar
'State De·part·ment Departamento m de Estado, *Ministerio de Asuntos Exteriores*
state·ment ['steɪtmənt] declaración f; (*bank statement*) extracto m
state of e'mer·gen·cy estado m de emergencia
state-of-the-'art *adj* modernísimo
states·man ['steɪtsmən] hombre m de estado
state 'troop·er policía m/f estatal
state 'vis·it visita f de estado
stat·ic (**e·lec·tric·i·ty**) ['stætɪk] electricidad f estática
sta·tion ['steɪʃn] **1** n RAIL estación f; RAD emisora f; TV canal m **2** v/t *guard etc* apostar; *be stationed in of soldier* estar destinado en
sta·tion·a·ry ['steɪʃənrɪ] *adj* parado
sta·tion·er ['steɪʃənər] papelería f
sta·tion·er·y ['steɪʃənərɪ] artículos *mpl* de papelería
sta·tion 'man·ag·er RAIL jefe m de estación
'sta·tion wag·on ranchera f
sta·tis·ti·cal [stə'tɪstɪkl] *adj* estadístico
sta·tis·ti·cal·ly [stə'tɪstɪklɪ] *adv* estadísticamente
sta·tis·ti·cian [stætɪs'tɪʃn] estadístico(-a) m(f)
sta·tis·tics [stə'tɪstɪks] (*nsg: science*) estadística f; (*npl: figures*) estadísticas *fpl*
stat·ue ['stætʃuː] estatua f
Stat·ue of 'Lib·er·ty Estatua f de la Libertad
sta·tus ['steɪtəs] categoría f, posición f; *women want equal status with men* las mujeres quieren igualdad con los hombres
'sta·tus bar COMPUT barra f de estado
'sta·tus sym·bol símbolo m de estatus
stat·ute ['stætuːt] estatuto m
staunch [stɒːntʃ] *adj supporter* incondicional; *friend* fiel
stay [steɪ] **1** n estancia f, *L.Am.* estadía f **2** v/i *in a place* quedarse; *in a condition* permanecer; *stay in a hotel* alojarse en un hotel; *stay right there!* ¡quédate ahí!; *stay put* no moverse
♦ **stay away** v/i: *tell the children to stay away* diles a los niños que no se acerquen
♦ **stay away from** v/t no acercarse a
♦ **stay behind** v/i quedarse
♦ **stay up** v/i (*not go to bed*) quedarse levantado
stead·i·ly ['stedɪlɪ] *adv improve etc* constantemente

stead·y ['stedɪ] **1** *adj* (*not shaking*) firme; (*continuous*) continuo; *beat* regular; *boyfriend* estable **2** *adv*: *they've been going steady for two years* llevan saliendo dos años; *steady on!* ¡un momento! **3** v/t (*pret & pp steadied*) afianzar; *voice* calmar
steak [steɪk] filete m
steal [stiːl] **1** v/t (*pret stole, pp stolen*) *money etc* robar **2** v/i (*be a thief*) robar; *he stole into the bedroom* entró furtivamente en la habitación
stealth bomb·er [stelθ] bombardero m invisible
stealth·y ['stelθɪ] *adj* sigiloso
steam [stiːm] **1** n vapor m **2** v/t *food* cocinar al vapor
♦ **steam up** v/i *of window* empañarse
steamed up [stiːmd'ʌp] *adj* F enojado, *Span* mosqueado F
steam·er ['stiːmər] *for cooking* olla f para cocinar al vapor
'steam i·ron plancha f de vapor
steel [stiːl] **1** n acero m **2** *adj* (*made of steel*) de acero
'steel·work·er trabajador(a) m(f) del acero
'steel·works acería f
steep¹ [stiːp] *adj hill etc* empinado; F: *prices* caro
steep² [stiːp] v/t (*soak*) poner en remojo
stee·ple ['stiːpl] torre f
'stee·ple·chase *in athletics* carrera f de obstáculos
steep·ly ['stiːplɪ] *adv*: *climb steeply of path* subir pronunciadamente; *of prices* dispararse
steer¹ [stɪr] n *animal* buey m
steer² [stɪr] v/t *car* conducir, *L.Am.* manejar; *boat* gobernar; *person* guiar; *conversation* llevar
steer·ing ['stɪrɪŋ] n MOT dirección f
'steer·ing wheel volante m, *S. Am.* timón m
stem¹ [stem] n *of plant* tallo m; *of glass* pie m; *of pipe* tubo m; *of word* raíz f
♦ **stem from** v/t (*pret & pp stemmed*) derivarse de
stem² [stem] v/t (*block*) contener
'stem·ware ['stemwer] cristalería f
stench [stentʃ] peste f, hedor m
sten·cil ['stensɪl] **1** n plantilla f **2** v/t (*pret & pp stenciled, Br stencilled*) *pattern* estarcir
step [step] **1** n (*pace*) paso m; (*stair*) escalón m; (*measure*) medida f; *step by step* paso a paso **2** v/i (*pret & pp stepped*): *step on sth* pisar algo; *step into a pud-*

dle pisar un charco; *I stepped back* di
un paso atrás; *step forward* dar un paso
adelante

◆ **step down** *v/i from post etc* dimitir
◆ **step up** *v/t* (*increase*) incrementar
'**step-broth-er** hermanastro *m*
'**step-daugh-ter** hijastra *f*
'**step-fa-ther** padrastro *m*
'**step-lad-der** escalera *f* de tijera
'**step-moth-er** madrastra *f*
step-ping stone ['stepɪŋ] pasadera *f*; *fig*
trampolín *m*
'**step-sis-ter** hermanastra *f*
'**step-son** hijastro *m*
ster-e-o ['steriou] *n* (*sound system*) equipo *m* de música
ster-e-o-type ['sterioutaip] *n* estereotipo
m
ster-ile ['sterəl] *adj* estéril
ster-il-ize ['sterəlaiz] *v/t woman* esterilizar; *equipment* esterilizar
ster-ling ['stɜːrlɪŋ] *n* FIN libra *f* esterlina
stern[1] [stɜːrn] *adj* severo
stern[2] [stɜːrn] *n* NAUT popa *f*
stern-ly ['stɜːrnlɪ] *adv* con severidad
ster-oids ['steroidz] *npl* esteroides *mpl*
steth-o-scope ['steθəskoup] fonendosco-
pio *m*, estetoscopio *m*
Stet-son® ['stetsn] sombrero *m* de vaquero
ste-ve-dore ['stiːvədɔːr] estibador(a)
m(f)
stew [stuː] *n* guiso *m*
stew-ard ['stuːərd] *n on plane* auxiliar *m*
de vuelo; *on ship* camarero *m*; *at demonstration, meeting* miembro *m* de la
organización
stew-ard-ess [stuːərˈdes] *on plane* auxiliar *f* de vuelo; *on ship* camarera *f*
stewed [stuːd] *adj apples, plums* en compota
stick[1] [stɪk] *n* palo *m*; *of policeman* porra
f; (*walking stick*) bastón *m*; **live out in
the sticks** F vivir en el quinto pino F, vivir
en el campo
stick[2] [stɪk] 1 *v/t* (*pret & pp* **stuck**) *with
adhesive* pegar; F (*put*) meter 2 *v/i* (*pret
& pp* **stuck**) (*jam*) atascarse; (*adhere*)
pegarse
◆ **stick around** *v/i* F quedarse
◆ **stick by** *v/t* F apoyar, no abandonar
◆ **stick out** *v/i* (*protrude*) sobresalir; (*be
noticeable*) destacar; *his ears stick out*
tiene las orejas salidas
◆ **stick to** *v/t* (*adhere to*) pegarse a; F
(*keep to*) seguir; F (*follow*) pegarse a F
◆ **stick together** *v/i* mantenerse unidos
◆ **stick up** *v/t poster, leaflet* pegar
◆ **stick up for** *v/t* F defender

stick-er ['stɪkər] pegatina *f*
'**stick-in-the-mud** F aburrido(-a) *m(f)* F,
soso(-a) *m(f)*
stick-y ['stɪkɪ] *adj hands, surface* pegajoso; *label* adhesivo
stiff [stɪf] 1 *adj cardboard, manner* rígido;
brush, penalty, competition duro; *muscle,
body* agarrotado; *mixture, paste* consistente; *drink* cargado 2 *adv*: **be scared
stiff** F estar muerto de miedo F; **be bored
stiff** F aburrirse como una ostra F
stiff-en ['stɪfn] *v/i of person* agarrotarse
◆ **stiffen up** *v/i of muscle* agarrotarse
stiff-ly ['stɪflɪ] *adv* con rigidez; *fig* forza-
damente
stiff-ness ['stɪfnəs] *of muscles* agarrota-
miento *m*; *fig*: *of manner* rigidez *f*
sti-fle ['staɪfl] *v/t yawn, laugh* reprimir;
criticism, debate reprimir
sti-fling ['staɪflɪŋ] *adj* sofocante; *it's sti-
fling in here* hace un calor sofocante
aquí dentro
stig-ma ['stɪgmə] estigma *m*
sti-let-tos [stɪˈletouz] *npl shoes* zapatos
mpl de tacón de aguja
still[1] [stɪl] 1 *adj* (*not moving*) quieto; *with
no wind* sin viento; *it was very still no
wind* no soplaba nada de viento 2 *adv*:
keep still! ¡estate quieto!; **stand still!**
¡no te muevas!
still[2] [stɪl] *adv* (*yet*) todavía, aún; (*nevertheless*) de todas formas; **do you still
want it?** ¿todavía *or* aún lo quieres?;
she still hasn't finished todavía *or*
aún no ha acabado; **I still don't understand** sigo sin entenderlo; **she might still
come** puede que aún venga; **they are
still my parents** siguen siendo mis padres; **still more** (*even more*) todavía más
'**still-born** *adj*: **be stillborn** nacer muerto
still 'life naturaleza *f* muerta, bodegón *m*
stilt-ed ['stɪltɪd] *adj* forzado
stim-u-lant ['stɪmjulənt] estimulante *m*
stim-u-late ['stɪmjuleɪt] *v/t person* estimular; *growth, demand* estimular, provocar
stim-u-lat-ing ['stɪmjuleɪtɪŋ] *adj* estimulante
stim-u-la-tion [stɪmjuˈleɪʃn] estimulación
f
stim-u-lus ['stɪmjuləs] (*incentive*) estímulo *m*
sting [stɪŋ] 1 *n from bee, jellyfish* picadura
f 2 *v/t* (*pret & pp* **stung**) *of bee, jellyfish*
picar 3 *v/i* (*pret & pp* **stung**) *of eyes,
scratch* escocer
sting-ing ['stɪŋɪŋ] *adj remark, criticism*
punzante
sting-y ['stɪndʒɪ] *adj* F agarrado F, rácano

F

stink [stɪŋk] **1** n (bad smell) peste f, hedor m; F (fuss) escándalo F; **kick up a stink** F armar un escándalo F **2** v/i (pret **stank**, pp **stunk**) (smell bad) apestar; F (be very bad) dar asco

stint [stɪnt] n temporada f; **do a stint in the army** pasar una temporada en el ejército

♦ **stint on** v/t F racanear F

stip·u·late ['stɪpjuleɪt] v/t estipular

stip·u·la·tion [stɪpju'leɪʃn] estipulación f

stir [stɜːr] **1** n: **give the soup a stir** darle vueltas a la sopa; **cause a stir** causar revuelo **2** v/t (pret & pp **stirred**) remover, dar vueltas a **3** v/i (pret & pp **stirred**) of sleeping person moverse

♦ **stir up** v/t crowd agitar; bad memories traer a la memoria

stir·cra·zy adj F majareta F

stir-fry v/t (pret & pp **stir-fried**) freír rápidamente y dando vueltas

stir·ring ['stɜːrɪŋ] adj music, speech conmovedor

stir·rup ['stɪrəp] estribo m

stitch [stɪtʃ] **1** n in sewing puntada f; in knitting punto m; **stitches** MED puntos mpl; **be in stitches** laughing partirse de risa; **have a stitch** tener flato **2** v/t sew coser

♦ **stitch up** v/t wound coser, suturar

stitch·ing ['stɪtʃɪŋ] (stitches) cosido m

stock [stɑːk] **1** n (reserves) reservas fpl; COM of store existencias fpl; (animals) ganado m; FIN acciones mpl; for soup etc caldo m; **in stock** en existencias; **out of stock** agotado; **take stock** hacer balance **2** v/t COM (have) tener en existencias; COM (sell) vender

♦ **stock up on** v/t aprovisionarse de

stock·breed·er ganadero(-a) m(f)

stock·brok·er corredor(a) m(f) de bolsa

stock cube pastilla f de caldo concentrado

stock ex·change bolsa f (de valores)

stock·hold·er accionista m/f

stock·ing ['stɑːkɪŋ] media f

stock·ist ['stɑːkɪst] distribuidor(a) m(f)

stock mar·ket mercado m de valores

'stock mar·ket crash crack m bursátil

stock·pile 1 n of food, weapons fpl **2** v/t acumular

stock·room almacén m

stock-still adv: **stand stock-still** quedarse inmóvil

stock·tak·ing inventario m

stock·y ['stɑːkɪ] adj bajo y robusto

stodg·y ['stɑːdʒɪ] adj food pesado

sto·i·cal ['stoʊɪkl] adj estoico

sto·i·cism ['stoʊɪsɪzm] estoicismo m

stole [stoʊl] pret → **steal**

stol·en ['stoʊlən] pp → **steal**

stom·ach ['stʌmək] **1** n estómago m, tripa f **2** v/t (tolerate) soportar

stom·ach·ache dolor m de estómago

stone [stoʊn] n piedra f; in fruit hueso m

stoned [stoʊnd] adj F (on drugs) colocado F

stone-deaf adj: **be stone-deaf** estar más sordo que una tapia

stone·wall v/i F andarse con evasivas

ston·y ['stoʊnɪ] adj ground, path pedregoso

stood [stʊd] pret & pp → **stand**

stool [stuːl] (seat) taburete m

stoop¹ [stuːp] **1** n: **have a stoop** estar encorvado **2** v/i (bend down) agacharse

stoop² [stuːp] n (porch) porche m

stop [stɑːp] **1** n for train, bus parada f; **come to a stop** detenerse; **put a stop to** poner fin a **2** v/t (pret & pp **stopped**) (put an end to) poner fin a; (prevent) impedir; (cease) parar; person in street parar; car, bus, train, etc: of driver detener; **check** bloquear; **stop doing sth** dejar de hacer algo; **it has stopped raining** ha parado or dejado de llover; **I stopped her from leaving** impedí que se fuera **3** v/i (pret & pp **stopped**) (come to a halt) pararse, detenerse; in a particular place: of bus, train parar

♦ **stop by** v/i (visit) pasarse

♦ **stop off** v/i hacer una parada

♦ **stop over** v/i hacer escala

♦ **stop up** v/t sink atascar

stop-gap solución f intermedia

stop·light (traffic light) semáforo m; (brake light) luz m de freno

stop·o·ver n parada f; in air travel escala f

stop·per ['stɑːpər] for bath, bottle tapón m

stop·ping ['stɑːpɪŋ]: **no stopping** sign prohibido estacionar

stop sign (señal f de) stop m

stop·watch cronómetro m

stor·age ['stɔːrɪdʒ] almacenamiento m; **put sth in storage** almacenar algo; **be in storage** estar almacenado

stor·age ca·pac·i·ty COMPUT capacidad f de almacenamiento

stor·age space espacio m para guardar cosas

store [stɔːr] **1** n tienda f; (stock) reserva f; (storehouse) almacén m **2** v/t almacenar; COMPUT guardar

store·front fachada f de tienda

store·house almacén m

S

'**store·keep·er** tendero(-a) *m(f)*
'**store·room** almacén *m*
sto·rey *Br* → **story²**
stork [stɔːk] cigüeña *f*
storm [stɔːrm] *n* tormenta *f*
'**storm drain** canal *m* de desagüe
'**storm warn·ing** aviso *m* de tormenta
storm 'win·dow contraventana *f*
storm·y ['stɔːrmɪ] *adj weather, relationship* tormentoso
sto·ry¹ ['stɔːrɪ] *(tale)* cuento *m; (account)* historia *f; (newspaper article)* artículo *m;* F *(lie)* cuento *m*
sto·ry² ['stɔːrɪ] *of building* piso *m,* planta *f*
stout [staʊt] *adj person* relleno, corpulento; *boots* resistente; *defender* valiente
stove [stəʊv] *for cooking* cocina *f, Col, Mex, Ven* estufa *f; for heating* estufa *f*
stow [stəʊ] *v/t* guardar
◆ **stow away** *v/i* viajar de polizón
'**stow·a·way** *n* polizón *m*
straggler ['stræglər] rezagado(-a) *m(f)*
straight [streɪt] **1** *adj line, back* recto; *hair* liso; *(honest, direct)* franco; *whisky* solo; *(tidy)* en orden; *(conservative)* serio; *(not homosexual)* heterosexual; *be a straight A student* sacar sobresaliente en todas las asignaturas; *keep a straight face* contener la risa **2** *adv (in a straight line)* recto; *(directly, immediately)* directamente; *(clearly)* con claridad; *stand up straight!* ¡ponte recto!; *look s.o. straight in the eye* mirar a los ojos de alguien; *go straight* F *of criminal* reformarse; *give it to me straight* F dímelo sin rodeos; *straight ahead* be situated todo derecho; *walk, drive* todo recto; *look hacia delante; carry straight on* of driver etc seguir recto; *straight away, straight off* en seguida; *straight out* directamente; *straight up without ice* solo
straight·en ['streɪtn] *v/t* enderezar
◆ **straighten out 1** *v/t situation* resolver; F *person* poner por el buen camino **2** *v/i of road* hacerse recto
◆ **straighten up** *v/i* ponerse derecho
straight'for·ward *adj (honest, direct)* franco; *(simple)* simple
strain¹ [streɪn] **1** *n on rope* tensión *f; on engine, heart* esfuerzo *m; on person* agobio *m* **2** *v/t fig: finances, budget* crear presión a; *strain one's back* hacerse daño en la espalda; *strain one's eyes* forzar la vista
strain² [streɪn] *v/t vegetables* escurrir; *oil, fat etc* colar
strain³ [streɪn] *n of virus* cepa *f*
strained [streɪnd] *adj relations* tirante

strain·er ['streɪnər] *for vegetables etc* colador *m*
strait [streɪt] estrecho *m*
strait-laced [streɪt'leɪst] *adj* mojigato
strand¹ [strænd] *n of wool, thread* hebra *f; a strand of hair* un pelo
strand² [strænd] *v/t* abandonar; *be stranded* quedarse atrapado *or* tirado
strange [streɪndʒ] *adj (odd, curious)* extraño, raro; *(unknown, foreign)* extraño
strange·ly ['streɪndʒlɪ] *adv (oddly)* de manera extraña; *strangely enough* aunque parezca extraño
strang·er ['streɪndʒər] *(person you don't know)* extraño(-a) *m(f),* desconocido(-a) *m(f); I'm a stranger here myself* yo tampoco soy de aquí
stran·gle ['stræŋgl] *v/t person* estrangular
strap [stræp] *n of purse, watch* correa *f; of brassiere, dress* tirante *m; of shoe* tira *f*
◆ **strap in** *v/t (pret & pp strapped)* poner el cinturón de seguridad a
◆ **strap on** *v/t* ponerse
strap·less ['stræplɪs] *adj* sin tirantes
stra·te·gic [strəˈtiːdʒɪk] *adj* estratégico
strat·e·gy ['strætɪdʒɪ] estrategia *f*
straw¹ [strɔː] *material* paja *f; that's the last straw!* ¡es la gota que colma el vaso!
straw² [strɔː] *for drink* pajita *f*
straw·ber·ry ['strɔːberɪ] *fruit* fresa *f, S. Am.* frutilla *f*
stray [streɪ] **1** *adj animal* callejero; *bullet* perdido **2** *n dog* perro *m* callejero; *cat* gato *m* callejero **3** *v/i of animal, child* extraviarse, perderse; *fig: of eyes, thoughts* desviarse
streak [striːk] **1** *n of dirt, paint* raya *f; in hair* mechón *m; fig: of nastiness etc* vena *f* **2** *v/i move quickly* pasar disparado
streak·y ['striːkɪ] *adj* veteado
stream [striːm] **1** *n* riachuelo *m; fig: of people, complaints* oleada *f; come on stream* entrar en funcionamiento **2** *v/i: there were tears streaming down my face* me bajaban ríos de lágrimas por la cara; *people streamed out of the building* la gente salía en masa
stream·er ['striːmər] serpentina *f*
'**stream·line** *v/t fig* racionalizar
'**stream·lined** *adj car, plane* aerodinámico; *fig: organization* racionalizado
street [striːt] calle *f*
'**street·car** *n* tranvía *m*
'**street·light** farola *f*
'**street peo·ple** *npl* los sin techo
'**street val·ue** *of drugs* valor *m* en la calle
'**street·walk·er** F prostituta *f*
'**street·wise** *adj* espabilado
strength [streŋθ] fuerza *f; (fig: strong*

point) punto *m* fuerte; *of friendship etc* solidez *f*; *of emotion* intensidad *f*; *of currency* fortaleza *f*

strength·en ['streŋθn] **1** *v/t muscles, currency* fortalecer; *bridge* reforzar; *country, ties, relationship* consolidar **2** *v/i of bonds, ties* consolidarse; *of currency* fortalecerse

stren·u·ous ['strenjuəs] *adj* agotador

stren·u·ous·ly ['strenjuəslɪ] *adv* deny tajantemente

stress [stres] **1** *n* (*emphasis*) énfasis *m*; (*tension*) estrés *m*; *on syllable* acento *m*; **be under stress** estar estresado **2** *v/t* (*emphasize: syllable*) acentuar; *importance etc* hacer hincapié en; *I must stress that ...* quiero hacer hincapié en que ...

stressed 'out [strest] *adj* F estresado

stress·ful ['stresfəl] *adj* estresante

stretch [stretʃ] **1** *n of land, water* extensión *m*; *of road* tramo *m*; *at a stretch* (*non-stop*) de un tirón **2** *adj fabric* elástico **3** *v/t material, income* estirar; F *rules* ser flexible con; *he stretched out his hand* estiró la mano; *my job stretches me* mi trabajo me obliga a esforzarme **4** *v/i to relax muscles, reach sth* estirarse; (*spread*) extenderse; *of fabric* estirarse, dar de sí

stretch·er ['stretʃər] camilla *f*

strict [strɪkt] *adj* estricto

strict·ly ['strɪktlɪ] *adv* con rigor; *it is strictly forbidden* está terminantemente prohibido

strid·den ['strɪdn] *pp* → **stride**

stride [straɪd] **1** *n* zancada *f*; *take sth in one's stride* tomarse algo con tranquilidad; *make great strides fig* avanzar a pasos agigantados **2** *v/t* (*pret strode*, *pp stridden*) caminar dando zancadas

stri·dent ['straɪdnt] *adj also fig* estridente

strike [straɪk] **1** *n of workers* huelga *f*; *in baseball* strike *m*; *of oil* descubrimiento *m*; *be on strike* estar en huelga; *go on strike* ir a la huelga **2** *v/i* (*pret & pp struck*) *of workers* hacer huelga; (*attack*) atacar; *of disaster* sobrevenir; *of clock* dar las horas; *the clock struck three* el reloj dio las tres **3** *v/t* (*pret & pp struck*) (*hit*) golpear; *fig: of disaster* sacudir; *match* encender; *oil* descubrir; *didn't it ever strike you that ...?* ¿no se te ocurrió que ...?; *she struck me as being ...* me dio la impresión de ser ...

◆ **strike out 1** *v/t in baseball* eliminar a, L.Am. ponchar **2** *v/i in baseball* quedar eliminado, L.Am. ponchar

'**strike·break·er** esquirol(a) *m(f)*

strik·er ['straɪkər] (*person on strike*) huelguista *m/f*; *in soccer* delantero(-a) *m(f)*

strik·ing ['straɪkɪŋ] *adj* (*marked*) sorprendente, llamativo; (*eye-catching*) deslumbrante

string [strɪŋ] *n also of violin, racket etc* cuerda *f*; *strings musicians* la sección de cuerda; *pull strings* mover hilos; *a string of* (*series*) una serie de

◆ **string along 1** *v/i* (*pret & pp strung*) F apuntarse F **2** *v/t* (*pret & pp strung*) F: *string s.o. along* dar falsas esperanzas a alguien

◆ **string up** *v/t* F colgar

stringed 'in·stru·ment [strɪŋd] instrumento *m* de cuerda

strin·gent ['strɪndʒnt] *adj* riguroso

'**string play·er** instrumentista *m/f* de cuerda

strip [strɪp] **1** *n of land* franja *f*; *of cloth* tira *f*; (*comic strip*) tira *f* cómica **2** *v/t* (*pret & pp stripped*) (*remove*) quitar; (*undress*) desnudar; *strip s.o. of sth* despojar a alguien de algo **3** *v/i* (*pret & pp stripped*) (*undress*) desnudarse; *of stripper* hacer striptease

'**strip club** club *m* de striptease

stripe [straɪp] raya *f*; *indicating rank* galón *m*

striped [straɪpt] *adj* a rayas

'**strip joint** F → **strip club**

'**strip·per** ['strɪpər] artista *m/f* de striptease; *male stripper* artista *m* de striptease

'**strip show** espectáculo *m* de striptease

strip'tease striptease *m*

strive [straɪv] *v/i* (*pret strove*, *pp striven*) esforzarse; *strive to do sth* esforzarse por hacer algo; *strive for* luchar por

striv·en ['strɪvn] *pp* → **strive**

strobe (**light**) [stroʊb] luz *f* estroboscópica

strode [stroʊd] *pret* → **stride**

stroke [stroʊk] **1** *n* MED derrame *m* cerebral; *when writing* trazo *m*; *when painting* pincelada *f*; (*style of swimming*) estilo *m*; *stroke of luck* golpe de suerte; *she never does a stroke* (*of work*) no pega ni golpe **2** *v/t* acariciar

stroll [stroʊl] **1** *n* paseo *m* **2** *v/i* caminar

stroll·er ['stroʊlər] *for baby* silla *f* de paseo

strong [strɔːŋ] *adj* fuerte; *structure* resistente; *candidate* claro, con muchos posibilidades; *support, supporter, views, objection* firme; *tea, coffee* cargado, fuerte

'**strong·hold** *fig* baluarte *m*

strong·ly ['strɔːŋlɪ] *adv* fuertemente, ro-

tundamente
strong-mind·ed [strɔːŋ'maɪndɪd] *adj* decidido
'strong point (punto *m*) fuerte *m*
'strong·room cámara *f* acorazada
strong-willed [strɔːŋ'wɪld] *adj* tenaz
strove [stroʊv] *pret* → **strive**
struck [strʌk] *pret & pp* → **strike**
struc·tur·al ['strʌktʃərl] *adj* estructural
struc·ture ['strʌktʃər] **1** *n* (*something built*) construcción *f*; *of novel, society etc* estructura *f* **2** *v/t* estructurar
strug·gle ['strʌgl] **1** *n* lucha *f* **2** *v/i with a person* forcejear; (*have a hard time*) luchar; *they struggled for the gun* forcejearon por conseguir la pistola; *he was struggling with the door* tenía problemas para abrir la puerta; *struggle to do sth* luchar por hacer algo
strum [strʌm] *v/t* (*pret & pp* **strummed**) *guitar* rasguear
strung [strʌŋ] *pret & pp* → **string**
strut [strʌt] *v/i* (*pret & pp* **strutted**) pavonearse
stub [stʌb] **1** *n of cigarette* colilla *f*; *of check* matriz *f*; *of ticket* resguardo *m* **2** *v/t* (*pret & pp* **stubbed**): *stub one's toe* darse un golpe en el dedo (del pie)
◆ **stub out** *v/t* apagar (apretando)
stub·ble ['stʌbl] *on man's face* barba *f* incipiente
stub·born ['stʌbərn] *adj person* testarudo, terco; *defense, refusal, denial* tenaz, pertinaz
stub·by ['stʌbɪ] *adj* regordete
stuck [stʌk] **1** *pret & pp* → **stick²** **2** *adj* F: *be stuck on s.o.* estar colado por alguien F
stuck-'up *adj* F engreído
stu·dent ['stuːdnt] *at high school* alumno(-a) *m(f)*; *at college, university* estudiante *m/f*
stu·dent 'nurse estudiante *m/f* de enfermería
stu·dent 'teach·er profesor(a) *m(f)* en prácticas
stu·di·o ['stuːdɪoʊ] *of artist, sculptor* estudio *m*; (*film studio, TV studio*) estudio *m*, plató *m*
stu·di·ous ['stuːdɪəs] *adj* estudioso
stud·y ['stʌdɪ] **1** *n* estudio *m*; (*room*) (cuarto *m* de) estudio *m* **2** *v/t & v/i* (*pret & pp* **studied**) estudiar
stuff [stʌf] **1** *n* (*things*) cosas *fpl* **2** *v/t* turkey rellenar; *stuff sth into sth* meter algo dentro de algo
stuffed 'toy [stʌft] muñeco *m* de peluche
stuff·ing ['stʌfɪŋ] relleno *m*
stuff·y ['stʌfɪ] *adj room* cargado; *person*

anticuado, estirado
stum·ble ['stʌmbl] *v/i* tropezar
◆ **stumble across** *v/t* toparse con
◆ **stumble over** *v/t* tropezar con; *words* trastrabillarse con
stum·bling-block ['stʌmblɪŋ] escollo *m*
stump [stʌmp] **1** *n of tree* tocón *m* **2** *v/t of question, questioner* dejar perplejo
◆ **stump up** *v/t* F aflojar, *Span* apoquinar F
stun [stʌn] *v/t* (*pret & pp* **stunned**) *of blow* dejar sin sentido; *of news* dejar atonito or de piedra
stung [stʌŋ] *pret & pp* → **sting**
stunk [stʌŋk] *pp* → **stink**
stun·ning ['stʌnɪŋ] *adj* (*amazing*) increíble, sorprendente; (*very beautiful*) imponente
stunt [stʌnt] *n for publicity* truco *m*; *in movie* escena *f* peligrosa
'stunt·man *in movie* doble *m*, especialista *m*
stu·pe·fy ['stuːpɪfaɪ] *v/t* (*pret & pp* **stupefied**) dejar perplejo
stu·pen·dous [stuː'pendəs] *adj* extraordinario
stu·pid ['stuːpɪd] *adj* estúpido; *what a stupid thing to say / do!* ¡qué estupidez!
stu·pid·i·ty [stuː'pɪdətɪ] estupidez *f*
stu·por ['stuːpər] aturdimiento *m*
stur·dy ['stɜːrdɪ] *adj person* robusto; *table, plant* resistente
stut·ter ['stʌtər] *v/i* tartamudear
sty [staɪ] *for pig* pocilga *f*
style [staɪl] *n* estilo *m*; (*fashion*) moda *f*; *go out of style* pasarse de moda
styl·ish ['staɪlɪʃ] *adj* elegante
styl·ist ['staɪlɪst] (*hair stylist*) estilista *m/f*
sub·com·mit·tee ['sʌbkəmɪtɪ] subcomité *m*
sub·com·pact (car) [sʌb'kɑːmpækt] utilitario de pequeño tamaño
sub·con·scious [sʌb'kɑːnʃəs] *adj* subconsciente; *the subconscious (mind)* el subconsciente
sub·con·scious·ly [sʌb'kɑːnʃəslɪ] *adv* inconscientemente
sub·con·tract [sʌbkən'trækt] *v/t* subcontratar
sub·con·trac·tor [sʌbkən'træktər] subcontratista *m/f*
sub·di·vide [sʌbdɪ'vaɪd] *v/t* subdividir
sub·due [səb'duː] *v/t rebellion, mob* someter, contener
sub·dued [səb'duːd] *adj* apagado
sub·head·ing ['sʌbhedɪŋ] subtítulo *m*
sub·hu·man [sʌb'hjuːmən] *adj* inhumano
sub·ject 1 *n* ['sʌbdʒɪkt] (*topic*) tema *m*; (*branch of learning*) asignatura *f*, mate-

ria *f*; GRAM sujeto *m*; *of monarch* súbdito(-a) *m(f)*; **change the subject** cambiar de tema 2 *adj* [ˈsʌbdʒɪkt]: **be subject to** have tendency to ser propenso a; *be regulated by* estar sujeto a; **subject to availability** *of goods* promoción válida hasta fin de existencias 3 *v/t* [səbˈdʒekt] someter

sub·jec·tive [səbˈdʒektɪv] *adj* subjetivo

sub·junc·tive [səbˈdʒʌŋktɪv] *n* GRAM subjuntivo *m*

sub·let [ˈsʌblet] *v/t* (*pret & pp* **sublet**) realquilar

sub·ma·chine gun metralleta *f*

sub·ma·rine [ˈsʌbməriːn] submarino *m*

sub·merge [səbˈmɜːrdʒ] 1 *v/t* sumergir 2 *v/i* *of submarine* sumergirse

sub·mis·sion [səbˈmɪʃn] (*surrender*) sumisión *f*; *to committee etc* propuesta *f*

sub·mis·sive [səbˈmɪsɪv] *adj* sumiso

sub·mit [səbˈmɪt] 1 *v/t* (*pret & pp* **submitted**) *plan, proposal* presentar 2 *v/i* (*pret & pp* **submitted**) someterse

sub·or·di·nate [səˈbɔːrdɪneɪt] 1 *adj* *employee, position* subordinado 2 *n* subordinado(-a) *m(f)*

sub·poe·na [səˈpiːnə] 1 *n* citación *f* 2 *v/t* *person* citar

◆ **sub·scribe to** [səbˈskraɪb] *v/t* *magazine etc* estar suscrito a; *theory* suscribir

sub·scrib·er [səbˈskraɪbər] *to magazine* suscriptor(a) *m(f)*

sub·scrip·tion [səbˈskrɪpʃn] suscripción *f*

sub·se·quent [ˈsʌbsɪkwənt] *adj* posterior

sub·se·quent·ly [ˈsʌbsɪkwəntli] *adv* posteriormente

sub·side [səbˈsaɪd] *v/i* *of flood waters* bajar; *of high winds* amainar; *of building* hundirse; *of fears, panic* calmarse

sub·sid·i·a·ry [səbˈsɪdɪeri] *n* filial *f*

sub·si·dize [ˈsʌbsɪdaɪz] *v/t* subvencionar

sub·si·dy [ˈsʌbsɪdɪ] subvención *f*

◆ **sub·sist on** *v/i* subsistir a base de

sub·sis·tence 'farm·er [səbˈsɪstəns] agricultor(a) *m(f)* de subsistencia

sub·sis·tence lev·el nivel *m* mínimo de subsistencia

sub·stance [ˈsʌbstəns] (*matter*) sustancia *f*

sub·stan·dard [sʌbˈstændərd] *adj* *performance* deficiente; *shoes, clothes* con tara

sub·stan·tial [səbˈstænʃl] *adj* sustancial, considerable

sub·stan·tial·ly [səbˈstænʃlɪ] *adv* (*considerably*) considerablemente; (*in essence*) sustancialmente, esencialmente

sub·stan·ti·ate [səbˈstænʃɪeɪt] *v/t* probar

sub·stan·tive [səbˈstæntɪv] *adj* significativo

sub·sti·tute [ˈsʌbstɪtuːt] 1 *n* *for person* sustituto(-a) *m(f)*; *for commodity* sustituto *m*; SP suplente *m/f* 2 *v/t* sustituir, reemplazar; **substitute X for Y** sustituir Y por X 3 *v/i*: **substitute for s.o.** sustituir a alguien

sub·sti·tu·tion [sʌbstɪˈtuːʃn] (*act*) sustitución *f*; **make a substitution** SP hacer un cambio *or* sustitución

sub·ti·tle [ˈsʌbtaɪtl] *n* subtítulo *m*

sub·tle [ˈsʌtl] *adj* sutil

sub·tract [səbˈtrækt] *v/t* *number* restar

sub·urb [ˈsʌbɜːrb] zona *f* residencial de la periferia

sub·ur·ban [səˈbɜːrbən] *adj* *housing* de la periferia; *attitudes, lifestyle* aburguesado

sub·ver·sive [səbˈvɜːrsɪv] 1 *adj* subversivo 2 *n* subversivo(-a) *m(f)*

sub·way [ˈsʌbweɪ] metro *m*

sub 'ze·ro *adj* bajo cero

suc·ceed [səkˈsiːd] 1 *v/i* (*be successful*) tener éxito; *to throne* suceder en el trono; **succeed in doing sth** conseguir hacer algo 2 *v/t* (*come after*) suceder

suc·ceed·ing [səkˈsiːdɪŋ] *adj* siguiente

suc·cess [səkˈses] éxito *m*; **be a success** *of book, play, idea* ser un éxito; *of person* tener éxito

suc·cess·ful [səkˈsesfəl] *adj* *person* con éxito; **be successful in business** tener éxito en los negocios; **be successful in doing sth** lograr hacer algo

suc·cess·ful·ly [səkˈsesfəlɪ] *adv* con éxito

suc·ces·sion [səkˈseʃn] sucesión *f*; **three days in succession** tres días seguidos

suc·ces·sive [səkˈsesɪv] *adj* sucesivo

suc·ces·sor [səkˈsesər] sucesor(a) *m(f)*

suc·cinct [səkˈsɪŋkt] *adj* sucinto

suc·cu·lent [ˈsʌkjulənt] *meat, fruit* suculento

suc·cumb [səˈkʌm] *v/i* (*give in*) sucumbir

such [sʌtʃ] 1 *adj* (*of that kind*) tal; **such men are dangerous** los hombres así son peligrosos; **I know of many such cases** conozco muchos casos así; **don't make such a fuss** no armes tanto alboroto; **I never thought it would be such a success** nunca imaginé que sería un éxito tal; **such as** como; **there is no such word as ...** no existe la palabra ... 2 *adv* tan; **as such** como tal

suck [sʌk] 1 *v/t* *candy etc* chupar; **suck one's thumb** chuparse el dedo 2 *v/i* P: **it sucks** (*is awful*) es una mierda P

◆ **suck up** *v/t* absorber 2 *v/i* F: **suck up to s.o.** hacer la pelota a alguien

suck·er [ˈsʌkər] F (*person*) primo(-a) *m/f* F, ingenuo(-a) *m/f*; F (*lollipop*) piruleta *f*

suc·tion ['sʌkʃn] succión f

sud·den ['sʌdn] adj repentino; **all of a sudden** de repente

sud·den·ly ['sʌdnlɪ] adv de repente

suds [sʌdz] npl (soap suds) espuma f

sue [suː] v/t demandar

suede [sweɪd] n ante m

suf·fer ['sʌfər] 1 v/i (be in great pain) sufrir; (deteriorate) deteriorarse; **be suffering from** sufrir 2 v/t loss, setback, heart attack sufrir

suf·fer·ing ['sʌfərɪŋ] n sufrimiento m

suf·fi·cient [sə'fɪʃnt] adj suficiente

suf·fi·cient·ly [sə'fɪʃntlɪ] adv suficientemente

suf·fo·cate ['sʌfəkeɪt] 1 v/i asfixiarse 2 v/t asfixiar

suf·fo·ca·tion [sʌfə'keɪʃn] asfixia f

sug·ar ['ʃʊgər] 1 n azúcar m or f; **how many sugars?** ¿cuántas cucharadas de azúcar? 2 v/t echar azúcar a; **is it sugared?** ¿lleva azúcar?

'**sug·ar bowl** azucarero m

'**sug·ar cane** caña f de azúcar

sug·gest [sə'dʒest] v/t I suggest that we stop now sugiero que paremos ahora

sug·ges·tion [sə'dʒestʃən] sugerencia f

su·i·cide ['suːɪsaɪd] suicidio m; **commit suicide** suicidarse

suit [suːt] 1 n traje m; in cards palo m 2 v/t of clothes, color sentar bien a; **suit yourself!** ¡haz lo que quieras!; **be suited for sth** estar hecho para algo

suit·a·ble ['suːtəbl] adj partner, words, clothing apropiado, adecuado; time apropiado

suit·a·bly ['suːtəblɪ] adv apropiadamente, adecuadamente

'**suit·case** maleta f, L.Am. valija f

suite [swiːt] of rooms, MUS suite f; furniture tresillo m

sul·fur ['sʌlfər] azufre m

sul·fur·ic ac·id [sʌl'fjuːrɪk] ácido m sulfúrico

sulk [sʌlk] v/i enfurruñarse; **be sulking** estar enfurruñado

sulk·y ['sʌlkɪ] adj enfurruñado

sul·len ['sʌlən] adj malhumorado, huraño

sul·phur etc Br → **sulfur etc**

sul·try ['sʌltrɪ] adj climate sofocante, bochornoso; sexually sensual

sum [sʌm] (total) total m, suma f; (amount) cantidad f; in arithmetic suma f; **a large sum of money** una gran cantidad de dinero; **sum insured** suma f asegurada; **the sum total of his efforts** la suma de sus esfuerzos

◆ **sum up** 1 v/t (pret & pp **summed**)

(summarize) resumir; (assess) catalogar 2 v/i (pret & pp **summed**) LAW recapitular

sum·mar·ize ['sʌməraɪz] v/t resumir

sum·ma·ry ['sʌmərɪ] n resumen m

sum·mer ['sʌmər] verano m

sum·mit ['sʌmɪt] of mountain cumbre f, cima f; POL cumbre f

'**sum·mit meet·ing** → **summit**

sum·mon ['sʌmən] v/t staff, ministers llamar; meeting convocar

◆ **summon up** v/t: **he summoned up his strength** hizo acopio de fuerzas

sum·mons ['sʌmənz] nsg LAW citación f

sump [sʌmp] for oil cárter m

sun [sʌn] sol m; **in the sun** al sol; **out of the sun** a la sombra; **he has had too much sun** le ha dado demasiado el sol

'**sun·bathe** v/i tomar el sol

'**sun·bed** cama f de rayos UVA

'**sun·block** crema f solar de alta protección

'**sun·burn** quemadura f (del sol)

'**sun·burnt** adj quemado (por el sol)

Sun·day ['sʌndeɪ] domingo m

'**sun·dial** reloj m de sol

sun·dries ['sʌndrɪz] npl varios mpl

sung [sʌŋ] pp → **sing**

'**sun·glass·es** npl gafas fpl or L.Am. anteojos mpl de sol

sunk [sʌŋk] pp → **sink**

sunk·en ['sʌŋkn] adj ship, cheeks hundido

sun·ny ['sʌnɪ] adj day soleado; disposition radiante; **it is sunny** hace sol

'**sun·rise** amanecer m

'**sun·set** atardecer m, puesta f de sol

'**sun·shade** sombrilla f

'**sun·shine** sol m

'**sun·stroke** insolación f

'**sun·tan** bronceado m; **get a suntan** broncearse

su·per ['suːpər] 1 adj F genial F, estupendo F 2 n (janitor) portero(-a) m(f)

su·perb [suː'pɜːrb] adj excelente

su·per·fi·cial [suːpər'fɪʃl] adj superficial

su·per·flu·ous [suː'pɜːrfluəs] adj superfluo

su·per·hu·man adj efforts sobrehumano

su·per·in·tend·ent [suːpərɪn'tendənt] of apartment block portero(-a) m(f); Br of police inspector(a) m(f) jefe

su·pe·ri·or [suː'pɪrɪər] 1 adj (better) superior; pej: attitude arrogante 2 n in organization superior m

su·per·la·tive [suː'pɜːrlətɪv] 1 adj superb excelente 2 n GRAM superlativo m

'**su·per·mar·ket** supermercado m

su·per·nat·u·ral adj powers sobrenatural **2** n: **the supernatural** lo sobrenatural

'su·per·pow·er POL superpotencia f

su·per·son·ic [su:pər'sɑːnɪk] adj flight, aircraft supersónico

su·per·sti·tion [su:pər'stɪʃn] superstición f

su·per·sti·tious [su:pər'stɪʃəs] adj person supersticioso

su·per·vise ['su:pərvaɪz] v/t class vigilar; workers supervisar; activities dirigir

su·per·vi·sor ['su:pərvaɪzər] at work supervisor(a) m(f)

sup·per ['sʌpər] cena f, L.Am. comida f

sup·ple ['sʌpl] adj person ágil; limbs, material flexible

sup·ple·ment ['sʌplɪmənt] (extra payment) suplemento m

sup·pli·er [sə'plaɪər] COM proveedor m

sup·ply [sə'plaɪ] **1** n suministro m, abastecimiento m; **supply and demand** la oferta y la demanda; **supplies of food** provisiones fpl; **office supplies** material f de oficina **2** v/t (pret & pp **supplied**) goods suministrar; **supply s.o. with sth** suministrar algo a alguien; **be supplied with ...** venir con ...

sup·port [sə'pɔːrt] **1** n for structure soporte m; (backing) apoyo m **2** v/t building, structure soportar, sostener; financially mantener; (back) apoyar

sup·port·er [sə'pɔːrtər] partidario(-a) m(f); of football team etc seguidor(a) m(f)

sup·port·ive [sə'pɔːrtɪv] adj comprensivo; **be supportive (toward, of a)**

sup·pose [sə'pouz] v/t (imagine) suponer; **I suppose so** supongo (que sí); **you are not supposed to ...** (not allowed to) no deberías ...; **it is supposed to be delivered today** (he meant to) se supone que lo van a entregar hoy; **it's supposed to be very beautiful** is said to be se supone que es hermosísimo

sup·pos·ed·ly [sə'pouzɪdlɪ] adv supuestamente

sup·pos·i·to·ry [sə'pɑːzɪtɔːrɪ] MED supositorio m

sup·press [sə'pres] v/t rebellion etc reprimir, sofocar

sup·pres·sion [sə'preʃn] represión f

su·prem·a·cy [su:'preməsɪ] supremacía f

su·preme [su:'priːm] adj supremo

sur·charge ['sɜːrtʃɑːrdʒ] n recargo m

sure [ʃʊr] **1** adj seguro; **I'm not sure** no estoy seguro; **be sure about sth** estar seguro de algo; **make sure that ...** asegurarse de que ... **2** adv: **sure enough** efectivamente; **it sure is hot today** F vaya calor que hace F; **sure!** F ¡claro!

sure·ly ['ʃʊrlɪ] adv (gladly) claro que sí; **surely you don't mean that!** ¡ no lo dirás en serio!; **surely somebody knows** alguien tiene que saberlo

sure·ty ['ʃʊrətɪ] for loan fianza f, depósito m

surf [sɜːrf] **1** n on sea surf m **2** v/t: **surf the Net** navegar por Internet

sur·face ['sɜːrfɪs] **1** n of table, object, water superficie f; **on the surface** fig a primera vista **2** v/i of swimmer, submarine salir a la superficie; (appear) aparecer

'sur·face mail correo m terrestre

'surf·board tabla f de surf

surf·er ['sɜːrfər] on sea surfista m/f

surf·ing ['sɜːrfɪŋ] surf m; **go surfing** ir a hacer surf

surge [sɜːrdʒ] n in electric current sobrecarga f; in demand etc incremento m repentino

◆ **surge forward** v/i of crowd avanzar atropelladamente

sur·geon ['sɜːrdʒən] cirujano(-a) m(f)

sur·ge·ry ['sɜːrdʒərɪ] cirugía f; **undergo surgery** ser intervenido quirúrgicamente

sur·gi·cal ['sɜːrdʒɪkl] adj quirúrgico

sur·gi·cal·ly ['sɜːrdʒɪklɪ] adv quirúrgicamente

sur·ly ['sɜːrlɪ] adj arisco, hosco

sur·mount [sər'maunt] v/t difficulties superar

sur·name ['sɜːrneɪm] apellido m

sur·pass [sər'pæs] v/t superar

sur·plus ['sɜːrpləs] **1** n excedente m **2** adj excedente

sur·prise [sər'praɪz] **1** n sorpresa f; **it came as no surprise** no me sorprendió **2** v/t sorprender; **be / look surprised** estar / parecer sorprendido

sur·pris·ing [sər'praɪzɪŋ] adj sorprendente; **it's not surprising that ...** no me sorprende que ...

sur·pris·ing·ly [sər'praɪzɪŋlɪ] adv sorprendentemente

sur·ren·der [sə'rendər] **1** v/i of army rendirse **2** v/t (hand in: weapons etc) entregar **3** n rendición f; (handing in) entrega f

sur·ro·gate 'moth·er ['sʌrəgət] madre f de alquiler

sur·round [sə'raund] **1** v/t rodear; **surrounded by** rodeado de or por **2** n of picture etc marco m

sur·round·ing [sə'raundɪŋ] adj circundante

sur·round·ings [sə'raundɪŋz] npl of village alrededores mpl; (environment) entorno m

sur·vey ['sɜːrveɪ] **1** n ['sɜːrveɪ] of modern

literature etc estudio m; of building tasación f, peritaje; poll encuesta f **2** v/t [sǝr-'veɪ] (look at) contemplar; building tasar, peritar

sur·vey·or [sǝr'veɪǝr] tasador(a) m(f) or perito (-a) m(f) de la propiedad

sur·viv·al [sǝr'vaɪvl] supervivencia f

sur·vive [sǝr'vaɪv] **1** v/i sobrevivir; **how are you? - I'm surviving** ¿cómo estás? - voy tirando; **his two surviving daughters** las dos hijas que aún viven **2** v/t accident, operation sobrevivir a; (outlive) sobrevivir

sur·vi·vor [sǝr'vaɪvǝr] superviviente m/f; **he's a survivor** fig es incombustible

sus·cep·ti·ble [sǝ'septǝbl] adj emotionally sensible, susceptible; **be susceptible to the cold/heat** ser sensible al frío/calor

sus·pect **1** n ['sʌspekt] sospechoso(-a) m(f) **2** v/t [sǝ'spekt] person sospechar de; (suppose) sospechar

sus·pect·ed [sǝ'spektɪd] adj murderer presunto; cause, heart attack etc supuesto

sus·pend [sǝ'spend] v/t (hang) colgar; from office, duties suspender

sus·pend·ers [sǝ'spendǝrz] npl for pants tirantes mpl, S. Am. suspensores mpl

sus·pense [sǝ'spens] Span suspense m, L.Am. suspenso m

sus·pen·sion [sǝ'spenʃn] MOT, from duty suspensión f

sus·pen·sion bridge puente m colgante

sus·pi·cion [sǝ'spɪʃn] sospecha f

sus·pi·cious [sǝ'spɪʃǝs] adj (causing suspicion) sospechoso; (feeling suspicion) receloso, desconfiado; **be suspicious of** sospechar de

sus·pi·cious·ly [sǝ'spɪʃǝslɪ] adv behave de manera sospechosa; ask con recelo or desconfianza

sus·tain [sǝ'steɪn] v/t sostener

sus·tain·a·ble [sǝ'steɪnǝbl] adj sostenible

swab [swɑːb] material torunda f; test muestra f

swag·ger ['swægǝr] n: **walk with a swagger** caminar pavoneándose

swal·low¹ ['swɑːloʊ] **1** v/t liquid, food tragar, tragarse **2** v/i tragar

swal·low² ['swɑːloʊ] n bird golondrina f

swam [swæm] pret → **swim**

swamp [swɑːmp] **1** n pantano m **2** v/t: **be swamped with** estar inundado de

swamp·y ['swɑːmpɪ] adj pantanoso

swan [swɑːn] cisne m

swap [swɑːp] **1** v/t (pret & pp **swapped**) cambiar; **swap sth for sth** cambiar algo por algo **2** v/i (pret & pp **swapped**) hacer un cambio

swarm [swɔːrm] **1** n of bees enjambre m **2** v/i: **the town was swarming with ...** la ciudad estaba abarrotada de ...

swar·thy ['swɔːrðɪ] adj face, complexion moreno

swat [swɑːt] v/t (pret & pp **swatted**) insect, fly aplastar, matar

sway [sweɪ] **1** n (influence, power) dominio m **2** v/i tambalearse

swear [swer] **1** v/i (pret **swore**, pp **sworn**) (use swearword) decir palabrotas or tacos; **swear at s.o.** insultar a alguien; **I swear** lo juro **2** v/t (pret **swore**, pp **sworn**) (promise), LAW jurar

◆ swear in v/t witnesses etc tomar juramento a

'swear·word palabrota f, taco m

sweat [swet] **1** n sudor m; **covered in sweat** empapado de sudor **2** v/i sudar

'sweat·band banda f (en la frente); on wrist muñequera f

sweat·er ['swetǝr] suéter m, Span jersey m

'sweat·shirt sudadera f

sweat·y ['swetɪ] adj hands sudoroso

Swede [swiːd] sueco(-a) m(f)

Swe·den ['swiːdn] Suecia f

Swe·dish ['swiːdɪʃ] **1** adj sueco **2** n sueco m

sweep [swiːp] **1** v/t (pret & pp **swept**) floor, leaves barrer **2** n (long curve) curva f

◆ sweep up v/t mess, crumbs barrer

sweep·ing ['swiːpɪŋ] adj statement demasiado generalizado; changes radical

sweet [swiːt] adj taste, tea dulce; F (kind) amable; F (cute) mono

sweet and 'sour adj agridulce

'sweet·corn maíz m, S. Am. choclo m

sweet·en ['swiːtn] v/t drink, food endulzar

sweet·en·er ['swiːtnǝr] for drink edulcorante m

'sweet·heart novio(-a) m(f)

swell [swel] **1** v/i of wound, limb hincharse **2** adj F (good) genial F, fenomenal F **3** n of the sea oleaje m

swell·ing ['swelɪŋ] n MED hinchazón f

swel·ter·ing ['sweltǝrɪŋ] adj heat, day sofocante

swept [swept] pret & pp → **sweep**

swerve [swɜːrv] v/i of driver, car girar bruscamente, dar un volantazo

swift [swɪft] adj rápido

swim [swɪm] **1** v/i (pret **swam**, pp **swum**) nadar; **go swimming** ir a nadar; **my head is swimming** me da vueltas la cabeza **2** n baño m; **go for a swim** ir a darse un baño

swim·mer ['swɪmər] nadador(a) *m(f)*

swim·ming ['swɪmɪŋ] natación *f*

'swim·ming cos·tume traje *m* de baño, bañador *m*

'swim·ming pool piscina *f*, *Mex* alberca *f*, *Rpl* pileta *f*

swin·dle ['swɪndl] **1** *n* timo *m*, estafa *f* **2** *v/t* timar, estafar; **swindle s.o. out of sth** estafar algo a alguien

swine [swaɪn] F (*person*) cerdo(-a) *m(f)* F

swing [swɪŋ] **1** *n* oscilación *f*; *for child* columpio *m*; **swing to the Democrats** giro favorable a los Demócratas **2** *v/t* (*pret & pp* **swung**) balancear; *hips* menear **3** *v/i* (*pret & pp* **swung**) balancearse; (*turn*) girar; *of public opinion etc* cambiar

swing-'door puerta *f* basculante *or* de vaivén

Swiss [swɪs] **1** *adj* suizo **2** *n person* suizo(-a) *m(f)*; **the Swiss** los suizos

switch [swɪtʃ] **1** *n for light* interruptor *m*; (*change*) cambio *m* **2** *v/t* (*change*) cambiar de **3** *v/i* (*change*) cambiar

♦ **switch off** *v/t lights, engine, PC, TV* apagar

♦ **switch on** *v/t lights, engine, PC, TV* encender, *L.Am.* prender

'switch·board centralita *f*, *L.Am.* conmutador

'switch·o·ver *to new system* cambio *m* (**to** a)

Swit·zer·land ['swɪtsərlənd] Suiza

swiv·el ['swɪvl] *v/i* (*pret & pp* **swiveled**, *Br* **swivelled**) *of chair, monitor* girar

swol·len ['swoulən] *adj* hinchado

swoop [swuːp] *v/i of bird* volar en picado

♦ **swoop down on** *v/t prey* caer en picado sobre

♦ **swoop on** *v/t of police etc* hacer una redada contra

sword [sɔːrd] espada *f*

'sword·fish pez *f* espada

swore [swɔːr] *pret* → **swear**

sworn [swɔːrn] *pp* → **swear**

swum [swʌm] *pp* → **swim**

swung [swʌŋ] *pret & pp* → **swing**

syc·a·more ['sɪkəmɔːr] plátano *m* (árbol)

syl·la·ble ['sɪləbl] sílaba *f*

syl·la·bus ['sɪləbəs] plan *m* de estudios

sym·bol ['sɪmbəl] símbolo *m*

sym·bol·ic [sɪm'bɑːlɪk] *adj* simbólico

sym·bol·ism ['sɪmbəlɪzm] simbolismo *m*

sym·bol·ist ['sɪmbəlɪst] simbolista *m/f*

sym·bol·ize ['sɪmbəlaɪz] *v/t* simbolizar

sym·met·ri·c(al) [sɪ'metrɪkl] *adj* simétrico

sym·me·try ['sɪmətrɪ] simetría *f*

sym·pa·thet·ic [sɪmpə'θetɪk] *adj* (*showing pity*) compasivo; (*understanding*) comprensivo; **be sympathetic toward a person / an idea** simpatizar con una persona / idea

♦ **sym·pa·thize with** ['sɪmpəθaɪz] *v/t person, views* comprender

sym·pa·thiz·er ['sɪmpəθaɪzər] POL simpatizante *m/f*

sym·pa·thy ['sɪmpəθɪ] (*pity*) compasión *f*; (*understanding*) comprensión *f*; **don't expect any sympathy from me!** no esperes que te compadezca

sym·pho·ny ['sɪmfənɪ] sinfonía *f*

'sym·pho·ny or·ches·tra orquesta *f* sinfónica

symp·tom ['sɪmptəm] *also fig* síntoma *f*

symp·to·mat·ic [sɪmptə'mætɪk] *adj:* **be symptomatic of** *fig* ser sintomático de

syn·chro·nize ['sɪŋkrənaɪz] *v/t* sincronizar

syn·o·nym ['sɪnənɪm] sinónimo *m*

sy·non·y·mous [sɪ'nɑːnɪməs] *adj* sinónimo; **be synonymous with** *fig* ser sinónimo de

syn·tax ['sɪntæks] sintaxis *f inv*

syn·the·siz·er ['sɪnθəsaɪzər] MUS sintetizador *m*

syn·thet·ic [sɪn'θetɪk] *adj* sintético

syph·i·lis ['sɪfɪlɪs] sífilis *f*

Syr·i·a ['sɪrɪə] Siria

Syr·i·an ['sɪrɪən] **1** *adj* sirio **2** *n* sirio(-a) *m(f)*

sy·ringe [sɪ'rɪndʒ] *n* jeringuilla *f*

syr·up ['sɪrəp] almíbar *m*

sys·tem ['sɪstəm] *also* COMPUT sistema *f*; **the braking system** el sistema de frenado; **the digestive system** el aparato digestivo

sys·te·mat·ic [sɪstə'mætɪk] *adj* sistemático

sys·tem·at·i·cal·ly [sɪstə'mætɪklɪ] *adv* sistemáticamente

sys·tems 'an·a·lyst ['sɪstəmz] COMPUT analista *m/f* de sistemas

S

T

tab [tæb] *n for pulling* lengüeta *f*; *in text* tabulador *m*; *bill* cuenta *f*; **pick up the tab** pagar (la cuenta)

ta·ble ['teɪbl] *n* mesa *f*; *of figures* cuadro *m*

'**ta·ble·cloth** mantel *m*

'**table lamp** lámpara *f* de mesa

table of 'con·tents índice *m* (de contenidos)

'**ta·ble·spoon** *object* cuchara *f* grande; *quantity* cucharada *f* grande

ta·blet ['tæblɪt] MED pastilla *f*

'**ta·ble ten·nis** tenis *m* de mesa

tab·loid ['tæblɔɪd] *n newspaper* periódico *m* sensacionalista (*de tamaño* tabloide)

ta·boo [tə'buː] *adj* tabú *inv*

ta·cit ['tæsɪt] *adj* tácito

ta·ci·turn ['tæsɪtɜːrn] *adj* taciturno

tack [tæk] **1** *n (nail)* tachuela *f* **2** *v/t (sew)* hilvanar **3** *v/i of yacht* dar bordadas

tack·le ['tækl] **1** *n (equipment)* equipo *m*; SP entrada *f*; **fishing tackle** aparejos *mpl* de pesca **2** *v/t* SP entrar a; *problem* abordar; *intruder* hacer frente a

tack·y ['tækɪ] *adj paint, glue* pegajoso; F *(cheap, poor quality)* chabacano, *Span* hortera F; *behavior* impresentable

tact [tækt] *n* tacto *m*

tact·ful ['tæktfəl] *adj* diplomático

tact·ful·ly ['tæktfəlɪ] *adv* diplomáticamente

tac·ti·cal ['tæktɪkl] *adj* táctico

tac·tics ['tæktɪks] *npl* táctica *f*

tact·less ['tæktlɪs] *adj* indiscreto

tad·pole ['tædpoʊl] *n* renacuajo *m*

tag [tæg] *n (label)* etiqueta *f*

◆ **tag along** *v/i (pret & pp* **tagged***)* pegarse

tail [teɪl] *n of bird, fish* cola *f*; *of mammal* cola *f*, rabo *m*

'**tail·back** *Br* caravana *f*

'**tail light** luz *f* trasera

tai·lor ['teɪlər] *n* sastre *m*

tai·lor-made [teɪlər'meɪd] *adj suit, solution* hecho a medida

'**tail·pipe** *of car* tubo *m* de escape

'**tail·wind** viento *m* de cola

taint·ed ['teɪntɪd] *adj food* contaminado; *reputation* empañado

Tai·wan [taɪ'wɑːn] Taiwán

Tai·wan·ese [taɪwɑn'iːz] **1** *adj* taiwanés **2** *n* taiwanés(-esa) *m(f)*; *dialect* taiwanés *m*

take [teɪk] *v/t (pret* **took***, pp* **taken***) (remo-* ve) llevarse; *Span* coger; *(steal)* llevarse; *(transport, accompany)* llevar; *(accept: money, gift, credit cards)* aceptar; *(study: maths, French)* hacer, estudiar; *photograph, photocopy* hacer, sacar; *exam, degree* hacer; *shower* darse; *stroll* dar; *medicine, s.o.'s temperature, taxi* tomar; *(endure)* aguantar; **how long does it take?** ¿cuánto tiempo lleva?; **I'll take it** *when shopping* me lo llevo; **it takes a lot of courage** se necesita mucho valor

◆ **take after** *v/t* parecerse a

◆ **take apart** *v/t (dismantle)* desmontar; F *(criticize)* hacer pedazos; F *(reprimand)* echar una bronca a F; F *in physical fight* machacar

◆ **take away** *v/t pain* hacer desaparecer; *(remove: object)* quitar; MATH restar; **take sth away from s.o.** quitar algo a alguien

◆ **take back** *v/t (return: object)* devolver; *person* llevar de vuelta; *(accept back: husband etc)* dejar volver; **that takes me back** *of music, thought etc* me trae recuerdos

◆ **take down** *v/t from shelf* bajar; *scaffolding* desmontar; *trousers* bajarse; *(write down)* anotar, apuntar

◆ **take in** *v/t (take indoors)* recoger; *(give accommodation to)* acoger; *(make narrower)* meter; *(deceive)* engañar; *(include)* incluir

◆ **take off 1** *v/t clothes, hat* quitarse; *10% etc* descontar; *(mimic)* imitar; *(cut off)* cortar; **take a day / week off** tomarse un día / una semana de vacaciones **2** *v/i of airplane* despegar, *L.Am.* decolar; *(become popular)* empezar a cuajar

◆ **take on** *v/t job* aceptar; *staff* contratar

◆ **take out** *v/t from bag, pocket* sacar; *tooth* sacar, extraer; *word from text* quitar, borrar; *money from bank* sacar; *insurance policy* suscribir; **he took her out to dinner** la llevó a cenar; **take the dog out** sacar al perro a pasear; **take the kids out to the park** llevar a los niños al parque; **don't take it out on me!** ¡no la pagues conmigo!

◆ **take over** *v/t company etc* absorber, adquirir; **tourists took over the town** los turistas invadieron la ciudad **2** *v/i of new management etc* asumir el cargo; *of new government* asumir el poder; *(do sth in s.o.'s place)* tomar el relevo

◆ **take to** *v/t (like)*: **how did they take to**

the new idea? ¿qué les pareció la nueva idea?; *I immediately took to him* me cayó bien de inmediato; *he has taken to getting up early* le ha dado por levantarse temprano; *she took to drink* se dio a la bebida

◆ **take up** *v/t carpet etc* levantar; *(carry up)* subir; *(shorten: dress etc)* acortar; *hobby* empezar a hacer; *subject* empezar a estudiar; *offer* aceptar; *new job* comenzar; *space, time* ocupar; *I'll take you up on your offer* aceptaré tu oferta

'**take-home pay** salario *m* neto

'**take-off** *of airplane* despegue *m*, L.Am. decolaje *m*; *(impersonation)* imitación *f*

'**take-o-ver** COM absorción *f*, adquisición *f*

'**take-o-ver bid** oferta *f* pública de adquisición, OPA *f*

tak-en ['teɪkən] *pp* → **take**

ta-kings ['teɪkɪŋz] *npl* recaudación *f*

tal-cum pow-der ['tælkəmpaʊdər] polvos *mpl* de talco

tale [teɪl] cuento *m*, historia *f*

tal-ent ['tælənt] talento *m*

tal-ent-ed ['tæləntɪd] *adj* con talento; *she's very talented* tiene mucho talento

'**tal-ent scout** cazatalentos *m inv*

talk [tɔːk] **1** *v/i* hablar; *can I talk to ...?* ¿podría hablar con ...?; *I'll talk to him about it* hablaré del tema con él **2** *v/t English etc* hablar; *talk business/politics* hablar de negocios / de política; *talk s.o. into sth* persuadir a alguien para que haga algo **3** *n (conversation)* charla *f*, C.Am., Mex plática *f*; *(lecture)* conferencia *f*, *give a talk on sth* dar una conferencia sobre algo; charla *f*; *talks* negociaciones *fpl*; *he's all talk pej* habla mucho y no hace nada

◆ **talk back** *v/i* responder, contestar

◆ **talk down to** *v/t* hablar con aires de superioridad a

◆ **talk over** *v/t* hablar de, discutir

talk-a-tive ['tɔːkətɪv] *adj* hablador

talk-ing-to ['tɔːkɪŋtuː] sermón *m*, rapapolvo *m*; *give s.o. a good talking-to* echar a alguien un buen sermón *or* rapapolvo

'**talk show** programa *m* de entrevistas

tall [tɔːl] *adj* alto; *it is ten meters tall* mide diez metros de alto

tall 'or-der: *that's a tall order* eso es muy difícil

tall 'sto-ry cuento *m* chino

tal-ly ['tælɪ] **1** *n* cuenta *f* **2** *v/i (pret & pp tallied)* cuadrar, encajar

◆ **tally with** *v/t* cuadrar con, encajar con

tame [teɪm] *adj animal* manso, domesticado; *joke etc* soso

◆ **tam-per with** ['tæmpər] *v/t lock* intentar forzar; *brakes* tocar

tam-pon ['tæmpɑːn] tampón *m*

tan [tæn] **1** *n from sun* bronceado *m*; *get a tan* ponerse moreno; *(color)* marrón *m* claro **2** *v/i (pret & pp tanned) in sun* broncearse **3** *v/t (pret & pp tanned) leather* curtir

tan-dem ['tændəm] *(bike)* tándem *m*

tan-gent ['tændʒənt] MATH tangente *f*

tan-ge-rine [tændʒəˈriːn] mandarina *f*

tan-gi-ble ['tændʒɪbl] *adj* tangible

◆ **tangle up:** *get tangled up of string etc* quedarse enredado

tan-go ['tæŋgoʊ] *n* tango *m*

tank [tæŋk] *for water* depósito *m*, tanque *m*; *for fish* pecera *f*; MOT depósito *m*; MIL, *for skin diver* tanque *m*

tank-er ['tæŋkər] *truck* camión *m* cisterna; *ship* buque *m* cisterna; *for oil* petrolero *m*

'**tank top** camiseta *f* sin mangas

tanned [tænd] *adj* moreno, bronceado

Tan-noy® ['tænɔɪ] megafonía *f*

tan-ta-liz-ing ['tæntəlaɪzɪŋ] *adj* sugerente

tan-ta-mount ['tæntəmaʊnt] *adj:* *be tantamount to* equivaler a

tan-trum ['tæntrəm] rabieta *f*

tap [tæp] **1** *n* grifo *m*, L.Am. llave *f* **2** *v/t (pret & pp tapped) (knock)* dar un golpecito en; *phone* intervenir

◆ **tap into** *v/t resources* explotar

'**tap dance** *n* claqué *m*

tape [teɪp] *n* cinta *f* **2** *v/t conversation etc* grabar; *with sticky tape* pegar con cinta adhesiva

'**tape deck** pletina *f*

'**tape drive** COMPUT unidad *f* de cinta

'**tape meas-ure** cinta *f* métrica

tap-er ['teɪpər] *v/i* estrecharse

◆ **taper off** *v/i of production, figures* disminuir

'**tape re-cor-der** magnetofón *m*, L.Am. grabador *m*

'**tape re-cor-ding** grabación *f* (magnetofónica)

ta-pes-try ['tæpɪstrɪ] *cloth* tapiz *m*; *art* tapicería *f*

'**tape-worm** tenia *f*, solitaria *f*

tar [tɑːr] *n* alquitrán *m*

tar-dy ['tɑːrdɪ] *adj* tardío

tar-get ['tɑːrgɪt] **1** *n in shooting* blanco *m*; *for sales, production* objetivo *m* **2** *v/t market* apuntar a

'**tar-get 'au-di-ence** audiencia *f* a la que está orientado el programa

'**tar-get date** fecha *f* fijada

'**tar-get 'fig-ure** cifra *f* objetivo

T

'tar·get group COM grupo *m* estratégico

'tar·get mar·ket mercado *m* objetivo

tar·iff ['tærɪf] (*price*) tarifa *f*; (*tax*) arancel *m*

tar·mac ['tɑːrmæk] *for road surface* asfalto *m*; *at airport* pista *f*

tar·nish ['tɑːrnɪʃ] *v/t metal* deslucir, deslustrar; *reputation* empañar

tar·pau·lin [tɑːr'pɔːlɪn] lona *f* (*impermeable*)

tart¹ [tɑːrt] *n* tarta *f*, pastel *m*

tart² [tɑːrt] *n* F *woman* fulana *f* F

tar·tan ['tɑːrtn] tartán *m*

task [tæsk] tarea *f*

'task force *for a special job* equipo *m* de trabajo; MIL destacamento *m*

tas·sel ['tæsl] borla *f*

taste [teɪst] **1** *n* gusto *m*; *of food etc* sabor *m*; *he has no taste* tiene mal gusto **2** *v/t also fig* probar

taste·ful ['teɪstfəl] *adj* de buen gusto

taste·ful·ly ['teɪstfəlɪ] *adv* con buen gusto

taste·less ['teɪstlɪs] *adj food* insípido; *remark* de mal gusto

tast·ing ['teɪstɪŋ] *of wine* cata *f*, degustación *f*

tast·y ['teɪstɪ] *adj* sabroso, rico

tat·tered ['tætərd] *adj clothes* andrajoso; *book* destrozado

tat·ters ['tætərz]: *in tatters clothes* hecho jirones; *reputation, career* arruinado

tat·too [tə'tuː] *n* tatuaje *m*

tat·ty ['tætɪ] *adj* sobado, gastado

taught [tɔːt] *pret & pp → teach*

taunt [tɔːnt] **1** *n* pulla *f* **2** *v/t* mofarse de

Tau·rus ['tɔːrəs] ASTR Tauro *m/f inv*

taut [tɔːt] *adj* tenso

taw·dry ['tɔːdrɪ] *adj* barato, cursi

tax [tæks] **1** *n* impuesto *m*; *before / after tax* sin descontar / descontado impuestos **2** *v/t people* cobrar impuestos a; *product* gravar

tax·a·ble 'in·come ingresos *mpl* gravables

ta·x·a·tion [tæk'seɪʃn] (*act of taxing*) imposición *f* de impuestos; (*taxes*) fiscalidad *f*, impuestos *mpl*

'tax avoid·ance elusión *f* legal de impuestos

'tax brack·et banda *f* impositiva

'tax de·duct·i·ble *adj* desgravable

'tax eva·sion evasión *f* fiscal

'tax free *adj* libre de impuestos

'tax ha·ven paraíso *m* fiscal

tax·i ['tæksɪ] *n* taxi *m*

'tax·i dri·ver taxista *m/f*

tax·ing ['tæksɪŋ] *adj* difícil, arduo

'tax in·spect·or inspector(a) *m(f)* de Hacienda

'tax·i rank, tax·i stand parada *f* de taxis

'tax ·pay·er contribuyente *m/f*

'tax re·turn *form* declaración *f* de la renta

'tax year año *m* fiscal

TB [tiː'biː] *abbr* (= *tuberculosis*) tuberculosis *f*

tea [tiː] *drink* té *m*; *meal* merienda *f*

'tea·bag ['tiːbæg] bolsita *f* de té

teach [tiːtʃ] **1** *v/t* (*pret & pp taught*) *person, subject* enseñar; *teach s.o. to do sth* enseñar a alguien a hacer algo **2** *v/i* (*pret & pp taught*): *I taught at that school* di clases en ese colegio; *he always wanted to teach* siempre quiso ser profesor

tea·cher ['tiːtʃər] *at primary school* maestro(-a) *m(f)*; *at secondary school, university* profesor(a) *m(f)*

tea·cher 'train·ing formación *f* pedagógica, magisterio *m*

tea·ching ['tiːtʃɪŋ] *profession* enseñanza *f*, docencia *f*

'tea·ching aid material *m* didáctico

'tea cloth paño *m* de cocina

'tea·cup taza *f* de té

'tea drink·er bebedor(a) *m(f)* de té

teak [tiːk] teca *f*

'tea leaf hoja *f* de té

team [tiːm] equipo *m*

'team·mate compañero(-a) *m(f)* de equipo

team 'spir·it espíritu *m* de equipo

team·ster ['tiːmstər] camionero(-a) *m(f)*

'team·work trabajo *m* en equipo

'tea·pot tetera *f*

tear¹ [ter] **1** *n in cloth etc* desgarrón *m*, rotura *f* **2** *v/t* (*pret tore, pp torn*) *paper, cloth* rasgar; *be torn between two alternatives* debatirse entre dos alternativas **3** *v/i* (*pret tore, pp torn*) (*run fast, drive fast*) ir a toda velocidad

♦ **tear down** *v/t poster* arrancar; *building* derribar

♦ **tear out** *v/t* arrancar

♦ **tear up** *v/t paper* romper, rasgar; *agreement* romper

tear² [tɪr] *in eye* lágrima *f*; *burst into tears* echarse a llorar; *be in tears* estar llorando

'tear·drop ['tɪrdrɑːp] lágrima *f*

tear·ful ['tɪrfəl] *adj* lloroso

'tear gas gas *m* lacrimógeno

tease [tiːz] *v/t person* tomar el pelo a, burlarse de; *animal* hacer rabiar

'tea serv·ice, 'tea set servicio *m* de té

'tea·spoon *object* cucharilla *f*; *quantity* cucharadita *f*

'tea strain·er colador *m* de té

teat [tiːt] teta *f*

'tea to·wel *Br* paño *m* de cocina

tech·ni·cal ['teknɪkl] *adj* técnico

tech·ni·cal·i·ty [teknɪ'kælətɪ] (*technical nature*) tecnicismo *m*; LAW detalle *m* técnico

tech·ni·cal·ly ['teknɪklɪ] *adv* técnicamente

tech·ni·cian [tek'nɪʃn] técnico(-a) *m(f)*

tech·nique [tek'niːk] técnica *f*

tech·no·log·i·cal [teknə'lɑːdʒɪkl] *adj* tecnológico

tech·nol·o·gy [tek'nɑːlədʒɪ] tecnología *f*

tech·no·phob·i·a [teknə'foʊbɪə] rechazo *m* de las nuevas tecnologías

ted·dy bear ['tedɪber] osito *m* de peluche

te·di·ous ['tiːdɪəs] *adj* tedioso

tee [tiː] *n* in golf tee *m*

teem [tiːm] *v/i*: **be teeming with rain** llover a cántaros; **be teeming with tourists / ants** estar abarrotado de turistas / lleno de hormigas

teen·age ['tiːneɪdʒ] *adj fashions* adolescente, juvenil; **teenage boy / girl** un adolescente / una adolescente

teen·ag·er ['tiːneɪdʒər] adolescente *m/f*

teens [tiːnz] *npl* adolescencia *f*; **be in one's teens** ser un adolescente; **reach one's teens** alcanzar la adolescencia

tee·ny ['tiːnɪ] *adj* F chiquitín F

teeth [tiːθ] *pl* → **tooth**

teethe [tiːð] *v/i* echar los dientes

'teething problems *npl* problemas *fpl* iniciales

tee·to·tal [tiː'toʊtl] *adj person* abstemio

tee·to·tal·er [tiː'toʊtlər] abstemio(-a) *m(f)*

tel·e·com·mu·ni·ca·tions [telɪkəmjuːnɪ'keɪʃnz] telecomunicaciones *fpl*

tel·e·gram ['telɪgræm] telegrama *m*

tel·e·graph pole ['telɪgræf] poste *m* telegráfico

tel·e·path·ic [telɪ'pæθɪk] *adj* telepático; **you must be telepathic!** ¡debes tener telepatía!

te·lep·a·thy [tɪ'lepəθɪ] telepatía *f*

tel·e·phone ['telɪfoʊn] **1** *n* teléfono *m*; **be on the telephone** (*be speaking*) estar hablando por teléfono; (*possess a phone*) tener teléfono **2** *v/t person* telefonear, llamar por teléfono a **3** *v/i* telefonear, llamar por teléfono

'tel·e·phone bill factura *f* del teléfono

'tel·e·phone book guía *f* telefónica, listín *m* telefónico

'tel·e·phone booth cabina *f* telefónica

'tel·e·phone call llamada *f* telefónica

'tel·e·phone con·ver·sa·tion conversación *f* por teléfono *or* telefónica

'tel·e·phone di·rec·to·ry guía *f* telefónica, listín *m* telefónico

'tel·e·phone ex·change central *f* telefónica, centralita *f*

'tel·e·phone mes·sage mensaje *m* telefónico

'tel·e·phone num·ber número *m* de teléfono

tel·e·pho·to lens [telɪ'foʊtoʊlenz] teleobjetivo *m*

tel·e·sales ['telɪseɪlz] televentas *fpl*

tel·e·scope ['telɪskoʊp] telescopio *n*

tel·e·thon ['telɪθɑːn] maratón *m* benéfico televisivo

tel·e·vise ['telɪvaɪz] *v/t* televisar

tel·e·vi·sion ['telɪvɪʒn] televisión *f*; *set* televisión *f*, televisor *m*; **on television** en *or* por (la) televisión; **watch television** ver la televisión

'tel·e·vi·sion au·di·ence audiencia *f* televisiva

'tel·e·vi·sion pro·gram programa *m* televisivo

'tel·e·vi·sion set televisión *f*, televisor *m*

'tel·e·vi·sion stu·di·o estudio *m* de televisión

tell [tel] **1** *v/t* (*pret & pp told*) *story* contar; *lie* decir, contar; **I can't tell the difference** no veo la diferencia; **tell s.o. sth** decir algo a alguien; **don't tell Mom** no se lo digas a mamá; **could you tell me the way to ...?** ¿me podría decir por dónde se va a ...?; **tell s.o. to do sth** decir a alguien que haga algo; **you're telling me!** ¡a mí me lo vas a contar! **2** *v/i* (*pret & pp told*) (*have effect*) hacerse notar; **the heat is telling on him** el calor está empezando a afectarle; **time will tell** el tiempo lo dirá

tell·er ['telər] cajero(-a) *m(f)*

tell·ing ['telɪŋ] *adj* contundente

tell·ing 'off regañina *f*

tell·tale ['telteɪl] **1** *adj signs* revelador **2** *n* chivato(-a) *m(f)*

temp [temp] **1** *n employee* trabajador(a) *m(f)* temporal **2** *v/i* hacer trabajo temporal

tem·per ['tempər] (*bad temper*) mal *humor m*; **be in a temper** estar de mal *humor*; **keep one's temper** mantener la calma; **lose one's temper** perder los estribos

tem·pe·ra·ment ['tempərəmənt] temperamento *m*

tem·pe·ra·men·tal [temprə'mentl] *adj* (*moody*) temperamental

tem·pe·rate ['tempərət] *adj* templado

tem·pe·ra·ture ['temprətʃər] temperatura *f*; (*fever*) fiebre *f*; **have a temperature** tener fiebre

tem·ple¹ ['templ] REL templo *m*

tem·ple² ['templ] ANAT sien f
tem·po ['tempou] tempo m
tem·po·rar·i·ly [tempə'rerɪlɪ] adv temporalmente
tem·po·rar·y ['tempərerɪ] adj temporal
tempt [tempt] v/t tentar
temp·ta·tion [temp'teɪʃn] tentación f
tempt·ing ['temptɪŋ] adj tentador
ten [ten] diez
te·na·cious [tɪ'neɪʃəs] adj tenaz
te·nac·i·ty [tɪ'næsɪtɪ] tenacidad f
ten·ant ['tenənt] of building inquilino(-a) m(f); of farm, land arrendatario m
tend¹ [tend] v/t (look after) cuidar (de)
tend² [tend]: **tend to do sth** soler hacer algo; **tend toward sth** tender hacia algo
ten·den·cy ['tendənsɪ] tendencia f
ten·der¹ ['tendər] adj (sore) sensible, delicado; (affectionate) cariñoso, tierno; steak tierno
ten·der² ['tendər] n COM oferta f
ten·der·ness ['tendərnɪs] (soreness) dolor m; of kiss etc cariño m, ternura f
ten·don ['tendən] tendón m
ten·nis ['tenɪs] tenis m
'**ten·nis ball** pelota f de tenis
'**ten·nis court** pista f de tenis; cancha f de tenis
'**ten·nis pla·yer** tenista m/f
'**ten·nis rack·et** raqueta f de tenis
ten·or ['tenər] MUS tenor m
tense¹ [tens] n GRAM tiempo m
tense² [tens] adj muscle, moment tenso; voice, person tenso, nervioso
◆ **tense up** v/i ponerse tenso
ten·sion ['tenʃn] of rope tensión f; in atmosphere, voice tensión f, tirantez f; in film, novel tensión f
tent [tent] tienda f
ten·ta·cle ['tentəkl] tentáculo m
ten·ta·tive ['tentətɪv] adj move, offer provisional
ten·ter·hooks ['tentərhuks]: **be on tenterhooks** estar sobre ascuas
tenth [tenθ] **1** adj décimo **2** n décimo m, décima parte f; of second, degree décima f
tep·id ['tepɪd] adj water, reaction tibio
term [tɜːrm] in office etc mandato m; EDU trimestre m; (condition) término m, condición f; (word) término m; **be on good/bad terms with s.o.** llevarse bien/mal con alguien; **in the long/short term** a largo/corto plazo; **come to terms with sth** llegar a aceptar algo
ter·mi·nal ['tɜːrmɪnl] **1** n at airport, for buses, for containers terminal f; ELEC, COMPUT terminal m; of battery polo m **2** adj illness terminal

ter·mi·nal·ly ['tɜːrmɪnəlɪ] adv: **terminally ill** en la fase terminal de una enfermedad
ter·mi·nate ['tɜːrmɪneɪt] **1** v/t contract rescindir; pregnancy interrumpir **2** v/i finalizar
ter·mi·na·tion [tɜːrmɪ'neɪʃn] of contract rescisión f; of pregnancy interrupción f
ter·mi·nol·o·gy [tɜːrmɪ'nɑːlədʒɪ] terminología f
ter·mi·nus ['tɜːrmɪnəs] for buses final m de trayecto; for trains estación f terminal
ter·race ['terəs] terraza f
ter·ra cot·ta [terə'kɑːtə] adj de terracota
ter·rain [te'reɪn] terreno m
ter·res·tri·al [te'restrɪəl] **1** n terrestre m **2** adj television por vía terrestre
ter·ri·ble ['terəbl] adj terrible, horrible
ter·ri·bly ['terəblɪ] adv (very) tremendamente
ter·rif·ic [tə'rɪfɪk] adj estupendo
ter·rif·i·cal·ly [tə'rɪfɪklɪ] adv (very) tremendamente
ter·ri·fy ['terɪfaɪ] v/t (pret & pp **terrified**) aterrorizar; **be terrified** estar aterrorizado
ter·ri·fy·ing ['terɪfaɪɪŋ] adj aterrador
ter·ri·to·ri·al [terɪ'tɔːrɪəl] adj territorial
ter·ri·to·ri·al 'wa·ters npl aguas fpl territoriales
ter·ri·to·ry ['terɪtɔːrɪ] territorio m; fig ámbito m, territorio m
ter·ror ['terər] terror m
ter·ror·ism ['terərɪzm] terrorismo m
ter·ror·ist ['terərɪst] terrorista m
'**ter·ror·ist at·tack** atentado m terrorista
'**ter·ror·ist or·gan·i·za·tion** organización f terrorista
ter·ror·ize ['terəraɪz] v/t aterrorizar
terse [tɜːrs] adj tajante, seco
test [test] **1** n prueba f; academic, for driving examen m **2** v/t probar, poner a prueba
tes·ta·ment ['testəmənt] to s.o.'s life etc testimonio m; **Old/New Testament** REL Viejo/Nuevo Testamento m
'**test-drive** v/t (pret **test-drove**, pp **test-driven**) car probar en carretera
tes·ti·cle ['testɪkl] testículo m
tes·ti·fy ['testɪfaɪ] v/i (pret & pp **testified**) LAW testificar, prestar declaración
tes·ti·mo·ni·al [testɪ'mounɪəl] n referencias fpl
tes·ti·mo·ny ['testɪmənɪ] LAW testimonio m
'**test-tube** tubo m de ensayo, probeta f
'**test-tube ba·by** niño(-a) m(f) probeta
tes·ty ['testɪ] adj irritable
te·ta·nus ['tetənəs] tétanos m
teth·er ['teðər] **1** v/t horse atar **2** n correa

f; *be at the end of one's tether* estar a la punto de perder la paciencia

text [tekst] texto *m*

'**text·book** libro *m* de texto

tex·tile ['tekstəl] textil *m*

tex·ture ['tekstʃər] textura *f*

Thai [taɪ] **1** *adj* tailandés **2** *n person* tailandés(-esa) *m(f)*; *language* tailandés *m*

Thai·land ['taɪlænd] Tailandia

than [ðæn] *adv que*; *bigger/faster than me* más grande / más rápido que yo; *more than 50* más de 50

thank [θæŋk] *v/t* dar las gracias a; *thank you* gracias; *no thank you* no, gracias

thank·ful ['θæŋkfəl] *adj* agradecido; *we have to be thankful that* ... tenemos que dar gracias de que ...

thank·ful·ly ['θæŋkfəlɪ] *adv (luckily)* afortunadamente

thank·less ['θæŋklɪs] *adj task* ingrato

thanks [θæŋks] *npl* gracias *fpl*; *thanks!* ¡gracias!; *thanks to* gracias a

Thanks·giv·ing (**Day**) [θæŋks'gɪvɪndeɪ] Día *m* de Acción de Gracias

that [ðæt] **1** *adj* cse *m*, esa *f*; *more remote* aquel *m*, aquella; *that one* **2** *pron* ése *m*, ésa; *more remote* aquél *m*, aquella *f*; *what is that?* ¿qué es eso?; *who is that?* ¿quién es ése?; *that's mine* ése es mío; *that's tea* es té; *that's very kind* qué amable; *I think that* ... creo que ...; *the person/car that you see* el coche / la persona que ves **3** *adv (so)* tan; *that big/expensive* tan grande / caro

thaw [θɔː] *v/i* of snow derretirse, fundirse; *of frozen food* descongelarse

the [ðə] el, la; *plural* los, las; *the sooner the better* cuanto antes, mejor

the·a·ter ['θɪətər] teatro *m*

'**the·a·ter crit·ic** crítico *m* teatral

the·a·tre *Br* → theater

the·at·ri·cal [θɪ'ætrɪkl] *also fig* teatral

theft [θeft] robo *m*

their [ðer] *adj* su; *(his or her)* su; *their brother* su hermano; *their books* sus libros

theirs [ðerz] *pron* el suyo, la suya; *theirs are red* los suyos son rojos; *that book is theirs* ese libro es suyo; *a friend of theirs* un amigo suyo

them [ðem] *pron direct object* los *mpl*, las *fpl*; *indirect object* les; *after prep* ellos *mpl*, ellas *fpl*; *I know them* los conozco; *I gave them the keys* les di las llaves; *I sold it to them* se lo vendí; *he lives with them* vive con ellos / ellas; *if a person asks for help, you should help them* hay que ayudarla, hay que ayudarla

theme [θiːm] tema *m*

'**theme park** parque *m* temático

'**theme song** tema *m* musical

them·selves [ðem'selvz] *pron reflexive* se; *emphatic* ellos mismos *mpl*, ellas mismas *fpl*; *they hurt themselves* se hicieron daño; *when they saw themselves in the mirror* cuando se vieron en el espejo; *they saw it themselves* lo vieron ellos mismos; *by themselves (alone)* solos; *(without help)* ellos solos, ellas solas

then [ðen] *adv (at that time)* entonces; *(after that)* luego, después; *deducing* entonces; *by then* para entonces

the·o·lo·gian [θɪə'loʊdʒɪən] teólogo *m*

the·ol·o·gy [θɪ'ɑːlədʒɪ] teología *f*

the·o·ret·i·cal [θɪə'retɪkl] *adj* teórico

the·o·ret·i·cal·ly [θɪə'retɪklɪ] *adv* en teoría

the·o·ry ['θɪrɪ] teoría *f*; *in theory* en teoría

ther·a·peu·tic [θerə'pjuːtɪk] *adj* terapéutico

ther·a·pist ['θerəpɪst] terapeuta *m/f*

ther·a·py ['θerəpɪ] terapia *f*

there [ðer] *adv* allí, ahí, allá; *over there* allí, ahí, allá; *down there* allí or ahí or allá abajo; *there is/are* ... hay ...; *there is/are not* ... no hay ...; *there you are giving sth* aquí tienes; *finding sth* aquí está; *completing sth* ya está; *there and back* ida y vuelta; *it's 5 miles there and back* entre ida y vuelta hay cinco millas; *there he is!* ¡ahí está!; *there, there!* ¡venga!

there·a·bouts [ðerə'haʊts] *adv* aproximadamente

there·fore ['ðerfɔːr] *adv* por (lo) tanto

ther·mom·e·ter [θər'mɑːmɪtər] termómetro *m*

ther·mos flask ['θɜːrməs] termo *m*

ther·mo·stat ['θɜːrməstæt] termostato *m*

these [ðiːz] **1** *adj* estos(-as) **2** *pron* éstos *mpl*, éstas *fpl*

the·sis ['θiːsɪs] (*pl theses* ['θiːsiːz]) tesis *f inv*

they [ðeɪ] *pron* ellos *mpl*, ellas *fpl*; *they are Mexican* son mexicanos; *they're going, but we're not* ellos van, pero nosotros no; *if anyone looks at this, they will see that* ... si alguien mira esto, verá que ...; *they say that* ... dicen que ...; *they are going to change the law* van a cambiar la ley

thick [θɪk] *adj soup* espeso; *fog* denso; *wall, book* grueso; *hair* poblado; *crowd* compacto; F *(stupid)* corto; *it's 3 cm thick* tiene 3 cm de grosor

thick·en ['θɪkən] *v/t sauce* espesar

thick·set ['θɪkset] *adj* fornido

thick·skinned [θɪk'skɪnd] *adj fig* insensible

thief [θiːf] (*pl* **thieves** [θiːvz]) ladrón(-ona) *m(f)*

thigh [θaɪ] muslo *m*

thim·ble ['θɪmbl] dedal *m*

thin [θɪn] *adj person* delgado; *hair* ralo, escaso; *soup* claro; *coat, line* fino

thing [θɪŋ] cosa *f*; **things** (*belongings*) cosas *fpl*; **how are things?** ¿cómo te va?; **it's a good thing you told me** menos mal que me lo dijiste; **what a thing to do / say!** ¡qué barbaridad!

thing·um·a·jig ['θɪŋʌmədʒɪg] F *object* chisme *m*; *person* fulanito *m*

think [θɪŋk] *v/t & v/i* (*pret & pp* **thought**) pensar; *hold an opinion* pensar, creer; **I think so** creo que sí; **I don't think so** creo que no; **I think so too** pienso lo mismo; **what do you think?** ¿qué piensas o crees?; **what do you think of it?** ¿qué te parece?; **I can't think of anything more** no se me ocurre nada más; **think hard!** ¡piensa más!; **I'm thinking about emigrating** estoy pensando en emigrar

◆ **think over** *v/t* reflexionar sobre

◆ **think through** *v/t* pensar bien

◆ **think up** *v/t plan* idear

'think tank grupo *m* de expertos

thin-skinned [θɪn'skɪnd] *adj* sensible

third [θɜːrd] **1** *adj* tercero **2** *n* tercero(a) *m(f)*; *fraction* tercio *m*, tercera parte *f*

third·ly ['θɜːrdlɪ] *adv* en tercer lugar

third 'par·ty tercero *m*

third-par·ty in'sur·ance seguro *m* a terceros

third 'per·son GRAM tercera persona *f*

'third-rate *adj* de tercera, de pacotilla F

Third 'World Tercer Mundo *m*

thirst [θɜːrst] sed *f*

thirst·y ['θɜːrstɪ] *adj* sediento; **be thirsty** tener sed

thir·teen [θɜːr'tiːn] trece

thir·teenth [θɜːr'tiːnθ] *n & adj* decimotercero

thir·ti·eth ['θɜːrtɪɪθ] *n & adj* trigésimo

thir·ty ['θɜːrtɪ] treinta

this [ðɪs] **1** *adj* este *m*, esta *f*; **this one** éste *m*, esta *f* **2** *pron* esto *m*, esta *f*; **this is good** esto es bueno; **this is ...** *introducing s.o.* éste / ésta es ...; TELEC soy ... **3** *adv*: **this big / high** así de grande / de alto

thorn [θɔːrn] espina *f*

thorn·y ['θɔːrnɪ] *adj also fig* espinoso

thor·ough ['θʌrou] *adj search* minucioso; *knowledge* profundo; *person* concienzudo

thor·ough·bred ['θʌroubred] *horse* pura-sangre *m*

thor·ough·ly ['θʌroulɪ] *adv* completa-mente; *clean up* a fondo; *search* minucio-samente; **I'm thoroughly ashamed** estoy avergonzadísimo

those [ðouz] **1** *adj* esos *mpl*, esas *fpl*; *more remote* aquellos *mpl*, aquellas *fpl* **2** *pron* ésos *mpl*, ésas *fpl*; aquéllos *mpl*, aquéllas *mpl*

though [ðou] **1** *conj* (*although*) aunque; **as though** como si **2** *adv* sin embargo; **it's not finished though** pero no está acabado

thought[1] [θɔːt] *single* idea *f*; *collective* pensamiento *m*

thought[2] [θɔːt] *pret & pp* → **think**

thought·ful ['θɔːtfəl] *adj* pensativo; *book* serio; (*considerate*) atento

thought·less ['θɔːtlɪs] *adj* desconsiderado

thou·sand ['θauznd] mil *m*; **thousands of** miles de; **a thousand and ten** mil diez

thou·sandth ['θauzndθ] *n & adj* milésimo

thrash [θræʃ] *v/t* golpear, dar una paliza a; SP dar una paliza a

◆ **thrash about** *v/i with arms etc* revol-verse

◆ **thrash out** *v/t solution* alcanzar

thrash·ing ['θræʃɪŋ] *also* SP paliza *f*

thread [θred] **1** *n* hilo *m*; *of screw* rosca *f* **2** *v/t needle* enhebrar; *beads* ensartar

thread·bare ['θredber] *adj* raído

threat [θret] amenaza *f*

threat·en ['θretn] *v/t* amenazar

threat·en·ing ['θretnɪŋ] *adj* amenazador

three [θriː] tres

three-'quar·ters tres cuartos *mpl*

thresh [θreʃ] *v/t corn* trillar

thresh·old ['θreʃhould] *of house, new age* umbral *m*; **on the threshold of** en el um-bral or en puertas del

threw [θruː] *pret* → **throw**

thrift [θrɪft] ahorro *m*

thrift·y ['θrɪftɪ] *adj* ahorrativo

thrill [θrɪl] **1** *n* emoción *f*, estremecimiento *m* **2** *v/t*: **be thrilled** estar entusiasmado

thrill·er ['θrɪlər] *movie* película *f* de *Span* suspense *or L.Am.* suspenso; *novel* novela *f* de *Span* suspense *or L.Am.* suspenso

thrill·ing ['θrɪlɪŋ] *adj* emocionante

thrive [θraɪv] *v/i of plant* medrar, crecer bien; *of business, economy* prosperar

throat [θrout] garganta *f*

'throat loz·enge pastilla *f* para la garganta

throb [θrɑːb] **1** *n of heart* latido *m*; *of music* zumbido *m* **2** *v/i* (*pret & pp* **throbbed**) *of heart* latir; *of music* zumbar

throm·bo·sis [θrɑːmˈboʊsɪs] trombosis *f*
throne [θroʊn] trono *m*
throng [θrɑːŋ] *n* muchedumbre *f*
throt·tle [ˈθrɑːtl] **1** *n on motorbike* acelerador *m; on boat* palanca *f* del gas; *on motorbike* mango *m* del gas **2** *v/t* (*strangle*) estrangular
◆ **throttle back** *v/i* desacelerar
through [θruː] **1** *prep* ◇ (*across*) a través de; ***go through the city*** atravesar la ciudad
◇ (*during*) durante; ***through the winter / summer*** durante el invierno / verano; ***Monday through Friday*** de lunes a viernes
◇ (*by means of*) a través de, por medio de; ***arranged through him*** acordado por él **2** *adv*: ***wet through*** completamente mojado; ***watch a film through*** ver una película de principio a fin; ***read a book through*** leerse un libro de principio a fin **3** *adj*: ***be through*** *of couple* haber terminado; (*have arrived: of news etc*) haber llegado; ***you're through*** TELEC ya puede hablar; ***I'm through with ...*** (*finished with*) he terminado con …
'**through flight** vuelo *m* directo
through·out [θruːˈaʊt] **1** *prep* durante, a lo largo de **2** *adv* (*in all parts*) en su totalidad
'**through train** tren *m* directo
throw [θroʊ] **1** *v/t* (*pret* **threw**, *pp* **thrown**) tirar; *of horse* tirar, desmontar; (*disconcert*) desconcertar; *party* dar **2** *n* lanzamiento *m*; ***it's your throw*** te toca tirar
◆ **throw away** *v/t* tirar, *L.Am.* botar
◆ **throw off** *v/t jacket etc* quitarse rápidamente; *cold* deshacerse de
◆ **throw on** *v/t clothes* ponerse rápidamente
◆ **throw out** *v/t old things* tirar, *L.Am.* botar; *from bar, job, home* echar; *from country* expulsar; *plan* rechazar
◆ **throw up 1** *v/t ball* lanzar hacia arriba; ***throw up one's hands*** echarse las manos a la cabeza **2** *v/i* (*vomit*) vomitar
'**throw·a·way** *adj remark* insustancial, pasajero; (*disposable*) desechable
'**throw-in** SP saque *m* de banda
thrown [θroʊn] *pp* → **throw**
thru [θruː] → **through**
thrush [θrʌʃ] *bird* zorzal *m*
thrust [θrʌst] *v/t* (*pret & pp* **thrust**) (*push hard*) empujar; *knife* hundir; ***thrust sth into s.o.'s hands*** poner algo en las manos de alguien; ***thrust one's way through the crowd*** abrirse paso a empujones entre la multitud
thud [θʌd] *n* golpe *m* sordo

thug [θʌg] matón *m*
thumb [θʌm] **1** *n* pulgar *m* **2** *v/t*: ***thumb a ride*** hacer autoestop
'**thumb·tack** [ˈθʌmtæk] chincheta *f*
thump [θʌmp] **1** *n blow* porrazo *m; noise* golpe *m* sordo **2** *v/t person* dar un porrazo a; ***thump one's fist on the table*** pegar un puñetazo en la mesa **3** *v/i heart* latir con fuerza; ***thump on the door*** aporrear la puerta
thun·der [ˈθʌndər] *n* truenos *mpl*
thun·der·ous [ˈθʌndərəs] *adj applause* tormenta *f*
thun·der·storm [ˈθʌndərstɔːrm] tormenta *f* (*con truenos*)
'**thun·der·struck** *adj* atónito
thun·der·y [ˈθʌndərɪ] *adj weather* tormentoso
Thurs·day [ˈθɜːrzdeɪ] jueves *m inv*
thus [ðʌs] *adv* (*in this way*) así
thwart [θwɔːrt] *v/t person, plans* frustrar
thyme [taɪm] tomillo *m*
thy·roid gland [ˈθaɪrɔɪdɡlænd] (glándula *f*) tiroides *m inv*
tick [tɪk] **1** *n of clock* tictac *m; in text* señal *f* de visto bueno **2** *v/i of clock* hacer tictac
'**tick·et** [ˈtɪkɪt] *for bus, train, lottery* billete *m*, *L.Am.* boleto *m; for airplane* billete *m*, *L.Am.* pasaje *m; for theater, concert, museum* entrada *f*, *L.Am.* boleto *m; for speeding etc* multa *f*
'**tick·et col·lec·tor** revisor(a) *m(f)*
'**tick·et in·spec·tor** revisor(a) *m(f)*
'**tick·et ma·chine** máquina *f* expendedora de billetes
'**ti okot of·fice** *at station* mostrador *m* de venta de billetes; THEA taquilla *f*, *L.Am.* boletería *f*
tick·ing [ˈtɪkɪŋ] *noise* tictac *m*
tick·le [ˈtɪkl] **1** *v/t person* hacer cosquillas a **2** *v/i of material* hacer cosquillas; ***stop that, you're tickling!*** ¡para ya, me haces cosquillas!
tickl·ish [ˈtɪklɪʃ] *adj person* tener cosquillas
ti·dal wave [ˈtaɪdlweɪv] maremoto *m* (*ola*)
tide [taɪd] marea *f*; ***high tide*** marea alta; ***low tide*** marea baja; ***the tide is in / out*** la marea está alta / baja
◆ **tide over** *v/t*: ***20 dollars will tide me over*** 20 dólares me bastarán
ti·di·ness [ˈtaɪdɪnɪs] orden *m*
ti·dy [ˈtaɪdɪ] *adj* ordenado
◆ **tidy away** *v/t* (*pret & pp* **tidied**) guardar
◆ **tidy up 1** *v/t room, shelves* ordenar; ***tidy o.s. up*** arreglarse **2** *v/i* recoger
tie [taɪ] **1** *n* (*necktie*) corbata *f*; SP (*even result*) empate *m*; ***he doesn't have any***

T

ties no está atado a nada **2** v/t *knot* hacer, atar; *hands* atar; **tie two ropes together** atar dos cuerdas **3** v/i empatar
◆ **tie down** v/t *also fig* atar
◆ **tie up** v/t *person, laces* atar; *boat* amarrar; *hair* recoger; **I'm tied up tomorrow** (*busy*) mañana estaré muy ocupado

tier [tɪr] *of hierarchy* nivel m; *in stadium* grada f

ti·ger ['taɪɡər] tigre m

tight [taɪt] **1** *adj clothes* ajustado, estrecho; *security* estricto; (*hard to move*) apretado; (*properly shut*) cerrado; (*not leaving much time*) justo de tiempo; **F** (*drunk*) como una cuba **F 2** *adv hold* fuerte; *shut* bien

tight·en ['taɪtn] v/t *screw* apretar; *control* endurecer; *security* intensificar; **tighten one's grip on sth** *on rope etc* asir algo con más fuerza; *on power etc* incrementar el control sobre algo
◆ **tighten up** v/i in *discipline, security* ser más estricto

tight-fist·ed [taɪt'fɪstɪd] *adj* agarrado
tight·ly ['taɪtlɪ] *adv* → **tight**
tight·rope ['taɪtroʊp] cuerda f floja
tights [taɪts] *npl Br* medias *fpl*, pantis *mpl*
tile [taɪl] *on floor* baldosa f; *on wall* azulejo m; *on roof* teja f
till[1] [tɪl] → **until**
till[2] [tɪl] *n* (*cash register*) caja f (registradora)
till[3] [tɪl] v/t *soil* labrar
tilt [tɪlt] **1** v/t inclinar **2** v/i inclinarse
tim·ber ['tɪmbər] madera f (de construcción)
time [taɪm] tiempo m; (*occasion*) vez f; **time is up** se acabó (el tiempo); **for the time being** por ahora, por el momento; **have a good time** pasarlo bien; **have a good time!** ¡que lo paséis bien!; **what's the time?, do you have the time?** ¿qué hora es?; **the first time** la primera vez; **four times** cuatro veces; **time and again** una y otra vez; **all the time** todo el rato; **two / three at a time** de dos en dos / de tres en tres; **at the same time** *speak, reply etc* a la vez; (*however*) al mismo tiempo; **in time** con tiempo; **on time** puntual; **in no time** en un santiamén
time bomb bomba f de relojería
time clock *in factory* reloj m registrador
time-con·sum·ing *adj* que lleva mucho tiempo
time dif·fer·ence diferencia f horaria
time-lag intervalo m
time lim·it plazo m
time·ly ['taɪmlɪ] *adj* oportuno
time out SP tiempo m muerto

tim·er ['taɪmər] *device* temporizador m; *person* cronometrador m
time-sav·ing *n* ahorro m de tiempo
time-scale *of project* plazo m (de tiempo)
time switch temporizador m
time-warp salto m en el tiempo
time zone huso m horario
tim·id ['tɪmɪd] *adj* tímido
tim·ing ['taɪmɪŋ] *of dancer* sincronización f; *of actor* utilización f de las pausas y del ritmo; **the timing of the announcement was perfect** el anuncio fue realizado en el momento perfecto
tin [tɪn] *metal* estaño m; *Br* (*can*) lata f
tin-foil ['tɪnfɔɪl] papel m de aluminio
tinge [tɪndʒ] *n of color, sadness* matiz m
tin·gle ['tɪŋɡl] *n* hormigueo m
◆ **tin·ker with** ['tɪŋkər] v/t enredar con
tin·kle ['tɪŋkl] *n of bell* tintineo m
tin·sel ['tɪnsl] espumillón m
tint [tɪnt] **1** *n of color* matiz m; *in hair* tinte m **2** v/t *hair* teñir
tint·ed ['tɪntɪd] *glasses* con un tinte; *paper* coloreado
ti·ny ['taɪnɪ] *adj* diminuto, minúsculo
tip[1] [tɪp] *n of stick, finger* punta f; *of mountain* cumbre f; *of cigarette* filtro m
tip[2] [tɪp] **1** *n advice* consejo m; *money* propina f **2** v/t (*pret & pp* **tipped**) *waiter etc* dar propina a
◆ **tip off** v/t avisar
◆ **tip over** v/t *jug* volcar; *liquid* derramar; **he tipped water all over me** derramó agua encima mío
tip-off soplo m
tipped [tɪpt] *adj cigarettes* con filtro
Tipp-Ex® *n* Tipp-Ex m
tip·py·toe ['tɪpɪtoʊ]: **on tippy-toe** de puntillas
tip·sy ['tɪpsɪ] *adj* achispado
tire[1] [taɪr] *n* neumático m, *L.Am.* llanta f
tire[2] [taɪr] **1** v/t cansar, fatigar **2** v/i cansarse, fatigarse; **he never tires of telling the story** nunca se cansa de contar la historia
tired [taɪrd] *adj* cansado, fatigado; **be tired of s.o./sth** estar cansado de algo / de alguien
tired·ness ['taɪrdnɪs] cansancio m, fatiga f
tire·less ['taɪrlɪs] *adj efforts* incansable, infatigable
tire·some ['taɪrsəm] *adj* (*annoying*) pesado
tir·ing ['taɪrɪŋ] *adj* agotador
tis·sue ['tɪʃuː] ANAT tejido m; (*handkerchief*) pañuelo m de papel, Kleenex® m
tis·sue pa·per papel m de seda
tit[1] [tɪt] *bird* herrerillo m

tit² [tɪt]: **give s.o. tit for tat** pagar a alguien con la misma moneda

tit³ [tɪt] V (*breast*) teta *f* V

ti·tle ['taɪtl] *of novel, person etc* título *m*; LAW título *m* de propiedad

'tit·tle·hold·er SP campeón(-ona) *m(f)*

tit·ter ['tɪtər] *v/i* reírse tontamente

to [tu:] *unstressed* [tə] **1** *prep* a; **to Japan / Chicago** a Japón / Chicago; **let's go to my place** vamos a mi casa; **walk to the station** camina a la estación; **to the north / south of ...** al norte / sur de ...; **give sth to s.o.** dar algo a alguien; **from Monday to Wednesday** de lunes a miércoles; **from 10 to 15 people** de 10 a 15 personas **2** *with verbs*: **to speak, to shout** hablar, chillar; **learn to swim** aprender a nadar; **nice to eat** sabroso; **too heavy to carry** demasiado pesado para llevarlo; **to be honest with you ...** para ser sincero ... **3** *adv*: **to and fro** de un lado para otro

toad [toʊd] sapo *m*

toad·stool ['toʊdstuːl] seta *f* venenosa

toast [toʊst] **1** *n* pan *m* tostado; *drinking* brindis *m inv*; **propose a toast to s.o.** proponer un brindis en honor de alguien **2** *v/t drinking* brindar por

toast·er ['toʊstər] tostador(a) *m(f)*

to·bac·co [tə'bækoʊ] tabaco *m*

to·bog·gan [tə'baːgən] *n* tobogán *m*

to·day [tə'deɪ] hoy

tod·dle ['taːdl] *v/i of child* dar los primeros pasos

tod·dler ['taːdlər] niño *m* pequeño

to do [tə'duː] F revuelo *m*

toe [toʊ] **1** *n* dedo *m* del pie; *of shoe* puntera *f* **2** *v/t*: **toe the line** acatar la disciplina

toe·nail ['toʊneɪl] uña *f* del pie

to·geth·er [tə'geðər] *adv* juntos(-as); **mix two drinks together** mezclar dos bebidas; **don't all talk together** no hablen todos a la vez

toil [tɔɪl] *n* esfuerzo *m*

toi·let ['tɔɪlɪt] *place* cuarto *m* de baño, servicio *m*; *equipment* retrete *m*; **go to the toilet** ir al baño

'toi·let pa·per papel *m* higiénico

toi·let·ries ['tɔɪlɪtrɪz] *npl* artículos *mpl* de tocador

'toi·let roll rollo *m* de papel higiénico

to·ken ['toʊkən] (*sign*) muestra *f*; *for gambling* ficha *f*; (*gift token*) vale *m*

told [toʊld] *pret & pp* → **tell**

tol·er·a·ble ['taːlərəbl] *adj pain etc* soportable; (*quite good*) aceptable

tol·er·ance ['taːlərəns] tolerancia *f*

tol·er·ant ['taːlərənt] *adj* tolerante

tol·er·ate ['taːləreɪt] *v/t noise, person* tolerar; **I won't tolerate it!** ¡no lo toleraré!

toll¹ [toʊl] *v/i of bell* tañer

toll² [toʊl] *n* (*deaths*) mortandad *f*, número *m* de víctimas

toll³ [toʊl] *n for bridge, road* peaje *m*; TELEC tarifa *f*

'toll booth cabina *f* de peaje

'toll-free *adj* TELEC gratuito

'toll road carretera *f* de peaje

to·ma·to [tə'meɪtoʊ] tomate *m*, *Mex* jitomate *m*

to·ma·to 'ketch·up ketchup *m*

to·ma·to 'sauce *for pasta etc* salsa *f* de tomate

tomb [tuːm] tumba *f*

tom·boy ['taːmbɔɪ] niña *f* poco femenina

'tomb·stone ['tuːmstoʊn] lápida *f*

tom·cat ['taːmkæt] gato *m*

to·mor·row [tə'mɔːroʊ] mañana; **the day after tomorrow** pasado mañana; **tomorrow morning** mañana por la mañana

ton [tʌn] tonelada *f* (*907 kg*)

tone [toʊn] *of color, conversation* tono *m*; *of musical instrument* timbre *m*; *of neighborhood* nivel *m*; **tone of voice** tono *m* de voz

◆ **tone down** *v/t demands, criticism* bajar el tono de

ton·er ['toʊnər] tóner *m*

tongs [taːnz] *npl* tenazas *fpl*; *for hair* tenacillas *fpl* de rizar

tongue [tʌn] *n* lengua *f*

ton·ic ['taːnɪk] MED tónico *m*

'ton·ic (wa·ter) (agua *f*) tónica *f*

to·night [tə'naɪt] esta noche

ton·sil ['taːnsl] amígdala *f*

ton·sil·li·tis [taːnsəˈlaɪtɪs] amigdalitis *f*

too [tuː] *adv* (*also*) también; (*excessively*) demasiado; **me too** yo también; **too big / hot** demasiado grande / caliente; **too much rice** demasiado arroz; **eat too much** comer demasiado

took [tʊk] *pret* → **take**

tool [tuːl] herramienta *f*

toot [tuːt] *v/t* F tocar

tooth [tuːθ] (*pl teeth* [tiːθ]) diente *m*

'tooth·ache dolor *m* de muelas

'tooth·brush cepillo *m* de dientes

'tooth·less ['tuːθlɪs] *adj* desdentado

'tooth·paste pasta *f* de dientes, dentífrico *m*

'tooth·pick palillo *m*

top [taːp] **1** *n of mountain* cima *f*; *of tree* copa *f*; *of wall, screen, page* parte *f* superior; (*lid: of bottle etc*) tapón *m*; *of pen* capucha *f*; *clothing* camiseta *f*, top *m*; (MOT: *gear*) directa *f*; **on top of** encima de, sobre; **at the top of the page** en la

T

parte superior de la página; **at the top of the mountain** en la cumbre; **the top of the class / league** person, team ser el primero de la clase / de la liga; **get to the top** of company, mountain llegar a la cumbre; of mountain; **be over the top** (exaggerated) ser una exageración **2** adj branches superior; **floor** de arriba, último; management, official alto; player mejor; speed, note máximo **3** v/t (pret & pp **topped**): **topped with ...** of cake etc con una capa de ... por encima

◆ **top up** v/t glass, tank llenar

top 'hat sombrero m de copa

top 'heav·y adj sobrecargado en la parte superior

top·ic ['tɑːpɪk] tema m

top·ic·al ['tɑːpɪkl] adj de actualidad

top·less ['tɑːplɪs] adj en topless

top·most ['tɑːpmoʊst] adj branches, floor superior

top·ping ['tɑːpɪŋ] on pizza ingrediente m

top·ple ['tɑːpl] **1** v/i derrumbarse **2** v/t government derrocar

top 'se·cret adj altamente confidencial

top·sy·tur·vy [tɑːpsɪ'tɜːrvɪ] adj (in disorder) desordenado; world al revés

torch [tɔːrtʃ] with flame antorcha f

tore [tɔːr] pret → **tear¹**

tor·ment **1** n ['tɔːrment] tormento m **2** v/t [tɔːr'ment] person, animal atormentar; **tormented by doubt** atormentado por la duda

torn [tɔːrn] pp → **tear¹**

tor·na·do [tɔːr'neɪdoʊ] tornado m

tor·pe·do [tɔːr'piːdoʊ] **1** n torpedo m also fig torpedear

tor·rent ['tɑːrənt] also fig torrente m; of lava colada f

tor·ren·tial [tə'renʃl] adj rain torrencial

tor·toise ['tɔːrtəs] tortuga f

tor·ture ['tɔːrtʃər] **1** n tortura f **2** v/t torturar

toss [tɑːs] **1** v/t ball lanzar, echar; rider desmontar; salad remover; **toss a coin** echar a cara o cruz **2** v/i: **toss and turn** dar vueltas

to·tal ['toʊtl] **1** n total m **2** adj sum, amount total; disaster rotundo, completo; idiot de tomo y lomo; stranger completo **3** v/t F car cargarse F; **the truck was totaled** el camión quedó destrozado

to·tal·i·tar·i·an [toʊtælɪ'terɪən] adj totalitario

to·tal·ly ['toʊtəlɪ] adv totalmente

tote bag ['toʊtbæg] bolsa f grande

tot·ter ['tɑːtər] v/i of person tambalearse

touch [tʌtʃ] **1** n toque m; sense tacto m; **lose touch with s.o.** perder el contacto

con alguien; **keep in touch with s.o.** mantenerse en contacto con alguien; **we kept in touch** seguimos en contacto; **be out of touch** no estar al corriente; **the leader was out of touch with the people** el líder estaba desconectado de lo que pensaba la gente; **in touch** SP fuera **2** v/t tocar; emotionally conmover **3** v/i tocar; of two lines etc tocarse

◆ **touch down** v/i of airplane aterrizar; SP marca un ensayo

◆ **touch on** v/t (mention) tocar, mencionar

◆ **touch up** v/t photo retocar; sexually manosear

touch·down ['tʌtʃdaʊn] of airplane aterrizaje m; SP touchdown m, ensayo m

touch·ing ['tʌtʃɪŋ] adj conmovedor

touch·line ['tʌtʃlaɪn] SP línea f de banda

'touch screen pantalla f táctil

touch·y ['tʌtʃɪ] adj person susceptible

tough [tʌf] adj person, meat, punishment duro; question, exam difícil; material resistente, fuerte

◆ **tough·en up** ['tʌfn] v/t person hacer más fuerte

'tough guy F tipo m duro F

tour [tʊr] **1** n of museum etc recorrido m; of area viaje m (**of** por); of band ecc gira f **2** v/t area recorrer **3** v/i of band etc estar de gira

'tour guide guía m/f turístico(-a)

tour·i·sm ['tʊrɪzm] turismo m

tour·i·st ['tʊrɪst] turista m/f

'tour·ist at·trac·tion atracción f turística

'tour·ist in·dus·try industria f turística

'tour·ist (in·for·ma·tion) of·fice oficina f de turismo

'tour·ist sea·son temporada f turística

tour·na·ment ['tʊrnəmənt] torneo m

'tour op·er·a·tor operador m turístico

tous·led ['taʊzld] adj hair revuelto

tow [toʊ] **1** v/t car, boat remolcar **2** n: **give s.o. a tow** remolcar a alguien

◆ **tow away** v/t car llevarse

to·ward [tɔːrd] prep hacia; **we are working toward a solution** estamos intentando encontrar una solución

tow·el ['taʊəl] toalla f

tow·er ['taʊər] n torre m

◆ **tower over** v/t of building elevarse por encima de; of person ser mucho más alto que

town [taʊn] ciudad f

town 'cen·ter centro m de la ciudad / del pueblo

town 'coun·cil ayuntamiento m

town 'hall ayuntamiento m

'tow·rope cuerda f para remolcar

tox·ic ['tɒksɪk] *adj* tóxico
tox·ic 'waste residuos *mpl* tóxicos
tox·in ['tɒksɪn] BIO toxina *f*
toy [tɔɪ] juguete *m*
'toy store juguetería *f*, tienda *f* de juguetes
◆ **toy with** *v/t object* juguetear con; *idea* darle vueltas a

trace [treɪs] **1** *n of substance* resto *m* **2** *v/t (find)* seguir el rastro a; *(follow: footsteps of)* seguir el rastro a; *(draw)* trazar
track [træk] *n (path)* senda *f*, camino *m*; *for horses* hipódromo *m*; *for cars* circuito *m*; *for athletics* pista *f*; *on CD* canción *f*, corte *m*; RAIL vía *f*; **track 10** RAIL vía 10; **keep track of sth** llevar la cuenta de algo
◆ **track down** *v/t* localizar
'track·suit chándal *m*
trac·tor ['træktər] tractor *m*
trade [treɪd] **1** *n (commerce)* comercio *m*; *(profession, craft)* oficio *m* **2** *v/i (do business)* comerciar; **trade in sth** comerciar en algo **3** *v/t (exchange)* intercambiar; **trade sth for sth** intercambiar algo por algo
◆ **trade in** *v/t when buying* entregar como parte del pago
'trade fair feria *f* de muestras
'trade·mark marca *f* registrada
'trade mis·sion misión *f* comercial
trad·er ['treɪdər] comerciante *m*
trade 'se·cret secreto *m* de la casa, secreto *m* comercial
trades·man ['treɪdzmən] *(plumber etc)* electricista, fontanero / plomero *etc*
tra·di·tion [trə'dɪʃn] tradición *f*
tra·di·tion·al [trə'dɪʃnl] *adj* tradicional
tra·di·tion·al·ly [trə'dɪʃnlɪ] *adv* tradicionalmente
traf·fic ['træfɪk] *n on roads, in drugs* tráfico *m*
◆ **traffic in** *v/t (pret & pp trafficked) drugs* traficar con
'traf·fic cir·cle rotonda *f*, *Span* glorieta *f*
'traf·fic cop F poli *m* de tráfico F
'traf·fic is·land isleta *f*
'traf·fic jam atasco *m*
'traf·fic light semáforo *m*
'traf·fic po·lice policía *f* de tráfico
'traf·fic sign señal *f* de tráfico
tra·ge·dy ['trædʒədɪ] tragedia *f*
tra·gic ['trædʒɪk] *adj* trágico
trail [treɪl] **1** *n (path)* camino *m*, senda *f*; *of blood* rastro *m* **2** *v/t (follow)* seguir la pista de; *(tow)* arrastrar **3** *v/i (lag behind)* ir a la zaga
trail·er ['treɪlər] *pulled by vehicle* remolque *m*; *(mobile home)* caravana *f*; *of film*

avance *m*, tráiler *m*
train[1] [treɪn] *n* tren *m*; **go by train** ir en tren
train[2] [treɪn] **1** *v/t team, athlete* entrenar; *employee* formar; *dog* adiestrar **2** *v/i of team, athlete* entrenarse; *of teacher etc* formarse
train·ee [treɪ'niː] aprendiz(a) *m(f)*
train·er ['treɪnər] SP entrenador(a) *m(f)*; *of dog* adiestrador(a) *m(f)*
train·ers ['treɪnərz] *npl Br shoes* zapatillas *fpl* de deporte
train·ing ['treɪnɪŋ] *of new staff* formación *f*; SP entrenamiento *m*; **be in training** SP estar entrenándose; **be out of training** SP estar desentrenado
'train·ing course cursillo *m* de formación
'train·ing scheme plan *m* de formación
'train sta·tion estación *f* de tren
trait [treɪt] rasgo *m*
trai·tor ['treɪtər] traidor(a) *m(f)*
tramp [træmp] **1** *n (vagabond)* vagabundo(-a) *m(f)* **2** *v/i* caminar con pasos pesados
tram·ple ['træmpl] *v/t* pisotear; **be trampled to death** morir pisoteado; **be trampled underfoot** ser pisoteado
◆ **trample on** *v/t person, object* pisotear
tram·po·line ['træmpəliːn] cama *f* elástica
trance [trɑːns] trance *m*; **go into a trance** entrar en trance
tran·quil ['træŋkwɪl] *adj* tranquilo
tran·quil·i·ty [træŋ'kwɪlətɪ] tranquilidad *f*
tran·quil·iz·er ['træŋkwɪlaɪzər] tranquilizante *m*
trans·act [træn'zækt] *v/t deal* negociar
trans·ac·tion [træn'zækʃn] *action* transacción *f*; *deal* negociación *f*
trans·at·lan·tic [trænzət'læntɪk] *adj* transatlántico
tran·scen·den·tal [trænsen'dentl] *adj* trascendental
tran·script ['trænskrɪpt] transcripción *f*
trans·fer 1 *v/t* [træns'fɜːr] *(pret & pp transferred)* transferir **2** *v/i (pret & pp transferred) in traveling* hacer transbordo; *from one language to another* pasar **3** *n* ['trænsfɜːr] transferencia *f*; *in travel* transbordo *m*; *of money* transferencia *f*
trans·fer·a·ble [træns'fɜːrəbl] *adj ticket* transferible
'trans·fer fee *for football player* traspaso *m*
trans·form [træns'fɔːrm] *v/t* transformar
trans·form·a·tion [trænsfər'meɪʃn] transformación *f*
trans·form·er [træns'fɔːrmər] ELEC transformador *m*
trans·fu·sion [træns'fjuːʒn] transfusión *f*

tran·sis·tor [træn'zıstər] transistor *m*; *(radio)* transistor *m*, radio *m* transistor

tran·sit ['trænzıt]: *in transit* en tránsito

tran·si·tion [træn'sıʒn] transición *f*

tran·si·tion·al [træn'sıʒnl] *adj* de transición

'tran·sit lounge *at airport* sala *f* de tránsito

'trans·it pas·sen·ger pasajero *m* en tránsito

trans·late [træns'leɪt] *v/t & v/i* traducir

trans·la·tion [træns'leɪʃn] traducción *f*

trans·la·tor [træns'leɪtər] traductor(a) *m(f)*

trans·mis·sion [trænz'mɪʃn] *of news, program* emisión *f*; *of disease* transmisión *f*; MOT transmisión *f*

trans·mit [trænz'mɪt] *v/t* (*pret & pp* **transmitted**) *news, program* emitir; *disease* transmitir

trans·mit·ter [trænz'mɪtər] *for radio, TV* emisora *f*

trans·par·en·cy [træns'pærənsɪ] PHOT diapositiva *f*

trans·par·ent [træns'pærənt] *adj* transparente; *(obvious)* obvio

trans·plant *v/t* [træns'plænt] MED transplantar **2** *n* ['trænsplænt] MED transplante *m*

trans·port 1 *v/t* [træn'spɔːrt] *goods, people* transportar **2** *n* ['trænspɔːrt] *of goods, people* transporte *m*

trans·por·ta·tion [trænspɔːr'teɪʃn] *of goods, people* transporte *m*; *means of transportation* medio *m* de transporte; *public transportation* transporte *m* público; *Department of Transportation* Ministerio *m* de Transporte

trans·ves·tite [træns'vestaɪt] travestí *m*, travestido *m*

trap [træp] **1** *n* trampa *f*; *set a trap for s.o.* tender una trampa a alguien **2** *v/t* (*pret & pp* **trapped**) atrapar; *be trapped by enemy, flames, landslide etc* quedar atrapado

trap·door ['træpdɔːr] trampilla *f*

tra·peze [trə'piːz] trapecio *m*

trap·pings ['træpɪŋz] *npl of power* parafernalia *f*

trash [træʃ] *(garbage)* basura *f*; *(poor product)* bazofia *f*; *(despicable person)* escoria *f*

trash·can ['træʃkæn] cubo *m* de la basura

trash·y ['træʃɪ] *adj goods, novel* barato

trau·mat·ic [trə'mætɪk] *adj* traumático

trau·ma·tize ['trɔːmətaɪz] *v/t* traumatizar

trav·el ['trævl] **1** *n* viajes *mpl*; *do you like travel?* ¿te gusta viajar?; *on my travels* en mis viajes **2** *v/i* (*pret & pp* **traveled**, *Br*

travelled) viajar **3** *v/t miles* viajar, recorrer

'trav·el a·gen·cy agencia *f* de viajes

'trav·el a·gent agente *m* de viajes

'trav·el bag bolsa *f* de viaje

trav·el·er, *Br* **trav·el·ler** ['trævələr] viajero(-a) *m(f)*

'trav·el·er's check, *Br* **'trav·el·ler's cheque** cheque *m* de viaje

'trav·el ex·pen·ses *npl* gastos *mpl* de viaje

'trav·el in·sur·ance seguro *m* de asistencia en viaje

'trav·el pro·gram, *Br* **'trav·el pro·gramme** *on TV etc* programa *m* de viajes

'trav·el·sick *adj* mareado

trawl·er ['trɔːlər] (barco *m*) arrastrero *m*

tray [treɪ] bandeja *f*

treach·er·ous ['tretʃərəs] *adj* traicionero

treach·er·y ['tretʃərɪ] traición *f*

tread [tred] **1** *n* pasos *mpl*; *of staircase* huella *f* (del peldaño); *of tyre* dibujo *m* **2** *v/i* (*pret* **trod**, *pp* **trodden**) andar; *mind where you tread* cuida dónde pisas

♦ **tread on** *v/t s.o.'s foot* pisar

trea·son ['triːzn] traición *f*

trea·sure ['treʒər] **1** *n* tesoro *m*; *person* tesoro *m* **2** *v/t gift etc* apreciar mucho

trea·sur·er ['treʒərər] tesorero(-a) *m(f)*

Trea·su·ry De·part·ment ['treʒərɪ] Ministerio *m* de Hacienda

treat [triːt] **1** *n* placer *m*; *it was a real treat* fue un auténtico placer; *I have a treat for you* tengo una sorpresa agradable para ti; *it's my treat* (*I'm paying*) yo invito **2** *v/t* tratar; *treat s.o. to sth* invitar a alguien a algo

treat·ment ['triːtmənt] tratamiento *m*

treat·y ['triːtɪ] tratado *m*

tre·ble¹ ['trebl] *n* MUS soprano *m*

tre·ble² ['trebl] **1** *adv*: *treble the price* el triple del precio **2** *v/i* triplicarse

tree [triː] árbol *m*

trem·ble ['trembl] *v/i* temblar

tre·men·dous [trɪ'mendəs] *adj* (*very good*) estupendo; (*enormous*) enorme

tre·men·dous·ly [trɪ'mendəslɪ] *adv* (*very*) tremendamente; (*a lot*) enormemente

trem·or ['tremər] *of earth* temblor *m*

trench [trentʃ] trinchera *f*

trend [trend] tendencia *f*; (*fashion*) moda *f*

trend·y ['trendɪ] *adj* de moda; *views* moderno

tres·pass ['trespæs] *v/i* entrar sin autorización; *no trespassing* prohibido el paso

♦ **trespass on** *v/t s.o.'s land* entrar sin autorización en; *s.o.'s privacy* entrometerse en

tres·pass·er ['trespæsər] intruso(-a) *m(f)*

tri·al ['traɪəl] LAW juicio *m*; *of equipment* prueba *f*; *be on trial* LAW estar siendo juzgado; *have sth on trial equipment* tener algo a prueba

tri·al 'pe·ri·od periodo *m* de prueba
tri·an·gle ['traɪæŋgl] triángulo *m*
tri·an·gu·lar [traɪ'æŋgjʊlər] *adj* triangular

tribe [traɪb] tribu *f*
tri·bu·nal [traɪ'bjuːnl] tribunal *m*
tri·bu·ta·ry ['trɪbjətərɪ] *of river* afluente *m*

trick [trɪk] **1** *n* (*to deceive, knack*) truco *m*; *play a trick on s.o.* gastar una broma a alguien **2** *v/t* engañar; *trick s.o. into doing sth* engañar a alguien para que haga algo

trick·e·ry ['trɪkərɪ] engaños *mpl*
trick·le ['trɪkl] **1** *n* hilo *m*, reguero *m*; *fig: of money* goteo *m* **2** *v/i* gotear, escurrir
trick·ster ['trɪkstər] embaucador(a) *m(f)*
trick·y ['trɪkɪ] *adj* (*difficult*) difícil
tri·cy·cle ['traɪsɪkl] triciclo *m*
tri·fle ['traɪfl] *n* (*triviality*) nadería *f*
tri·fling ['traɪflɪŋ] *adj* insignificante
trig·ger ['trɪgər] *n on gun* gatillo *m*; *on camcorder* disparador *m*
◆ **trigger off** *v/t* desencadenar
trim [trɪm] **1** *adj* (*neat*) muy cuidado; *figure* delgado **2** *v/t* (*pret & pp trimmed*) *hair, hedge* recortar; *budget, costs* recortar, reducir; (*decorate: dress*) adornar **3** *n* (*light cut*) recorte *m*; *just a trim, please to hairdresser* corto sólo las puntas, por favor; *in good trim* en buenas condiciones
trim·ming ['trɪmɪŋ] *on clothes* adorno *m*; *with all the trimmings dish* con la guarnición clásica; *car* con todos los extras
trin·ket ['trɪŋkɪt] baratija *f*
tri·o ['triːoʊ] MUS trío *m*
trip [trɪp] **1** *n* (*journey*) viaje *m* **2** *v/i* (*pret & pp tripped*) (*stumble*) tropezar **3** *v/t* (*pret & pp tripped*) (*make fall*) poner la zancadilla a
◆ **trip up 1** *v/t* (*make fall*) poner la zancadilla a; (*cause to go wrong*) confundir **2** *v/i* (*stumble*) tropezar; (*make a mistake*) equivocarse
tripe [traɪp] mondongo *m*, *Span* callos *mpl*
tri·ple ['trɪpl] → **treble²**
trip·lets ['trɪplɪts] *npl* trillizos *mpl*
tri·pod ['traɪpɑːd] PHOT trípode *m*
trite [traɪt] *adj* manido
tri·umph ['traɪʌmf] *n* triunfo *m*
triv·i·al ['trɪvɪəl] *adj* trivial
triv·i·al·i·ty [trɪvɪ'ælətɪ] trivialidad *f*

trod [trɑːd] *pret* → **tread**
trod·den ['trɑːdn] *pp* → **tread**
trol·ley ['trɑːlɪ] (*streetcar*) tranvía *f*
trol·ley·bus ['trɑːlɪbʌs] trolebús *m*
trom·bone [trɑːm'boʊn] trombón *m*
troops [truːps] *npl* tropas *fpl*
tro·phy ['troʊfɪ] trofeo *m*
trop·ic ['trɑːpɪk] trópico *m*
trop·i·cal ['trɑːpɪkl] *adj* tropical
trop·ics ['trɑːpɪks] *npl* trópicos *mpl*
trot [trɑːt] *v/i* (*pret & pp trotted*) trotar
trou·ble ['trʌbl] **1** *n* (*difficulties*) problema *m*, problemas *mpl*; (*inconvenience*) molestia *f*; (*disturbance*) conflicto *m*, desorden *m*; *go to a lot of trouble to do sth* complicarse mucho la vida para hacer algo; *no trouble!* no es molestia; *get into trouble* meterse en líos **2** *v/t* (*worry*) preocupar, inquietar; (*bother, disturb*) molestar

'trou·ble-free *adj* sin complicaciones
'trou·ble-mak·er alborotador(a) *m(f)*
'trou·ble-shoot·er (*mediator*) persona encargada de resolver problemas
'trou·ble-shoot·ing resolución *f* de problemas
trou·ble·some ['trʌblsəm] *adj* problemático
trou·sers ['traʊzərz] *npl* pantalones *mpl*
trout [traʊt] (*pl trout*) trucha *f*
tru·ant ['truːənt]: *play truant* hacer novillos, *Mex* irse de pinta, *S. Am.* hacer la rabona
truce [truːs] tregua *f*
truck [trʌk] camión *m*
'truck driv·er camionero(-a) *m(f)*
'truck farm huerta *f*
'truck farm·er horticultor(a) *m(f)*
'truck stop restaurante *m* de carretera
trudge [trʌdʒ] **1** *v/i* caminar fatigosamente **2** *n* caminata *f*
true [truː] *adj* verdadero, cierto; *friend, American* auténtico; *come true of hopes, dream* hacerse realidad
tru·ly ['truːlɪ] *adv* verdaderamente, realmente; *Yours truly* le saluda muy atentamente
trum·pet ['trʌmpɪt] trompeta *f*
trum·pet·er ['trʌmpɪtər] trompetista *m/f*
trunk [trʌŋk] *of tree, body* tronco *m*; *of elephant* trompa *f*; (*large case*) baúl *m*; *of car* maletero *m*, *C.Am.*, *Mex* cajuela *f*, *Rpl* baúl *m*
trunks [trʌŋks] *npl Br for swimming* bañador *m*
trust [trʌst] **1** *n* confianza *f*; FIN fondo *m* de inversión **2** *v/t* confiar en
trusted ['trʌstɪd] *adj* de confianza
trust·ee [trʌs'tiː] fideicomisario(-a) *m(f)*

T

trust·ful, trust·ing ['trʌstfʊl, 'trʌstɪŋ] adj confiado

trust·wor·thy ['trʌstwɜːrðɪ] adj de confianza

truth [truːθ] verdad f

truth·ful ['truːfəl] adj person sincero; account verdadero

try [traɪ] **1** v/t (pret & pp **tried**) probar; LAW juzgar; **try to do sth** intentar hacer algo, tratar de hacer algo **2** v/i (pret & pp **tried**): **he didn't even try** ni siquiera lo intentó; **you must try harder** debes esforzarte más **3** n intento m; **can I have a try?** of food ¿puedo probar?; at doing sth ¿puedo intentarlo?

◆ **try on** v/t clothes probar

◆ **try out** v/t new machine, new method probar

try·ing ['traɪɪŋ] adj (annoying) molesto, duro

T-shirt ['tiːʃɜːrt] camiseta f

tub [tʌb] (bath) bañera f, L.Am. tina f; for liquid cuba f; for yoghurt, ice cream envase m

tub·by ['tʌbɪ] adj rechoncho

tube [tuːb] tubo m

tube·less ['tuːblɪs] adj tire sin cámara de aire

tu·ber·cu·lo·sis [tuːbɜːrkjəˈloʊsɪs] tuberculosis f

tuck [tʌk] **1** n in dress pinza f **2** v/t (put) meter

◆ **tuck away** v/t (put away) guardar; F (eat quickly) zamparse F

◆ **tuck in 1** v/t children arropar; sheets remeter **2** v/i (start eating) ponerse a comer

◆ **tuck up** v/t sleeves etc remangar; **tuck s.o. up in bed** meter a alguien en la cama

Tues·day ['tuːzdeɪ] martes m inv

tuft [tʌft] of hair mechón m; of grass mata f

tug [tʌg] **1** n (pull) tirón m; NAUT remolcador m **2** v/t (pret & pp **tugged**) (pull) tirar de

tu·i·tion [tuːˈɪʃn] clases fpl

tu·lip ['tuːlɪp] tulipán m

tum·ble ['tʌmbl] v/i caer, caerse

tum·ble-down ['tʌmbldaʊn] adj destartalado

tum·ble-dry·er ['tʌmbldraɪər] secadora f

tum·bler ['tʌmblər] for drink vaso m; in circus acróbata m/f

tum·my ['tʌmɪ] F tripa f F, barriga f F

'tum·my ache dolor m de tripa or barriga

tu·mor ['tuːmər] tumor m

tu·mult ['tuːmʌlt] tumulto m

tu·mul·tu·ous [tuːˈmʌltʊəs] adj tumultuoso

tu·na ['tuːnə] atún m

tune [tuːn] **1** n melodía f; **be in tune** of instrument estar afinado; **sing in tune** cantar sin desafinar; **be out of tune** of singer desafinar; of instrument estar desafinado **2** v/t instrument afinar

◆ **tune in** v/t Radio, TV sintonizar

◆ **tune in to** v/t Radio, TV sintonizar (con)

◆ **tune up 1** v/i of orchestra, players afinar **2** v/t engine poner a punto

tune·ful ['tuːnfəl] adj melodioso

tun·er ['tuːnər] hi-fi sintonizador m

tune-up ['tuːnʌp] of engine puesta f a punto

tun·nel ['tʌnl] n túnel m

tur·bine ['tɜːrbaɪn] turbina f

tur·bu·lence ['tɜːrbjələns] in air travel turbulencia f

tur·bu·lent ['tɜːrbjələnt] adj turbulento

turf [tɜːrf] césped m; piece tepe m

Turk [tɜːrk] turco(-a) m(f)

Tur·key ['tɜːrkɪ] Turquía

tur·key ['tɜːrkɪ] pavo m

Turk·ish ['tɜːrkɪʃ] **1** adj turco **2** n language turco m

tur·moil ['tɜːrmɔɪl] desorden m, agitación f

turn [tɜːrn] **1** n (rotation) vuelta f; in road curva f; junction giro m; in vaudeville número m; **take turns in doing sth** turnarse para hacer algo; **it's my turn** me toca a mí; **it's not your turn yet** no te toca todavía; **take a turn at the wheel** turnarse para conducir or L.Am. manejar; **do s.o. a good turn** hacer un favor a alguien **2** v/t wheel girar; corner dar la vuelta a; **turn one's back on s.o.** dar la espalda a alguien **3** v/i of driver, car, wheel girar; of person: turn around volverse; **turn left / right here** gira aquí a la izquierda/a la derecha; **it has turned sour/cold** se ha cortado / enfriado; **it turned blue** se volvió or puso azul; **he has turned 40** ha cumplido cuarenta años

◆ **turn around 1** v/t object dar la vuelta a; company dar un vuelco a; (COM: deal with) procesar, preparar **2** v/i of person volverse, darse la vuelta; of driver dar la vuelta

◆ **turn away 1** v/t (send away) rechazar; **the doorman turned us away** el portero no nos dejó entrar **2** v/i (walk away) marcharse; (look away) desviar la mirada

◆ **turn back 1** v/t edges, sheets doblar **2** v/i of walkers etc volver; in course of action echarse atrás

◆ **turn down** v/t offer, invitation rechazar; volume, TV, heating bajar; edge, collar doblar

◆ **turn in 1** *v/i* (*go to bed*) irse a dormir **2** *v/t to police* entregar
◆ **turn off 1** *v/t* TV, *engine* apagar; *tap* cerrar; *heater* apagar; *it turns me off* F *sexually* me quita las ganas F **2** *v/i of car, driver* doblar
◆ **turn on 1** *v/t* TV, *engine, heating* encender, *L.Am.* prender; *tap* abrir; F *sexually* excitar F **2** *v/i of machine* encenderse, *L.Am.* prenderse
◆ **turn out 1** *v/t lights* apagar **2** *v/i: it turned out well* salió bien; *as it turned out* al final; *he turned out to be ...* resultó ser ...
◆ **turn over 1** *v/i in bed* darse la vuelta; *of vehicle* volcar, dar una vuelta de campana **2** *v/t* (*put upside down*) dar la vuelta a; *page* pasar; FIN facturar
◆ **turn up 1** *v/t collar* subirse; *volume, heating* subir **2** *v/i* (*arrive*) aparecer
turn·ing ['tɜːrnɪŋ] giro *m*
'**turn·ing point** punto *m* de inflexión
tur·nip ['tɜːrnɪp] nabo *m*
'**turn·out** *of people* asistencia *f*
'**turn·o·ver** FIN facturación *f*; *staff turnover* rotación *f* de personal
'**turn·pike** autopista *f* de peaje
'**turn sig·nal** *on car* intermitente *m*
'**turn·stile** torniquete *m* (de entrada)
'**turn·ta·ble** *of record player* plato *m*,
tur·quoise ['tɜːrkwɔɪz] *adj* turquesa
tur·ret ['tʌrɪt] *of castle* torrecilla *f*; *of tank* torreta *f*
tur·tle ['tɜːrtl] tortuga *f* (marina)
tur·tle·neck '**sweater** suéter *m* de cuello alto
tusk [tʌsk] colmillo *m*
tu·tor ['tuːtər] *at university* tutor *m*; (*private*) *tutor* profesor(a) *m(f)* particular
tu·xe·do [tʌk'siːdoʊ] esmoquin *m*
TV [tiː'viː] televisión *f*; *on TV* en la televisión
TV din·ner menú *m* precocinado
TV guide guía *f* televisiva
TV pro·gram programa *m* de televisión
twang [twæŋ] **1** *n in voice* entonación *f* nasal **2** *v/t guitar string* puntear
tweez·ers ['twiːzərz] *npl* pinzas *fpl*
twelfth [twelfθ] *n & adj* duodécimo
twelve [twelv] doce
twen·ti·eth ['twentɪɪθ] *n & adj* vigésimo
twen·ty ['twentɪ] veinte
twice [twaɪs] *adv* dos veces; *twice as*

much el doble
twid·dle ['twɪdl] *v/t* dar vueltas a; *twiddle one's thumbs* holgazanear
twig [twɪg] *n* ramita *f*
twi·light ['twaɪlaɪt] crepúsculo *m*
twin [twɪn] gemelo *m*
'**twin beds** *npl* camas *fpl* gemelas
twinge [twɪndʒ] *of pain* punzada *f*
twin·kle ['twɪŋkl] *v/i of stars* parpadeo *m*; *of eyes* brillo *m*
twin 'room habitación *f* con camas gemelas
'**twin town** ciudad *f* hermana
twirl [twɜːrl] **1** *v/t hacer girar* **2** *n of cream etc* voluta *f*
twist [twɪst] **1** *v/t* retorcer; *twist one's ankle* torcerse el tobillo **2** *v/i of road, river* serpentear **3** *n in rope, road* vuelta *f*; *in plot, story* giro *m* inesperado
twist·y ['twɪstɪ] *adj road* serpenteante
twit [twɪt] F memo(-a) *m(f)* F
twitch [twɪtʃ] **1** *n nervous* tic *m* **2** *v/i* (*jerk*) moverse (ligeramente)
twit·ter ['twɪtər] *v/i of birds* gorjear
two [tuː] dos; *the two of them* los dos, ambos
two-faced ['tuːfeɪst] *adj* falso
'**two-piece** (*woman's suit*) traje *m*
'**two-stroke** *adj engine* de dos tiempos
two-way '**traf·fic** tráfico *m* en dos direcciones
ty·coon [taɪ'kuːn] magnate *m*
type [taɪp] **1** *n* (*sort*) tipo *m*, clase *f*; *what type of ...?* ¿qué tipo *or* clase de ...? **2** *v/i* (*use a keyboard*) escribir a máquina **3** *v/t with a typewriter* mecanografiar, escribir a máquina
type·writ·er ['taɪpraɪtər] máquina *f* de escribir
ty·phoid ['taɪfɔɪd] fiebre *f* tifoidea
ty·phoon [taɪ'fuːn] tifón *m*
ty·phus ['taɪfəs] tifus *m*
typ·i·cal ['tɪpɪkl] *adj* típico; *that's typical of you / him!* ¡típico tuyo / de él!
typ·i·cal·ly ['tɪpɪklɪ] *adv* típicamente; *typically American* típicamente americano
typ·ist ['taɪpɪst] mecanógrafo(-a) *m(f)*
ty·ran·ni·cal [tɪ'rænɪkl] *adj* tiránico
ty·ran·nize ['tɪrənaɪz] *v/t* tiranizar
ty·ran·ny ['tɪrənɪ] tiranía *f*
ty·rant ['taɪrənt] tirano(-a) *m(f)*
tyre *Br* → **tire¹**

T

U

ug·ly [ˈʌglɪ] *adj* feo
UK [juːˈkeɪ] *abbr* (= **United Kingdom**) RU *m* (= Reino *m* Unido)
ul·cer [ˈʌlsər] úlcera *f*; *in mouth* llaga *f*
ul·ti·mate [ˈʌltɪmət] *adj* (*final*) final; (*basic*) esencial; *the ultimate car* (*best, definitive*) lo último en coches
ul·ti·mate·ly [ˈʌltɪmətlɪ] *adv* (*in the end*) en última instancia
ul·ti·ma·tum [ʌltɪˈmeɪtəm] ultimátum *m*
ul·tra·sound [ˈʌltrəsaʊnd] MED ultrasonido *m*; (*scan*) ecografía *f*
ul·tra·vi·o·let [ʌltrəˈvaɪələt] *adj* ultravioleta
um·bil·i·cal cord [ʌmˈbɪlɪkl] cordón *m* umbilical
um·brel·la [ʌmˈbrelə] paraguas *m inv*
um·pire [ˈʌmpaɪr] *n* árbitro *m*; *in tennis* juez *m/f* de silla
ump·teen [ʌmpˈtiːn] *adj* F miles de F
UN [juːˈen] *abbr* (= **United Nations**) ONU *f* (= Organización *f* de las Naciones Unidas)
un·a·ble [ʌnˈeɪbl] *adj*: *be unable to do sth* (*not know how to*) no saber hacer algo; (*not be in a position to*) no poder hacer algo
un·ac·cept·a·ble [ʌnəkˈseptəbl] *adj* inaceptable; *it is unacceptable that* es inaceptable que
un·ac·count·a·ble [ʌnəˈkaʊntəbl] *adj* inexplicable
un·ac·cus·tomed [ʌnəˈkʌstəmd] *adj*: *be unaccustomed to sth* no estar acostumbrado a algo
un·a·dul·ter·at·ed [ʌnəˈdʌltəreɪtɪd] *adj* (*fig: absolute*) absoluto
un·A·mer·i·can [ʌnəˈmerɪkən] *adj* poco americano; *activities* antiamericano
u·nan·i·mous [juːˈnænɪməs] *adj verdict* unánime; *be unanimous on* ser unánime respecto a
u·nan·i·mous·ly [juːˈnænɪməslɪ] *adv vote, decide* unánimemente
un·ap·proach·a·ble [ʌnəˈprəʊtʃəbl] *adj person* inaccesible
un·armed [ʌnˈɑːrmd] *adj person* desarmado; *unarmed combat* combate *m* sin armas
un·as·sum·ing [ʌnəˈsuːmɪŋ] *adj* sin pretensiones
un·at·tached [ʌnəˈtætʃt] *adj* (*without a partner*) sin compromiso, sin pareja
un·at·tend·ed [ʌnəˈtendɪd] *adj* desatendi-

do; *leave sth unattended* dejar algo desatendido
un·au·thor·ized [ʌnˈɔːθəraɪzd] *adj* no autorizado
un·a·void·a·ble [ʌnəˈvɔɪdəbl] *adj* inevitable
un·a·void·a·bly [ʌnəˈvɔɪdəblɪ] *adv*: *be unavoidably detained* entretenerse sin poder evitarlo
un·a·ware [ʌnəˈwer] *adj*: *be unaware of* no ser consciente de
un·a·wares [ʌnəˈwerz] *adv* desprevenido; *catch s.o. unawares* agarrar *or Span* coger a alguien desprevenido
un·bal·anced [ʌnˈbælənst] *adj also* PSYCH desequilibrado
un·bear·a·ble [ʌnˈberəbl] *adj* insoportable
un·beat·a·ble [ʌnˈbiːtəbl] *adj team* invencible; *quality* insuperable
un·beat·en [ʌnˈbiːtn] *adj team* invicto
un·be·knownst [ʌnbɪˈnəʊnst] *adj*: *unbeknownst to her* sin que ella lo supiera
un·be·liev·a·ble [ʌnbɪˈliːvəbl] *adj also* F increíble; *he's unbelievable* F (*very good / bad*) es increíble
un·bi·as·(s)ed [ʌnˈbaɪəst] *adj* imparcial
un·block [ʌnˈblɑːk] *v/t pipe* desatascar
un·born [ʌnˈbɔːrn] *adj* no nacido
un·break·a·ble [ʌnˈbreɪkəbl] *adj plates* irrompible; *world record* inalcanzable
un·but·ton [ʌnˈbʌtn] *v/t* desabotonar
un·called-for [ʌnˈkɔːldfɔːr] *adj*: *be uncalled-for* estar fuera de lugar
un·can·ny [ʌnˈkænɪ] *adj resemblance* increíble, asombroso; *skill* inexplicable; (*worrying: feeling*) extraño, raro
un·ceas·ing [ʌnˈsiːsɪŋ] *adj* incesante
un·cer·tain [ʌnˈsɜːrtn] *adj future, origins* incierto; *be uncertain about sth* no estar seguro de algo; *what will happen? - it's uncertain* ¿qué ocurrirá? - no se sabe
un·cer·tain·ty [ʌnˈsɜːrtntɪ] incertidumbre *f*; *there is still uncertainty about his health* todavía hay incertidumbre en torno a su estado de salud
un·checked [ʌnˈtʃekt] *adj*: *let sth go unchecked* no controlar algo
un·cle [ˈʌŋkl] tío *m*
un·com·for·ta·ble [ʌnˈkʌmftəbl] *adj chair, hotel* incómodo; *feel uncomfortable about sth* no estar tranquilo con su decisión etc sentirse incómodo con algo; *I feel uncomfortable with him* me siento incómodo

con él

un·com·mon [ʌnˈkɑːmən] *adj* poco corriente, raro; *it's not uncommon* no es raro *or* extraño

un·com·pro·mis·ing [ʌnˈkɑːmprəmaɪzɪŋ] *adj* inflexible

un·con·cerned [ʌnkənˈsɜːrnd] *adj* indiferente; *be unconcerned about s.o./sth* no preocuparse por alguien / algo

un·con·di·tion·al [ʌnkənˈdɪʃnl] *adj* incondicional

un·con·scious [ʌnˈkɑːnʃəs] *adj* MED, PSYCH inconsciente; *knock unconscious* dejar inconsciente; *be unconscious of sth* (*not aware*) no ser consciente de algo

un·con·trol·la·ble [ʌnkənˈtroʊləbl] *adj anger, children* incontrolable; *desire* incontrolable, irresistible

un·con·ven·tion·al [ʌnkənˈvenʃnl] *adj* poco convencional

un·co·op·er·a·tive [ʌnkoʊˈɑːpərətɪv] *adj*: *be uncooperative* no estar dispuesto a colaborar

un·cork [ʌnˈkɔːrk] *v/t bottle* descorchar

un·cov·er [ʌnˈkʌvər] *v/t remove cover from* destapar; *plot, ancient remains* descubrir

un·dam·aged [ʌnˈdæmɪdʒd] *adj* intacto

un·daunt·ed [ʌnˈdɔːntɪd] *adj* impertérrito; *carry on undaunted* seguir impertérrito

un·de·cid·ed [ʌndɪˈsaɪdɪd] *adj question* sin resolver; *be undecided about s.o./ sth* estar indeciso sobre / acerca de alguien / algo

un·de·ni·a·ble [ʌndɪˈnaɪəbl] *adj* innegable

un·de·ni·a·bly [ʌndɪˈnaɪəblɪ] *adv* innegablemente

un·der [ˈʌndər] **1** *prep* (*beneath*) debajo de, bajo; (*less than*) menos de; *under the water* bajo el agua; *it is under review / investigation* está siendo revisado / investigado **2** *adv* (*anesthetized*) anestesiado

un·der·age *adj*: *underage drinking* el consumo de alcohol por menores de edad

'un·der·arm *adv*: *throw a ball underarm* lanzar una pelota soltándola por debajo de la altura del hombro

'un·der·car·riage tren *m* de aterrizaje

'un·der·cov·er *adj agent* secreto

'un·der·cut *v/t* (*pret & pp undercut*) COM vender más barato que

'un·der·dog *n*: *support the underdog* apoyar al más débil

un·der·done *adj meat* poco hecho

un·der·es·ti·mate *v/t* subestimar

un·der·ex·posed *adj* PHOT subexpuesto

un·der·fed *adj* malnutrido

un·der·go *v/t* (*pret underwent, pp undergone*) *surgery, treatment* ser sometido a; *experiences* sufrir; *the hotel is undergoing refurbishment* se están efectuando renovaciones en el hotel

un·der·grad·u·ate *Br* estudiante *m/f* universitario(-a) (*todavía no licenciado(a)*)

'un·der·ground 1 *adj passages etc* subterráneo; POL *resistance, newpaper etc* clandestino **2** *adv work* bajo tierra; *go underground* POL pasar a la clandestinidad

'un·der·growth maleza *f*

'un·der·hand *adj* (*devious*) poco honrado

un·der·lie *v/t* (*pret underlay, pp underlain*) (*form basis of*) sostentar

un·der·line *v/t text* subrayar

un·der·ly·ing *adj causes, problems* subyacente

un·der·mine *v/t s.o.'s position, theory* minar, socavar

un·der·neath [ʌndərˈniːθ] **1** *prep* debajo de, bajo **2** *adv* debajo

'un·der·pants *npl* calzoncillos *mpl*

'un·der·pass *for pedestrians* paso *m* subterráneo

un·der·priv·i·leged [ʌndərˈprɪvɪlɪdʒd] *adj* desfavorecido

un·der·rate *v/t* subestimar, infravalorar

'un·der·shirt camiseta *f*

un·der·sized [ʌndərˈsaɪzd] *adj* demasiado pequeño

'un·der·skirt enaguas *fpl*

un·der·staffed [ʌndərˈstæft] *adj* sin suficiente personal

un·der·stand [ʌndərˈstænd] **1** *v/t* (*pret & pp understood*) entender, comprender; *language* entender; *I understand that you ...* tengo entendido que ...; *they are understood to be in Canada* se cree que están en Canadá **2** *v/i* (*pret & pp understood*) entender, comprender

un·der·stand·a·ble [ʌndərˈstændəbl] *adj* comprensible

un·der·stand·a·bly [ʌndərˈstændəblɪ] *adv* comprensiblemente

un·der·stand·ing [ʌndərˈstændɪŋ] **1** *adj person* comprensivo **2** *n* of *problem, situation* interpretación *f*; (*agreement*) acuerdo *m*; *on the understanding that ...* (*condition*) a condición de que ...

'un·der·state·ment *n*: *that's an understatement* ¡y te quedas corto!

un·der·take *v/t* (*pret undertook, pp undertaken*) *task* emprender; *undertake to do sth* (*agree to*) encargarse de hacer algo

U

un·der·tak·er [ˈʌndərˈteɪkər] *Br* encargado *m* de una funeraria

'un·der·tak·ing (*enterprise*) proyecto *m*, empresa *f*; *give an undertaking to do sth* comprometerse a hacer algo

un·der·val·ue *v/t* infravalorar

'un·der·wear ropa *f* interior

un·der·weight *adj*: *be underweight* pesar menos de lo normal

'un·der·world *criminal* hampa *f*; *in mythology* Hades *m*

un·der·write *v/t* (*pret* **underwrote**, *pp* **underwritten**) FIN asegurar, garantizar

un·de·served [ʌndɪˈzɜːrvd] *adj* inmerecido

un·de·sir·a·ble [ʌndɪˈzaɪrəbl] *adj* *features, changes* no deseado; *person* indeseable; *undesirable element person* persona *f* problemática

un·dis·put·ed [ʌndɪˈspjuːtɪd] *adj* *champion, leader* indiscutible

un·do [ʌnˈduː] *v/t* (*pret* **undid**, *pp* **undone**) *parcel, wrapping* abrir; *buttons, shirt* desabrochar; *shoelaces* desatar; *s.o. else's work* deshacer

un·doubt·ed·ly [ʌnˈdaʊtɪdlɪ] *adv* indudablemente

un·dreamt-of [ʌnˈdremtəv] *adj* *riches* inimaginable

un·dress [ʌnˈdres] **1** *v/t* desvestir, desnudar; *get undressed* desvestirse, desnudarse **2** *v/i* desvestirse, desnudarse

un·due [ʌnˈduː] *adj* (*excessive*) excesivo

un·du·ly [ʌnˈduːlɪ] *adv* *punished, blamed* injustamente; (*excessively*) excesivamente

un·earth [ʌnˈɜːrθ] *v/t* descubrir; *ancient remains* desenterrar

un·earth·ly [ʌnˈɜːrθlɪ] *adv*: *at this unearthly hour* a esta hora intempestiva

un·eas·y [ʌnˈiːzɪ] *adj* *relationship, peace* tenso; *feel uneasy about* estar inquieto por

un·eat·a·ble [ʌnˈiːtəbl] *adj* incomible

un·e·co·nom·ic [ʌniːkəˈnɑːmɪk] *adj* antieconómico, no rentable

un·ed·u·cat·ed [ʌnˈedʒəkeɪtɪd] *adj* inculto, sin educación

un·em·ployed [ʌnɪmˈplɔɪd] *adj* desempleado, *Span* parado

un·em·ploy·ment [ʌnɪmˈplɔɪmənt] desempleo *m*, *Span* paro *m*

un·end·ing [ʌnˈendɪŋ] *adj* interminable

un·e·qual [ʌnˈiːkwəl] *adj* desigual; *be unequal to the task* no estar a la altura de lo que requiere el trabajo

un·er·ring [ʌnˈerɪŋ] *adj* *judgment, instinct* infalible

un·e·ven [ʌnˈiːvn] *adj* *quality* desigual; *surface, ground* irregular

un·e·ven·ly [ʌnˈiːvnlɪ] *adv* *distributed, applied* de forma desigual; *be unevenly matched of two contestants* no estar en igualdad de condiciones

un·e·vent·ful [ʌnɪˈventfəl] *adj* *day, journey* sin incidentes

un·ex·pec·ted [ʌnɪkˈspektɪd] *adj* inesperado

un·ex·pec·ted·ly [ʌnɪkˈspektɪdlɪ] *adv* inesperadamente, de forma inesperada

un·fair [ʌnˈfer] *adj* injusto; *that's unfair* eso no es justo

un·faith·ful [ʌnˈfeɪθfəl] *adj* *husband, wife* infiel; *be unfaithful to s.o.* ser infiel a alguien

un·fa·mil·i·ar [ʌnfəˈmɪljər] *adj* desconocido, extraño; *be unfamiliar with sth* desconocer algo

un·fas·ten [ʌnˈfæsn] *v/t belt* desabrochar

un·fa·vo·ra·ble, *Br* **un·fa·vou·ra·ble** [ʌnˈfeɪvərəbl] *adj* desfavorable

un·feel·ing [ʌnˈfiːlɪŋ] *adj* *person* insensible

un·fin·ished [ʌnˈfɪnɪʃt] *adj* inacabado; *leave sth unfinished* dejar algo sin acabar

un·fit [ʌnˈfɪt] *adj*: *be unfit physically* estar en baja forma; *be unfit to eat* no ser apto para el consumo; *be unfit to drink* no ser potable; *he's unfit to be a parent* no tiene lo que se necesita para ser padre

un·fix [ʌnˈfɪks] *v/t* soltar, desmontar

un·flap·pa·ble [ʌnˈflæpəbl] *adj* F impasible

un·fold [ʌnˈfoʊld] **1** *v/t sheets, letter* desdoblar; *one's arms* descruzar **2** *v/i of story etc* desarrollarse; *of view* abrirse

un·fore·seen [ʌnfɔːrˈsiːn] *adj* imprevisto

un·for·get·ta·ble [ʌnfərˈgetəbl] *adj* inolvidable

un·for·giv·a·ble [ʌnfərˈgɪvəbl] *adj* imperdonable; *that was unforgivable of you* eso ha sido imperdonable

un·for·tu·nate [ʌnˈfɔːrtʃənət] *adj* *people* desafortunado; *event* desgraciado; *choice of words* desafortunado, desacertado; *that's unfortunate for you* has tenido muy mala suerte

un·for·tu·nate·ly [ʌnˈfɔːrtʃənətlɪ] *adv* desgraciadamente

un·found·ed [ʌnˈfaʊndɪd] *adj* infundado

un·friend·ly [ʌnˈfrendlɪ] *adj* *person* antipático; *place* desagradable; *welcome* hostil; *software* de difícil manejo

un·fur·nished [ʌnˈfɜːrnɪʃt] *adj* sin amueblar

un·god·ly [ʌnˈgɑːdlɪ] *adj*: *at this ungodly hour* a esta hora intempestiva

U

un·grate·ful [ʌnˈgreɪtfəl] *adj* desagradecido

un·hap·pi·ness [ʌnˈhæpɪnɪs] infelicidad *f*

un·hap·py [ʌnˈhæpɪ] *adj person, look* infeliz; *day* triste; *customer etc* descontento

un·harmed [ʌnˈhɑːrmd] *adj* ileso; *be unharmed* salir ileso

un·health·y [ʌnˈhelθɪ] *adj person* enfermizo; *conditions, food, economy* poco saludable

un·heard-of [ʌnˈhɜːrdɒv] *adj* inaudito

un·hurt [ʌnˈhɜːrt] *adj*: *be unhurt* salir ileso

un·hy·gi·en·ic [ʌnhaɪˈdʒiːnɪk] *adj* antihigiénico

u·ni·fi·ca·tion [juːnɪfɪˈkeɪʃn] unificación *f*

u·ni·form [ˈjuːnɪfɔːrm] 1 *n* uniforme *m* 2 *adj* uniforme

u·ni·fy [ˈjuːnɪfaɪ] *v/t* (*pret & pp* **unified**) unificar

u·ni·lat·e·ral [juːnɪˈlætərəl] *adj* unilateral

un·i·ma·gi·na·ble [ʌnɪˈmædʒɪnəbl] *adj* inimaginable

un·i·ma·gi·na·tive [ʌnɪˈmædʒɪnətɪv] *adj* sin imaginación

un·im·por·tant [ʌnɪmˈpɔːrtənt] *adj* poco importante

un·in·hab·i·ta·ble [ʌnɪnˈhæbɪtəbl] *adj* inhabitable

un·in·hab·it·ed [ʌnɪnˈhæbɪtɪd] *adj building* deshabitado; *region* desierto

un·in·jured [ʌnˈɪndʒərd] *adj*: *be uninjured* salir ileso

un·in·tel·li·gi·ble [ʌnɪnˈtelɪdʒəbl] *adj* ininteligible

un·in·ten·tion·al [ʌnɪnˈtenʃnl] *adj* no intencionado; *sorry, that was unintentional* lo siento, ha sido sin querer

un·in·ten·tion·al·ly [ʌnɪnˈtenʃɪlɪ] *adv* sin querer

un·in·te·rest·ing [ʌnˈɪntrəstɪŋ] *adj* sin interés

un·in·ter·rupt·ed [ʌnɪntəˈrʌptɪd] *adj sleep, two hours' work* ininterrumpido

u·nion [ˈjuːnjən] POL unión *f*; (*labor union*) sindicato *m*

u·nique [juːˈniːk] *adj* único

u·nit [ˈjuːnɪt] unidad *f*; *unit of measurement* unidad *f* de medida; *power unit* fuente *f* de alimentación

u·nit 'cost COM costo *m or Span* coste *m* unitario *or* por unidad

u·nite [juːˈnaɪt] 1 *v/t* unir 2 *v/i* unirse

u·nit·ed [juːˈnaɪtɪd] *adj* unido

U·nit·ed 'King·dom Reino *m* Unido

U·nit·ed 'Na·tions *fpl* Naciones Unidas

U·nit·ed 'States (of A'mer·i·ca) Estados *mpl* Unidos (de *América*)

u·ni·ty [ˈjuːnɪtɪ] unidad *f*

u·ni·ver·sal [juːnɪˈvɜːrsl] *adj* universal

u·ni·ver·sal·ly [juːnɪˈvɜːrsəlɪ] *adv* universalmente

u·ni·verse [ˈjuːnɪvɜːrs] universo *m*

u·ni·ver·si·ty [juːnɪˈvɜːrsətɪ] 1 *n* universidad *f*; *he is at university* está en la universidad 2 *adj* universitario

un·just [ʌnˈdʒʌst] *adj* injusto

un·kempt [ʌnˈkempt] *adj appearance* descuidado; *hair* revuelto

un·kind [ʌnˈkaɪnd] *adj* desgradable, cruel

un·known [ʌnˈnoʊn] 1 *adj* desconocido 2 *n*: *a journey into the unknown* un viaje hacia lo desconocido

un·lead·ed [ʌnˈledɪd] *adj* sin plomo

un·less [ənˈles] *conj* a menos que, a no ser que; *don't say anything unless you're sure* no digas nada a menos que *or* a no ser que estés seguro

un·like [ʌnˈlaɪk] *prep* (*not similar to*) diferente de; *it's unlike him to drink so much* él no suele beber tanto; *that photograph is so unlike you* has salido completamente diferente en esa fotografía

un·like·ly [ʌnˈlaɪklɪ] *adj* (*improbable*) improbable; *explanation* inverosímil; *he is unlikely to win* es improbable *or* poco probable que gane

un·lim·it·ed [ʌnˈlɪmɪtɪd] *adj* ilimitado

un·list·ed [ʌnˈlɪstɪd] *adj*: *be unlisted* no aparecer en la guía telefónica

un·load [ʌnˈloʊd] *v/t* descargar

un·lock [ʌnˈlɑːk] *v/t* abrir

un·luck·i·ly [ʌnˈlʌkɪlɪ] *adv* desgraciadamente, por desgracia

un·luck·y [ʌnˈlʌkɪ] *adj day, choice* aciago, funesto; *person* sin suerte; *that was so unlucky for you!* ¡qué mala suerte tuviste!

un·manned [ʌnˈmænd] *adj spacecraft* no tripulado

un·mar·ried [ʌnˈmærɪd] *adj* soltero

un·mis·ta·ka·ble [ʌnmɪˈsteɪkəbl] *adj* inconfundible

un·moved [ʌnˈmuːvd] *adj*: *he was unmoved by her tears* sus lágrimas no lo conmovieron

un·mu·si·cal [ʌnˈmjuːzɪkl] *adj person* sin talento musical; *sounds* estridente

un·nat·u·ral [ʌnˈnætʃrəl] *adj* anormal; *it's not unnatural to be annoyed* es normal estar enfadado

un·ne·ces·sa·ry [ʌnˈnesəserɪ] *adj* innecesario

un·nerv·ing [ʌnˈnɜːrvɪŋ] *adj* desconcertante

un·no·ticed [ʌnˈnoʊtɪst] *adj*: *it went un-*

noticed pasó desapercibido

un·ob·tain·a·ble [ʌnəb'teɪnəbl] *adj goods* no disponible; TELEC desconectado

un·ob·tru·sive [ʌnəb'truːsɪv] *adj* discreto

un·oc·cu·pied [ʌn'ɑːkjʊpaɪd] *adj building, house* desocupado; *post* vacante

un·of·fi·cial [ʌnə'fɪʃl] *adj* no oficial; *this is still unofficial but ...* esto todavía no es oficial, pero ...

un·of·fi·cial·ly [ʌnə'fɪʃlɪ] *adv* extraoficialmente

un·or·tho·dox [ʌn'ɔːrθədɑːks] *adj* poco ortodoxo

un·pack [ʌn'pæk] **1** *v/t* deshacer **2** *v/i* deshacer el equipaje

un·paid [ʌn'peɪd] *adj work* no remunerado

un·pleas·ant [ʌn'pleznt] *adj* desagradable; *he was very unpleasant to her* fue muy desagradable con ella

un·plug [ʌn'plʌg] *v/t* (*pret & pp unplugged*) TV, *computer* desenchufar

un·pop·u·lar [ʌn'pɑːpjələr] *adj* impopular

un·pre·ce·dent·ed [ʌn'presɪdentɪd] *adj* sin precedentes; *it was unprecedented for a woman to ...* no tenía precedentes que una mujer ...

un·pre·dict·a·ble [ʌnprɪ'dɪktəbl] *adj person, weather* imprevisible, impredecible

un·pre·ten·tious [ʌnprɪ'tenʃəs] *adj person, style, hotel* modesto, sin pretensiones

un·prin·ci·pled [ʌn'prɪnsɪpld] *adj* sin principios

un·pro·duc·tive [ʌnprə'dʌktɪv] *adj meeting, discussion* infructuoso; *soil* improductivo

un·pro·fes·sion·al [ʌnprə'feʃnl] *adj* poco profesional

un·prof·it·a·ble [ʌn'prɑːfɪtəbl] *adj* no rentable

un·pro·nounce·a·ble [ʌnprə'naʊnsəbl] *adj* impronunciable

un·pro·tect·ed [ʌnprə'tektɪd] *adj borders* desprotegido, sin protección; *unprotected sex* sexo *m* sin preservativos

un·pro·voked [ʌnprə'voʊkt] *adj attack* no provocado

un·qual·i·fied [ʌn'kwɑːlɪfaɪd] *adj worker, doctor etc* sin titulación

un·ques·tio·na·bly [ʌn'kwestʃnəblɪ] *adv* (*without doubt*) indiscutiblemente

un·ques·tion·ing [ʌn'kwestʃnɪŋ] *adj attitude, loyalty* incondicional

un·rav·el [ʌn'rævl] *v/t* (*pret & pp unraveled, Br unravelled*) *string, knitting* desenredar; *mystery, complexities* desentrañar

un·rea·da·ble [ʌn'riːdəbl] *adj book* ilegible

un·re·al [ʌn'rɪəl] *adj* irreal; *this is unreal!* F ¡esto es increíble! F

un·rea·lis·tic [ʌnrɪə'lɪstɪk] *adj* poco realista

un·rea·so·na·ble [ʌn'riːznəbl] *adj person* poco razonable, irrazonable; *demand, expectation* excesivo, irrazonable; *you're being unreasonable* no estás siendo razonable

un·re·lat·ed [ʌnrɪ'leɪtɪd] *adj issues* no relacionado; *people* no emparentado

un·re·lent·ing [ʌnrɪ'lentɪŋ] *adj* implacable

un·re·li·a·ble [ʌnrɪ'laɪəbl] *adj car, machine* poco fiable; *person* informal

un·rest [ʌn'rest] malestar *m*; (*rioting*) disturbios *mpl*

un·re·strained [ʌnrɪ'streɪnd] *adj emotions* incontrolado

un·road·wor·thy [ʌn'roʊdwɜːrðɪ] *adj* que no está en condiciones de circular

un·roll [ʌn'roʊl] *v/t carpet, scroll* desenrollar

un·ru·ly [ʌn'ruːlɪ] *adj* revoltoso

un·safe [ʌn'seɪf] *adj* peligroso; *it's unsafe to drink / eat* no se puede beber / comer

un·san·i·tar·y [ʌn'sænɪterɪ] *adj conditions, drains* insalubre

un·sat·is·fac·to·ry [ʌnsætɪs'fæktərɪ] *adj* insatisfactorio

un·sa·vo·ry [ʌn'seɪvərɪ] *adj person, reputation* indeseable; *district* desagradable

un·scathed [ʌn'skeɪðd] *adj* (*not injured*) ileso; (*not damaged*) intacto

un·screw [ʌn'skruː] *v/t top* desenroscar; *shelves, hooks* desatornillar

un·scru·pu·lous [ʌn'skruːpjələs] *adj* sin escrúpulos

un·self·ish [ʌn'selfɪʃ] *adj* generoso

un·set·tled [ʌn'setld] *adj issue* sin decidir; *weather, stock market, lifestyle* inestable; *bills* sin pagar

un·shav·en [ʌn'ʃeɪvn] *adj* sin afeitar

un·sight·ly [ʌn'saɪtlɪ] *adj* horrible, feo

un·skilled [ʌn'skɪld] *adj* no cualificado

un·so·cia·ble [ʌn'soʊʃəbl] *adj* insociable

un·so·phis·ti·cat·ed [ʌn'fɪstɪkeɪtɪd] *adj person, beliefs* sencillo; *equipment* simple

un·sta·ble [ʌn'steɪbl] *adj* inestable

un·stead·y [ʌn'stedɪ] *adj hand* tembloroso; *ladder* inestable; *be unsteady on one's feet* tambalearse

un·stint·ing [ʌn'stɪntɪŋ] *adj* generoso; *be unstinting in one's efforts / generosity* no escatimar esfuerzos / generosidad

un·stuck [ʌn'stʌk] *adj:* **come unstuck** F *of plan etc* irse al garete F

un·suc·cess·ful [ʌnsək'sesfəl] *adj writer etc* fracasado; *candidate* perdedor; *party, attempt* fallido; **he tried but was unsuccessful** lo intentó sin éxito

un·suc·cess·ful·ly [ʌnsək'sesfəlɪ] *adv try, apply* sin éxito

un·suit·a·ble [ʌn'suːtəbl] *adj partner, film, clothing* inadecuado; *thing to say* inoportuno

un·sus·pect·ing [ʌnsəs'pektɪŋ] *adj* confiado

un·swerv·ing [ʌn'swɜːrvɪŋ] *adj loyalty, devotion* inquebrantable

un·think·a·ble [ʌn'θɪŋkəbl] *adj* impensable

un·ti·dy [ʌn'taɪdɪ] *adj room, desk* desordenado; *hair* revuelto

un·tie [ʌn'taɪ] *v/t knot, laces, prisoner* desatar

un·til [ən'tɪl] **1** *prep* hasta; **from Monday until Friday** desde el lunes hasta el viernes; **I can wait until tomorrow** puedo esperar hasta mañana; **not until Friday** no antes del viernes; **it won't be finished until July** no estará acabado hasta julio **2** *conj* hasta que; **can you wait until I'm ready?** ¿puedes esperar hasta que esté listo?; **they won't do anything until you say so** no harán nada hasta que (no) se lo digas

un·time·ly [ʌn'taɪmlɪ] *adj death* prematuro

un·tir·ing [ʌn'taɪrɪŋ] *adj efforts* incansable

un·told [ʌn'toʊld] *adj suffering* indecible; *riches* inconmensurable; *story* nunca contado

un·trans·lat·a·ble [ʌntræns'leɪtəbl] *adj* intraducible

un·true [ʌn'truː] *adj* falso

un·used[1] [ʌn'juːzd] *adj goods* sin usar

un·used[2] [ʌn'juːst] *adj:* **be unused to sth** no estar acostumbrado a algo; **be unused to doing sth** no estar acostumbrado a hacer algo

un·u·su·al [ʌn'juːʒl] *adj* poco corriente; **it is unusual …** es raro *or* extraño …

un·u·su·al·ly [ʌn'juːʒəlɪ] *adv* inusitadamente; **the weather's unusually cold** hace un frío inusual

un·veil [ʌn'veɪl] *v/t memorial, statue etc* desvelar

un·well [ʌn'wel] *adj* indispuesto, mal; **be unwell** sentirse indispuesto *or* mal

un·will·ing [ʌn'wɪlɪŋ] *adj* poco dispuesto, reacio; **be unwilling to do sth** no estar dispuesto a hacer algo, ser reacio a hacer

algo

un·will·ing·ly [ʌn'wɪlɪŋlɪ] *adv* de mala gana, a regañadientes

un·wind [ʌn'waɪnd] **1** *v/t* (*pret & pp* **unwound**) *tape* desenrollar **2** *v/i* (*pret & pp* **unwound**) *of tape* desenrollarse; *of story* irse desarrollando; F (*relax*) relajarse

un·wise [ʌn'waɪz] *adj* imprudente

un·wrap [ʌn'ræp] *v/t* (*pret & pp* **unwrapped**) *gift* desenvolver

un·writ·ten [ʌn'rɪtn] *adj law, rule* no escrito

un·zip [ʌn'zɪp] *v/t* (*pret & pp* **unzipped**) *dress etc* abrir la cremallera de; COMPUT descomprimir

up [ʌp] **1** *adv position* arriba; *movement* hacia arriba; **up in the sky / up on the roof** (arriba) en el cielo / tejado; **up here / there** aquí / allí arriba; **be up** (*out of bed*) estar levantado; *of sun* haber salido; (*be built*) haber sido construido, estar acabado; *of shelves* estar montado; *of prices, temperature* haber subido; (*have expired*) haber acabado; **what's up?** F ¿qué pasa?; **up to the year 1989** hasta el año 1989; **he came up to me** se me acercó; **what are you up to these days?** ¿qué es de tu vida?; **what are those kids up to?** ¿qué están tramando esos niños?; **be up to something** (*bad*) estar tramando algo; **I don't feel up to it** no me siento en condiciones de hacerlo; **it's up to you** tú decides; **it is up to them to solve it** (*their duty*) les corresponde a ellos resolverlo, **be up and about** *after illness* estar recuperado **2** *prep:* **further up the mountain** más arriba de la montaña; **he climbed up a tree** se subió a un árbol; **they ran up the street** corrieron por la calle; **the water goes up this pipe** el agua sube por esta tubería; **we traveled up to Chicago** subimos hasta Chicago **3** *n:* **ups and downs** altibajos *mpl*

'up·bring·ing *n* educación *f*

'up·com·ing *adj* (*forthcoming*) próximo

up'date[1] *v/t file, records* actualizar; **update s.o. on sth** poner a alguien al corriente de algo

'up·date[2] *n* actualización *f*; **can you give me an update on the situation?** ¿me puedes poner al corriente de la situación?

up'grade *v/t computers etc* actualizar; (*replace with new versions*) modernizar; *product* modernizar; **upgrade s.o. to business class** cambiar a alguien a clase ejecutiva

up·heav·al [ʌp'hiːvl] *emotional* conmoción *m*; *physical* trastorno *m*; *political*, *social* sacudida *f*

up·hill 1 *adv* [ʌp'hɪl] *walk* cuesta arriba **2** *adj* ['ʌphɪl] *struggle* arduo, difícil

up'hold *v/t (pret & pp* **upheld)** *traditions*, *rights* defender, conservar; *(vindicate)* confirmar

up·hol·ster·y [ʌp'houlstərɪ] *(coverings of chairs)* tapicería *f*; *(padding of chairs)* relleno *m*

'up·keep *of buildings*, *parks etc* mantenimiento *m*

'up·load *v/t* COMPUT cargar

up'mar·ket *adj restaurant*, *hotel* de categoría

up·on [ə'pɑːn] *prep →* **on**

up·per ['ʌpər] *adj part of sth* superior; *stretches of a river* alto; *deck* superior, de arriba

up·per 'class *adj accent*, *family* de clase alta

up·per 'clas·ses *npl* clases *fpl* altas

'up·right 1 *adj citizen* honrado **2** *adv sit* derecho

up·right ('pi·an·o) piano *m* vertical

'up·ris·ing levantamiento *m*

'up·roar *(loud noise)* alboroto *m*; *(protest)* tumulto *m*

up'set 1 *v/t (pret & pp* **upset)** *drink*, *glass* tirar; *emotionally* disgustar **2** *adj emotionally* disgustado; **get upset about sth** disgustarse por algo; **have an upset stomach** tener el estómago mal

up'set·ting *adj* triste

'up·shot *(result*, *outcome)* resultado *m*

up·side 'down *adv* boca abajo; **turn sth upside down** *box etc* poner algo al revés *or* boca abajo

up'stairs 1 *adv* arriba **2** *adj room* de arriba

'up·start advenedizo(-a) *m(f)*

up'stream *adv* río arriba

'up·take FIN respuesta *f (of* a); **be quick / slow on the uptake** F ser / no ser muy espabilado F

up'tight *adj* F *(nervous)* tenso; *(inhibited)* estrecho

up-to-'date *adj information* actualizado; *fashions* moderno

'up·turn *in economy* mejora *f*

up·ward ['ʌpwərd] *adv fly*, *move* hacia arriba; **upward of 10,000** más de 10.000

u·ra·ni·um [jʊ'reɪnɪəm] uranio *m*

ur·ban ['ɜːrbən] *adj* urbano

ur·ban·i·za·tion [ɜːrbənaɪ'zeɪʃn] urbanización *f*

ur·chin ['ɜːrtʃɪn] golfillo(-a) *m(f)*

urge [ɜːrdʒ] **1** *n* impulso *m*; **I felt an urge to hit her** me entraron ganas de pegarle; **I**

have an urge to do something new siento la necesidad de hacer algo nuevo **2** *v/t*: **urge s.o. to do sth** rogar a alguien que haga algo

◆ **urge on** *v/t (encourage)* animar

ur·gen·cy ['ɜːrdʒənsɪ] *of situation* urgencia *f*

ur·gent ['ɜːrdʒənt] *adj job*, *letter* urgente; **be in urgent need of sth** necesitar algo urgentemente; **is it urgent?** ¿es urgente?

u·ri·nate ['jʊrəneɪt] *v/i* orinar

u·rine ['jʊrɪn] orina *f*

urn [ɜːrn] urna *f*

U·ru·guay ['jʊrəgwaɪ] *n* Uruguay

U·ru·guay·an [jʊrə'gwaɪən] **1** *adj* uruguayo **2** *n* uruguayo(-a) *m(f)*

us [ʌs] *pron* nos; *after prep* nosotros(-as); **they love us** nos quieren; **she gave us the keys** nos dio las llaves; **he sold it to us** nos lo vendió; **that's for us** eso es para nosotros; **who's that? - it's us** ¿quién es? - ¡somos nosotros!

US [juː'es] *abbr (= United States)* EE.UU. *mpl* (= Estados *mpl* Unidos)

USA [juːes'eɪ] *abbr (= United States of America)* EE.UU. (= Estados Unidos)

us·a·ble ['juːzəbl] *adj* utilizable; **it's not usable** no se puede utilizar

us·age ['juːzɪdʒ] uso *m*

use 1 *v/t* [juːz] *tool*, *word* utilizar, usar; *skills*, *knowledge*, *car* usar; *a lot of gas*, *pej: person* consumir; **I could use a drink** F no me vendría mal una copa **2** *n* [juːs] uso *m*, utilización *f*; **be of great use to s.o.** ser de gran utilidad para alguien; **it's of no use to me** no me sirve; **is that of any use?** ¿eso sirve para algo?; **it's no use** no sirve de nada; **it's no use trying / waiting** no sirve de nada intentarlo / esperar

◆ **use up** *v/t* agotar

used¹ [juːzd] *adj car etc* de segunda mano

used² [juːst] *adj*: **be used to s.o./sth** estar acostumbrado a alguien / algo; **get used to s.o./sth** acostumbrarse a alguien / algo; **be used to doing sth** estar acostumbrado a hacer algo; **get used to doing sth** acostumbrarse a hacer algo

used³ [juːst]: **I used to like him** antes me gustaba; **they used to meet every Saturday** solían verse todos los sábados

use·ful ['juːsfəl] *adj* útil

use·ful·ness ['juːsfʊlnəs] utilidad *f*

use·less ['juːslɪs] *adj* inútil; *machine*, *computer* inservible; **be useless** F *person* ser un inútil F; **it's useless trying** *(there's no point)* no vale la pena intentarlo

us·er ['ju:zər] *of product* usuario
us·er-'friend·ly *adj software, device* de
fácil manejo
ush·er ['ʌʃər] *n (at wedding)* persona que
se encarga de indicar a los asistentes dónde se deben sentar
♦ **usher in** *v/t new era* anunciar
ush·er·ette [ʌʃə'ret] acomodadora *f*
u·su·al ['ju:ʒl] *adj* habitual, acostumbrado; *as usual* como de costumbre; *the
usual, please* lo de siempre, por favor
u·su·al·ly ['ju:ʒəlɪ] *adv* normalmente; *I
usually start at 9* suelo empezar a las 9
u·ten·sil [ju:'tensl] *n* utensilio *m*

u·te·rus ['ju:tərəs] útero *m*
u·til·i·ty [ju:'tɪlətɪ] *(usefulness)* utilidad *f*;
public utilities servicios *mpl* públicos
u·til·ize ['ju:tɪlaɪz] *v/t* utilizar
ut·most ['ʌtmoust] **1** *adj* sumo **2** *n*: *do
one's utmost* hacer todo lo posible
ut·ter ['ʌtər] **1** *adj* completo, total **2** *v/t
sound* decir, pronunciar
ut·ter·ly ['ʌtərlɪ] *adv* completamente, totalmente
U-turn ['ju:tɜːrn] cambio *m* de sentido;
do a U-turn fig: in policy etc dar un giro
de 180 grados

V

va·can·cy ['veɪkənsɪ] *at work* puesto *m*
vacante
va·cant ['veɪkənt] *adj building* vacío; *position* vacante; *look, expression* vago, distraído
va·cant·ly ['veɪkəntlɪ] *adv* distraídamente
va·cate [veɪ'keɪt] *v/t room* desalojar
va·ca·tion [veɪ'keɪʃn] *n* vacaciones *fpl*; *be
on vacation* estar de vacaciones; *go to
... on vacation* ir de vacaciones a ...
va·ca·tion·er [veɪ'keɪʃənər] turista *m/f; in
summer* veraneante *m/f*
vac·cin·ate ['væksɪneɪt] *v/t* vacunar; *be
vaccinated against ...* estar vacunado
contra ...
vac·cin·a·tion [væksɪ'neɪʃn] *action* vacunación *f; (vaccine)* vacuna *f*
vac·cine ['væksi:n] vacuna *f*
vac·u·um ['vækjʊəm] **1** *n* PHYS, *fig* vacío
m **2** *v/t floors* pasar el aspirador por, aspirar
'vac·u·um clean·er aspirador *m*, aspiradora *f*
'vac·u·um flask termo *m*
vac·u·um-'packed *adj* envasado al vacío
vag·a·bond ['vægəbɑːnd] vagabundo(-a)
m(f)
va·gi·na [və'dʒaɪnə] vagina *f*
va·gi·nal ['vædʒɪnl] *adj* vaginal
va·grant ['veɪgrənt] vagabundo(-a) *m(f)*
vague [veɪg] *adj* vago; *he was very vague about it* no fue muy preciso
vague·ly ['veɪglɪ] *adv answer, (slightly)*
vagamente; *possible* muy poco

vain [veɪn] **1** *adj person* vanidoso; *hope*
vano **2** *n: in vain* en vano; *their efforts
were in vain* sus esfuerzos fueron en vano
val·en·tine ['væləntaɪn] *card* tarjeta *f* del
día de San Valentín; *Valentine's Day* día
de San Valentín *or* de los enamorados
val·et **1** *n* ['væleɪ] *person* mozo *m* **2** *v/t*
['vælət] *car* lavar y limpiar
'val·et ser·vice *for clothes* servicio *m* de
planchado; *for cars* servicio *m* de lavado
y limpiado
val·iant ['væljənt] *adj* valiente, valeroso
val·iant·ly ['væljəntlɪ] *adv* valientemente,
valerosamente
val·id ['vælɪd] *adj* válido
val·i·date ['vælɪdeɪt] *v/t with official
stamp* sellar; *s.o.'s alibi* dar validez a
va·lid·i·ty [və'lɪdətɪ] validez *f*
val·ley ['vælɪ] valle *m*
val·u·a·ble ['væljʊbl] **1** *adj* valioso **2** *n:
valuables* objetos *mpl* de valor
val·u·a·tion [væljʊ'eɪʃn] tasación *f*, valoración *f*
val·ue ['vælju:] **1** *n* valor *m; be good value* ofrecer buena relación calidad-precio; *get value for money* recibir una
buena relación calidad-precio; *rise / fall
in value* aumentar / disminuir de valor
2 *v/t s.o.'s friendship, one's freedom* valorar; *I value your advice* valoro tus consejos; *have an object valued* pedir la
valoración *or* tasación de un objeto
valve [vælv] válvula *f*
van [væn] camioneta *f*, furgoneta *f*

van·dal ['vændl] vándalo m, gamberro(-a) m(f)

van·dal·ism ['vændəlɪzm] vandalismo m

van·dal·ize ['vændəlaɪz] v/t destrozar (intencionadamente)

van·guard ['vænɡɑːrd] vanguardia f; **be in the vanguard of** fig estar a la vanguardia de

va·nil·la [vəˈnɪlə] 1 n vainilla f 2 adj de vainilla

van·ish ['vænɪʃ] v/i desaparecer

van·i·ty ['vænətɪ] of person vanidad f

'van·i·ty case neceser m

van·tage point ['væntɪdʒ] on hill etc posición f aventajada

va·por ['veɪpər] vapor m

va·por·ize ['veɪpəraɪz] v/t of atomic bomb, explosion vaporizar

'va·por trail of airplane estela f

va·pour Br → **vapor**

var·i·a·ble ['verɪəbl] 1 adj variable 2 n MATH, COMPUT variable f

var·i·ant ['verɪənt] n variante f

var·i·a·tion [verɪˈeɪʃn] variación f

var·i·cose vein ['værɪkoʊs] variz f

var·ied ['verɪd] adj variado

va·ri·e·ty [vəˈraɪətɪ] (variedness, type) variedad f; **a variety of things to do** (range, mixture) muchas cosas para hacer

var·i·ous ['verɪəs] adj (several) varios; (different) diversos

var·nish ['vɑːrnɪʃ] 1 n for wood barniz m; for fingernails esmalte m 2 v/t wood barnizar; fingernails poner esmalte a, pintar

var·y ['verɪ] 1 v/i (pret & pp **varied**) variar; **it varies** depende 2 v/t (pret & pp **varied**) variar

vase [veɪz] jarrón m

vas·ec·to·my [vəˈsektəmɪ] vasectomía f

vast [væst] adj desert, knowledge vasto; number, improvement enorme

vast·ly ['væstlɪ] adv enormemente

VAT [viːeɪˈtiː, væt] Br abbr (= **value-added tax**) IVA m (= impuesto m sobre el valor añadido)

Vat·i·can ['vætɪkən]: **the Vatican** el Vaticano

vau·de·ville ['vɒdvɪl] adj vodevil m

vault¹ [vɒlt] n in roof bóveda f; **vaults** (cellar) sótano m; of bank cámara f acorazada

vault² [vɒlt] 1 n SP salto m 2 v/t beam etc saltar

VCR [viːsiːˈɑːr] abbr (= **video cassette recorder**) aparato m de Span vídeo or L.Am. video

VDU [viːdiːˈjuː] abbr (= **visual display unit**) monitor m

veal [viːl] ternera f

veer [vɪr] v/i girar, torcer

ve·gan ['viːɡn] 1 n vegetariano(-a) m(f) estricto (-a) (que no come ningún producto de origen animal) 2 adj vegetariano estricto

vege·ta·ble ['vedʒtəbl] hortaliza f; **vegetables** verduras fpl

ve·ge·tar·i·an [vedʒɪˈterɪən] 1 n vegetariano(-a) m(f) 2 adj vegetariano

ve·ge·tar·i·an·ism [vedʒɪˈterɪənɪzm] vegetarianismo m

veg·e·ta·tion [vedʒɪˈteɪʃn] vegetación f

ve·he·mence ['viːəməns] vehemencia f

ve·he·ment ['viːəmənt] adj vehemente

ve·he·ment·ly ['viːəməntlɪ] adv vehementemente

ve·hi·cle ['viːɪkl] also fig vehículo m

veil [veɪl] 1 n velo m 2 v/t cubrir con un velo

vein [veɪn] ANAT vena f; **in this vein** fig en este tono

Vel·cro® ['velkroʊ] velcro m

ve·loc·i·ty [vɪˈlɑːsətɪ] velocidad f

vel·vet ['velvɪt] n terciopelo m

vel·vet·y ['velvɪtɪ] adj aterciopelado

ven·det·ta [venˈdetə] vendetta f

vend·ing ma·chine ['vendɪŋ] máquina f expendedora

vend·or ['vendər] LAW parte f vendedora

ve·neer [vəˈnɪr] on wood chapa f; of politeness etc apariencia f, fachada

ven·e·ra·ble ['venərəbl] adj venerable

ven·e·rate ['venəreɪt] v/t venerar

ven·e·ra·tion [venəˈreɪʃn] veneración f

ve·ne·re·al dis·ease [vɪˈnɪrɪəl] enfermedad f venérea

ve·ne·tian 'blind persiana f veneciana

Ven·e·zue·la [venɪzˈweɪlə] n Venezuela

Ven·e·zue·lan [venɪzˈweɪlən] 1 adj venezolano 2 n venezolano(-a) m(f)

ven·geance ['vendʒəns] venganza f; **with a vengeance** con ganas

ven·i·son ['venɪsn] venado m

ven·om ['venəm] also fig veneno m

ven·om·ous ['venəməs] adj snake venenoso; fig envenenado

vent [vent] n for air respiradero m; **give vent to** feelings dar rienda suelta a

ven·ti·late ['ventɪleɪt] v/t ventilar

ven·ti·la·tion [ventɪˈleɪʃn] ventilación f

ven·ti·la·tion shaft pozo m de ventilación

ven·ti·la·tor ['ventɪleɪtər] ventilador m; MED respirador m

ven·tril·o·quist [venˈtrɪləkwɪst] ventrílocuo(-a) m(f)

ven·ture ['ventʃər] 1 n (undertaking) iniciativa f; COM empresa f 2 v/i aventurarse

ven·ue ['venjuː] for meeting lugar m; for concert local m, sala f

ve·ran·da [vəˈrændə] porche *m*
verb [vɜːrb] verbo *m*
verb·al [ˈvɜːrbl] *adj* (*spoken*) verbal
verb·al·ly [ˈvɜːrbəlɪ] *adv* de palabra
ver·ba·tim [vɜːrˈbeɪtɪm] *adv* literalmente
ver·dict [ˈvɜːrdɪkt] LAW veredicto *m*;
  what's your verdict? ¿qué te parece?,
  ¿qué opinas?
verge [vɜːrdʒ] *n* of road arcén *m*; **be on
  the verge of** ruin estar al borde de; *tears*
  estar a punto de
◆ **verge on** *v/t* rayar en
ver·i·fi·ca·tion [verɪfɪˈkeɪʃn] (*checking*)
  verificación *f*; (*confirmation*) confirmación *f*
ver·i·fy [ˈverɪfaɪ] *v/t* (*pret & pp* **verified**)
  (*check*) verificar; (*confirm*) confirmar
ver·mi·cel·li [vɜːrmɪˈtʃelɪ] *nsg* fideos *mpl*
ver·min [ˈvɜːrmɪn] *npl* bichos *mpl*, alima-
  ñas *fpl*
ver·mouth [vɜːrˈmuːθ] vermut *m*
ver·nac·u·lar [vərˈnækjələr] *n* lenguaje *m*
  de la calle
ver·sa·tile [ˈvɜːrsətəl] *adj* polifacético,
  versátil
ver·sa·til·i·ty [vɜːrsəˈtɪlətɪ] polivalencia *f*,
  versatilidad *f*
verse [vɜːrs] verso *m*
versed [vɜːrst] *adj*: **be well versed in a
  subject** estar muy versado en una materia
ver·sion [ˈvɜːrʃn] versión *f*
ver·sus [ˈvɜːrsəs] *prep* SP, LAW contra
ver·te·bra [ˈvɜːrtɪbrə] vértebra *f*
ver·te·brate [ˈvɜːrtɪbreɪt] *n* vertebra-
  do(-a) *m(f)*
ver·ti·cal [ˈvɜːrtɪkl] *adj* vertical
ver·ti·go [ˈvɜːrtɪɡou] vértigo *m*
ver·y [ˈverɪ] **1** *adv* muy; **was it cold? - not
  very** ¿hizo frío? - no mucho; **the very
  best** el mejor de todos **2** *adj*: **at that very
  moment** en ese mismo momento; **that's
  the very thing I need** (*exact*) eso es precisamente lo que necesito; **the very
  thought** (*mere*) sólo de pensar en; **right
  at the very top / bottom** arriba / al fondo
  del todo
ves·sel [ˈvesl] NAUT buque *m*
vest [vest] chaleco *m*
ves·tige [ˈvestɪdʒ] vestigio *m*; vestigio *m*
vet[1] [vet] *n* (*veterinary surgeon*) veterina-
  rio(-a) *m(f)*
vet[2] [vet] *v/t* (*pret & pp* **vetted**) *applicants
  etc* examinar, investigar
vet[3] [vet] MIL veterano(-a) *m(f)*
vet·e·ran [ˈvetərən] **1** *n* veterano(-a) *m(f)*
  2 *adj* veterano
vet·e·ri·nar·i·an [vetərəˈnerɪən] veteri-
  nario(-a) *m(f)*

ve·to [ˈviːtou] **1** *n* veto *m* **2** *v/t* vetar
vex [veks] *v/t* (*concern, worry*) molestar,
  irritar
vexed [vekst] *adj* (*worried*) molesto, irritado; **the vexed question of** la polémica
  cuestión de
vi·a [ˈvaɪə] *prep* vía
vi·a·ble [ˈvaɪəbl] *adj* viable
vi·brate [vaɪˈbreɪt] *v/i* vibrar
vi·bra·tion [vaɪˈbreɪʃn] vibración *f*
vic·ar [ˈvɪkər] vicario *m*
vic·ar·age [ˈvɪkərɪdʒ] vicaría *f*
vice[1] [vaɪs] vicio *m*; **the problem of vice**
  el problema del vicio
vice[2] *Br* → **vise**
vice pres·i·dent vicepresidente(-a) *m(f)*
vice squad brigada *f* antivicio
vi·ce ver·sa [vaɪsɪˈvɜːrsə] *adv* viceversa
vi·cin·i·ty [vɪˈsɪnətɪ] zona *f*; **in the vicinity of ...** the church etc en las cercanías
  de ...; *$500 etc* rondando ...
vi·cious [ˈvɪʃəs] *adj* dog fiero; *attack, temper, criticism* feroz
vi·cious 'cir·cle círculo *m* vicioso
vi·cious·ly [ˈvɪʃəslɪ] *adv* con brutalidad
vic·tim [ˈvɪktɪm] víctima *f*
vic·tim·ize [ˈvɪktɪmaɪz] *v/t* tratar injustamente
vic·tor [ˈvɪktər] vencedor(a) *m(f)*
vic·to·ri·ous [vɪkˈtɔːrɪəs] *adj* victorioso
vic·to·ry [ˈvɪktərɪ] victoria *f*; **win a victory over ...** obtener una victoria sobre
  ...
vid·e·o [ˈvɪdɪou] **1** *n* Span vídeo *m*, L.Am.
  video *m*; **have X on video** tener a X en
  Span vídeo *or* L.Am. video **2** *v/t* grabar
  en Span vídeo *or* L.Am. video
'vid·e·o cam·e·ra videocámara *f*
vid·e·o cas'sette videocasete *m*
'vid·e·o con·fer·ence TELEC videoconferencia *f*
'vid·e·o game videojuego *m*
'vid·e·o·phone videoteléfono *m*
'vid·e·o re·cord·er aparato *m* de Span
  vídeo *or* L.Am. video
'vid·e·o re·cord·ing grabación *f* en Span
  vídeo *or* L.Am. video
'vid·e·o·tape cinta *f* de Span vídeo *or*
  L.Am. video
vie [vaɪ] *v/i* competir
Vi·et·nam [vɪetˈnɑːm] Vietnam *m*
Vi·et·nam·ese [vɪetnəˈmiːz] **1** *adj* vietnamita **2** *n* vietnamita *m/f*; *language* vietnamita *m*
view [vjuː] **1** *n* vista *f*; *of situation* opinión
  f; **in view of** teniendo en cuenta; **be on
  view** of paintings estar expuesto al público; **with a view to** con vistas a **2** *v/t
  events, situation* ver, considerar; TV *pro-*

gram, house ver **3** v/i *(watch* TV) ver la televisión

view·er ['vju:ər] TV telespectador(a) *m(f)*

'**view·find·er** PHOT visor *m*

'**view·point** punto *m* de vista

vig·or ['vɪɡər] *(energy)* vigor *m*

vig·or·ous ['vɪɡərəs] *adj shake* vigoroso; *person* enérgico; *denial* rotundo

vig·or·ous·ly ['vɪɡərəslɪ] *adv shake* con vigor; *deny, defend* rotundamente

vig·our *Br →* **vigor**

vile [vaɪl] *adj smell* asqueroso; *thing to do* vil

vil·la ['vɪlə] chalet *m*; *in the country* villa *f*

vil·lage ['vɪlɪdʒ] pueblo *m*

vil·lag·er ['vɪlɪdʒər] aldeano(-a) *m(f)*

vil·lain ['vɪlən] malo(a) *m(f)*

vin·di·cate ['vɪndɪkeɪt] v/t *(show to be correct)* dar la razón a; *(show to be innocent)* vindicar; *I feel vindicated* los hechos me dan ahora la razón

vin·dic·tive [vɪn'dɪktɪv] *adj* vengativo

vin·dic·tive·ly [vɪn'dɪktɪvlɪ] *adv* vengativamente

vine [vaɪn] vid *f*

vin·e·gar ['vɪnɪɡər] vinagre *m*

vine·yard ['vɪnjɑːrd] viñedo *m*

vin·tage ['vɪntɪdʒ] **1** *n of wine* cosecha *f* **2** *adj (classic)* clásico *m*

vi·o·la [vɪ'oʊlə] MUS viola *f*

vi·o·late ['vaɪəleɪt] v/t violar

vi·o·la·tion [vaɪə'leɪʃn] violación *f*; *(traffic violation)* infracción *f*

vi·o·lence ['vaɪələns] violencia *f*; *outbreak of violence* estallido de violencia

vi·o·lent ['vaɪələnt] *adj* violento; *have a violent temper* tener muy mal genio

vi·o·lent·ly ['vaɪələntlɪ] *adv react* violentamente; *object* rotundamente; *fall violently in love with s.o.* enamorarse perdidamente de alguien

vi·o·let ['vaɪələt] *n color, plant* violeta *m*

vi·o·lin [vaɪə'lɪn] violín *m*

vi·o·lin·ist [vaɪə'lɪnɪst] violinista *m/f*

VIP [vi:aɪ'pi:] *abbr (= very important person)* VIP *m*

vi·per ['vaɪpər] *snake* víbora *f*

vi·ral ['vaɪrəl] *adj infection* vírico, viral

vir·gin ['vɜːrdʒɪn] virgen *m/f*

vir·gin·i·ty [vɜːr'dʒɪnətɪ] virginidad *f*; *lose one's virginity* perder la virginidad

Vir·go ['vɜːrɡoʊ] ASTR Virgo *m/f inv*

vir·ile ['vɪrəl] *adj man* viril; *prose* vigoroso

vi·ril·i·ty [vɪ'rɪlətɪ] virilidad *f*

vir·tu·al ['vɜːrtʃʊəl] *adj* virtual

vir·tu·al·ly ['vɜːrtʃʊəlɪ] *adv (almost)* virtualmente, casi

vir·tu·al re·'al·i·ty realidad *f* virtual

vir·tue ['vɜːrtʃuː] virtud *f*; *in virtue of* en

virtud de

vir·tu·o·so [vɜːrtʃuː'oʊzoʊ] MUS virtuoso(-a) *m(f)*

vir·tu·ous ['vɜːrtʃʊəs] *adj* virtuoso

vir·u·lent ['vɪrʊlənt] *adj* virulento

vi·rus ['vaɪrəs] MED, COMPUT virus *m inv*

vi·sa ['viːzə] visa *f*, visado *m*

vise [vaɪs] torno *m* de banco

vis·i·bil·i·ty [vɪzə'bɪlətɪ] visibilidad *f*

vis·i·ble ['vɪzəbl] *adj object, difference* visible; *anger* evidente; *not visible to the naked eye* no ser visible a simple vista

vis·i·bly ['vɪzəblɪ] *adv different* visiblemente; *he was visibly moved* estaba visiblemente conmovido

vi·sion ['vɪʒn] *also* REL visión *f*

vis·it ['vɪzɪt] **1** *n* visita *f*; *pay a visit to the doctor / dentist* visitar al doctor / dentista; *pay s.o. a visit* hacer una visita a alguien **2** v/t visitar

vis·it·ing card ['vɪzɪtɪŋ] tarjeta *f* de visita

'**vis·it·ing hours** *npl at hospital* horas *fpl* de visita

vis·it·or ['vɪzɪtər] *(guest)* visita *f*; *(tourist)*, *to museum etc* visitante *m/f*

vi·sor ['vaɪzər] visera *f*

vis·u·al ['vɪʒʊəl] *adj* visual

vis·u·al 'aid medio *m* visuale

vis·u·al dis·play u·nit monitor *m*

vis·u·al·ize ['vɪʒʊəlaɪz] v/t visualizar; *(foresee)* prever

vis·u·al·ly ['vɪʒʊlɪ] *adv* visualmente

vis·u·al·ly im·'paired *adj* con discapacidad visual

vi·tal ['vaɪtl] *adj (essential)* vital; *it is vital that ...* es vital que ...

vi·tal·i·ty [vaɪ'tælətɪ] *of person, city etc* vitalidad *f*

vi·tal·ly ['vaɪtəlɪ] *adv*: *vitally important* de importancia vital

vi·tal 'or·gans *npl* órganos *mpl* vitales

vi·tal sta·'tis·tics *npl of woman* medidas *fpl*

vit·a·min ['vaɪtəmɪn] vitamina *f*

'**vit·a·min pill** pastilla *f* vitamínica

vit·ri·ol·ic [vɪtrɪ'ɑːlɪk] *adj* virulento

vi·va·cious [vɪ'veɪʃəs] *adj* vivaz

vi·vac·i·ty [vɪ'væsətɪ] vivacidad *f*

viv·id ['vɪvɪd] *adj color* vivo; *memory, imagination* vívido

viv·id·ly ['vɪvɪdlɪ] *adv (brightly)* vivamente; *(clearly)* vívidamente

V-neck ['viːnek] cuello *m* de pico

vo·cab·u·la·ry [voʊ'kæbjʊlərɪ] vocabulario *m*

vo·cal ['voʊkl] *adj to do with the voice* vocal; *expressing opinions* ruidoso; *a vocal opponent* un declarado adversario '**vo·cal cords** *npl* cuerdas *fpl* vocales

'**vo·cal group** MUS grupo *m* vocal

'**vo·cal·ist** ['vəʊkəlɪst] MUS vocalista *m/f*

vo·ca·tion [və'keɪʃn] (*calling*) vocación *f*; (*profession*) profesión *f*

vo·ca·tion·al [və'keɪʃnl] *adj guidance* profesional

vod·ka ['vɑːdkə] vodka *m*

vogue [vəʊg] moda *f*; *be in vogue* estar en boga

voice [vɔɪs] **1** *n* voz *f* **2** *v/t opinions* expresar

'**voice mail** correo *m* de voz

void [vɔɪd] **1** *n* vacío *m* **2** *adj*: *void of* carente de

vol·a·tile ['vɑːlətəl] *adj personality, moods* cambiante; *markets* inestable

vol·ca·no [vɑːl'keɪnoʊ] volcán *m*

vol·ley ['vɑːlɪ] *n of shots* ráfaga *f*; *in tennis* volea *f*

'**vol·ley·ball** voleibol *m*, balonvolea *m*

volt [vəʊlt] voltio *m*

volt·age ['vəʊltɪdʒ] voltaje *m*

vol·ume ['vɑːljəm] volumen *m*; *of container* capacidad *f*; *of book* volumen *m*, tomo *m*

vol·ume con'trol control *m* del volumen

vol·un·tar·i·ly [vɑːlən'terɪlɪ] *adv* voluntariamente

vol·un·ta·ry ['vɑːlənterɪ] *adj* voluntario

vol·un·teer [vɑːlən'tɪr] **1** *n* voluntario(-a) *m(f)* **2** *v/i* ofrecerse voluntariamente

vo·lup·tu·ous [və'lʌptʃʊəs] *adj woman, figure* voluptuoso

vom·it ['vɑːmɪt] **1** *n* vómito *m* **2** *v/i* vomitar

◆ **vomit up** *v/t* vomitar

vo·ra·cious [və'reɪʃəs] *adj appetite* voraz

vo·ra·cious·ly [və'reɪʃəslɪ] *also fig* vorazmente

vote [vəʊt] **1** *n* voto *m*; *have the vote* (*be entitled to vote*) tener el derecho al voto **2** *v/i* POL votar; *vote for / against* votar a favor / en contra **3** *v/t*: *they voted him President* lo votaron presidente; *they voted to stay behind* votaron (a favor de) quedarse atrás

◆ **vote in** *v/t new member* elegir en votación

◆ **vote on** *v/t issue* someter a votación

◆ **vote out** *v/t of office* rechazar en votación

vot·er ['vəʊtər] POL votante *m/f*

vot·ing ['vəʊtɪŋ] POL votación *f*

'**vot·ing booth** cabina *f* electoral

◆ **vouch for** [vaʊtʃ] *v/t truth of sth* dar fe de; *person* responder por

vouch·er ['vaʊtʃər] vale *m*

vow [vaʊ] **1** *n* voto *m* **2** *v/t*: *vow to do sth* prometer hacer algo

vow·el [vaʊl] vocal *f*

voy·age ['vɔɪɪdʒ] *n* viaje *m*

vul·gar ['vʌlgər] *adj person, language* vulgar, grosero

vul·ne·ra·ble ['vʌlnərəbl] *adj to attack, criticism* vulnerable

vul·ture ['vʌltʃər] buitre *m*

W

wad [wɑːd] *n of paper, absorbent cotton etc* bola *f*; *a wad of \$100 bills* un fajo de billetes de 100 dólares

wad·dle ['wɑːdl] *v/i of duck* caminar; *of person* anadear

◆ **wade** [weɪd] *v/i* caminar en el agua

◆ **wade through** *v/t book, documents* leerse

wa·fer ['weɪfər] *cookie* barquillo *m*; REL hostia *f*

'**wa·fer-thin** *adj* muy fino

waf·fle[1] ['wɑːfl] *n to eat* gofre *m*

waf·fle[2] ['wɑːfl] *v/i* andarse con rodeos

wag [wæg] **1** *v/t* (*pret & pp wagged*) *tail, finger* menear **2** *v/i* (*pret & pp wagged*)

of tail menearse

wage[1] [weɪdʒ] *v/t*: *wage war* hacer la guerra

wage[2] [weɪdʒ] *n* salario *m*, sueldo *m*; *wages* salario *m*, sueldo *m*

'**wage earn·er** asalariado(-a) *m(f)*

'**wage freeze** congelación *f* salarial

'**wage ne·go·ti·a·tions** *npl* negociación *f* salarial

'**wage pack·et** *fig* salario *m*, sueldo *m*

wag·gle ['wægl] *v/t hips* menear; *ears, loose screw etc* mover

wag·gon, *Br* **wag·on** ['wægən] RAIL vagón *m*; *be on the wagon* F haber dejado la bebida

W

wail [weɪl] **1** *n of person, baby* gemido *m*; *of siren* sonido *m*, aullido *m* **2** *v/i of person, baby* gemir; *of siren* sonar, aullar

waist [weɪst] cintura *f*

'waist·coat *Br* chaleco *m*

'waist·line cintura *f*

wait [weɪt] **1** *n* espera *f*; *I had a long wait for a train* esperé mucho rato el tren **2** *v/i* esperar; *have you been waiting long?* ¿llevan mucho rato esperando? **2** *v/t*: *don't wait supper for me* no me esperéis a cenar; *wait table* trabajar de camarero
◆ *wait for v/t* esperar; *wait for me!* ¡esperadme!
◆ *wait on v/t* (*serve*) servir; (*wait for*) esperar
◆ *wait up v/i* esperar levantado

wait·er ['weɪtər] camarero *m*

wait·ing ['weɪtɪŋ] *n* espera *f*; *no waiting sign* señal *f* de prohibido estacionar

'wait·ing list lista *f* de espera

'wait·ing room sala *f* de espera

wait·ress ['weɪtrɪs] camarera *f*

waive [weɪv] *v/t right* renunciar; *requirement* no aplicar

wake¹ [weɪk] **1** *v/i* (*pret* **woke**, *pp* **woken**): *wake* (*up*) despertarse **2** *v/t* (*pret* **woke**, *pp* **woken**): *wake* (*up*) despertar

wake² [weɪk] *n of ship* estela *f*; *in the wake of* fig tras; *missionaries followed in the wake of the explorers* a los exploradores siguieron los misioneros

'wake-up call: *could I have a wake-up call at 6.30?* ¿me podrían despertar a las 6.30?

Wales [weɪlz] *n* Gales

walk [wɔːk] **1** *n* paseo *m*; *longer* caminata *f*; (*path*) camino *m*; *it's a long / short walk to the office* hay una caminata / un paseo hasta la oficina; *go for a walk* salir a dar un paseo, salir de paseo; *it's a five-minute walk* está a cinco minutos a pie **2** *v/i* caminar, andar; *she walked over to the window* se acercó a la ventana; *I walked over to her place* fui a su casa **3** *v/t dog* sacar a pasear; *walk the streets* (*walk around*) caminar por las calles
◆ *walk out v/i of spouse* marcharse; *from theater etc* salir; (*go on strike*) declararse en huelga
◆ *walk out on v/t*: *walk out on s.o.* abandonar a alguien

walk·er ['wɔːkər] (*hiker*) excursionista *m/f*; *for baby, old person* andador *m*; *be a slow / fast walker* caminar *or* andar despacio / rápido

walk·ie·'talk·ie [wɔːkɪ'tɔːkɪ] walkie-talkie *m*

walk-in 'clos·et vestidor *m*, armario *m* empotrado

walk·ing ['wɔːkɪŋ] *n* (*hiking*) excursionismo *m*; *walking is one of the best forms of exercise* caminar es uno de los mejores ejercicios; *it's within walking distance* se puede ir caminando *or* andando

'walk·ing stick bastón *m*

'walk·ing tour visita *f* a pie

'Walk·man® walkman *m*

'walk·out *n* (*strike*) huelga *f*

'walk·over (*easy win*) paseo *m*

'walk-up *n* apartamento *m* en un edificio sin ascensor

wall [wɔːl] *external, fig* muro *m*; *of room* pared *m*; *go to the wall of company* quebrar; *drive s.o. up the wall* F hacer que alguien se suba por las paredes

wal·let ['wɑːlɪt] cartera *f*

wal·lop ['wɑːləp] **1** *n* F *blow* tortazo *m* F, galletazo *m* F **2** *v/t* F dar un golpetazo a F; *opponent* dar una paliza a F

'wall·pa·per 1 *n* papel *m* pintado **2** *v/t* empapelar

wall-to-wall 'car·pet *Span* moqueta *f*, *L.Am.* alfombra *f*

wal·nut ['wɔːlnʌt] nuez *f*; *tree, wood* nogal *m*

waltz [wɔːlts] *n* vals *m*

wan [wɑːn] *adj face* pálido *m*

wan·der ['wɑːndər] *v/i* (*roam*) vagar, deambular; (*stray*) extraviarse; *my attention began to wander* empecé a distraerme
◆ *wander around v/i* deambular, pasear

wane [weɪn] *v/i of interest, enthusiasm* decaer, menguar

wan·gle ['wæŋgl] *v/t* F agenciarse F

want [wɑːnt] **1** *n*: *for want of* por falta de **2** *v/t* querer; (*need*) necesitar; *want to do sth* querer hacer algo; *I want to stay here* quiero quedarme aquí; *do you want to come too?* - *no, I don't want to* ¿quieres venir tú también? - no, no quiero; *you can have whatever you want* toma lo que quieras; *it's not what I wanted* no es lo que quería; *she wants you to go back* quiere que vuelvas; *he wants a haircut* necesita un corte de pelo **3** *v/i*: *he wants for nothing* no le falta nada

'want ad anuncio *m* por palabras (*buscando algo*)

want·ed ['wɑːntɪd] *adj by police* buscado por la policía

want·ing ['wɑːntɪŋ] *adj*: *the team is wanting in experience* al equipo le falta experiencia

wan·ton ['wɑːntən] *adj* gratuito

war [wɔːr] n also fig guerra f; **be at war** estar en guerra

war-ble ['wɔːrbl] v/i of bird trinar

ward [wɔːrd] n in hospital sala f; child pupilo(-a) m(f)

♦ ward off v/t blow parar; attacker rechazar; cold evitar

war-den ['wɔːrdn] of prison director(-a) m(f), alcaide(sa) m(f); Br of hostel vigilante m/f

'ward-robe for clothes armario m; (clothes) guardarropa m

ware-house ['werhaus] almacén m

'war-fare guerra f

'war-head ojiva f

war-i-ly ['werɪlɪ] adv cautelosamente

warm [wɔːrm] 1 adj hands, room, water caliente; weather, welcome cálido; coat de abrigo; it's warmer than yesterday hace más calor que ayer 2 v/t → warm up

♦ warm up 1 v/t calentar 2 v/i calentarse; of athlete etc calentar

warm-heart-ed ['wɔːrmhɑːrtɪd] adj cariñoso, simpático

warm-ly ['wɔːrmlɪ] adv welcome, smile calurosamente; warmly dressed abrigado

warmth [wɔːrmθ] calor m; of welcome, smile calor m, calidez m

'warm-up SP calentamiento m

warn [wɔːrn] v/t advertir, avisar

warn-ing ['wɔːrnɪŋ] n advertencia f, aviso m; **without warning** sin previo aviso

warp [wɔːrp] 1 v/t wood combar; character corromper 2 v/i of wood combarse

warped [wɔːrpt] adj fig retorcido

'war-plane avión m de guerra

war-rant ['wɔːrənt] 1 n orden f judicial 2 v/t (deserve, call for) justificar

war-ran-ty ['wɔːrəntɪ] (guarantee) garantía f; **be under warranty** estar en garantía

war-ri-or ['wɔːrɪər] guerrero(-a) m(f)

'war-ship buque m de guerra

wart [wɔːrt] verruga f

'war-time tiempos mpl de guerra

war-y ['werɪ] adj cauto, precavido; **be wary of** desconfiar de

was [wʌz] pret → be

wash [wɑːʃ] 1 n lavado m; **have a wash** lavarse; that shirt needs a wash hay que lavar esa camisa 2 v/t lavar 3 v/i lavarse

♦ wash up v/i (wash one's hands and face) lavarse

wash-a-ble ['wɑːʃəbl] adj lavable

'wash-ba-sin, 'wash-bowl lavabo m

'wash-cloth toallita f

washed out [wɑːʃt'aut] adj agotado

wash-er ['wɑːʃər] for faucet etc arandela f; → washing machine

wash-ing ['wɑːʃɪŋ] (clothes washed) ropa f limpia; (dirty clothes) ropa f sucia; **do the washing** lavar la ropa, hacer la colada

'wash-ing ma-chine lavadora f

wash-ing-'up liq-uid Br lavavajillas m inv

'wash-room lavabo m, aseo m

wasp [wɑːsp] insect avispa f

waste [weɪst] 1 n desperdicio m; from industrial process desechos mpl; **it's a waste of time / money** es una pérdida de tiempo / dinero 2 adj residual; **waste land** erial m 3 v/t derrochar; money gastar; time perder

♦ waste away v/i consumirse

'waste dis-pos-al (unit) trituradora f de basuras

waste-ful ['weɪstfəl] adj despilfarrador, derrochador

'waste-land erial m

'waste-pa-per papel m usado

waste-pa-per 'bas-ket papelera f

'waste pipe tubería f de desagüe

'waste prod-uct desecho m

watch [wɑːtʃ] 1 n timepiece reloj m; **keep watch** hacer la guardia, vigilar 2 v/t film, TV ver; (look after) vigilar 3 v/i mirar, observar

♦ watch for v/t esperar

♦ watch out v/i tener cuidado; **watch out!** ¡cuidado!

♦ watch out for v/t tener cuidado con

watch-ful ['wɑːtʃfəl] adj vigilante

'watch-mak-er relojero(-a) m(f)

wa-ter ['wɑːtər] 1 n agua f; **waters** NAUT aguas fpl 2 v/t plant regar 3 v/i. **my eyes are watering** me lloran los ojos; **my mouth is watering** se me hace la boca agua

♦ water down v/t drink aguar, diluir

'water can-non cañón m de agua

'wa-ter-col-or, Br 'wa-ter-col-our acuarela f

'wa-ter-cress berro m

watered 'down ['wɔːtərd] adj fig dulcificado

'wa-ter-fall cascada f, catarata f

'wa-ter-ing can ['wɔːtərɪŋ] regadera f

'wa-ter-ing hole hum bar m

'wa-ter lev-el nivel m del agua

'wa-ter lil-y nenúfar m

'wa-ter-line línea f de flotación

wa-ter-logged ['wɔːtərlɑːgd] adj earth, field anegado; boat lleno de agua

'wa-ter main tubería f principal

'wa-ter-mark filigrana f

'wa-ter mel-on sandía f

'wa-ter pol-lu-tion contaminación f del agua

W

'wa·ter po·lo waterpolo *m*

'wa·ter·proof *adj* impermeable

'wa·ter·shed *fig* momento *m* clave

'wa·ter·side *n* orilla *f*; **at the waterside** en la orilla

'wa·ter·ski·ing esquí *m* acuático

'wa·ter·tight *adj compartment* estanco; *fig* irrefutable

'wa·ter·way curso *m* de agua navegable

'wa·ter·wings *npl* flotadores *mpl* (*para los brazos*)

wa·ter·works F: *turn on the waterworks* ponerse a llorar como una magdalena F

wa·ter·y ['wɔːtərɪ] *adj* aguado

watt [wɑːt] vatio *m*

wave¹ [weɪv] *n in sea* ola *f*

wave² [weɪv] **1** *n of hand* saludo *m* **2** *v/i with hand* saludar con la mano; *wave to s.o.* saludar con la mano a alguien **3** *v/t flag etc* agitar

'wave·length RAD longitud *f* de onda; *be on the same wavelength fig* estar en la misma onda

wa·ver ['weɪvər] *v/i* vacilar, titubear

wav·y ['weɪvɪ] *adj hair, line* ondulado

wax [wæks] *n for floor, furniture* cera *f*; *in ear* cera *f*, cerumen

way [weɪ] **1** *n (method)* manera *f*, forma *f*; *(manner)* manera *f*, modo *m*; *(route)* camino *m*; *I don't like the way he behaves* no me gusta cómo se comporta; *can you tell me the way to …?* ¿me podría decir cómo se va a …?; *this way (like this)* así; *(in this direction)* por aquí; *by the way (incidentally)* por cierto, a propósito; *by way of (via)* por; *(in the form of)* a modo de; *in a way (in certain respects)* en cierto sentido; *be under way* haber comenzado, estar en marcha; *give way* MOT ceder el paso; *(collapse)* ceder; *give way to (be replaced by)* ser reemplazado por; *have one's (own) way* salirse con la suya; *OK, we'll do it your way* de acuerdo, lo haremos a tu manera; *lead the way* abrir (el) camino; *fig* marcar la pauta; *lose one's way* perderse; *be in the way (be an obstruction)* estar en medio; *it's on the way to the station* está camino de la estación; *I was on my way to the station* iba camino de la estación; *no way!* ¡ni hablar!, ¡de ninguna manera!; *there's no way he can do it* es imposible que lo haga **2** *adv* F *(much)*: *it's way too soon to decide* es demasiado pronto como para decidir; *they are way behind with their work* van atrasadísimos en el trabajo

way 'in entrada *f*

way of 'life modo *m* de vida

way 'out *n* salida *f*; *fig: from situation* salida *f*

we [wiː] *pron* nosotros *mpl*, nosotras *fpl*; *we are the best* somos los mejores; *they're going, but we're not* ellos van, pero nosotros no

weak [wiːk] *adj* débil; *tea, coffee* poco cargado

weak·en ['wiːkn] **1** *v/t* debilitar **2** *v/i* debilitarse

weak·ling ['wiːklɪŋ] *morally* cobarde *m/f*; *physically* enclenque *m/f*

weak·ness ['wiːknɪs] debilidad *f*; *have a weakness for sth (liking)* sentir debilidad por algo

wealth [welθ] riqueza *f*; *a wealth of* abundancia de

wealth·y ['welθɪ] *adj* rico

wean [wiːn] *v/t* destetar

weap·on ['wepən] arma *f*

wear [wer] **1** *n*: *wear (and tear)* desgaste *m*; *clothes for everyday / evening wear* ropa *f* de diario / de noche **2** *v/t (pret wore, pp worn) (have on)* llevar; *(damage)* desgastar **3** *v/i (pret wore, pp worn) (wear out)* desgastarse; *(last)* durar

◆ **wear away 1** *v/i* desgastarse **2** *v/t* desgastar

◆ **wear down** *v/t* agotar

◆ **wear off** *v/i of effect, feeling* pasar

◆ **wear out 1** *v/t (tire)* agotar; *shoes* desgastar **2** *v/i of shoes, carpet* desgastarse

wea·ri·ly ['wɪrɪlɪ] *adv* cansinamente

wear·ing ['werɪŋ] *adj (tiring)* agotador

wear·y ['wɪrɪ] *adj* cansado

weath·er ['weðər] **1** *n* tiempo *m*; *what's the weather like?* ¿qué tiempo hace?; *be feeling under the weather* estar pachucho **2** *v/t crisis* capear, superar

'weath·er-beat·en *adj* curtido

'weath·er chart mapa *m* del tiempo

'weath·er fore·cast pronóstico *m* del tiempo

'weath·er·man hombre *m* del tiempo

weave [wiːv] **1** *v/t (pret wove, pp woven)* tejer **2** *v/i (pret wove, pp woven) move* zigzaguear

web [web] *of spider* tela *f*; *the Web* COMPUT la Web

webbed 'feet patas *fpl* palmeadas

'web page página *f* web

'web site sitio *m* web

wed·ding ['wedɪŋ] boda *f*

'wed·ding an·ni·ver·sa·ry aniversario *m* de boda

'wed·ding cake pastel *m or* tarta *f* de boda

'wed·ding day día *f* de la boda

'wed·ding dress vestido *m* de boda *or*

novia

'wed·ding ring anillo m de boda

wedge [wedʒ] 1 n to hold sth in place cuña f; of cheese etc trozo m 2 v/t: **wedge a door open** calzar una puerta para que se quede abierta

Wed·nes·day ['wenzdeɪ] miércoles m inv

weed [wiːd] 1 n mala hierba 2 v/t escardar
◆ weed out v/t (remove) eliminar; candidates descartar

'weed·kill·er herbicida m

weed·y ['wiːdɪ] adj F esmirriado, enclenque

week [wiːk] semana f; **a week tomorrow** dentro de una semana

'week·day día m de la semana

week'end fin m de semana; **on the weekend** el fin de semana

week·ly ['wiːklɪ] 1 adj semanal 2 n magazine semanario m 3 adv semanalmente

weep [wiːp] v/i (pret & pp **wept**) llorar

'weep·ing wil·low sauce m llorón

weep·y ['wiːpɪ] adj: **be weepy** estar lloroso

wee-wee 1 n F pipí m; **do a wee-wee** hacer pipí 2 v/i F hacer pipí

weigh[1] [weɪ] 1 v/t pesar 2 v/i pesar; **how much do you weigh?** ¿cuánto pesas?

weigh[2] [weɪ] v/t: **weigh anchor** levar anclas
◆ weigh down v/t cargar; **be weighed down with** bags ir cargado con; worries estar abrumado por
◆ weigh on v/t preocupar
◆ weigh up v/t (assess) sopesar

weight [weɪt] peso m; **put on weight** engordar, ganar peso; **lose weight** adelgazar, perder peso
◆ weight down v/t sujetar (con pesos)

'weight·less ['weɪtləs] adj ingrávido

'weight·less·ness ['weɪtləsnəs] ingravidez f

'weight·lift·er levantador(a) m(f) de pesas

'weight·lift·ing halterofilia f, levantamiento m de pesas

weight·y ['weɪtɪ] adj (fig: important) serio

weir [wɪr] presa f (rebasadero)

weird [wɪrd] adj extraño, raro

weird·ly ['wɪrdlɪ] adv extrañamente

weird·o ['wɪrdoʊ] n F bicho m raro F

wel·come ['welkəm] 1 adj bienvenido; **you're welcome!** ¡de nada!; **you're welcome to try some** prueba algunos, por favor 2 n bienvenida f 3 v/t guests etc dar la bienvenida a; fig: decision etc acoger positivamente

weld [weld] v/t soldar

weld·er ['weldər] soldador(a) m(f)

wel·fare ['welfer] bienestar m; financial assistance subsidio m estatal; **be on welfare** estar recibiendo subsidios del Estado

'wel·fare check cheque con el importe del subsidio estatal

wel·fare 'state estado m del bienestar

'wel·fare work trabajo m social

'wel·fare work·er asistente m/f social

well[1] [wel] n for water, oil pozo m

well[2] [wel] 1 adv bien; **as well** (too) también; **as well as** (in addition to) así como; **it's just as well you told me** menos mal que me lo dijiste; **very well** muy bien; **well, well!** surprise ¡caramba!; **well ...** uncertainty, thinking bueno ...; **you might as well spend the night here** ya puestos quédate a pasar la noche aquí; **you might as well throw it out** yo de ti lo tiraría 2 adj: **be well** estar bien; **how are you? - I'm very well** ¿cómo estás? - muy bien; **feel well** sentirse bien; **get well soon!** ¡ponte bueno!, ¡que te mejores!

well-'bal·anced adj person, diet equilibrado

well-be'haved adj educado

well-'be·ing bienestar m

well-'built adj also euph fornido

well-'done adj meat muy hecho

well-'dressed adj bien vestido

well-'earned adj merecido

well-'heeled adj F adinerado, Span con pasta F

well-in'formed adj bien informado

well-'known adj fact conocido; person conocido, famoso

well-'made adj bien hecho

well-'man·nered adj educado

well-'mean·ing adj bienintencionado

well-'off adj acomodado

well-'paid adj bien pagado

well-'read adj: **be well-read** haber leído mucho

well-'timed adj oportuno

well-to-'do adj acomodado

'well-wish·er admirador(a) m(f)

well-'worn adj gastado

Welsh [welʃ] 1 adj galés 2 n language galés; **the Welsh** los galeses

went [went] pret → **go**

wept [wept] pret & pp → **weep**

were [wɜr] pret → **be**

west [west] 1 n oeste m; **the West** (Western nations) Occidente m; (western part of a country) el oeste 2 adj del oeste; **west Africa** África occidental 3 adv travel hacia el oeste; **west of** al oeste de

West 'Coast of USA Costa f Oeste

West In·di·an 1 *adj* antillano **2** *n* antillano(-a) *m(f)*

West In·dies ['ɪndɪz] *npl*: **the West Indies** las Antillas

west·er·ly ['westərlɪ] *adj wind* del oeste; *direction* hacia el oeste

west·ern ['westərn] **1** *adj* occidental; **Western** occidental **2** *n movie* western *m*, película *f* del oeste

West·ern·er ['westərnər] occidental *m/f*

west·ern·ized ['westərnaɪzd] *adj* occidentalizado

west·ward ['westwərd] *adv* hacia el oeste

wet [wet] *adj* mojado; (*damp*) húmedo; (*rainy*) lluvioso; **get wet** mojarse; **wet paint** as sign recién pintado; **be wet through** estar empapado

wet 'blan·ket F aguafiestas *m/f inv*

'wet suit *for diving* traje *m* de neopreno

whack [wæk] **1** *n* F (*blow*) porrazo *m* F; F (*share*) parte *f* **2** *v/t* F dar un porrazo a F

whacked [wækt] *adj* F hecho polvo F

whale [weɪl] ballena *f*

whal·ing ['weɪlɪŋ] caza *f* de ballenas

wharf [wɔːrf] *n* embarcadero *m*

what [wɑːt] **1** *pron* qué; **what is that?** ¿qué es eso?; **what is it?** (*what do you want*) ¿qué quieres?; **what?** (*what do you want*) ¿qué?; (*what did you say*) ¿qué?, ¿cómo?; *astonishment* ¿qué?; **what about some dinner?** ¿os apetece cenar?; **what about heading home?** ¿y si nos fuéramos a casa?; **what for?** (*why*) ¿para qué?; **so what?** ¿y qué?; **what is the book about?** ¿de qué trata el libro?; **take what you need** toma lo que te haga falta **2** *adj* qué; **what university are you at?** ¿en qué universidad estás?; **what color is the car?** ¿de qué color es el coche?

what·ev·er [wɑːt'evər] **1** *pron*: **I'll do whatever you want** haré lo que quieras; **whatever gave you that idea?** ¿se puede saber qué te ha dado esa idea?; **whatever the season** en cualquier estación; **whatever people say** diga lo que diga la gente **2** *adj* cualquier; **you have no reason whatever to worry** no tienes por qué preocuparte en absoluto

wheat [wiːt] trigo *m*

whee·dle ['wiːdl] *v/t*: **wheedle sth out of s.o.** camelar algo a alguien

wheel [wiːl] **1** *n* rueda *f*; (*steering wheel*) volante *m* **2** *v/t bicycle* empujar **3** *v/i of birds* volar en círculos

◆ **wheel around** *v/i* darse la vuelta

'wheel·bar·row carretilla *f*

'wheel·chair silla *f* de ruedas

'wheel clamp cepo *m*

wheeze [wiːz] *n* resoplido *m*

when [wen] **1** *adv* cuándo; **when do you open?** ¿a qué hora abren? **2** *conj* cuando; **when I was a child** cuando era niño

when·ev·er [wen'evər] *adv* (*each time*) cada vez que; **call me whenever you like** llámame cuando quieras; **I go to Paris whenever I can afford it** voy a París siempre que me lo puedo permitir

where [wer] **1** *adv* dónde; **where from?** ¿de dónde?; **where to?** ¿a dónde? **2** *conj* donde; **this is where I used to live** aquí es donde vivía antes

where·a·bouts [werə'bauts] **1** *adv* dónde **2** *npl* **nothing is known of his whereabouts** está en paradero desconocido

where·as *conj* mientras que

wher·ev·er [wer'evər] **1** *conj* dondequiera que; **sit wherever you like** siéntate donde prefieras **2** *adv* dónde

whet [wet] *v/t* (*pret & pp* **whetted**) *appetite* abrir

wheth·er ['weðər] *conj* si; **I don't know whether to tell him or not** no sé si decírselo o no; **whether you approve or not** te parezca bien o no

which [wɪtʃ] **1** *adj* qué; **which one is yours?** ¿cuál es tuyo? **2** *pron interrogative* cuál; *relative* que; **take one, it doesn't matter which** toma uno, no importa cuál

which·ev·er [wɪtʃ'evər] **1** *adj*: **whichever color you choose** elijas el color que prefieras **2** *pron*: **whichever you like** el que quieras; **use whichever of the methods you prefer** utiliza el método que prefieras

whiff [wɪf] (*smell*) olorcillo *m*

while [waɪl] **1** *conj* mientras; (*although*) si bien **2** *n* rato *m*; **a long while** un rato largo; **for a while** durante un tiempo; **I lived in Tokyo for a while** viví en Tokio una temporada; **I'll wait a while longer** esperaré un rato más

◆ **while away** *v/t* pasar

whim [wɪm] capricho *m*

whim·per ['wɪmpər] **1** *n* gimoteo *m* **2** *v/i* gimotear

whine [waɪn] *v/i of dog* gimotear; F (*complain*) quejarse

whip [wɪp] **1** *n* látigo *m* **2** *v/t* (*pret & pp* **whipped**) (*beat*) azotar; *cream* batir, montar; F (*defeat*) dar una paliza a F

◆ **whip out** *v/t* F sacar rápidamente

◆ **whip up** *v/t* (*arouse*) agitar; F *meal* improvisar

whipped cream [wɪpt] nata *f* montada

whip·ping ['wɪpɪŋ] (*beating*) azotes *mpl*; F (*defeat*) paliza *f* F

'whip·round F colecta f; **have a whip-round** hacer una colecta

whirl [wɜːrl] **1** n: **my mind is in a whirl** me da vueltas la cabeza **2** v/i dar vueltas

'whirl·pool in river remolino m; for relaxation bañera f de hidromasaje

whirr [wɜːr] v/i zumbar

whisk [wɪsk] **1** n kitchen implement **2** v/t eggs batir

◆ **whisk away** v/t retirar rápidamente

whis·kers ['wɪskərz] npl of man patillas fpl; of animal bigotes mpl

whis·key, whis·ky ['wɪskɪ] whisky m

whis·per ['wɪspər] **1** n susurro m; (rumor) rumor m **2** v/i susurrar **3** v/t susurrar

whis·tle ['wɪsl] **1** n sound silbido m; device silbato m **2** v/t & v/i silbar

white [waɪt] **1** n color blanco m; of egg clara f; person blanco(-a) m(f) **2** adj blanco; **her face went white** se puso blanca

white 'Christ·mas Navidades fpl blancas

white 'cof·fee Br café m con leche

white-col·lar 'work·er persona que trabaja en una oficina

'White House Casa f Blanca

white 'lie mentira f piadosa

white 'meat carne f blanca

'white·wash **1** n cal f; fig encubrimiento m **2** v/t encubrir

white 'wine vino m blanco

whit·tle ['wɪtl] v/t wood tallar

◆ **whittle down** v/t reducir

whiz(z) [wɪz] n: **be a whiz(z) at** F ser un genio de

◆ **whizz by, whizz past** v/i of time, car pasar zumbando

'whizz-kid F joven m/f prodigio

who [huː] pron interrogative ¿quién?; relative que; **who do you want to speak to?** ¿con quién quieres hablar?; **I don't know who to believe?** no sé a quién creer

who·dun·(n)it [huː'dʌnɪt] libro o película centrados en la resolución de un caso

who·ev·er [huː'evər] pron quienquiera; **whoever can that be calling at this time of night?** ¿pero quién llama a estas horas de la noche?

whole [hoʊl] **1** adj entero; **the whole town / country** toda la ciudad / todo el país; **he drank / ate the whole lot** se lo bebió / comió todo; **it's a whole lot easier / better** es mucho más fácil / mucho mejor **2** n totalidad f; **the whole of the United States** la totalidad de los Estados Unidos; **on the whole** en general

whole-heart·ed [hoʊl'hɑːrtɪd] adj incondicional

whole-heart·ed·ly [hoʊl'hɑːrtɪdlɪ] adv incondicionalmente

whole·meal 'bread pan m integral

'whole·sale **1** adj al por mayor; fig indiscriminado **2** adv al por mayor

whole·sal·er ['hoʊlseɪlər] mayorista m/f

whole·some ['hoʊlsəm] adj saludable, sano

whol·ly ['hoʊlɪ] adv completamente

whol·ly owned 'sub·sid·i·ar·y subsidiaria f en propiedad absoluta

whom [huːm] pron fml quién; **whom did you see?** ¿a quién vio?; **the person to whom I was speaking** la persona con la que estaba hablando

whoop·ing cough ['huːpɪŋ] tos f ferina

whop·ping ['wɑːpɪŋ] adj F enorme

whore [hɔːr] n prostituta f

whose [huːz] **1** pron interrogative de quién; relative cuyo(-a); **whose is this?** ¿de quién es esto?; **a country whose economy is booming** un país cuya economía está experimentando un boom **2** adj de quién; **whose bike is that?** ¿de quién es esa bici?

why [waɪ] adv interrogative por qué; relative por qué; **that's why** por eso; **why not?** ¿por qué no?

wick [wɪk] pabilo m

wick·ed ['wɪkɪd] adj malvado, perverso

wick·er ['wɪkər] adj de mimbre

wick·er 'chair silla f de mimbre

wick·et ['wɪkɪt] in station, bank etc ventanilla f

wide [waɪd] adj ancho; experience, range amplio, **be 12 feet wide** tener 12 pies de ancho

wide a'wake adj completamente despierto

wide·ly ['waɪdlɪ] adv used, known ampliamente

wid·en ['waɪdn] **1** v/t ensanchar **2** v/i ensancharse

wide-'o·pen adj abierto de par en par

wide-'rang·ing adj amplio

'wide·spread adj extendido, muy difundido

wid·ow ['wɪdoʊ] n viuda f

wid·ow·er ['wɪdoʊər] viudo m

width [wɪdθ] anchura f, ancho m

wield [wiːld] v/t weapon empuñar; power detentar

wife [waɪf] (pl wives [waɪvz]) mujer f, esposa f

wig [wɪg] peluca f

wig·gle ['wɪgl] v/t menear

wild [waɪld] **1** adj animal salvaje; flower silvestre; teenager, party descontrolado; (crazy: scheme) descabellado; applause arrebatado; *be wild about ...* (*keen on*) estar loco por ...; *go wild* (*express enthusiasm*) volverse loco; (*become angry*) ponerse hecho una furia; *run wild of children* descontrolarse 2 *n*: *the wilds* los parajes remotos

wil·der·ness ['wɪldərnɪs] (*empty place*) desierto *m*, yermo *m*; (*fig: garden etc*) jungla *f*

'**wild·fire**: *spread like wildfire* extenderse como un reguero de pólvora

wild-'goose chase búsqueda *f* infructuosa

'**wild·life** flora *f* y fauna; *wildlife program* TV documental *f* sobre la naturaleza

wild·ly ['waɪldlɪ] *adv applaud* enfervorizadamente; *I'm not wildly enthusiastic about the idea* la idea no me emociona demasiado

wil·ful *Br* → **willful**

will[1] [wɪl] *n* LAW testamento *m*

will[2] [wɪl] *n* (*willpower*) voluntad *f*

will[3] [wɪl] *v/aux*: *I will let you know tomorrow* te lo diré mañana; *will you be there?* ¿estarás allí?; *I won't be back until late* volveré tarde; *you will call me, won't you?* me llamarás, ¿verdad?; *I'll pay for this - no you won't* esto lo pago yo - no, ni hablar; *the car won't start* el coche no arranca; *will you tell her that ...?* ¿le quieres decir que ...?; *will you have some more tea?* ¿quiere más té?; *will you stop that!* ¡basta ya!

will·ful ['wɪlfəl] *adj person* tozudo, obstinado; *action* deliberado, intencionado

will·ing ['wɪlɪŋ] *adj* dispuesto

will·ing·ly ['wɪlɪŋlɪ] *adv* gustosamente

will·ing·ness ['wɪlɪŋnɪs] buena disposición *f*

wil·low ['wɪloʊ] sauce *m*

'**will·pow·er** fuerza *f* de voluntad

wil·ly-nil·ly ['wɪlɪ'nɪlɪ] *adv* (*at random*) a la buena de Dios

wilt [wɪlt] *v/i of plant* marchitarse

wi·ly ['waɪlɪ] *adj* astuto

wimp [wɪmp] F enclenque *m/f* F, blandengue *m/f* F

win [wɪn] **1** *n* victoria *f*, triunfo *m* **2** *v/t* & *v/i* (*pret* & *pp* **won**) ganar

◆ **win back** *v/t* recuperar

wince [wɪns] *v/i* hacer una mueca de dolor

winch [wɪntʃ] *n* torno *m*, cabestrante *m*

wind[1] [wɪnd] **1** *n* viento *m*; (*flatulence*) gases *mpl*; *get wind of ...* enterarse de ... **2** *v/t*: *be winded* quedarse sin respiración

wind[2] [waɪnd] **1** *v/i* (*pret* & *pp* **wound**) zigzaguear; serpentear; *wind around*

enrollarse en **2** *v/t* (*pret* & *pp* **wound**) enrollar

◆ **wind down 1** *v/i of party etc* ir finalizando **2** *v/t car window* bajar, abrir; *business* ir reduciendo

◆ **wind up 1** *v/t clock* dar cuerda a; *car window* subir, cerrar; *speech, presentation* finalizar; *business, affairs* concluir; *company* cerrar **2** *v/i* (*finish*) concluir; *wind up in hospital* acabar en el hospital

'**wind-bag** F cotorra *f* F

'**wind·fall** *fig* dinero *m* inesperado

wind·ing ['waɪndɪŋ] *adj* zigzagueante, serpenteante

'**wind in·stru·ment** instrumento *m* de viento

'**wind·mill** molino *m* de viento

win·dow ['wɪndoʊ] *also* COMPUT ventana *f*; *of car* ventana *f*, ventanilla *f*; *in the window of store* en el escaparate *or* L.Am. la vidriera

'**win·dow box** jardinera *f*

'**win·dow clean·er** *person* limpiacristales *m/f inv*

'**win·dow·pane** cristal *f* (*de una ventana*)

'**win·dow seat** *on plane, train* asiento *m* de ventana

'**win·dow-shop** *v/i* (*pret* & *pp* **window-shopped**): *go window-shopping* ir de escaparates *or* L.Am. vidrieras

win·dow-sill ['wɪndoʊsɪl] alféizar *m*

'**wind·pipe** tráquea *f*

'**wind·screen** *Br*, '**wind·shield** parabrisas *m inv*

'**wind·shield wip·er** limpiaparabrisas *m inv*

'**wind·surf·er** *person* windsurfista *m/f*; *board* tabla *f* de windsurf

'**wind·surf·ing** el windsurf

wind·y ['wɪndɪ] *adj* ventoso; *a windy day* un día de mucho viento; *it's very windy today* hoy hace mucho viento; *it's getting windy* está empezando a soplar el viento

wine [waɪn] vino *m*

'**wine bar** *bar* especializado en vinos

'**wine cel·lar** bodega *f*

'**wine glass** copa *f* de vino

'**wine list** lista *f* de vinos

'**wine mak·er** viticultor(a) *m(f)*

'**wine mer·chant** comerciante *m/f* de vinos

win·er·y ['waɪnərɪ] bodega *f*

wing [wɪŋ] *n* ala *f*; SP lateral *m/f*, extremo *m/f*

'**wing-span** envergadura *f*

wink [wɪŋk] **1** *n* guiño *m*; *I didn't sleep a wink* F no pegué ojo **2** *v/i of person* guiñar, hacer un guiño; **wink at s.o.** guiñar *or* hacer un guiño a alguien

win·ner ['wɪnər] ganador(a) *m(f)*, vencedor(a) *m(f)*; *of lottery* acertante *m/f*

win·ning ['wɪnɪŋ] *adj* ganador

'win·ning post meta *f*

win·nings ['wɪnɪŋz] *npl* ganancias *fpl*

win·ter ['wɪntər] *n* invierno *m*

win·ter 'sports *npl* deportes *mpl* de invierno

win·try ['wɪntrɪ] *adj* invernal

wipe [waɪp] *v/t* limpiar; *tape* borrar

◆ **wipe out** *v/t* (*kill, destroy*) eliminar; *debt* saldar

wip·er ['waɪpər] → **windshield wiper**

wire [waɪr] *n* alambre *m*; ELEC cable *m*

wire·less ['waɪrlɪs] radio *f*

wire 'net·ting tela *f* metálica

wir·ing ['waɪrɪŋ] *n* ELEC cableado *m*

wir·y ['waɪrɪ] *adj* person fibroso

wis·dom ['wɪzdəm] *of person* sabiduría *f*; *of action* prudencia *f*, sensatez *f*

'wis·dom tooth muela *f* del juicio

wise [waɪz] *adj* sabio; *action, decision* prudente, sensato

wise·crack *n* F chiste *m*, comentario *m* gracioso

'wise guy *pej* sabelotodo *m*

wise·ly ['waɪzlɪ] *adv act* prudentemente, sensatamente

wish [wɪʃ] **1** *n* deseo *m*, **best wishes** un saludo cordial; **make a wish** pedir un deseo **2** *v/t* desear; **I wish that you could stay** ojalá te pudieras quedar; **wish s.o. well** desear a alguien lo mejor; **I wished him good luck** le deseé buena suerte **3** *v/i*: **wish for** desear

'wish·bone espoleta *f*

wish·ful 'think·ing ['wɪʃfəl] ilusiones *fpl*; **that's wishful thinking on her part** que no se haga ilusiones

wish·y-wash·y ['wɪʃɪwaːʃɪ] *adj person* anodino; *color* pálido

wisp [wɪsp] *of hair* mechón *m*; *of smoke* voluta *f*

wist·ful ['wɪstfəl] *adj* nostálgico

wist·ful·ly ['wɪstfəlɪ] *adv* con nostalgia

wit [wɪt] (*humor*) ingenio *m*; *person* ingenioso(-a) *m(f)*; **be at one's wits' end** estar desesperado; **keep one's wits about one** mantener la calma; **be scared out of one's wits** estar aterrorizado

witch [wɪʧ] bruja *f*

'witch·hunt *fig* caza *f* de brujas

with [wɪð] *prep con; **shivering with fear** temblando de miedo; **a girl with brown eyes** una chica de ojos castaños; **are you with me?** (*do you understand*) ¿me sigues?; **with no money** sin dinero

with·draw [wɪð'drɔː] **1** *v/t* (*pret withdrew, pp withdrawn*) *complaint, money, troops* retirar **2** *v/i* (*pret withdrew, pp withdrawn*) *of competitor, troops* retirarse

with·draw·al [wɪð'drɔːəl] *of complaint, application, troops* retirada *f*; *of money* reintegro *m*

with·draw·al symp·toms *npl* síndrome *m* de abstinencia

with·drawn [wɪð'drɔːn] *adj person* retraído

with·er ['wɪðər] *v/i* marchitarse

with·hold *v/t* (*pret & pp withheld*) *information* ocultar; *payment* retener; *consent* negar

with·in *prep* (*inside*) dentro de; *in expressions of time* en menos de; **within five miles of home** a cinco millas de casa; **we kept within the budget** no superamos el presupuesto; **it is well within your capabilities** lo puedes conseguir perfectamente; **within reach** al alcance de la mano

with·out *prep* sin; **without looking / asking** sin mirar / preguntar

with·stand *v/t* (*pret & pp withstood*) resistir, soportar

wit·ness ['wɪtnɪs] **1** *n* testigo *m/f* **2** *v/t accident, crime* ser testigo de; *signature* firmar en calidad de testigo

'wit·ness stand estrado *m* del testigo

wit·ti·cism ['wɪtɪsɪzm] comentario *m* gracioso *or* agudo

wit·ty ['wɪtɪ] *adj* ingenioso, agudo

wob·ble ['waːbl] *v/i* tambalearse

wob·bly ['waːblɪ] *adj* tambaleante

wok [waːk] wok *m*, sartén *típica de la cocina china*

woke [wouk] *pret* → **wake[1]**

wok·en ['woukn] *pp* → **wake[1]**

wolf [wulf] **1** *n* (*pl wolves* [wulvz]) *animal* lobo *m*; (*fig: womanizer*) don juan *m* **2** *v/t*: **wolf** (**down**) engullir

'wolf whis·tle *n* silbido *m*

'wolf-whis·tle *v/i*: **wolf-whistle at s.o.** silbar a alguien (*como piropo*)

wom·an ['wumən] (*pl women* ['wɪmɪn]) mujer *f*

wom·an 'doc·tor médica *f*

wom·an 'driv·er conductora *f*

wom·an·iz·er ['wumənaɪzər] mujeriego(-a) *m(f)*

wom·an·ly ['wumənlɪ] *adj* femenino

wom·an 'priest mujer *f* sacerdote

womb [wuːm] matriz *f*, útero *m*

wom·en ['wɪmɪn] *pl* → **woman**

wom·en's lib [wɪmɪnz'lɪb] la liberación de la mujer

wom·en's lib·ber [wɪmɪnz'lɪbər] partidario(-a) *m(f)* de la liberación de la mujer

won [wʌn] *pret & pp* → **win**

won·der ['wʌndər] **1** *n* (*amazement*) asombro *m*; **no wonder!** ¡no me sorprende!; **it's a wonder that ...** es increíble que ... **2** *v/i* preguntarse; **I've often wondered about that** me he preguntado eso a menudo **3** *v/t* preguntarse; **I wonder if you could help** ¿le importaría ayudarme?

won·der·ful ['wʌndərfəl] *adj* maravilloso

won·der·ful·ly ['wʌndərfəlɪ] *adv* (*extremely*) maravillosamente

won't [wount] → **will³**

wood [wud] *n* madera *f*; *for fire* leña *f*; (*forest*) bosque *m*

wood·ed ['wudɪd] *adj* arbolado

wood·en ['wudn] *adj* (*made of wood*) de madera

wood·peck·er ['wudpekər] pájaro *m* carpintero

'**wood·wind** MUS sección *f* de viento de madera

'**wood·work** carpintería *f*

wool [wul] lana *f*

wool·en, *Br* **wool·len** ['wulən] **1** *adj* de lana **2** *n* prenda *f* de lana

word [wɜːrd] **1** *n* palabra *f*; **I didn't understand a word of what she said** no entendí nada de lo que dijo; **is there any word from ...?** ¿se sabe algo de ...?; **I've had word from my daughter** (*news*) he recibido noticias de mi hija; **you have my word** tienes mi palabra; **have words** (*argue*) discutir; **have a word with s.o.** hablar con alguien; **the words** *of song* la letra **2** *v/t* **article, letter** redactar

word·ing ['wɜːrdɪŋ]: **the wording of a letter** la redacción de una carta

word 'pro·cess·ing procesamiento *m* de textos

word 'pro·ces·sor *software* procesador *m* de textos

wore [wɔːr] *pret* → **wear**

work [wɜːrk] **1** *n* (*job*) trabajo *m*; (*employment*) trabajo *m*, empleo *m*; **out of work** desempleado, *Span* en el paro; **be at work** estar en el trabajo; **I go to work by bus** voy al trabajo en autobús **2** *v/i* *of person* trabajar; *of machine*, (*succeed*) funcionar; **how does it work?** *of device* ¿cómo funciona? **3** *v/t* **employee** hacer trabajar; **machine** hacer funcionar, utilizar

◆ **work off** *v/t* **bad mood, anger** desahogarse de; **flab** perder haciendo ejercicio

◆ **work out 1** *v/t* **problem, puzzle** resolv-

er; **solution** encontrar, hallar **2** *v/i* *at gym* hacer ejercicios; *of relationship etc* funcionar, ir bien

◆ **work out to** *v/t* (*add up to*) sumar

◆ **work up** *v/t* **appetite** abrir; **work up enthusiasm** entusiasmarse; **get worked up** (*get angry*) alterarse; (*get nervous*) ponerse nervioso

work·a·ble ['wɜːrkəbl] *adj* **solution** viable

work·a·hol·ic [wɜːrkə'hɑːlɪk] *n* F **persona obsesionada con el trabajo**

work·er ['wɜːrkər] trabajador(a) *m(f)*; **she's a good worker** trabaja bien

'**work·day** (*hours of work*) jornada *f* laboral; (*not a holiday*) día *m* de trabajo

'**work·force** trabajadores *mpl*

'**work hours** *npl* horas *fpl* de trabajo

work·ing ['wɜːrkɪŋ] *n* funcionamiento *m*

'**work·ing class** clase *f* trabajadora

'**work·ing-class** *adj* de clase trabajadora

'**work·ing con·di·tions** *npl* condiciones *fpl* de trabajo

work·ing 'day → **workday**

work·ing hours → **work hours**

work·ing 'knowl·edge conocimientos *mpl* básicos

work·ing 'moth·er madre *f* que trabaja

'**work·load** cantidad *f* de trabajo

'**work·man** obrero *m*

'**work·man·like** *adj* competente

'**work·man·ship** factura *f*, confección *f*

work of 'art obra *f* de arte

'**work·out** sesión *f* de ejercicios

'**work per·mit** permiso *m* de trabajo

'**work·shop** (*also seminar*) taller *m*

'**work sta·tion** estación *f* de trabajo

'**work·top** encimera *f*

world [wɜːrld] mundo *m*; **the world of computers / the theater** el mundo de la informática / del teatro; **out of this world** F sensacional

World 'Cup Mundial *m*, Copa *f* del Mundo

world·ly ['wɜːrldlɪ] *adj* mundano

world-'class *adj* de categoría mundial

world-'fa·mous *adj* mundialmente famoso

world 'pow·er potencia *f* mundial

world 're·cord récord *m* mundial *or* del mundo

world 'war guerra *f* mundial

'**world·wide 1** *adj* mundial **2** *adv* en todo el mundo

worm [wɜːrm] *n* gusano *m*

worn [wɔːrn] *pp* → **wear**

worn-'out *adj* **shoes, carpet, part** gastado; **person** agotado

wor·ried ['wʌrɪd] *adj* preocupado

wor·ried·ly ['wʌrɪdlɪ] *adv* con preocupación

wor·ry ['wʌrɪ] **1** *n* preocupación *f* **2** *v/t* (*pret & pp* **worried**) preocupar **3** *v/i* (*pret & pp* **worried**) preocuparse; ***don't worry, I'll get it!*** ¡no te molestes, ya respondo yo!

wor·ry·ing ['wʌrɪɪŋ] *adj* preocupante

worse [wɜːrs] **1** *adj* peor; ***get worse*** empeorar **2** *adv* peor

wors·en ['wɜːrsn] *v/i* empeorar

wor·ship ['wɜːrʃɪp] **1** *n* culto *m* **2** *v/t* (*pret & pp* **worshipped**) adorar, rendir culto a; *fig* adorar

worst [wɜːrst] **1** *adj & adv* peor **2** *n*: ***the worst*** lo peor; ***if the worst comes to the worst*** en el peor de los casos

worst-case sce·nar·i·o el peor de los casos

worth [wɜːrθ] *adj*: ***$20 worth of gas*** 20 dólares de gasolina; ***be worth ...*** *in monetary terms* valer ...; ***the book's worth reading*** valer la pena leer el libro; ***be worth it*** valer la pena

worth·less ['wɜːrθlɪs] *adj person* inútil; ***be worthless*** *of object* no valer nada

worth·while *adj* que vale la pena; ***be worthwhile*** valer la pena

worth·y ['wɜːrðɪ] *adj* digno; *cause* justo; ***be worthy of*** (*deserve*) merecer

would [wud] *v/aux*: ***I would help if I could*** te ayudaría si pudiera; ***I said that I would go*** dije que iría; ***I told him I would not leave unless ...*** le dije que no me iría a no ser que ...; ***would you like to go to the movies?*** ¿te gustaría ir al cine?; ***would you mind if I smoked?*** ¿le importa si fumo?; ***would you tell her that ...?*** ¿le podrías decir que ...?; ***would you close the door?*** ¿podrías cerrar la puerta?; ***I would have told you but ...*** te lo habría dicho pero ...; ***I would not have been so angry if ...*** no me habría enfadado tanto si ...

wound¹ [wuːnd] **1** *n* herida *f* **2** *v/t with weapon, remark* herir

wound² [waund] *pret & pp* → **wind**²

wove [wouv] *pret* → **weave**

wov·en ['wouvn] *pp* → **weave**

wow [wau] *int* ¡hala!

wrap [ræp] *v/t* (*pret & pp* **wrapped**) *parcel, gift* envolver; ***he wrapped a scarf around his neck*** se puso una bufanda al cuello

◆ **wrap up** *v/i against the cold* abrigarse

wrap·per ['ræpər] envoltorio *m*

wrap·ping ['ræpɪŋ] envoltorio *m*

'wrap·ping pa·per papel *m* de envolver

wrath [ræθ] ira *f*

wreath [riːθ] corona *f* de flores

wreck [rek] **1** *n* restos *mpl*; ***be a nervous wreck*** ser un manojo de nervios **2** *v/t ship* hundir; *car* destrozar; *plans, marriage* arruinar

wreck·age ['rekɪdʒ] *of car, plane* restos *mpl*; *of marriage, career* ruina *f*

wreck·er ['rekər] grúa *f*

wreck·ing com·pa·ny ['rekɪŋ] empresa *f* de auxilio en carretera

wrench [renʃ] **1** *n tool* llave *f* **2** *v/t* (*pull*) arrebatar; ***wrench one's wrist*** hacerse un esguince en la muñeca

wres·tle ['resl] *v/i* luchar

◆ **wrestle with** *v/t problems* combatir

wres·tler ['reslər] luchador(a) *m(f)* (*de lucha libre*)

wrest·ling ['reslɪŋ] lucha *f* libre

'wres·tling match combate *m* de lucha libre

wrig·gle ['rɪgl] *v/i* (*squirm*) menearse; *along the ground* arrastrarse; *into small space* escurrirse

◆ **wriggle out of** *v/t* librarse de

◆ **wring out** *v/t* (*pret & pp* **wrung**) *cloth* escurrir

wrin·kle ['rɪŋkl] **1** *n* arruga *f* **2** *v/t clothes* arrugar **3** *v/i of clothes* arrugarse

wrist [rɪst] muñeca *f*

'wrist watch reloj *m* de pulsera

writ [rɪt] LAW mandato *m* judicial

write [raɪt] **1** *v/t* (*pret* **wrote**, *pp* **written**) escribir; *check* extender **2** *v/i* (*pret* **wrote**, *pp* **written**) escribir

◆ **write down** *v/t* escribir, tomar nota de

◆ **write off** *v/t debt* cancelar, anular; *car* destrozar

writ·er ['raɪtər] escritor(a) *m(f)*; *of book, song* autor(a) *m(f)*

'write-up reseña *f*

writhe [raɪð] *v/i* retorcerse

writ·ing ['raɪtɪŋ] *words, text* escritura *f*; (*hand-writing*) letra *f*; ***in writing*** por escrito

'writ·ing desk escritorio *m*

'writ·ing pa·per papel *m* de escribir

writ·ten ['rɪtn] *pp* → **write**

wrong [rɒːŋ] **1** *adj answer, information* equivocado; *decision, choice* erróneo; ***be wrong*** *of person* estar equivocado; *of answer* ser incorrecto; *morally* ser injusto; ***what's wrong?*** ¿qué pasa?; ***there is something wrong with the car*** al coche le pasa algo; ***you have the wrong number*** TELEC se ha equivocado **2** *adv* mal; ***go wrong*** *of person* equivocarse; *of marriage, plan etc* fallar **3** *n* mal *m*; ***right a wrong*** deshacer un entuerto; ***he knows right from wrong*** sabe distinguir entre el bien y el mal; ***be in the***

wrong tener la culpa
wrong·ful ['rɔːŋfəl] *adj* ilegal
wrong·ly ['rɔːŋlɪ] *adv* erróneamente
wrote [rout] *pret* → **write**

wrought 'i·ron [rɔːt] hierro *m* forjado
wrung [rʌŋ] *pret & pp* → **wring**
wry [raɪ] *adj* socarrón

X, Y

xen·o·pho·bi·a [zenou'foubɪə] xenofobia *f*
X-ray ['eksreɪ] **1** *n* rayo *m* X; *picture* radiografía *f* **2** *v/t* radiografiar, sacar una radiografía de
xy·lo·phone [zaɪlə'foun] xilófono *m*
yacht [jɑːt] yate *m*
yacht·ing ['jɑːtɪŋ] vela *f*
yachts·man ['jɑːtsmən] navegante *m/f* (*en embarcación de vela*)
Yank [jæŋk] F yanqui *m/f*
yank [jæŋk] *v/t* tirar de
yap [jæp] *v/i* (*pret & pp* **yapped**) *of small dog* ladrar (*con ladridos agudos*); F (*talk a lot*) parlotear F, largar F
yard[1] [jɑːrd] *of prison, institution etc* patio *m*; *behind house* jardín *m*; *for storage* almacén *m* (*al aire libre*)
yard[2] [jɑːrd] *measurement* yarda *f*
'**yard·stick** patrón *m*
yarn [jɑːrn] *n* (*thread*) hilo *m*; F (*story*) batallita *f* F
yawn [jɔːn] **1** *n* bostezo *m* **2** *v/i* bostezar
year [jɪr] *n* año *m*; **I've know her for years** la conozco desde hace años; **we were in the same year** *at school* éramos del mismo curso; **be six years old** tener seis años (de edad)
year·ly ['jɪrlɪ] **1** *adj* anual **2** *adv* anualmente
yearn [jɜːrn] *v/i* anhelar
◆ **yearn for** *v/t* ansiar
yearn·ing ['jɜːrnɪŋ] *n* anhelo *m*
yeast [jiːst] levadura *f*
yell [jel] **1** *n* grito *m* **2** *v/i* gritar **3** *v/t* gritar
yel·low ['jelou] **1** *n* amarillo *m* **2** *adj* amarillo
yel·low 'pag·es *npl* páginas *fpl* amarillas
yelp [jelp] **1** *n* aullido *m* **2** *v/i* aullar
yes [jes] *int* sí; **she said yes** dijo que sí
'**yes-man** *pej* pelotillero *m*
yes·ter·day ['jestərdeɪ] **1** *adv* ayer; **the day before yesterday** anteayer; **yesterday afternoon** ayer por la tarde **2** *n* ayer *m*

yet [jet] **1** *adv* todavía, aún; **as yet** aún, todavía; **have you finished yet?** ¿has acabado ya?; **he hasn't arrived yet** todavía *or* aún no ha llegado; **is he here yet?** ¿ya ha llegado?; **has he arrived yet? - not yet** ¿ha llegado ya? - todavía *or* aún no; **yet bigger / longer** aún más grande / largo; **the fastest one yet** el más rápido hasta el momento **2** *conj* sin embargo; **yet I'm not sure** sin embargo no estoy seguro
yield [jiːld] **1** *n* *from fields etc* cosecha *f*; *from investment* rendimiento *m* **2** *v/t* *fruit, good harvest* proporcionar; *interest* rendir, devengar **3** *v/i* (*give way*) ceder; *of driver* ceder el paso
yo·ga ['jougə] yoga *m*
yog·hurt ['jougərt] yogur *m*
yolk [jouk] yema *f*
you [juː] *pron singular* tú, *L.Am.* usted, *Rpl, C.Am.* vos; *formal* usted; *plural*: *Span* vosotros, vosotras, *L.Am.* ustedes; *formal* ustedes; **you are clever** eres / es inteligente; **do you know him?** ¿lo conoces / conoce?; **you go, I'll stay** tú ve / usted vaya, yo me quedo; **never know** nunca se sabe; **you have to pay** hay que pagar; **exercise is good for you** es bueno hacer ejercicio
young [jʌŋ] *adj* joven
young·ster ['jʌŋstər] joven *m/f*
your [jʊr] *adj singular*: tu, *L.Am.* su; *formal* su; *plural*: *Span* vuestro, *L.Am.* su; *formal* su; **your house** tu / su casa; **your books** tus / sus libros
yours [jʊrz] *pron singular* el tuyo, la tuya, *L.Am.* el suyo, la suya; *formal* el suyo, la suya; *plural* el vuestro, la vuestra, *L.Am.* el suyo, la suya; *formal* el suyo, la suya; **a friend of yours** un amigo tuyo / suyo / vuestro; **yours ...** *at end of letter* un saludo
your·self [jʊr'self] *pron reflexive* te, *L.Am.* se; *formal* se; *emphatic* tú mismo *m*, tú misma *f*, *L.Am.* usted mismo, usted misma; *Rpl, C.Am.* vos mismo, vos mis-

ma; *formal* usted mismo, usted misma; *did you hurt yourself?* ¿te hiciste / se hizo daño?; *when you see yourself in the mirror* cuando te ves / se ve en el espejo; *by yourself* (*alone*) solo; (*without help*) tú solo, tú mismo, *Am* usted solo, usted mismo; *formal* usted solo, usted mismo

your·selves [jʊr'selvz] *pron reflexive* os, *L.Am.* se; *formal* se; *emphatic* vosotros mismos, vosotras mismas *fpl, Am* ustedes mismos, ustedes mismas; *formal* ustedes mismos, ustedes mismas; *did you hurt yourselves?* ¿os hicisteis / se hicieron daño?; *when you see your-*

selves in the mirror cuando os veis / se ven en el espejo; *by yourselves* (*alone*) solos; (*without help*) vosotros solos, *Am* ustedes solos, ustedes mismos; *formal* ustedes solos, ustedes mismos

youth [juːθ] *n* juventud *f*; (*young man*) joven *m/f*

'**youth club** club *m* juvenil

youth·ful ['juːθfəl] *adj* joven; *fashion, idealism* juvenil

'**youth hos·tel** albergue *m* juvenil

Yu·go·sla·vi·a [juːgə'slɑːvɪə] Yugoslavia

Yu·go·sla·vi·an [juːgə'slɑːvɪən] **1** *adj* yugoslavo **2** *n* yugoslavo(-a) *m(f)*

yup·pie ['jʌpɪ] F yupi *m/f*

Z

zap [zæp] *v/t* (*pret & pp* **zapped**) F (COMPUT: *delete*) borrar; (*kill*) liquidar F; (*hit*) golpear; (*send*) enviar

◆ **zap along** *v/i* F (*move fast*) volar F

zapped [zæpt] *adj* F (*exhausted*) hecho polvo F

zap·per ['zæpər] *for changing* TV *channels* telemando *m*, mando *m* a distancia

zap·py ['zæpɪ] *adj* F *car, pace* rápido; (*lively, energetic*) vivo

zeal [ziːl] celo *m*

ze·bra ['zebrə] cebra *f*

ze·ro ['zɪrəʊ] cero *m*; *10 degrees below zero* 10 bajo cero

ze·ro '**growth** crecimiento *m* cero

◆ **zero in on** *v/t* (*identify*) centrarse en

zest [zest] entusiasmo *m*

zig·zag ['zɪgzæg] **1** *n* zigzag *m* **2** *v/i* (*pret & pp* **zigzagged**) zigzaguear

zilch [zɪltʃ] F nada de nada

zinc [zɪŋk] cinc *m*

zip [zɪp] *Br* cremallera *f*

◆ **zip up** *v/t* (*pret & pp* **zipped**) *dress, jacket* cerrar la cremallera de; COMPUT com-

pactar

'**zip code** código *m* postal

zip·per ['zɪpər] cremallera *f*

zit [zɪt] F *on face* grano *m*

zo·di·ac ['zəʊdɪæk] zodiaco *m*; *signs of the zodiac* signos *mpl* del zodiaco

zom·bie ['zɑːmbɪ] F (*idiot*) estúpido(-a) *m(f)* F; *feel like a zombie* (*exhausted*) sentirse como un zombi

zone [zəʊn] zona *f*

zonked [zɑːŋkt] *adj* F (*exhausted*) molido P

zoo [zuː] zoo *m*

zo·o·log·i·cal [zuːə'lɑːdʒɪkl] *adj* zoológico

zo·ol·o·gist [zuː'ɑːlədʒɪst] zoólogo(-a) *m(f)*

zo·ol·o·gy [zuː'ɑːlədʒɪ] zoología *f*

zoom [zuːm] *v/i* F (*move fast*) ir zumbando F

◆ **zoom in on** *v/t* PHOT hacer un zoom sobre

zoom '**lens** zoom *m*

zuc·chi·ni [zuː'kiːnɪ] calabacín *m*

APPENDIX

Spanish verb conjugations

In the following conjugation patterns verb stems are shown in normal type and verb endings in *italic* type. Irregular forms are indicated by **bold** type.

Notes on the formation of tenses.

The following stems can be used to generate derived forms.

Stem forms	Derived forms
I. From the **Present indicative**, *3rd pers sg* (mand*a*, vend*e*, recib*e*)	**Imperative** *2nd pers. sg* (¡mand*a*! ¡vend*e*! ¡recib*e*!)
II. From the **Present subjunctive**, *2nd* and *3rd pers sg* and all plural forms (mand*es*, mand*e*, mand*emos*, mand*éis*, mand*en* – vend*as*, vend*a*, vend*amos*, vend*áis*, vend*an* – recib*as*, recib*a*, recib*amos*, recib*áis*, recib*an*)	**Imperative** *1st pers pl*, *3rd pers sg* and *pl* as well as the negative imperative of the *2nd pers sg* and *pl* (no mand*es*, mand*e* Vd., mand*emos*, no mand*éis*, mand*en* Vds. – no vend*as*, vend*a* Vd., vend*amos*, no vend*áis*, vend*an* Vds. – no recib*as* etc)
III. From the **Preterite**, *3rd pers pl* (mand*aron*, vend*ieron*, recib*ieron*)	a) **Imperfect Subjunctive I** by changing ...ron to ...*ra* (mand*ara*, vend*iera*, recib*iera*) b) **Imperfect Subjunctive II** by changing ...ron to ...*se* (mand*ase*, vend*iese*, recib*iese*) c) **Future Subjunctive** by changing ...ron to ...*re* (mand*are*, vend*iere*, recib*iere*)
IV. From the **Infinitive** (mand*ar*, vend*er*, recib*ir*)	a) **Imperative** *2nd pers pl* by changing ...r to ...*d* (mand*ad*, vend*ed*, recib*id*) b) **Present participle by** changing ...ar to ...*ando*, ...er and ...ir to ...*iendo* (or sometimes ...*yendo*) (mand*ando*, vend*iendo*, recib*iendo*) c) **Future** by adding the *Present* tense endings of **haber** (mand*aré*, vend*eré*, recib*iré*) d) **Conditional** by adding the *Imperfect* endings of **haber** (mand*aría*, vend*ería*, recib*iría*)

> **V.** From the **Past participle** (mand*ado*, vend*ido*, recib*ido*) | all **compound tenses** by placing a form of **haber** or **ser** in front of the participle.

First Conjugation

⟨1a⟩ **mandar.** No change to the written or spoken form of the stem.

Simple tenses

Indicative

	Present	Imperfect	Preterite
sg	mando	mandaba	mandé
	mandas	mandabas	mandaste
	manda	mandaba	mandó
pl	mandamos	mandábamos	mandamos
	mandáis	mandabais	mandasteis
	mandan	mandaban	mandaron

	Future	Conditional
sg	mandaré	mandaría
	mandarás	mandarías
	mandará	mandaría
pl	mandaremos	mandaríamos
	mandaréis	mandaríais
	mandarán	mandarían

Subjunctive

Present		Imperfect I	Imperfect II
sg	mande	mandara	mandase
	mandes	mandaras	mandases
	mande	mandara	mandase
pl	mandemos	mandáramos	mandásemos
	mandéis	mandarais	mandaseis
	manden	mandaran	mandasen

	Future	Imperative
sg	mandare	—
	mandares	manda (no mandes)
	mandare	mande Vd.
pl	mandáremos	mandemos
	mandareis	mandad (no mandéis)
	mandaren	manden Vds.

Infinitive: mandar
Present participle: mandando
Past participle: mandado

Compound tenses

1. **Active forms:** the conjugated form of **haber** is placed before the *Past participle* (which does not change):

Indicative

Perfect	*he* mand*ado*	**Future perfect**	*habré* mand*ado*
Pluperfect	*había* mand*ado*	**Past conditional**	*habría* mand*ado*
Past anterior	*hube* mand*ado*		
Past infinitive	*haber* mand*ado*	**Past gerundive**	*habiendo* mand*ado*

Subjunctive

Perfect	*haya* mand*ado*	**Future perfect**	*hubiere* mand*ado*
Pluperfect	*hubiera* mand*ado*		
	hubiese mand*ado*		

2. **Passive forms:** the conjugated form of **ser** (or **haber**) is placed before the *Past participle* (which does not change):

Indicative

Present	*soy* mand*ado*	**Past anterior**	*hube sido* mand*ado*
Imperfect	*era* mand*ado*	**Future**	*seré* mand*ado*
Preterite	*fui* mand*ado*	**Future perfect**	*habré sido* mand*ado*
Perfect	*he sido* mand*ado*	**Conditional**	*sería* mand*ado*
Pluperfect	*había sido* mand*ado*	**Past conditional**	*habría sido* mand*ado*

Infinitive		Gerundive	
Present	*ser* mand*ado* etc	**Present**	*siendo* mand*ado*
Past	*haber sido* mand*ado*	**Past**	*habiendo sido* mand*ado*

Subjunctive

Present	*sea* mand*ado*	**Pluperfect**	*hubiera sido* mand*ado*
			hubiese sido mand*ado*
Imperfect	*fuera* mand*ado*		
	fuese mand*ado*		
Future	*fuere* mand*ado*	**Future perfect**	*hubiere sido* mand*ado*
Past	*haya sido* mand*ado*		

	Infinitive	Present Indicative	Present Subjunctive	Preterite
⟨1b⟩	cambiar. Model for all ...*iar* verbs, unless formed like *variar* ⟨1c⟩.			
		cambio	cambie	cambié
		cambias	cambies	cambiaste
		cambia	cambie	cambió
		cambiamos	cambiemos	cambiamos
		cambiáis	cambiéis	cambiasteis
		cambian	cambien	cambiaron
⟨1c⟩	variar. *i* becomes *í* when the stem is stressed.			
		varío	varíe	varié
		varías	varíes	variaste
		varía	varíe	varió
		variamos	variemos	variamos
		variáis	variéis	variasteis
		varían	varíen	variaron
⟨1d⟩	evacuar. Model for all ...*uar* verbs, unless formed like *acentuar* ⟨1e⟩.			
		evacuo	evacue	evacué
		evacuas	evacues	evacuaste
		evacua	evacue	evacuó
		evacuamos	evacuemos	evacuamos
		evacuáis	evacuéis	evacuasteis
		evacuan	evacuen	evacuaron
⟨1e⟩	acentuar. *u* becomes *ú* when the stem is stressed.			
		acentúo	acentúe	acentué
		acentúas	acentúes	acentuaste
		acentúa	acentúe	acentuó
		acentuamos	acentuemos	acentuamos
		acentuáis	acentuéis	acentuasteis
		acentúan	acentúen	acentuaron
⟨1f⟩	cruzar. Final *z* in the stem becomes *c* before *e*. Model for all ...*zar* verbs.			
		cruzo	cruce	crucé
		cruzas	cruces	cruzaste
		cruza	cruce	cruzó
		cruzamos	crucemos	cruzamos
		cruzáis	crucéis	cruzasteis
		cruzan	crucen	cruzaron

	Infinitive	Present Indicative	Present Subjunctive	Preterite

⟨1g⟩ **tocar.** Final *c* in the stem becomes *qu* before *e*. Model for all …*car* verbs.

	toco	toque	toqué
	tocas	toques	tocaste
	toca	toque	tocó
	tocamos	toquemos	tocamos
	tocáis	toquéis	tocasteis
	tocan	toquen	tocaron

⟨1h⟩ **pagar.** Final *g* in the stem becomes *gu* (*u* is silent) before *e*. Model for all …*gar* verbs.

	pago	pague	pagué
	pagas	pagues	pagaste
	paga	pague	pagó
	pagamos	paguemos	pagamos
	pagáis	paguéis	pagasteis
	pagan	paguen	pagaron

⟨1i⟩ **fraguar.** Final *gu* in the stem becomes *gü* before *e* (*u* with dieresis is pronounced). Model for all …*guar* verbs.

	fraguo	fragüe	fragüé
	fraguas	fragües	fraguaste
	fragua	fragüe	fraguó
	fraguamos	fragüemos	fraguamos
	fraguáis	fragüéis	fraguasteis
	fraguan	fragüen	fraguaron

⟨1k⟩ **pensar.** Stressed *e* in the stem becomes *ie*.

	pienso	piense	pensé
	piensas	pienses	pensaste
	piensa	piense	pensó
	pensamos	pensemos	pensamos
	pensáis	penséis	pensasteis
	piensan	piensen	pensaron

⟨1l⟩ **errar.** Stressed *e* in the stem becomes *ye* (because it comes at the beginning of the word).

	yerro	yerre	erré
	yerras	yerres	erraste
	yerra	yerre	erró
	erramos	erremos	erramos
	erráis	erréis	errasteis
	yerran	yerren	erraron

	Infinitive	Present Indicative	Present Subjunctive	Preterite

⟨1m⟩ **contar.** Stressed *o* of the stem becomes *ue* (*u* is pronounced).

		cuento	cuente	conté
		cuentas	cuentes	contaste
		cuenta	cuente	contó
		contamos	contemos	contamos
		contáis	contéis	contasteis
		cuentan	cuenten	contaron

⟨1n⟩ **agorar.** Stressed *o* of the stem becomes *üe* (*u* with dieresis is pronounced).

		agüero	agüere	agoré
		agüeras	agüeres	agoraste
		agüera	agüere	agoró
		agoramos	agoremos	agoramos
		agoráis	agoréis	agorasteis
		agüeran	agüeren	agoraron

⟨1o⟩ **jugar.** Stressed *u* in the stem becomes *ue*; final *g* of the stem becomes *gu* before *e*: (*see* ⟨1h⟩); *conjugar, enjugar* and *enjugarse* are regular.

		juego	juegue	jugué
		juegas	juegues	jugaste
		juega	juegue	jugó
		jugamos	juguemos	jugamos
		jugáis	juguéis	jugasteis
		juegan	jueguen	jugaron

⟨1p⟩ **estar.** *Present indicative 1st pers sg* in *...oy*, otherwise regular, but note the stressed *a*; the *Present subjunctive* has a stress on the *e* in the endings (apart from *1st pers pl*); *Preterite etc* as ⟨21⟩. Otherwise regular.

		estoy	esté	estuve
		estás	estés	estuviste
		está	esté	estuvo
		estamos	estemos	estuvimos
		estáis	estéis	estuvisteis
		están	estén	estuvieron

⟨1q⟩ **andar.** *Preterite* and derived forms like *estar* as in ⟨21⟩. Otherwise regular.

		ando	ande	anduve
		andas	andes	anduviste
		anda	ande	anduvo
		andamos	andemos	anduvimos
		andáis	andéis	anduvisteis
		andan	anden	anduvieron

601

	Infinitive	Present Indicative	Present Subjunctive	Preterite
⟨1r⟩	dar. *Present indicative 1st pers sg in …oy, otherwise regular. Present subjunctive 1st and 3rd pers sg takes an accent. Preterite etc follow the regular second conjugation. Otherwise regular.*			
		doy	dé	di
		das	des	diste
		da	dé	dio
		damos	demos	dimos
		dáis	deis	disteis
		dan	den	dieron

Second Conjugation

⟨2a⟩ **vender.** No change to the written or spoken form of the stem.

Simple tenses

Indicative

	Present	Imperfect	Preterite
sg	vendo	vendía	vendí
	vendes	vendías	vendiste
	vende	vendía	vendió
pl	vendemos	vendíamos	vendimos
	vendéis	vendíais	vendisteis
	venden	vendían	vendieron

	Future	Conditional
sg	venderé	vendería
	venderás	venderías
	venderá	vendería
pl	venderemos	venderíamos
	venderéis	venderíais
	venderán	venderían

Subjunctive

	Present	Imperfect I	Imperfect II
sg	venda	vendiera	vendiese
	vendas	vendieras	vendieses
	venda	vendiera	vendiese
pl	vendamos	vendiéramos	vendiésemos
	vendáis	vendierais	vendieseis
	vendan	vendieran	vendiesen

	Future	Imperative
sg	vendiere	—
	vendieres	vende (no vendas)
	vendiere	venda Vd.
pl	vendiéremos	vendamos
	vendiereis	vended (no vendáis)
	vendieren	vendan Vds.

Infinitive: vender
Present participle: vendiendo
Past participle: vendido

Compound tenses

Formed with the *Past participle* together with **haber** and **ser**, see ⟨1a⟩.

Infinitive	Present Indicative	Present Subjunctive	Preterite

⟨2b⟩ **vencer.** Final *c* of the stem becomes *z* bevore *a* and *o*. Model for all ...*cer* verbs where the ...*cer* is proceded by a consonant.

	venz*o*	venz*a*	venc*í*
	venc*es*	venz*as*	venc*iste*
	venc*e*	venz*a*	venc*ió*
	venc*emos*	venz*amos*	venc*imos*
	venc*éis*	venz*áis*	venc*isteis*
	venc*en*	venz*an*	venc*ieron*

⟨2c⟩ **coger.** Final *g* of the stem becomes *j* before *a* and *o*. Model for all ...*ger* verbs.

	co*jo*	co*ja*	cog*í*
	co*ges*	co*jas*	cog*iste*
	co*ge*	co*ja*	cog*ió*
	co*gemos*	co*jamos*	cog*imos*
	co*géis*	co*jáis*	cog*isteis*
	co*gen*	co*jan*	cog*ieron*

⟨2d⟩ **merecer.** Final *c* of the stem becomes *zc* before *a* and *o*.

	merez*co*	merez*ca*	merec*í*
	merec*es*	merez*cas*	merec*iste*
	merec*e*	merez*ca*	merec*ió*
	merec*emos*	merez*camos*	merec*imos*
	merec*éis*	merez*áis*	merec*isteis*
	merec*en*	merez*can*	merec*ieron*

⟨2e⟩ **creer.** Unstressed *i* between two vowels becomes *y*. Past participle: *creído*. Present participle: *creyendo*.

	cre*o*	cre*a*	cre*í*
	cre*es*	cre*as*	cre*íste*
	cre*e*	cre*a*	cre*yó*
	cre*emos*	cre*amos*	cre*ímos*
	cre*éis*	cre*áis*	cre*ísteis*
	cre*en*	cre*an*	cre*yeron*

⟨2f⟩ **tañer.** Unstressed *i* is omitted after *ñ* and *ll*; compare ⟨3h⟩ Present participle: *tañendo*.

	tañ*o*	tañ*a*	tañ*í*
	tañ*es*	tañ*as*	tañ*iste*
	tañ*e*	tañ*a*	**taño**
	tañ*emos*	tañ*amos*	tañ*imos*
	tañ*éis*	tañ*áis*	tañ*isteis*
	tañ*en*	tañ*an*	**tañ**e*ron*

	Infinitive	Present Indicative	Present Subjunctive	Preterite

⟨**2g**⟩ **perder.** Stressed *e* in the stem becomes *ie*; model for many other verbs.

	pier*do*	pier*da*	perd*í*
	pier*des*	pier*das*	perd*iste*
	pier*de*	pier*da*	perd*ió*
	perd*emos*	perd*amos*	perd*imos*
	perd*éis*	perd*áis*	perd*isteis*
	pier*den*	pier*dan*	perd*ieron*

⟨**2h**⟩ **mover.** Stressed *o* in the stem becomes *ue*. ...*olver* verbs form their *Past participle* with ...*uelto*.

	mue*vo*	mue*va*	mov*í*
	mue*ves*	mue*vas*	mov*iste*
	mue*ve*	mue*va*	mov*ió*
	mov*emos*	mov*amos*	mov*imos*
	mov*éis*	mov*áis*	mov*isteis*
	mue*ven*	mue*van*	mov*ieron*

⟨**2i**⟩ **oler.** Stressed *o* in the stem becomes *hue*... (when it comes at the beginning of the word).

	huelo	**hue**la	ol*í*
	hueles	**hue**las	ol*iste*
	huele	**hue**la	ol*ió*
	ol*emos*	ol*amos*	ol*imos*
	ol*éis*	ol*áis*	ol*isteis*
	huelen	**hue**lan	ol*ieron*

⟨**2k**⟩ **haber.** Many irregular forms. In the *Future* and *Conditional* the *e* after the stem *hab*... is dropped. Future: *habré*. Imperative *2nd pers sg: he*.

	he	ha*ya*	hu*be*
	has	ha*yas*	hu*biste*
	ha	ha*ya*	hu*bo*
	he*mos*	ha*yamos*	hu*bimos*
	hab*éis*	ha*yáis*	hu*bisteis*
	han	ha*yan*	hu*bieron*

⟨**2l**⟩ **tener.** Irregular in most forms. In the *Future* and *Conditional* the *e* coming after the stem is dropped and a *d* is inserted. Future: *tendré*. Imperative *2nd pers sg: ten*.

	teng*o*	teng*a*	tuv*e*
	tie*nes*	teng*as*	tuv*iste*
	tie*ne*	teng*a*	tuv*o*
	ten*emos*	teng*amos*	tuv*imos*
	ten*éis*	teng*áis*	tuv*isteis*
	tie*nen*	teng*an*	tuv*ieron*

	Infinitive	Present Indicative	Present Subjunctive	Preterite

⟨2m⟩ **caber.** Irregular in many forms. In the *Future* and *Conditional* the *e* coming after the stem is dropped. Future: *cabré.*

		quepo	**quep**a	**cup**e
		cab*es*	**quep***as*	cup*iste*
		cab*e*	**quep**a	cup*o*
		cab*emos*	**quep***amos*	cup*imos*
		cab*éis*	**quep***áis*	cup*isteis*
		cab*en*	**quep***an*	cup*ieron*

⟨2n⟩ **saber.** Irregular in many forms. In the *Future* and *Conditional* the *e* coming after the stem is dropped. Future: *sabré.*

		sé	**sep**a	**sup**e
		sab*es*	**sep***as*	**sup***iste*
		sab*e*	**sep**a	**sup**o
		sab*emos*	**sep***amos*	**sup***imos*
		sab*éis*	**sep***áis*	**sup***isteis*
		sab*en*	**sep***an*	**sup***ieron*

⟨2o⟩ **caer.** In the *Present* ...*ig*... is inserted after the stem. Unstressed *i* between vowels changes to *y* as with ⟨2e⟩. Past participle: *caído.* Present participle: *cayendo.*

		ca**ig**o	ca**ig**a	ca*í*
		ca*es*	ca**ig***as*	ca*íste*
		ca*e*	ca**ig**a	ca*yó*
		ca*emos*	ca**ig***amos*	ca*ímos*
		ca*éis*	ca**ig***áis*	ca*ísteis*
		ca*en*	ca**ig***an*	ca*yeron*

⟨2p⟩ **traer.** In the *Present* ...*ig*... is inserted after the stem. The *Preterite* ends in ...*je*. In the *Present participle i* changes to *y*. Past participle: *traído.* Present participle: *trayendo.*

		tra**ig**o	tra**ig**a	tra**j**e
		tra*es*	tra**ig***as*	tra**j***iste*
		tra*e*	tra**ig**a	tra**j**o
		tra*emos*	tra**ig***amos*	tra**j***imos*
		tra*éis*	tra**ig***áis*	tra**j***isteis*
		tra*en*	tra**ig***an*	tra**j***eron*

Infinitive	Present Indicative	Present Subjunctive	Preterite

⟨2q⟩ valer. In the *Present* …g… is inserted after the stem. In the *Future* and *Conditional* the e coming after the stem is dropped and a …d… inserted. Future: *valdré.*

	valgo	valga	valí
	vales	valgas	valiste
	vale	valga	valió
	valemos	valgamos	valimos
	valéis	valgáis	valisteis
	valen	valgan	valieron

⟨2r⟩ poner. …g… is inserted in the *Present*. Irregular in the *Preterite* and *Past participle*. In the *Future* and *Conditional* the e coming after the stem is dropped and a …d… inserted. Future: *pondré.* Past participle: *puesto.* Imperative *2nd pers sg*: *pon.*

	pongo	ponga	puse
	pones	pongas	pusiste
	pone	ponga	puso
	ponemos	pongamos	pusimos
	ponéis	pongáis	pusisteis
	ponen	pongan	pusieron

⟨2s⟩ hacer. In the *1st* person of the *Present Indicative* and *Subjunctive* g replaces c. Irregular in the *Preterite* and *Past participle*. In the *Future* and *Conditional* the ce is dropped. In the *Imperative sg* just the stem is used with …c changing to …z. Future: *haré.* Imperative *2nd pers sg*: *haz.* Past participle: *hecho.*

	hago	haga	hice
	haces	hagas	hiciste
	hace	haga	hizo
	hacemos	hagamos	hicimos
	hacéis	hagáis	hicisteis
	hacen	hagan	hicieron

⟨2t⟩ poder. Stressed o in the stem changes to …ue… in the *Present* and the *Imperative*. Irregular in the *Preterite* and *Present participle*. In the *Future* and *Conditional* the e coming after the stem is dropped. Future: *podré.* Present participle: *pudiendo.*

	puedo	pueda	pude
	puedes	puedas	pudiste
	puede	pueda	pudo
	podemos	podamos	pudimos
	podéis	podáis	pudisteis
	pueden	puedan	pudieron

	Infinitive	Present Indicative	Present Subjunctive	Preterite

⟨2u⟩ **querer.** *Stressed* e *in the stem changes to* ie *in the Present and Imperative. Irregular in the Preterite. In the Future and Conditional the* e *coming after the stem is dropped. Future:* querré.

	quiero	quiera	quise
	quieres	quieras	quisiste
	quiere	quiera	quiso
	queremos	queramos	quisimos
	queréis	queráis	quisisteis
	quieren	quieran	quisieron

⟨2v⟩ **ver.** *Present indicative 1st pers sg, Present subjunctive and Imperfect are formed on the stem* ve..., *otherwise formation is regular using the shortened stem* v... *Irregular in the Past participle. Past participle:* visto.

	veo	vea	vi
	ves	veas	viste
	ve	vea	vio
	vemos	veamos	vimos
	veis	veáis	visteis
	ven	vean	vieron

	Infinitive	Present Indicative	Present Subjunctive	Imperfect Indicative	Preterite

⟨2w⟩ **ser.** Totally irregular with several different stems being used. Past participle: *sido*. Imperative *2nd pers sg*: *sé*. *2nd pers pl*: *sed*.

soy	s**ea**	**er**a	**fui**
eres	s**ea**s	**er**as	**fui**ste
es	s**ea**	**er**a	**fue**
so**mos**	s**ea**mos	**éra**mos	**fui**mos
so**is**	s**eá**is	**er**ais	**fui**steis
so**n**	s**ea**n	**er**an	**fue**ron

⟨2x⟩ **placer.** Used almost exclusively in the *3rd pers sg*. Irregular forms: *Present subjunctive* pl**ega** and pl**egue** egue as well as *plazca*; *Preterite* pl**ugo** (or *plació*), pl**uguieron** (or *placieron*); *Imperfect subjunctive* pl**uguiera**, pl**uguiese** (or *placiera*, *placiese*); *Future subjunctive* pl**uguiere** (or *placiere*).

⟨2y⟩ **yacer.** Used mainly on gravestones and so used primarily in the *3rd pers*. The *Present indicative 1st pers sg* and *Present subjunctive* have three forms. The *Imperative* is regular; just the stem with *c* changing to *z*. *Present indicative*: ya**zc**o, ya**zg**o, ya**g**o, ya**c**es etc; *Present subjunctive*: ya**zc**a, ya**zg**a, ya**g**a etc; *Imperative* ya**c**e and ya**z**.

⟨2z⟩ **raer.** The regular forms of the *Present indicative 1st pers sg* and *Present subjunctive* are less common than the forms with inserted ...*ig*... as in ⟨2o⟩: ra**ig**o, ra**ig**a; but also ra**y**o, ra**y**a (less common). Otherwise regular.

⟨2za⟩ **roer.** As well as their regular forms the *Present indicative 1st pers sg* and *Present subjunctive* have the less common forms: ro**ig**o, ro**ig**a, ro**y**o, ro**y**a.

Third Conjugation

⟨3a⟩ **recibir.** No change to the written or spoken form of the stem.

Simple tenses

Indicative

	Present	**Imperfect**	**Preterite**
sg	recibo	recibía	recibí
	recibes	recibías	recibiste
	recibe	recibía	recibió
pl	recibimos	recibíamos	recibimos
	recibís	recibíais	recibisteis
	reciben	recibían	recibieron

	Future	**Conditional**
sg	recibiré	recibiría
	recibirás	recibirías
	recibirá	recibiría
pl	recibiremos	recibiríamos
	recibiréis	recibiríais
	recibirán	recibirían

Subjunctive

	Present	**Imperfect I**	**Imperfect II**
sg	reciba	recibiera	recibiese
	recibas	recibieras	recibieses
	reciba	recibiera	recibiese
pl	recibamos	recibiéramos	recibiésemos
	recibáis	recibierais	recibieseis
	reciban	recibieran	recibiesen

	Future	**Imperative**
sg	recibiere	—
	recibieres	recibe (no recibas)
	recibiere	reciba Vd.
pl	recibiéremos	recibamos
	recibiereis	recibid (no recibáis)
	recibieren	reciban Vds.

Infinitive: recibir
Present participle: recibiendo
Past participle: recibido

Compound tenses

Formed with the *Past participle* together with **haber** and **ser**, see ⟨1a⟩.

	Infinitive	Present Indicative	Present Subjunctive	Preterite

⟨**3b**⟩ **esparcir.** Final *c* of the stem becomes *z* before *a* and *o*.

		esparz*o*	esparz*a*	esparcí
		esparc*es*	esparz*as*	esparc*iste*
		esparc*e*	esparz*a*	esparc*ió*
		esparc*imos*	esparz*amos*	esparc*imos*
		esparc*ís*	esparz*áis*	esparc*isteis*
		esparc*en*	esparz*an*	esparc*ieron*

⟨**3c**⟩ **dirigir.** Final *g* of the stem becomes *j* before *a* and *o*.

		diri*jo*	diri*ja*	dirigí
		dirig*es*	diri*jas*	dirig*iste*
		dirig*e*	diri*ja*	dirig*ió*
		dirig*imos*	diri*jamos*	dirig*imos*
		dirig*ís*	diri*jáis*	dirig*isteis*
		dirig*en*	diri*jan*	dirig*ieron*

⟨**3d**⟩ **distinguir.** Final *gu* of the stem becomes *g* before *a* and *o*.

		disting*o*	disting*a*	distinguí
		distingu*es*	disting*as*	distingu*iste*
		distingu*e*	disting*a*	distingu*ió*
		distingu*imos*	disting*amos*	distingu*imos*
		distingu*ís*	disting*áis*	distingu*isteis*
		distingu*en*	disting*an*	distingu*ieron*

⟨**3e**⟩ **delinquir.** Final *qu* of the stem becomes *c* before *a* and *o*.

		delin*co*	delin*ca*	delinquí
		delinqu*es*	delin*cas*	delinqu*iste*
		delinqu*e*	delin*ca*	delinqu*ió*
		delinqu*imos*	delin*camos*	delinqu*imos*
		delinqu*ís*	delin*cáis*	delinqu*isteis*
		delinqu*en*	delin*can*	delinqu*ieron*

⟨**3f**⟩ **lucir.** Final *c* of the stem becomes *zc* before *a* and *o*.

		luz*co*	luz*ca*	lucí
		luc*es*	luz*cas*	luc*iste*
		luc*e*	luz*ca*	luc*ió*
		luc*imos*	luz*camos*	luc*imos*
		luc*ís*	luz*cáis*	luc*isteis*
		luc*en*	luz*can*	luc*ieron*

	Infinitive	Present Indicative	Present Subjunctive	Preterite

⟨3g⟩ **concluir.** A *y* is inserted after the stem unless the ending begins with *i*. Past participle: *concluido*. Present participle: *concluyendo*.

conclu**yo**	conclu**ya**	conclu**í**
conclu**yes**	conclu**yas**	conclu**iste**
conclu**ye**	conclu**ya**	conclu**yó**
conclu**imos**	conclu**yamos**	conclu**imos**
conclu**ís**	conclu**yáis**	conclu**isteis**
conclu**yen**	conclu**yan**	conclu**yeron**

⟨3h⟩ **gruñir.** Unstressed *i* is dropped after *ñ*, *ll* and *ch*. Likewise *mullir*: *mulló*, *mulleron*, *mullendo*; *henchir*: *hinchó*, *hincheron*, *hinchendo* Present participle: *gruñendo*.

gruñ**o**	gruñ**es**	gruñ**e**
gruñ**imos**	gruñ**ís**	gruñ**en**
gruñ**a**	gruñ**í**	gruñ**as**
gruñ**iste**	gruñ**a**	gruñ**ó**
gruñ**amos**	gruñ**imos**	gruñ**áis**
gruñ**isteis**	gruñ**an**	gruñ**eron**

⟨3i⟩ **sentir.** Stressed *e* of the stem becomes *ie*; unstressed *e* remains unchanged before endings starting with *i*, but before other endings it changes to ...*i*...; likewise *adquirir*: stressed *i* of the stem becomes *ie*; unstressed *i* remains unchanged in all forms. Present participle: *sintiendo*.

s**ie**nt**o**	s**ie**nt**a**	sent**í**
s**ie**nt**es**	s**ie**nt**as**	sent**iste**
s**ie**nt**e**	s**ie**nt**a**	s**i**nt**ió**
sent**imos**	s**i**nt**amos**	sent**imos**
sent**ís**	s**i**nt**áis**	sent**isteis**
s**ie**nt**en**	s**ie**nt**an**	s**i**nt**ieron**

⟨3k⟩ **dormir.** Stressed *o* of the stem becomes *ue*; unstressed *o* is unchanged when the ending starts with *i*; otherwise it changes to ...*u*... Present participle: *durmiendo*.

d**ue**rm**o**	d**ue**rm**a**	dorm**í**
d**ue**rm**es**	d**ue**rm**as**	dorm**iste**
d**ue**rm**e**	d**ue**rm**a**	d**u**rm**ió**
dorm**imos**	d**u**rm**amos**	dorm**imos**
dorm**ís**	d**u**rm**áis**	dorm**isteis**
d**ue**rm**en**	d**ue**rm**an**	d**u**rm**ieron**

Infinitive	Present Indicative	Present Subjunctive	Preterite

⟨3l⟩ **medir.** The *e* of the stem is kept if the ending contains an *i*. Otherwise it changes to ...*i*... whether stressed or unstressed. Present participle: *midiendo*.

mid*o*	mid*a*	med*í*
mid*es*	mid*as*	med*iste*
mid*e*	mid*a*	mid*ió*
med*imos*	mid*amos*	med*imos*
med*ís*	mid*áis*	med*isteis*
mid*en*	mid*an*	mid*ieron*

⟨3m⟩ **reír.** As *medir* ⟨3l⟩; when *e* changes to *i* any second *i* belonging to the ending is dropped. Past participle: *reído*. Present participle: *riendo*.

r*í*o	r*í*a	re*í*
r*í*es	r*í*as	re*íste*
r*í*e	r*í*a	ri*ó*
re*imos*	ri*amos*	re*ímos*
re*ís*	ri*áis*	re*ísteis*
r*í*en	r*í*an	ri*eron*

⟨3n⟩ **erguir.** As *medir* in the *Present indicative*, *Subjunctive* and *Imperative*. Other forms follow *sentir* with initial *ie*... changing to *ye*... Present participle: *irguiendo*. Imperative: *irgue, yergue*.

irgo, yergo	**irga, yerga**	ergu*í*
irgues, yergues	**irgas, yergas**	erguiste
irgue, yergue	**irga, yerga**	irgu*ió*
ergu*imos*	irg*amos*, yerg*amos*	erguimos
ergu*ís*	irg*áis*, yerg*áis*	erguisteis
irguen, yerguen	**irgan, yergan**	irgu*ieron*

⟨3o⟩ **conducir.** Final *c* of the stem, as with *lucir* ⟨3f⟩, becomes *zc* before *a* and *o*. *Preterite* is irregular with ...*je*.

conduz*co*	conduz*ca*	conduj*e*
conduces	conduz*cas*	conduj*iste*
conduce	conduz*ca*	conduj*o*
conduc*imos*	conduz*camos*	conduj*imos*
conduc*ís*	conduz*cáis*	conduj*isteis*
conduc*en*	conduz*can*	conduj*eron*

Infinitive	Present Indicative	Present Subjunctive	Preterite

⟨3p⟩ **decir.** In the *Present* and *Imperative e* and *i* are changed, as with *medir*; in the *Present indicative 1st pers sg* and in the *Present subjunctive c* becomes *g*. Irregular *Future* and *Conditional* based on a shortened *Infinitive*. *Preterite* has *je*. Future: *diré*. Past participle: *dicho*. Present participle: *diciendo*. Imperative *2nd pers sg: di*.

di**g**o	di**g**a	di**j**e
di**c**es	di**g**as	di**j**iste
di**c**e	di**g**a	di**j**o
de**c**imos	di**g**amos	di**j**imos
de**c**ís	di**g**áis	di**j**isteis
di**c**en	di**g**an	di**j**eron

⟨3q⟩ **oír.** In the *Present indicative 1st pers sg* and *Present subjunctive ...ig...* is inserted after the *o...* of the stem. Unstressed *...i...* changes to *...y...* when coming between two vowels. Past participle: *oído*. Present participle: *oyendo*.

oi**g**o	oi**g**a	oí
o**y**es	oi**g**as	oíste
o**y**e	oi**g**a	o**y**ó
oímos	oi**g**amos	oímos
oís	oi**g**áis	oísteis
o**y**en	oi**g**an	o**y**eron

⟨3rk⟩ **salir.** In the *Present indicative 1st pers sg* and the *Present subjunctive a ...g...* is inserted after the stem. In the *Future* and *Conditional* the *i* is replaced by *d*. Future: *saldré*. Imperative: *2nd pers sg: sal*.

sal**g**o	sal**g**a	salí
sales	sal**g**as	saliste
sale	sal**g**a	salió
salimos	sal**g**umos	salimos
salís	sal**g**áis	salisteis
salen	sal**g**an	salieron

	Infinitive	Present Indicative	Present Subjunctive	Imperfect Indicative	Preterite

⟨3s⟩ venir. In the *Present* two changes: either a ...g... is inserted after the stem or *e*, *ie* and *i* follow the same changes as *sentir*. In the *Future* and *Conditional* the *i* is dropped and replaced by *d*. Future: *vendré*. Present participle: *viniendo*. Imperative *2nd pers sg*: *ven*.

		vengo	venga	venía	vine
		vienes	vengas	venías	viniste
		viene	venga	venía	vino
		venimos	vengamos	veníamos	vinimos
		venís	vengáis	veníais	vinisteis
		vienen	vengan	venían	vinieron

⟨3t⟩ ir. Totally irregular with several different stems being used. Present participle: *yendo*

		voy	vaya	iba	fui
		vas	vayas	ibas	fuiste
		va	vaya	iba	fue
		vamos	vayamos	íbamos	fuimos
		vais	vayáis	ibais	fuisteis
		van	vayan	iban	fueron

Imperative: **ve** (no **vayas**), **vaya** Vd, **vamos**, *id* (no **vayáis**), **vayan** Vds.

Notas sobre el verbo inglés

a) Conjugación

1. **El tiempo presente** tiene la misma forma que el infinitivo en todas las personas menos la **3ª** del singular; en ésta, se añade una *-s* al infinitivo, p.ej. *he brings*, o se añade *-es* si el infinitivo termina en sibilante (ch, sh, ss, zz), p.ej. *he passes*. Esta *s* tiene dos pronunciaciones distintas: tras consonante sorda se pronuncia sorda, p.ej. *he paints* [peɪnts]; tras consonante sonora se pronuncia sonora, *he sends* [sendz]; *-es* se pronuncia también sonora, sea la *e* parte de la desinencia o letra final del infinitivo, p.ej. *he washes* [wɑːʃɪz], *he urges* [ˈɜːrdʒɪz]. Los verbos que terminan en *-y* la cambian en *-ies* en la tercera persona, p.ej. *he worries, he tries*, pero son regulares los verbos que en el infinitivo tienen una vocal delante de la *-y*, p.ej. *he plays*. El verbo *to be* es irregular en todas las personas: *I am, you are, he is, we are, you are, they are*. Tres verbos más tienen forma especial para la tercera persona del singular: *do-he does, go-he goes, have-he has*.

   En los demás tiempos, todas las personas son iguales. **El pretérito y el participio del pasado** se forman añadiendo *-ed* al infinitivo, p.ej. *I passed, passed*, o añadiendo *-d* a los infinitivos que terminan en *-e*, p.ej. *I faced, faced*. (Hay muchos verbos irregulares: v. abajo). Esta *-(e)d* se pronuncia generalmente como [t]: *passed* [pæst], *faced* [feɪst]; pero cuando se añade a un infinitivo que termina en consonante sonora o en sonido consonántico sonoro o en *r*, se pronuncia como [d]: *warmed* [wɔːrmd], *moved* [muːvd], *feared* [fɪrd]. Si el infinitivo termina en *-d o -t*, la desinencia *-ed* se pronuncia [ɪd]. Si el infinitivo termina en *-y*, ésta se cambia en *-ie*, antes de añadirse la *-d*: *try-tried* [traɪd], *pity-pitied* [pɪtɪd]. **Los tiempos compuestos del pasado** se forman con el verbo auxiliar *have* y el participio del pasado, como en español: **perfecto** *I have faced*, **pluscuamperfecto** *I had faced*. Con el verbo auxiliar *will* (*shall*) y el infinitivo se forma **el futuro**, p.ej. *I shall face*; y con el verbo auxiliar *would* (*should*) y el infinitivo se forma **el condicional**, p.ej. *I should face*. En cada tiempo existe además una forma continua que se forma con el verbo *be* (= estar) y el participio del presente (v. abajo): *I am going, I was writing, I had been staying, I shall be waiting*, etc.

2. **El subjuntivo** ha dejado casi de existir en inglés, salvo en algún caso especial (*if I were you, so be it, it is proposed that a vote be taken*, etc.). En el presente, tiene en todas las personas la misma forma que el infinitivo, *that I go, that he go*, etc.

3. **El participio del presente** y **el gerundio** tienen la misma forma en inglés, añadiéndose al infinitivo la desinencia *-ing*: *painting, sending*. Pero **1)** Los verbos cuyo infinitivo termina en *-e* muda la pierden al añadir *-ing*, p.ej. *love-loving, write-writing* (excepciones que conservan la *-e*: *dye-dyeing, singe-singeing*); **2)** El participio del presente de los verbos *die, lie, vie*, etc. se escribe *dying, lying, vying*, etc.

4. Existe una clase de verbos ligeramente irregulares, que terminan en consonante simple precedida de vocal simple acentuada; en éstos, antes de añadir la desinencia *-ing* o *-ed*, se dobla la consonante:

lob	lob*bed*	lob*bing*	compel	compel*led*	compel*ling*
wed	wed*ded*	wed*ding*	control	control*led*	control*ling*
beg	beg*ged*	beg*ging*	bar	bar*red*	bar*ring*
step	step*ped*	step*ping*	stir	stir*red*	stir*ring*
quit	quit*ted*	quit*ting*			

Los verbos que terminan en *-l*, *-p*, aunque precedida de vocal átona, tienen doblada la consonante en los dos participios en el inglés escrito en Gran Bretaña, aunque no en el de Estados Unidos:

| travel | traveled, | traveling, |
| | *Br* travel*led*, | *Br* travel*led* |

Los verbos que terminan en *-c* la cambian en *-ck* al añadirse las desinencias *-ed*, *-ing*:

| traffic | traffi*cked* | traffi*cking* |

5. **La voz pasiva** se forma exactamente como en español, con el verbo *be* y el participio del pasado: *I am obliged, he was fined, they will be moved*, etc.

6. Cuando se dirige uno directamente a otra(s) persona(s) en inglés se emplea únicamente el pronombre *you*. *You* se traduce por el *tú*, *vosotros*, *usted* y *ustedes* del español.

b) Los verbos irregulares ingleses

Se citan las tres partes principales de cada verbo: infinitivo, pretérito, participio del pasado.

alight - alighted, alit - alighted, alit
arise - arose - arisen
awake - awoke - awoken, awaked
be (am, is, are) - was (were) been
bear - bore - borne
beat - beat - beaten
become - became - become
begin - began - begun
behold - beheld - beheld
bend - bent - bent
beseech - besought, beseeched - besought, beseeched
bet - bet, betted - bet, betted
bid - bid - bid
bind - bound - bound
bite - bit - bitten
bleed - bled - bled

blow - blew - blown
break - broke - broken
breed - bred - bred
bring - brought - brought
broadcast - broadcast - broadcast
build - built - built
burn - burnt, burned - burnt, burned
burst - burst - burst
bust - bust(ed) - bust(ed)
buy - bought - bought
cast - cast - cast
catch - caught - caught
choose - chose - chosen
cleave (*cut*) - clove, cleft - cloven, cleft
cleave (*adhere*) - cleaved - cleaved
cling - clung - clung

come - came - come
cost (v/i) - cost - cost
creep - crept - crept
crow - crowed, crew - crowed
cut - cut - cut
deal - dealt - dealt
dig - dug - dug
do - did - done
draw - drew - drawn
dream - dreamt, dreamed - dreamt, dreamed
drink - drank - drunk
drive - drove - driven
dwell - dwelt, dwelled - dwelt, dwelled
eat - ate - eaten
fall - fell - fallen
feed - fed - fed
feel - felt - felt
fight - fought - fought
find - found - found
flee - fled - fled
fling - flung - flung
fly - flew - flown
forbear - forbore - forborne
forbid - forbad(e) - forbidden
forecast - forecast(ed) - forecast(ed)
forget - forgot - forgotten
forgive - forgave - forgiven
forsake - forsook - forsaken
freeze - froze - frozen
get - got - got, gotten
give - gave - given
go - went - gone
grind - ground - ground
grow - grew - grown
hang - hung, (v/t) hanged - hung, (v/t) hanged
have - had - had
hear - heard - heard
heave - heaved, NAUT hove - heaved, NAUT hove
hew - hewed - hewed, hewn
hide - hid - hidden
hit - hit - hit
hold - held - held
hurt - hurt - hurt

keep - kept - kept
kneel - knelt, kneeled - knelt, kneeled
know - knew - known
lay - laid - laid
lead - led - led
lean - leaned, leant - leaned, leant
leap - leaped, leapt - leaped, leapt
learn - learned, learnt - learned, learnt
leave - left - left
lend - lent - lent
let - let - let
lie - lay - lain
light - lighted, lit - lighted, lit
lose - lost - lost
make - made - made
mean - meant - meant
meet - met - met
mow - mowed - mowed, mown
pay - paid - paid
plead - pleaded, pled - pleaded, pled
prove - proved - proved, proven
put - put - put
quit - quit(ted) - quit(ted)
read - read [red] - read [red]
rend - rent - rent
rid - rid - rid
ride - rode - ridden
ring - rang - rung
rise - rose - risen
run - ran - run
saw - sawed - sawn, sawed
say - said - said
see - saw - seen
seek - sought - sought
sell - sold - sold
send - sent - sent
set - set - set
sew - sewed - sewed, sewn
shake - shook - shaken
shear - sheared - sheared, shorn
shed - shed - shed
shine - shone - shone
shit - shit(ted), shat - shit(ted), shat
shoe - shod - shod
shoot - shot - shot
show - showed - shown
shrink - shrank - shrunk

shut - shut - shut
sing - sang - sung
sink - sank - sunk
sit - sat - sat
slay - slew - slain
sleep - slept - slept
slide - slid - slid
sling - slung - slung
slink - slunk - slunk
slit - slit - slit
smell - smelt, smelled - smelt, smelled
smite - smote - smitten
sow - sowed - sown, sowed
speak - spoke - spoken
speed - sped, speeded - sped, speeded
spell - spelt, spelled - spelt, spelled
spend - spent - spent
spill - spilt, spilled - spilt, spilled
spin - spun, span - spun
spit - spat - spat
split - split - split
spoil - spoiled, spoilt - spoiled, spoilt
spread - spread - spread
spring - sprang, sprung - sprung
stand - stood - stood
stave - staved, stove - staved, stove
steal - stole - stolen
stick - stuck - stuck
sting - stung - stung

stink - stunk, stank - stunk
strew - strewed - strewed, strewn
stride - strode - stridden
strike - struck - struck
string - strung - strung
strive - strove - striven
swear - swore - sworn
sweep - swept - swept
swell - swelled - swollen
swim - swam - swum
swing - swung - swung
take - took - taken
teach - taught - taught
tear - tore - torn
tell - told - told
think - thought - thought
thrive - throve - thriven
throw - threw - thrown
thrust - thrust - thrust
tread - trod - trodden
understand - understood - understood
wake - woke, waked - woken, waked
wear - wore - worn
weave - wove - woven
wed - wed(ded) - wed(ded)
weep - wept - wept
wet - wet(ted) - wet(ted)
win - won - won
wind - wound - wound
wring - wrung - wrung
write - wrote - written

Numbers – Numerales

Cardinal Numbers – Números cardinales

0	*zero, Br tb nought* cero	40	*forty* cuarenta
1	*one* uno, una	50	*fifty* cincuenta
2	*two* dos	60	*sixty* sesenta
3	*three* tres	70	*seventy* setenta
4	*four* cuatro	80	*eighty* ochenta
5	*five* cinco	90	*ninety* noventa
6	*six* seis	100	*a hundred, one hundred* cien(to)
7	*seven* siete		
8	*eight* ocho	101	*a hundred and one* ciento uno
9	*nine* nueve	110	*a hundred and ten* ciento diez
10	*ten* diez	200	*two hundred* doscientos, *-as*
11	*eleven* once	300	*three hundred* trescientos, -as
12	*twelve* doce	400	*four hundred* cuatrocientos, -as
13	*thirteen* trece	500	*five hundred* quinientos, -as
14	*fourteen* catorce	600	*six hundred* seiscientos, -as
15	*fifteen* quince	700	*seven hundred* setecientos, -as
16	*sixteen* dieciséis	800	*eight hundred* ochocientos, *-as*
17	*seventeen* diecisiete	900	*nine hundred* novecientos, -as
18	*eighteen* dieciocho	1000	*a thousand, one thousand* mil
19	*nineteen* diecinueve	1959	*one thousand nine hundred and fifty-nine* mil novecientos cincuenta y nueve
20	*twenty* veinte		
21	*twenty-one* veintiuno		
22	*twenty-two* veintidós	2000	*two thousand* dos mil
30	*thirty* treinta	1 000 000	*a million, one million* un millón
31	*thirty-one* treinta y uno	2 000 000	*two million* dos millones

Notas:

i) In Spanish numbers a comma is used for decimals:

   1.25 **one point two five** una coma veinticinco

ii) A period is used where, in English, we would use a comma:

   1.000.000 = 1,000,000

   Numbers like this can also be written using a space instead of a comma:

   1 000 000 = 1,000,000

Ordinal Numbers – Números ordinales

1st	*first*	1°	primero
2nd	*second*	2°	segundo
3rd	*third*	3°	tercero
4th	*fourth*	4°	cuarto
5th	*fifth*	5°	quinto
6th	*sixth*	6°	sexto
7th	*seventh*	7°	séptimo
8th	*eighth*	8°	octavo
9th	*ninth*	9°	noveno, nono
10th	*tenth*	10°	décimo
11th	*eleventh*	11°	undécimo
12th	*twelfth*	12°	duodécimo
13th	*thirteenth*	13°	decimotercero
14th	*fourteenth*	14°	decimocuarto
15th	*fifteenth*	15°	decimoquinto
16th	*sixteenth*	16°	decimosexto
17th	*seventeenth*	17°	decimoséptimo
18th	*eighteenth*	18°	decimoctavo
19th	*nineteenth*	19°	decimonoveno, decimonono
20th	*twentieth*	20°	vigésimo
21st	*twenty-first*	21°	vigésimo prim(er)o
22nd	*twenty-second*	22°	vigésimo segundo
30th	*thirtieth*	30°	trigésimo
31st	*thirty-first*	31°	trigésimo prim(er)o
40th	*fortieth*	40°	cuadragésimo
50th	*fiftieth*	50°	quincuagésimo
60th	*sixtieth*	60°	sexagésimo
70th	*seventieth*	70°	septuagésimo
80th	*eightieth*	80°	octogésimo
90th	*ninetieth*	90°	nonagésimo
100th	*hundredth*	100°	centésimo
101st	*hundred and first*	101°	centésimo primero
110th	*hundred and tenth*	110°	centésimo décimo
200th	*two hundredth*	200°	ducentésimo
300th	*three hundredth*	300°	trecentésimo
400th	*four hundredth*	400°	cuadringentésimo
500th	*five hundredth*	500°	quingentésimo
600th	*six hundredth*	600°	sexcentésimo
700th	*seven hundredth*	700°	septingentésimo
800th	*eight hundredth*	800°	octingentésimo
900th	*nine hundredth*	900°	noningentésimo
1000th	*thousandth*	1000°	milésimo
2000th	*two thousandth*	2000°	dos milésimo
1,000,100th	*millionth*	1 000 100°	millonésimo
2,000,000th	*two millionth*	2 000 000°	dos millonésimo

Fractions and other Numerals – Números quebrados y otros

$^1/_2$	one half, a half	medio, media
$1^1/_2$	one and a half	uno y medio
$2^1/_2$	two and a half	dos y medio
$^1/_3$	one third, a third	un tercio, la tercera parte
$^2/_3$	two thirds	dos tercios, las dos terceras partes
$^1/_4$	one quarter, a quarter	un cuarto, la cuarta parte
$^3/_4$	three quarters	tres cuartos, las tres cuartas partes
$^1/_5$	one fifth, a fifth	un quinto
$3^4/_5$	three and four fifths	tres y cuatro quintos
$^1/_{11}$	one eleventh, an eleventh	un onzavo
$^5/_{12}$	five twelfths	cinco dozavos
$^1/_{1000}$	one thousandth, a thousandth	un milésimo
	seven times as big, seven times bigger	siete veces más grande
	twelve times more	doce veces más
	first(ly)	en primer lugar
	second(ly) etc	en segundo lugar
8 = 15	seven and (or plus) eight are (or is) fifteen	siete y (or más) ocho son quince
3 = 7	ten minus three is seven, three from ten leaves seven	diez menos tres resta siete, de tres a diez van siete
× 3 = 6	two times three is six	dos por tres son seis
4 = 5	twenty divided by four is five	veinte dividido por cuatro es cinco

Dates – Fechas

1996	nineteen ninety-six	mil novecientos noventa y seis
2005	two thousand (and) five	dos mil cinco

10th of November, November 10 (ten)
ez de noviembre, el 10 de noviembre

1st of March, March 1 (first)
o de marzo, L.Am. el primero de marzo, el 1o de marzo

Headword in blue

A·mer·i·ca [əˈmerɪkə] *continent* América; *USA* Estados *mpl* Unidos

International Phonetic Alphabet

in·sult **1** *n* [ˈɪnsʌlt] insulto *m* **2** *v/t* [ɪnˈsʌlt] insultar

Translation in normal characters with gender shown in *italics*

'break·down *of vehicle, machine* avería *f*; *of talks* ruptura *f*; (*nervous breakdown*) crisis *f inv* nerviosa; *of figures* desglose *m*

Hyphenation points

con·sum·er 'con·fi·dence confianza *f* de los consumidores
con'sum·er goods *npl* bienes *mpl* de consumo
con'sum·er so·ci·e·ty sociedad *f* de consumo

ress shown in headwords

'mov·ie thea·ter cine *m*, sala *f* de cine

Examples and phrases in *bold italics*

i·deal·ly [aɪˈdiːəlɪ] *adv*: *ideally situated* en una posición ideal; *ideally, we would do it like this* lo ideal sería que lo hiciéramos así

dicating words in *italics*

stub·born [ˈstʌbərn] *adj person* testarudo, terco; *defense, refusal, denial* tenaz, pertinaz
busi·ness [ˈbɪznɪs] negocios *mpl*, (*company*) empresa *f*; (*sector*) sector *m*; (*affair, matter*) asunto *m*; *as subject of study* empresariales *fpl*; *on business* de negocios